UNIVERSITY CASEBOOK SERIES®

SALES LAW: DOMESTIC AND INTERNATIONAL

CASES, PROBLEMS, AND MATERIALS

by

STEVEN D. WALT
Percy Brown, Jr., Professor of Law
University of Virginia School of Law

FOUNDATION
PRESS

University Casebook Series is a trademark registered in the U.S. Patent and Trademark Office.

© 2014 LEG, Inc. d/b/a West Academic
    444 Cedar Street, Suite 700
    St. Paul, MN 55101
    1-877-888-1330

Printed in the United States of America

ISBN: 978-1-59941-186-6

Mat #40510471

PREFACE

This book describes the law of sales under Article 2 of the Uniform Commercial Code ("UCC") and the United Nations Convention on the International Sales of Goods ("CISG"). It also covers aspects of documentary sales and letters of credit, and makes reference to the law of leases under Article 2A of the UCC. Article 2 of the UCC is the predominant law applicable to domestic sales transactions, and CISG to international sales. Although a course on international business transactions touches on international sales, the subject cannot usefully be left out of a course on sales law. The increasing globalization of trade makes knowledge of international sales law necessary. In addition, because the rules of sales law are almost all default rules, parties can select Article 2 or the CISG, or elements of both, to govern their transaction when Article 2 or the CISG's rules do not otherwise apply to it. The fact that the transaction is domestic or international therefore is unimportant. Accordingly, to plan a sales contract or analyze the parties' rights and obligations under one already concluded requires an understanding of Article 2 and the CISG. For both reasons, this book integrates domestic and international sales law.

Casebooks in the area differ in their approach and emphasis. This book takes a "bottom up" approach to the subject. It focuses on statutory or treaty provisions and their language, taking into account their relation to other provisions. Where useful the material includes domestic or foreign decisions construing relevant provisions. Often a provision's language, supplemented by case law, is enough to decide an issue. In many instances it is not enough. On a continuum running from vague common law rules to the more precise provisions of ERISA, Article 2 and the CISG's provisions tend to be toward the vague end of the range. Vague or open-ended language of the provisions by themselves will not dictate a result in some cases. This means that other considerations must be introduced to resolve an issue or at least frame its resolution. The book's "bottom up" approach relies on more abstract resources when necessary to apply or evaluate Article 2 and the CISG's provisions.

The materials that follow are presented in a particular steamlined format. Rather than intimating salient issues through a collage of disparate materials, a discursive description introduces each topic. The description gives needed background to the topic and identifies the general features of provisions relevant to it. Cases, notes and problems following the description then explore specific aspects of the provisions. Citations to cases and secondary literature are kept to a bare minimum. The discursive material and notes try to be transparent: there is no attempt to submerge or obscure issues. Both serve the problems and reproduced cases, which are intended to be the focus of discussion. The mix of problems and cases accommodates different teaching styles.

I thank William Warren for his advice, Rena Kelley for valuable research and Anne Lippett for carefully reviewing the manuscript. I am particularly grateful to Clayton Gillette for his comments on an earlier draft of the book.

Steven Walt

November 2013

SUMMARY OF CONTENTS

TABLE OF CONTENTS

TABLE OF CASES

The principal cases are in bold type.

UNIVERSITY CASEBOOK SERIES ®

SALES LAW: DOMESTIC AND INTERNATIONAL

CASES, PROBLEMS, AND MATERIALS

CHAPTER 1

SALES LAW AND SALES TRANSACTIONS

A sale is the transfer of ownership in an asset for a price. The asset sold may be a good or intangible property such as a payment rights or intellectual property. Although both tangible and intangible assets can be sold, the law of sales is a distinct body of commercial law with a more limited subject matter. "Sales law" generally refers to the law regulating the sale of goods. Because a sale of goods involves a contract, sales law is a subset of contract law. The law of sales, however, differs from general contract law in one important respect. General contract law is the result of common law doctrine created by an accretion of judicial decisions. By contrast, sales law is largely governed by state or federal statute, and in some cases treaty.

Domestic sales transactions are governed primarily by state statutory law. Federal law, although applicable to some aspects of sales of goods, does not regulate most sales transaction. The principal state statute governing domestic sales is Article 2 of the Uniform Commercial Code (the "UCC"). The UCC is a comprehensive set of commercial law statutes produced jointly by two non-legislative bodies: the National Conference of Commissioners on Uniform State Law ("NCCUSL," later renamed the "Uniform Law Commission") and the American Law Institute ("ALI"). The first version of the UCC appeared in 1952 and was comprised of 11 Articles. Nine of the Articles contained substantive rules on different subject matters of commercial law: sales of goods (Article 2), negotiable instruments (Article 3), bank deposits and collections (Article 4), letters of credit (Article 5), bulk sales (Article 6), documents of title (Article 7), investment securities (Article 8), and secured transactions (Article 9). Two further Articles were added in the late 1980s governing leases in personal property (Article 2A) and wire transfers (Article 4A). Every state except Louisiana has adopted all of the Articles of the UCC, sometimes with some nonuniform amendments. Louisiana has adopted all of the Articles except Articles 2, 6 and 7. Congress has enacted the UCC for the District of Columbia, Guam, Puerto Rico (in part), and the Virgin Islands. To date every Article has been revised at least once and in some cases several times. The revisions have varied in the extent of changes made, ranging from the cosmetic to the radically different. The pace of state adoptions of revisions to Articles of the UCC has varied. The current state enactments of the UCC and adoption of its revisions is reported in 1–2 Unif. L. Ann. 1 (2005).

Much of this text is focused on the law of domestic sales under Article 2 of the UCC. Accordingly, a more detailed description of the present state of Article 2 might be useful. Aside from minor amendments in 1962, 1966 and 2001, changes have not been made to Article 2 since its adoption in 1952. By 1990 NCCUSL and a study group appointed by the ALI both felt that Article 2 had become outdated and merited revision. Between 1994 and 2002 two different drafting committees produced a number of drafts proposing significant changes in Article 2. A number of the drafts contained controversial revisions of key provisions. Although modest but still significant revisions were approved by the ALI in 1999, NCCUSL refused to allow its membership to consider the draft. In 2003 a draft containing some corrections and adjustments but almost no significant changes to Article 2 was approved by both the ALI and NCCUSL as Amended Article 2. Some trade groups, consumer representatives and commentators opposed Amended Article 2, and no jurisdiction has enacted it. Critics found that the modesty of the amendments either did not justify their enactment or threatened to undermine well-settled parts of Article 2. Judging that it was unlikely to be enacted, the ALI and NCCUSL withdrew proposed Article 2 in 2011, and the official text of the UCC now includes only the unamended version of the Article. The text below therefore focuses entirely on unamended Article 2. Unprefixed references by Article and section number are to unamended Article 2 (e.g., 2–207, 7–309). A few of the proposed amendments to Article 2 nonetheless are worth considering, as they sometimes reflect trends in judicial interpretations of the current version of Article 2 or propose specific changes to Article 2. References to relevant provisions in the proposed amendments to Article 2 appear as "Proposed" followed by the Article and section number (e.g., Proposed 2–207). All references to other Articles in the UCC are to the 2013 Official Text and Comments and appear by Article followed by section number.

A. THE UCC AND ITS OFFICIAL COMMENTS

The UCC is a special sort of codification of commercial law. It is different from commercial codes familiar in civil law countries. Civil law codes typically share three features: they are comprehensive, unified and systematic. See Bruce W. Frier, Symposium: One Hundred Years of Uniform State Laws: Interpreting Codes, 89 Mich. L. Rev. 2201 (1991). In principle these codes provide a set of interconnected explicit legal principles sufficient to resolve any issue that arises within their scope. The exclusive sources of resulting legal entitlements are the principles contained in the code. By contrast, the UCC, including Article 2, is not comprehensive, unified and systematic. It is not comprehensive because it does not supply all of the legal principles needed to resolve all issues. To resolve some issues, resort to extra-UCC law is needed. Section 1–103(b), for instance, supplements the UCC with principles of equity where a UCC provision does not displace them. Because the UCC does not state all of its operative principles or attempt to prioritize stated principles, its codification is neither unified nor systematic. For instance, 1–103(a) enumerates some of the UCC's underlying purposes without stating the connection between them. And 2–302's regulation of contracts by unconscionability leaves the working notion of unconscionability completely unspecified. Although 1–104 states that the UCC is intended as a unified coverage of its subject matter, it is unified only in that the provisions covering the subject matter appear in a single statute. The incomplete and nonexclusive nature of the UCC reflects the jurisprudential views of its Chief Reporter, Karl Llewellyn.

Given the character of the UCC as a code, the Official Comments accompanying each UCC provision play an important role in its interpretation. The Comments elaborate on the intended application of each provision. Although the 1952 version of the UCC contained a provision allowing Comments to be consulted in construction of the text, the provision was later removed from the Official Text of the UCC. Thus, Official Comments generally do not have the force of law, not being enacted along with their accompanying provisions. (Nonuniform enactments in several states consider Comments as evidence of the legislative intent behind the enacted UCC text; e.g., Iowa Code § 554.11109 (2005).) Courts use the Comments in three ways. First, Comments assist courts in explaining the meaning of the provisions they accompany. Although not law, courts understandably rely on Comments in a way somewhat comparable to their reliance on statutes. What better evidence are they to rely upon? Judicial reliance on the Comments also is unavoidable. Judge Learned Hand's reported reaction to the provision in the 1952 version of the UCC allowing resort to Comments was: "Well, what this comes to is to say that we may do what we shall do anyway." In rare cases some courts even have given priority to Comment over statutory text.

Second, courts use Comments to fill gaps not addressed by the text of specific provision. Take 2–504, for instance, which creates certain delivery and notification duties for a seller when the sales contract calls for a carrier to transport the goods to the buyer. The section imposes these duties only when "the contract does not require the seller to deliver [the goods] at a particular destination." This clearly implies that the seller's duties of delivery are different under a sales contract requiring delivery at a particular destination. But 2–504 is silent about when a sales contract requires the seller to deliver goods to a particular destination and when it does not. Thus, 2–504 contains a gap. Official Comment 5 to 2–504 fills this gap by providing that "under this Article the 'shipment' contract is regarded as the normal one and the 'destination' contract as the variant type." A "shipment" contract does not require the seller to deliver goods to a particular destination. It merely requires the seller to deliver them to the carrier for transport to the place named in the sales contract. According to Comment 5, 2–504 applies to a sales contract that simply calls for transport by a carrier. A sales contract requiring the seller to "send the merchandise" to a named place is an example. See Stampede Presentation Products, Inc. v. Productive Transportation, Inc., 80 UCC Rep. Serv.2d 927 (W.D.N.Y. 2013); Pestana v. Karinol Corp., 367 So.2d 1096 (Fla. Ct. App. 1979). Given the Comment, such a contract calls for seller to enter into a shipment contract, not a destination contract.

A third use of Official Comments is to confirm a view of a provision that a court endorses on independent grounds. Section 2–504 again serves as an example. A court might believe that costs of carriage might be lower if the buyer bears transit risk of the goods than if the seller bears it. Buyers usually have a range of different preferences for the details of delivery to the destination. More important, they have better information than their sellers about the condition of the goods when the carrier delivers them. The costs of litigating against the carrier might also be lower for buyers than for their sellers, because buyers are in closer proximity to the goods at the time of the carrier's delivery. The court therefore might conclude that carriage costs are lower for most buyers when sellers enter into "shipment" contracts. Having reached this conclusion independently of 2–504, the court might further support its conclusion as consistent with Official Comment 5: "shipment" contracts are the "normal" contracts while "destination" contracts are "deviant." Use of Comments to confirm independently reached conclusions is important because Article 2's provisions frequently are vague in their content. Their application to specific facts requires independent judgments of policy, and Comments sometimes can support policy judgments.

B. INTERNATIONAL SALES AND THE CISG

Article 2 is the predominant law governing domestic sales of goods. However, as international sales of goods have increased along with international trade generally, many sales transactions are beyond Article 2's scope. Since the middle of the twentieth century world trade has grown at many times the rate of increase in world gross domestic product. A rough measure of the level of international trade in goods is the dollar value of imports and exports of merchandise. In 2000 the United States accounted for about 15 percent of world exports and about 19 percent of world imports. In that year it exported goods valued at about $781 billion while importing goods valued at $1.257 trillion. WTO, International Trade Statistics Table 1.6 (2001), available at www.wto.org/english/res_e/statis_e/its2001_e/stats2001_e.pdf.   The economics of the geographic patterns of trade is not well understood. Although transport costs generally have declined over time, the distance over which trade occurs also has decreased during the same period (with the exception of the United States). See Celine Carrere & Maurice Shiff, On the Geography of Trade: Distance is Alive and Well (2005), M. Obstfeld & Kenneth Rogoff, The Six Major Puzzles in International Economics: Is there a Common Cause?, NBER Working Paper 777 (2000). This trend shows increased trade across shorter distances. However, even international trade over shorter distances still requires contracts for the sale and transport of goods across borders. Such trade simply may be with a buyer in an adjacent nation rather than one in a remote nation. International sales of goods create uncertainty in the law applicable to the sales transaction. They also create a risk of a lack of uniformity in the applicable domestic sales law. As international trade in goods increases, the problem of uncertainty and nonuniformity in sales law becomes more important.

The United Nations Convention on Contracts for the International Sale of Goods ("the CISG") was produced in response to the expansion of global trade and the uncertainty resulting from reliance on nonuniform domestic sales law. It has become the predominant law governing the international sales of goods. The CISG is the product of the United Nations Commission on International Trade Law (UNCITRAL), organized in 1966. UNCITRAL is dedicated to modernizing commercial law rules and unifying the law of international commerce. Between 1968 and 1980 UNCITRAL organized meetings and drafting groups to produce a uniform sales law. In 1980 in Vienna, a diplomatic conference attended by 62 countries unanimously approved the adoption of the CISG. The CISG entered into force, open for adoption by countries, on January 1, 1988. It is a multilateral treaty that is effective in nations that have adopted the convention by depositing instruments of adoption with the United Nations. To date 80 countries have done so. Almost all of the developed countries, including the United States, Japan and most of the member states of the European Union (but not the United Kingdom), and many developing countries such as China, Russia and Brazil have adopted it. In the future the CISG is likely to become the uniform law of sales governing most international trade in goods—the international counterpart of Article 2 of the UCC. To date signatory countries to the treaty represent over 60 percent of world trade. Already national courts have decided thousands of cases applying the CISG. The relevant diplomatic history and drafts of the CISG are collected in Documentary History of the Uniform Law for International Sales (J. Honnold ed., 1989). For detailed descriptions of the CISG's provisions, see Clayton P. Gillette & Steven D. Walt, The UN Convention on Contracts for the International Sale of Goods: Practice and Theory (2013); UN Convention on Contracts for the International Sales of Goods (CISG) (S. Kröll, L. Mistelis & P.P. Viscasillas eds., 2011); Schlechtriem & Schwenzer: Commentary on the UN Convention on the International Sales of Goods (CISG) (I. Schwenzer ed., 3d ed. 2010); and John O. Honnold, Uniform Law for International Sales Under the 1980 United Nations Convention (H.M. Flechtner ed., 4th ed. 2009).

The CISG does not provide for an international system of courts or other bodies for its interpretation or enforcement. This leaves its interpretation and enforcement to national courts or other tribunals. Arbitral tribunals in different countries will frequently be called on to construe the CISG because international sales contracts often provide for arbitration of disputes. These contracts might be governed by the CISG. Thus, there is a risk of significant diversity in the construal of the CISG by courts and arbitrators. Article 7(1) of the CISG tries to foster uniformity in interpretation. It expressly directs tribunals to recognize and adhere to CISG's international character and to promote uniformity in its interpretation. How successful Article 7(1)'s directive will be remains to be seen. One source of diversity in interpretation is the vagueness of a number of the CISG's provisions, discussed later in these materials. Tribunals can reach different but reasonable conclusions about what vague provisions require. Early interpretations of some of the CISG's provisions suggest a "homeward trend" whereby the forum court's construction of the CISG is influenced by its own domestic law. See, e.g., Obergericht des Kantons Luzern (Switzerland), 8 January 1997, available at http://cisgw3.law.pace.edu/cases/970108s1.html. Another factor driving this diversity is the degree of deference tribunals give interpretations offered by other judicial or arbitral tribunals. Uniformity requires coordination of interpretations of the CISG and therefore deference to the earlier resolution of an issue by a tribunal.

As a practical matter, tribunals might not defer to each other, despite the benefits of increased uniformity. For one thing, the deference given by other courts probably will depend on the identity of the precedent court. Put bluntly, a United States court is unlikely to adopt the interpretation of the CISG given by a Honduran or Ugandan court weight simply because the latter decided an issue first. In addition, the rank of the foreign court within its own legal system likely will matter. Although the Supreme Court has repeatedly said that foreign law interpreting a treaty is entitled to considerable weight, it also has added that only interpretations by a foreign country's highest court are entitled to this weight. See Olympic Airlines v. Husain, 540 U.S. 644, 655 n.9 (2004).

Finally, there is a problem of access to decisions of tribunals construing the CISG. The problem, however, is less serious than in the past. UNCITRAL created the CLOUT ("case law on UNCITRAL texts") reporting system in 1988. CLOUT collects and publishes abstracts of court decisions and arbitral awards interpreting the CISG, where available, as well as some complete reports. Selected CLOUT abstracts are reproduced in several of the chapters that follow. CLOUT also collects reports relating to all of the texts produced by UNCITRAL, not just the CISG. CLOUT's abstracts and reports are submitted by national correspondents who monitor, collect and summarize decisions in one of the United Nations' official languages. To date CLOUT has published several summaries of relevant case law, as part of the UNCITRAL "Digests" of case law under the CISG. The latest Digest collects case law through 2012; see UNCITRAL Digest of Case Law on the United Nations Convention on Contracts for the International Sale of Goods: 2012 Edition, available at http://www.uncitral.org/pdf/english/clout/CISG-digest–2012–e.pdf. The Digest also appears in hardcopy form in Special Issue, 30 J.L. & Comm. 1 (2013). To encourage uniformity in interpretation, UNCITRAL is considering establishing an editorial board in the CLOUT system. Material collected by CLOUT is available at http://www.uncitral.org/uncitral/en/case_law.html.

C. DEFAULT RULES AND SALES LAW

Contracts do not provide for every future contingency that might occur during the term of the contract. They also do not fully specify the obligations of the parties when these contingencies occur. As it is sometimes put, the contracts we observe are "incomplete." Parties fail to complete contracts for good reasons. For one thing, contracting is expensive and fully specifying the contract's terms might not be worth it for the parties. Some contingencies are so remote that, discounted by the probability of their occurrence, the expected savings from assigning obligations to the contingency is less than the cost of doing so. A contract price of $50 probably does not warrant addressing the seller's delivery obligation if a meteor shower prevents a Saturday morning delivery. Other contingencies might be so costly to discover as to not be worth even discovering in the first place. Finally, the practicalities of negotiation might preclude completion of a contract. Insistence that the contract provide for every contingency can signal unreliability as a contracting partner. A party who demands that every contingency be addressed by the contract risks being seen as a potentially difficult contracting partner. The barriers that prevent the production of a complete contract are transaction costs broadly understood: the costs of negotiating, executing and enforcing a contract.

Two questions arise about incomplete contracts: (1) should certain obligations be part of the contract, whatever the parties' agreement has provided?, and (2) how should the law provide terms to fill in gaps left by the parties' contract? The first question asks whether certain terms should be mandatory and could be asked even about complete contracts. Mandatory terms are terms that the parties cannot deviate from; they are part of any contract to which they apply, whatever the desires of the contracting parties. Mandatory terms are justifiable on the grounds of paternalism or the impact of a contract on third parties. Paternalism justifies a mandatory term as being in the best interests of the contracting parties in some specified sense of "best interest." Alternatively, a contract can create costs for persons not party to the contract which are not taken into account by contracting parties or reflected in the market price of the good for which they are contracting. These are costs that a contract "externalizes" onto others outside of the contract. When a contract externalizes costs, its enforcement might serve the interests of the contracting parties while not maximizing social welfare. A possible example of externalized costs concern judicial interpretations of contract terms. A judicial interpretation of a term in a parties' Contract 1 might make it more likely that another court will apply the same interpretation of the same term in other parties' Contract 2. If the interpretation frustrates the desires of the parties to Contract 2, adjudication of Contract 1 reduces the value of Contract 2 to its parties. The effect of judicial interpretation of terms on all contracts might justify making certain terms mandatory across contracts.

The UCC contains few mandatory terms. Section 1–302(a) allows the parties' agreement to vary the provisions of the UCC. There are only two limits placed on their power to do so. Parties cannot opt out of rules that "elsewhere in the UCC" are made mandatory. In addition, 1–302(b) does not allow variation by agreement of statutorily prescribed duties of good faith, diligence, reasonableness and care. However, it allows the parties' agreement to set standards by which these duties are measured, if not "manifestly unreasonable." This concession arguably qualifies the mandatory nature of the duties of good faith and the like under the UCC. Although some of the UCC's Articles contain some significant mandatory terms (e.g., 3–104(d), 4–403(a), 4A–402, 4A–404, 4A–405), Article 2 contains very few mandatory terms. This is unsurprising because Article 2 governs a wide range of sales transactions between firms and commercially sophisticated parties. Paternalistic concerns are out of place here. Externalities created by contracts also arguably are infrequent or not serious enough in their impact to warrant a broad swath of mandatory terms in Article 2.

The second question asks how the law should fill in gaps in the parties' contract. Rules that apply to a contract unless the parties' agreement provides otherwise are "default rules." Almost all of Article 2's rules can be varied by agreement. For instance, Article 2's rules set price (2–305(a)), time and place of delivery (2–308, 2–310(a)), excuse performance (2–615), and fix remedies (2–719(1)), unless altered by the parties' agreement. The CISG contains a similar range of default rules. Under Article 6 of the CISG, the parties can opt out of any of its provisions, except for certain formal requirements enforceable under the applicable domestic law of a contracting state. If the parties do not agree otherwise, the CISG's rules apply. Chapter 2, section D discusses this point. By supplying terms for agreements, default rules reduce transaction costs.

There are two possible standards for selecting default rules: the majoritarian standard and the penalty default standard. One recommendation is that the law select terms that most parties prefer.

More accurately, the law should select terms that most parties prefer, if the cost of contracting for different terms is the same for all parties. This is a "majoritarian" default standard. Providing terms that most parties want minimizes the sum of transaction costs in contracting for different terms (if the cost of contracting for different terms is the same for all parties). In saving most parties the cost of obtaining terms they desire, the joint surplus realized from their contracts is increased. The joint surplus is the difference between the returns to both parties from performance of the contract and the total cost to them of the contract, its performance and enforcement. Of course, each party is only concerned about its own contractual surplus, not the surplus realized by the other party. But a larger joint surplus is a larger "pie" to be allocated between the parties, so that each has an interest in reducing the transaction costs associated with the contract. Although a majoritarian default standard forces contracting parties with idiosyncratic—or minority—desires to incur costs to avoid being bound by unsuitable terms, the standard reduces transaction costs across similar contracts. For discussion of the majoritarian default standard, see Robert E. Scott & Jody S. Kraus, Contract Law and Theory 72 (5th ed. 2013); Charles J. Goetz & Robert E. Scott, the Limits of Expanded Choice: An Analysis of the Interaction Between Express and Implied Contract Terms, 73 Cal. L. Rev. 283 (1985).

A different standard for selecting default rules is a "penalty" or information-forcing standard. This standard advocates rules that supply terms that contracting parties would not have wanted. Default rules that supply such terms penalize these parties: the parties are bound by the terms unless their agreement provides otherwise. In order to contract for different terms, the rule encourages parties to reveal information to their contracting partners. Once the information is disclosed, both parties are equally well informed and can conclude an efficient contract on that basis. See Ian Ayres & Robert Gertner, Filling Gaps in Incomplete Contracts: An Economic Theory of Default Rules, 99 Yale L. J. 87 (1989). Thus, disclosure of information by one party can prevent a party from taking advantage of its information to obtain an inefficient contract. Penalty default rules are appropriate when one party has more information about a transaction than its contracting partner. In these circumstances of asymmetric information, disclosure of information allows contractual obligations to be allocated optimally to minimize the costs of performance. By contrast, a majoritarian standard would select a rule that most parties would prefer, even if the rule allows the party with more information to obtain a contract on inefficient but profitable terms.

An often-cited example of a penalty default is the foreseeability limitation on consequential damages. Under the limitation, damages are not recoverable for loss that the breaching party could not reasonably foresee at the conclusion of the contract as a likely result of its breach. A close variant on the facts of the well-known case of *Hadley v. Baxendale* illustrates the penalty character of the limitation. Assume that a common carrier transports goods under contracts with shippers. Assume also that the shippers are of two types: "low-value" and "high-value" shippers. "Low-value" shippers suffer few consequential damages if the carrier fails to deliver their goods. "High-value" shippers suffer significant consequential damages if their goods are not delivered.

Finally, assume that the carrier cannot identify a shipper's type without information supplied by the shipper.

The price the carrier charges a shipper includes the cost of carriage. This cost in turn reflects the risk that it will be liable for the shipper's loss in the event that the goods are not delivered. Because the carrier cannot identify a shipper as a low- or high-value shipper, the price it charges all shippers is the blended price for shipping the goods of both types of shippers. Correspondingly, it will take precautions for each shipment commensurate with the blended price it charges. If high-value shippers are atypical, so that the shipment of high-value goods is not reasonably foreseeable, the foreseeability limitation limits the carrier's liability. The carrier will be liable only for the extent of consequential damages suffered by low-value shippers if the goods are not delivered. These damages, by assumption, are few and high-value shippers therefore are undercompensated for their loss. As a result, *Hadley*'s foreseeability limitation is a penalty default: it sets a term high-value shippers do not prefer. High-value shippers wanting to increase the carrier's potential liability can disclose information about the extent of their loss if the goods are not delivered. Once disclosed their loss is reasonably foreseeable to the carrier. In response it can adjust the price of carriage upward to take into account its increased potential liability. Correspondingly, the carrier can take the precautions appropriate for high-value shipments. Thus, by "penalizing" the better informed party, the foreseebility limitation induces it to disclose information to get the terms it prefers.

Majoritarian and penalty default standards need not compete with each other. Nothing requires that there be a single standard for selecting rules to fill gaps in contracts under all circumstances. A majoritarian standard can be favored in some circumstances and a penalty default standard in others. A penalty default standard might be appropriate in cases of asymmetric information between contracting parties where the cost of opting out of a default rule are low. Majoritarian defaults are favored when parties are equally well informed or when the cost of aggregate contracting around a rule is high. In fact, penalty defaults can be understood as recommended by a majoritarian default standard. Most parties would prefer a rule that encourages a party with superior information to disclose it. This is because disclosure allows the contracting parties to optimally allocate obligations under the contract. In this way the joint surplus from performance of the contract is maximized. Of course, the party with superior information would rather not disclose the information once the party has acquired it: She instead prefers to use the information strategically to obtain a larger profit for itself. However, most parties selecting a rule before they transact (and without the superior information) prefer a rule that forces disclosure of information. Disclosure allows the selection of contract terms that will produce a larger joint surplus than otherwise. Article 2 of the UCC contains a mix of both majoritarian and penalty defaults.

D. DEFAULT STANDARDS VERSUS DEFAULT RULES

Most of Article 2 and the CISG's provisions apply unless varied by the parties' agreement. Cf. 1–302(a); CISG Article 6. They therefore are default rules. Almost all of Article 2 and the CISG's default rules are of a certain sort. These defaults do not prescribe in advance specific conduct required of the contracting parties. Instead, they prescribe a standard of conduct that is determinable only by taking into account the specific circumstances in which conduct occurs. The scholarly literature often refers to the former sort of prescription as a "rule" and the latter sort as a "standard." Put in these terms, Article 2 and the CISG's defaults are almost entirely standards, not rules. For instance, 2–309(1) provides that, if not otherwise provided for in Article 2 or in the agreement, the time in which delivery is to be made is a reasonable time. Article 33(c) of the CISG states a similar requirement. What constitutes a reasonable time obviously depends on the particular circumstances of the contract and the parties. Section 2–309(1) and Article 33(c) of the CISG therefore state a default standard for timely delivery. In fact, "reasonable" or its close counterpart "seasonable" are terms that appear in Article 2's provisions more than 30 times. For its part, the CISG also contains numerous provisions cast in similar terms. By one count, provisions appealing to "reasonableness" appear about 40 times in the CISG's 101 mostly brief Articles.

From the point of view of a majoritarian approach to default rules, default standards potentially are objectionable. The majoritarian approach favors terms that most contracting parties would agree to if they had bargained over them. These are terms that save most parties transaction costs in providing the terms of their agreements. Default standards, however, make it difficult for contracting parties to know in advance exactly how courts will apply them should litigation occur. Standards are not transparent in their application at the formation of the contract. Nor for that matter are standards transparent to the court applying them. To determine whether contractual performance satisfies the standard, the trier of fact must take particular circumstances into account. Opacity in a default term also allows parties to game contractual performance, especially if one party is sufficiently confident that its conduct will be found ex post not to be in breach of default terms. Because default standards are opaque, they increase parties' cost of enforcing contractual obligations. For these reasons, most parties would not prefer vague standards to apply to their contract. They would prefer instead precise rules determinable in advance. In addition, given their vagueness and simplicity, standards do not save on many transaction costs because parties could quite cheaply provide for themselves the same standards.

This criticism of default standards, if correct, condemns most (but not all) of Article 2's provisions. See Robert E. Scott, The Death of Contract Law, 54 U. Toronto L. J. 369 (2004); Alan Schwartz & Robert E. Scott, Contract Theory and the Limits of Contract Law, 113 Yale L. J. 541, 594–609 (2003). It has some indirect empirical support in the observed frequency with which parties in some industries or trade groups opt out of Article 2 or the CISG. For instance, the North Amercian Export Grain Association's standard form contract makes the CISG inapplicable. See NAEGA Contract No. 2, para. 27. However, Article 2's default standards still may be defensible. Article 2's scope is broad. It applies to a wide range of different sales transactions among an equally wide range of transactors, from organizations and natural persons, and across isolated and repeated sales. Low-value sales may not justify the same precise rule justified by a high-value sale; sophisticated transactors might prefer a rule to a standard to regulate their transaction. A low-value sale could justify the very modest reduction in transaction costs produced by a standard that would not be justified by a high-value sale. Article 2's default standards are justified if they provide terms most parties in a very diverse population of transactors and contracts would prefer. The minority of more sophisticated parties in specialized or complex sales transactions may have different preferences. If so, they can and will contract around Article 2 entirely or particular default standards within it. Parties may opt because their preference are unrepresentative of the populations of contracting parties whose contracts are subject to Article 2. The evidence of observed opting out of Article 2 therefore is consistent with Article 2's default standards being majoritarian standards. Ultimately, whether Article 2's default standards are justified turns on such empirical issues. See Steven Walt, The State of Debate Over the Incorporation Strategy in Commercial Law, 38 UCC L. J. 205 (2006).

A separate question is why Article 2 and the CISG contain mostly default standards, not precise rules, especially when contracting parties usually prefer precise rules to govern their contract. Even if the optimal defaults for sales law are standards, the organizations that produce defaults governing sales might select rules. Conversely, even if the optimal defaults are rules, they might select default standards to govern sales contracts. There is no guarantee that default-producing organizations select the optimal form of defaults. It therefore is worth asking why the organizations that produce Article 2 and the CISG choose to include mostly default standards in them. Focusing on the CISG, Professors Gillette and Scott explain the selection of default standards by the preferences of the participants and institutional processes through which the CISG was produced. The ALI and NCCUSL generate the UCC, including Article 2, while UNCITRAL, an organization of the United Nations, produced the CISG. See Clayton P. Gillette & Robert E. Scott, The Political Economy of International Sales Law, 25 Int'l Rev. L. & Econ. 446 (2005). Alan Schwartz and Robert E. Scott, The Political Economy of Private Legislation, 143 U. Pa. L. Rev. 595 (1995), provides a similar explanation of Article 2's production through the ALI and NCCUSL. The description below concerns Professors Gillette and Scott's explanation of the CISG's production.

The participants appointed by countries to draft the CISG were legal academics and governmental officials. Commercial interests were not represented and had an attenuated stake in the outcome of the drafting. Neither legal academics nor government officials has direct or indirect pecuniary interest in the type of default drafted; the primary motivation for both is to enhance their reputation and prestige within their professions. A successful drafting effort that is widely adopted enhances their reputation more than a failed drafting effort or a product that is adopted by few countries. Their professional reputation also is enhanced more by producing a draft covering a broader range of transactions than one covering a narrower range of transactions. For its part, UNCITRAL's objective also is to have uniform laws produced under its auspices be widely adopted. Although UNCITRAL officially does not require that their drafters all agree on a draft or consensus at the diplomatic conference at which the draft is approved, in practice consensus at both stages is the rule. Without consensus, the prospect of eventual widespread adoption of the CISG would have been jeopardized. Consensus requires the draft to be found acceptable by all participants from a wide range of different legal systems. Professors Gillette and Scott argue that the combination of the participant's desire to enhance their professional reputations and the need for consensus makes the production of a sales law with default standards likely and default rules unlikely.

A close examination reveals why cross-border consensus in developing defaults rules. A default rule conditions an outcome on facts that the contracting parties can determine in advance of litigation. For instance, the requirement that, unless otherwise agreed, the seller is obligated to deliver the goods at its place of business is a default rule. See, e.g., 2–308(a); CISG Article 31(c). The seller's place of business usually can be determined easily without the help of a court. By comparison, the default standard that obligates the seller to deliver at a reasonable location is applied with certainty only after litigation. Because default rules condition on specific and determinable facts, they risk being inconsistent with national sales laws. Representatives from these countries therefore might object to them. Even if UNCITRAL's participants found the default rules acceptable, the countries they represent might choose not to ratify a treaty containing them. Default standards are more likely to be find favor with the participants, because the vague language in which their terms are cast makes them unlikely to be inconsistent with national law. After all, national law is unlikely to have defaults that condition obligations on what is unreasonable or unseasonable or inconsistent with trade practice. Because the professional reputation of CISG's drafters is enhanced by drafting defaults that are likely enjoy widespread adoption, they prefer default standards to default rules. The CISG therefore contains default standards rather than rules.

True, the drafters might have supplied default rules while providing reservations that allowed adopting countries to avoid their application. However, this strategy risks the possibility that countries unhappy with the default rules will choose to make these reservations. A wide use of reservations leaves the application of the default rules to only a limited range of sales transactions. The limited application does not do much to enhance the reputation of the CISG's participants. Preferable to them are default standards that apply to a wider range of sales transactions than default rules that apply in a limited range of transactions.

E. A NOTE ON EFFICIENCY

At points in this book reference will be made to efficient and inefficient contract terms. Implicit in these references is a notion of efficiency and a standard for evaluating the law of sales. The notion of efficiency used is simple: efficiency is the greatest difference between gains and costs. How that difference is distributed between contracting parties is irrelevant from the standpoint of efficiency. Gains and costs often are financial gains and costs. Where the contracting parties are businesses, this is likely to be true. Where a party is a consumer, gain and cost may be partly nonfinancial. Although gains and costs may be hard to measure in such cases, gain and cost can be defined even there.

A contract term can be efficient either because it increases gains or reduces costs, compared to other alternative terms. In evaluating the law of sales, this book focuses on the effect of contract terms on the allocation of costs between the seller and buyer. The gains from the transaction are assumed to be unaffected by the allocation. The book's focus therefore is on a partial analysis of efficiency only. Of course, realistically the law regulating sales affects not just the cost of performing a sales contract and therefore the contract price. It also can affect the willingness to enter into a particular contract in the first place, the care with which a sales contract is performed, as well as the willingness to litigate or settle disputes arising from the sales contract. For example, a right to specific relief, where available, decreases the buyer's risk that a remedy for the seller's breach undercompensates her. At the same time, the remedy reduces the seller's expected profit from breach and therefore its incentive to search for profitable alternatives to contracts it has undertaken. The seller also incurs negotiation costs in arranging to "bribe" a buyer to waive its specific performance right. A complete analysis of the law of sales must be general, not partial. Such an analysis is infeasible.

Both the legal literature and this book sometimes evaluate the efficiency of a contract term by asking whether the contracting parties would prefer it to an alternative term. This is a roundabout but convenient way of asking about efficiency. Contracting parties prefer a term when it minimizes the relevant costs of the contract because by minimizing contracting costs for their transaction, the contract produces the largest difference between gains and costs. The larger the difference, the greater the net gain to be distributed among themselves under the contract. Thus, contracting parties prefer a term when and only when the term is efficient. One can assess the efficiency of a term directly. Alternatively, one can assess its efficiency indirectly, by asking whether the contracting parties prefer the term to an alternative term. The basis of the different assessments is the same—efficiency.

Finally, efficiency is a defensible normative criterion to use to evaluate the law of sales. The welfare of the contracting parties is a value, and gains and costs of a transaction affect their welfare. Efficiency is an instrumental value because it evaluates contract terms by their capacity to maximize the welfare of the contracting parties. This book uses efficiency as the only criterion to assess sales law. There are non-instrumental values, such as autonomy or perhaps community, and non-instrumental normative criteria associated with them. In the law of sales such criteria do not compete with efficiency. This is true for three principal reasons. First, these non-instrumental values often are inapplicable to the predominant parties to sales contracts. Concerns of autonomy, for instance, are inapplicable to business buyers and sellers. And not all the terms in a sales contract need affect the autonomy (suitably defined) of even consumer buyers or sellers. By contrast, efficiency is a criterion that is applicable to all sales transactions and parties. Second, non-instrumental values have nothing to say about the vast range of sales law. It is completely unclear how risk of loss, particular damages measures or the Statute of Frauds implicates autonomy, for instance. Third, as noted above, almost all of the law of sales consists of default rules. Rules that can be altered by agreement do not affect the autonomy of contracting parties. If parties do not like a particular rule, they can contract around it. In fact, if they dislike even the mandatory rules of a jurisdiction they can arrange to have their contract made subject to the law of another jurisdiction. True, a default rule parties dislike adds some cost to them in contracting for terms they prefer. But the same is true of all default rules, by their nature. Unless every party finds default terms satisfactory, at least some of them will prefer different terms. A rule that forces parties to incur costs in avoiding the application of default terms to their contracts therefore by itself cannot count as an interference with autonomy. See Richard Craswell, Contract Law, Default Rules, and the Philosophy of Promising, 88 Mich. L. Rev. 489 (1989).

PROBLEM 1.1

Article 2's Statute of Frauds requirements (discussed in Chapter 3) makes unenforceable qualifying contracts that do not satisfy 2–201's writing requirements. These requirements impose costs on contracting parties in memorializing their agreements. Section 2–201's requirements can be justified as a penalty default rule: Although the contracting parties prefer not to incur the cost of memorializing their agreement, 2–201 induces them to do so. By satisfying 2–201, the parties provide information about their contract that reduces proof costs otherwise imposed on the trier of fact and taxpayers. Ayres & Gertner, supra, at 95–96. Can 2–201 be justified as a majoritarian default rule?

PROBLEM 1.2

Section 2–608(1) permits a buyer to revoke its acceptance of a nonconforming good only if the nonconformity substantially impairs its value "to the buyer." Thus, the standard of revocation is subjective: A buyer's idiosyncratic and possibly undisclosed preferences can affect the extent to which a nonconformity in the goods impairs value. Because idiosyncratic preferences can justify revocation, a seller likely would either incur higher bargaining costs in setting a higher standard for revocation (or precluding revocation entirely) or take precautions against tendering nonconforming goods that allow revocation. In either case all sellers would charge their buyers a higher contract price to reflect these added costs. Accordingly, a majoritarian default rule might select a higher, objective standard for revocation. Can the same higher, objective standard be justified as a penalty default rule?

CHAPTER 2

THE SCOPE OF ARTICLE 2

The Uniform Commercial Code ("UCC") covers a range of commercial transactions, from sales, leases, checks, and promissory notes to wire transfers, investment securities and secured transactions. Each of its Articles regulates a particular type of transaction and provides mandatory and default rules peculiar to that transaction. Thus, it is important to determine the scope of each of the UCC's Articles. Of course, a transaction need not be regulated by only one of the UCC's Articles; many will governed by more than one Article. For instance, a sale of goods may be on credit whereby the good sold secures its purchase price. The sale creates a security interest in favor of the seller. Accordingly, Article 2 governs the sale and Article 9 the security interest aspects of transaction. To determine which Articles of the UCC apply, the characteristics of the transaction (e.g., sale, security interest) must be determined. Classification of the different aspects of the transaction for purposes of the UCC therefore still is necessary. Three basic but important questions about classification are common: when is a sales transaction governed by Article 2?, when is a transaction a lease rather than a sale regulated by Article 2A?, and when is an international sales transaction governed by the CISG and not Article 2? This Chapter deals with the scope of Article 2, Article 2A (leases), and the CISG, respectively.

A. SALES OF GOODS

Although Article 2 is entitled "Sales," 2–102 provides that "this Article applies to transactions in goods." "Transactions in goods" seems to include a broader range of dealings than just sales. A sale, as defined in 2–106(1), is a transfer of title in goods for a price. But 2–102's quoted language is expansive enough to cover transactions other than sales. A gift of a good is a type of "transaction" in goods, although it is not a sale or even an exchange. Article 2 has been held not to cover gift transactions; see Neuhoff v. Marvin Lumber and Cedar Co., 370 F.3d 197 (1st Cir. 2004). "Transaction" is not defined in Article 2 or elsewhere in the UCC. There are some limitations on Article 2's scope even if Article 2 applies to non-sales transactions. A number of Article 2's provisions by their terms apply only to sellers and buyers, including sections on warranties (2–314–2–316), tender of delivery (2–503) and remedies (2–714–2–719). These provisions therefore cannot apply to non-sales transactions, except by analogy. Other Articles of the UCC also limit Article 2's application to a non-sale transaction. A bailment of goods covered by a warehouse receipt and a lease of goods are "transactions" covered by Articles 7 and 2A, respectively. These transactions therefore are not governed by Article 2.

A sale of goods clearly is the most important "transaction in goods" covered by Article 2. A transaction can either call for the present sale of goods or the sale of goods in the future. Article 2 covers both sorts of transaction through a connected set of definitions. Under these definitions, a "present" sale of goods is a sale, and a sale of "future" goods is a contract of sale. According to 2–106(1), a sale is the passage of title to the good for a price. Section 2–401(1) in turn provides that title cannot pass until the goods have been identified to the contract. And under 2–501(1)(a) goods are "identified" to the contract when the contract is made if the goods are existing and identified. Thus, if existing goods are identified, their identification to the contract has occurred. Under 2–106(1) title to the good therefore can pass and the transaction passing it is a sale.

Sales of future goods are brought under Article 2 through other definitions. Section 2–106(1) provides that, unless context suggests otherwise, " 'contract' and 'agreement' are limited to those relating to the present or future sale of goods." Section 2–105(1) in turn defines "goods" as "things . . . which are movable at the time of identification to the contract for sale . . . " Thus, goods that have not been produced at the time of the contract cannot be identified as of that date. Under 2–105(1) they therefore cannot be "goods." Instead, they apparently are "future" goods. Section 2–106(1) defines a sale of "future goods" to be a contract for the sale of goods. Section 2–105(2) confirms this result: "A purported present sale of future goods . . . operates as a contract to sell." Therefore, "a sale of goods" includes sales of both present and future goods.

This sequence of definitions does not work perfectly. It has the odd result that future goods are not goods. Section 2–105(1)'s defines "goods" as that "things" that are moveable at the time of their "identification" to the contract. According to this definition "things" that have not been produced to date cannot be "goods." Thus, under this definition, "future" goods are not "goods." Because Article 2 covers transactions in goods, 2–105(1)'s definition of goods, read literally, means that contracts to sell goods not in existence are not covered by Article 2. This result is an unintended consequence: the drafting history of Article 2 clearly shows that it is meant to apply to wholly executory contracts for the sale of goods not yield procured or produced. See PEB Study Group: Uniform Commercial Code—Article 2 Preliminary Report 46 (1990). It also is meant to govern breaches of sales contracts in which the seller never procures or produces the goods. The unintended consequence is easily avoided by interpreting 2–105(1) so that "goods" are "things that are moveable at the time of identification to the contract for sale or that *would be moveable* were they to come into existence." Proposed 2–103(1)(k) expands the definition of "goods" to include future goods.

The difficulties in determining Article 2's scope have not primarily concerned contracts for the sale "future" goods. Rather, they have involved the items included in 2–105(1)'s definition of a good. The question has been whether a particular sales transaction is one for the sale of "goods." Regardless of whether Article 2 applies only to sales of goods or more broadly to other transactions in goods, the sale or other transaction must be one of "goods." The following case illustrates the consequences of finding a transaction not to involve a sale of goods.

Adel v. Greensprings of Vermont

United States District Court, District of Vermont, 2005
363 F. Supp.2d 692

■ Opinion By: WILLIAM K. SESSIONS III

Plaintiffs Leslie and Joanne Adel are a married couple from Vineland, New Jersey. Defendant Greensprings of Vermont, Inc. ("Greensprings") is a Vermont corporation with its principle place of business in Vermont. Greensprings owns and operates the Greenspring at Mt. Snow resort in West Dover, Vermont.

* * *

Together with their two children and eight friends, Leslie and Joanne Adel went on a ski vacation in southern Vermont from February 3 through February 7, 1999. The vacationers stayed in Unit 24 at Greenspring. Greenspring is a townhouse condominium owned by Thomas and Charlene Fallarco. The townhouse condominium is part of a larger complex developed by defendant Greensprings. Greensprings owns and maintains the water supply for the Greenspring condominiums. Greensprings also owns and maintains common areas of the complex such as a swimming pool and spa at the Greenspring recreation center. While he was in Vermont, Leslie Adel used the swimming pool and spa at the Greenspring recreation center as well as the bathrooms, showers and a bathtub Jacuzzi in Unit 24.

On February 9, 1999, two days after he returned from his ski vacation, Adel began to experience flu-like symptoms. Unfortunately, his condition steadily worsened and he was transferred to the Hospital of the University of Pennsylvania on February 16.

On February 17, a physician took a sputum specimen from Adel's lungs. The hospital laboratory cultured Legionnella pneumonphila from that specimen on February 23. As a result, Adel was diagnosed as suffering from Legionnaires' disease. Adel was hospitalized at the Hospital of the University of Pennsylvania for six weeks. His bout with Legionnaires' disease was serious and included 45 days in a coma. Adel claims to have suffered permanent injuries as a result of contracting Legionnaires' disease.

On February 23, 1999, Nancy Thayer of the epidemiology division of the Vermont Department of Health ("DOH") received a report that Adel had Legionnaires' disease. Ms. Thayer began an investigation into the possible sources of Adel's illness.

The primary means of transmission of Legionnaires' disease is the inhalation of aerosolized water droplets containing the Legionnella pneumonphila bacteria. The incubation period for Legionnaires' disease is usually between 2 and 14 days. Thus, Adel's Vermont vacation fell within the potential incubation period.

On February 24, 1999, the DOH sent sanitarian Alfred Burns to Greenspring to collect swabs and water samples. Burns collected 33 samples from locations at the Greensprings complex. These included seven samples from the spa in the recreation center and nine samples from inside unit 24. Of all the samples taken, two returned positive tests for Legionella pneumophila. The positive tests were from a jug of water collected from a bathroom on the lower floor of unit 24 and a jug of water collected in the upstairs master bathroom in Unit 24.

Burns also inspected the spa in the recreation center. This inspection revealed many deficiencies. Burns found that there was no written operating manual as required by DOH regulations. Similarly, there was no written log of hourly and weekly tests. More seriously, the free chlorine/bromine levels were not within the required range of between 2 and 5 parts per million. Burns found a free chlorine/bromine level of 0.00 parts per million. Burns gave the spa an overall rating of unsatisfactory.

On June 7, 1999, the DOH sent cultures from the positive samples from Unit 24 to the United States Centers for Disease Control and Prevention ("CDC") for further testing. On June 24, 1999, the CDC performed a test known as monoclonal antibody subtyping. This test revealed that both cultures were Legionella pneumophila serogroup 1, monoclonal antibody pattern 1,2,5,6. The CDC also tested a culture from the sputum specimen taken from Adel on February 17, 1999. On August 3, 1999, the CDC identified that culture as Legionella pneumophila serogroup 1, monoclonal antibody pattern 1,2,5,6.

The plaintiffs have disclosed Dr. Jennifer Clancy ("Clancy") as an expert on liability and causation. Clancy concludes that "to a reasonable degree of scientific certainty, negligent operation and maintenance of the Greensprings water system caused the growth of legionellae in the system and the subsequent infection of Mr. Adel." In support of her view that Greensprings was negligent in maintaining the water system, Clancy points to evidence of reporting violations, failures to conduct required testing, inadequate well vents and inadequate storage overflow at Greensprings. The defendants claim that this evidence is insufficient to support a conclusion that any negligence on their part led to the presence of Legionella in the Greensprings water supply.

* * *

Greensprings owns and operates the water system that provides water to the Greenspring apartment complex and to the public recreation center. Although this water system is privately owned, it is regulated by the State of Vermont as a public system.

Apartment owners at Greenspring have water meters at their apartments. They do not get billed according to the meter readings, however. Greensprings sends a monthly bill to the Greenspring at Mt. Snow Homeowners' Association for all of its water services. The Homeowners' Association then sends a bill to each condo owner. These bills are calculated on a per-capita basis.

In 1999, Rubin had primary responsibility for the water system at the Greensprings complex. Among other duties, Rubin was responsible for the maintenance and testing of the water supply. Defendant Glennon is licensed as a water system operator by the State of Vermont. He acquired this license so that there would be someone available with a license if other operators left Greensprings. Nevertheless, Glennon did not play any direct role in managing the water supply and he did not closely supervise Rubin's work in this regard.

* * *

The Warranty of Merchantability

A warranty of merchantability is implied only "if the seller is a merchant with respect to goods of that kind." Vt. Stat. Ann. tit. 9A § 2–314 (2004). The Vermont Supreme Court has not decided whether a water supplier is a "seller" of a "good" under Vermont's version of the UCC. This Court must therefore predict how the Vermont Supreme Court would rule if it were faced with this question. This is a difficult task as decisions from other state courts are divided. Nevertheless, the Court is persuaded by the reasoning of those decisions finding that water suppliers are sellers of goods under Article 2 of the UCC.

The Court and the parties have identified eight cases that consider whether water suppliers are sellers of goods under Article 2 of the UCC. Six courts have held that water is a good and that water suppliers are merchants. In contrast, only two courts have held that the furnishing of water is not a sale of goods under the UCC. Thus, a clear majority of the jurisdictions that have considered the issue hold that water is a good under the UCC.

The situation is less clear when we turn to the question of whether water suppliers can be held liable for a breach of the warranty of merchantability. The issue is complicated by the fact that two courts have held that, even though the furnishing of water is covered by the UCC, the warranty of merchantability does not apply. The Court finds the reasoning of these cases very unpersuasive. In Sternberg v. N.Y. Water Serv. Corp., 548 N.Y.S.2d 247, 248 (N.Y. App. Div. 1989), the court followed, without any further analysis, Canavan v. City of Mechanicville, 229 N.Y. 473, 128 N.E. 882 (N.Y. 1920). However, Canavan does not even consider the UCC, which is unsurprising considering that it was decided many decades prior to New York's adoption of the UCC. As Sternberg simply relies on *Canavan*, it provides little guidance on the scope of the UCC's warranty of merchantability. Dakota Park Indus. v. City of Huron, 638 N.W.2d 884 (S.D. 2002), is also unpersuasive. The *Dakota Pork* court follows *Sternberg* and *Canavan* without noting that this line of cases rests on authority that predates the UCC.

This Court rejects the approach of *Dakota Pork* and *Sternberg*. If the furnishing of water is covered by Vermont's version of the UCC then the warranty of merchantability should apply. The statute clearly states that "unless excluded or modified (§ 2–316), a warranty that the goods shall be merchantable is implied in a contract for their sale if the seller is a merchant with respect to goods of that kind." Vt. Stat. Ann. tit. 9A § 2–314 (2004). Thus, if a seller of water is a merchant with respect to water, there is an implied warranty. The statute provides no basis to grant a special exemption for sellers of water.

This means that the key issue is whether or not sellers of water are merchants with respect to water. As noted above, a majority of courts have found that they are. Nevertheless, the defendants ask the Court to follow the recent decision by the Appeals Court of Massachusetts in Mattoon v. City of Pittsfield, 775 N.E.2d 770 (Mass Ct. App. 2002). The *Mattoon* court held that water providers are not merchants because the provision of water is primarily the rendition of services rather than the sale of goods.

The *Mattoon* court argued as follows:

Here, the city did not create or manufacture the water. Rather, the city, by a system of reservoirs, captured the water from brooks, streams, and rainfall. It treated the water and then distributed it to its citizens. Although the city charged a sum for the water, that rate reflected the cost of storage, treatment and distribution. Thus, it is clear that the predominant factor, thrust, or purpose of the activity was the rendition of services and not the sale of goods. *Mattoon*, 775 N.E.2d at 784. The defendants claim that this argument can be applied directly to the facts of this case. Just like the city in *Mattoon*, the defendants merely captured, treated and distributed the water. Thus, the defendants ask the Court to conclude that they were simply providing a service.

There are a number of reasons for rejecting the reasoning of *Mattoon*. First, the argument starts with an irrelevant premise. An item can be a "good" under the UCC even if the seller did not create or manufacture it. This is made clear by Vt. Stat. Ann. tit. 9A § 2–107 (2004) which provides that a contract for the sale of minerals or the like (including oil and gas) . . . to be removed from realty is a contract for the sale of goods within this article if they are to be severed by the seller." See also *Gall*, 555 A.2d at 789 n.2 (noting that crude oil is considered a good under Article 2 of the UCC); Restatement (Second) of Torts § 402A, cmt. e (noting that strict liability could apply to someone who sold a toxic mushroom). Thus, *Mattoon* is incorrect in so far as it suggests that water is not a good because it is captured rather than manufactured. Moreover, even if this were a relevant factor, the defendants alter the water when they treat it.

Mattoon also places undue emphasis on the fact that the cost of water reflects the cost of storage, treatment and distribution. The provision of goods always includes service elements such as storage and distribution. Thus, all sellers of goods will incur such costs and water providers are not unique in this regard.

The Supreme Court of Pennsylvania has taken a better approach to this question. See Gall v. Allegheny County Health Dep't., 555 A.2d 786, 788–90 (Pa. 1989). When deciding whether water is a "good" under Article 2 of the UCC, the *Gall* court focused on the UCC's definition of "good." Under the UCC, " 'Goods' means all things (including specially manufactured goods) which are movable at the time of identification to the contract for sale." Water satisfies these requirements. As the Gall court notes, "all who have paid bills for water can attest to its movability." *Gall*, 555 A.2d at 789. In this case, the defendants extract water from an underground aquifer. Thus, their sale may also qualify as a sale of goods under Vt. Stat. Ann. tit. 9A § 2–107 which provides that the "the sale of minerals or the like (including oil and gas)" is a sale of goods within Article 2 of the UCC.

The defendants regularly provide water to the homeowners at the Greensprings complex. These homeowners pay for the water on a per-capita basis. As water is a good, the defendants are merchants with respect to water. Thus, a warranty of merchantability is implied in the defendants' sale of water. Consequently, the defendants are not entitled to summary judgment on Count II of the complaint. * * *

NOTES

1. *Adel* is one of a number of cases that ask whether a particular item of personal property is a "good." The same inquiry arises when the subject matter of the transaction is electricity or gas; see GFI Wisconsin v. Reedsbury Hill Utility Commission, 440 B.R. 791 (W.D. Wis. 2010) (collecting cases). Because under 2–102 Article 2 applies to "transactions in goods," the character of personal property must be determined. Aside from sheer accuracy, it is worth asking why determining Article 2's scope is important. The answer concerns Article 2's default rules. Article 2 contains default rules that may be different from the rules that apply under general contract law or other law. So the rules applicable to a transaction can depend on the law applicable to it. The parties in *Adel* are fighting over the law applicable to their sale of water because of the implied warranties made in connection with a sale. One of the implied warranties central in *Adel* is the implied warranty of merchantability. Section 2–314 creates an implied warranty of merchantability if (1) the contract is for the sale of goods and (2) the seller is a merchant with respect to good of the kind sold. To be merchantable, the goods inter alia must be fit for the ordinary purposes for which good of that description are used. 2–314(2)(c). General contract law does not create an implied warranty of merchantability. Thus, although the issue as presented in *Adel* is whether water is a good, at bottom the issue of concern is the application of an implied warranty of merchantability to a transaction involving water.

2. Matoon v. City of Pittsfield, 775 N.E.2d 770 (Mass. Ct. App. 2002), on facts similar to those in *Adel*, finds Article 2 to be inapplicable to a sale of water by a city. At issue in *Matoon* also is the application of an implied warranty of merchantability to the sale. *Matoon* concluded that water is not a good and, alternatively, a contract providing for the city's supply of water a contract predominantly for services. *Adel* criticizes *Matoon*'s assumption that a good must be created or manufactured. In a part of the opinion in *Matoon* not referred to by *Adel* the court adds that "[s]ound public policy helps dictate our result . . . The cost to protect the water in the reservoirs would be prohibitive. Therefore, we hold that the code [Article 2] did not cover in this instance the city's provision of water to its citizens." *Matoon*, 775 N.E.2d 770 at 784. The *Matoon* court believed that the burden to the city of taking precautions to detect impurities in its water is greater ("prohibitive") than the reduction in expected risk to the buyers of receiving impure water. The city's burden is a cost to it, and the reduction in risk to the buyers is an expected benefit to them. *Matoon* concludes that Article 2 is inapplicable to the sale in part because imposing the obligation to detect impurities in the water is not cost-justified. The seller's cost of detecting impurities exceeds its buyers' expected benefit of receiving impure water. Because Article 2 is inapplicable, the city's sale of water does not create an implied warranty of merchantability.

Matoon need not have deemed Article 2 inapplicable to the sale in order to find that the sale did not create the warranty. It instead could have found the city not to be a "merchant" with respect to the water. 2–104(1), Comment 1 to 2–104. If the city is not a merchant seller of water, no implied warranty of merchantability arises in connection with the sale. Thus, *Adel* and *Matoon* can be understood as disagreeing over whether a seller of water is a "merchant." Notice that not all sellers of water need be "merchants" with respect to it. To be a merchant under 2–104(1), the seller must "deal in goods of the kind." The sellers in *Adel* and *Matoon* arguably are different with respect to their capacity to undertake cost-justified precautions. The defendant in *Adel* owned and operated a spa; the city in *Matoon* supplied water to its residents obtained from other reservoirs. The spa owner in *Adel* provided water in the rooms rented to guests and spa facilities available to them. It had fewer water-producing facilities and customers than the city in *Matoon*. These differences might affect the sellers' respective costs of taking precautions against delivering contaminated water. They can bear on whether a seller is considered a "merchant" for purposes of 2–314's implied warranty of merchantability. Chapter 4 discusses this point in more detail. The merchant status of a seller frequently is in issue; see The Andersons, Inc. v. Drobny, 1998 U.S. Dist. LEXIS 5146, at *1 (W.D. Mich. 1998) (farmers), Cook v. Downing, 891 P.2d 611 (Okla. Ct. App. 1994) (dentists).

3. The issue of Article 2's scope arises in connection with information technology. Agreements to distribute electronic data, including computer software, interactive media and databases, call for the transfer of data. The transfer may occur through the sale of a diskette containing the data or transmission of the data to the purchaser's computer. In both cases the data are embodied ultimately in a tangible form. Agreements to distribute electronic data typically call for the sale of computer diskette or computer to the purchaser. The purchaser, however, only is licensed to use the information on the diskette or computer: The seller continues to own the rights to the information. A sale of goods occurs when computer information is sold in a tangible form. The question is whether Article 2 also governs the computer information embedded in goods sold. A number of courts have found software to be goods when embedded in disc form or computer hardware; see, e.g., Advent Systems Ltd. v. Unisys Corp., 925 F.2d 670 (3d Cir. 1991); Multi–Tech Systems, Inc. v. Floreat, Inc., 47 UCC Rep. Serv.2d 924 (D. Minn. 2002). Judicial opinion is more divided over whether Article 2 governs the online sale of "virtual goods" such as software programs. "Virtual goods" consist of electronic codes stored in a data base. They are not embedded in physical objects and have no physical location. Software programs sold over the internet therefore do not easily fall under 2-105(1)'s definition of "goods," which requires that the item be "moveable at the time of identification to the contract." Compare Rottner v. AVG Technologies USA, Inc., 80 UCC Rep. Serv.2d 730, 737 (D. Mass. 2013) (sale of standardized computer program comparable to a sale of tangible good) with Specht v. Netscape Commc'ns. Corp., 306 F.3d 17, 29 n.13 (2d Cir. 2002) (Article 2 does not obviously apply to downloaded software).

In 1999 NCCUSL approved the Uniform Computer Information Act (UCITA) for adoption by states. See Uniform Computer Information Transactions Act (UCITA) (1999), available at http://www.law.upenn. edu/bll/archives/ulc/ucita/ucita200.pdf. UCITA does not govern an agreement merely because the agreement calls for the transmission of electronic data. Instead, UCITA basically applies to a transaction in computer information only if the primary purpose of the transaction is to obtain access to the information. UCITA § 103(b)(1). It also applies to copies or documentation containing computer information. UCITA § 102(10). Accordingly, UCITA does not govern goods or computer information embedded in them where the purchaser's primary purpose is to buy the goods. An example is the purchase of a car containing a computerized braking system. UCITA considers such information part of the car and subject to Article 2. UCITA, Comment to § 103. At the same time, where UCITA applies computer information embodied in goods is not subject to Article 2. To date only two states (Maryland and Virginia) have adopted UCITA. Several states even have enacted "bombshelter" provisions which make agreements selecting UCITA unenforceable against their residents. In most states the question of whether Article 2 governs computer information embedded in goods therefore remains open.

4. The controversy over Article 2's application to computer information is reflected in Proposed Article 2, which was withdrawn in 2011. UCITA draws a distinction between types of goods embodying computer information, to which UCITA applies, and other types of goods also embodying computer information, to which UCITA is inapplicable. UCITA § 103(b)(1). This requires distinguishing roughly between goods that are computers or contain computer programs and goods that contain computer programs but are not computers or computer peripherals. The distinction is hard to draw in practice. When is a good a "smart good" rather than a computer or computer peripheral containing computer information? Draft versions of Proposed Article 2 proposed to extend Article 2's scope to computer programs embedded in goods in prescribed ways. The difficulty of identifying these prescribed ways led to the elimination of the proposal from the final version of Proposed Article 2.

Proposed Article 2 did not make Article 2's regulation of computer information less uncertain. In fact, the proposed amendments arguably increased the uncertainty. Proposed 2–102 left 2–102 unchanged. For its part, Proposed 2–103(1)(k) expressly excluded "information" from the definition of "goods." Thus, by excluding computer information from the definition of "goods," seemingly Proposed Article 2 did not regulate information embedded in goods. However, Comment 7 to Proposed 2–103 created doubt: ". . . [T]his article has been amended to exclude information not associated with goods. Thus, this article does not directly apply to an electronic transfer of information . . . However, transactions often include both goods and information . . . For example, the sale of 'smart goods' such as an automobile contains many computer programs. . . . When a transaction includes both the sale of goods and the transfer of rights in information, it is up to courts to determine whether the transaction is entirely within or outside of this article . . . " The first two sentences quoted excluded information from Proposed Article 2's scope. However, the next two sentences left the question of Article 2's regulation of transactions involving information to the courts (as does current Article 2). This presupposes that Proposed Article 2 did not exclude information from its scope. Professor Henning recounts the history of Proposed Article 2's treatment of embedded software; see

William H. Henning, Amended Article 2: What Went Wrong?, 11 Duq. Bus. L.J. 134, 136–38 (2008).

PROBLEM 2.1

To which of the following transactions does Article 2 of the UCC apply? Consult 2–102, 2–105(1)–(2), 2–107(1)–(2), 2–304(2), 2–401, 2–501(1).

(a) A contract for the sale of wood that the buyer is to cut.

(b) A contract for the sale of a Honda Accord in exchange for a year's lease of the buyer's lawnmower.

(c) A contract for widget to be produced within three months.

(d) A contract to write a casebook on sales law.

(e) A contract to purchase 10 French 100 franc bank notes.

(f) A contract to sell both a compact disc containing music and the music on it.

(g) A contract to purchase an option to buy a Honda Accord at a specified price.

(h) A contract for the sale of electricity, the amount used to be calculated by meter readings.

B. HYBRID TRANSACTIONS

Transactions often consist of both a sale of goods and the undertaking of other contractual obligations. These are hybrid transactions. Hiring a photographer to take wedding pictures and supply copies of the photos taken or an electrician to install light fixtures she provides are examples. They involve contracts for the sale of goods along with the hire of services. Another sort of hybrid transaction is a sale of goods in which computer information is embedded, such as the sale of a "smart good." The contract here calls for the sale of goods and the license of information embedded in the goods. Almost all sales contracts involve some element of a service, at least in the uninteresting sense that labor is required to produce or procure a manufactured good. The invoice price of my customized widget might reflect the cost of labor expended by the manufacturer to meet my order. The presence of labor as an input into the production of a good does not make a contract a hybrid transaction. My contract with the manufacturer is for the delivery of a customized widget, not for the labor needed to customize it. A hybrid transaction is one in which the contract calls for the sale of a good along with the undertaking of other contractual obligations, such as the supply of services or computer information. Because 2–102 makes Article 2 applicable to "transactions in goods," courts must determine when a hybrid transaction is a transaction in goods.

AAF–McQuay, Inc. v. MJC, Inc.

United States District Court, Western District of Virginia, 2002
47 UCC Rep. Serv.2d 48

■ Memorandum Opinion JUDGE JAMES H. MICHAEL, JR.

* * *

The following facts are undisputed, unless otherwise noted. The plaintiff, AAF–McQuay, Inc., a Delaware corporation with its principal place of business in Kentucky, manufactures, sells and services heating, ventilating and air conditioning equipment. At its plant in Staunton, Virginia, the plaintiff manufactures air conditioning units known as "chillers." The chillers are cooled through an internal system of 20–foot–long finned tube condenser coils with as many as 16 metal fins per inch of coil. The plaintiff offers its customers the option of having an anti-corrosive coating applied to the condenser coils in the chiller. One such option was to purchase Heresite P–413, a baked phenolic coating, developed by Heresite Protective Coatings, Incorporated.

Under an agreement with Heresite Protective Coatings, the defendant, MJC, Inc., a Georgia corporation, held the exclusive regional license for use of the coating and the special application technique. The application process involved several stages. In the initial stage, the coils are degreased, sandblasted and etched. Afterwards, the coils are immersed multiple times in vats of the Heresite P–413 coating. After each of the first three immersions, the coating is partially cured by baking the coil in an oven. After the fourth immersion, the coil is sprayed with an additional coating and then cured.

From January 1995 until May 1998, the plaintiff sent those coils which required Heresite P–413 coating to the defendant. The plaintiff shipped the coils together with a corresponding purchase order. Certain terms and conditions were printed on the back of the purchase order, including, inter alia, that upon acceptance by seller, the purchase order constituted a contract, and that the seller expressly warranted the product or services to be delivered or performed. Upon receipt of the shipment, the defendant would issue a confirmation form which contained no additional terms and conditions and then proceed to coat the coils. The resulting invoice which the defendant subsequently sent to the plaintiff also contained no additional terms or conditions.

The plaintiff's coils, at 20 feet in length, were longer than the defendant's vats, which were 16 feet long. The defendant used a process, known as flooding, which involved spraying the coating onto the coils. The plaintiff maintains that the correct coating process in such cases involves dipping half of the coil, revolving it, and dipping the other half. The defendant recognizes that special procedures are necessary to coat oversized coils, but argues that its approach, of spraying the coating onto the coils, was an acceptable application technique.

In January 1997, the plaintiff states that it received reports that the Heresite P–413 coating was peeling off the condenser coils of one of its units in Hawaii. The coating itself was being pulled into the condenser and restricting air flow. Moreover, the impact on the performance of the condenser caused failures in other parts of the unit, including condenser fan motors and compressors. Similar complaints were made by other customers two years later. According to plaintiff, problems have been reported on at least 31 units. The plaintiff attributes these problems to the defendant's improper preparation and application of the coating. The plaintiff further contends that the defendant failed to respond in a timely manner when the plaintiff contacted it about the coating failures.

The defendant asserts that its spray technique was a proper application process under its licensing agreement with Heresite Protective Coatings. It further represents that the plaintiff failed to provide it with specifics as to which coils had problems. Nevertheless, the defendant states it offered to perform field fixes with a new coating product, but before this could be arranged, the defendant learned that the plaintiff had filed a lawsuit against it.

* * *

The defendant moves for summary judgment on several grounds, including that the statute of limitations has run; that no meeting of the minds occurred between the parties; that even if a contract existed, no general breach occurred because it was fully performed; and that the only applicable warranty in this case is the defendant's written one-year express warranty. The defendant bases its arguments on the premise that the common law of contracts, and not the Virginia version of the Uniform Commercial Code is the applicable law in this case. To reach this conclusion, the defendant contends that the transactions at issue in this case were for services, namely, for the service of applying the Heresite P–413 coating to the coils.

Thus, the threshold question for the court to address is whether the transaction was one for the sale of goods or the provision of services. While the UCC is intended to apply to transactions in goods, the Code may also apply to a transaction which involves a mixture of goods and services. A court must examine the transactions and determine "whether their predominant factor, their thrust, their purpose, reasonably stated, is the rendition of service, with goods incidentally involved (e.g., contract with artist for painting) or is a transaction of sale, with labor incidentally involved (e.g., installation of a water heater in a bathroom)." See Princess Cruises, Inc. v. General Electric Co., 143 F.3d 828, 833 (4th Cir. 1998). Among the factors for the court to consider are: "(1) the language of the contract, (2) the nature of the business of the supplier, and (3) the intrinsic worth of the materials." See Coakley & Williams, Inc. v. Shatterproof Glass Corp., 706 F.2d 456, 460 (4th Cir. 1983).

In analyzing the language of the contract, a court looks for terms peculiar to goods. These terms include "purchase order," "buyer" or "seller," as well as such references as "defects in workmanship and materials." In contrast, references to "service engineer" or "quotation for services" have lead to the logical conclusion that a contract was for services.

In this case, the plaintiff issued a purchase order for the coils which were to be shipped to the defendant. The forms provided columns for "quantity," "product description" and "unit price." The invoices issued by the defendant for the work done contain the same terms. Thus, the

vocabulary of the documentation in this case suggests terms peculiar to
transactions in goods. The court recognizes the difficulty in ascertaining
the significance of words found on a standard form. While the court will
certainly weigh this factor in its analysis, it is an examination of the
second factor which the court finds most helpful in determining what
the predominant purpose of this transaction was.

The defendant contends that no goods were sold in the transactions
with the plaintiff; rather, only the service of applying the Heresite
coating was provided. However, an analysis of the defendant's own
marketing and sales literature reveals that the nature of the
defendant's business was more than that of a service provider. First,
the defendant issued an estimated pricing schedule for "Heresite
Coating for Coils" and offered the price of coating per square feet of
tubes. No separate calculation of cost for application of the coating is
made. Second, in its marketing literature, the defendant promoted the
coating with claims such as: "Heresite P413 is the only pure phenolic
coils coating on the market with a plasticizer. The plasticizer allows for
thermal expansion and contraction of the coil without cracking the
coating." The defendant advertised that such coating "extends the life of
any coil by at least three (3) times as compared to a non-Heresite coil"
and claimed such a coating "is the BEST protection for your finned
coils." Based on these representations, the court finds that the
defendant is soliciting business as a provider of the Heresite coating.
The court recognizes that the defendant offered a package deal in that a
customer could not separately purchase the coating. The court further
acknowledges that the application process of the coating is critical to
making the coating as effective as is claimed. However, things are "not
the less 'goods' within the definition of the act because service may play
a role in their ultimate use." Bonebrake v. Cox, 499 F.2d 951, 958 (8th
Cir. 1974). As the *Bonebrake* court reasoned, the fact that the
transactions involved substantial amounts of labor, here in the form of
applying the Heresite coating, does not remove them from inclusion
under the Code.

The defendant believes a different conclusion is required based on
the third factor, the intrinsic worth of the materials, and in particular
on how the Fourth Circuit analyzed this factor in *Princess Cruises*. In
that case, the court noted that the value of the materials was never
separately itemized on the purchase orders and price quotes. Instead,
these documents "blended the cost of materials into the final price of a
services contract, thereby confirming that services rather than
materials predominated in the transaction." See *Princess Cruises, Inc.*,
143 F.3d at 833–34. The defendant argues that because the purchase
orders and invoices in this case fail to differentiate the cost of the
coating from the cost of its application, this court should likewise find
that services predominated in the transaction.

However, the failure to separate the cost of materials from the cost
of application on a purchase order does not automatically mean that
services predominate in a transaction. In *Princess Cruises*, the Fourth
Circuit viewed the failure to list on the contract the small number of
parts involved in that transaction as further support for its finding that
services predominated in the case (having already noted that the price
quote stated in large print, "Quotation for Services," and actually listed

the service functions to be performed). Thus, the *Princess Cruises* court looked at the third factor within the context of the other factors. This court shall do the same.

It is true that the purchase orders and invoices in this case do not provide separate prices for the coating and its application. However, the failure to provide a price for the application of coating only bolsters the court's finding that it was the good, that is, the Heresite coating, which was the predominant thrust of the transaction. As was already discussed above, the defendant indicated on its price list that the price being quoted was for coating. Moreover, the defendant's marketing materials clearly sell Heresite P–413 coating, not the application process. In *Princess Cruises*, the plaintiff purchased services which required the provision of some parts, while here, the plaintiff purchased a good, the coating, which required application.

The defendant also argues that the failure to differentiate the cost of the coating from the application costs provides proof that the coating is not a good because it is not "movable at the time of identification to the contract for sale . . . " Va. Code. Ann. § 8.2–105(1). According to the defendant, no unit of measure can be identified for the coating at the time of contracting, and as such, it does not fall under the definition of a good under the UCC. The court disagrees. Although the plaintiff could not purchase the coating separately, for example, by the gallon, the good itself at the time of the contract is in a movable form. Indeed, the defendant's own licensing agreement stipulates that the defendant shall purchase the coating from Heresite Protective Coating at a price of $26.00 for a U.S. gallon.

Accordingly, the court finds that the transactions at issue in this case were for goods, and as such, that the Virginia UCC applies. This finding moots the defendant's claim that the three-year statute of limitations for breach of an unwritten contract had run. Under Va. Code Ann. § 8.2–725(1), a claim for breach of a sales contract must be brought within four years after the cause of action accrued. Accrual occurs when the breach is or should have been discovered. As such, those claims of plaintiff, which accrued on or after May 22, 1997, are properly before the court.

With the defendant's contractual law grounds for summary judgment moot, what remains is a record replete with genuine issues of material fact. The court reiterates that it must examine the facts in a light most favorable to the non-movant. As such, the plaintiff argues that it never received the express written warranty which the defendants argue applies in this case. The defendant is free to dispute the plaintiff's claim at trial, but for the purposes of a summary judgment motion, the court considers that the issue concerning possible breach of the UCC warranties still exists. Furthermore, the central factual issues remain; namely, whether the spray technique was a proper method for application of the coating and whether this was responsible for the problems with the plaintiff's coils. Therefore, the court does not find that only one conclusion can be reached based on the facts and law of this case.

Ole Mexican Foods, Inc. v. Hanson Staple Company

Supreme Court of Georgia, 2009
676 S.E.2d 169

■ Opinion by: CARLEY, JUSTICE

Appellee Hanson Staple Company brought suit for breach of contract, alleging that Appellant Ole Mexican Foods, Inc. failed to purchase over $300,000 worth of packaging which was specially manufactured by Appellee for Appellant. In its answer, Appellant denied all liability and asserted in a counterclaim that Appellee had "breached its agreement with [Appellant] by shipping defective product." Thereafter, the parties negotiated a handwritten "agreement reached in settlement," outside the presence of counsel, which provided, in relevant part, that Appellant would "purchase a minimum of $130,000 worth of current inventory from" Appellee and would "test the remainder of inventory and . . . purchase additional inventory if it meets quality expectations." On a motion to enforce the settlement agreement, the trial court ordered Appellant to "purchase a minimum of $130,000 worth of [certain of Appellee's] product inventory" and that such purchases would "be governed by the Georgia Uniform Commercial Code [UCC], and [Appellant] shall retain the right to reject [Appellee's] product pursuant to the Georgia [UCC]."

On appeal, the Court of Appeals reversed, ruling that the trial court erred in applying the implied warranties of the UCC to the settlement agreement, because the primary purpose of the settlement, construed as a whole, "was to resolve a dispute between the parties about (1) whether [Appellant] was obligated to purchase any goods from [Appellee] and (2) whether [Appellee's] goods were merchantable." Hanson Staple Co. v. Ole Mexican Foods, 293 Ga. App. 4, 7 (666 S.E.2d 398) (2008). * * * Having granted certiorari to clarify if and when the implied warranties found in the UCC apply to settlement agreements involving the sale of goods, we hold that those implied warranties are applicable to such an agreement only if its predominant purpose is the sale of goods and not the settlement of litigation. * * *

When difficulties in interpreting the UCC arise, it "shall be liberally construed and applied to promote its underlying purposes and policies." OCGA § 11–1–102 (1). Those purposes and policies are

(a) To simplify, clarify, and modernize the law governing commercial transactions; (b) To permit the continued expansion of commercial practices through custom, usage, and agreement of the parties; [and] (c) To make uniform the law among the various jurisdictions. OCGA § 11–1–102 (2). * * *

[U]nder Georgia law, "[t]o determine whether a sales contract is governed by the UCC, 'we must look to the primary or overall purpose of the transaction.'" Crews v. Wahl, 238 Ga. App. 892, 900 (4) (a) (520 S.E.2d 727) (1999).

"When presented with two elements of a contract, each absolutely necessary if the subject matter is to be of any significant value to the [parties], it is a futile task to attempt to determine which component is 'more necessary.' Thus, (we must look) to the predominant purpose, the thrust of the contract as it would exist in the minds of reasonable parties. There is no surer way to provide for predictable results in the face of a highly artificial classification system." J. Lee Gregory, Inc. v. Scandinavian House, 209 Ga. App. 285, 288 (Ga. App. 1993). Therefore, the "predominant purpose" test is a way, consistent with the text of the UCC, to "simplify, clarify, and modernize the law governing commercial transactions. . . ." OCGA § 11–1–102 (2) (a).

"Although the present settlement agreement is not a mixed goods/services contract, the same analysis is applicable to determine whether it should be treated as a contract for the sale of goods." Novamedix v. NDM Acquisition Corp., 166 F.3d 1177, 1183 (Fed. Cir. 1999). We adopt that analysis for settlement agreements involving the sale of goods, as it is most consistent with the weight of authority and with Georgia law. * * *

The fact that the document at issue is labeled "agreement reached in settlement" "is a good barometer of the parties' intentions. Though the label that contracting parties affix to an agreement is not necessarily determinative of the agreement's predominant purpose, it can constitute potent evidence of that purpose." Ross–Simons of Warwick v. Baccarat, 102 F.3d 12 (1st Cir. 1996). Furthermore, the agreement involves a sale of the very same goods which were the subject of a previous alleged sales contract and ensuing litigation between the parties.

An additional indication of the essential nature of the agreement as a settlement is the fact that it arose out of litigation which involved more than the mere obligation vel non to purchase goods. In the litigation, Appellant complained of defective goods and, indeed, submitted an affidavit asserting that it had suffered damages from packaging which had "problems with color, with sticking (during delivery and the shelf life of the product), failure to seal, label discoloration, incorrect or inadequate labeling, incorrect or outdated art work and melting during the packaging process." Thus, the litigation being settled included the issue of whether the goods were merchantable and fit for a particular purpose. As the Court of Appeals properly determined, the parties' aim to settle this very issue creates strong doubt that the primary purpose of their agreement was a sale of goods subject to application of the same implied warranties of Article 2. Application of those warranties would frustrate the settlement purpose of the agreement.

Furthermore, the $130,000 sale of goods constituted less than half the value of the inventory specified in Appellee's complaint. The Court of Appeals correctly recognized that the parties' agreement validly permitted Appellant to determine well over half of its alleged purchase obligation in accordance with its own subjective quality expectations. A sale of goods pursuant to Article 2 clearly was not the predominant purpose for at least that provision of the agreement which dealt with the larger proportion of the inventory in dispute. At most, only the smaller, $130,000 proportion could be deemed a sale of goods, which would suggest that the parties' agreement was a contract to settle litigation with any sale of goods merely incidental.

* * * Therefore, we affirm the holding of the Court of Appeals that, "[c]onstruing the settlement agreement as a whole, we find that the

implied warranties of the UCC should not be applied to it." *Hanson Staple Co. v. Ole Mexican Foods*, supra at 7. * * *

NOTES

1.   Suppose the court in *AFF–McQuay* had determined that the contract was one predominantly for the service of applying the Heresite coating, not for the sale of the coating. Based on the facts of the case, might the following issues be decided differently at trial: whether a contract had been concluded (2–204(1)), whether AFF's claim was time-barred (2–725(2)), and whether implied warranties applied to the provision of services (2–313, 2–314)? In other cases, on appropriate facts the result will be the same whether Article 2 of the UCC or general contract law applies. For example, if the settlement agreement in *Ole Mexican Foods* had disclaimed implied warranties of merchantability, the seller would not be liable for unmerchantable boxes it delivered to the buyer as part of that agreement. This is the same result that would be reached if general contract law governs the settlement agreement, because it does not impose an implied warranty of merchantability. Thus, to avoid liability the seller need not disclaim the warranty. On *Ole Mexican Foods'* facts, the settlement agreement did not contain the disclaimer; see 2–316(2) and (3). The law applicable to the agreement therefore matters.

2.   The predominant purpose "test" used by the *AFF–McQuay* court is the test used by most courts to characterize a hybrid transaction. As the court recites, the test employs three factors to determine a transaction's nature as a sale of goods or a non-sale: (1) the language of the contract, (2) the nature of the supplier's business, and (3) the intrinsic worth of the materials. The first two factors are determined by the seller's representations to customers in either its contracts or business, and the court considers them particularly important in determining the predominant purpose of the transaction. In other areas of law, the language of parties' contracts often are ignored or minimized. It is effectively treated as a label that does not drive the characterization of a transaction. The predominant purpose test, as applied, gives the opposite effect to contractual language. It uses the supplier's contractual and business representations to determine predominant purpose. The difference in treatment is justifiable generally. Contractual language can be used for strategic effect or simply to signal to courts the likely intent of the parties (or sometimes both). In areas of law where contracts might benefit the contracting parties at the expense of third parties, strategic effects are a concern. In the circumstances, contract language is properly ignored in characterizing the nature of the transaction contracted for. It is treated merely as a label for the transaction, not its substance. Strategic effects are not present systematically in most hybrid contracts because what the contracting parties do has no effects on others. In these circumstances, contractual and other representations are likely to signal to courts the law the parties want applied to their contract.

3.   An alternative approach used by a minority of courts is the "gravaman of the action" test. This test asks whether the source of the buyer's complaint is the seller's services or a defect in the goods. See, e.g., Anthony Pools v. Sheehan, 455 A.2d 434 (Md. 1983); Data

Processing Services, Inc. v. L.H. Smith Oil Corp., 492 N.E.2d 314 (Ind. Ct. App. 1986). Similarly, where the hybrid transaction involves computer information embedded in goods, the approach asks whether the complaint goes to the information or to the defects in the goods. If the complaint goes to the services provided, the transaction isn't in goods and Article 2 therefore doesn't apply. If it goes to the goods provided, the transaction is in goods and Article 2 applies. Thus, the gravaman test does not ask after the purpose of the transaction; instead it focuses on the aspect of the transaction to which the buyer's complaint is directed. UCITA applies the gravaman test to transactions that fall within its scope. UCITA § 103(b)(1) (implication), Comment 4(b)(1) to § 103.

The gravaman test has some defects. For one thing, sometimes it is difficult to apply. A buyer complaining of breach may not allege or even know the source of the seller's defective performance—whether it arises from defectively performed labor or defective goods, or both. These are matters that may be resolvable only at trial, after a court has selected the law applicable to the dispute. Doesn't the predominant purpose test have its own problems in application? Another difficulty is that some complaints, such as defects in contract formation or matters of parol evidence, may go to the entire contract. These complaints are not based on either the services or goods aspects of the transaction. A final difficulty is strategic. The test allows a complainant effectively to select law favorable to it by suitably framing its complaint as directed to an aspect of the transaction. The law selected might not be the law the parties preferred at the time they contracted. Of course, parties could avoid this risk simply by selecting applicable law in their contract. But transaction costs might discourage parties from doing so.

4. It is fair to ask why the characterization of a hybrid transaction matters. The answer is default rules. With enough time and expense, contracting parties can specify all of the terms applicable to their hybrid transaction. The terms selected replicate those provided by Article 2 or non-Article 2 law, or a combination of the two sets of rules. Because the parties have selected all the terms of the contract, characterizing their transaction as within or outside Article 2's scope doesn't matter. However, contracts are incompletely specified. Default rules complete contracts. Article 2's default rules differ from defaults applicable to transactions other than those in goods. Thus, the characterization of hybrid transactions selects the default rules applicable to it.

Although the majority of courts adopt the predominant purpose test to characterize hybrid transactions, a strong argument can be made against it. The test selects a single set of laws to apply to an entire transaction: If the predominant purpose is to provide services, general contract law applies to all aspects of the transaction; if it is to provide goods, Article 2 applies to all aspects of the transaction. A "one law" approach is inappropriate for hybrid transactions. This is because the default rules efficient for sales of goods arguably are inefficient for other transactions. Article 2's rules concerning delivery, transfer of title, acceptance and inspection, implied warranties and recoverable damages are examples. These rules may reflect the preferences of the majority of parties contracting for the sale of goods, but parties' preferences might be different when other sorts of contracts are involved. For instance, a warranty places the risk of nonconformity on the seller. If the provision of a service is uncertain in its outcome, or the preferences of recipients unpredictable, most parties might prefer to allocate the risk of nonconformity in the services to the recipient. In that case a warranty for the outcome of services is inefficient as a default rule for service contracts. A test that applies a single set of default rules to a hybrid transaction risks applying inefficient rules to some aspects of the transaction.

For example, consider a contract to provide computer software under a non-exclusive license. The contract calls for the software to be packaged with hardware supplied by a software provider. The software and hardware constitute a database processing system. The obligations of the software provider also include technical support in installing the software and training the buyer's personnel to operate it. This transaction involves the sale of goods (hardware), a license of intellectual property (software) and the provision of services (technical support). Software is intellectual property that typically is licensed, as it is here; it is not sold. Licensing allows the licensor to charge different prices to the different users of the software. A sale price also might be hard to determine where the value of the software to the users is unknown. Warranties of merchantability usually do not extend to services, such as supplying and training personnel. Given the uncertainties in software design, such warranties might be undesirable when software is licensed. Because software is not sold, remedies that measure damages by a cover or market price are inapplicable. For all of these reasons, Article 2's default rules may not be the efficient set of default rules for the intellectual property and services aspects of the transaction. The predominant purpose test is unable to recognize this possibility because it applies a single set of default rules to the entire transaction. By comparison, the gravaman test is an improvement. It applies different law to different aspects of transaction, according to the aspect to which the complaint is directed. Thus, the test can apply different sets of default rules to the intellectual property, services and goods aspects of the contract.

PROBLEM 2.2

(a) Jones sold 1000 shares of common stock in ABC Corp. to Smith for $100,000. The stock is in certificated form and traded at $100 per share at the time of the sale. (Consult 8–102(a)(4), (15), (17).) The sales contract calls for Jones to deliver the certificates to Smith. In the course of doing so, Jones accidentally spilled ink on the certificate. The spilled ink makes the print on the certificates indecipherable. Smith sued Jones for breach of contract after finding that transfer of the certificates has become difficult as a result. Does Article 2 of the UCC apply to Smith's lawsuit against Jones? 2–102(a), 2–105(a).

(b) Suppose the above accident did not occur. Instead, Smith delivered the stock certificates to Jones without incident. However, the stock certificates are printed on paper which is defective. The defect causes the print on the face of the certificates to run so that the print becomes indecipherable. As before, Jones finds transfer of the certificates in this condition to be difficult and sues Smith for breach of contract. Does Article 2 of the UCC apply to Smith's lawsuit against Jones? 2–102, 2–105(a)

PROBLEM 2.3

Beer Inc. operates a homemade beer store in Charlottesville. Customers wanting custom beer in small quantities place orders with Beer. The deal they enter into calls for them to select and purchase their choice of yeast and hops on display at Beer's place of business. These ingredients represent $10 of the $50 price Beer charges to produce a batch of beer. Apart from combining the ingredients customers have selected, Beer provides only the water needed to produce the batch ordered. The results are quite variable, due to variations in room temperature and the experience of Beer's staff. Three years ago Dan, a visitor from France, ordered and paid $50.00 Beer for a batch of beer after selecting his yeast and hops. Dan picked up the batch a few days after placing his order and immediately sampled it. According to Dan, the batch Beer produced for him is "undrinkable." Beer refused Dan's demand for a refund. Assume that the poor taste of Dan's batch of beer could have resulted from either a sudden increase in humidity in Beer's production facility or the inexperience of its employees. Does Dan have a cause of action under Article 2 of the UCC?

C. LEASES

Almost all law governing leases is domestic law, and the applicable domestic law in the United States is almost entirely state law. The only significant exception concerns leases in aircrafts, aircraft engines and helicopters, which the Cape Town Convention on International Interests in Mobile Equipment and its Protocol controls. http://www.unidroit.org/english/conventions/mobile-equipment/main.htm. Article 2A of the UCC applies to leases in goods. Because a lease is not a sale (2A–103(1)(j)), Article 2 does not govern lease transactions. Equipment leases constitute an increasingly important type of capital investment, ranging from computer, medical and transportation products. In 2009 $518 billion was invested in equipment leases in the United States. Equipment and Leasing Finance Association, The Economic Contribution of Equipment Leasing to the U.S. Economy: Growth, Investment & Jobs–Update, 2005 4 (2005), available at http://www.finance-equipment.com/forms/Leasing%20Report%202005.pdf. This constituted about 20 percent of the value of all domestic business investment in equipment. All of the states have adopted Article 2A, either in its initial or revised versions. For the most part, Article 2A and Article 2 are very similar, since Article 2A applies many of Article 2's sales concepts to leases. Comment to 2A–101. However, there are differences between the two Articles. For instance, a lessor has a right to recover leased goods from a transferee of the lessee upon the lessee's default. This right is greater than the corresponding seller's right of recovery upon its buyer's default. Compare 2A–525(2) with 2–702. Thus, the distinction between a sale and lease sometimes remains important.

There are significant accounting, tax and legal differences between leases and sales. Accounting standards distinguish between two sorts of leases: capital and operating leases. See Financial Accounting

Standards Board (FASB), Accounting Standards No. 13: Accounting for Leases (1976). The distinction turns basically on whether the lessee enjoys the risks and benefits of ownership for most of the asset's useful life. For example, leases typically are classified as capital leases rather than operating leases when the lease time equals or exceeds 75% of the asset's estimated useful life. A capital lease makes the lessee the owner of the asset, and the transaction a type of financed sale to her. Accordingly, the lessee must record the asset and the payment obligations as if the asset had been purchased with financing. The leased good is recorded as an asset and the total lease payments due (discounted to present value) are recorded as a liability. This treatment acknowledges the reality that lease payments effectively are installment payments on the good's purchase price. By contrast, an operating lease leaves the important incidents of ownership with the lessor. Under accounting standards for an operating lease, the leased asset is not recorded on the balance sheet as an asset and lease payments are not recorded as a liability. Instead, rent is recorded as an expense only on the lessee's income statement in the period it becomes due. This treatment allows the lessee to maintain a more favorable debt-to-equity ratio on its balance sheet. By contrast, a capital lease treats the lease as type of financed sale, requiring the buyer to record the entire purchase price as a liability. Capitalizing a lease therefore can detrimentally affect the lessee's debt-to-equity or other financial ratios. FASB is revising its accounting standards for leases to eliminate the distinction between capital and operating leases. The revised standards will require that a lease be recorded as both an asset and liability. See FASB, Proposed Accounting Standards Update, Leases (Topic 842) (May 16, 2013).

For tax purposes, a lessee may deduct rent payments as ordinary business expenses. By contrast, the buyer of a good may not deduct the purchase price paid at the time of the purchase. Instead, the price may be deducted as an expense through a prescribed depreciation schedule. The allowable depreciation schedule usually is based on an estimate of the economic life of the asset that is shorter than the asset's actual useful life. Thus, the periodic depreciation expense allowed to a buyer usually is greater than the deductible rental payments allowed to the lessee. Tax law has its own criteria for determining when a transaction is a lease. See Rev. Proc. 2001–28 C.B. 1156 (2001). Because accounting standards, sales law and tax law each use different criteria to determine the character of a lease, a transaction can be a lease for accounting purposes or sales law but not for tax purposes, and vice versa.

A lease and a sale have different legal consequences. A lease transfers a possessory interest in the goods, not title to them. The lessee therefore generally cannot transfer title to the goods to a purchaser. 2A–305(1). Accordingly, the lessor can recover leased goods sold by the lessee to a third party. By contrast, a sale transfers title. 2–106(1). Thus, the seller cannot recover goods in turn sold by the buyer to a third party, unless the seller has a security interest in the goods enforceable against that party. Bankruptcy law also attaches significantly different consequences to leases and sales. In a lessee's bankruptcy, the lessee's trustee must abide by the terms of the lease or return the leased goods to the lessor. By contrast, an unpaid seller cannot recover the goods from the buyer's bankruptcy trustee. If the seller is unsecured, it instead is given an unsecured claim against the buyer's bankruptcy estate. Even if the seller has an enforceable security interest, bankruptcy law generally entitles the seller to be paid an amount equal to the value of its collateral. This value of collateral may be less than the amount the buyer owes the seller. Classifying a transaction as a credit sale therefore is more favorable to the buyer's bankruptcy estate than classifying it as a lease is to the lessee's bankruptcy estate.

Distinguishing between a lease and a sale can be difficult. This is particularly true when a sale is secured. In a secured sale the seller usually finances the buyer's purchase of the good. The buyer in turn grants the seller a security interest in the good purchased to secure its price. 9–103(a), (b)(1). Objectively, there is no observable difference between the obligations under a lease and a secured sale. For instance, assume that a transaction calls for the transferee of the good to make monthly payments of $100 to the transferor for one year. The $100 periodic payments may be characterized as rental payments under a one-year lease with $1,200 in total lease payments. Alternatively, the $100 payments may be deemed installment payments on a $1,200 purchase price. If the lessee fails to make the rental payments, the lessor can retrieve the leased good. Correspondingly, if the buyer-debtor fails to make its installment payments on the purchase price, the seller-secured creditor can repossess the good. Obligations to maintain the good or pay taxes and insurance on it affect only the size of the periodic payments, not their character as rental or installments payments. The lessor, for instance, could make the lessee responsible for these expenses or incur the expenses and increase the monthly rental payments due in their amount. The seller can do the same in the case of an installment sale.

Whether a transaction involves a lease or a sale requires a judgment about who owns the goods. In a lease transaction, the lessor has a residual interest in the goods and is entitled to get them back at the end of the term of the lease. It remains the owner of the good. In a sale, the buyer becomes the owner of the good. Where the sale is secured, when the buyer pays the purchase price to the seller, the security interest ends and the buyer owns the good unencumbered. If a transaction transfers possession for the useful life of a good having no salvage value, the transferee gets the benefits and bears the risks of fluctuations in the value of the good during that time. Because an owner gets the benefits and bears the burdens of an asset, the transferee effectively owns the good. Regardless of whether this transaction is described as a lease with a purchase option price of $0 or an installment sale, the transferee owns the good. In substance the transaction is a sale, even if the parties label their agreement a "lease."

Purchase options complicate judgments about the character of a transaction as a lease or sale. This is because purchase options make the determination of ownership difficult. By splitting the risks normally associated with ownership, a purchase option sometimes makes it hard to identify the owner of the good. Suppose an agreement gives the transferee the option to purchase the good at the end of a specified term. If the price at which the purchase option may be exercised is less than the current market value of the good, the optionee will exercise the option and own the good. If the purchase option price is more than the current market value, the optionee will not exercise the option. In that case the optionor will continue to own the good. Thus, there is no answer to the question as to who will be the owner of the good at the end of the specified term of the transaction. The only accurate answer is "it depends." In this case the test of ownership requires asking whether the transferee is likely to become the owner of the good at the end of the term. If the transferee likely will exercise the purchase option, it will come to own the good and the transaction is a sale. If not, the transferor will continue to own the good and the transaction is a lease. Whether the transferee likely will exercise the purchase option depends on the price at which the purchase option can be exercised and the market value of the good (ignoring interests rates). For the ownership test to be serviceable with purchase options, the market value of the good must be the market value of the good at the time the option can be exercised, as estimated at the inception of the agreement. Otherwise, the result of the ownership test would change over time according to when the estimate of market value is made. Judgments about the character of a transaction would be uncertain.

Articles 1 and 2A contain provisions that courts use to distinguish leases from sales. Section 2A–103(1)(j) defines a lease as "a transfer of the right to possession and use of goods for a term." The definition expressly excludes both sales and security interests. Section 1–203 provides some standards that determine when a transaction structured as a lease will be interpreted instead as a security interest. (Revised Article 1 divides former 1–201(b)(37) into 1–201(b)(35) and 1–203 without changing its content. Section 1–203 contains the standards contained in former 1–201(b)(37).) Transactions structured as leases that 1–203 does not deem security interests are called genuine or "true" leases. These leases are governed by Article 2A. Transactions deemed security interests by 1–203 are governed by Article 9. Because almost all such transactions will involve a secured sale, Article 2 will govern the sales portion of transactions that create security interests. Courts therefore use 1–203 to distinguish a secured sale from a true lease.

Section 1–203 states two different standards for determining whether a transaction creates a true lease or a security interest. One standard states a sufficient condition for a lease being a disguised security interest. 1–203(b). It is sometimes called a "bright-line test." According to this standard, a transaction structured as a lease is a sale subject to a security interest if (1) the lessee has an obligation to continue paying consideration for the term of the lease, (2) the lease cannot be terminated, and (3) either the lessor retains no meaningful reversionary interest in the leased good or the lessee will acquire the reversionary interest at the end of the lease term. 1–203(b)(1)–(4). The lessor retains no meaningful reversionary interest when the original lease term is equal to or greater than the remaining economic life of the good. 1–203(b)(1). The same is true when the lessee is obligated to renew the lease for the remaining economic life of the good. 1–203(b)(2). The lessee will acquire the reversionary interest when it has the option to renew the lease for the remaining economic life of the goods or become the owner of the goods for no consideration or additional nominal consideration. 1–203(b)(3)–(4). Additional consideration is nominal if the purchase or renewal price at the end of the lease term is less than the fair market or fair rental value, respectively. 1–203(d). Courts often call this last condition the "economic realities" test. See In re Worldcom, Inc. v. General Electric Global Asset Management Services, 339 B.R. 56, 66 (Bankr. S.D.N.Y. 2006). The test essentially asks whether at the end of the lease term the only economically sensible course for the lessee is to exercise the option to renew the lease or purchase the goods. Where consideration for exercising a purchase or renewal option is nominal, the only economically sensible course is for the lessee to exercise the option. If the price for exercising a purchase option is nominal, the lessee will exercise it and become the owner of the good.

The second standard applies only when the first standard does not apply. According to this standard, whether a transaction in the form of a lease is a security interest is "determined by the facts of each case." 1–203(a). Of course, strictly 1–203(a) does not really describe a standard at all. It does not direct courts to any particular facts, or features of leases, in classifying a lease as a true lease or a security interest. Section 1–203(c) lists some common provisions of leases that do not by themselves make the transaction a security interest. For instance, a provision requiring the lessee to pay taxes, insurance or maintenance by itself does not require classifying the transaction as a security interest. 1–203(c)(3). But aside from the first standard described, 1–203 does not tell a court which facts require classification of a lease as a security interest. In applying 1–203(a), courts frequently use the economic realities test to characterize the transaction, as in *In re Pillowtex, Inc.* below. The two following cases apply the standards contained in 1–203 to classify a transaction the parties deem a lease. *In re Pillowtex, Inc.* applies 1–203(a) and *Gangloff Industries, Inc. v. Generic Financing and Leasing Corp.* 1–203(b).

In re Pillowtex, Inc.

United States Court of Appeals, Third Circuit, 2003
349 F.3d 711

■ FUENTES, CIRCUIT JUDGE:

Duke Energy Royal LLC ("Duke") appeals from an order of the District Court denying a motion to compel Pillowtex Corporation ("Pillowtex" or "debtor") to make lease payments owing under the Master Energy Services Agreement ("MESA"), an agreement its predecessor entered into with Pillowtex. The District Court denied Duke's motion on the grounds that the MESA was not a true lease, but rather a secured financing arrangement. The sole issue in this appeal is whether the District Court correctly determined that the MESA entered into between Pillowtex and Duke prior to Pillowtex's bankruptcy filing was a secured financing arrangement rather than a true lease. We affirm because we agree with the District Court that, based on the economic realities of the underlying transaction, the MESA was a secured financing arrangement.

Facts and Procedural Background

Because the nature of the MESA is at issue, we first turn to its provisions and the transaction underlying the agreement. Pillowtex and

Duke entered into the MESA on June 3, 1998. Pursuant to the MESA, Duke agreed to install certain equipment "for the purpose of improving the efficiency of energy consumption or otherwise to reduce the operating costs" incurred by Pillowtex at its facilities. The MESA covered two different sets of energy services projects, one involving production equipment and the other energy-savings equipment. The production equipment was provided to Pillowtex by Duke pursuant to separate stand-alone agreements, which were recorded as true leases on Pillowtex's books, and which the parties agree constituted true leases. Therefore, only the nature of the parties' arrangements concerning the energy-savings equipment is at issue in this appeal.

The energy-savings equipment included certain lighting fixtures, T8 lamps and electronic ballasts (collectively the "lighting fixtures"), which were installed in nine of Pillowtex's facilities and a new wastewater heat recovery system that included hot water heating equipment (the "wastewater system" and together with the lighting fixtures, the "energy fixtures"), which was installed at Pillowtex's Columbus, Georgia plant. The lighting fixtures were selected, and the wastewater system was constructed, specifically for Pillowtex's facilities.

In order to induce Pillowtex to enter into the energy services projects, Duke offered to originate funding for the production equipment "on a two-to-one basis (i.e., for every $1 million of energy projects Duke would originate $2 million for funding of equipment) with a minimum of $28 million in funding for equipment leasing or financing." Another incentive Pillowtex had for entering into the agreement was "that the energy projects would be cost neutral to Pillowtex for the term of the agreement; that is, Pillowtex's payments to Duke would be equivalent to Pillowtex's actual savings . . . and Pillowtex would then reap the benefits from the cost savings after the end of the term of the project." In keeping with this arrangement, Pillowtex accounted for its payments to Duke under the MESA as a utility expense.

The MESA provided that the cost of acquiring and installing the energy fixtures would be paid by Duke, which incurred total costs of approximately $10.41 million. Of this amount, approximately $1.66 million was for material and labor costs for the wastewater system. Approximately $4.46 million was for labor to install the lighting fixtures and $4.29 million was for material costs for the lighting fixtures, which is to say that the cost of labor to install the fixtures was higher than the cost of the actual materials themselves. Also, Duke paid approximately $223,000 to dispose of light fixtures and related equipment that it removed from Pillowtex's facilities.

In exchange, Pillowtex was to pay Duke on a monthly basis one-twelfth of Pillowtex's annual energy savings, in an amount the parties agreed to in advance, until the end of the MESA's 8 year term. In addition, the parties agreed that the simple payback of all of Duke's costs was not to exceed 5 years. "Simple payback" is synonymous with "payback period," an accounting term which refers to "the length of time required to recover a venture's initial cash investment, without accounting for the time value of money." BLACK'S LAW DICTIONARY 1150 (7th ed. 1999). In other words, the payments were structured to ensure that Pillowtex would make predetermined, equal monthly payments and that Duke would recover its costs 3 years prior to the end of the term of the MESA. Although the MESA was for an 8 year term, the parties agree that the useful life of the energy fixtures was 20–25 years.

It is undisputed that Duke and Pillowtex intended to structure the MESA to have the characteristics of a lease and that the parties were trying to create a true lease. Indeed, Pillowtex's counsel conceded during oral argument before the District Court, "I don't disagree that [the MESA] was structured to have those characteristics for tax purposes and, you know, to [the] extent they could, the parties were trying to create a true lease, I would admit that." The parties intended for the MESA to be structured as a true lease, in large part, because Pillowtex was subject to capital expenditure limitations under its senior credit facility and did not wish to have the energy-savings equipment count as capital expenditures under that facility. Nevertheless, the MESA is not labeled a lease and it does not refer to the parties as lessee and lessor. Also, Duke alleges that the parties were concerned with structuring the MESA's provisions relating to energy-savings equipment in accordance with the requirements of Financial Accounting Standard 13, which sets the standards for financial accounting and reporting for leases. However, the MESA fails to qualify as a true lease under P 7 of that standard because the present value of the total payments due under the MESA exceeds the value of the original cost of the energy fixtures.

In keeping with their intent to structure the transaction as a lease, the MESA provides that title to the equipment would remain with Duke. Also, Pillowtex agreed not to claim ownership of the equipment for income tax purposes, and Pillowtex was not obligated to purchase the equipment at the end of the term of the MESA. Rather, the MESA provided the following four options to Duke at the conclusion of its term, if Pillowtex was not then in default:

(i) remove the Equipment installed and replace those [sic] Equipment with equipment comparable to those originally in place, provided that no such replacement shall be required with respect to Production Equipment; or,

(ii) abandon the Equipment in place; or,

(iii) continue this Agreement until the expiration of the term hereof and then extend the term of this Agreement for such additional period(s) and payment terms as the parties may agree upon; or,

(iv) give the Customer the option of purchasing all (but not less than all) of the Equipment at a mutually agreed upon price.

If Duke elected to exercise option (I), it was bound to "be responsible for all costs and expenses in removing such Equipment, including costs to repair any damage to [Pillowtex's] Facility caused by such removal." Despite the existence of the option for Duke to repossess the equipment, Pillowtex's Vice President for Engineering, Michael Abba, testified that in his understanding, there was no chance of that option being exercised:

It was clearly my understanding that Duke would abandon the Lighting Fixtures and the Wastewater System at the conclusion of the

MESA and in fact statements were made to me by Duke sales personnel to that effect. Moreover, because the energy projects were of no economic benefit to Pillowtex until the end of the term when Pillowtex would reap the energy savings going forward, I would not have signed off on the projects if the Lighting Fixtures and Wastewater System were not to be abandoned. I also believe that, based on the prohibitive cost of removing and replacing the Lighting Fixtures and the Wastewater System for Pillowtex, Duke [had] no choice but to abandon the Lighting Fixtures and the Wastewater System at the end of the term of the MESA.

After Duke and Pillowtex executed the MESA, Duke entered into a Master Lease Agreement ("Master Lease") with General Electric Capital Corporation ("GECC"), dated August 2, 1999, pursuant to which GECC agreed to finance the lighting fixtures for four of the nine Pillowtex facilities in which Duke was to install new fixtures pursuant to the MESA. Concurrently with the execution of the Master Lease and the execution of an equipment schedule listing lighting fixtures subject to the Master Lease, Duke and GECC entered into a Collateral Assignment Agreement through which Duke granted GECC a security interest in all of Duke's rights and interests in the MESA, including Duke's right to payment under the MESA, as security for Duke's obligations under the Master Lease. Also, in connection with the Master Lease transaction, Pillowtex executed an Acknowledgment Letter which provides that its interest in the MESA and equipment covered by it "is subject and subordinate to [GECC's] rights under . . . the Master Lease Agreement . . . between GECC and Duke." Shortly after Duke and GECC entered into the Master Lease, on August 12, 1999, GECC and SouthTrust Bank executed a Master Assignment Agreement, pursuant to which GECC assigned all of its rights and interests in the Master Lease and the Collateral Assignment it had with Duke, as well as the MESA and certain other documents, to SouthTrust. Therefore, with respect to the lighting fixtures, SouthTrust holds the rights and interests under the MESA for the lighting fixtures at four of Pillowtex's facilities and Duke holds the rights and interests under the MESA for the lighting fixtures at the other five facilities.

On November 14, 2000, Pillowtex and certain of its subsidiaries filed petitions for relief under Chapter 11 of the Bankruptcy Code. Thereafter, Pillowtex stopped making payments due under the MESA. On February 21, 2002, Duke filed a motion under section 365(d)(10) of the Bankruptcy Code to compel Pillowtex to make lease payments on the equipment it had provided to Pillowtex under the MESA. Section 365(d)(10) requires debtors-in-possession, such as Pillowtex, to "timely perform all of the obligations of the debtor . . . first arising from or after 60 days after the order for relief in a case under Chapter 11 . . . under an unexpired lease of personal property . . . until such lease is assumed or rejected. . . . " 11 U.S.C. § 365(d)(10). In response to Duke's motion, Pillowtex filed an objection in which it argued that Duke was not entitled to payment of post-petition monthly obligations, which Pillowtex represented amounted to $1.8 million, because the MESA was not a true lease. After a hearing on the matter, the District Court, sitting in Bankruptcy, denied Duke's motion. Duke timely appealed. * * *

Analysis

Whether an agreement is a true lease or a secured financing arrangement under the Bankruptcy Code is a question of state law. In this case, the parties agreed that the MESA would be interpreted, performed, and enforced in accordance with the laws of the State of New York. Accordingly, we turn to New York law in order to resolve whether the MESA constitutes a secured financing arrangement or a lease. Under New York law, because Pillowtex is seeking to characterize the MESA as a secured financing arrangement rather than a lease, Pillowtex bears the burden of proof on that issue.

Article 2A of the New York Uniform Commercial Code explains that a lease is "a transfer of the right to possession and use of goods for a term in return for consideration, but a sale . . . or retention or creation of a security interest is not a lease." N.Y. U.C.C. § 2–A–103(1)(j) (McKinney 2002). Thus, the definition of a lease expressly excludes security interests. The exclusion of security interests from the definition of a lease requires that we turn to the U.C.C. definition of a security interest.

Section 1–201(37) [1–201(b) (35)] of the U.C.C. provides that a security interest "means an interest in personal property or fixtures which secures payment or performance of an obligation." After defining the term "security interest," section 1–201(37) [1–203] sets out a test for determining whether a transaction creates a lease or a security interest. Section 1–201(37) [1–203] begins by noting that whether a transaction creates a lease or a security interest is to be determined on a case-by-case basis. After indicating that courts are to examine the facts of each case in order to characterize a transaction, the statute sets out a bright-line test, sometimes referred to as a per se rule, for determining whether a transaction creates a security interest as a matter of law. Specifically, section 1–201(37) [1–203] provides:

> (a) Whether a transaction creates a lease or security interest is determined by the facts of each case; however, a transaction creates a security interest if the consideration the lessee is to pay the lessor for the right to possession and use of the goods is an obligation for the term of the lease not subject to termination by the lessee, and:
>
> > (i) the original term of the lease is equal to or greater than the remaining economic life of the goods,
> >
> > (ii) the lessee is bound to renew the lease for the remaining economic life of the goods or is bound to become the owner of the goods,
> >
> > (iii) the lessee has an option to renew the lease for the remaining economic life of the goods for no additional consideration or nominal additional consideration upon compliance with the lease agreement, or
> >
> > (iv) the lessee has an option to become the owner of the goods for no additional consideration or nominal additional consideration upon compliance with the lease agreement.

N.Y. U.C.C. § 1–201(37) [1–203]. Thus, under the two-part test set out in New York's U.C.C., if Pillowtex did not have the right to terminate the MESA prior to the end of its term, and any of the four factors set out in section 1–201(37)(a)(i)–(iv) [1–203(b)(1)–(4)] are met, then the MESA would be considered to create a security interest as a matter of law. If, on the other hand, it is determined that "the transaction is not a disguised security agreement per se, [we] must then look at the specific facts of the case to determine whether the economics of the transaction suggest such a result." In re Taylor, 209 B.R. 482, 484 (Bankr. S.D. Ill. 1997). In this case, the District Court went directly to the economic realities of the transaction memorialized in the MESA. In doing so the Court seems to have implicitly held that the MESA was not a disguised security agreement under the bright-line test of section 1–102(37) [1–203(b)]. We agree.

On appeal, Pillowtex argues that the MESA is a secured financing agreement both under this bright-line test and also based on the economics of the MESA transaction. Specifically, Pillowtex argues that the second and fourth factors set out in the second part of the statutory two-part test are present: (1) that at the end of the MESA's term Pillowtex was bound to become the owner of the energy fixtures and (2) that it was bound to become the owner of the fixtures for no or nominal additional consideration upon compliance with the terms of the MESA. Duke concedes that the first part of the two-part test is satisfied: that the MESA prohibits Pillowtex from terminating its obligation to pay Duke the full cost of the energy fixtures before the termination of the MESA's term. However, Duke maintains that none of the four factors in section 1–102(37)(a)(i)–(iv) [1–203(b)(1)–(4)] are present. These factors are hereafter referred to as "residual value factors" because they relate to whether residual value will remain for the purported lessor, Duke, at the end of the term of the MESA.

As an initial matter, we note that the first and third residual value factors are not satisfied. The first factor is whether "the original term of the lease is equal to or greater than the remaining economic life of the goods." N.Y. U.C.C. § 1–201(37)(a)(i) [1–203(b)(1)]. Here, the term of the MESA is eight years and Pillowtex concedes that the expected useful life of the equipment is 20–25 years. Thus, the economic life of the equipment exceeds the term of the MESA by a factor of three and the first residual value factor set out in section 1–201(37)(a) [1–203(b)] is not met. The third factor indicative of a security interest is met where "the lessee has an option to renew the lease for the remaining economic life of the goods for no additional consideration or nominal additional consideration upon compliance with the lease agreement." N.Y. U.C.C. § 1–102(37)(a)(iii) [1–203(b)(3)]. This factor is not met because the terms of the MESA do not give Pillowtex the option to renew the lease for the remaining life of the equipment for no or nominal consideration.

As to the second factor, Pillowtex argues that it was bound, if not formally then in a de facto sense, to become the owner of the energy fixtures because the only way that the fixtures would be removed from Pillowtex's facilities is if Duke paid millions of dollars to acquire and install replacements. Along the same lines, Pillowtex argues with respect to the fourth residual value factor that, although the MESA does not expressly give it the option to become the owner of the energy fixtures for no or nominal consideration, in effect it has this option because it can compel Duke to abandon the energy fixtures by refusing to negotiate an extension of the MESA or a purchase of the energy fixtures at the end of the MESA's term.

We agree with Duke that neither the second nor the fourth residual value factors are present here because Pillowtex is not contractually bound to become the owner of the energy fixtures, nor does the MESA provide Pillowtex with the option to become the owner of the energy fixtures for no or nominal consideration. Rather, the existing options as to how to proceed at the end of the term of the MESA were to be exercised only by Duke. Pillowtex provides no authority for the proposition that a de facto arrangement is enough to satisfy the requirements of section 1–102(37)(a)(ii) and (iv) [1–203(b)(2) and (4)]. If anything, the relevant caselaw points us to the opposite conclusion. See *In re Edison Bros. Stores*, 207 B.R. at 810 ("If the lease agreement explicitly provides that the lessee has an option to purchase the leased goods for nominal consideration (e.g., for $1), the agreement is presumed to be a disguised security agreement"). Accordingly, we conclude that none of the four residual value factors set forth in N.Y. U.C.C. § 1–201(37)(a)(i)–(iv) [1–203(b)(1)–(4)] are met.

The parties agree that, where none of the four factors set out in section 1–201(37)(a) [1–203(b)] are present, courts are to consider the economic reality of the transaction in order to determine, based on the particular facts of the case, whether the transaction is more fairly characterized as a lease or a secured financing arrangement. They also agree that the District Court applied the correct standard for evaluating the economic reality of their transaction. As the District Court explained:

Under relevant case law, courts will look to various factors in evaluating the "economic reality of the transaction . . . in determining whether there has been a sale or a true lease," Pactel Fin. v. D.C. Marine Serv. Corp., 136 Misc. 2d 194, 518 N.Y.S.2d 317, 318 (N.Y. Dist. Ct. 1987), including the following: "[a] whether the purchase option is nominal; [b] whether the lessee is required to make aggregate rental payments having a present value equaling or exceeding the original cost of the leased property; and [c] whether the lease term covers the total useful life of the equipment." In re Edison Bros. Stores, 207 B.R. 801, 809–10 and n.8, 9, 10 (Bankr. D. Del. 1997). "In this regard, courts are required to examine the intent of the parties and the facts and circumstances which existed at the time the transaction was entered into." *In re Edison Bros.*, 207 B.R. at 809.

The District Court found that the MESA was substantively better characterized as a security agreement than a true lease because the second Edison Bros. factor clearly weighed in Pillowtex's favor, and the first and third factors were largely neutral. We agree with the District Court's conclusion in this regard.

Specifically, with respect to the second factor, Duke concedes that the aggregate rental payments owing by Pillowtex under the MESA had a present value equal to or exceeding the cost of the energy fixtures. The *Edison Bros.* court cogently explained the importance of such a fact in showing the existence of a security agreement:

The rationale behind this second factor is that if the alleged lessee is obligated to pay the lessor a sum equal to or greater than the full purchase price of the leased goods plus an interest charge over the term of the alleged lease agreement, a sale is likely to have been intended since what the lessor will receive is more than a payment for the use of the leased goods and loss of their value; the lessor will receive a consideration that would amount to a return on its investment.

Applying that logic to this case, Duke has already been well-compensated for the transferral of the lighting fixtures to Pillowtex, undercutting the proposition that the fixtures were merely leased.

Like the District Court, we are unpersuaded by Duke's attempt to rely on the first and third *Edison Bros.* factors. With respect to the first factor, Duke points out that the MESA provides that it "has the option to . . . give [Pillowtex] the option of purchasing all (but not less than all) of the Equipment at a mutually agreed price." Based on this provision of the MESA, Duke asserts that "Pillowtex does not have the option to purchase the Equipment unless Duke offers it such option, and even then only if Pillowtex agrees on a satisfactory price with Duke." Duke concludes that, therefore, the first economic realities factor weighs in favor of a finding that the MESA is a lease. We agree, however, with Pillowtex's contention that, although the MESA nominally required Pillowtex to bargain for an option price, Pillowtex could essentially ensure a nominal option price by refusing to bargain. This refusal would "effectively compel Duke to abandon the energy fixtures to avoid the exorbitant expense of acquiring and installing replacements." Thus, as an economic reality the option price at the end of the MESA was illusory, nullifying the weight of this factor.

With respect to the third factor, Duke observes that the useful life of the energy fixtures is longer than the term of the MESA, and cites to *Edison Bros.* for the proposition that the long life of the fixtures is indicative of a true lease. In relevant part, the *Edison Bros.* court explained that:

An essential characteristic of a true lease is that there be something of value to return to the lessor after the term. Where the term of the lease is substantially equal to the life of the lease property such that there will be nothing of value to return at the end of the lease, the transaction is in essence a sale. Conversely, if the lessor expected a remaining useful life after the expiration of the lease term, it can be reasonably inferred that it expected to retain substantial residual value in the leased property at the end of the lease term and that it therefore intended to create a true lease. *Edison Bros.,* 207 B.R. at 818 (citations omitted).

We agree that under certain circumstances, the fact that transferred goods have a useful life extending beyond the term of the transferring agreement could reveal the transferor's expectation of retaining residual value in those goods. Such an inference would only be proper, however, where the evidence showed a plausible intent by the transferor to repossess the goods.

The economic realities of the particular transaction in this case belie any such intent. Although the useful life of the lighting fixtures is 20–25 years, eclipsing the MESA's 8–year term, it would be unreasonable for Duke to incur the high costs necessary to repossess the fixtures: namely, the costs associated with removing, scrapping, and replacing the fixtures. Also, the uncontroverted evidence in this case establishes that there is little (if any) market value for used lighting fixtures. In short, it would have made no economic sense for Duke to spend large amounts of money to reclaim the fixtures, especially in the face of poor resale prospects. We therefore conclude that the District Court did not err by discounting the significance of the useful life of the lighting fixtures as compared to the length of the MESA when conducting its analysis of the economic realities of the transaction underlying the MESA. On balance, then, applying the three Edison Bros. factors to this case leads us to conclude that the MESA was not a true lease.

Beyond reiterating its arguments on the three factors, Duke argues that (1) the mutual subjective intent of the parties was to structure the MESA as a lease; (2) Pillowtex's accounting for the MESA payments as a utility expense is evidence that it did not treat the MESA as a repayment of debt incurred to purchase the energy fixtures; (3) it is of no consequence that the MESA is not labeled a lease; and (4) Duke maintained a meaningful reversionary interest in the fixtures at the end of the MESA's term. None of these arguments is persuasive to us.

First, Duke argues that the District Court erred by failing to analyze the intent of the parties. Duke asserts that the record shows that the parties structured the MESA so that it would qualify as a lease under relevant accounting standards. That way, Pillowtex would not reduce the amount of credit available to it under its senior credit facility. Duke also cites a statement that counsel for Pillowtex made to the District Court, which Duke characterizes as a concession: "I don't disagree that it was structured to have that, those characteristics for tax purposes and, you know, to the extent that they could, the parties were trying to create a lease, I would admit that."

Duke's intent argument fails, however, because the New York U.C.C. no longer looks to the intent of the drafting parties to determine whether a transfer is a lease or a security agreement. Specifically, the 1992 version of § 1–201(37) [1–203(a)] directed courts to determine "whether a lease is intended as security"; this language was amended in 1995 to read "whether a transaction creates a lease or security interest". In this way, the reference to parties' intent was explicitly omitted. The Official Comment to the amended version confirms the importance of the changed language:

> Prior to this amendment, section 1–201(37) [1–203(a)] provided that whether a lease was intended as security (i.e., a security interest disguised as a lease) was to be determined from the facts of each case . . . Reference to the intent of the parties to create a lease or security agreement has led to unfortunate results. In discovering intent, courts have relied upon factors that were thought to be more consistent with sales or loans than leases. Most of these criteria, however, are as applicable to true leases as to security interests . . . Accordingly, amended section 1–201(37) [1–203(a)] deletes all references to the parties' intent.

* * *

Based on the foregoing authority, we are unwilling to characterize the MESA as a lease on the basis that the parties intended it to appear to be one for tax purposes. Duke admonishes the Court in its brief that "equipment leasing between sophisticated commercial entities dealing at arms length for their mutual benefit is an important commercial activity and one that should not be lightly recharacterized." This admonition rings hollow in the context of bankruptcy cases, however, because every dollar that is used to pay a purported lessor depletes the pool of assets available to pay other constituencies of the estate. In other words, refusing to defer to the intent of contracting parties in resolving whether their agreement is a lease is particularly appropriate in bankruptcy, as otherwise the costs of the agreement would be externalized to third-party creditors.

* * *

Next, Duke argues that the District Court erred by taking into consideration that the MESA was not labeled a lease. The District Court merely observed in passing, however, that "the MESA is not labeled a lease," and that there is no indication that the court relied heavily on this observation. Even if it did rely to some extent on this fact, this reliance was harmless since the economic realities independently dictate that the MESA was in fact not a lease. Accordingly, we do not believe that the District Court committed reversible error by mentioning the labeling of the MESA.

Duke goes on to insist that it had a "meaningful residual interest" in the fixtures, such an interest being "the fundamental characteristic distinguishing a lease from a security interest." As discussed earlier, however, Duke only has a nominal residual interest, not a meaningful one: the combination of the cost of retrieving the fixtures and their poor market value renders the residual interest negligible. Duke claims that we should not "speculate" as to what it might do for economic reasons at the end of the MESA's term, and instead look to the parties' intent at the time of drafting the agreement. As we have mentioned above, however, Duke's argument is backwards: the Court must subordinate the parties' intent to the economic reality that Duke would not have plausibly reclaimed the fixtures at the end of MESA's term. This is not mere speculation on our part. The uncontroverted evidence shows that removal of the fixtures would be prohibitively expensive, and that the fixtures' value on the market would not make it worth Duke's while to reclaim them. In short, the economic realities analysis not only permits, but requires us to examine the state of affairs at the end of the MESA's term.

* * *

Conclusion

After carefully considering the arguments discussed above and all other arguments advanced by appellant, we conclude that the District Court correctly determined that the MESA was not a lease and, therefore, that Duke was not entitled to lease payments under 11 U.S.C. § 365(d)(10). We will remand this case to the District Court so that it may determine whether Duke is entitled to adequate protection.

Gangloff Industries, Inc. v. Generic Financing and Leasing, Corp.

Indiana Court of Appeals, 2009
907 N.E.2d 1059

■ Opinion by: ROBB, JUDGE

Gangloff Industries, Inc. appeals the trial court's judgment on Generic Financing and Leasing Corp.'s complaint for immediate possession and damages filed after Gangloff took possession of a certain truck of which Generic claimed ownership. Gangloff raises six issues for our review, which we consolidate and restate as two: 1) whether the agreement between Generic and Robert Bougher was a lease or a security interest in the truck, and 2) if it was a security interest, whether the possessory lien Gangloff asserted took priority. Concluding that the agreement is a security interest and that Gangloff's possessory lien had priority, we reverse and remand.

Facts and Procedural History

On September 23, 2005, Robert Bougher entered into an agreement titled "Lease Agreement" with Generic concerning a 2000 Western Star semi-truck. The agreement provides, in relevant part, as follows:

This lease agreement made on this 23rd day of September 2005 between Generic Financing and Leasing, Corp. (hereinafter called Lessor) and Robert N. Bougher Jr. (hereinafter called lessee). . . .

1. Lease: Lessor hereby leases to and lessee hereby leases from Lessor a certain motor vehicles [sic], hereinafter referred to as the "Leased Property," described as follows:

* * *

2000 Western Star

2. Lease Term: This lease shall become effective upon the day and date above and shall continue until the 23rd of November 2008.

3. Rental: Lessee shall pay to Lessor a Rental of $43,051.95 payable in installments of $1,099.00 per month, the first payment being due and payable on the 23rd day of October 2005, and a like sum due and payable on the same date of each succeeding month during the term of this lease. . . .

Should Lessee be in default of any payments including taxes, insurance, licensing, rent, and any other under this lease, said delinquent payment shall bear interest at the rate of 18% per annum.

4. Ownership: It is expressly understood that this is an agreement for lease only, and that the Lessee acquires no right, title, or interest in or to the Leased property other than the right to the possession and use of the same in accordance with the terms of this lease.

* * *

6. Repair: Lessee shall, at it's [sic] own expense, provide suitable and adequate garage space and service for said truck . . . and shall maintain said truck in good repair, mechanical condition, and running order. . . . Repair shall include any and all work needed to be done on

the truck completely overhaul if the engine blows or any other, all at the expense of the Lessee.

* * *

9. Licenses: Lessee shall provide and maintain, at his own expense, all necessary owner's vehicle licenses and license tags for said truck. Lessee shall be responsible for all permits regarding the truck or it's [sic] operation.

10. Highway Use Tax and Licenses: Lessee shall provide and maintain, at his own expense, all necessary owner's vehicle licenses and license tags for said truck and shall also be responsible for the highway use tax and all permits regarding the truck or it's [sic] operation.

* * *

12. Insurance:

A) Lessee will, at it's [sic] own expense, provide and maintain for the term of this lease, public liability and physical damage insurance on the Leased Property covering both the Lessee and the Lessor . . .

Such policies of insurance shall be carried with a company or companies approved by the Lessor. Such policies of insurance shall also be issued in the name of the Lessor and the Lessee, as their respective interests may appear. . . .

13. Default: That if there is any default by the Lessee in the payments required hereunder when due or any breach of covenants or conditions in this agreement by the Lessee . . . the Lessor may hold, take possession of, or repossess the vehicle(s) until such default is cured. . . . In case of any such default or breach, the Lessor shall also have the right, to terminate this agreement. . . . The Lessor shall be entitled to repossess the vehicle and to dispose of the vehicle in any reasonably commercial fashion. . . . The Lessor shall be entitled to reimbursement for expenses including reasonable attorney fees in enforcing this lease.

* * *

26. Option to Purchase: Upon the expiration of this lease and with the exercising of the option of purchase, the lessee may purchase from the Lessor the vehicle for the amount of $3,190.00.

On September 27, 2005, Bougher's wife, Kathy, and Gangloff entered into an "Owner Operator Service Contract" by which Kathy agreed to "furnish to [Gangloff], exclusively and continuously, during the term of this contract, the [2000 Western Star 3–axle semi-truck]," to pay all costs of operation, including maintenance costs and repairs; and to operate the equipment herself or "furnish sufficient employees to operate said equipment." Thereafter, Bougher began operating the truck to haul goods for Gangloff.

On March 13, 2007, the truck broke down and required repairs costing over $6,000. Gangloff paid for the repairs and Bougher was to re-pay Gangloff. On July 19, 2007, Bougher was re-fueling his truck at a truck stop when he suffered a heart attack from which he ultimately died. Kathy contacted Gangloff to recover the truck and trailer from the truck stop, which it did. Gangloff took possession of the truck and placed it in a secure location pending Kathy's removal of the truck and payment for its recovery and storage. Gangloff retained possession of the truck until January 7, 2008, on which date a court order granted Generic immediate possession.

On August 3, 2007, Generic filed in Steuben County a Complaint for Immediate Possession and Damages against Gangloff, alleging that it was the owner of the truck, that Bougher had defaulted under the terms of the lease, and that Gangloff was unlawfully holding the truck for debts Bougher owed it. Generic sought treble damages and attorney fees for theft and conversion. The case was subsequently transferred to Cass County as a preferred venue. Gangloff filed a counterclaim alleging that it had a possessory lien on the truck for the repairs it paid for and for the recovery and storage of the truck. Gangloff also asserted a claim for quantum meruit. On January 7, 2008, the trial court issued an order for immediate possession, finding that Generic was likely to prevail at trial and should be awarded possession of the truck. Gangloff ceded possession of the truck to Generic as ordered.

* * *

II. Generic and Bougher's Agreement

Gangloff first contends that the agreement between Generic and Bougher, though labeled a lease, was in fact a security interest. A security interest is defined by Indiana Code section 26–1–1–201(37) [1–201(b)(35)] as "an interest in personal property or fixtures which secures payment or performance of an obligation." "The primary issue to be decided in determining whether a lease is 'intended as security' is whether it is in effect a conditional sale in which 'lessor, retains an interest in the 'leased' goods as security for the purchase price." United Leaseshares, Inc. v. Citizens Bank & Trust Co., 470 N.E.2d 1383, 1386 (Ind. Ct. App. 1984). Including a lease intended as security in the statutory definition of a security interest "represents the drafter's refusal to recognize form over substance." Id. The definition itself provides guidance for distinguishing a true lease from a lease intended as security:

Whether a transaction creates a lease or security interest is determined by the facts of each case. However, a transaction creates a security interest if the consideration the lessee is to pay the lessor for the right to possession and use of the goods is an obligation for the term of the lease not subject to termination by the lessee and:

(a) the original term of the lease is equal to or greater than the remaining economic life of the goods;

(b) the lessee is bound to renew the lease for the remaining economic life of the goods or is bound to become the owner of the goods;

(c) the lessee has an option to renew the lease for the remaining economic life of the goods for no additional consideration or nominal additional consideration upon compliance with the lease agreement; or

(d) the lessee has an option to become the owner of the goods for no additional consideration or nominal additional consideration upon compliance with the lease agreement.

* * *

For purposes of this subsection:

(x) Additional consideration is not nominal if:

(i) when the option to renew the lease is granted to the lessee the rent is stated to be the fair market rent for the use of the goods for the term of the renewal determined at the time the option is to be performed; or

(ii) when the option to become the owner of the goods is granted to the lessee the price is stated to be the fair market value of the goods determined at the time the option is to be performed.

Additional consideration is nominal if it is less than the lessee's reasonably predictable cost of performing under the lease agreement if the option is not exercised.

(y) "Reasonably predictable" . . . [is] to be determined with reference to the facts and circumstances at the time the transaction is entered into. Ind. Code § 26–1–1–201(37) [1–203]

The statute unequivocally states that an agreement is a security interest if (1) the consideration the lessee is to pay the lessor is an obligation for the term of the lease and the lessee may not terminate the obligation; and (2) one of four enumerated conditions applies. Here, the only potentially relevant condition is (d) [1–203(b)(4)], that the lessee has the option to become the owner of the goods for no additional consideration or nominal additional consideration upon compliance with the lease agreement. Under the agreement, Bougher was obligated to pay Generic a total of $43,051.95 in monthly installments of $1,099.00 per month over a period of thirty-eight months.[1] A Generic representative testified at the hearing that the consideration was based on "the price of the truck plus the interest . . . [d]ivided by the months to get the payments." Generic alone had the option to terminate the agreement prior to the term fixed therein. Thus, the agreement meets part (1) of the statutory test.

As for part (2) of the statutory test—that the lessee has the option to become the owner of the goods for nominal additional consideration upon compliance with the agreement—additional consideration is nominal if it is less than the lessee's reasonably predictable cost of performing under the lease agreement if the option is not exercised. Ind. Code § 26–1–1–201(37) [1–203(d)(2)]. The "reasonably predictable cost" is to be determined by reference to the facts and circumstances at the time the agreement was made. Id. However the test is articulated, "the courts are clear upon one thing, which is that where the terms of the lease and option purchase are such that the only sensible course of action for the lessee at the end of the term is to exercise the option to purchase and become the owner of the goods, then the lease is one intended to create a security interest." *United Leaseshares, Inc.*, 470 N.E.2d at 1387. At the conclusion of the term of the agreement, Bougher had the option to purchase the truck for $3,190.00, which was "10% of the financed amount."[2] Had Bougher seen the agreement

---

[1]   Multiplying the monthly payment by the number of payments does not yield the total amount cited as due under the agreement, even considering the $4,000 down payment Bougher made.

[2]   Again, the math does not seem to be accurate. By our calculation, the "financed amount" is $41,762.00 ($1,099.00 x 38 months) and the option price is 7.6% of that amount. Using the numbers in the agreement, the option price is 7.4% of the total rental. However, our result is the same regardless of which figures are used.

through to its conclusion, he would have paid a total of $45,762.00 (by our calculation including the down payment) for use of the truck for approximately three years. The only sensible course of action would have been to exercise the option and purchase the truck for a fraction of the total rental price.[3] We therefore conclude that the agreement created a security interest rather than a true lease.[4]

* * *

[Discussion of Gangloff's asserted possessory lien and its priority omitted]

Conclusion

The trial court's judgment and award of damages in favor of Generic is reversed and the case is remanded for further proceedings.

Reversed and remanded.

NOTES

1.   A "full payout" lease is a lease in which the lessor recovers the entire cost of the leased asset, including profit, in lease payments from the lessee. Leases in which the present value of total lease payments are equal or greater than the fair market value of the leased assets are full payout leases. The lease in *Pillowtex* apparently had a full payout term. The *Pillowtex* court considered this term to "undercut[ ] the proposition that the fixtures were merely leased." Section 1–203(c)(1) disagrees. Subsection (c) lists a set of terms that by themselves ("merely because") do not create a security interest. Section 1–203(c)(1) describes a full payout term. Thus, an agreement in the form of a lease does not create a secured transaction merely because it contains a full payout term. See Comment 2 (paragraph 8) to 1–203. Some courts find (c)(1)'s ban puzzling. See, e.g., Gibraltor Financial Corp. v. Prestige Equipment Corp., 949 N.E.2d 314, 325 n.11 (Ind. 2011). Subsection (c)(1) nonetheless has an economic justification. Lessees might agree to a full payout term for either of two reasons. First, they might operate under liquidity constraints. A lessee might have insufficient cash to purchase an asset. It might have only enough funds to make period lease payments, even if the sum of those payments equal the fair market value of the asset. Second, a lessee's inferior bargaining power might compel it to agree to a full payout term. For instance, an immediate need for goods sold in a thin market could force a lessee to lease them under a full payout term rather than having to wait to find suitable

---

[3]   The parties did not introduce any evidence regarding what the fair market value of the semi-truck would be at the expiration of the agreement.

[4]   Prior to the 1991 amendment, our courts considered the following facts relevant to the determination of whether an agreement was a true lease or a security interest: a) the total amount of rent the lessee is required to pay; b) whether the lessee acquires any equity in the property; c) the useful life of the leased goods; d) which party is responsible for the payment of taxes, insurance and other expenses normally associated with ownership; e) which party bears the risk of loss; and f) the extent of the lessee's liability upon default. Although Indiana Code section 26–1–1–201(37) as amended provides that an agreement does not create a security interest merely because it contains certain provisions which our courts previously considered probative, it does not prohibit consideration of them. Here, Bougher had the risk of loss, was required to pay all expenses normally associated with ownership, and was liable for the entire unpaid amount in the event of default.

goods to buy. A lessor's bargaining power does not transform an otherwise true lease into a security interest.

2. Both the economic realties test and the "nominality" of the exercise price of a purchase option require an estimate of fair market value. Because the market value of a good can change between the inception of a lease and the date on which an option to purchase is exercisable under the lease, the date at which fair market value is estimated is crucial. Inflation and unpredictable increases in demand may increase the market price of a good above the estimate of fair market value made at the time a lease is entered into. Fair market value may be determined on an ex ante basis, at the time the lease was concluded, or an ex post basis, at the time the option is exercisable. Although 1–203(d) does not explicitly select between them, 1–203(e) suggests an ex ante estimation. Courts tend to agree; see, e.g., In re Marhoefer Packing Co., 674 F.2d 1139 (7th Cir. 1982); In re UNI Imaging Holdings, LLC, 423 B.R. 406 (Bankr. S.D.N.Y. 2010).

3. Section 1–203(d)(2) provides that an option to purchase the goods is not nominal if the purchase price is stated to be the fair market value of the goods at the time the option is to be performed. Its negative implication is that a purchase option price is nominal if the exercise price is less than the fair market value at the time the option is exercised. In applying (d)(2), the court in *Gangloff Industries* found that the lease required the lessee (Bougher) to pay the lessor (Generic) a total of $43,052 over the 38 months of the lease. Because the lessee had the option to purchase the semi-truck at the end of the lease term for $3,190, the purchase option represented about 7.4% of the total payments required by the lease. The court concluded, based on (d)(2), that the option price therefore was nominal. Is this a correct application of (d)(2)? To evaluate the court's reasoning, assume that a lease gave the lessee the option to purchase the leased asset for $3,190. The lease requires the lessee to make total of $43,052 in rental payments. At the time the lease permits the lessee to exercise the purchase option, the leased asset has a fair market value of $3,000. Does (d)(2) consider this option price nominal? In footnote 3, the *Gangloff* court observes that the parties did not produce evidence of the fair market value of the sem-truck at the end of the lease term.

In re Marhoefer Packing Co., supra, the court characterized an option price of almost 50% of the estimated fair market value of the goods as "significant" and "not nominal." Cases have found that an option price considerably less than fair market value is nominal; see, e.g., In re Royal Food Markets, Inc., 121 B.R. 913 (Bankr. Fla. 1990) (concluding that purchase prices below 25% are nominal). These cases do not reveal when the percentage of option price to fair market value is sufficiently "low" to make the option price is nominal. Findings of nominality based on percentages get some support from Comment 2 to 1–203, which states: "There is a set of purchase options whose fixed price is less than fair market value but greater than nominal that must be determined on the facts of each case to ascertain whether the transaction in which the option is included creates a lease or security interest." Section 1–203(d) appears to define when a purchase option price is nominal while the Comment assumes that "nominality" is defined independently of the subsection. No generally accepted meaning of "nominal price" has emerged in the case law; see In re QDS Components, Inc., 292 B.R. 313 (Bankr. S.D. Ohio 2002).

4. Another source of litigation under 1–203 focuses on the termination condition in 1–203(b)'s bright-line test. Section 1–203(b) applies only if the lease is "not subject to termination by the lessee." The question arises as to whether leases that give the lessee a right of termination effectively are terminable when termination is not economically sensible for the lessee. The argument is that a right of termination that will not be exercised in effect makes the lease not terminable. This argument often has been made in connection with rent-to-own contracts (RTOs). RTOs are an economically important type of transaction in which characterization has been an issue. An RTO is a terminable lease with an option to purchase. No down payment or security deposit is required and the credit history or financial state of the lessee is not checked. The term of the lease typically is short, from one week to a month, and the rent for the period is paid in advance. Small rental payments usually are required. The lease permits the lessee to renew the lease for an additional term simply by paying in advance for the term. If the lessee continues to rent the asset for a stipulated period (typically about 78 weeks), it becomes the owner at the end of the period. RTOs usually also include an option allowing the lessee to purchase the asset within the period for a cash price determined in part by the amount of rent payments previously made. The effective exercise price of purchase option is two to four times the retail cash price. The assets rented through RTO contracts are mostly new and used furniture, appliances and electronic equipment. Although the RTO industry reports that most RTO customers do not end up owning the merchandise rented, an FTC survey finds that 70 percent of RTO customers purchase the merchandise. See Federal Trade Commission Bureau of Economics Staff Report, Executive Summary, Survey of Rent–To–Own Customers (2000).

In the last 15 years RTOs have become the focus of legislative efforts, pitting consumer groups and bankruptcy trustees against the RTO industry. At the federal level, the National Bankruptcy Review Commission in 1994 recommended that the Bankruptcy Code be amended to deem RTOs installment sales contracts. The recommendation was not adopted. The RTO industry has prevailed at the state level. Almost all states have enacted statutes providing that RTOs terminable by the lessee are true leases, not installment sales contracts. Even in the few states that have not enacted such legislation, 1–203 [former 1–201(b)(37)] arguably does not consider a terminable RTO a "security interest." In Perez v. Rent–A–Center, Inc., 892 A.2d 1255 (N.J. 2006), the New Jersey Supreme Court relied on its finding that a vast majority of RTO customers purchase the merchandise rented to conclude that a terminable RTO is a type of conditional sales contract. According to the court, this propensity among RTO customers makes an RTO in substance an installment sale, notwithstanding the customer's right of termination. Although the *Perez* court did not consider 1–203 [former 1–201(b)(37)], its "conditional sale" characterization commits it to characterizing the transaction as creating a security interest. Other courts disagree, concluding that a termination right is economically valuable to RTO customers even if they terminate infrequently. See In re Powers, 983 F.2d 88 (7th Cir.

1993); W.H. Paige & Co. v. State Board of Tax Commissioners, 711 N.E.2d 552 (Tax Ct. Ind. 1999). For analysis of survey data suggesting that customers find termination a valuable feature of an RTO, see Brian J. Zikmund–Fisher & Andrew M. Parker, Demand for Rent–To–Own Contracts: A Behavioral Economic Explanation, 38 J. Econ. Behav. & Org. 199 (1999).

PROBLEM 2.4

Characterize the transactions described below by consulting 1–201(b)(35), 1–203 and 2–401(1). In doing so, assume where relevant that a straight-line rate of depreciation accurately reflects reduction in value of goods. A straight-line rate allocates depreciation per period by the formula:

$$\text{Per period depreciation} \quad = \quad \frac{\text{Cost of asset} - \text{Salvage value}}{\text{Useful life of asset}}$$

Assume also that goods involved in the transactions below have no salvage value at the end of their useful life.

(a) Susan and Bill execute a written agreement concerning a machine with a useful life of 20 years. Machines of the type subject to their agreement normally sell for $100,000. The terms of the agreement recite that "Susan agrees to lease the machine to Bill for 20 years at a rent of $1,000 per month. At the end of that time, Bill is required to return the machine to Susan. Neither Bill nor Susan have the right to terminate this lease." Lease or secured sale? Would the characterization change if the agreement recited that "Susan retains title to the machine throughout the lease term"? 1–201(b)(35).

(b) Bill "leases" a machine from Susan for five years. Their agreement calls for him to make annual payments as "rent" and does not allow either party to cancel the arrangement. Machines of the sort Bill leased can be purchased for $20,000 and have a six-year useful life, and no scrap value. The industry has a strong preference for new machines, so that the machine Bill leased will decline in value to $12,000 on delivery. The machine's value declines by $2,000 in each subsequent year. For instance, at the end of the first year after delivery the machine's value is $10,000. Bill's agreement with Susan gives him the right to purchase the machine at the end of each of the years of the five-year arrangement. The purchase price is set by a schedule calculated according to a straightline depreciation rate over the five-year period of the transaction. For example, at the end of the first year Bill could purchase the machine for $16,000. True lease or security interest? Would the result change if the machine turns out no value after the third year? 1–203(d). Would the result change if Bill had the right to purchase the machine at the end of the first four years of the five-year arrangement according to the calculated purchase prices?

(c) Suppose the agreement in (b) gives Bill the right to cancel the "lease" at any time, without penalty. Lease or secured sale? Would the characterization change if the agreement gave Bill the right to cancel the "lease" only during the last week of the fifth year?

PROBLEM 2.5

(a) Susan and Bill enter into an agreement described as a "lease." It calls for Bill to lease a car from Susan for a period of two years. The lease payments are based on the difference between the car's estimated residual value at the end of the period and the original purchase price. At the end of the two-year period Susan is required to sell the car in a commercially reasonable manner. The car has a 10–year useful life. If the sale proceeds are less than the car's estimated residual value, Bill must pay Susan the deficiency. If the sale proceeds exceed the estimated residual value, Susan must credit Bill for the excess. Bill does not have the right to cancel or extend the term of the agreement, or to purchase the car from Susan. Lease or secured sale?

(b) Assume that the agreement described above does not call for Susan to sell the car at the end of the two-year "lease" term. Instead, Bill is to return the car to Susan at the end of the term. In addition, Bill drives the car more than a specified number of miles during the two-year period, the excess mileage is charged to him at a per mile charge of 50 cents. If he drives fewer miles than the estimate, he is credited for the unutilized miles on the same per mile basis. Lease or secured sale?

(c) Assume that the Susan and Bills' agreement requires Susan to sell the car in a commercially reasonable manner at the end of the two-year term. Susan is to receive a maximum of $1,000 of the sale proceeds. Proceeds in any amounts above that maximum are surplus, to be credited to Bill as a "rent rebate." If the sale proceeds are less than $1,000, Bill is liable for one half of the deficiency. Under the agreement this portion of the deficiency is a "rent adjustment." The current Industry Standards Manual puts a $8,000 resale price on two year old cars of the sort Bill "leased." Lease or secured sale? Would the characterization change if the Manual put a $1,000 resale price on the car?

D. THE CISG AND INTERNATIONAL SALES OF GOODS

The scope of the CISG is limited. It does not apply to all commercial transactions. Instead, it applies to contracts for the sale of goods that are international as defined by the CISG. Under the CISG contracts for such sales are international if they are made between parties whose places of business are in different countries. Article 1(1)(a). The CISG applies to these contracts in two different circumstances: either when the different countries have ratified the CISG or when the forum's choice of law rules ("rules of private international law") select the law of a country that has ratified the CISG. Article 1(1)(a), (b). This basic scope provision not only describes the type of transactions to which the CISG's substantive rules apply. It also constitutes a conflict of laws provision that determines the conditions under which these substantive rules apply. Conflict of laws provisions are rules that a forum uses to select the law applicable to a particular dispute. The CISG's basic scope provision is Article 1. Article 1 is a conflict of laws provision. It provides that the CISG applies either when a contract for the sale of goods is between parties with places of business in different countries that have ratified the CISG or the forum's conflicts principles select the law of a country that has ratified the CISG.

To see the value of the CISG's conflict of laws provision, consider briefly some other conflict of laws rules in use today. Section 1–301(b) is the UCC's general conflict of law provision. It permits the forum state to apply its own law when the parties' agreement has not selected another law and transaction bears an "appropriate relation" to the forum state. Obviously this is a vague standard for the selection of substantive law. Some courts have interpreted an "appropriate relation" as requiring the application of the law of the state having the most significant relationship to the transaction and parties. The "most significant relationship" standard is the conflict of laws rule adopted by the Restatement (Second) of Conflict of Laws. See Restatement (Second) of Conflict of Laws § 188(1) (1969). Even if these courts are right that 1–301(b) permits the choice of forum law only when the forum bears the most significant relationship to the transaction and parties, the "most significant relationship" is as vague as "appropriate relation." For its part, the European Community, by regulation, has adopted its own conflicts rules governing contracts. See Law Applicable to Contractual Obligations, Regulation (EC) No. 593/2008 (Rome I). The default rule of the Regulation is that the law of the country of the seller's habitual residence governs the contract for the sale of goods. Article 4(1)(a). (A legal person's habitual residence is the place of its central administration. Article 19(1).) However, the rule does not apply where the contract bears a "manifestly" closer connection to another country. In this case Article 4(3) makes applicable the law of the country that bears the closest connection to the contract. The vagueness of the "manifestly closest connection" standard makes it difficult to apply in many international sales contracts involving negotiation or performance in different countries. Vague conflicts rules produce legal uncertainty. Reducing this uncertainty requires contracting parties to incur transaction costs either to select law or litigate the issue of applicable law.

1. THE CISG'S TEST OF INTERNATIONALITY

Article 1(1)(a)'s scope provision is easily applied in most instances. This is because its application turns on mostly verifiable facts that make a sales contract international. Under Article 1(1)(a) the CISG applies to contracts for the sale of goods between parties whose places of business are in different contracting states. The identity of the parties usually can be easily determined from the written agreement, when one exists, or by determining who concluded the agreement. In many instances the location of the place of business of the parties also can be identified easily; *Asante Technologies, Inc., v. PMC–Sierra, Inc.*, reproduced below, is an exception. Although the CISG might have used a more cheaply verifiable variable to locate the contracting parties, such as their place of registration, not all contracting parties are corporations or other registered entities. Even registered entities can change their place of registration relatively easily, making ongoing verification burdensome. Whether a country has ratified the CISG can be determined by consulting the declarations on record with the United Nations Treaty Section. Importantly, unlike previous sales treaties, the CISG's application does not turn on whether performance of the contract occurs in more than one country. This fact, although objective, is more difficult to verify than the contracting parties' place of business. The scope of the various treaties and model laws produced by UNCITRAL also turns on the location of a party's place of business in a contracting state.

Article 1(1)(b) is less easily applied. Under Article 1(1)(b), the CISG applies if the forum's conflict of laws principles select the law of a contracting state. As just noted, a forum's conflicts principles sometimes are vague and therefore uncertain in their application. Partly for this reason, Article 95 allows ratifying countries to make a reservation declaring that they will not be bound by Article 1(1)(b). To date the United States, China, Singapore, the Czech Republic and Slovakia have made the reservation.

Article 1(1)(b) contains an important ambiguity that makes its application even more difficult. It is unclear from the Article's language whether it states a conflict of laws rule of the forum or merely a substantive rule of the law of the contracting state selected by the forum's conflicts rules. An example illustrates the ambiguity. Assume that a contract for the sale of goods is concluded by a seller located in country A and a buyer located in country B. Country A has ratified the CISG while making an Article 95 reservation opting out of Article 1(1)(b); country B has not ratified the CISG. Litigation on the contract is initiated in the courts of country F, which has ratified the CISG. Country F has not made an Article 95 reservation opting out of Article 1(1)(b). Finally, assume that F's conflicts principles select the law of Country A as applicable to the contract. If Article 1(1)(b) is part of the forum's (F's) conflicts principles, the CISG applies under Article 1(1)(b), as Country F has not made an Article 95 reservation. On the other hand, if Article 1(1)(b) is part of the substantive law of the country ratifying the CISG, the result is different. F's conflicts principles have selected country A's law, which includes the CISG. Because Country A has made an Article 95 reservation, the reservation deems A "not to be bound" by Article 1(1)(b). Article 1(1)(b) therefore is not part of Country A's substantive law. Accordingly, the CISG applies to the litigated contract only if Article 1(1)(a) is satisfied. Because B is non-contracting state, the Article is not satisfied and the CISG therefore does not apply to the contract dispute.

The relevant diplomatic history surrounding Article 1(1)(b)'s intended interpretation does not resolve the ambiguity. Uniformity in the interpretation of the CISG probably favors reading the Article as stating a rule of substantive law. Countries making an Article 95 reservation intend the CISG not to apply when their law is selected by a forum's conflicts principles. If the forum were their own courts, these countries would not be bound by Article 1(1)(b) and their courts would find the Article inapplicable. Understanding Article 1(1)(b) as part of the conflicts rules of the forum simply encourages forum shopping for a forum that will apply Article 1(1)(b) when courts in reservation-countries would not. This forum shopping produces a nonuniformity in the CISG's interpretation. On the other hand, viewing Article 1(1)(b) as part of the forum's conflicts rules results in a more frequent application of the CISG, because only five ratifying countries have made an Article

95 reservation. In every other ratifying country, the CISG will apply under Article 1(1)(b) if the forum's conflicts principles select the law of a contracting state. The ambiguity in Article 1(1)(b)'s interpretation and its consequences are discussed in John O. Honnold, Uniform Law for International Sales Under the 1980 United Nations Convention 44–46 (H.M. Flechtner ed., 4th ed. 2009); Ingeborg Schwenzer & Pascal Hachem, Article 1, in Schlechtriem & Schwenzer: Commentary on the UN Convention on the International Sale of Goods (CISG) 41–43 (I. Schwenzer ed., 3d ed. 2010).

Asante Technologies, Inc. v. PMC–Sierra, Inc.

United States District Court, Northern District of California, 2001
164 F. Supp.2d 1142

■ James Ware, United States District Judge

* * * The Complaint in this action alleges claims based in tort and contract. Plaintiff contends that Defendant failed to provide it with electronic components meeting certain designated technical specifications. Defendant timely removed the action to this Court on March 16, 2001.

Plaintiff is a Delaware corporation having its primary place of business in Santa Clara County, California. Plaintiff produces network switchers, a type of electronic component used to connect multiple computers to one another and to the Internet. Plaintiff purchases component parts from a number of manufacturers. In particular, Plaintiff purchases application-specific integrated circuits ("ASICs"), which are considered the control center of its network switchers, from Defendant.

Defendant is also a Delaware corporation. Defendant asserts that, at all relevant times, its corporate headquarters, inside sales and marketing office, public relations department, principal warehouse, and most design and engineering functions were located in Burnaby, British Columbia, Canada. Defendant also maintains an office in Portland, Oregon, where many of its engineers are based. Defendant's products are sold in California through Unique Technologies, which is an authorized distributor of Defendant's products in North America. It is undisputed that Defendant directed Plaintiff to purchase Defendant's products through Unique, and that Defendant honored purchase orders solicited by Unique. Unique is located in California. Determining Defendant's "place of business" with respect to its contract with Plaintiff is critical to the question of whether the Court has jurisdiction in this case.

Plaintiff's Complaint focuses on five purchase orders. Four of the five purchase orders were submitted to Defendant through Unique as directed by Defendant. However, Plaintiff does not dispute that one of the purchase orders, dated January 28, 2000, was sent by fax directly to Defendant in British Columbia, and that Defendant processed the order in British Columbia. Defendant shipped all orders to Plaintiff's headquarters in California. Upon delivery of the goods, Unique sent invoices to Plaintiff, at which time Plaintiff tendered payment to Unique either in California or in Nevada.

The Parties do not identify any single contract embodying the agreement pertaining to the sale. Instead, Plaintiff asserts that acceptance of each of its purchase orders was expressly conditioned upon acceptance by Defendant of Plaintiff's "Terms and Conditions," which were included with each Purchase Order. Paragraph 20 of Plaintiff's Terms and Conditions provides "APPLICABLE LAW. The validity [and] performance of this [purchase] order shall be governed by the laws of the state shown on Buyer's address on this order." The buyer's address as shown on each of the Purchase Orders is in San Jose, California. Alternatively, Defendant suggests that the terms of shipment are governed by a document entitled "PMC–Sierra TERMS AND CONDITIONS OF SALE." Paragraph 19 of Defendant's Terms and conditions provides "APPLICABLE LAW: The contract between the parties is made, governed by, and shall be construed in accordance with the laws of the Province of British Columbia and the laws of Canada applicable therein, which shall be deemed to be the proper law hereof. . . . "

Plaintiff's Complaint alleges that Defendant promised in writing that the chips would meet certain technical specifications. Defendant asserts that the following documents upon which Plaintiff relies emanated from Defendant's office in British Columbia: (1) Defendant's August 24, 1998 press release that it would be making chips available for general sampling; (2) Defendant's periodic updates of technical specifications; and (3) correspondence from Defendant to Plaintiff, including a letter dated October 25, 1999. It is furthermore undisputed that the Prototype Product Limited Warranty Agreements relating to some or all of Plaintiff's purchases were executed with Defendant's British Columbia facility.

Defendant does not deny that Plaintiff maintained extensive contacts with Defendant's facilities in Portland Oregon during the "development and engineering" of the ASICs. These contacts included daily email and telephone correspondence and frequent in-person collaborations between Plaintiff's engineers and Defendant's engineers in Portland. Plaintiff contends that this litigation concerns the inability of Defendant's engineers in Portland to develop an ASIC meeting the agreed-upon specifications.

Plaintiff now requests this Court to remand this action back to the Superior Court of the County of Santa Clara pursuant to 28 U.S.C. section 1447(c), asserting lack of subject matter jurisdiction. In addition, Plaintiff requests award of attorneys fees and costs for the expense of bringing this motion. * * *

The Convention on Contracts for the International Sale of Goods ("CISG") is an international treaty which has been signed and ratified by the United States and Canada, among other countries. The CISG was adopted for the purpose of establishing "substantive provisions of law to govern the formation of international sales contracts and the rights and obligations of the buyer and the seller." U.S. Ratification of 1980 United Nations Convention on Contracts for the International Sale of Goods: Official English Text, 15 U.S.C. App. at 52 (1997). The CISG applies "to contracts of sale of goods between parties whose places of business are in different States . . . when the States are Contracting States." 15 U.S.C. App., Art. 1 (1)(a). Article 10 of the CISG provides that "if a party has more than one place of business, the place of business is that which has the closest relationship to the contract and its performance." 15 U.S.C. App. Art. 10.

Defendant asserts that this Court has jurisdiction to hear this case pursuant to 28 U.S.C. section 1331, which dictates that the "district courts shall have original jurisdiction of all civil actions arising under the Constitution, laws, or treaties of the United States." Specifically, Defendant contends that the contract claims at issue necessarily implicate the CISG, because the contract is between parties having their places of business in two nations which have adopted the CISG treaty. The Court concludes that Defendant's place of business for the purposes of the contract at issue and its performance is Burnaby, British Columbia, Canada. Accordingly, the CISG applies. Moreover, the parties did not effectuate an "opt out" of application of the CISG. Finally, because the Court concludes that the CISG preempts state laws that address the formation of a contract of sale and the rights and obligations of the seller and buyer arising from such a contract, the well-pleaded complaint rule does not preclude removal in this case.

A.   Federal Jurisdiction Attaches to Claims Governed By the CISG

Although the general federal question statute, 28 U.S.C. § 1331(a), gives district courts original jurisdiction over every civil action that "arises under the . . . treaties of the United States," an individual may only enforce a treaty's provisions when the treaty is self-executing, that is, when it expressly or impliedly creates a private right of action. See Tel–Oren v. Libyan Arab Republic, 726 F.2d 774, 808 (D.C. Cir. 1984). The parties do not dispute that the CISG properly creates a private right of action. U.S. Ratification of 1980 United Nations Convention on Contracts for the International Sale of Goods: Official English Text, 15 U.S.C. App. at 52 (1997) ("The Convention sets out substantive provisions of law to govern the formation of international sales contracts and the rights and obligations of the buyer and seller. It will apply to sales contracts between parties with their places of business in different countries bound by Convention, provided the parties have left their contracts silent as to applicable law."). Therefore, if the CISG properly applies to this action, federal jurisdiction exists.

B.   The Contract in Question Is Between Parties from Two Different Contracting States

The CISG only applies when a contract is "between parties whose places of business are in different States." 15 U.S.C. App., Art. 1(1)(a). If this requirement is not satisfied, Defendant cannot claim jurisdiction under the CISG. It is undisputed that Plaintiff's place of business is Santa Clara County, California, U.S.A. It is further undisputed that during the relevant time period, Defendant's corporate headquarters, inside sales and marketing office, public relations department, principal warehouse, and most of its design and engineering functions were located in Burnaby, British Columbia, Canada. However, Plaintiff contends that, pursuant to Article 10 of the CISG, Defendant's "place of business" having the closest relationship to the contract at issue is the United State.[1]

The Complaint asserts inter alia two claims for breach of contract and a claim for breach of express warranty based on the failure of the delivered ASICS to conform to the agreed upon technical specifications. In support of these claims, Plaintiff relies on multiple representations allegedly made by Defendant regarding the technical specifications of the ASICS products at issue. Among the representations are: (1) an August 24, 1998 press release; (2) "materials" released by Defendant in September, 1998; (3) "revised materials" released by Defendant in November 1998; (4) "revised materials" released by Defendant in January, 1999; (5) "revised materials" released by Defendant in April, 1999; (6) a September, 1999 statement by Defendant which included revised specifications indicating that its ASICS would comply with 802.1q VLAN specifications; (7) a statement made by Defendant's President and Chief Executive Officer on October 25, 1999; (8) a communication of December, 1999; and (9) "revised materials" released by Defendant in January, 2000. It appears undisputed that each of these alleged representations regarding the technical specifications of the product was issued from Defendant's headquarters in British Columbia, Canada.

Rather than challenge the Canadian source of these documents, Plaintiff shifts its emphasis to the purchase orders submitted by Plaintiff to Unique Technologies, a nonexclusive distributor of Defendant's products. Plaintiff asserts that Unique acted in the United States as an agent of Defendant, and that Plaintiff's contacts with Unique establish Defendant's place of business in the U.S. for the purposes of this contract.

Plaintiff has failed to persuade the Court that Unique acted as the agent of Defendant. Plaintiff provides no legal support for this proposition. To the contrary, a distributor of goods for resale is normally not treated as an agent of the manufacturer. Restatement of the Law of Agency, 2d § 14J (1957) ("One who receives goods from another for resale to a third person is not thereby the other's agent in the transaction."); Stansifer v. Chrysler Motors Corp., 487 F.2d 59, 64–65 (9th Cir. 1973) (holding that nonexclusive distributor was not agent of manufacturer where distributorship agreement expressly stated "distributor is not an agent"). Agency results "from the manifestation of consent by one person to another that the other shall act on his behalf and subject to his control, and consent by the other so to act." Restatement of the Law of Agency, 2d, § 1 (1957).

Plaintiff has produced no evidence of consent by Defendant to be bound by the acts of Unique. To the contrary, Defendant cites the distributorship agreement with Unique, which expressly states that the contract does not "allow Distributor to create or assume any obligation on behalf of [Defendant] for any purpose whatsoever." Furthermore, while Unique may distribute Defendant's products, Plaintiff does not

---

[1]   Article 10 of the CISG states inter alia:

For the purposes of this Convention:(a) If a party has more than one place of business, the place of business is that which has the closest relationship to the contract and its performance, having regard to the circumstances known to or contemplated by the parties at any time before or at the conclusion of the contract.

allege that Unique made any representations regarding technical specifications on behalf of Defendant. Indeed, Unique is not even mentioned in the Complaint. To the extent that representations were made regarding the technical specifications of the ASICs, and those specifications were not satisfied by the delivered goods, the relevant agreement is that between Plaintiff and Defendant. Accordingly, the Court finds that Unique is not an agent of Defendant in this dispute. Plaintiff's dealings with Unique do not establish Defendant's place of business in the United States.

Plaintiff's claims concern breaches of representations made by Defendant from Canada. Moreover, the products in question are manufactured in Canada, and Plaintiff knew that Defendant was Canadian, having sent one purchase order directly to Defendant in Canada by fax. Plaintiff supports its position with the declaration of Anthony Contos, Plaintiff's Vice President of Finance and Administration, who states that Plaintiff's primary contact with Defendant "during the development and engineering of the ASICs at issue . . . was with [Defendant's] facilities in Portland, Oregon." The Court concludes that these contacts are not sufficient to override the fact that most if not all of Defendant's alleged representations regarding the technical specifications of the products emanated from Canada. Moreover, Plaintiff directly corresponded with Defendant at Defendant's Canadian address. Plaintiff relies on all of these alleged representations at length in its Complaint. In contrast, Plaintiff has not identified any specific representation or correspondence emanating from Defendant's Oregon branch. For these reasons, the Court finds that Defendant's place of business that has the closest relationship to the contract and its performance is British Columbia, Canada. Consequently, the contract at issue in this litigation is between parties from two different Contracting States, Canada and the United States. This contract therefore implicates the CISG.

C.   The Effect of the Choice of Law Clauses

Plaintiff next argues that, even if the Parties are from two nations that have adopted the CISG, the choice of law provisions in the "Terms and Conditions" set forth by both Parties reflect the Parties' intent to "opt out" of application of the treaty. 6 Article 6 of the CISG provides that "the parties may exclude the application of the Convention or, subject to Article 12, derogate from or vary the effect of any of its provisions." 15 U.S.C. App., Art. 6. Defendant asserts that merely choosing the law of a jurisdiction is insufficient to opt out of the CISG, absent express exclusion of the CISG. The Court finds that the particular choice of law provisions in the "Terms and Conditions" of both parties are inadequate to effectuate an opt out of the CISG.[2]

---

[2]   Plaintiff's Terms and Conditions provide "APPLICABLE LAW. The validity [and] performance of this [purchase] order shall be governed by the laws of the state shown on Buyer's address on this order." The buyer's address as shown on each of the Purchase Orders is San Jose, California. Defendant's Terms and Conditions provides "APPLICABLE LAW: The contract between the parties is made, governed by, and shall be construed in accordance with the laws of the Province of British Columbia and the laws of Canada applicable therein, which shall be deemed to be the proper law hereof. . . . " It is undisputed that British Columbia has adopted the CISG.

Although selection of a particular choice of law, such as "the California Commercial Code" or the "Uniform Commercial Code" could amount to implied exclusion of the CISG, the choice of law clauses at issue here do not evince a clear intent to opt out of the CISG. For example, Defendant's choice of applicable law adopts the law of British Columbia, and it is undisputed that the CISG is the law of British Columbia. Furthermore, even Plaintiff's choice of applicable law generally adopts the "laws of" the State of California, and California is bound by the Supremacy Clause to the treaties of the United States. U.S. Const. art. VI, cl. 2 ("This Constitution, and the laws of the United States which shall be made in pursuance thereof; and all treaties made, or which shall be made, under the authority of the United States, shall be the supreme law of the land.") Thus, under general California law, the CISG is applicable to contracts where the contracting parties are from different countries that have adopted the CISG. In the absence of clear language indicating that both contracting parties intended to opt out of the CISG, and in view of Defendant's Terms and Conditions which would apply the CISG, the Court rejects Plaintiff's contention that the choice of law provisions preclude the applicability of the CISG.

D.   Federal Jurisdiction Based Upon the CISG Does Not Violate the Well–Pleaded Complaint Rule

The Court rejects Plaintiff's argument that removal is improper because of the well-pleaded complaint rule. The rule states that a cause of action arises under federal law only when the plaintiff's well-pleaded complaint raises issues of federal law. Anticipation of a federal preemption defense, such as the defense that federal law prohibits the state claims, is insufficient to establish federal jurisdiction. Even where both parties concede that determination of a federal question is the only issue in the case, removal is improper unless the plaintiff's complaint establishes that the case "arises under" federal law.

It is undisputed that the Complaint on its face does not refer to the CISG. However, Defendants argue that the preemptive force of the CISG converts the state breach of contract claim into a federal claim. Indeed, Congress may establish a federal law that so completely preempts a particular area of law that any civil complaint raising that select group of claims is necessarily federal in character.

It appears that the issue of whether or not the CISG preempts state law is a matter of first impression. In the case of federal statutes, "the question of whether a certain action is preempted by federal law is one of congressional intent. The purpose of Congress is the ultimate touchstone." Pilot Life Ins. Co. v. Dedeaux, 481 U.S. 41, 45 (1987). Transferring this analysis to the question of preemption by a treaty, the Court focuses on the intent of the treaty's contracting parties.

In the case of the CISG treaty, this intent can be discerned from the introductory text, which states that "the adoption of uniform rules which govern contracts for the international sale of goods and take into account the different social, economic and legal systems would contribute to the removal of legal barriers in international trade and promote the development of international trade." 15 U.S.C. App. at 53. The CISG further recognizes the importance of "the development of international trade on the basis of equality and mutual benefit." These objectives are reiterated in the President's Letter of Transmittal of the

CISG to the Senate as well as the Secretary of State's Letter of Submittal of the CISG to the President. The Secretary of State, George P. Shultz, noted:

> Sales transactions that cross international boundaries are subject to legal uncertainty—doubt as to which legal system will apply and the difficulty of coping with unfamiliar foreign law. The sales contract may specify which law will apply, but our sellers and buyers cannot expect that foreign trading partners will always agree on the applicability of United States law. * * * The Convention's approach provides an effective solution for this difficult problem. When a contract for an international sale of goods does not make clear what rule of law applies, the Convention provides uniform rules to govern the questions that arise in making and performance of the contract.

The Court concludes that the expressly stated goal of developing uniform international contract law to promote international trade indicates the intent of the parties to the treaty to have the treaty preempt state law causes of action.

The availability of independent state contract law causes of action would frustrate the goals of uniformity and certainty embraced by the CISG. Allowing such avenues for potential liability would subject contracting parties to different states' laws and the very same ambiguities regarding international contracts that the CISG was designed to avoid. As a consequence, parties to international contracts would be unable to predict the applicable law, and the fundamental purpose of the CISG would be undermined. Based on very similar rationale, courts have concluded that the Warsaw Convention preempts state law causes of action. The conclusion that the CISG preempts state law also comports with the view of academic commentators on the subject. See William S. Dodge, Teaching the CISG in Contracts, 50 J. Legal Educ. 72, 72 (March 2000) ("As a treaty the CISG is federal law, which preempts state common law and the UCC."); David Frisch, Commercial Common Law, The United Nations Convention on the International Sale of Goods, and the Inertia of Habit, 74 Tul. L. Rev. 495, 503–04 (1999) ("Since the CISG has the preemptive force of federal law, it will preempt article 2 when applicable.").

Furthermore, the Court has considered Plaintiff's arguments and finds them unpersuasive. Plaintiff argues that the CISG is incomparable to preemption under the Warsaw Convention, because "the CISG leaves open the possibility of other, concurrent causes of action." This argument merely begs the question by assuming that the state law causes of action asserted by Plaintiff are properly brought. Based on the proper applicable legal analysis discussed above, the Court concludes that the pleaded state law claims are preempted.

Plaintiff next claims that the CISG does not completely supplant state law, because the CISG is limited in scope to the formation of the contract and the rights and obligations of the seller and buyer arising from the contract. Plaintiff's correct observation that the CISG does not concern the validity of the contract or the effect which the contract may have on the property in the goods sold fails to support Plaintiff's conclusion that the CISG does not supplant any area of state contract law. Although the CISG is plainly limited in its scope (15 U.S.C. App.,

Art. 4.), the CISG nevertheless can and does preempt state contract law to the extent that the state causes of action fall within the scope of the CISG. Compare Franchise Tax Bd., 463 U.S. at 22–23 (holding that ERISA did not preempt the state tax collection suit at issue, because the state causes of action did not fall within the scope of § 502(a) of ERISA) and Metropolitan Life Ins. Co., 481 U.S. at 66 (relying on Franchise Tax Bd. and holding that ERISA preempts all state causes of action within the scope of § 502(a)).

Finally, Plaintiff appears to confuse the matter of exclusive federal jurisdiction with preemption. Plaintiff first asserts that "if . . . the CISG is 'state law' . . . then the California courts have jurisdiction to adjudicate a case arising under these laws." The matter of whether California courts may have jurisdiction to interpret the CISG is irrelevant to the determination of whether the CISG preempts state law and establishes federal jurisdiction over the case. Even where federal law completely preempts state law, state courts may have concurrent jurisdiction over the federal claim if the defendant does not remove the case to federal court. This Court does not hold that it has exclusive jurisdiction over CISG claims. Hence, the Court's conclusion that the CISG preempts state claims is not inconsistent with Plaintiff's examples of the adjudication of CISG-based claims in state court. Plaintiff further asserts that "if the CISG so completely supplants state law as to deny the California courts the opportunity to rule on a CISG cause of action, then the reference to 'state law' in Asante's choice-of-law provision is unambiguous, and the CISG also does not apply." The Court also rejects this claim, as the determination of CISG preemption is wholly independent of the question of whether a choice-of-law clause in a particular contract is ambiguous or not.

The Court concludes that the well-pleaded complaint rule does not preclude federal jurisdiction in this case, because the CISG preempts state law causes of action falling within the scope of the CISG.

NOTES

1. The seller in *Asante Technologies* had multiple places of business. For purposes of Article 1(1)(a), the seller must be located in only one of its places of business. Under Article 10(a), if a party has more than one place of business, its place of business is that which has the closest relationship to "the contract and its performance." Article 10(a) does not locate a party at its principal place of business or its head office. Instead, the party is located at the place most closely connected to the transaction as a whole. See Secretariat Commentary on the [1978] Draft Convention on Contracts for the International Sale of Good, in Diplomatic History of the Uniform Law for International Sales 409 (para. 6) (J. Honnold ed., 1989). Locating a party's place of business when it has multiple places of business is unproblematic when both the contract and its performance occur at one location or within one country. In Bezirksgericht der Saane (Switzerland), 20 February 1997, available at http://www.cisg.law.pace.edu/cases/970220s1.html, an Austrian buyer concluded a contract for the sale of liquor from a Swiss branch office of a firm with its head office in Liechtenstein. The contract required the seller to transport the liquor by truck from Switzerland. Switzerland had ratified the CISG; Liechtenstein had not. Finding that both the contract and its performance occurred at the seller's Swiss branch office, the court concluded that the seller's place of business was in Switzerland. *Asante Technology* is more difficult because elements of the parties' contract and its performance occur in different countries. Some of the buyer's purchase orders were received by the seller's California distributor, which in turn forwarded them to the seller in Canada. The electronic components were delivered to the buyer in California, and the buyer paid the seller's California distributor. In locating the seller's place of business, the *Asante Technology* court considers important the representations made by the seller from its headquarters in Canada. It therefore apparently assumes that a party's location is at the place at which its conduct occurred for which it is allegedly liable. In *Asante Technology* the seller's alleged liability is based on warranties it made to the buyer in communications from its Canadian headquarters. Article 10(a) does not support this claim-based way of locating a contracting party. The Article locates a place of business by its connection to the "contract and its performance," not to the place in which conduct occurs which gives rise to breach.

2. Article 6 allows contracting parties to opt out of ("derogate from") all of the CISG's provisions, except for certain formal requirements enforceable by applicable domestic law. This makes the CISG almost entirely a set of default rules. Article 6's application raises two questions: (1) Is an express exclusion of the CISG or specific provisions required, or does an implicit exclusion suffice?, and (2) If an express exclusion is required, what language constitutes an express exclusion? None of the CISG's provisions answer either question. The Uniform Law on the International Sale of Goods (1964) was a treaty that served as a template in the drafting of the CISG. Article 3 of that treaty allowed parties to exclude its application expressly or implicitly. Early drafts of the CISG eliminated comparable language in Article 6, and the national representatives were unable to agree on a position to be reflected in the CISG's text. So both questions just identified have been left to national courts and arbitral tribunals.

Both questions are in play in *Asante Technology*. The buyer argued that the parties' agreement selects British Columbian provincial law as well as Canadian law. This choice of law, according to the buyer, displaces the CISG. In rejecting the buyer's argument, the *Asante Technology* court requires the parties' agreement to evince a "clear intent" to opt out of the CISG. Because Canada has ratified the CISG, it is part of the federal law of Canada. Thus, in selecting Canadian law the court concludes that the parties have not shown a clear intent to derogate from the CISG. Most courts are in accord with *Asante Technology* in giving effect only to express exclusions from the CISG. See Hanwha Corp. v. Cedar Petrochemicals, Inc., 760 F. Supp.2d 426 (S.D.N.Y. 2011); BP Oil Int'l, Ltd. v. Empresa Estatal Petroleos de Ecuador, 332 F.3d 333 (5th Cir. 2003); Valero Marketing & Supply Co. v. Greeni, 373 F. Supp.2d 475 (D.N.J. 2005); but cf. American Biophysics Corp. v. Dubois Marine Specialties, 411 F.Supp.2d 61 (D.R.I. 2006).

It can be argued that the language of the parties' agreement in *Asante Technology* expressly excluded the CISG. Rational contracting parties do not incur contracting costs to provide terms that applicable default rules already make applicable to their agreement. Providing such terms is a waste of resources. Given the court's conclusion that the seller's place of business was in Canada and the buyer's in California, under Article 1(1)(a) the CISG governs their sales contract. Both the seller and buyers' forms they exchanged contained an applicable law clause calling for British Columbian provincial law and Canadian law. Canadian federal law already incorporates the CISG. Thus, assuming that parties do not waste resources in providing for terms already applicable to their contract, the parties in *Asante Technology* clearly intended to exclude the CISG and make Canadian federal and provincial law applicable to their contract. Why else would they provide the applicable law clause they did? True, the CISG does not contain rules governing all aspects of the sales contract, as noted below, and the parties might have intended merely to have Canadian domestic law supplement the CISG's rules. The applicable law clause need not be read as an intention to exclude the CISG. This is possible but unlikely. Parties wanting Canadian domestic law merely to supplement the CISG, not displace it entirely, probably would go out of their way to articulate their desire. Otherwise, they risk having a court interpret their applicable law clause merely as calling for the CISG. This leaves the selection of supplementing applicable domestic law entirely up to the court. In addition, the novelty of the CISG itself subjects the parties' contract to a good deal of legal uncertainty. For both reasons, the parties more likely intended their applicable law clause to exclude the CISG entirely. A fairly recent survey of American business lawyers found that most choose to opt out the CISG; see George V. Philippopoulos, Awareness of the CISG Among American Attorneys, 40 UCC L. J. 357 (2008).

3. In Ho Myung Moolsan, Co. Ltd. v. Manitou Mineral Water, Inc., 73 UCC Rep. Serv.2d 313 (S.D.N.Y. 2010), both parties litigated a sales contract on the assumption that the UCC applied to it. In fact the contract was governed by the CISG. Finding that the parties either waived the CISG's application or were estopped from asserting it, the court concluded that the UCC applied. The court's conclusion is in tension with the dominant view that the CISG is a set of default rules and that derogation from its application under Article 6 must be express. If the CISG becomes inapplicable only when the parties expressly opt out of its application, why is it inapplicable when the parties waive or are estopped from asserting its application? Strictly, the court's view is internally consistent: expressly opting out can be required as part of the sales contract, while implicitly opting out is allowed later when the contract is litigated. However, the position is questionable. Expressly opting out is more costly than implicitly opting out by waiver or estoppel. There seems to be no good reason to require parties to bear higher transaction costs at the contract formation stage to opt out of the CISG than at the litigation stage. True, waiver or estoppel might send a particularly clear signal that the parties do not want the CISG to be applied to their contract. But so too can particularly entrenched trade usage or course of dealing to the same effect.

PROBLEM 2.6

(a) Seller Corp., located in Charlottesville, contracts to sell steel tubing to Buyer Corp., located in Tokyo. The contract calls for Seller to manufacture the tubing in Seller's Charlottesville factory and deliver it Buyer in New York City for installation in a building there under construction. Does the CISG apply to the sales contract? CISG Article 1(1)(a).

(b) Suppose Buyer is a homeowner whose home is located in Tokyo. Buyer contracts with Seller to purchase steel piping for incorporation in his home. The steel piping almost always is used for industrial applications in factories. Although the contract gives Buyer's Tokyo address, it calls for Seller to deliver the piping to Buyer in New York City. Based on these facts, does the CISG apply to the sales contract? CISG Article 2(a).

(c) Suppose in (a) that Buyer Corp. changed its installation plans so that Seller's steel piping was no longer needed. Accordingly, Buyer took delivery of the piping and resold it to Buyer 2, located in New York City, who installed the piping in its building there. After discovering that the piping was defective, Buyer 2 sued Seller. (Buyer Corp. proved to be an inconvenient defendant for Buyer 2.) Does the CISG control Buyer 2's rights against Seller, if any? CISG Articles 1(1)(a), 4.

PROBLEM 2.7

Material Corp. is a multinational corporation headquartered and incorporated in Delaware, with corporate subsidiaries and factories in the United Kingdom and Columbia ("Material UK" and "Material Columbia," respectively). Opt is a Columbian corporation that manufactures computers. After consulting the Delaware headquarters, Material's London office contracted with Opt to sell it a specially designed computer. Delivery was to be made at Opt's office in Columbia. The sales contract called for Opt to provide Material with crucial components for the computer. These components amount to 40 percent of the parts comprising the computer Material is to deliver. In addition, the contract required Material to use it "good faith efforts" to market Opt's computers in the United Kingdom. Material was obligated to purchase from Opt computers that Material could resell in the United Kingdom through its "good faith best efforts."

The agreement was complex and Material UK throughout negotiations sought advice and acted on instructions from Material's Delaware headquarters. Material Columbia took no part in the transaction. Near the close of the deal, some executives from the Delaware office traveled to Columbia to oversee the details of a final agreement. A protracted series of negotiations required Material's executives to rent offices in Columbia for three weeks. To finalize the agreement, Material UK's chief contracting officer flew to Columbia to initial the formal agreement. A dispute later arises over the computer Material UK delivered to Opt and Material UK's failure to buy any of Opt's computers. As to the latter, Opt alleges that Material UK made no effort to market Opt's computers in the United Kingdom. Columbia and the United States have ratified the CISG; the United Kingdom has not. What law governs the dispute? CISG Articles

1(1)(a), 3(1), 10(a), 14(1); cf. 2–102, 2–306(2). Would the applicable law change if Material Delaware contracted with Opt?

PROBLEM 2.8

Seller located in France contracted to sell machinery to Buyer located in the United Kingdom. The contract is negotiated in Paris and calls for delivery there as well. In addition, Seller's French plant will produce the computers. Accordingly, when the parties litigate over the contract, the forum court determines that French law applies to the dispute. France has ratified the CISG without making an Article 95 reservation; the United Kingdom has not ratified the CISG.

     (a) Does the CISG govern? Articles 1(1)(b), 95.

     (b) Assume that the forum court selects the law of the United States as applicable to the contract. Does the CISG govern the contract? The United States has made a reservation under Article 95.

     (c) Assume that the country in which the forum court is located has ratified the CISG without making an Article 95 reservation. Assume also that the court determines that United States law governs the contract. Does the CISG apply?

PROBLEM 2.9

Seller is located in the United Kingdom and Buyer in India. Their agreement requires Seller to deliver a quantity of widgets to be manufactured by it in New Delhi to Buyer in London. The price and delivery dates are specified, and the contract's applicable law clause calls for "the CISG to apply to all aspects of this agreement, to the exclusion of otherwise applicable local law. All disputes relating to this agreement will be litigated only in American or British courts." Every state other than Louisiana has enacted 1–301(a) (or pre-2001 1–105(1)), which in relevant part provides that "when a transaction bears a reasonable relation to this state and also to another state or nation the parties may agree that the law either of this state or of such other state or nation shall govern their rights and obligations." The relevant portion of Article 3(1) of the Law Applicable to Contractual Obligations, effective in the United Kingdom, provides that "[a] contract shall be governed by the law chosen by the parties . . . By their choice the parties can select the law applicable to the whole or part only of their contract." Regulation (EC) No. 593/2008 (Rome I). Neither the United Kingdom nor India has ratified the CISG. If suit arising from the sales contract is filed in an American or British court, will these courts apply the CISG?

2. COVERED CONTRACTS

The CISG governs only contracts for the sale of goods. Article 1(1). A contract therefore fall outside the CISG's scope for either of two reasons: the contract does not involve a sale or it involves the sale of a non-good. Consider these points in order. A variety of contracts, including distributorship, agency, and franchise agreements, are not governed by the CISG. Such agreements are not sales contracts. Instead, they set the general terms and some specific terms within which sales of goods are to be concluded. For instance, a joint venture agreement might set payment dates, marketing obligations and prices for goods ordered by the venture, and call for trademark protection. Such agreements state the ground rules within which contracts of sale are to be concluded without themselves being contracts of sale. Thus, the CISG does not apply to them. Courts have held that framework agreements by themselves are not contracts for the sale of goods when they do not call for a particular sale of goods and lack definite terms as to price and quantity of these goods. See, e.g., Amco Ukservice & Prompriladamco v. American Meter Co., 312 F. Supp.2d 681 (E.D. Pa. 2004); Viva Vino Import Co. v. Farnese Vini S.r.l., 2000 WL 1224903, at *1 (E.D. Pa. 2000); Helen Kaminski PTY Ltd. v. Marketing Australian Products, 1997 WL 414137, at *1 (S.D.N.Y. 1997). Other national courts have reached the same result; see e.g., Bundesgerichtshof (Germany), 23 July 1997, available at http://cisgw3.law.pace.edu/cases/970723g2.html. However, particular sales of goods concluded under framework agreements are subject to the CISG. Thus, different law applies to the enforceability and entitlements under a framework agreement and under a sales contract concluded within it. This difference in law does not matter when the domestic law applicable to the framework agreement is the same as the CISG. However, some domestic law formal requirements and definiteness of terms can be more demanding than under the CISG.

Article 1 limits the CISG's scope to contracts for the sale of goods. The CISG therefore is inapplicable to contracts for the sale of assets other than goods. The CISG does not define the term "goods." Instead, Article 2 makes the CISG inapplicable to certain sorts of sales. Some of these sales involve goods, such as sales of consumer goods or ships. CISG Articles 2(a), (e). Other sales may or may not involve goods, such as sales by auction or sales electricity. Article 2(b), (f). Clearly goods are tangible assets that are moveable, because the CISG's provisions regulating delivery, shipment and risk of loss (e.g., Articles 31, 60, 67) contemplate such assets. In most instances the character of an asset as a good under the CISG will be uncontroversial. However, sometimes its character will be difficult to determine. Is a contract for the sale of unmined ore by a U.S. seller to a Japanese buyer a contract for the sale of a good? Under Article 2 of the UCC, unmined ore is a good; see 2–107(1). The answer, however, is unclear under the CISG. A more salient example involves the sale of tangible assets in which intangible rights are embedded, such as intellectual property rights. Is the sale of the flash drive in which the software program is embedded a sale of a good under the CISG? As noted in section A. above, the answer is important because it determines the set of default rules applicable to the contract. Following are abstracts of two German cases addressing the issue.

Uncitral Clout Case 131

Germany: Landgericht Munchen I (8 February 1995)

The German defendant ordered a computer programme from the French plaintiff. The programme was delivered and installed. The parties also intended to conclude a second contract concerning the use of the programme, but the negotiations on that contract failed. The defendant then refused to pay the purchase price of the programme, which was delivered and installed.

The court held that the CISG was applicable as the parties had their place of business in different CISG Contracting States and as the CISG applies to standard software. The court further found also that the parties had agreed on all particulars of the sale of the programme and therefore had concluded a sales contract.

It was held that the defendant could not rely on a possible lack of conformity of the software programme, since it had not effectively given notice of the defect but had only asked for assistance in addressing the problems identified. As a result, the court ordered the defendant to pay the purchase price and interest at the rate of 5%.

Uncitral Clout Case 122

Germany: Oberlandesgericht Koln (26 August 1994)

The plaintiff, a Swiss market research institute, had elaborated and delivered a market analysis, which had been ordered by the defendant, a German company. The defendant refused to pay the price alleging that the report did not comply with the conditions agreed upon by the parties.

The court held that the CISG was not applicable, since the underlying contract was neither a contract for the sale of goods (article 1(1) CISG) nor a contract for the production of goods (article 3(1) CISG). Noting that the sale of goods is characterized by the transfer of property in an object, the court found that, although a report is fixed on a piece of paper, the main concern of the parties is not the handing over of the paper but the transfer of the right to use the ideas written down on such paper. Therefore, the court held that the agreement to prepare a market analysis is not a sale of goods within the meaning of articles 1 or 3 CISG.

PROBLEM 2.10

Seller Corp., incorporated in France, is located in New York City and Buyer Corp., incorporated in France, is located in Paris. Seller and Buyer reach an agreement for the sale of drilling machines ("the agreement"). The terms of the agreement give Buyer the right to purchase from Seller these machines, according to its needs. Buyer also has the right to use Seller's trademark for machines it produces with Seller's specifications. The agreement requires Buyer to get Seller's approval for advertisements in places for the machines it produces with Seller's trademark. It also places a lower limit on the price at which Buyer can sell both any machines it purchases from Seller as well as those it produces with Seller's trademark. (Assume the limitation does not violate applicable antitrust laws.) Finally, the agreement calls for Buyer to provide special metal drill fittings to Seller for incorporation in the machines Seller produces for Buyer. The drill fittings, which only Buyer can supply, cost $100. Drilling machines of the sort described in the agreement cannot be produced without drill fittings.

Buyer orders 100 drilling machines from Seller at $10,000 per machine and supplies Seller with drill fittings to be incorporated in them. Seller produces and delivers the machines to Buyer, who later discovers that they do not work. Buyer sues Seller for breach of contract. At the same time, Buyer advertises the machines without getting Seller's approval and resells machines previously purchased from Seller for a price below the limit set by its agreement with Seller. Seller sues Buyer for breach of contract. Does the CISG apply to Buyer's suit against Seller? Does it apply to Seller's suit against Buyer? See CISG Articles 1(1)(a), 3(1), (2), 4.

PROBLEM 2.11

At Buyer Corp.'s request, Data Corp. designed a software program suitable for Buyer's specific inventory control system. Data registered a copyright in the software naming itself as owner. To deliver the program, Data sold to Buyer flash drives containing it. The sales agreement Data gave Buyer a nonexclusive license to use the program indefinitely while restricting the conditions of its use. Buyer is located in the U.S. and Seller in France. Does the CISG apply to licensed software? See CISG Articles 1, 3(2). What result if the parties are both located in the U.S.? For the treatment of computer information embedded in tangible objects, see supra Notes 2 and 3.

3. THE CISG'S LIMITED SCOPE

The CISG is not a comprehensive law of international sales contracts. It does not address a number of issues that can arise in connection with such contracts. Article 4 limits CISG's scope, even when it applies to a transaction, to the formation of the sales contract and the rights and obligations of the contracting parties arising from such a contract. Thus, the CISG does not govern the rights of third parties in the contract or the goods. Issues not controlled by the CISG are left to applicable national sales law.

Important among the issues the CISG does not address, and therefore does not govern, is the "validity" of the contract or its provisions. Article 4(a). Because the CISG does not contain definitions of operative terms, including "validity," its scope ultimately depends on whether an issue is characterized as one of "validity," as opposed to, say, one of contract formation, which the CISG does govern. The CISG also does not apply to the seller's liability for death or personal injury caused by the goods to any person. Article 5. Even when the CISG applies to a matter, it does not contain all the resources to resolve it. The CISG does not contain a counterpart to 1–103(b) of the UCC, which supplements the UCC with principles of law and equity. This means that some matters within the CISG's scope are resolved under domestic law, not the CISG. Article 7(2) provides that matters not "expressly settled" in the CISG are to be settled by "general principles on which [the CISG] is based." The CISG nowhere identifies these "general principles." Where such principles are inapplicable to a matter, Article 7(2) directs that domestic law selected by conflict of laws rules resolve it.

PROBLEM 2.12

Seller Corp., located in Shanghai, contracted to sell air conditioning units to Buyer Corp., located in Atlanta. Before Seller shipped the units to Buyer, it discovered that they did not confirm to the specifications required by the contract. It said nothing to Buyer even after obtaining an inspection certificate that attested to the conformity of the units. On delivery Buyer tested the units and discovered the nonconformity. Buyer sued Seller alleging breach of contract as well as negligence and fraud. Does Buyer have a cause of action in negligence and fraud? CISG Preamble, Articles 4, 7; cf. Electrocraft Arkansas, Inc. v. Super Electric Motors, Ltd., 70 UCC Rep. Serv.2d 716 (E.D. Ark. 2009).

PROBLEM 2.13

X Corporation, headquarted in New York City, had an overstock of computer hardware in its warehouses. Rather than finding buyers in the United States, X Corporation had Selco, its wholly owned subsidiary located in Berlin, arrange for sales with European buyers. Selco sold some of X's overstock to Buyer, located in Paris. The computer hardware Selco delivered to Buyer malfunctioned and Selco is insolvent. Accordingly, Buyer has sued only X Corporation for breach of contract. It argues that X is liable under the CISG. Does the CISG govern X's liability, if any? CISG Articles, 1(1)(a), 4; Restatement (Third) of Agency § 2.06 (2006) (liability of undisclosed principal).

CHAPTER 3

CONTRACT FORMATION AND THE MECHANICS OF ASSENT

A. ARTICLE 2'S TWO APPROACHES TO CONTRACT FORMATION

In general, two different approaches can be taken to the formation of a contract. One is to analyze contract formation in terms of a formal offer and acceptance. A contract, on this approach, is a bargain initiated by an offer and concluded by an acceptance. Rules concerning the lapse, rejection and revocation of an offer are part of this approach. A second approach is simply to find a contract where there is consent to an agreement. Civil law systems adopt this approach, deeming a contract concluded when there is an accordance of wills or consent among parties. See, e.g., French Civil Code Article 1108(1). As traditionally understood, civil law codes do not require that mutual consent be the product of an acceptance of an offer.

Article 2 of the Uniform Commercial Code ("UCC") adopts both approaches to contract formation. It takes the second, "agreement" approach while at the same time preserving elements of the "offer and acceptance" approach. This makes sense because, although textbook examples of contracts concluded by an acceptance following a formal offer exist, many bargains can only be artificially analyzed as offers and acceptances. A series of interconnected UCC provisions show Article 2's adoption of the "agreement" approach. Section 2–204(1) provides that "a contract for sale of goods may be made in any manner sufficient to show agreement, including conduct of both parties which recognizes the existence of such a contract." Section 1–201(b)(3) in turn defines "agreement" as ". . . the bargain of the parties in fact as found in their language or inferred from other circumstances . . ." Thus, under 2–204(1) the agreement of the parties is sufficient to create a contract for sale. Notice that "agreement" does not require an acceptance of an offer to conclude a contract. It requires only a bargain, however the bargain is indicated ("shown"). An "agreement" need not be concluded by an acceptance following an offer. Section 2–204(2) supports this conclusion. It provides that "an agreement sufficient to constitute a contract for sale may be found even though the moment of its making is undetermined." If a contract could be concluded only by an acceptance, then in principle the moment at which the contract was concluded would be determined.

At the same time, Article 2 also adopts the "offer and acceptance" approach to contract formation. It does this by presupposing the continued operation of some common law mechanics of formation. Section 1–103(b) incorporates into Article 2 extra-UCC principles of law consistent with that Article, and therefore the common law rules of offer and acceptance still apply to Article 2. For the same reason, 1–103(b) makes applicable to Article 2 common law rules of lapse, revocation and effectiveness of offers. Article 2 also contains specific formation rules that presuppose the continued operation of the common law mechanics of assent. For instance, 2–207(1), by allowing an acceptance that varies the terms of an offer to conclude a contract, presupposes that an acceptance concludes a contract. Section 2–206(1) presupposes the same thing. Subsection (1)(a) of 2–206 rejects the common law default formation rule to the effect that an offer invites acceptance through the same medium by which the offer was communicated. It instead provides that "an offer to make a contract shall be construed as inviting acceptance in any manner and by any medium reasonable in the circumstances . . . " Section 2–206(1)(a) therefore alters only the acceptable medium of acceptance invited by the offer. It preserves the common law requirement that a contract be concluded by an acceptance of an offer.

Rules of offer and acceptance are applicable, but less important, when a contract is concluded by electronic communication. Electronic communications replace oral or written offers and acceptances with computer messages. This is the case with orders for goods placed by email or on the seller's internet web site. With internet orders, the seller's web site displays a description or identification of specific goods along with their price, leaving the quantity ordered to be entered by the buyer. The buyer completes its order by entering the quantity desired and sending the order. Typically the seller responds with a computer-generated confirmation of the order and an indication of the estimated shipping date. Common law notions of an offer are broad enough to consider the buyer's onsite order an offer. Under 2–606(1)(b) an offer to buy goods invites acceptance either by prompt shipment of goods, whether conforming or nonconforming, or by a promise to ship goods. As a promise to ship, the seller's confirmation therefore is an acceptance of the buyer's order. Because the buyer's onsite order and the seller's order confirmation are identical in terms (other than shipment) and usually are exchanged quickly, characterizing the buyer's order as an offer and the seller's confirmation as an acceptance does not matter. No legal consequences turn on which electronic message deemed the offer and which the acceptance. But the common law mechanics of assent are easily applied to contracts formed by electronic communications.

Bio–Tech Pharmacal, Inc. v. International Business Connections, LLC

Arkansas Court of Appeals, 2004
184 S.W.3d 447

■ **OPINION BY:** SAM BIRD, JUDGE

Following a bench trial in Washington County, the trial court awarded appellee $12,951.87 on its complaint against appellant to recover for goods sold. Appellant argues on appeal that the trial judge erred in 1) denying its motion for a directed verdict, and 2) finding that it waived the right to rely on a contractual term that required appellee to immediately confirm all orders by fax or email. Finding no error, we affirm.

Appellant is a manufacturer of nutritional supplements. In September 1999, it began purchasing raw materials from appellee, which operated through its president, Detleff Fuhrmann. Over a period of four months, appellant placed approximately seventeen orders with appellee.

According to Detleff Fuhrmann, the parties transacted most of their business by telephone. He explained that he was in almost daily telephone contact with appellant and that if he could locate material that appellant was interested in purchasing, he would telephone one of appellant's personnel and advise of the material's availability and price. If agreeable, appellant would then issue a purchase order to appellee. Each purchase order would recite the material being ordered, the quantity, the unit price, the total price, appellant's shipping address, and six "Terms of Contract," including the following: Order/price confirmation w/ship date must be faxed/e-mailed immediately. Upon receiving the purchase order, appellee would order the material from its supplier and pay for it in advance. When the material became available, it would be shipped to appellant, and appellee would send appellant an invoice that referenced appellant's purchase order number. It is undisputed that appellee never faxed or emailed a confirmation to appellant on any order. According to Fuhrmann, confirmations were handled by telephone.

Despite the lack of written confirmation, appellant received and paid for several orders from appellee without protest or complaint. However, in January and February 2000, appellant attempted to cancel numerous orders by writing "CANCEL" across the orders and faxing them to appellee. During this same period, appellant also requested return authorizations for some of the materials that it had received. All but one of these return requests listed "Inadequate Purchase Order Confirmation" as a reason for return.

Fuhrmann testified that he was surprised to receive the cancellation notices and return requests because he had never had any previous complaints from appellant. He told appellant that he did not want to accept a return of the goods that had already been shipped, and he asked appellant to pay for those goods. At one point appellant paid appellee $8,000, which apparently covered only part of the outstanding balance. No further payments were made.

On August 10, 2000, appellee sued appellant to collect the balance due on three purchase orders. Appellant defended on the ground that appellee had not confirmed the purchase orders as required. Following a bench trial, the circuit judge entered a verdict in appellee's favor for $12,951.87. Appellant now appeals from that verdict.

  * * *

At the close of appellee's evidence, appellant sought a directed verdict on two of the purchase orders, arguing that appellee's failure to fax or email a confirmation of those orders meant that appellee had not "accepted" the purchase order "offers" in accordance with their terms, and thus no contract was formed. The trial court denied the motion, ruling that a question remained as to whether appellee had the right to rely on the parties' course of dealing in not faxing or emailing a confirmation. Ultimately, the court found that a contract had been formed as to the two orders.

Appellant argues on appeal, as it did below, that its purchase orders were offers and that they required acceptance by one means only—faxing or emailing a confirmation; thus, when appellee failed to accept in the required manner, no contract was formed. We hold that appellant was not entitled to a directed verdict on this point.

We note first that it is true that a purchase order is generally considered an offer. However, even if we consider appellants' purchase orders to be offers, we disagree with appellant that they clearly invited acceptance by only one means. Under the Uniform Commercial Code, an offer may generally be accepted in any manner and by any medium reasonable in the circumstances. However, as appellant points out, an offeror may specify a particular manner in which the offer may be accepted. When that occurs, the offeree must comply in the manner specified in order to accept the offer. See also Ark. Code Ann. § 4–2–206(1)(a), which reads:

(1) Unless otherwise unambiguously indicated by the language or circumstances:

(a) an offer to make a contract shall be construed as inviting acceptance in any manner and by any medium reasonable in the circumstances[.]

The purpose of this statutory language is to make it clear that any reasonable manner of acceptance is intended to be regarded as available unless the offeror has made it quite clear that it will not be acceptable.

The confirmation requirement contained in appellant's purchase orders is, by the orders' express language, a term of the parties' contract. It is not unambiguously set out as a means of accepting an offer. In fact, nothing is said in the purchase order regarding a specific means of acceptance. Therefore, we cannot say that the purchase orders expressly require acceptance by only one means.

Further, purchase orders may sometimes be considered an acceptance rather than an offer. The circumstances of this case would allow for that possibility, given the parties' course of dealing. Fuhrmann testified that he was in constant telephone contact with appellant and that prior to appellant's issuance of a purchase order, he provided appellant with information about the price and availability of the materials appellant sought. Thus, it is possible that appellant's purchase order actually operated as an acceptance of appellee's offer. It is also possible that appellant's purchase order was simply confirmation of a contract that had already been made. The UCC contemplates that parties may enter into oral agreements that are subsequently confirmed in writing. Ark. Code Ann. § 4–2–201(2). Appellant's purchase orders identified the product to be shipped and contained the quantity, price, terms of payment, and shipping information. Further, the orders contained several "terms of contract." Therefore, it would be reasonable to infer, given the parties' regular course of dealings, that they had already made an oral contract and that Fuhrmann was simply awaiting confirmation in the form of appellant's purchase order before obtaining the materials. In light of these reasonable inferences, which our standard of review requires us to consider, we conclude that the trial court did not err in refusing to grant a directed verdict on the ground that no contract had been formed.

* * *

Affirmed.

Remapp International Corp. v. Comfort Keyboard Co.

United States Court of Appeals, Seventh Circuit, 2009
560 F.3d 628

■ KAPALA, DISTRICT COURT JUDGE.

In this diversity action, plaintiff, ReMapp International Corporation, filed a complaint alleging that defendant, Comfort Keyboard Company, Inc., breached the parties' contract for the sale of goods by failing to pay for the items it ordered from plaintiff. Following a bench trial, the magistrate judge entered judgment in favor of plaintiff on its breach of contract claim in the amount of $67,560. Defendant now appeals.

I. Background

At trial, Hal Edmonds, the president of plaintiff, testified that plaintiff provides contract manufacturing services of electronic materials, including printed circuit boards. Edmonds testified that plaintiff had done business with defendant for about six or seven years. When plaintiff and defendant started doing business, defendant would submit a written purchase order for goods. However, within a very short time, defendant would just call plaintiff and say what parts it needed. Edmonds testified that since 2004, the payment terms for all board assemblies were 50% "ARO" (after receipt of the pro forma order) and 50% thirty days after receipt of the shipment.

Edmonds recalled that in April 2006 defendant ordered 1,000 USB boards, and in May 2006, defendant placed an order for 1,000 HUB boards. In July 2006, both orders were increased to 2,000. According to Edmonds, the defendant's president, Khalil "Charles" Afifi verbally placed each order directly with Edmonds, as was the practice for some years. In addition to the boards, Afifi verbally asked plaintiff to buy microprocessors for all the boards if plaintiff could buy the microprocessors for less than six dollars. Plaintiff was able to find microprocessors for $5.85. Plaintiff then called Afifi and obtained Afifi's verbal authorization to purchase 4,100 microprocessors at the $5.85 price.

According to Edmonds, after Afifi placed the orders for the boards, plaintiff provided defendant with a pro forma invoice, which was essentially "what the final invoice would look like when the product is finished and delivered." This would assure that defendant knew exactly what it would be paying when the bill was due. The pro forma invoice contains conditions and includes the freight, "it documents what's transpired, and has built into it a request for the payment conditions." Edmonds explained that a pro forma invoice is not a quotation, but "a follow-up to an agreement to an acceptance." As to the microprocessors, plaintiff issued a standard invoice dated July 19, 2006, which stated "100% Payment at time of purchase."

Edmonds recounted that from April through August 2006 the parties had continuing dialog on various aspects of the orders. At no time did defendant tell Edmonds not to proceed with the orders. According to Edmonds, he and Afifi had discussed the invoices for the boards numerous times, and Afifi encouraged plaintiff to keep going and make whatever changes were necessary. On May 2, 2006, Edmonds sent an e-mail to Afifi stating that plaintiff was finishing "the USB" and the "HUB can move quickly, as well." On May 19, 2006, Edmonds sent Afifi an e-mail stating that he found a program in a sample board that was used to program a component of the USB board and stated that he had attached the pro forma invoice for the USB boards. Afifi replied, "YOU ARE THE BEST. . . . GREAT NEWS . . . 'THANK YOU.'" Edmonds explained that on August 17, 2006, he sent Afifi an e-mail asking if Afifi wanted one USB connector on 1,000 HUB boards, and two USB connectors on the other 1,000 HUB boards. Later that day, Afifi responded with an e-mail stating, "1500 with two and 500 with one." On August 18, 2006, Edmonds sent Afifi an e-mail about a design change defendant had requested. In that e-mail Edmonds states, in part, "[F]or the 1000 boards already made the engineer says he can put an SMT pad on the backside using the existing pads. Will that work for you?" Later that day, Afifi replied, "GREAT. . . . PLEASE HAVE THEM DO THAT . . ."

On July 28, 2006, Edmonds sent Afifi an e-mail requesting payment for the invoices for the USB and HUB boards. Edmonds explained that plaintiff deviated slightly from its normal procedure by ordering the products prior to pre-payment. On cross-examination, Edmonds admitted that in his history of working with defendant, this was the first time that defendant had not paid at least 50% before plaintiff placed an order with the supplier.

Edmonds sent Afifi several more e-mails in August and September requesting payment. Edmonds estimated that between May and October 2006, he had approximately twenty conversations with Afifi in which Afifi promised that the payments were forthcoming. On September 26, 2006, Afifi sent an e-mail to Edmonds stating that his investors wanted to use a different supplier. Edmonds responded with an e-mail requesting that Afifi pay the balance of his account.

Edmonds further testified that on October 6, 2006, plaintiff issued an invoice to defendant for the parts that had been manufactured. Edmonds testified that both the USB and HUB boards had been manufactured, but the microprocessors had not yet been put on the boards when production was stopped. According to Edmonds, the printed boards are unique for each customer because they are designed for each customer's particular need. If the customer did not take what they ordered, the boards would be scrapped. The microprocessors, on the other hand, were purchased, but could be sold and used elsewhere. At the time of the trial, the boards and the microprocessors remained in China undelivered because defendant had not paid plaintiff.

Afifi testified that the parties first started doing business around 2001–2002. Afifi described the parties' purchasing practice up until May 2006 as follows. Purchases would begin by Edmonds calling Afifi and asking if Afifi needed anything. Afifi would then ask for a price and Edmonds would issue a pro forma invoice, which was "technically like a quote." Sometimes they would go back and forth, and Edmonds would send multiple pro forma invoices with adjustments. If the price was acceptable to Afifi, he would send Edmonds 50% of the payment for the order. Once the job was done, Edmonds would call Afifi to inform him that the boards were ready to ship, and the other 50% was required. Afifi identified several previous pro forma invoices where he paid 50% at the time he placed the order and 50% at the time the order was ready to be shipped. According to Afifi, the 50% payment was an approval by defendant to proceed with the job.

Afifi further testified that he never authorized invoices for the USB boards, HUB boards or the microprocessors. Specifically, Afifi testified that he never asked Edmonds to see how much it would be to increase the original board orders to 2,000 boards. As to the microprocessors, Afifi testified that he never authorized the purchase of the microprocessors because he could get them in the United States for a cheaper price. Afifi also claimed he never paid 50% down on any of the orders as he had done in the past, and denied having any conversation with Edmonds that plaintiff would order any of the items on credit. Afifi denied receiving several of Edmonds' e-mails seeking payment and averred that many of the e-mails that Edmonds claimed were from Afifi were fraudulent.

The magistrate judge entered judgment in favor of plaintiff on plaintiff's breach of contract claim concluding that three oral contracts existed between plaintiff and defendant. The first was for defendant to purchase 2,000 USB boards at a price of $21.65 each for a total cost of $43,300. The second was for defendant to purchase 2,000 HUB boards at a price of $23.60 each for a total cost of $47,200. The third was for defendant to purchase 4,100 microprocessors at a price of $5.85 each for a total of $23,985.

The magistrate judge noted that because the sale of goods in each contract was in excess of $500, Wisconsin's codification of the Uniform Commercial Code's Statute of Frauds required the contract to be in writing. However, the magistrate judge concluded that the parties' oral contracts fell within exceptions to the Statute of Frauds. First, he found that the evidence established that the USB and HUB boards were custom manufactured for defendant and were not suitable for resale to others. As such, he held that the first two contracts were enforceable under Wisconsin Statute § 402.201(3)(a), which provides an exception to the Statute of Frauds for specially manufactured goods. Second, the magistrate judge found that defendant failed to object to plaintiff's July 19, 2006 invoice for the 4,100 processors within ten days after receipt of the invoice. Accordingly, he held that this third contract was enforceable under Wisconsin Statute § 402.201(2), which provides an exception to the Statute of Frauds where a merchant sends another merchant a written confirmation of the parties' contract, and no written objection is made within ten days of receipt.

The magistrate judge awarded damages to plaintiff for the USB and HUB board contracts, but not for the microprocessor contract. The magistrate judge held that plaintiff was not entitled to damages for defendant's breach of the microprocessor contract because plaintiff failed to show that it mitigated its damages by attempting to resell the microprocessors which could be resold at the full price. As to damages for the USB and HUB boards, the magistrate judge found these could not be resold, deducted freight charges and additional unproven charges as well as the $.10 per pound that plaintiff could obtain as scrap for the boards, and awarded plaintiff a total of $67,560.00 in damages.

II.   Discussion

On appeal, defendant argues that the magistrate judge erred in his findings of fact by concluding that oral contracts existed, that those oral contracts were outside of the Statute of Frauds and that plaintiff was entitled to damages. Defendant also argues that plaintiff assumed the risk of ordering all of these electronic components by proceeding without any assurance defendant would accept the product. * * *

A.   Formation of a Contract

Defendant's first argument is that the magistrate judge erred in his finding of facts by holding that the parties had three oral contracts. Defendant contends that the facts do not demonstrate any acceptance of the contracts by defendant. Specifically, defendant asserts that the testimony regarding the parties' course of dealing shows that plaintiff's pro forma invoice was a written offer, that acceptance of the offer required 50% pre-payment, and that defendant never accepted the offer because it never paid the 50% pre-payment.

However, this court cannot find that the magistrate judge clearly erred in finding that the pro forma invoice was a written confirmation of the parties' earlier oral agreement rather than a written offer requiring payment for acceptance. Under Wisconsin law, "[a] contract for sale of goods may be made in any manner sufficient to show agreement, including conduct by both parties which recognizes the existence of such a contract." Wis. Stat. § 402.204(1). In this case, Edmonds testified that Afifi called him and placed orders for the USB boards and the HUB boards, after which Edmonds created a pro forma invoice. Edmonds explained that in place of the purchase orders defendant submitted to plaintiff at the beginning of the parties' relationship, plaintiff had created a pro forma invoice after defendant placed an order to assure defendant knew exactly what the final invoice would look like. Edmonds further testified that the pro forma invoice was not a quotation, but occurred after the acceptance of the agreement.

Moreover, both parties' conduct indicated they had formed a contract. In response to Edmonds' e-mail sending the pro forma invoice for the USB boards, Afifi replied affirmatively. Later in the summer, Afifi sent e-mails to Edmonds responding to a question about how he wanted the HUB boards constructed. In addition, Edmonds' e-mails to Afifi frequently indicated that the boards were either made or being made, and the record shows no response by Afifi informing Edmonds that he did not think the parties had a contract.

Although defendant argues that Afifi should be believed when he testified that the pro forma invoice was a "quote", the trial court is entitled to significant deference as to its credibility determinations. Afifi's testimony that he believed he had not accepted Edmonds' offer was contradictory to the emails he sent to Edmonds and his overall silence in response to clear indications that plaintiff was producing his order.

Defendant has not developed a separate argument as to the microprocessors, but the magistrate judge's finding that the parties entered a third contract for 4,100 microprocessors is also supported by the record. Edmonds testified that Afifi verbally asked him to buy the microprocessors for the boards if he could find them for under $6.00. He further testified that when he found the microprocessors for $5.85 he obtained Afifi's verbal authorization to purchase them. Because Edmonds needed to contract for the microprocessors quickly to maintain the price, he entered the contract and issued Afifi an invoice for 100% of the payment. Neither party testified as to a pro forma invoice for the microprocessors. Thus, it is unclear if defendant is contending the invoice was plaintiff's offer which required 100% payment for acceptance. In any event, although Afifi denied placing any oral order, again, the magistrate judge credited Edmonds' testimony. This testimony supports the magistrate judge's conclusion that the parties had an oral agreement for the microprocessors.

Defendant is correct that the evidence reflects that up until these orders plaintiff always required a 50% down payment prior to commencing manufacture of the products. However, this fact does not necessarily indicate that the parties did not have a contract. According to Edmonds, when defendant placed an order and plaintiff orally accepted, plaintiff then created a pro forma invoice outlining the terms of the parties' agreement. One of the terms of the agreement was 50% payment upon receipt of the invoice. Simply because the payment terms of a contract go unfilled does not mean there is no contract. Here, the magistrate judge's finding that there was an oral offer and acceptance is not clearly erroneous.

* * *

III. Conclusion

Accordingly, we affirm the district court's judgment in favor of plaintiff.

B. OFFER-VARYING ACCEPTANCE: THE BATTLE OF THE FORMS

A purported acceptance may contain terms not included in the offer. It may be conveyed orally, in electronic form or in writing. Although the terms of both the offer and the purported acceptance often are in standard forms, they sometimes may be contained in communications containing terms formulated for a specific transaction. When the purported acceptance contains terms not in the offer, two questions arise. One is whether a contract exists at all. The second question assumes that a contract exists and asks what its terms include. A third question arises when the purported acceptance does not conclude a contract but the parties' behavior evidences a contract. In this case, there is a question as to the terms of that contract. Section 2–207 addresses all three questions.

Section 2–207 is poorly drafted and continues to generate litigation over its application. One of the UCC's drafters later described the section as a "miserable, bungled, patched-up job." Richard E. Speidel, Robert S. Summers & James J. White, Commercial Law 467 (4th ed.

1987) (reproduced letter from Grant Gilmore to Robert Summers). Subsection (1) of 2–207 determines when a purported acceptance concludes a contract. The subsection provides that an offeree's response constitutes an "acceptance" if it is "[a] definite and seasonable expression of acceptance . . . even though it states terms additional to or different from those offered or agreed upon." Thus, a response containing terms additional to or different from those contained in the offer does not constitute a rejection and a counteroffer. This part of subsection (1) is a rejection of the common law mirror image rule for acceptance. By deeming a contract concluded even when a purported acceptance varies the terms of the offer, 2–207(1) prevents the offeror from strategically avoiding liability on a purely executory contract. Very little litigation has involved this part of subsection (1). Offerees whose offerors seek to rely on 2–207(1) to deny that a purported acceptance concludes a contract usually make other arrangements. Rather than litigate the issue, they usually find other offerors.

The other part of 2–207(1) addresses a completely different "battle." This occurs when an agreement already has been reached. Later, a written confirmation is sent by one or both of the parties reciting terms that vary the terms of the earlier agreement. In this case 2–207(1) provides that "a written confirmation which is sent . . . operates as an acceptance even though it states terms additional to or different from those offered or agreed upon . . . ." So, for instance, the earlier agreement might contain terms just relating to quantity, price and delivery date. The later written confirmation might contain consistent further terms ("additional" terms) or conflicting terms ("different" terms). Subsection (1) provides that in both cases the confirmation remains an "acceptance," not a rejection and counteroffer.

This part of 2–207(1) is odd. A confirmation containing additional or different terms from those contained in the earlier agreement obviously cannot constitute a rejection and counteroffer. The earlier agreement already exists. The confirming party cannot unilaterally alter the existence or terms of the agreements by sending the confirmation. In fact, a confirmation is not a purported acceptance at all. At most the confirmation operates as a proposal to modify the terms of a contract already concluded. In providing the language just quoted, the probable intent of 2–207(1)'s drafters has nothing to do with contract formation. Instead, the intent likely is to allow the terms contained in the confirmation to become part of the terms of the earlier agreement under some circumstances. Subsection (2) of 2–207 determines when "additional terms" become part of a contract formed under subsection (1). Although an agreement followed by a confirmation need not be formed under 2–207(1), subsection (2) likely applies to the "additional terms" contained in a confirmation that varies the terms of the agreement. Section 2–207(2)'s interpretation itself is problematic, as discussed in *Reilly Foam Corp. v. Rubbermaid Corp.*, reproduced in part below, and in the notes following the case.

Section 2–207(3) is fairly straightforward. As with subsection (2), subsection (3) provides the terms of a contract. But subsection (3) applies only if 2–207(1) does not apply and where the parties' conduct indicates that they have contracted: "Conduct by both parties which recognizes the existence of a contract is sufficient to establish a contract for sale although the writings of the parties do not otherwise establish a contract." Subsection (1) applies where the writings of the parties *do* establish a contract. Under subsection (1), the writings establish a contract when two conditions are met: The offeree's response is a definite and seasonable expression of acceptance, and the acceptance is not made expressly conditional on the offeror's assent to the additional terms contained in the offeree's response. If the "writings do establish a contract" under 2–207(1), the terms of that contract are determined by 2–207(2), not 2–207(3). Because subsection (2) provides the terms of a contract formed or recognized under subsection (1), 2–207(3) applies to set contract terms only if subsection (2) does not apply. A common instance in which 2–207(3) applies is when the offeror and offeree perform after the offeree has sent the offeror a standard form stating that its acceptance is made expressly conditional on the offeror's assent to the terms in its form. The "expressly conditional" language in the offeree's response prevents a contract from being formed under 2–207(1). Because the parties' performance recognizes a contract, the terms of the contract are determined by subsection (3).

The terms of the contract governed by 2–207(3) falls into two categories. One consists of the terms on which the offeror and offeree's offer and purported acceptance agree. These are terms common to the parties' writings. Terms that are not common to the writings drop out: They are "knocked out" and are not part of the resulting contract. Thus, both different and additional terms in the offeror and offeree's writings are eliminated. Subsection (3) therefore rejects the corollary of the mirror image rule: the "last shot" doctrine, under which the terms of the resulting contract are those of the last writing dispatched prior to performance. A second category of terms consists of gap filling terms provided by the UCC where the parties have been silent. These gap fillers include such terms as price (2–305), place of delivery (2–308), time of performance (2–309), implied warranties of quality (2–314–2–315) and title (2–312). Subsection (3) refers to them as "supplementary terms": the UCC gap fillers supplement the terms common to the parties' writings. Two consequences follow. One is that a UCC gap filler does not become part of the resulting contract under subsection (3) when the parties' writings both exclude it. This is case, for example, when the both the seller and buyer's writings agree to a term that differs from the UCC gap filler. A second consequence is that where the terms in the parties' writings differ and one of the differing terms is identical to a UCC-supplied gap filler, the UCC gap filler "supplements" the terms common to both parties' writings. In this case the term identical to the UCC-supplied gap filler governs the contract and the other term falls away under the knockout rule. The UCC-supplied term therefore reintroduces into the contract a term that subsection (3)'s knockout rule would otherwise have eliminated.

This second consequence arguably is objectionable. A party whose writing excludes a UCC-gap filler signals that it prefers a different term. It is indicating that a different term is appropriate for the transaction even if the gap filler is optimal for most the contracts of the majority of contracting parties. For instance, the offeror's writing might disclaim a 2–314 implied warranty of merchantability while the offeree's writing provides for the warranty. By supplementing the parties' contract with UCC gap fillers, subsection (3) saddles the offeror with a term it provided against while giving the offeree the UCC gap filler it provided for. Although the offeror prefers an enforceable contract without an implied warranty to not having a contract at all, it might prefer having no contract to having one with an implied warranty (at the stated price). In these circumstances there is no guarantee that the parties get an optimal set of terms for their contract.

Reilly Foam Corp. v. Rubbermaid Corp.

United States District Court, Eastern District of Pennsylvania, 2002
206 F. Supp. 2d 643

■ BERLE M. SCHILLER, DISTRICT JUDGE

* * *

Background

Reilly Foam manufactures custom-order sponges and other foam products. Defendant Rubbermaid manufactures home products, including mops nationwide. Before its agreement with Reilly Foam, Rubbermaid obtained sponges for its mop products from a company known as Tek Pak, a competitor of Reilly Foam.

In 1997, Rubbermaid launched its "Tidal Wave Project" to introduce new and improved sponge mops into the marketplace. The new sponge mops were named for a wave pattern which would be cut into the sponges. There were to be two basic designs for the Tidal Wave mops: a butterfly sponge and a roller sponge. The butterfly sponge mop included a mechanism which folded in half like the wings of a butterfly in order to wring out water. The roller sponge would be squeezed by a roller mechanism.

Target Stores agreed to stock cobalt blue and yellow laminate versions of the Tidal Wave sponge mop line at its stores nationwide. Rubbermaid initially sought to obtain sponges for the mops from Tek Pak. However, Tek Pak could not make timely deliveries of sponges to meet Target's needs.

Rubbermaid contacted Reilly Foam on March 4, 1999 to determine if it could fulfill Rubbermaid's need for sponges. Rubbermaid's immediate objective with Reilly Foam was to satisfy Target's current demand. Reilly Foam submitted a price quotation to Rubbermaid on March 8, 1999 for Pattern Butterfly sponges and Pattern Roller Mop sponges on an expedited basis. Reilly Foam then manufactured and delivered the sponges.

Between March 8 and March 30, the parties discussed a longer-term relationship in which Reilly Foam would supply sponges for Rubbermaid's Tidal Wave Project. But the parties now vigorously dispute what the terms of the relationship were. According to Joseph Reilly of Reilly Foam, his company was to be the exclusive supplier of Butterfly and Roller Mop sponges with a Tidal Wave design. Rubbermaid was to purchase a minimum of 300,000 Butterfly, 300,000 Roller Mop, and 300,000 yellow ester Tidal Wave sponges each year. Rubbermaid also submitted written estimates to Reilly Foam of its requirements for Butterfly and Roller Mop sponges. Reilly Foam needed to retool its equipment and to license technology from a corporation named Foamex to produce the sponges with a "tidal wave" effect carved into their bottoms. Reilly Foam expressed concern that its profits on the contract permit it to recoup its costs.

On March 26, 1999, Reilly Foam forwarded a letter to Tony Ferrante of Rubbermaid signed by Joseph Reilly. The letter read:

This letter details the proposal that we briefly spoke about last evening. This includes the two laminates that we are currently working on, the roller mop and the butterfly mop. There are other products that we are familiar with through Kendo/New Knight, which would be the brown large celled ester, the pattern yellow ester and the yellow ether and white scrubmate. All of these are priced on the ensuing quotation. Our proposal is that Rubbermaid Cleaning Products commit to two million pieces of product under the sub-heading Other Affected Products. There would be a surcharge of $.015 per part in an effort to amortize the cost of tooling for the wave pattern. The two million products would need to be taken over a two year period. We would also require a commitment for all of the butterfly and roller mop laminates that include the Rubbermaid Cleaning Products design. I have also spoken to Foamex and they have agreed to run their "sample" tool for the short term until the production tool is complete, which would be approximately eight weeks. Please keep in mind that this is a proprietary pattern and we would need your design should this project move forward. Finally, we appreciate the opportunity and understand the price sensitive nature of your products. Reilly Foam Corporation has made various concession to keep this program moving forward. Tony, after reviewing the quotation and the conditions of this letter, please respond through a letter stating Rubbermaid Cleaning Products intentions. I look forward to your response./s/ Joseph G. ReillyJoseph G. Reilly * * *

Tony Ferrante responded by letter on March 30, 1999. The letter, addressed to "Joe" Reilly, read in relevant part:

This letter is to serve as Rubbermaid's commitment and authorization to procure tooling so that Reilly Foam will be in a position to make sponge products with Rubbermaid's patent pending Tidal Wave TM design. I understand that $.015 will be added to the cost of the sponge purchase price until we have made purchases of 2 million sponges, thereby covering the tooling cost of $30,000. Referencing the attached quotation, our commitment is as follows: 1. Any sponge mop product produced by New Knight, Inc., on behalf of Rubbermaid Home Products, will source the sponge component from Reilly Foam. This includes the current product offering, as referenced in your quotation, as well as any future new products that New Knight will produce for us.2. Should any cost savings arise from productivity improvements, Rubbermaid is entitled to share in those benefits.* * *Best Regards/s/ Tony Ferrante Tony Ferrante Product Manager Rubbermaid Home Products

New Knight, an independent corporation, assembled mops on behalf of Rubbermaid. Attached to his letter was Reilly Foam's price list, marked "Approved" and signed by Mr. Ferrante. Shortly thereafter, Rubbermaid supplied Reilly Foam with a forecast of how many sponges of each variety it would need. Following the exchange of letters, Rubbermaid instructed New Knight to purchase sponges solely from Reilly Foam. New Knight complied and used Reilly Foam as its exclusive source of sponges until New Knight entered bankruptcy in August 2001. Rubbermaid itself made purchases of sponges listed under the "other affected products" category. At the same time, Rubbermaid continued to purchase sponges from Tek Pak for use in the Tidal Wave line of mops. Moreover, Rubbermaid did not purchase two million sponges within the two-year window which Reilly Foam sought.

Reilly Foam contends that Rubbermaid has breached the contract by failing to use Reilly Foam as Rubbermaid's exclusive supplier for the Tidal Wave Project (including roller mop and butterfly mop sponges) and making purchases from Plaintiff's competitors, by failing to purchase the minimum annual quantities of sponges in the "other affected products category" set forth in the price list which Joseph Reilly sent on March 26, 1999, and by failing to purchase two million "other affected sponges" within two years with a $0.015 surcharge.

Choice of Law

Reilly Foam contends that Pennsylvania law applies to all claims in this action. In its briefs, Rubbermaid has relied heavily on Pennsylvania's Uniform Commercial Code, 13 PENN. CONS. STAT. ANN. § 1101 et seq. . . . * * *

1. Whether the March 26, 1999 Letter Was an Offer Within the Meaning of Pa.UCC 2206

The parties first dispute whether the March 26, 1999 correspondence was merely a price quote or an "offer" within the meaning of the Pa.U.C.C. The Pa.U.C.C. does not expressly define 'offer,' but it has been defined based on common law principles as "the manifestation of willingness to enter into a bargain, so made as to justify another person in understanding that his assent to that bargain is invited and will conclude it." Bergquist Co. v. Sunroc Corp., 777 F. Supp. 1236, 1248 (E.D. Pa. 1991) (Ditter, J.); see also RESTATEMENT (SECOND) OF CONTRACTS §§ 24 (1979). Documents reflecting preliminary negotiations between the parties do not evince an enforceable contract.

In the U.C.C. context, courts have encountered difficulty determining whether a document that quotes a seller's prices constitutes an offer. Generally, price quotes are not considered an offer, but rather "mere invitations to enter into negotiations or to submit offers." Bergquist, 777 F. Supp. at 1248. The buyer's purchase order— which sets such terms as product choice, quantity, price, and terms of delivery—is usually the offer.

However, some price quotes are sufficiently detailed to be deemed offers, which turns a subsequent document from a buyer containing a positive response into an acceptance. What transforms a quotation into an offer cannot be neatly defined; it depends on the manifestation of intent by the seller and the "unique facts and circumstances of each case." Rich Prods. Corp. v. Kemutec, Inc., 66 F. Supp. 2d 937, 956 (E.D. Wis. 1999). As is the case with a purported offer under the common law, the seller "must intend that the contract exist upon acceptance of the offer; that is, it must reasonably appear from the price quotation that assent to that quotation is all that is needed to ripen the offer into a contract." Bergquist, 777 F. Supp. at 1249.

Reviewing Reilly Foam's March 26 correspondence and its treatment by Rubbermaid, both parties treated the price quote as an offer and not merely a price quote. First, the March 26 letter did not merely list price. The letter refers to itself as a "proposal" in its opening paragraph. The attached list also includes a number of specific terms including the identification of products, their quantities, the licensing of needed technology, and details for the special manufacture of the sponges. Rubbermaid treated the letter as an offer at least with respect to quantities and prices of "other affected products." Mr. Ferrante's March 30 response merely noted that the terms states on the price list were "approved" and stated in his letter that the $0.015 surcharge for the first two million sponges purchased was acceptable.

While it may have been desirable to include additional terms in the March 26, 1999 letter to clarify its status as an offer, contract formation depends on the manifestation of intent by the parties to be bound rather than the presence or absence of specific terms. Moreover, Joseph Reilly's March 26 letter described the price list as a quotation, no such appellation is given to the letter itself. In any event, a party's description of a document as a price quote or offer is not determinative. The Court finds the March 26 correspondence contains sufficient detail and is deemed an offer as a matter of law.

2.   Effect of Different Terms in Rubbermaid's March 30 Acceptance

Once Reilly Foam's March 26 letter is deemed an offer, there can be no doubt that Rubbermaid's March 30 response accepted it. See Pa.U.C.C. § 2207(a) (expression of acceptance operates to form contract even if it states additional or different terms).[1] However, Rubbermaid argues that even if the March 26 letter is deemed an offer, its March 30 acceptance contained a number of different terms which modified the contract under the Pa.U.C.C.'s purported "knockout rule." Reilly Foam retorts that the Court should not follow the knockout rule and permit the terms of its offer to govern. If the knockout rule does apply, it argues, Rubbermaid's acceptance did not contain any different terms. * * *

Terms of the Contract

If Reilly Foam's March 26 letter operates as an offer and Rubbermaid's March 30 correspondence acts as an acceptance, the Court is left with the task of determining the terms of the agreement between these merchants under Pa.U.C.C. § 2207, commonly called the "Battle of the Forms" provision.

Section 2207

Frequently, businessmen do not set forth all of the terms of their agreements in a single, comprehensive document. Rather, deals are

---

[1]   Rubbermaid does argue that its March 30, 1999 letter was not an acceptance but a rejection and counteroffer because it constituted a conditional acceptance. However, to be deemed a rejection due to conditional acceptance, the offeree must do more than allude to preferred terms. It must make its acceptance "expressly . . . conditional on assent to the additional or added terms." Pa.U.C.C. § 2207(a). In other words, it must demonstrate an unwillingness to proceed with the transaction unless its conditions are met. Rubbermaid's March 30 letter evinces a willingness to proceed with the transaction and therefore cannot be deemed a rejection or counteroffer

made on the basis of conversations and letters exchanged between the parties. Ultimately, one party reduces the terms of a proposed deal to writing, which is deemed an offer. Under the common law, a document qualifying as an offer could only be 'accepted' by a second document expressing acceptance on terms identical to the offer.

The rule changed with the enactment of the Battle of the Forms provision of the Pa. U.C.C., which permits an expression of acceptance to operate as an acceptance even if it contains additional or different terms. See Pa.U.C.C. § 2207(a). The additional terms become part of the contract unless: (1) the offer expressly limits acceptance to the terms of the offer; (2) the inserted term materially alters the offer; or (3) notification of objection to the inserted terms has been given or is given within a reasonable time. Pa.U.C.C. § 2207(b)(1)–(3).[2] The fate of different terms is less clear. Section 2207(b) does not directly address different terms in an acceptance, and the question remains: if the offer is accepted on different terms, should the terms of the offer control or should the acceptance be followed, or should the conflicting terms cancel each other out, to be replaced by gap fillers provided by the U.C.C.? The question has divided courts and scholars.

One approach considers any expression of acceptance with differing terms as actually a rejection and counter-offer. Thus, the terms outlined in the acceptance would govern. This view has been widely discredited as a revival of the common law rule, and the Court is not aware of any jurisdiction in which it is currently in force.

The minority view permits the terms of the offer to control. Because there is no rational distinction between additional terms and different terms, both are handled under § 2207(b). For support, advocates of this position point to Official Comment 3: "Whether or not additional or different terms will become part of the agreement depends upon the provisions of subsection [b]."[3] Professor Summers, the leading advocate of the minority rule, reasons that offerors have more reason to expect that the terms of their offer will be enforced than the recipient of an offer can hope that its inserted terms will be effective. The offeree at least had the opportunity to review the offer and object to its contents; if the recipient of an offer objected to a term, it should not have proceeded with the contract. Following this approach, Reilly Foam urges that the terms of its March 26, 1999 letter and price list, as the offer, would control. Because each of Rubbermaid's new terms posed material alterations to the parties' contract, they would have no effect.

The final approach, held by a majority of courts, is now known as the "knockout rule." Under this approach, terms of the contract include those upon which the parties agreed and gap fillers provided by the U.C.C. provisions. This approach recognizes the fundamental tenet behind U.C.C. § 2207: to repudiate the "mirror-image" rule of the

---

[2] For the sake of consistency, all citations to the U.C.C. use Pennsylvania's format. Section 2207 is the equivalent of in the original version promulgated by the American Law Institute and the National Conference of Commissioners of Uniform States Laws. Section 2207(b) corresponds to § 2–207(2).

[3] Judge Posner, speaking for himself, has advocated a similar rule: that the terms of the offer prevail over different terms set forth in the acceptance only if the different terms do not materially alter the contract. See Northrop Corp. v. Litronic Indus., 29 F.3d 1173, 1178 (7th Cir. 1994). However, as noted below, he predicted that Illinois would adopt the knockout rule.

common law. One should not be able to dictate the terms of the contract merely because one sent the offer. Indeed, the knockout rule recognizes that merchants are frequently willing to proceed with a transaction even though all terms have not been assented to. It would be inequitable to lend greater force to one party's preferred terms than the other's. As one court recently explained, "An approach other than the knock-out rule for conflicting terms would result in . . . [ ] any offeror . . . [ ] always prevailing on its terms solely because it sent the first form. That is not a desirable result, particularly when the parties have not negotiated for the challenged clause." Richardson v. Union Carbide Indus. Gases Inc., 790 A.2d 962, 968 (N.J. Super. Ct. App. Div. 2002). Support for this view is also found in the Official U.C.C. Comments:

Where clauses on confirming forms sent by both parties conflict each party must be assumed to object to a clause of the other conflicting with one on the confirmation sent by himself. As a result the requirement that there be notice of objection which is found in subsection [b] is satisfied and the conflicting terms do not become a part of the contract. The contract then consists of the terms originally expressly agreed to, terms on which the confirmations agree, and terms supplied by this Act, including subsection [b]. U.C.C. § 2207 cmt. 6.

Advocates of the knockout rule interpret Comment 6 to require the cancellation of terms in both parties' documents that conflict with one another, whether the terms are in confirmation notices or in the offer and acceptance themselves. A majority of courts now favor this approach.

The Court's task today is to predict how the Pennsylvania Supreme Court would rule if confronted with the issue. In making this determination, federal courts should examine, if available: "(1) what the Pennsylvania Supreme Court has said in related areas; (2) the decisional law of the Pennsylvania intermediate courts; (3) federal appeals and district court cases interpreting state law; and (4) decisions from other jurisdictions that have discussed the issues we face here." Werwinski v. Ford Motor Co., 286 F.3d 661, 675 (3d Cir. 2002).The Pennsylvania Supreme Court has never addressed the issue. The Court has unearthed only one intermediate court opinion, but it does not directly address the question, contains self-contradictory comments, and does little to aid in prediction. See United Coal & Commodities Co. v. Hawley Fuel Coal, Inc., 525 A.2d 741, 743–44 (Pa. Super. Ct. 1987). The court circumnavigated the issue. Therefore, *United Coal* provides little guidance.

I next turn to federal courts within Pennsylvania. My colleagues seem to be comfortable with application of the knockout rule, but to date, no one has expressly held it to be the law. One court applied the knockout rule, but did so upon the agreement of the parties. See Titanium Metals Corp. v. Elkem Mgmt., 191 F.R.D. 468, 470 (W.D. Pa. 1998) (Smith, J.). Another described the debate in some detail but never specifically adopted a rule. See Pennsylvania Power & Light Co. v. Joslyn Corp., Civ. A. No. 87–2027, 1988 U.S. Dist. LEXIS 12073, at *6 (E.D. Pa. 1988). A third court has expressed a preference for the knockout rule, but it ultimately rested on the ground that the offeror had expressly objected to the offeree's insertion of a different delivery term into the contract, barring the term under Pa.U.C.C. § 2207(b)(3)).

See Reaction Molding Technologies, Inc. v. General Electric Co., 588 F. Supp. 1280, 1289 (E.D. Pa. 1984).

The Tenth Circuit has predicted that the Pennsylvania Supreme Court would opt for the knockout rule. See Daitom Inc. v. Pennwalt Corp., 741 F.2d 1569, 1578–79 (10th Cir. 1984). In light of the superior policy reasons behind the knockout rule, its fit with the text of the statute, and the vast majority of jurisdictions adopting it, I concur with the Tenth Circuit and conclude that the Pennsylvania Supreme Court would adopt the knockout rule.

Application of § 2207 to the Exchange of Letters Between Reilly Foam and Rubbermaid

The parties have concluded a contract for the sale of sponges. Both Reilly Foam's proposal and Rubbermaid's response call for the sale of sponges of differing varieties, and they agree on the identification of particular sponges, along with dimensions and prices for each. Rubbermaid also agreed to add $0.015 to price of each sponge until Rubbermaid had made purchases of 2 million sponges to cover Reilly Foam's tooling costs of $30,000.00.

As to annual purchases of "other affected products," the price list accompanying Reilly Foam's March 26 letter set a minimum annual quantity requirement for each type of sponge. Rubbermaid's March 30 response contains no term at odds with that requirement. To the contrary, Mr. Ferrante wrote "approved" on the page. Furthermore, while Mr. Ferrante's letter does not expressly mention "Other Affected Products," Mr. Ferrante did consent to the $0.015 surcharge on the first two million sponges, implying that he accepted an obligation to purchase sponges in the "other affected products" category.As noted above, the March 26, 1999 correspondence sets those numbers at 340,000 for Brown sponges, 350,000 for Yellow Ester with Wave Pattern sponges, and 300,000 for the Yellow Ether to White Scrubmate sponges.

The March 26 and March 30 letters also do not differ with respect to the time period within which Rubbermaid was to purchase two million sponges with a $0.015 surcharge. Reilly Foam sought a two-year time frame, and Rubbermaid omitted that term in its acceptance. Rubbermaid therefore argues the two terms drop out under the knockout rule, giving Rubbermaid an infinite period of time in which to make its purchases. However, Mr. Ferrante's March 30 letter is silent as to the time period within which Rubbermaid had to make its purchases. Thus, the offer and acceptance do not differ and the two-year requirement is part of the contract.

However, as to the requirements contract clause that Reilly Foam sought respecting the butterfly and roller mop sponges, the knockout rule applies. Rubbermaid's acceptance of a requirements contract was limited to Tidal Wave project sponges produced by New Knight on behalf of Rubbermaid for current products listed in Reilly Foam's March 26 letter. The parties agree that New Knight assembled only the butterfly sponge mop; Rubbermaid manufactured the roller mop "in-house." Thus, Rubbermaid's commitment only related to the butterfly sponges. In addition, any new products that New Knight might produce in the future for Rubbermaid would be subject to the same arrangement. However, Rubbermaid did not commit to purchase all of its direct requirements for sponges from Reilly Foam. Therefore, the term creating a requirements contract for all of Rubbermaid's needs for the Tidal Wave brand of sponges falls out of the contract. Rubbermaid did commit to ensuring that its purchases from New Knight are manufactured with Reilly Foam sponges. Both letters agreed on that point. * * *

In summary, Rubbermaid has breached the contract in failing: (1) to make minimum annual purchases of "other affected products" as set forth on the March 26 price list; (2) to purchase two million sponges under the "other affected products" category with a $0.015 surcharge within two years of the contract date. Reilly Foam may also sue for Rubbermaid's alleged failure to make good faith efforts to ensure that New Knight purchased all of its requirements of butterfly mop sponges for Rubbermaid products from Reilly Foam until New Knight went bankrupt in August 2001. Plaintiff must also establish the extent of its damages at trial. * * *

Conclusion

In summary, Rubbermaid has breached the contract in failing: (1) to make minimum annual purchases of "other affected products" as set forth on the March 26 price list; (2) to purchase two million sponges under the "other affected products" category with a $0.015 surcharge within two years of the contract date. * * *

NOTES

1. The status of the contracting parties as merchants or non-merchants may affect whether terms in the offeree's response become part of the contract. Section 2–207(2) regulates "additional terms . . . to the contract" formed under 2–207(1). Additional terms in a confirmation or purported acceptance are terms that are consistent with the terms of an initial agreement or offer, respectively. Subsection (1) refers to two sorts of contracts: an agreement followed by a written confirmation and an offer and a purported acceptance containing non-identical terms. These are "the contract" to which 2–207(2) supplies the terms. Under 2–207(2) additional terms included in a written confirmation are not part of the contract. If at least one of the parties is not a merchant (2–104(1)), they merely are "proposals for addition to the contract." The terms become part of the contract only if the offeror agrees to them. This part of 2–207(2) adopts a "first shot" rule: an offer-varying acceptance can operate as an acceptance under 2–207(1), and the contract thereby created is on the terms of the first writing or oral communication sent. If both parties are merchants, the additional terms serve as "proposals" for inclusion in the contract. They do not become part of the contract if (a) the offer restricts acceptance to the terms of the offer, (b) the additional terms materially alter the contract, or (c) if the offeror makes a timely objection to their inclusion in the contract. 2–207(2)(a)–(c). Thus, unless one of (a)–(c) applies, the additional terms become part of the contract.

2. Section 2–207(2)'s treatment of terms in a purported acceptance that differ from terms in the offer is unclear. Different terms in a purported acceptance are terms that either are contrary to or inconsistent with the terms in an offer. "Blue widget" is a contrary term when the offer is for a "green widget." "Sold subject to all implied warranties" is an inconsistent term when the offer states that "all implied warranties are disclaimed." The *Reilly Foam* court follows the majority of courts in interpreting 2–207(2) to apply the knockout rule to different terms. This interpretation is questionable. For one thing, the knockout rule appears only in 2–207(3), not 2–207(2). Section 2–207(3) provides that the terms of a contract under the subsection consist of terms on which the writings agree together with terms supplemented by the UCC. Terms that differ between the purported acceptance and the offer therefore are not part of the contract. The different terms in both the offeror and offeree's writings drop out. Section 2–207(2) does not contain language similar to 2–207(3) or language which has the same consequence. If the drafters of 2–207(2) had intended different terms in the offer and purported acceptance to cancel each other out, it is likely that they would have included language similar to that in 2–207(3). In addition, reading the knockout rule into 2–207(2) lacks statutory support. Under 2–207(2), either the terms in the offeree's purported acceptance are included in the contract or they drop out. None of the terms of the *offeror's* offer drop out. Section 2–207(2)'s language is very clear in this respect: "Between merchants *such terms* become part of the contract unless . . ." (emphasis added). "Such terms" refers to the terms of the offeree's purported acceptance. Comment 6, on which the *Reilly Foam* court relies, does not support the court's position. The Comment discusses conflicting terms in confirmations sent by both the offeror and offeree. These are conflicting confirmations of a prior oral agreement. The Comment has no application where an oral agreement on terms is not already present. Thus, it has no application to cases in which a contract is formed under 2–207(1) by an exchange of writings, as in *Reilly Foam*. In these cases Comment 6 does not support dropping the offer's term when a term in the offeree's purported acceptance differs from it.

3. Good contract law rules have two features: They reduce transaction costs and provide efficient contract terms. While 2–207(1) reduces transaction costs, 2–207(2) arguably sometimes provides inefficient terms. Under 2–207(1) contracting parties save transaction costs in dispatching writings or other communications without bothering to assure themselves that the terms in their communications are identical. The benefits of agreeing on all terms before performance commences must be discounted by the probability of litigation over different or additional terms. Because in many cases the chance of litigation is remote, the expected benefit of reaching agreement on all terms is low. In these circumstances the parties are better off commencing performance without reaching an agreement on all terms. By providing that an offer-varying acceptance can conclude a contract, 2–207(1) relieves parties of the need to agree on all terms before commencing performance.

However, interpreting 2–207(2) to incorporate the knockout rule arguably produces an inefficient set of contract terms. Although contracting parties prefer to have their agreement enforced even when their communications contain different terms, they might not be indifferent as to how additional or different terms are treated by courts ex post. Because the knockout rule eliminates the different terms in both the offer and purported acceptance, a court must supply a term.

The term 2–207(2) supplies need not be the term in the offeror or the offeree's communications. This makes it possible for a 2–207(2) to supply the parties' contract with inefficient terms. For example, suppose the seller purchases goods from a third party to fill a contract with its buyer. The goods are in the third party's hands. Assume that the seller's offer calls for the buyer to take delivery at that party's place of business while the buyer's purported acceptance calls for the seller to deliver the goods to the buyer. If the buyer's costs of obtaining delivery are lower than the seller's delivery costs, allocating delivery costs to the seller is inefficient: Both parties are better off if the buyer takes delivery from the third party. The knockout rule eliminates the different delivery terms in the seller and buyer's communications. The UCC-supplied delivery term under 2–308(a) sets the place of delivery as the seller's place of business. Given the buyer's lower delivery costs, both the seller and buyer prefer that the buyer take delivery from the third party, not at the seller's place of business. The parties nonetheless might prefer an enforceable contract with an inefficient delivery term to not having an enforceable contract at all.

4. Section 2–207's knockout rule rejects the common law "last shot" rule: the rule that the terms of a contract concluded by performance following an offer-varying acceptance are those contained in the last communication prior to performance. The criticism of the last shot rule is this last communication will contain terms favorable only to the sender. The recipient, who is usually the buyer and who accepts the goods without reading the terms of the offer, nonetheless is bound by terms unfavorable to it. Some early literature on 2–207 rejected the assumption of unilaterally favorable terms. If all buyers inform themselves of the terms in an offer before they begin performance, they obviously will not be saddled with terms in offers unfavorable to them. Informed buyers will reject such offers and sellers making them will lose sales. Competitive pressures therefore will force sellers to offer terms favorable to buyers (at a competitive price) or exit the product market. If only some buyers inform themselves of the terms of offers and sellers cannot discriminate between "informed" and "uninformed" buyers, sellers will offer a single set of terms to all buyers. Because sellers know that they will lose sales to informed buyers when their offers contain terms unfavorable to them, their offers may contain terms favorable to both informed and uninformed buyers. In this way uninformed buyers may receive favorable terms even though unaware of the terms of an offer before beginning performance. Douglas G. Baird & Robert Weisberg, Rules, Standards, and the Battle of the Forms: A Reassessment of § 2–207, 68 Va. L. Rev. 1217, 1254–1259 (1982).

This argument is sensitive to its assumptions about the product markets in which offers are made. The seller will offer terms favorable to all buyers if the risk of losing a sale is high when an offer contains terms unfavorable to the buyer and the extra profit on a sale containing terms unfavorable to the buyer is small. The conclusion follows only if three assumptions hold: (1) sellers cannot reliably discriminate between informed and uniformed buyers, (2) the proportion of informed buyers among the population of buyers is great, and (3) the per sale extra profit from setting terms unfavorable to uninformed buyers is small. If sellers can reliably distinguish between informed and uniformed buyers, it can select between two different strategies. One is maximize the number of sales. This requires making offers on terms likely to be accepted by both informed and uninformed buyers. Such offers therefore include terms favorable to all buyers and a competitive price. A second strategy is to maximize revenues. This requires offers directed only at uninformed buyers and setting prices above competitive levels—a term unfavorable to buyers. The seller loses sales to informed buyers (and therefore profits on these sales) but earns additional profit on sales made to uninformed buyers. Which of the two strategies is best for a seller depends on which one earns it the greatest aggregate profit over all the sales it makes. See Ezra Friedman, Competition and Unconscionability, 15 Am. L. & Econ. Rev. 443 (2013). Although there are assertions in the literature that both business and consumer buyers fail to read offers, no systematic studies on point exist. Some empirical evidence finds favorable terms presented to all buyers in a number of product markets. See Alan Schwartz & Louis L. Wilde, Intervening in Markets on the Basis of Imperfect Information: A Legal and Economic Analysis, 127 U. Pa. L. Rev. 630 (1979).

The last shot rule can be defended and the knockout rule criticized in a different way: by identifying the decision maker best positioned to regulate the terms of a contract. The question of which terms control when the terms an offer and purported acceptance differ asks which terms regulate the contract. As with other issues of regulation, one can ask which decision maker is most likely to further the interests that will benefit from the regulation. With sales contracts, the relevant interests are those of the seller and buyer. In the usual case the choice of decision makers is between those subject to regulation—courts, regulators, and legislators. Section 2–207(2)'s knockout rule implicitly assumes that courts best protect the interests of the contracting parties. The different terms drop out, and the court must supply the contract with either a UCC-supplementary term or some other term. But courts have limited information about the parties' interests, as is often recognized in matter of regulation. They also can be subject to cognitive bias and might not be motivated to further the parties' interests. For these reasons, a court might select inefficient contract terms.

Legislatures and regulators potentially have available to them more information about the interests of typical contracting parties. However, as with most types of regulation, both institutions are subject to capture by interest groups. The risk of capture therefore is present with regulatory or legislative alternatives to 2–207(2)'s knockout rule. For instance, particular consumer groups may obtain regulation of contract terms favorable to them but harmful to other consumers. The last shot rule in effect allows the contract to be regulated by terms selected by one of the parties—the offeror. This form of regulation is not subject to problems about limited information about the contracting parties' interests, because the terms of the contract are those of the last communication sent prior to commencement of performance. The last shot rule does not require determining which terms the parties' interests favor. Although it might enforce terms unilaterally favorable to the offeror, the risk is limited to the particular contract. By contrast, the terms set by regulation or legislation apply to all contracts within the scope of a regulation or statute. Thus, the risk of regulatory or legislative capture affects all contracts and therefore the interests of a wide range of contracting parties. From a regulatory perspective, the last shot rule arguably is the best rule among feasible regulatory alternatives.

PROBLEM 3.1

Is a contract concluded by the exchange of the following communications under 2–207? Under common law?

(a) Buyer sends a letter to Seller stating: "We offer to buy 10 widgets at $10 per widget to be delivered to us on January 1." Seller responds by letter: "We accept you terms; we will deliver the widgets by February 1." Would the result change if Buyer's letter had instead stated in relevant part "and we would appreciate delivery of the widgets on January 1"?

(b) Buyer sends a letter to Seller stating: "We offer to buy 10 widgets at $10 per widget." Seller responds by letter: "We accept your terms; we will deliver the widgets by February 1."

(c) Buyer sends a letter to Seller stating: "We offer to buy 10 widgets at $10 per widget, delivery on January 1." Seller responds by letter: "We accept your terms, except that the price will be $15 per widget."

PROBLEM 3.2

(a) Buyer sent a letter to Seller requesting that Seller ship two ABC trucks to it as soon as possible. Seller did not respond immediately. Instead, two days later it shipped two ABC trucks to Buyer by carrier. The trucks were lost in transit to Buyer and Buyer never received them. Four days after the shipment Buyer received a purchase acknowledgement from Seller with shipping information. Buyer does not want to pay for goods it has not received, and Seller would like to recover the contract price. (Ignore the carrier's liability, if any, to either Buyer or Seller.) Has a contract been concluded between Buyer and Seller? 2–206(1)(b).

(b) Assume that Seller responded immediately to Buyer's letter by telephone. In doing so it accepted all of the terms of Buyer's offer. Does the telephone call conclude a contract? 2–206(1)(a); cf. 1–103(b).

PROBLEM 3.3

Buyer sent Seller a purchase order that stated: "We would like to purchase 10 XYZ machines at $5,000 per machine for installation in our factory. The machines are to come with full warranties. In addition, you will be liable for any business loss we suffer if the machines fail to work as warranted." Seller responded by a purchase acknowledgement, which read in relevant part: "We acknowledge receipt of your purchase order. This acceptance is made expressly conditional on the terms in this acknowledgment." The terms disclaimed all warranties and liability for loss resulting from the failure of the machines to operate as warranted.

(a) Has a contract been concluded by the exchange of these communications? 2–207(1).

(b) Assume that Seller shipped the machines after sending Buyer its purchase acknowledgement. Is Seller liable to Buyer if the machines don't work properly? 2–206(1)(b).

(c) Assume that Seller shipped the machines, which Buyer received, before it sent its purchase acknowledgement to Buyer. Is Seller liable to Buyer if the machines do not work properly? 2–207(3).

(d) Assume that Buyer's purchase order stated that it is "expressly conditioned on Seller's acceptance of all terms contained in this order that are additional or different from the terms in this order. Seller's shipment of goods in response to this order constitutes its acceptance of the terms of this order." Buyer's purchase order otherwise contained the terms described above, while Seller responded with the purchase acknowledgement above before it shipped the XYZ machines. If the machines Seller delivers do not work, is Seller liable to Buyer? 2–207(3), 2–206(1). Suppose Buyer's purchase order called for it to pay Seller 90 days after delivery. Does it matter whether the terms of the resulting contract are determined by 2–206(1) or 2–207(3)?

PROBLEM 3.4

Buyer's purchase order called for "AAA widgets at $10 per widget, payment within 30 days of delivery." Seller's order acknowledgement stated that "this acknowledgement assents to the terms of Buyer's purchase order, except that payment is due within 7 days of delivery and Seller is entitled to attorney's fees incurred in connection with recovery of damages arising from Buyer's breach of this contract." Buyer paid for the widgets Seller delivered 10 days after delivery, and Seller incurred $1,000 in attorney's fees in a successful breach of contract suit against Buyer (unrelated to Buyer's date of payment). Does Seller's contract with Buyer require Buyer to pay Seller within 10 days of Seller's delivery of the widgets? Does it entitle Seller to recover the $1,000 in attorney's fees? 2–207(2); Comments 3 & 5 to 2–207.

C. PROPOSED 2–207

Although Proposed Article 2 has been withdrawn from consideration for adoption, its proposed redrafting of 2–207 is worth considering briefly. Proposed 2–207 altered 2–207 in important respects. A portion of Proposed 2–206 and all of Proposed 2–207 appear below.

§ 2–206(3) A definite and seasonable expression of acceptance in a record operates as an acceptance even if it contains terms additional or different from the offer.

§ 2–207 Subject to Section 2–202 [Article 2's parol evidence rule], if (i) conduct by both parties recognizes the existence of a contract although their records do not otherwise establish a contract, (ii) a contract is formed by an offer and acceptance, or (iii) a contract formed in any manner is confirmed by a record that contains terms additional to or different from those in a contract being confirmed, the terms of the contract are:

(a) terms that appear in the records of both parties;

(b) terms, whether in a record or not, to which both parties agree;

(c) terms supplied or incorporated under any provision of the Act.

Part of the proposed amendment to 2–207 is merely statutory book-keeping, as it were. In contrast to 2–207, Proposed 2–207 separated questions of contract formation from questions about the terms of a contract. Proposed 2–206 dealt with contract formation. Within Proposed 2–206, Proposed 2–206(3) replaced current 2–207(1) in providing that a purported acceptance that contains additional or different terms from the offer operates as an acceptance. There is no change in 2–206(3)'s recognition of the rule of offer-varying acceptance. In addition, by its terms Proposed 2–207 applied to contracts concluded by "records." This allowed Proposed 2–207 to cover contracts concluded through electronic media, not just through writings (see Proposed 2–103(m)). Proposed 2–207 also makes regulates the terms of a contract, however the contract is formed. Thus, under Proposed 2–207 the same terms apply to a contract whether it is formed by conduct, offer and acceptance or followed by a confirmation.

Some of Proposed 2–207's changes in 2–207 are substantive. Current 2–207(2)(b) makes additional terms in an offer-varying acceptance part of the contract between merchants when they do not materially alter the contract. Terms that do not materially alter the contract become part of the contract unless either of subsection (2)(a) or (2)(c)'s conditions are met. Unsurprisingly, there continues to be considerable litigation over the sorts of additional terms that are materially altering. See Vultan Automative Equip., Ltd. v. Global Marine Engines & Parts, Inc., 49 UCC Rep. Serv.2d 743 (D. R.I. 2003) (interest or other credit terms); Vanlab v. Blossum Valley Foods Corp., 55 UCC Rep. Serv.2d 765 (W.D.N.Y. 2005) (nonarbitral forum selection clauses); Sibcoltrex, Inc. v. Am. Food Grp., Inc., 241 F. Supp.2d 104 (D. Mass. 2003) (arbitration clauses). By eliminating reference to the materiality of additional terms in a purported acceptance, Proposed 2–207 sets the terms of the contract without regard to their materiality. This excision makes the section simpler to apply. Proposed 2–207's most significant change is that it expressly applies the knockout rule to all contracts, however they are formed. Under Proposed 2–207(a) and (b), the only terms that become part of the parties' contract are those common to their records or otherwise agreed upon. Additional or different terms in a purported acceptance therefore are excluded if not agreed upon because they are not common to the parties' records. Proposed 2–207(c) continues to supplement the terms of a contract with UCC-supplied terms.

D. THE CISG'S FORMATION RULES

1. MECHANICS OF ASSENT: OFFER AND ACCEPTANCE

The CISG's formation rules are based on offer and acceptance. A contract is concluded when an acceptance of an offer becomes effective. See Article 23. Most of the CISG's formation rules are consistent with those of the common law. Two important differences concern the point at which an acceptance becomes effective and the irrevocability of offers. Article 18(2) provides that an acceptance becomes effective when it reaches the offeror. This civil law "receipt" rule of acceptance is in contrast to the common law rule deeming an acceptance effective upon its dispatch. The CISG's treatment of the irrevocability of offers also differs from the common law. Article 16(1) implicitly deems an offer irrevocable after the offeree has dispatched an acceptance.

It follows from the combination of Article 18(2) and Article 16(1)'s rules that the offeree is not bound by its acceptance until the acceptance is received by the offeror while the offeror cannot revoke its offer after the acceptance has been dispatched. Because Article 18(2) deems the acceptance to have occurred only on the offeror's receipt, the offeree can reject the offer as long as the rejection reaches the offeror before the acceptance arrives. As under common law, rejection terminates the offer. Cf. Article 17.

Article 16(2) provides that an offer cannot be revoked if it either indicates that it is irrevocable or the offeree reasonably relies on its irrevocability. There is some doubt about the circumstances in which Article 16(2) deems an offer irrevocable. Article 16(2)(a) states that an offer is irrevocable if it indicates, "whether by stating a fixed time for acceptance or otherwise," that is it is irrevocable. The quoted language is unclear. It may mean that the mere setting of a time past which an offer lapses makes the offer irrevocable. Alternatively, the quoted language could be read to mean that an offer "indicates" that it is irrevocable if the offer states that it remains open for a fixed time. The latter understanding of Article 16(2)(a) puts the CISG's rule on irrevocability close to 2–205's firm offer rule with respect to merchants. There still remain differences. Unlike 2–205, Article 16(2) does not apply only to written offers and does not limit the irrevocability of an offer to three months.

The CISG's treatment of open price terms also is unclear and controversial. A proposal that is otherwise definite in terms may not explicitly or implicitly set a price. The question arises as to whether a proposal lacking a price term can be an offer. For convenience, call the demand that an offer expressly or implicitly provide for price "the definite price requirement." Section 2–305(a) does not incorporate the requirement. Where an agreement fails to set price, 2–305(a) fixes the price of the goods as a "reasonable" price at the time of delivery. A "reasonable" price can be market price, and market price is a variable that is verifiable by a court. By contrast, Article 14(1) seems to incorporate the definite price requirement. It does so indirectly, by requiring that the terms of an offer be sufficiently definite. According to Article 14(1), an offer in turn is sufficiently definite "if it indicates the goods and expressly or implicitly fixes . . . the price." This condition appears to require that an offer fix price. At the same time, Article 55 seems to deny the definite price requirement. It provides that a "validly concluded" contract which does not expressly or implicitly fix the price is to have "impliedly made reference" to the price generally charged in the trade at the time of the conclusion of the contract. Article 55 therefore presupposes that a contract can be "validly concluded" with an open price term. The two Articles appear to be inconsistent with each other.

Several tribunals have found that Article 14(1) in fact incorporates the definite price requirement. United Technologies Int'l Pratt & Whitney Commercial Engine Bus. v. Malev Hungarian Airlines, 13 J. L. & Comm. 31 (1993) (Hungary); Tribunal of International Commercial Arbitration at the Russian Federation Chamber of Commerce and

Industry (Russia), 3 March 1995, available at http://www.cisg.law.pace. edu/cisg/wais/db/cases2/950303r1.html. The reasoning of other tribunals accepts the same conclusion. These courts have determined that the CISG is inapplicable to framework contracts, such as distributorship agreements, relying in part on the absence of a price term in some of these contracts. See Viva Vino Import Corp. v. Franese Vini S.r.l., 2000 WL 1224903 (E.D. Pa. 2000); Helen Kaminski Pty. Ltd. v. Australian Prods., 1997 WL 414137 (S.D.N.Y. 1997). They therefore assume that a contract for the sale of goods must have a price term.

A strong argument can be made that Article 14(1) incorporates the definite price requirement. Closely considered, the Article merely states a sufficient condition for a proposal being sufficiently definite in a price term—that it expressly or implicitly fixes price (". . . if it indicates the goods and expressly fixes . . . the price"). That is, it merely states that *if* a proposal fixes price and quantity, it is sufficiently definite in terms. Article 14(1) does not state a necessary condition for a proposal being sufficiently definite in terms. That is, the Article does not say that a proposal can be an offer, and therefore sufficiently definite, *only if* it fixes the price term. This reading of Article 14(1) not only is true to the Article's language. It also avoids the inconsistency between Articles 14 and 55 described above. To date no court has accepted the argument. A more detailed discussion of Articles 14's treatment of open price terms appears in Clayton P. Gillette & Steven D. Walt, Sales Law: Domestic and International 129–134 (2d. ed. 2009).

PROBLEM 3.5

Seller, located in New York City, and Buyer, located in Paris, have never dealt with each other before and no trade usage is applicable to their transaction. They exchange communications in the circumstances described below. Do the communications conclude a contract in each case? See CISG Articles 16, 18, 23, 24.

(a) Seller dispatches an offer which is received by Buyer on January 1. Buyer responds on that date by dispatching a letter which reads "I accept your offer . . . " Seller receives Buyer's letter on January 6. It opens the letter on January 8, the first business day after receipt.

(b) On January 1 Buyer dispatches a letter to Seller stating "I accept your offer . . . " Buyer later changes its mind and send a fax on January 2 stating "I reject your offer . . . Ignore my previous dispatch." Seller receives the fax on January 2 and Buyer's letter on January 4.

(c) On January 1 Buyer dispatched a letter to Seller stating: "I reject your offer . . . " On January 2 Buyer changed its mind and sent a fax stating "I accept your offer . . . Ignore my letter of January 1."

(d) On January 1 Buyer receives an offer previously dispatched by Seller stating "I offer you . . . " Buyer dispatches to Seller on January 2 an acceptance by letter. On January 3 Seller send a letter to Buyer stating "I revoke my offer of January 1; ignore it." Buyer receives Seller's January 3 letter on January 4. Seller receives Buyer's letter of acceptance on January 5.

(e) On January 1 Seller dispatches a letter to Buyer which states: "I offer to sell you . . . , but you must let me know by the end of the month whether you accept this offer." Seller notifies Buyer on January 5 that it revokes the offer. On January 6 Buyer faxes an acceptance to Seller, which it receives the same day.

2. ARTICLE 19'S QUALIFIED MIRROR IMAGE RULE

The CISG's treatment of offer-varying acceptances differs from both 2–207 and Proposed 2–207. Article 19, the CISG's counterpart to 2–207, adopts a slightly modified mirror image rule. Article 19(1) states the mirror image rule for acceptance: "A reply to an offer which purports to be an acceptance but contains additions, limitations or other modifications is a rejection of the offer and constitutes a counter-offer." Thus, for a reply to operate an acceptance under Article 19(1) it must contain only the terms of the offer. A reply containing additional or different terms, or limitations on the terms in the offer, is not an acceptance and therefore does not conclude a contract. Instead it operates as a rejection and a counteroffer. In this way Article 19(1) rejects the result under 2–207(1), in which an offer-varying acceptance can conclude a contract.

Article 19(2) qualifies Article 19(1)'s mirror image rule: "However, a reply to an offer which purports to be an acceptance but contains additional or different terms which do not materially alter the terms of the offer constitutes an acceptance, unless the offer, without undue delay, objects orally to the discrepancy or dispatches a notice to that effect." This subsection applies only to non-material alterations of the terms of the offer. Replies containing material altering terms therefore remain subject to Article 19(1). And under Article 19(1), such replies operate as rejections and counteroffers, not acceptances.

Nothing need be done by the offeror to prevent the formation of a contract. The offeror must take action only if the response contains a non-material alteration of the offer's terms. If the offeror timely objects, the reply still does not constitute an acceptance. The reply constitutes an acceptance only if the offeror does not timely object to the non-material alterations in it. In this case Article 19(2) modifies Article 19(1)'s mirror image rule.

Article 19(2)'s qualification of Article 19(1)'s mirror image rule is slight. This is because almost any additional or different terms in a reply will constitute a material alteration of the terms of the offer. Unlike 2–207(2)(b), Article 19(3) enumerates the sorts of alterations that are "material": "Additional or different terms relating, among other things, to the price, payment, quality and quantity of the goods, place and time of delivery, extent of one party's liability to the other or the settlement of disputes are considered to alter the terms of the offer materially." This enumeration includes almost all types of matters covered by a contract. To test Article 19(3)'s breadth, ask yourself what likely terms in a reply are not "material" under Article 19(3)'s enumeration. There are very few. Further, the enumeration is not exhaustive; subsection (3) states that the enumerated matters, "among other things," are material. Additional or different terms relating to matters not enumerated therefore still can be considered "material" under Article 19(3). Because the breadth of Article 19(3)'s enumeration of material terms is so broad, the range of non-material alterations in replies is correspondingly narrow. Thus, Article 19(2) modification of Article 19(1)'s mirror image rule is slight: the modification seldom will apply.

The "last shot" corollary to the mirror image rule remains applicable to Article 19 when an offer or counteroffer is accepted by conduct. A reply containing materially altering terms of the offer operates under Article 19(1) as a rejection and counteroffer, not an acceptance. The counteroffer is itself an offer because it invites acceptance of its terms; see Article 14(1). Performance by the party receiving the counteroffer constitutes acceptance of the counteroffer. Article 18(1) is clear that conduct can constitute acceptance: "A statement made or other conduct of the offeree indicating assent to an offer is an acceptance." Thus, performance by the offeree after receipt of the counteroffer constitutes its acceptance of the counteroffer and concludes a contract. Article 23. The terms of the contract are those contained in the counteroffer. For instance, where a seller's reply to its buyer is a rejection and counteroffer, and the buyer performs by taking delivery and using the goods, the buyer's conduct constitutes acceptance. The terms of the contract are those in the seller's counteroffer—the "last shot" before the buyer's performance. Correspondingly, where Article 19(2) modifies Article 19(1)'s mirror image rule, the last shot doctrine does not apply: The offer-varying acceptance creates a contract under terms that include the non-materially altering terms in the offeree's reply.

Courts applying Article 19 have held that replies which change or add a term affecting price, quantity or quality, the place of delivery or selection of forum are material alterations of offers. See, e.g., Oberster Gerichtshof (Austria), 9 March 2000, available at http://www.cisg.law. pace.edu/cases/000309a3.html; Oberlanesgericht Frankfurt am Main (Germany), 23 May 1995, available at http://www.cisg.law.pace.edu/ cases/950523g1.html, Cour de Cassation (France), 16 July 1998, available at http://www.cisg.law.pace.edu/cases/980716f1.html. For instance, an additional term in an order confirmation requiring credit insurance or a guarantee if payment is not made in advance is a material alteration of the terms of an offer. See Roser Technologies, Inc. v. Carl Schreiber GmbH, 2013 U.S. Dist. LEXIS 129242, at *1 (W.D. Pa. 2013).

Consider whether the terms in the following two replies constitute material alterations of the respective two offers: (1) A buyer's purchase order for tiles contains no term dealing with notice of any nonconformities in tile delivered by the seller. The seller's order acknowledgment repeats the terms of the buyer's purchase order and adds a term requiring notice of nonconformities within 30 days of delivery. Under these facts a German court found the term requiring notice not to be a material alteration of the terms of the buyer's purchase order; Landgericht Baden–Baden (Germany), 14 August 1991, available at http://www.cisg.law.pace.edu/cases/910814g1.html. (2) A buyer's offer set a delivery date of no later than March 15, 1997. The seller responded by accepting the offer but adding that the date of delivery was to be "April, time of delivery remains reserved." A German court reasoned that the delivery date in the seller's response was not a material alteration in part because "it did not regard the goods sold." Oberlandesgericht Naumburg (Germany), 27 April 1999, available at http://www.cisg.law.pace.edu/cases/990427g1.html.

Article 19(3) arguably states a bright-line rule of sorts as to matters enumerated in the subsection. Additional or different terms in a reply relating to the enumerated matters materially alter the offer's terms. Matters referred to but not enumerated ("among other things") presumably are subject to a fact-specific standard of materiality. The Austrian Supreme Court in effect held that Article 19(3)'s enumeration states a fact-specific standard, not a bright-line rule. According to a report of the case, the Court held that ". . . the alterations listed in article 19(3) CISG are not to be considered as altering the terms of the offer 'materially' in the sense of article 19(2) CISG if, in the light of usages, the negotiations and the very circumstances of the case, they are not deemed essential. In particular, it was held that alterations merely in favour of the other party do not require an express acceptance." Oberster Gerichtshof (Austria), 20 March 1997, available at http://cisgw3.law.pace.edu/cases/970320a3.html.

In evaluating the Court's reading of Article 19(3), two issues need to be separated. One is the interpretation of the parties' communications. Trade usage, course of dealing and circumstantial evidence might show that the term in reply does not alter a term in the offer. Articles 8 and 9 of the CISG interpret the communications of the parties against the background of these considerations. If a reply, properly interpreted, does not alter the terms of the offer, a contract is concluded on the basis of Article 23. Because the reply does not alter the offer's terms, Article 19 in general and Article 19(3) in particular is inapplicable. This is because the reply does not contain additional or different terms from the offer in the first place. The other issue is the treatment of a term in a reply that, properly interpreted, alters the terms of the offer. Article 19(3) considers terms relating to the matters enumerated in the subsection "material" alterations. It does not create a mere presumption that can be rebutted by evidence that the parties do not consider the alteration "essential." The Court seems to confuse the issue of interpretation and the separate issue of the character of an alteration in the reply. It is correct about the issue of interpretation but wrong about Article 19(3)'s treatment of additional or different terms in a reply. Trade usage and circumstantial evidence are relevant to whether a term in the reply alters a term in the offer. However, if the reply alters a term in the offer, whether the altering term essential to the parties or favorable to the offeror are irrelevant. Rather than a fact-specific inquiry into the effect of an alteration on the value of the contract to the offeror, Article 19(3) adopts a simple rule that avoids this inquiry: if an alteration relates the enumerated matters, the alteration is per se "material."

CSS Antenna, Inc. v. Amphenol–Tuchel Electronics, GmbH

United Stated District Court, District of Maryland, 2011
764 F. Supp.2d 745

■ Opinion by: CATHERINE C. BLAKE, DISTRICT JUDGE

CSS Antenna, Inc. ("CSS") has sued Amphenol–Tuchel Electronics, GmbH ("ATE") for breach of contract, breach of express warranty, and breach of implied warranty of fitness for a particular purpose. Now pending before the court is the defendant's motion to dismiss for lack of personal jurisdiction and improper venue. In the alternative, the defendant moves to transfer venue to the United States District Court for the Eastern District of Michigan or for dismissal under the doctrine of forum non conveniens. The motion has been fully briefed, and oral argument was heard on January 21, 2011. For the following reasons, the defendant's motion will be denied.

Background

ATE, which is based in Heilbronn, Germany, manufactures and supplies cable assemblies and related components. Although ATE manufactures the majority of its goods in Germany, it operates an office in the United States located in Canton, Michigan. The office handles customer service, engineering, and quality control for ATE and processes sales, purchase confirmations, and invoices for ATE's United States operations. The Canton office does not manufacture any goods for ATE.

CSS, which is based in Maryland, designs and manufactures cellular and PCS antennae. In 2004, CSS informed Softronics, Ltd. ("Softronics"), a company based in Cedar Rapids, Iowa, that it was searching for components for its cellular towers. On September 24, 2004, Brian Klosterman, an employee at Softronics, sent an inquiry to ATE via its global website. Mr. Klosterman requested samples of ATE connectors that he believed might be suitable for CSS's project. The inquiry was routed to Fred Bolick, ATE's Major Account Manager in ATE's Canton, Michigan office. Mr. Bolick contacted Mr. Klosterman at Softronics, who provided Mr. Bolick with contact information for Dave Sobczak, an employee at CSS. Mr. Bolick then directly contacted Mr. Sobczak at CSS.

In October 2004, Mr. Bolick requested and was granted permission to visit CSS's offices in Maryland to discuss the application of ATE's components with CSS's antennae. No contract was formed at that time. Following this visit, however, Mr. Bolick continued negotiations with CSS over the telephone, via e-mail, and through facsimile transmissions between ATE's Michigan office and CSS's Maryland office. In late 2004, CSS began placing purchase orders for various ATE components with Mr. Bolick. ATE responded to each of these orders by sending a purchase confirmation form to CSS's billing department. The parties conducted business through this purchase order, purchase confirmation arrangement until April 2005, when they signed an Inventory and Supply Agreement. Even after April 2005, however, the parties continued to conduct business through the purchase order, purchase confirmation system. During the course of their dealings, ATE representatives made four additional trips to CSS's office in Edgewood, Maryland.

In 2006, CSS began experiencing cellular site failures where ATE cables were installed. CSS alleges that these failures were caused by the infiltration of water into ATE's cables despite ATE's assurance that its components would remain watertight even after exposure to normal weather cycles. On July 30, 2009, CSS commenced this civil action against ATE. On June 7, 2010, ATE filed a motion to dismiss CSS's complaint. CSS has opposed the motion.

Analysis

* * *

B. Forum Selection Clause

ATE also has moved to dismiss CSS's complaint based on a forum selection clause contained in its General Conditions for the Supply of Products and Services of the Electrical and Electronics Industry ("General Conditions"). A motion to dismiss based on a forum selection clause is treated under Rule 12(b)(3) as a motion to dismiss on the basis of improper venue. Treating a motion to dismiss based on a forum selection clause under 12(b)(3) "allows the court to freely consider evidence outside the pleadings." Id. at 549–50.

The forum selection clause contained in ATE's General Conditions states: "If the Purchaser is a businessperson, sole venue for all disputes arising directly or indirectly out of the contracts shall be the Supplier's place of business. However, the Supplier may also bring an action at the Purchaser's place of business."[1] ATE contends that its contract with CSS was subject to this forum selection clause because ATE's purchase confirmation forms referenced the General Conditions. CSS argues that it was never aware of ATE's General Conditions and never agreed to the forum selection clause contained in the General Conditions.

The parties agree that the United Nations Convention on the Contract for the International Sale of Goods ("CISG") governs the question of whether the forum selection clause is binding upon CSS. Under the CISG, "[a] reply to an offer which purports to be an acceptance but contains additions, limitations or other modifications is a rejection of the offer and constitutes a counter-offer." CISG, art. 19(1). If, however, the additional or different terms contained in the purported acceptance do not materially alter the terms of the offer, and if the offeror fails to object without undue delay, then the terms of the contract include the additional or different terms contained in the acceptance. CISG art. 19(2). The CISG defines additional or different terms that materially alter an offer to include terms relating to "price, payment, quality and quantity of the goods, place and time of delivery, extent of one party's liability to the other or the *settlement of disputes*." CISG, art. 19(3) (emphasis added).

CSS contends that the April 2005 "KANBAN" Agreement signed by the parties memorialized their business relationship and represents the sole contractual agreement between CSS and ATE. Because the KANBAN Agreement did not reference the General Conditions, CSS argues that the forum selection clause never became part of their

---

[1] The Supplier's, or ATE's, place of business is Canton, Michigan.

contract. The KANBAN Agreement, however, contains only terms relating to inventory, replenishment, and delivery specifications. No information regarding price or quantity is included in the KANBAN Agreement. Moreover, the parties continued to carry on their business dealings through their purchase order and purchase confirmation arrangement even after signing the KANBAN Agreement. Thus, the court finds that the KANBAN Agreement was intended by the parties to serve as a supplemental agreement between the parties, not to memorialize their entire contractual relationship.

Instead, it appears that the parties formed multiple, separate contracts with each other through their purchase order, purchase confirmation arrangement. Pursuant to this arrangement, CSS would send a purchase order form to ATE's office in Canton, Michigan. The parties agree that this constituted an initial offer to purchase components from ATE. In response, ATE would send a purchase confirmation form, which included a reference to ATE's General Conditions, back to CSS. Under the CISG, ATE's purchase confirmation form did not constitute an acceptance of CSS's offer because ATE's General Conditions included terms, such as the forum selection clause, that related to the settlement of disputes. Thus, by including the General Conditions in its purchase confirmation form, ATE materially altered CSS's offer. Accordingly, ATE's purchase confirmation form constituted a counteroffer.[2] See CISG, art. 19. ATE contends that CSS then accepted its counteroffer, including the forum selection clause, by receiving its components and paying for the goods. CSS argues that, although it accepted ATE's components, it did not accept the General Conditions for two reasons: (1) under the CISG, a party's express acceptance to a forum selection clause contained in a order confirmation form is necessary for it to become part of a contract, and (2) the language on ATE's purchase confirmation form was not sufficient to put CSS on notice that ATE intended to incorporate the General Conditions into their contract.

CSS relies on two cases to support its argument that a forum selection clause contained in a seller's order confirmation form does not become part of a contract unless the buyer affirmatively assents to the provision. See Chateau des Charmes Wines Ltd. v. Sabate USA Inc., 328 F.3d 528, 531 (9th Cir. 2003) (holding that a seller's inclusion of a forum selection clause in its invoice and the buyer's failure to object did not mean that the clause became part of the contract); Solae, LLC v. Hershey Canada Inc., 557 F. Supp. 2d 452, 457–458 (D. Del. 2008) (concluding that a forum selection clause did not become part of the contract even though multiple invoices and confirmations contained the Conditions of Sale because the buyer never affirmatively assented to the proposed modification). In both of these cases, however, a purchase order and purchase confirmation form did not form the basis of the contract between the parties, as is the case here. Instead, the parties in *Chateau des Charmes Wines* and *Solae* had formed an oral agreement relating to the price and quantity terms of the contract prior to the exchange of purchase orders and purchase confirmations. The court in

---

[2] Even if the General Conditions did not materially alter CSS's offer under the Article 19 of CISG, the General Conditions would have become part of the contract because CSS did not object to the additional terms without undue delay. See CISG, art. 19(2).

both cases, therefore, treated the seller's invoice containing the forum selection clause as a proposal to modify the oral contract already established by the parties. Under the CISG, modification of a contract requires the agreement of both parties. See CISG, art. 29(1). Because the buyer in each case did not affirmatively assent to the modification, both courts held that the forum selection clause did not become part of the parties' contract. In contrast, at least on the present record, CSS and ATE did not have an existing oral or written contract when ATE sent its order confirmation form to CSS. The order confirmation, therefore, was not a proposed modification that would require CSS's affirmative assent under the CISG. As discussed above, it was a counteroffer that CSS accepted. Thus, these cases do not support CSS's argument that affirmative acceptance was necessary for ATE's forum selection clause to be part of their contract. Whether the language in ATE's purchase confirmation form was sufficient to put CSS on notice that ATE intended the General Conditions to apply, however, is a separate question.

Article 8 of the CISG provides that "[f]or the purposes of this Convention statements made by and other conduct of a party are to be interpreted according to his intent where the other party knew or could not have been unaware what that intent was." CISG, art. 8(1). Statements made by a party are interpreted according to the understanding of a reasonable person, and "[i]n determining the intent of a party or the understanding a reasonable person would have had, due consideration is given to all relevant circumstances of the case including the negotiations, any practices which the parties have established between themselves, usages and any subsequent conduct of the parties." CISG, art. 8(2)–(3). Based on the facts currently on the record, the court cannot conclude that CSS knew or should have known that ATE intended the General Conditions to apply to their contract.

First, the language referencing ATE's General Conditions was insufficient to put CSS on notice that ATE intended to incorporate the General Conditions into its contract. ATE's purchase confirmation form does not mention a forum selection clause on its face. Instead, page two of ATE's purchase confirmation form states:

May we point out that for all deliveries and services only the known general conditions of supply and delivery for products and services of the electrical industry (ZVEI) in their latest editions are valid.

. . . .

Please take note:

According to our general conditions for the supply of products and services to the electrical and electronics industry based on the [ZVEI] from Jan. 2002, we allow, as a supplier of components, defect claims up to 12 months after the date of the transfer of risk.

Our general conditions of delivery can be viewed or downloaded as .pdf file from our homepage: http://www.amphenol.de.

This language is ambiguous at best. The phrase "may we point out" is neither clear nor specific regarding ATE's intent that the General Conditions should control the terms of the sale. The ambiguity of the language referencing the General Conditions is further highlighted by the specificity of the surrounding language in the purchase confirmation form. The language alerting buyers to ATE's limitation on defect claims states: "[a]ccording to our general conditions for the supply of products and services to the electrical and electronics industry based on the [ZVEI] from Jan. 2002, we allow, as a supplier of components, defect claims up to 12 months after the date of the transfer of risk." This language is unambiguous. Indeed, in an abundance of caution, CSS filed separate actions against ATE and Amphenol Corporation, an affiliate of ATE, to ensure that it preserved its claim against both entities in accordance with ATE's clear statement regarding its limitation on defect claims. Compared with this unambiguous language, the court cannot conclude that CSS should have been aware from the broad language referencing the General Conditions that ATE intended to incorporate them into their contract.

Second, there is no evidence on the record to show that [CSS] had actual knowledge of ATE's General Conditions. The record shows that ATE sent its purchase confirmation forms directly to CSS's billing department, where no one with authority to enter into, modify, or otherwise accept any contracts worked. Both David Sobczak and Keith Barbalace, two CSS representatives responsible for negotiating with ATE, stated that ATE's General Conditions were never discussed during their negotiations and that they did not become aware of them until the defendant filed its motion to dismiss. Thus, at this time, the court cannot conclude that CSS had knowledge that ATE intended to incorporate its General Conditions into their contract.

Accordingly, on the present record, the defendant's motion to dismiss for improper venue will be denied without prejudice. If further evidence is developed during discovery demonstrating the terms of the contracts and whether CSS had knowledge of ATE's intent, then the court may reconsider the defendant's motion. Cf. Belcher–Robinson, L.L.C. v. Linamar Corp., 699 F. Supp. 2d 1329, 1338 (M.D. Ala. 2010) (explaining that, under the standard for ruling on a motion to dismiss and based upon the evidence on the record at the time, the court could not conclude that the forum selection clause was part of the contract).

* * *

Conclusion

For the foregoing reasons, the defendant's motion to dismiss for lack of personal jurisdiction, motion to transfer venue, and motion to dismiss based on the doctrine of forum non conveniens will be denied. The defendant's motion to dismiss for improper venue will be denied without prejudice.

NOTES

1. In concluding that CSS's conduct did not indicate its intent to accept ATE's counteroffer, the court makes two findings: (1) that ATE's purchase confirmation form containing terms in its General Conditions constituted a counteroffer, and (2) that CSS lacked sufficient notice of these terms. In finding that CSS lacked notice, the court deemed the language in ATE's purchase confirmation incorporating its General Conditions to be ambiguous. The language was "neither clear nor specific regarding ATE's intent that the General Conditions should

control the terms of the sale." Is the court's conclusion here consistent with its first finding? If ATE's confirmation is ambiguous, it does not sufficiently indicate ATE's intent to be bound in the case of CSS's acceptance. Thus, under Article 14(1), the confirmation cannot be an offer and therefore not a counteroffer. Because ATE's response cannot be a counteroffer, CSS's conduct cannot indicate assent to it under Article 18(1). Whether CSS had notice of the terms incorporated into ATE's confirmation is irrelevant. More generally, is CSS not bound by the terms ATE incorporated by reference into its confirmation because the confirmation is not an offer? Or because CSS's conduct does not indicate assent to ATE's counteroffer, when it lacked sufficient notice of one of the counteroffer's terms?

2.   In light of the court's conclusion that CSS lacked sufficient notice of ATE's counteroffer, the court's discussion of Article 8(2) is misplaced. Article 8(2) states an unexceptional rule of contract interpretation: statements made by a party are to be interpreted according to the understanding of a reasonable person. If CSS did not have notice of ATE's counteroffer so that its conduct does not indicate assent to it, the interpretation a reasonable person in CSS's position would put on the statements in ATE's confirmation is irrelevant. Even if a reasonable person would find the statements unambiguous, CSS still lacked sufficient notice of them. Put another way, given the court's application of Article 18(1), Article 8(2)'s application is superfluous.

3.   The CISG's rules of interpretation are unclear as to when an offer incorporates by reference terms available on the offeror's website. An Austrian case requires the offeror to send its standard terms to the offeree, even when the offeror communicates that they are available on its website. See Oberlandesgericht Celle (Austria), 24 July 2009, http://cisgw3.law.pace.edu/cases/090724g1.html.   Accord   Bundesgerichtshof (Germany), 31 October 2001, available at http://cisgw3.law.pace.edu/cases/011031g1.html. On the other hand, a Chinese arbitral tribunal held the offeree to the offeror's terms available on its website when the offer incorporated them by reference. See China International Economic & Trade Arbitration Commission (CIETAC), 17 September 2003, available at http://cisgw3.law.pace.edu/cases/030917c1.html. In *Roser Technologies, Inc. v. Carl Schreiber GmbH*, 2103 U.S. Dist. LEXIS 129242, at *1 (W.D. Pa. 2013), the seller's purchase order confirmations stated that "[t]his order confirmation is subject to our standard conditions of sale as known (www.csnmetals.de)." Although the court concluded that the confirmations constituted counteroffers and not acceptances of the buyer's offers, it relied on *CSS Antenna* to find that the counteroffers did not incorporate these standard terms: "In the case at bar, all of the factors that weigh against a finding that CSN's [the seller's] standard conditions were properly incorporated into the contract are present while none of the factors weigh in favor of incorporation are present. The language included on the order confirmations were ambiguous at best, as the language merely directed the other party to a website which needs to be navigated in order for the standard conditions to be located. See *CSS Antenna,* 764 F. Supp.2d, at 754. There is no evidence that RIT [the buyer] had actual knowledge of the attempted inclusion of CSN's standard conditions. See *id.* There is no evidence that the parties had discussed incorporation of the standard conditions during contract negotiations. See *id.* There is no

evidence that RTI actually received CSN's standard conditions. Further, no employee of RTI initialed next to the statement attempting to incorporate the standard conditions. *Id.*" *Roser Technologies*, 2013 U.S. Dist. LEXIS 129242, at *8.

4. A party who fails to timely object to the terms in a counteroffer will be taken to have assented to the terms. Under Article 18(1) its conduct constitutes acceptance of the counteroffer. The buyer in Magellan Int'l Corp. v. Salzgitter Handel GmbH, 76 F. Supp.2d 919 (N.D. Ill. 1999), opened a letter of creditor in the seller's favor after the seller's order confirmation had altered the terms of the buyer's order. In these circumstances the court found that the resulting contract was concluded on the terms of the seller's confirmation. In Filanto v. Chilewich, 789 F. Supp. 1229 (S.D.N.Y. 1992), the buyer's offer contained an arbitration clause and obligated the buyer to open a letter of credit in the seller's favor. Months later, after the buyer opened the letter of credit, the seller objected to the arbitration clause. The court determined that the seller had accepted the buyer's offer when, after the buyer had opened a letter of credit, it failed to timely object to the arbitration clause.

5. Courts are often required to decide only whether the parties have agreed to arbitrate their disputes, not whether a sales contract has been concluded. Although an arbitration clause is frequently part of the sales contract, the court must determine only whether there is a written agreement to arbitrate the issue in dispute. If there is a written agreement to arbitrate, the arbitrators decide the existence and terms of the sales contract. This is because Article II(3) of the United Nations Convention on the Recognition and Enforcement of Foreign Arbitral Awards (the "New York Convention"), 330 U.N.T.S. 3 (1958), requires a court in a contracting state to refer parties to arbitration if they have made an agreement in writing to arbitrate. Article II(2) in turn provides that "the term 'agreement in writing' shall include an arbitral clause in a contract or an arbitration agreement, signed by the parties or contained in an exchange of letters or telegrams." Although some courts consider this language merely to illustrate the term's application without defining it, most courts understand Article II(3) to define the term "agreement in writing."

A straightforward reading of Article II(3)'s language is that an "agreement in writing" must satisfy two requirements. First, the arbitration clause in a contract or an arbitration agreement must be in writing. Second, the written clause or agreement must be signed by both parties or be contained in an exchange of letters or telegrams. There is considerable dispute over these "agreement in writing" requirements. Some United States courts find an "agreement in writing" under Article II(2) is satisfied by an exchange of letters, where only one of the letters contains an arbitration clause and the party receiving it does not object. See Imtex Int'l Corp. v. Lorprint Inc., 625 F. Supp. 1572 (S.D.N.Y. 1986). Filanto v. Chilewich, 789 F. Supp. 1229 (S.D.N.Y. 1992), an early case applying the CISG's formation rules, implicitly takes this position. It finds the New York Convention applicable even though the seller's written correspondence did not accept arbitration proposed in the buyer's written correspondence. Other courts require both a written agreement to arbitrate and either the parties' signatures or an exchange of letters or telexes containing the clause. See Kahn Lucas, Lancaster v. Lark International Ltd., 186 F.3d 210 (2d Cir. 1999); cf. Sphere Drake Insurance PLC v. Marine Towing, Inc., 16 F.3d 669 (5th Cir. 1994) (only arbitration agreement must either be signed or contained in exchange of letters or telegrams; contract containing arbitration clause is enforceable unsigned).

PROBLEM 3.6

Buyer, located in New York City, submitted a purchase order to Seller, located in Berlin, for 10 generators at Seller's quoted price. Seller responded with its order confirmation, which made the confirmation subject to its standard terms and required Buyer to establish a letter of credit in its favor. The confirmation referred to the standard terms but did not provide them. Buyer was unaware of Seller's standard terms and its purchase order did not incorporate them or provide for the establishment of a letter of credit. Seller subsequently asked Buyer for certain specifications relating to the shipment of the generators, which Buyer supplied. When Seller later insisted that Buyer establish the letter of credit, as required by Seller's order confirmation, it refused. Does the parties' exchange of communications conclude a contract? See Article 19(1), (3). If not, is a contract concluded on another basis? Article 18(2). If so, does the concluded contract require Buyer to establish a letter of credit in Seller's favor? Article 19(1). What result under 2-207? See Roser Tech. v. Carl Schreiber GmbH, 2013 U.S. Dist. LEXIS 129242, at *1 (W.D. Pa., 2013).

E. ROLLING CONTRACTS UNDER ARTICLE 2

A rolling contract is a contract under which additional terms are presented, often at the time of delivery, which the buyer can accept by using the goods or reject by returning them. Usually rolling contracts require the buyer to pay the purchase price before it takes delivery of the goods. These contracts also are called "layered contracts" or "pay now, terms later contracts." Rolling contracts are not new sorts of agreements, although they are used increasingly with internet sales. Airlines, insurers and credit card issuers regularly provide products or services under terms that arrive after the purchaser has agreed to pay or has paid for the service. Rolling contracts also increasingly are used to license intellectual property. In such contracts the issue is not whether a contract has been concluded; the parties' conduct manifests an agreement. Instead two legal issues arise: when is the contract concluded?; and do the additional terms accompanying delivery of the goods become part of the contract?

Rolling contracts can be distinguished from two other sorts of agreements. One is an agreement in which the terms are individually negotiated. Where the agreement allows for additional terms to accompany the goods, there is no difficulty in finding assent by the buyer to the additional terms. The buyer has agreed to these terms even if it is unaware of their content at the time the contract was negotiated. Section 2–204(1) allows a contract to be formed on this basis: "A contract for sale of goods may be made in any manner sufficient to show agreement, including conduct by both parties which recognizes the existence of a contract." Another sort of agreement involves standard terms presented to the buyer on a take-it-or-leave it basis. This too is an easy case: A buyer generally is bound by the standard terms in an offer she accepts, even if she is not aware of these terms at the time of her acceptance. Rolling contracts present a third sort of agreement, in which the buyer is presented with terms after she has ordered and paid for the goods. For some courts enforcing the terms of rolling contracts, the buyer is bound by these later-arriving terms even without prior notice of them, unless she returns the goods within a stipulated period. The buyer's assent to the later-arriving terms is inferred from inaction: the buyer's failure to timely return the goods. Other courts apparently enforce them because they believe most buyers gain from the enforcement of terms in rolling contracts. See Clayton P. Gillette, Rolling Contracts as an Agency Problem, 2004 Wis. L. Rev. 679, 686–687. Although the difference between a buyer's ignorance of a term presented to it and its ignorance of a term presented later is a matter of degree, for these courts the difference matters. These courts reject rolling contracts by denying that the buyer's assent to later-arriving terms can be inferred from her inaction. For academic support of this view, see Mark A. Lemley, Terms of Use, 91 Minn. L. Rev. 459 (2006); James J. White, Autistic Contracts, 45 Wayne L. Rev. 1693, 1721 (2000).

Doctrinally, rolling contracts can be analyzed in two different ways, with different results. The difference turns on when the sales contract was formed. One view, adopted by some courts, considers the contract to be concluded at the time the promise to ship is made or the goods are shipped. 2–206(2)(b). The buyer's purchase order is the offer and the seller's promise to ship or the shipment of the goods is the acceptance. See Klocek v. Gateway, Inc., 104 F. Supp.2d 1332, 1338–1339 (D. Kan. 2000). According to this analysis, a contract is formed on terms the parties agreed to at the time the order is placed and accepted. Terms the seller adds that accompany delivery of the goods are regulated by 2–207. Under 2–207(2), if one of the parties is a non-merchant, these terms serve as mere proposals for addition to the contract. They do not become part of the contract unless the buyer accepts them. If both parties are merchants, the additional terms do not become part of the contract if they materially alter it or the offeree timely objects to them. Thus, in either case, the later-arriving terms are unlikely to become part of the contract.

Continuing this analysis, later-arriving terms cannot be deemed enforceable modifications of an initial contract. Section 2–209 allows an enforceable modification even when not supported by consideration, provided that the modification is made in good faith. However, a modification of a contract requires the agreement of both parties to the contract. Unilateral modifications are not enforceable. See 2–209(1) ("An agreement modifying a contract. . . ."). Where the contract is formed at the time the seller promises to ship or when shipment occurs, the terms accompanying the goods serve merely as a proposal for a modification. The buyer still must indicate its assent to the terms modifying the earlier agreement. Her failure to return the goods within the time stipulated by the later-arriving terms does not by itself indicate the buyer's assent to the terms. Of course, there could be circumstances in which the buyer's inaction could constitute an agreement to modify a contract. For instance, a clause in an initial contract could provide for modifications by later-arriving terms. But these circumstances do not generally hold for all or most rolling contracts.

The alternative doctrinal analysis considers the sales contract to be formed at the point performance has begun. On this analysis the seller is the offeror and the buyer the offeree; see *Hill v. Gateway 2000*, below. Performance has begun usually after the buyer has taken delivery of the goods and inspected them, not when the buyer's acceptance of the offer occurred. After inspecting the goods, the buyer is or should be aware that the terms accompanying delivery call for rejection of the goods by returning them. In these circumstances the buyer's retention of the goods allows an inference of its assent to the additional terms accompanying the delivery. For the result to follow, 2–207 must be inapplicable to rolling contracts. Otherwise, the later-arriving terms likely will not be part of the contract. This is because under 2–207 the later-arriving terms will either constitute a "confirmation" under 2–207(1) or additional terms under 2–207(2). The terms cannot plausibly be considered a "confirmation" of a prior oral agreement, as 2–207(1) requires, because the analysis assumes that the contract is formed when performance has begun, not before. Thus, they must be considered additional terms. But, as additional terms, the later-arriving terms likely will not become part of the contract under 2–207(2). As noted above, 2–207(2) treats additional terms as mere proposals for inclusion in the contract if one of the parties is a non-merchant. Even if both parties are merchants, 2–207(2) excludes the additional terms from the contract unless they do not materially alter the contract of the offeree timely objects to their inclusion. Later-arriving terms probably contain some materially altering terms. For these reasons, if 2–207 is applicable to rolling contracts, later-arriving terms do not become part of the contract. *Hill v. Gateway 2000*, reproduced below, takes the view that 2–207 is inapplicable to the rolling contract formed there. An assessment of this view appears in the Note 1 following the case.

Hill v. Gateway 2000

United States Court of Appeals, Seventh Circuit, 1997
105 F.3d 1147

■ Opinion by: EASTERBROOK, CIRCUIT JUDGE

A customer picks up the phone, orders a computer, and gives a credit card number. Presently a box arrives, containing the computer and a list of terms, said to govern unless the customer returns the computer within 30 days. Are these terms effective as the parties' contract, or is the contract term-free because the order-taker did not read any terms over the phone and elicit the customer's assent?

One of the terms in the box containing a Gateway 2000 system was an arbitration clause. Rich and Enza Hill, the customers, kept the computer more than 30 days before complaining about its components and performance. They filed suit in federal court arguing, among other things, that the product's shortcomings make Gateway a racketeer (mail and wire fraud are said to be the predicate offenses), leading to treble damages under RICO for the Hills and a class of all other purchasers. Gateway asked the district court to enforce the arbitration clause; the judge refused, writing that "the present record is insufficient to support a finding of a valid arbitration agreement between the parties or that the plaintiffs were given adequate notice of the arbitration clause." Gateway took an immediate appeal, as is its right. 9 U.S.C. § 16(a)(1)(A).

The Hills say that the arbitration clause did not stand out: they concede noticing the statement of terms but deny reading it closely enough to discover the agreement to arbitrate, and they ask us to conclude that they therefore may go to court. Yet an agreement to arbitrate must be enforced "save upon such grounds as exist at law or in equity for the revocation of any contract." 9 U.S.C. § 2. Doctor's Associates, Inc. v. Casarotto, 134 L. Ed. 2d 902, 116 S. Ct. 1652 (1996), holds that this provision of the Federal Arbitration Act is inconsistent with any requirement that an arbitration clause be prominent. A contract need not be read to be effective; people who accept take the risk that the unread terms may in retrospect prove unwelcome. Terms inside Gateway's box stand or fall together. If they constitute the parties' contract because the Hills had an opportunity to return the computer after reading them, then all must be enforced.

ProCD, Inc. v. Zeidenberg, 86 F.3d 1447 (7th Cir. 1996), holds that terms inside a box of software bind consumers who use the software after an opportunity to read the terms and to reject them by returning the product. Likewise, Carnival Cruise Lines, Inc. v. Shute, 499 U.S. 585, 113 L. Ed. 2d 622, 111 S. Ct. 1522 (1991), enforces a forum-selection clause that was included among three pages of terms attached to a cruise ship ticket. *ProCD* and *Carnival Cruise Lines* exemplify the many commercial transactions in which people pay for products with terms to follow; *ProCD* discusses others. 86 F.3d at 1451–52. The district court concluded in *ProCD* that the contract is formed when the consumer pays for the software; as a result, the court held, only terms known to the consumer at that moment are part of the contract, and provisos inside the box do not count. Although this is one way a contract could be formed, it is not the only way: "A vendor, as master of the offer, may invite acceptance by conduct, and may propose limitations on the kind of conduct that constitutes acceptance. A buyer may accept by performing the acts the vendor proposes to treat as acceptance." Id. at 1452. Gateway shipped computers with the same sort of accept-or-return offer *ProCD* made to users of its software. *ProCD* relied on the Uniform Commercial Code rather than any peculiarities of Wisconsin law; both Illinois and South Dakota, the two states whose law might govern relations between Gateway and the Hills, have adopted the UCC; neither side has pointed us to any atypical doctrines in those states that might be pertinent; *ProCD* therefore applies to this dispute.

Plaintiffs ask us to limit *ProCD* to software, but where's the sense in that? *ProCD* is about the law of contract, not the law of software. Payment preceding the revelation of full terms is common for air transportation, insurance, and many other endeavors. Practical considerations support allowing vendors to enclose the full legal terms with their products. Cashiers cannot be expected to read legal documents to customers before ringing up sales. If the staff at the other end of the phone for direct-sales operations such as Gateway's had to read the four-page statement of terms before taking the buyer's credit card number, the droning voice would anesthetize rather than enlighten many potential buyers. Others would hang up in a rage over the waste of their time. And oral recitation would not avoid customers' assertions (whether true or feigned) that the clerk did not read term X to them, or that they did not remember or understand it. Writing provides benefits for both sides of commercial transactions. Customers as a group are better off when vendors skip costly and ineffectual steps such as telephonic recitation, and use instead a simple approve-or-return device. Competent adults are bound by such documents, read or unread. For what little it is worth, we add that the box from Gateway was crammed with software. The computer came with an operating system, without which it was useful only as a boat anchor. Gateway also included many application programs. So the Hills' effort to limit *ProCD* to software would not avail them factually, even if it were sound legally—which it is not.

For their second sally, the Hills contend that *ProCD* should be limited to executory contracts (to licenses in particular), and therefore does not apply because both parties' performance of this contract was complete when the box arrived at their home. This is legally and factually wrong: legally because the question at hand concerns the formation of the contract rather than its performance, and factually because both contracts were incompletely performed. *ProCD* did not depend on the fact that the seller characterized the transaction as a license rather than as a contract; we treated it as a contract for the sale of goods and reserved the question whether for other purposes a "license" characterization might be preferable. All debates about characterization to one side, the transaction in *ProCD* was no more executory than the one here: Zeidenberg paid for the software and walked out of the store with a box under his arm, so if arrival of the box with the product ends the time for revelation of contractual terms, then the time ended in *ProCD* before Zeidenberg opened the box. But of course ProCD had not completed performance with delivery of the box, and neither had Gateway. One element of the transaction was the warranty, which obliges sellers to fix defects in their products. The Hills have invoked Gateway's warranty and are not satisfied with its response, so they are not well positioned to say that Gateway's obligations were fulfilled when the motor carrier unloaded the box. What is more, both ProCD and Gateway promised to help customers to use their products. Long-term service and information obligations are common in the computer business, on both hardware and software sides. Gateway offers "lifetime service" and has a round-the-clock telephone hotline to fulfil this promise. Some vendors spend more money helping customers use their products than on developing and manufacturing them. The document in Gateway's box includes promises of future performance that some consumers value highly; these promises bind Gateway just as the arbitration clause binds the Hills.

Next the Hills insist that *ProCD* is irrelevant because Zeidenberg was a "merchant" and they are not. Section 2–207(2) of the UCC, the infamous battle-of-the-forms section, states that "additional terms [following acceptance of an offer] are to be construed as proposals for addition to a contract. Between merchants such terms become part of the contract unless . . . ". Plaintiffs tell us that *ProCD* came out as it did only because Zeidenberg was a "merchant" and the terms inside

ProCD's box were not excluded by the "unless" clause. This argument pays scant attention to the opinion in *ProCD,* which concluded that, when there is only one form, "§ 2–207 is irrelevant." 86 F.3d at 1452. The question in *ProCD* was not whether terms were added to a contract after its formation, but how and when the contract was formed—in particular, whether a vendor may propose that a contract of sale be formed, not in the store (or over the phone) with the payment of money or a general "send me the product," but after the customer has had a chance to inspect both the item and the terms. *ProCD* answers "yes," for merchants and consumers alike. Yet again, for what little it is worth we observe that the Hills misunderstand the setting of *ProCD.* A "merchant" under the UCC "means a person who deals in goods of the kind or otherwise by his occupation holds himself out as having knowledge or skill peculiar to the practices or goods involved in the transaction," § 2–104(1). Zeidenberg bought the product at a retail store, an uncommon place for merchants to acquire inventory. His corporation put ProCD's database on the Internet for anyone to browse, which led to the litigation but did not make Zeidenberg a software merchant.

At oral argument the Hills propounded still another distinction: the box containing ProCD's software displayed a notice that additional terms were within, while the box containing Gateway's computer did not. The difference is functional, not legal. Consumers browsing the aisles of a store can look at the box, and if they are unwilling to deal with the prospect of additional terms can leave the box alone, avoiding the transactions costs of returning the package after reviewing its contents. Gateway's box, by contrast, is just a shipping carton; it is not on display anywhere. Its function is to protect the product during transit, and the information on its sides is for the use of handlers ("Fragile!" "This Side Up!") rather than would-be purchasers.

Perhaps the Hills would have had a better argument if they were first alerted to the bundling of hardware and legal-ware after opening the box and wanted to return the computer in order to avoid disagreeable terms, but were dissuaded by the expense of shipping. What the remedy would be in such a case—could it exceed the shipping charges?—is an interesting question, but one that need not detain us because the Hills knew before they ordered the computer that the carton would include some important terms, and they did not seek to discover these in advance. Gateway's ads state that their products come with limited warranties and lifetime support. How limited was the warranty—30 days, with service contingent on shipping the computer back, or five years, with free onsite service? What sort of support was offered? Shoppers have three principal ways to discover these things. First, they can ask the vendor to send a copy before deciding whether to buy. The Magnuson–Moss Warranty Act requires firms to distribute their warranty terms on request, 15 U.S.C. § 2302(b)(1)(A); the Hills do not contend that Gateway would have refused to enclose the remaining terms too. Concealment would be bad for business, scaring some customers away and leading to excess returns from others. Second, shoppers can consult public sources (computer magazines, the Web sites of vendors) that may contain this information. Third, they may inspect the documents after the product's delivery. Like Zeidenberg, the Hills took the third option. By keeping the computer beyond 30 days, the Hills accepted Gateway's offer, including the arbitration clause.

The Hills' remaining arguments, including a contention that the arbitration clause is unenforceable as part of a scheme to defraud, do not require more than a citation to Prima Paint Corp. v. Flood & Conklin Mfg. Co., 388 U.S. 395, 18 L. Ed. 2d 1270, 87 S. Ct. 1801 (1967). Whatever may be said pro and con about the cost and efficacy of arbitration (which the Hills disparage) is for Congress and the contracting parties to consider. Claims based on RICO are no less arbitrable than those founded on the contract or the law of torts. The decision of the district court is vacated, and this case is remanded with instructions to compel the Hills to submit their dispute to arbitration.

NOTES

1. In *Hill* Gateway included a form containing an arbitration clause along with a computer after the buyers placed an order by telephone. Judge Easterbrook repeats the position he takes in ProCD, Inc. v. Zeidenberg, 86 F.3d 1447 (7th Cir. 1996), that 2–207 is inapplicable when only one form is involved. Section 2–207's language does not support this view. By its terms, 2–207(1) allows a confirmation of previous agreement that contains additional or different terms to operate as an "acceptance." A single form therefore can confirm a previous oral agreement. See Step–Saver Data Systems, Inc. v. Wyse Tech., 939 F.2d 91 (3d Cir. 1991); Klocek v. Gateway, Inc., 104 F.Supp.2d 1332 (D. Kan. 2000). There is a split in authority as to whether a document received after delivery of the goods constitutes a confirmation that contains additional terms. See Rocheux Int'l of New Jersey, Inc. v. U.S. Merchants Fin. Grp. Inc., 741 F. Supp.2d 651, 678 (D.N.J. 2010). Courts either find that 2–207(2) governs the later-arriving additional terms or that 2–207 does not apply and the contract does not include these terms. *Hill* is unusual in finding that 2–207 does not apply but that the contract includes later-arriving additional terms.

2. Enforcement of the terms of rolling contracts is controversial because contract doctrine is at odds with broadly practical concerns. Contract doctrine requires assent to the terms of a contract. To find assent, there must a reasonable inference from the behavior of the offer indicating its acceptance. But acceptance cannot reasonably be inferred from the offeree's inaction in response to later-arriving terms. Except in the unusual case where the offeree's costs of rejection are zero, inaction may indicate merely sound budgeting, not assent. For instance, assume that the offeree is a buyer who values the good at $90. Assume also that the contract price of the good is $100, and the buyer's cost of returning the goods is $15. The buyer will retain the goods because the cost of returning them is greater than the net cost to the buyer of retaining them ($90 − $100 = -$10). In these circumstances the buyer's retention of the goods in the face of a later-arriving term deeming retention of the goods to be acceptance does not constitute acceptance. This is because no reliable inference can be drawn from the inaction of the buyer to show assent to the later-arriving term. Instead, retention of the goods merely is a rational decision. Slightly more controversial examples are clickwrap and browsewrap formats deeming a click or browsing of a website to indicate acceptance. Traditional contract doctrine also makes

it difficult to find acceptance in circumstances in which opening a box or attaching a plug constitute acceptance.

Much of the recent case law involving rolling contracts concerns electronic contracts for the licensing of software. Two types of terms figure in these contracts: "clickwrap" and "browsewrap" terms. A clickwrap term calls for the offeree to signal assent by entering electronically a stroke ("clicking") on an entry on a computer screen before receiving licensed software. Browsewrap terms state that the use ("browsing") of a website amounts to acceptance of its terms. In recent years a number of courts have enforced browsewrap and clickwrap licenses. Cases requiring the licensee to have notice of the terms clicking or browsing subjects it to include Register.com, Inc. v. Verio, Inc., 356 F.3d 393 (2d Cir. 2004) (repeat visit to site gave licensee reason to know of browsewrap terms); Specht v. Netscape Commc'ns. Corp., 306 F.3d 35 (2d Cir. 2002) (single visit to site gave licensee no reason to know of terms); Cairo, Inc. v. Crossmedia Servs., Inc., 2005 WL 756610, at *1 (N.D. Cal. 2005) (terms in site inconspicuously located); Novak v. Overture Servs., Inc., 309 F.Supp.2d 446 (E.D.N.Y. 2004). Cases finding acceptance of terms of license by a click with notice that terms apply but without requiring disclosure of the terms, include Mortgage Plus, Inc. v. DocMagic, Inc., 55 UCC Rep. Serv.2d 58 (D. Kan. 2004).

Savings in contracting and agency costs is a practical concern that favors including later-arriving terms in a contract. As Judge Easterbrook points out in *Hill*, a rolling contract saves the seller the effort of communicating all the terms of the contract to its buyer at the time it makes its offer or invites one. Rolling contracts also save sellers the cost of having to monitor their employees to assure that the employees convey to the buyer accurately all the terms of the agreement. Agency costs therefore also are reduced. The contract price buyers pay is reduced as a result of these reductions in contracting and agency costs. Savings in contracting and agency costs must be offset against the cost buyers must incur in subsequently discovering an unfavorable term and rejecting the offer. However, in well-functioning product markets, buyers are unlikely to receive unfavorable terms. Sellers in such markets will suffer financial and reputational harms from offering terms unfavorable to many buyers. (The conditions under which this is true are rehearsed above in section B.) Because rolling contracts reduce relevant costs and likely contain efficient contract terms, later-arriving terms should be enforced. This conclusion holds without regard to whether the offeree has assented to later-arriving terms. Savings in contracting and agency costs justify holding the offeree to these terms, whether or not the offer has assented to them. See Bischoff v. DirectTV, Inc., 180 F. Supp.2d 1097 (C.D. Cal. 2002); Gillette, supra (collecting cases).

3.   UCITA's formation rules provide for rolling contracts for the provision of computer information. See Uniform Computer Information Transaction Act, available at www.nccusl.org. UCITA § 202(a) allows contracts to be formed "in any manner sufficient to show agreement." Cf. 2–206(2). These contracts can include terms provided after performance has begun. Terms later provided are binding on a party if it assents to them, and it in turn assents to the terms if it adopts them.

Adoption occurs if a party fails to reject terms. Thus, under UCITA contract terms provided after performance are be accepted simply by a party's failure to reject them. In fact, this can occur even if the party has not actually reviewd the post-performance terms. Under UCITA § 208(2), a party adopts terms in a record provided after performance has begun if it has reason to know that the terms would later be provided and it lacked the opportunity to review them prior to beginning performance. Most business licensees will have reason to know that further terms will follow after the license has been made available to it even before they contract for the license. UCITA § 208(2) follows *Hill* with respect to terms provided after a license has been made available and the licensing fee paid. Comment 3 to UCITA § 208.

However, additional restrictions apply with respect to acceptance of post-performance terms in consumer contexts. UCITA § 209 adds restrictions regulating a "mass market license," which includes licenses to consumer licensees. Under UCITA § 209(b), the licensee who rejects the terms of the license must be reimbursed for the cost of returning the computer information, if the licensee previously paid for the license and did not have the opportunity to review its terms prior to payment. UCITA § 209(b) adds to *Hill* the requirement that the mass market licensee be reimbursed for the cost of returning the computer information. The rationale underlying UCITA § 209 is that non-business licensees often may be unaware that further terms will follow after the license has been made available. These licensees therefore can be held to have manifested assetn to such terms prior to payment. This rationale is consistent with traditional contract doctrine requiring a manifestation of assent as a condition of being bound. Given UCITA § 209(b)'s right of reimbursement, a mass market licensee who fails to return computer information presumptively accepts the later-arriving terms of a license. For criticisms of the restrictive definition of a mass market license, see Jean Braucher, The Failed Promise of the UCITA Mass–Market Concept and Its Lessons for Policing of Standard Form Contracts, 7 J. Small & Emerging Bus. L. 393 (2003).

PROBLEM 3.7

(a) Seller sent Buyer a catalogue describing items for sale. No other terms of sale were included. Buyer sent Seller its order form ordering 100 items X from the catalogue at $10 per item. Buyer's form called for delivery to be made within 10 days of Seller's acceptance of the order and that payment was due within 30 days of delivery. Seller responded by email in a form which stated: "We agree to a sale to you of 100 items X at $15 per item; delivery to be within 15 days of our agreement and payment due within 30 days of delivery." Neither Seller nor Buyer has performed. Have Seller and Buyer contracted for the sale of 100 items X? If they have contracted, what are the terms of their contract? 2–207(1), (2).

(b) Suppose in (a) Seller's response stated: "We agree to sale you 100 items X at $15 per item; delivery and payment on terms of your purchase order." Is the result different from the result in (a)? 2–207(1), (2).

(c) Suppose in (a) Seller responded as follows: "We agree to sell you 100 items X at $10, but delivery is to be within 12 days of our acceptance and payment with 30 days of delivery." Is the result different than in (a)? 2–207(1), (2).

(d) Would the result in (a) change if Seller was located in New York City and Buyer in Paris? CISG Articles 1, 19.

(e) Suppose in (a) Buyer's order form made no mention of price while Seller's response called for a sale at $15 per item X. The parties have never done business together before and item X is specially manufactured and sold only by Seller. Also suppose that the terms of the order and response are otherwise as in (a) and that Seller is located in New York City and Buyer in Paris. Is the result different from the result in (a)? CISG Articles 1, 14, 8, 9, 19, 23, 55; cf. 2–305(a).

PROBLEM 3.8

Buyer sent Seller purchase order by letter for 100 items X at $10 and Seller accepted by telephone. No other relevant terms were mentioned in the letter and telephone conversation. Several days later Buyer received from Seller a letter stating: "This letter accepts your purchase order. Terms: 100 items X at $10; we hereby disclaim all liability for consequential damages resulting from our breach in connection with this order; Buyer's sole recourse against Seller is limited to a refund of $1 per item for each defective item delivered."

(a) If Seller fails to deliver any items X and Buyer loses sales before it obtains substitute goods from other sellers, is Seller liable for the lost sales?

(b) Suppose Seller delivers the items but they turn out to be defective and Buyer refuses Seller's refund of $1 per widget. Is Seller liable for damages in an amount in excess of this sum? 2–207(2), Comment 3 to 2–207, 2–715, 2–719(1).

PROBLEM 3.9

Seller is located in New York City and Buyer in Paris. Buyer sends Seller a purchase order calling for the goods ordered to be shipped to Paris by airplane. Seller responds with an order acknowledgment stating that shipment will be by ocean carrier. In the relevant trade it is common for sellers to allow their buyers to select between air and ocean carriage. The cost of delivery by air is greater than the cost of ocean carriage, and both Seller and Buyers' communications require Seller to bear all delivery costs. When the price of air carriage increases, Seller refuses to deliver the goods to Paris by air. Is there a contract between Seller and Buyer? If so, does it require Seller to deliver the goods by air? CISG Articles 8(1), 9(2), 19.

PROBLEM 3.10

Buyer sends a letter to Seller ordering a widget on January 1. The price of widgets fluctuates significantly over short periods. Accordingly, Seller on January 5, the day it receives Buyer's letter, accepts Buyer's order in its own letter sent that day. Widget prices drop on January 6 and Buyer sends Seller a note stating that "I have decided not to purchase the widget described in my January 1 letter." Is Buyer bound by the terms of its January 1 letter? Make assumptions needed to answer the question. 1–103(b), 2–204, 2–206(1); CISG Articles 1, 14(1), 16(1), (2), 18(2), 23. What can Seller do to protect itself? CISG Article 6.

PROBLEM 3.11

Suppose in *Hill* that several days after the Hills ordered their computer they received a letter from Gateway. Gateway's letter stated: "We are pleased that you have ordered from us a computer at a price of $1,000. However, we must insist on receiving from you $1,200 for the order; otherwise, we will not deliver."

(a) Are the terms of this letter enforceable against the Hills? 2–204(1), 2–206(1), 2–207(1), (2), 2–209.

(b) Assume in *Hill* that the documentation accompanying the computer Gateway delivered contained a term stating that the Hills are deemed to accept all of Gateway's terms contained in the documentation unless they call Gateway and reject the terms immediately upon opening the box containing the computer. If the Hills do not contact Gateway immediately on opening the box, are they bound by the arbitration clause in *Hill*? 2–204(1), 2–206(1).

F. ELECTRONIC CONTRACTING

Unsurprisingly, contracts increasingly are concluded and administered through electronic media, such as email or the internet. Federal and state law in the United States accommodates and encourages electronic commerce by legally recognizing it. The Uniform Electronic Transactions Act (UETA), adopted by 47 states, and the federal Electronic Signatures in Global and National Commerce Act (E–Sign), 15 U.S.C. §§ 7001–7031 (2011), are the main domestic legislation governing electronic contracting. Common to both pieces of legislation is a central principle: medium-neutrality. This is the idea that paper-based and electronically-based transactions are to be treated in the same way. Put another way, electronically-based transactions are not to be treated differently just because they are concluded or conducted in an electronic form. See, e.g., UETA § 7; E–Sign § 7001(a). Amendments to UCC provisions also make changes that reflect the principle of medium-neutrality (e.g., 9–203(b)(3)(A), 9–102(a)(70); 1–201(b)(16), (31)). The principle of medium-neutrality prohibits a contract or signature from being denied legal effect solely because it is in electronic form. In addition, the UETA contains rules for attributing an electronic signature to a person, the treatment of errors in the electronic record that occur during transmission, and default rules as to the time an electronic communication is sent and received.

Domestic electronic contracts governed by United States law are subject to UETA or E–Sign. Similarly, international contracts subject to European Union law or some national law recognizes contracting through electronic media. See, e.g., Council Directive 2000/31, Directive on Electronic Commerce, 2000 O.J. (L 178) (EC); Council Directive 1999/93, Directive on a Community Framework for Electronic Signatures, 1999 O.J. (L 013) (EC). However, the recognition of electronic contracts is uncertain when a contracting party is from a country that does not have legal rules applicable to electronic contracts. In such instances a uniform law on international electronic contracting is useful. In 2005 the United Nations adopted the Convention on the Use of Electronic Communications in International Contracts, http://www.uncitral.org/uncitral/en/uncitral_texts/electronic_commerce/2005Convention.html. ("Convention"). The Convention applies to contracts between parties whose places of business are in different States. Where applicable it regulates the use of electronic communications in connection with these contracts. "Electronic communication" includes both communications that conclude a contract as well as those made in its performance. The term is defined broadly to include information sent, received or stored electronically as well as telegram, telex and telecopy. The Convention governs, with some exceptions, only business-to-business and business-to-government contracts. It entered into force on March 1, 2013, six months after three States ratified the Convention.

The Convention makes the legal rules applicable to electronic contracts more predictable. Article 8 deems electronic communications, such as those over the internet, valid and enforceable, and Article 9 allows an electronic communication to satisfy a legal requirement of a writing and signature. Both Articles implement the principle of medium-neutrality. Article 12 treats as valid contracts formed through interactive communication systems between a natural person and an automated message system or between such systems. Article 14 deals with input errors made by a natural person on an interactive website. It allows the person making the error to withdraw it on timely notification when it has not materially benefitted from the goods or services provided by the party not in error. By its terms, the Article limits the right to correct errors to the buyer. Finally, Article 20 makes the Convention applicable to contracts to which any enumerated treaties apply, including the CISG. One of the practical consequences of the Article is that any "writing" requirements in these treaties will be satisfied by electronic communications. See, e.g., CISG Articles 11, 12, 96.

CHAPTER 4

FORMAL REQUIREMENTS

Almost all of Article 2's rules are default rules. Most of its rules set terms that the contracting parties can alter by agreement. See 1–302(a). Two of Article 2's few formal requirements governing the sales contract are mandatory: the Statute of Frauds and the doctrine of unconscionability. They set requirements that the parties cannot contract around. Nonetheless, in a sense even these formal requirements are default rules too. This is because the contracting parties, with some inconvenience, can arrange to have their sales contract regulated by law that does not insist on the formal requirements. For example, the parties can select the CISG as applicable to their contract, and the CISG has neither a Statute of Frauds nor a parol evidence rule. They can even structure their sales transaction to assure that law that does not insist on these formalities will apply. However, Article 2's formal requirements are mandatory in the recognizable sense that they cannot be contracted around if Article 2 applies to the sales contract. A third formal requirement is the parol evidence rule. It is a default rule: Even if Article 2 governs the sales contract, contracting parties can avoid application of Article 2's parol evidence rule simply by not reducing their agreement to writing.

A. ARTICLE 2'S STATUTE OF FRAUDS

1. SECTION 2–201(1)'S GENERAL RULE

Even if a sales contract is concluded, it may not be enforceable as a contract. The Statute of Frauds states a formal requirement that must be satisfied for certain contracts within its scope to be enforced. The Uniform Commercial Code ("UCC") contains different Statute of Frauds provisions, governing different sorts of contracts. Section 2A–201(1) applies to leases of personal property, and 9–203(b)(3)(A) to the creation of security interests in personal property. Section 2–201(1) contains Article 2's Statute of Frauds. It requires that a contract for the sale of goods with a price of $500 or more is enforceable against a party to the contract only if the party signed a legally sufficient memorandum. The memorandum could be created before or after the sales contract is concluded, as long as it evidences the contract and contains the terms required by 2–201(1). Of course, the memorandum may but need not itself constitute the sales contract. A memorandum satisfying 2–201(1) need be created only by the time enforcement is sought against a party to the sales contract. It could be created but destroyed or unavailable, although proof of its creation might be difficult in these circumstances. For the sales contract to be enforceable, such a memorandum is necessary. Otherwise, the contract is unenforceable, unless one of the exceptions in 2–201(2) or (3) is satisfied.

Section 2–201(1) contains three fairly minimal requirements. First, the writing must be "sufficient to indicate that a contract for sale has been made." A "writing" is any "intentional reduction to tangible form."

1–201(b)(43). Thus, printed emails, video tapes, and tape recordings each count as a "writing." Comment 1 to 2–201 weakens the demand of "sufficiency" just quoted, by merely requiring that the writing "afford a basis for believing that the offered oral evidence rests on a real transaction." A writing may "afford a basis" for inferring that a sales contract was concluded even if it is not "sufficient to indicate" this fact. Even so, a written purchase order or price schedule, for instance, will not by itself indicate that a sales contract was made. They are consistent with no contract being concluded. Second, the writing must be signed by the party against whom enforcement is sought. A "signature" includes any symbol adopted by the party with a present intent to authenticate. 1–201(b)(38) ("signed"). Accordingly, a letterhead, a statement on a video tape or even a personal identification number on an electronically stored record all can count as a "signature." Third, 2–201(1) arguably requires that the writing state the quantity of goods or at least allow for the calculation of a quantity. Although not expressly demanded by 2–201(1)'s language, the requirement is fairly implied from 2–201(1)'s restriction that a contract is not enforceable beyond the quantity mentioned in the writing. Comment 1 to 2–201 explicitly requires that the writing specify a quantity of goods. A decent contrary argument, however, can be made that 2–201(1) does not demand a quantity term be in the writing. Rather, 2–201(1) can be read simply to say that *if* the writing mentions a quantity of goods, the sales contract is enforceable beyond the quantity mentioned. In addition, 2–201(1) does not imply that a legally sufficient memorandum must contain a quantity term. Proposed 2–201(1) takes this position, providing that "[a] record is not insufficient because it omits . . . a term agreed upon . . . "

By it terms, a legally sufficient memorandum must be a signed writing. Although some courts find stored electronic transmissions to be "signed writings," the issue (but not its resolution) is controversial. Proposed 2–201(1) and other UCC Statute of Frauds provisions now require that a memorandum be "signed record" or an "authenticated record." See, e.g., 9–203(b)(3)(A). A "record" includes a writing as well information "stored in an electronic or other medium and . . . retrievable in perceivable form." Proposed 2–102(m); 1–201(b)(31). Proposed 2–103(p)(ii) amends the definition of "sign" to include the attachment of an electronic sound, symbol or process to a record with the present intent to authenticate or adopt it. The purpose of the change is to achieve medium-neutrality in enforcement. Medium-neutrality requires that the terms of a document will not be denied enforcement solely because the document is in non-paper form or contains a non-manually produced signature. This allows enforcement of electronic records containing electronic signatures.

Section 2–201(1)'s retention of the requirement that the signed memorandum be a writing no longer matters; an electronic record with an electronic signature suffices. This is because both predominant state law as well as federal law adopts medium-neutrality applicable for contracts within Article 2's scope. At the state level, 48 of the 50 states have adopted the Uniform Electronic Transactions Act ("UETA"). See 7A Unif. L. Ann. 211 (1999). The UETA provides that a record or signature cannot be denied legal effect solely because it is in electronic form. UETA § 7(a). The UETA applies to sales contracts governed by

Article 2. UETA § 3(b)(2). Federal law requires the same treatment. Under the Electronic Signatures in Global and National Commerce Act ("E–Sign"), transactions in interstate or foreign commerce involving signatures or contracts cannot be denied effect solely because they are in electronic form. 15 U.S.C. § 7001(a)(1), (2). In general E–Sign requires that state and other law be medium-neutral. Thus, as federal law, E–Sign preempts 2–201(1)'s non-media-neutral writing requirement. E–Sign does not preempt state law enactments of the UETA. 15 U.S.C. § 7002(a)(1). In addition, E–Sign limits it own preemptive effect by allowing state or other law to "modify, limit or supersede" the requirement of medium-neutrality. The limitation basically applies only when state or other law itself requires medium-neutrality and makes specific reference to E–Sign. Because UETA and E–Sign both require medium-neutrality, there is no need to amend 2–201 to allow for electronic records with electronic signatures.

A couple of points about 2–201(1) are worth noting. First, satisfaction of 2–201(1) does not mean that there is an enforceable contract. Its simply means that a party can go forward to prove the existence and terms of the sales contract. The fact finder still may determine that no agreement had been made or that the terms of the agreement are different from those in the legally sufficient memorandum. Section 2–201(1) only bars a party from enforcing a contract within 2–201(1) without a legally sufficient memorandum. Thus, 2–201(1) states only a necessary not a sufficient condition for the enforceability of certain sales contracts as contracts. Second, the qualification "as a contract" is important. Failure to satisfy the Statute of Frauds does not mean that the sales contract is unenforceable. A contracting party still may recover "off the contract," on an extra-contractual basis. The most likely extra-contractual basis of recovery is restitution to the extent of the value of benefits conveyed to a contracting party. Another "off the contract" remedy, although less likely, is in tort on the basis of conversion.

Section 2–201(1)'s requirements apply to certain modifications of contracts. A modification of a contract alters the terms of a previous agreement. The previous agreement may or may not fall within the scope of 2–201(1). Nonetheless, if the modification of that agreement brings the contract within 2–201(1), the modified contract must satisfy its requirements. Section 2–209(3) so provides: "The requirements of the statute of frauds section of this Article (Section 2–201) must be satisfied if the contract as modified is within its provisions." Therefore, the modification is unenforceable unless 2–201(1) is met or one of its exceptions applies.

Section 2–209(3) is easy to apply in cases involving modifications to price or quantity. For instance, if the initial contract has a price of $100, it falls outside of 2–201(1). Once modified to raise the price to $600, 2–201(1) now applies. Harder cases involve the modification of terms other than price or quantity. Suppose the initial contract is evidenced by a writing satisfying 2–201(1). The contract is modified orally to change the date of delivery or the place payment is to be made. Must the modified terms themselves be evidenced by a writing? Courts and commentators tend to divide. On the one hand, the writing contains price, quantity and a basis for believing that an initial contract was concluded. See Comment 1 to 2–201. The modification leaves these terms unaltered; only the delivery and payment terms were changed. So seemingly the writing evidencing the initial contract also serves to satisfy 2–201 with respect to the modified contract. Requiring a writing to evidence these changed terms increases 2–201(1)'s requirements for modified contracts. Section 2–209(3)'s language seemingly does not do so. This is the conclusion many commentators take. On the other hand, 2–209(3) requires 2–201 to be satisfied when "the contract as modified" is within its scope. The delivery and payment terms are terms of the contract "as modified." Thus, seemingly 2–209(3) requires that a writing evidence the contract "as modified," including the modified terms. Many courts take this position.

PROBLEM 4.1

(a) Buyco received a catalogue sent by Sellco describing Sellco's products with associated prices. The catalogue contained a purchase order form with Sellco's letterhead and address, and space left for quantities ordered. Buyco's manager completed the order form by filling in the quantities of the products needed and mailed the form before the March 1 expiration date on the catalogue. The order came to $10,000. Sellco received Buyco's order form on February 15, but not before Sellco had raised its prices. When Buyco's manager called to ask when Buyco could expect delivery of the items ordered, Sellco refused to deliver at the prices listed in Buyco's order form. In Buyco's later suit, Sellco takes the position that its communications with Buyco did not conclude a contract and, even if had one been concluded, it is unenforceable against Sellco. Focusing only on Sellco's latter position, is the contract unenforceable? 2–201(1).

(b) Assume in (a) that Buyco responded with a purchase order under its letterhead acknowledging receipt of the order. The facts are otherwise the same as in (a). Is the contract unenforceable if one was concluded?

(c) Assume in (a) that Sellco regularly filled purchase orders sent by Buyco on receiving them. Is the result different? 2–201, 1–201(b)(3), (12), 1–303(d), Comment 1 to 2–201.

PROBLEM 4.2

(a) In 2007 Seller, a Texas computer manufacturer, and Buyer, a Virginia retailer, met at a trade show and agreed that Seller would supply Buyer with 100 computers for a total price of $15,000. The agreement was concluded with a handshake. Later, Seller sent Buyer an email which read in relevant part: "This is to confirm our agreement reached at the trade show that we will supply you with 100 computers at $15,000 total price. Seller." In subsequent litigation with Buyer over the contract, Seller argues that the contract is unenforceable. Is it? See 2–201(1), Electronic Signatures in Global and National Commerce Act ("E–Sign"), 15 U.S.C. §§ 7001(a), 7002, 7003(a)(3), 7006(4), (5); cf. UETA § 7(b), (c).

(b) What result in (a) if Seller's email had simply read in relevant part: "this is to confirm our agreement reached at the trade show that we will supply you with 100 computers at $15,000 total price"? E–Sign §§ 7000(a), 7006(5).

(c) Suppose in litigation under (a)'s facts Seller sought to enforce the contract against Buyer. Is the contract enforceable against it?

2.   SECTION 2–201(1)'S JUSTIFICATION

A Statute of Frauds requires that there by some written evidence that a contract has been concluded. The writing serves an evidentiary purpose: it provides information that has some evidentiary value concerning the existence of a contract. A writing provides evidentiary value to the extent that it allows a reliable inference that a contract was concluded. How much evidentiary value a particular Statute of Frauds provides depends on the requirements of the particular Statute. Different Statutes of Frauds require written evidence that has different degrees of evidentiary value. To fix ideas, consider a spectrum with two extremes: no Statute of Frauds requirement at one end and the requirement that the contract and its essential terms be concluded in writing at the other end. For example, a contract to sell an investment security is enforceable even without a memorandum evidencing the sale or its terms; see 8–113. On the other hand, an employment contract for a term of two years is within the Statute of Frauds, and its enforcement requires a memorandum containing the essential terms of the agreement. See Restatement (Second) of Contracts §§ 130, 131(c) (1981). The requirement that the memorandum include the essential terms gives the writing high evidentiary value, because the existence and terms of an agreement can be inferred from a writing with fair reliability. This is because such a requirement encourages parties to memorialize agreements and their terms in writings. In fact, some former communist countries required that certain contracts be concluded in writing to facilitate central control of economic activity. At the other extreme, where no Statute of Frauds is in force, an inference that a contract was concluded cannot be made reliably from an allegation to that effect. Put another way, the probability that a contract was concluded is not increased by the allegation (taking the incentives to litigate into account).

Section 2–201(1) is closer to the "in writing" side of the spectrum. Its requirement that a writing be sufficient to indicate a sales contract provides some evidence that one was concluded. The quantity term in the writing gives some information about an important term of the contract. By comparison, unrevised (pre-2001) 1–206's Statute of Frauds governs the sale of personal property other than goods—an assignment of a contract, for instance. It requires mention of a price term, a "reasonable" identification of the subject matter of the sale, and a signature. Unlike 2–201(1), the failure to mention price limits enforcement of the contract to $5,000. For its part, 2A–201(1), which applies to personal property leases, requires that the leased goods and lease term be "described." These Statute of Frauds requirements differ from 2–201(1)'s requirements and allow more reliable inferences about some matters and less about others. For instance, 1–206 provides a more reliable inference about price than 2–201(1), which does not require mention of price. Some non-UCC Statutes of Frauds require the memorandum to contain all the material terms of the contract. See, e.g., Ohio Rev. Code § 1335.05 (2006) (as interpreted). Because 2A–201(1)'s writing requirements only apply when total lease payments are at least

$1,000, they do not allow reliable inferences for leases with leases payments of less than that amount. Although hard to compare along a common metric, the different Statutes of Frauds supply require writings with different minimum evidentiary value.

The traditional justification for the Statute of Frauds is that the writing requirement prevents fraudulent allegations that a contract was concluded. However, this justification is unsupported by evidence. There is an almost complete absence of data backing the empirical assumption on which the justification is based. Comparative data about the rate of fraud in jurisdictions with and without a Statute of Frauds, controlling for other variables such as rates of criminality, legal costs and value of the underlying sales contract, would be helpful. In principle the data is available because civil law systems do not generally have a Statute of Frauds. The price of sale of goods contracts in these systems could be compared with the price of comparable contracts in jurisdictions that have a Statute of Frauds. Controlling for other variables affecting price, the measurement of the price effects of different formal requirements would support or weaken the case for the requirement.

A more convincing justification is that the Statute of Frauds reduces the proof costs that a contract would otherwise impose on nonparties. Without 2–201(1)'s requirements, part of the cost of adjudicating a contract falls on courts and ultimately taxpayers. Even contracting parties who agree that a contract was concluded may disagree about its terms. In litigating terms, the parties incur part of the costs of proving them. But the rest of the proof costs are incurred by nonparties, such as judges, court officials and other litigants whose cases are delayed as a result. In deciding whether to contract and litigate, parties only take into account their costs of doing so, not the full costs of their activity. Thus, they will undertake an efficient number of contracts and litigated disputes. By requiring a legally sufficient memorandum as a condition of enforceability, 2–201(1) shifts some of the proof costs to the contracting parties that would otherwise be borne by third parties. It thereby forces them to incur the cost of producing a statutorily specified amount of evidence of a contract and its terms before litigation. Further, the parties can more cheaply produce this evidence ex ante than can courts and triers of fact ex post. As a result of the parties internalizing some of the costs of contracting and litigation, the parties are more likely to calibrate more of the full marginal costs and the benefits to them to obtain efficient contracts (and litigation).

Obviously, a Statute of Frauds does not force contracting parties to fully internalize proof costs. The portion of proof costs borne by them depends on the stringency of the Statute's writing requirement. A requirement that the contract and its terms itself be written and signed, for instance, reduces the cost of proving its terms ex post significantly. As noted above, 2–201(1)'s demands that there be a signature, a quantity term and some indication that a contract was made are minimal requirements. They provide information having much less evidentiary value than a requirement that the contract and its terms be written, because contract terms not in the writing must still be proven. Accordingly, 2–201(1) continues to leave a large portion of the proof costs associated with establishing a contract and its terms on third parties. But 2–201(1)'s justification is that the size of the externalities associated with proof costs is reduced at little cost to the contracting parties ex ante. Considered as devices for reducing externalities, the different Statute of Frauds provisions in the UCC require the contracting parties to internalize proof costs ex ante to different extents. Cf. pre-2001 1–206(1); 9–203(b)(3)(A). It might be that 2–201(1)'s minimal requirements are too minimal: They reduce externalities in proof costs by so little an amount that the full cost of litigation and contracting over their satisfaction is not justified.

3. EXCEPTIONS TO 2–201(1)'S STATUTE OF FRAUDS

Section 2–201(2)–(3) contain exceptions to 2–201(1)'s Statute of Frauds requirements. The exceptions allow for the enforcement of a contract falling within 2–201(1) even when 2–201(1)'s requirements are not satisfied. Although the exceptions are in parts difficult to interpret, their rationale is clear. Section 2–201(2)–(3) describe circumstances giving information with the same evidentiary value as 2–201(1). In other words, they provide as reliable an inference that a contract exists, as well as its terms, as is provided by a legally sufficient memorandum that satisfies 2–201(1). Thus, the exceptions serve as evidentiary substitutes for 2–201(1)'s writing requirements. Although some courts take seriously 2–201(1)'s introductory language ("Except as otherwise provided in this section . . . ") to limit exceptions to 2–201(1) to those listed in 2–201(2)–(3), a number of courts allow promissory estoppel as an exception, applicable to 2–201 via 1–103(b). Proposed 2–201(1) and its associated Comment 2 allow for exceptions to 2–201(1) not listed in 2–201(2)–(3). The conditions for promissory estoppel, when met, probably also allow an inference that a contract exists.

Section 2–201(2) describes what is often referred to as the "merchant's exception" to 2–201(1). The exception allows enforcement of a sales contract, even when 2–201(1) is not satisfied, if (i) a written confirmation is received, (ii) the confirmation is "sufficient against the sender" under 2–201(1), (iii) the recipient does not object in writing to the confirmation within 10 days of receiving it, and (iv) both the sender and recipient are merchants. Condition (ii)'s language is slightly opaque. To be "sufficient against the sender" under 2–201(1), the sender must have a signed a writing that is "sufficient to indicate that a contract for sale has been made." Unsurprisingly, courts disagree over what is required for writing to "sufficiently indicate" a contract for sale. The majority and dissent in *Bazak International Corp.*, appearing below, illustrate the disagreement. The opacity of 2–201(2)'s conditions aside, its justification is straightforward: The inference from the failure of a merchant-recipient to timely object to a confirmation enforceable against the merchant-sender under 2–201(1) is as reasonable as the inference from a legally sufficient memorandum signed by the recipient. Often when decisional law divides over an interpretation of the language of 2–201's exceptions, the disagreement is over the evidentiary value provided by 2–201(1)'s requirements.

Section 2–201's other exceptions work in the same way as 2–201(2). They too provide evidence of a sales contract that is reliable as a legally sufficient memorandum meeting 2–201(1)'s requirements. Section 2–

201(3)(a) makes a sales contract that does not satisfy 2–201(1) enforceable if the goods are to be specially manufactured and unsuitable for sale to others, provided that the seller either has made a substantial beginning of their manufacture or has committed to do so. Section 2–201(3)(c) makes enforceable sales contracts not satisfying 2–201(1) with respect to goods which have been accepted by the buyer or for which payment has been made. Under 2–201(3)(b), a contract that does not satisfy 2–201(1) is enforceable if the party against whom enforcement is sought "admits in his pleadings, testimony or otherwise in court that a contract for sale has been made . . . " Payment made, an in-court admission, or the production of goods suitable only for the buyer allow as reasonable an inference that a contract exists as is provided by a legally sufficient memorandum. In fact, in 2–201(3)(c)'s exception, Comment 2 to Proposed 2–201 finds that payment and receipt of goods amounts to an admission of a contract: "Receipt and acceptance either of the goods or the price constitutes an unambiguous overt admission by both parties that a contract actually exists."

Bazak International Corp. v. Mast Industries, Inc.

New York Court of Appeals, 1989
73 N.Y.2d 113

■ Opinion By: KAYE, JUDGE

This dispute between textile merchants concerning an alleged oral agreement to sell fabric centers on the "merchant's exception" to the Statute of Frauds (UCC 2–201 [2]). We conclude that annotated purchase order forms signed by the buyer, sent to the seller and retained without objection, fall within the merchant's exception, satisfying the statutory requirement of a writing even without the seller's signature. It was therefore error to dismiss the buyer's breach of contract action on Statute of Frauds grounds, and deny it any opportunity to prove that the alleged agreement had indeed been made.

For purposes of this dismissal motion, we accept the facts as stated by plaintiff buyer (Bazak International). On April 22, 1987 Karen Fedorko, marketing director of defendant seller (Mast Industries), met with Tuvia Feldman, plaintiff's president, at Feldman's office. Fedorko offered to sell Feldman certain textiles that Mast was closing out, and the two negotiated all the terms of an oral agreement except price. At a meeting the following day, Fedorko and Feldman agreed on a price of $103,330. Fedorko told Feldman that Bazak would receive written invoices for the goods the next day and that the textiles would be delivered shortly. When no invoices arrived, Feldman contacted Fedorko, who assured him that everything was in order and that the invoices were on the way. However, on April 30, 1987, Fedorko had Feldman come to the New York City offices of Mast's parent company where, following Fedorko's instructions, Feldman sent five purchase orders by telecopier to Mast's Massachusetts office. That same day Feldman received written confirmation of Mast's receipt of the orders. Mast made no objection to the terms set forth in the telecopied purchase orders, but never delivered the textiles despite Bazak's demands.

Bazak then filed a complaint alleging breach of contract and fraud, which Mast moved to dismiss for failure to state a cause of action, based upon the lack of documentary evidence (CPLR 3211[a][7]). Mast contended that the only writings alleged in the complaint—the purchase orders sent by Bazak to Mast, and Mast's confirmation of receipt of the purchase orders—were insufficient under UCC 2–201 to satisfy the Statute of Frauds. In addition, Mast argued that the complaint did not make out a cause of action for fraud, but merely duplicated the contract allegations.

Supreme Court denied the motion to dismiss, but the Appellate Division reversed, holding that the breach of contract claim was barred by the Statute of Frauds, and that the fraud claim merely disguised a flawed breach of contract claim. The focal issue before us on Bazak's appeal from that order is whether the disputed documents qualified as confirmatory writings within the "merchant's exception" to the Statute of Frauds (UCC 2–201[2]). We conclude that they did, and therefore reverse the Appellate Division order.

At the heart of the dispute are two issues involving the telecopied purchase orders. First, the parties disagree as to the standard for determining whether the purchase orders are confirmatory documents: Mast asserts that there is a presumption against application of UCC 2–201(2)—if the memorandum on its face is such that a reasonable merchant could reasonably conclude that it was not a confirmation, then the claim is barred as a matter of law by the Statute of Frauds. Bazak, on the other hand, argues for a less restrictive standard—that is, a requirement only that the writings afford a belief that the alleged oral contract rests on a real transaction, a requirement Bazak contends that it has met. Second, the parties disagree as to the application of the governing standard to this complaint. Bazak contends that the purchase orders were sent in confirmation of the agreement already reached, and that there is sufficient support for that interpretation in the documents themselves; Mast argues that on their face, the purchase orders are no more than offers to enter into an agreement, and thus inadequate to satisfy the Statute of Frauds.

As to both issues, we are essentially in agreement with Bazak, and therefore reverse the order dismissing its complaint. * * *

Description of the Writings

A total of five printed purchase order forms, all of them on Bazak's letterhead, were telecopied by Feldman to Mast from the offices of Mast's parent company. The first four are individual orders for various quantities of different types of fabric, while the fifth summarizes the orders and states the total price. All are dated April 23, 1987—the date of the alleged oral contract. On each form, are the handwritten words "As prisented [sic] by Karen Fedorko." At the bottom of each form are several lines of small type reading: "All claims must be made within 5 days after receipt of goods. No allowances or returns after goods are cut. This is only an offer and not a contract unless accepted in writing by the seller, and subject to prior sale." Each form concludes with two signature lines, one for "Bazak International Corp." and one for "customers acceptance." Each form is signed by Bazak, but the space for "customers acceptance" remains blank.

An interoffice memorandum confirms that the purchase orders were telecopied to Mast's Massachusetts office from the premises of Mast's parent company on April 30, 1987.

The Writings as Confirmations of a Contract

The Statute of Frauds remains a vital part of the law of this State. A contract for the sale of goods for the price of $500 or more is not enforceable "unless there is some writing sufficient to indicate that a contract for sale has been made between the parties and signed by the party against whom enforcement is sought or by his authorized agent or broker." (UCC 2–201[1].) That section further provides that the only indispensable term in such a writing is quantity.

Undisputedly, the alleged oral contract in this case was for the sale of more than $500 worth of goods, and the only writings were not signed by Mast, against whom enforcement is sought. Bazak claims, however, that the orders fall under the merchant's exception to the signature requirement contained in UCC 2–201(2): "Between merchants if within a reasonable time a writing in confirmation of the contract and sufficient against the sender is received and the party receiving it has reason to know its contents, it satisfies the requirements of subsection (1) against such party unless written notice of objection to its contents is given within 10 days after it is received." Bazak contends that the purchase orders are writings in confirmation of the oral agreement reached between Fedorko and Feldman, and that having failed to object to their contents Mast cannot now assert the Statute of Frauds defense.

At the outset, we are called upon to define the standard to be applied in determining whether a document can be construed as a confirmatory writing under UCC 2–201(2): are explicit words of confirmation necessary? Should there be a presumption against application of the section? Relying on a New Jersey case, Trilco Term. v. Prebilt Corp. (167 NJ Super 449, 400 A2d 1237, affd without opn 174 NJ Super 24, 415 A2d 356), and a subsequent Federal case applying *Trilco*, Norminjil Sportswear Corp. v. T G & Y Stores Co. (644 F Supp 1 [SD NY]), Mast argues that confirmatory language is necessary, and that an exacting standard should be imposed.

The cases cited by Mast do stand for the proposition that a writing offered as confirmatory in satisfaction of UCC 2–201(2) is insufficient unless it explicitly alerts the recipient to the fact that it is intended to confirm a previous agreement. In *Trilco*, the lower court stated its belief that as a policy matter, a more stringent test was appropriate under UCC 2–201(2) than that applied under UCC 2–201(1) to determine if a writing was "sufficient to indicate that a contract for sale has been made", because under the merchant's exception, a party could be bound by a writing it had not signed. The Federal District Court in *Norminjil* found this reasoning persuasive in what it perceived to be the absence of any New York case law on the point.

We disagree. Cases dealing with the sufficiency of a confirmatory writing between merchants are hardly legion, but this is not the first time any New York court has interpreted the confirmatory writing requirement. In B & R Textile Corp. v. Domino Textiles (77 AD2d 539), the Appellate Division found that an invoice specifying the parties to the sale, the goods, prices and quantities involved, and the terms of payment constituted a writing in confirmation of an oral contract. Moreover, although the Appellate Division did not articulate the standard it had applied in reaching that result, there was no mention of any express language of confirmation in the invoice, suggesting that a more liberal test was employed.

But even writing on a clean slate, we reject the exacting standard proposed by *Trilco* and *Norminjil* as inconsistent with the letter and spirit of the relevant UCC sales provisions.

UCC 2–201(1) requires that the writing be "sufficient to indicate" a contract, while UCC 2–201(2) calls for a writing "in confirmation of the contract." We see no reason for importing a more stringent requirement of explicitness to the latter section, and holding merchants engaged in business dealings to a higher standard of precision in their word choices. The official comment describes UCC 2–201(1) as simply requiring "that the writing afford a basis for believing that the offered oral evidence rests on a real transaction." As Karl Llewellyn, a principal drafter of UCC 2–201, explained to the New York Law Revision Commission: "What the section does * * * is to require some objective guaranty, other than word of mouth, that there really has been some deal." (1954 Report of NY Law Rev Commn, at 119.) We hold that the same standard applies under UCC 2–201(1) and 2–201(2), noting that this conclusion accords with the majority of courts and commentators that have considered the issue.

Special merchant rules are sprinkled throughout article 2 of the Uniform Commercial Code, distinguishing the obligations of business people from other (see, UCC 2–103[1][b]; 2–205, 2–207[2]; 2–209[2]; 2–312[3]; 2–314[1]; 2–327[1][c]; 2–402[2]; 2–403[2]; 2–509[3]; 2–603 [1]; 2–605[1][b]; and 2–609[2]). Among the suggested motivations was to state clear, sensible rules better adjusted to the reality of what commercial transactions were (or should be), thereby promoting predictable, dependable, decent business practices. Section 2–201 (2) recognized the common practice among merchants, particularly small businesses, to enter into oral sales agreements later confirmed in writing by one of the parties. Absent such a provision, only the party receiving the confirmatory writing could invoke the Statute of Frauds, giving that party the option of enforcing the contract or not, depending on how advantageous the transaction proved to be. UCC 2–201(2) was intended to address that inequity; it encourages the sending of confirmatory writings by removing the unfairness to the sender.

In imposing a requirement that the writing explicitly state that it is sent in confirmation, the understandable concern of the New Jersey court in *Trilco* was that the effect of UCC 2–201 (2) was "to bind a merchant to a writing that he did not sign" (167 NJ Super, at 455, 400 A2d, at 1240, supra), and thus to create a new potential unfairness: a merchant might unilaterally create a binding contract simply by dispatching unsolicited purchase orders, thus unfairly disadvantaging the recipient. Consequently, the court perceived it was necessary to require that the writing contain explicit language of confirmation or reference to the prior agreement, so the recipient could know that the sender was asserting the existence of a contract, and hence had a "meaningful opportunity" to exercise the right of objection found in UCC 2–201(2) (id., at 454, 400 A2d, at 1240). This argument is not without merit. However, in our view it overlooks other protections provided by UCC 2–201.

A confirmatory writing does not satisfy the requirements of UCC 2–201(2) unless it is "sufficient against the sender." This alone provides some protection against abuse, for the sending merchant itself runs the risk of being held to a contract. Moreover, while we hold that explicit words of confirmation are not required, the writing still must satisfy the test articulated in UCC 2–201(1) that it be "sufficient to indicate that a contract for sale has been made". A purchase order, standing alone, is unlikely to meet this test. On the other hand, if the writing contains additional evidence that it is based upon a prior agreement, then as a policy matter it is not unfair to require the recipient to make written objection where there is an intent to disavow it. True, a rule requiring explicit confirmatory language or an express reference to the prior agreement could be applied mechanically and would afford the broadest possible protection to recipients of unsolicited orders. But that rigidity and breadth also could work unnecessary injustice and be unresponsive to the realities of business practice, which was a likely motivation for the merchant's exception in the first instance. Indeed, such a rule would reintroduce the very unfairness addressed by the reform, for the sending merchant still would be bound by the writing while the recipient could ignore it or enforce it at will.

Finally, as additional protection against abuse and inequity, we note that the consequence of a failure to give timely written notice of objection to a confirmatory writing is only to remove the bar of the Statute of Frauds. The burden of proving that a contract was indeed made remains with the plaintiff, as does the burden of proving the terms of the contract. By the same token, the defendant remains free to urge that no contract was made, or that it differed from the one claimed by plaintiff (UCC 2–201, official comment 3). Thus, UCC 2–201(2) neither binds the receiving merchant to an agreement it has not made nor delivers an undeserved triumph to the sending merchant. It does no more than permit the sender to proceed with an attempt to prove its allegations.

We therefore conclude that, in determining whether writings are confirmatory documents within UCC 2–201(2), neither explicit words of confirmation nor express references to the prior agreement are required, and the writings are sufficient so long as they afford a basis for believing that they reflect a real transaction between the parties.

It remains for us to apply this standard to the facts and determine whether the documents in issue satisfy the requirements of UCC 2–201(2).

Of the various requirements of UCC 2–201(2), four are not in controversy. There is no dispute that both parties are merchants, that the writing was sent within a reasonable time after the alleged agreement, that it was received by someone with reason to know of its contents, and that no written objection was made. If the writings can be construed as confirming the alleged oral agreement, they are sufficient under UCC 2–201(1) against Bazak—the sender—since Bazak signed them. Thus, the open question is whether, applying the governing standard, the documents here were sufficient to indicate the existence of a prior agreement.

Cases considering whether writings containing the words "order" or "purchase order" could satisfy the "confirmatory" requirement of UCC 2–201(2) fall into two categories. In some, the writings on their face contemplated only a future agreement, and they were held insufficient to overcome the Statute of Frauds defense (see, e.g., Arcuri v. Weiss, 198 Pa Super 506, 184 A2d 24); in others, there was language clearly indicating that a contract had already been made, and the writings were deemed sufficient (see, e.g., Dura–Wood Treating Co. v. Century Forest Indus., 675 F2d 745, supra; Perdue Farms v. Motts, Inc., 459 F Supp 7, supra). The writings here do not fit neatly into either group. However, taken as a whole, there is sufficient evidence that the writings rest on a real transaction, and therefore satisfy the Statute of Frauds.

We first address Mast's contention—apparently decisive in the Appellate Division—that the small print at the foot of the forms to the effect that they are "only an offer and not a contract unless accepted in writing by the seller" must be given literal effect and precludes the possibility that the writings were confirmatory of an agreement. While an express disclaimer generally would suffice to disqualify a memorandum as confirmatory of an oral agreement, it is plain from the face of these documents that the printed matter was entirely irrelevant to the dealings between these parties. The forms themselves bespeak their purpose: to record a sale by Bazak as seller, not a purchase by Bazak as buyer. The language regarding claims, allowances and returns are clearly all referable to a transaction in which Bazak was the seller, as is the signature line for Bazak. Read literally, these forms would not even have allowed for Mast's signature; the line for "customers acceptance" is obviously inapplicable—Bazak, not Mast, was the customer. In short, though Mast is free to argue at trial that different inferences should be drawn, the forms indicate that Bazak simply used its seller's documents to record its confirmation of the alleged contract, and that the small print at the bottom of the page was no part of that communication.

The handwritten notations on the purchase order forms provide a basis for believing that the documents were in furtherance of a previous agreement. The terms set forth are highly specific; precise quantities, descriptions, prices per unit and payment terms are stated. The documents refer to an earlier presentation by defendant's agent Karen Fedorko. The date April 23, 1987 is written on the forms and the date April 30 on the transmission, indicating reference to a transaction that took place a week before they were sent. Finally, Mast itself relayed Bazak's forms. The telecopier transmittal sheet shows that the forms were sent to Mast by defendant's own parent company in New York, using its facilities—obviously suggesting that the forms were not merely unsolicited purchase orders from Bazak, but that their content reflected an agreement that had been reached between the parties.

While no one of these factors would be sufficient under UCC 2–201(2), considered together they adequately indicate confirmation of a preexisting agreement so as to permit Bazak to go forward and prove its allegations.

Finally on this issue, addressing the dissent, it is apparent that a philosophical difference divides the court. The plain implication of the

dissent is that express confirmatory language is needed because
"ambiguous" confirmatory writings unfairly burden receiving
merchants. The majority, by contrast, perceives that the Code intended
to place such a burden on the receiving merchant because there is less
unfairness in requiring it to disavow than in denying the sending
merchant who has failed to use any magic words an opportunity to
prove the existence of a contract. A merchant bent on fraud, of course,
can easily send documents containing express confirmation of a
nonexistent oral contract, so it is difficult to see how our reading of the
statute "weakens" its protection against fraud (dissenting opn, at 131).
The protection consists of requiring a writing that provides a basis for
belief that it rests on a real transaction—no more, no less. If the writing
is sufficient to indicate the existence of a contract, it is also sufficient at
the pleading stage to support an inference that the receiving merchant
knew full well what it was. * * *

■ **DISSENT:** ALEXANDER, JUDGE

In my view, the purchase orders at issue here, which describe
themselves as offers and do not otherwise indicate the existence of a
completed agreement are not "sufficient against the sender" (UCC 2–
201[2]) because they fail to "indicate that a contract for sale has been
made between the parties" (UCC 2–201[1]). Consequently they are not
confirmatory memoranda sufficient to satisfy the Statute of Frauds and
plaintiff's contract cause of action was properly dismissed.
Furthermore, plaintiff has failed to plead facts sufficiently independent
of its contract claim to sustain its second cause of action for fraud. Thus,
contrary to the view taken by the majority, I would affirm the order of
the Appellate Division dismissing the complaint. Accordingly, I dissent.

I.

As alleged by Bazak International Corp. (Bazak), on April 22 and
23, 1987, Ms. Karen Fedorko, marketing director of defendant Mast
Industries, Inc. (Mast), met with Bazak's corporate officer, Tuvia
Feldman, and allegedly negotiated all the terms of an oral agreement,
pursuant to which Bazak was to purchase certain knitted textiles from
Mast at a price of $103,330.

Approximately one week later, on or about April 30, 1987, Bazak
sent Mast five purchase orders prepared by Bazak and bearing Bazak's
signature. These orders recite the description, quantity and price terms
of the goods and four of the orders are also inscribed "As prisented [sic]
by Karen Fedorko", presumably a reference to the meetings of April 22
and 23. None of the orders, however, refer to any "agreement",
"contract", "sale", "purchase" or anything else to indicate that an
agreement had been reached by the parties on that date or thereafter.
Indeed, near the bottom of each order, a disclaimer states: "this in [sic]
only an offer and not a contract unless acceptec in writing by the seller".
Further, the orders include two signature lines, one signed by Bazak,
and the other, which is blank, labeled "CUSTOMERS ACCEPTANCE".
It is undisputed that Mast received the orders but did not sign them or
object to them within 10 days.

When Mast did not deliver the subject goods, Bazak commenced
this action alleging breach of contract and fraud. Mast's motion to
dismiss the complaint, which asserted the Statute of Frauds defense

(UCC 2–201), was denied by Supreme Court. The Appellate Division reversed, holding that the purchase orders, which were not signed by Mast, did not constitute confirmatory documents sufficient to take this alleged agreement between merchants out of the Statute of Frauds (see, UCC 2–201[2]) since the orders, by their terms, were merely offers. The majority of this court now reverses and denies Mast's motion to dismiss.

II.

The majority concludes that the merchant's exception of UCC 2–201(2) does not require that writings contain express confirmatory language and that writings satisfy both UCC 2–201(1) and (2) when they are "sufficient to indicate that a contract for sale has been made between the parties" (UCC 2–201[1]) and are therefore "sufficient against the sender" (UCC 2–201[2]). In my view, however, it is unnecessary to reach the question of whether UCC 2–201(2) requires that writings "in confirmation of the contract" contain express confirmatory language because Bazak's purchase orders do not satisfy UCC 2–201(1). As the only proper inference to be drawn from the plain language of the purchase orders is that they are offers, the majority's determination that they evidence a completed contract is nothing more than speculation. These purchase orders expressly state that they are offers, and even if this plain language can be disregarded, the remaining language of the orders is ambiguous at best. By holding that the requirements of UCC 2–201 are satisfied by these writings, the majority undermines the very protections the statute was intended to afford. * * *

The official comment explains that a writing sufficiently "[indicates] that a contract for sale has been made" (UCC 2–201[1]) when it [affords] a basis for believing that the offered oral evidence rests on a real transaction" (UCC 2–201, official comment 1). While the majority correctly articulates this standard, it misapplies this standard by holding that these writings, which are at best ambiguous, satisfy the statute. Even a most liberal construction of UCC 2–201 (1) requires at least that the writing indicate that the existence of a contract is more probable than not. This construction serves the statute's purpose of preventing fraud without unduly burdening commercial transactions and comports with the operation of the merchant's exception of UCC 2–201(2). That subsection denies the Statute of Frauds defense to only those merchants who "unreasonably [fail] to reply to a letter of confirmation" (Hawkland, Sales and Bulk Sales Under the Uniform Commercial Code, at 28–29). Significantly, UCC 2–201(2) binds the receiving merchant only when it "has reason to know of [the] contents" of the writing, indicating that the contents of the writing must at least put the receiving merchant on notice that the sender believes that a contract was made. Thus, to satisfy UCC 2–201(1) and therefore be "sufficient against the sender" (UCC 2–201[2]), the writing must at least allow for the reasonable inference that a contract was made and therefore that the writing rests on a real transaction. * * *

Here, the majority's conclusion that there is sufficient evidence that Bazak's purchase orders evidence a completed contract is refuted by the writings themselves. As indicated earlier, the writings are at best ambiguous, allowing for equally probable inferences that the parties either engaged only in negotiations or entered a contract. They do not demonstrate that the existence of a contract is more probable than not and therefore cannot satisfy the statute. Indeed, in view of this manifest ambiguity, a finding that these purchase orders "indicate that a contract for sale has been made" would require resort to the extraneous evidence of the practices and intentions of the parties offered by Bazak. Consideration of such evidence outside the terms of the documents themselves, however, is clearly precluded by the Statute of Frauds (UCC 2–201).

The purchase orders, by their own terms, are only offers. Each form states "this in [sic] only an offer and not a contract unless accepted in writing by the seller". The plain import of this language, in this action where defendant was a seller, was that defendant would not be bound unless it signed the form. The majority attempts to avoid the import of this plain language, urging that it should be disregarded because this printed statement is on a form plaintiff usually used when acting as a seller and thus is meaningless in this alleged transaction where plaintiff was acting as a buyer. Significantly, plaintiff, who prepared the documents, never indicated on any of the forms that this disclaimer should be disregarded and, fully aware of the existence of the disclaimer, signed each form on the line provided beneath it. Moreover, the fact that plaintiff usually used these forms in its capacity as a seller is not properly considered in evaluating the sufficiency of the documents on their face.

Even if the "offer" language properly could be disregarded, the purchase orders nevertheless are ambiguous and therefore insufficient to "indicate that a contract for sale has been made" (UCC 2–201[1]). Four of the purchase orders merely list quantities of goods and prices, with the additional notation "as prisented [sic] by Karen Fedorko". This reference to a presentation by defendant's employee is simply that— there is no indication that an agreement was reached at that presentation. Additionally, the list of goods and prices, as well as the totals contained in the fifth purchase order similarly provide no basis for inferring that a contract was made before the orders were drafted. They do not list delivery terms or other special requirements of the seller which might indicate that an agreement had been reached. The fact that the purchase orders were transmitted from defendant's home office, while possibly unusual, sheds no light on whether the parties had reached an agreement. Thus, nothing in the purchase orders reasonably leads to the conclusion that the existence of a completed contract is more probable than not.

Finally, the majority's holding that these purchase orders satisfy UCC 2–201(1) and (2) substantially weakens the statute's protection against fraud. To assert the Statute of Frauds defense, merchants will be required to promptly respond to writings which provide no notice that the sender believes that they have a contract and which may in fact indicate to the contrary: that the sender has submitted an offer. Such a rule unfairly burdens the receiving merchants and effectively negates the very purpose and intent of UCC 2–201(2): to put both the sending merchant and the receiving merchant on equal footing. * * *

NOTES

1. Whether Bazak's purchase orders are "sufficient against the sender" under 2–201(2) depends on whether they satisfy 2–201(1)'s requirements. The majority and dissent in *Bazak International* disagree over the sufficiency of Bazak's documentation because they disagree over the legal standard governing when a writing is "sufficient to indicate" that a contract for sale has been made. The majority, relying on Comment 1 to 2–201(1), requires that a writing merely provide a basis for believing that a contracts exists. Accord Bazak Int'l Corp. v. Tarrant Apparel Grp., 378 F.Supp.2d 377 (S.D.N.Y. 2005); GPL Treatment, Ltd. v. Louisiana Pacific Corp., 914 P.2d 682 (Or. 1996). This is a low standard of sufficiency. The dispatch of purchase orders provides some basis for concluding that a sale contract was concluded. Although the dissent argues that the majority misapplies its own standard, the dissent in fact adopts a higher standard of sufficiency. This standard requires that a writing is "sufficient to indicate" a sales contract only if its language allows a reasonable inference that a sales contract exists. Language in the writing that indicates that a sales contract has been made easily satisfies the standard. See Vision Sys., Inc. v. EMC Corp., 56 UCC Rep. Serv.2d 875, 880 (Mass. Super. Ct. 2005). A purchase order does not contain such language or allow a reasonable inference that a sales contract exists.

2. Section 2–201(2)'s merchant's exception is one of 13 provisions in Article 2 which state a special rule for merchants. The merchant status of the sender or recipient of a confirmation of a contract sometimes is at issue under 2–201(2). Section 2–104(1)'s definition of "merchant" employs two different tests. A person is a merchant if he meets either of the tests. Under one test, a person is a merchant if he "deals" in the goods involved. Although Article 2 does not define the term "dealing," courts consider a dealer as one in the business of buying or selling goods involved in the litigated transaction. The term's application often turns on the frequency with which a party has bought or sold goods of the sort. See, e.g., Sierens v. Clausen, 328 N.E.2d 559 (Ill. 1975); Chisolm v. Cleveland, 741 S.W.2d 619 (Tex. Ct. App. 1987). Under the second test a person is a merchant if the person "by his occupation holds himself out as having knowledge or skill peculiar to the practices or goods involved in the transaction . . . " This test makes 2–104(1)'s definition of a merchant broadly applicable.

Section 2–104(1)'s definition does not limit the "practices" involved in a transaction to practices relating to the goods. The practices can be conventions related to the transaction. A person having knowledge of these behavioral regularities therefore can be a "merchant" even if ignorant of the goods involved. Consider the practice of opening one's mail and timely responding to letters containing an alleged confirmation of a sale. Most people engage in this practice even if they do not deal in goods that are the subject of a sale alleged in the confirmation. For that reason, most buyers and sellers are "merchants" with respect to 2–201(2)'s merchant's exception. Comment 2 to 2–104 agrees: "Section[ ] 2–201(2) . . . dealing with . . . confirmatory memoranda . . . rest[s] on normal business practices which are or ought to be typical of and familiar to any person in business. For purposes of these sections almost every person in business would, therefore, be deemed a 'merchant' . . . since the practices involved in the transaction are non-specialized business practices such as answering mail." Courts tend to consider most persons merchants for purposes of 2–201(2); see Smith v. General Mills Inc., 39 UCC Rep. Serv.2d 57 (Mont. 1998); Nelson v. Union Equity Co-operative Exch., 548 S.W.2d 352 (Tex. 1977).

This conclusion makes sense. Deeming most people merchants for purposes of 2–201(2)'s merchant's exception reduces contracting costs in the majority of contracts. Contracting costs include the cost of assuring enforcement if a dispute arises. A narrower definition of "merchant" would make the exception inapplicable to many transactions. Thus, to assure the enforceability of their sales contracts, many parties would have to obtain a legally sufficient memorandum from the party against whom enforcement is sought. This could be costly. A broad definition of "merchant" gives a contracting party the less costly alternative of sending a confirmation. True, in order to avoid 2–201(2)'s application to a transaction, the recipient is put to the cost of timely responding to it. But the cost of detecting a confirmation received and responding to it is low: most recipients read their mail and the cost of a written response almost always is insignificant. By comparison, the cost to the sender of obtaining a legally sufficient memorandum from the recipient satisfying 2–201(2) is higher than the cost to the recipient of responding so as to avoid 2–201(2)'s application. Contracting costs for most parties therefore are reduced if most persons are deemed merchants under 2–201(2). The same need not be true under other provisions of Article 2 where merchant status is relevant. Section 2–104(1)'s definition of "merchant" is indeterminate enough to require an argument for deeming someone a merchant for purposes of a relevant provision. Thus, a person may be a merchant for purposes of 2–201(2) without being a merchant for purposes of Article 2's other merchant provisions.

PROBLEM 4.3

Sidley Corp. manufactured and sold steel wheels, and Brake Corp., which sold mufflers, had long contemplated expanding its sales activities to include wheels. Sidley sent Brake the following letter:

Dear Brake Corp.:

This is to confirm our agreement for us to supply you with the steel wheels we discussed at $1,000 per wheel (including delivery). We are looking forward to working with you.

Signed /Sidley Corp.

(a) The morning Brake received Sidley's letter it called Sidley and denied that their negotiations had resulted in an agreement. Brake was not quite ready to enter the wheel market yet, it told Sidley. If Sidley sues Brake to enforce their alleged agreement, does 2–201 prevent its enforcement? 2–201(2), 1–204(1), Comment 2 to 2–104.

(b) Assume that the content of Brake's response in (a) was contained in a return letter to Sidley mailed the morning Brake received it. Does 2–201 prevent enforcement of the alleged agreement?

(c) Assume that Brake's letter in (b) read as follows:

Dear Sidley Corp.:

Our respective recollections differ. I recall that we had a deal on 20 steel wheels, but frankly we just aren't sure about anything. In any event, we have decided not to begin selling wheels. Thanks for your willingness to supply us with them.

Signed/Brake Corp.

Does 2–201 prevent enforcement of the alleged agreement? 2–201(1), (2), 1–204(1).

PROBLEM 4.4

Although Susan and Bill both work full-time as accountants, they also buy and sell at the annual swap meet in town. At this year's swap meet Bill saw a set of 10 antique champagne glasses Susan was offering for sale and on the spot agreed to buy them for $60 each. Because Bill was leaving for a vacation immediately after the swap meet ended, Susan promised to deliver the glasses to his office three weeks later. Before Bill left town he emailed Susan a message thanking her for "the wonderful deal for both of us at $60 per champagne glass; thanks also for agreeing to deliver the 10 glasses to me as we discussed. I owe you." Susan printed out the email and placed it in her files. Two weeks after receiving Bill's email, Susan had second thoughts about the deal and refuses to deliver the glasses to Bill. She is prepared to deny that a deal was made.

(a) Can Bill enforce the agreement against Susan? 2–201(2); 2–104(1); 1–201(b)(43).

(b) Suppose in (a) Bill's email read as follows: "Thanks for the wonderful deal on the glasses for both of us; thanks too for delivering glasses to me when I wasn't able to take them away on the spot." Does the result in (a) change? 2–201(1), 2–201(2).

(c) Assume that Susan did not just file the printed copy of Bill's email. She also immediately sent Bill a letter stating: "My memory of our conversation at the swap meet is hazy. I thought that we agreed that you would buy my 10 plates for sale at $50 per plate. But it doesn't matter. I've decided to keep the glasses; I can use them." Is the agreement at the swap meet enforceable against Susan? 2–201(2), 2–201(1).

(d) Suppose in (c) Susan's letter had stated: "The information in your email is mistaken. I agreed to sell you the 10 champagne glasses for $65 per glass; you also agreed to pick them up at my office on your return from vacation."

DF Activities Corp. v. Brown

United States Court of Appeals, Seventh Circuit, 1988
851 F.2d 920

■ Opinion: POSNER, CIRCUIT JUDGE.

This appeal in a diversity breach of contract case raises an interesting question concerning the statute of frauds, in the context of a dispute over a chair of more than ordinary value. The plaintiff, DF

Activities Corporation (owner of the Domino's pizza chain), is controlled by a passionate enthusiast for the work of Frank Lloyd Wright. The defendant, Dorothy Brown, a resident of Lake Forest (a suburb of Chicago) lived for many years in a house designed by Frank Lloyd Wright—the Willits House—and became the owner of a chair that Wright had designed, the Willits Chair. This is a stark, high-backed, uncomfortable-looking chair of distinguished design that DF wanted to add to its art collection. In September and October 1986, Sarah–Ann Briggs, DF's art director, negotiated with Dorothy Brown to buy the Willits Chair. DF contends—and Mrs. Brown denies—that she agreed in a phone conversation with Briggs on November 26 to sell the chair to DF for $60,000, payable in two equal installments, the first due on December 31 and the second on March 26. On December 3 Briggs wrote Brown a letter confirming the agreement, followed shortly by a check for $30,000. Two weeks later Brown returned the letter and the check with the following handwritten note at the bottom of the letter: "Since I did not hear from you until December and I spoke with you the middle of November, I have made other arrangements for the chair. It is no longer available for sale to you." Sometime later Brown sold the chair for $198,000, precipitating this suit for the difference between the price at which the chair was sold and the contract price of $60,000. Brown moved under Fed. R. Civ. P. 12(b)(6) to dismiss the suit as barred by the statute of frauds in the Uniform Commercial Code. See UCC § 2–201. (The Code is, of course, in force in Illinois, and the substantive issues in this case are, all agree, governed by Illinois law.) Attached to the motion was Brown's affidavit that she had never agreed to sell the chair to DF or its representative, Briggs. The affidavit also denied any recollection of a conversation with Briggs on November 26, and was accompanied by both a letter from Brown to Briggs dated September 20 withdrawing an offer to sell the chair and a letter from Briggs to Brown dated October 29 withdrawing DF's offer to buy the chair.

The district judge granted the motion to dismiss and dismissed the suit. DF appeals, contending that although a contract for a sale of goods at a price of $500 or more is subject to the statute of frauds, the (alleged) oral contract made on November 26 may be within the statutory exception for cases where "the party against whom enforcement is sought admits in his pleading, testimony or otherwise in court that a contract for sale was made." UCC § 2–201(3)(b). DF does not argue that Brown's handwritten note at the bottom of Briggs' letter is sufficient acknowledgment of a contract to bring the case within the exemption in section 2–201(1).

At first glance DF's case may seem quite hopeless. Far from admitting in her pleading, testimony, or otherwise in court that a contract for sale was made, Mrs. Brown denied under oath that a contract had been made. DF argues, however, that if it could depose her, maybe she would admit in her deposition that the affidavit was in error, that she had talked to Briggs on November 26, and that they had agreed to the sale of the chair on the terms contained in Briggs' letter of confirmation to her.

There is remarkably little authority on the precise question raised by this appeal—whether a sworn denial ends the case or the plaintiff may press on, and insist on discovery. In fact we have found no authority at the appellate level, state or federal. Many cases hold, it is true, that the defendant in a suit on an oral contract apparently made unenforceable by the statute of frauds cannot block discovery aimed at extracting an admission that the contract was made, simply by moving to dismiss the suit on the basis of the statute of frauds or by denying in the answer to the complaint that a contract had been made. See, e.g., Boylan v. G.L. Morrow Co., 468 N.W.2d 681, 682 (N.Y. 1984). The clash of views is well discussed in Triangle Marketing, Inc. v. Action Industries, Inc., 630 F. Supp. 1578, 1581–83 (N.D. Ill. 1986), which, in default of any guidance from Illinois courts, adopted the *Boylan* position. We need not take sides on the conflict. When there is a bare motion to dismiss, or an answer, with no evidentiary materials, the possibility remains a live one that, if asked under oath whether a contract had been made, the defendant would admit it had been. The only way to test the proposition is for the plaintiff to take the defendant's deposition, or, if there is no discovery, to call the defendant as an adverse witness at trial. But where as in this case the defendant swears in an affidavit that there was no contract, we see no point in keeping the lawsuit alive. Of course the defendant may blurt out an admission in a deposition, but this is hardly likely, especially since by doing so he may be admitting to having perjured himself in his affidavit. Stranger things have happened, but remote possibilities do not warrant subjecting the parties and the judiciary to proceedings almost certain to be futile.

A plaintiff cannot withstand summary judgment by arguing that although in pretrial discovery he has gathered no evidence of the defendant's liability, his luck may improve at trial. The statement in a leading commercial law text that a defense based on the statute of fraud must always be determined at trial because the defendant might in cross-examination admit the making of the contract, reflects a misunderstanding of the role of summary judgment; for the statement implies, contrary to modern practice, that a party unable to generate a genuine issue of fact at the summary judgment stage, because he has no evidence with which to contest an affidavit of his adversary, see Fed. R. Civ. P. 56(e), may nevertheless obtain a trial of the issue. He may not. By the same token, a plaintiff in a suit on a contract within the statute of frauds should not be allowed to resist a motion to dismiss, backed by an affidavit that the defendant denies the contract was made, by arguing that his luck may improve in discovery. Just as summary judgment proceedings differ from trials, so the conditions of a deposition differ from the conditions in which an affidavit is prepared; affidavits in litigation are prepared by lawyers, and merely signed by affiants. Yet to allow an affiant to be deposed by opposing counsel would be to invite the unedifying form of discovery in which the examining lawyer tries to put words in the witness's mouth and construe them as admissions.

The history of the judicial-admission exception to the statute of frauds, well told in Stevens, Ethics and the Statute of Frauds, 37 Cornell L.Q. 355 (1952), reinforces our conclusion. The exception began with common-sense recognition that if the defendant admitted in a pleading that he had made a contract with the plaintiff, the purpose of the statute of frauds—protection against fraudulent or otherwise false contractual claims—was fullfilled. (The situation would be quite otherwise, of course, with an oral admission, for a plaintiff willing to testify falsely to the existence of a contract would be equally willing to testify falsely to the defendant's having admitted the existence of the contract.) Toward the end of the eighteenth century the courts began to reject the exception, fearing that it was an invitation to the defendant to perjure himself. Later the pendulum swung again, and the exception is now firmly established. The concern with perjury that caused the courts in the middle period to reject the exception supports the position taken by Mrs. Brown in this case. She has sworn under oath that she did not agree to sell the Willits Chair to DF. DF wants an opportunity to depose her in the hope that she can be induced to change her testimony. But if she changes her testimony this will be virtually an admission that she perjured herself in her affidavit (for it is hardly likely that her denial was based simply on a faulty recollection). She is not likely to do this. What is possible is that her testimony will be sufficiently ambiguous to enable DF to argue that there should be still further factual investigation—perhaps a full-fledged trial at which Mrs. Brown will be questioned again about the existence of the contract.

With such possibilities for protraction, the statute of frauds becomes a defense of meager value. And yet it seems to us as it did to the framers of the Uniform Commercial Code that the statute of frauds serves an important purpose in a system such as ours that does not require that all contracts be in writing in order to be enforceable and that allows juries of lay persons to decide commercial cases. The methods of judicial fact finding do not distinguish unerringly between true and false testimony, and are in any event very expansive. People deserve some protection against the risks and costs of being hauled into court and accused of owing money on the basis of an unacknowledged promise. And being deposed is scarcely less unpleasant than being cross-examined—indeed, often it is more unpleasant, because the examining lawyer is not inhibited by the presence of a judge or jury who might resent hectoring tactics. The transcripts of depositions are often very ugly documents.

Some courts still allow the judicial-admission exception to be defeated by the defendant's simple denial, in a pleading, that there was a contract; this is the position well articulated in Judge Shadur's opinion in the *Triangle Marketing* case. To make the defendant repeat the denial under oath is already to erode the exception (as well as to create the invitation to perjury that so concerned the courts that rejected the judicial-admission exception altogether), for there is always the possibility, though a very small one, that the defendant might be charged with perjury. But, in any event, once the defendant has denied the contract under oath, the safety valve of section 2–201(3)(b) is closed. The chance that at a deposition the defendant might be badgered into withdrawing his denial is too remote to justify prolonging an effort to enforce an oral contract in the teeth of the statute of frauds. If Dorothy Brown did agree on November 27 to sell the chair to DF at a bargain price, it behooved Briggs to get Brown's signature on the dotted line, posthaste.

Affirmed.

■ **Dissent:** JOEL M. FLAUM, CIRCUIT JUDGE, dissenting.

Because I disagree with the majority's holding that additional discovery is prohibited whenever a defendant raises a statute of frauds defense and submits a sworn denial that he or she formed an oral contract with the plaintiff, I respectfully dissent. Neither would I hold, however, that a plaintiff is automatically entitled to additional discovery in the face of a defendant's sworn denial that an agreement was reached. Rather, in my view district courts should have the authority to exercise their discretion to determine the limits of permissible discovery in these cases. This flexibility is particularly important where, as here, the defendant's affidavit does not contain a conclusive denial of contract formation. While district courts have broad discretion in discovery matters, I believe the district court abused that discretion in the present case.

I.

The purpose of the statute of frauds "is to protect a party from the fraudulent and perjurious claim of another that an oral contract was made and not to prevent an oral contract admittedly made from enforcement." URSA Farmers Coop. Co. v. Trent, 374 N.E.2d 1123, 1125 (Il. 1978) [citation omitted]). The statute is also designed to protect innocent parties from the expense of defending against allegations that they breached a contract that is not evidenced by a writing. As the majority notes, there is no Illinois case law conclusively deciding a plaintiff's right to obtain further discovery when a defendant denies the existence of an oral contract in a sworn affidavit. Relevant case law in other jurisdictions is split between the position that the majority adopts today and a rule permitting additional discovery (and in some cases full trials) in statute of frauds cases.

A.

Although it is difficult to give full effect to both the statute of frauds and the admissions exception thereto, that is what we must attempt to do. In my view, these provisions can best be reconciled by allowing district courts to exercise their discretion to determine when additional discovery is likely to be fruitful and when it is being sought just to improperly pursue a defendant who is clearly entitled to the protection of the statute of frauds.

If a denial is a complete bar to additional discovery, the exception to the statute of frauds for admissions made in a "pleading, *testimony* or otherwise in court that a contract for sale was made" would be rendered virtually meaningless. Ill. Rev. Stat. ch. 26, para. 2–201(3)(b) (emphasis added). In Illinois involuntary admissions can satisfy the admissions exception to the statute of frauds. Such involuntary admissions will be almost impossible under the majority's rule because the plaintiff will never have an opportunity to examine the defendant in order to elicit an involuntary admission. Either the defendant will make a fatal admission in his or her affidavit and the statute of frauds exception will be satisfied without resort to the testimony component, or the defendant will deny the contract in his or her pleadings and the case will be dismissed before a testimonial admission is possible. A blanket rule prohibiting any further discovery once the defendant denies under oath that a contract was formed is therefore too inflexible.

Similarly, I would not adopt a rule that requires district courts to allow additional discovery in every one of these cases. I would leave the decision to the discretion of the district judge. In cases where a defendant does not explicitly deny under oath that an oral contract was reached, or where there is some indication that the statute of frauds is being used to perpetrate a fraud, it would be permissible to allow the plaintiff to question the defendant under oath to ensure that he or she personally denies that the parties formed an oral contract. This does not mean, however, that summary judgment is never appropriate when the statute of frauds is raised as an affirmative defense. If a defendant who conditionally denies contract formation in his or her pleadings or affidavit specifically denies that an agreement was reached in a deposition, summary judgment might well be appropriate at that stage of the litigation. A simple denial in an affidavit, however, should not trigger foreclosure of further discovery in every case.

B.

In the present case I think the district court abused its discretion by disallowing any additional discovery once Brown filed her motion to dismiss and accompanying affidavit. The majority argues that it would be futile for DF Activities Corporation ("DF") to take Brown's deposition. Brown is unlikely to admit any facts from which a reasonable trier of fact could conclude that an oral contract was formed because, in the face of her affidavit, such admissions would leave her exposed to perjury charges. In my view, this overstates the content of Brown's affidavit. While Brown denied that any oral or written agreement was reached in both her answer and motion to dismiss, such a blanket denial is curiously missing from her affidavit. Rather, in her affidavit Brown stated only that she did not accept any offer from Domino's Farms or Sarah Briggs for the sale of the Willits chair and that she does not recall having a conversation with Sarah Briggs on November 26, 1988. Deposing Brown therefore would not necessarily be a futile effort. It is possible that under questioning during a deposition Brown would remember the November 26 conversation during which Briggs claims she and Brown reached an agreement for the sale of the chair. Although any convenient prior memory lapse might be viewed with suspicion if a deposition elicited additional information, it is highly unlikely that it would lead to perjury charges. On the facts of this case, I believe the district court abused its discretion when it refused to allow DF to take Brown's deposition.

II.

I share the majority's concern that one of the purposes of the statute of frauds is to protect litigants from the cost of defending breach of contract claims based on alleged agreements that are not supported by written documentation. The statute of frauds, however, contains a specific exception for cases in which a party admits in a pleading, testimony, or otherwise in court that an oral contract was reached, and that provision must be given some effect. The testimonial admissions provision would be virtually meaningless if a district court could never exercise its discretion to permit additional discovery in the face of a defendant's sworn denial in an affidavit.

Because in my view the district court abused its discretion when it prohibited further discovery, I would remand this case to the district court with instructions to permit discovery to continue at least to the point where DF is given an opportunity to depose Brown. If Brown then denies under oath during her deposition that any oral contract was made, summary judgment might well be appropriate at that time.

NOTES

1.   Section 2–201(3)(b)'s exception applies if a party against whom enforcement of a sales contract is sought "admits in his pleading, testimony or otherwise in court" that the contract was made. Although depositions and other pre-trial proceedings are not "otherwise in court," *BF Activities* follows other courts in allowing admissions in depositions to fall under 2–201(3)(b). Proposed 2–201(3)(b) makes the exception applicable to admissions made "otherwise under oath."

Subsection (3)(b)'s admissions exception remains unclear in several respects. It is unclear whether the exception merely states the consequence of a party admitting a contract or whether it gives a party the right to obtain an admission from the other party. If the former, then 2–201(3)(b) almost never applies. The party's denial ends the case. The only occasion in which the exception would apply is in the rare case in which the party accidentally admits a contract in its pleadings. Because the subsection almost never applies, it would be effectively useless. On the other hand, if subsection (3)(b) gives a party the right to obtain an admission, it suggests no limit on the point in litigation at which the admission can be obtained. The absence of a limit risks undermining the Statute of Fraud's purpose. Both the majority and dissent in *BF Activities* reject the view of Triangle Marketing, Inc. v. Action Indus., Inc., 630 F. Supp. 1578 (N.D.Ill. 1986), that the exception merely states the consequence of a party obtaining an admission. But they set different limits on the right to obtain an admission from a party. Understanding the Statute of Fraud's purpose to reduce litigation costs, the majority stops a party from obtaining an admission when the opposing party denies a contract in a sworn affidavit. The denial in the affidavit ends the case. The dissent relies on 2–201(3)(b)'s reference to admissions made in "testimony" to give a court discretion to allow further proceedings to elicit an admission, even when the contract is denied in a sworn affidavit. It does not, however, explain how this discretion is consistent with one of the Statute of Fraud's purposes: "to protect innocent parties from the expense of defending against allegations that they breached a contract that is not evidenced by a writing." For its part, the majority fails to explain how 2–201(3)(b)'s reference to "testimony" is consistent with its limit ending a case on a sworn denial of a contract. Proposed 2–201(3)(b) does not settle the matter. It leaves unresolved whether a party has a right to elicit "testimony" for the purpose of getting an admission even when a sworn affidavit denies the contract.

2.   The other vagueness in 2–201(3)(b) concerns what constitutes an "admission." A defendant's acknowledgment can raise the issue in different ways. The defendant might concede that several terms were agreed to but others were left open. Alternatively, she might concede certain facts but deny that an enforceable agreement was made. Or a defendant might simply acknowledge uncertainty about the course of events. The prevailing view is that an admission occurs when facts are admitted that as a matter of law indicate a contract. See Wehry v.

Daniels, 784 N.E.2d 532 (Ind. Ct. App. 2003); Jackson v. Meadows, 264 S.E.2d 503 (Ga. Ct. App. 1980).

PROBLEM 4.5

Seller negotiated with Mr. Buyer to supply it with 1000 pounds of rock salt for his driveway for $1,000. After his last telephone call with Mr. Buyer, Seller thought it had a deal and delivered the salt to him. Mr. Buyer quickly rejected the salt, believing that the negotiations hadn't produced an agreement. In response to Seller's suit to enforce the agreement, Mr. Buyer moved to dismiss. His motion denied that there was an agreement while conceding that Seller had made an "offer," which he had "accepted." If deposed Mr. Buyer will have the same response. Does Mr. Buyer's denial end the case? 2–201(3)(b).

PROBLEM 4.6

Alpha and Zeta are neighbors who used to be friends. Alpha had put his car up for sale at $20,000 and was waiting for a buyer. In a conversation one day with Alpha, Zeta, who had always admired the care with which Alpha gave the car, agreed to buy it for $18,000. This was a very fair price because Alpha's car had a resale value of $25,000. The two agreed that Zeta would pay Alpha at the end of the month, when Zeta received his paycheck. In the first week after their conversation, Alpha turned away several offers to buy his car for $20,000 even when presented with the cash. Two weeks before Zeta was to pay Alpha, he decided that he needed a truck, not a car. Zeta told Alpha to make other arrangements. In the meantime, an unfavorable report on Alpha's type of car was published, and its resale price now has fallen to $15,000. Nothing further has happened to date.

(a) Can Alpha enforce the terms of his conversation against Zeta? 2–201(1); see 1–103(b), International Products & Technologies, Inc. v. Iomega Corp., 10 UCC Rep. Serv.2d 694 (E.D.Pa. 1989); Warder & Lee Elevator, Inc. v. Britten, 274 N.W.2d 339 (Iowa 1979).

(b) Suppose Alpha sues Zeta to enforce their agreement and that Zeta attaches an affidavit to its answer that reads in relevant part: "We had agreed on price but on nothing else about my offer to buy Alpha's car. But we didn't have an agreement." Is their agreement enforceable? May Zeta continue proceedings to enforce the agreement? 2–201(3)(b).

(c) Suppose Zeta's affidavit in (b) read in relevant part: "We agreed on price I was to pay for Alpha's car as well as when I was to make payment. But I deny that we ever had a deal." Is their agreement enforceable? 2–201(3)(b).

(d) Suppose Zeta gave Alpha a check for $5,000, which Alpha cashed, on which Zeta's entry "down payment on Alpha's car" appeared. Would the result in (a) change? Suppose the check did not contain this statement. Is the result different? 2–201(3)(c), Comment 2 to 2–201.

4. ESTOPPEL AND THE STATUTE OF FRAUDS

Suppose a seller tells her buyer that their sales contract is enforceable without a legally sufficient memorandum. In fact, this is false and the seller knows it. Relying on the seller's statement, the buyer does not insist on a memorandum. Or suppose the seller promises to deliver specified goods under a sales contract, and the buyer acts on the promise by not seeking the goods elsewhere. No legally sufficient memorandum is executed. In the first case the buyer detrimentally relies on the seller's misrepresentation of fact; in the second it detrimentally relies on the seller's promise. Courts divide over whether the seller is equitably estopped in the first case and promissorily estopped in the second case from raising 2–201(1) as a defense to enforcement of the sales contract. Compare Allied Grape Growers v. Bronco Wine Co., 203 Cal.App.3d 432 (Cal. Ct. App. 1988) (recognizing estoppel) with Lige Dickson Co. v. Union Oil Co. of California, 635 P.2d 103 (Wash. 1981) (refusing recognition). Courts recognizing the estoppel exception require a showing that a sales contract was concluded. In addition, promissory estoppel requires proof that the promisee detrimentally relied on the promise and that an injustice can be avoided only by enforcement of the promise.

There are decent arguments on both sides of the debate. Section 2–201(1)'s introductory language ("Except as otherwise provided in this section") seemingly limits the exceptions to 2–201(1)'s requirements to those described in 2–201(2)–(4). Estoppel is not among those exceptions. Courts recognizing the estoppel exception argue that the language nonetheless does not displace principles of estoppel made applicable to Article 2 via 1–103(b). See *Warder & Lee Elevator*, supra. They also reason that the refusal to recognize estoppel effectively allows the fraud or unfair advantage which the Statute of Frauds was intended to protect against. Opponents of estoppel take the opposite position, howeiver, arguing that estoppel in fact allows the sort of fraud the Statute was designed to avoid. A party asserting a contract can lie about its existence and terms. It will present evidence of supposed detrimental reliance on the other party's representation or promise. True, to find estoppel the court must find that the representation or promise the party asserting the contract alleges was made. Estoppel also requires a showing of reliance of a definite and substantial nature. But courts nonetheless can make mistakes about these matters and parties can manufacture credible evidence. The Statute of Frauds is designed to avoid these mistakes. Case law reflects this close division of opinion. Although a majority of courts allow the estoppel exception, a sizable minority do not. See *Allied Grape Growers*, supra (compiling decisions as of 1988).

B. THE CISG AND THE STATUTE OF FRAUDS

The CISG eliminates all formal writing requirements, not just the Statute of Frauds. These include the requirements of some legal systems that certain contracts be concluded in writing. At the same time the CISG allows signatory nations to make a reservation opting out of the CISG's elimination of formal writing requirements. Article 11 allows a sales contract to be enforceable without a writing: "A contract of sale need not be concluded in or evidenced by writing and is not subject to any other requirement as to form." However, a writing requirement can arise from trade usage or course of performance. Article 9(2), for instance, provides that "[t]he parties are considered, unless otherwise agreed, to have impliedly made applicable to their contract or its formation a usage of which the parties knew or ought to have known and which in international trade is widely known...." Article 9(1) subjects the parties to practices established between themselves. Trade usage or a course of dealing are implied terms of the parties' contract; they arise from the behavior of the parties or from the behavioral regularities of the trade in which they are involved. A writing requirement created by trade usage or course of dealing is limited to the parties' contract. Where such trade usage or course of performance is absent, Article 11 makes a sales contract enforceable even if it is not concluded or evidenced by a writing.

Courts and lawyers occasionally miss Article 11's impact on the enforceability of sales contracts not evidenced by a legally sufficient memorandum. GPL Treatment Ltd. v. Louisiana–Pacific Corp., 914 P.2d 682 (Or. 1996) is a notable example. There, the plaintiffs were Canadian sellers of wooden shakes and the defendant-buyer was an American corporation whose place of business was in the United States. The alleged sales were concluded by an exchange of telephone calls and purchase orders. When the sellers sued the buyer, the buyer denied the contracts and moved to dismiss based on the sellers' failure to satisfy 2–201(1)'s Statute of Frauds requirements. The trial court granted the motion, finding that an order confirmation sent by the sellers did not satisfy 2–201(2)'s merchant's exception. It rejected as untimely the sellers' attempt to argue that the CISG applied, rather than Article 2 of the UCC. Both the Oregon Court of Appeals and Supreme Court affirmed the trial court's dismissal. The majority, concurring and dissenting opinions in the Supreme Court did not consider the issue of applicable law or whether the trial court abused its discretion in rejecting the sellers' argument.

Clearly the CISG, not Article 2 of the UCC, applied to the sales contracts in *GPL Treatment*. The sellers' places of business were in British Columbia, a province of a contracting state; the buyer's place of business was in the United States. (Although a member of a family controlling one of the sellers had an office in Portland, the appeals court recited that the sellers operated in British Columbia.) Both Canada and the United States are signatory nations to the CISG. Thus, under Article 1(1)(a) the CISG governs the sales contracts. Article 11 eliminates all Statute of Frauds requirements for such contracts, and neither Canada nor the United States have made reservations making Article 11 inapplicable. The alleged contracts in *GPL Treatment* therefore are enforceable even without a legally sufficient memorandum. Thus, the Oregon court's determination that the sellers did not satisfy 2–201(2)'s merchant's exception to 2–201(1) is beside the point. Because the CISG eliminates formal writing requirements as a condition of enforceability, sales contracts not evidenced by writings need not satisfy the exception. The Oregon courts' incorrect selection of applicable law led it to subject the alleged contracts to requirements and exceptions inapplicable to them.

The effect of a signatory state opting out of Article 11 is somewhat controversial. Article 12 allows a contracting state to declare under Article 96 that it will not be bound by inter alia Article 11. Article 96 in turn allows a contracting state whose domestic legislation requires contracts to be concluded in or evidenced by a writing to declare that Article 11 "does not apply where any party has his place of business in that State." To date 10 countries have made the reservation allowed under Article 96, mostly countries of the former Soviet Union. The difficult question concerns the applicability of writing requirements under domestic law when a contracting state has made the reservation.

The following example illustrates the problem. Assume that Seller is located in Argentina and Buyer in France. Their sales contract is not in evidenced by a writing. Argentina has made an Article 96 reservation while France has not. Finally, assume that France has no writing requirements for enforcement of the sales contract at issue. There are two opposing interpretations of the effect of Argentina's Article 96 reservation. One is that Argentina's domestic law writing requirements apply to the contract. If so, the contract is unenforceable even under the CISG. By making an Article 96 reservation, Argentina declares that Article 11 "does not apply when any party has its place of business" in Argentina. Argentina's domestic law writing requirements therefore apply. An opposing interpretation denies this conclusion. By making an Article 96 reservation, Argentina merely declares that Article 11 "does not apply." If Article 11 does not apply, the issue of the law applicable to the enforcement of a contract not evidenced by a writing is not addressed by the CISG. Instead, the issue is addressed by applicable domestic law. The forum's conflict of laws principles select this law. If the applicable domestic law is the law of Argentina, writing requirements under Argentinian law regulate the contract and therefore it is unenforceable. If applicable law is French domestic law, the contract is enforceable because French law has no applicable writing requirements.

The second interpretation probably is the better one. By its terms, the effect of an Article 96 reservation is simply that Article 11 "does not apply" where any party has its place of business in the contracting state making the reservation. Article 96 does not further provide that the law governing writing requirements is the law of that contracting state. At the same time, Article 96 does not provide that the applicable law is not that state's law. Article 96 simply is *silent* as to which law is applicable. Interpreting Article 96 to make the reservation state's domestic law always applicable gives such states more than the treaty gives them: a unilateral selection of their own domestic law. The interpretation also can yield indeterminate results when parties are located in different contracting states, both of which have made Article 96 reservations. Where the domestic laws of these states have different writing requirements, which writing requirements control? An earlier proposal to the CISG that the writing requirements of the reservation state's law governed was rejected. Assuming that contracting states that have not made an Article 96 reservation want their own domestic law to apply sometimes, Article 96 is not best read to foreclose the possibility. Thus, when an Article 96 reservation makes Article 11 inapplicable, conflict of laws rules probably select the applicable domestic law writing requirements governing the sales contract. See Forestal Guarani S.A. v.

Daros Int'l, Inc., 613 F.3d 395 (3d Cir. 2010); Juzgado Nacional de Primera Instancia en lo Comercial No. 18 (Argentina), 20 October 1989, available at http://cisgw3.law.pace.edu/cases/891020a1.html (dicta); Metropolitan Court of Budapest, 24 March 1992 (Hungary), available at http://cisgw3.law.pace.edu/cases/920324h1.html.

PROBLEM 4.7

Seller Corp. is located in Country X and Buyer Corp. in Country Y. Their representatives meet at a trade convention and agree that Seller will sell Buyer ten customized tractors at $10,000 per tractor. After Buyer relates to Seller the very unusual features it requires for the tractors, the representatives close the deal with a handshake. Buyer later regrets its purchase and calls Seller to cancel the agreement before Seller makes a start on the manufacture of the tractors. Can Seller enforce the agreement against Buyer? In answering the question, state any needed assumptions. 2–201(3)(a); CISG Articles 1(1), 11, 12, 96.

C. THE PAROL EVIDENCE RULE

When parties to a sales contract put their agreement in writing, terms of the agreement that do not appear in the writing may not be enforceable because of the parol evidence rule. The parol evidence rule controls their enforceability by restricting the admission of evidence of terms not contained in the written agreement. The rule states a formal requirement for the admissibility of such evidence. It therefore has a different function than the Statute of Frauds. The Statute of Frauds determines whether a contract is enforceable if it falls within 2–201(1). It restricts the enforceability of certain contracts. If a contract is unenforceable under 2–201, the case ends. By contrast, the parol evidence rule regulates the evidence that is admissible to prove the terms of an otherwise enforceable contract. It restricts the admissibility of evidence of the terms of a contract, not the contract's enforceability. The rule economizes on the costs parties have to incur in administering their contract. By limiting the sort of evidence that can be introduced to prove the terms of the agreement if litigation occurs, the parol evidence rule enables parties to reliably predict the evidence that will be introduced to prove these terms. This in turn allows them confidence in how their contract likely will be interpreted by the trier of fact. As a result, the parties have to incur fewer costs in taking precautions ex ante to assure that the trier of fact accurately determines the contract's terms ex post. For instance, they do not have to include a clause in their contract listing the sorts of evidence that cannot be introduced to prove the terms of their agreement. By restricting the admissible evidence at trial, the parol evidence rule also reduces the parties' expected litigation costs. Because part of the full cost of the contract includes expected litigation costs, the rule therefore reduces the price of the contract.

1. SECTION 2–202

Article 2's parol evidence rule, 2–202, differs in important respects from the common law parol evidence rule. The common law rule makes inadmissible evidence of prior or contemporaneous agreement to contradict an integrated writing: a writing intended to be a final expression of the parties' agreement. Evidence of prior or contemporaneous agreement to terms consistent with terms contained in the writing is admissible, unless the writing is intended to be a complete expression of the parties' agreement. Where the writing is intended to be a complete expression of the parties' agreement—a complete integration—such evidence of consistent terms is inadmissible. The evidence the parol rule makes inadmissible is not limited to oral evidence; it can include prior written agreements. In addition, the terms of the parol evidence rule limit its scope. By its terms, the rule does not bar evidence of subsequent agreements, including modifications, or waivers of contractual rights referenced in a writing. The rule also does not exclude the introduction of evidence directed at establishing fraud, lack of consideration or mistake. It too does not exclude evidence aimed at showing that a writing is not a final or complete expression of the parties' agreement. The rationale for these limitations on the parol evidence rule is in the purpose for which the evidence is introduced: such evidence is not introduced to establish the terms of the contract.

Section 2–202 replicates in part the contours of the common law parol evidence rule. Terms in an integrated writing "may not be contradicted by evidence of any prior agreement or of a contemporaneous oral agreement." Section 2–202(b) bars evidence of consistent terms when the writing is completely integrated: The terms of the integration "may be explained or supplemented. . . . (b) by evidence of consistent additional terms unless the court finds the writing to have been intended also as a complete and exclusive statement of the terms of the agreement." But 2–202 treats evidence about trade usage, course of performance and course of dealing differently from "consistent additional terms." Section 2–202(a) provides that the terms of an integrated writing "may be explained or supplemented . . . (a) by course of dealing, or usage of trade . . . or by course of performance . . . " There is no restriction on their admissibility under 2–202(a) comparable to the restriction on admissibility in 2–202(b) when a writing is integrated. This means that trade usage, course of performance and course of dealing "may explain or supplement" the terms of even a completely integrated writing. Thus, under 2–202(a) evidence of trade usage and the like are barred only when inconsistent with the terms of a complete integration or when the integration excludes these terms. In this respect 2–202 differs from the common law parol evidence rule. Comment 2 to 2–202 sets a high standard of exclusion, requiring that trade usage, course of performance and course of dealing be "carefully negated." Section 2A–202's parol evidence rule, which applies to leases in goods, replicates 2–202, and the amendments to Article 2 leave 2–202 almost entirely unchanged.

Another way to understand 2–202's special treatment of evidence concerning trade usage and the like is through a pair of UCC definitions of words appearing in 2–202. Section 2–202 bars certain evidence of "terms." Section 1–201(b)(40) defines a "term" as "that portion of an agreement" relating to a particular matter. "Agreement" in turn is defined as the parties' bargain, as found by circumstances that include trade usage and the like. 1–201(b)(3). Thus, trade usage and like, where applicable, are among the "terms" of an agreement. Section 2–202 treats the admissibility of evidence about terms differently depending on the type of term. Section 2–202(b) excludes evidence of "consistent additional terms" in a completely integrated writing. Because 2–202(a) does not contain a similar exclusion for trade usage and the like, the "terms" referred to in 2–202(a)—trade usage and the like—cannot be the "terms" referred to in 2–202(b). Evidence of trade usage and the like therefore is admissible to "explain or supplement" even when a writing is a complete integration. Again, it is inadmissible only when inconsistent with the terms contained in the writing.

Section 2–202's different treatment of trade usage, course of performance and course of dealing reflects the belief of Article 2's drafters that parties usually want these terms to apply even to their completely integrated agreements. Where they do not want it to apply, the integration will exclude it. Comment 2 to 2–202 takes this view of the preferences of most parties: "Such writings are to be read on the assumption that the course of prior dealings between the parties and the usages of trade were taken for granted when the document was phrased." Assuming most parties usually want trade usage and the like to apply to their agreements, they probably want these terms to "supplement" the terms even of completely integrated agreements. Trade usage and like are "taken for granted." Parties who do not want this will exclude trade usage and the like in the integration. In interpreting an agreement, 1–303(e) (unrevised 1–205(4)) makes the same assumption: The express terms of the agreement are to be construed whenever reasonable as consistent with trade usage and the like; they control over trade usage and the like only where the construction is unreasonable. Where an integration "carefully negates" trade usage, course of performance and course of dealing, it is unreasonable to "explain" the meaning of express terms in light of them. Note 2 following the cases below evaluates the assumption that most parties want trade usage, course of dealing and course of performance to apply to their contracts.

Section 2–202 continues to generate litigation, much of it concerning the admissibility of evidence of trade usage under 2–202(a). By its terms, 2–202 excludes evidence that contradicts the terms of the integrated writing. Section 2–202(a) therefore does not apply in that case to allow trade usage and the like to "explain or supplement" the terms of the writing. Such evidence also is excluded as contradicting a term of the integration when the integration itself excludes such evidence. Two issues in particular produce most of the disagreement in the courts: the proper standard of contradiction under 2–202, and the required degree of specificity needed to prevent the interpretation of terms in an integration by trade usage and the like.

<h1 style="text-align:center">C–Thru Container Corp. v. Midland
Manufacturing Co.</h1>

Supreme Court of Iowa, 1995
533 N.W.2d 542

■ Opinion: TERNUS, JUSTICE

This case requires us to interpret and apply the trade-usage exception to the parol evidence rule embodied in Iowa Code chapter 554,

Iowa's Uniform Commercial Code (U.C.C.). The trial court held that parol evidence of trade usage was inadmissible and granted summary judgment to the defendant, Midland Manufacturing Company. We agree with the contrary decision of the court of appeals that the challenged evidence was admissible and generated a question of fact that prevented summary judgment. Therefore, we affirm the decision of the court of appeals and reverse the judgment of the district court.

I.   Background Facts and Proceedings.

C–Thru Container Corporation entered into a contract with Midland Manufacturing Company in March of 1989. In this contract, Midland agreed to purchase bottle-making equipment from C–Thru and to make commercially acceptable bottles for C–Thru. Midland was to pay for the equipment by giving C–Thru a credit against C–Thru's bottle purchases. The contract stated that C–Thru expected to order between 500,000 and 900,000 bottles in 1989. Finally, the contract also provided that if Midland failed to manufacture the bottles, C–Thru could require Midland to pay the entire purchase price plus interest within thirty days.

Midland picked up the equipment as agreed and later sent a notice to C–Thru that it was ready to begin production. C–Thru never ordered any bottles from Midland, but instead purchased its bottles from another supplier at a lower price. C–Thru claims that in numerous phone conversations between the parties Midland indicated that it was unable to produce commercially acceptable bottles for C–Thru.

In 1992, Midland gave C–Thru notice that it was rescinding the 1989 contract based on C–Thru's failure to order any bottles. C–Thru did not respond to this notice. Midland later sent C–Thru notice that it was claiming an artisan's lien [f]or the expenses of moving, rebuilding and repairing the machinery. Midland eventually foreclosed the artisan's lien and sold the machinery.

Approximately one month later, C–Thru notified Midland that Midland had failed to comply with the terms of the contract and that the full purchase price plus interest was due and payable within thirty days. When Midland failed to pay C–Thru the amount requested, C–Thru Filed a petition alleging that Midland had breached the contract by being incapable of producing the bottles as agreed to in the contract.

Midland filed a motion for summary judgment. It contended that the contract did not require that it demonstrate an ability to manufacture commercially acceptable bottles as a condition precedent to C–Thru's obligation to place an order. Midland asserted that the contract merely required that it manufacture commercially acceptable bottles in response to an order from C–Thru. Because C–Thru never placed an order, Midland argued that it had not breached the contract by failing to manufacture any bottles.

C–Thru resisted Midland's motion. It argued that a material issue of fact existed on whether Midland was unable to manufacture the bottles, thereby excusing C–Thru's failure to place an order. As proof that Midland could not manufacture the bottles, C–Thru pointed to Midland's failure to provide sample bottles. C–Thru relied on deposition testimony that the practice in the bottle-making industry was for the bottle manufacturer to provide sample bottles to verify that it could make commercially acceptable bottles before the purchaser placed any orders.In ruling on Midland's motion for summary judgment, the trial court found no sample container requirement in the written contract. The court also held that the parol evidence rule precluded consideration of any evidence that the practice in the trade was to provide sample bottles before receiving an order. It concluded that no genuine issue of material fact existed and granted Midland summary judgment. The court of appeals reversed the district court's ruling, concluding that evidence regarding the trade practice should have been considered. We granted Midland's application for further review.

* * *

III. Should Usage-of-Trade Evidence Be Allowed?

Under the common law of Iowa, parol evidence is admissible to shed light on the parties' intentions but it may not be used to modify or add to the contract terms. Nevertheless, sale-of-goods contracts, such as the agreement here, are governed by Iowa Code chapter 554, the Iowa Uniform Commercial Code. Section 554.2202 contains the applicable U.C.C. parol evidence rule and it states:

Terms with respect to which the confirmatory memoranda of the parties agree or which are otherwise set forth in a writing intended by the parties as a final expression of their agreement with respect to such terms as are included therein may not be contradicted by evidence of any prior agreement or of a contemporaneous oral agreement but may be explained or supplemented

a.   by course of dealing or usage of trade (section 554.1205) or by course of performance (section 554.2208); and

b.   by evidence of consistent additional terms unless the court finds the writing to have been intended also as a complete and exclusive statement of the terms of the agreement.

Iowa Code § 554.2202 (1993) (emphasis added). Thus, unlike the common law, parol evidence may be used to supplement a fully integrated agreement governed by the U.C.C. if the evidence falls within the definition of usage of trade.

The Iowa U.C.C. includes the following definition of usage of trade:

2.   A usage of trade is any practice or method of dealing having such regularity of observance in a place, vocation or trade as to justify an expectation that it will be observed with respect to the transaction in question. The existence and scope of such a usage are to be proved as facts. . . . Id. § 554.1205(2).

Section 554.1205 goes on to provide that any usage of trade of which the parties are or should be aware supplements their agreement. Id. § 554.1205(3)

Midland does not dispute that a trier of fact could find that the alleged practice in the bottling industry of providing samples to a prospective purchaser is a usage of trade. However, Midland argues usage-of-trade evidence may not be used to add a new term to a contract that is complete and unambiguous.

We first reject Midland's argument that evidence of trade usage is admissible only when the contract is ambiguous. There is no such requirement in section 554.2202. Moreover, the official comment to section 2–202 of the Uniform Commercial Code, which is identical to section 554.2202, states that this section "definitely rejects" a requirement that the language of the contract be ambiguous as a condition precedent to the admission of trade-usage evidence. U.C.C. § 2–202 cmt. I (1977). We also hold that even a "complete" contract may be explained or supplemented by parol evidence of trade usages. As the official comment to section 2–202 states, commercial sales contracts "are to be read on the assumption that the course of prior dealings between the parties and the usages of trade were taken for granted when the document was phrased." U.C.C. § 2–202 cmt. 2 (1977). Therefore, even a completely integrated contract may be supplemented by practices in the industry that do not contradict express terms of the contract.

That brings us to the remaining argument made by Midland—that C–Thru may not use parol evidence to add a new term to the agreement. Section 554.2202 says that when parol evidence shows a usage of trade that does not contradict a contract term, the evidence is admissible to "supplement" the contract. We look to the common meaning of the word "supplement." State v. Simmons, 500 N.W.2d 58, 59 (Iowa 1993) (we give words used in a statute their ordinary meaning, including reference to the dictionary definition). "Supplement" means "to add . . . to." Webster's Third New Int'l Dictionary 2297 (1993). Consequently, the trade-usage evidence upon which C–Thru relies is admissible even though it adds a new term to the contract. White & Summers, § 3–3 (usage of trade may itself constitute a contract term).

IV. Summary.

The usage-of-trade evidence offered by C–Thru does not contradict any explicit contractual term. It supplements the written agreement which is permitted under section 554.2202. Taking this evidence in a light most favorable to C–Thru, we conclude there exists a genuine issue of fact concerning the performance required of Midland as a prerequisite to C–Thru's obligation to place an order. Therefore, summary judgment is not appropriate. We affirm the decision of the court of appeals, reverse the judgment of the district court and remand for further proceedings.

Alaska Northern Development, Inc. v. Alyeska Pipeline Service Co.

Supreme Court of Alaska, 1983
666 P.2d 33

■ Opinion by: COMPTON, JUSTICE

Alaska Northern Development, Inc. ("AND") appeals a judgment in favor of Alyeska Pipeline Service Co. ("Alyeska") in a dispute involving contract formation and interpretation. For the reasons stated below, we affirm.

I. Factual and Procedural Background

In late October or early November 1976, David Reed, a shareholder and corporate president of AND, initiated discussion with Alyeska personnel in Fairbanks regarding the purchase of surplus parts. The

Alyeska employees with whom Reed dealt were Juel Tyson, Clarence Terwilleger and Donald Bruce.

After a series of discussions, Terwilleger indicated that Reed's proposal should be put in writing so it could be submitted to management. With the assistance of AND's legal counsel, Reed prepared a letter of intent dated December 10, 1976. In this letter, AND proposed to purchase "the entire Alyeska inventory of Caterpillar parts." The place for the purchase price was left blank.

Alyeska responded with its own letter of intent dated December 11, 1976. The letter was drafted by Bruce and Tyson in consultation with William Rickett, Alyeska's manager of Contracts and Material Management. Again, the price term was absent. The letter contained the following language, which is the focus of this lawsuit: "Please consider this as said letter of intent, subject to the final approval of the owner committee." (Emphasis added.)

Reed was given an unsigned draft of the December 11 letter, which was reviewed by AND's legal counsel. Reed then met with Rickett, and they agreed on sixty-five percent of Alyeska's price as the price term to be filled in the blank on the December 11 letter. Rickett filled in the blank as agreed and signed the letter. In March 1977, the owner committee rejected the proposal embodied in the December 11 letter of intent.

AND contends that the parties understood the subject to approval language to mean that the Alyeska owner committee would review the proposed agreement only to determine whether the price was fair and reasonable. Alyeska contends that Reed was never advised of any such limitation on the authority of the owner committee. In April 1977, AND filed a complaint alleging that there was a contract between AND and Alyeska, which Alyeska breached. The complaint was later amended to include counts for reformation and punitive damages.

Alyeska moved for summary judgment on the punitive damages and breach of contract counts. The superior court granted summary judgment in favor of Alyeska on the punitive damages count. The court initially denied Alyeska's motion for summary judgment on the breach of contract claim; however, based on a review of the case after discovery had closed, the court announced at a hearing on September 26, 1980, that it would reverse its earlier ruling and grant Alyeska's motion. The court confirmed this ruling at a hearing on November 5, 1980, after consideration of AND's Motion for Clarification.

The superior court explained its rationale for granting summary judgment against AND on the breach of contract claim as follows. The court recognized that AND predicated its breach of contract claim on the theory that Reed's letter of December 10th was an offer and that Rickett's letter of December 11th was an acceptance of that offer. Viewed in that light, the court addressed "four theoretical possibilities in analyzing the interplay between the December 11th letter and the December 10th letter." First, the writings could be construed as an offer with a responding promise to pass the offer on to the owner committee, which was responsible for making such determinations. Second, the letters could be construed as an offer and a counter-offer that AND rejected. Third, the letters could be considered as an offer with a responding counter-offer containing, among other things, the unlimited right of the owner committee to review and approve. The court ruled that if the letters were ultimately found to fall into one of these three categories, AND would not prevail, either because the offer embodied in the December 10 letter was never accepted, or because the owner committee never approved the proposal.

The only way in which AND might prevail was on the fourth possibility, i.e., the letters could be construed as an offer followed by a counter-offer limiting the authority of the owner committee to review only the contract price. The court ruled that AND could not establish a breach of contract claim under the fourth construction of the letters because the parol evidence rule barred the admission of extrinsic evidence that might limit the scope of the owner committee's approval power. The only recourse for AND, therefore, was to seek reformation of the December 11 letter that limited the owner committee approval clause.

The case proceeded to trial on the reformation claim. After a six-week trial, the superior court concluded that AND had failed to establish that a specific agreement was not properly reduced to writing and therefore rejected its request to reform the December 11 letter. Attorney's fees were awarded to Alyeska.

On appeal, AND does not challenge the superior court's denial of reformation. Instead, it contends that the superior court erred in granting summary judgment on the breach of contract and punitive damages counts, erred in denying a trial by jury on the reformation count, erred in not permitting cross-examination for purposes of impeachment, and erred in awarding attorney's fees to Alyeska.

II. Application of the Parol Evidence Rule

The superior court held that the parol evidence rule of the Uniform Commercial Code, section 2–202, codified as AS 45.02.202, applied to the December 11 letter and therefore no extrinsic evidence could be presented to a jury which limited the owner committee's right of approval. AND contends that the court erred in applying the parol evidence rule. We disagree.

In order to exclude parol evidence concerning the inclusion of additional terms to a writing, a court must make the following determinations. First, the court must determine whether the writing under scrutiny was integrated, i.e., intended by the parties as a final expression of their agreement with respect to some or all of the terms included in the writing. Second, the court must determine whether evidence of a prior or contemporaneous agreement contradicts or is inconsistent with the integrated portion. If the evidence is contradictory or inconsistent, it is inadmissible. If it is consistent, it may nevertheless be excluded if the court concludes that the consistent term would necessarily have been included in the writing by the parties if they had intended it to be part of their agreement.

A. Was the December 11 Letter a Partial Integration?

An integrated writing exists where the parties intend that the writing be a final expression of one or more terms of their agreement. Whether a writing is integrated is a question of fact to be determined by the court in accordance with all relevant evidence. In granting summary judgment on the breach of contract claim, the superior court stated that it had carefully considered all relevant evidence, including oral and written records of all facets of the business deal in question, to arrive at its finding that the agreement was partially integrated. After the six-week trial on the reformation issue, the superior court reaffirmed this finding:

35. The plaintiff initially contends that the letter of December 11, 1976 (the letter) was not integrated or partially integrated and therefore the court was in error in granting summary judgment in favor of defendant on the contract counts of the plaintiff's complaint on September 26, 1980.

36. After considering the evidence submitted at trial, the court reaffirms its prior conclusion that the letter was integrated as to the Owners Committee's approval clause.

37. The parties intended to write down their discussions in a comprehensive form which allowed Reed to seek financing and allow the primary actors (Tyson, Bruce, Terwilleger, Rickett) to submit the concept embodied by the letter to higher management. . . .

38. There are three subjects upon which plaintiff seeks reformation. . . . As to the first, [limiting the Owner Committee to a consideration of price] which has been plaintiff's primary focus, the court finds that such reference was integrated such that the parole [sic] evidence rule would bar any inconsistent testimony. Testimony that the owners were limited to "price" in their review is inconsistent. . . .

41. With respect to the Owners Committee's approval clause, according to the plaintiff's contention the owners were entitled to review the transaction, on whatever basis, only one time. This was testified to by both Mr. Reed and argued by plaintiff in closing. . . . It was also conceded in closing that the review by the owners, on whatever standard, would occur prior to any formal contract being negotiated and executed. . . . This is also consistent with the testimony of each of the participants.

42. In addition, Mr. Reed, in consultation with Ed Merdes and Henry Camarot, his attorneys, tendered the letter of March 4, 1977, as a document which could serve as "the contract". . . . The March 4 letter contains no further reference to the Owners Committee's approval function. . . . Therefore, I find that as to the Owners Committee's approval. . . . the letter of December 11 constitutes an integration or partial integration. . . . This having been established, the analysis outlined by the court on September 26, 1980, when granting defendant's motion for summary judgment on the contract claims is applicable.

After reviewing the record, we cannot say that this finding of a partial integration was clearly erroneous. * * *

B.   Does the Excluded Evidence Contradict the Integrated Terms?

Having found a partial integration, the next determination is whether the excluded evidence contradicts the integrated portion of the writing * * *

AND contends that the superior court erred in granting summary judgment because the evidence conflicted as to the meaning of the owner committee approval clause. It concludes that under Alyeska it was entitled to a jury trial on the interpretation issue. Alyeska contends, and the superior court ruled, that a jury trial was inappropriate because, as a matter of law, AND's asserted meaning of the clause at issue was not reasonably susceptible to the language of the writing. The superior court stated:

The Court is making the. . . . ruling that the offer of evidence to show that Rickett's letter really meant to limit owner committee approval to the price term alone. . . . is not reasonably susceptible—or the writing is not reasonably susceptible to that purpose. And therefore, that extrinsic evidence operates to contradict the writing, not specific words in the writing, but the words in the context of the totality of the writing and the totality of the extrinsic evidence.

We agree that the words used in the December 11 letter are not reasonably susceptible to the interpretation advanced by AND. Therefore, we find no merit to AND's contention that it was entitled to a jury trial on the interpretation issue.

After rejecting the extrinsic evidence for purposes of interpretation, the superior court found AND's offered testimony, that the owner committee's approval power was limited to approval of the price, to be inconsistent with and contradictory to the language used by the negotiators in the December 11 letter. AND contends that the offered testimony did not contradict, but rather explained or supplemented the writing with consistent additional terms. For this contention, AND relies on the standard articulated in Hunt Foods & Industries, Inc. v. Doliner, 270 N.Y.S.2d 937 (N.Y. App. 1966). In *Hunt Foods*, the defendant signed an option agreement under which he agreed to sell stock to Hunt Foods at a given price per share. When Hunt Foods attempted to exercise the option, the defendant contended that the option could only be exercised if the defendant had received offers from a third party. The court held that section 2–202 did not bar this evidence from being admitted because it held that the proposed oral condition to the option agreement was not "inconsistent" within the meaning of section 2–202; to be inconsistent, "the term must contradict or negate a term of the writing. A term or condition which has a lesser effect is provable." Id. at 940.

The narrow view of consistency expressed in *Hunt Foods* has been criticized. In Snyder v. Herbert Greenbaum & Associates, Inc., 380 A.2d 618 (Md. App. 1977), the court held that the parol evidence of a contractual right to unilateral rescission was inconsistent with a written agreement for the sale and installation of carpeting. The court defined "inconsistency" as used in section 2–202(b) as "the absence of reasonable harmony in terms of the language *and* respective obligations of the parties." Id. at 623 (emphasis in original) (citing U.C.C. § 1–205(4)).

We agree with this view of inconsistency and reject the view expressed in Hunt Foods. Under this definition of inconsistency, it is clear that the proffered parol evidence limiting the owner committee's right of final approval to price is inconsistent with the integrated term that unconditionally gives the committee the right to approval. Therefore, the superior court was correct in refusing to admit parol evidence on this issue. * * *

For the foregoing reasons, the judgment of the superior court is affirmed.

NOTES

1. Section 2–202 bars evidence of trade usage, course of performance and course of dealing ("trade usage" below) that contradicts the terms of an integrated writing. A contradiction is an inconsistency, so trade usage contradicts a term when it is inconsistent with the term. Two different standards of inconsistency are apparent in the case law applying 2–202. A broad standard of contradiction finds a contradiction when parol evidence is inconsistent with the plain meaning of a term in the integration. For example, if a quantity term in the integration calls for 50 tons while a prior agreement called for 40 tons, the latter quantity term is inconsistent with the former quantity term. Similarly, evidence that "7" means "12" and "12" means "15" is inconsistent with a term in the integration allowing for impurities between 7 and 12 percent. See Deerfield Commodities, Ltd. v. Nerco, Inc., 696 P.2d 1096 (Or. App. Ct. 1985). In finding that evidence that the term providing that the owners' committee's power of approval was limited to price was inconsistent with the term that provided for "final approval of the owner committee" in the integration, the *Alaska Northern* adopts the broad standard.

A narrow standard of contradiction finds a contradiction only when parol evidence "totally negates" a term in the integration. Parol evidence that qualifies the term without negating it does not contradict the term. *Hunt Foods* adopts the narrow standard of contradiction: "the term must contradict or negate a term in the writing. A term or condition which has lesser effect is provable." For example, if a term in the integration calls for "blue widgets" and trade usage allows for the delivery of blue or red widgets, parol evidence to this effect is not inconsistent with the term. By contrast, trade usage that allowed delivery of any color of widget other than blue would contradict the term "blue widgets" and therefore "totally negate" it. A textbook example of the narrow standard in operation is Columbia Nitrogen Corp. v. Royster Co., 451 F.2d 3 (4th Cir. 1971). There, the integration obligated the buyer to order a minimum of 31,000 tons of phosphate per year. The court allowed trade usage to the effect that the quantity term was an estimate, not a required minimum.

Choosing between the two standards of contradiction is difficult. The choice depends on empirical assumptions about the costs of excluding trade usage from an integration and the likelihood of judicial error in interpreting agreements. To see this, notice the different effects that the broad and narrow standards of contradiction have on these variables. A narrow standard requires parties who prefer not to have trade usage apply to their written contract to very clearly signal their preference. Otherwise, trade usage will apply to the written contract, unless it "totally negates" the terms of the writing. A very clear signal is costly for the parties to send. To be sure that trade usage will be inapplicable their agreement, they must take care to expressly provide for the exclusion of trade usage in the integration. See Comment 2 to 2–202 (trade usage becomes part of the meaning of the terms unless "carefully negated"). At the same time, this very clear signal reduces the risk of judicial error in interpreting the terms of their agreement. For this reason, the narrow standard increases specification costs for the parties while reducing the risk of judicial error in interpretation. A broad standard of contradiction has the opposite effect on these two variables. Parties who prefer that trade usage not apply to their written contracts need not signal their preference. This is because the broad standard treats as inconsistent trade usage that contradicts the plain meaning of the terms in their integration. Thus, the parties avoid incurring the specification costs of excluding trade usage. At a minimum, the specification costs incurred are lower than they are under the narrow standard. However, the broad standard increases the risk of judicial error in the interpretation of their written agreement. The parties' failure to clearly signal to a court their preferences increases the likelihood that the court will not interpret the terms in accordance with the parties' intentions. Thus, the broad standard of contradiction reduces specification costs to the parties while increasing the risk of judicial interpretive error.

Ideally, the efficient standard of contradiction is the standard that optimally minimizes the sum of specification and judicial error costs. Reducing the risk of judicial interpretive error produced by a standard of contradiction increases the expected value of the contract. This is because the contract's expected value is the product of the probability of an accurate judicial interpretion of the contract and the value of the contract as accurately interpreted. Specification of the contract's terms reduces the risk that a court will misinterpret them. However, specifying contract terms in detail is costly for the parties. Judicial interpretive error and specification costs are minimized when the marginal increase in specification costs equals the marginal reduction in judicial error costs produced by specifying the contract terms in more detail. The optimal standard of contradiction is one in which, for a given term, the marginal specification cost balance the marginal cost of judicial error. Obviously, courts and commentators are not in a position to observe these variables reliably. For one thing, the specification costs of excluding trade usage vary between small and large firms; cf. Janet W. Steverson, I Mean What I Say, I Think: The Danger to Small Businesses of Entering into Legally Enforceable Agreements That May Not Reflect Their Intentions, 7 J. Small & Emerg. Bus. L. 283, 310–316 (2003). Even if the marginal effects of specification costs and their impact on judicial error were observable, it would be miraculous if a single standard of contradiction were always optimal. For instance, where a writing spells out in detail the terms of the agreement, the marginal decrease in the risk of judicial error from further specification probably is slight. In this case the marginal specification costs of excluding trade usage in the writing probably exceed this benefit. A narrow standard therefore would be preferable to a broad standard in this case. However, the marginal reduction in judicial error from further specification is likely to be high when the writing is sparsely elaborated and contains few terms. In this situation, marginal increases in specification costs incurred in excluding trade usage might well be cost-justified. The broad standard of contradiction in this case would be preferable to a narrow standard.

Although the case is a close one, a respectable argument can be made in favor of the narrow standard of contradiction. The inability of courts to observe transaction costs and reductions in judicial interpretive error argues for a single standard. The narrow standard increases specification costs for parties who prefer to exclude trade usage from their written agreements. They must send a very clear signal to do so. However, contracting parties who prefer trade usage to be applicable to their agreements need not incur the transaction costs doing so. This is because the narrow standard makes trade usage applicable unless it "totally negates" the terms of their written agreement. If trade usage reflects the preferences of most contracting parties, and the cost of contracting in and out of trade usage is the same, the narrow standard of contraction reduces aggregate specification costs. Although it increases the contracting costs of a minority of parties wanting to exclude trade usage, it reduces these costs for the majority of contracting parties. The narrow standard therefore probably is the better standard of contradiction.

2.   Section 2–202(a)'s assumption that most contracting parties want trade usage to be applicable to the contract can be questioned. Some trade associations, such as the National Grain and Feed Association (NGFA) and organizations of cotton merchants and millers ("cotton associations"), offer standard form contracts incorporate rules promulgated by these associations. The rules are mostly precise, brightline directives and definitions, not business norms such as trade usage. Most significantly, arbitral rules or practice in both the NGFA and cotton associations prohibit arbitrators from taking into account trade usage when inconsistent with the express terms of a contract. See Lisa Bernstein, Private Commercial Law in the Cotton Industry: Creating Cooperation Through Rules, Norms, and Institutions, 99 Mich. L. Rev. 1724 (2001); Lisa Bernstein, Merchant Law in a Merchant Court: Rethinking the Code's Search for Immanent Business Norms, 144 U. Pa. L. Rev. 1765 (1996). This data suggest that members of the NGFA and cotton associations prefer not to have trade usage apply to their contracts in most cases.

The problem with drawing inferences about the preferences of typical contracting parties is that the data might be unrepresentative. The general population of contracting parties might not share the characteristics of the members of the NGFA and cotton associations, and their contracting environments. If so, inferences from the preferences of these members to contracting parties generally are unjustified. Some features of the contracting environment and goods sold by members of the NGFA and cotton associations are different from the range of sales contracts governed by Article 2. NGFA and cotton association members transact by standardized contracts whose terms are precisely defined by regularly updated rules. The commodities sold also are standardized, making a precise set of rules and definitions desirable. In addition, members of such associations frequently enter into repeated, small-profit sales with other association members. This makes reputation for performance an important constraint on breach of contract. Article 2 applies to a much broader and more diverse range of sales contracts than are governed by the NGFA and cotton association rules. The parties may be individuals or firms, and the goods may not be standardized. The parties to a sales contract may not engage in repeat transactions with each other or with a compact group of parties. Under these conditions reputation is unlikely to constrain breach.

Finally, most of the sales contracts under Article 2 are not subject to rules of any association. For these reasons, an inference from the preferences of trade association members to most parties contracting under Article 2 is unsound. Most parties contracting under Article 2 might prefer trade usage to apply to their sales contracts even if trade association members do not. Inferences about the preference for the incorporation of trade usage into the sale contract must be drawn from a representative sample of sales contracts under Article 2.

PROBLEM 4.8

Rug Corp., a wholesale seller of new and antique tribal carpets, and Buy Corp. entered into long and detailed negotiations that produced an oral agreement. A handshake was enough to conclude the bargain because the parties often had done business with each on similar terms in the past. The agreement called for Buy to take delivery of 100 antique tribal carpets each month, over a period of two years. Price was set at $25,000 for each allotment of carpets delivered. No mention was made of the fact that in previous agreements Rug had on occasion adjusted the price of monthly deliveries downward to reflect market conditions in the antique tribal carpet market. Several days after Rug and Buys' representatives had shaken hands, at the urging of Rug's legal counsel, Rug sent Buy a document under its letterhead which read in part: "This is to confirm the terms of our agreement with you of several days ago. We agree to deliver to you 50 antique tribal carpets each month, over a two year period. The total price per delivery is $25,000." When Rug offered to deliver a lot of 50 carpets, Buy demanded delivery of a further 50 carpets. It also insisted on a 5% reduction in price in light of declining demand for antique tribal carpets. Buy was unsatisfied with Rug's response to the effect that price reductions were a thing of the past: the agreement set price at $25,000 without any adjustment. (a) Is their agreement enforceable? (b) If so, what terms does it include? 2–201(1), 2–202, 2–207.

PROBLEM 4.9

Assume that in Problem 4.8 Rug and Buy had memorialized their agreement in a signed document. Assume also that the document memorializing the agreement recited that Rug was to deliver 100 antique tribal carpets each month and that the price for each delivery was $25,000. The agreement was detailed in its terms, reflecting the extensive negotiations on which it was based, and contained the following provision: "This writing constitutes the complete and exclusive expression of the parties' agreement. It supersedes all prior agreements and understandings." Will the jury hear evidence of the occasions on which Rug reduced its contract price? 2–202(a), 1–303(b), (d), Comment 2 to 2–202.

PROBLEM 4.10

Stone Corp. negotiated with City to supply it with gravel needed to pave or repair roads throughout the year. The parties came to an agreement on price, the quantity of gravel to be supplied in each delivery, and the delivery dates. During negotiations, to get City to sign the detailed agreement drawn up by both parties, Stone agreed to delivery on first business day of each month of the year. Although the written agreement recited this delivery date, it merely provided that delivery was to be "during the first week of each month." Stone also agreed to deliver additional loads of gravel as needed by City. This understanding too was not reflected in the parties' written agreement. After the agreement was signed by both parties, City approached Stone and asked for assurances that the gravel deliveries would be on the first day of the month. Stone gave the assurances in a later telephone conversation. Due to a shortage of gravel, Stone has made clear to City its intention to make delivers at the end of the first week of each month. Stone also has stated that it will not have sufficient access to gravel to deliver additional loads should City need them.

(a) Assume that City's written agreement with Stone contains a clause reciting that "this agreement represents the full and final understanding of the parties and contains an exclusive statement of all of the terms of that agreement. It supersedes prior or contemporaneous agreements between the parties." Can City introduce evidence concerning Stone's agreement to make deliveries on the first business day of each month? 2–202(b). If so, evidence based on which of Stone's communications to City? 2–202. Can City introduce evidence concerning Stone's agreement to deliver additional loads of gravel as needed by City? 2–202(b).

(b) Assume that the written agreement simply states that it "represents the final understanding of the parties." Can City introduce evidence concerning Stone's agreement to make deliveries on the first day of each month? Can it introduce evidence concerning Stone's agreement to delivery additional loads of gravel? 2–202, 2–202(b).

(c) Assume that the written agreement contains the clause appearing in (a). Also assume that it is overwhelming practice in delivering gravel for suppliers to made deliveries on the first day of each month. Is evidence about Stone's agreement to deliver on the first business day of the first week of each month admissible? 2–202(a). What if the clause contained language to the effect that "trade usage is inapplicable to this agreement unless expressly incorporated by its terms"? See Comment 2 to 2–202 (third sentence).

2. THE CISG AND THE PAROL EVIDENCE RULE

The parol evidence rule is peculiar to common law legal systems; it is not part of civil law systems. Adjudication in civil law systems usually occurs without juries. Although the wide availability of jury trials in common law systems sometimes is used to explain the presence of the parol evidence rule in these systems, the explanation is unconvincing. The rule applies in bench trials too. The trial judge also must abide by the self-denying ordinance not to consider parol evidence where a writing is integrated. A more plausible explanation is a concern about testimony given by witnesses. Common law and civil law systems evaluate the reliability of parol evidence offered by witnesses differently. In a contract dispute over terms, an important sort of evidence usually is testimony by witnesses, and the witnesses often are the contracting parties or their employees. Civil law systems are more optimistic than common law systems about the ability of the trier of fact (usually the court) to discern the veracity of the witnesses. This relative optimism might extend to the ability to determine the bearing of written prior agreements on the terms of a contract when the contract is integrated. With such optimism, there is no reason to withhold parol evidence from the trier of fact.

The CISG does not deal expressly with the evidence that is admissible to prove the terms of a contract. As with many of the CISG's provisions, the pertinent diplomatic history is inconclusive. A 1977 draft of Article 8(3) included the italicized portion of the following part of the Article: "In determining the intent of a party or the understanding a reasonable person would have had, due consideration is to be given to all relevant circumstances of the case including . . . *any applicable legal rules for contracts of sale*" (emphasis added). The draft was rejected, partly because Article 8(3) itself was thought unnecessary. One reason Article 8(3) could be thought unnecessary is that the CISG's provisions did not upset domestic law rules governing the interpretation of a contract, including the parol evidence rule. However, later events in the CISG's diplomatic history suggest that the CISG displaces the parol evidence rule. Canada's proposal to incorporate in Article 11 a version of the rule was rejected by the Austrian representative to the Vienna Conference because it denied the judge "the free appreciation of evidence." Diplomatic History of the Uniform Law of International Sales 483 (para. 51) (J. Honnold ed., 1989). From the failure of the Conference to act on Canada's proposal, it could be concluded that the CISG rejects the parol evidence rule. Taken as whole, the diplomatic history simply is too sparse to settle the question conclusively.

Three Articles are central to the CISG's treatment of parol evidence. Article 11 provides that a contract "may be proved by any means, including witnesses." This seems to allow proof of contract terms by testimony of witnesses offering parol evidence about prior written or oral agreements. Article 8(3) provides in relevant part that "[i]n determining the intent of a party . . . due consideration is to be given to all relevant circumstances of the case including the negotiations, any practices which the parties have established between themselves, usages . . . " The Article appears broad enough to require admission of parol evidence to prove the terms the parties' understood their agreement to include ("the intent of a party"). And Article 7(2) requires that where the CISG does not "expressly settle" a matter governed by it, the matter is settled by the CISG's "underlying principles," or, if none are applicable, by applicable domestic law. Article 4 includes within the CISG's scope the rights and obligations of contracting parties arising from the sales contract. Because these are defined by the terms of the parties' agreement, the sort of evidence admissible to prove these terms arguably is within the CISG's scope. Although the CISG does not "expressly settle" the admissibility of parol evidence or identify underlying principles for settling the matter, a plausible underlying principle is freedom of contract: The terms of an agreement are those provided by the parties or by the CISG's default rules. This principle supports the admissibility of parol evidence aimed at proving these terms. Based on Articles 7, 8 or 11, courts have concluded that sales contracts governed by the CISG are not subject to the parol evidence rule. See, e.g., Beijing Metals v. Minerals Import/Export Corp. v. American Business Ctr., Inc., 993 F.2d 1178 (5th Cir. 1993); Shuttle Packaging Sys. v. Tsonakis, 2001 U.S. Dist. LEXIS 21630, at *1 (S.D. Mich. 2001). *MCC–Marble* below provides the most detailed argument to date for the conclusion that the CISG rejects the parol evidence rule.

A case can be made against this conclusion, also based on Articles 7, 8 and 11. These Articles can be read to leave to domestic law rules governing the admissibility of evidence about contract terms. Article 7(2) arguably allows the continued application of the parol evidence rule under domestic law. This is because the parol evidence rule deals with an issue not covered by any of the CISG's underlying principles: the admissibility of evidence to prove the terms of a contract. The CISG and its animating principle deal only with substantive rights and obligations arising from the sales contract, not evidence about them. Cf. Zapata Hermanos Sucesores, S.A. v. Hearthside Baking Co., 313 F.3d 385 (7th Cir. 2002) (no "principles" underlying the CISG determine whether attorney's fees are recoverable as "loss"). Thus, Article 7(2) leaves to applicable domestic law the regulation of evidence about the terms of the contract. Articles 8(3) and 11 both are consistent with the parol evidence rule. Under the rule, parol evidence can be used to determine whether a writing is integrated. For this purpose, Article 8(3) can be read to require "due consideration" of "all relevant circumstances," including parol evidence, to determine the parties' intent with respect to a writing. Even when the integrated character of a writing is not at issue, Article 8(3) does not specify the "due consideration" to be given to these circumstances. Because the parol evidence rule specifies the "due consideration" to be given to parol evidence, it is not inconsistent with Article 8(3). Where the issue arises as to whether a writing is integrated, Article 11 allows that it "may be proved by any means, including witnesses." More generally, Article 11 says nothing about the conditions under which the testimony of witness is admissible. If parties intended the writing to be integrated, the exclusion of evidence of prior or contemporaneous agreements inconsistent with the terms of the integration is consistent with all three Articles.

MCC–Marble Ceramic Center, Inc. v. Ceramica Nuova D'Agostino, S.P.A.

United States Court of Appeals, Fifth Circuit, 1998
144 F.3d 1384

■ Opinion: Birch, Circuit Judge

This case requires us to determine whether a court must consider parol evidence in a contract dispute governed by the United Nations Convention on Contracts for the International Sale of Goods ("CISG"). The district court granted summary judgment on behalf of the defendant-appellee, relying on certain terms and provisions that appeared on the reverse of a pre-printed form contract for the sale of ceramic tiles. The plaintiff-appellant sought to rely on a number of affidavits that tended to show both that the parties had arrived at an oral contract before memorializing their agreement in writing and that they subjectively intended not to apply the terms on the reverse of the contract to their agreements. The magistrate judge held that the affidavits did not raise an issue of material fact and recommended that the district court grant summary judgment based on the terms of the contract. The district court agreed with the magistrate judge's reasoning and entered summary judgment in the defendant-appellee's favor. We REVERSE.

Background

The plaintiff-appellant, MCC–Marble Ceramic, Inc. ("MCC"), is a Florida corporation engaged in the retail sale of tiles, and the defendant-appellee, Ceramica Nuova d'Agostino S.p.A. ("D'Agostino") is an Italian corporation engaged in the manufacture of ceramic tiles. In October 1990, MCC's president, Juan Carlos Mozon, met representatives of D'Agostino at a trade fair in Bologna, Italy and negotiated an agreement to purchase ceramic tiles from D'Agostino based on samples he examined at the trade fair. Monzon, who spoke no Italian, communicated with Gianni Silingardi, then D'Agostino's commercial director, through a translator, Gianfranco Copelli, who was himself an agent of D'Agostino. The parties apparently arrived at an oral agreement on the crucial terms of price, quality, quantity, delivery and payment. The parties then recorded these terms on one of D'Agostino's standard, pre-printed order forms and Monzon signed the contract on MCC's behalf. According to MCC, the parties also entered into a requirements contract in February 1991, subject to which D'Agostino agreed to supply MCC with high grade ceramic tile at specific discounts as long as MCC purchased sufficient quantities of tile. MCC completed a number of additional order forms requesting tile deliveries pursuant to that agreement.

MCC brought suit against D'Agostino claiming a breach of the February 1991 requirements contract when D'Agostino failed to satisfy orders in April, May, and August of 1991. In addition to other defenses, D'Agostino responded that it was under no obligation to fill MCC's orders because MCC had defaulted on payment for previous shipments. In support of its position, D'Agostino relied on the pre-printed terms of the contracts that MCC had executed. The executed forms were printed in Italian and contained terms and conditions on both the front and reverse. According to an English translation of the October 1990 contract, the front of the order form contained the following language directly beneath Monzon's signature:

The buyer hereby states that he is aware of the sales conditions stated on the reverse and that he expressly approves of them with special reference to those numbered 1–2–3–4–5–6–7–8.

Clause 6(b), printed on the back of the form states:

Default or delay in payment within the time agreed upon gives D'Agostino the right to . . . suspend or cancel the contract itself and to cancel possible other pending contracts and the buyer does not have the right to indemnification or damages.

D'Agostino also brought a number of counterclaims against MCC, seeking damages for MCC's alleged nonpayment for deliveries of tile that D'Agostino had made between February 28, 1991 and July 4, 1991. MCC responded that the tile it had received was of a lower quality than contracted for, and that, pursuant to the CISG, MCC was entitled to reduce payment in proportion to the defects. D'Agostino, however, noted that clause 4 on the reverse of the contract states, in pertinent part:

Possible complaints for defects of the merchandise must be made in writing by means of a certified letter within and not later than 10 days after receipt of the merchandise. . . .

Although there is evidence to support MCC's claims that it complained about the quality of the deliveries it received, MCC never submitted any written complaints.

MCC did not dispute these underlying facts before the district court, but argued that the parties never intended the terms and conditions printed on the reverse of the order form to apply to their agreements. As evidence for this assertion, MCC submitted Monzon's affidavit, which claims that MCC had no subjective intent to be bound by those terms and that D'Agostino was aware of this intent. MCC also filed affidavits from Silingardi and Copelli, D'Agostino's representatives at the trade fair, which support Monzon's claim that the parties subjectively intended not to be bound by the terms on the reverse of the order form. The magistrate judge held that the affidavits, even if true, did not raise an issue of material fact regarding the interpretation or applicability of the terms of the written contracts and the district court accepted his recommendation to award summary judgment in D'Agostino's favor. MCC then filed this timely appeal.

* * *

Discussion

The parties to this case agree that the CISG governs their dispute because the United States, where MCC has its place of business, and Italy, where D'Agostino has its place of business, are both States Party to the Convention. See CISG, art. 1. Article 8 of the CISG governs the interpretation of international contracts for the sale of goods and forms the basis of MCC's appeal from the district court's grant of summary judgment in D'Agostino's favor. MCC argues that the magistrate judge and the district court improperly ignored evidence that MCC submitted regarding the parties' subjective intent when they memorialized the terms of their agreement on D'Agostino's pre-printed form contract, and that the magistrate judge erred by applying the parol evidence rule in derogation of the CISG.

I.   Subjective Intent Under the CISG

Contrary to what is familiar practice in United States courts, the CISG appears to permit a substantial inquiry into the parties' subjective intent, even if the parties did not engage in any objectively ascertainable means of registering this intent. Article 8(1) of the CISG instructs courts to interpret the "statements . . . and other conduct of a party . . . according to his intent" as long as the other party "knew or could not have been unaware" of that intent. The plain language of the Convention, therefore, requires an inquiry into a party's subjective intent as long as the other party to the contract was aware of that intent.

In this case, MCC has submitted three affidavits that discuss the purported subjective intent of the parties to the initial agreement concluded between MCC and D'Agostino in October 1990. All three affidavits discuss the preliminary negotiations and report that the parties arrived at an oral agreement for D'Agostino to supply quantities of a specific grade of ceramic tile to MCC at an agreed upon price. The affidavits state that the "oral agreement established the essential terms of quality, quantity, description of goods, delivery, price and payment." The affidavits also note that the parties memorialized the terms of their oral agreement on a standard D'Agostino order form, but all three affiants contend that the parties subjectively intended not to be bound by the terms on the reverse of that form despite a provision directly below the signature line that expressly and specifically incorporated those terms.[1]

The terms on the reverse of the contract give D'Agostino the right to suspend or cancel all contracts in the event of a buyer's non-payment and require a buyer to make a written report of all defects within ten days. As the magistrate judge's report and recommendation makes clear, if these terms applied to the agreements between MCC and D'Agostino, summary judgment would be appropriate because MCC failed to make any written complaints about the quality of tile it received and D'Agostino has established MCC's non-payment of a number of invoices amounting to $108,389.40 and 102,053,846.00 Italian lira.

Article 8(1) of the CISG requires a court to consider this evidence of the parties' subjective intent. Contrary to the magistrate judge's report, which the district court endorsed and adopted, article 8(1) does not focus on interpreting the parties' statements alone. Although we agree with the magistrate judge's conclusion that no "interpretation" of the contract's terms could support MCC's position, article 8(1) also requires a court to consider subjective intent while interpreting the conduct of the parties. The CISG's language, therefore, requires courts to consider evidence of a party's subjective intent when signing a contract if the other party to the contract was aware of that intent at the time. This is precisely the type of evidence that MCC has provided through the Silingardi, Copelli, and Monzon affidavits, which discuss not only Monzon's intent as MCC's representative but also discuss the intent of D'Agostino's representatives and their knowledge that Monzon did not intend to agree to the terms on the reverse of the form contract. This acknowledgment that D'Agostino's representatives were aware of Monzon's subjective intent puts this case squarely within article 8(1) of the CISG, and therefore requires the court to consider MCC's evidence as it interprets the parties' conduct.

II.   Parol Evidence and the CISG

Given our determination that the magistrate judge and the district court should have considered MCC's affidavits regarding the parties'

---

[1]   MCC makes much of the fact that the written order form is entirely in Italian and that Monzon, who signed the contract on MCC's behalf directly below this provision incorporating the terms on the reverse of the form, neither spoke nor read Italian. This fact is of no assistance to MCC's position. We find it nothing short of astounding that an individual, purportedly experienced in commercial matters, would sign a contract in a foreign language and expect not to be bound simply because he could not comprehend its terms. We find nothing in the CISG that might counsel this type of reckless behavior and nothing that signals any retreat from the proposition that parties who sign contracts will be bound by them regardless of whether they have read them or understood them.

subjective intentions, we must address a question of first impression in this circuit: whether the parol evidence rule, which bars evidence of an earlier oral contract that contradicts or varies the terms of a subsequent or contemporaneous written contract, plays any role in cases involving the CISG. We begin by observing that the parol evidence rule, contrary to its title, is a substantive rule of law, not a rule of evidence. See II E. Allen Farnsworth, Farnsworth on Contracts, § 7.2 at 194 (1990). The rule does not purport to exclude a particular type of evidence as an "untrustworthy or undesirable" way of proving a fact, but prevents a litigant from attempting to show "the fact itself—the fact that the terms of the agreement are other than those in the writing." Id. As such, a federal district court cannot simply apply the parol evidence rule as a procedural matter—as it might if excluding a particular type of evidence under the Federal Rules of Evidence, which apply in federal court regardless of the source of the substantive rule of decision.

The CISG itself contains no express statement on the role of parol evidence. It is clear, however, that the drafters of the CISG were comfortable with the concept of permitting parties to rely on oral contracts because they eschewed any statutes of fraud provision and expressly provided for the enforcement of oral contracts. Compare CISG, art. 11 (a contract of sale need not be concluded or evidenced in writing) with U.C.C. § 2–201 (precluding the enforcement of oral contracts for the sale of goods involving more than $500). Moreover, article 8(3) of the CISG expressly directs courts to give "due consideration . . . to all relevant circumstances of the case including the negotiations . . . " to determine the intent of the parties. Given article 8(1)'s directive to use the intent of the parties to interpret their statements and conduct, article 8(3) is a clear instruction to admit and consider parol evidence regarding the negotiations to the extent they reveal the parties' subjective intent.

Despite the CISG's broad scope, surprisingly few cases have applied the Convention in the United States, see Delchi Carrier SpA v. Rotorex Corp., 71 F.3d 1024, 1027–28 (2d Cir. 1995) (observing that "there is virtually no case law under the Convention"), and only two reported decisions touch upon the parol evidence rule, both in dicta. One court has concluded, much as we have above, that the parol evidence rule is not viable in CISG cases in light of article 8 of the Convention. In Filanto S.p.A. v. Chilewich Int'l Corp., 789 F. Supp. 1229 (S.D.N.Y. 1992), a district court addressed the differences between the UCC and the CISG on the issues of offer and acceptance and the battle of the forms. See 789 F. Supp. at 1238. After engaging in a thorough analysis of how the CISG applied to the dispute before it, the district court tangentially observed that article 8(3) "essentially rejects . . . the parol evidence rule." Id. at 1238 n.7. Another court, however, appears to have arrived at a contrary conclusion. In Beijing Metals & Minerals Import/Export Corp. v. American Bus. Ctr., Inc., 993 F.2d 1178 (5th Cir. 1993), a defendant sought to avoid summary judgment on a contract claim by relying on evidence of contemporaneously negotiated oral terms that the parties had not included in their written agreement. The plaintiff, a Chinese corporation, relied on Texas law in its complaint while the defendant, apparently a Texas corporation, asserted that the CISG governed the dispute. Id. at 1183 n.9. Without resolving the choice of law question, the Fifth Circuit cited *Filanto* for the proposition that there have been very few reported cases applying the CISG in the United States, and stated that the parol evidence rule would apply regardless of whether Texas law or the CISG governed the dispute. *Beijing Metals*, 993 F.2d at 1183 n.9. The opinion does not acknowledge Filanto's more applicable dictum that the parol evidence rule does not apply to CISG cases nor does it conduct any analysis of the Convention to support its conclusion. In fact, the Fifth Circuit did not undertake to interpret the CISG in a manner that would arrive at a result consistent with the parol evidence rule but instead explained that it would apply the rule as developed at Texas common law. See id. at 1183 n.10. As persuasive authority for this court, the Beijing Metals opinion is not particularly persuasive on this point.

Our reading of article 8(3) as a rejection of the parol evidence rule, however, is in accordance with the great weight of academic commentary on the issue. As one scholar has explained:

The language of Article 8(3) that "due consideration is to be given to all relevant circumstances of the case" seems adequate to override any domestic rule that would bar a tribunal from considering the relevance of other agreements. . . . Article 8(3) relieves tribunals from domestic rules that might bar them from "considering" any evidence between the parties that is relevant. This added flexibility for interpretation is consistent with a growing body of opinion that the "parol evidence rule" has been an embarrassment for the administration of modern transactions. Honnold, Uniform Law for International Sales § 110 at 170–71 (1989).

* * * [A]lthough jurisdictions in the United States have found the parol evidence rule helpful to promote good faith and uniformity in contract, as well as an appropriate answer to the question of how much consideration to give parol evidence, a wide number of other States Party to the CISG have rejected the rule in their domestic jurisdictions. One of the primary factors motivating the negotiation and adoption of the CISG was to provide parties to international contracts for the sale of goods with some degree of certainty as to the principles of law that would govern potential disputes and remove the previous doubt regarding which party's legal system might otherwise apply. Courts applying the CISG cannot, therefore, upset the parties' reliance on the Convention by substituting familiar principles of domestic law when the Convention requires a different result. We may only achieve the directives of good faith and uniformity in contracts under the CISG by interpreting and applying the plain language of article 8(3) as written and obeying its directive to consider this type of parol evidence.

This is not to say that parties to an international contract for the sale of goods cannot depend on written contracts or that parol evidence regarding subjective contractual intent need always prevent a party relying on a written agreement from securing summary judgment. To the contrary, most cases will not present a situation (as exists in this case) in which both parties to the contract acknowledge a subjective intent not to be bound by the terms of a pre-printed writing. In most cases, therefore, article 8(2) of the CISG will apply, and objective evidence will provide the basis for the court's decision. See Honnold, Uniform Law § 107 at 164–65. Consequently, a party to a contract governed by the CISG will not be able to avoid the terms of a contract and force a jury trial simply by submitting an affidavit which states that he or she did not have the subjective intent to be bound by the contract's terms. Cf. Klopfenstein v. Pargeter, 597 F.2d 150, 152 (9th Cir. 1979) (affirming summary judgment despite the appellant's submission of his own affidavit regarding his subjective intent: "Undisclosed, subjective intentions are immaterial in [a] commercial transaction, especially when contradicted by objective conduct. Thus, the affidavit has no legal effect even if its averments are accepted as wholly truthful."). Moreover, to the extent parties wish to avoid parol evidence problems they can do so by including a merger clause in their agreement that extinguishes any and all prior agreements and understandings not expressed in the writing.

Considering MCC's affidavits in this case, however, we conclude that the magistrate judge and the district court improperly granted summary judgment in favor of D'Agostino. Although the affidavits are, as D'Agostino observes, relatively conclusory and unsupported by facts that would objectively establish MCC's intent not to be bound by the conditions on the reverse of the form, article 8(1) requires a court to consider evidence of a party's subjective intent when the other party was aware of it, and the Silingardi and Copelli affidavits provide that evidence. This is not to say that the affidavits are conclusive proof of what the parties intended. A reasonable finder of fact, for example, could disregard testimony that purportedly sophisticated international merchants signed a contract without intending to be bound as simply too incredible to believe and hold MCC to the conditions printed on the reverse of the contract. Nevertheless, the affidavits raise an issue of material fact regarding the parties' intent to incorporate the provisions on the reverse of the form contract. If the finder of fact determines that the parties did not intend to rely on those provisions, then the more general provisions of the CISG will govern the outcome of the dispute.
* * *

Conclusion

MCC asks us to reverse the district court's grant of summary judgment in favor of D'Agostino. The district court's decision rests on pre-printed contractual terms and conditions incorporated on the reverse of a standard order form that MCC's president signed on the company's behalf. Nevertheless, we conclude that the CISG, which governs international contracts for the sale of goods, precludes summary judgment in this case because MCC has raised an issue of material fact concerning the parties' subjective intent to be bound by the terms on the reverse of the pre-printed contract. The CISG also precludes the application of the parol evidence rule, which would otherwise bar the consideration of evidence concerning a prior or contemporaneously negotiated oral agreement. Accordingly, we REVERSE the district court's grant of summary judgment and remand this case for further proceedings consistent with this opinion.

NOTES

1. *MCC–Marble*'s conclusion that the CISG displaces the parol evidence rule is based on two considerations: Article 8(3)'s plain language and the desire for uniformity in contract law rules that motivated the CISG's adoption. Article 8(3)'s language does not displace the parol evidence rule. As noted above, Article 8(3) requires "due consideration" of "all relevant circumstances" but does not define or restrict the consideration "due" to these circumstances, including parol evidence. The parol evidence rule's restrictions on the admissibility of parol evidence arguably provide the consideration "due" to parol evidence. Even if Article 8(3) somehow defines the "due consideration" to be given to evidence, it is not apparent that the definition makes parol evidence always admissible to prove the terms of a contract. The court's invocation of uniformity also is questionable. The CISG leaves to applicable domestic law a number of important issues relating to contract terms. Consider Article 4(a). It provides that the CISG is not concerned with issues of "validity," except as expressly provided for in its provisions. Issues of validity therefore generally are left to applicable domestic law. Because domestic laws can differ over the contract terms they consider invalid and so unenforceable, Article 4(a) allows different results depending on the applicable domestic law. The CISG therefore fails to achieve complete uniformity in contract law. Given the CISG's allowance of a degree of diversity in contract law, the court cannot conclude that the putative desire for uniformity in contract requires displacement of the parol evidence rule. Chapter 6 discusses the issue of validity under the CISG more fully.

2. *MCC–Marble* did not need to decide whether the CISG makes the parol evidence rule inapplicable to sales contracts within its scope. It could have reached the same result even if the rule applies. The parol evidence rule does not bar evidence introduced for the purpose of showing that the writing was not a final expression of the parties' agreement. For this purpose, evidence is being introduced to show that the writing was not integrated. It is not being offered to prove the terms of the contract. The buyer in *MCC–Marble* claimed that the seller's standard form did not reflect the parties' final agreement. The affidavit of the buyer's president stating that the buyer did not intend to be bound by the seller's standard form supports the buyer's claim. Thus, the buyer's argument was that it was not bound by the seller's form because the form is not the contract. The court rejected the buyer's argument, finding that the agreement was the final expression of the parties' agreement. In finding the writing to be integrated, the court did not need to pass on whether the CISG displaced the parol evidence rule. Even if the rule continues to apply to contracts governed by the CISG, parol evidence is inadmissible to restrict a term of the integration.

The buyer's counsel failed to make its argument clear. The court observes that the buyer "makes much" of its president's inability to understand Italian. Apparently the buyer's counsel argued on the basis of the buyer's affidavit that the buyer was not bound by the terms of the standard form its president signed in a language he could not read. The court rejects this argument as "astounding." The buyer's actual argument, however, is different. It is that, given the inability of the buyer's representative to understand Italian, the buyer did not intend the seller's standard form to be an integration. Although the case recites that the seller's representative served as a translator for an oral agreement on price and the like, the facts do not state that the representative translated the terms of the standard form for the buyer. In these circumstances a reasonable person in the seller's position would not have concluded that the buyer intended the standard form to be integrated. This argument ultimately may be unconvincing, but it is not astounding.

3. The parol evidence rule does not bar evidence introduced for the purpose of proving mistake, fraud or a lack of consideration. The rule also does not bar evidence aimed at proving the meaning of the terms of an integration. The difficulty presented by these exceptions is that they risk undermining the parol evidence rule itself. This is because evidence introduced under these exceptions can allow the trier of fact to conclude that the terms of an agreement are not reflected in the integration. For example, to prove fraud extrinsic evidence about the circumstances under which the agreement was concluded must be introduced. Even if the trier of fact finds no fraud, it might use the extrinsic evidence introduced to conclude that the terms of the agreement are different from terms in the integration. This result defeats the purpose of the parol evidence rule. A more frequent example of the problem involves the introduction of evidence bearing on the meaning of terms in the integration. In *Alaska Northern*, for instance, the buyer sought to introduce evidence that "final approval of the owner committee" in the integration meant "final approval of the owner committee limited to price." The introduction of evidence to explain the meaning of terms in the integration risks adding or changing the terms of the agreement. Courts frequently follow *Alaska Northern* in barring such evidence unless the terms in the integration are reasonably susceptible of the meaning sought to be introduced. See, e.g., Brinderson–Newberg Joint Venture v. Pacific Erector, 971 F.2d 272 (9th Cir. 1992); Richard L. Cohn v. Taco Bell Corp., 1994 U.S. Dist. LEXIS 334, at *1 (N.D. Ill. 1994).

PROBLEM 4.11

Seller, located in Atlanta, and Buyer, located in Paris, conclude a sales contract governed by the CISG. Both parties prefer that all trade usage, course of dealing and course of performance not be made in any way applicable to their contract. Accordingly, they would like to draft a provision that best assures that their contract will not be subject to trade usage and the like. Which of the following four provisions does so? Do any guarantee the desired result? See CISG Articles 6, 8, 9.

(a) "Article 9 of the CISG, and all of the usages referred to in that Article, shall not govern this contract."

(b) "The CISG is inapplicable to this contract; instead local law applies to all aspects of the contract."

(c) "All trade usage, course of dealing or performance shall be inapplicable to this contract, including all of the usages referred to in Article 9 of the CISG."

(d) "All trade usage, course of dealing or performance shall be inapplicable to all aspects of this contract, including the interpretation of its terms. In addition, Articles 8 and 9 are inapplicable to the contract."

PROBLEM 4.12

Rug, located in Los Angeles, and Buy, located in Berlin, are going to conclude a contract for the sale of rugs. They want to assure that certain evidence relating to their contract is kept from the trier of fact should litigation occur. The parties do not want measures taken that create uncertainty about the rules applicable to their sales contract. Which of the following provisions in their written agreement is likely to best achieve this result?

(a) "The law applicable to all aspects of this contract does not include the CISG or any of its provisions." CISG Article 6.

(b) "Evidence of prior or contemporaneous negotiations or agreements may not be introduced to vary or add to the terms of this writing." CISG Articles 6, 8, 9.

(c) "The law governing the admissibility of evidence of the terms of the agreement is governed by applicable domestic law." CISG Article 6.

(d) Draft a provision that improves on (a)–(c), taking into account the parties' desires. In doing so consider CISG Article 6, 1–301(a) and 2–202.

D. UNCONSCIONABILITY

An otherwise enforceable sales contract will not be enforced if it is unconscionable. Borrowing the notion of unconscionability from pre-UCC common law, 2–302 regulates its application to sales contracts. Section 2A–108, which is identical to 2–302, regulates the conscionability of leases of goods. Section 2–302 does not define the notion of unconscionability; it merely regulates its judicial use. According to 2–302(1), a finding of unconscionability is made by the court, and 2–302(2) gives the contracting parties the opportunity to submit evidence relevant to the issue. The subsection requires the finding to be made on an ex ante basis: An unconscionable contract or any its terms must be unconscionable at the time the contract was made. Later events that make a contract unprofitable or oppressive do not make a contract or its terms unconscionable. If the court finds a contract unconscionable, it may refuse to enforce the entire contract or just the offending term. The court also may limit enforcement of the offending term so that the result of its application is conscionable. Section 2–302 does not give the victim of an unconscionable contract or term a right to recover damages.

In applying 2–302, courts rely heavily on Comment 2 to 2–302's description of the section's animating principle. Comment 2 in relevant part provides: "The principle [underlying 2–302] is one of the prevention of oppression and unfair surprise . . . and not of disturbance of allocation of risks because of superior bargaining power." This provision identifies two components of a bargain: a procedural and a substantive element. A contract is substantively unconscionable if its terms are "oppressive" or otherwise unreasonably unfavorable to a party. Procedural unconscionability is present if the process by which the contract was made is defective in some way. The defect may be in the capacities or understanding of a contracting party, or in the particular circumstances in which the bargain was concluded. According to

Comment 2, superior bargaining power alone does not make a bargain procedurally unconscionable. See Williams v. Walker–Thomas Furniture Co., 350 F.2d 445, 449 (D.C.Cir. 1965), a well-known pre-UCC case applying the doctrine of unconscionability, identifies both the substantive and procedural components of unconscionability: "Unconscionability has generally been recognized to include an absence of meaningful choice on the part of one of the parties together with contracts terms which are unreasonably favorable to the other party."

According to most courts, unconscionability contains substantive and procedural components. A contract or a term is unconscionable only if it is both substantively and procedurally unconscionable. A few courts adopt a mathematical analogy, setting a "sliding scale" of the two components. If the analogy is taken seriously, it allows a finding of unconscionability when only one of the components is present, if the unconscionability present is sufficiently serious. Some cases have found unconscionability on substantive grounds alone. Claims of unconscionability are relatively infrequent and seldom succeed. Note 1 following *Brower* below describes a partial exception to this generalization.

Findings of unconscionability are rare, probably because 2–302 is difficult to apply. This is so for two reasons. First, and obviously, the standards of substantive and procedural unconscionability are vague. For instance, a term often is difficult to identify as substantive unconscionable if the governing standard requires that it be unfairly one-sided. Applying the commonly listed menu of procedural defects that include an absence of meaningful choice or gross disparities in bargaining power is hard when these items are as vague as the governing standard of procedural unconscionability. Second, 2–302's application depends on information to which courts have limited access. For example, a commonly used indication of substantive unconscionability is the disparity between the market price of a good and its contract price. A contract price that is higher than market price suggests unfairness—and probably a procedural defect in bargaining too. However, the higher price might not mean that the buyer paid too much for the goods. Instead, the higher price might reflect the greater risk of payment or the higher cost the seller must incur in performing the sales contract with the particular buyer. To exclude this possibility, a court must accurately identify the price of goods in the comparable market. It therefore must compare the price of goods offered to buyers presenting similar risks to their sellers that the buyer presents to its seller. Courts usually lack this information.

As an illustration, consider what might at first appear as an easy case. In Maxwell v. Fidelity Financial Services, Inc., 907 P.2d 51 (Ariz. 1995), a lender financed the buyer's purchase of a home water heater. The sale price of about $6,500 was financed with a ten-year loan at 19.5 percent interest, with a total cost of nearly $15,000. The court found that the disparity between the cash sale price and the credit price raised a question of substantive unconscionability. It did not base its finding on a disparity between the interest rate normally charged for such loans and the interest rate the lender charged its debtor. Instead, the court compared the cash price of the goods and the credit price of the loan. On remand the trial court apparently had to determine whether the price of loan was grossly excessive. Even if the trial court looked to the interest rates normally charged for comparable consumer loans to decide, it would have to take into account the risks of default presented by the particular debtor. The court might have trouble obtaining accurate information about default risk. Of course, sometimes an interest rate or sale price might be so high that a court is confident that the price (or interest rate) disparity is grossly excessive. But to decide whether to strike down the price term or interest rate, or simply reduce it instead, the court must determine the extent of the price or interest rate disparity. It therefore must measure the extent to which the price or interest rate charged is excessive. *Brower* below raises the question of the one-sidedness of a choice of forum clause, a nonprice term.

Even if unconscionability doctrine were judicially manageable, its application does not alter the economic situation of those ostensibly protected by it. A party's poor bargaining position results from her lack of alternatives. She accepts an offer with a high credit price because she cannot feasibly pay cash. Given her alternatives, a contract with a high credit price is the best she can do. The party's financial situation gives her no "meaningful" alternative. Finding such contracts unconscionable does not help her. While relieving the party of a contract or term she finds burdensome ex post, the result does not improve her poor financial situation. It still leaves her with no alternative to accepting contracts on terms deemed unconscionable. See Amoco Oil Co. v. Ashcraft, 791 F.2d 519 (7th Cir. 1986). In fact, nonenforcement might leave her or others in her financial situation worse off. Contracting parties offering contracts that are struck down as unconscionable will no longer offer them. Withdrawing these contracts leaves potential contracting parties with few contracting alternatives with even fewer alternatives.

Brower v. Gateway 2000, Inc.

Supreme Court of New York, Appellate Division, 1998
246 A.D.2d 246

■ Opinion: MILONAS, J.P.

Appellants are among the many consumers who purchased computers and software products from defendant Gateway 2000 through a direct-sales system, by mail or telephone order. As of July 3, 1995, it was Gateway's practice to include with the materials shipped to the purchaser along with the merchandise a copy of its "Standard Terms and Conditions Agreement" and any relevant warranties for the products in the shipment. The Agreement begins with a "Note to the Customer," which provides, in slightly larger print than the remainder of the document, in a box that spans the width of the page: "This document contains Gateway 2000's Standard Terms and Conditions. By keeping your Gateway 2000 computer system beyond thirty (30) days after the date of delivery, you accept these Terms and Conditions." The document consists of 16 paragraphs, and, as is relevant to this appeal, paragraph 10 of the agreement, entitled "dispute resolution," reads as follows: "Any dispute or controversy arising out of or relating to this Agreement or its interpretation shall be settled exclusively and finally by arbitration. The arbitration shall be conducted in accordance with the Rules of Conciliation and Arbitration of the International Chamber of Commerce. The arbitration shall be conducted in Chicago, Illinois, U.S.A. before a sole arbitrator. Any award rendered in any such arbitration proceeding shall be final and binding on each of the parties, and judgment may be entered thereon in a court of competent jurisdiction."

Plaintiffs commenced this action on behalf of themselves and others similarly situated for compensatory and punitive damages, alleging deceptive sales practices in seven causes of action, including breach of warranty, breach of contract, fraud and unfair trade practices. In particular, the allegations focused on Gateway's representations and advertising that promised "service when you need it," including around-the-clock free technical support, free software technical support and certain on-site services. According to plaintiffs, not only were they unable to avail themselves of this offer because it was virtually impossible to get through to a technician, but also Gateway continued to advertise this claim notwithstanding numerous complaints and reports about the problem.

Insofar as is relevant to appellants, who purchased their computers after July 3, 1995, Gateway moved to dismiss the complaint based on the arbitration clause in the Agreement. Appellants argued that the arbitration clause is invalid under UCC 2–207, unconscionable under UCC 2–302 and an unenforceable contract of adhesion. Specifically, they claimed that the provision was obscure; that a customer could not reasonably be expected to appreciate or investigate its meaning and effect; that the International Chamber of Commerce (ICC) was not a forum commonly used for consumer matters; and that because ICC headquarters were in France, it was particularly difficult to locate the organization and its rules. To illustrate just how inaccessible the forum was, appellants advised the court that the ICC was not registered with the Secretary of State, that efforts to locate and contact the ICC had been unsuccessful and that apparently the only way to attempt to contact the ICC was through the United States Council for International Business, with which the ICC maintained some sort of relationship.

In support of their arguments, appellants submitted a copy of the ICC's Rules of Conciliation and Arbitration and contended that the cost of ICC arbitration was prohibitive, particularly given the amount of the typical consumer claim involved. For example, a claim of less than $50,000 required advance fees of $4,000 (more than the cost of most Gateway products), of which the $2,000 registration fee was nonrefundable even if the consumer prevailed at the arbitration. Consumers would also incur travel expenses disproportionate to the damages sought, which appellants' counsel estimated would not exceed $1,000 per customer in this action, as well as bear the cost of Gateway's legal fees if the consumer did not prevail at the arbitration; in this respect, the ICC Rules follow the "loser pays" rule used in England. Also, although Chicago was designated as the site of the actual arbitration, all correspondence must be sent to ICC headquarters in France.

The IAS Court dismissed the complaint as to appellants based on the arbitration clause in the Agreements delivered with their computers. We agree with the court's decision and reasoning in all respects but for the issue of the unconscionability of the designation of the ICC as the arbitration body.

* * *

Finally, we turn to appellants' argument that the IAS Court should have declared the contract unenforceable, pursuant to UCC 2–302, on the ground that the arbitration clause is unconscionable due to the unduly burdensome procedure and cost for the individual consumer. The IAS Court found that while a class action lawsuit, such as the one herein, may be a less costly alternative to the arbitration (which is generally less costly than litigation), that does not alter the binding effect of the valid arbitration clause contained in the agreement.

As a general matter, under New York law, unconscionability requires a showing that a contract is "both procedurally and substantively unconscionable when made" (Gillman v. Chase Manhattan Bank, 73 NY2d 1, 10). That is, there must be "some showing of 'an absence of meaningful choice on the part of one of the parties together with contract terms which are unreasonably favorable to the other party' [citation omitted]" (Matter of State of New York v. Avco Fin. Servs., 50 NY2d 383, 389). The Avco Court took pains to note, however, that the purpose of this doctrine is not to redress the inequality between the parties but simply to ensure that the more powerful party cannot " 'surprise' " the other party with some overly oppressive term (supra, at 389).

As to the procedural element, a court will look to the contract formation process to determine if in fact one party lacked any meaningful choice in entering into the contract, taking into consideration such factors as the setting of the transaction, the experience and education of the party claiming unconscionability, whether the contract contained "fine print," whether the seller used "high-pressured tactics" and any disparity in the parties' bargaining power (Gillman v. Chase Manhattan Bank, supra, at 11). None of these factors supports appellants' claim here. Any purchaser has 30 days within which to thoroughly examine the contents of their shipment, including the terms of the Agreement, and seek clarification of any term therein. The Agreement itself, which is entitled in large print "Standard Terms and Conditions Agreement," consists of only four pages and 16 paragraphs, all of which appear in the same size print. Moreover, despite appellants' claims to the contrary, the arbitration clause is in no way "hidden" or "tucked away" within a complex document of inordinate length, nor is the option of returning the merchandise, to avoid the contract, somehow a "precarious" one. We also reject appellants' insinuation that, by using the word "standard," Gateway deliberately meant to convey to the consumer that the terms were standard within the industry, when the document clearly purports to be no more than Gateway's "standard terms and conditions."

With respect to the substantive element, which entails an examination of the substance of the Agreement in order to determine whether the terms unreasonably favor one party (Gillman v. Chase Manhattan Bank, supra, 73 NY2d, at 12), we do not find that the possible inconvenience of the chosen site (Chicago) alone rises to the level of unconscionability. We do find, however, that the excessive cost factor that is necessarily entailed in arbitrating before the ICC is unreasonable and surely serves to deter the individual consumer from invoking the process. Barred from resorting to the courts by the arbitration clause in the first instance, the designation of a financially prohibitive forum effectively bars consumers from this forum as well; consumers are thus left with no forum at all in which to resolve a dispute. In this regard, we note that this particular claim is not mentioned in the *Hill* decision, which upheld the clause as part of an enforceable contract.

While it is true that, under New York law, unconscionability is generally predicated on the presence of both the procedural and substantive elements, the substantive element alone may be sufficient to render the terms of the provision at issue unenforceable. Excessive fees, such as those incurred under the ICC procedure, have been grounds for finding an arbitration provision unenforceable or commercially unreasonable. In *Filias* previously mentioned [*Filias v. Gateway 2000* (unreported case)], the Federal District Court stated that it was "inclined to agree" with the argument that selection of the ICC rendered the clause unconscionable, but concluded that the issue was moot because Gateway had agreed to arbitrate before the American Arbitration Association (AAA) and sought court appointment of the AAA pursuant to Federal Arbitration Act (9 USC) § 5. The court accordingly granted Gateway's motion to compel arbitration and appointed the AAA in lieu of the ICC. Plaintiffs in that action (who are represented by counsel for appellants before us) contend that costs associated with the AAA process are also excessive, given the amount of the individual consumer's damages, and their motion for reconsideration of the court's decision has not yet been decided. While the AAA rules and costs are not part of the record before us, the parties agree that there is a minimum, nonrefundable filing fee of $500, and appellants claim each consumer could spend in excess of $1,000 to arbitrate in this forum.

Gateway's agreement to the substitution of the AAA is not limited to the *Filias* plaintiffs. Gateway's brief includes the text of a new arbitration agreement that it claims has been extended to all customers, past, present and future (apparently through publication in a quarterly magazine sent to anyone who has ever purchased a Gateway product). The new arbitration agreement provides for the consumer's choice of the AAA or the ICC as the arbitral body and the designation of any location for the arbitration by agreement of the parties, which "shall not be unreasonably withheld." It also provides telephone numbers at which the AAA and the ICC may be reached for information regarding the "organizations and their procedures."

As noted, however, appellants complain that the AAA fees are also excessive and thus in no way have they accepted defendant's offer (see, UCC 2–209); because they make the same claim as to the AAA as they did with respect to the ICC, the issue of unconscionability is not rendered moot, as defendant suggests. We cannot determine on this record whether the AAA process and costs would be so "egregiously oppressive" that they, too, would be unconscionable. Thus, we modify the order on appeal to the extent of finding that portion of the arbitration provision requiring arbitration before the ICC to be unconscionable and remand to Supreme Court so that the parties have the opportunity to seek appropriate substitution of an arbitrator pursuant to the Federal Arbitration Act (9 USC § 1 et seq.), which provides for such court designation of an arbitrator upon application of either party, where, for whatever reason, one is not otherwise designated (9 USC § 5).

* * *

Accordingly, the order of Supreme Court, New York County (Beatrice Shainswit, J.), entered October 21, 1997, which, to the extent appealed from, granted defendants' motion to dismiss the complaint as to appellants on the ground that there was a valid agreement to arbitrate between the parties, should be modified, on the law and the facts, to the extent of vacating that portion of the arbitration agreement as requires arbitration before the International Chamber of Commerce, with leave to the parties to seek appointment of an arbitrator pursuant to 9 USC § 5 and remanding the matter for that purpose, and otherwise affirmed, without costs. * * *

NOTES

1. Courts apparently tend to find arbitration clauses unconscionable more frequently than they have other sorts of contract terms. A study comparing federal and state cases in 1982–1983 and 2002–2003 found more than a four-fold increase in the number of unconscionability claims brought between the two periods. Two thirds of these claims in 2002–2003 involved arbitration agreements compared to about a sixth of the claims in the 1982–1983 period. In 1982–1983 courts were slightly less likely to find arbitration agreements unconscionable than nonarbitration agreements; in 2002–2003 arbitration agreements were found unconscionable at twice the rate of nonarbitration agreements. Significantly, in 2002–2003 courts struck down one half of the arbitration agreements as unconscionable when claims of unconscionability were raised. See Susan Randall, Judicial Attitudes Toward Arbitration and the Resurgence of Unconscionability, 52 Buffalo L. Rev. 185 (2004).

Many cases strike down arbitration clauses based on the costs a party must bear to arbitrate. These costs include filing fees, payment of arbitrators, contractually assigned attorneys' fees, and travel expenses. In *Brower* Gateway's buyers had to incur fees and other expenses to arbitrate their claims against Gateway under the ICC's rules, in accordance with ICC procedures. *Brower* struck down Gateway's arbitration clause as substantively unconscionable because it found that the buyer's arbitral costs were excessive. According to the court, the costs of arbitration made the buyers' vindication of their contractual rights financially infeasible. The Supreme Court in American Express Co. v. Italian Colors Restaurant, 133 S. Ct. 2304 (2013), drastically limited the "effective vindication" rationale for invalidating an arbitration clause as substantively unconscionable. *Italian Colors* holds that the economic infeasibility of pursuing a statutory right does not by itself invalidate an arbitration agreement. The Court nonetheless allowed that there might be an exception for arbitration fees and administrative costs that make arbitration financially infeasible. *Brower*, decided before *Italian Colors*, finds that the arbitration clause at issue is substantively unconscionable, in part based on arbitral fees that make arbitration financially infeasible for Gateway's buyers. The Supreme Court has not decided whether a "fees and costs" exception survives *Italian Colors.*

2.   Courts scrutinizing arbitration clauses for excessive cost variously compare the difference between arbitration and litigation costs, the likelihood that arbitration costs will deter a party from arbitrating claims, and the financial capacity of a party to incur these costs. The *Brower* court finds that "the excessive cost factor that is necessarily entailed in arbitrating before the ICC is unreasonable and surely serves to deter the individual consumer from invoking the process." It does not elaborate on the finding. *Brower* appears to test the excessive nature of Gateway's buyer's arbitration costs by their tendency to deter their arbitration of claims. The test of deterrence is not a particularly good test of excessive cost. Courts have difficulty obtaining information needed to calibrate a party's costs and benefits of arbitrating a claim. In addition, the test fails to regulate terms that can substitute for arbitration clauses. An enforceable warranty disclaimer places the risk of nonconformity in the goods on the buyer. More generally, a disclaimer can disclaim almost all elements of loss. The buyer has no right to recover from the seller for loss resulting from nonconformities covered by the disclaimer. An arbitration clause that deters the buyer from arbitrating produces the same result as an enforceable disclaimer: by not arbitrating, the buyer bears the risk of the nonconformity. Thus, a disclaimer of warranties and liability for other losses can serve as a substitute for an arbitration clause that deters the buyer from arbitrating claims. These disclaimers are not judicially regulated by the excessive cost imposed on the buyer. Unless there is a procedural flaw in the bargain, the seller will offer the buyer an efficient contract with either a warranty disclaimer or an arbitration clause.

3.   A peculiarity of the law of arbitration bears on the regulation of arbitration clauses for unconscionability. Section 2 of the Federal Arbitration Act (FAA) provides in relevant part that a written arbitration agreement "shall be valid, irrevocable, and enforceable, save upon such grounds as exist at law or in equity for the revocation of any contract." 9 U.S.C. § 2 (2000). The Supreme Court in Doctor's Associates, Inc. v. Casarotto, 517 U.S. 681 (1996), held that the section's "saving" clause prevents state law from treating arbitration clauses less favorably than other terms in a contract. As a matter of federal and most state law, forum selection clauses are considered to be presumptively valid. These clauses are unenforceable if they work to deprive a party of an effective judicial forum in which to vindicate its contractual claims. An arbitration clause is a nonjudicial forum selection clause. In general, nonarbitral forum selection clauses are not vetted according to their impact on a party's effective vindication of its contractual rights. *Brower* and similar cases arguably subject arbitration clauses to a form of judicial scrutiny that is not applied to nonarbitral forum selection clauses. Thus, regulation of these clauses for substantive unconscionability seems to violate *Doctor's Associates's* holding. To date no court has reached this conclusion.

It is not always easy to tell when a rule invalidating an agreement as unconscionable violates section 2 of the FAA. A rule that, although applicable generally to both arbitration agreements and other contracts, may have its predominant impact on arbitration agreements. If the general rule is judged by its potential sphere of application, it does not discriminate against arbitration. If it is judged by the agreements to which it most frequently is applicable, the rule can have a disproportionate impact on arbitration agreements. Measured by impact, the rule can discriminate against arbitration agreements. This difference in the standard for determining discrimination divided the Supreme Court in AT & T Mobility v. Concepcion, 131 S. Ct. 1740 (2011). *Concepcion* holds that the section 2 of the FAA preempts a California rule that deemed waivers of consumer class action arbitrations unconscionable. Justice Scalia, writing for the majority, found that the rule, as applied, disfavors class waivers in arbitration agreements as against waivers of class litigation in agreements that do not call for arbitration. By contrast, Justice Breyer in dissent viewed the California rule as stating a general unconscionability rule that applies to class actions waivers in all contracts. He concluded that the rule does not discriminate against arbitration agreements.

4. Section 2–302 continues to apply to sales contracts governed by the CISG. Article 4(a) provides that the CISG is not concerned with issues of the "validity" of the contract or of any of its provisions. Although the CISG does not define validity (or other any term), the enforceability of a contract term clearly is a matter of validity. Thus, applicable domestic law of unconscionability regulates sales contracts under the CISG. Accord Berry v. Ken M. Spooner Farms, Inc., 59 UCC Rep. Serv.2d 443 (W.D. Wash. 2006).

PROBLEM 4.13

Time Watches, a subsidiary of a French multinational corporation, is incorporated and does business in New York. In urgent need of parts for watches it is producing, Time asked its distributor for the name of a likely supplier who could deliver on short notice. The distributor referred Time to Movement, a large California supplier of parts for watches. Time's immediate need for parts prevented it from searching for suppliers, and it acted on the reference. The distributor failed to tell Time that it held a controlling interest in Movement. Time's French representatives, who could only speak basic English, were offered a standard form sales contract by Movement. One of Movement's employees translated into French the contents of the contract. Movement refused Time's proposal that it alter a provision setting a 75% restocking fee for returned parts. The terms of the contract were "nonnegotiable," according to Movement. In fact this was true: Movement sold its parts only according to the terms of its standard form contract. Some smaller suppliers of watch parts did not have a restocking fee. Time decided to make the purchase after Movement's employee stated that "I'll work with you and make some adjustment to the restocking fee in your case." Needing Movement's parts immediately, Time and Movement signed the standard form contract, which recited "This writing constitutes the complete and exclusive expression of the parties' agreement. It supersedes all prior agreements or negotiations." Later, Time returned some parts Movement had delivered and Movement charged Time a 75% restocking fee on the parts. Time had paid for the parts and now demands the return of the full price paid. It offers two arguments in support: (1) that the terms of agreement do not allow Movement to charge a 75% restocking fee, and (2) even if the agreement called for the fee, it is unenforceable. Will Time prevail on either argument? 2–202, 2–302(1), Comment 2 to 2–302. Would the result change if Mr. Time were an individual who bought the parts for his own watch?

PROBLEM 4.14

Jones Corp. agreed to buy an air conditioning unit from Cool Corp. for $1,000. The terms of the agreement gave Jones two options: a cash payment and a credit option. If Jones paid cash on delivery of the unit, the purchase price was $1,000. If Jones paid for the unit six months after delivery, the price was $1,300. Cool set the credit price taking into account Jones' very poor credit history and dim financial prospects. For customers in better financial circumstances Cool offers a credit price of $1,050 for the unit, for payment 6 months after delivery. No other supplier would sell Jones a unit on credit, and Jones' operations could not function well without air conditioning. Strapped for cash, Jones purchased the air conditioning unit under the credit option. A month after Jones made the agreement with Cool, Jones' financial prospects improved dramatically: Its credit rating was raised to that of Cool's best customers, and it is now flush with cash. Accordingly, Jones now seeks to pay Cool $1,050 for the unit. When Cool refused to accept anything less than $1,300, Jones sued Cool seeking to have the payment term of the sales contract declared unenforceable. Alternatively, Jones claims that it is entitled to pay $1,050. Will Jones succeed? 2–302. Would the result be different if the unit had been purchased by Mr. Jones for use in his home? (Assume that usury laws are inapplicable.)

CHAPTER 5

WARRANTIES

A. WARRANTIES AS TO THE GOODS

The seller is financially responsible to the buyer if the goods do not conform to the contract. Article 2 deals with the seller's responsibility for the quality of the goods delivered through various warranties. A warranty allocates the risk of nonconformity in the goods to the seller. If a warranty is not created, or created but effectively disclaimed, the buyer bears the risk of nonconformity. Some warranties are express. If the sales contract calls for delivery of "five all cotton shirts" and the seller delivers five polyester shirts, the seller has breached its express warranty as to the shirts' material. Other warranties are not express. Instead, they are implied because most parties would have provided for them explicitly in their sales contract if doing so were not costly. For instance, most sellers who are merchants with respect to the goods they are selling would agree to warrant that the goods are fit for the purposes to which they are ordinarily put. Compare 2–314(2)(c).

Article 2 recognizes four warranties: an express warranty (2–313), an implied warranty of merchantability (2–314), an implied warranty of fitness for a particular purpose (2–315), and an implied warranty of good title (2–312). Article 2 prefers not to call the latter warranty an implied warranty only because this warranty has separate rules governing its disclaimer. See Comment 6 to 2–312. Nonetheless, the warranty of good title is an implied warranty. All of Article 2's warranties go to the quality of the goods. Even the warranty of good title warrants a quality: the quality of title in the goods conveyed. None of Article 2's warranties are mandatory terms of the sales contract. The seller can avoid creating an express warranty by not making promises or representations as to the goods. She can effectively disclaim any implied warranties created; see 2–316, 2–312(2). In this case the buyer bears the cost if the goods do not conform. Buyers will prefer a contract without warranties when her cost of bearing that risk is lower than the seller's charge for bearing it.

Article 2's warranties do not always all apply to a sales contract. Sometimes some warranties will apply while other warranties are inapplicable. For instance, no express warranty is created if the seller makes no representations as to the goods. Nonetheless, an implied warranty of fitness for a particular purpose arises if the seller knows of the buyer's atypical purpose for the goods and has reason to know that the buyer is relying on his judgment that the goods are suitable for the purpose. Conversely, the implied warranty of fitness does not arise where the buyer's purpose for the goods is ordinary. Nonetheless, the seller's representations as to the goods create an express warranty. Some of the warranties overlap in their coverage when they jointly apply. For instance, under 2–313(1)(b) the seller's promise or affirmation of fact creates an express warranty. For its part, to be merchantable under 2–314(2)(f) the goods must conform to "the promise or affirmations of fact made on the container or label if any." Thus, promises or affirmations of facts on labels of goods sold by a merchant seller create both an express warranty and an implied warranty of merchantability. An overlap in warranty coverage usually does not matter when warranties can be disclaimed. All warranties other than express warranties can be disclaimed. 2–316(2), 2–312(2). The overlap matters only when a seller's representations create an express warranty, because express warranties once made cannot be disclaimed. 2–316(1).

A breach of warranty action has five elements. All but the last element have close counterparts to a negligence action in tort. First and obviously, there must be a warranty as to the goods. Second, the goods delivered must breach the relevant warranty. Because warranty liability is strict, the seller's breach need not be the result of its negligence. Third, the breach must result in injury to the buyer. Fourth, it must proximately cause the injury. Cf. Comment 13 to 2–314. Fifth, the buyer must give the seller timely notice of the breach. 2–607(3)(a). Article 2 assigns the burden of proving these elements according to whether the buyer has accepted the goods. If the buyer has accepted them, she bears the relevant burden of proof. 2–607(4). To recover, she therefore must prove all of the elements of the action. If she has rejected the goods or effectively revoked her acceptance, the seller must prove that the buyer does not have a breach of warranty action. In this case the seller therefore must prove that one or more of the elements of the action are missing.

Warranty litigation often focuses on the existence and scope of the seller's warranty as to the goods. Do the seller's statements as to the goods create an express warranty? Or do they instead merely express the seller's opinion or commendation? If a breach of implied warranties is at issue, the purposes to which the goods are "ordinarily" put under 2–314(2)(c) or whether the buyer's purpose is "particular" under 2–315 can be disputed. The meaning of the terms in these legal standards is not obvious or self-applying. To apply Article 2's warranty provisions in hard cases, a rationale for warranties is needed. An old rationale, sometimes still stated in some case law, is one of honoring the buyer's reasonable expectations. The buyer, it is said, is entitled to receive goods with qualities that she was reasonably led to expect. This rationale does not make Article 2's warranties easier to apply because it does not say what makes her expectations "reasonable." The seller can offer the buyer different priced sales contracts, according to how the risk of nonconformity in the goods is allocated between them. The sales contract concluded by the seller and buyer will have a price that reflects this allocation of risk. As a result, the buyer's "reasonable" expectations as to quality therefore will be sensitive to the contract price. These expectations do not determine what warranties the seller has made to the buyer. Because the buyer's expectations are determined at least in part by the warranties or other risk-allocation provisions it pays for, it is circular to say that the warranties determine the buyer's expectations. For this reason, the buyer's reasonable expectation is not a standard that helps apply Article 2's warranty provisions.

A more helpful rationale for warranties is comparative risk-reduction. Warranties have an economic function. The risk of a nonconformity in the goods is a cost that either the seller or the buyer must bear (at least between themselves). The parties prefer to allocate that risk to the party who can reduce or eliminate it at the least cost, because doing so reduces the cost of the contract and therefore increases the joint surplus from the contract. The risk of nonconformity in the goods can be reduced or eliminated in either of two ways: by reducing or preventing the nonconformity from occurring in the first place or by insuring against loss resulting from its occurrence. Allocating the nonconformity risk to the party better able to reduce or prevent the risk clearly reduces its cost. But insuring against the risk does not merely shift the cost of the nonconformity. It reduces cost too by shifting the nonconformity risk away from the party for whom the risk is a disutility. See George L. Priest, A Theory of Consumer Product Warranty, 90 Yale L. J. 1297 (1981). Nonconformity risk is a disutility to parties who are risk-averse with respect to it. Risk-averse parties prefer to incur a fixed and certain cost (the insurance premium) to a cost having the same expected value but which is variable and uncertain (the insured-against event). The disutility of the expected cost to them is greater than the disutility of the certain cost. A .5 chance of losing $10 and a .5 chance of losing nothing has the same expected value ($5) as the certainty of losing $5. A party who prefers to pay $5 rather than bear a risk of loss with an expected value of $5 is risk-averse with respect to the $5 loss. Nonconformity risk is reduced when the risk-averse party incurs a certain cost (the premium) and the variance of the actual cost is shifted away from her. Although consumer buyers usually are thought to be risk-averse with respect to purchases that risk large-dollar loss, commercial buyers can be too. Not all commercial buyers are corporations, which have limited liability. In addition, managers of commercial buyers can have undiversified investments in their firms which make them risk-averse with respect to the firm's losses.

The rationale of comparative risk-reduction finds a warranty when the seller has a comparative advantage over the buyer at reducing or eliminating a risk of nonconformity in the goods. Sellers often have superior information about the qualities of the goods they are selling. They know the capacities of the goods and their suitability to meet the ordinary needs of buyers. In addition, sellers are in a better position than their buyers to take measures to improve the qualities of the goods they sell. Finally, sellers are more likely than buyers to know the overall defect rates of their goods based on multiple sales of the same type of good. Thus, sellers can include in the price of every good they sell a cost that reflects the risk that the good will be defective. That cost serves as an insurance premium that buyers pay when they purchase the good. Buyers for whom nonconformity risk is a disutility prefer to reduce the risk by paying the seller the premium to bear it. For these reasons, unless otherwise indicated, sellers warrant qualities in the goods for which they have a comparative advantage at risk-reduction. The rationale of risk-reduction, however, does not resolve all cases in which a warranty or its content is at issue, and most courts do not rely explicitly on the rationale. But it provides some basis for applying Article 2's warranty provisions in some hard cases.

B. EXPRESS WARRANTIES

Section 2–313 governs express warranties. Under 2–313 an express warranty is created when two requirements are met. First, the seller must make a representation or promise which relates to the goods. The representation may be an affirmation of fact, a description of the goods, or a sample or model. 2–313(1)(a)–(c). Opinions or commendations of the goods, or affirmations about the good's value, are not representations that create an express warranty. 2–313(2). Second, the representation or promise relating to the goods must form the "basis of the bargain." 2–313(1)(a)–(c). Neither requirement is transparent, and litigation frequently focuses on both conditions.

The first requirement requires that representations or promises relating to the goods be distinguished from opinions or commendations about the goods ("puffing"). To draw the distinction, courts often look to features of the seller's language, including its generality and formality. General statements about the goods, other things being equal, express opinions or commendations, while specific statements as to the goods are representations. A statement that the goods are for "today, tomorrow and beyond" might not be specific enough to create an express warranty as to future performance. See, e.g., In re Toshiba America HD DVD Marketing and Sales Practices Litig., 69 UCC Rep. Serv.2d 1085 (D.N.J. 2009). Oral statements are less likely than written statements to be representations or promises and more likely to express the seller's opinion. See, e.g., Federal Signal Corp. v. Safety Factors, Inc., 886 P.2d 172, 179 (Alaska 1994). None of these linguistic features is decisive. Courts also look to the context in which the language is used. A manufacturer's statement that its computer monitor displayed "millions of colors" is a representation relating to the goods when the statement appears among the technical specifications in the manufacturer's web site, even when the phrase was not itself specific. See Sanders v. Apple, Inc., 672 F.Supp.2d 978 (N.D. Cal. 2009). And a manufacturer of amplifiers' statement that the goods are "free from defects in materials and workmanship" appears to be specific. Nonetheless, the statement does not create an express warranty against low frequency oscillations when the buyer had submitted electrical specifications for the amplifiers and was aware that the material used was prone to the oscillations. See Scientific Components Corp. v. Sirenza Microdevices, Inc., 73 UCC Rep. Serv.2d 1 (2d Cir. 2010).

In distinguishing representations from opinions, the comparative risk-reduction rationale for warranties sometimes is helpful. The rationale asks whether the buyer could infer that the seller was agreeing to bear the risk of nonconformity in the goods, based on its statement about them. Where the seller's statement relates to qualities in the goods about which the seller has superior information or risk-reducing capacity, the statement is a representation relating to the goods. Otherwise, it is an expression of the seller's opinion or commendation about them. A manufacturer of computer monitors has superior knowledge about the color resolution of its monitors. At the same time, the amplifier manufacturer is no better position than its buyer at eliminating low frequency oscillations that apparently can accompany amplifiers made according to the buyer's specifications. So the former seller's statement ("millions of colors") is a representation relating to the computer monitors, while the latter seller's statement ("free from defects in materials and workmanship") is not a representation that the amplifiers will be free of low frequency oscillations.

Section 2–313's second requirement, that the representation form the "basis of the bargain," is opaque. Courts basically take three different positions on the meaning of this phrase. One position interprets "the basis of the bargain" as reliance. The seller's affirmation of fact, description or promise is part of the basis of the bargain if the buyer relies on it by agreeing to the contract or by acting on the promise. This understanding fits with the conventional meaning given to the phrase. Most courts adopt this "reliance required" view. The second position is that "the basis of the bargain" does not mean reliance. Rather, all affirmations of fact, descriptions or promises made as part of the contract form the basis of the bargain. The view is supported by some history. The relevant language was drafted against the background of language in the express warranty provision in section 12 of the Uniform Sales Act. This provision stated in relevant part: "[a]ny affirmation of act or any promise by the seller relating to the goods is an express warranty if the natural tendency of such affirmation or promise is to induce the buyer to purchase the goods, and if the buyer purchases the goods *relying thereon*" (emphasis added). In substituting "the basis of the bargain" language for "relying thereon," 2–313's drafters signaled that reliance was not needed to create an express warranty. The difficulty with this view is that it does not say what "the basis of the bargain" requires. The phrase cannot just mean that the seller's affirmation, description or promise relates to the goods. After all, an affirmation, description or promise relating to the goods does not by itself create an express warranty. In addition, 2–313 requires that they form "the basis of the bargain." It is not apparent what the phrase means other than reliance.

The third position understands "the basis of the bargain" to create a presumption of reliance that the seller must rebut by a showing of non-reliance. The view does not deny that "the basis of the bargain" means reliance. By requiring the seller to show the buyer's non-reliance, it simply eases the buyer's burden of proving reliance. Comment 3 to 2–313 supports a presumption of reliance: "In actual practice affirmations of fact made by the seller about the goods during a bargain are regarded as part of the description of those goods; hence no particular reliance on such statements need be shown in order to weave them into the fabric of the agreement. Rather, any fact which is to take such affirmations, once made, out of the agreement requires clear affirmative proof." See also Comment 8 to 2–313. Views that take this position vary according to when the seller must rebut the buyer's reliance. For instance, according to Cippolone v. Liggett Group, Inc., 893 F.2d 541 (3d Cir. 1990), the buyer must establish that it was aware of the seller's representation or promise at the time of the agreement. It must demonstrate reliance on the seller's representation or promise relating to the goods only if the seller has established that the buyer did not believe the representation or promise. If the buyer has shown that it was aware of the seller's representation or promise, and the seller does not establish the buyer's non-belief, the case ends. The buyer does not have to demonstrate its reliance on the seller's representation or promise it did not believe.

Requiring reliance has an economic justification: the requirement encourages the seller to disclose information about the goods that is potentially valuable to the buyer. The seller's representations or promises relating to the goods give the buyer information it might lack. This information can increase the value the buyer places on the goods, by apprizing her of qualities of which she might otherwise be unaware or have difficulty discovering. Without a reliance requirement, the seller's representations or promises are enough to create an express warranty. This increases the seller's expected liability under the contract because she bears the risk that the goods will not conform to her representations or promises. A reliance requirement reduces the seller's expected liability because it creates an additional barrier to the creation of an express warranty. Because the seller's liability is a cost to it, reducing the seller's cost from making representations or promises about the goods encourages her to make more of them. As a result, a reliance requirement encourages the seller's representations or promises, which gives valuable information to the buyer. Without a reliance requirement, the seller will reduce its expected liability by making fewer representations or promises and therefore giving the buyer less information.

The two cases below concern 2–313's two requirements for an express warranty, respectively. *Boud v. SDNCO, Inc.* applies 2–313's requirement that the seller make representations or promises relating to the goods, and *Rogath v. Siebenmann* interprets 2–313's "basis of the bargain" requirement.

Boud v. SDNCO, Inc.

Supreme Court of Utah, 2002
54 P.3d 1131

■ DURRANT, ASSOCIATE CHIEF JUSTICE:

Introduction

Appellant Joseph Boud seeks rescission of his contractual agreement to purchase a luxury yacht from appellee KCS International, Inc., dba Cruisers Yachts ("Cruisers"), because of mechanical and electrical problems with the yacht. Boud appeals the district court's grant of summary judgment in favor of Cruisers. This case presents three main questions. First, did a sales brochure containing a photograph of the model Boud purchased and an accompanying caption describing the yacht create an express warranty, and if so, was that express warranty disclaimed? Second, did Cruisers engage in deceptive sales practices by including the photograph and caption in its sales brochure? Third, did the photograph and accompanying caption constitute negligent misrepresentations?

We conclude that an express warranty was not created by the brochure and that even were this the case, the parties' written contract effectively disclaimed any warranty other than the limited warranty provided for in the contract itself. Because no express warranty was created, we further conclude that Boud's allegations that Cruisers engaged in deceptive sales practices or made negligent misrepresentations also fail. We therefore affirm the district court's decision granting summary judgment in favor of Cruisers.

Background

* * *

In December 1998, Boud visited Wasatch Marine, a Salt Lake City retailer run by SDNCO, Inc., that sells yachts manufactured by Cruisers. Wasatch Marine gave Boud a copy of Cruisers' 1999 sales brochure. Boud read and reviewed this brochure, paying particular attention to a page that contained a photograph of Cruisers' 3375 Esprit model apparently moving at a high rate of speed. Accompanying the photograph was a caption that read as follows:

Offering the best performance and cruising accommodations in its class, the 3375 Esprit offers a choice of either stern drive or inboard power, superb handling and sleeping accommodations for six.

Due in part to the depictions in the brochure, Boud agreed to buy a 3375 Esprit model yacht for over $150,000. In late December 1998, he put down a $15,000 deposit and agreed to take delivery of the yacht in the spring of 1999. On May 10, 1999, Boud paid the balance of the sales price; he then took the yacht for a test drive and signed a sales contract on May 20. This contract indicated that Boud would receive a $476 refund, as he had overpaid. During the test drive on May 20, 1999, and a subsequent test drive approximately a week later, the yacht manifested several electrical and mechanical problems. Pursuant to a limited warranty that accompanied the written contract, Wasatch Marine serviced the yacht and attempted to fix the problems.

A subsequent test drive of the yacht in early June revealed that problems still existed with the yacht. Boud claims that these problems included (1) difficulty shifting gears, (2) the system alarm going off at idling speed, (3) partial failure of the air conditioning system, (4) unexplained sounding of the carbon monoxide detector, (5) a malfunctioning generator, and (6) misalignment of the rear door. Due to these mechanical problems, Boud sought to rescind the sales agreement. Cruisers responded by offering to repair or replace any defective parts as per the limited warranty. Boud then commenced this action.

In his amended complaint, Boud relied on three independent theories. First, he argued that the photograph and caption were themselves an express warranty, and that Cruisers and Wasatch Marine failed to provide him with a yacht that satisfied that warranty. Second, he asserted that, by putting forth the photograph and caption, Cruisers had engaged in deceptive sales practices in violation of section 13–11–4 of the Utah Code. Finally, Boud alleged that the photograph and accompanying language amounted to negligent misrepresentations made by Cruisers.

The district court heard arguments on Cruisers' motion for summary judgment and granted the motion on the ground that the materials in the brochure amounted to mere sales talk, or puffery, which could not give rise to an express warranty. The court further concluded that because the referenced portion of the brochure was not specific enough to create an express warranty, Boud's alternative arguments also failed. Boud appeals these rulings, and we have jurisdiction pursuant to Utah Code section 78–2–2(3)(j) (1996).

Analysis

I.   Issues Presented/Standard of Review

On appeal, Boud claims that the district court erred in three respects. First, he argues that the district court erred in ruling that the photograph and caption in Cruisers' sales brochure did not amount to an express warranty. Second, he maintains that the district court should have found that Cruisers engaged in deceptive sales practices in violation of section 13–11–4 of the Utah Commercial Code. Finally, Boud contends that the district court incorrectly concluded that the photograph and caption did not constitute negligent misrepresentations. * * *

II.   Boud May Not Rely on the Photograph and Caption As an Express Warranty

The district court concluded that the photograph and caption contained in Cruisers' brochure did not provide an express warranty on which Boud could rely. We agree for two reasons.

A.   The Photograph and Accompanying Caption Did Not Create an Express Warranty

The creation of express warranties by affirmation or promise is governed by section 70A–2–313 of the Utah Code, which adopts the Uniform Commercial Code's provisions governing express warranties. Subsection 70A–2–313(1)(a), which governs promotional materials, states that an "affirmation of fact or promise made by [a] seller . . . [that] becomes part of the basis of [a] bargain creates an express warranty." Utah Code Ann. § 70A–2–313(1)(a) (1999). The next subsection places a limitation on this rule, however; it states that an "affirmation merely of the value of the goods or a statement purporting to be merely the seller's opinion or commendation of the goods does not create [an express] warranty."[1] Id. § 70A–2–313(2) (emphasis added). Thus, the determination of whether an express warranty has been created ultimately hinges upon an examination of whether representations made by the seller were mere statements of opinion or were, rather, promises or affirmations of fact. In order to make this determination, we must examine the actual language and images set forth in Cruisers' brochure.

To qualify as an affirmation of fact, a statement must be objective in nature, i.e., verifiable or capable of being proven true or false. Similarly, to be relied upon as a promise, a statement must be highly specific or definite. The photograph and caption contained in Cruisers' brochure are not objective or specific enough to qualify as either facts or promises; the statements made in the caption are merely opinions, and

---

[1]   At the district court's hearing on Cruisers' motion for summary judgment, counsel for Cruisers quoted Hirschberg Optical Co. v. Dalton, Nye & Cannon Co., 7 Utah 433, 27 P. 83 (1891), for a definition of the term "puffing." The quoted section of that case reads as follows: The general praise of his own wares by a seller, commonly called "puffing," for the purpose of enhancing them in the buyer's estimation, has always been allowed; provided it is kept within reasonable bounds; that is, provided the praise is general, and the language is not the positive affirmation of a specific fact affecting the quality, so as to be an express warranty . . . Id. at 436 (internal quotation and citation omitted).

the photograph makes no additional assertions with regard to the problems of which Boud has complained.

Thus, Hirschberg Optical set forth a test that distinguishes an express warranty from puffing on the basis of whether the seller's statements were specific or general. Under the Utah Commercial Code, which was adopted after Hirschberg Optical and governs this case, the dispositive test focuses on whether the statements qualify as fact or mere opinion. See Utah Code Ann. § 70A–2–313 (1999). Often, looking at the specificity of the statements will prove useful in applying this test. In the present case, however, objective measurability is the dispositive factor in distinguishing fact from opinion.

Cruisers' brochure contains language characteristic of an opinion. Specifically, its assertions that the 3375 Esprit offers the "best performance" and "superb handling" rely on inherently subjective words. See Royal Bus. Machs., Inc. v. Lorraine Corp., 633 F.2d 34, 42 (7th Cir. 1980) ("General statements to the effect that goods are 'the best' . . . are generally regarded as expressions of the seller's opinion or 'the puffing of his wares' and do not create an express warranty." While representations that a boat is "fastest in its class" or "most powerful in its class" could be objectively tested for their truth and could therefore qualify as affirmations of fact, an assertion that a boat is "best in its class" cannot. See id. The word "best" is a description that must ultimately be measured against some opinion or other imprecise standard, and "superb" is a near synonym subject to the same qualification. Cf. Martin Rispens & Son v. Hall Farms, Inc., 621 N.E.2d 1078, 1083 (Ind. 1993) ("The statement 'top quality seeds' is a 'classic example of puffery.'). Similarly, "performance" is not a single quality, but rather embodies numerous qualities a boat may possess, and different people may place different weight on each individual quality. Reasonable people could therefore disagree and legitimately argue that several different boats in a given class perform "best" based on personal preferences that would be impossible to discount or disprove. As such, it would be unreasonable as a matter of law for anyone to rely on such a statement as one of fact. Accordingly, the language contained in the caption at issue is a mere statement of opinion.

Moreover, because the photograph does not make any factual representations with respect to the problems Boud has alleged, it does not create an express warranty on which Boud could sustain his claims. While the photograph depicts a boat moving across a body of water, it makes no representations regarding mechanical or electrical systems; nor does it provide any representations as to quality or reliability.

Consequently, we agree with the district court that the brochure lacks the specificity necessary to have created an express warranty. The proper source of redress for the yacht's mechanical and electrical problems is the limited warranty.

B. By Signing the Contract, Boud Disclaimed Any Express Warranty That Might Have Been Created and Agreed That the Contract Was an Integration of the Final Terms of the Parties' Agreement

Even if we were to conclude that the photograph and caption created an express warranty, Boud disclaimed any express warranty that might have been created during the negotiation process by signing the written sales agreement. This court has held that "terms that might otherwise be considered a basis of the bargain are not express warranties if the final written contract effectively disclaims and/or excludes any such warranties." Rawson v. Conover, 2001 UT 24, P56, 20 P.3d 876 (Utah 2001).

The contract entered into between the parties included the following language directly above the signature line on which Boud signed:

Purchaser agrees that his contract includes all of the terms, conditions and warranties on both the face and reverse side hereof, that this agreement cancels and supersedes any prior agreement and as of the date hereof comprises the complete and exclusive statement of the terms of the agreement relating to the subject matter covered hereby. PURCHASER BY HIS/HER EXECUTION OF THIS AGREEMENT ACKNOWLEDGES THAT HE/SHE HAS READ ITS TERMS, CONDITIONS AND WARRANTIES BOTH ON THE FACE AND THE REVERSE SIDE HEREOF AND A [SIC] HAS RECEIVED A TRUE COPY OF THIS AGREEMENT, AND FURTHER AGREES TO PAY THE 'BALANCE DUE' SET FORTH ABOVE ON OR BEFORE THE DATE SPECIFIED.

Further, the contract clearly stated the following in bold capital letters:

NO WARRANTIES, EXPRESS OR IMPLIED, ARE MADE OR WILL BE DEEMED TO HAVE BEEN MADE BY EITHER SELLER OR THE MANUFACTURER OF THE NEW MOTOR VEHICLE . . . EXCEPTING ONLY THE CURRENT PRINTED WARRANTY . . . WHICH WARRANTY IS INCORPORATED HEREIN AND . . . A COPY OF WHICH WILL BE DELIVERED TO PURCHASER AT THE TIME OF DELIVERY . . . AND THE REMEDIES SET FORTH IN SUCH WARRANTY WILL BE THE ONLY REMEDIES AVAILABLE . . . . .

Boud argues that he is not bound by this disclaimer because (1) evidence of prior terms should replace the limited warranty, (2) he signed the contract under duress, and (3) the contract was not accompanied by adequate consideration. We reject each of these arguments. We conclude that, by signing the sales contract, Boud certified that he accepted the limited warranty provision and disclaimed any prior express warranty that might have been created.

1.   The Parole Evidence Rule Precludes the Introduction of Contradictory Terms

To begin with, Boud's attacks on the validity of the sales contract fail because the parole evidence rule precludes a search for additional or contradictory terms outside of the four corners of a written contract absent some proof of fraud or mistake. See Semenov v. Hill, 1999 Utah 58, P12, 982 P.2d 578 ("The general rule pertaining to acceptance of an offer by signing is that 'where a person signs a document, he is not permitted to show that he did not know its terms, and in the absence of fraud or mistake he will be bound by all its provisions, even though he has not read the agreement and does not know its contents.' ").

No evidence of fraud or mistake has been presented in this case; Boud therefore cannot avoid the effect of the parol evidence rule nor claim that the parties agreed to any terms other than those included in the written contract. * * *

III. Because the Photograph and Caption Fail to Create an Express Warranty, They do not Constitute Material Representations That Would Implicate Deceptive Sales Practices or Negligent Misrepresentations.

With respect to his assertions that Cruisers engaged in deceptive sales practices and made negligent misrepresentations, Boud has conceded in this appeal as well as to the district court that the validity of all three of his arguments hinges on his claim that the language and photograph in the brochure were specific enough to create an express warranty. Because we have determined that the photograph and caption did not create an express warranty, Boud's alternative arguments fail as a result of his concession.[2] We therefore affirm the district court's decision to grant summary judgment in favor of Cruisers.

Conclusion

We conclude that the photograph and caption contained in Cruisers' sales brochure were mere statements of opinion and did not create an express warranty. Moreover, even if they did, because Boud signed the written sales contract and thereby accepted the limited warranty associated with it, he expressly disclaimed any prior express warranty. Finally, because Boud has conceded that his alternative arguments depend upon his claim that the brochure created an express warranty, we hold that his causes of action for deceptive sales practices under the Utah Consumer Sales Practices Act and negligent misrepresentation also fail. For all these reasons, the decision of the district court is affirmed. * * *

NOTES

1.   Does the *Boud* court find the statements in Cruiser's brochure, "best performance" and "superb handling," to be general statements and therefore presumptively to express Cruiser's opinions about the yacht it was selling? Or does it find that the Cruiser's statements depend on subjective standards and therefore presumptively to express Cruiser's opinion about the yacht's qualities? Suppose Cruiser in its brochure had called its yacht "the fastest yacht being sold." Is the statement any less general than "best performance" or "superb handling"? The court in Keith v. Buchanan, 173 Cal.App.3d 13 (1985), deemed the seller's statement that its yacht was "seaworthy" an affirmation of fact. Is the seller's representation a general statement? Or is it a statement dependent on an objective standard?

---

[2]   Because we base our conclusion regarding Boud's alternative arguments on Boud's concession that his alternative claims fail if the brochure did not create an express warranty, we do not reach the issues of whether deceptive sales practices and negligent misrepresentation claims can exist in the absence of an express warranty or whether a signed disclaimer such as the one contained in this contract is sufficient to preclude deceptive sales practices or negligent misrepresentation claims.

By making general statements, sellers might be undertaking to bear the risk of nonconformity if the goods lack the qualities represented in those statements. A general statement simply increases a seller's prospective liability compared with a specific statement. By contrast, a statement whose verification depends on a subjective standard exposes the seller to ex post strategic exploitation by the buyer should litigation occur. Subjective standards are hard to verify, and the seller therefore runs the risk that the buyer might convince a trier of fact to erroneously conclude that the goods didn't meet that standard. This allows the buyer largely to control the extent of the seller's prospective liability. Sellers are unlikely to agree to terms which expose them to exploitation ex post by the buyer. Absent contrary evidence, sellers therefore are unlikely to agree to bear nonconformity risks that depend on subjective standards. Thus, buyers cannot reasonably infer from seller's statements dependent on these standards that the statements are affirmations of fact relating to the goods.

2.   Courts sometimes recite the proposition that whether a statement constitutes a warranty or merely an opinion depends on the circumstances of the sale and the type of goods. See, e.g., Sessa v. Riegle, 427 F. Supp. 760, 765 (E.D. Pa. 1977). This obvious observation acknowledges that nonlinguistic factors are relevant to the character of a statement as a warranty or an opinion. Two nonlinguistic factors important for courts are the buyer's expertise in dealing with goods of the type it is purchasing and the predictability of the product or detectability of defects in it. One or both of these factors explain most (but not all) case outcomes in which the character of a statement is at issue. For cases involving sales of horses in which these factors appear relevant to whether the seller's statements create an express warranty, see *Sessa*, supra ("the horse is sound" not an express warranty; buyer experienced and defects in horse difficult to detect), Nelson v. Heuckeroth, 1978 U.S. Dist. LEXIS 14996, at *1 (S.D.N.Y. 1978) ("suitable for use as a show horse" creates express warranty; buyer inexperienced); but see Simpson v. Widget, 709 A.2d 1366 (N.J. Super. Ct. 1998) ("sound horse" creates express warranty that horse is "servicably sound;" buyer experienced).

3.   To create an express warranty under 2–313(1), the affirmation of fact, description or promise must "relate to the goods." Thus, a breach of representation or promise under the sales contract that is unrelated to the goods is not a breach of an express warranty. For instance, a promise that replacement products will be readily available is unrelated to the product being sold. See Royal Business Machs. v. Lorraine Corp., 633 F.2d 34 (7th Cir. 1980). It therefore does not create an express warranty under 2–313(1). Closer cases involve a seller's remedial promises related to the goods sold, such as a promise to repair or replace defective goods. While the promise "relates to the goods," it does not promise that the goods will perform or have particular qualities. Rather, a repair or replace clause simply promises to remedy a nonconformity if the goods fail to perform or have particular qualities promised. Although 2–313(1) does not expressly require that the promise relating to the goods undertake that the goods have particular qualities, the majority of courts understand 2–313(1) to do so. Accordingly, they hold that remedial promises do not create express warranties of quality. See Cosman v. Ford Motor Co., 674 N.E.2d 61, 67 (Ill. Ct. App. 1996).

The distinction between warranties and remedial promises matters because of Article 2's statute of limitations. Article 2's limitations period is four years. See 2–725(1). Under 2–725(1) this period begins to run when a cause of action accrues. A cause of action accrues, according to 2–725(2), when breach occurs. For most breaches of warranty, breach occurs on tender of deliver to the buyer. 2–725(2). The exception to this general rule is for warranties that explicitly extend to future performance. In this case the cause of action accrues when the breach is or should have been discovered. If remedial promises are warranties, the accrual of the cause of action for breach is determined by either 2–725(2)'s general rule (tender of delivery) or its future performance exception (discovery of breach). However, if they are not warranties, 2–725(2)'s exception does not apply and the cause of action therefore accrues on breach. Breach probably occurs on the seller's refusal or failure to perform the remedial promise.

The result has a practical consequence. Because remedial promises usually come with time limits, a cause of action for breach of the remedial promise accrues at a later date than if the promise were a warranty with the same time limits. To illustrate, assume that the seller of a refrigerator warrants the refrigerator's motor against failure for one year after purchase. The warranty explicitly extends to future performance and 2–725(2)'s future performance exception therefore applies. Thus, 2–725(1)'s limitation period begins to run from the time of discovery of breach within one year of the purchase. Now assume instead that the seller promises to repair or replace the refrigerator's motor if it fails within one year of the refrigerator's purchase. The seller gives no warranty. Section 2–725(2)'s future performance exception does not apply because the seller's remedial promise is not a warranty. Instead, according to 2–725(2), the buyer's cause of action accrues on breach. Breach probably occurs when the seller refuses or is unable to repair or replace the refrigerator's motor on failure within the year of the refrigerator's purchase. Section 2–725(1)'s four-year limitations period begins to run from this date. The seller's refusal or failure to honor its remedial promise occurs after the buyer discovers that the refrigerator's motor has failed. Thus, the buyer's cause of action for breach of the seller's remedial promise accrues after its cause of action for breach of the seller's warranty. For a concise description of the division in judicial interpretations of 2–725, see Larry T. Garvin, Uncertainty and Error in the Law of Sales: The Article Two Statute of Limitations, 83 B.U. L. Rev. 345 (2003).

4. It is common for buyers to seek recovery based on various tort theories as alternatives to warranty liability. Frequently the buyer's complaint includes allegations of fraud, negligent or innocent misrepresentation, and sometimes strict liability. Tort and express warranty liability overlap because facts that create liability also can create tort liability. For instance, a seller is liable for fraudulently misrepresenting a fact about the goods if the buyer suffers financial loss resulting from its reliance on the seller's intentional misrepresentation of the fact. See Restatement (Second) of Torts § 525 (1977). The seller also is liable for breach of an express warranty on the same facts. Even if the seller's misrepresentations are unintended, the buyer can recover in tort based on the seller's innocent misrepresentations. The same facts constitute a breach of the seller's express warranty. See Restatement (Second) of Torts § 552C Comment b (1977) ("[M]ost of the innocent misrepresentations made actionable by this Section would also be actionable under the Code [i.e., Article 2 of the UCC] on the theory of breach of warranty"). In *Boud* the buyer's allegation that Cruiser was liable for negligently misrepresenting the yacht's condition failed for the same reason its warranty allegation failed: Cruiser's statements were expressions of opinion, not representations of fact. The overlap between tort and warranty liability can be harmless, as in *Boud*. It matters when burdens of proof, limitations periods and recoverable damages differ. Chapter 6 takes up this issue in connection with the economic loss rule.

Rogath v. Siebenmann

United States Court of Appeals, Second Circuit, 1997
129 F.3d 261

■ MCLAUGHLIN, CIRCUIT JUDGE:

Background

This case revolves around a painting, entitled "Self Portrait," supposedly painted in 1972 by a well-known English artist, Francis Bacon.

In July 1993, defendant Werner Siebenmann sold the Painting to plaintiff David Rogath for $570,000. In the Bill of Sale, Siebenmann described the provenance of the Painting and warranted that he was the sole owner of the Painting, that it was authentic, and that he was not aware of any challenge to its authenticity.

Problems arose three months later when Rogath sold the Painting to Acquavella Contemporary Art, Inc., in New York, for $950,000. Acquavella learned of a challenge to the Painting's authenticity and, on November 1, 1993, requested that Rogath refund the $950,000 and take back the Painting. Rogath did so, and then sued Siebenmann in the Southern District of New York (Batts, J.) for breach of contract, breach of warranty and fraud.

Rogath moved for partial summary judgment on the breach of warranty claims, and the district court granted his motion. The court concluded that (1) Siebenmann was unsure of the provenance of the Painting when he sold it to Rogath; (2) he was not the sole owner of the Painting; and (3) when he sold the Painting to Rogath he already knew of a challenge to the Painting's authenticity by the Marlborough Fine Art Gallery in London. The court awarded Rogath $950,000 in damages, the price at which he had sold it to Acquavella. The court dismissed, sua sponte, Rogath's remaining claims for fraud and breach of contract "in light of the full recovery on the warranties granted herein." Finally, a few days later, the court denied Rogath's motion to attach the money that Siebenmann had remaining from the proceeds of the initial sale to Rogath.

Siebenmann appeals the grant of partial summary judgment. Rogath cross-appeals the denial of his motion for attachment and the dismissal of his fraud and breach of contract claims.

Discussion

Siebenmann concedes that his promises and representations set forth in the Bill of Sale constitute warranties under New York law. He claims, however, that Rogath was fully aware when he bought the Painting that questions of authenticity and provenance had already been raised regarding the Painting. He maintains that, under New York law, Rogath therefore cannot rest claims for breach of warranty on the representations made in the Bill of Sale.

We review de novo the district court's disposition of Rogath's motion for partial summary judgment. The parties agree that New York law applies.

A.   Breach of Warranty under New York Law

The Bill of Sale provides:

In order to induce David Rogath to make the purchase, Seller . . . makes the following warranties, representations and covenants to and with the Buyer.

1.   That the Seller is the sole and absolute owner of the painting and has full right and authority to sell and transfer same; having acquired title as described in a copy of the Statement of Provenance signed by Seller annexed hereto and incorporated herein; [and] that the Seller has no knowledge of any challenge to Seller's title and authenticity of the Painting. . . .

Because the Bill of Sale was a contract for the sale of goods, Rogath's breach of warranty claims are governed by Article Two of the Uniform Commercial Code ("UCC"). See N.Y.U.C.C. § 2–102. Section 2–313 of the UCC provides that "any description of the goods which is made part of the basis of the bargain creates an express warranty that the goods shall conform to the description." N.Y.U.C.C. § 2–313(1)(b).

Whether the "basis of the bargain" requirement implies that the buyer must rely on the seller's statements to recover and what the nature of that reliance requirement is are unsettled questions. Not surprisingly, this same confusion haunted the New York courts for a time.

Some courts reasoned that the buyer must have relied upon the accuracy of the seller's affirmations or promises in order to recover. See, e.g., City Mach. & Mfg. Co. v. A. & A. Mach. Corp., 1967 U.S. Dist. LEXIS 11140 (E.D.N.Y. 1967); Scaringe v. Holstein, 477 N.Y.S.2d 903, 904 (App. Div. 1984); Crocker Wheeler Elec. Co. v. Johns–Pratt Co., 51 N.Y.S. 793, 794 (App. Div. 1898).

Other courts paid lip service to a "reliance" requirement, but found that the requirement was met if the buyer relied on the seller's promise as part of "the basis of the bargain" in entering into the contract; the buyer need not show that he relied on the truthfulness of the warranties.

Finally, some courts reasoned that there is a "reliance" requirement only when there is a dispute as to whether a warranty was in fact given by the seller. These courts concluded that no reliance of any kind is required "where the existence of an express warranty in a contract is conceded by both parties." CPC Int'l, Inc. v. McKesson Corp., 513 N.Y.S.2d 319, 322 (Sup. Ct. 1987); see Ainger v. Michigan Gen. Corp., 476 F. Supp. 1209, 1226–27 (S.D.N.Y. 1979). In these cases, the buyer need establish only a breach of the warranty.

In 1990 New York's Court of Appeals dispelled much of the confusion when it squarely adopted the "basis of the bargain" description of the reliance required to recover for breach of an express warranty. In CBS Inc. v. Ziff–Davis Publishing Co., 553 N.E.2d 997 (N.Y. 1990), the court concluded that "this view of 'reliance'—i.e., as requiring no more than reliance on the express warranty as being a part of the bargain between the parties—reflects the prevailing perception of an action for breach of express warranty as one that is no longer grounded in tort, but essentially in contract." 553 N.E.2d at 1001. The court reasoned that "the critical question is not whether the buyer believed in the truth of the warranted information . . . but whether [he] believed [he] was purchasing the [seller's] promise [as to its truth]."

CBS was not decided on the basis of the UCC, probably because the sale of the magazine business at issue did not constitute the sale of goods. Nevertheless, the court relied heavily on UCC authorities, see *CBS*, 553 N.E.2d at 1000–001, expressly noting that "analogy to the Uniform Commercial Code is 'instructive'."

In 1992, in a case also involving the sale of a business, we followed the New York Court of Appeals and delineated fine factual distinctions in the law of warranties: a court must evaluate both the extent and the source of the buyer's knowledge about the truth of what the seller is warranting. "Where a buyer closes on a contract in the full knowledge and acceptance of facts disclosed by the seller which would constitute a breach of warranty under the terms of the contract, the buyer should be foreclosed from later asserting the breach. In that situation, unless the buyer expressly preserves his rights under the warranties . . . , we think the buyer has waived the breach." Galli v. Metz, 973 F.2d 145, 151 (2d Cir. 1992). The buyer may preserve his rights by expressly stating that disputes regarding the accuracy of the seller's warranties are unresolved, and that by signing the agreement the buyer does not waive any rights to enforce the terms of the agreement.

On the other hand, if the seller is not the source of the buyer's knowledge, e.g., if it is merely "common knowledge" that the facts warranted are false, or the buyer has been informed of the falsity of the facts by some third party, the buyer may prevail in his claim for breach of warranty. In these cases, it is not unrealistic to assume that the buyer purchased the seller's warranty "as insurance against any future claims," and that is why he insisted on the inclusion of the warranties in the bill of sale. *Galli*, 973 F.2d at 151.

In short, where the seller discloses up front the inaccuracy of certain of his warranties, it cannot be said that the buyer—absent the express preservation of his rights—believed he was purchasing the seller's promise as to the truth of the warranties. Accordingly, what the buyer knew and, most importantly, whether he got that knowledge from the seller are the critical questions.

1.   What Siebenmann Knew

Here, as the district court pointed out, Siebenmann, the seller, produced no evidence to contradict Rogath's evidence that Siebenmann knew of the cloud that hung over the Painting's authenticity before he sold it to Rogath. Siebenmann admits that he was told that the Marlborough Gallery was troubled by certain peculiarities of the Painting—including shiny black paint (as opposed to the matte black that Bacon apparently preferred) and the use of pink paint (which Bacon evidently did not use)—that suggested that Bacon was not the painter.

Siebenmann also admits that Julian Barran, a London art dealer, had earlier refused to buy the Painting because of doubts harbored by the Marlborough Gallery. Moreover, there was uncontroverted evidence that, on a prior occasion, Siebenmann's attempted sale of the Painting to a client of Robert Peter Miller, the owner of an art gallery in New York, was aborted when (1) Miller learned that the Marlborough had concerns about the Painting's authenticity, and (2) David Sylvester, a British art critic, advised Miller not to proceed with the purchase because of the Marlborough objection and because Sylvester himself was not sure of the authenticity of the Painting.

Finally, Siebenmann does not deny that in June 1993 he received a fax from Anita Goldstein, an art dealer in Zurich, Switzerland, stating that "everybody is afraid of the authenticity" of the Painting.

2.   What Siebenmann Told Rogath: Reasonable Inferences

In an affidavit in opposition to Rogath's motion for partial summary judgment, Siebenmann stated that "I spoke directly with David Rogath about the controversy created by the Marlborough Gallery towards this painting." He also said that, in a phone conversation with Rogath on July 13, 1993, "I specifically mentioned Marlborough Gallery and the 'problems' or the 'controversy' that it had produced for this painting. . . . Mr. Rogath brushed aside the Marlborough Gallery controversy. He told me he had experienced difficulties with this particular gallery in the past and did not consider them to be especially reputable." In his deposition, Siebenmann added that he told Rogath on the phone "that I had problems with the Marlborough Gallery."

Siebenmann also filed an affidavit from Ronald Alley, the curator of the Tate Gallery in London, England, and the author of a survey of Bacon's work as well as several other writings about Bacon. Alley stated:

> I was phoned by Mr David Rogath, hitherto unknown to me, who said that he was thinking of buying the painting and asked whether it was correct that I had seen it and thought it to be authentic. My reply, to the best of my recollection, can be summarized as follows: "It is a picture which did not pass through Marlborough Fine Art and is said to have a provenance which sounds quite plausible but is more or less impossible to check. Both Ms Beston of Marlborough Fine Art and David Sylvester say they don't think it is by Bacon, but Sylvester knows it only from a photograph. I flew to Geneva for the day to look at it in a warehouse and felt convinced it was genuine."

For his part, Rogath denied that he was aware of any challenges to the authenticity or provenance of the Painting before entering into the Bill of Sale. He stated in his affidavit:

> During our telephone conversation, Mr. Siebenmann did not tell me that the Marlborough Gallery had "questioned" or "reserved judgment" about the Painting, or had caused any "problems" or "controversy" concerning the Painting. He said nothing at all like that during the conversation. Neither did Mr. Alley, in our subsequent conversation, refer to any such matters. He certainly did not tell me that Ms. Beston and Mr. Sylvester "don't think it is by Bacon." In fact, I spoke with Mr. Alley after the inauthenticity of the Painting had become known to me. . . . Had either Mr. Siebenmann or Mr. Alley hinted to me that the Painting was of questioned authenticity, it would have been a "red flag" for me, as I had no desire to spend some $600,000 dollars to purchase a painting the authenticity of which was in dispute. . . .

Here, the Bill of Sale states that the warranties induced Rogath to buy the Painting, but Rogath did not "expressly preserve his rights" under the Bill of Sale, as required by Galli. See 973 F.2d at 150. Accordingly, exactly what Siebenmann told Rogath is clearly crucial. On the other hand, what Alley may have told Rogath about the authenticity and provenance of the Painting is immaterial. Only if the seller, Siebenmann himself, informed Rogath of doubts about the provenance or challenges to authenticity will Rogath be deemed to have waived any claims for breach of warranty arising from the written representations appearing in the Bill of Sale.

As Rogath emphasizes, Siebenmann nowhere specifically alleges that he informed Rogath of his doubts about the authenticity and provenance of the Painting. He merely alluded to the "controversy" or "problems" with the Marlborough Gallery. Still, Siebenmann's testimony, however ambiguous, may justify the inference that Rogath knew more than he now claims to have known when he entered into the Bill of Sale.

At the very least, there is indisputable ambiguity in the affidavits about the pivotal exchange between Rogath and Siebenmann. We are satisfied that genuine issues of fact persist. In this posture, we must draw all reasonable inferences in Siebenmann's favor. Accordingly, as regards the Marlborough challenge, summary judgment on Rogath's claims for breach of the warranties of provenance and no challenges to authenticity is inappropriate.

3.   What Sylvester Said

Sylvester's doubts about the Painting also cannot justify summary judgment for Rogath, but for different reasons. Siebenmann was aware that "Sylvester advised Miller not to proceed with the purchase of the Painting because of the 'Marlborough objection and that he wasn't sure himself of the authenticity of the painting.'" Siebenmann did not claim to have disclosed to Rogath Sylvester's statement. Indeed, in his affidavit opposing Rogath's summary judgment motion, Siebenmann stated that he did not consider Sylvester's doubts to be a challenge. Siebenmann's nondisclosure could constitute a breach of warranty—but only if Sylvester's statement was a "challenge" to authenticity. We conclude that the question of whether Sylvester's statement constituted a challenge poses factual issues for trial.

A contractual term is ambiguous where it may be ascribed "conflicting reasonable interpretations." Mellon Bank, N.A. v. United Bank Corp. of N.Y., 31 F.3d 113, 116 (2d Cir. 1994). "As a general matter, we have held that when a contract is ambiguous, its interpretation becomes a question of fact and summary judgment is inappropriate."

Although the parties apparently agree as to what Sylvester said, reasonable minds could differ as to whether what he said constituted a challenge apart from the Marlborough challenge. Sylvester's recommendation that the buyer not proceed "because of the Marlborough objection" could reasonably be interpreted as merely advice to heed the Marlborough challenge. Further, a rational juror could interpret the statement that "[Sylvester] wasn't sure" as evincing an ambivalence on the part of Sylvester that did not rise to the level of a challenge, especially given that Sylvester himself had not seen the Painting, but only photographs of it.

In this context, moreover, the term may well be a specialized one. It is hardly clear as a matter of law that "challenge" includes every mention by one person of the fact that a challenge has been made by another person (or, for example, that it would include Anita Goldstein's statement that "everybody is afraid of the authenticity" of the Painting). Nor is it clear as a matter of law whether the term "challenge" would include an expression of uncertainty by someone who had never seen the painting in question. If Siebenmann proffers art-industry or other evidence as to the meaning of this ambiguous contract term, its meaning will be a question for the jury at trial.

B.   No Alternate Basis for the Damages Award

The district court also concluded that Siebenmann breached the warranty of ownership of the Painting. The court did not specify, however, whether this breach contributed to the collapse of the resale to Acquavella. Was there a cause and effect relationship? We cannot say, based on the evidence before us, that the breach of this warranty resulted in the failed Acquavella sale and caused Rogath's damages.

It appears from the record that Acquavella was more concerned over whether Bacon was the painter than whether Siebenmann was the owner of the Painting. In aborting the sale, Acquavella sent to Rogath a copy of a fax from Valerie Beston, the managing director of the Marlborough Gallery, in which Beston opines at the outset of her letter that the Painting is an "outright fake." There is also some evidence that the Acquavella may have been concerned with the provenance of the Painting. In her letter, Beston goes on to describe the provenance as "dubious."

There is no evidence, however, that Acquavella's concern about Siebenmann's title to the Painting fueled the failed sale.

C.   Rogath's Cross–Appeal

The district court dismissed, sua sponte, Rogath's claims for fraud and breach of contract "in light of the full recovery on the warranties granted herein." In light of our vacatur of Rogath's award for breach of warranty, on remand to the district court we reinstate Rogath's claims for fraud and breach of contract. Finally, on remand Rogath, if so advised, is free to move for attachment, under Federal Rule of Civil Procedure 64.

Conclusion

The order granting Rogath's motion for partial summary judgment is vacated, and the case is remanded to the district court for disposition not inconsistent with this opinion.

NOTES AND QUESTIONS

1. The *Rogath* court relies on CBS v. Ziff–Davis Publishing, Inc. 553 N.E.2d 997 (N.Y. 1990) for the proposition that 2–313(1)'s "basis of the bargain" language requires reliance on the seller's representation or promise, not on the truth of the information in the representation or promise. Thus, the buyer can believe that the information is false but still rely on the seller's representation or promise as to its truth. As the court sees it, the critical issue is whether the buyer believed he was "purchasing the seller's promise." In purchasing the seller's promise, the buyer insures against the consequences of the information in the promise being false. The buyer relies on the seller to indemnify it if the information in the promise is false. It is not relying on the truth of the information in the promise.

Is the court's understanding of 2–313(1)'s "basis of the bargain" language consistent with principles of the general common law of contracts? In answering this question, consider the basic principle of the common law of contracts that contract liability is strict. This principle makes a seller potentially liable to its buyer for representations that are false or promises that are unfulfilled. Whether the buyer has relied on these representations or promises does not affect the seller's potential liability for breach. According to the *Rogath* court, only the promises that the buyer purchases form the basis of the bargain. Which of the seller's promises the buyer has purchased is a question of fact. By contrast, the common law of contracts makes the seller potentially liable for all its promises or representations in a valid contract.

2. The *Rogath* court identifies the seller's promises that the buyer purchases according to the source of the buyer's knowledge about the truth of the information in the promise. If the seller personally has disclosed facts that made representations in the contract untrue, the buyer has not purchased the seller's promise as to the truth of the representation. The buyer has "waived the breach," as the court puts it. A buyer who learns that the seller's representation is false from sources other than the seller still purchases the seller's promise. It has a breach of warranty action against the seller.

This distinction based on the buyer's source of knowledge seems questionable. Either the buyer has purchased the seller's promise as to the truth of information or not. If the promise has been purchased, the seller has insured the buyer against the consequences of the information in the promise being false. As a result, the buyer is indifferent as to the truth of the information. The source of the buyer's knowledge that the information in the seller's promise is false has no effect on its welfare or the likelihood it has purchased the seller's promise. On the other hand, if the buyer has not purchased the seller's promise, it remains uninsured (or remains self-insured) against the consequences of the information in the promise being false. Because it has "waived the breach," the buyer must take precautions or insure against the possibility that the information is false. The source of the buyer's knowledge that the information is false also does not affect its incentive to take precautions or obtain insurance. For these reasons, the buyer's source of knowledge does not identify the seller's promises the buyer has purchased.

3. In Coastal Power International Ltd. v. Transcontinental Capital Corp., 10 F. Supp.2d 345 (S.D.N.Y. 1998), Coastal Power purchased substantially all of the stock of CCEP, which owned a floating power plant. The purchase agreement contained the seller's representations and warranties, including the representation that no fact or condition has occurred before closing that could be expected to have a material adverse change. The purchase agreement required the seller to notify the buyer if any of the representations became untrue and conditioned the buyer's obligation to close on the accuracy of the representations. Coastal Power and CCEP signed the purchase agreement on December 30, 1994. On May 12, 1995 CCEP informed Coastal Power that the power plant's insurer was unlikely to continue to insure the plant past May 31 unless the plant's moorings were upgraded. Upgrading would be expensive. On May 30 Coastal Power and CCEP closed the purchase agreement. Later, Coastal Power modified the moorings and sued the seller of the stock in CCEP and others to recover for breach of the seller's representation. The court held that the buyer had waived its rights. Although the purchase agreement was not governed by Article 2 of the UCC, the court relied on *Rogath* as authority for its holding. Did Coastal Power waive its rights if the *Rogath* court's holding is applied to *Coastal Power*'s facts?

4. *Rogath*'s holding initially may seem inconsistent with the objective of placing the nonconformity risk on the party best positioned to avoid it. It discourages the efficient exchange of information because the buyer will fear that getting information from the seller will result in it bearing the risk of nonconformity. And if the buyer has already discovered that the information in the seller's representation or promise is false, it is well placed to avoid the risk. Nothing is gained by requiring the seller to disclose the information in order for it to avoid warranty liability. However, this conclusion is a bit too quick. From the point of view of contract administration, the *Rogath* court's distinction based on the buyer's source of knowledge makes some sense. The distinction provides a legal test for reliance that is easily verifiable and administrable. If courts must adjudicate what the buyer knew and when the buyer knew it, warranty litigation becomes complex and costly. A court can more easily determine what the seller personally disclosed to the buyer about the information in its promise. Promises accompanied by the seller's disclosure that information in them is false do not form the basis of the bargain; promises not accompanied by the disclosure form the basis of the bargain. The court's "disclosure" rule sometimes will place the nonconformity risk on a seller who is in the inferior position to avoid it. If the proof costs were zero, a better rule that looked to the buyer's knowledge could be devised. But *Rogath*'s disclosure rule might be defensible when proof costs are significant.

PROBLEM 5.1

XT mini computers have recently become the rage and are in short supply. Seller, an electronics dealer, was contacted by Buyer who was looking for XTs. Seller told Buyer that currently it did not have any in stock and getting Manufacturer to fill orders it had accepted for XTs was not guaranteed. However, Manufacturer had shipped 100 computers in route to Seller in response to Seller's order for XT mini computers. Seller offered to redirect the shipment to Buyer at a prepaid price of $400 per shipped computer. Because Buyer had to meet its own orders for XTs quickly, it agreed to Seller's offer and paid for the computers. When the shipment arrived in boxes marked "XT computers," Buyer discovered that the boxes contained only AB computers. AB computers have exactly the same capabilities as the XTs but somehow are not in demand. Has Seller made an express warranty as to the computers it redirected to Buyer? 2–313(1)(b). If so, what is the content of that warranty? If Seller has not expressly warranted that the computers Buyer received are XTs, has Seller made any other warranties to Buyer? 2–314(2)(a).

PROBLEM 5.2

Buyer bought a lawnmower from Seller. In negotiating the sale, Buyer asked Seller about the amount of oil that needed to be added to the gas used in the lawnmower. Seller told him that amount X was needed. Buyer was intent on purchasing the lawnmower, and Seller's information did not affect his decision to purchase in any way. In fact, the correct amount of oil to be added to lawnmower was Y, which is less than X. Buyer faithfully added amount X to the gas in its lawnmower. Doing so may or may not have reduced the lawnmower's resale value and may or may not have affected its useful life. What barriers are there to Buyer recovering from Seller based on a breach of express warranty? 2–313(1). Cf. Texsun Feed Yards, Inc. v. Ralston Purina Co., 447 F.2d 660 (5th Cir. 1971) (seller should have same liability for statements concerning use of product that it has for statements concerning the quality of the product sold). On another theory?

PROBLEM 5.3

Assume that in the sale described in Problem 5.2 neither the bill of sale nor the Seller said anything about the capacity of the lawnmower to cut tall grass. Buyer had no reason to inquire because dry weather kept her lawn short. When she later read the owner's manual that accompanied the lawnmower, she first learned that the mower had a setting that enabled it "to cut grass up to one foot tall." Buyer was disappointed when her mower was unable to cut her lawn when an unexpected wet season caused her grass to grow to 10 inches high. Has Seller expressly warranted the capacity of the lawnmower to cut grass of that height? 2–313(1), Comments 7 and 9 to 2–313, 2–209.

C. IMPLIED WARRANTY OF MERCHANTABILITY

Section 2–314 describes standards of quality that goods sold by a merchant seller must meet. These are standards of merchantability, and 2–314 defines a warranty of merchantability. The warranty of merchantability is implied. It therefore does not arise from any representation or promise made by the seller. Instead, the warranty arises from the seller's status as a merchant seller. Section 2–314(1) narrows the required merchant status. The seller must be a merchant "with respect to goods" of the kind sold. Not every seller engaged in business will be a merchant with respect to the goods of the kind it is selling. Section 2–314's warranty of merchantability only arises in sales made by sellers who are "professionals" in the goods they sell. See Comment 1 (third paragraph) to 2–104. The implied warranty of merchantability differs from 2–313's express warranty in two respects. First, unlike an express warranty, the implied warranty depends on the seller's merchant status. Second, unlike 2–313's express warranty, the implied warranty of merchantability does not require reliance by the buyer or "form the basis of the bargain."

Section 2–314(2) states the minimum quality standards the goods must meet. See 2–314(2) ("at least"), Comment 6 to 2–314. The subsection does not crisply define the standards of merchantability. By their terms, 2–314(2)'s required standards are conjunctive. Thus, to be merchantable the goods must meet all of the standards described in 2–314(2)(a)–(f). Section 2–314(2)'s two basic standards of merchantability are subsection (a)'s requirement that the goods "pass without objection in the trade under the contract description," and subsection (c)'s requirement that the goods "are fit for the ordinary purposes for which such goods are used." The standards described in the other subsections are redundant. Cf. 1 N.Y. Law Revision Commission, Report: Study of the Uniform Commercial Code 398–399 (1955). Subsection (f) is superfluous given 2–313: An express warranty is breached if the goods do not conform to the promise or affirmations of fact made on the container or label. Also, goods fail to meet subsection (e)'s standard because they are inadequately packaged or labeled or they will not pass without objection in the trade under the contract description. They therefore fail also to meet subsection (a)'s standard. Finally, goods that are below average quality under the contract description violate subsection (b)'s standard. But they therefore also violate subsection (a)'s "pass without objection in the trade" standard. In addition, goods that are below average quality under the contract description breach an express warranty created by description.

Subsections (a) and (c)'s standards probably are not redundant. Usually goods will meet or violate both standards at the same time. For instance, a good that is unfit for the ordinary purposes to which it is used usually will not pass without objection in the trade. This is because trade practice will likely reflect the preferences of buyers, and buyers want goods that serve the ordinary purposes for which they are bought. Trade practice that allows goods unsuitable for ordinary purposes risks a migration of buyers away from the product or a reduction in its price. However, the temporary unavailability of close substitutes could force buyers to continue to purchase goods that do not satisfy all of the ordinary purposes to which they are put but which now pass as unobjectionable in the trade. Industry-friendly inefficient regulations also could do so. Such possibilities are rare. Most cases litigated under 2–314 involve 2–314(2)(a) and (c). The choice of subsection remains useful when available evidence more directly goes to one subsection rather than the other. For instance, trade practice might be more precise than the vague contours of ordinary purposes. If so, goods might be more easily shown to be objectionable in the relevant trade than to be unsuited for ordinary purposes. For the same reason, available evidence sometimes makes one or more of the other subsections useful.

The comparative risk reduction rationale suggests that 2–314's implied warranty efficiently allocates nonconformity risk. By dealing in goods of the kind it is selling, the merchant seller learns a fair amount about the capacities of the goods. Certainly it usually knows more about their capacities than the buyer. At the same time, common knowledge informs the seller about the ordinary purposes to which the goods it is selling are put. Because the seller has superior knowledge with respect to the goods' capabilities, it is in a better position than the buyer to avoid or eliminate the risk that the goods will not suit the ordinary purposes to which goods of the type are put. It can invest to increase the quality of the goods so that they are more likely to suit those purposes. Risk-averse buyers will prefer their sellers to bear nonconformity risk, thereby reducing its cost by shifting the risk from a risk-averse to a risk-neutral party. For both reasons, most merchant sellers and their buyers prefer the merchant seller to bear the risk that the goods do not meet 2–314(2)'s standards of merchantability. Merchant sellers who for some reason know comparatively little about goods they are selling, or are otherwise disadvantaged at taking precautions against nonconformities in them, can shift nonconformity risk by disclaiming implied warranties.

Hodges v. Johnson

Supreme Court of Kansas, 2009
199 P.3d 1251

■ Opinion: DAVIS J.:

The small claims court granted judgment against a used-car dealer for the cost of replacing a defective air conditioner in a vehicle purchased by a consumer. The used-car dealer appealed the monetary award; the district court affirmed but denied the plaintiffs' request for attorney fees. Both parties appealed. The Court of Appeals reversed the district court, concluding that the implied warranty of merchantability "warrants the operation of major components that are necessary for the vehicle to operate" and that the air conditioner is not a major component of the used vehicle. We reverse the Court of Appeals, affirm the district court's decision affirming the small claims court, reverse the district court's decision regarding attorney fees, and remand the case to the district court for an assessment of those fees.

Facts

Jim Johnson owns a car dealership in Saline County that sells high-end, used vehicles. In January 2005, Johnson sold Dr. Merle Hodges and Melissa Hodges a 1995 Mercedes S320 with 135,945 miles for $17,020 (the sales price of $15,900 plus tax). Johnson had been driving the Mercedes as his personal vehicle for roughly 2 years before the sale. Johnson testified before the district court in this case that he told the Hodgeses when they purchased the Mercedes that it was a nice car in good condition. Dr. Hodges testified that Johnson said the car "was just pretty much a perfect car" and that Johnson "loved driving it."

At the time the Hodgeses bought the Mercedes from Johnson, there was no discussion about the operation of the air conditioning, heating, or other components of the vehicle. Both Dr. Hodges and Johnson testified that they had no reason to believe that the air conditioner did not work when the Mercedes was sold to the Hodgeses.

In February 2005, about a month after he had bought the car from Johnson, Dr. Hodges noticed that the vent in the Mercedes did not circulate cool air and that the car emitted a strange smell. In March of the same year, the Hodgeses noticed that the Mercedes' air conditioning did not work and contacted the Hodgeses' mechanic, Virgil Anderson. Anderson added Freon to the air conditioner. About a month later, the air conditioner again was not working; Anderson added more Freon. The Hodgeses contacted Johnson to notify him of the air conditioning problem, and Johnson told them that some older vehicles may need a yearly boost of Freon to work properly.

In May 2005, the air conditioner failed a third time. After checking the air conditioning system for leaks, Anderson informed the Hodgeses that the Mercedes' evaporator, condenser, and compressor needed to be replaced. Anderson explained that these repairs would cost approximately $3,000 to $4,000.

At some time around May 2005, a mechanic who worked for Anderson told the Hodgeses that Johnson had requested that the mechanic put a product called Super Seal into the Mercedes' air conditioner in May 2003 (when he was using the car as his personal vehicle). The mechanic explained that the use of Super Seal complicated the current repair of the air conditioner and that the mechanic personally would not recommend Super Seal or apply it unless requested.

Johnson testified that he did not recall any problems with the Mercedes' air conditioner after the mechanics added Super Seal in May 2003, though he could not recall whether additional Freon was added during that time. Johnson further testified that the air conditioning problem in 2003 only involved the car's evaporator.

Anderson identified the condenser as the main problem with the Mercedes' air conditioner in 2005. Anderson testified during the pendency of this case that he could not determine whether the problem with the Mercedes' air conditioner existed at the time that the Hodgeses bought the car from Johnson or occurred at some time later.

The Hodgeses asked Johnson to pay to repair the air conditioning unit in the Mercedes. Johnson refused.

Shortly thereafter, the Hodgeses filed an action in small claims court against Johnson, alleging he caused them damages of $3,474—Anderson's estimate of the repair costs. The small claims court found in favor of the Hodgeses and awarded them $3,474 damages, plus $56 in costs and interest.

Johnson appealed to the district court. After holding a de novo hearing, the district court also found in favor of the Hodgeses, noting that "while [Johnson] may not have known of the failure of the air conditioning unit[,] . . . there is an implied warranty of merchantability," and Johnson "is responsible to the plaintiffs to provide a car that is merchantable." The court therefore entered a judgment in favor of the Hodgeses for $3,474, together with costs of $56 plus interest. The court found that attorney fees were not warranted because Johnson's actions did not rise "to a level of misrepresentation."

The Hodgeses appealed the denial of attorney fees to the Court of Appeals. Johnson filed a cross-appeal, arguing that the implied warranty of merchantability does not extend to air conditioning units on used vehicles. The Court of Appeals reversed in a divided opinion and held as a matter of law that the implied warranty of merchantability on a used vehicle extends only to "the operation of major components that are necessary for the vehicle to operate, such as the engine and transmission." The court further held that "it is the responsibility of the buyer to ensure that the components incidental to operation are in working condition." Because it found that a car's air conditioning unit is not a major component of its operation, the court held as a matter of law that the implied warranty of merchantability did not hold Johnson accountable for the failure of the air conditioner in this case.

Because the majority held that the implied warranty of merchantability did not apply to the Mercedes' air conditioning system as a matter of law, the majority declined to reach Johnson's other arguments that the Hodgeses bought the car at a significant discount and that the Hodgeses had failed to prove the exact amount of damages.
* * *

Judge Leben dissented, stating that the majority applied the wrong standard for evaluating whether the implied warranty of merchantability applied in this case. According to Judge Leben, the question in this case was not whether the implied warranty of merchantability applied—a question of law—but whether the specific air conditioner in this Mercedes was covered by that warranty—a question of fact. Judge Leben stated that because this case involved a question of fact, it should be reviewed for substantial competent evidence. Judge Leben further found that substantial evidence existed to support the district court's decision in this case.

This court granted the Hodgeses' petition for review.

Implied Warranty of Merchantability

Kansas' implied warranty of merchantability is contained in K.S.A. 84–2–314, which states that "a warranty that the goods shall be merchantable is implied in a contract for their sale if the seller is a merchant with respect to goods of that kind." K.S.A. 84–2–314(1). The statute further states that in order for goods to be "merchantable," they must be "at least such as . . . are fit for the ordinary purposes for which such goods are used." K.S.A. 84–2–314(2)(c).

The implied warranty in K.S.A. 84–2–314 "set[s] minimum standards of merchantability." International Petroleum Services, Inc. v. S & N Well Service, Inc., 230 Kan. 452, 454, 639 P.2d 29 (1982).

Although "more may be required by the parties' agreement, course of dealing, or usage of trade," the minimum standards contained in K.S.A. 84–2–314 "assure a buyer that if the goods received do not conform at least to normal commercial expectations, the buyer will have a cause of action by which he or she can secure compensation for losses suffered." 230 Kan. at 454. This court has explained that the warranty seeks to strike a balance between "two extremes":

"Even though the seller may be careful not to make a single assertion of fact or promise about the goods, the ordinary buyer in a normal commercial transaction has a right to expect that the goods which are purchased will not turn out to be completely worthless. The purchaser cannot be expected to purchase goods offered by a merchant for sale and use and then find the goods are suitable only for the junk pile. On the other hand, a buyer who has purchased goods without obtaining an express warranty as to their quality and condition cannot reasonably expect that those goods will be the finest of all possible goods of that kind. . . . If an item is used or is secondhand, surely less can be expected in the way of quality than if the item is purchased new.

A buyer seeking "[t]o establish a breach of the implied warranty of merchantability under 84–2–314(2)(c) . . . must prove first, the ordinary purpose of the type of goods involved, and second, the particular goods sold were not fit for that purpose." Black v. Don Schmid Motor, Inc., 232 Kan. 458, 467 (1983). In Kansas, this requirement has been interpreted to mean that "the buyer must show the goods were defective and the defect existed at the time of the sale. [Citations omitted.]" 232 Kan. at 467; see also Dieker v. Case Corp., 276 Kan. 141, 162 (2003) ("To demonstrate a breach of the implied warranty of merchantability, plaintiff must show that the goods were defective, that the defect was present when the goods left the manufacturer's control, and that the defect caused the injury sustained by plaintiff.").

The extent of a merchant's obligation to a buyer "depends on the circumstances of the transaction." *International Petroleum Services*, 230 Kan. at 457. This flexibility is essential because "any number of things can foul the operation of complex machinery, and in the case of used goods, not all of these problems amount to a breach of the warranty of merchantability. The buyer's knowledge that the goods are used, the extent of their prior use, and whether the goods are significantly discounted may help determine what standards of quality should apply to the transaction." 230 Kan. at 457.

In sales of used automobiles, this principle has been more specifically interpreted to mean that a "late model, low mileage car, sold at a premium price, is expected to be in far better condition and to last longer than an old, high mileage, 'rough' car that is sold for little above its scrap value." Dale v. King Lincoln–Mercury, Inc., 234 Kan. 840, 844 (1984).

Relevant Case Law

The Kansas Supreme Court has considered the application of the implied warranty of merchantability to the sale of used automobiles on two separate occasions. In Black, the plaintiffs had purchased a 1–year–old Peugeot with slightly under 23,000 miles on it from the defendant. Shortly after the purchase, the plaintiff noticed that the

Peugeot was leaking transmission fluid, that the accelerator would stick when the car was driven over 40 miles per hour, that the radio malfunctioned, and that the air conditioner leaked cold water when the car turned corners. The plaintiff made numerous attempts to have the seller fix the problem over the first 5 months that the plaintiff owned the vehicle, but the transmission problem worsened significantly during that time. The plaintiff eventually stopped driving the Peugeot after the clutch on the air conditioner fell out of the car onto the highway when the plaintiff was driving to work one morning.

The plaintiff sued to revoke his acceptance of the Peugeot from the defendant seller, arguing breach of express warranty and implied warranty of merchantability. A jury returned a verdict in favor of the plaintiff for the purchase price plus consequential damages.

On appeal, the defendant claimed that the plaintiff failed to present sufficient evidence to establish a breach of the implied warranty of merchantability. The *Black* court affirmed the district court's award, noting that a claim for breach of implied warranty may be proved by circumstantial evidence. 232 Kan. at 467. The court found that the jury "could have inferred from the evidence presented the plaintiff's reasonable expectations as to the use of the Peugeot" and "could also have found that the defect existed when the car left [the defendant's] control." 232 Kan. at 467.

About a year after the court decided *Black*, it had the opportunity to again consider a case involving the implied warranty in a used-car sale in *Dale*. The plaintiff in that case purchased a 3–year–old Buick LeSabre Custom with about 33,000 miles from the defendant car dealer. The defendant had described the car to the plaintiff as "a 'cream puff,' meaning that it was excellent and in tip top condition." 234 Kan. at 840. Less than a month after the plaintiff purchased the vehicle, the transmission failed. The defendant paid for a new transmission under the dealership's express warranty. About a month later, the engine failed. Because the time period for the express warranty had expired, the defendant refused to cover the cost of replacing the engine block. The plaintiff sued for breach of implied warranty of merchantability.

The *Dale* court affirmed the judgment for the plaintiff, stating:

"A 'cream puff,' a relatively low mileage General Motors full-size automobile, represented by the dealer as being in excellent condition when sold, certainly can be expected to contain a motor and transmission which will give the new purchaser more than a few days' service. Such a vehicle, with defective major components, is patently unmerchantable. The fact that the seller in this case was unaware of the true condition of the car is immaterial, for the act imposes no requirement of intent or prior knowledge on the part of a supplier. 234 Kan. at 843.

Analysis

The comments to K.S.A. 84–2–314 make clear that this implied warranty of merchantability applies by operation of law to "all sales by merchants" and "arises from the fact of the sale." K.S.A. 84–2–314, Kansas Comment 1. Applying this standard to the facts before us, it is clear that the transaction in this case—the sale of the Mercedes by Johnson to the Hodgeses—fits within the implied warranty. There is no dispute that Johnson is a merchant dealing in the sale of used vehicles or that the Mercedes is a "good" within the meaning of the statute. Thus, when Johnson sold the Mercedes to the Hodgeses, he implicitly warranted that the Mercedes would be "merchantable." See K.S.A. 84–2–314(1).

While a court's initial determination as to whether the implied warranty of merchantability applies to a particular transaction (based on the court's determination as to whether the case involves a sale of goods by a merchant) is a question of law, the subsequent determination as to whether that implied warranty has been breached is a question of fact. An appellate court generally reviews a district court's findings of fact to determine if the findings are supported by substantial competent evidence and are sufficient to support the district court's conclusions of law. Substantial competent evidence is such legal and relevant evidence as a reasonable person might regard as sufficient to support a conclusion.

In evaluating the evidence to support the district court's factual findings, an appellate court does not weigh conflicting evidence, evaluate witnesses' credibility, or redetermine questions of fact. A court ordinarily presumes that the district court found all facts necessary to support its judgment. A claim for breach of implied warranty may be proved by circumstantial evidence.

The Court of Appeals majority recognized that the sale of the Mercedes triggered the implied warranty but concluded as a matter of law under K.S.A. 84–2–314(2) that the vehicle's air conditioner was not covered by the warranty because the air conditioner did not affect the vehicle's merchantability. To reach this conclusion, the majority employed a three-part syllogism: First, for goods to be merchantable under the statute, they must be "fit for the ordinary purposes for which such goods are used." K.S.A. 84–2–314(2)(c). Second, the majority concluded that the primary purpose for which used vehicles are used is transportation; thus only the major components of a vehicle that bear upon its ability to effectively transport people from one location to another affect the vehicle's merchantability. Finally, the majority interpreted our past cases involving the warranty of merchantability in the sale of used vehicles to suggest that the warranty may not apply "unless a major component or several components are defective, causing the vehicle to become virtually inoperable."

Applying this syllogism, the Court of Appeals majority determined that the air conditioner was not a major component of the Mercedes and thus did not impair the primary purpose for which used cars vehicles are employed:

"An air conditioner is not a major component of a car that is 10 years old with over 135,000 miles on it, and does not fall within the implied warranty of merchantability. We find no implied warranty of merchantability, considering the age of the car, the high mileage, and the fact that the Hodges provided no proof that the air conditioner did not work when they purchased the vehicle."

This conclusion is not supported by the case law. Although it may be that the implied warranty of merchantability does not extend to some components of a used vehicle in a particular transaction, this is a case-by-case determination in most cases—not a question of law. The Court of Appeals correctly acknowledged that the transaction involved in this case was subject to the statutory provisions of K.S.A. 84–2–314. But the Court of Appeals erred when it attempted to determine the extent of Johnson's obligation to the Hodgeses as a matter of law.

The Court of Appeals majority's approach is similarly unsupported by the statutes. K.S.A. 84–2–314(2)(c) defines merchantable goods as goods that are "fit for the ordinary purposes for which such goods are used." The Court of Appeals interpreted this provision to mean that a used vehicle must be fit for the primary purpose of transportation. This interpretation is inconsistent with the plain language of K.S.A. 84–2–314(2)(c), which clearly contemplates goods that may be put to more than one use. Although there can be little doubt that the primary purpose of a vehicle is transportation, the Court of Appeals' opinion ignores the reality that a buyer may purchase a particular vehicle for a number of other purposes—among which may be safety, fuel economy, utility, or comfort in traveling to and from various destinations.

Contrary to the Court of Appeals' conclusion, the extent of a merchant's obligation under the implied warranty of merchantability depends on the circumstances of a transaction. International Petroleum Services noted that not all problems that arise in "the operation of complex machinery" result in "a breach of the warranty of merchantability." 230 Kan. at 457. The determination as to whether the implied warranty has been breached turns on a number of factors, including "[t]he buyer's knowledge that the goods are used, the extent of their prior use, and whether the goods are significantly discounted." 230 Kan. at 457.

The broad range of used goods that may be covered by the implied warranty of merchantability underscores the wisdom of this court's previous recognition that a "late model, low mileage car, sold at a premium price, is expected to be in far better condition and to last longer than an old, high mileage, 'rough' car that is sold for little above its scrap value." Dale, 234 Kan. at 844. In this case, we have a 1995 Mercedes S320 with 135,945 miles selling for $17,020 in 2005. Johnson related to the buyer that it was a nice car in good condition; Dr. Hodges testified that he was told the car "was pretty much a perfect car." In short, this vehicle falls somewhere between the extremes of a "late model, low mileage car, sold at a premium price" and "an old, high mileage, 'rough' car . . . sold for little above its scrap value." 234 Kan. at 844.

The implied warranty of merchantability applies to the transaction in this case as a matter of law under K.S.A. 84–2–314. The question remaining to be resolved is not the existence of this warranty, but rather the extent of the seller's obligation under the warranty. Because this case does not involve either extreme on the spectrum of used vehicles, the resolution of this question is not a question of law, but rather a factual determination. The attempt by the Court of Appeals to convert this question into a legal determination amounts to error, and its decision in this regard must be reversed.

After hearing the evidence in this case, the district court determined that the Hodgeses were entitled to judgment against Johnson for the sum of $3,474, together with costs of $56 and interest, and thus affirmed the award of the small claims court. The question we confront in our review of the district court's decision is whether its factual finding that Johnson breached the implied warranty of merchantability is supported by substantial competent evidence.

To demonstrate a breach of the implied warranty of merchantability, a plaintiff must show that the purchased goods were defective, that the defect was present when the goods left the seller's control, and that the defect caused the injury sustained by the plaintiff. The circumstantial evidence in this case is sufficient to establish that the defect in the air conditioner existed at the time of sale. In 2003, 2 years before the Hodgeses purchased the vehicle, the Mercedes' air conditioner failed while Johnson was using it as his personal vehicle. Johnson insisted that his mechanic, against the mechanic's advice, use a product called Super Seal to fix the problem. The Hodgeses discovered that the air conditioner was again defective as soon as the weather became warm enough to require climate control. The use of the Super Seal, the strong odor emanating from the vehicle's ventilation system immediately after the sale, and the complete breakdown of the air conditioner when the buyer first attempted to use it all tend to establish that it was defective at the time of sale. While Johnson may not have known that the Mercedes' air conditioner was defective when he sold the vehicle to the Hodgeses, there is no requirement that a buyer establish that the seller knew of a defective component at the time of sale to trigger the implied warranty.

With regard to damages, there is no question that the complete failure of the air conditioner's operation led to the buyer replacing it. As this court has concluded:

"The general measure of damages for breach of warranty is the difference at the time and place of acceptance between the value of the goods accepted and the value they would have had if they had been as warranted, unless special circumstances show proximate damages of a different amount. K.S.A. 84–2–714(2). As concerns used or secondhand goods it is generally understood that the measure of damages is the cost of repair when repair is possible." *International Petroleum Services*, 230 Kan. at 460.

The district court heard evidence concerning the cost of the necessary repairs to the Mercedes' air conditioner. While there was testimony that employing used parts rather than new parts would reduce the cost of repairs and that the estimate quoted was too high, the court based its decision of monetary damages on the evidence of record. We will not substitute our judgment for that of the district court when the district court's decision is supported by substantial competent evidence.

We find that there is substantial competent evidence to support the district court's conclusion that the implied warranty of merchantability in this transaction was not limited to only the Mercedes' major components affecting transportation, but rather extended at a minimum to the vehicle's air conditioning unit. We also find that there was substantial competent evidence to demonstrate that the air conditioning unit was defective at the time of sale and that the required repairs would cost $3,474. Accordingly, we reverse the Court of Appeals' reversal of the district court's judgment in favor of the Hodgeses and affirm the district court's decision. * * *

NOTES

1. As *Hodges* emphasizes, to be merchantable under 2–314(2)(c) the goods must be fit at the time of tender for the ordinary purposes to which they are put. Goods can and usually have more than one purpose to which they are ordinarily put. Thus, the fact that the good are suitable for an ordinary purpose does not mean that it is suitable for other ordinary purposes. Sometimes it is difficult to identify the purpose or range of purposes to which the good ordinarily is put. Cars ordinarily are used for transportation, but a comfortable ride at a comfortable interior temperature also ordinary purposes to which cars are put. See, e.g., Green v. Green Mountain Coffee Roasters, Inc., 76 UCC Rep. Serv.2d 346 (D.N.J. 2011) (coffee machine fit for ordinary purposes to which it is put when capable of brewing coffee; brewing correct amounts of coffee not among its ordinary purposes); Carey v. Chaparrel Boats, Inc., 514 F. Supp. 2d 1152 (D. Minn. 2007) (cracks in boat's finish a "cosmetic problem" with no effect on the boat's ordinary use; no breach of 2–314(2)(c)). Used goods make the problem even harder. Goods that are suitable for some ordinary purposes when new might no longer serve some of those purposes when used. Courts have reached different results about the merchantability of used goods. Compare Regan Purchase & Sales Corp. v. Primavera, 328 N.Y.S.2d 490 (N.Y. Civ. Ct. 1972) (used commercial ice maker and dishwasher suitable for ordinary purposes even it they are inoperable when purchased), with Isip v. Mercedes–Benz USA, LLC, 65 Cal.Rptr.3d 695 (Cal. Ct. App. 2007) (used car that smells, lurks, clanks and emits smells not fit for intended purpose), Krack v. Action Motors Corp., 87 Conn.App. 687 (Conn. Ct. App. 2006) (used salvaged car unmerchantable when sold for the price of a used unsalvaged car).

2. *Hodges* does not identify the merchantability standard applicable to a used car. Because the 1995 Mercedes in the case was neither a late model, low mileage car sold at a premium nor an old, high mileage car sold close to scrap value, the court found that the standard depended on the circumstances of the transaction. It therefore deemed the applicable standard of merchantability to be a question of fact, not law. As a result, the court reviewed the lower court's judgment based on whether it was supported by substantial evidence. The court therefore did not itself have to identify the merchantability standard applicable to the transaction. Nor did the lower court. What might that standard be? Price. Goods sold have greater or lesser quality depending on their price. In *Hodges* the difficulty is not in knowing whether a working air conditioner is among the ordinary purposes to which used cars are put. Of course it depends on the price paid for the used car. The difficulty is determining whether that purpose is among the ordinary purposes to which a used 1995 Mercedes purchased a particular price. Accordingly, used car price arguably is a reliable indicator of quality. See Comment 7 to 2–314. The 1995 Mercedes purchased could be compared to other used 1995 Mercedes with similar mileage and condition sold or held for sale at a similar price. If all or most of these comparable cars came with working air conditioners, working air conditioning is presumptively an ordinary purpose to which the 1995 Mercedes purchased is put. Otherwise, it is not among the car's ordinary purposes. Cf. Regan Purchase & Sales Corp. v. Primavera, 328 N.Y.S.2d 490 (N.Y. Civ. Ct. 1972) (inoperable used commercial equipment merchantable when purchased at a significant discount from new equipment).

Greene v. Boddie–Noell Enterprises, Inc.

United States District Court, Western District of Virginia, 1997
966 F. Supp. 416

■ Opinion by: JAMES P. JONES, UNITED STATES DISTRICT JUDGE

In this products liability case, the plaintiff contends that she was badly burned by hot coffee purchased from the drive-through window of a fast food restaurant, when the coffee spilled on her after it had been handed to her by the driver of the vehicle. The defendant restaurant operator moves for summary judgment on the ground that the plaintiff cannot show a prima facie case of liability. I agree, and dismiss the case.

I.

The circumstances surrounding the accident in which the plaintiff, Katherine Greene, was injured are set forth in the depositions submitted in support of the motion for summary judgment.

Greene was a passenger in a car driven by her boyfriend, Chris Blevins, on the morning of December 31, 1994, when he purchased food and drink from the drive-through window of the Hardee's restaurant in Wise, Virginia, operated by the defendant. Blevins paid the Hardee's employee and received an order of gravy and biscuits, a steak biscuit, juice for Greene, and coffee for himself. He immediately handed the food and beverages to Greene. The food was on a plate, and the beverages were in cups. Greene placed the plate on her lap and held a cup in each hand. According to Greene, the Styrofoam coffee cup was comfortable to hold, and had a lid on the top, although she did not notice whether the lid was fully attached.

Blevins drove out of the restaurant parking lot, and over a "bad dip" at the point at which the lot meets the road. When the front tires of the car went slowly across the dip, the coffee "splashed out" on Greene, burning her legs through her clothes. Blevins remembers Greene exclaiming, "the lid came off." She did not look at the cup until the coffee burned her, and does not know whether the cup was tilted in one direction or another when the coffee spilled out.

As soon as the coffee burned her, Greene threw the food and drink to the floor of the car, and in the process stepped on the coffee cup. When the cup was later retrieved from the floor of the car, the bottom of the cup was damaged, and the lid was at least partially off of the top of the cup. After Greene was burned by the coffee, Blevins drove her to the emergency room of a local hospital, where she was treated. She missed eleven days of work, and suffered permanent scarring to her thighs.

Both Greene and Blevins testified that they had heard of the "McDonald's coffee case" prior to this incident[1] and Greene testified that while she was not a coffee drinker, she had been aware that if coffee spilled on her, it would burn her. After the accident, Greene gave a recorded statement to a representative of the defendant in which she stated, "I know the lid wasn't on there good. It came off too easy."

The plaintiff filed an action against the defendant as a result of this accident in state court on October 21, 1996, and the defendant removed the case to this court, based on the court's diversity jurisdiction. In her suit, the plaintiff contends that the defendant impliedly warranted that the coffee sold was fit for consumption and that because of its extreme heat and improperly attached cup lid, it was not as warranted.[2] It is also alleged that the defendant was negligent in failing to warn the plaintiff of the heat of the coffee and of the improperly attached cup lid.

Following discovery depositions of the plaintiff and Blevins, the defendant has moved for summary judgment in its favor. Oral argument has been presented and the motion is ripe for decision.

* * *

III.

To prove a case of liability in Virginia, a plaintiff must show that a product had a defect which rendered it unreasonably dangerous for ordinary or foreseeable use. In order to meet this burden, a plaintiff must offer proof that the product violated a prevailing safety standard, whether the standard comes from business, government or reasonable consumer expectation.

Here the plaintiff has offered no such proof. There is no evidence that either the heat of the coffee or the security of the coffee cup lid violated any applicable standard. Do other fast food restaurants serve coffee at a lower temperature, or with lids which will prevent spills even when passing over an obstruction in the road? Do customers expect cooler coffee, which may be less tasty, or cups which may be more secure, but harder to unfasten?

In fact, the plaintiff testified that she knew, and therefore expected, that the coffee would be hot enough to burn her if it spilled. While she also expressed the opinion that the cup lid was too loose, that testimony does not substitute for evidence of a generally applicable standard or consumer expectation, since "[the plaintiff's] subjective

---

[1] On August 17, 1994, a state court jury in Albuquerque, New Mexico, awarded 81–year old Stella Liebeck $160,000 in compensatory damages and $2.7 million in punitive damages, after she was burned by coffee purchased from a drive-through window at a McDonald's restaurant. The trial judge later reduced the punitive damages to $480,000, and the parties settled the case before an appeal. According to news reports, Mrs. Liebeck contended that for taste reasons McDonald's served coffee about 20 degrees hotter than other fast food restaurants, and in spite of numerous complaints, had made a conscious decision not to warn customers of the possibility of serious burns. The jury's verdict received world-wide attention.

[2] Under the Virginia Uniform Commercial Code, the sale of food or drink implies a warranty of merchantability, meaning that the goods are fit for the purposes for which such goods are used and are adequately contained, packaged, and labeled "as the agreement may require." Va. Code Ann. § 8.2–314 (Michie 1991). The suit papers also allege a breach of express warranty, but no such express warranty has been identified.

expectations are insufficient to establish what degree of protection . . . society expects from [the product]."

The plaintiff argues that the mere fact that she was burned shows that the product was dangerously defective, either by being too hot or by having a lid which came off unexpectedly. But it is settled in Virginia that the happening of an accident is not sufficient proof of liability, even in products cases. This is not like the case of a foreign substance being found in a soft drink bottle, where a presumption of negligence arises.

To be merchantable, a product need not be foolproof, or perfect. As one noted treatise has expressed, "it is the lawyer's challenging job to define the term 'merchantability' in [the] case in some objective way so that the court or jury can make a determination whether that standard has been breached." James J. White & Robert S. Summers, Handbook of the Law Under the Uniform Commercial Code § 9.7, at 356 (2d ed. 1980).

In the present case, there has been no showing that a reasonable seller of coffee would not conclude that the beverage must be sold hot enough to be palatable to consumers, even though it is hot enough to burn other parts of the body. A reasonable seller might also conclude that patrons desire coffee lids which prevent spillage in ordinary handling, but are not tight enough to avert a spill under other circumstances, such as when driving over a bump. It was the plaintiff's obligation to demonstrate that she had proof that the defendant breached a recognizable standard, and that such proof is sufficient to justify a verdict in her favor at trial. She has not done so, and accordingly the motion for summary judgment must be granted.[3]

An appropriate final judgment will be entered.

For the reasons set forth in the opinion accompanying this final judgment, it is ordered and adjudged that the defendant's motion for summary judgment is granted and final judgment on the merits is entered in favor of the defendant. . . .

NOTES

1. In addition to a negligence claim, the plaintiff alleged a breach of an express warranty and an implied warranty of merchantability. However, as the court notes, she failed to identify the express warranty made by the seller. Why do you think she failed to do so? What evidence could she produce and what would it likely at most establish?

2. *Greene* is somewhat unusual in that the plaintiff's implied warranty claim is based only on a breach of 2–314(2)(e) (see footnote 2). On what other subsections might she have based her claim? The court found that the plaintiff failed to prove that the lid of the cup in which the seller delivered hot coffee was inadequate to contain or package the coffee. In doing so it suggested that the standard of adequacy is a cost-benefit standard: "A reasonable seller might also conclude that patrons desire coffee lids which prevent spillage in ordinary handling, but are not tight enough to avert a spill under other circumstances, such as when driving over a bump." Patrons want lids that give prevent spills

---

[3] The plaintiff has also alleged a failure to warn, but without proof of actual or constructive notice of a dangerous product, there was no such duty.

while giving them easy access to their coffee (the benefit), at a risk that a bump while driving might result in spills (the cost). Suppose the plaintiff had established that the coffee lid was inadequate to contain hot coffee. Would she prevail under 2–314(2)(e)? Reread subsection (e).

3. The plaintiff, as part of her negligence claim, alleged that the seller failed to warn that the coffee to burn part of the body if the lid of the coffee cup became detached. The allegation also could have been made part of her warranty claim, based on 2–314(2)(e)'s standard that the goods be "adequately . . . labeled as the agreement may require." In McMahon v. Bunn–O–Matic, 150 F.3d 651 (7th Cir. 1998), a buyer of a coffee machine burned by coffee prepared with it alleged that the machine's manufacturer (Bunn) had a duty to warn that hot coffee can cause bodily burns if spilled. The court denied that the manufacturer had the duty:

> What would this warning have entailed? A statement that coffee is served hot? That it can cause burns? They already knew these things and did not need to be reminded . . . That this coffee was unusually hot and therefore capable of causing severe burns? Warning consumers about a surprising feature that is potentially dangerous yet hard to observe could be useful, but the record lacks any evidence that 179 degrees °F is unusually hot for coffee. What remains is the argument that Bunn should have provided a detailed warning about the severity of burns that hot liquids can cause, even if 179 degrees °F is a standard serving temperature . . . Bunn can't deliver a medical education with each cup of coffee. Any person severely injured by any product could make a claim, at least as plausible as the McMahons', that they did not recognize the risks ex ante as clearly as they do after the accident. Insistence on more detail can make any warning, however elaborate, seem inadequate. Indiana courts have expressed considerable reluctance to require ever-more detail in warnings. Extended warnings present several difficulties, first among them that, the more text must be squeezed onto the product, the smaller the type, and the less likely is the consumer to read or remember any of it. Only pithy and bold warnings can be effective. Long passages in capital letters are next to illegible, and long passages in lower case letters are treated as boilerplate. Plaintiff wants a warning in such detail that a magnifying glass would be necessary to read it. To be useful, warnings about burns could not stop with abstract information about the relation among a liquid's temperature and volume (which jointly determine not only the number of calories available to impart to the skin but also the maximum rate of delivery), contact time (which determines how many of the available calories are actually delivered), and the severity of burns. It would have to address the risk of burns in real life, starting with the number of cups of coffee sold annually, the number of these that spill (broken down by location, such as home, restaurant, and car), and the probability that any given spill will produce a severe (as opposed to a mild or average) burn. Only after understanding these things could the consumer determine whether the superior taste of hot coffee justifies the incremental risk. Tradeoffs are complex. Few consumers could understand the numbers and reach an intelligent decision on the spot at a checkout counter. Yet such a detailed

warning (equivalent to the package insert that comes with drugs) might obscure the principal point that precautions should be taken to avoid spills. Indiana does not require vendors to give warnings in the detail plaintiffs contemplate. It expects consumers to educate themselves about the hazards of daily life—of matches, knives, and kitchen ranges, of bones in fish, and of hot beverages—by general reading and experience, knowledge they can acquire before they enter a mini mart to buy coffee for a journey. Id. at 655–657.

4.   Section 2–314(2)'s merchantability standards can overlap both with each other and express warranties when trade usage is applicable. Ambassador Steel Co. v. Ewald Steel Co., 190 N.W.2d 275 (Mich. 1971) is illustrative. There the buyer ordered a shipment of steel without specifying the desired carbon content of the product. The steel the seller delivered cracked because it had a carbon content below that of "commercial quality" steel, which has a carbon content of between 1010 and 1020. Applicable trade usage was to the effect that an order for steel without a specific quality calls for delivery of "commercial quality" steel. Based on this custom, the court found that the seller had breached 2–314(2)(b)'s standard that fungible goods delivered be of the average quality within the contract description. Given the trade usage, the court also could have found a breach of both 2–314(2)(a)'s "pass without objection in the trade" standard and (c)'s "ordinary purposes" standard. Notice that on the case's facts the seller also breached its express warranty as to carbon content. Under revised 1–303(d), trade usage may give meaning to specific terms of the agreement. Thus, given the applicable trade usage, an order for "steel," without specification of carbon content, is an order for "commercial quality" steel—steel with a carbon content of between 1010 and 1020. As a result, in agreeing to deliver "steel" the seller has described the steel to be delivered as "commercial quality" steel. The seller therefore expressly warrants the steel's carbon content under 2–313(1)(b) to be that of commercial quality steel. In delivering steel with a lower carbon content, the seller's breached its express warranty.

5.   One area in which the vagueness of 2–314(2)'s merchantability standards cause problems concerns goods whose ingredients create risk even when the goods are well made. Properly produced alcohol, cigarettes, sugar products and fat in foods can cause injury to purchasers. Tobacco litigation has focused on subsection (2)(c)'s fitness for ordinary purposes standard. Predictably, two different understandings of the standard are possible. One is that the product is fit for ordinary purposes to which it is put if it is not defective in its ingredients or production, even if the ingredients risk injury. The other is that the product is fit for ordinary purposes if its use does not result in injury. A properly produced cigarette with the usual ingredients meets the former standard of fitness; it may not meet the latter standard. Although a majority of courts judge merchantability according to the former standard, some courts do so using the latter standard. Compare Green v. American Tobacco Co., 409 F.2d 1166 (5th Cir. 1969) (cigarettes merchantable if nondefective in ingredients or production) with Wright v. Brooke Group Ltd., 114 F. Supp.2d 797 (N.D. Iowa 2000) (unmerchantable if manufacturer knowingly produced cigarettes presenting risk of carcinogens and addiction). Adding to the divergence of interpretation, courts occasionally invoke the purchaser's

assumption of risk to find no implied warranty against a risk of injury; see Allgood v. R.J. Reynolds Tobacco Co., 80 F.3d 168, 172 (5th Cir. 1996).

PROBLEM 5.4

Jones wanted to sell some furniture he has just inherited. Wanting to get the highest price for it, Jones engaged Ace Auction House. Ace is experienced in selling a variety of furniture at auction. Although Ace sometimes auctions items it has purchased, usually it puts up for sale others' goods. It followed its usual practice and placed Jones' furniture in its monthly auction. Ace advertised the event as "Ace's monthly auction" but provided no other information. At the auction Smith made the highest bid for Jones' furniture. When he took delivery from Ace, he discovered that the furniture was badly scratched and was ridden with termites. Has Ace made an implied warranty to Smith regarding the furniture? 2–314(1), (2). Suppose Ace stated in its advertisement that the auction included Jones' furniture. What result? 1–103(b).

PROBLEM 5.5

Manufacturer produces airline engines and recently won a contract to produce a new series. Needing to operate its factory for longer periods of time, Manufacturer replaced its current air conditioning units with units having greater cooling capacity. Rather than throw away the replaced units, Manufacturer sold them to Buyer. The sales contract recited that the air conditioning units were being sold "without any representations of quality." When Buyer installed them in its own factory two months after delivery, it discovered that the units did not work. Although Manufacturer acknowledges that the installed units do not work, it insists (truthfully) that its elaborate pre-sale inspection did not reveal any defects in the units. Has Manufacturer breached an obligation to Buyer for which it might be liable? 2–314(2), Comment 13 to 2–314.

PROBLEM 5.6

Buyer, an extreme sports enthusiast and bungee jumping expert, saw an XY bungee cord in Seller's store and had to have it. Handing Seller's salesman the XY bungee cord along with the purchase price, Buyer received a sales receipt and left the store pleased with his purchase. Seller is a leading retailer offering bungee cords. The XY cord was made according to Seller's highest standards, which are recognized as the best in the industry. The sales receipt Seller gave Buyer listed the item as "1 XY bungee cord." Unfortunately, after using the cord on a number of jumps, the XY cord failed Buyer during a jump. Later examination revealed that the cord was not defectively produced; it simply "wore out," according to the examination report. Buyer's executor is unmoved on learning that Buyer's cord would not have failed had he purchased Seller's higher priced AB cord. Has Seller breached an implied warranty to Buyer? 2–314(2)(a), (c), (e).

D. IMPLIED WARRANTY OF FITNESS FOR A PARTICULAR PURPOSE

Section 2–315 creates a warranty that the goods will be fit for the particular purpose to which they will be put by the buyer. As with a warranty of merchantability, the warranty of fitness for a particular purpose is implied. It arises by law when its conditions are met, not by contract. This means that the seller need make no statement or perform any act to create the warranty. Under 2–315 the warranty of fitness arises when three conditions are met: (1) the seller has reason to know of the particular purpose for which the buyer requires the goods; (2) the seller has reason to know that the buyer is relying on its skill or judgment in furnishing the buyer with goods suitable for the buyer's particular purpose, and (3) that the buyer in fact relies on the seller's skill or judgment. None of these conditions require that the seller be a merchant with respect to the goods it is selling. Nor do they require that the seller actually know of the buyer's particular purpose or its reliance. Section 2–315 requires only that the seller have reason to know these matters. Usually the seller will know the buyer's particular purpose at the time the contract is concluded because the buyer will have disclosed it. However, sometimes trade usage, a course of dealing or an inference from other information disclosed by the buyer is enough to give the seller reason to know of the buyer's particular purpose and reliance on the seller's skill or judgment.

A warranty of fitness can arise even where the seller makes no express warranty as to the goods. Assume that the seller knows of the buyer's particular purpose as well as its reliance on the seller's skill or judgment in supplying suitable goods. To make the sale, the seller commends the goods it offers to the buyer but says nothing else. If seller's statement merely commends the goods, the statement creates no express warranty under 2–313. Nonetheless, an implied warranty of fitness arises under 2–315. A warranty of fitness also can arise even where a warranty of merchantability is not created. Assume on the same facts that the seller is not a merchant with respect to the goods and that the goods are not customarily put to the use intended by the buyer. The sale creates a 2–315 warranty but not a warranty of merchantability because the seller is not a merchant. Finally, the warranties of fitness and merchantability can overlap and therefore both arise in the same sales transaction. Assume that the seller is a merchant and that the above facts apply. The sale creates a warranty of merchantability under 2–314 that the goods are suitable for customary uses to which they are put. Section 2–314 does not create a warranty that the goods are suitable for the buyer's particular, nonstandard purpose. However, on the above facts 2–315 creates a warranty that the goods are fit for the buyer's particular purpose. If the goods are unsuitable all purposes, both the warranty of merchantability and fitness are breached.

Section 2–315 does not say when the buyer's purpose for a good is "particular." This omission makes applying the section difficult. To illustrate, suppose a buyer has a computer program that requires substantial amounts of memory. The buyer asks her seller for a computer that will operate that program. The seller sells her a computer that will not operate it. In these circumstances the seller knew that the buyer had a particular purpose in mind for the computer and, by her question, was relying on its judgment to supply a computer suitable for this purpose. It may seem obvious that the seller has created (and breached) its 2–315 warranty of fitness to the buyer. But it is not obvious. A "particular" purpose might be one specific to the buyer: the purpose the buyer intends to put the good. In this sense, only the rare buyer making a completely random purchase lacks a particular purpose. Alternatively, a "particular" purpose could be a nonstandard, atypical or idiosyncratic purpose—a purpose to which the goods are not ordinarily put. In the illustration just given, the buyer certainly has a particular purpose in mind for the computer in the sense of a specific purpose for it. However, the buyer's purpose may or may not be particular in the sense of the purpose being nonstandard, atypical or idiosyncratic. To know this, we need to know the memory needs of programs buyers usually run on computers.

Comment 2 to 2–315 interprets "particular" to mean atypical or idiosyncratic. It contrasts a "particular purpose" with an "ordinary purpose" for which goods are used. A warranty of merchantability covers goods suitable for the ordinary purposes to which they are put, not a warranty of fitness. The Comment speaks of the uses which are "customarily" made of goods in contrast to "specific uses" which are "peculiar" to the buyer's business. It observes that the concept of merchantability covers customary uses to which goods are put. This suggests that the warranty of fitness is limited only to circumstances in which a buyer has a nonstandard or idiosyncratic use intended for the good. The 2–314 warranty is not available for this use, although it remains available for the fitness of the good for ordinary, standard purposes.

Courts continue to divide over the meaning of "particular purpose." Some courts understand the phrase to mean the buyer's specific purpose, without wondering about Comment 2 or 2–314's bearing on the matter. See Outlook Windows P'ship v. York Int'l Corp., 112 F. Supp.2d 877 (D. Neb. 2000). The buyer's specific purpose may be ordinary or idiosyncratic. Others require the purpose to be nonstandard or idiosyncratic, based on Comment 2. See Franulovic v. Coca Cola, 64 UCC Rep. Serv.2d 370 (D.N.J. 2007). At least one court finds the interpretation of "particular purpose" as the buyer's specific purpose to be "ridiculous." See DiIenno v. Libbey Glass Div. v. Owens–Illinois, Inc., 668 F. Supp. 373, 376 (D. Del. 1987). However, there is no good statutory reason to limit a warranty of fitness to buyers with nonstandard or idiosyncratic purposes. Section 2–315's language does not require this limitation, and Comment 2 goes beyond the statute.

As important, limiting "particular purposes" to nonstandard or idiosyncratic purposes leaves buyers without an implied warranty when they arguably should have one. To see this, assume that a buyer purchases a good for an ordinary purpose from a nonmerchant seller. The buyer makes known to its seller its purpose before the sale and that it is counting on the seller's judgment of suitability. The good is unsuitable for the buyer's purpose. On these assumptions 2–315 does not imply a warrant of fitness because the buyer's purpose is ordinary, not nonstandard or idiosyncratic. No implied warranty of merchantability arises under 2–314 either, because the seller is not a merchant with respect to the good. The seller is liable to the buyer only if it has made an express warranty as to the suitability for the buyer's purpose.

This is a bad result and 2–315's relevant language does not require it. Although the nonmerchant seller might not be an expert about the capacities of the good, prior experience often will give it more knowledge than its buyer. At least it will usually be more ignorant about the good's suitability for ordinary purposes than the buyer. In addition, the buyer has disclosed to the seller the purpose to which it intends to put the good. The disclosure reduces the seller's costs in acquiring information about the buyer's purpose for the goods. For both reasons, the seller usually is in a better position than the buyer to take measures to assure that the good suits the buyer's purpose. Because these measure increase the seller's cost of providing a suitable good, the seller will increase the contract price to reflect them. Buyers will prefer the higher priced cost contract if their costs of assuring suitability of the goods for their particular purposes is higher than their sellers' costs of doing so. If the buyer knows more about the goods than the seller, so that it can take measures to assure fitness at less cost than the seller, the seller will offer a lower priced contract that disclaims the 2–315 warranty. See 2–316(2). The disclaimer shifts to the buyer the risk that the goods will be unfit for the buyer's particular purpose.

Another complaint about 2–315's warranty of fitness is its requirement that the buyer in fact rely on the seller's skill or judgment. This reliance requirement allows a seller to knowingly sell good unsuitable for the buyer's particular purpose without liability. For example, suppose the buyer gives the seller specifications for fabricating a good at the same time it informs the seller of the purpose of the purchase. The buyer's purpose is nonstandard or idiosyncratic. Suppose too that goods fabricated according to the buyer's specifications are fit for customary purposes. Finally, suppose that the seller knows that the good fabricated according to the buyer's specifications will produce a good unsuitable for the buyer's purpose. The goods are merchantable because they are fit for the customary purposes to which they are put. Section 2–315 does not create a warranty of fitness because the buyer has relied on its own judgment as to suitability of the goods, not the seller's judgment. Nonetheless, the seller knows that the goods are unsuitable. Thus, 2–315's reliance requirement allows the seller to sell unsuitable goods to a non-relying buyer without warranty liability.

A better rule would eliminate 2–315's reliance requirement. At present the requirement gives the seller no incentive to disclose to the non-relying buyer information that would enable it to avoid loss resulting from purchase of unsuitable goods. This encourages the inefficient use of information that would avoid loss to the buyer. In tort law, under a contributory negligence rule, the last clear chance rule makes the last person who could reasonably have avoided the injury liable for it. This gives the person in the best position to avoid the injury an incentive to do so. By contract, 2–315 does not give the seller a similar incentive. Because 2–315 does not create a warranty of fitness in a purchase by a non-relying buyer, the buyer bears the risk that the goods will prove unsuitable. By disclosing information the seller risks losing a sale—a cost to it—while benefitting only the buyer, who avoids loss resulting from purchasing unsuitable goods. The seller has no incentive to bear a cost without receiving an offsetting benefit.

An efficient rule for warranty assigns the risk of nonconformity (unsuitability of the goods) to the party best positioned to reduce or eliminate it. See generally Robert Cooter, Unity in Tort, Contract, and Property: The Model of Precaution, 73 Cal. L. Rev. 1 (1985). The seller can disclose the information about the unsuitability of the goods at less cost than the non-relying buyer otherwise would incur in discovering this fact. After all, the seller already has the information, so that its cost of disclosing the information is close to zero. Without 2–315's reliance requirement, a warranty of fitness arises when the seller has reason to know of the buyer's particular purpose. To avoid warranty liability, the seller can disclaim the warranty in accordance with 2–316(2). Because the disclaimer shifts the nonconformity risk to the buyer, it signals to her the need to take measures to reduce or eliminate the risk. Alternatively, the seller can offer the buyer another product better suited for the buyer's particular purpose. Finally, the seller can refuse to sell the unsuitable good to the buyer. By disclaiming the warranty of fitness, the seller thereby effectively "discloses" to the buyer the information about unsuitability. By insisting on selling a different product or not making a sale, the seller takes measures to avoid the buyer's purchase of unsuitable goods.

Lewis v. Mobil Oil Corp.

United States Court of Appeals, Eighth Circuit, 1971
438 F.2d 500

■ GIBSON, CIRCUIT JUDGE.

In this diversity case the defendant appeals from a judgment entered on a jury verdict in favor of the plaintiff in the amount of $89,250 for damages alleged to be caused by use of defendant's oil.

Plaintiff Lewis has been doing business as a sawmill operator in Cove, Arkansas, since 1956. In 1963, in order to meet competition, Lewis decided to convert his power equipment to hydraulic equipment. He purchased a hydraulic system in May 1963, from a competitor who was installing a new system. The used system was in good operating condition at the time Lewis purchased it. It was stored at his plant until November 1964, while a new mill building was being built, at which time it was installed. Following the installation, Lewis requested from Frank Rowe, a local Mobil oil dealer, the proper hydraulic fluid to operate his machinery. The prior owner of the hydraulic system had used Pacemaker oil supplied by Cities Service, but plaintiff had been a customer of Mobil's for many years and desired to continue with Mobil. Rowe said he didn't know what the proper lubricant for Lewis' machinery was, but would find out. The only information given to Rowe by Lewis was that the machinery was operated by a gear-type pump; Rowe did not request any further information. He apparently contacted a Mobil representative for a recommendation, though this is not entirely clear, and sold plaintiff a product known as Ambrex 810. This is a straight mineral oil with no chemical additives.

Within a few days after operation of the new equipment commenced, plaintiff began experiencing difficulty with its operation. The oil changed color, foamed over, and got hot. The oil was changed a number of times, with no improvement. By late April 1965, approximately six months after operations with the equipment had begun, the system broke down, and a complete new system was installed. The cause of the breakdown was undetermined, but apparently by this time there was some suspicion of the oil being used. Plaintiff Lewis requested Rowe to be sure he was supplying the right kind of oil. Ambrex 810 continued to be supplied.

From April 1965 until April 1967, plaintiff continued to have trouble with the system, principally with the pumps which supplied the pressure. Six new pumps were required during this period, as they continually broke down. During this period, the kind of pump used was a Commercial pump which was specified by the designer of the hydraulic system. The filtration of oil for this pump was by means of a metal strainer, which was cleaned daily by the plaintiff in accordance with the instruction given with the equipment.

In April 1967, the plaintiff changed the brand of pump from a Commercial to a Tyrone pump. The Tyrone pump, instead of using the metal strainer filtration alone, used a disposable filter element in addition. Ambrex 810 oil was also recommended by Mobil and used with this pump, which completely broke down three weeks later. At this point, plaintiff was visited for the first time by a representative of Mobil Oil Corporation, as well as a representative of the Tyrone pump manufacturer.

On the occasion of this visit, May 9, 1967, plaintiff's system was completely flushed and cleaned, a new Tyrone pump installed, and on the pump manufacturer's and Mobil's representative's recommendation, a new oil was used[1] which contained certain chemical additives, principally a "defoamant." Following these changes, plaintiff's system worked satisfactorily up until the time of trial, some two and one-half years later.

Briefly stated, plaintiff's theory of his case is that Mobil supplied him with an oil which was warranted fit for use in his hydraulic system, that the oil was not suitable for such use because it did not contain certain additives, and that it was the improper oil which caused the mechanical breakdowns, with consequent loss to his business. The defendant contends that there was no warranty of fitness, that the breakdowns were caused not by the oil but by improper filtration, and that in any event there can be no recovery of loss of profits in this case.

I.   The Existence of Warranties

Defendant maintains that there was no warranty of fitness in this case, that at most there was only a warranty of merchantability and that there was no proof of breach of this warranty, since there was no proof that Ambrex 810 is unfit for use in hydraulic systems generally. We find it unnecessary to consider whether the warranty of

---

[1] Upon recommendation of Mobil, plaintiff used Mobil's DTE 23 and Del Vac Special after the second Tyrone was installed in May 9, 1967, until July 25, 1967, when plaintiff changed to Pacemaker XD–15. All of the above oils contained certain chemical additives for anti-wear, anti-oxidation and anti-foaming.

merchantability was breached, although there is some proof in the record to that effect, since we conclude that there was a warranty of fitness.

Plaintiff Lewis testified that he had been a longtime customer of Mobil Oil, and that his only source of contact with the company was through Frank Rowe, Mobil's local dealer, with whom he did almost all his business. It was common knowledge in the community that Lewis was converting his sawmill operation into a hydraulic system. Rowe knew this, and in fact had visited his mill on business matters several times during the course of the changeover. When operations with the new machinery were about to commence, Lewis asked Rowe to get him the proper hydraulic fluid. Rowe asked him what kind of a system he had, and Lewis replied it was a Commercial pump type. This was all the information asked or given. Neither Lewis nor Rowe knew what the oil requirements for the system were, and Rowe knew that Lewis knew nothing more specific about his requirements. Lewis also testified that after he began having trouble with his operations, while there were several possible sources of the difficulty the oil was one suspected source, and he several times asked Rowe to be sure he was furnishing him with the right kind.

Rowe's testimony for the most part confirmed Lewis'. It may be noted here that Mobil does not contest Rowe's authority to represent it in this transaction, and therefore whatever warranties may be implied because of the dealings between Rowe and Lewis are attributable to Mobil. Rowe admitted knowing Lewis was converting to a hydraulic system and that Lewis asked him to supply the fluid. He testified that he did not know what should be used and relayed the request to a superior in the Mobil organization, who recommended Ambrex 810. This is what was supplied.

When the first Tyrone pump was installed in April 1967, Rowe referred the request for a proper oil recommendation to Ted Klock, a Mobil engineer. Klock recommended Ambrex 810. When this pump failed a few weeks later, Klock visited the Lewis plant to inspect the equipment. The system was flushed out completely and the oil was changed to DTE–23 and Del Vac Special containing several additives. After this, no further trouble was experienced.

This evidence adequately establishes an implied warranty of fitness. Arkansas has adopted the Uniform Commercial Code's provision for an implied warranty of fitness:

> "Where the seller at the time of contracting has reason to know any particular purpose for which the goods are required and that the buyer is relying on the seller's skill or judgment to select or furnish suitable goods, there is unless excluded or modified under the next section an implied warranty that the goods shall be fit for such purpose." 7C Ark.Stat.Ann. § 85–2–315 (1961).

Under this provision of the Code, there are two requirements for an implied warranty of fitness: (1) that the seller have "reason to know" of the use for which the goods are purchased, and (2) that the buyer relies on the seller's expertise in supplying the proper product. Both of these requirements are amply met by the proof in this case. Lewis' testimony, as confirmed by that of Rowe and Klock, shows that the oil was purchased specifically for his hydraulic system, not for just a hydraulic system in general, and that Mobil certainly knew of this specific purpose. It is also clear that Lewis was relying on Mobil to supply him with the proper oil for the system, since at the time of his purchases, he made clear that he didn't know what kind was necessary.

Mobil contends that there was no warranty of fitness for use in his particular system because he didn't specify that he needed an oil with additives, and alternatively that he didn't give them enough information for them to determine that an additive oil was required. However, it seems that the circumstances of this case come directly within that situation described in the first comment to this provision of the Uniform Commercial Code:

> "1. Whether or not this warranty arises in any individual case is basically a question of fact to be determined by the circumstances of the contracting. Under this section the buyer need not bring home to the seller actual knowledge of the particular purpose for which the goods are intended or of his reliance on the seller's skill and judgment, if the circumstances are such that the seller has reason to realize the purpose intended or that the reliance exists." 7C Ark.Stat.Ann. § 85–2–315, Comment 1 (1961).

Here Lewis made it clear that the oil was purchased for his system, that he didn't know what oil should be used, and that he was relying on Mobil to supply the proper product. If any further information was needed, it was incumbent upon Mobil to get it before making its recommendation. That it could have easily gotten the necessary information is evidenced by the fact that after plaintiff's continuing complaints, Mobil's engineer visited the plant, and, upon inspection, changed the recommendation that had previously been made.

Additionally, Mobil contends that even if there were an implied warranty of fitness, it does not cover the circumstances of this case because of the abnormal features which the plaintiff's system contained, namely an inadequate filtration system and a capacity to entrain excessive air. There are several answers to this contention. First of all, the contention goes essentially to the question of causation—i. e., whether the damage was caused by a breach of warranty or by some other cause—and not to the existence of a warranty of fitness in the first place. Secondly, assuming that certain peculiarities in the plaintiff's system did exist, the whole point of an implied warranty of fitness is that a product be suitable for a specific purpose, and that a seller should not supply a product which is not so suited. Thirdly, there is no evidence in the record that the plaintiff's system was unique or abnormal in these respects. It operated satisfactorily under the prior owner, and the new system has operated satisfactorily after it was adequately cleaned and an additive type oil used.

While we will discuss these problems more completely in the question of causation, it may be briefly noted here that the proof shows that plaintiff's filtration system was installed and maintained in strict accordance with the manufacturer's recommendations, that this was a standard system, and that any hydraulic system has a certain unavoidable capacity to entrain air. While a "perfect" system which is run 24 hours a day might not have any air in it, in actual practice there are at least two sources of air. One is from minute leaks in "packing glands." The other source arises from the fact that when the system is shut down, as at night and over the lunch hour, as well as for repairs, the oil drains out of the system and into the reservoir. When the system is started up again, air which has entered the system to replace the drained oil must be dissipated. This dissipation occurs by running the system for a few minutes and is affected by the capacity of the oil to rid itself of air bubbles. It is sufficient to note here that there was no evidence that the plaintiff's system was in any way unique in this respect. Thus, Mobil's defense that there was no warranty of fitness because of an "abnormal use" of the oil is not appropriate here.

II.   Breach of Warranty As the Cause of Plaintiff's Damage

The primary controversy in this case is whether the damage done to the plaintiff's hydraulic system was caused by the defendant's breach of warranty in failing to provide a proper oil. This issue primarily presents a question of the sufficiency of the evidence to support the jury's verdict that the cause of the plaintiff's damage was the use of Ambrex 810 and that Ambrex 810 was an improper oil for his system. Of course, on appeal the evidence must be viewed in the light most favorable to the jury verdict, and we think there was sufficient evidence to support the verdict on the breach of warranty issue. An understanding of the evidence in this case will be facilitated by a brief explanation of each party's theory of the cause of damage.

Plaintiff's theory was that the damage was caused by pump cavitation induced by the failure of the oil to expurgate air bubbles quickly enough from its body, and that this characteristic of the oil could have been prevented by the addition of proper additives, principally a defoamant additive, but also anti-wear, anti-oxidation, and anti-rust additives.

Pump cavitation occurs when air bubbles in the body of the oil are sucked into the pump along with the hydraulic fluid. The moving parts within the pump have very small tolerances and must be kept lubricated at all times by the hydraulic fluid. Due to the exceedingly high pressures within the pump, when there are air bubbles in the fluid, they become compressed into larger bubbles and at some point interfere with the lubricating qualities of the oil, permitting the metal parts of the pump to come in contact. When this contact occurs, small metal pieces flake off and get into the fluid, which then disperses these metal contaminants throughout the system. These metal particles can in turn be responsible for causing other problems in the system which would result in the introduction of atmospheric contamination—i. e., dirt—into the system. As the metal particles, plus the other contamination, are circulated throughout the system by means of the hydraulic fluid and returned to the pump intake, serious damage is caused to the pump which cannot tolerate these contaminants.

According to the plaintiff's theory, this process can be prevented by the addition of an anti-foamant additive in the oil which aids it in expurgating air quickly so that air bubbles are not sucked into the pump in the first place.

Defendant's theory of the cause of damage was that plaintiff failed to maintain his equipment properly, failed to have a proper filtration system, and failed to flush the system after pump failures. Defendant also contested plaintiff's allegations that a defoamant additive in the oil would prevent damage from pump cavitation.

The following brief summary of the evidence on these theories demonstrates that there was adequate proof in the record to sustain the jury's verdict on the breach of warranty issue.

The above description of the theory of cavitation was testified to in substance by plaintiff's expert witness Edwards. This witness also testified that it was his opinion that plaintiff's trouble with his system was caused by pump cavitation, and the cavitation damage was caused by the use of Ambrex 810. It was his further opinion that Ambrex 810 caused pump cavitation because of its failure to have suitable additives which could have prevented this damage and that Ambrex 810 was unsuitable for use in equipment of this type. Edwards' credentials as an expert are not challenged in this case, and this opinion evidence was entitled to be considered by the jury.

Another expert witness for the plaintiff also testified that a non-additive oil such as Ambrex 810 was unsuitable for use in plaintiff's equipment and that an additive oil was necessary. The manufacturer of plaintiff's equipment testified similarly. The jury was also entitled to consider the fact that when a Mobil engineer actually visited plaintiff's mill and saw the equipment, he changed his oil recommendation to one containing additives. Further circumstantial evidence that the oil was the cause of the problems was the fact that once the system was flushed and additive oil was used, the system thereupon functioned satisfactorily.

Against the foregoing evidence, the defendant presented the following evidence. First, two expert witnesses testified that, using new samples of oil, Ambrex 810 performed as well as or better than an additive oil on certain standard laboratory tests of foam dissipation and air release qualities. Plaintiff's expert witness testified in rebuttal that such tests were not indicative of how the two oils would perform in actual operation, because once they had actually been "worked" the non-additive oil (Ambrex 810) underwent certain chemical changes which would affect these qualities, while the chemicals in the additive oil would counteract these changes so as not to affect the qualities so much.

Defendant also presented testimony from a sawmill operator using equipment made by the same manufacturer as plaintiff's that he used "pipeline drip" as his hydraulic fluid and that his equipment operated satisfactorily. Apparently the inference to be drawn here was that the quality of oil used as hydraulic fluid was not important to the proper operation of the equipment. However, plaintiff was able to establish on rebuttal that this "pipeline drip" was in fact a lubricating oil which contained all the chemical additives which were needed and missing in Ambrex 810.

The defendant contended that the cause of the plaintiff's trouble was his failure to have an adequate filtration process on his equipment to clean the oil. Some of the defense witnesses testified that metal strainers were not sufficient and that paper filters were necessary. The evidence on this point is somewhat unsatisfactory, because no attempt was made by the defense to make distinctions between the kinds of pumps used by the plaintiff. Plaintiff admits that as to the Tyrone pumps which were used in the later stages of operation, paper filters were required by the manufacturer, but it is uncontested that they were used on these pumps. The system originally operated with Commercial pumps. The manufacturer of that equipment testified that with these pumps only metal strainers were used, not paper filters, and that he had installed many systems which worked satisfactorily under these circumstances so long as the proper oil was used. While the evidence on this issue is conflicting, we think the jury was entitled to conclude, as it obviously did, that inadequate filtration was not the cause of plaintiff's trouble.

The defendant also contended that plaintiff's trouble was caused by a failure to flush his system thoroughly after a pump failure, and that sufficient contaminants remained in the system to cause the subsequent failures, instead of the oil being the cause. Again the evidence on this point is not entirely clear, but the force of this contention is considerably vitiated by the fact that one of the failures occurred shortly after the installation of an entirely new system. It seems evident that this system was cleaner than one which would have been merely flushed, and yet it did not operate satisfactorily with Ambrex 810.

We conclude that there was adequate evidence to sustain the jury's verdict that plaintiff's damage was caused by the breach of warranty. * * *

To summarize our decision in this case, having reviewed the evidence as a whole and the instructions of the able trial judge, we conclude that there was a warranty of fitness for a particular purpose in this case, that the warranty was breached, and that the defendant was liable for the damages caused by this breach, including loss of profits during the time plaintiff was using Ambrex 810. * * * The jury's verdict was in the single amount of $89,250. We are unable to determine from the record what would be a proper amount to award for direct damages plus loss of profits for the appropriate time period. Therefore, the judgment must be reversed and remanded for a new trial on the issue of damages. * * *

NOTES

1. The *Lewis* court found that there was "ample proof" that Mobile Oil's local dealer had reason to know the particular purpose for which Lewis was purchasing Ambrex 810 hydraulic fluid. Lewis asked the dealer to supply him with the proper hydraulic fluid for his pump. On being asked what kind of pump he had, Lewis identified his system as a "Commercial-pump type." According to the court, what makes Lewis' purpose in purchasing the hydraulic fluid "particular"? That Lewis purchased the hydraulic fluid specifically for his hydraulic system? Or that his hydraulic system was of a nonstandard or atypical sort? Lewis' description of his system as a "Commercial-pump type" gives enough information for the local dealer to know the specific purpose for which Lewis wanted hydraulic fluid. He told the dealer about his specific purpose. However, if a purpose is "particular" only if nonstandard or atypical, Mobile Oil needs to know how rare Commercial pumps are among hydraulic pumps. If Commercial pumps

are common, Lewis' purpose is ordinary and therefore not particular. More recent cases show a weak trend requiring that a particular purpose be nonstandard or atypical; see, e.g., McDonald Bros., Inc. v. Tinder Wholesale, LLC, 395 F. Supp.2d 255 (M.D.N.C. 2005); Arndt v. Extreme Motorcycles, 2007 U.S. Dist. LEXIS 95625, at *1 (W.D.N.C. 2007); Franulovic v. Coca Cola, 64 UCC Rep. Serv.2d 370 (D.N.J. 2007).

2. Lewis' local Mobile dealer supplied him with Ambrex 810 between November 1964 and April 1967. Because the court found that the dealer had reason to know of Lewis' particular purpose when he first began purchasing the product, it concluded that a 2–315 warranty accompanied each sale of the Ambrex 810. Lewis had to replace several pumps damaged by use of this product over the three year period, and the court upheld a jury verdict that Mobile Oil had breached its 2–315 warranties in sales of the product during this time. Suppose the court had held that a buyer's purpose is particular only if it is not ordinary— nonstandard or idiosyncratic. Suppose too that Lewis' Commercial-type pump was a nonstandard pump. Then, to apply 2–315, the trier of fact would need to determine the date on which Mobile's local dealer first had reason to know that Lewis' purpose in purchasing hydraulic fluid was particular. This date is needed to determine when Mobile's 2–315 warranty first arose.

Assume that the seller knows or has reason to know of the buyer's particular purpose in purchasing the goods. Apart from sheer mistake, why might the buyer prefer to argue that the sale creates a warranty of fitness rather than a warranty of merchantability? 2–316(2).

3. The issue of the buyer's reliance on the seller's skill or judgment arises when the buyer orders a specific brand or provides its own specifications. Reliance is present if the buyer would respond to the seller's communication that the brand ordered or the specification is unsuitable for the buyer's particular purpose. A finding of reliance forces the seller to bear the cost of either investigating whether the order or specification is suitable for the buyer's particular purpose or disclaiming the warranty of fitness. Courts generally do not find reliance in these circumstances. See, e.g., Duffy v. Idaho Crop Improvement Ass'n, 895 P.2d 1195 (Idaho 1995) (type of product); Blockhead v. The Plastic Forming Co., 402 F. Supp. 1017 (D. Conn. 1975) (specifications); Conservation Load Switch Inc. v. Ohio Univ., 2004 WL 596244, at *1 (Ohio Ct. Cl. 2004) (model). Their implicit judgment is that the buyer has more expertise than the seller in selecting the brand or specification that suits its purposes. A finding of no reliance gives the buyer an incentive either to use this expertise in selection or ask the seller to select a particular brand or specifications.

PROBLEM 5.7

Jones, a professional artist, had a commission to construct a sculpture. Requiring steel for the piece, Jones approached Works, a national manufacturer of steel products, and told it of her commission. Works recommended its flexible steel, a general purpose steel product. Jones acted on Works' advice and in January ordered 10 sheets of the steel at a total price of $1,000, which Works delivered. Before beginning her sculpture, Jones placed further orders for 10 sheets of the steel at the same price in

February and March. In March Jones began constructing her sculpture using all of the steel Works had delivered. The sculpture collapsed because the steel was insufficiently rigid to support the significant weight of the sculpture's other materials. Jones visited Works in April to complaint about the sculpture's collapse. Works assured her that the steel it delivered contained no defects, which was true, and Jones ordered 10 more sheets of Works' flexible steel at $1,000, which Works delivered, to make a smaller version of the same sculpture. This version of the sculpture also collapsed because the steel was insufficiently rigid. In May Works' sales representive visited Jones' studio seeking further orders of steel. On being shown Jones' design and her failed efforts, the representative recommended that she order a more rigid brand of Works' steel. Jones ordered 10 sheets of Works's rigid steel at $1,000, which Works delivered, and fashioned the sculpture containing it. This time her efforts were successful. Jones is satisfied with her sculpture's stability. However, she is unhappy that she was forced to throw away the steel sheets she used in her unsuccessful attempts at producing a stable sculpture. The steel is worthless. Jones wants Works to refund her $5,000, the amount she paid for all of the steel Works delivered between January and May. In what amount, if any, is Jones entitled to a refund? 2–315, 2–314, 2–711.

E. WARRANTY OF TITLE

Under 2–312 a warranty of title is implied in the sale of goods. The seller warrants that "the title conveyed shall be good, and its transfer rightful." 2–312(1)(a). In addition, under 2–312(1)(b) the seller warrants that the goods are "delivered free from any security interest or other lien or encumbrance of which the buyer at the time of contracting had no knowledge." The merchant seller dealing in goods of the kind sold also warrants that the goods delivered are free of a third party's rightful infringement claims to intellectual property. 2–312(3). The seller's ignorance of defects in title is no defense to a breach of warranty of title claim. As with other warranties, the seller's warranty liability is strict. The underlying justification for the warranty of title is the same as Article 2's other warranties: The seller is in a comparatively better position than its buyer in determining the quality of title it is conveying.

The warranty of title is a guarantee that title to the goods is "good" and "clean." A buyer of stolen goods receives void title—no title, not good title. Its seller therefore breaches 2–312(a)(1). Even a seller who delivers good title still can breach 2–312(1)(a). Section 2–312(1)(a) warrants that the transfer of title is "rightful." A seller who transfers title in breach of covenants to its own lender, for instance, still might convey good title to the buyer. Nonetheless, the transfer is wrongful and the sale therefore breaches 2–312(1)(a). Title transferred subject to liens or encumbrances, while good, is "unclean." A lien is a property right of another in an asset. Security interests are consensual liens on assets, while judgment and statutory liens are nonconsensual liens. The sale of goods subject to a security interest or other lien transfers unclean title to the goods. If the buyer lacks of knowledge of the lien, the seller breaches 2–312(1)(b).

Two different problems arise in 2–312's interpretation. One concerns the extent of the warranty of title. Although 2–312(1)'s language does not cover ultimately invalid claims, most courts construe the warranty of title to extend to them. See, e.g., Pacific Sunwear of California, Inc. v. Olaes Enterprises, Inc., 67 UCC Rep. Serv.2d 62 (Cal. App. 4th Dist. 2008). Case law has asked whether the seller warrants not just that title is good but that the goods also are free of a "cloud on title." A "cloud on title" (or a "substantial shadow over title") is a non-spurious claim to title or interest in the goods by another, whether or not the claim ultimately is found superior to the buyer's title. If the seller warrants that against a cloud on title, the warranty is breached when the buyer must defend against a colorable claim to the goods. *Sabor v. Dan Angelone Chevrolet, Inc.*, reproduced below, illustrates the reasoning of these cases. Proposed 2–312 adopted this construction of 2–312.

The second problem concerns the buyer's remedies for the seller's breach of the warranty of title. To see the difficulty, recognize first that the injured buyer generally can select among the remedies described in 2–711. (Chapter 10 describes the buyer's remedies in more detail.) These include recovery of the purchase price paid to the seller. In addition, when available, the buyer can use "cover" (2–712) and "market price" measures (2–713) to calculate its damages. The cover measure allows the buyer to recover the difference between its cost of obtaining a substitute purchase and the contract price. The market price measure allows recovery of the difference between the market price at the time the buyer learned of the warranty of title breach and the contract price. However, these measures are available only if the buyer has not accepted the goods or effectively revoked its acceptance. In many instances the buyer learns of the seller's breach of the warranty of title a considerable time after it is in possession of the goods. The goods have been accepted and revocation will come too late. As a result, in many cases the buyer cannot measure its damages by "cover" or "market price." Instead, it must measure its damages according to 2–714.

Section 2–714(2) provides the general formula for measuring damages for breach of warranty: "The measure of damages for breach of warranty is the difference at the time and place of acceptance between the value of the goods accepted and the value they would have had if they been as warranted, unless special circumstances who proximate damages of a different amount." One difficulty is that the general formula sometimes gives a poor result. Courts have held in breach of title warranty cases that the value of accepted goods is zero, even when the buyer has gotten some use out of the goods. See, e.g, Jerry Parks Equipment Co. v. Southeast Equip. Co., 817 F.2d 340 (5th Cir. 1987). Where the purchase price is reliable evidence of the market price of the goods if they had been as warranted, and where the market of accepted goods is deemed to be zero, 2–714(2)'s general measure allows the buyer to recover its purchase price. This measure overcompensates the buyer because it takes no account of the buyer's use of the goods before it was dispossessed of them. The temporary use of the goods is of some value to the buyer. Overcompensation also occurs where the market price of the good falls between the time the goods were accepted and the time the goods were taken from the buyer.

For these reasons, the majority of courts rely on 2–714(2)'s "unless" clause to measure damages by the market value of the goods at the time they were taken from the buyer, rather than using 2–714(2)'s formula. See, e.g., Metalcraft, Inc. v. Pratt, 500 A.2d 329 (Md. Ct. App. 1985). Fixing market price as of this time puts on the buyer the risk of appreciation and depreciation in market price after acceptance of the goods. As a result, the buyer's damages place it in approximately the position it would have been in had the seller not breached the title warranty. However, measuring damages by the time of dispossession still does not assure that the buyer is neither overcompensated nor undercompensated. This is because the market price of the goods can appreciate or depreciate even after the time they are taken from the buyer. Setting a time at which to measure damages inevitably ignores the possibility of fluctuations in market price after this time. By ignoring fluctuations in market price over the entire life of the good, a "time of dispossession" measure of damages cannot guarantee that the buyer is neither overcompensated nor undercompensated. Finally, even ignoring fluctuations in market price after dispossession, undercompensation still remains possible. This is because the buyer might value the goods in excess of the market (or purchase) price. Section 2–714(2)'s formula for damages, based on market price does not make such buyers whole.

Saber v. Dan Angelone Chevrolet

Supreme Court of Rhode Island, 2002
811 A.2d 644

■ WILLIAMS, CHIEF JUSTICE.

In this case, the defendant, Dan Angelone Chevrolet, Inc. (defendant), appeals from a Superior Court judgment, challenging several rulings made by the trial justice. Before closing arguments, the trial justice determined as a matter of law that the defendant, a Rhode Island corporation, breached the warranty of title of a car sold to the plaintiff, George Saber (plaintiff), a resident of the Commonwealth of Massachusetts. The jury found that the plaintiff provided the defendant with sufficient notice of the breach and awarded the plaintiff damages in the amount of $14,900. On appeal, the defendant alleges that the trial justice committed a variety of errors. For the reasons set out below, we deny and dismiss the defendant's appeal and affirm the trial justice's rulings.

I.   Facts and Travel

On February 7, 1990, plaintiff bought a used 1985 Chevrolet Corvette (Corvette or car), from defendant for $14,900. The Corvette was red, had an automatic transmission, and its odometer said 34,744 miles. At that time plaintiff also purchased an extended warranty to cover certain problems that might arise with the car. Between March 1990 and April 1992, plaintiff experienced several mechanical problems with the car and brought it to defendant for service. Because of the series of problems he was experiencing, plaintiff decided to research the car's history. In conducting a title search on the car, he discovered that a title application for the Corvette described it as black and equipped with a manual transmission. In light of his discovery, plaintiff, through an attorney, contacted the Massachusetts State Police (state police).

In response to plaintiff's call, state police Lieutenant Joseph Costa (Lt. Costa) examined the Corvette and discovered some discrepancies with respect to its vehicle identification number (VIN) and major components. The plate located on the window downpost, which contained the VIN, was blistered and painted over. Additionally, derivative identification numbers on the car's frame, engine and transmission did not correspond to the VIN on the window downpost. Further, a Mylar sticker, which is typically located on the door of the car and also has the same VIN as the window downpost, was missing. Finally, the Corvette was equipped with a third brake light, which was manufactured one year after the car supposedly was manufactured. Based on those observations, Lt. Costa believed that some of the car parts were stolen.

After the inspection, plaintiff drove the Corvette home. The next day, plaintiff drove the car to the North Dartmouth barracks of the state police. There, he voluntarily left the car in the parking lot, dropped off the keys and took a ride home from an employee. Lieutenant Costa testified that the car was impounded and that plaintiff could not have it back.

Later, the Corvette was delivered to Danny's Autobody, a privately owned business located in New Bedford, Massachusetts, that the state police used as an impound facility. A subsequent investigation revealed that the Corvette was neither stolen nor composed of stolen parts. Rather, according to defendant's brief, the Corvette was destroyed in a fire and subsequently rebuilt using parts from various other cars. The frame was replaced with one from an "identical type" car, the motor was replaced, the engine block was taken from a Chevrolet Camaro and the car was painted red. According to defendant, it received the Corvette in its current, refurbished condition as a trade-in and later sold it to plaintiff. None of those facts were disclosed to plaintiff when he purchased the car, and it is not clear whether defendant was aware of them when it sold the Corvette to plaintiff.

In 1992, plaintiff filed a lawsuit against defendant in Massachusetts District Court, which later was dismissed for lack of jurisdiction. In 1995, plaintiff filed the instant action in Superior Court seeking damages for negligence and breach of contract. The plaintiff's amended complaint added counts for deceptive trade practices, misrepresentation, revocation of acceptance, and violations of the Magnuson Moss Warranty Act, 15 U.S.C. §§ 2301–2312, but did not expressly allege breach of warranty of title. To support his claim for negligence, however, plaintiff alleged in his complaint that he was not given good title to the car.

The trial began in April 2000. At the close of plaintiff's case, defendant moved for judgment as a matter of law, arguing that there could be no breach of the warranty of title because the car was not stolen. The trial justice, however, denied defendant's motion, stating that the warranty of title may be breached by law enforcement impoundment. Before closing arguments, both parties moved for judgment as a matter of law. The trial justice determined that, based on Lt. Costa's testimony, the car was impounded and because of that impoundment, defendant breached the warranty of title owed to plaintiff. The trial justice granted plaintiff's motion on that issue. The trial justice, however, charged the jury with the task of determining whether plaintiff provided defendant with sufficient notice of the breach as required under G.L. 1956 § 6A–2–607. The jury returned a verdict in plaintiffs favor. The defendant later renewed its motion for judgment as a matter of law and moved for a new trial. Both motions were denied. The defendant timely appealed.

II.   Judgment as a Matter of Law

* * * The defendant argues that the trial justice erred in granting plaintiffs motion for judgment as a matter of law for three reasons. First, defendant claims that the trial justice unfairly allowed plaintiff to amend his complaint to establish liability for breach of warranty of title based on the fact that the Corvette was impounded. Second, defendant challenges the trial justice's finding that the car was indeed impounded. Finally, according to defendant, even if the car was impounded, the trial justice erred in finding that the impoundment constituted a breach of warranty of title. We conclude that each of defendant's claims are without merit and address each seriatim.

A.   "Amendment" of Plaintiff's Complaint

The defendant argues that the trial justice erred in granting plaintiffs motion for judgment as a matter of law because the trial justice predicated his decision on a theory that was not properly raised in plaintiffs complaint. According to defendant, allowing plaintiff to proceed on the "new" theory constituted an unfair amendment of plaintiffs complaint.[1]

B.   Impoundment

Next, defendant argues that the trial justice erred in finding that the Corvette was impounded. A car is impounded if it is placed "in the custody of the police or the court." Black's Law Dictionary 760 (7th ed. 1999).

The trial justice found it undisputed that "law enforcement authorities of the Commonwealth of Massachusetts impounded [the Corvette]." At trial, Lt. Costa testified that after he inspected the car, he suspected that it was composed of stolen parts. Lieutenant Costa further testified that, based on his suspicion, the car was seized and impounded and that plaintiff could not have it back.

According to defendant, because plaintiff voluntarily relinquished custody of the Corvette to the state police, the car never was impounded. We deem that argument unpersuasive. Lieutenant Costa testified that plaintiff's consent was irrelevant to the impoundment. We agree that plaintiff's failure to oppose the impoundment in this case should have no impact on the trial justice's finding. The defendant did not offer any testimony to contest the fact that plaintiff was dispossessed of the car by the state police. In fact, the state police still possessed the car at the time of the trial. Based on the facts presented

---

[1]   According to defendant, plaintiff never put defendant "on 'fair and adequate notice' that 'the type of claim being asserted' was one of breach of warranty of title due to vehicle dispossession, reliquishment and/or impoundment. Had [defendant known] this would be an issue in the case it would have conducted discovery addressing the breach of warranty of title issue." . . .

at trial, there was no dispute that the car was impounded and the trial justice did not err in so finding.

C. Breach as a Matter of Law

Under § 6A–2–312(1) of the Rhode Island Uniform Commercial Code (UCC), "there is in a contract for sale a warranty by the seller that: (a) the title conveyed shall be good, and its transfer rightful." The UCC does not define "good title." Thus, to determine what is required of a seller to convey "good title" under § 6A–2–312(1)(a), we apply our well settled canons of statutory construction.

" 'Generally when a statute expresses a clear and unambiguous meaning, the task of interpretation is at an end and this Court will apply the plain and ordinary meaning of the words set forth in the statute.' State v. Bryant, 670 A.2d 776, 779 (R.I. 1996). However, when the statutory language is ambiguous, 'the primary object of the Court is to ascertain the legislative intention from a consideration of the legislation in its entirety, viewing the language used therein in the light, nature, and purpose of the enactment thereof.' Mason v. Bowerman Bros., Inc., 95 R.I. 425, 431, 187 A.2d 772, 776 (1963)." Pierce v. Pierce, 770 A.2d 867, 871 (R.I. 2001).

The term "good title" as it is used in § 6A–2–312(1)(a) is ambiguous. The UCC does not provide whether a seller's obligation under § 6A–2–312(1)(a) is limited to transferring legally valid title or whether "good title" assumes some other associated qualities.

Unlike most other statutory enactments, the UCC is accompanied by official commentary. "While these comments are not controlling authority and may not be used to vary the plain language of the [UCC]," they are useful for determining the purpose of its provisions and ascertaining the intent of its drafters. Jefferson v. Jones, 286 Md. 544, 408 A.2d 1036, 1039 (Md. 1979). Official comment 1 to § 6A–2–312 declares that one of the purposes of the warranty of title is to provide "for a buyer's basic needs in respect to a title which he in good faith expects to acquire by his purchase, namely, that he receive a good, clean title transferred to him so that he will not be exposed to a lawsuit in order to protect it." That comment goes on to state that the warranty of quiet possession is abolished, but that a "disturbance of quiet possession is one way, among many, in which the breach of the warranty of title may be established." Id.

The language in official comment 1 evidences the General Assembly's intent to allow a buyer to establish a breach of warranty of title even if a seller did indeed deliver legally valid title. Without ruling on the official comment's abolition of the warranty of quiet possession, we do adopt its position that a buyer may establish a breach of warranty of title by showing a disturbance of quiet possession. After reading the official comment we conclude that disturbance of quiet possession does not depend on a buyer's ability to show that a seller transferred legally invalid title. Were we to limit the scope of § 6A–2–312 to those situations where title lawfully rested in a third party, buyers would be attempting to establish, rather than protect, their title and the language in official comment 1 would be rendered nugatory. Thus, the General Assembly apparently intended to "provide a remedy for the buyer who successfully defends a title suit." James J. White &

Robert S. Summers, Uniform Commercial Code, § 9–12 at 536 (4th ed. 1995).

There is, however, a split of authority concerning the scope of the warranty of title. Cf. Jefferson, 408 A.2d at 1039–40 (holding that proof of superior title in third party is not required to establish breach of warranty of title); American Container Corp. v. Hanley Trucking Corp., 268 A.2d 313, 318 (N.J. Super. Ct. 1970) ("The mere casting of a substantial shadow over his title, regardless of the ultimate outcome, is sufficient to violate a warranty of good title."); Colton v. Decker, 540 N.W.2d 172, 176 (S.D. 1995) (holding that a seller breached its warranty of title by selling buyer a truck with conflicting vehicle identification numbers that was seized by the police under the mistaken belief that it was stolen) with C.F. Sales, Inc. v. Amfert, Inc., 344 N.W.2d 543, 555 (Iowa 1983) (holding that warranty of title is not breached unless superior title is established in a third party). We conclude that we are giving effect to the General Assembly's stated intention by aligning ourselves with those jurisdictions that allow a buyer to establish breach of warranty of title if a substantial shadow is cast over a title, even if the buyer's title ultimately is proven to be legally valid.

By adopting this position, we do acknowledge that "there is some point at which [a] third party's claim against the goods becomes so attenuated that we should not regard it as an interference against which the seller has warranted." White & Summers, § 9–12 at 537. Here, the car and its parts were not stolen and defendant did indeed have and deliver a legally valid title to plaintiff. We are satisfied, however, that under the facts in this case, the claim made against plaintiffs car—the state police's impoundment—was not too far attenuated. Lieutenant Costa's inspection of the Corvette revealed that it had contradicting VINs and a missing Mylar sticker. Based on those facts Lt. Costa reasonably, albeit mistakenly, believed that the car was composed of stolen parts, and therefore impounded it. By doing so, the state police called plaintiffs ownership into question, thereby "casting a substantial shadow over his title." *American Container Corp.*, 268 A.2d at 318.

The Corvette in this case reminds us of a passage attributed to Abraham Lincoln when he asked, "how many legs does a dog have if you count his tail as a leg? Four. You can call a tail a leg if you want to, but that doesn't make it a leg." Just as a dog's tail is not a leg, this car is not a typical 1985 Corvette. Although defendant argues that the car is a 1985 Corvette, the car has several "unique" qualities that distinguish it from most other 1985 Corvettes. Without knowing the colorful past associated with this car, plaintiff could not get the benefit of his bargain when he made his purchase. The Corvette was rebuilt after having previously been declared a total loss because of fire damage. Various parts were replaced from an assortment of other vehicles. Vehicle identification numbers embossed on certain parts did not correspond to one another. We conclude that those distinctive characteristics associated with the car and its title would lower its value in the eyes of a reasonably prudent purchaser. By imposing liability for breach of warranty of title in this scenario, the trial justice allayed buyers' fears of encountering a similar situation. Thus, we uphold the trial justice's ruling that defendant breached the warranty of title. * * *

IV. Motion for a New Trial

* * *

After the trial justice determined that defendant breached the warranty of title as a matter of law, he explained to the parties that the only remaining issue was whether plaintiff provided defendant with reasonable notice of the breach under § 6A–2–607(3). The defendant now argues that there was insufficient evidence for the jury to find that plaintiff provided defendant with sufficient notice of the breach of warranty of title.

The plaintiff testified that he called defendant on the telephone to give him notice that he considered the warranty breached. Although plaintiff later testified on cross-examination that his attorney, rather than plaintiff personally, was the one who called defendant, the combination of testimony was evidence that defendant received notification that it breached the warranty owed to plaintiff. Indeed, defendant substantiated plaintiff's claim when Dan Angelone, the defendant's owner, acknowledged that he did receive a phone call from plaintiff's attorney, even though he stated that he could not recall the contents of the conversation. Thus, the trial justice did not overlook or misconceive material or relevant evidence in rejecting defendant's motion. He commented on the evidence adduced at trial and discussed what he perceived were potential problems. Noting his concerns with plaintiff's credibility, the trial justice determined that it was the jury's function to resolve those issues. If the jury believed plaintiff, there was sufficient evidence to satisfy the notice requirement [of § 6A–2–607(3)]. * * *

Conclusion

For the foregoing reasons, the defendant's appeal is denied and dismissed. The judgment of the Superior Court is affirmed. Upon satisfaction of the judgment, title of the car shall revert to the defendant. The papers may be returned to the Superior Court.

NOTES

1. The buyer in *Saber* apparently added a breach of warranty of title claim to support his negligence claim against the car dealer. His breach of contract claim was not expressly based on a breach of the warranty. Is there another sort of warranty that the buyer could have relied on to support his breach of contract claim? See 2–313(1)(b), 2–314(2)(a). The buyer bought a used 1985 Chevrolet Corvette. Later investigation revealed that the car's frame was from an "identical type" of car and the engine block came from a Chevrolet Camaro. The trial court found for the buyer on its breach of warranty of title claim. On different facts, might the buyer prefer to rely on the dealer's breach of a different warranty?

2. *Saber* and most courts rely on Comment 1 to 2–312 to extend 2–312 to create a warranty against colorable claims to title in the goods by third parties. The relevant portion of the Comment provides that the 2–312(1) meets the buyer's need to receive a "good, clean title transferred to him . . . so that he will not be exposed a lawsuit in order to protect it . . . Disturbance of quiet possession, although not mentioned specifically, is one way, among many, in which the breach of warranty of title may be established." Section 2–312(1) implies a warranty that the title is "good" and free of "lien and other encumbrances . . ." Colorable but ultimately invalid claims to title do not fall under these statutory terms. Although not inconsistent with 2–312(1)'s language, nothing in the language signals a legislative intent to extend 2–312(1) warranty to colorable claims. The *Saber* court finds the "apparent" legislative intent from the quoted portion of Comment 1. Rhode Island, whose law the *Saber* court applied, has not incorporated the Official Comments to Article 2. The finding of a legislative intent to incorporate the Comments is less plausible in jurisdictions whose legislatures do not enact the Official Comments to Article 2 of the UCC along with the statute. Very few states incorporate by statute the UCC's Official Comments; see, e.g. Ky. Rev. Stat. § 335.1–103(3) (2011). At least one state statute directs that no implication of legislative intent be drawn from the Comments to the UCC; Colo. Rev. Stat. 2–5–102(3) (2011).

3. In *Saber* the buyer's car remained with the car dealer. The trial court measured his damages by 2–714(2)'s "unless" clause, awarding him the purchase price. Is the award likely to overcompensate the buyer? Why might it not? In some breach of title warranty cases the buyer is only temporarily dispossessed of the goods. Section 2–714(2)'s general formula for warranty damages does not apply because it measures loss of the goods, not the temporary interference with use of them. Buyers temporarily dispossessed of the goods can recover damages under either 2–714(2)'s "unless" clause, 2–714(1)'s "reasonable determination" measure or 2–715's allowance of incidental expenses and consequential damages. See, e.g., Colton v. Decker, 540 N.W.2d 172 (S.D. 1995) (costs of recovering vehicle incidental expenses); Universal C.I.T. Credit Corp. v. State Farm Mut. Auto. Ins. Co., 493 S.W.2d 385 (Mo. Ct. App. 1973) (attorneys fees in defending title recoverable as consequential damages).

4. Article 41 of the CISG requires the seller to deliver goods which are free from "any right or claim of a third party." The Article's reference to "right or claim" means that a third party's claim does not have to be based on a legal interest in the goods. Apparently its claim to title is enough for the seller to be in breach of Article 41. In addition, "claim" is unqualified, so that the seller breaches its obligation even when a third party's claim to title in the goods is frivolous. The little diplomatic history on the point agrees. See Secretariat Commentary on the [1978] Draft Convention on Contracts for the International Sale of Goods, in Diplomatic History of the Uniform Law for International Sales 426 (then-Article 39, para. 3) (J. Honnold ed., 1989). Thus, unlike under 2–312(1), under Article 41 there is no need for the line-drawing exercise of distinguishing colorable from frivolous claims to title.

PROBLEM 5.8

X Corporation borrowed money from Bank to buy some factory equipment, granting Bank a security interest in the equipment to secure the loan. Later, X granted Finance a security interest in the equipment in exchange for Finance's loan. Both Bank and Finance properly recorded their security interests. X defaulted on its loan obligations to Finance and Finance had the local sheriff seize the equipment and dispose of it at a judicial sale. Ace bought the equipment unaware of Bank's security interest. After Bank recovered the equipment from Ace, Ace sued X Corp., the local sheriff and Finance. (You may assume that Bank has superior title in the goods it recovered.) From whom can Ace recover under 2–312, if anyone? 2–312(2), Comment 5 to 2–312, 2–103(1)(d), 9–610(d).

PROBLEM 5.9

Buyer bought an expensive refrigerator from Best Store and took it home. Five years later Buyer read an article in the local paper that described Best's poor financial situation. The article reported that Best had for the last decade granted Bank a security interest in all of its inventory and was currently in default on all of its loans. To verify the information about Bank, the reporter related that she had confirmed that it had properly recorded its security interest throughout the last decade. The article indicated that Bank was considering its options in enforcing its security interest. On reading the news story Buyer became concerned and demanded that Store refund the refrigerator's purchase price, less an adjustment reflecting Buyer's use to date. Store truthfully explained that its sale to Buyer eliminated Bank's security interest in Buyer's refrigerator. Unconvinced, Buyer immediately sued Store alleging a breach of its 2–312 warranty. Why will Buyer's suit be unsuccessful? 2–312(1), Comment 1 to 2–312, 2–725(2).

F. WARRANTIES IN FINANCE LEASES

A sale is not a lease. While a sale transfers ownership, a lease gives the lessee only a right of possession for a term. Compare 2–106(1) with 2A–103(1)(j). As a result, Article 2's warranties do not apply to leases of goods. Nonetheless, the common law imposed warranties of quality on lessors in commercial transactions that were similar to 2–314 and 2–315's warranties. Article 2A's drafters found these warranties to be uncertain in their scope; see Comment to 2A–101. For this reason, Article 2A creates a set of warranties for leases of goods that are the counterpart of Article 2's warranties. Section 2A–210 recognizes an express warranty with respect to leased goods, while 2A–211 creates a warranty against interference with the lessee's enjoyment of leased goods. Section 2A–212 recognizes an implied warranty of merchantability of leased goods when the lessor is a merchant with respect to them. For its part, under 2A–213 the lessor warrants that the leased goods are fit for the particular purpose for which the goods are required. The requirements for the warranty of fitness are the same as those described by 2–315.

Article 2A warranties are easy to justify. Like Article 2's warranties, Article 2A's warranties apply to transactions in which the person supplies the goods. In Article 2A's case, the transaction is a lease and the supplier a lessor. A lessee, no less than a buyer, is harmed when it receives nonconforming goods. From the perspective of efficiency, the risk of nonconformity should be assigned to the party that has an advantage at taking precautions to reduce or eliminate the risk. The lessor generally can take these precautions at less cost than can the lessee, just as the seller can do so at less cost than its buyer. However, in some cases the lessor is not the supplier of leased goods. Rather, it provides the financing that enables the lessee to lease them. For instance, User wants to lease equipment rather than buy it. Supplier sells equipment needed by User but is unwilling to lease them. Financer can satisfy User's desire for a lease and Supplier's desire for a sale. It will provide funds which accommodate the desires of both parties. To do so, Financer can enter into a particular three-party transaction between it, Supplier and User that Article 2A calls a "finance lease."

To understand what a finance lease involves (and does not involve), consider three different possible three-party transactions between Financer, Supplier and User.

Transaction 1: Financer lends User the purchase price of the equipment it needs. User uses the money to buy the equipment from Supplier. To secure Financer's loan, User grant it security interest in the equipment purchased with Financer's funds. This transaction describes a secured sale. User has bought the equipment from Supplier with secured financing provided by Financer. The transaction transfers ownership in the equipment to User. Thus, the transaction between Supplier and User is a sale, not a lease. 2A–103(1)(j). The transaction between User and Financer creates a security interest that secures User's obligation to Financer to repay the loan. The transaction does not satisfy User's desire for a lease.

Transaction 2: Supplier sells the equipment User needs to Financer. Financer in turn transfers possession of the equipment to User for its entire useful economic life. User agrees to make periodic payments to Financer that their agreement calls "rent" and to return the equipment to Financer at the end of its useful life. User has no right to cancel the transaction with Financer.

This transaction describes two sales. In addition to Supplier's sale to Financer, Financer's transaction with User is a secured sale. Because the term of the transaction is for the economic life of the equipment, the transaction creates a security interest, not a true lease. 1–203(b)(1); consult supra Chapter 2, section C. Financer's security interest in the equipment secures the purchase price owed by User to Financer. The fact that Financer's agreement with User labels the periodic payments User owes as "rent" is irrelevant. In substance the transaction is a secured sale and the payments installments on the equipment's purchase price. As in Transaction 1, the transaction does not satisfy User's desire for a lease.

Transaction 3: After User has selected the equipment, Financer buys it from Supplier. At the same time User "leases" the equipment from Financer and has Supplier deliver the equipment to User. The "lease agreement" makes its effectiveness conditional on User's approval of the terms of Financer's sales contract with Supplier. The agreement calls for User to make periodic payments of "rent" over the term of the "lease" and does not give User the right to cancel the agreement.

Transaction 3 may or may not describe a finance lease. (The terms describing the transaction are put in quotation marks so that questions about its legal character are not begged.) If the Financer–User transaction is for the economic life of the equipment, the transaction creates a security interest, not a lease. In this case, as in Transaction 2, the transaction between Financer and User is secured sale and the payments of "rent" are installment payments on the equipment's purchase price. Alternatively, if the Financer-User transaction is for less than the economic life of the equipment and otherwise passes 1–203's tests, the transaction is a true lease and the periodic payments are rent. In this case, the lease in Transaction 3 is a finance lease. It satisfies both Supplier and User's desires.

Section 2A–103(1)(g) defines the conditions a lease must meet to be a finance lease. To be a finance lease, obviously the transaction must be a true lease. See Comment (g) to 2A–103(1). In addition, the lessor must not select the goods. Instead, the lessee must select them. In addition, Section 2A–103(1)(g)'s definition requires that the lessor acquire the goods or right to possession and use of the goods in connection with the lease. Finally, (g) includes a slightly complex disjunctive condition. One of these conditions is that effectiveness of the lease agreement is conditional on the lessee's approval of the lessor's sales contract with the supplier or the right to possess or use the goods. 2A–103(1)(g)(iii)(B). Assuming that the Financer–User transaction is a true lease, the lease meets 2A–103(1)(g)'s conditions. User has selected Supplier's equipment, not Financer. Financer also purchased the equipment from Supplier contemporaneously with its lease agreement with User. Finally, the lease agreement's effectiveness was made conditional on User's approval of the terms of Financer's sales contract with Supplier. Thus, the Financer–User lease is a finance lease. Financer has provided the financing enabling User to lease the equipment. By contrast, in Transactions 1 and 2 Finance provides the financing enabling User to buy it.

The character of a lease as a finance lease is important for the lessor's warranties. A finance lessor is not a warrantor under Article 2A. Section 2A–212 and 2A–313's implied warranties of merchantability and fitness, respectively, and 2A–211(2)'s implied warranty against infringement do not apply to finance leases. This means that, unless the lease agreement provides otherwise, these warranties are not implied in a finance lease. As a result, in a finance lease, risk of the nonconformities described in 2A–211(2), 2A–312 and 2A–313 remain with the lessee. This is unlike non-finance leases, in which these sections place the relevant risk on the lessor under their prescribed conditions.

The special allocation of risk for finance leases is justified. The finance lessor acquires goods for lease at the direction of its lessee. Its acquisition finances the lessee's lease. As some courts puts it, the finance lessor deals in funds, not goods. Finance lessors typically finance the lease of a wide variety of goods selected by their lessees. Usually, the lessee, not the lessor, takes delivery of the asset leased. For these reasons, the finance lessor has no expertise in the goods it is leasing. Its lack of relevant expertise makes it unlike the typical merchant lessor, who deals in goods of the kind leased and has possession of them for some period. The lessee who selects the goods the finance lessor is to buy will know more about them than the finance lessor. Because the finance lessor is a relative stranger to the goods it leases, the lessor is in an inferior position to its lessee to take precautions to reduce or eliminate a risk of nonconformities in the leased goods. An efficient allocation of nonconformity risk therefore places the risk on the finance lessee. Article 2A's special exception for finance leases does this.

Although the finance lessor is not a warrantor of the goods, the finance lessee gets the benefit of any warranties the supplier of the goods makes to the finance lessor. 2A–209(1). Under 2A–209(1), as a beneficiary of the warranties, the lessee remains subject to the terms of these warranties. Because the finance lessor purchases the goods from the supplier, Article 2's warranty provisions apply. Thus, Article 2's express and implied warranties apply to the sales contract under their prescribed conditions. Section 2A–209(1) passes these warranties through to the finance lessee. The lessee will have notice of them, because 2A–103(1)(g)(iii)'s disjunctive conditions assure that it gets information about the terms of the sales contract between the supplier and the finance lessor. The result is that although the finance lessee bears the nonconformity risk as against the finance lessor, the supplier ultimately bears this risk as against the finance lessee. This allocation of risk makes sense for the reason given above: As a dealer in the goods, the supplier is better positioned than the lessee to take precautions against the risk of nonconformity in the leased goods.

PROBLEM 5.10

Needing special tractors for a short-term project, Construction found the right ones at Tractor Corporation, a seller of construction equipment. However, Tractor was unwilling to rent tractors and Construction did not want to purchase them. Accordingly, Tractor recommended that Construction contact TracFin, its wholly owned subsidiary that financed purchases or leases of Tractor's construction equipment. Construction did so. After TractFin bought the tractors Construction had picked out and presented Construction with the sales contract, Construction signed a lease agreement with TracFin. The tractors Construction rented would not start. Tractor has gone into bankruptcy while TracFin has not. TracFin refuses to do anything to remedy the situation and insists that Construction continue paying rent on the tractors (see 2A–407). Does TracFin have any warranty liability to Construction? 2A–103(1)(g), Comment (g) to 2A–103 (final paragraph), 2A–212, 2A–213. Is this a good result?

PROBLEM 5.11

Expeditions was looking for a GPS system to provide to clients it took on tours in the wilderness. After discussions with Global, Expeditions decided that Global's "small box" GPS system was right for it. Accordingly, Expeditions signed a detailed sales contract and purchased 100 small boxes from Global. A year later Global's accountant advised it that renting its 100 small boxes had significant tax advantages over owning them. Acting on the advice, Expeditions convinced Bank to purchase Expeditions' small boxes and rent them to Expeditions. This occurred after Bank had investigated in detail Enterprises' business and its creditworthiness. The terms of their agreement called for Bank to buy the small boxes and lease them to Expeditions for two years. Expeditions was required to make monthly payments to Global during this period. At the end of the two year period Expeditions would deliver the small boxes to Bank. Neither party had a right to cancel the agreement. The small boxes have a five-year useful life from the date of their purchase from Global. During the first year of the agreement, the small boxes failed due to a manufacturing defect. Global has gone out of business and Expeditions is looking to Bank for satisfaction.

(a) Assume that the agreement between Expeditions and Bank gives Expeditions the option to purchase the small boxes from Bank at the end of the first year of their agreement for the fair market value of the boxes on that date. Does the agreement create any warranties of Bank to Expeditions? 1–203(a), (b)(4), 2A–103(1)(g), Comment (g) to 2A–103, 2A–212, 2A–213.

(b) What result if the agreement gave Expeditions the option of purchasing the small boxes at the end of the first year of the agreement for one dollar? 1–203(b)(4), 2–314, 2–315.

G. WARRANTIES UNDER THE CISG

The CISG's provisions covering product quality do not speak of "warranty." Instead, they refer to the seller's obligations. Article 30, for instance, requires the seller to deliver the goods as required by the contract and the CISG's provisions ("this Convention"). Nonetheless, in everything but name, relevant CISG provisions create warranties. Article 35(1) provides that the seller must deliver goods of the quantity, quality and description required by the contract. The requirement that the goods conform to the contract description puts the risk that the goods do not so conform on the seller. Article 35(1) therefore recognizes an express warranty, the counterpart of 2–313(1)(b). Like 2–313(1)(b), a "description" of the goods in the contract creates the relevant obligation. Statements by the seller that are not "descriptions" of them, such as opinions or commendations, do not. The CISG nowhere distinguishes between "descriptions" and "opinions" or "commendations." However, Article 35(1)'s reference to "description" requires this distinction. In an international context, the classification of a statement sometimes will be hard to make. This is particularly true when a seller's statements are made during negotiations or otherwise are not incorporated into a formal document. Article 8(2) helps a bit. Where a contracting party does not know the intended interpretation of the other party's statements, the statements are to be interpreted according to the understanding of a reasonable person in the party's position. Linguistic and social conventions among international contracting parties sometimes can determine the character of a statement as a "description" or an "opinion."

Article 35(1) differs from 2–313(1) in one important respect. Unlike 2–313(1), Article 35(1) does not require that a description form "the basis of the bargain." It only requires that the seller deliver goods that conform to the "description required by the contract." Thus, a description creates an express warranty as long as it is part of the contract. To avoid a finding of an express warranty under Article 2 of the UCC, the seller can argue that a contract description did not form the basis of the bargain. For courts that understand that requirement as one of reliance, the seller can try to establish that the buyer did not rely on the description. This tack is not available to the seller under the CISG. Instead, the seller must argue that the contested representation of the goods is not within the contract description of them. The seller's positions therefore must be that either the representation is not a description of the goods at all or, if descriptive of them, not part of the contract description. Accordingly, Article 35(1) requires identifying which descriptions are part of the contract and which are not. The CISG's elimination of the parol evidence rule (see Chapter 4, Section C, supra) can make doing so difficult.

Article 35(2) creates both implied warranties and an express warranty not covered by Article 35(1). Article 35(2)(a) tracks 2–314(2)(c)'s implied warranty of merchantability, requiring that the goods be fit "for the purposes for which goods of the same description would ordinarily be used." See Norfolk Southern R.R. Co. v. Power Source Supply, 66 UCC Rep. Serv.2d 680 (W.D. Pa. 2008). However, it is less specific than 2–314(2)'s standards of merchantability in that, unlike 2–314(2)(b), the subsection does not require that the goods be of fair average quality within the contract description. This leaves open the possibility that goods might be fit for the ordinary purposes to which they are put while still being of less than average quality. Article 35(2)(b) creates a warranty of fitness for a particular purpose, the counterpart of 2–315. It requires the goods to be fit for any particular purpose made "known to the seller at the time of the conclusion of the contract." Article 35(2)(b)'s warranty of fitness, unlike 2–315, arises even if the seller does not know or have reason to know of the buyer's reliance. However, the warranty does not arise if the buyer did not rely or relied unreasonably on the seller's skill and judgment. Article 35(2)(c) requires the goods to possess the qualities that the seller has held out as a sample or model. This express warranty is the counterpart of 2–313(1)(c). Unlike 2–313(1)(c), Article 35(2)(c) does not require does not require that the sample or model form the basis of the bargain.

Article 35(2)(a)'s standard of merchantability is vague, and courts and arbitrators have been called on to interpret it. The vagueness is particularly difficult to resolve under the CISG. While courts can rely on common law and pre-Code statute to clarify unclear components of the UCC's warranty provisions, they cannot do the same with the CISG's warranty provisions. A key provision of the CISG effectively prohibits national courts from adopting a "homeward trend" whereby they interpret the CISG's provisions through the lens of their domestic law. Article 7(2) describes a rule of interpretation for construing the CISG's provisions. It essentially provides that matters governed by the CISG but not expressly addressed by its provisions are to be settled according to the "general principles" underlying the CISG. If these principles do not settle the matter, applicable domestic law is to settle it. Article 7(2) therefore requires courts to construe Article 35(2)(a)'s standard of merchantability based on the CISG's underlying "general principles," not notions of merchantability borrowed from domestic law.

To date U.S. courts have only given passing attention to the CISG's merchantability standard. Netherlands Arbitration Institute (Netherlands), 15 October 2002, available at http://www.cisg.law.pace.edu/cases/021015n1.html remains the most careful discussion of the matter. The arbitration there involved the sale of condensate, a byproduct of natural gas, to a buyer who refined or resold it. The condensate in dispute was the "Rijn Blend." After buying the Rijn Blend from the sellers for a few years, the buyer refused a shipment because it contained a mercury level high enough to make the condensate unacceptable for refining or reselling. The sales contract said nothing about the mercury level permitted in the shipment of Rijn Blend. The arbitral tribunal also concluded that the sellers did not know or have reason to know of the buyer's particular purpose of refining or reselling the shipment. Instead, the tribunal viewed the case as presenting the issue as to whether the shipment breached the seller's warranty of merchantability under Article 35(2)(a). To resolve the issue, the tribunal therefore had to determine the standard of merchantability implicit in the Article.

The tribunal identified three alternative tests of fitness under Article 35(2)(a). One was that the goods be of "merchantable" quality so as to be saleable in a substitute market at the contract price. This test asks whether a buyer would have purchased the Rijn Blend at the contract price if it had been aware of the mercury levels in the shipment. The tribunal concluded that the Rijn Blend shipped did not meet the merchantability test. A second test of fitness is one of "average quality": The goods must be of the average quality of goods of the same description. The tribunal decided that the buyer had not proved that the mercury levels rendered the shipment below average quality. However, the tribunal rejected both tests of fitness under Article 35(2)(a). Instead, it found that a third test—the "reasonable quality" test—applied. This test asks whether a buyer would reasonably expect the product to have certain qualities. Applying the test, the tribunal concluded that a buyer purchasing the Rijn Blend at the contract price would reasonably expect it to contain mercury levels below the shipment the seller tendered.

The tribunal relied on Article 7(2) of the CISG to reject both the merchantability and average quality tests of fitness. It found that "national notions regarding quality of goods are not controlling in CISG cases. For that reason, the average quality standard cannot be accepted. It is a theory, which imports a domestic notion [ed.: from some civil law countries] which is not sufficiently universal into the CISG system in violation of Article 7(2) CISG." The tribunal used the same reasoning to reject the merchantability standard. This reasoning is questionable. It does not consider Article 7(2)'s rule of interpretation carefully enough. Article 7(2) does not prohibit the use of the warranty standards of domestic law in interpreting Article 35(2)(a)'s merchantability standard. It only bars using domestic law standards to ignore the "general principles" underlying the CISG to determine that standard. If a domestic law standard, such as merchantability or average quality, helps identify these principles, the fact that it is domestic law does not disqualify the standard from being used to construe Article 35(2)(a). The few U.S. courts to have considered the matter have used the UCC warranty provisions to inform the Article 35(2)'s interpretation. See, e.g., Chicago Prime Packers, Inc. v. Northam Food Trading Co., 408 F.3d 894 (7th Cir. 2005). This practice does not violate Article 7(2)'s directive.

The tribunal's adoption of the reasonable quality test is itself dubious, for different reasons. This test requires determining what the buyer would reasonably expect from a shipment of Rijn Blend. The tribunal found that buyer's rejection of the shipment of Rijn Blend was reasonable because the seller on resale could only get a price heavily discounted from the contract price. The discount apparently reflected the high mercury levels in the shipment. But the failure to be able to sell in a substitute market at the same price is the merchantability test the tribunal rejected earlier. This suggests that the two tests are in fact the same. The only difference is in the perspective from which the presence of a substitute market is tested. The reasonable quality standard tests it from the seller's "supply" side: The sellers of the Rijn Blend would get a lower price for their condensate than the prevailing market price of condensate. The merchantability standard test the presence of a substitute market from the buyer's "demand" side: the buyer of the Rijn Blend with high mercury levels would offer a lower price for it than for other condensate.

Finally, the tribunal's discussion of Article 35(2)(a)'s merchantability standard is unnecessary to the result. The same result could be reached more directly, and with stronger justification, in another way, based on the buyer's prior dealings in Rijn Blend with the sellers. Apparently the buyer had ordered and received previous shipments of the condensate from the sellers with lower levels of mercury than in the contested shipment. The tribunal takes this fact to support the finding that the buyer reasonably expected a shipment of condensate with similar mercury levels. In effect, the tribunal's finding acknowledges that the parties had a course of dealing between themselves regarding permissible mercury levels. Article 9(1) binds the parties to "any practices which they have established between themselves." Thus, the buyer could have recovered on the basis of Article 9(1) alone. The question as whether a particular mercury levels in the condensate rendered it unfit for "ordinary purposes" under Article 35(2)(a) does not need to be answered.

Medical Marketing International v. Internazionale Medico

United States District Court, Eastern District of Louisiana, 1999
1999 WL 311945

■ Order and Reasons: DUVAL, DISTRICT J.

Before the court is an Application for Order Conforming Arbitral Award and Entry of Judgment, filed by plaintiff, Medical Marketing International, Inc. ("MMI"). Having considered the memoranda of plaintiff, and the memorandum in opposition filed by defendant, Internazionale Medico Scientifica, S.r.l. ("IMS"), the court grants the motion.

Factual Background

Plaintiff MMI is a Louisiana marketing corporation with its principal place of business in Baton Rouge, Louisiana. Defendant IMS is an Italian corporation that manufactures radiology materials with its principal place of business in Bologna, Italy. On January 25, 1993, MMI and IMS entered into a Business Licensing Agreement in which IMS granted exclusive sales rights for Giotto Mammography H.F. Units to MMI.

In 1996, the Food and Drug Administration ("FDA") seized the equipment for noncompliance with administrative procedures, and a dispute arose over who bore the obligation of ensuring that the Giotto equipment complied with the United states Governmental Safety Regulations, specifically the Good Manufacturing Practices (GMP) for Medical Device Regulations. MMI formally demanded mediation on October 28, 1996, pursuant to Article 13 of the agreement. Mediation was unsuccessful, and the parties entered into arbitration, also pursuant to Article 13, whereby each party chose one arbitrator and a third was agreed upon by both.

An arbitration hearing was held on July 13–15, July 28, and November 17, 1998. The hearing was formally closed on November 30, 1998. The arbitrators rendered their decision on December 21, 1998, awarding MMI damages in the amount of $357,009.00 and legal interest on that amount from October 28, 1996. The arbitration apportioned 75% of the $83,640.45 cost of arbitration to MMI, and the other 25% to IMS. IMS moved for reconsideration on December 30, 1998, and this request was denied by the arbitrators on January 7, 1999. Plaintiff now moves for an order from this court confirming the arbitral award and entering judgment in favor of the plaintiff under 9 U.S.C. § 9 * * *

Analysis

The scope of this court's review of an arbitration award is "among the narrowest known to law." Denver & Rio Grande Western Railroad Co. v. Union Pacific Railroad Co., 119 F.3d 847, 849 (10th Cir.1997). The FAA outlines specific situations in which an arbitration decision may be overruled: (1) if the award was procured by corruption, fraud or undue means; (2) if there is evidence of partiality or corruption among the arbitrators; (3) if the arbitrators were guilty of misconduct which prejudiced the rights of one of the parties; or (4) if the arbitrators exceeded their powers. Instances in which the arbitrators "exceed their powers" may include violations of public policy or awards based on a "manifest disregard of the law." See W.R. Grace & Co. v. Local Union 759, 461 U.S. 757, 766 (1983), Walcha v. Swan, 346 U.S. 427, 436–37 (1953).

IMS has alleged that the arbitrators' decision violates public policy of the international global market and that the arbitrators exhibited "manifest disregard of international sales law." Specifically, IMS argues that the arbitrators misapplied the United Nations Convention on Contracts for the International Sales of Goods, commonly referred to as CISG, and that they refused to follow a German Supreme Court Case interpreting CISG.

MMI does not dispute that CISG applies to the case at hand. Under CISG, the finder of fact has a duty to regard the "international character" of the convention and to promote uniformity in its application. CISG Article 7. The Convention also provides that in an international contract for goods, goods conform to the contract if they are fit for the purpose for which goods of the same description would ordinarily be used or are fit for any particular purpose expressly or impliedly made known to the seller and relied upon by the buyer. CISG Article 35(2). To avoid a contract based on the non-conformity of goods, the buyer must allege and prove that the seller's breach was "fundamental" in nature. CISG Article 49. A breach is fundamental when it results in such detriment to the party that he or she is substantially deprived of what he or she is entitled to expect under the contract, unless the party in breach did not foresee such a result. CISG Article 25.

At the arbitration, IMS argued that MMI was not entitled to avoid its contract with IMS based on non-conformity under Article 49, because IMS's breach was not "fundamental." IMS argued that CISG did not require that it furnish MMI with equipment that complied with the United States GMP regulations. To support this proposition, IMS cited a German Supreme Court case, which held that under CISG Article 35, a seller is generally not obligated to supply goods that conform to public laws and regulations enforced at the buyer's place of business. Entscheidunger des Bundersgerichtshofs in Zivilsachen (BGHZ) 129, 75 (1995). In that case, the court held that this general rule carries with it exceptions in three limited circumstances: (1) if the public laws and regulations of the buyer's state are identical to those enforced in the seller's state; (2) if the buyer informed the seller about those regulations; or (3) if due to "special circumstances," such as the existence of a seller's branch office in the buyer's state, the seller knew or should have known about the regulations at issue.

The arbitration panel decided that under the third exception, the general rule did not apply to this case. The arbitrators held that IMS was, or should have been, aware of the GMP regulations prior to entering into the 1993 agreement, and explained their reasoning at length. IMS now argues that the arbitration panel refused to apply CISG and the law as articulated by the German Supreme Court. It is clear from the arbitrators' written findings, however, that they carefully considered that decision and found that this case fit the exception and not the rule as articulated in that decision. The arbitrators' decision was neither contrary to public policy nor in manifest disregard of international sales law. This court therefore finds that the arbitration panel did not "exceed its powers" in violation of the FAA. Accordingly,

It is ordered that the Application for Order Conforming Arbitral Award is hereby granted.

NOTES

1. Article 35(2)(a)'s notion of fitness for ordinary use is in one respect underspecified. While the subsection requires that the goods be "fit for the purposes for which goods of the same description would ordinarily be used," it does not say where. In domestic sales the ordinary uses will usually be the same in the locations of both the seller and buyer. In international sales ordinary uses can differ according to the location of the parties, sometimes due to different regulations governing the goods, as in *Medical Marketing*. The Austrian Supreme Court in Oberster Gerichtshof (Austria), 13 April 2000, available at http://cisgw3.law.pace.edu/cases/000413a3.html, had to decide which country's uses govern when they regulatory standards differed between the seller and buyer's countries. There, an Austrian buyer purchased four machines from a German seller for resale. Austrian law required for resale that the machines be labeled, while German law did not. The machines delivered did not contain the necessary labeling. The contract said nothing about labeling, and apparently no trade usage or course of dealing controlled the matter. On these facts the Court decided the standards of the seller's country determine the fitness of the goods for the purposes to which they ordinarily are put. The seller would be charged with knowledge of standards of the buyer's country, the Court held, only in one of three circumstances: when the standards in the buyer's country were the same as in the seller's country, when the standards in the buyer's country were bargained for explicitly, or when the seller knew or had reason to know of the standards in the buyer's country. In that case, failure to comply with standards in the buyer's country makes the goods unfit for the ordinary purposes to which they are used. The arbitral tribunal whose award the *Medical Marketing* court confirmed relied on the same rule that the Austrian Supreme Court announced. More recent case law follows the Court's "seller's country" rule. See, e.g., Oberster Gerichtshof (Austria), 25 January 2006, available at http://cisgw3.law.pace.edu/cases/060125a3.html.

The Austrian Supreme Court's rule and its exception are defensible. A seller usually will not know the regulations applicable to the goods in the buyer's country. This is particularly true when the seller does not know the ultimate destination of the goods. By contrast, the buyer likely knows the regulations in its own country or can easily find out. This situation in which the seller and buyer find themselves is one of asymmetric information: The buyer knows or is a position to know something the seller does not. The Court's "seller's country" rule imposes on the buyer the costs of discovering information about regulations in its own country and disclosing the information to its seller. Failure to do so puts the risk of nonconformity of the goods with local regulations on the buyer. Because the buyer has cheaper access to the relevant information, the risk allocation produces a lower priced contract than under a "buyer's country" rule. The buyer's informational advantage disappears when one of the exceptions to the rule apply. For example, if the contract expressly provides that the goods will conform to regulations in the buyer's country, presumably the seller is a position to determine the content of the regulations. Thus, the exceptions to the "seller's country" rule put the burden of delivering goods that conform to regulations in the buyer's country.

2. Courts and arbitral tribunals generally agree that Article 35(2)(a) requires that the goods be fit for the ordinary purposes as determined by standards in the seller's country, unless an exception applies. See e.g. Oberlandesgericht Saarbrücken (Germany), 17 January 2007, available at http://cisgw3.law.pace.edu/cases/070117g1.html; Oberster Gerichtshof (Austria), 13 April 2000, available at http://www.cisg.law.pace.edu/cases/000413a3.html. The Article, however, does not expressly so provide. It is therefore worth asking how Article 7(2)'s interpretive rule supports this construction of the Article. Article 7(2) in relevant part requires that matters not expressly settled by the CISG are to be settled by the CISG's underlying general principles. Note 1 above suggests that the "seller's country" rule makes good sense. However, Article 7(2) requires something more: that one or more "general principles" underlying the CISG supports it. It is unclear what those general principles are and how they support the dominant interpretation of Article 35(2)(a). The European courts that have construed the Article have relied on scholarly commentary and their domestic law, not principles underlying the CISG. See, e.g., Oberster Gerishtchof (Austria), 25 January 2006, available at http://cisgw3.law. pace.edu/cases/060125a3.html.

3.   International sales contracts, such as the contract in *Medical Marketing*, often contain an arbitration clause. The typical arbitration clause is an agreement between the seller and buyer to have disputes they cannot resolve themselves resolved by a non-governmental decision maker. The decision of the arbitrator is an arbitral "award." Arbitral awards are not self-executing, unlike judgments by courts. The award instead becomes a judgment of a court only if the court where the award was issued "confirms" it. Once confirmed, the award can be enforced in the same way, and to the same extent, as a judicial judgment. In the United States a federal statute, the Federal Arbitration Act ("FAA"), enables the federal court in the place where the arbitral award was issued to confirm the award. 9 U.S.C. § 201 et seq. (2011). (Almost all states have their own arbitration acts, often modeled on the FAA.) Section 9 of the FAA requires the court to confirm the award unless a statutory basis for refusing to confirm it applies under section 10. Section 10 enumerates very limited statutory grounds for refusing confirmation. An award procured by corruption or fraud is one such ground, as is partiality or corruption in the arbitrators. Another ground is that the arbitrators have exceeded their powers, which are defined by the scope of the arbitration clause. Section 9 does not allow a court to refuse to confirm an award on grounds other than the limited ones listed in section 10. In particular, courts cannot refuse confirmation just because the arbitrators made the wrong decision.

Judicial doctrine recognizes a non-statutory ground for refusing to enforce an award. It permits a court to refuse enforcement under the FAA when awards show a "manifest disregard of the law." An award manifestly disregards the law when the arbitrators knowingly ignore a law that is unambiguous and applicable to the facts. In contesting confirmation of the arbitral award in *Medical Marketing*, the seller alleged that the award was based on a manifest disregard of the law. The court tested the award by this nonstatutory basis. Some federal courts have questioned the doctrine, and the Supreme Court recently has put it in doubt. In Hall Street Associates v. Mattel Inc., 128 S. Ct. 1396 (2008), the Court stated that section 10 of the FAA provides the exclusive grounds for invalidating an arbitral award. However, at the same time it assumed without deciding that manifest disregard of the law is a valid ground for challenging an arbitral award under the FAA. Lower federal courts are divided over whether *Hall Street* ends the manifest disregard doctrine.

Chicago Prime Packers, Inc. v. Northam Food Trading Co.

United States Court of Appeals, Seventh Circuit, 2005
408 F.3d 894

■ FLAUM, CHIEF JUDGE.

Defendant-appellant Northam Food Trading Company ("Northam") contracted with plaintiff-appellee Chicago Prime Packers, Inc. ("Chicago Prime") for the purchase of 40,500 pounds of pork back ribs. Following delivery, Northam refused to pay Chicago Prime the contract price, claiming that the ribs arrived in an "off condition." Chicago Prime filed this diversity action for breach of contract against Northam. Following a bench trial, the district court awarded Chicago Prime $178,200.00, the contract price, plus prejudgment interest of $27,242.63. Northam appeals the award. For the reasons stated herein, we affirm.

I.   Background

The district court found the following facts based on the stipulations of the parties and the evidence presented at trial. Because neither party contends that any of the findings of fact in this section are "clearly erroneous," we accept them as established for purposes of this appeal. See Fed. R. Civ. P. 52(a).

Chicago Prime, a Colorado corporation, and Northam, a partnership formed under the laws of Ontario, Canada, are both wholesalers of meat products. On March 30, 2001, Chicago Prime contracted to sell Northam 1,350 boxes (40,500 pounds) of pork back ribs. Northam agreed to pay $178,200.00 for the ribs, with payment due within seven days of receipt of the shipment. The contract also set forth a description of the ribs, the price, and the date and location for pick-up.

Chicago Prime purchased the ribs specified in the contract from meat processor Brookfield Farms ("Brookfield"). When a pork loin is processed at Brookfield, it is broken into various segments, one of which is the back rib. After processing, Brookfield packages back ribs "flat" (horizontally), layer by layer, in 30–pound boxes. The ribs are placed first in a blast freezer and then transferred to an outside freezer where they remain until shipped.

In addition to its own freezers, Brookfield stored the ribs at issue in this case in as many as two independent cold storage facilities: B&B Pullman Cold Storage ("B&B"), and Fulton Market Cold Storage ("Fulton"). According to Brookfield's temperature logs and quality control records for its own facilities, the ribs were maintained at acceptable temperatures and were processed and maintained in accordance with Brookfield's procedures. Records presented at trial also indicate that the ribs were stored at or below acceptable temperatures during the entire time they were in B&B's possession. The parties offered no evidence regarding storage of the ribs at Fulton.

On April 24, 2001, Brown Brother's Trucking Company ("Brown"), acting on behalf of Northam, picked up 40,500 pounds of ribs from B&B. Chicago Prime, the seller, never possessed the ribs. When Brown accepted the shipment, it signed a bill of lading, thereby acknowledging that the goods were "in apparent good order." The bill of lading also indicated, however, that the "contents and condition of contents of packages [were] unknown." The next day, Brown delivered the shipment to Northam's customer, Beacon Premium Meats ("Beacon"). Like Chicago Prime, Northam, the buyer, never possessed the ribs. Upon delivery, Beacon signed a second bill of lading acknowledging that it had received the shipment "in apparent good order," except for some problems not at issue in this case.

Under the terms of the contract, Northam was obligated to pay Chicago Prime by May 1, 2001. Sandra Burdon, who negotiated the contract on behalf of Northam, testified that, on that date, Northam had no basis for withholding payment. In fact, she thought that a check had been sent to Chicago Prime prior to May 1, 2001, but subsequently discovered that the check had not been mailed. On May 2, 2001, Chicago Prime, not having heard from Northam, demanded payment.

On May 4, 2001, Beacon began "processing" a shipment of ribs and noticed that the product appeared to be in an "off condition." Beacon asked Inspector Ken Ward of the United States Department of Agriculture ("USDA") to examine the product. Ward inspected the ribs at the Beacon facility, found that the meat "did not look good," and ordered Beacon to stop processing it. Ward then placed a "U.S. Retained" tag on the shipment, noting "yellow, green, temperature, abused, spoiled," and had the ribs placed in Beacon's freezer. The same day, Northam and Chicago Prime learned of a potential problem with the ribs.

Inspector Ward returned to Beacon on May 7 and 8, 2001 and examined both frozen and thawed samples of the product. On May 23, 2001, Dr. John Maltby, Ward's supervisor, also conducted an on-site inspection of the ribs. When Dr. Maltby arrived, Beacon employees were "reworking" the ribs, trying to salvage any good portions. Dr. Maltby reviewed Beacon's shipping records and temperature logs from the relevant time period and found no "anomalies" or "gaps." In addition, he examined approximately 20 cases of ribs and prepared a written report. According to this report, Beacon gave Dr. Maltby two pallets of frozen ribs untouched by Beacon, as well as some of the product that Beacon had reworked. Looking inside the intact pallets, Dr. Maltby found ribs stacked both horizontally and vertically, with some frozen individually and others frozen together in larger units. The individually frozen ribs were "putrid," while the ribs frozen in larger units were "good."

Examining samples of the thawed, reworked product, Dr. Maltby found putrid, green, slimy ribs, but no sign of temperature abuse. He concluded in his report that the inspected product was rotten, that it arrived at Beacon in a rotten condition, and that it appeared to have been "assembled from various sources." Dr. Maltby also concluded that there was no opportunity for salvage and that all of the product should be condemned. The same day, the USDA issued a Notice of Receipt of Adulterated or Misbranded Product and the entire shipment of 1,350 boxes of ribs was condemned. After Northam informed it of the results of Dr. Malby's inspection, Chicago Prime continued to demand payment and eventually filed suit.

At trial, it was undisputed that the parties entered into a valid and enforceable contract for the sale and purchase of ribs, that Chicago Prime transferred a shipment of ribs to a trucking company hired by Northam, and that Northam had not paid Chicago Prime for the ribs.

Northam argued that it was relieved of its contractual payment obligation because the ribs were spoiled when its agent, Brown, received them. The district court concluded that it was Northam's burden to prove nonconformity, and held that Northam had failed to prove that the ribs from Chicago Prime were spoiled at the time of transfer to Brown. The court went on to state alternative holdings in favor of Chicago Prime based on its finding that, "even if the ribs were spoiled at the time of transfer, Northam . . . failed to prove that it examined the ribs, or caused them to be examined, within as short a period as is practicable under the circumstances, or that it rejected or revoked its acceptance of the ribs within a reasonable time after it discovered or should have discovered the alleged non-conformity." Chi. Prime Packers, Inc. v. Northam Food Trading Co., 320 F. Supp. 2d 702, 711 (N.D. Ill. 2004). The court awarded Chicago Prime the contract price of $178,200.00, plus prejudgment interest of $27,242.63.

II. Discussion

The district court held, and the parties do not dispute, that the contract at issue is governed by the United Nations Convention on Contracts for the International Sale of Goods ("CISG"), reprinted at 15 U.S.C.A. Appendix (West 1997), a self-executing agreement between the United States and other signatories, including Canada. Under the CISG, "the seller must deliver goods which are of the quantity, quality and description required by the contract," and "the goods do not conform with the contract unless they . . . are fit for the purposes for which goods of the same description would ordinarily be used." CISG Art. 35(1)–(2). The risk of loss passes from the seller to the buyer when the goods are transferred to the buyer's carrier. CISG Art. 67(1). While the seller is liable "for any lack of conformity which exists at the time when risk passes to the buyer," CISG Art. 36(1), the buyer bears the risk of "loss of or damage to the goods after the risk has passed to the buyer . . . unless the damage is due to an act or omission of the seller." CISG Art. 66. In other words, Chicago Prime is responsible for the loss if the ribs were spoiled (nonconforming) at the time Northam's agent, Brown, received them from Chicago Prime's agent, Brookfield, while Northam is responsible if they did not become spoiled until after the transfer.

The parties agree that the main factual issue before the district court was whether the ribs were spoiled at the time of transfer. On appeal, Northam makes two arguments: (1) that the district court erred in placing upon Northam the burden of proving that the ribs were spoiled at the time of transfer, and (2) that the evidence presented at trial does not support the district court's finding that the ribs became spoiled after Brown received them from Brookfield.

A. Burden of Proof

Northam asserts that Chicago Prime should bear the burden of proving that the ribs were not spoiled at the time of transfer because the quality of the goods is an essential element of Chicago Prime's breach of contract claim. Chicago Prime counters that nonconformity is an affirmative defense for which Northam, as the defendant-buyer, has the burden of proof. Proper assignment of the burden of proof is a question of law that we review de novo.

The CISG does not state expressly whether the seller or buyer bears the burden of proof as to the product's conformity with the contract. Because there is little case law under the CISG, we interpret its provisions by looking to its language and to "the general principles" upon which it is based. See CISG Art. 7(2); see also Delchi Carrier SpA v. Rotorex Corp., 71 F.3d 1024, 1027–28 (2d Cir. 1995). The CISG is the international analogue to Article 2 of the Uniform Commercial Code ("UCC"). Many provisions of the UCC and the CISG are the same or similar, and "caselaw interpreting analogous provisions of Article 2 of the [UCC], may . . . inform a court where the language of the relevant CISG provision tracks that of the UCC." Delchi Carrier SpA, 71 F.3d at 1028. "However, UCC caselaw 'is not per se applicable.' " Id.

A comparison with the UCC reveals that the buyer bears the burden of proving nonconformity under the CISG. Under the UCC, the buyer may plead breach of the implied warranty of fitness for ordinary purpose as an affirmative defense to a contract action by the seller for the purchase price. See Comark Merch., Inc. v. Highland Group, Inc., 932 F.2d 1196, 1203 (7th Cir. 1991); Alberts Bonnie Brae, Inc. v. Ferral, 188 Ill. App. 3d 711, 544 N.E.2d 422, 423, 135 Ill. Dec. 926 (Ill. App. 1989); see also 77A CORPUS JURIS SECUNDUM SALES § 287 (2004) ("The buyer, when sued for the purchase price, may set up a breach of warranty as a defense to the seller's action."). In such an action it is the defendant-buyer's burden to prove the breach of the warranty.

Section 2–314 of the UCC provides that a warranty that goods are "fit for the ordinary purpose for which such goods are used" is implied unless the contract states otherwise. Mirroring the structure and content of this section, Article 35(2) of the CISG provides that unless the contract states otherwise, "goods do not conform with the contract unless they . . . are fit for the purposes for which goods of the same description would ordinarily be used." Accordingly, just as a buyer-defendant bears the burden of proving breach of the implied warranty of fitness for ordinary purpose under the UCC, under the CISG, the buyer-defendant bears the burden of proving nonconformity at the time of transfer. See Larry A. DiMatteo et al., The Interpretive Turn in International Sales Law: An Analysis of Fifteen Years of CISG Jurisprudence, 24 NW. J. INT'L L. & BUS. 299, 400 (2004) (Under the CISG, "the buyer is allocated the burden of proving that the goods were defective prior to the expiration of the seller's obligation point."). The district court was correct to conclude that Northam bears the burden of proving that the ribs were spoiled at the time of transfer.

B.   Conformity of the Ribs at the Time of Transfer

The district court held that Northam failed to prove that the ribs were spoiled, or nonconforming, at the time of transfer. First, the court found that other evidence undermined Dr. Maltby's testimony that the ribs were rotten when they arrived at Beacon:

Chicago Prime points out several problems with Northam's reliance on Dr. Maltby's conclusion. Most significantly, neither Dr. Maltby nor anyone else could confirm that the meat Dr. Maltby inspected was in fact the product that was sold to Northam by Chicago Prime, and evidence was produced at trial to suggest that they were not the same ribs. Even though the rib boxes were labeled with Brookfield establishment numbers, the evidence showed that Beacon had purchased and received other loads of ribs originating from Brookfield prior to April 25, 2001. Furthermore, some of the ribs examined by Dr. Maltby (from one of the Intact Pallets) were stacked both horizontally and vertically. Brookfield pack-ages its loin back ribs only horizontally. Dr. Maltby had no personal knowledge of how or where the meat was stored from April 25, 2001 to May 23, 2001, and the first time any government inspector viewed the meat was on May 4, 2001. According to Dr. Maltby, loin back ribs, if kept at room temperature, could spoil in five to seven days. Surprisingly, Northam did not present any witness affiliated with Beacon to address those issues.

Next, the district court found that three witnesses had credibly testified that "the ribs delivered by Brookfield were processed and stored in acceptable conditions and temperatures from the time they were processed until they were transferred to Northam on April 24, 2001." Despite Northam's attempts to discredit the testimony of these witnesses by pointing to deficiencies in Brookfield's record-keeping during the relevant period, the district court found "nothing in the evidence demonstrating that Brookfield, B&B or Fulton did anything improper with respect to the ribs or that the ribs were spoiled prior to being transferred to Northam." Based on these factual findings, the district court concluded that Northam had not met its burden of demonstrating that the ribs were spoiled at the time of transfer.

By highlighting Dr. Maltby's testimony and potential gaps in Chicago Prime's evidence, Northam suggests that the opposite holding is also supportable. This, however, is not the correct inquiry. On appeal from a bench trial, we will not set aside the factual conclusions of the district court "unless clearly erroneous." Fed. R. Civ. P. 52(a). "Under this standard, one who contends that a finding is clearly erroneous has an exceptionally heavy burden to carry on appeal." Spurgin–Dienst v. United States, 359 F.3d 451, 453 (7th Cir. 2004). This is especially true when the appellant argues that the district court erred in crediting or discrediting a witness's testimony.

Northam argues that the district court erred in discrediting Dr. Maltby's testimony, and contends that Dr. Maltby's conclusion that the ribs were rotten before the transfer should be determinative. Even if the district court could have given Dr. Maltby's conclusion more weight, however, Northam has not shown that the court clearly erred in finding the evidence undermining his conclusion to be more persuasive.

The evidence supporting Northam's position was not so overwhelming that it was clear error to find in favor of Chicago Prime. Northam offered no credited evidence showing that the ribs were spoiled at the time of transfer or excluding the possibility that the ribs became spoiled after the transfer. In addition, it presented no evidence that Brookfield stored the ribs in unacceptable conditions that could have caused them to become spoiled before the transfer. Finally, Northam did not present a witness from Beacon to respond to the evidence suggesting that the ribs examined by Dr. Maltby were not those sold to Northam by Chicago Prime. Upon this record, the district court did not clearly err in finding that Northam did not meet its burden of proof as to its affirmative defense of nonconformity.

Because we hold that the district court correctly assigned to Northam the burden of proving nonconformity and did not clearly err in finding that Northam had not met this burden, we need not reach the district court's alternative holdings.

III. Conclusion

We affirm the district court's award to Chicago Prime.

NOTES

1. The CISG only addresses the burden of proof in one provision—Article 79, which exempts a party from performance of its obligations under prescribed conditions. Article 79(1) requires the party seeking the exemption to prove that these conditions obtain. The CISG nowhere else expressly assign burdens of proof. Nonetheless, most courts and commentators find that the CISG implicitly allocates the burden of proof to the buyer. Articles 4 and 7 might support the finding. Article 4 provides in relevant part that the CISG governs the rights and obligations of the contracting parties arising from the contract. Conceivably among these "obligations" is the burden of the buyer to persuade the trier of facts that the goods do not conform to the contract. Alternatively, Article 7(2) could support the assignment of the burden to the buyer. Although the burden of proof is not expressly settled by the CISG, the assignment of the burden to the buyer is based on its underlying "general principles." *Chicago Prime Packers* takes this view, as do most courts and commentators. See, e.g., Bundesgerichtshof (Germany), 9 January 2002, available at http://www.cisg.law.pace.edu/cases/020109g1.html; Tribunale di Vigevano (Italy), 12 July 2000, available at http://www.cisg.law.pace.edu/cases/000712i3.html; Franco Ferrari, in The Draft UNCITRAL Digest and Beyond—Cases, Analysis and Unresolved Issues in the U.N. Sales Convention 167 (R. Brand, F. Ferrari & H. Flechtner eds., 2003).

The court in *Chicago Prime Packers* invokes the CISG's underlying "general principles" to conclude that the CISG implicitly assigns the burden of proof. It then notes that Article 35 is similar to 2–314(2)'s implied warranty of merchantability. Because 2–314 assigns the burden of proving nonconformity on the buyer who has accepted the goods, the court concludes that Article 35 also assigns the burden to the buyer. What role do the CISG's "general principles" play in the court's argument? Does the court identify principles that allow the inference putting the burden on the buyer?

2. Some courts and arbitral tribunals disagree as to the CISG's implicit burden of proof assignment. The seller has the burden of proving that the goods conform at the time the risk of loss passes to the buyer. Most courts have concluded that the buyer bears the burden of proving nonconformity after risk of loss passes to it. However, a few decisions put the burden on the seller. See Rechtbank van koophandel Kortrijk (Belgium), 6 October 1997, available at http://cisgw3.law.pace.edu/cases/971006b1.html; Rechtbank van koophandel Kortrijk (Belgium), 16 December 1996 available at http://cisgw3.law.pace.edu/cases/961216b1.html. And at least one court has held that equitable considerations allow placing on the seller the burden of proving conformity even after risk has passed to the buyer. See Hof van Beroep Antwerpen, 14 April 2004 (Belgium), available at http://cisgw3.law.pace.edu/cases/040414b1.html; cf. Oberster Gerichtshof (Austria), 12

September 2006, available at http://cisgw3.law.pace.edu/cases/ 060912a3.html. For a proposal recommending a burden-shifting scheme, see Ann L. Linne, Burden of Proof Under Article 35 CISG, 20 Pace Int'l L. Rev. 31 (2008). Do the CISG's underlying general principles support a particular burden of proof assignment?

3. The Fourth Circuit in Schmitz–Werke GmbH & Co. v. Rockland Industries, Inc., 37 Fed. App'x 687 (4th Cir. 2002) takes a different view on the matter:

> Courts interpreting the CISG should look to the language of the CISG and to the general principles on which the Convention is based. * * * Case law interpreting provisions of Article 2 of the Uniform Commercial Code that are similar in the CISG can also be helpful in interpreting the convention. * * *

> The parties agree that private international law would apply the choice of law rules of the forum state (Maryland), which in this case would choose to apply the law of the contracting state. * * * However, a court should only reach private international law if the CISG's text, interpreted in conformity with the general principles on which the CISG is based, does not settle the issue at hand. * * * Schmitz [the German buyer] agrees that Maryland law applies to issues on which the CISG is silent, but notes that Maryland law should not be reached unless the CISG fails to provide a resolution of the issue.

> Under Maryland law, Rockland [the Maryland seller] is correct that a plaintiff in a products liability case must show that the product in question is defective, even if the cause of action is for breach of an express or implied warranty. Id. at 692.

Is the court using Maryland law that is similar to Article 35 to interpret Article 35? Or does the court rely on Maryland law because it finds none of the CISG's "general principles" allocate burden? In other words, is the Fourth Circuit relying on the first portion of the sentence in Article 7(2) or the last portion of the sentence? Assuming that Maryland law properly allocates burden, is Maryland's product liability law the best source for assigning it in a breach of warranty suit? What would the assignment be if the court had consulted Maryland's version of 2–607(4)?

Most commentators detest the court's reasoning in *Schmitz–Werke*. See, e.g., Larry A. DiMatteo et al., The Interpretive Turn in International Sales Law: An Analysis of Fifteen Years of CISG Jurisprudence, 24 Nw. J. Int'l L. & Bus. 299, 400 (2004). In their view the opinion takes no notice of the views of foreign courts and commentators about the CISG's implicit burden assignment. This omission ignores Article 7(1)'s injunction that the CISG be interpreted to promote uniformity in its application.

4. A strong case can be made that the CISG does not allocate the burden of proving that the goods do not conform to the contract. For one thing, the CISG's drafters believe that the Convention does not generally address burden of proof. The drafters are unlikely to have unintentionally addressed the matter. In addition, the CISG arguably lacks underlying general principles allocating burden of proof. Article 79(1) is the only instance in which the CISG expressly allocates burden.

Some European courts have found the principle underlying the Article to require that a party attempting to benefit from a provision prove the facts required by the provision. See Tribunale di Vigevano (Italy), 12 July 2000, available at http://www.cisg.law.pace.edu/cases/000712i3.html; Oberlandesgericht Innsbruck (Austria), 1 July 1994, available at http://www.cisg.law.pace.edu/cases/940701a3.html. A principle extracted from a single provision is insufficiently general in scope to underlie the CISG, as Article 7(2) requires. The better inference is that the principle applies only to Article 79(1). Courts and commentators have not produced principles that are both sufficiently general in scope and embedded in the CISG.

Finally, contracting states that participated in drafting the CISG had good reason to exclude burden of proof from the CISG's scope. Burden of proof is an important component of litigation cost. The party bearing the burden incurs the cost of acquiring and presenting information in litigation. Correspondingly, the other party is saved the costs of supplying this information. However, presumptions and rules allowing discovery or information gathering by a court or arbitral tribunal also affect a party's cost of acquiring and presenting information. As a result, different legal systems can assign burden differently. As important, they can disagree over which burden assignment minimizes total litigation costs. Given the divergence in practice between adversarial and inquisitorial legal systems, the participants in the CISG's drafting understandably might have decided to leave burden assignments outside the CISG's scope.

CHAPTER 6

WARRANTY DISCLAIMERS AND ADDITIONAL WARRANTY ISSUES

A significant amount of litigation under the UCC involves warranties. To recover for breach of warranty, the buyer must prove that the seller made and breached a warranty and that the breach proximately caused loss to it. In addition, the buyer must establish that it gave the seller adequate notice of the breach. It also must establish that the sales contract does not limit or exclude the remedy it seeks. Finally, the buyer must prove that it stands in a relationship to the seller that allows it to recover under Article 2. These requirements are potential barriers to the buyer's warranty claims against the seller. If the buyer cannot meet them, its warranty claim fails. Thus, the buyer's case fails if the seller has not made an express warranty or has effectively disclaimed implied warranties regarding the goods. At the same time, federal law and some states law restrict or prohibit warranty disclaimers in certain consumer sales contracts. Even if the warranty is not disclaimed, tardy or insufficient notice of breach bars the buyer's recovery for the breach. Privity requirements also might apply so that the buyer does not stand in the requisite relationship to the seller to recover. And even if the buyer is in privity with the seller, remedy limitations in the sales contract might limit or exclude certain remedies. Given these barriers to recovery for breach of warranty under Article 2, buyers sometimes attempt to rely on tort law to recover for their loss. This Chapter describes warranty disclaimers and additional issues common in warranty litigation.

A. WARRANTY DISCLAIMERS

As discussed in Chapter 5, warranties allocate the risk of nonconformities in the goods to the seller. The underlying rationale for the allocation is that seller is in a better position than the buyer to avoid the loss or insuring against it. The contract price reflects the price of the warranty in addition to the seller's production costs. The seller charges the buyer a price for the warranty that is less than the buyer's cost of having to be financially responsible for nonconformities in the goods. However, there are occasions on which the seller is not in superior position with respect to loss. For instance, the buyer might have an atypical use for the goods that presents a low risk that they will prove unsuitable. The rowboat that a buyer purchases to exhibit in a contemporary art show does not need to be seaworthy. Or the buyer might take above average care in its use of the goods. In both cases the buyer's cost of bearing the risk that the goods will be nonconforming is less than the implicit price the seller charges for the warranty.

Article 2 of the UCC enables the contracting parties to allocate the risk of nonconformities in the goods to the buyer. The seller need make no express warranties with respect to qualities of the goods. Realistically, in most circumstances the seller will make some statements in concluding the sales contract. The question then is whether the statements create an express warranty under 2–313(1). This is important because, according to 2–316(1), negations or limitations of express warranties are inoperative. As a result, an express warranty once made cannot be disclaimed. The most difficult cases are ones in which the seller's statements concern qualities of the goods while the sales contract disclaims warranties as to these qualities. The question here is whether the seller's statements describe the goods or merely identify them. For example, suppose the seller refers to the goods it is selling as "flexglue," a term common in the trade for a particular type of adhesive. If "flexglue" simply identifies the product being sold (a type of adhesive), the term does not purport to describe the product's flexibility. The term simply serves to identify the type of adhesive being sold. On the other hand, "flexglue" could describe the glue as being flexible.

Implied warranties arise when the seller satisfies 2–314 or 2–315. Sections 2–316(2) and (3) allows disclaimers of implied warranties, but places significant restrictions on them. Courts have tended to read those restrictions narrowly to disfavor disclaimers. Sections 2–316(2) and (3) provide two different means by which implied warranties can be disclaimed. Section 2–316(2) requires that the exclusion or modification of the warranty of merchantability mention merchantability. Thus, the exclusion of "all implied warranties" is ineffective, as is "no guarantees of any sort." Merchantability must be mentioned whether the disclaimer is oral or written. In addition, where the disclaimer is written, it must conspicuous. Section 1–201(b)(10) defines "conspicuous." Conspicuousness is a matter for the court. Disclaimers of the implied warranty of fitness for a particular purpose must be in writing and conspicuous. Subsection (2) gives language that suffices to disclaim the warranty ("There are no warranties which extend beyond the description on the face hereof"). Other language therefore also can disclaim the warranty of fitness. Presumably "The warranty of fitness for a particular purpose is disclaimed" suffices.

There are, however, certain situations in which the requirements for disclaiming warranties are partly relaxed. Section 2–316(2)'s restrictions on disclaimers is prefaced by "subject to subsection (3)." Correspondingly, 2–316(3) applies "notwithstanding subsection (2)." Section 2–316(3) imposes different limitations on disclaimers of implied warranties. Thus, a disclaimer that meets these limitations is effective even if it does not satisfy 2–316(2)'s limitations. Under subsection (3)(a), a seller can exclude all implied warranties with language such as "as is," or "with all faults," or other language from which a reasonable buyer would infer that the warranties are being disclaimed. Unlike 2–316(2), the disclaimer of merchantability does not have to mention merchantability. Subsection (3)(a) has two restrictions. First, the disclaiming language must "make[ ] plain that there is no implied warranty." Second, subsection (3)(a)'s ways of disclaiming implied warranties apply "unless the circumstances indicate otherwise." An example where circumstances might indicate otherwise might apply where consumer buyers do not often understand the legal consequences of language such as "as is" or "with all faults." Section 2–316(3)(b) allows implied warranties to be excluded by the buyer's examination of the goods prior to contracting, and 2–316(3)(c) allows exclusion by course of dealing or performance, or usage of trade. Finally, 2–312(2) has separate requirements for disclaimers of the warranty of title.

A question that has bothered courts is whether a written disclaimer under 2–316(3)(a) must be conspicuous. While 2–316(2) requires that written disclaimers be conspicuous, subsection (3)(a) does not have the same requirement. Two different positions can be taken on this omission. One is that the omission is intended and subsection (3)(a)'s limitations do not include "conspicuousness." While the requirement of conspicuousness is among subsection (2)'s limitations, subsection (3) applies "notwithstanding subsection (2)," and subsection (2) is "subject to subsection (3)." Thus, these provisions make subsection (3)'s requirements independent of subsection (2)'s requirements. In addition, Comment 1 to 2–316's reference to "conspicuous language or other circumstances" appears to recognize the separate requirements of the two subsections. Thus, subsection (2)'s conspicuousness limitation does not apply to subsection (3). The other position is that the omission of conspicuousness from subsection (3) is unintended and should be implied. The reasoning is that the use of language approved by subsection (3) serves the same purpose as language approved by subsection (2): to protect buyers from unwittingly agreeing to disclaimers. Subsection (2)'s conspicuousness requirements helps accomplish this purpose. For this reason, requiring conspicuous language in subsection (2) but not in subsection (3) makes no sense. See Gindy Mfg. Corp. v. Cardinale Trucking Corp., 268 A.2d 345 (N.J. Super. Ct. 1970). Most courts accept this conclusion and require that written disclaimers under 2–316(3)(a) also be conspicuous. Proposed 2–316(3)(a) and 2A–214(3)(a) both require that written disclaimers be conspicuous.

The extension of a conspicuousness requirement to 2–316(3)(a) might be too quick. Comment 6 to 2–316 describes 2–316(2)'s requirements for disclaimers as the "general rule." This suggests that subsection (2)'s requirements are specific to it and therefore do not apply to subsection (3), which provides exceptions to subsection (2) ("[n]otwithstanding subsection (2)"). Subsection (3)(a)'s language confirms the separateness of the limitations in the two subsections. It allows disclaimers that meet its requirements "unless the circumstances indicate otherwise." In some circumstances the inconspicuousness of a disclaimer might make it ineffective. However, in other circumstances the inconspicuousness of a disclaimer might not affect its effectiveness, such as when the buyer knows of its contents. A conspicuousness requirement therefore is not needed in subsection (3) in order to protect the buyer from surprise. Subsection (3)(a)'s catch all, "unless the circumstances indicate otherwise," accomplishes this.

Article 2's regulation of warranty disclaimers probably is only a limited success. Section 2–316's drafters might be concerned with the buyer's ignorance of the legal consequences of the disclaimer. Section 2–316 only partly remedies this ignorance. Subsection (2) merely insists that the disclaimer use certain canonical language, and subsection (3) requires that the disclaiming language make plain that there is no implied warranty. While disclaimers complying with either subsection give buyers some information about nonconformity risk, the information still can be cast in legal jargon. Buyers unfamiliar with legal language or its consequences will not understand that they bear nonconformity risk. In response to this problem, Proposed 2–316(2) proposes that the disclaimer of an implied warranty of merchantability in a consumer contract be in a record and recite that "the seller undertakes no responsibility for the goods, except as otherwise provided in the contract."

Section 2–316 does nothing to overcome the buyer's burden of processing information about the disclaimer or the possibility that buyers suffer from cognitive error in processing the information in the disclaimer. An effective disclaimer can be complex. Nothing in 2–316 assures that buyers are not faced with disclaimers so detailed that they are unable to gauge the risks the contract assigns to them. Cf. Ellen M. Moore & F. Kelly Shuptrine, Warranties: Continued Readability Problems After the 1975 Magnuson–Moss Warranty Act, 27 Consumer Aff. 23 (1993) (warranties in study not easily understood by half of American adult population). Unlike the Federal Trade Commission's rules for advertisements, warranty disclaimers need not be "clear" to be effective. Nor need they accommodate the propensity of some buyers to underestimate the probability or impact of the goods not conforming. A handful of states apparently regard the consumer buyer as incompetent in understanding the legal consequences of a warranty disclaimer. They have adopted nonuniform versions of 2–316 which ban disclaimers of implied warranties in sales transactions with consumer buyers, with some exceptions. See, e.g., Ala. Code 7–2–316(5), Me. Rev. Stat. Ann., title 11, 2–316(5), W.Va. Code 46A–6–107.

Universal Drilling Co. v. Camay Drilling Co.

United States Court of Appeals, Tenth Circuit, 1984
737 F.2d 869

■ McKAY, CIRCUIT JUDGE.

The parties to this lawsuit are "experienced, sophisticated, intelligent business[men] with vast education and experience in petroleum engineering, . . . oil and gas exploration, and . . . [the] makeup and operation of oil drilling rigs and equipment." In June 1977 they entered into negotiations for the purchase and sale of two drilling rigs referred to by the parties as the Marthens Rig and Rig 10.

The negotiations resulted in a contract dated July 1, 1977, and an amendment to that contract dated August 8, 1977.[1] Despite the dates

---

[1]   The July 1, 1977 contract contained the following clauses:

     18.01   The assets being purchased and sold hereunder are being sold by [defendant] in an "as-is" condition and without any warranty of operability or fitness.

     * * *

     26.01   This Agreement and the exhibits hereto and the agreements referred to herein set forth the entire agreement and understanding of the parties in respect of the transactions contemplated hereby and supersede all prior agreements, arrangements and understandings relating to the subject matter hereof. No representation, promise, inducement or statement of intention has been made by [defendant] or [plaintiffs] which is not embodied in this Agreement or in the documents referred to herein, and neither [defendant] nor [plaintiffs] shall be bound by or liable for any alleged representation, promise, inducement or statements of intention not so set forth.

written on the documents, plaintiffs contend that there was no contract until the amendment was actually executed on August 19, 1977. Defendant does not challenge that contention.

The contract defines the property to be sold as the personal property listed in Exhibits A, B and C to the contract. Rig 10 is defined as the property in Exhibit A and the Marthens Rig is defined as the property in Exhibits B and C.

Subsequent to the delivery of the property, plaintiffs complained that the property they received did not conform to the contract alleging that they were to receive two used but nevertheless operable drilling rigs. Defendant, however, relying on the contract, argued that it delivered all of the property listed in the specific exhibits. This diversity lawsuit resulted.

At trial plaintiffs sought to introduce extrinsic evidence to establish certain representations and warranties made by defendant. The trial court applying the parol evidence rule embodied in Colo. Rev. Stat. § 4–2–202 (1973), excluded the evidence despite plaintiffs' claims that the evidence was admissible under the fraud exception to the parol evidence rule. The trial court also rejected plaintiffs' theory that there were breaches of express warranties based on the description of the goods contained in the contract. Plaintiffs appeal those rulings as well as the court's award of attorneys' fees. * * *

Breach of Express Warranties by Description

Approaching this issue it must again be remembered that the parties to this suit are experienced in the field of oil and gas exploration and drilling. Furthermore, none of the parties allege that they were in an inferior bargaining position.

Plaintiffs do not dispute the trial court's finding that the contract, specifically paragraph 18.01, effectively disclaimed all implied warranties. Plaintiffs do allege, however, that the description of the assets contained in the contract created an express warranty that the assets would conform to that description. In addition, plaintiffs argue that such an express warranty of description cannot be disclaimed, or at least was not effectively disclaimed.

Section 2–316 of the Uniform Commercial Code as adopted in Colorado provides for the modification and exclusion of warranties. Colo. Rev. Stat. § 4–2–316 (1973). In particular it provides that words or conduct relevant to the creation of an express warranty and words or conduct tending to negate or limit warranty shall be construed wherever reasonable as consistent with each other; but subject to the provisions of this article on parol or extrinsic evidence (section 4–2–202), negation or limitation is inoperative to the extent such construction is unreasonable. Id. § 4–2–316(1). Accordingly, the initial inquiry must be whether express warranties were created under section 4–2–313 and if so how they are affected by section 18.01 of the contract.

Plaintiff argues that this case is controlled by section. 4–2–313(b) which provides that "any description of the goods which is made part of the basis of the bargain creates an express warranty that the goods shall conform to the description." Colo. Rev. Stat. § 4–2–313(b). The principles underlying section 4–2–313 are set out in comment four to that section:

4. In view of the principle that the whole purpose of the law of warranty is to determine what it is that the seller has in essence agreed to sell, the policy is adopted of those cases which refuse except in unusual circumstances to recognize a material deletion of the seller's obligation. Thus, a contract is normally a contract for a sale of something describable and described. A clause generally disclaiming "all warranties, express or implied" cannot reduce the seller's obligation with respect to such description and therefore cannot be given literal effect under Section 2–316.

This is not intended to mean that the parties, if they consciously desire, cannot make their own bargain as they wish. But in determining what they have agreed upon good faith is a factor and consideration should be given to the fact that the probability is small that a real price is intended to be exchanged for a pseudo-obligation. Id. § 4–2–313 comment 4.

Similarly, Professors White and Summers argue that a seller should not be able to disclaim a warranty created by description.

We hope courts will reach similar conclusions and strike down attempted disclaimers in cases in which the seller includes a description of the article which amounts to a warranty and then attempts to disclaim all express warranties. To illustrate further: assume that the sales contract describes machinery to be sold as a "haybaler" and then attempts to disclaim all express warranties. If the machine failed to bale hay and the buyer sued, we would argue that the disclaimer is ineffective. In our judgment, the description of the machine as a "haybaler" is a warranty that the machine will bale hay and, in the words of 2–316, a negation or limitation ought to be "inoperative" since it is inconsistent with the warranty.

Plaintiff relies principally on two cases that follow this rationale. Century Dodge Inc. v. Mobley, 272 S.E.2d 502, 504 (1980) (cert. denied); Blankenship v. Northtown Ford, Inc., 420 N.E.2d 167, 170–71 (1981). In both cases automobile dealers had sold "new" cars which for various reasons did not meet the description of a "new" car. Consequently the courts held that the boilerplate disclaimer provisions of the consumer sales contracts did not relieve the dealers of their responsibility to deliver a "new" car.

We do not question the rationale of the above authorities. Nonetheless, we find them not controlling in the instant case. If in this case we were dealing with a consumer transaction, as in the cases just cited, we would be more inclined to follow those authorities. However, as noted in subsequent cases, "the courts are less reluctant to hold educated businessmen to the terms of contracts to which they have entered than consumers dealing with skilled corporate sellers." Bowers Manufacturing Co. v. Chicago Machine Tool Co., 453 N.E.2d 61, 66 (1983).

Furthermore, both sections 4–2–313 and 4–2–316 express the policy of the statutory scheme to allow parties to make any bargain they wish. Comment four to section 4–2–313 states that if parties consciously desire they can disclaim whatever warranties they wish. Colo. Rev. Stat. § 4–2–313 comment 4 (1973). In addition, comment one to section 4–2–316 explains that its purpose is to "protect a buyer from unexpected and unbargained language of disclaimer." Id. § 4–2–316 comment 1. Consequently, we will not rewrite the contract in this case. The exhibits to the contract which described the goods must be read in conjunction with the contract itself. The contract states that the goods are used and there is no guarantee that they are fit or even operable.

If we were to hold that the contract in the instant case created undisclaimable express warranties by description, we cannot think of alternative language that would memorialize the intent of the parties— to purchase and sell used "as is" equipment which has value but which may need repairs or additional parts to be fit and operable.

Our holding on this issue does not leave plaintiffs in general without remedy in similar contexts or the plaintiffs in this case with an "empty bargain." If the goods delivered do not meet the description in the contract there is a breach of the contract. In short, if no mast were delivered or if what was delivered was junk metal which in no way resembled a mast, plaintiffs would have a cause of action for breach of the contract.

Finally, plaintiffs did not receive an empty bargain. An appraisal which plaintiffs commissioned valued the goods received at an amount in excess of $3,000,000. The purchase price for the assets was $2,925,000.

The trial court did not err in excluding plaintiffs' evidence regarding breach of warranty. * * *

NOTES

1. The court determined that an express warranty by description was not created by the contract description of the assets sold as two drilling rigs ("the Marthens Rig and Rig 10"). The description of the assets as drilling rigs therefore is not a warranty that the rigs will operate. So although an express warranty once created cannot be disclaimed (2–316(1)), the contract's language did not create one. In finding no express warranty, the court considered the contract language referring to the assets being sold merely as a way of identifying them. The language does not describe qualities of those assets. Otherwise, the court noted, the parties could not use language to identify the assets without upsetting their intent to assign the risk that the drilling rigs will not function to the buyer.

Do you find the court's handling of relevant legal authority persuasive? The court acknowledges two cases that support the buyer's position that a contract description imports a warranty (*Century Dodge Inc. v. Mobley* and *Blankenship v. Northtown Ford, Inc.*). It distinguishes the cases from its case on the basis of the characteristics of the buyers. The buyers in those cases were consumers, while the buyer in *Universal Drilling* is a commercial buyer. Section 2–313's regulation of express warranties does not turn on the status of the contracting parties. Even if courts sometimes are more solicitous of consumer buyers than commercial buyers, who are generally knowledgeable, 2–313 does not allow them to do so. The seller creates an express warranty only if 2–313's requirements are met, and not otherwise. Is there a better way to distinguish *Century Dodge* and *Blankenship* from *Universal Drilling*? Consider that the car dealers in the former two cases sold cars that they described as "new." The adjective describes a quality of the cars. By contrast, the contract language in *Universal Drilling* identified the assets sold as Rig 10 and the Marthens Rig. This language does not describe a quality of the rigs (other than being a rig).

2.   The suggestion just made is that whether contract language describes the goods depends on the understanding of the parties. The test is how a reasonable person in the buyer's position would understand the contract's terms. Here the commercial status of the buyer can matter. If the buyer in *Universal Drilling* (implausibly) had been a consumer in search of a drilling rig, she might well understand the reference to "Rig 10" and "Marthens Rig" to mean "operable Rig 10" and "operable Marthens Rig." The commercial buyer in *Universal Drilling* arguably did not have same understanding. It likely understood the terms merely to pick out the assets being sold. By contrast, the consumer buyers in *Century Dodge* and *Blankenship* almost certainly understood that a "new" car meant a new car.

3.   Section 2–316(1) makes a warranty disclaimer "inoperative" when the express warranty and the disclaimer are inconsistent. The subsection is expressly made subject to the parol evidence rule (2–202). This proviso risks allowing a fully integrated written agreement to exclude an express warranty made by the seller before the agreement was executed. Section 2–202's parol evidence rule bars evidence or prior representations or promises, or contemporaneous written representations or promises that are inconsistent with a writing the parties intend to be complete with respect to a particular matter. Thus, the rule bars evidence of an express warranty when the integrated written agreement disclaims warranties not contained in the integration. In effect the parol evidence rule works to allow the seller to do indirectly what 2–316(1) prevents it from doing directly: disclaim express warranties. Courts and commentators struggle with the proper relation between 2–202's parol evidence rule and 2–316(1). Fraud is an exception to the parol evidence rule, allowing the buyer in *Universal Drilling* to argue unsuccessfully that a seller's prior representations were fraudulent. Some courts admit evidence of prior express warranties under the guise of determining whether the written contract is integrated. A few courts simply declare that the parol evidence rule has no application where a prior express warranty is contradicted by a written disclaimer. See, e.g., Carpetland, U.S.A. v. Payne, 536 N.E.2d 306 (Ind. Ct. App. 1989). To insure that the buyer has no expectations created by a prior express warranty, a UCC study recommends that the parol evidence rule (2–202) be revised to require that a merger clause in the integration be separately signed by the buyer. See PEB Study Group: Uniform Commercial Code Article 2 105 (1990).

Rinaldi v. Iomega Corp.

Delaware Superior Court, 1999
41 U.C.C. Rep. Serv.2d 1143

■ Memorandum Opinion: COOCH, J.

I. Introduction: Factual and Procedural History

This proposed class action was commenced in September 1998 on behalf of all persons who have purchased purportedly defective "Zip drives" from January 1, 1995 to the present. The Zip drives are manufactured by defendant Iomega Corporation, a computer storage device maker incorporated in Delaware and based in Utah. A Zip drive is a large capacity personal computer data storage drive. The complaint alleges inter alia that the alleged defect, said by Plaintiffs to be commonly known as the "Click of Death," causes irreparable damage to the removable magnetic media storage disks on which the drives store data. Plaintiffs also allege that the defect renders the data on the disks unreadable and that when another drive attempts to read the data from a disk that has been infected, the defect transfers to the second drive, causing further damage.

Plaintiffs' complaint has four counts. Count I alleges that Defendant breached the implied warranty of merchantability by manufacturing a product that was not fit for the ordinary purpose for which such products are used and that Defendant's disclaimer of the implied warranty of merchantability contained in the packaging of the product was ineffective because it was not sufficiently "conspicuous" as required by 6 Del. C.2–316(2). Count II alleges that Defendant was negligent in manufacturing and designing the Zip drive without using the reasonable care, skill, and diligence required when placing such a product into the stream of commerce. Count III alleges that Defendant committed consumer fraud in violation of the Delaware Consumer Fraud Act by falsely misrepresenting through advertising to the consuming public that the Zip drives were suitable for their intended purpose. Count IV alleges that Defendant was negligent in failing to warn the consuming public about the risks of its product when it knew or should have known that the product could cause damage when used for its intended purpose.

Before this Court is Defendant's Motion to Dismiss the complaint in its entirety based on (1) Plaintiffs' alleged failure in Count I to state a claim for breach of the implied warranty of merchantability, (2) Plaintiffs alleged failure in Count II to state a claim that Defendant negligently designed and manufactured its Zip drives in that Plaintiffs have not pled allegations of negligence with sufficient "particularity" pursuant to Superior Court Civil Rule 9(b), (3) Plaintiffs' alleged failure in Count III to state a claim that Defendant violated the Delaware Consumer Fraud Act in that they have not pled fraud with sufficient "particularity" pursuant to Superior Court Civil Rule 9(b) and (4) Plaintiffs alleged failure to state a claim that Defendant negligently failed to warn users of its Zip drives about the claimed potential problems in that they have not pled negligence with sufficient "particularity" pursuant to Superior Court Civil Rule 9(b).

For the reasons set forth below, Defendant's Motion to Dismiss is granted in part, denied in part and deferred in part. Defendant's Motion to Dismiss Count I on the grounds that Plaintiffs have failed to state a claim for breach of the implied warranty of merchantability is granted since the Court finds that the disclaimer is "conspicuous." Defendant's Motion to Dismiss Count II on the grounds that Plaintiffs have failed to state a claim for negligent design and manufacture is denied. Defendant's Motion to Dismiss Count III on the grounds that Plaintiffs have failed to plead fraud with sufficient particularity under the Delaware Consumer Fraud Act is granted, but dismissal now is deferred because Plaintiffs are granted potential leave to amend Count Ill pursuant to Superior Court Civil Rule 15(a) on or before a date that will be established at a later time. Defendant's Motion to Dismiss Count IV on the grounds that Plaintiffs have failed to state a claim for negligent failure to warn is denied.

* * *

III. Discussion

A. Count I of the Complaint is Dismissed Because Defendant's Disclaimer of the Implied Warranty of Merchantability Has Satisfied the Conspicuousness Requirement Despite The Disclaimer's Location Within the Zip Drive Package.

Defendant contends that Plaintiffs' claim for breach of the implied warranty of merchantability has failed to state a claim because Defendant's disclaimer of the implied warranty of merchantability, contained within the packaging of the Zip drive, effectively disclaimed all Liability. The sole issue to be resolved here is whether Count I of the complaint should be dismissed because Defendant's disclaimer of the implied warranty of merchantability was not "conspicuous," as required by 6 Del. C. § 2–316, because the disclaimer was contained within the packaging of the Zip drive product itself and therefore not "discovered" by the purchaser prior to the purchaser's purchase of the product.

Defendant's disclaimer inside the Zip drive package provides:

EXCEPT AS STATED ABOVE IN THIS PARAGRAPH, THE FOREGOING WARRANTIES ARE IN LIEU OF ALL OTHER CONDITIONS OR WARRANTIES, EXPRESS, IMPLIED, OR STATUTORY, INCLUDING, WITHOUT LIMITATION, ANY IMPLIED CONDITION OR WARRANTY OF MERCHANTABILITY OR FITNESS FOR A PARTICULAR PURPOSE AND OF ANY OTHER WARRANTY OBLIGATION ON THE PART OF IOMEGA (capitals in original).

The above disclaimer appears near the bottom of a document labeled "IOMEGA LIMITED WARRANTY" located inside the packaging.

6 Del. C. § 2–316(2) provides, in pertinent part, ". . . to exclude or modify the implied warranty of merchantability or any part of it the language must mention merchantability and in the case of a writing must be conspicuous. . . . " 6 Del. C. § 2–316(2) is identical to § 2–316(2) of the Uniform Commercial Code.

The usual arguments concerning the conspicuousness requirement of U.C.C. § 2–316(2) have been based on issues such as the size of the type set and the location of the disclaimer in the warranty itself. Defendant contends that the conspicuousness requirement has been met regardless of the location of the disclaimer inside the Zip drive package so long as the disclaimer is "noticeable and easily readable." Defendant asserts that "modern commercial realities of how contracts are formed with consumers of prepackaged products necessitates that the terms of [its] warranty disclaimer be given effect."

Plaintiffs do not claim that the disclaimer was improperly worded, that the text of the disclaimer was improperly placed in the rest of the warranty or that the typeface of the disclaimer was too small, but instead argue that the disclaimer, located in the packaging of the product, could not realistically be called to the attention of the consumer until after the sale had been consummated, thus rendering the disclaimer not "conspicuous" as a matter or law and therefore ineffective.

Although similar issues of additional terms to a contract such as a shrinkwrap license, an arbitration clause and a license agreement, each physically located within the packaging of the product, has been litigated in other jurisdictions, the parties have cited no case directly addressing the effectiveness, under U.C.C. § 2–316(2), of a disclaimer of the implied warranty of merchantability by virtue of its location within the packaging of a product itself, nor has the Court found any such case.

The issue of conspicuousness, generally, under § 2–316 has been the topic of various law review articles, periodicals and texts, and has been the subject of much litigation. As stated, however, no authorities have been located that squarely addressed the issue in this case. The traditional focus has been on the "mention" of merchantability and the visible characteristics of the disclaimer, such as type set and location within the warranty document itself. In determining if a disclaimer of the implied warranty of merchantability is effective as being "conspicuous," the secondary authorities and courts have often looked to the purpose of § 2–316. The purpose of that section is to "protect a buyer from unexpected and unbargained for language of disclaimer." [Comment 1 to 2–316]. That purpose is the real backbone in determining if a disclaimer is conspicuous when looking at factors beyond the mentioning of merchantability and type set.

Analogous support for this Court's conclusion that the physical location of the disclaimer of the implied warranty of merchantability inside the Zip drive packaging does not make the disclaimer inconspicuous can be found in some cases from other jurisdictions. In ProCD, Inc. v. Zeidenberg, 86 F.3d 1447 (7th Cir. 1996), the Seventh Circuit held that a shrinkwrap license located inside the packaging of the computer program was enforceable as an additional term of the contract, and stated that the commercial practicalities of modern retail purchasing dictate where terms such as a shrinkwrap license should be located. The *ProCD* court held that it would be otherwise impractical for these additional terms to be located on the outside of the box in "microscopic" type. The *ProCD* court stated, "transactions in which the exchange of money precedes the communication of detailed terms are common." The *ProCD* court then looked to other sections of the U.C.C. that dealt with the issue in terms of acceptance and rejection of goods: "A buyer accepts goods under § 2–606(1)(b) when, after an opportunity to inspect, [the buyer] fails to make an effective rejection under § 2–602(1). [The seller] extended an opportunity to reject if a buyer should find the license unsatisfactory." The *Pro CD* court continued its analysis and observed that

Consumer goods work the same way. Someone who wants to buy a radio set visits a store, pays and walks out with a box. Inside the box is a leaflet containing some terms, the most important of which usually is the warranty, read for the first time in the comfort of home. By [the buyer's] lights, the warranty in the box is irrelevant; every consumer gets the standard warranty implied by the UCC in the event the contract is silent; yet so far as we are aware no state disregards warranties furnished with consumer products.

Plaintiffs argue that *ProCD* is inapposite because it specifically concerned the validity of a shrinkwrap license which is not governed by U.C.C. § 2–316(2). Although that is correct, ProCd stressed that "the U.C.C. . . . permits parties to structure their relations so that the buyer has a chance to make a final decision after a detailed review" of the contract terms. All of the additional terms, which included the shrinkwrap license, became part of the contract in *ProCD.*

In Hill v. Gateway 2000, Inc., 105 F.3d 1147 (7th Cir. 1997), the Seventh Circuit relied on *ProCD* in holding that an arbitration clause located inside the packaging of a computer was enforceable as an additional term to the contract, and stated, "practical considerations support allowing vendors to enclose the full legal terms with their products . . . Customers as a group are better off when vendors skip costly and ineffectual steps such as telephonic recitation, and use instead a simple approve-or-return device." In holding that the arbitration clause was effective, the Hill court concluded that an additional term physically located outside of the contract was nevertheless an enforceable term of the contract.

In M.A. Mortenson Co. v. Timberline Software Corp., 970 P.2d 803 (Wash. Ct. App. 1999), the Washington Court of Appeals relied on *ProCD* and *Hill* and held that a licensing agreement located inside the packaging of a software program was enforceable as an additional term to the contract. In *Mortenson* the court stated, ". . . the terms of the present license agreement are part of the contract as formed between parties. We find that [the purchaser's] installation and use of the software manifested its assent to the terms of the license. . . . " As in *ProCD* and *Hill*, the *Mortenson* court held that a licensing agreement located within the packaging of the product, not in the contract itself, was an enforceable additional term of the contract.

Other courts have also addressed the issue of the physical location of the disclaimer of the implied warranty of merchantability from different perspectives. Thus in Step–Saver Data Systems., Inc. v. Wyse Technology, 1990 U.S. Dist. LEXIS 7709 (E.D. Pa. 1990), the United States District Court for the Eastern District of Pennsylvania discussed the location of a disclaimer of the implied warranty of merchantability inside computer software packaging and held the location of an additional term (in *Step–Saver*, a disclaimer) is to be considered independently of conspicuousness. The *Step–Saver* court held that "there is no question that pursuant to the U.C.C., limitation of warranty and remedies are valid when packaged with the product so long as the limitation is clear, conspicuous and one that a reasonable person would have noticed and understood." The holding in *Step–Saver* that conspicuousness and location are to be considered independently is not directly on point with the issue at bar. However, the *Step–Saver* court relied on the purpose behind § 2–316 in finding that so long as a disclaimer of the implied warranty of merchantability is one that could be noticed and understood, the disclaimer is conspicuous.

This Court has addressed the issue of conspicuousness under § 2–316(2) in Lecates v. Hertrich Pontiac Buick Co., 515 A.2d 163 (Del. Super. Ct. 1986). In *Lecates*, a case on which Plaintiffs rely, the issue was whether the implied warranties were effectively disclaimed by an automobile dealer when the car that was sold malfunctioned, causing physical injuries. The court held that the seller's disclaimer of the implied warranty of merchantability located in a sales invoice satisfied the conspicuous requirement of § 2–316(2). In *Lecates*, the specific question was whether or not the disclaimer had been delivered by the seller to the buyer only after the sale had already been consummated. The *Lecates* court addressed this narrow issue in light of the specific facts in that case and observed that disclaimer clauses have been held ineffective "if it appeared that the documents in which such clauses appeared were given to the buyer after the sale had been consummated." *Lecates* addressed the issue of what terms and conditions were a part of the contract at the point of contract consummation, but here, Defendant's disclaimer of the implied warranty of merchantability was an additional term of each contract between each plaintiff and Defendant to purchase the Zip drives. Defendant's sales of the Zip drives to the six plaintiffs were each not "consummated" until after each plaintiff had had an opportunity to inspect and then to reject or to accept the product with the additional terms that were enclosed within the packaging of the Zip drive.

The commercial practicalities of modem retail purchasing make it eminently reasonable for a seller of a product such as a Zip drive to place a disclaimer of the implied warranty of merchantability within the plastic packaging. The buyer can read the disclaimer after payment for the Zip drive and then later have the opportunity to reject the contract terms (i.e., the disclaimer) if the buyer so chooses. This Court concludes that Defendant's disclaimer of the implied warranty of merchantability was effective despite its physical placement inside the packaging of the Zip drive and has satisfied the conspicuousness requirement of 6 Del. C. § 2–316(2).

Defendant's Motion to Dismiss Count I on the grounds that Plaintiffs have failed to state a claim for breach of the implied warranty of merchantability is granted. * * *

IV. Conclusion

For the reasons explained below, Defendant's to Dismiss is granted in part, denied in part and deferred in part. Defendant's Motion to Dismiss Count I on the grounds that Plaintiffs have failed to state a claim for breach of the implied warranty of merchantability is granted since the Court finds that the disclaimer is "conspicuous." Defendant's Motion to Dismiss Count II on the grounds that Plaintiffs have failed to state a claim for negligent design and manufacture is denied. Defendant's Motion to Dismiss Count III on the grounds that Plaintiffs have failed to plead fraud with sufficient particularity under the Delaware Consumer Fraud Act is granted, but dismissal now is deferred Plaintiffs are granted leave to amend Count III pursuant to Superior Court Civil Rule 15(a) on or before a date that will be established at a later time. Defendant's Motion to Dismiss Count IV on grounds that Plaintiffs have failed to state a claim for negligent failure to warn is denied.

NOTES

1. The sales contract in *Rinaldi* is a "rolling" or "layered" contract. As described in Chapter 3, rolling or layered contracts are contracts in which some of the terms are provided by the seller after the goods are delivered. In the typical rolling contract of the sort in *Rinaldi*, the buyer has the right to reject the goods if it is finds these terms unacceptable. The terms that arrived in *Rinaldi* were contained in the packaging of the product and included a warranty disclaimer. Although the disclaimer was in bold type close to a heading that signaled a warranty limitation, it was not visible until the package was opened. The plaintiff-buyers argued that the disclaimer of implied warranties did not satisfy 2–316(2) because it was not conspicuous until after the buyers purchased the product. If the contract was not a rolling contract, what result? 2–316(2), Comment 1 to 2–316.

2. The court relied on well-known cases involving rolling contracts for the proposition that commercial practicalities dictate where additional terms delivered to the buyer with the goods are placed. It concluded that the seller's placement of the warranty disclaimer within the packaging does not make the disclaimer inconspicuous. None of the cases the court relies on for "analogous support" deal with a warranty disclaimer that arrives after the buyer places its purchase order, as the court concedes. Given the concession, is its reliance on those cases safe? Consider this statement from ProCD v. Zeidenberg, 86 F.3d 1447, 1453 (7th Cir. 1996), one of the cases: "Some portions of the UCC impose additional requirements on the way parties agree on terms. A disclaimer of the implied warranty of merchantability must be 'conspicuous.' UCC § 2–316(2), incorporating UCC § 1–201(10). Promises to make firm offers, or to negate oral modifications, must be 'separately signed.' UCC §§ 2–205, 2–209(2). These special provisos reinforce the impression that, so far as the UCC is concerned, other terms may be as inconspicuous as the forum-selection clause on the back of the cruise ship ticket in *Carnival Lines*."

3. The court determined that "[t]he buyer can read the disclaimer after payment for the Zip drive and then later have the opportunity to reject the contract terms (i.e., the disclaimer) if the buyer so chooses." On this finding it concluded that the location of the disclaimer in the packaging made the disclaimer conspicuous under 2–316(2). Has the court applied the correct standard of conspicuousness? 1–201(b)(10). Is there an alternative basis on which the court could have found the disclaimer effective? 2–316(3)(a). What is the advantage of doing so? For recognition of the need for a legal standard to determine how extensive the buyer's search for terms in rolling contracts must be, see Eric A. Posner, *ProCD v. Zeidenberg* and Cognitive Overload in Contractual Bargaining, 77 U. Chi. L. Rev. 1181, 1187 (2011).

4. Judge Kozinski, when required to interpret the Bankruptcy Code's undefined standard of conspicuousness, had this to say about 1–201(b)(10)'s standard:

The [Bankruptcy Appellate Panel] borrowed the UCC's definition of "conspicuous," but looked to caselaw from the District of South Carolina to interpret it. It needn't have reached quite so far. Interpreting Nevada's version of the UCC, we held that a term is conspicuous if "a reasonable person in the buyer's position would not have been surprised to find the [term] in the contract." Sierra Diesel Injection Service, Inc. v. Burroughs Corp., 890 F.2d 108, 114 (9th Cir. 1989).

We decide conspicuousness as a matter of law. This is not because judges are experts at graphic design, but because subjecting conspicuousness to fact-finding would introduce too much uncertainty into the drafting process. See Smith v. Check–N–Go of Illinois, Inc., 200 F.3d 511, 515 (7th Cir. 1999) ("No matter what a lender did, a borrower could say that to his eyes the combination of color, typeface, spacing, size, style, underlining, capitalization, border, and placement . . . emphasized one disclosure over another.").

Lawyers who think their caps lock keys are instant "make conspicuous" buttons are deluded. In determining whether a term is conspicuous, we look at more than formatting. A term that appears in capitals can still be inconspicuous if it is hidden on the back of a contract in small type. Terms that are in capitals but also appear in hard-to-read type may flunk the conspicuousness test. A sentence in capitals, buried deep within a long paragraph in capitals will probably not be deemed conspicuous. Formatting does matter, but conspicuousness ultimately turns on the likelihood that a reasonable person would actually see a term in an agreement. Thus, it is entirely possible for text to be conspicuous without being in capitals. In re Bassett, 285 F.3d 882, 885–886 (9th Cir. 2002).

PROBLEM 6.1

Dealer has on display a set of colored glass bowls under a sign "Ideal glass." Buyer, at Dealer's invitation, inspected the glass bowls on display before purchasing a set and found them satisfactory. Unfortunately, Buyer was distracted by her cell phone while inspecting them and failed to notice scratches on the display bowls. After using the bowls for week, Buyer discovered that some of the bowls developed color blemishes. The blemishes are the result of production defects and appear only with use. Buyer is unhappy about both the scratches and the blemishes. Is Dealer liable to Buyer? 2–313(1)(a), (c), 2–316(3)(b). Would your answer change if the sign read "Perfect glass"?

PROBLEM 6.2

Seller and Buyer's sales contract contained two pages. The top of the first page was headed "TERMS AND CONDITIONS BELOW." The middle of the second page contained an italicized paragraph disclaiming all implied warranties. The disclaimer mentioned merchantability and fitness for a particular purpose. A place for Buyer's signature appeared on the bottom of the first page.

(a) Is the disclaimer effective? 2–316(2), 1–201(b)(10).

(b) Assume that the heading on the first page read "TERMS AND CONDITIONS STATED ON PAGES 1 AND 2 BELOW." Is the disclaimer effective?

(c) Assume that the disclaimer came in the final paragraph on the second page just above the space for Buyer's signature. Is the disclaimer effective?

(d) Assume in (c) that the disclaimer was not italicized. Is it still effective?

(e) Assume that Seller and Buyer negotiated and jointly drafted every paragraph of the agreement. The first page of the agreement was headed "TERMS AND CONDITIONS BELOW," the disclaimer came in the middle of the second page, and Buyer's signature appeared on the bottom of the first page. Is the disclaimer effective?

PROBLEM 6.3

Seller and Buyer executed a twenty page standard form contract in small type drafted by Seller. A warranty disclaimer appeared in the middle of page 10 in an undistinguished type font. Unlike other buyers in contracts of this type, Buyer was unusually thorough and took the time to read through the entire contract carefully. Is the warranty disclaimer effective according to how most courts construe 2–316(3)(a)? Compare In re Mesa Business Equipment, 1991 U.S. App. LEXIS 8625, at *1 (9th Cir. 1991) (rationale underlying conspicuousness evaporates if the buyer is aware of the disclaimer). Is this a good result?

B. WARRANTY DISCLAIMERS UNDER THE CISG

None of the CISG's provisions expressly addresses the disclaimer of warranties. Nonetheless, a number of provisions clearly allow the sales contract to waive them. Article 6 allows the parties to opt out of ("derogate from") almost all of the CISG's provisions, including the Articles that create warranties. See Ajax Tool Works, Inc. v. Can–Eng Mfg. Ltd., 2003 U.S. Dist. LEXIS 1306, at *1 (D. Ill. 2003). For its part, Article 35(2) makes the warranties described in the Article subject to contrary agreement by the parties ("Except where the parties have agreed otherwise"). Article 41 contains comparable language. Article 35(3) relieves the seller of liability based on particular circumstances in which the contract was concluded. It provides that the seller is not liable under Article 35(2) if the buyer knew or could not have been unaware of a lack of conformity with Article 35(2) at the conclusion of the contract. Even the express warranty created by Article 35(1) can be disclaimed by an appropriate contractual provision. If the contract disclaims express warranties going to description, for instance, then the contract does not require the seller to deliver goods of a certain description. In that case Article 35(1) does not obligate the seller to deliver goods "which are . . . of the description required by the contract."

Initially, it might appear that the CISG also governs how warranties are disclaimed. This is because Article 8 provides familiar rules of interpretation for understanding the parties' statements and conduct. A warranty disclaimer allocates to the buyer the risk that the goods do not conform to the contract. So whether the contract disclaims warranties seemingly is a matter only of contract interpretation. Article 8(1), for instance, provides that the statements or conduct of a party is to be interpreted according to his intent when the other party knew or could not have been aware of that intent. If Article 8(1) is inapplicable, Article 8(2) provides that the statements or conduct is to be interpreted according to the understanding of a reasonable person in the other party's circumstances. Thus, seemingly the enforceability of a disclaimer turns only on interpreting the language of the contract, according to the intended or reasonable meaning given to its terms.

The trouble is that there is another issue that must be resolved that the CISG does not resolve: whether disclaimer is a matter of "validity" of a provision of the contract. Article 4(a) states that, except as otherwise expressly provided, the CISG is not concerned with "the validity of the contract or any of its provisions." Instead, issues of validity are left to applicable domestic law. Although excluding validity from the CISG's scope risks losing the uniformity that the CISG purports to achieve, Article 4(a) has this consequence. The CISG does not define "validity," and the sparse relevant diplomatic history suggests that the terms include matters of contractual capacity, duress, fraud and illegality. It is unclear whether the term extends to warranty disclaimers.

This uncertainty in coverage is a problem because the enforcement of disclaimers can be characterized in two different ways, with two different consequences. On the one hand, the enforceability of a disclaimer can be considered merely a question of contract interpretation, as just suggested. As a question of contract interpretation, the only issue is the parties' allocation of nonconformity risk between themselves. If the disclaimer reflects the parties' intent to put the risk of nonconformity of the goods on the buyer, the parties' intent controls. The CISG's rules of interpretation apply to construe the disclaimer clause in the contract. On the other hand, the enforceability of a disclaimer can be characterized as a question of validity. The question here is whether legal effect is to be given to the contract's allocation of risk. For this purpose, the parties' allocation of risk is not determinative.

It is tempting to argue the CISG in fact addresses the validity of warranty disclaimers. Article 4(a) excludes issues of validity from the CISG's scope "except as otherwise expressly provided" in the CISG. One might therefore contend that since Articles 35 and 41 "expressly provide" for agreements to alter the warranties created by Articles 35 or 41, the validity of a disclaimer is addressed by Article 35. Thus, even if enforcement of the disclaimer is a matter of validity, the CISG addresses the matter in Articles 35 and 41. The weakness of the argument is in the "expressly provided." Article 35 and 41 do not label agreements altering these warranties "valid" and therefore do not expressly provide for the validity of disclaimers. By contrast, in another context, Article 55 labels a contract "valid." The CISG therefore does not address the validity of warranty disclaimers. As a result, their validity is determined by applicable domestic law.

The CISG's drafters might well have considered the enforceability of warranty disclaimers to be a matter of validity. National laws treat disclaimers differently, especially (but not only) in consumer contracts. In the United States, some state laws ban the disclaimer of implied warranties in consumer sales, as does federal law when the seller makes a written warranty under the Magnuson–Moss Act. Other law, such as 2–316(2), requires disclaimers to be stated in mandated language or format. The CISG's drafters understandably could have purchased consensus at the price of leaving the enforceability of disclaimers outside of the CISG's scope. Although some early commentators considered disclaimers to be a matter only of contract interpretation, most of the more recent commentary and almost all of the sparse case law considers them a matter of validity. See, e.g., Oberlandesgericht Köln 22 (Germany), 21 May 1996, available at http://cisgw3.law.pace.edu/cases/960521g1.html; cf. Oberster Gerichtshof (Austria), 7 September 2000, available at http://cisgw3.law.pace.edu/cases/000907a3.html (validity of standard clauses restricting right to withhold payment governed by applicable domestic law). A U.S. court has held that "validity" for purposes of Article 4 includes issues that under domestic law render the contract void or unenforceable. See Geneva Pharm. Tech. Corp. v. Barr Labs., 201 F.Supp.2d 236 (S.D.N.Y. 2002) rev'd on other grounds, 386 F.2d 485 (2d Cir. 2004). Warranty disclaimers fit within this definition. As a result, whether a warranty disclaimer is enforceable requires asking two questions: (1) has the contract allocated the risk of the relevant nonconformity to the buyer?, and (2) will this allocation be given legal effect under applicable domestic law? Question (1) is a matter of contract interpretation, usually easily answered, and question (2) a matter of validity.

A recent U.S. case, Norfolk Southern R.R. Co. v. Power Source Supply, Inc., 66 UCC Rep. Serv.2d 680 (W.D. Pa. 2008), is illustrative. The sales contract in *Norfolk Southern* between a Virginia seller with a Pennsylvania presence and a Canadian buyer disclaimed all implied warranties other than a warranty of good title. The disclaimer on the second page of the two page document was in capital letters in the same font size as the rest of the document. It expressly disclaimed warranties of merchantability and fitness for a particular purpose. When the seller demanded the full contract price, the buyer defended by alleging that the seller had breached implied warranties of merchantability and fitness for a particular purpose. After determining that the CISG governed the sales contract, the court found that the contract effectively disclaimed the implied warranties. The following passage from the opinion contains the court's reasoning:

> The validity of the disclaimer cannot be determined by reference to the CISG itself. CISG art 4(a). It is therefore necessary to turn to the forum's choice of law rules. Geneva Pharm. Tech. Corp. v. Barr Lab., 201 F.Supp.2d 236, 282–83 (S.D.N.Y. 2002) rev'd on other grounds, 386 F.3d 485 (2d Cir. 2004); see also Zapata Hermanos Sucesores, S.A. v. Hearthside Baking Co., Inc., 313 F.3d

385, 390 (7th Cir. 2002) (using, in a CISG case involving an Illinois firm, "choice of law principles" to determine that the common law of Illinois applied "to any issues . . . not covered in express terms by the Convention"); Pescatore v. Pan Am. World Airways, Inc., 97 F.3d 1, 12–13 (2d Cir. 1996) (applying state choice of law rules to an action brought under the Warsaw Convention).

Under Pennsylvania law, the first step in a choice of laws analysis is to determine whether "there is an actual or real conflict between the potentially applicable laws." Hammersmith v. TIG Ins. Co., 480 F.3d 220, 230 (3d Cir. 2007). Alberta law allows disclaimer of implied terms as follows:

Where any right, duty or liability would arise under a contract of sale by implication of law, it may be negatived or varied by express agreement or by the course of dealing between the parties or by usage if the usage is such as to bind both parties to the contract. R.S.A. 2000, c. S–2, s. 54. Pennsylvania law requires that the disclaimer be "conspicuous" and, if the warranty of merchantability is being disclaimed or modified, the "mention" of the word "merchantability." 13 Pa C.S.A. § 2316(b). Whether a disclaimer is conspicuous is a question of law, to be determined by "whether a reasonable person against whom the modification or exclusion is to operate ought to have noticed it." Hornberger v. Gen. Motors Corp., 929 F.Supp. 884, 889 (E.D. Pa. 1996) (citations omitted). Under Pennsylvania law, factors to consider include: "(1) the placement of the clause in the document; (2) the size of the disclaimer's print; and (3) whether the disclaimer was highlighted or called to the reader's attention by being in all caps. . . ." Id. Expressions such as "as is" or "with all faults" are approved by statute as language of exclusion. 13 Pa C.S.A. § 2316(c)(1).

After examining the final, executed bills of sale, under the standards set forth above, the Court finds the disclaimer to be valid under either the laws of Pennsylvania or Alberta. There is no conflict, and hence no need for a conflict of laws analysis. *Norfolk Southern,* 66 UCC Rep. Serv.2d, at 685–86.

The step in the court's reasoning relying on Pennsylvania's 2–316(2) might well be questionable. Article 4(a) directs a court to the applicable domestic law governing the disclaimer. However, which part of domestic law controls the disclaimer is a separate and harder question to answer. In testing the disclaimer by 2–316(2), the *Norfolk Southern* court assumes that Pennsylvania's Article 2 of the UCC's disclaimer provision applies to a contract governed by the CISG. But there is another possibility. General contract principles governing disclaimers under Pennsylvania common law instead might apply. The selection of different Pennsylvania law matters because Pennsylvania's common law might not enforce a disclaimer that does not mention "merchantability" or meet the other requirements of 2–316(2) or (3). To decide which part of domestic law applies, perhaps the following counterfactual question should be asked: If the sales contract were not governed by the CISG, which part of applicable domestic law would govern it? If this question were asked on *Norfolk Southern's* facts, the answer would be Pennsylvania's Article 2 of the UCC (or Alberta's Sale of Goods Act). Thus, although the *Norfolk Southern* court does not ask the question, it tested the warranty disclaimer by the correct part of potentially applicable domestic law.

On the other hand, the way in which the court implicitly determines the applicable domestic law of disclaimers is not inevitable. The part of domestic law regulating warranty disclaimers could be selected in a different way. An alternative determines that the law of disclaimers within domestic law controls when it continues to apply to a sales contract governed by the CISG. This requires asking the following noncounterfactual question: Given that the CISG governs the sales contract, which part of applicable domestic law that the CISG does not displace controls the enforceability of the warranty disclaimer? If the question had been asked by the *Norfolk Southern* court, the result in the case might have been different. Because the CISG governed the sales contract, Pennsylvania's Article 2 of the UCC (or Alberta's Sale of Goods Act) did not apply to it. This means that Article 2's provisions regulating warranty disclaimers also were inapplicable. Thus, Pennsylvania or Alberta's common law of disclaimers, which are not displaced by the CISG, governed the sales contract. Pennsylvania or Alberta's common law of disclaimers therefore would determine whether the seller's warranty disclaimer was enforceable.

C. REMEDY LIMITATIONS AND DAMAGE EXCLUSIONS

In addition to warranty disclaimers, sales contracts frequently contain remedy limitations and damage exclusions. A remedy limitation, as the term suggests, restrict the remedies of the nonbreaching party. It operates to liquidate damages, thereby fixing the breaching party's liability. For example, on the seller's breach 2–711(1) entitles the buyer to reject or revoke its acceptance of the goods and recover both the contract price paid and damages. A very common contractual provision makes the buyer's exclusive remedy to have the seller repair or replace the goods. This provision eliminates the buyer's access to the range of remedies otherwise available under 2–711(1), limiting her to repair or replacement. The exclusive remedy sets a limit on the seller's liability. If the seller repairs or replaces the goods, the buyer cannot reject them or revoke its acceptance. Nor can a court award damages from the seller's breach.

A damage exclusion (sometimes also called a "damage limitation") excludes the liability of the breaching party for certain sorts of damages. By excluding liability for damages of particular sorts, the risk of these damages is allocated to the nonbreaching party. The most frequent sort of excluded damages are consequential damages. Shifting the risk of consequential damages to the buyer is sensible when it has a comparative advantage at reducing or eliminating consequential damages resulting from the seller's breach. The seller's expected liability from breach is part of the cost of the its performance and therefore is reflected in the contract price. A damage exclusion clause allows the parties to shift the risk of consequential damages to reduce the contract price by reducing the seller's expected breach costs.

The following is an example of a typical provision that combines a warranty disclaimer, remedy limitation and damage exclusion.

NO IMPLIED WARRANTIES, INCLUDING A WARRANTY OF MERCHANTABILITY AND FITNESS FOR A PARTICULAR PURPOSE, APPLIES TO THIS SALE, AND THE SELLER MAKES NO EXPRESS WARRANTIES OTHER THAN THOSE EXPRESSLY STATED.

Seller's liability arising out of warranties, representations or defects from any cause shall be limited solely to repairing or replacing the good sold.

IN NO EVENT WILL THE SELLER BE LIABLE BY VIRTUE OF THIS WARRANTY, OR OTHERWISE, FOR ANY CONSEQUENTIAL OR INCIDENTAL LOSS OR DAMAGE (INCLUDING LOST PROFITS OR OTHER COMMERCIAL LOSS).

The warranty disclaimer in the first sentence allocates the risk of nonconformity in the goods between the seller and the buyer. The buyer bears the risk of the all nonconformities in the goods other than the risk that they do not conform to the seller's express statements. The seller continues to bear the risk that the goods do not conform to its express statements. The buyer therefore bears the risk that the goods are unsuitable for the ordinary purposes to which they are put or the buyer's particular purposes. The second sentence is an exclusive remedy limitation. It fixes the seller's liability in the event of its breach. Section 2–719(2) permits exclusive remedy limitations. The seller's liability in effect is limited to its cost of repairing or replacement the nonconforming goods. The damage exclusion in the third sentence puts the risk of consequential damages resulting from the seller's breach on the buyer. An exclusive remedy limitation is not enough to do this. Without the damage exclusion, the seller would be obligated to repair or replace the nonconforming goods, but the buyer still could recover consequential damages resulting from the nonconformity. Section 2–719(3) permits the exclusion of consequential damages.

Article 2 of the UCC's regulation of remedy limitations and damage exclusions is vague. In fact, there are two different sorts of vagueness. One concerns the standard by which remedy limitations are judged to be invalid; the other concerns the relation between damage exclusions and remedy limitations when they are found to be invalid. Consider the two sorts of vagueness in turn. The first vagueness in 2–719 relates to the standard of invalidity for remedy limitations. Section 2–719(2) deems a remedy limitation invalid when it "fails of its essential purpose." If the remedy limitation fails this "test," 2–719(2) allows the nonbreaching party to resort to Article 2's remedies. Where the buyer is the nonbreacher, this means that it has available to it the remedies described in 2–711(1). The obvious question is when a remedy fails of its "essential purpose." Section 2–719(2) does not provide a "test" because neither it nor Comment 1 to 2–719 says anything informative about the matter. The subsection presupposes that an exclusive remedy limitation has an "essential" purpose. This is true but unhelpful. Remedy limitations against the buyer are reflected in the price of the good: A more extensive limitation reduces the seller's expected cost from breach and therefore the contract price offered to the buyer, while a lesser limitation increases its expected breach cost and therefore the contract price. At the same time, a remedy limitation reduces the value of the good to the buyer because its recourse against the seller is limited. Thus, from the buyer's perspective, the "essential" purpose of a remedy limitation is to reduce the contract price more than or as much as it reduces the value of the good to the buyer. Otherwise, the buyer would not agree to the limitation. The trouble is that 2–709(2) is silent as to when a remedy fails of its "essential purpose."

Comment 1 states that "it is of the very essence of a sales contract that at least a minimum adequate remedy is available." This seems to suggest that a valid remedy limitation must give a minimum of protection in the event of breach. However, the suggestion is wrong. As just noted, the contract price varies inversely according to the extent of the remedy limitation. Higher contract prices reflect fewer limitations; lower prices more extensive limitations. There is no "minimum" remedy that is of the "essence" in a sales contract any more than there is a minimum price or quantity that is the essence of a sales contract. For this reason, a remedy limitation cannot fail just because it leaves the nonbreacher with limited protection.

Some courts implicitly acknowledge this conclusion. They instead ask what the parties bargained for, considering the goods, price and the characteristics of the parties themselves. See, e.g., Riegel Power v. Voith Hydro, 888 F.2d 1043 (4th Cir. 1989). Most cases in which the validity of a remedy limitation clause is in contention involve a limitation of the buyer's remedies to have nonconforming goods repaired or replaced. The seller has either failed to repair or replace them, or has done so after delay. The buyer in these cases could have agreed to limit its remedies to repair or replacement in exchange for one of the three following promises by its seller:

    1.   The seller will try to repair or replace the goods if it feasible to do so.

    2.   The seller will try to repair or replace the goods in a timely fashion.

    3.   The seller will successfully repair or replace the goods in a timely fashion.

Promises 1–3 differ according to the burden the seller undertakes. As with any contract term, the trier of fact must determine which promise the buyer bargained for. A buyer might seek promise 1, which places a light burden on the seller, because a concern for reputation or ongoing relations with the buyer might make her likely to accommodate the buyer. On the other hand, a consumer buying a predictable product is likely to seek the seller's promise of successful and timely repair or replacement of nonconforming goods. Evidence of trade usage or the price of similar contracts without the remedy limitation is relevant. So too are characteristics of the goods that might make the seller reluctant to guarantee success.

The second vagueness in 2–719 is the relation between subsections (2) and (3). The question is whether the invalidity of a remedy limitation contained in subsection (2) renders the damage exclusion in subsection (3) invalid. Section 2–719(2) invalidates an exclusive remedy limitation when it fails of its essential purpose. In that case 2–719(2) allows the nonbreaching party to resort to remedies available under Article 2. See 2–711 (buyer's remedies); 2–703 (seller's remedies).

Section 2–719(3) allows the limitation or exclusion of consequential damages if conscionable. Thus, the damage limitation or exclusion is invalid if unconscionable, without regard to whether the remedy limitation is invalid because it fails of its essential purpose. The issue is whether the invalidity of a remedy limitation renders invalid a conscionable damage exclusion. Section 2–719 does not say. Courts take three positions on the issue. One position is that the damage exclusion is dependent on the remedy limitation, so that the invalidity of the latter makes the former invalid too. Under this view, if the remedy limitation is found to fails of its essential purpose, the damage exclusion is also invalid. Many early cases adopted this "dependent" position. A second position is that the two provisions are independent of each other. This leaves the validity of the damage exclusion regulated only by 2–719(3), so that it is invalid only if unconscionable. Under this view, even if the remedy limitation is deemed to fail of its essential purpose, the damage exclusion remains valid as long as it is conscionable. Recent cases tend to take this "independent" position.

The third position is described by some courts as a "case-by-case" approach. A more accurate term for the position is a "bargained-for" position. According to it, the parties' bargain establishes whether the remedy limitation is conditioned on the damage exclusion, so that the invalidity of the former makes the latter invalid. See Milgard Tempering, Inc. v. Selas Corp. of America, 902 F.2d 703 (9th Cir. 1990); AES Technology Systems, Inc. v. Coherent Radiation, 583 F.2d 933 (7th Cir. 1978). Unlike the other two positions, the agreement determines whether the damage exclusion is dependent or independent of the remedy limitation. By contrast, the dependent and independent approaches adopt different per se rules on the matter. In looking to the terms of the bargain, the bargained-for approach requires a court to determine the conditions of the parties' respective promises. For instance, the buyer's agreement to exclude consequential damages could be based on two different conditions, as in the following two promises:

    1.   I will bear consequential damages resulting from your delivery of nonconforming goods only if you repair or replace them.

    2.   I will bear consequential damages resulting from your delivery of nonconforming goods whether or not you repair or replace them.

Promises 1 or 2 can both serve as consideration for the bargain. In promise 1 the buyer agrees to exclude consequential damages in exchange for the seller repairing or replacing nonconforming goods. In promise 2 its agreement to exclude them is made not made conditional on the seller's repair or replacement and so is not in exchange for the remedy limitation. The damage exclusion therefore is independent of the remedy limitation. Buyers will not always make promise 1. For instance, a buyer might have a comparative advantage over its seller at reducing or eliminating consequential damages whether or not the seller succeeds at repair or replacement. To receive a lower priced contract, the buyer will agree to a damage exclusion not conditioned on the remedy limitation. It will make promise 2. As with any bargain, the promises exchanged between the contracting parties must be determined on a case-by-case basis.

Rheem Manufacturing Co. v. Phelps Heating & Air Conditioning

Supreme Court of Indiana, 2001
746 N.E.2d 941

■ Opinion by: SULLIVAN, JUSTICE

* * * Phelps expended considerable sums repairing Rheem furnaces that Phelps had sold and installed. We hold that the language of the UCC precludes Phelps from recovering consequential damages from Rheem for breach of express warranty and that the language of the express warranty at issue precludes Phelps from recovering for labor expenses. However, Phelps may still have valid claims for indemnity and breach of implied warranty.

Background

* * * Rheem Manufacturing Company ("Rheem") makes furnaces for use in homes and offices. During the late 1980s and early 1990s, Rheem sold its furnaces through a distributor, Federated Supply Corporation ("Federated"). Federated in turn sold Rheem furnaces to Phelps Heating and Cooling ("Phelps"), a central Indiana contractor.

The box in which every furnace was shipped contained the following warranty:

Manufacturer, RHEEM AIR CONDITIONING DIVISION, warrants ANY PART of this furnace against failure under normal use and service within the applicable periods specified below, in accordance with the terms of this warranty.

This express warranty was limited by three clauses that are at the heart of this appeal. First, Rheem limited the remedies available for breach of the warranty to replacement of parts:

Under this Warranty, RHEEM will furnish a replacement part that will be warranted for only the unexpired portion of the original warranty. . . . [1]

Second, Rheem disclaimed consequential and incidental damages:

ANY CLAIMS FOR INCIDENTAL OR CONSEQUENTIAL DAMAGES ARE EXPRESSLY EXCLUDED.

Finally, Rheem disclaimed any liability for the cost of servicing the furnaces:

This Warranty does not cover any labor expenses for service, nor for removing or reinstalling parts. All such expenses are your responsibility unless a service labor agreement exists between you and your contractor.

During the early 1990s, several types of Rheem furnaces malfunctioned after Phelps installed them. A Phelps executive testified that from "late 1989 until 1993, Rheem had virtually no high efficiency furnaces on the market that were not experiencing reliability problems. . . ." While Rheem issued numerous "technical service

---

[1]   On its face, it is unclear if this remedy is exclusive, but this ambiguity is clarified by a subsequent term: "RHEEM'S SOLE LIABILITY WITH RESPECT TO DEFECTIVE PARTS SHALL BE AS SET FORTH IN THIS WARRANTY. . . ."

bulletins" offering instructions on how to fix these problems, Phelps customers experienced difficulties for another three to four years.

Phelps executives met with a Rheem service representative on May 11, 1994. At this meeting, Phelps requested between $40,000 and $65,000 to compensate it for the cost involved in servicing the furnaces. Rheem rejected this request.

Phelps brought suit against Rheem and Federated on August 8, 1994, claiming that Rheem breached its express and implied warranties and was negligent in its manufacture of the furnaces. Underlying all of these claims is Phelps's assertion that the furnaces "shut down and were not operational after installation. Among other things, the pilot assemblies, hot surface ignitors, flame sensors and ignition controls failed." The complaint first contended that Rheem breached the implied warranty of fitness for a particular purpose because Rheem and Federated "knew that Phelps intended to use the furnaces and install them in properties serviced by Phelps" but the furnaces were "defective, and after they had been installed . . . they failed to function properly." (Id.) Similarly, Phelps sought damages for breach of the implied warranty of merchantability, contending that Rheem and Federated were merchants but that the defects in the furnaces made them "unsuitable and posed a risk of personal injury and property damages to customers serviced by Phelps . . . Phelps also asserted a claim under the express warranty, arguing that it "incurred substantial expenses and other damages in remedying the problems caused by the defective furnaces." Finally, Phelps claimed that "Rheem and Federated Supply were negligent and careless in their design and sale of the furnaces by failing to manufacture and provide furnaces which were operational and in reasonable working order."

Phelps described its damages as including "but not limited to, lost customers, lost profits, and the additional cost of servicing the defective furnaces and remedying the defects therein." In answers to interrogatories, Phelps listed its warranty damages as "lost service charges," "lost labor charges," "lost profits" from two customers who would no longer do business with Phelps, and the "approximate value of office time spent . . . comput[ing] damages."

Rheem moved for summary judgment on all of these claims. Rheem's brief in support of its motion asserted that the damages Phelps sought on the warranty theories were precluded by the limitations in the express warranty and by lack of privity on the implied warranties. Rheem also argued that Phelps could not claim tort damages for the purely economic injuries that resulted from the failure of the furnaces to operate as intended. The trial court granted Rheem's motion for summary judgment in regards to negligence, but denied it as to the warranties.

Rheem sought an interlocutory appeal on the warranty claims and the trial court certified its order. The Court of Appeals affirmed the denial of summary judgment. Rheem Mfg. Co. v. Phelps Heating & Air Conditioning, Inc., 714 N.E.2d 1218 (Ind. Ct. App. 1999). As for the express warranties, the Court of Appeals found a genuine issue of material fact as to "whether the cumulative effect of Rheem's actions was commercially *reasonable*." Id. at 1228 (emphasis in original). On the implied warranty claims, the court stated that the evidence establishing privity was "slight." The court nevertheless held that "perfect vertical privity is not necessary in this case" and then found a genuine issue of material fact as to whether Rheem breached its implied warranties and whether its conduct in doing so was "reasonable." Id. at 1231.

Discussion

* * *

Rheem's appeal raises three issues which require us to analyze the operation of express and implied warranties under Indiana's version of the Uniform Commercial Code ("the UCC").

I.

Rheem first argues that the trial court should have granted summary judgment as to Phelps's claim for lost profits under the express warranty because the warranty excluded consequential damages.[2] This argument requires us to examine the interplay between Indiana Code §§ 26–1–2–719(2) and (3), the UCC subsections pertinent to damage exclusions and remedy limitations in express warranties:

> (2) Where circumstances cause an exclusive or limited remedy to fail of its essential purpose, remedy may be had as provided in IC 26–1. (3) Consequential damages may be limited or excluded unless the limitation or exclusion is unconscionable. Limitation of consequential damages for injury to the person in the case of consumer goods is prima facie unconscionable, but limitation of damages where the loss is commercial is not.

These arguments pose the question of whether an exclusion of consequential damages survives when a separate contract provision limiting a buyer's remedies has failed of its essential purpose. The courts that have faced this issue have fallen into two camps that are divided along the lines of the parties' arguments in this case. One group takes what is known as the "dependent" view and reads § 2–719(2)'s reference to remedies "provided in [the UCC]" as overriding a contract's consequential damage exclusion. This gloss on § 2–719 makes an exclusion of consequential damages dependent on whether a limited remedy fails of its essential purpose. Other courts take an "independent" view and reason that because §§ 2–719(2) and (3) are separate subsections with separate language and separate standards, the failure of a limited remedy has no effect on an exclusion of consequential damages.

The Court of Appeals accepted the independent view. However, the court also grafted onto § 2–719 a requirement of "commercial

---

[2]   While Phelps seeks both consequential and incidental damages, the same analysis applies to each and we will discuss only consequential damages. Rheem and Phelps present conflicting constructions of these subsections. Both parties appear to accept that the remedy provided by Rheem failed of its essential purpose and that Phelps is entitled to the benefits of the express warranty. But Phelps contends that, under § 2–719(2), where a limited remedy "fail[s] of its essential purpose, remedy may be had as provided in IC 26–1," which includes consequential damages. Phelps argues that because Rheem's repair attempts failed for roughly four years, the limited remedy of replacement of parts failed of its essential purpose and Phelps could claim all buyer's remedies provided by the UCC, including consequential damages. Rheem counters that its exclusion of consequential damages is controlled by § 2–719(3). Rheem argues that despite the failure of the limited remedy under § 2–719(2), § 2–719(3) allows an exclusion of consequential damages to operate unless it is unconscionable.

reasonableness" and affirmed the denial of summary judgment on the ground that a triable issue existed as to whether Rheem's consequential damages exclusion and limited remedy were commercially reasonable.

We hold that Indiana Code § 26–1–2–719(2) does not categorically invalidate an exclusion of consequential damages when a limited remedy fails of its essential purpose. Our first step in interpreting any Indiana statute is to determine whether the legislature has spoken clearly and unambiguously on the point in question. A statute is ambiguous when "it is susceptible to more than one interpretation." In re Lehman, 690 N.E.2d 696, 702 (Ind. 1997).

In light of the depth of disagreement among the courts that have faced this issue, it is evident that the UCC is ambiguous on this point. The UCC subsections at issue are susceptible to two interpretations— one dependent, one independent—and as such we have no plain language to apply.

Faced with an ambiguous statute, we turn next to other applicable canons of construction. First, we note that our main objective in statutory construction is to determine, effect and implement the intent of the legislature." Melrose v. Capitol City Motor Lodge, Inc., 705 N.E.2d 985, 989 (Ind. 1998). In ascertaining this intent, we "presume that the legislature did not enact a useless provision" such that "where statutory provisions are in conflict, no part of a statute should be rendered meaningless but should be reconciled with the rest of the statute." Robinson v. Wroblewski, 704 N.E.2d 467, 474–75 (Ind. 1998).

Several aspects of Indiana Code §§ 26–1–2–719(2) and (3) point to a legislative intent consistent with the independent view. First, as many independent courts have noted, the drafters of the UCC inserted distinct legal standards into each provision. A limited remedy will be struck when it fails of its essential purpose; an exclusion of consequential damages fails when it is unconscionable. Moreover, these subsections are distinct in who applies the standards they set out. Whether a limited remedy fails of its essential purpose is an issue of fact that a jury may determine. Conversely, an exclusion of consequential damages stands unless it is unconscionable, and unconscionability is determined by a court as a matter of law. See Ind. Code § 26–1–2–302 (1993).[3] These facial distinctions between §§ 2–719(2) and (3) suggest a legislative intent that the provisions should function independently of one another.

Second, the independent view is consistent with the principle of statutory interpretation that "where possible, we interpret a statute such that every word receives effect and meaning and no part is rendered 'meaningless if it can be reconciled with the rest of the

---

[3] The two sections also aim at distinct contractual functions: A contract may well contain no limitation on breach of warranty damages but specifically exclude consequential damages. Conversely, it is quite conceivable that some limitation might be placed on a breach of warranty award, but consequential damages would expressly be permitted.

The limited remedy of repair and consequential damages exclusion are two discrete ways of attempting to limit recovery for breach of warranty. The Code, moreover, tests each by a different standard. . . . We therefore see no reason to hold, as a general proposition, that the failure of the limited remedy provided in the contract, without more, invalidates a wholly distinct term in the agreement excluding consequential damages. The two are not mutually exclusive. Chatlos Systems v. National Cash Register Corp., 635 F.2d 1081, 1086 (3rd Cir. 1980).

statute.'" Bagnall v. Town of Beverly Shores, 726 N.E.2d 782, 786 (Ind. 2000). The dependent view renders § 2–719(3) inoperative by deleting an exclusion of consequential damages without any analysis of its unconscionability. See id. ("If we were to read subparts (2) and (3) as dependent, we would effectively read out the unconscionability test of subpart (3). . . ."). On the other hand, the independent view allows both provisions to operate: § 2–719(2) will strike a failed limited remedy, allowing the buyer to claim damages, but not consequential damages if a valid clause excludes them under § 2–719(3). This construction harmonizes the language in § 2–719(2) that "remedy may be had as provided in IC 26–1" with the unconscionability test imposed by § 2–719(3). The "remedy" clause in § 2–719(2), which is crucial to the dependent argument, must be taken in its fullest sense. On its face, the phrase refers to all of the UCC, not merely its remedy provisions. Therefore "remedy may be had" under subsection (2) only to the extent that it is not limited by subsection (3), which is part of "IC 26–1."

Third, the UCC instructs us to construe its provisions with three specific legislative purposes in mind, all of which comport with the independent view:

(1) IC 26–1 shall be liberally construed and applied to promote its underlying purposes and policies.

(2) Underlying purposes and policies of IC 26–1 are:

(a) to *simplify, clarify, and modernize* the law governing commercial transactions;

(b) to permit the continued expansion of commercial practices through custom, usage, and agreement of the parties;

(c) to make uniform the law among the various jurisdictions.

Ind. Code § 26–1–1–102 (1993) (emphasis added). The independent view serves all of the enumerated purposes. The independent view supplies simplicity and clarity by allowing a clearly expressed agreement to control a transaction. The independent view is also the modern trend. The independent view aids sound commercial practice by allowing the parties to anticipate clearly the results of their transaction, while the dependent view retains the specter of unknown damages for the seller despite the parties' explicit understanding to the contrary. See Ind. Code § 26–1–1–102(2)(b) (1993).[4] The fact that courts are divided on this issue indicates that precise uniformity is impossible. However, as we have noted, the modern trend is towards the independent view.

---

[4] Sound commercial practice may require sellers in certain industries to exclude exposure to possibly expansive consequential damages:

[T]he potential significance of liability for consequential damages in commercial transactions undoubtedly prompted the Code's drafters, consistent with the Code's endorsement of the principle of freedom of contract, to make express provision for the limitation or exclusion of such damages. For certain sellers, exposure to liability for consequential damages could drastically affect the conduct of their business, causing them to increase their prices or limit their markets. . . . In a commercial setting, the seller's right to exclusion of consequential damages is recognized as a beneficial risk-allocation device that reduces the seller's exposure in the event of breach. Kearney & Trecker Corp. v. Master Engraving Co., 527 A.2d 429, 433 (N.J. 1987). A Rheem executive testified that such exclusions of consequential damages are standard in the gas-powered furnace industry.

Finally, the legislature's intent to follow the independent view is also supported by the UCC's general policy favoring the parties' freedom of contract. The UCC tells us that one of its paramount concerns is enabling contracting parties to control their own relationships. See. e.g., Ind. Code § 26–1–1–102(3) (1993) ("The effect of provisions of IC 26–1 may be varied by agreement, except as otherwise provided in IC 26–1. . . . "). Official Comment One to Indiana Code § 26–1–2–719 states that "under this section parties are left free to shape their remedies to their particular requirements and reasonable agreements limiting or modifying remedies are to be given effect." However, the dependent view ignores the intent of the parties and allows a buyer to recover consequential damages despite an explicit contract term excluding them. The dependent courts essentially presume that the parties intended the exclusion of consequential damages to depend on the limited remedy. On the other hand, the independent view refuses to override categorically an exclusion of consequential damages and will give effect to the terms of the contract. Indeed, consistent with the principle of freedom of contract, the independent view allows the parties to agree to a dependent arrangement.

This freedom to set contract terms is especially important in the context of a commercial transaction. Sophisticated commercial actors should be free to allocate risks as they see fit, and courts should not interfere simply because such risks have materialized. This is the view shared by Professors White and Summers:

In general we favor the [independent] line of cases. Those cases seem most true to the Code's general notion that the parties should be free to contract as they please. When the state intervenes to allocate the risk of consequential loss, we think it more likely that the loss will fall on the party who cannot avoid it at the lowest cost. This is particularly true when a knowledgeable buyer is using an expensive machine in a business setting. It is the buyer who operates the machine, adjusts it, and understands the consequences of its failure. Sometimes flaws in such machines are inherent and attributable to the seller's faulty design or manufacture. But the fault may also lie in buyer neglect, in inadequate training and supervision of the operators or even in intentional use in ways forbidden by the seller. Believing the parties to know their own interests best, we would leave the risk allocation to the parties. White & Summers, Uniform Commercial Code § 12–10, at 605 (3rd ed. 1988) (hereinafter "White & Summers").

Phelps attempts to escape this conclusion by arguing that the furnace sales were not a sophisticated commercial transaction worthy of such deference. Phelps notes that the warranties were simply found inside of the furnace box and were not the product of detailed negations. Phelps's argument here may prove too much, i.e., that only the ultimate customer, and not Phelps at all, was to benefit from the warranty. If Phelps is a beneficiary of the warranty (as we have noted both parties appear to assume), Phelps cannot escape the conclusion that these goods were relatively sophisticated and flowed between businesses entities. This context is far different than those confronted in the many dependent cases that focus on losses suffered by consumers at the hands of large commercial entities.

The Court of Appeals applied the independent view, but found a genuine issue of material fact as to whether "the cumulative effect of Rheem's actions was commercially reasonable." Rheem Mfg. Co. v. Phelps Heating & Air Conditioning, Inc., 714 N.E.2d 1218, 1228 (Ind. Ct. App. 1999). The court pointed to no statutory authority that requires these exclusions or limitations to be "commercially reasonable," nor did it define this term. The court did make some passing references to Official Comment One to § 2–719, which assures a buyer an "adequate" remedy in the face of a breach of warranty. Id. at 1228 ("We remain mindful that even as Comment 1 to Ind. Code § 26–1–2–719 advises that 'reasonable agreements limiting or modifying remedies are to be given effect,' the next sentence also cautions that 'it is of the very essence of a sales contract that at least minimum adequate remedies be available.'"). This comment, however, makes no reference to commercial reasonableness. Indeed, the court stated frankly that its primary concern was with the "fairness of the outcome" and reaching an "equitable result." Id. In light of our conclusion that the legislature intended the independent view to apply to these circumstances, we are constrained to reject the commercial reasonableness test applied by the Court of Appeals and to reverse the trial court's denial of summary judgment on Phelps's claims for incidental and consequential damages.

II.

Rheem next argues that the trial court erred by denying summary judgment on Phelps's claims for labor expenses incurred in fixing its customers' furnaces. The record shows that Phelps lost nearly $100,000 by servicing Rheem furnaces under a service labor warranty that Phelps gave to its customers. Rheem argues that a "service labor exclusion" found in the express warranty prevents Phelps from claiming damages in this form: "This Warranty does not cover any labor expenses for service, nor for removing or reinstalling parts. All such expenses are your responsibility unless a service labor agreement exists between you and your contractor." Phelps counters by arguing that this remedy clause failed of its essential purpose and therefore Phelps could claim all UCC damages.

The first step in determining whether a limited remedy failed of its essential purpose is to parse out exactly what purpose the remedy was to serve. While the parties, the trial court, and the Court of Appeals make no reference to this inquiry, both the terms of the warranty and the record illuminate the remedy's purpose. The limitation is addressed to the end-user, warning them that they must look to the contractor for repairs: "All such expenses are your responsibility unless a service labor agreement exists between you and your contractor." Further, a Rheem officer testified that the "custom, practice and standard method of dealing in the gas furnace industry is that the manufacturer's warranty is for parts only and excludes reimbursement for labor expenses for service or for removing or installing parts, consequential and incidental damages." Similarly, the president of Phelps testified that "standard procedure throughout the industry was that a dealer would supply a one-year warranty for labor. And then the parts, depending on the manufacture[r] . . . usually had a one-year warranty. . . . " In addition,

Phelps at one time marketed extended service warranties as part of its business.

These facts demonstrate that the limited remedy was intended to maintain a reasonable division of responsibilities between the manufacturer and the contractor when customers experienced problems. Rheem's parts-only warranty worked in tandem with Phelps's labor warranties to let customers know that they had to seek repair service from the local contractor, not the distant manufacturer. Phelps benefited from this relationship by marketing extended warranties on top of its one-year service warranty. If the warranty held Rheem liable for repairs, Rheem would naturally skip over Phelps and sell extended service warranties directly to the customer. For its part, the limited remedy gave Rheem the reassurance that it would not be liable for repairs on its furnaces at distant locations around the country. With this limitation in place, customers could rely on local repair service, Phelps could market extended warranties, and Rheem could be sure it would not be obligated to make repairs. Thus the apparent purpose of this limited remedy was to facilitate the manufacturer/contractor distinction for the benefit of all parties.

We must next determine whether circumstances caused the remedy to fail of this purpose. We set out the basic framework for analyzing the failure of essential purpose in *Martin Rispens*:

Commentators have suggested that § 2–719, as it relates to failure of essential purpose, is not concerned with arrangements which were oppressive at the inception which is a question of unconscionability, but with the application of an agreement to "novel circumstances not contemplated by the parties." White & Summers, § 10–12. In addition, they have suggested that this provision should be triggered when the remedy fails of its essential purpose, not the essential purpose of the UCC, contract law, or of equity. Id. One author suggests that the method used to decide whether a particular limitation fails of its essential purpose is to identify the purpose underlying the provision and determine whether application of the remedy in the particular circumstances will further that purpose. If not, then, and only then, is there a failure of essential purpose. Jonathan A. Eddy, On The "Essential" Purposes of Limited Remedies: The Metaphysics of UCC § 2–719(2), 65 Cal.L.Rev. 28, 36–40 (1978).

Using this analysis, we hold that the remedy served its purpose. Rheem, as the manufacturer, had technical expertise in the functioning of its product. It was reasonable for Phelps to expect Rheem to use this expertise to supply replacement parts and technical guidance in the event of malfunctions. Phelps, as the contractor, had the manpower and facilities to implement these fixes in the field. It was reasonable for Rheem to expect Phelps to use these tools to go into local homes and offices to fix the furnaces. With the extended warranties, Phelps could even profit through this process. By supplying technical guidance and replacement parts. Rheem's limited remedy lived up to the purpose it was designed to serve.

Phelps' main argument as to the failure of essential purpose is that the furnaces experienced problems for roughly four years. However, the purpose of the limited remedy was not to guarantee that every furnace would be easily fixed, but to guarantee that the most logical party would be charged with making the repairs. Phelps was that party, and under this limitation it accepted the risk that repairs would be difficult and labor intensive. In Martin Rispens, we stated that a limited remedy fails only in the face of " 'novel circumstances not contemplated by the parties.' " 621 N.E.2d at 1085 (citation omitted). As Comment One to Indiana Code § 26–1–2–719 puts it, a limited remedy fails when its application "operates to deprive either party of the substantial value of the bargain." Thus a limited remedy fails of its essential purpose when an unexpected circumstance arises and neither party accepted the risk that such circumstance would occur.

Even if we were to find that this remedy failed of its essential purpose, Phelps would not be entitled to the damages it seeks under the warranty. The parties characterize these service repair costs as either consequential damages or direct damages. In either event, Phelps is not entitled to recovery under the warranty and summary judgment should be entered.

The parties characterize the service labor as a form of consequential damage because Rheem should have foreseen that its failure to provide functioning furnaces would have caused Rheem to make multiple repairs under its service warranty. See Ind. Code § 26–1–2–715 (1993). To the extent these repair costs were consequential damages, they are excluded by Rheem's warranty as discussed in Part I, supra.

The parties also characterize the repair costs as a form of direct damages. A buyer's remedy for breach of warranty is typically the difference between the goods as warranted and the goods as accepted. See Ind. Code § 26–1–2–714(2) (1993). However, the cost of repair may serve as a proxy for direct damages. See, e.g., Jones v. Abriani, 169 Ind. App. 556, 350 N.E.2d 635, 646 (1976) ("In this case, one reasonable way of measuring the difference in the value of the goods between what was actually delivered (a defective mobile home) and what was warranted (a mobile home with the defects repaired) is the cost of repairing the defects."). Phelps argues that it should be able to recover the cost of repairing the furnaces in the event that the limited remedy failed of its essential purpose.

We hold, however, that Phelps is not in a position to claim this form of remedy. Typically, a buyer claiming repair damages is suing its immediate seller. Recovering the repair cost replicates the typical warranty damages—value of goods as warranted minus value of goods as delivered—by awarding the amount spent to put the goods in the warranted condition. This measure of damages reflects the fact that a properly functioning market would deduct from the price of the item the cost of repairs a purchaser would have to make. The repair costs that Phelps seeks to recoup serve no such purpose because Phelps is not in possession of the goods.

We conclude by noting that, while Phelps, as an intermediate seller, is not entitled to these direct warranty damages, it may have a claim sounding in indemnity or subrogation for damages suffered by those with which it shared privity. Whether or not Phelps can recover on an indemnity theory is an issue to be decided on remand.

III.

We summarily affirm the Court of Appeals as to Phelps's implied warranty claims.

Conclusion

Having previously granted transfer, we reverse the order of the trial court on Phelps's express warranty claims and remand this case for proceedings consistent with this opinion.

* * *

NOTES

1. The buyer urged the court to adopt the "dependent" approach, while the seller urged it to embrace the "independent" approach. The court gives as a reason for its adoption of the independent approach that the approach is "more line with the UCC and with contract law in general." To test this, assume that the sales contract contains a clause limiting the buyer's remedy to repair or replacement and a damage exclusion clause. Assume also that the damage exclusion clause is made expressly conditional on the seller repairing or replacing the nonconforming goods. Finally, assume that the damage exclusion clause is conscionable. In these circumstances the independent approach validates the damage exclusion even if the seller fails to repair or replace the nonconforming goods. Is this result consistent with general contract law? Now suppose the dependent approach were applied in the same circumstances. Is the result it reaches consistent with contract law? Don't both approaches produce a result that frustrates the expressed intention of both parties to the sales contract? Milgard Tempering, Inc. v. Selas Corp. of America, 902 F.2d 703 (9th Cir. 1990) evaluated the validity of a damage exclusion clause when the remedy limitation failed, based on the parties' bargained-for allocation of risk. In concluding that the damage exclusion clause was invalid, the court found that the buyer "did not agree to pay $1.45 million in order to participate in a science experiment." Id. at 709.

2. Razor v. Hyundai American Motor, 854 N.E.2d 607 (Ill. 2006) concludes that the case-by-case approach to damage exclusions, described in the text, is unsupported by Code provision or Official Comment and makes the enforceability of damage exclusions uncertain. These are two separate criticisms. First, 2–719(3) and its Comments say nothing about the validity of a damage exclusion being dependent on the parties' allocation of risk. However, subsection (3) and its Comments are silent about the relation between 2–709(2) and subsection (3) generally. Thus, all three possible approaches to the relation between remedy limitations and damages exclusions are unsupported by them. Perhaps it is wrong to expect the UCC to say anything about the relation between the two sorts of provisions. Instead, the terms of the sales contract controls the matter, if at all. After all, 2–719(1) allows parties by contract to provide exclusive remedies, and 2–719(3) allows them to exclude damages. If the contract can provide for these matters, it also can provide for the effect of the invalidity of the remedy limitation on the damage exclusion. It is unsurprising that 2–719(3) and its Comments do not address a matter of contract interpretation. For a suggested revision to 2–719 requiring the contract to specifically address the damage exclusion on the failure of the limited remedy, see Note, Sections 2–719(2) & 2–719(3) of the Uniform Commercial Code: The Limited Warranty Package & Consequential Damages, 21 Val. U. L. Rev. 111, 141, 143 (1996).

Second, as to the uncertainty produced by the case-by-case approach, both the dependent and independent approaches would give more predictable outcomes than the case-by-case approach. Both are per se rules which deem a damage exclusion enforceable or unenforceable without regard to the bargain of which it is a part. The contracting parties therefore can easily forecast their results in advance. On the other hand, the application of these per se rules can produce inefficient contracts by making it more costly for the parties to produce an enforceable bargain that reflects their desires. As a result, there is a familiar tradeoff between the predictability of the approaches and the increased burdens they put on contracting parties. Although the results of the case-by-case approach are more unpredictable than those of the dependent and independent approaches, the former approach might reduce the cost to the parties of getting what they want.

3. How unpredictable are the results under the case-by-case approach? It depends on how explicitly the contract allocates the risk of consequential damages. AES Technology Systems, Inc. v. Coherent Radiation, 583 F.2d 933 (7th Cir. 1978), involved a contract in which the buyer's only remedy was repair or replacement. The warranty provision in the contract recited that this was the buyer's "sole remedy and seller's sole liability on the contract . . ." The *AES* court found a damage exclusion was implied in this language. When the seller failed to repair or replace the nonconforming goods, it concluded, based on this language and the "factual background" of the transaction, that the buyer continued to bear the risk of consequential damages. Id. at 941. Razor v. Hyundai Motor America, 854 N.E.2d 607 (Il. 2006) describes the court's reasoning in *AES* as follows: "The court inferred a consequential damages disclaimer where none existed, struck the language from which the disclaimer was inferred, then enforced the disclaimer against the buyer anyway, based on the court's understanding of 'the factual background.'" Id. at 618. A more charitable description of the reasoning is that the *AES* court inferred a damage exclusion ("disclaimer") from the contract's express language, invalidated the remedy limitation based on the seller's failure to repair or replace, and enforced the damage exclusion based on the parties' intended risk allocation and the background of the transaction. Where the contract expressly conditions the damage exclusion, the parties' risk allocation can easily be discerned by the court. Cf. Smith v. Navstar Int'l Transp. Corp., 957 F.2d 1439, 1444 (7th Cir. 1992) (measure of certainty provided by contractual allocation of risk of consequential damages).

4. The division among courts in interpreting 2–719 was reflected in proposals to amend 2–719 as part of Proposed Article 2. A 1998 proposed amendment gave adopting states the option to select among alternatives. These alternatives essentially either invalidated the damage exclusion on failure of the remedy limitation or validated it on the parties' agreement that the nonbreacher assumed the risk of consequential damages on the failure of the remedy limitation. The 1999 proposed amendment of 2–719 replaced this proposal, altering 2–719 to incorporate the independent approach. This proposal too was rejected, and the final version of Proposed Article 2 left 2–719 unchanged.

PROBLEM 6.4

Seller contracted to supply equipment to be used by Buyer in its business. The contract provided that within one year Seller would repair or replace defective parts of the equipment. It also provided: "This remedy is the sole remedy available to Buyer, and Seller is not responsible for the costs of business interruption or other consequential damages." At the time of contracting, Seller informed Buyer that it was operating to capacity and that it had delayed honoring some of its commitments to its customers. The day Seller delivered the equipment to Buyer, it broke. Buyer immediately notified Seller of this fact. Seller's repair staff was occupied and did not reach Buyer until the end of the first week. The defective part was replaced a week later (at the end of the second week), but the replacement proved to be defective too. Seller was unable to install a replacement part until the end of the third week. Replacing the equipment was out of the question during the entire period because Seller did not have a replacement available. It is established that replacing the part usually takes a week. Buyer sued Seller for breach of warranty and proves that its net sales lost from the equipment's failure were $100,000 per week. How much, if any, of its $300,000 in net lost sales (3 × $100,000) is Buyer entitled to recover from Seller? 2–719(1)(a), (2).

D. NOTICE OF BREACH

1. THE UCC

To recover for breach of warranty, the buyer must give notice of the breach. Section 2–607(3)(a) provides that the buyer who has accepted tender of the goods must give notice of breach to the seller within a reasonable time after it has discovered or should have discovered the breach or be barred from any remedy. The buyer asserting a breach of warranty typically has accepted tender of the goods. Section 2–607(3)(a) bars any remedy for the breach, including revocation of acceptance or remedy provided by the contract. See 1–201(b)(32). Although 2–607(3)(a)'s notice requirement applies to all breaches, the section usually is contested in breach of warranty cases.

Section 2–607(3)(a)'s apparently simple notice requirement raises three main questions. Courts continue to disagree about each of them. First, what constitutes adequate notice of breach under the subsection? The subsection requires the buyer to "notify the seller . . . of breach." Courts disagree about the content of required notice. Some courts consider notice to be sufficient if the buyer informs the seller that it is having difficulty with the goods. The notice need not state the buyer considers the seller in breach. This is the "lenient" standard of notice referred to by the *American Bumper* court in the opinion reproduced below. Comment 4 to 2–607 supports the lenient standard, stating that "[t]he content of the notification need merely be sufficient to let the seller know that the transaction is still troublesome and must be watched." See Daigle v. Ford Motor, 713 F.Supp.2d 822 (D. Minn. 2010). There is nothing in 2–607(3)(a)'s language that reinforces this statement. A number of courts stick to 2–607(3)(a)'s plain language and require the buyer's notice to state that it considers the seller's performance to be in breach. See, e.g., In re Bausch & Lomb Contact Lens Solutions, 2008 U.S. Dist. LEXIS 119056, at *1 (D.S.C. 2008). This is the "strict" standard of notice referred to in *American Bumper*. Several states have adopted nonuniform amendments to 2–607(3)(a) waiving notice when the breach causes personal injury to the consumer buyer. See, e.g., 11 Maine Rev. Stat. § 2–607(7) (2011) ("Subsection (3) paragraph (a) shall not apply where the remedy is for personal injury resulting from any breach"); S.C. Code Ann. § 36–2–607(3)(a) (2011) (". . . however, no notice of injury to the person in the case of consumer goods shall be required").

The second question concerns the notice requirement when the seller already has notice of its breach. Does 2–607(3)(a) in these circumstances require the buyer to give notice of the seller's breach? Although some early cases required it, many courts excuse the buyer when the seller has actual knowledge of its breach. See Agrarian Grain Co. v. Meeker, 526 N.E.2d 1189 (Ind. Ct. App. 1988). The rationale for this exception to 2–607(3)'s notice requirement is that the seller's actual knowledge already provides the benefit the buyer's notice would provide. Its knowledge of breach already puts it in a position to salvage the nonconforming goods or negotiate with the buyer. No purpose is served by requiring the buyer to inform the seller of a fact it already knows.

A third question is raised by 2–607(3)(a)'s requirement that the buyer give notice within a "reasonable time" after it discovers or should discover the breach. What is the "reasonable time" within which notice must be given? The question asks about the standard of timeliness. Here courts tend to judge the timeliness of notice by the purposes underlying 2–607(3)(a). *American Bumper* identifies the same purposes identified by almost all courts. Although identification of these purposes does not produce a "calendar count" of timeliness, it helps determine the reasonableness of the time in which the buyer must give notice. To see this, recognize that all of the purposes identified go to the seller's interests, such as its opportunity to cure or prepare a defense. These interests are reflected in the contract price the seller charges. This is because the price includes not just the seller's production costs and profit. It also includes the seller's cost of salvaging nonconforming goods, accommodating the buyer or litigating contentions of breach. The sooner the seller receives notice that the goods are nonconforming, the sooner it can begin to take measures to reduce loss from goods with which the buyer is unhappy. Timely notice avoids waste. A timely notice requirement therefore produces a lower priced contract that the seller offers its buyer than one without the requirement. Both parties prefer this contract to the higher priced alternative contract. This of course does not tell a court whether the buyer's delay of 32 days in giving notice, for example, rather than 10 or 27 days, is "reasonable." The "reasonable" time is one in which the marginal cost to the buyer of giving notice at a particular time equals the seller's marginal benefit from receiving notice at that time. Obviously this time varies according to characteristics of the parties and the transaction, and courts lack precise information about the values of these variables. But the standard helps in focusing on the impact of events after the buyer's acceptance of the goods and on the seller's costs in salvaging the deal if the buyer becomes unhappy with the goods.

A final matter concerns a proposal to improve 2–607(3)(a). Under current 2–607(3)(a) the failure to give adequate and timely notice of breach bars the buyer from all remedies. This is so whether or not the buyer's inadequate or tardy notice harms the seller. As a result, the consequence of violating 2–607(3)(a) can be disproportionate to the damage caused by the buyer's failure to give proper notice. The buyer recovers nothing even if the breaching seller is not harmed or is harmed little. To eliminate this remedial "penalty" to the nonbreacher, Proposed 2–607(3)(a) revises the subsection to bar the buyer who give inadequate or untimely notice from a remedy only to the extent that the seller is prejudiced by this failure. The proposed amendment arguably ignores the costs of administering 2–607(3)(a) and its impact on contract price. As under current 2–607(3)(a), to determine the timeliness of notice courts implicitly must calibrate over time the buyer's costs of giving notice and the seller's benefit from receiving it. However, Proposed 2–607(3)(a) also requires the court to determine the impact of inadequate or tardy notice on the seller. For instance, it must gauge the costs the seller bears by losing the opportunity to cure the nonconformity in the goods. This is a considerable informational burden that sellers will take into account in setting contract price. True, judicially created presumptions could be set to favor the seller, thereby effectively placing the burden on the buyer to prove that the seller is not prejudiced by the defective notice. But presumptions are blunt tools for protecting the seller's interests. By comparison, contractual provisions specifying the time in which notice must be given seem superior. The contracting parties are better placed than a court to calibrate the impact of notice on their interests. Clauses setting the time in which the buyer must give notice of breach have been common in contracts in some industries. See Bomze v. M. Schwarz Textile Corp., 100 Pa. Super. 588 (Pa. Super. Ct. 1931) (red cloth); Van Gelder Yarn Co. v. Mauney, 228 N.C. 99 (N.C. 1947) (cotton yarns).

American Bumper & Manufacturing Co. v. Transtechnology Corp.

Michigan Court of Appeals, 2002
652 N.W.2d 252

■ Per Curiam.

Plaintiff appeals as of right from the trial court's order granting summary disposition in favor of defendants under MCR 2.116(C)(10). We affirm.

In April 1989, plaintiff entered into an agreement with the Ford Motor to manufacture the front bumpers for Ford F-series pickup trucks. According to plaintiff's complaint, at all times Ford controlled the material specifications, processes, checking procedures, and finishes for the fasteners used in manufacturing the bumpers. Ford provided a list of approved sub-suppliers to plaintiff, which included defendants. From the suppliers of fasteners approved by Ford, plaintiff requested quotes for U-nuts that plaintiff would use to fasten the bumpers to the Ford bumper assemblies. In November 1990, the Palnut Company (first a division of defendant TRW, Inc., and later a division of defendant TransTechnology Corporation) responded to plaintiff's request by issuing a quotation for its U-nuts. In February 1991, plaintiff submitted a "blanket" purchase order, which allowed plaintiff to fill its need for U-nuts over the course of its contract with Ford.

From 1991 to 1993, Palnut provided plaintiff with many U-nuts used in the bumper assemblies for Ford's F-series pickup trucks. The U-nuts that were initially supplied to plaintiff had a phosphate-based coating. In 1992, in response to Ford's requirements, Palnut changed the coating on the U-nuts to a zinc organic-based coating called Dorroflake. Late in 1992, plaintiff expressed concerns about Palnut's slow delivery performance. In response, a Palnut employee suggested changing the fastener coating to Dacromet because that coating could be done in house. Dacromet is a zinc water-based coating manufactured by Metal Coatings International. Palnut sent samples of the Dacromet-coated U-nuts to plaintiff and in April 1993, plaintiff notified Palnut that the Dacromet-coated U-nuts were approved by its quality assurance department. Ford also approved Dacromet as a coating and in August 1993, Ford required that only Dacromet be used as a coating on the U-nuts and that Dorroflake was no longer an approved coating.

In late November 1993, Ford received reports from its dealers that the U-nuts were failing, causing the bumpers to become loose or fall off the trucks. Ford relayed this information to plaintiff on November 28, 1993. Plaintiff then notified Palnut of the U-nut failure and on December 6, 1993, plaintiff canceled its contract with Palnut. In February 1994, Ford initiated a recall campaign to replace the defective U-nuts, an endeavor that cost Ford more than $9 million.

On February 25, 1994, Ford issued a report, purportedly identifying what it believed to be the causes of the failure of the U-nuts. Ford believed that plaintiff and Palnut were at fault and that plaintiff should bear the financial responsibility because it was the end item supplier. Plaintiff and Palnut conducted independent investigations regarding why the U-nuts were failing. Ultimately, it was found that the cause of the failure was stress corrosion cracking. The U-nuts, which are made of high-strength steel, would crack or corrode when the zinc coating was exposed to a salt water environment (such as when roads are salted in the winter) and when the U-nuts are stressed (by inserting and tightening a bolt). One of the experts stated that it is "bad engineering" to put zinc on high-strength steel and that this was the cause of the U-nut failure.

In June 1994, plaintiff presented its response to Ford's report. In the response, plaintiff carefully dismissed each charge against it and Palnut and instead concluded that the root cause of the failure of the U-nuts was associated with the change to Dacromet from Dorroflake. Plaintiff clearly stated that the fault was with Ford and Metal Coatings International because Ford directed Palnut and all the approved fastener suppliers to change to Dacromet, but neither Ford nor Metal

Coatings International had properly tested Dacromet when Ford directed this change.

Nothing more happened between plaintiff and Palnut until plaintiff filed suit against defendants in August 1997. In the meantime, in 1995, Ford and plaintiff entered into settlement negotiations and an agreement was reached in May 1995. Plaintiff had initially paid $900,000 to Ford as part of the recall campaign, and also agreed to a one-time price reduction of $2.2 million. Palnut was not aware of or involved in the settlement negotiations.

Plaintiff's amended complaint alleges breach of express warranty, breach of implied warranties of fitness and merchantability, express indemnification, and implied indemnification. Defendants moved for summary disposition, arguing that plaintiff failed to comply with the notice provision of MCL 440.2607(3)(a) of the Uniform Commercial Code, MCL 440.2607(3)(a), requiring a buyer to notify a seller of a breach of contract within a reasonable time of discovering the breach, and that plaintiff was barred from any remedy. Defendants also argued that the breach of express warranty and express indemnification claims should be dismissed because the language in plaintiff's purchase orders that supported those claims never became part of the parties' contract. Finally, defendants argued that the implied indemnification claim should be dismissed because defendants were not given notice of, or an opportunity to participate in, the settlement negotiations between plaintiff and Ford. The trial court agreed and granted summary disposition under MCR 2.116(C)(10) in defendants' favor "for the reasons set forth in the defendant[s'] brief and for the arguments made in court today." * * *

This case involves application of the Uniform Commercial Code, MCL 440.1101 et seq. Specifically, the trial court ruled that plaintiff had failed to give notice of breach of the contract to Palnut and, therefore, was barred from any remedy. MCL 440.2607(3)(a) provides:

(3) Where a tender has been accepted

(a) the buyer must within a reasonable time after he discovers or should have discovered any breach notify the seller of breach or be barred from any remedy[.]

The burden of establishing a breach is on the buyer. MCL 440.2607(4). The parties disagree regarding whether there is a "strict" or "lenient" standard in Michigan relative to the adequacy of notice. Comment four to MCL 440.2607 states that the "content of the notification need merely be sufficient to let the seller know that the transaction is still troublesome and must be watched." This sentence has been used to justify a lenient standard. Comment four, however, further states that "the notification which saves the buyer's rights . . . need only be such as informs the seller that the transaction is claimed to involve a breach, and thus opens the way for normal settlement through negotiation." This sentence has been used to justify the strict standard.

Regardless of whether a strict or lenient standard is applied, we find that the notice was not adequate in this case because the notice did not satisfy the policies underlying the UCC's notice provision and plaintiff's conduct did not satisfy the UCC's standard of commercial good faith. Here, the undisputed facts are that Ford notified plaintiff in late November 1993 of the problems that Ford was experiencing with the U-nuts. Immediately thereafter, plaintiff informed Palnut that Ford was experiencing problems with the U-nuts. About one week later, plaintiff recommended, and Ford agreed, to change the fastener supplier from Palnut to California Industrial Products. On December 6, 1993, plaintiff notified Palnut that it would no longer purchase U-nuts from Palnut. Ford, plaintiff, and Palnut then began to investigate the problem to determine why the U-nuts were failing. Ford's report was issued in February 1994. Ford assigned blame to plaintiff and Palnut, but believed that plaintiff should be assigned financial responsibility because it was the end item supplier. In June 1994, plaintiff responded to Ford's conclusions with its own report exonerating itself and Palnut from responsibility for the failure of the U-nuts. Plaintiff's report clearly assigned blame to Ford and Metal Coatings International. From March to May of 1995, Ford and plaintiff entered into settlement negotiations where plaintiff agreed to a settlement of $3.1 million and future price reductions to Ford totaling about $8 million. Palnut was not involved in any way in the settlement negotiations. It was not until August 1997 that plaintiff filed suit against defendants.

The purposes of the UCC's notice requirement are (1) to prevent surprise and allow the seller the opportunity to make recommendations how to cure the nonconformance, (2) to allow the seller the fair opportunity to investigate and prepare for litigation, (3) to open the way for settlement of claims through negotiation, and (4) to protect the seller from stale claims and provide certainty in contractual arrangements. Aqualon Co. v. MAC Equipment, Inc., 140 F.3d 262, 269 (4th Cir. 1998). Here, rather than allowing Palnut to attempt to cure the defect, plaintiff recommended purchasing the U-nuts from another manufacturer and simply canceled the contract. Once the parties investigated the problem with the U-nuts, plaintiff determined that Palnut was not at fault. Further, there was no overture of negotiation or settlement between plaintiff and Palnut. Indeed, there is no evidence that plaintiff ever considered Palnut to be in breach after the June 1994 report was presented to Ford. Ultimately, plaintiff did not bring suit against defendants until more than 3 1/2 years after the defect with the U-nuts was first discovered.

We find that plaintiff has not presented a genuine issue of material fact that would preclude summary disposition for defendants. In this case, plaintiff did nothing more than initially notify defendants that there was a problem with the U-nuts, and never notified defendants that they were in breach. Some courts have made clear that it is not enough for the buyer to only notify the seller that it is having difficulty with the goods. Clearly, plaintiff's conduct after the problem with the U-nuts was discovered is completely contrary to a finding that plaintiff considered defendants to be in breach because plaintiff's own investigation exonerated defendants from fault. Eastern Airlines, Inc. v. McDonnell Douglas Corp., 532 F.2d 957, 978 (5th Cir. 1976) (even if adequate notice is given at some point, subsequent actions by the buyer may negate its effect and the buyer's conduct, taken as a whole, must constitute timely notification that the transaction is claimed to involve a breach). The purposes of the notice requirement were not served in this case; therefore, MCL 440.2607(3)(a) bars plaintiff from any remedy.

To the extent that plaintiff argues that the "any remedy" language applies only to any remedy under the UCC and does not include its claims of express and implied indemnification, we disagree. MCL 440.1201(34) broadly defines "remedy" as "any remedial right to which an aggrieved party is entitled with or without resort to a tribunal." Further, MCL 440.2607(3)(a) also clearly states that if notice of the breach is not given within a reasonable time, the buyer is "barred from any remedy." It does not state "any remedy under the UCC" as plaintiff contends. Here, the statute plainly and unambiguously states that notice must be given or the buyer is barred from any remedy. Further, the indemnification claims here should be included as "any remedy" where the indemnification claims are based on the underlying breach of warranty claims for which the buyer also seeks a remedy.

Accordingly, the trial court did not err in granting summary disposition in favor of defendants under MCR 2.116(C)(10) because plaintiff failed to give adequate notice under MCL 440.2607(3)(a) for the alleged breach, thus barring plaintiff from pursuing any remedy.

NOTES

1. American Bumper sued Palent over three years after notifying it of the U-nut's failure. Why do you think American Bumper did not notify Palent before suit that the U-nuts Palent delivered in 1994 were nonconforming? Might it have something to do with the settlement it reached with Ford over the U-nuts? What does the court appear to think about the delay? Cf. 1–304.

2. Suppose American Bumper had timely notified Palent of any of the following: (a) the U-nuts Palent had delivered came in damaged packages; (b) it was having a hard time installing the U-nuts on the bumper assemblies; or (c) the U-nuts were not properly constructed. Does the notification in (a)–(c) give sufficient notice under 2–607(3)(a)? Compare 2–607(3)(a) with Comment 4 to 2–607. Why didn't the court have to decide whether adequate notice under 2–607(3)(a) must meet the lenient standard or the strict standard?

3. Probably a majority of courts find that filing a lawsuit is not adequate notice. See, e.g., Armco Steel Corp. v. Isaacson Structural Steel Co., 611 P.2d 507(Alaska 1980); Whitesell Corp. v. Whirlpool Corp., 2009 WL 3327243, at 2* (W.D. Mich. 2009). Their rationale is that none of 2–607(3)(a)'s underlying policies identified in *American Bumper* are served by considering suit as notice. Some of the cases that recognize suit as notice involve sales of consumer goods by consumer sellers. The concern is with the seller's bad faith flight on receiving notice before suit. See Mullins v. Wyatt, 887 S.W.2d 356 (Ky. 1997).

4. Section 2–607(3)(a)'s timeliness requirement puts on the buyer the cost of giving notice of discovering breach. The "reasonableness" of the period in which it must give notice therefore depends in part on the buyer's characteristics. This is particularly true for consumer buyers. Courts usually are sensitive to the consumer status of the buyer. In Buzadzhi v. Bexso, 2011 U.S. Dist. LEXIS 905, at *1 (N.D. Okla. 2011), the buyers sued the seller when the dresser it sold fell on their child killing him. The buyer brought a breach of warranty action two and a half years after the incident without previously notifying the seller. The court had to decide whether two and a half years after breach was reasonable in a retail consumer injury case. In rejecting the seller's argument that timeliness of notice should not depend on the character of the injury from breach, the court stated: "[The seller] argues that 'the fact that this lawsuit involves personal injuries should not alter the conclusion [that plaintiffs failed to give reasonably timely notice].' The distinction recognized in the case law, however, is not between lawsuits that involve personal injury and those that do not. Rather, the distinction is between suits brought by retail consumers and commercial purchasers. The court is persuaded that the "reasonable notice" requirement of Section 2–607(3)(a) should be viewed under a more relaxed standard than that expected of commercial purchasers. This is so because a retail consumer is not likely to be aware of the notice requirement, is not primarily concerned with replacement of nonconforming shipment of goods, and because there can be no issue of commercial bad faith on the part of the retail consumer." Id. at *6.

5. Wholesaler sold a car battery to Retailer covered by a warranty. Retailer in turn sold the battery covered by the same warranty to Buyer. The battery malfunctioned while Buyer was using it, thereby breaching the warranty. Buyer immediately notified Retailer of the breach. Later, Buyer sued Wholesaler only without giving notice to it. Assuming that suit is not notice, is Buyer's remedy against Wholesaler for breach of warranty barred by 2–607? See 2–103(1)(d), 2–607(3)(a), (5)(a), Comment 5 to 2–607. Compare Ace American Ins. Co. v. Fountain Powerboats, Inc., 63 UCC Rep. Serv.2d 924 (D.N.H. 2007) with Compac Computer Corp. v. Lapray, 135 S.W.3d 657 (Tex. 2004).

2. THE CISG

The CISG has its own requirements for notice of breach, which differ in some respects from the UCC's requirements. Article 39(1) bars the buyer from a remedy unless it notifies the seller of the nonconformity in the goods within a reasonable time after it discovers or ought to have discovered it. The notice must specify the nature of the nonconformity. Its required content differs from that required by 2–607(3)(a) in two respects. First, unlike 2–607(3)(a), the notice need not declare breach. Mention of the specific nonconformity of the goods with contract apparently suffices. Second, unlike Comment 4 to 2–607(3)(a), mere notice that signals that the "transaction must be watched" is insufficient. According to Article 39(1), the notice must specify the nonconformity in the goods. Article 40 excuses the buyer from giving sufficient and timely notice if the seller knew or could not have been unaware of the conformity in the goods. Article 39(2) sets a time limit of two years from the date the goods have been handed to the buyer within which it must give the required notice to the seller. Finally, Article 44 gives the buyer some limited remedies against the seller even when proper notice has not been given, if the buyer has a reasonable excuse for the failure. The Article's limited reprieve remains subject to Article 39(2)'s two-year time bar.

By its terms, the notice period begins to run from the time of discovery, not from the time the buyer comes into possession of the goods. Compare Article 38(1). While the buyer usually will be in a position to discover nonconformities once it possesses the goods, sometimes the discovery will take longer. Latent defects, for example, may only be revealed once the goods are in use for a period. Article 39(1) gives the buyer a "reasonable" time after it discovered or ought to have discovered the defect. See Shuttle Packaging Sys. LLC v. Tsonakis, 2001 U.S. Dist. LEXIS 21630, at *1 (W.D. Mich. 2001). "Ought to have discovered" is an ambiguous phrase. The phrase indicates that the standard is an objective one. However, Article 39(1) does not say from whose perspective the buyer ought to have discovered the nonconformity—the seller or the buyer's perspective.

The main problem in Article 39(1) concerns its vague requirement that the buyer give notice within a "reasonable" time of discovery. Comparable domestic law, such as 2–607(3)(a), sets a similarly imprecise period. Article 39(1)'s time period represents a compromise between different standards of timeliness between legal systems. Legal systems tend to adopt three different approaches to the matter. CISG Advisory Council Opinion No. 2, Examination of the Goods and Notice of Non–Conformity: Articles 38 and 39 (2004), available at http://cisgw3. law.pace.edu/cisg/CISG–AC-op2.html. Some legal systems require the buyer to give notice within a short time of taking possession of the goods. See LG Stuttgart (Germany), 31 August 1989, available at http:// www.cisg.law.pace.edu/cases/890831g1.html (shoes: 16 days beyond a "reasonable time"); Oberster Gerichtshof (Austria), 15 October 1998, available at http://www.cisg.law.pace.edu/cases/981015a3.html (total notice period of 14 days); HG Zürich (Switzerland), 30 November 1998, available at http://www.cisg.law.pace.edu/cases/981130s1.html (lambswool jackets: more than 14 days beyond a "reasonable time"). A second set of legal systems require notice within a more extended period, such as under 2–607(3)(a). The third set requires no notice within any particular period or notice only when the buyer relies on particular remedies. See English Sale of Goods Act § 35(1). Although Article 39(1)'s time period appears closer to 2–607(3)(a)'s "reasonable time" standard than the standards operating in the other two sorts of legal systems, Article 7(1) requires that the reasonableness of the notice period be set in light of "international character" of the CISG. Domestic law standards of timely notice at most can inform, but not determine, Article 39(1)'s time period. Courts have had a mixed record in setting this period, as the Abstracts of an early German and Austrian cases, reproduced below, illustrate.

Fairly obviously, the reasonableness of the time period turns on different factors. Some concern the characteristics of the nonconformity, such as whether it is a manifest or latent defect. Others concern the characteristics of the goods themselves, such as whether they are perishable or durable. Finally, the reasonableness of the notice period can turn on the sophistication or experience of the buyer itself. The reasonable time for giving notice has varied between several days and several months, depending on the durability of the good and the nature of the defect. See CISG Advisory Council Opinion No. 2, supra (collecting cases). An Italian case decided by the Tribunale di Vigevano (Italy), 12 July 2000, available at http://www.cisg.law.pace.edu/cases/ 000712i3.html, after reciting some of these factors, concluded that the buyer's notice four months after receiving the goods came too late. There the buyer purchased rubber to fabricate into the soles of shoes.

The rubber was defective and the buyer gave the seller notice of the defect only after the buyer's downstream customers affixed the soles to shoes. The court noted that the defect in the rubber might have been detectable at the time the rubber was fabricated into soles, even if it was not apparent earlier at the time the buyer took delivery of the rubber. In that case the buyer's notice four months after delivery was untimely. However, the court also noted that the buyer might have had to wait for the downstream customers' complaints to detect the defect in the rubber. In this case the four-month time period for notice might be reasonable. Because the court found that the buyer bore the burden of proof on timeliness, and had not retained any of the shoes containing the defective rubber, it could not demonstrate that the defect in the rubber could only be detected through complaints from downstream customers. The buyer in that case therefore could not establish the reasonableness of a delay of four months in giving notice.

As noted above, Article 44 gives the buyer who fails to give timely notice limited remedies against its seller, if it has a reasonable excuse for the failure. The buyer who qualifies can recover damages (other than lost profits), but it cannot avoid the contract, for example, and put the nonconforming goods back on the seller. It is hard to understand how Article 44's condition that requires the buyer to have a reasonable excuse for failing to give timely notice ever applies. After all, if the buyer has a reasonable excuse, the reasonable period within which it must give notice seemingly takes this into account. In that case the buyer's notice would not be untimely. As a result, Article 44 does not apply. Perhaps the following is a rare example in which it applies: assume that the buyer gives the seller notice of the nonconformity in the seller's language. The translation the buyer uses to do so, provided by a reputable translator, is inaccurate and fails to specify the nonconformity the buyer is relying on. The buyer's notice, even if timely, is insufficient and therefore ineffective under Article 39(1). Nonetheless, the buyer might have a reasonable excuse for the faulty translation. If so, Article 44 gives the buyer limited remedies against the seller, "notwithstanding the provisions of paragraph (1) of Article 39."

Uncitral Clout Case 319

Germany: Bundesgerichtshof (3 November 1999)

A German manufacturer of paper, plaintiff, purchased semi-finished articles from a Swiss seller, for the purpose of producing humid tissue-paper. The semi-finished articles had been treated in a paper machine furnished with a grinding equipment, delivered by X, defendant, to the seller. This paper machine suffered a total loss a few days after being used. The buyer gave notice to the seller that rust stains were found on the humid tissue-paper, and that a large portion of the delivered semifinished articles also tended to develop brown stains. Upon receipt of an examination report carried out by an expert company, the seller made X liable for the damage, as it suspected that such damage had been caused by the defective grinding equipment. The seller assigned its rights to the buyer and the buyer claimed damages from X.

The appellate court left open the issue whether the semi-finished articles were in conformity with the contract. It held that the notice of lack of conformity was not timely given, and that therefore the buyer had lost its right to rely on a lack of conformity. Accordingly, the claim was dismissed. The buyer appealed to the Supreme Court.

The court found that the grinding equipment had a hidden defect, as it was not possible for the seller to notice the defect neither upon delivery nor after examination of the equipment (article 38(1) CISG). The court did not decide on the issue whether under CISG, a hidden defect must be notified as soon as it is detected, so that the period set for giving notice pursuant to article 39(1) CISG would commence when the defect is actually established, or whether such period should commence as soon as the hidden defect would objectively be recognized as such.

The court held that the total loss of the paper machine was due either to an operating fault or to the defective grinding equipment. It further held that, even if, through internal investigations and without specific expertise, an operating fault could have been excluded in a short period of time, a period of about one week had to be granted to the seller, allowing it to decide which further steps to take, such as the choice and appointment of an expert. Additionally, a period of two weeks had to be accorded for the expert's examination to be followed by a one month-period of time for notification, which according to the court, it was a reasonable time as required by article 39(1) CISG. Therefore, the seller's notice of lack of conformity was not untimely given.

Furthermore, the court stated that, in case of defective technical equipment, a description of the symptoms should suffice in order to satisfy the requirements of article 39 (1) CISG. A specification of the reasons causing the defect is not required. By giving notice to X that the buyer had found rust stains on the humid tissue-paper treated with X's alleged defective equipment, the seller complied with the requirements of article 39 (1) CISG.

The court remanded the case to the appellate court, as it found that this court had not decided on the possible limitation of X's liability regarding the lack of conformity of the semi-finished articles as well as on the extent of the damages suffered by the buyer.

Uncitral Clout Case 423

Austria: Oberster Gerichtshof (27 August 1999)

The Italian plaintiff (seller) sold to the Austrian defendant (buyer) hiking shoes which were resold and directly delivered to a Scandinavian enterprise. About three weeks after the last partial delivery, the buyer informed the seller of defects which had not been detectable upon initial inspection. The seller refused to take back the shoes and demanded payment of the price. The buyer asserted that due to the failure of the seller to deliver goods in conformity with the contract it had suffered loss of profit and asserted its right to set-off its damages.

The court of first instance dismissed the claim. The Court of Appeal set aside the judgment and remanded the case to the court of first instance. The Supreme Court confirmed the decision of the court of appeal. It found that according to article 38(1) CISG the buyer must examine the goods within a short period. This time frame varies according to the circumstances, e.g. the size of the firm of the buyer, the kind of goods and their complexity. Each partial delivery has to be examined separately. The Court stated that normally, in the absence of special circumstances the buyer should notify the seller of any lack of conformity pursuant to article 39(1) CISG within about 14 days from delivery.

Under the facts, the Supreme Court found no reason to extend this time-limit, particularly given that the shoes were seasonal goods and the seller's need to sell them during the season must be considered. Thus the notice was delayed and the buyer lost the right to rely on the lack of conformity, unless the defects could not be discovered by an examination pursuant to normal business practice. The Court found that in the absence of any applicable business practice the goods must be examined thoroughly and in a professional manner. The Court noted that in any case the burden of proof regarding notification of non-conformity in due form and time lies with the buyer.

As the findings of the court of first instance were not sufficient to assess whether the mere visual inspection of the delivered shoes was in line with the relevant business practices and whether the notification was in time or not, the case was remanded to the court of first instance.

BP Oil International Ltd. v. Empresa Estatal Petroleos de Ecuador

United States Court of Appeals, Fifth Circuit, 2003
332 F.3d 333

■ JERRY E. SMITH, CIRCUIT JUDGE:

Empresa Estatal Petroleos de Ecuador ("PetroEcuador") contracted with BP Oil International, Ltd. ("BP"), for the purchase and transport of gasoline from Texas to Ecuador. PetroEcuador refused to accept delivery, so BP sold the gasoline at a loss. BP appeals a summary judgment dismissing PetroEcuador and Saybolt, Inc. ("Saybolt"), the company responsible for testing the gasoline at the port of departure. We affirm in part, reverse in part, and remand.

I.

PetroEcuador sent BP an invitation to bid for supplying 140,000 barrels of unleaded gasoline deliverable "CFR" to Ecuador. "CFR," which stands for "Cost and Freight," is one of thirteen International Commercial Terms ("Incoterms") designed to "provide a set of international rules for the interpretation of the most commonly used trade terms in foreign trade." Incoterms are recognized through their incorporation into the Convention on Contracts for the International Sale of Goods ("CISG").

BP responded favorably to the invitation, and PetroEcuador confirmed the sale on its contract form. The final agreement required that the oil be sent "CFR La Libertad–Ecuador." A separate provision, paragraph 10, states, "Jurisdiction: Laws of the Republic of Ecuador." The contract further specifies that the gasoline have a gum content of less than three milligrams per one hundred milliliters, to be determined at the port of departure. PetroEcuador appointed Saybolt, a company specializing in quality control services, to ensure this requirement was met.

To fulfill the contract, BP purchased gasoline from Shell Oil Company and, following testing by Saybolt, loaded it on board the M/T TIBER at Shell's Deer Park, Texas, refinery. The TIBER sailed to La Libertad, Ecuador, where the gasoline was again tested for gum content. On learning that the gum content now exceeded the contractual limit, PetroEcuador refused to accept delivery. Eventually, BP resold the gasoline to Shell at a loss of approximately two million dollars.

BP sued PetroEcuador for breach of contract and wrongful draw of a letter of guarantee. After PetroEcuador filed a notice of intent to apply foreign law pursuant to FED. R. CIV. P. 44.1, the district court applied Texas choice of law rules and determined that Ecuadorian law governed. BP argued that the term "CFR" demonstrated the parties' intent to pass the risk of loss to PetroEcuador once the goods were delivered on board the TIBER. The district court disagreed and held that under Ecuadorian law, the seller must deliver conforming goods to the agreed destination, in this case Ecuador. The court granted summary judgment for PetroEcuador.

BP also brought negligence and breach of contract claims against Saybolt, alleging that the company had improperly tested the gasoline. Saybolt moved for summary judgment, asserting a limitation of liability defense and waiver of claims based on the terms of its service contract with BP. The court granted Saybolt's motion, holding that BP could not sue in tort, that BP was bound by the waiver provision, and that Saybolt did not take any action causing harm to BP. Pursuant to FED. R. CIV. P. 54(b), the court entered final judgment in favor of PetroEcuador and Saybolt.

III.

BP and PetroEcuador dispute whether the domestic law of Ecuador or the CISG applies. After recognizing that federal courts sitting in diversity apply the choice of law rules of the state in which they sit, the district court applied Texas law, which enforces unambiguous choice of law provisions . . . Paragraph 10, which states "Jurisdiction: Laws of the Republic of Ecuador," purports to apply Ecuadorian law. Based on an affidavit submitted by PetroEcuador's expert, Dr. Gustavo Romero, the court held that Ecuadorian law requires the seller to deliver conforming goods at the agreed destination, making summary judgment inappropriate for BP.

A.

The CISG, ratified by the Senate in 1986, creates a private right of action in federal court. The treaty applies to "contracts of sale of goods between parties whose places of business are in different States . . . when the States are Contracting States." CISG art. 1(1)(a). BP, an American corporation, and PetroEcuador, an Ecuadorian company, contracted for the sale of gasoline; the United States and Ecuador have ratified the CISG. * * *

B.

The CISG incorporates Incoterms through article 9(2), which provides: "The parties are considered, unless otherwise agreed, to have impliedly made applicable to their contract or its formation a usage of which the parties knew or ought to have known and which in international trade is widely known to, and regularly observed by, parties to contracts of the type involved in the particular trade concerned." CISG art. 9(2). Even if the usage of Incoterms is not global, the fact that they are well known in international trade means that they are incorporated through article 9(2).

PetroEcuador's invitation to bid for the procurement of 140,000 barrels of gasoline proposed "CFR" delivery. The final agreement, drafted by PetroEcuador, again specified that the gasoline be sent "CFR La Libertad–Ecuador" and that the cargo's gum content be tested pre-shipment. Shipments designated "CFR" require the seller to pay the costs and freight to transport the goods to the delivery port, but pass title and risk of loss to the buyer once the goods "pass the ship's rail" at the port of shipment. The goods should be tested for conformity before the risk of loss passes to the buyer. In the event of subsequent damage or loss, the buyer generally must seek a remedy against the carrier or insurer.

In light of the parties' unambiguous use of the Incoterm "CFR," BP fulfilled its contractual obligations if the gasoline met the contract's qualitative specifications when it passed the ship's rail and risk transferred to PetroEcuador. CISG art. 36(1). Indeed, Saybolt's testing confirmed that the gasoline's gum content was adequate before departure from Texas. Nevertheless, in its opposition to BP's motion for summary judgment, PetroEcuador contends that BP purchased the gasoline from Shell on an "as is" basis and thereafter failed to add sufficient gum inhibitor as a way to "cut corners." In other words, the cargo contained a hidden defect.

Having appointed Saybolt to test the gasoline, PetroEcuador "ought to have discovered" the defect before the cargo left Texas. CISG art. 39(1). Permitting PetroEcuador now to distance itself from Saybolt's test would negate the parties' selection of CFR delivery and would undermine the key role that reliance plays in international sales agreements. Nevertheless, BP could have breached the agreement if it provided goods that it "knew or could not have been unaware" were defective when they "passed over the ship's rail" and risk shifted to PetroEcuador. CISG art. 40.

Therefore, there is a fact issue as to whether BP provided defective gasoline by failing to add sufficient gum inhibitor. The district court should permit the parties to conduct discovery as to this issue only.

IV.

BP raises negligence and breach of contract claims against Saybolt, alleging that the company improperly tested the gasoline's gum content before shipment. These claims amount to indemnification for BP's losses suffered on account of PetroEcuador's refusal to accept delivery. Our conclusion that PetroEcuador is liable so long as BP did not knowingly provide deficient gasoline renders these claims moot.

Summary judgment was therefore proper, though we need not review the district court's reasoning.

If PetroEcuador improperly refused CFR delivery, it is liable to BP for any consequential damages. In its claims against Saybolt, BP pleaded "in the alternative"; counsel also acknowledged, at oral argument, that beyond those damages stemming from PetroEcuador's refusal to accept delivery, BP has no collateral claims against Saybolt. If Saybolt negligently misrepresented the gasoline's gum content, PetroEcuador (not BP) becomes the party with a potential claim.

Even if PetroEcuador is not liable because BP knowingly presented gasoline with an inadequate gum content, BP's claims drop out. BP alleges that Saybolt "negligently misrepresented the quality" of the gasoline before its loading in Texas; it also claims that Saybolt's improper testing was "a proximate cause of the gasoline to be refused by PetroEcuador and/or the gum content to increase which caused BP to suffer pecuniary loss." BP's claims depend on the fact that Saybolt misrepresented the quality of the gasoline. It goes without saying, however, that if BP knew that the gasoline was deficient, it could not have relied on Saybolt's report to its detriment.

The judgment dismissing PetroEcuador is reversed and remanded for proceedings consistent with this opinion. The judgment dismissing Saybolt is affirmed.

NOTES

1.   Both CLOUT 319 and CLOUT 423 create a presumption that a particular time is reasonable, although they differ over the particular period. CLOUT 319 gives a four week period while CLOUT 423's period is 14 days, and other courts have stated different presumptively reasonable periods. See, e.g., CLOUT 230, CLOUT 280, available at http://www.uncitral.org/uncitral/en/case_law.html. The presumptive period can be rebutted by a showing that a different period was reasonable in the particular case. Clearly a presumptively reasonable period gives contracting parties some certainty in structuring their performance of the contract. The particular presumptively reasonable period for notice set by a court is less important. A survey of cases up to 2005 finds German and Swiss courts tending to converge on a period of one month, with some deviation; see Daniel Girsberger, The Time Limits of Article 39 CISG, 25 J. L. & Comm. 241 (2006).

Professor Harry Flechtner objects to decisions which create a presumption of timely notice because they "invade the function of the Convention's drafters and the sovereign prerogatives of the Contracting States." John O. Honnold, Uniform Law for International Sales Under the 1980 United Nations Convention 372 (H.M. Flechtner ed., 4th ed. 2009) (editorial commentary). Is the objection convincing? Consider in this regard Article 7(1), which instructs courts in interpreting the CISG's provisions to take into account the need for uniformity in its application. The Article arguably authorizes courts in signatory countries to coordinate their interpretations of the CISG's provisions so that the provisions are applied in the same way. Creating a presumptively reasonable time period is an effective way to coordinate interpretations of Article 39(1) among national courts. Because signatory countries understand Article 7(1)'s potential to facilitate coordination in interpreting the CISG, the judicial creation of a presumptively reasonable period does not invade their "sovereign prerogative."

2.   The sales contract in *BP Oil* required the oil to be sent "CFR La Libertad–Ecuador." "CFR" stands for "cost and freight." It is a delivery term frequently used when the contract calls for an ocean carrier to transport the goods to the buyer. The contract left the term "CFR" undefined. The International Chamber of Commerce (ICC), International Commercial Terms ("Incoterms") defines the term, and international sales contracts frequently incorporate Incoterms, either explicitly or implicitly. As Incoterms defines "CFR," the contract price includes the cost ("C") and ocean freight charges ("FR") of bringing the goods to the port of destination—here, La Libertad, Ecuador. Under the definition, the seller's obligation of delivery ends when it places the goods on board the named vessel at the loading port. At that point the risk of loss of the goods also passes to the buyer. See ICC, Incoterms 2010 (Doc. 715) A4 ("Delivery"). Article 2 of the UCC has its own definition of the same term; see 2–319 ("C&F").

The *BP Oil* court states that "Incoterms are recognized through their incorporation into the Convention on Contracts for the International Sale of Goods ("CISG") . . . " The CISG does not incorporate Incoterms by reference. Although the court does not refer to a specific Article of the CISG which implicitly incorporates Incoterms, the court probably considers Article 9(2) to do so. Read Article 9(2) carefully. What facts must the court assume obtain for Incoterms to apply the sales contract in *BP Oil*?

3.   Where the sales contract involves carriage, as in *BP Oil*, Article 38(2) allows the buyer to defer inspecting the goods until they arrive at their destination. Thus, although under the CFR delivery term BP delivered the oil to PetroEcuador when it passed the ship's rail in Deer Park, Texas (the port of shipment), PetroEcuador could wait until the oil arrived in La Libertad to inspect it. Why, then, did the Fifth Circuit conclude that PetroEcuador should have discovered the defect in the oil shipment earlier and given notice to BP before the oil arrived in La Libertad? See Article 39(1). Given the court's conclusion, why didn't the court find that PetroEcuador might retain a remedy under the CISG? See CISG Article 40.

PROBLEM 6.5

Seller, located in Charlottesville, sold and delivered some electronic equipment to Buyer, located in Canada, on March 1, 2003. The contract warranted the equipment against failures in its performance. Buyer experienced no problems with the equipment until February 15, 2006 when it stopped working. Although Buyer immediately informed Seller of the problem, Seller refused to do anything about it. Worse, Buyer later discovered that Seller's employees had documented and related to Seller failures in the equipment that occur only after years of use. Buyer sued Seller on March 1, 2006 seeking to recover damages from Seller's breach of contract. The suit is filed within the applicable four year statute of limitations. Buyer can establish that the equipment's failure was due to a design failure, not improper use. Can Buyer recover anything from Seller? CISG Articles 1(1)(a), 35, 36, 39(1),(2), 40.

E. PRIVITY AND THE CONTRACT–TORT DIVIDE

1. PRIVITY

Sales law originally followed the common law of contracts and required privity for the plaintiff to recover from the seller. Privity exists when there is a contractual relationship between parties. The rationale underlying the notion is that the agreement creates rights and imposes obligations only between the parties to it. Thus, to maintain suit against the seller, the plaintiff must be a party to the contract with the seller. The requirement of privity therefore is a barrier to the buyer's recovery for breach of warranty. More recent sales law relaxes without eliminating the privity requirement.

Modern sales law identifies two different issues of privity: vertical and horizontal privity. Vertical privity refers to a connection within the distribution chain of sellers. It exists when there is a contractual relationship between the buyer and the defendant-seller in the distribution chain. Vertical privity is absent when the defendant-seller in that chain is not the buyer-plaintiff's seller. For instance, suppose the buyer purchases a good from a seller, who in turn purchased the good from its manufacturer. There is no vertical privity between the buyer and the manufacturer, who is the remote seller of the good. The issue here is whether the buyer can maintain a warranty action against the remote seller. Article 2 of the UCC arguably says nothing about this issue. The decisional law of most states allows the warranty action even without vertical privity when the buyer is personally injured or its property damaged by the remote seller's product. Courts are divided as to when the buyer does not suffer personal injury or property damage. Some courts allow the warranty action when there is a breach of an express warranty. Courts that do not require vertical privity allow the buyer to recover direct damages from the remote seller. They tend to disagree as to whether consequential damages are also recoverable. Courts are more divided when breach is of an implied warranty. A number of courts have eliminated vertical privity with respect to actions for breach of implied warranties of merchantability. Fewer courts have done so with respect to warranty actions for breach of implied warranties of fitness for a particular purpose.

Horizontal privity exists when there is a contract between the plaintiff and the retail seller. It is absent when the plaintiff has not purchased the product. For instance, nonpurchasing users of the product or members of the buyer's household are not in horizontal privity with the buyer's seller. These persons are outside the chain of distribution of the product. The issue of horizontal privity is whether non-buyers can maintain a warranty action against the defendant-retail seller. Section 2–318 addresses horizontal privity. It offers states three alternatives (Alternatives A–C) from which to select. A few states have enacted nonuniform versions of 2–318 or its counterpart, or left the matter entirely to decisional law. Although 2–318's heading refers to "third party beneficiaries of warranties," these "beneficiaries" bear little relation to third party beneficiaries under general contract law. Under contract law an agreement can call for performance to be tendered to a third party and give that party a right to sue. By contrast, 2–318 gives specified "beneficiaries" a right to sue, whatever the contract provides. See Alternatives A–C (final sentence). Thus, unlike third-party beneficiary contracts, 2–318 does not allow contracting parties to limit their liability to third parties.

Section 2–318 deals with two different questions about horizontal privity. One question concerns who can be a proper plaintiff in a warranty action. Alternatives A–C give different answers to this question. About half the states have adopted Alternative A, which extends warranty coverage to "any natural person who is in the family or household of his buyer or who is a guest in his home if it is reasonable to expect that such person may use, consume or be affected by the goods and who is injured in person by the breach of the warranty." The rest of the states that have adopted 2–318 are divided between Alternatives B and C. Alternative B extends coverage to "any natural person who may reasonably be expected to use, consume or be affected by the goods and who is injured in person by breach of the warranty." Alternative C extends warranty coverage to "any person who may reasonably be expected to use, consume or be affected by the goods and who is injured by breach of the warranty." Unlike Alternatives A and B, the beneficiary in Alternative C need not be a natural person. Comment 3 to 2–318 states that Alternative A is "not intended to enlarge or restrict the developing case law on whether the seller's warranties, give to his buyer who resells, extend to other persons in the distributive chain." Although some courts have used this Comment to extend Alternative A's categories to nonhousehold members, the case law generally interprets the Alternative narrowly.

The second question about horizontal privity concerns the type of injury for which non-privity plaintiffs can recover. Alternatives A–C differ in the restrictiveness of covered injury. Alternatives A and B allow actions to recover for personal injury. These Alternatives, read strictly, therefore do not allow recover for purely commercial loss or property damage. Alternative C is more expansive, allowing recovery for "injury" from breach of warranty.

Because Alternative C allows persons "affected" by the goods to recover, courts have had to determine whether affected persons can recover when their only injury is economic. The question arises when the affected party has neither used nor purchased the goods. For instance, it might lose profits as a result of the seller's breach of warranty, even though it is not a party to the sales contract or an intended beneficiary of that contract. Some courts have not allowed this non-privity plaintiff to recover its purely economic loss, while allowing non-privity users or purchasers to recover. See, e.g., Paramount Aviation Corp. v. Gruppo Agusta, 288 F.3d 67 (3d Cir. 2002); 3M. v. Nishika Ltd., 565 N.W.2d 16 (Minn. 1997). The limitation has an economic rationale. It is difficult for the seller in advance to accurately estimate its potential liability on breach to non-parties to the contract, particularly when they neither use nor purchase the product. Their different circumstances make the variance in liability wide and uncertain. The seller lacks information about their businesses and therefore about the economic losses they will suffer on breach. The uncertainty in potential liability therefore makes it hard for the seller to take efficient precautions to avoid breaching its warranty. By contrast, non-parties to the contract who potentially are affected by breach know the details of their businesses, including the impact of breach on their profits. They are better positioned to take precautions to avoid the resulting economic loss to them. See Richard A. Posner, Common–Law Economic Torts: An Economic and Legal Analysis, 48 Ariz. L. Rev. 735, 737–38 (2006).

The CISG does not address issues of privity. Article 4 limits the CISG's scope to "the formation of the contract of sale and the rights and obligations of the seller and the buyer arising from such a contract." The CISG therefore does not govern the rights of those who are not parties to the contract, such as the ultimate buyer in the distributive chain. Article 35(1) reinforces this conclusion. It requires the seller to deliver goods of the quantity, quality and description "required by the contract." Because the seller's obligations are set by the contract, and these obligations are owed to its buyer, the seller's obligations under Article 35(1) are not owed to those with whom it is not in privity. For both reasons, the CISG leaves issues of privity to applicable domestic law. This result is unsurprising because domestic law differs with respect to privity, both within the United States and in other countries. See, e.g., German Civil Code (BGB) § 437 (buyer's remedies apply only against its seller); Mathias Reimann, Liability for Defective Products at the Beginning of the Twenty–First Century: The Emergence of a Worldwide Standard, 51 Am. J. Comp. L. 751, 793 (2003). Relevant European Union Directives appear to require privity; see, e.g., Consumer Guarantee Directive, Article 2, Directive 99/44/EC, OJ 1999 7.7.99 J171/12. By leaving the matter to domestic law, the CISG's drafters avoided addressing a controversial issue. See Richard E. Speidel, The Revision of UCC Article 2, Sales in Light of the United Nations Convention on Contracts for the International Sale of Goods, 16 Nw. J. Int'l L. & Bus. 165 (1995).

Tex Enterprises, Inc. v. Brockway Standard, Inc.

Supreme Court of Washington, 2003
66 P.3d 625

■ OWENS, J.

A commercial purchaser seeks to recover economic damages from a manufacturer for breach of implied warranties under article 2 of the Uniform Commercial Code, Title 62A RCW (UCC). The plaintiff asserts that implied warranties arose out of the manufacturer's verbal assurances as to the quality of his product, made directly to the plaintiff. However, the plaintiff ultimately purchased the product from an intermediate distributor, not the manufacturer. Furthermore, an agreement between the manufacturer and the distributor contained a disclaimer of all warranties. Thus, absent privity between the plaintiff and the manufacturer, and without reliance on the contract between the manufacturer and the distributor as a third party beneficiary, we hold that such assurances do not give rise to implied warranties.

Facts

Brockway Standard, Inc. (Brockway) is a Georgia corporation that manufactures three- and five-gallon unlined steel containers, treated only with a rust inhibitor. J.F. Shelton Company (Shelton) is a Washington distributor of Brockway products. Tex Enterprises, Inc. (Tex) is a Washington corporation that purchases three- and five-gallon containers in which it ships and stores Spantex, a liquid coating used to seal decks and other exterior surfaces. Brockway sells its containers to Shelton, who in turn sells them to Washington purchasers like Tex.

Shelton did not have a negotiated distributorship contract with Brockway. Generally, Shelton's practice was to place phone or fax orders for Brockway products, and Brockway would ship the goods and mail an invoice. On the back of the invoice, terms and conditions were printed which warranted only that the goods would be free from defects in workmanship and materials. The terms explicitly disclaimed all other warranties, express or implied, and limited damages to refund of the purchase price and cost of return shipping. An additional clause required that Georgia law govern the agreement. Although Shelton had received multiple invoices over the course of its relationship with Brockway, these terms were never negotiated, and Shelton was unaware of their existence until the inception of this lawsuit.

Similarly, Tex's practice was to place verbal orders with Shelton for Brockway products. No party has referred to any written agreement between Tex and Shelton. Furthermore, because Tex never ordered directly from Brockway, Tex was unaware of the disclaimer, remedy limitation clause, and choice of law clause printed on Brockway's invoices. No similar disclaimers or limitations were printed anywhere on Brockway products or their packaging, and Shelton never notified Tex that the disclaimers existed.

Prior to September 1997, Tex used Brockway one-gallon tin cans to store and ship Spantex, but used another company's three- and five-gallon steel containers. In September 1997, a Shelton representative (Mr. Garrett) and a Brockway representative (Mr. Egan) visited Tex's president (Mr. Pieratt), with the objective of persuading him to switch to Brockway three- and five-gallon containers for storing and shipping Spantex. Mr. Garrett and Mr. Egan toured the Tex facility and examined the containers that Tex was using. Mr. Egan told Mr. Pieratt that Brockway containers were "just as good" for storing Spantex as the containers Tex was using. Furthermore, Mr. Egan arranged for Shelton to receive a "chargeback" (similar to a rebate) as an incentive to price the Brockway containers competitively and to facilitate the Tex deal. Relying on these representations, Mr. Pieratt agreed to switch to Brockway containers. Ultimately, Tex purchased 4,800 Brockway containers in which it stored and shipped more than 22,000 gallons of Spantex to its customers.

In the spring of 1998, Tex began to receive complaints from retail and consumer customers. The Spantex that was stored in the three- and five-gallon Brockway containers had begun to thicken and solidify, rendering it useless. Tex claims that the problem was caused by a reaction between the Spantex and the rust inhibitor with which the containers were treated. Tex expected that its costs for replacing the ruined Spantex would exceed $440,000.

Tex sued both Brockway and Shelton, claiming that it was entitled to recovery under a variety of theories including breach of express warranty, breach of implied warranty of merchantability, breach of implied warranty of fitness for a particular purpose, and breach of contract (against Shelton only). Tex sought to recover its costs for replacing the ruined product, incidental and consequential damages, disposal costs, and attorney fees. Shelton settled with Tex and is no longer a party to this lawsuit.

Brockway responded that the language on its invoices limited the claims and remedies available to Tex. In multiple orders, the trial court applied Georgia law and eventually dismissed all claims based upon the disclaimers printed on the Brockway invoices and lack of privity.

The Court of Appeals agreed that any third party beneficiary claims would depend upon Shelton's agreement with Brockway, which was limited by the language on Brockway's invoices. Still, the court reversed and remanded, holding instead that "direct representations to the purchaser can create express and implied warranties that run to the purchaser independent of any contract between the manufacturer and distributor."

Brockway petitioned for review only on the limited question of whether, as a matter of law, an implied warranty can arise from a manufacturer's direct representation to a remote commercial purchaser, without reliance on an underlying contract as a third party beneficiary.

Issue

Can an implied warranty arise from a manufacturer's direct representation to a remote commercial purchaser, absent a contract between the parties or reliance as a third party beneficiary on the contract between the manufacturer and its immediate buyer?

Analysis

* * *

Article 2 of the UCC, as adopted in Washington, governs warranties arising from the sale of goods. Unless excluded or modified, a warranty that goods are merchantable "is implied in a contract for their sale," so long as the seller is a "merchant with respect to goods of that kind." RCW 62A.2–314(1). This implied warranty of merchantability assures that the goods "are fit for the ordinary purposes for which such goods are used." RCW 62A.2–314(2)(c). Similarly, unless excluded or modified, an implied warranty of fitness for a particular purpose arises "[w]here the seller at the time of contracting has reason to know any particular purpose for which the goods are required and that the buyer is relying on the seller's skill or judgment to select or furnish suitable goods." RCW 62A.2–315.

RCW 62A.2–316 allows exclusion or modification of implied warranties so long as the limiting language meets the formal requirements of that section. See RCW 62A.2–316(2), (3). RCW 62A.2–719 also allows sellers to limit available remedies to the return of the goods and repayment of the purchase price or to repair and replacement of the goods. These provisions provide one method for sellers to limit their liability under the UCC.

In addition, lack of privity has historically been a defense to claims of breach of warranty. There are two types of plaintiffs for whom lack of privity has been a concern. A " 'horizontal' non-privity plaintiff" is not a buyer of the product in question, but is one who consumes or is affected by the goods. The " 'vertical' non-privity plaintiff" is a buyer who is in the distributive chain, but who did not buy the product directly from the defendant. Id. Tex is a vertical nonprivity plaintiff.

By adopting alternative A of section 2–318 of The American Law Institute, Uniform Commercial Code 1972 Official Text, the Washington Legislature chose to eliminate the privity requirement for horizontal nonprivity plaintiffs under certain circumstances. UCC comment 3 to section 2–318, as adopted in Washington, notes that this provision is silent with regard to vertical privity, but the section "is not intended to enlarge or restrict the developing case law on whether the seller's warranties, given to his buyer who resells, extend to other persons in the distributive chain." Thus, questions regarding the extension of warranties to vertical nonprivity plaintiffs are left to the courts.

In Baughn v. Honda Motor Co., 107 Wn.2d 127, 727 P.2d 655 (1986), this court upheld a trial court's summary judgment order in favor of a manufacturer, dismissing the remote purchasers' claims for breach of implied warranty. The *Baughn* court adopted the traditional rule that a plaintiff may not bring an implied warranty action under the UCC without contractual privity. It is important to note that the *Baughn* court would have allowed a plaintiff's express warranty claim to proceed because "[t]he privity requirement is relaxed . . . when a manufacturer makes express representations, in advertising or otherwise, to a plaintiff."

A few years later in Touchet Valley Grain Growers, Inc. v. OPP & Seibold Gen. Constr., Inc., 119 Wn.2d 334, 831 P.2d 724 (Wash. 1992), this court created an exception to the privity requirement for implied warranties. The *Touchet Valley* court allowed a vertical nonprivity plaintiff to recover where the plaintiff was the intended third party beneficiary of the implied warranty that the manufacturer gave to its intermediate dealer. Notably, the *Touchet Valley* court did not overturn *Baughn*. Id. at 346. Instead, it distinguished *Baughn* based in part on the fact that "the analysis was not based on a third party beneficiary argument." Thus, we conclude that *Touchet Valley* carved a third party beneficiary exception out of the general rule that a vertical nonprivity plaintiff cannot recover from a remote manufacturer for breach of implied warranty.

The Court of Appeals in this case held that a manufacturer's direct verbal representations to a remote purchaser can create express and implied warranties that run to the remote purchaser, independent of any contract between the manufacturer and the intermediate distributor. Tex Enters., Inc. v. Brockway Standard, Inc., 39 P.3d 362 (Wash. Ct. App. 2002). However, allowing implied warranties to arise without reliance on an underlying contract is inconsistent with both the plain language of RCW 62A.2–314 and –315 and this court's prior approach to implied warranties.

First, the plain language of both RCW 62A.2–314 and –315 requires that implied warranties arise only out of contractual relationships. RCW 62A.2–314 states that the warranty that goods shall be merchantable is "implied in a contract for their sale." Similarly, RCW 62A.2–315 explains that the implied warranty of fitness for a particular purpose arises based on the seller's understanding "at the time of contracting." This language can be contrasted with RCW 62A.2–313 (express warranties), the language of which does not refer to an underlying "contract." Thus, the plain meaning of this statutory language forecloses application of implied warranties where there is no underlying contract to which the purchaser is a party or an intended third party beneficiary.

In addition, Tex has failed to cite to any case in which this court has allowed a vertical nonprivity plaintiff to recover economic damages for breach of implied warranty without reliance on some underlying contract. Such a restriction is justified because, to be enforceable, contractual relationships under the UCC must be formed according to the code's safeguards, making contractual relationships comparatively formalized. See, e.g., RCW 62A.2–201 (statute of frauds). In contrast, express representations, made in advertisements or otherwise, require no formalities. Thus, we recognize that allowing implied warranties to arise out of express representations could leave a manufacturer unable to adequately predict when implied warranties will attach.

This court has also distinguished between express and implied warranties, restricting recovery for breach of implied warranty where it would have allowed recovery for breach of express warranty. See *Baughn*, 107 Wn.2d at 151–52. Because implied warranties arise by operation of law without specific adoption by the seller, we recognize that such warranties must be more closely guarded than express warranties, whose adoption requires some voluntary action.

The combination of the plain language of the statutory scheme and this court's prior treatment of implied warranties overcomes the reasoning of the Court of Appeals in this case. To support its conclusion, the Court of Appeals relied first upon Dobias v. Western Farmers Ass'n, 491 P.2d 1346 (Wisc. Ct. App. 1971), in which the manufacturer of an herbicide made representations to Western Farmers salesmen about its product's compatibility with corn. The salesmen in turn communicated that representation to farmers. Although the *Dobias* court ultimately held the manufacturer liable to the plaintiffs, it never clearly based the manufacturer's liability on implied warranties. Thus, reliance on *Dobias* for the proposition that implied warranties may arise out of a remote manufacturer's representations is tenuous at best. Furthermore, the Court of Appeals failed to recognize this court's subsequent adoption of the traditional privity rule for vertical implied warranty plaintiffs.

The Court of Appeals also adopted the reasoning of the Florida Court of Appeals in Cedars of Lebanon Hospital Corp. v. European X–Ray Distributors of America, Inc., 444 So. 2d 1068 (Fla. Ct. App. 1984), a case involving a fact pattern similar to this one. The *Cedars* court reasoned that it would be "fundamentally unfair . . . to allow the manufacturer to hide behind the doctrine of privity when the product, which it induced the purchaser to buy, turns out to be worthless." *Cedars*, 444 So. 2d at 1072. The *Cedars* court also hoped to avoid prolonged indemnity litigation, gradually advancing up the chain of privity. However, both of these concerns are easily alleviated where the plaintiff is allowed to pursue a claim under breach of express warranty, something that Washington law clearly allows in this case. Therefore, we find the *Cedars* reasoning unconvincing.

It is important to note that Tex and future vertical nonprivity plaintiffs are not left without recourse. We emphasize that this court has already clearly established that the privity requirement is relaxed where a manufacturer makes express representations to a plaintiff. *Baughn*, 107 Wn.2d at 151–52. In fact, the issue of whether an express warranty was made in this case still remains to be decided by the trial court. Furthermore, because Brockway has correctly conceded that Tex's express warranty claims are not dependent upon the Brockway–Shelton contract, there is no question that Washington law governs the determination of whether Brockway's statements amounted to an express warranty. Finally, where a commercial plaintiff can show that it is the intended third party beneficiary of a contract between the manufacturer and its direct purchaser, recovery may be available under a third party beneficiary analysis.

For all of the reasons discussed above, we hold that implied warranties do not arise out of express representations made by a manufacturer to a remote commercial purchaser absent privity or reliance on some underlying contract.

Conclusion

We reverse the Court of Appeals with regard to the implied warranty claim and hold that in cases where a commercial purchaser seeks to recover economic damages from a remote manufacturer, implied warranties do not arise absent privity or an underlying contract to which the remote commercial purchaser is a third party beneficiary.

Hyundai Motor America, Inc. v. Goodin

Supreme Court of Indiana, 2005
822 N.E.2d 947

■ BOEHM, JUSTICE.

We hold that a consumer may sue a manufacturer for economic loss based on breach of the implied warranty of merchantability even if the consumer purchased the product from an intermediary in the distribution chain. There is no requirement of "vertical" privity for such a claim.

Facts and Procedural Background

On November 18, 2000, Sandra Goodin test drove a Hyundai Sonata at AutoChoice Hyundai in Evansville, Indiana. The car was represented as new and showed nineteen miles on the odometer. Goodin testified that when she applied the brakes in the course of the test drive she experienced a "shimmy, shake, pulsating type feel." The AutoChoice salesperson told her that this was caused by flat pots on the tires from extended inactivity and offered to have the tires rotated and inspected. After this explanation, Goodin purchased the Sonata for $22,710.00.

The manufacturer, Hyundai, provided three limited warranties: 1 year/12,000 miles on "wear items;" 5 years/60,000 miles "bumper to bumper;" and 10 years/100,000 miles on the powertrain.[1] Hyundai concedes that brake rotors, brake calipers, and brake caliper slides were subject to the 5 year/60,000 mile warranty covering "repair or replacement of any component originally manufactured or installed by [Hyundai] that is found to be defective in material or workmanship under normal use and maintenance." To claim under this warranty, a vehicle must be serviced by an authorized Hyundai dealer who is then reimbursed by Hyundai for any necessary parts or labor.

Three days after the car was purchased, Goodin's husband, Steven Hicks, took it back to AutoChoice for the promised tire work. Goodin testified that she continued to feel the shimmy but did nothing further for a month. On December 22, she took the car to a different Hyundai dealer, Bales Auto Mall, in Jeffersonville, Indiana, for an unrelated problem and also made an appointment six days later for Bales to inspect the brakes. Bales serviced the brake rotors for warping, but on May 1, 2001, Goodin returned to Bales complaining that the vehicle continued to vibrate when the brakes were applied. Bales found the rotors to be out of tolerance and machined them. Eighteen days later Goodin again returned to Bales, reporting that she still felt vibrations and for the first time also heard a "popping" noise. Goodin told the service advisor at Bales that she thought there may be a problem with the suspension, and Bales changed and lubed the strut assembly. Eleven days later Goodin once more brought the car to Bales reporting continued shimmy and also a "bed spring type" noise originating from the brakes. The Bales mechanic was unable to duplicate the brake problem, but balanced and rotated the tires as Goodin had requested. One week later Goodin returned to Bales where she and Jerry Hawes, Bales's Service Manager, test drove the Sonata. The brake problem did not occur during the test drive, but Hawes identified a noise from the direction of the left front tire and repaired the rubber mounting bracket.

Goodin told Hawes that the brake problem had occurred about seventy percent of the time. The problem was worse when it was wet or cool, was consistently occurring when she drove down a steep hill near her home, and was less frequent when a passenger's weight was added. Goodin made arrangements to leave the car with Hawes at Bales, but, according to Hawes, over a several day period he could not duplicate the symptoms Goodin reported.

On August 24, 2001, Goodin took her car back to her original dealer, AutoChoice, reporting that the brakes "squeak and grind when applied." Goodin left the car with AutoChoice where the left front rotor was machined and loose bolts on the front upper control arm were tightened. Goodin testified that after this five-day procedure the brakes

---

[1] On the "Buyers Order," AutoChoice Hyundai included the following preprinted language in capital letters:

ALL WARRANTIES, IF ANY, BY A MANUFACTURER OR SUPPLIER OTHER THAN DEALER ARE THEIRS, NOT DEALER'S, AND ONLY SUCH MANUFACTURER OR OTHER SUPPLIER SHALL BE LIABLE FOR PERFORMANCE UNDER SUCH WARRANTIES, UNLESS DEALER FURNISHES BUYER WITH A SEPARATE WRITTEN WARRANTY MADE BY DEALER ON ITS OWN BEHALF. DEALER HEREBY DISCLAIMS ALL WARRANTIES, EXPRESS OR IMPLIED, INCLUDING ANY IMPLIED WARRANTIES OF MERCHANTABILITY OR FITNESS FOR A PARTICULAR PURPOSE, ON ALL GOODS AND SERVICES SOLD BY DEALER. . . .

began to make the same noises and vibrations even before she arrived home.

In October 2001 Goodin hired an attorney who faxed a letter to Hyundai Motor America giving notice of her complaint and requesting a refund of the purchase price. On November 13, 2001, Goodin filed a complaint against Hyundai Motor America, Inc. alleging claims under the Magnuson–Moss Warranty Act, 15 U.S.C. §§ 2301–2312, for breach of express warranty, breach of implied warranty, and revocation of acceptance. On April 23, 2002, in anticipation of litigation, Goodin hired William Jones to inspect her car. Jones noted that the odometer read 57,918 miles and the car was still under warranty. Jones drove the car approximately five miles and found "severe brake pulsation on normal stops" which "was worse on high speed stops." Although he did not remove the tires to inspect the brake rotors, Jones opined that the rotors were warped and defective or there was "a root cause that has not been discovered and corrected by the repair facilities." His ultimate conclusion was that the "vehicle was defective and unmerchantable at the time of manufacture and unfit for operation on public roadways." Three weeks later, after the 5 year/60,000 mile warranty had expired, Goodin's husband, Hicks, replaced the rotors with new rotors from a NAPA distributor. After this repair, according to Hicks, the pulsation went from "very bad" to "mild" and "less frequent."

Steven Heiss, District Parts and Service Manager for Hyundai Motor America served as the liaison between Hyundai and the dealers and provided warranty training. If a dealer is not performing repairs correctly, Hyundai, through its liaisons, addresses the problem. Heiss inspected Goodin's Sonata on October 21, 2002. At that point the Sonata had been driven 77,600 miles. He testified that during his twenty-three mile test drive he neither heard the noise described by Goodin nor felt any vibration from the brakes. However, Heiss did hear a "droning noise" which he later concluded was due to a failed left rear wheel bearing. He regarded this as a serious problem and not one caused by abuse or misuse of the vehicle. The wheel bearing would have been covered by the 5 year/60,000 mile warranty. Before his inspection, Heiss had been told that the rotors had been changed by Hicks five months earlier, and when Heiss measured the rotors he found that they were out of standard. Heiss testified a miscast from the factory was one of a number of possible reasons for damaged rotors.

At the conclusion of a two day trial, the jury was instructed on all claims. Over defendants' objection, the instructions on implied warranties made no reference to a privity requirement. The jury returned a verdict for Hyundai on Goodin's breach of express warranty claim, but found in favor of Goodin on her claim for breach of implied warranty of merchantability. Damages of $3,000.00 were assessed and Goodin's counsel was later awarded attorneys' fees of $19,237.50 pursuant to the fee shifting provisions of the Magnuson–Moss Warranty Act.

Hyundai orally moved to set aside the verdict as contrary to law on the ground that Goodin purchased the car from AutoChoice and therefore did not enjoy vertical privity with Hyundai. The court initially denied that motion, but the following day set aside the verdict, holding lack of privity between Goodin and Hyundai precluded a cause of action for breach of implied warranty. Goodin then moved to reinstate the verdict, and, after briefing and oral argument, the trial court granted that motion on the ground that Hyundai was estopped from asserting lack of privity.

Hyundai appealed, asserting: (1) it was not estopped from asserting a defense of lack of privity; and (2) lack of vertical privity barred Goodin's recovery for breach of implied warranty of merchantability. The Court of Appeals agreed on both points, holding that Hyundai was not estopped from asserting that privity was an element of Goodin's prima facie case, and, because privity was lacking, Goodin did not prove her case. The Magnuson–Moss Warranty Act looks to state law for the contours of implied warranties. The Court of Appeals was "not unsympathetic" to Goodin's claims but regarded itself as bound by a footnote in Martin Rispens & Son v. Hall Farms, Inc., 621 N.E.2d 1078, 1084 n.2 (Ind. 1993), where this Court stated: "In Indiana, privity between the seller and the buyer is required to maintain a cause of action on the implied warranties of merchantability." Id. at 784. We granted transfer.

Vertical Privity

A.   The Relationship Between Federal and State Law in Claims Based on Implied Warranty of Merchantability

This case is brought under a federal statute. The Magnuson–Moss Warranty Act, 15 U.S.C. §§ 2301–2312 (2000), provides a federal right of action for consumers to enforce written or implied warranties where they claim to be damaged by the failure of a supplier, warrantor, or service contractor to comply with any obligation under that statute or under a written warranty, implied warranty, or service contract. The Act also limits the extent to which manufacturers who give express warranties may disclaim or modify implied warranties, but looks to state law as the source of any express or implied warranty. As the Seventh Circuit recently put it: "Because §§ 2308 and 2304(a) do not modify, or discuss in any way, a state's ability to establish a privity requirement, whether privity is a prerequisite to a claim for breach of implied warranty under the Magnuson–Moss Act therefore hinges entirely on the applicable state law." Voelker v. Porsche Cars N. Am., Inc., 353 F.3d 516, 525 (7th Cir. 2003).

Goodin's claim is for breach of the implied warranty of merchantability, not for violation of any substantive provision of the federal statute. Accordingly, her claim lives or dies on the resolution of an issue of state law, specifically whether Indiana requires privity between buyer and manufacturer for a claim of breach of implied warranty.

B.   Standard of Review

Hyundai does not dispute that under circumstances applicable here Indiana recognizes implied warranties of fitness for a particular purpose and implied warranties of merchantability. Ind. Code §§ 26–1–2–314, 315 (2003). Rather, Hyundai contends that under Indiana law, a buyer must be in vertical privity with a seller to impose liability on the seller for breach of an implied warranty. Whether Indiana law requires privity to sustain an action for breach of an implied warranty is purely a question of law and therefore is reviewed under a de novo standard.

An implied warranty of merchantability imposed by operation of law is to be liberally construed in favor of the buyer.

C. Origins of Privity

Indiana has adopted the Uniform Commercial Code, notably its provision that: "A warranty that the goods shall be merchantable is implied in a contract for their sale if the seller is a merchant with respect to goods of that kind. . . . " Ind. Code § 26–1–2–314(1) (2004). Hyundai asserts, and the Court of Appeals found, Indiana law requires vertical privity between manufacturer and consumer when economic damages are sought. Hyundai Motor America, Inc. v. Goodin, 804 N.E.2d 784, 783 (Ind. Ct. App. 2004). Goodin argues that traditional privity of contract between the consumer and manufacturer is not required for a claim against a manufacturer for breach of the implied warranty of merchantability, especially if the manufacturer provides a Magnuson–Moss express warranty with the product.

Privity originated as a doctrine limiting tort relief for breach of warranties. The lack of privity defense was first recognized in Winterbottom v. Wright, 10 M. & W. 109, 152 Eng. Rep. 402 (Ex. 1842). In that case, the court sustained a demurrer to a suit by an injured coachman for breach of warranty by a third party who contracted with the owner to maintain the coach. In this century, however, MacPherson v. Buick Motor Co., 111 N.E. 1050 (1916), and Henningsen v. Bloomfield Motors, Inc., 161 A.2d 69 (1960), established that lack of privity between an automobile manufacturer and a consumer would not preclude the consumer's action for personal injuries and property damage caused by the negligent manufacture of an automobile. "Vertical" privity typically becomes an issue when a purchaser files a breach of warranty action against a vendor in the purchaser's distribution chain who is not the purchaser's immediate seller. Simply put, vertical privity exists only between immediate links in a distribution chain. A buyer in the same chain who did not purchase directly from a seller is "remote" as to that seller. Id. "Horizontal" privity, in contrast, refers to claims by nonpurchasers, typically someone who did not purchase the product but who was injured while using it. Goodin purchased her car from a dealership and is thus remote from the manufacturer and lacks "vertical" privity with Hyundai.

"Although warranty liability originated as a tort doctrine, it was assimilated by the law of contracts and ultimately became part of the law of sales." Hawkland, supra, at 771. But "privity is more than an accident of history. It permitted manufacturers and distributors to control in some measure their risks of doing business." Richard W. Duesenberg, The Manufacturer's Last Stand: The Disclaimer, 20 Bus. Law 159, 161 (1964). Because vertical privity involves a claim by a purchaser who voluntarily acquired the goods, it enjoys a stronger claim to justification on the basis of freedom of contract or consensual relationship. It nevertheless has come under criticism in recent years, and this is the first opportunity for this Court to give full consideration to this issue.

D. Indiana Case Law

Although this Court did not address the issue, even before the Products Liability Act, both the Court of Appeals and federal courts applying Indiana law held that a claimant was not required to prove privity to succeed in a personal injury action in tort based on breach of implied warranties. Three federal court decisions drew on these decisions to conclude that privity of contract is not required in Indiana to maintain a cause of action for personal injury based on breach of an implied warranty.

However, several Court of Appeals decisions subsequently held that recovery of economic loss for alleged failure of the expected benefit of the bargain based on breach of implied warranty under the UCC required a buyer to be in privity of contract with the seller. Corbin v. Coleco Industries, 748 F.2d 411, 415 (7th Cir. 1984), took the view that "subsequent Indiana cases have shed new light on Indiana's interpretation of implied warranty under the UCC, thus making it clear that privity is indeed required."

This Court has mentioned the common law privity requirement in the context of actions sounding in contract only once, and that in a footnote. Martin Rispens & Son v. Hall Farms, Inc., 621 N.E.2d 1078 (Ind. 1993), addressed negligence and express and implied warranty claims by a farmer against both the direct seller and the grower of seed that allegedly damaged the farmer's crops. The footnote cited to the UCC and two Court of Appeals decisions and other courts have taken the footnote as settled Indiana law on this issue. As the Court of Appeals put it in its decision in this case:

> The [footnote] indicates our supreme court's unequivocal acceptance that privity between a consumer and a manufacturer is required in order to maintain a cause of action for breach of an implied warranty of merchantability. . . . Any change in the law removing the privity requirement in implied warranty actions should be left to that court. . . . To the extent Goodin argues that this result is inequitable, we are not entirely unsympathetic. Whether the cons of the vertical privity rule outweigh the pros is something for either our supreme court or the General Assembly to address.

Hyundai, 804 N.E.2d at 788. In *Martin Rispens*, the implied warranty claims were rejected based on an effective disclaimer of implied warranty, under Indiana Code section 26–1–2–316(2) which permits parties to agree to exclude or modify implied warranties if done in a particular manner. The farmer did not present privity as an issue on transfer to this Court and neither party briefed it. It was not necessary to the decision. Accordingly, the language in *Martin Rispens*, though often cited, is dicta and we accept the invitation from the Court of Appeal to reconsider it.

Indiana law, as developed in the Court of Appeals, has already eroded the privity requirement to some degree. In Thompson Farms, Inc. v. Corno Feed Products, Inc., 366 N.E.2d 3 (1977), the Court of Appeals permitted the plaintiff to recover on an implied warranty where it was shown that the contractual arrangements between the manufacturer and the dealer who sold to the plaintiff created an agency relationship; and the manufacturer's agents participated significantly in the sale both through advertising and personal contact with the buyer. Under those circumstances the Court of Appeals held that the manufacturer was a "seller" within the meaning of Indiana Code section

26–1–2–314. *Richards*, 384 N.E.2d at 1092, involved a defective boat sold by a dealer where the manufacturer's agents also engaged in personal contact with the buyer by giving demonstrations and attempting to adjust the loss after the sale. The Court of Appeals then, following *Thompson Farms, Inc.*, held that the participation in the sale by the manufacturer was sufficient to bring it into the transaction as a seller within the requirements of Indiana Code section 26–1–2–314. However, if the plaintiff could not show perfect vertical privity or an exception to the rule, then the plaintiff could not prove the claim.

E.   Statutory Developments in Indiana

The Product Liability Act, Indiana Code § 34–20–2–1 et seq. (1999), does not require a personal injury plaintiff to prove vertical privity in order to assert a products liability claim against the manufacturer. Even before the Product Liability Act in 1978, the requirement of privity of contract in warranty actions in Indiana began to erode in 1963 with the passage of the Uniform Commercial Code under section 2–318:

> A seller's warranty whether express or implied extends to any natural person who is in the family or household of his buyer or who is a guest in his home if it is reasonable to expect that such person may use, consume or be affected by the goods and who is injured in person by breach of the warranty. A seller may not exclude or limit the operation of this section. I.C. § 26–1–2–318. Section 2–318 was taken verbatim from the UCC as originally prepared by the Uniform Code Committee Draftsmen in 1952. It eliminated "horizontal" privity as a requirement for warranty actions. However, that version of 2–318 took no position on the requirement of vertical privity.

The purpose of the original version of section 2–318, which remains unchanged in Indiana today, was to give standing to certain non-privity plaintiffs to sue as third-party beneficiaries of the warranties that a buyer received under a sales contract. Hawkland, supra, at 769. That version of section 2–318 provided only that the benefit of a warranty automatically extended to the buyer's family, household, and houseguests, supra, at 775. It was intended to, and did, accomplish its goal of "freeing any such beneficiaries from any technical rules as to [horizontal] privity." U.C.C. § 2–318 cmt. 2. Some states refused to enact this version of section 2–318, and others adopted nonuniform versions of the statute. In 1966, in response to this proliferation of deviant versions of a purportedly uniform code, the drafters proposed three alternative versions of section 2–318. Only California, Louisiana, and Texas have failed to adopt one of these three versions of section 2–318.

> The majority of states, including Indiana, retained or adopted the 1952 version of section 2–318, which now appears in the Uniform Commercial Code as "Alternative A." Alternative B provides that "any natural person who may reasonably be expected to use, consume or be affected by the goods and who is injured in person by breach of warranty" may institute a breach of warranty action against the seller. U.C.C. § 2–318 cmt. 3. Alternative B expands the class of potential plaintiffs beyond family, household, and guests, and also implicitly abolishes the requirement of vertical privity because the seller's

warranty is not limited to "his buyer" and persons closely associated with that buyer. Alternative B is applicable only to claims for personal injury.

Because Alternatives A and B of 2–318 are limited to cases where the plaintiff is "injured in person," they do not authorize recovery for such loss. But neither do they bar a non-privity plaintiff from recovery against such a remote manufacturer for direct economic loss. . . . Thus, Alternatives A and B of 2–318 do not prevent a court from abolishing the vertical privity requirement even when a non-privity buyer seeks recovery for direct economic loss.

Alternative C is the most expansive in eliminating the lack-of-privity defense. It provides that: "A seller's warranty whether express or implied extends to any person who may reasonably be expected to use, consume or be affected by the goods and who is injured by breach of the warranty." Alternative C expands the class of plaintiffs to include other nonpurchasers such as the buyer's employees and invitees, and bystanders. Alternative C also eliminates the vertical privity requirement, but is not restricted to "personal" injury. Because Alternative C refers simply to "injury," plaintiffs sustaining only property damage or economic loss in some states have been held to have standing to sue under this language. This is consistent with the stated objective of the drafters that the third alternative follow "the trend of modern decisions as indicated by Restatement of Torts 2d § 402A (Tentative Draft No. 10, 1965) in extending the rule beyond injuries to the person." Hawkland, supra, at 770.

The commentaries to the UCC were careful to explain that the these alternatives were not to be taken as excluding the development of the common law on the issue of vertical privity:

[Alternative A] expressly includes as beneficiaries within its provisions the family, household and guests of the purchaser. Beyond this, the section in this form is neutral and is not intended to enlarge or restrict the developing case law on whether the seller's warranties, given to his buyer who resells, extend to other persons in the distributive chain. U.C.C § 2–318, cmt. n.3.

F.   Privity as an Obsolete Requirement as Applied to Consumer Goods

There is a split of authority in other jurisdictions with similar or identical versions of section 2–318 on the availability of implied warranty claims by remote purchasers, particularly if only economic loss is claimed, as in the present case.[2] Courts of other jurisdictions that have retained or adopted Alternative A note that the statute speaks only to horizontal privity, and is silent as to vertical privity. As the Pennsylvania Supreme Court put it: "Merely to *read* the language [of § 2–318] is to demonstrate that the code simply fails to treat this problem. . . . There thus is nothing to prevent this court from joining in the growing number of jurisdictions which, although bound by the code, have nevertheless abolished vertical privity in breach of warranty cases." Kassab v. Central Soya, 246 A.2d 848, 856 (Pa. 1968) (emphasis in original). Indiana has not legislated on this issue since 1966 when

---

[2]   Several jurisdictions that have adopted Alternative A have abolished privity. Others have retained the common law privity rule.

the UCC adopted these three alternatives. More recently, the "Buyback Vehicle Disclosure" statute eliminated the lack-of-privity defense for actions under that section. See I.C. § 24–5–13.5–13(c) (1995). In short, the General Assembly in keeping Alternative A left to this Court the issue of to what extent vertical privity of contract will be required.

Courts that have abolished vertical privity have cited a variety of reasons. Principal among these is the view that, in today's economy, manufactured products typically reach the consuming public through one or more intermediaries. As a result, any loss from an unmerchantable product is likely to be identified only after the product is attempted to be used or consumed. Hininger v. Case Corp. 23 F.3d 124, 127 (5th Cir. 1994) (In Texas, the privity requirement is not needed to assert a claim for breach of an implied warranty against a remote manufacturer of a finished product); Reed v. City of Chicago, 263 F. Supp. 2d 1123, 1125 (N.D. Ill. 2003) (Under Alternative A of 2–318, privity is no longer an absolute requirement for breach of warranty actions. Since benefit of paper gowns were for the protection of potentially suicidal detainees privity between the detainee and the manufacturer was not required for the warranty to apply); Hubbard v. General Motors Corp., 39 UCC Serv.2d 83 (S.D.N.Y. 1996) (buyer from dealer could sue manufacturer for direct economic loss for defective braking system in truck). Others have cited the concern that privity encourages thinly capitalized manufacturers by insulating them from responsibility for inferior products. Yet others have focused on the point that if implied warranties are effective against remote sellers it produces a chain of lawsuits or crossclaims against those up the distribution chain. And some focus on the reality in today's world that manufacturers focus on the consumer in communications promoting the product. See Spring Motors Distribs., Inc. v. Ford Motor Co., 98 N.J. 555, 489 A.2d 660, 676–77 (N.J. 1985) ("Eliminating the requirement of vertical privity is particularly appropriate in the present action where Spring Motors read advertisements published by Clark, specifically requested Clark transmissions, expected the transmissions to be incorporated into trucks to be manufactured by Ford, contracted with Ford only, and now seeks to recover its economic loss.").

Finally, some jurisdictions have abolished privity in warranty actions where only economic losses were sought based on the notion that there is "no reason to distinguish between recovery for personal and property injury, on the one hand, and economic loss on the other." Hiles Co. v. Johnston Pump Co., 560 P.2d 154, 157 (Nev. 1977). A variance on this theme is the view that abolishing privity "simply recognizes that economic loss is potentially devastating to the buyer of an unmerchantable product and that it is unjust to preclude any recovery from the manufacturer for such loss because of a lack of privity, when the slightest physical injury can give rise to strict liability under the same circumstances." *Groppel*, 616 S.W.2d at 59. One court preserving the privity requirement expressed the view that "there may be cases where the plaintiff may be unfairly prejudiced by the operation of the economic loss rule in combination with the privity requirement." Ramerth v. Hart, 983 P.2d 848, 852 (Idaho 1999).

In Indiana, the economic loss rule applies to bar recovery in tort "where a negligence claim is based upon the failure of a product to perform as expected and the plaintiff suffers only economic damages." *Martin Rispens*, 621 N.E.2d at 1089. Possibly because of the economic loss rule, Goodin did not raise a negligence claim here. Furthermore, at oral argument Goodin's attorney pointed to the warranty disclaimer in the Buyer's Order as a bar to Goodin's ability to sue her direct seller, AutoChoice, which could then have sued Hyundai for reimbursement. This disclaimer, Goodin contends, precluded a chain of claims ultimately reaching the manufacturer. Therefore, Goodin claims that if this Court does not abolish the vertical privity requirement she will be left without a remedy for Hyundai's breach of its implied warranty of merchantability, and Hyundai's implied warranty becomes nonexistent in practical terms.

The basis for the privity requirement in a contract claim is essentially the idea that the parties to a sale of goods are free to bargain for themselves and thus allocation of risk of failure of a product is best left to the private sector. Otherwise stated, the law should not impose a contract the parties do not wish to make. The Court of Appeals summarized this view well:

Generally privity extends to the parties to the contract of sale. It relates to the bargained for expectations of the buyer and seller. Accordingly, when the cause of action arises out of economic loss related to the loss of the bargain or profits and consequential damages related thereto, the bargained for expectations of buyer and seller are relevant and privity between them is still required. Implied warranties of merchantability and fitness for a particular use, as they relate to economic loss from the bargain, cannot then ordinarily be sustained between the buyer and a remote manufacturer. *Richards*, 384 N.E.2d at 1092. We think that this rationale has eroded to the point of invisibility as applied to many types of consumer goods in today's economy. The UCC recognizes an implied warranty of merchantability if "goods" are sold to "consumers" by one who ordinarily deals in this product. Warranties are often explicitly promoted as marketing tools, as was true in this case of the Hyundai warranties. Consumer expectations are framed by these legal developments to the point where technically advanced consumer goods are virtually always sold under express warranties, which, as a matter of federal law run to the consumer without regard to privity. 15 U.S.C. § 2310. Magnuson–Moss precludes a disclaimer of the implied warranty of merchantability as to consumer goods where an express warranty is given. 15 U.S.C. § 2308. Given this framework, we think ordinary consumers are entitled to, and do, expect that a consumer product sold under a warranty is merchantable, at least at the modest level of merchantability set by UCC section 2–314, where hazards common to the type of product do not render the product unfit for normal use.

Even if one party to the contract—the manufacturer—intends to extend an implied warranty only to the immediate purchaser, in a consumer setting, doing away with the privity requirement for a product subject to the Magnuson–Moss Warranty Act, rather than rewriting the deal, simply gives the consumer the contract the consumer expected. The manufacturer, on the other hand is encouraged to build quality into its products. To the extent there is a cost of adding uniform or standard quality in all products, the risk of a lemon is passed to all buyers in the form of pricing and not randomly distributed among those unfortunate enough to have acquired one of the lemons. Moreover, elimination of privity requirement gives consumers such as Goodin the value of their expected bargain, but will rarely do more than duplicate the Products Liability Act as to other consequential damages. The remedy for breach of implied warranty of merchantability is in most cases, including this one, the difference between "the value of the goods accepted and the value they would have had if they had been as warranted." 714 I.C. § 26–1–2–714(2). This gives the buyer the benefit of the bargain. In most cases, however, if any additional damages are available under the UCC as the result of abolishing privity, Indiana law would award the same damages under the Products Liability Act as personal injury or damage to "other property" from a "defective" product. Gunkel v. Renovations, Inc., 822 N.E.2d 150 (Ind. 2005).

For the reasons given above we conclude that Indiana law does not require vertical privity between a consumer and a manufacturer as a condition to a claim by the consumer against the manufacturer for breach of the manufacturer's implied warranty of merchantability.

Conclusion

The judgment of the trial court is affirmed.

NOTES

1. *Tex Enterprises* and *Goodin* disagree as to whether a non-privity plaintiff can recover from a remote seller for economic loss resulting from the seller's breach of an implied warranty. *Tex Enterprises* relies on 2–314 and 2–315's warranties to support its requirement of vertical privity. Both 2-314 and 2-315's warranties arise from an underlying contract between the seller and buyer. The court concludes that the "plain meaning" of these provisions bar recovery when the plaintiff is not a party to that contract or an intended beneficiary of it. Is the court's conclusion too quick? Consider Alternative A of 2–318, which is in effect in Washington. It allows a family member or guest of the buyer not in privity to recover from the buyer's seller breach of implied warranties. The family member or guest is not party to the sales contract and need not be an intended beneficiary of it. Given Alternative A, the plain language of 2–314 and 2–315 does not bar the non-privity plaintiff from recovering when not a party to the contract. Comment 3 to 2–318 warns that Alternative A "is not intended to enlarge or restrict the developing case law on whether the seller's warranties, given to his buyer who resells, extend to other persons in the distributive chain." The Comment signals that Alternative A takes no position on the requirement of vertical privity. If 2–314 and 2–315 barred the non-privity plaintiff from recovering, Comment 3 could not allow developing case law to abolish vertical privity.

2. In jurisdictions that require vertical privity the non-privity plaintiff must rely on two alternative theories of recovery. One theory is the contractual assignment. On appropriate facts, the plaintiff can argue that the immediate seller assigned all of its rights under the contract with the remote seller to it (the plaintiff). If the assigned contract contains implied warranties, the plaintiff as an assignee acquires the assignor's rights given by the warranties. See e.g. Tunison v. Hollow Oak Props., LLC, 2010 Conn. Super. LEXIS 2655, at *35 (Conn. Super. Ct. 2010). The second theory of recovery is as a third party beneficiary. The plaintiff's argument here is that it was the intended beneficiary of the remote seller's contract with its immediate seller. It therefore has a right to enforce the terms of that contract, including any implied warranties that arose from the contract. See, e.g., Harris Moran Seed v. Phillips, 949 So.2d 916 (Ala. Ct. App. 2006).

3. As *Tech Enterprises* and *Goodin* illustrate, courts disagree about the efficiency of the requirement of vertical privity. The disagreement reflects the difficulty of determining whether abolishing vertical privity produces a net benefit for the non-privity plaintiff. The matter cannot be settled by focusing only on the ultimate purchaser's expectations, as the court does in *Goodin*. The question is whether the ultimate purchaser gets a contract at a price it believes is worth paying for. This requires estimating both the benefits and costs of abolishing vertical privity to the purchaser. Clearly, abolishing vertical privity increases the value of the ultimate purchaser's contract with its immediate seller. This is because the purchaser can look to the remote seller to recover loss resulting from the seller's breach of warranties. Sometimes the remote seller is the purchaser's only recourse when its immediate seller has disclaimed all warranties, as was the case in *Goodin*, or is insolvent. Abolishing privity in these circumstances gives the purchaser a source of compensation it would not otherwise have. This makes the ultimate purchaser's contract with its immediate seller more valuable to it.

On the other hand, abolition of vertical privity increases the remote seller's expected liability for breach of warranty. This is because seller now bears the risk of nonconformity in the goods not only as against its immediate buyer but also as against all buyers of the goods in the distributive chain. In addition, the seller incurs litigation costs in defending against the ultimate buyer's warranty claim. The seller's increased expected liability increases the cost of performing the contract and therefore the contract price it offers its buyer. This increased price in turn is reflected in the contracts downstream that sellers offer their buyers. An important element of the seller's liability is its responsibility for consequential damages resulting from breach. Often consequential damages dwarf direct damages in the form of diminution in value of the product. The variance in consequential damages is high, depending on the buyer's particular circumstances. While sellers might have tolerably reliable information about their immediate buyer's circumstances, so that they can estimate the size of consequential damages resulting from breach of warranty, their information about the circumstances of remote buyers of their products is sparse and unreliable. If the ultimate buyers are better positioned to manage their own damages from the remote seller's breach, they might not benefit on balance from the increased contract price resulting from abolishing vertical privity.

Even some of the courts that have rejected vertical privity appear to be sensitive to this consideration. They have not required privity for plaintiffs seeking to recover direct economic loss (i.e., diminution in value of the good). See Morrow v. New Moon Homes, Inc., 548 P.2d 279 (Alaska 1976), *Goodin*. However, courts that otherwise allow the non-privity plaintiff to recover direct damages from its remote seller have not allowed recovery of indirect economic loss, such as lost profits. See Garden Gate, Inc. v. Northstar Freeze–Dry Mfg., Inc., 526 N.W.2d 305 (Iowa 1995); Beard Plumbing and Heating, Inc., v. Thompson Plastics, Inc., 152 F.3d 313 (4th Cir. 1998).

4. Courts that have rejected vertical privity have had to decide whether, and how, Article 2's provisions that apply to the ultimate purchaser's contract with its immediate seller also apply to the remote seller. The issue arises particularly with respect to the buyer's right of revocation, notice of breach, and the running of the applicable statute of limitations. Authority is sharply split on these matters. Courts have disagreed as to whether the ultimate purchaser can revoke its acceptance of nonconforming goods as against the remote seller. Compare Deere & Co. v. Johnston, 67 Fed. Appx. 253 (5th Cir. 2003) (revocation permissible), with AG Connection Sales, Inc. v. Greene County Motor Co., 67 UCC Rep. Serv.2d 312 (D. Kan. 2008) (buyer cannot revoke). Some courts require the ultimate purchaser to give notice to the remote seller in accordance with 2–607(3)(a); others do not. Compare Hobbs v. General Motors Corp., 134 F. Supp.2d 1277 (M.D. Ala. 2001) (notice required) with Firestone Tire & Rubber Co. v. Cannon, 452 A.2d 192 (Md. Ct. App. 1982) (notice not required). Finally, courts disagree over whether 2–725(1)'s four-year limitations period begins to run from the remote seller's tender of delivery to its immediate buyer, rather than from the immediate seller's tender of delivery to the ultimate purchaser. Compare Wilson v. Class, 1992 Del. Super. LEXIS 105, at *7 (Del. Super. Ct. 1992) (tender of delivery to the immediate buyer) with Coady v. Marvin Lumber & Cedar Co., 167 F. Supp. 2d 166, 167 (D. Mass. 2001) (tender to ultimate purchaser). Courts are even divided over whether the remote seller's effective warranty disclaimer against an immediate buyer are effective against the ultimate purchaser. Compare Wenner Petroleum Corp. v. Mitsui & Co. (USA), Inc., 748 P.2d 356 (Colo. Ct. App. 1987) (remains effective) with Prof'l. Lens Plan, Inc. v. Polaris Leasing Corp., 234 Kan. 742 (Kan. 1984) (ineffective).

5. Article 2A, applicable to leases, states the three alternatives that 2–318 offers for sales of goods. 2A–216. Although possible, states are unlikely to adopt different alternatives for sales and leases. As with 2–316, 2A–216 leaves to courts the question as to whether the non-privity plaintiff can bring an action against the lessor for breach of lease warranties. Suppose Lessee enters into a lease with Lessor after selecting the goods from Manufacturer and instructing Lessor to purchase them. Manufacturer's goods come with an implied warranty of merchantability. Later, after Manufacturer has become insolvent, the goods prove unfit for the ordinary purposes to which they are put and Lessee sues Lessor for breach of an implied warranty of merchantability. Will Lessee's suit be dismissed? See 2A–103(1)(g), 2A–209, Comment 1 to 2A–209, 2A–212; cf. 2A–216.

2. THE CONTRACT–TORT DIVIDE

A breach of warranty often presents facts that potentially make the seller liable in tort. For instance, the seller's breach of an express warranty can be recast as negligence, fraud, or negligent or innocent misrepresentation. Or the sale of nonconforming goods can make the seller strictly liable under the law of products liability. Whether the seller is liable in contract or tort would not matter if the limitations of the two areas of law were the same. But they are not. Contract and tort law differ in at least five respects relevant to warranties. (1) *Notice.* Notice of breach is required to recover for breach of warranty. Notice is not required for tort recovery. (2) *Statutes of limitation.* Although 2–725(2)'s four-year limitation period is longer than the typical limitation period for torts, tort law often delays the running of the period until the injury is discoverable. (3) *Disclaimers.* Warranty law enforces warranty disclaimers that allocate risk by contract. Disclaimers either are not enforceable in tort or given extremely limited effect. (4) *Damages.* The sales contract can limit or exclude types of damage that are recoverable on breach of warranty. These contractual limitations on damages are not enforceable in tort. (5) *Privity.* While privity sometimes is required for a breach of warranty action, privity is not required for recovery in tort. Given these differences, buyers typically add tort counts to their warranty claims.

a. THE UCC

The issue of the relationship between contract and tort liability frequently arises where personal injury occurs. In most cases the plaintiff will have alternative causes of action for breach of warranty and strict products liability in tort. Strict products liability makes the seller liable without fault when it sells a product in a defective condition rendering the product unreasonably dangerous to the user or its property. Restatement (Second) of Torts, § 402A (1965). To recover, the user (buyer) need only prove its injury resulted from the unreasonably dangerous condition of the product. The buyer need not establish privity or breach of warranty. In addition, the seller is liable without regard to contractually allocated risks.

Most courts apply the economic loss doctrine to determine whether the seller's liability for tendering a nonconforming good must be established in tort or contract. Under a strict version of the doctrine, the plaintiff who suffers only monetary loss as a result of the seller's breach cannot recover in tort. The plaintiff must recover its losses in contract, if at all. Economic loss includes loss in the value of the good, repair costs, incidental expenses and consequential damages such as lost profit. Courts tend to adopt a modest version of the economic loss doctrine, which allows a limited exception. The modest version of the doctrine does not allow tort liability for economic loss unless the loss is accompanied by physical injury or property damage other than to the purchased product. "Other property damage" is a legal term of art. Damage to the purchased product results in the loss of its value. This sort of damage is not considered "property damage." Instead, the doctrine considers the damage to the product itself to be a type of economic loss. The exception for property damage applies when breach results in damage to property other than the product itself. If breach results in personal injury or "other" property damage, the plaintiff can recover all of its loss (including economic loss) in tort. The Restatement (Third) of Torts (1998) follows the modest version of the economic loss rule, as does some state statutes. See Restatement (Third) of Torts §§ 1, 21; Minn. § 604.101 (2010).

A pair of influential Supreme Court cases illustrates what counts as other property damage. The Court endorsed the modest version of the economic loss doctrine in East River S.S. Corp. v. Transamerica Delaval, Inc., 476 U.S. 858 (1986). There, a contractor agreed to build and install turbines in four of the shipbuilder's ships under construction. The turbines failed after being installed and the shipbuilder incurred costs in repairing them and lost income while the ships were out of service. The shipbuilder sued the contractor in tort, alleging negligence and strict liability for design defects. In rejecting the shipbuilder's tort claims, the Supreme Court found that damage to the turbines resulted in their not meeting the shipbuilder's expectations. The Court held that this loss was economic and recoverable only as a claim for breach of warranty. The fact that the failure of the turbines damaged the ship's propulsion system did not allow suit in tort. Id. at 467. Thus, in barring the tort suit, the Court concluded that damage to a system of which the defective good is a part does not count as "other" property.

The second case is Saratoga Fishing Co. v. J.M. Martinac & Co., 520 U.S. 875 (1997). In *Saratoga Fishing*, a fishing vessel sank as a result of a defective hydraulic system. The owner of the vessel at the time it sank had purchased it from a previous owner. Before the previous owner sold the ship, he had added equipment to the vessel. The Supreme Court had to decide whether the owner's tort suit against the manufacturer was barred by the economic loss doctrine. To do so, it had to decide whether the equipment added by the previous owner was "other" property. The Court found that the added equipment counted as other property for purposes of the economic loss doctrine. To the manufacturer's worry that tort law does not limit potential liability, the Court thought that the doctrines of foreseeability, proximate cause and the economic loss doctrine itself limit liability for economic loss. Id. at 884. Although *East River* and *Saratoga Fishing* are admiralty cases and not binding authority for state law, courts tend to have accepted the conclusions these cases reach.

The distinction between the product itself and "other" property is clear, and identifying when the product is a component of an integrated system in most cases is relatively easy. But the question is why the distinction and identification should matter. The contract can and does allocate loss between the parties and, if the parties prefer, can distinguish between types of property damage. The same is true for loss from personal injury. The cost of negotiating for these types of loss is low because the parties are already contracting for other terms of the sales agreement. This is not a many-person, high-negotiation cost environment where tort law rules are suitable. For example, parties to a security agreement can and do provide for a security interest in both existing and after-acquired collateral. See 9–204(a). Merely because the debtor does not have rights in after-acquired collateral at the time the security agreement is concluded does not prevent it from in advance granting rights in the collateral acquired later. Similarly, the fact that "other" property is involved should not prevent parties from allocating the risk of damage to it by in advance by contract. The same goes for the risk of personal injury. Section 2–719(3) already allows this, subject to the usual limitation of unconscionability. More generally, the contract, not the economic loss doctrine, can determine whether recovery can be in contract. While a few cases adopt a contractual approach to recovery (e.g., *Idaho Power Co. v. Westinghouse Electric Corp.*, 596 F.2d 924 (9th Cir. 1979)), most do not. Consider in this regard *Coach USA, Inc. v. Van Hool N.V.*, reproduced below.

Coach USA, Inc. v. Van Hool N.V.

United States District Court, Western District of Wisconsin, 2006
2006 U.S. Dist. LEXIS 88783

■ Opinion and order: CRABB, DISTRICT JUDGE

In this civil action for monetary relief, plaintiffs Coach USA, Inc. and Keeshin Charter Services, Inc. contend that defendants Van Hool N.V. and ABC Bus Companies, Inc. are liable in tort for damage caused when a bus manufactured by Van Hool and leased to plaintiffs by Coach USA caught fire on July 15, 2005. Jurisdiction is present under 28 U.S.C. § 1332.

Presently before the court is defendant ABC Bus Companies, Inc.'s motion to dismiss plaintiffs' claims against it under Fed. R. Civ. P. 12(b)(6). (Defendant Van Hool is not a party to the pending motion. Therefore, all references to "defendant" will be to defendant ABC Bus Company.) The motion will be granted because the parties' contract expressly bars the claims plaintiffs have brought against defendant in this lawsuit. * * *

Factual Allegations

A.   Parties

Plaintiff Coach USA, Inc. is a Delaware corporation with its principal place of business in Paramus, New Jersey. Plaintiff Keeshin Charter Service, Inc. is an Illinois corporation with its principal place of business in Chicago, Illinois. It is a wholly owned subsidiary of plaintiff Coach USA. Defendant Van Hool, N.V. is a foreign corporation organized under the laws of Belgium. Defendant ABC Bus Company is a Minnesota corporation with its principal place of business in Faribault, Minnesota.

B.   Lease Agreement

On February 1, 2002, plaintiff Coach USA entered into a lease agreement with defendant ABC Bus Company in which the bus company leased to plaintiff Coach USA for a period of 60 months a 1997 Van Hool T945 bus, manufactured by defendant Van Hool. Under the terms of the lease, plaintiff was obligated to lease the bus for the full 60 months, after which it would be given the option of purchasing the vehicle for the price of $41,000.

The lease agreement provided:

> This agreement creates a lease of Equipment only and does not create a sale thereof or the creation of any other interest in or to the Equipment by Lessee. Lessor shall remain the sole owner of the Equipment, and nothing contained in this agreement or in the payment of rent hereunder shall enable Lessee to acquire any right, title or interest in or to the Equipment not specifically set forth herein.

Contained in the lease agreement was a warranty clause, which stated:

> Except as otherwise provided ... LESSOR MAKES NO WARRANTY, REPRESENTATION, OR GUARANTEE, EXPRESS OR IMPLIED, WRITTEN OR ORAL, OF MECHANICAL CONDITION, RELIABILITY, CAPACITY, MERCHANTIBILITY, OR FITNESS FOR ANY PARTICULAR PURPOSE WHATSOEVER. THE EQUIPMENT IS LEASED AND ACCEPTED BY LESSEE STRICTLY "AS IS." LESSOR SPECIFICALLY DISCLAIMS ANY WARRANTY OF MERCHANTABILITY OR FITNESS FOR ANY PARTICULAR PURPOSE AND ANY LIABILITY FOR ANY CONSEQUENTIAL OR INCIDENTAL DAMAGES ARISING OUT OF THE USE OF OR INABILITY TO USE THE EQUIPMENT. FURTHER, LESSEE SPECIFICALLY ACKNOWLEDGES THAT IT HAS HAD FULL OPPORTUNITY TO INSPECT SAID EQUIPMENT TO ITS FULL AND COMPLETE SATISFACTION. . . .

In addition, the agreement contained the following indemnity clause:

> Lessee hereby agrees to defend, indemnify and hold Lessor harmless from any and all liability arising out of the ownership, leasing, use, unauthorized use, licensing, maintenance, condition, or operation of the Equipment during the term of this Lease or as long as lessee has control over the Equipment . . .

> It is the parties' intention to shift all liability from lessor to Lessee whether the liability was, or may have been, caused in whole or in part by Lessor, Lessee, or both. The foregoing covenants of indemnity are absolute and unconditional and shall continue in full force and effect regardless of where, how or by whom the subject Equipment is operated . . .

> In addition to their customary meaning, the following definitions are provided: "liability" means but is not limited to, responsibility for any claim sounding in tort, contract or otherwise, for death, injury or damage to person, property, real or personal, tangible or intangible, or any other claim, loss or damage. "Indemnify" means, but is not limited to, the shifting of liability from lessor to lessee whether the liability was, or may have been, caused in whole or in part by Lessor, lessee or both. . . .

C. Accident

Plaintiffs used the leased bus to transport passengers and their personal property. On July 15, 2005, the bus caught fire while being driven on Interstate 90 North in Janesville, Wisconsin. The fire caused substantial damage to the vehicle and to passengers' personal property.

D. Lawsuit

On July 11, 2006, plaintiffs filed a lawsuit against defendants ABC Bus Companies and Van Hool in the Circuit Court for Rock County, Wisconsin. On August 18, 2006, defendants removed to this court. In their complaint, plaintiffs allege that defendant ABC Bus Companies owed plaintiffs a duty "to use reasonable care in the sale and distribution of the [bus]" leased to plaintiffs and that ABC breached that duty by:

a. S[elling] the subject vehicle which ABC knew was prone to a foreseeable hazard of an electrical malfunction which posed an unreasonable fire hazard;

b. Failing to properly inspect the subject vehicle for defects prior to certifying the subject vehicle as worthy to be placed in the stream of commerce;

c. Failing to properly route, secure, fasten, and protect battery cables and ground wires to avoid movement, abrasion and vibration;

d. Fail[ing] to provide, use and install adequate clamps, ties or securing devices to be [sic] fasten, hold and secure the battery cables and ground wires in a fixed position to prevent vibration and abrasion;

e. Fail[ing] to properly inspect the subject vehicle and ensure that the battery cables and ground wires in the motor coach were assembled and installed pursuant to SAEJ1292 Oct 1981 standards for motor coaches.

In the complaint, plaintiffs requested relief in the form of (1) "contribution and/or indemnification" for all damages plaintiffs paid to their passengers for the destruction of the passengers' personal property and (2) damages for the value of the bus and the loss of its use.

Opinion

A. Claims against Defendant ABC Bus Company

Although plaintiffs allege that defendant ABC Bus Companies, Inc. committed various torts against them, this is not a tort case. Rather, it is a case governed by the plain, unequivocal, unambiguous language of the parties' lease agreement. Under that agreement, defendant disclaimed all warranties and plaintiffs agreed that defendants would not be liable for any damages arising out of plaintiffs' use of the leased vehicle. Moreover, the agreement defines liability to include "responsibility for any claim sounding in tort, contract or otherwise, for death, injury or damage to person, property, real or personal, tangible or intangible, or any other claim, loss or damage." In short, the agreement precludes plaintiffs from raising any of the claims they are asserting against defendant in this lawsuit.

Plaintiffs seek to recover for damage to the bus and to the personal property of plaintiffs' passengers. Defendant points out (and by their silence on the matter, plaintiffs appear to concede) that plaintiffs do not and never have owned the vehicle in question. Under the terms of the lease agreement, defendant is the "sole owner" of the vehicle. Of course, it would be absurd to require the owner of the damaged vehicle to compensate the lessee for the value of the vehicle in which the lessee has no proprietary interest. Because plaintiffs have made no attempt to rebut defendant's argument on this point, I understand them to have withdrawn their request for money damages for harm caused to the bus itself.

That leaves plaintiffs' request for damage caused to their passengers' personal property. Plaintiffs contends that defendant is liable for this damage because it acted negligently by failing to inspect the vehicle and secure the bus's battery cables and ground wires. In its motion, defendant asserts alternate grounds upon which to dismiss plaintiffs' claims. First, it asserts, plaintiffs' tort claims are barred by the plain language of the lease agreement. In the alternative, defendant suggests that plaintiffs' claims are barred by the economic loss doctrine, which seeks "to preserve the distinction between contract and tort law and to prevent parties from eschewing agreed-upon contract remedies and seeking broader remedies under tort theory than the contract would have permitted." Cerabio LLC v. Wright Medical Technology, Inc., 410 F.3d 981, 987–988 (7th Cir. 2005).

In their response brief, plaintiffs ignore defendant's primary allegation, that the contract bars plaintiffs' claims. Instead, plaintiffs assert that an exception to Wisconsin's economic loss doctrine permits them to continue litigating their tort claims. They are mistaken.

The economic loss doctrine prevents "commercial contracting parties . . . [from] escalat[ing] their contract dispute into a charge of tortious misrepresentation if they could easily have protected themselves from the misrepresentation of which they now complain." All–Tech Telecom, Inc. v. Amway Corp., 174 F.3d 862, 866 (7th Cir. 1999) (applying Wisconsin law). For purposes of the doctrine, "economic loss" is "the loss in a product's value which occurs because the product is inferior in quality and does not work for the purposes for which it was manufactured and sold." Daanen & Janssen, Inc. v. Cedarapids, Inc., 573 N.W.2d 842, 845 (1998). The doctrine prevents "end runs" around a contract by prohibiting parties from reworking a disclaimed contract warranty into a legitimate tort claim, when the underlying complaint is the same: a product was defective. The economic loss doctrine applies primarily when a contract is silence with respect to tort claims, but is clear in its prohibition of contract warranties.

It is doubtful that reliance on the doctrine is necessary in cases like this one, in which the parties' contract disclaims expressly "any claim sounding in tort, contract or otherwise, for death, injury or damage to person, property, real or personal, tangible or intangible, or any other claim, loss or damage." See, e.g., Restatement (Third) of Torts, § 2 (1999) ("[A] contract between the plaintiff and another person absolving the person from liability for future harm bars the plaintiff's recovery from that person for harm."). When signing the lease agreement, the plaintiffs and defendant anticipated the possibility of future tort claims. Plaintiffs expressly disclaimed their ability to bring such actions. In the absence of any suggestion by the parties that the lease agreement is unenforceable, plaintiffs are not free to ignore the plain terms of their contract. To permit them to do so would be contrary to the parties' legitimate expectations at the time the lease agreement was signed and would violate the terms of their freely-negotiated agreement.

Even if I were to apply the economic loss doctrine to the facts of this case, the result would be the same. Under the doctrine, a party unhappy with the performance of a product may not seek in tort remedies that are unavailable to it under the terms of its contract. The reason for this is simple:

> Contract law, and the law of warranty in particular, is well suited to commercial controversies . . . because the parties may set

the terms of their own agreements. The manufacturer can restrict its liability, within limits, by disclaiming warranties or limiting remedies. In exchange, the purchaser pays less for the product. Since a commercial situation generally does not involve large disparities in bargaining power, [there is] no reason to intrude into the parties' allocation of the risk. East River S.S. Corp. v. Transamerica Delaval, Inc., 476 U.S. 858, 872–873 (1986) (applying economic loss doctrine in context of federal maritime law).

Plaintiffs assert that insofar as they are seeking damages for harm caused to their passengers' luggage, they are not complaining about the failure of the bus, but rather the damage the bus's failure caused to other property. Under Wisconsin law, when an allegedly defective product damages "other property," tort claims are not barred by the economic loss doctrine. Wausau Tile, Inc. v. County Concrete Corp., 593 N.W.2d 445 (1999) ("The economic loss doctrine does not preclude a product purchaser's claims of personal injury or damage to property other than the product itself.")

To determine whether damaged property is "other property," Wisconsin courts employ two tests: the "integrated system" test and the "disappointed expectations" test. Grams v. Milk Products, Inc., 699 N.W.2d 167 (Wisc. 2005). Under the "integrated system" test, courts determine whether the allegedly defective product is a component in a larger system. Id., P 27. "[O]nce a part becomes integrated into a completed product or system, the entire product or system ceases to be 'other property' for purposes of the economic loss doctrine." Selzer v. Brunsell Bros., 652 N.W.2d 806 (Wisc. Ct. App. 2002). However, if a product has no function apart from its value as a part of a larger system, the larger system and its component parts are not "other property." *Grams*, 699 N.W.2d 167. In this case, the luggage and other personal property for which plaintiffs are seeking damages were not integrated into the bus plaintiffs leased from defendant. Consequently, the integrated system test does not bar plaintiffs' tort claims. The next question is whether the disappointed expectations test does.

Under the disappointed expectations test, the "determination of whether particular damage qualifies as damage to 'other property' turns on the parties' expectations of the function of the bargained-for product." When "prevention of the subject risk was one of the contractual expectations motivating the purchase of the defective product," the economic loss doctrine applies to bar tort claims, even when the damages sought relate to property other than that which was the direct subject of the parties' contract.

Plaintiffs leased a bus from defendant for the purpose of transporting passengers and their personal property from one location to another. Given the fact that the parties' lease agreement made specific mention of "real or personal property," explicitly transferring all liability for damage from defendant to plaintiffs, it is clear that the type of property damage for which plaintiffs are seeking recovery was contemplated by the parties at the time they entered into the lease agreement. As a result, the "other property" exception cannot be used to defeat Wisconsin's economic loss doctrine.

Plaintiffs' claims against defendant are barred by the parties' lease agreement and by the doctrine of economic loss; therefore, defendant's motion to dismiss will be granted.

Order

It is ordered that the motion to dismiss of defendant ABC Bus Companies, Inc. is granted. Defendant ABC Bus Companies, Inc. is dismissed from this lawsuit, as are plaintiffs' claims against it.

NOTES

1.   In the lease agreement in *Coach USA* the lessor disclaimed liability for any tort claim for personal injury or damage to real or personal property. The court found that the agreement prevents the plaintiffs from suing the lessor in tort. It reasons that allowing suit "would be contrary to the parties' legitimate expectations at the time the lease agreement was signed and would violate the terms of their freely-negotiated agreement." The court is thereby suggesting that the contract, not the economic loss doctrine, determines whether recovery in tort is permitted. Would the court reach the same conclusion if the plaintiff had sued the lessor in tort to recover for personal injury? Very few courts have taken a contractual approach when personal injury is involved.

2.   Although the court doubts that reliance on the economic loss doctrine is necessary on the case's facts, it goes on to ask whether the economic loss doctrine applies to the lease of the bus. While the extension of the doctrine to service contracts has been controversial, courts and applicable statutes have applied it to leases of goods. See Minn. Stat. § 604.101 (2010); generally Reeder R. Fox & Patrick J. Loftus, Riding the Choppy Waters of East River: Economic Loss Doctrine Ten Years Later, 64 Def. Counsel J. 260, 266–268 (1997). The fire on the leased bus damaged both the bus and its passengers' personal property. In a non-technical sense, the latter obviously is "other" property. However, the court has to determine whether the passengers' possessions are "other" property for purposes of the economic loss doctrine. According to the *Coach USA* court, one of the tests Wisconsin courts employ to determine whether "other" property is damaged turns on disappointed expectations. Property is not "other" property if the parties have allocated the risk of damage to the property to the plaintiff. In this case the plaintiff's expectations with respect to the damage are not disappointed. Is Wisconsin's disappointed expectations test in fact a test to determine whether damage is to the product itself or to other property? Or is it simply a test to determine whether the parties have allocated the risk of damage to a type of property (product itself or other property) among themselves? The latter test determines whether the contract has allocated the risk. It makes application of the economic loss doctrine irrelevant.

3.   Although case law has tended to apply the modest version of the economic loss doctrine, some courts allow exceptions to it. One of the more popular is the "sudden and calamitous" exception. Courts which recognize the exception allow recovery in tort when economic loss results from a sudden and calamitous failure in the product. Damage to other property is unnecessary. Contrast Bailey Farms Inc. v. Nor–Am

Chem. Co., 27 F.3d 188 (6th Cir. 1994); Consumer Power Co. v. Curtis–Wright Corp., 780 F.2d 1093 (3d Cir. 1986) (exception recognized) with East River S.S. Corp. v. Transamerica Delaval Inc., 476 U.S. 858, 870 (1986) (rejected). Some courts also allow recover in tort for pure economic loss when the sales contract reflects a disparity in bargaining power between the parties. See AIG Aviation Ins. v. Avco Corp., 71 UCC Rep. Serv.2d 737 (D.N.M. 2010). A recent study of the judicial application of the economic loss doctrine in construction cases finds a significant increase in exceptions to the modest version of the doctrine; see Anthony Niblett, Richard A. Posner & Andrei Shleifer, The Evolution of a Legal Rule, 39 J. Legal Stud. 325 (2010).

PROBLEM 6.6

Manufacturer sold expensive drill bits to Bank after Customer Corp. had selected the products and directed Bank to purchase them. Prior to Bank's purchase, Customer approved the terms of the sale and agreed to in turn "lease" the drill bits from Bank. The agreement gave Customer the right to purchase the bits from Bank for $100 during the first year of the agreement. The bits proved to be unsuitable for drilling and injured Customer's employee who used them on a job site. Manufacturer had gone out of business and Customer's employee elected to sue only Bank. Assume that the applicable law adopts Alternative A of 2–318 and 2A–216. Can Customer recover damages from Bank for breach of an implied warranty of merchantability? See General Electric Credit Corp. v. Ger–Beck Machine Co., 806 F.2d 1207 (3d Cir. 1986); Northwest Collectors v. Gerritsen, 446 P.2d 197 (Wash. 1968). Would the result change if Bank and Customer's agreement did not give Customer the right to purchase the bits from Bank? Can Customer recover based on strict products liability or other tort theory? Compare Arriaga v. CitiCapital Commercial Corp., 167 Cal. App. 4th 1527, 1534 (Cal. Ct. App. 2008) (finance lessor not strictly liable) with Nath v. National Equipment Leasing, 439 A.2d 633, 682 (Pa. 1981) (dissent would find liability).

b. THE CISG

The relationship between contract and tort also causes trouble under the CISG. The question under domestic sales law is whether warranty or other contract liability displaces tort liability. When the CISG is applicable the question is whether it displaces domestic tort law. Article 4 provides in part that the CISG "governs only . . . the rights and obligations of the seller and buyer arising from such a contract." The implication of this language is that the CISG does not govern their rights and obligations that arise independently of the contract. Tort liability arises apart from the sales contract. Thus, Article 4's language suggests that applicable domestic tort law may continue to control tort liability, even when the CISG governs the sales contract.

This conclusion is controversial and too quick. There are two plausible views about the proper relationship between the CISG and tort law. One view adopts the position just given: tort law continues to apply at the same time the CISG applies to an issue arising under the contract. It "competes" with the CISG. The idea supporting this view is that the sales agreement creates contractual interests, while tort law creates non-contractual interests. See Peter Schlechtriem, The Borderline of Tort and Contract–Opening a New Frontier?, 21 Cornell Int'l L. J. 467, 474 (1988). For example, tort law's purpose is to protect against personal injury and property damage. It therefore gives individuals rights not to suffer personal injury. Because these rights do not depend on contract, they give individuals a non-contractual interest in bodily integrity. Similarly, tort law gives people a non-contractual interest in avoiding damage to their property. Although the risk of personal injury or property damage can be allocated by contract, the "competition" view allows the contractual allocation to leave these interests unaffected. For instance, assume that the seller's breach results in damage to the buyer's property. Assume also that applicable tort law gives the buyer a cause of action for this damage. Article 74 allows the injured party to recover consequential damages resulting from breach of contract, and Article 6 allows the contract to limit or exclude this recovery. Nonetheless, applicable domestic tort law continues to apply. As a result, the buyer can recover for its property damage in tort, even if it cannot recover under the sales contract.

The obvious consequence of the "competition" view is that the CISG's application will be limited. If a party benefits from its application, it will not rely on controlling tort law. However, if controlling tort law gives the party more extensive rights than under the contract and the CISG, it will not rely on the CISG. Instead, it will sue in tort. Two consequences follow. One is that the CISG will be applicable less frequently than if it displaces tort law. The other consequence is that, when tort law applies, the parties' rights will vary depending on the content of national tort law. In these cases divergent national laws replace the CISG's uniform rules. These consequences do not establish that the "competition" view is wrong. But they do suggest that the view frustrates the CISG's announced purpose of supplying uniform rules that govern international sales contracts; see Preamble (third paragraph).

An alternative view is that the CISG displaces applicable tort law when it addresses an issue also addressed by that law. This is the "issue displacement" view. Under Article 4 the CISG governs the rights and obligations of contracting parties arising from the contract. Other Articles define those rights and obligations. At the same time, Article 4(a) and (b) exclude certain issues that arise from the contract from the CISG's scope. As a result, if the CISG identifies and addresses an issue arising from the sales contract, it displaces tort and other non-CISG law addressing the same issue. If the CISG either does not identify an issue or identifies but does not address the issue, tort or other non-CISG law continues to control it. The legal terms in which domestic law describes the issue are irrelevant. Instead, whether the CISG identifies and addresses the issue alone matters. See Clayton P. Gillette & Steven D. Walt, Sales Law: Domestic and International 56–58 (2d ed. 2009). For example, assume again that the nonconformity in the good sold damages the buyer's property. Assume also this sort of damage was reasonably foreseeable by the seller in advance. Article 74 considers this loss consequential damage and includes it in the buyer's recoverable damages. Thus, the CISG identifies an issue (liability for foreseeable property damage resulting from breach) and addresses it (the damage is recoverable consequential damages). Domestic law which, on the same facts, allows the buyer to recover in tort for property damage therefore is preempted. The buyer's tort action is barred.

The CISG identifies some issues but does not address them either expressly or implicitly. Instead, it excludes these issues from the CISG's scope. For instance, Article 4(b) excludes from the CISG's scope the effect the contract may have on property in the goods sold. If the seller sells a good that is subject to a security interest, the CISG does not determine whether the buyer takes title to the good free of the security interest. The resolution of this issue is left to applicable domestic sales or secured transactions law. Finally, the CISG neither identifies some issues nor addresses them. In these cases domestic law again controls. For example, assume that the nonconformity in the goods render them unreasonably dangerous. Applicable products liability law holds the seller strictly liable in the circumstances. The seller is liable under that law not because the goods do not conform to the contract. It is liable because the goods as sold are unreasonably dangerous. This additional fact makes the seller's liability turn on an issue not identified or addressed by the CISG (the seller's liability for tendering unreasonably dangerous goods). Under the issue-displacement view, the CISG therefore does not preempt domestic tort law.

Electrocraft Arkansas, Inc. v. Super Electric Motors, Ltd.

United States District Court, Eastern District of Arkansas, 2009
70 UCC Rep. Serv.2d 716

■ Memorandum and order: WRIGHT, DISTRICT JUDGE

Electrocraft Arkansas, Inc. (Electrocraft) brings this action against Super Electric Motors, LTD (Super Electric) asserting the following claims in connection with allegedly defective refrigerator motors that Electrocraft purchased from Super Electric: violations of the United Nations Convention on Contracts for the International Sale of Goods (CISG); violations of Article 2 of the Uniform Commercial Code (UCC), codified in Ark. Code Ann. §§ 4–2–101 et seq.; breach of express warranty; breach of implied warranty of merchantability; negligence/strict liability; violations of the Arkansas Deceptive Trade Practices Act (ADTPA), codified in Ark. Code Ann. §§ 4–88–101 et seq.; tortious interference with a business expectancy; and unjust enrichment and restitution. Super Electric has counterclaimed against Electrocraft under the CISG and seeks judgment against Electrocraft for unpaid invoices in the amount of $1,126,077.92 and lost profits in excess of $1,000,000.

The matter is before the Court on motion of Super Electric to dismiss Electrocraft's complaint. Electrocraft has responded in opposition to Super Electric's motion and Super Electric has filed a reply to Electrocraft's response. For the reasons that follow, the Court grants in part and denies in part Super Electric's motion to dismiss.

I.

Electrocraft is a Delaware corporation doing business in the State of Arkansas and supplies electric refrigerator motors to manufacturers of refrigerators. Super Electric is a company engaged in the manufacture of refrigerator motors. Super Electric was formed under the laws of Hong Kong and its manufacturing facilities are located in Shenzhen, China.

Electrocraft states it has been purchasing refrigerator motors from Super Electric since approximately 2002 and that the motors were able to be utilized for their intended purpose after being inspected by Electrocraft. The motors would then be delivered to Electrocraft's customers, including Whirlpool and other manufacturers.

Electrocraft states that in July 2008, it began to receive notices from its customers that the motors supplied by Super Electric were failing at an unacceptable rate. Electrocraft states that it confirmed there were incurable problems with the motors as a result of manufacturing defects and that due to their failure to operate in the intended fashion, the defective motors have been returned to Electrocraft by the end user, causing Electrocraft to be unable to fulfill its contractual obligations to its customers. Electrocraft states it is currently in possession of approximately 300,000 defective motors manufactured and delivered by Super Electric without having any productive use.

Electrocraft states that representatives of Super Electric confirmed that the motors were defective but still demanded payment for the motors that had been delivered. Electrocraft states that despite demand, Super Electric has been unwilling or unable to cure the situation, to refund for paid invoices, or to void the unpaid invoices for the defective motors, and that Super Electric has caused it damage by way of the loss of existing customers, being forced to pay significant amounts to resolve customer claims and remedy customer complaints, and damage to its business reputation.

II.

Super Electric moves to dismiss Electrocraft's complaint on the following grounds: (1) count one of Electrocraft's complaint, asserting violations of the CISG, does not set forth sufficient facts to state a claim upon which relief can be granted under the CISG; (2) the CISG preempts and subsumes the breach of warranty claims contained in counts two and three of Electrocraft's complaint; (3) the CISG preempts and subsumes the negligence/strict liability claim in count four of Electrocraft's complaint; (4) the ADTPA claim in count five of Electrocraft's complaint is preempted by the CISG and must in any case be dismissed as the ADTPA applies only to actions brought by consumers; (5) the tortious interference with business expectancy claim in count six of Electrocraft's complaint is preempted by the CISG and Electrocraft additionally cannot plead facts to meet the elements of such a cause of action; and (6) the unjust enrichment and restitution claims in count seven of Electrocraft's complaint are preempted and subsumed by the CISG and, moreover, such claims under Arkansas law are not cognizable in circumstances in which the parties' rights and remedies are borne of a contract. * * *

B.

1.

The Court first addresses application of the CISG to this action. The CISG is an international treaty, ratified by the United States in 1986, that sets out substantive provisions of law to govern the formation of international sales contracts and the rights and obligations of the buyer and seller. The aim of the CISG is to promote worldwide uniformity in dealing with sales disputes arising from international sales. The CISG applies to international sales contracts between parties that are located in signatory countries, and who have not opted out of CISG coverage at the time of contracting. The People's Republic of China ratified the CISG in 1986 and Hong Kong is a Contracting State under the CISG. Neither Electrocraft nor Super Electric have opted out of the CISG with respect to the contract at issue in this action and both parties have their places of business in different Contracting States under the Convention. Accordingly, the Court finds that the CISG is the applicable law in this action.

2.

Having determined that the CISG is the applicable law in this action, the Court turns to Super Electric's arguments concerning application of the CISG to the claims in Electrocraft's complaint.

i.

Super Electric first argues that count one of Electrocraft's complaint, asserting violations of the CISG, does not set forth sufficient facts to state a claim upon which relief can be granted under the CISG. Super Electric argues that Electrocraft's CISG claim makes general and conclusory statements of liability under the CISG but does not set forth applicable CISG provisions so as to provide a legal framework for evaluating the allegations of the complaint, such as setting forth details about the notice of nonconformity or articulating whether Electrocraft inspected the goods within a reasonable amount of time. Electrocraft, however, explained its course of dealing with Super Electric and noted that the parties had a contract for the sale of goods, that Electrocraft inspected the goods, and that Electrocraft notified Super Electric of the nonconformity of the goods as soon as it learned of the nonconformity from customers (and that Super Electric confirmed the goods' nonconformity). The Court finds that Electrocraft has set forth at this juncture sufficient details underlying its CISG claim. While it may be that Electrocraft's CISG claim will not survive summary judgment or trial, Electrocraft has pled in count one of the complaint "enough facts to state a claim to relief that is plausible on its face."

ii.

Super Electric argues that even if a claim under the CISG has been stated, the CISG preempts Electrocraft's state law causes of action. Certainly, as a treaty to which the United States is a signatory, the CISG is federal law; thus, under the Supremacy Clause, it preempts inconsistent provisions of state law where it applies. The issue is one of scope. State law causes of action that fall within the scope of federal law are preempted. Id. Conversely, state law causes of action that fall outside the scope of federal law will not be preempted. Thus, the CISG preempts Electrocraft's state law claims only if such claims fall within the scope of the CISG.

a.

Concerning Electrocraft's breach of express and implied warranties under Article 2 of the Arkansas UCC as set forth in counts two and three of the complaint, Electrocraft "concedes that its breach of contract and warranty claims are rooted in the CISG" and essentially agrees that its breach of warranty claims under Article 2 of the Arkansas UCC are preempted by the CISG. Electrocraft states it asserted claims under the UCC only in the event this Court determined that Hong Kong was not a signatory of the CISG and that the CISG thus was not the applicable law. As previously noted, however, the Court today finds that Hong Kong is a Contracting State under the CISG and that the CISG is the applicable law to this action. Accordingly, Electrocraft's warranty claims under Article 2 of the Arkansas UCC—counts two and three of the complaint—are preempted and subsumed by the CISG. Electrocraft may, however, assert, consistent with its complaint, all rights and remedies under the CISG (as may Super Electric), including warranty provisions under CISG Article 35.

b.

Whether Electrocraft's negligence/strict liability claim in count four of the complaint falls within the scope of the CISG and is preempted presents a more difficult question given the relationship of tort and contract and their respective remedies. The CISG is exclusively concerned with the contractual relationship between the seller and the buyer. However, under most legal systems the mere existence of contractual remedies does not preclude a party from relying on other remedies, particularly those based on tort. In this respect, "[l]iability based on breach of an international sales contract falling under CISG may 'collide' or 'concur' with liability based on domestic tort law rules." Schlechtriem, The Borderland of Tort and Contract: Opening a New Frontier?, 21 Cornell Int'l L. J. at 467.

Commentators differ on the preemptive effect of the CISG on tort remedies. For example, one pair of commentators argue that "[i]f one seeks to achieve the greatest level of uniformity, it cannot be left to individual states to apply their domestic laws, whether contractual or based on tort" and that the need to promote uniformity as it is laid down in CISG Article 7(1) thus requires that "the CISG displaces any domestic rules if the facts that invoke such rules are the same that invoke the Convention." Schwenzer, Hachem, The CISG—Successes and Pitfalls, 57 Am. J. Comp. L. at 471. "In other words, wherever concurring domestic remedies are only concerned with the non-conformity of the goods—such as negligence in delivering nonconforming goods, negligent misrepresentation of their qualities, or mistake as to their substance—such remedies must be pre-empted by the CISG." Id.[1]

---

[1]   Although the aim of the CISG is to promote worldwide uniformity in dealing with sales disputes arising from international sales, obstacles to a uniform interpretation of the CISG have been noted, including the absence of a supranational body empowered to review and resolve conflicting decisions, and a tendency by some to interpret the CISG in conformity with the background assumptions and conceptions that the interpreter, trained in a particular domestic legal tradition, brings to the task, a tendency that has been labeled the "homeward

Another commentator argues that contractual and delictual remedies have coexisted in many jurisdictions for centuries, and a given State's ratification of the sales Convention does not imply its intention to merge contract with tort. Joseph Lookofsky, In Dubio Pro Conventione? Some Thoughts About Opt–Outs, Computer Programs, and Preemption Under the 1980 Vienna Sales Convention (CISG), 13 Duke J. Comp. & Int'l L. 263, 286 (2003). It is argued that "[t]he possibility that some domestic rules might be allowed to compete with (also applicable) CISG rules represents little threat to the global goal of achieving a uniform Convention interpretation, and the application of domestic rules should not be preempted simply because the operative facts of a given case seem 'covered' by a given CISG rule."

Despite differing viewpoints concerning the preemptive effect of the CISG on tort remedies, there is agreement that concurring state contractual claims are preempted by the CISG. Ingeborg Schwenzer, Buyers Remedies in the Case of Non–Conforming Goods: Some Problems in a Core Area of the CISG, 101 Am. Soc'y Int'l L. Proc. 416, 421 (2007). See also Forestal Guarani, S.A. v. Daros International, Inc., Civil Action No. 03–4821 (JAG), 2008 U.S. Dist. LEXIS 79734, at *2 n.4 (D.N.J. Oct. 08, 2008) (the CISG, a treaty of the United States, preempts state contract law and common law, to the extent those causes of action fall within the scope of the CISG). Thus, a tort that is in essence a contract claim and does not involve interests existing independently of contractual obligations (such as goods that cause bodily injury) will fall within the scope of the CISG regardless of the label given to the claim, see Schlechtriem, The Borderland of Tort and Contract: Opening a New Frontier?, 21 Cornell Int'l L. J. at 473, and therefore not require a determination concerning the preemptive effect of the CISG on tort remedies. See also Geneva Pharmaceuticals Tech. Corp. v. Barr Labs, Inc., 201 F.Supp.2d 236, 286 n.30 (S.D.N.Y. 2002) ("Just because a party labels a cause of action a 'tort' does not mean that it is automatically not pre-empted by the CISG. A tort that is actually a contract claim, or that bridges the gap between contract and tort law may very well be pre-empted") (citing Schlechtriem, The Borderland of Tort and Contract: Opening a New Frontier?, 21 Cornell Int'l L. J. at 474), aff'd in part, rev'd in part on other grounds, 386 F.3d 485 (2nd Cir. 2004). The question for this Court, then, is whether Electrocraft's negligence/strict liability claim is, as argued by Super Electric, "actually . . . a breach-of-contract claim in masquerade."

The difference between an action in contract and one in tort is not always exact. Damages prayed for are a factor to consider in determining whether an action is in contract or tort. The purpose of the law of contract is to see that promises are performed, whereas the law of torts provides redress for various injuries. Owing to that distinction, the measure of damages in contract cases differs from that in tort cases. In tort cases, the purposes of the law is to compensate the plaintiff for the injury inflicted even though it may have been unexpected, but in contract cases the special damages must have been in contemplation of the parties when the agreement was made.

---

trend." Harry Flechtner, Article 79 of the United Nations Convention on Contracts for the International Sale of Goods (CISG) as Rorschach Test: The Homeward Trend and Exemption for Delivering Non–Conforming Goods, 19 Pace Int'l L. Rev. 29, 30–31 (2007).

The Court has considered the matter and determines that Electrocraft's negligence/strict liability claim is based on contract. As previously noted, Electrocraft "concedes that its breach of contract and warranty claims are rooted in the CISG," and "it further concedes that its negligence [and, necessarily, strict liability] claim is based on the same factual allegations: that [Super Electric] had a duty to provide conforming goods to Electrocraft, it failed to do so and such failure caused Electrocraft to sustain damages." But these are not allegations of wrongdoing that are extra-contractual or otherwise amount to a breach of a duty distinct from or in addition to the breach of contract claim at issue in this action. Rather, the obligation of the seller to deliver goods conforming to the contract and the interests of the buyer to use, consume, or to resell the goods purchased, and therefore to receive them conforming to the contract, as alleged by Electrocraft, are economic interests that are basically contractual and regulated by the CISG and its rules and remedies for international sales. In addition, Electrocraft seeks identical damages for its negligence/strict liability claim as it seeks for its breach of contract and warranty claims. It is clear, then, that Electrocraft's negligence/strict liability claim is based on breach of contract, not breach of a non-contractual duty, and Electrocraft's negligence/strict liability claim in count four of the complaint is thus preempted by and subsumed within the CISG. Electrocraft may, however, assert, consistent with its complaint, all rights and remedies under the CISG, as may Super Electric.

c.

Concerning Electrocraft's unjust enrichment and restitution claims in count seven of the complaint, Electrocraft essentially agrees that to the extent Super Electric would concede or this Court would determine the existence of a valid contract, the unjust enrichment claim is preempted by the CISG. Super Electric does not dispute the existence of a valid contract, however, and so Electrocraft's unjust enrichment claim is preempted and subsumed by the CISG. In addition, Electrocraft states that its restitution claim is a remedy under the CISG. Accordingly, the Court finds that Electrocraft's unjust enrichment and restitution claims in count seven of the complaint are preempted and subsumed by the CISG. Electrocraft may, however, assert, consistent with its complaint, all rights and remedies under the CISG, as may Super Electric.

3.

The Court now turns to Super Electric's argument that Electrocraft's ADTPA claim in count five of the complaint is preempted by the CISG and must in any case be dismissed as that Act applies only to actions brought by consumers. The Court rejects both of these arguments.

First, the Court finds that the matters for which the ADTPA provides redress do not fall within the scope of the CISG as the CISG does not preempt claims for "misrepresentation, fraud, betrayal and intentional harm to economic interests." Schlechtriem, The Borderland of Tort and Contract: Opening a New Frontier?, 21 Cornell Int'l L.J. at 474. Accordingly, the CISG does not preempt Electrocraft's ADTPA claim.

The Court additionally finds that the ADTPA is not limited to actions brought by consumers. In support of its argument that the ADTPA is so limited, Super Electric cites Mosby v. International Paper Co., Inc., No. 5:07cv00314–WRW, 2008 U.S. Dist. LEXIS 50327, 2008 WL 2669148, at *2 (E.D.Ark. July 1, 2008). The Court does not find Mosby to be persuasive authority for the issue cited, however.

Mosby involved a situation in which the plaintiff alleged breach of contract and deceptive trade practices by International Paper Company, with which plaintiff had entered into a contract to be a contract logger. In determining that the plaintiff failed to state a cause of action under the ADTPA upon which relief can be granted, the court in *Mosby* quoted the Preamble to the ADTPA and concluded that "[a]pplying the ADTPA in a situation where the provider of services, rather than the consumer, was allegedly injured seems out of line with both the ADTPA's purpose, and case law under the ADTPA," and that "[b]ecause the ADTPA was enacted to protect consumers, the facts alleged under Plaintiff's ADTPA cause of action do not appear to be of the type that give rise to a cause of action under that Act." 2008 U.S. Dist. LEXIS 50327, 2008 WL 2669148, at *2. But even though it may initially seem or appear that the ADTPA does not apply to non-consumers, the plain and unambiguous language of the ADTPA is controlling, and in that regard, the ADTPA makes clear that (1) the Act is meant to protect both the consumer public and the legitimate business community, see Ark. Code Ann. § 4–88–105(c) (Act creates Consumer Protection Division to protect legitimate business community and the general public as consumers), and (2) Ark. Code Ann. § 4–88–113(f) allows a cause of action for any person who suffers damages as a result of an unconscionable, false or deceptive act or practice in business, commerce, or trade, with "person" being defined in Ark. Code Ann. § 4–88–102(5) as an "individual, organization, group, association, partnership, corporation, or any combination of them." The ADTPA "does not state that business entities or non-consumers cannot utilize its provisions as a basis for recovery" and, "[t]hus, one does not have to be a consumer to recover under the ADTPA." Valor Healthcare, Inc. v. Pinkerton, No. 08–6015, 2008 U.S. Dist. LEXIS 105988, 2008 WL 5396622, at *3 (W.D.Ark. Dec. 23, 2008). Accordingly, the Court denies Super Electric's motion to dismiss Electrocraft's ADTPA claim in count five of the complaint.

4.

Finally, Super Electric argues that Electrocraft's tortious interference with business expectancy claim in count six of the complaint is preempted by the CISG and that Electrocraft in any case cannot plead facts to meet the elements of such a cause of action. The Court disagrees.

First, being a tort claim alleging intentional harm to economic interests, the Court concludes that Electrocraft's tortious interference with business expectancy claim is not preempted by the CISG, which only concerns the sales of goods between merchants in different countries.

The Court additionally finds that Electrocraft has sufficiently pled a tortious interference with business expectancy claim. The elements of tortious interference that must be proved are: (1) the existence of a valid contractual relationship or a business expectancy; (2) knowledge of the relationship or expectancy on the part of the interfering party; (3) intentional interference inducing or causing a breach or termination of the relationship or expectancy; and (4) resultant damage to the party whose relationship or expectancy has been disrupted. The conduct of the defendant must be at least "improper." In determining whether an actor's conduct in intentionally interfering with a contract or a prospective contractual relation of another is improper or not, consideration is given to the following factors: (a) the nature of the actor's conduct; (b) the actor's motive; (c) the interests of the other with which the actor's conduct interferes; (d) the interests sought to be advanced by the actor; (e) the social interests in protecting the freedom of action of the actor and the contractual interests of the other; and (f) the proximity or remoteness of the actor's conduct to the interference and the relations between the parties. Intentional torts involve consequences which the actor believes are substantially certain to follow his actions. The defendant must have either desired to bring about the harm to the plaintiff or have known that this result was substantially certain to be produced by his conduct.

Super Electric argues that Electrocraft cannot plead facts supporting the third element of a tortious interference claim, i.e., that Super Electric engaged in any intentional, improper interference with Electrocraft's relationships or expectancies. Electrocraft alleges, however, that Super Electric knowingly supplied defective motors despite the knowledge that Electrocraft was dependent upon Super Electric to supply conforming motors, and that as a direct and proximate result of Super Electric's tortious interference, and because Super Electric's conduct in this matter was willful and malicious, it caused the termination of Electrocraft's business expectancy with Whirlpool and another manufacturer. The Court finds that Electrocraft has sufficiently pled at this juncture a tortious interference claim. While it may be that Electrocraft's tortious interference claim will not survive summary judgment or trial, Electrocraft has pled in count six of the complaint "enough facts to state a claim to relief that is plausible on its face."

III.

For the foregoing reasons, the Court grants in part and denies in part Super Electric's motion to dismiss.

PROBLEM 6.7

Assume that the CISG governs the sales contracts described below. Does the CISG preempt applicable domestic law described in the following cases? CISG Articles 4, 5.

(a) Seller expressly warranted that the widgets it delivers to Buyer will remain operable. Three years later Buyer discovered that the widgets do not work. It immediately notified Seller that the widgets have failed. Buyer was not in a position to discover this fact before that date. A state Buyer Protection Statute entitles a buyer who receives nonconforming goods to return them to its seller on timely notification of the nonconformity.

(b) At the time Seller delivered the widgets in (a) it knew that they would not continue to work. State tort law makes Seller liable to Buyer based on fraud.

(c) Seller's sale of widgets to Buyer violated export control restrictions under the U.S. Export Administration Act.

(d) The widgets Seller delivered failed, injuring Buyer.

F. THE MAGNUSON–MOSS WARRANTY ACT

Law other than the UCC increasingly governs warranties previously governed exclusively by the UCC. Both state and federal law regulates warranties in some sales transactions, particularly in consumer sales. Some state consumer protection acts prohibit disclaimers of implied warranties in consumer transactions. See, e.g., Mass. Ann. Laws ch. 106, § 2–316A, Md. Com. Law Ann. § 2–316, Vt. Stat. Ann. tit. 9A, § 2–316(5). Much more prevalent are state "lemon" laws, which apply to sales of new motor vehicles to consumer buyers. These laws give the buyers rights when the manufacturer has made an applicable express warranty covering the car. The most important right concerns the buyer's remedies when the car does not conform to warranties. Nonconformity is defined as a defect that substantially impairs the use, value or safety of the vehicle. Lemon laws give the buyer a right to a refund or replacement car when the manufacturer cannot fix the nonconformity after a reasonable number of attempts or time. In one respect, this remedy replicates remedies available to the buyer under 2–711. Section 2–711's remedies are available to it when a remedy limitation fails of its essential purpose, as when the seller fails to make a successful and timely repair. However, lemon laws provide an objective standard for an untimely repair, typically after four attempts at repair.

The Magnuson–Moss Warranty Act ("the Act"), 12 U.S.C. §§ 2301–2312, is the most important federal law affecting warranties. The Act applies when, as part of the sale, a warrantor gives a written warranty to a consumer on a consumer product. Because the Act is triggered only when a written warranty has been made, it applies most often to manufacturers of goods who include such warranties in the sales materials or packaging that accompanies the goods. The Act is principally a disclosure statute. Its drafters believed that disclosure would induce market competition resulting in consumer products being covered by extensive warranties. The Act does not require anyone to make a warranty at all. In fact, the Act states that the Federal Trade Commission ("FTC") does not have the authority to mandate warranties or their duration. § 2302(b)(2). It merely requires the person making the written warranty to do so in a prescribed way that makes it less likely to deceive consumers. In addition, the Act prevents the warrantor from disclaiming implied warranties. As authorized by the Act, the FTC has produced rules regulating warranties covered by it. 16 C.F.R. Parts 700–703. The Act's provisions may be enforced by the Attorney General and the FTC. § 2310(c)(1). Finally, a consumer damaged by a breach of a written warranty or implied warranty may sue. § 2310(d)(1). The latter creates a federal right of action for breach of a written or implied warranty. The consumer who prevails in an action brought under the

Act may recover attorney's fees. This makes bringing suit under the Act more attractive to consumers than suing under the UCC.

By its terms, the Act governs "written warranties" made by warrantors to "consumers" who purchase "consumer products." Each of the terms in quotation marks has a specific meaning peculiar to the Act. Because the Act's definition of a "written warranty" differs from 2–313's definition of an express warranty, a written warranty under the Act may not be a 2–313 express warranty. In general, the Act's definition is narrower than 2–313's definition. A written promise or affirmation that the product had no defects in material or workmanship is a "written warranty" if the promise forms the basis of the bargain. § 2301(6)(A). The promise or affirmation also is an express warranty under 2–313(1). However, a written representation about characteristics of the product other than defects in materials or workmanship, while an express warranty under 2–313(1), is not a written warranty under the Act. Oral express warranties also obviously are not written warranties. At least one influential case has held that "written warranties" do not include promises or affirmations made in documents associated with the written warranty, such as advertisements and brochures. See Skelton v. General Motors Corp., 660 F.2d 311 (7th Cir. 1981). These collateral promises or affirmations can be express warranties under 2–313.

In one respect a written warranty under the Act is broader than a 2–313 express warranty. The Act counts as a written warranty certain written service contracts offered in connection with the sale of a consumer product. In particular, a written undertaking to remedy a defect in the product stated in the undertaking is a written warranty. § 2301(6)(B). By comparison, 2–313(1) does not consider a remedial promise to be an express warranty. For example, the car manufacturer in *Hyundai Motor America, Inc. v. Goodin*, reproduced above, gave a written promise to repair or replace defective parts of the brake system within 5 years or 60,000 miles. When the manufacturer's dealer failed to fix the car's brake system after repeated attempts, the buyer sued under the Magnuson-Moss Act for inter alia breach of an "express warranty." Strictly, the buyer's allegation is that the manufacturer breached its written warranty. Because the buyer's theory of breach is that the manufacturer failed to perform its remedial promise, the allegation is not that it breached its 2–313 express warranty. The breach of the remedial promise puts the buyer's suit within the Act's scope.

The Act applies only to consumer goods distributed in commerce. Warranties on services relating to these goods are not covered. FTC § 700.1(g). "Consumer products" are tangible personal property normally used for personal, family or household purposes. § 2301(1). They remain consumer products even if they become affixed to realty, as with certain stoves and air conditioning units. In looking to the normal purpose to which a product is put, the definition of "consumer product" uses an objective standard. The normal use is the statistically frequent use. As a result, the peculiar purpose to which a consumer buyer might put a product does not determine whether it is a "consumer product." For example, a consumer might purchase a helicopter for a family vacation. The helicopter nonetheless is not a consumer product, because helicopters normally are not purchased for personal, family or household purposes. See FTC § 700.1(a). Conversely, a product normally used for these purposes but purchased for commercial purposes remains a consumer product. If Google buys home computers for its headquarters, the computers remain consumer products in Google's hands. By contrast, the definition of consumer goods in the UCC uses a subjective standard. Under 9–102(a)(23), for example, a good is a consumer good if it is used or bought primarily for personal, household or family purposes. For purposes of the UCC, the helicopter is a consumer product.

The Act's definition of "consumer" is broad. It covers three types of persons. § 2301(3). One is a buyer of the consumer product for purposes other than resale. This is the original purchaser of the product. A second type is the person to whom the product is transferred while the written or implied warranty continues to cover it. The third type of consumer is one whom state law entitles to enforce the warranty. Courts have had difficulty determining the people who fall within the third category. *Parrot v. DaimlerChrysler Corp.*, reproduced below, and the notes following it address the difficulty.

The Act requires that written warranties on consumer products actually costing the consumer $10 or more be clearly and conspicuously designated as either a "full warranty" or a "limited warranty." § 2303(a). (The FTC by regulation has increased the relevant threshold cost to $15 or more; FTC § 701.3.) In the designation the full warranty must state the duration of the warranty, while a limited warranty need not. A full warranty is one that meets the federal minimum standards for warranty. A limited warranty does not meet those requirements. The warrantor can offer both full and limited warranties on different parts of the same product, as long as the warranties are clearly and conspicuously designated. § 2305. For instance, a car manufacturer may offer a full 3–year warranty on a car's power train and a limited warranty on other car's other parts. The car manufacturer in *Hyundai Motor America, Inc.* v. *Goodin*, supra, gave three different limited warranties.

The designation is intended to supply consumers with a quick and easy way of learning about the extent of warranty protection on products they are purchasing. Because the Act allows the warrantor to decide whether to make a full or limited warranty (or no warranty at all), the warrantor can choose whether or not the warranty will meet federal minimum standards for warranty. A warranty that does not meet those standards does not violate the Act, assuming that the Act's designation and disclosure requirements are met. The Act's drafters believed that consumers prefer products with full warranties, thereby inducing warrantors to offer full rather than limited warranties.

To meet the federal minimum standards, the written warranty must contain certain provisions and not impose certain conditions on the consumer. § 2304. The warrantor must provide an effective and timely remedy in the event that the product fails to conform to the warranty. It generally cannot impose requirements on the consumer, other than notification, as a condition of obtaining the remedy. If the warrantor fails to timely fix the nonconformity, the warrantor must allow the consumer to elect either a refund or replacement without charge. The warranty cannot disclaim or limit the duration of implied warranties that arise under state law, such as warranties of merchantability and fitness for a particular purpose. It also cannot exclude or limit consequential damages for breach of warranty (written or implied), unless the exclusion or limitation is conspicuously indicated on the face of the written warranty. The Act does not preempt state law that disallows such exclusions or limitations. Accordingly, FTC regulation requires that the written warranty conspicuously indicate in a separate statement that applicable state law might not give effect to them. FTC § 701.3(9). The warranties of warrantors doing business at a national level will have potentially different damage limitations depending on where its products are sold.

A "limited warranty" is a written warranty that does not meet the federal minimum standards. Because the Act does not specify the content of limited warranties, warrantors have greater choice about their contents. Nonetheless, even a limited warranty cannot disclaim or modify implied warranties. § 2308(a). However, unlike a full warranty, a limited warranty can limit the duration of implied warranties to the duration of a written warranty of reasonable duration. § 2308(b). This allowance creates uncertainty in enforcement. The reasonableness of the duration of a limited warranty is not transparent and probably depends on the product. Because a limitation on duration of implied warranties is effective only if the duration of the written warranty is reasonable, warrantors will have difficulty determining whether the limitation is enforceable.

None of the Act's provisions require that the terms of a written warranty be simple and easy for the consumer to understand. Although the Act authorizes the FTC to prescribe rules making warranties readable (§ 2302), it has not done so. Instead, the FTC has taken a "softer" approach and offered suggestions for writing simple and understandable warranty terms. See FTC Staff, Writing Readable Warranties (June, 1993). The impact of the Act on frequency and content of written warranties has been modest. Most warrantors offer limited warranties when they offer Magnuson-Moss written warranties at all. A 1993 study found that the terms of warranties on both small and large appliances studied are not understandable by the 50 percent of the American adult population unable to read at an eighth-grade level. The majority of warranties studied required some college education to understand. In addition, the complexity of some warranties increased over time. See Ellen M. Moore & F. Kelly Shuptrine, Warranties: Continued Readability Problems After the 1975 Magnuson–Moss Warranty Act, 27 Cons. Affairs 23 (1993); cf. Michael J. Wisdom, An Empirical Study of the Magnuson–Moss Warranty Act, 31 Stan. L. Rev. 1117 (1979).

The Act is silent on privity requirements imposed under the law of many states. Where applicable, privity requires a plaintiff seeking to recover damages from the seller for breach of warranty to be in a contractual relation with the seller. The Act does not say whether it preempts state law privity requirements or continues to recognize the requirements where applicable. Courts have disagreed about the matter in the case of implied warranties. Decent arguments support both views. On the one hand, the Act gives the consumer a cause of action against a warrantor or supplier who has breached a written or implied warranty. § 2311(d)(1). A remote seller who makes a written warranty is a "warrantor," as is one who in its business makes the product covered by the warranty available to the consumer. A "consumer" is a person to whom the product is transferred while the warranty remains effective. Finally, a warrantor cannot disclaim implied warranties associated with the consumer product which comes into the consumer's hands. Seemingly, the consumer has a right of action against the warrantor for breach of implied warranties, even without privity. Some courts have relied on this reasoning to conclude that the Act displace state law requirements of privity. See Szajna v. General Motors Corp., 503 N.E.2d 760 (Ill. 1986). Other courts disagree. The Act defines "implied warranty" by reference to state law. § 2301(7). Although the Act prevents a warrantor from disclaiming implied warranties and requires it to take specified remedial actions when they are breached, the Act does not otherwise restrict state law regulating implied warranties. A requirement of privity therefore continues to apply. *Abraham v. Volkswagon of America,* reproduced below, finds this reasoning persuasive.

Abraham v. Volkswagon of America

United States Court of Appeals, Second Circuit, 1986
795 F.2d 238

■ WINTER, CIRCUIT JUDGE:

This litigation originated as a class action suit brought under the Magnuson–Moss Warranty Act, 15 U.S.C. §§ 2301–2312 (1982) ("Magnuson–Moss," "the Act"), involving alleged defects in the oil systems of Volkswagen Rabbits. The district court dismissed the class action for lack of subject matter jurisdiction. It concluded that only 75 of the 119 named plaintiffs had viable claims for relief, and thus that the Act's unique jurisdictional provision requiring a minimum of 100 named plaintiffs to bring a class action in a federal court had not been satisfied. The remaining individual claims were dismissed on the ground that they did not meet the joinder requirements of Rule 20(a), Fed. R. Civ. P., and thus could not be aggregated to satisfy another of the Act's jurisdictional provisions requiring a total amount in controversy of at least $50,000.

We hold that: (i) the district court used an improper procedure in resolving the 100 named plaintiffs jurisdictional question; (ii) implied warranty claims brought under the Magnuson–Moss Act are subject to state law privity rules; (iii) the express warranties in this case do not cover automobile defects manifesting themselves after expiration of the time/mileage limits of the relevant warranties; (iv) joint owners of automobiles may be counted only once toward satisfaction of the 100 named plaintiffs requirement; and (v) joinder of the remaining plaintiffs should have been allowed under Rule 20(a). We affirm in part, reverse in part, and remand.

Background

The 119 plaintiffs are owners of Volkswagen Rabbits, model years 1975–79. They brought a class action lawsuit against the manufacturer, Volkswagen of America ("VWOA") alleging, inter alia, breach of the express warranty given in connection with the sale of each car and breach of the implied warranty of merchantability. Their claim, as originally stated, was that the oil system in the 1975–79 Rabbits was defective, causing excessive oil consumption, engine damage and failure, and decreased resale value of the cars. Not all plaintiffs claim to have suffered each form of damage, but all claim to have suffered at least one of the varieties specified. The complaint, as later amended, alleged that the damages claimed resulted from a single defective part, the valve stem seal, which is supposed to prevent oil from leaking into the engine's combustion chamber. The seal allegedly was made of an inferior material that caused it to harden and crack prematurely, which in turn led to oil leakage and the other types of damage claimed.

Federal jurisdiction was invoked under the Magnuson–Moss Act. 15 U.S.C. §§ 2301–2312 (1982). This Act applies to all sales of consumer products in which a written warranty is given. Section 2310(d)(1) of the Act provides that "a consumer who is damaged by the failure of a supplier, warrantor, or service contractor to comply with any obligation under [the Act], or under a written warranty, implied warranty, or service contract, may bring suit for damages and other legal and equitable relief. . . ." 15 U.S.C. § 2310(d)(1). Federal and state courts have concurrent jurisdiction over Magnuson–Moss actions, id. § 2310(d)(1)(A), (B), but no claim is cognizable by a federal court if: (i) the amount in controversy of any individual claim is less than $25; (ii) the total amount in controversy is less than $50,000; or (iii) the action is brought as a class action by fewer than 100 named plaintiffs. 15 U.S.C. § 2310(d)(3)(A), (B), (C).

VWOA moved to dismiss the class action claims on the ground that the 100 named plaintiffs requirement was not satisfied and that the court thus lacked subject matter jurisdiction. It also moved to sever, and then dismiss for lack of subject matter jurisdiction, the individual damage claims on the ground that they did not satisfy the joinder requirements of Fed. R. Civ. P. 20(a) and thus could not be aggregated toward the $50,000 requirement.

VWOA sought discovery in connection with its motion to dismiss the class action for failing to comply with the 100 named plaintiffs requirement. The plaintiffs opposed discovery on the ground that it was a "merits inquiry" that was improper in determining a subject matter jurisdiction question. Following Walsh v. Ford Motor Co., 588 F. Supp. 1513, 1519–21 (D.D.C. 1984), the district court held, however, that the 100 named plaintiffs requirement could not be determined merely by examining the face of the complaint. 103 F.R.D. at 360–61. The district court stated that if individual claims could not be examined on the merits at the jurisdiction stage, "plaintiff could simply open up the local telephone directory and find 99 other individuals willing to place their names on a complaint and thereby defeat a motion to dismiss and permit the lone individual to proceed with discovery." The district court thus required the 119 named plaintiffs to answer interrogatories and comply with document requests regarding the details of their individual damage claims, such as place of purchase and mileages at which breakdowns had occurred.

The district court then proceeded to determine which individual claims should be counted. Again following Walsh, 588 F. Supp. at 1521, it held that joint owners named in the complaint as owners of Rabbits could be counted only once toward satisfaction of the 100 named plaintiffs threshold. 103 F.R.D. at 361–62. Thirteen pairs of plaintiffs fell into this category. The district court also ruled that express warranty claims for damage that occurred outside the time/mileage limits of the warranty were barred as a matter of law. 103 F.R.D. at 362. For 1975 Rabbits, the manufacturer's warranty covered the first 24 months or 24,000 miles, whichever came first. For 1976–79 Rabbits, the relevant coverage was 12 months or 20,000 miles. Evidence obtained during discovery revealed that 59 plaintiffs had claims for damage occurring after their respective express warranties had expired. Finally, the district court held that implied warranty claims were subject to the privity requirements of the law of the state in which the particular vehicle was purchased. The court determined that at least five relevant states—New York, New Jersey, Illinois, Indiana, Wisconsin (and perhaps Ohio)—required privity as an element of a valid implied warranty claim. Thirty-one plaintiffs had purchased their Rabbits in these five states and were not in privity with VWOA.

The final step in the district court's jurisdictional inquiry was a compilation of the named plaintiffs who possessed no valid claim. The court read the Act as requiring 100 named plaintiffs with either a valid express or implied warranty claim. 103 F.R.D. at 361. This holding is not challenged on appeal.

The named plaintiff count was reduced from 119 to 106 after subtraction of 13 joint owners. Fifty-nine plaintiffs were also found to have invalid express warranty claims. Of these 59, 31 were not in privity with VWOA and had purchased Rabbits in states requiring privity. These 31 thus had neither a valid express nor implied warranty claim against VWOA. The further subtraction of 31 yielded a final named plaintiff count of 75. The district court thus dismissed the class action for failure to meet the 100 named plaintiffs jurisdictional threshold of Section 2310(d)(3)(C).

The court next addressed the second element of the motion to dismiss—the motion to sever all remaining individual claims, and then to dismiss each one for lack of federal jurisdiction. This question turned on whether the $50,000 amount in controversy requirement of Section 2310(d)(3)(B) was satisfied. None of the 75 remaining plaintiffs claimed individual damage of that magnitude. However, individual claims may be aggregated toward satisfaction of the $50,000 requirement if the claims satisfy the requirements for joinder under Rule 20. 15 U.S.C. § 2310(d)(3)(B). The aggregate damage claims of the 75 remaining plaintiffs did exceed $50,000, but the court concluded that Rule 20 had not been satisfied. 103 F.R.D. at 363–64.

In denying joinder, the district court focused on Paragraph 22 of the First Amended Complaint, which alleged defects in a variety of components in the oil system, such as the oil pan, valve stem seals, and oil warning light. The answers to interrogatories revealed that some of the alleged defects had occurred on some cars but not others, and that some plaintiffs had needed repairs at 20,000 miles while others had not needed them until 80,000 miles. The court concluded that this disparity in timing of problems made the driving and maintenance history of each car vitally important to proof of each individual claim, 103 F.R.D. at 364, and thus held that the 75 plaintiffs had not satisfied the "same transaction or occurrence" test of Rule 20. It then dismissed all of the remaining individual claims.

Plaintiffs moved for reconsideration on the joinder issue, and for permission to amend the complaint to clarify the nature of the defect alleged. Permission to amend was granted. The substituted paragraphs of the complaint are set out in the margin. [Omitted.] They were designed to make clear that the same defect—the faulty valve stem seal—was alleged to be at fault in every case, and that the differences noted by the court, such as mileage disparities, went only to the amount of damage and not to the basis of liability. The district court was unpersuaded, however, and on June 25, 1985, again dismissed the action "for substantially the reasons set forth" in its earlier decision.

On appeal, the plaintiffs claim that the district court erred (i) in scrutinizing the merits of individual claims before ruling on the 100 named plaintiffs jurisdictional issue; (ii) in holding that state law privity rules apply to implied warranty claims under Magnuson–Moss; (iii) in holding that no valid written warranty claim can be made for damage occurring outside the applicable time/mileage limits of the warranty; (iv) in holding that joint owners of automobiles may only be counted as one plaintiff for jurisdictional purposes; and (v) in holding that the 75 remaining plaintiffs did not meet the Rule 20 requirement for joinder. For reasons stated infra, we address all these issues.

Discussion

* * *

2.   Implied Warranty and State Law Privity

The district court held that state law privity rules are applicable to implied warranty claims brought under Magnuson–Moss. 103 F.R.D. at 362. The effect of this holding was to dismiss implied warranty claims by owners who purchased used Rabbits and whose claims are governed by the law of a state that requires privity to enforce an implied warranty.

The language of the statute would seem to support the conclusion reached by the district court. An "implied warranty" is defined as "an implied warranty arising under State law (as modified by sections 2308 and 2304(a) . . .) in connection with the sale by a supplier of a consumer product." 15 U.S.C. § 2301(7). The "arising under" phrase strongly suggests that the obligations of the warranty are solely the creation of state law, an inference further strengthened by the explicit reference to "modifications" of such state law elsewhere in the Act, none of which deal with privity.

Plaintiffs counter with an argument based on other statutory language, however. Section 2308 provides that a "supplier" may not disclaim an "implied warranty" for the duration of any written warranty that it extends, while Section 2310(d)(1) provides in relevant part that "a consumer who is damaged by the failure of a supplier, warrantor, or service contractor to comply with any obligation under this chapter, or under an . . . implied warranty . . . may bring suit for damages and other legal and equitable relief." 15 U.S.C. § 2310(d)(1). The statutory definition of "consumer" includes "any person to whom [the] product is transferred during the duration of an implied or written warranty." 15 U.S.C. § 2301(3). Similarly, under the Act's definition of "supplier," a consumer can sue any party in the chain of production and distribution regardless of privity. 15 U.S.C. § 2301(4); House Report, supra, 1974 U.S. Code Cong. & Ad. News at 7717. Reading these provisions literally, they appear to provide for an action by a consumer without privity against a supplier on an implied warranty arising under the law of a state that does not allow transferees without privity to sue.

Conceding the anomaly, we turn to the legislative history. First, it is clear that Congress intended to restrict the ability of sellers to disclaim the warranties implied under state law. Prior to passage of Magnuson–Moss, the common practice of many sellers was to provide a written warranty that offered minimal protection and disclaimed all implied warranties. This practice often placed the consumer in a worse contractual position than if no warranty at all had been given, because implied warranty protection under the Uniform Commercial Code is often more extensive than the express warranty given by a seller. House Report, supra, 1974 U.S. Code Cong. & Ad. News at 7706. Because the very term "warranty" implies an increase in contractual protection to consumers, warranties that were largely disclaimers were in a real sense misleading.

Several sections of the Act thus ensure that a consumer with a written warranty also enjoys implied warranty protection. Id. at 7721– 22. Implied warranties: (i) may not be disclaimed if a written warranty, "full" or "limited," is given, 15 U.S.C. § 2308(a); (ii) may not be limited in duration if a full warranty is given, 15 U.S.C. § 2304(a)(2); and (iii) may be limited to the duration of a limited warranty only if the time limitation is not unreasonable or unconscionable, 15 U.S.C. § 2308(b). A seller is thus still free to offer a relatively worthless written warranty, 15 U.S.C. § 2303(a)(2), but by doing so is barred from disclaiming implied warranties arising under state law. 15 U.S.C. § 2308(a). The restrictions on a seller's power to disclaim implied warranty protection while giving a written warranty is thus a major change in the law of warranties.

Second, it is clear that with regard to written warranties, full or limited, privity is not required and transferees of the original purchaser may enforce them during their effective period. This result flows directly from the statutory definitions of "consumer," "supplier" and "warrantor," and from the enforcement provisions authorizing actions by consumers for breach of a written warranty. 15 U.S.C. § 2310(d). The 1971 bills did not contain such broad definitions and thus allowed sellers to restrict written warranties to original purchasers. See 1971 Hearings, supra, at 7–9, 22, 58, 62–63, 78. The definitions were altered during the legislative process prior to enactment. In making these changes, however, Congress did not focus on the privity requirements of state law regarding implied warranties but considered only the effect on written warranties. See House Report, 1974 U.S. Code Cong. & Ad. News 7717 ("where a warranty or service contract on a consumer product is given for a specified duration it would cover transferees who use the product"). The legislative history thus adequately explains the limits on a supplier's power to disclaim implied warranties and the abolition of privity with regard to written warranties. This explanation does not, however, illumine the import of the anomaly in the statutory language described above.

The legislative history of the provisions regarding implied warranties is more explicit and supports the view that state privity requirements applicable to such warranties were not supplanted by Magnuson–Moss. Section 2301(7), the "arising under State law" definition of implied warranty, was added to the House bill after the 1973 hearings. See H.R. 20, reprinted in 1973 Hearings, supra, at 3–28. The Senate bill as passed did not define implied warranty. See Senate Report, supra, at 11–14. However, it did include a version of what eventually became 15 U.S.C. § 2308, the section limiting a seller's power to disclaim implied warranties. The Senate Report states:

It is not the intent of the Committee to alter in any way the manner in which implied warranties are created under the Uniform Commercial Code. For instance, an implied warranty of fitness for particular purpose which might be created by an installing supplier is not, in many instances, enforceable by the consumer against the manufacturing supplier. The Committee does not intend to alter currently existing state law on these subjects. Senate Report, supra, at 21.

Because the Conference did not modify Section 2308 in a way relevant to the question we are considering—it adopted the House version allowing a warrantor to limit the duration of an implied warranty to the duration of the written limited warranty, H.R. Rep. No. 1606, 93d Cong., 2d Sess. 1–2 (1974) (conference report)—and because the Conference's adoption of the House's "arising under state law" definition of implied warranty is fully consistent with the statement in the Senate Report, id. at 2, we believe that state law, including privity requirements, governs implied warranties except where explicitly modified by Sections 2308 and 2304(a).

Plaintiffs argue that privity is an "antiquated" defense and that the Act's definitional provisions reflect a general purpose to do away with it. The statement in the Senate Report wholly undercuts these arguments. The Uniform Commercial Code creates two implied warranties pertinent to our inquiry: (i) of merchantability, § 2–314, and (ii) of fitness for a particular purpose, § 2–315. The controversy over privity, however, exists only in the case of the implied warranty of merchantability, which arises automatically in every sale of goods by one who is a merchant in those goods. U.C.C. § 2–314. In contrast, the implied warranty of fitness for a particular purpose, U.C.C. § 2–315, does not arise in every consumer sale, but only when a seller knows or has reason to know the particular purpose for which a buyer requires goods, and also knows or should know that the buyer is relying on his special knowledge. To have a cause of action for breach of an implied warranty of fitness, therefore, privity must necessarily exist because the creation of the warranty requires a direct exchange between buyer and seller. The Senate Report recognized this and explicitly stated that state law was to govern. However, the Report in no way limited the proposition stated to the implied warranty of fitness. Rather it used the implied warranty of fitness as an example illustrating the proposition that state law governed implied warranties generally.

Both the statutory language and the legislative history, therefore, indicate that Congress did not intend to supplant state law with regard to privity in the case of implied warranties.

3.   Time/Mileage Limits on Express Warranties

Plaintiffs also argue that a defect discovered outside the time or mileage limits of the applicable written warranty, but latent before that time, may be the basis of a valid express warranty claim if the warrantor knew of the defect at the time of sale. The district court, relying again on *Walsh*, concluded that a buyer holding a warranty with an express limitation as to the time or mileage bears the risk of repairs that become necessary beyond that period. The *Walsh* court, in a more extensive discussion of the issue, relied on several state court cases in holding that "latent defects" discovered after the term of the warranty are not actionable under the warranty. *Walsh*, 588 F. Supp. at 1536.

Relying on Alberti v. General Motors Corp., 600 F. Supp. 1026 (D.D.C. 1985), plaintiffs seek to distinguish the present case on the ground that the post-warranty failures alleged here resulted from latent defects known to VWOA at the time of sale. The court in *Alberti* held that the plaintiffs there stated valid express warranty claims, without regard to when breakdowns had occurred, because General Motors allegedly knew at the time of sale that the brake system on the cars in question was flawed and might cause control problems for drivers. 600 F. Supp. at 1028. The alleged defect thus "did not remain 'latent' . . . but, rather, was patent—at least to GM." Id. Plaintiffs here allege similar knowledge on VWOA's part as to the inferior nature of the valve stem seals.

The general rule is that an express warranty does not cover repairs made after the applicable time or mileage periods have elapsed. Plaintiffs argue, however, that the present case falls within the limited exception recognized in *Alberti*. We do not find the reasoning of *Alberti* persuasive and decline to follow it. The language of the decision itself suggests that the court confused concepts of implied and express warranty. The decision thus speaks of General Motors breaching its warranty that the cars would be "merchantable and fit for the purpose of providing the ordinary transportation . . . expected of them." *Alberti*, 600 F. Supp. at 1028. These terms and concepts are usually associated with the implied warranty of merchantability, as opposed to the type of limited express warranty at issue in this case and actually at issue in *Alberti*.

Moreover, virtually all product failures discovered in automobiles after expiration of the warranty can be attributed to a "latent defect" that existed at the time of sale or during the term of the warranty. All parts will wear out sooner or later and thus have a limited effective life. Manufacturers always have knowledge regarding the effective life of particular parts and the likelihood of their failing within a particular period of time. Such knowledge is easily demonstrated by the fact that manufacturers must predict rates of failure of particular parts in order to price warranties and thus can always be said to "know" that many parts will fail after the warranty period has expired. A rule that would make failure of a part actionable based on such "knowledge" would render meaningless time/mileage limitations in warranty coverage.
* * *

Conclusion

Although we hold that the district court used an improper procedure in addressing the 100 named plaintiffs requirement, it is clear that many plaintiffs must be dismissed and that the remaining plaintiffs amount to substantially fewer than 100. We believe it would serve no purpose to reverse those dismissals only to remand them to the certainty of another dismissal. We direct the parties to confer and seek to agree upon which dismissals must be affirmed under the guidelines established in this opinion. The clerk should be so informed within 10 days of this opinion. Upon remand, however, plaintiffs should be given an opportunity to substitute new named plaintiffs in an effort to satisfy the 100 named plaintiffs threshold requirement. Had the class been certified and the number of plaintiffs subsequently reduced to 75, plaintiffs would have had a right to notify members of the class of the opportunity to become a named plaintiff. On remand, a substantially equivalent opportunity should be made available to plaintiffs to make such a notification if they choose. Thereafter, proceedings should proceed in a manner consistent with this opinion.

Affirmed in part, reversed in part and remanded.

NOTES

1. As noted, the Act does not address whether contractual privity is needed to enforce warranties. This statutory silence is not a problem for express warranties which qualify as written warranties. State law has not required privity in the case of express warranties. Thus, whether the Act's allowance of an action for their breach preempts relevant state privity requirements is unimportant. Privity is not required for express warranties whether or not preemption operates. The issue of privity matters with implied warranties because some state law requires it. Although some state courts find that the Act displaces state privity requirements (e.g., Szajna v. General Motors Corp., 503 N.E.2d 760 (Ill. 1986)), federal courts tend to conclude that these requirements continue to apply. See, e.g., Voekler v. Porsche Cars N. Am., Inc., 353 F.3d 516 (7th Cir. 2003); Larry J. Soldinger Associates, Ltd. v. Aston Martin Lagonda of N. Am., Inc., 1999 WL 756174, at *1 (N.D.Ill. 1999).

2. In *Hyundai Motor America, Inc. v. Goodin*, supra p. 324, the car manufacturer gave a limited warranty covering the repair or replacement of defective parts in the car. The warranty extended to the buyer who purchased the car from a dealer. When the dealer failed to repair the defects in the car's brake system after repeated attempts, the buyer sued the manufacturer for breach of an "express warranty" and an implied warranty of merchantability under the Act. (As noted above, strictly the manufacturer's written remedial promise does not create a 2–313 express warranty. Nonetheless, it is a written warranty under the Act.) The jury found that the manufacture had not breached the former warranty, even though its repeated attempts as repair failed. While a full warranty requires the warrantor to remedy defects in the product within a reasonable time (§ 2304(a)(1)), the Act does not impose a similar requirement on limited warranties. See Ocana v. Ford Motor Co., 992 So.2d 319 (Fla. Dist. Ct. App. 2008). The jury in *Goodin* apparently believed that the manufacturer's limited warranty did not require timely and successful repair. To determine whether the buyer's breach of implied warranty claim against the manufacturer was properly brought, the court took itself as having to decide whether state law required vertical privity. The court therefore implicitly shares the view of courts which find that the Act does not preempt state law privity requirements.

3. Section 2310(d)(1) entitles a consumer damaged by a warrantor or supplier's breach "under a written warranty, implied warranty or service contract" to sue for damages or equitable relief. Does § 2310(d)(1) create a federal cause of action for breach of all implied warranties, whether or not they are accompanied by "written warranties" as defined by the Act? Assume that a seller has made an express warranty to a consumer that is not a written warranty under the Act. Assume also that the seller breaches an implied warranty that arises from the sale. May the buyer recover from the seller under the Act? Courts are divided. Compare Gross v. Shep Brown's Boat Basin, 2000 WL 1480373 (D.N.H. 2000) with McCurdy v. Texar, Inc., 575 So.2d 299 (Fla. Ct. App. 1991). On the one hand, when read alone, § 2310(d)(1) seemingly entitles a consumer to sue for breach of an "implied warranty." It does not require that the warrantor have given a written warranty. On the other hand, read together with § 2308(a), which regulates disclaimers of implied warranties accompanying a written warranty, § 2310(d)(1) appears to be limited to suits for breach of implied warranties when the consumer has received a written warranty. In this case § 2310(d)(1) allows suit under the Act for breach of a written warranty or implied warranty only if a written warranty has been made.

4. The Act allows a consumer to "bring suit" for breach of a written warranty, implied warranty or service contract in state or federal court. § 2310(d)(1). Suit may be "brought" only if the warrantor has been given a reasonable opportunity to cure the breach. § 2310(e). To sue in federal court, the consumer must have individual claims of at least $25 and aggregate claims of at least $50,000. § 2310(d)(3)(A), (B). The consumer who prevails in an action "brought under" the Act may recover attorney's fees. § 2310(d)(2). To "bring" suit under the Act requires adding a count in the complaint under the Act for breach of warranty. When suit is brought in federal court the complaint will include this count, in order to establish that the court has subject matter jurisdiction over the warranty suit. However, a complaint filed in state court might omit a Magnuson-Moss count. Some courts have been fairly strict in requiring the count as a condition of awarding attorney's fees to a plaintiff who prevails under the Act. See Baldwin v. Jarrett Bay Yacht Sales, LLC, 683 F. Supp. 2d 385 (E.D.N.C. 2009); but cf. Barton v. Hertz Corp., 35 F. Supp. 2d 1377 (M.D. Fla. 1999).

Parrot v. DaimlerChrysler Corp.

Supreme Court of Arizona, 2006
130 P.3d 530

■ RYAN, JUSTICE

In this case, we must determine whether an automobile lessee can maintain an action under the Magnuson–Moss Warranty Act

("Warranty Act" or "Act"), 15 U.S.C. §§ 2301–2312 (2000), and whether the lessee has a right to pursue remedies under the Arizona Motor Vehicle Warranties Act ("Lemon Law"), Ariz. Rev. Stat. ("A.R.S.") §§ 44–1261 to –1267 (2003 & Supp. 2005). We hold that, under the circumstances of this case, a lessee neither can sue under the Warranty Act nor have remedies under the Lemon Law.

I.

Bill Parrot leased a 2000 Jeep Cherokee from Pitre Chrysler Plymouth Jeep Eagle ("Pitre") in Scottsdale, Arizona. The Jeep came with "Chrysler's standard limited warranty." Simultaneously with executing its lease with Parrot, Pitre assigned the lease to the lender, Chrysler Financial Company, L.L.C. Pitre apparently retained title to the vehicle.

Parrot alleges that while he possessed the vehicle, he had to bring it to various dealerships at least thirteen times for repairs including: at least eleven times for suspension/axle defects; four times for alignment defects; three times for a windshield leak; three times for brake defects; and once for an exhaust system defect.

Dissatisfied with the repair work done on the Jeep, Parrot filed suit in superior court alleging that DaimlerChrysler had breached its written warranty and seeking remedies under the Warranty Act and the Lemon Law. The parties filed cross motions for summary judgment. The trial court granted DaimlerChrysler's motion for summary judgment.

Parrot appealed. The court of appeals reversed, concluding that Parrot was a consumer subject to protection under both the Warranty Act and the Lemon Law.

We granted DaimlerChrysler's petition for review because the applicability of the Warranty Act and the Lemon Law to lessees is an issue of first impression for this Court. We have jurisdiction under Article 6, Section 5(3), of the Arizona Constitution and A.R.S. § 12–120.24 (2003).

II.

This matter concerns the interpretation of the Warranty Act and the Lemon Law. Statutory interpretation is an issue of law and is decided de novo. "We interpret statutes to give effect to the legislature's intent. When a statute is clear and unambiguous, we apply its plain language" to find the legislature's intent and do "not engage in other means of statutory interpretation." Kent K. v. Bobby M., 210 Ariz. 279, 283, P14, 210 Ariz. 279, 110 P.3d 1013, 1017 (2005). A statute is clear and unambiguous when it admits of only one meaning.

We first examine the Warranty Act and then turn to Arizona's Lemon Law. Under neither is Parrot entitled to relief.

III.

A.

In response to complaints "from irate owners of motor vehicles complaining that automobile manufacturers and dealers were not performing in accordance with the warranties on their automobiles," Motor Vehicle Mfrs. Ass'n of U.S. v. Abrams, 899 F.2d 1315, 1317 (2d

Cir. 1990), Congress enacted the Warranty Act in 1975. The purpose of the Warranty Act is "to prevent warranty." Milton R. Schroeder, Private Actions under the Magnuson–Moss Warranty Act, 66 Cal. L. Rev. 1, 9 (1978) ("Schroeder"). To further that purpose, the Act requires conspicuous disclosure of the "terms and conditions" of warranties "in simple and readily understood language." 15 U.S.C. § 2302(a). And, "to enforce its requirements, the Act permits 'a consumer who is damaged by the failure of a supplier, warrantor, or service contractor to comply with any obligation under this chapter, or under a written warranty, implied warranty, or service contract' to sue warrantors for damages and other relief in any court of competent jurisdiction." DiCintio v. DaimlerChrysler Corp., 97 N.Y.2d 463, 768 N.E.2d 1121, 1123, 742 N.Y.S.2d 182 (N.Y. 2002) (quoting 15 U.S.C. § 2310(d)(1)). To bring a cause of action under the Warranty Act, a person must be a consumer of a consumer product and have a written warranty, implied warranty, or service contract, as those terms are defined by the Warranty Act.

The Warranty Act defines "consumer product" as "any tangible personal property which is distributed in commerce and which is normally used for personal, family or household purposes." 15 U.S.C. § 2301(1). The parties agree that the Jeep is a consumer product. Therefore, the dispositive issue is whether Parrot is a consumer as defined by the Act.

The Act creates three categories of consumers. Id. § 2301(3). The first category includes "a buyer . . . of any consumer product," other than for purposes of resale. Id. The second encompasses "any person to whom [a consumer product] is transferred during the duration of . . . [a] written warranty." Id. The third category includes "any other person who is entitled by the terms of such warranty . . . or under applicable State law to enforce against the warrantor . . . the obligations of the warranty." Id.

Each category requires a qualifying sale—a sale in which a person buys a consumer product for purposes other than resale. The first category necessarily involves a qualifying sale by its own terms, requiring that a consumer be a "buyer . . . of any consumer product." The necessity of a qualifying sale for categories two and three consumers arises from the Warranty Act's definition of "written warranty." DiCintio, 768 N.E.2d at 1124.

The Warranty Act defines "written warranty" as:

(A) any written affirmation of fact or written promise made in connection with the sale of a consumer product by a supplier to a buyer which relates to the nature of the material or workmanship and affirms or promises that such material or workmanship is defect free or will meet a specified level of performance over a specified period of time, or

(B) any undertaking in writing in connection with the sale by a supplier of a consumer product to refund, repair, replace, or take other remedial action with respect to such product in the event that such product fails to meet the specifications set forth in the undertaking, which written affirmation, promise, or undertaking becomes part of the basis of the bargain between a supplier and a buyer for purposes other than resale of such product. 15 U.S.C. § 2301(6).

Subsections (A) and (B) each expressly require a sale of a consumer product by a supplier. Id. In addition, both subsections are modified by the qualifying phrase at the end of 15 U.S.C. § 2301(6). That qualifying phrase calls for the underlying sale to be to a buyer "for purposes other than resale" and for the written affirmation, promise, or undertaking to be part of the basis of the bargain. Id.

Consequently, the existence of a written warranty, as defined by the Warranty Act, is a requirement for both category two and category three "consumer" status. A person cannot be a category two consumer unless some person purchased the vehicle for purposes other than resale and the written warranty was "part of the basis of the bargain between a supplier and a buyer."

Similarly, a person cannot be a category three consumer unless a qualifying sale has occurred. The category three definition of "consumer" has two parts. Both parts require that a qualifying sale occur—that a person purchased the vehicle for purposes other than resale and that the warranty was "part of the basis of the bargain between a supplier and a buyer."

The first part states that, in addition to meeting the foregoing requirements, a consumer must be a person "entitled by the terms of such warranty . . . to enforce against the warrantor . . . the obligations of the warranty." 15 U.S.C. § 2301(3) (emphasis added). The use of the word "such" to modify "warranty" logically refers to the previous use of "warranty" in the statute. The previous use of "warranty" occurs in category two when it defines a consumer as a person to whom the product is "transferred during the duration of . . . [a] written warranty." Id. Thus, the first part of the definition of a category three consumer means any person entitled by the terms of a written warranty to enforce the obligations of the warranty against the warrantor. As discussed above, the term "written warranty," as defined in the Warranty Act, is a "written affirmation, promise, or undertaking [that] becomes part of the basis of the bargain between a supplier and a buyer for purposes other than resale of such product." § 2301(6). Accordingly, to be a category three consumer under the first part of the definition, a qualifying sale as defined by the Warranty Act must have occurred.

The second part of category three defines a consumer as "any other person who is entitled . . . under applicable State law to enforce against the warrantor . . . the obligations of the warranty." § 2301(3). In this second part, the phrase "the warranty" should not be interpreted in the generic sense as meaning any warranty. Such an interpretation would be inconsistent with the statutory scheme as a whole.

We presume that Congress uses terms consistently. Other than references to an implied warranty, every other use of the term "warranty" in 15 U.S.C. § 2301(3) is either a direct reference to "written warranty" or a short-hand reference to "written warranty." Thus, a consistent reading of the second part of section 2301(3)'s definition of a category three consumer requires interpreting "warranty" as a written warranty as defined by the Warranty Act.

We therefore conclude that to be a category three consumer, a written warranty as defined by the Warranty Act must exist. Because a written warranty requires a qualifying sale, to meet the requirements under this category there must be evidence of such a sale.

B.

Parrot claims that he is a category two or three consumer with a written warranty governed by the Warranty Act. He is neither because no qualifying sale—a purchase for purposes other than resale—has occurred.

Parrot conceded at oral argument that Pitre purchased the Jeep from DaimlerChrysler for the purpose of resale. The only identifiable sale in the record before this Court is to the lessor, Pitre, whose ultimate goal is to resell the vehicle. Consequently, the only sale here was for purposes of resale.

Even though the language defining a category two consumer appears to reach beyond sales of consumer products to include transactions in which a merchant leases goods to consumers or in which the consumer is only a bailee, such a reading is erroneous. The definition[ ] of [a] written . . . warranty still require[s] a sale between a supplier and a buyer. Thus, this portion of the definition of "consumer" must be viewed as referring to transferees after an initial sale of the product. There must be an initial buyer who buys "for purposes other than resale" of the product. Schroeder at 11. Parrot concedes that there is no such sale here. Thus, we hold that because the only sale in this case was for purposes of resale, Parrot does not have a written warranty governed by the Warranty Act.

C.

Parrot relies on several recent cases to support his claim that he is either a category two or three consumer. We do not find these cases persuasive. For example, in Cohen v. AM General Corp., the court concluded that "the purpose of the transaction . . . was not for resale, but for the lease of the vehicle." 264 F. Supp. 2d 616, 619 (N.D. Ill. 2003). The court based its conclusion on the following factors: the leasing company would not have purchased the vehicle but for the fact that the car dealer had entered into a leasing agreement with the plaintiff; the leasing company did not "intend[ ] to add the vehicle to its inventory or advertise it for sale to other parties"; and it profited through the lease agreement. Id. In Peterson v. Volkswagen of America, Inc., 697 N.W.2d 61, 71–73 (Wis. 2005), the court concluded that when a lessor purchased a vehicle for purposes of leasing the vehicle instead of reselling it, the lessee came within the purview of the Act as a category three consumer.

But here, Parrot conceded that Pitre, the dealer-lessor, had purchased the Jeep for resale. Thus, both *Cohen* and *Peterson*, in which the purpose of the purchase of the motor vehicle was found to be for leasing, are inapposite.

Parrot also relies heavily on opinions that have held that interpreting the Warranty Act as not applying to leases "is inconsistent with the purposes of the [Warranty] Act—to protect the ultimate user of the product." Szubski v. Mercedes–Benz, U.S.A., L.L.C., 796 N.E.2d 81, 88, P28 (Ct. Com. Pl. Ohio 2003). Although this interpretation of the Act has a certain attraction, it does not comport with the plain language of the Act. As discussed above, a person must be a consumer as defined under the Warranty Act, which requires that there be a qualifying sale. See 15 U.S.C. § 2301(3), (6). In the absence of such a sale, Parrot simply does not qualify as a consumer under the Act.

Finally, a few courts, including our court of appeals, have concluded that if state law permits enforcement of a written warranty, then the Warranty Act governs that warranty even if the written warranty does not otherwise meet the requirements of the Warranty Act.

We find the reasoning of these courts flawed in two respects. First, they rely upon an incorrect reading of 15 U.S.C. § 2301(6). Second, they rely upon the mistaken assumption that the use of the term "the warranty" in the second part of category three's definition of "consumer" means that the Warranty Act governs any warranty enforceable under state law.

For instance, in *Parrot*, the court mistakenly limited the qualifying phrase "which written affirmation, promise, or undertaking becomes part of the basis of the bargain between a supplier and a buyer for purposes other than resale of such product" to subsection (B) of 15 U.S.C. § 2301(6). Instead, as set forth in paragraphs 13 and 14, above, the qualifying phrase applies to both subsection (A) and (B) of § 2301(6). See also 16 C.F.R. § 700.11(b) ("A written warranty must be 'part of the basis of the bargain.' This means that it must be conveyed at the time of sale of the consumer product. . . . ").

This error led the court to conclude that, to be a category two consumer, one need only have a "written warranty . . . 'made in connection with the sale' of a consumer product by 'a supplier' to 'a buyer.' Likewise, the court's conclusion that Parrot is a category three consumer rests in part on its mistaken reading of 15 U.S.C. § 2301(6).

In Dekelaita v. Nissan Motor Corp., 799 N.E.2d 367 (Ill. Ct. App. 2003), the court concluded that the lessee was a category three consumer because the lessee was entitled to enforce the warranty under state law. This conclusion rested on the premise that "the third [category] does not exclusively require that the warranty meet[ ] the Act's definition if in fact it is enforceable under state law."

But *Dekelaita* comes to this conclusion without any discussion of the statute or reference to "warranty" as used in the definition of a category three consumer. Instead, the court simply assumed that a category three consumer may obtain remedies under the Warranty Act if a warranty is enforceable under state law. See id. But this is an incorrect reading of the reference to warranty in the definition of a category three consumer. Under 15 U.S.C. § 2301(6), for the Act to apply, a purchase for purposes other than resale is required. *Dekelaita* simply does not address these requirements.

The court in *Dekelaita* nevertheless went on to conclude that a written warranty, as defined by the Warranty Act, existed in that case. This conclusion, however, relies upon the same mistaken reading of 15 U.S.C. § 2301(6) as was made in *Parrot*.

Because the court in *Dekelaita* relied on this misreading of 15 U.S.C. § 2301(6), it ignored the issue of whether the sale was for purposes other than resale and whether the written warranty was part of the basis of the bargain between the supplier and the buyer.

Dekelaita's holding that all that is necessary to be a category three consumer is to have some warranty that is enforceable under state law is based upon a mistaken premise.

In Voekler v. Porsche Cars North America, Inc., 353 F.3d 516 (7th Cir. 2003), the court depended upon the holding in *Dekelaita* to conclude that because the lessee could enforce the warranty under state law, the lessee was a category three consumer. 353 F.3d at 524. Because we do not find *Dekelaita* persuasive precedent for this proposition, we decline to follow *Voelker*.

We therefore hold that because Pitre purchased the vehicle for purposes of resale, and there is no other qualifying sale on the record before us, Parrot does not qualify as a consumer under the Warranty Act. As a result, he cannot maintain an action against DaimlerChrysler under the Warranty Act.

IV.

The Warranty Act "apparently was not successful in resolving consumer problems with chronically defective automobiles." *Abrams*, 899 F.2d at 1317. As a result, a number of states enacted so-called lemon laws. Id.; see also Joan Vogel, Squeezing Consumers: Lemon Laws, Consumer Warranties, and a Proposal for Reform, 1985 Ariz. St. L.J. 589, 592 ("Due to the inadequacy of the UCC and the Magnuson–Moss Warranty Act, thirty seven states have now passed lemon laws to deal with automobile warranty disputes."). Arizona enacted its version of a lemon law in 1984. See 1984 Ariz. Sess. Laws, ch. 265, § 1 (codified as amended at A.R.S. §§ 44–1261 to –1265).

The Lemon Law definition of "consumer" parallels the definition in the Warranty Act: "Consumer" means the purchaser, other than for purposes of resale, of a motor vehicle, any person to whom the motor vehicle is transferred during the duration of an express warranty applicable to the motor vehicle or any other person entitled by the terms of the warranty to enforce the obligations of the warranty. A.R.S. § 44–1261(A)(1). An important difference between the Lemon Law and the Warranty Act is that the Lemon Law does not define the term "warranty." Accordingly, the requirement that there be a sale for purposes other than resale does not apply to warranties under the Lemon Law. Thus, although Parrot would not qualify as a category one consumer under the Lemon Law because he did not purchase the Jeep, he may qualify as a category two or three consumer under A.R.S. § 44–1261(A)(1). However, we need not decide whether Parrot would qualify as a category two or three consumer because of the limited remedies afforded by the Lemon Law.

The Lemon Law's remedies for the failure of a manufacturer "or its authorized dealers" to correct or repair "any defect or condition which substantially impairs the use . . . of the motor vehicle," are replacing the vehicle "or accepting return of the motor vehicle from the consumer and refunding to the consumer the full purchase price, including all collateral charges, less a reasonable allowance for the consumer's use of the vehicle." A.R.S. § 44–1263(A).

Both remedies assume that the consumer has the right to transfer title to the vehicle back to the manufacturer. Only the owner of the vehicle or holder of title can transfer title. See A.R.S. § 28–2058 (2004).

This record, however, establishes that Pitre is the owner and title holder; at oral argument Parrot conceded that he did not have title in the vehicle. A person who neither owns a vehicle nor has title to it cannot return the vehicle to the manufacturer, nor is he entitled to have the defective vehicle replaced by another. Therefore, under the Lemon Law, Parrot has no remedy.

That the statute's remedies are inapplicable to lessees is implicit in A.R.S. § 44–1263(A), which provides express protection of a "lienholder," requiring that "the manufacturer shall make refunds to the consumer and lienholder, if any, as their interests appear," without providing protection for lessors.

Our conclusion is bolstered by a 1992 amendment to the section of Arizona's version of the Uniform Commercial Code 7 pertaining to leases. See 1992 Ariz. Sess. Laws, ch. 226, § 4 (codified as amended at A.R.S. §§ 47–2A101 to –2A532 (2005)). In the section governing revocation of acceptance of a lease, lessors and lessees may agree to be bound by the Lemon Law and not by the Uniform Commercial Code:

> The lessee and lessor may, by a conspicuous writing contained in the lease or elsewhere, provide that the provisions of this section will not apply to a new motor vehicle which is otherwise subject to the provisions of title 44, chapter 9, article 5 [the Lemon Law]. . . . When the parties have so agreed, then for the purposes of title 44, chapter 9, article 5, the lessee shall be deemed the consumer of the motor vehicle, with the lessor having all the rights of a lienholder in such motor vehicle.

A.R.S. § 47–2A517(F). Subsection F recognizes that although leases may be "otherwise subject" to the Lemon Law, the remedies provided in section 44–1263(A) are, as a practical matter, simply not available to the lessee. As the latter part of subsection F makes clear, for such remedies to be available, the lessee and lessor have to be made the functional equivalents of a consumer and a lienholder. There is no "conspicuous writing" evidencing such an agreement in this case.

Furthermore, a proponent of the amendment noted that "unlike a buyer, a lessee normally does not have the right to sell or otherwise alienate title to the leased goods, an important reason why it may often be inappropriate to allow the lessee the remedies available under the lemon law." State Bar of Ariz., Corp., Banking and Commercial Loan Section, Comm. on U.C.C. Article 2A, Report of the Comm. on Article 2A (Oct. 1, 1991). Accordingly, unless the lessor and lessee have expressly provided in writing to permit the lessee "to 'sell' the vehicle back to the manufacturer or other responsible party or to exercise other remedies under the lemon law," a lessee has no remedy under the Lemon Law. Because Parrot and Pitre did not expressly provide for such a contingency, Parrot's claim under the Lemon Law fails.

V.

For the foregoing reasons, we vacate the decision of the court of appeals and affirm the summary judgment entered by the superior court.

NOTE

On facts close to those in *Parrot*, Voekler v. Porsche Cars North America, Inc., 353 F.3d 516 (7th Cir. 2003) reached a different conclusion. Voekler leased a Porsche from a Porsche dealer, which had previously purchased the car from Porsche. The Porsche came with a limited warranty requiring Porsche to repair or replace any part defective in material or workmanship. Voekler's lease gave him a purchase option in the car and assigned to him all of the dealer's rights against Porsche. After Porsche failed to repair the car, Voekler sued it and others for breach of a written warranty and implied warranty of merchantability under the Magnuson–Moss Act. The Seventh Circuit had to decide whether the Act applied to the written warranty assigned in the lease of the car to Voekler. The court found that Voekler was not a "category one" or "category two" consumer. A category one consumer must be a buyer, which requires a sale. Voekler was a lessee, not a buyer. Voekler also was not a category two consumer because Porsche's warranty did not begin to run until Voekler took possession. Thus, the car was not transferred to him "during" the warranty's duration, as the relevant part of the Act's definition of "consumer" requires. The court made the following statement about Voekler's status as a category three consumer:

> Finally, we consider whether Voelker has stated a claim as a category three consumer. That is, we ask whether he is "any other person who is entitled by the terms of such warranty (or service contract) *or under applicable State law* to enforce against the warrantor (or service contractor) the obligations of the warranty (or service contract)." 15 U.S.C. § 2301(3) (emphasis added). Copans, as the defendants assert, assigned to Voelker "all its rights under the Porsche Limited Warranty." Under the state law of Illinois, as an assignee of that warranty, a lessee like Voelker was entitled to enforce the rights arising from the warranty. Therefore, Voelker qualifies as a category three consumer.

> The defendants nonetheless argue that, even if Voelker satisfied the definition of consumer, because the only sale of the car was for purposes of resale, he does not have a written warranty as defined in the statute and therefore may not proceed with his claim for breach of written warranty.

> Having concluded above that the sale of the auto from Porsche to Copans was for the purpose of resale, we agree with the defendants that the New Car Limited Warranty does not satisfy the statute's definition of a written warranty because it was not made to a "buyer for purposes other than resale."

> For Voelker to state a valid claim, however, the New Car Limited Warranty need not meet the definition of written warranty contained in § 2301(6). Because Voelker is a category three consumer *entitled under state law* to enforce the New Car Limited Warranty, he is a consumer allowed under the Magnuson–Moss Act to enforce the New Car Limited Warranty. See 15 U.S.C. § 2301(3) (including as consumers those entitled to enforce a warranty "under applicable State law").

In short, because Voelker, under the assignment from Copans, is a person entitled to enforce the New Car Limited Warranty under the applicable state law, the Court holds that Voelker may proceed as a category three consumer regarding his claim for breach of written warranty under the Magnuson–Moss Act. Id. at 525.

PROBLEM 6.8

Jones, the owner of Fit Inc., a fitness club, needed some exercise bicycles for the club. He saw what he needed at Seller's exhibit of XX bikes at a trade fair. In conversation Seller told Jones that the XX bike was constructed only from parts made in the USA and worked as well as the AA bike (a higher priced exercise bicycle). Jones was impressed and placed an order on Fit Inc.'s behalf with Seller for bikes for the club. Seller presented Jones with a document for his signature that read in relevant part: "LIMITED 2–YEAR WARRANTY: Seller guarantees your satisfaction with the XX bike. The XX bike will work in any indoor environment, including fitness clubs. SELLER MAKES NO FURTHER WARRANTIES, EITHER EXPRESS OR IMPLIED, INCLUDING BUT NOT LIMITED TO A WARRANTY OF MERCHANTABILITY." Jones, who was pleased with his find, readily signed the document. A month after Fit Inc. received the bikes, Jones discovered in the course of cleaning them that they contained some parts made in Canada. The XX bikes also soon began to malfunction. A trade paper reported (accurately) that the XX bikes were suitable only for home use and were in many respects inferior to the AA bike.

(a) Fit Inc. would like to recover damages from Seller for breach of warranty under the Magnuson–Moss Act. Can it? §§ 2310(d)(1), 2301(1), (3), (6); FTC § 700.5.

(b) Suppose the document Seller presented to Jones included the following additional language: "Seller warrants that the parts of the XX bikes are free of defects and will, at its option, repair or replace any defective part within two years of delivery of the bikes." May Fit Inc. recover under the Magnuson–Moss Act if the XX bikes delivered prove to be unsuitable for use in a fitness club? On what basis? §§ 2310(d)(1), 2308(a).

(c) Suppose Fit Inc. replaced its XX exercise bikes. In doing so it sold the bikes to Sports Second, who put the bikes in its inventory of used exercise equipment for sale. Assume that Seller's document contained the provision appearing in (b). If parts in the XX bikes were defective, may Sports Second recover damages from Seller under the Magnuson–Moss Act? §§ 2310(d)(1), 2301(3).

(d) Suppose the XX bikes failed to work three years after Fit Inc. put them to use. May Fit Inc. recover for breach of an implied warranty under the Magnuson–Moss Act? § 2308(b).

PROBLEM 6.9

Write, a pen manufacturer, sold a shipment of expensive pens to Ace, a pen retailer. The sale was accompanied by a warranty which stated in relevant part: "LIMITED ONE YEAR WARRANTY. Write warrants to the purchaser that the pen is free of defects in materials and workmanship. It will repair or replace the pen sold if the pen contains defects in material and workmanship, if and only if it receives notice of these defects within one year of the original purchase." Ace in turn sold one of Write's pens to Smith under its own sales contract a month after buying it from Write. The only writing accompanying this sales contract stated that "Ace hereby delivers to Smith one pen at a price of $300." Smith's pen stopped working two days after his purchase. After complaining to Ace and Write and receiving no satisfaction, Smith sued both Write and Ace. He wants to return the pen and get a refund. Can Smith get the relief he wants against Ace under the Magnuson–Moss Act? Under the UCC? Against Write? §§ 2310(d)(1), (f), 2301(4), (10); FTC § 700.4; 2–608, 2–711.

CHAPTER 7

PERFORMANCE OF THE CONTRACT

Article 2's performance rules govern the procedure under which the parties perform their sales agreement. They determine what the parties must do and when, and the consequences of their performance or failure to perform. Unlike formation rules, performance rules do not determine the procedure for concluding a valid sales contract. They also do not allocate various risks of performance of the contract between the parties. The contract's express and implied terms do this. For instance, Article 2's warranties assign the risk of nonconformity in the goods on delivery, and risk of loss assigns the risk of damage, destruction or theft of the goods before delivery. The price term allocates the risk of fluctuations in market price between the conclusion of the contract and its performance. Liability limits or exclusions allocate the risk of damage from breach between the parties. All are substantive terms in the parties' agreement. Article 2's performance rules, like almost all of Article 2's other rules, are default rules: they apply unless the parties' agreement provides different rules for performance. Although the CISG's performance rules are for the most part the same as Article 2's rules, they differ in some important respects.

Section 2–301 states the technical requirements for performance. The seller is obligated to deliver the goods or documents required by the contract and the buyer is obligated to pay for and accept goods that conform to the contract. The seller and buyer's respective obligations are conditions of the other. This means that the parties must perform at the same time: the seller must deliver and the buyer must accept and pay the contract price. Their respective obligations are concurrent conditions of exchange. Comment 2 to 2–511. Because the parties' respective obligations of performance are dependent on each other, the failure of one party's performance excuses the other party's performance. This fits with the parties' presumptive desire not to have to invest in performance if the other party fails to perform. The typical seller does not want to deliver if the buyer does not pay, and the typical buyer does not want to pay if the seller does not deliver.

Other provisions qualify slightly the seller and buyer's respective obligations. Under 2–507(1), the buyer's obligation to accept the goods and pay for them is conditioned on the seller's tender of delivery. Tender of delivery does not require that seller actually deliver the goods. Instead, it requires the seller to hold conforming goods at the buyer's disposal and give it any notice reasonably necessary to enable it to take delivery. 2–503(1). Similarly, under 2–511(1), the seller's obligation to tender delivery of the goods is conditioned on the buyer's tender of payment. Tender of payment requires that the payment be made available to the seller. It does not require that payment be made.

The buyer is obligated to pay for the goods at the time and place where the buyer is to receive them. 2–310(a). To "receive" the goods means to take possession of them. 1–201(1)(c). Under 2–308(a) the seller's place of business is the place at which the buyer is to receive the goods. Taken together, 2–310(a) and 2–308(a) require the buyer to pay at the seller's place of business. Section 2–310(a)'s payment on receipt rule has an immediate consequence when the contract calls for shipment. In this case the seller must arrange for carriage and deliver the goods to the carrier. 2–504(a). Although the seller's satisfies its obligation of delivery by putting the goods into the carrier's hands, 2–310(a)'s payment on receipt rule does not obligate the buyer to pay until it obtains the goods. Few sellers want to part with the goods before they receive the contract price, unless they trust the buyer or have taken a security interest. For this reason, many contracts requiring shipment call for payment against tender of documents of title covering the goods. See 2–513(3)(b). Nonetheless, absent contrary agreement, 2–310(a)'s payment on receipt rule applies. This default rule is fairly easy to justify. Most buyers do not want to pay until they have are certain that they have received the goods (or, strictly, tender of the goods) they ordered. Sellers, who control the production and delivery, are in a position to ensure that their buyers get the goods they ordered. By delaying payment until the buyer receives the goods, the rule gives seller an incentive to supply their buyers with conforming goods.

Section 2–308(a)'s place of receipt rule is a bit harder to justify. Most buyers probably are not well positioned to take delivery at the seller's place of business or do not want to do so. Many contracts call for the buyer to make payment elsewhere, by requiring payment against presentation of documents of title covering the goods or payment on a collect-on-delivery ("C.O.D.") basis. However, more buyers arguably prefer 2–308(a)'s place of receipt rule to any alternative default rule. Would more buyers prefer to receive the goods at their place of business? Their factory or residence? Some other location? None seem likely to be attractive to more buyers than receipt at the seller's place of business. Thus, 2–308(a)'s place of receipt rule is best justified as a rule more buyers prefer to other possible places to receive the goods.

A. INSPECTION AND ITS IMPORTANCE

Where goods are tendered, delivered or identified to the contract for sale, the buyer has a right before payment or acceptance to inspect them. 2–513(1). Inspection must be at a reasonable time and place and in a reasonable manner. The buyer bears the expense of inspection but these may be recovered from the seller if the goods are rejected and do not conform to the contract. 2–513(2). The buyer's right to inspect prior to payment applies even when the contract calls for shipment of the goods. Although the seller under the contract may tender documents of title, the buyer may delay payment until the goods have arrived and it has an opportunity to inspect them. 2–310(b). For example, assume the contract is on a "F.O.B. Sellerville" basis. The seller delivers the goods to the carrier at Sellerville and receives a bill of lading in turn. It presents the bill to the buyer and demands payment of the contract price before the good arrive at Buyerville. The buyer is entitled to refuse to make payment until the goods have arrived and it has had an opportunity to inspect them. This is because the buyer has a right to inspect the goods prior to payment unless the contract's terms exclude that right. 2–310(b). A term requiring payment against tender of documents of title covering the goods excludes the right to pre-payment inspection. So too do delivery terms such as C.O.D. or C.I.F., since contracts using those terms will often require payment against documents of title covering the goods while they are in transit. Consult 2–513(3). The F.O.B. delivery term is not inconsistent with the buyer's right of pre-payment inspection. See 2-319(1).

Pre-payment inspection is important to the contracting parties for some obvious reasons. It allows the buyer to discover nonconformities early and notify the seller of them. In response the seller can take timely remedial action, such as tendering replacement goods, curing nonconformities in the goods originally tendered or accommodating the buyer in some other way. Inspection also enables the buyer to establish that the nonconformities existed at the time the goods were tendered and did not occur at some later time. This saves the buyer some of the expense of proving breach in litigation. For both reasons, pre-payment inspection reduces costs that arise from the seller's breach.

As important are three strictly legal consequences of the buyer's right to pre-payment inspection. First, the right triggers acceptance of the goods if not timely exercised. Section 2–606(1)(b) deems acceptance to occur when the buyer fails to effectively reject the goods after it has had a reasonable opportunity to inspect them. A rejection in turn is ineffective if not made within a reasonable time after delivery or tender. 2–602(1). Thus, the buyer accepts goods if it fails to make an effective rejection after a reasonable time and opportunity to inspect them. A buyer who has accepted the goods is liable for the contract price. 2–709(1). Second, tardy inspection affects the allocation of the burden of proving breach. Section 2–607(4) puts the burden of proof of breach on the buyer with respect to goods accepted. The buyer whose inspection comes too late and does not reject the goods within a reasonable time after delivery or tender accepts them. 2–606(1)(b). As a result, under 2–607(4) the buyer must prove that the goods are nonconforming. Third, tardy inspection bars remedies against the seller for breach. Section 2–607(3)(a) bars the buyer from any remedy if it fails to notify the seller within a reasonable time after he discovers or should have discovered the breach. A buyer who does not timely inspect the goods therefore cannot recover for nonconformities that timely inspection would have revealed.

Article 2 does not state the precise time within which inspection must occur. Instead, 2–606(1)(b) deems acceptance to occur after the buyer has had a reasonable opportunity to inspect the goods. Courts have had to determine what constitutes a reasonable time to inspect. To determine this time, case law considers the perishability of the goods, the difficulty of discovering the defect, and the terms of the contract. See Figueroa v. Kit San Co., 845 P.2d 567, 576 (Idaho Ct. App. 1992). The length of time that has passed after delivery by itself is not determinative. An inspection that occurred nine months after delivery has been found reasonable, while inspection close to 24 hours after delivery was judged unreasonable. Cf. La Villa Fair v. Lewis Carpet Mills, Inc., 548 P.2d 825 (Kan. 1976); Miron v. Yonkers Raceway, Inc., 400 F.2d 112 (2d Cir. 1968). In considering factors other than the mere passage of time, courts appear to allow implicit cost-benefit judgments to inform their findings of timeliness. They balance the costs to the buyer of early discovery of the defect against the cost to the seller in delaying discovery. See George L. Priest, Breach and Remedy for the Tender of Nonconforming Goods Under the Uniform Commercial Code: An Economic Approach, 91 Harv. L. Rev. 960, 984–988 (1978). If detection of defects is protracted because requiring extensive testing or interaction with other materials, early inspection might not be cost-effective. See *Figueroa*. Similarly, if the goods do not deteriorate quickly, so that defects can be revealed by a delayed inspection, early inspection is not advantageous. In both instances a long period in which to inspect is reasonable. See *Figueroa*. On the other hand, if the qualities of the goods are unstable so that there is a risk of deterioration, the delay in inspection might not be cost-effective. A leisurely inspection comes too late to preserve evidence of a defect or allow the seller to salvage the goods. A short inspection period therefore is reasonable. See *Miron*, 400 F.2d at 119 (inspection of race horse the day after sale came too late).

PROBLEM 7.1

Buyer selected a humidifier at Seller's showroom and signed a sales contract for its purchase and installation. Payment was due after the unit was installed. The contract indicated the humidifier's serial number, and Seller set aside the designated humidifier for delivery and installation in Buyer's home. Although the contract called for Seller to install the humidifier within a week of its sale, Buyer's changed plans forced Seller to delay installation until six weeks after the sale. Soon after the humidifier was installed, Buyer noticed that it failed to work properly. It immediately notified Seller of the failure. When Buyer refused to pay the contract price, Seller sued Buyer for it. Is Seller entitled to the price (with or without a deduction for Buyer's damages)? 2–709(1)(a), 2–513(1), 2–501.

B. REJECTION: GROUNDS AND PROCEDURE

The inspecting buyer must make a choice: accept or reject the goods. If the buyer accepts them, it must pay the seller the contract price. 2–607(1). It still may recover damages if the goods are nonconforming or the seller has breached its other obligations of performance. If the buyer rejects the goods, the seller is ultimately responsible for their disposition. It must arrange to resell them or be bound by the buyer's reasonable disposition when permitted. The seller nonetheless may recover damages or obtain other relief if the buyer's rejection is wrongful. 2–703. Thus, acceptance puts the responsibility for the goods on the buyer while rejection puts it on the seller. Accordingly, acceptance and rejection function as signals from the buyer to the seller as to who is to dispose of the goods. To see this, realize that even a buyer who obtains conforming goods it no longer wants need not breach by rejecting them. Instead, it can accept the goods and resell them itself. Thus, the buyer has to decide whether to retain the goods and resell them itself or have the seller resell them (breach). It will choose the cheaper avenue for disposing of goods it does not want because it is responsible for the costs of disposition. The buyer will decide to retain the goods if its resale costs disposing of the goods, net of proceeds of its resale, are lower than the seller's cost of doing so. If its disposal costs are higher than the seller's disposal costs, the buyer will have the seller resell the goods. Acceptance is the buyer's signal to the seller that it has decided to retain the goods; rejection its signal that the seller is to dispose of them.

1. THE PERFECT TENDER RULE

Section 2–601 states the grounds on which goods can be rightfully rejected. According to it, the buyer is entitled to reject the goods or the tender if they fail to conform to the contract "in any respect." Unless the seller's performance complies exactly with its obligations under the contract, the buyer's rejection is proper. Comment 2 to 2–106. This standard for rightful rejection is called the "perfect tender rule."

The perfect tender rule means that the extent of the nonconformity is not a condition of rejection. The rule entitles the buyer to reject the goods even if they do not conform to the contract only in an immaterial respect. In this respect 2–601's rule differs from the rule that operates in general contract law. The operative rule there is one of substantial performance. According to this rule, a party who has substantially performed its contractual obligations is entitled to the other party's performance. Its failure to perform all of its obligations does not discharge the other party's obligations to perform. See Restatement (Second) of Contracts § 237 (1981). Unlike the substantial performance rule, the perfect tender rule entitles the buyer to reject the goods if they do not conform exactly ("perfectly") to the contract.

The perfect tender rule does not apply to installment contracts. 2–612. Its operation also is limited when the seller has a right to cure a nonconforming tender. 2–508. Both limitations are discussed below.

Two factors soften 2–601's generous grounds for rejection even when it applies. First, the parties' agreement can restrict or qualify the basis upon which the buyer can reject a tender. It can allow rejection only if the goods do not substantially conform to the sales contract. The sales contract can even prevent the buyer from rejecting the goods at all in the face of a nonconforming tender. In fact, many standard form contracts do just this. Article 2 considers rejection to a type of remedy. 2–711(1). Many standard form contracts limit the buyer's remedies to repair or replacement of the goods, as permitted by 2–719(1)(b). The repair or replacement remedy is in this case is exclusive. As a result, the buyer who receives nonconforming goods cannot reject them. Agreements containing exclusive repair or replace clauses contract around the perfect tender rule. Second, trade usage, course of performance or course of dealing inform what the contract requires. Section 2–601 entitles the buyer to reject goods that do not conform to the contract. "Contract" means the sum of legal obligations resulting from the parties' agreement. 1–201(b)(12). The parties' "agreement" in turn means their bargain, as found in trade usage, course of dealing and course of performance. 1–201(b)(3). Thus, applicable trade usage and the like inform the parties' agreement or are among its terms. This allows a tender which does not appear to comply with the contract's terms nonetheless to be "perfect." For instance, assume that the contract calls for the seller to deliver hides having individual weights of between 13 pounds and 20 pounds per hide. The seller delivers a few hides that weigh less than 13 pounds and a few others that weigh more than 20 pounds. Assume also that applicable trade usage allows some variation in the weight of a few hides delivered. Given this usage, the contract description calling for individual weights of "between 13 pounds and 20 pounds" means something like "between 13 pounds and 20 pounds, give or take some variance." The hides seller delivered conform to the contract if they fall within the variance in individual weight allowed by trade usage. See Schmoll Fils & Co. v. Agoos Tanning Co., 152 N.E. 630 (Mass. 1926) (pre-Code case).

The perfect tender rule may initially appear to be inefficient. An efficient rule minimizes the cost of the seller's breach. Where the buyer is allowed to reject nonconforming goods, there are broadly two sorts of costs to consider: the seller's cost of retrieving and reselling the nonconforming goods, and the buyer's cost of adapting the goods or obtaining substitute goods. If the seller's costs of retrieval and resale are less than the buyer's costs of adapting or obtaining substitute goods, rejection minimizes the costs from breach because it returns the goods to the seller. However, where the breach is immaterial, the buyer's costs in retaining or disposing of the goods are low. After all, an immaterial breach does not affect the buyer's ability to use or resell the goods. Rejection nonetheless forces the seller to retrieve and resell even when its costs of doing so exceed the buyer's cost of retaining or disposing of the goods and recovering damages. This is particularly true when the nonconforming goods have been customized for the buyer, because the buyer likely values them more than other potential buyers. The possibility of rejection following an immaterial breach therefore might suggest that the perfect tender rule is inefficient. Of course, the right to reject might not be exercised. This is because the breaching seller in this position can bargain for its buyer, for a price, to retain the goods and not reject them. But the question is whether the perfect tender rule is efficient as a default rule.

Further consideration suggests that the perfect tender rule might after all be efficient. The rule allows a buyer in a declining market to seize on an immaterial nonconformity to reject the goods. Rejection followed by cancellation shifts market risk borne by the buyer under the contract back to the seller. This is a sort of ex post strategic behavior by the buyer. To prevent the shifting of risk, the seller has to bargain with the buyer to persuade it not to reject. However, the substantial performance rule also allows for strategic behavior. It encourages the seller to cut corners by tendering goods that are immaterially nonconforming. The substantial performance rule forces the buyer in these circumstances to retain the goods, limiting its relief to damages. This is a sort of ex ante strategic breach by the seller. If the measurement of the buyer's damages is inaccurate, the seller's nonconforming tender effectively increases the price of the goods to the buyer. Both rules for rejection therefore encourage different sorts of strategic behavior. However, although the perfect tender and substantial performance rules both induce undesirable behavior, arguably the risk of the seller's ex ante strategic behavior is more pronounced. Reputational restraints can limit a buyer's ability to strategically reject immaterially nonconforming goods. A buyer who wants future dealings with the same seller, or different sellers in the same product market, will think twice about making a strategic rejection. Article 2's drafters apparently believe that similar restraints do not operate to limit the seller's incentive to offer immaterially nonconforming goods. The perfect tender rule is thought necessary to discipline sellers who might otherwise strategically breach. The case for the rule remains controversial, and commentators before and after Article 2's enactment have urged adoption of the substantial performance rule for rejection. See Karl N. Llewellyn, On Warranty of Quality, and Society: II, 37 Colum. L. Rev. 341, 378 (1937); ABA Task Force, Preliminary Report on the Uniform Commercial Code Article 2 Study Group, 16 Del. J. Corp. L. 981, 1160 (1991).

2. THE MECHANICS OF REJECTION

Article 2 has two requirements for rejection. First, the rejection must be timely. Section 2–602(1) requires that the rejection be "within a reasonable time" after delivery or tender of the goods. Section 1–205(a) provides that whether a time for taking an action required by the UCC is reasonable "depends on the nature, purpose, and circumstances of the action." This is a completely unhelpful piece of advice. No reader of the 2–602(1) would think that the reasonableness of an action does not depend on the factors mentioned. As noted above in section B.1., courts are a bit more helpful and determine the reasonableness of a delay in rejection by the difficulty of discovering the defect, the terms of the contract, the perishability of the goods and the course of performance or dealing between the parties.

The second requirement is one of content of notice of rejection. Section 2–602(1) provides that a rejection is ineffective unless the buyer "seasonably notifies" the seller. The notice need not be written. However, it must be enough to inform the seller that the buyer is rejecting the goods. See 1–202(d). The buyer's notice need not state the specific grounds on which the buyer is rejecting them. However, 2–607(3)(a) bars a buyer who rejects without notifying the seller of breach from any remedy. Because rejection is a remedy (2–711), the rejection must at least notify the seller of the breach. See Comment 4 to 2–607. Failure to do so renders the rejection ineffective. As with the reasonableness of time, Article 2 leaves unspecified the seasonableness of notice. Section 1–205(b) unhelpfully provides that an action is taken seasonably if it is taken within an agreed upon time or, if none is agreed, "at or within a reasonable time." Presumably the same factors that determine whether a rejection is timely also determine the timeliness of notice of rejection.

Section 2–602(1)'s requirements for rejection has two important consequences. One is that a buyer who fails to give proper and timely notice has not effectively rejected the goods; it has merely attempted to reject. Under 2–606(1)(b), an ineffective rejection is an acceptance. The other consequence is that a buyer can make a wrongful but effective (proper) rejection. This is because 2–602(1)'s procedure for an effective rejection applies without regard to whether the rejection is rightful or wrongful. According to the procedure, a rejection is effective if it is timely and provides sufficient notice to the seller. Thus, even if a buyer's rejection of a conforming tender is wrongful, it still is effective as a rejection. Because the wrongful rejection is effective, it does not operate as an acceptance. In other words, the Code distinguishes very clearly between the effectiveness of a rejection and its rightfulness.

Unfortunately, 2–602 is not as clear as it should be that a wrongful rejection nonetheless may be effective. The section's heading is "Manner and Effect of Rightful Rejection," and headings are part of the Code. See 1–107. In addition, Comment 3 describes 2–602 as applying only to rightful rejections. This statutory material makes it appear that 2–602(1)'s procedure for an effective rejection does not apply to wrongful rejections. However, the material is misleading and does not accurately reflect 2–602(1)'s content. By its terms, 2–602(1)'s procedure for an effective rejection applies without regard to whether the rejection is rightful. In addition, 2–602(3)'s reference to the seller's right with respect to goods "wrongfully rejected" presupposes that the rejection is effective. And Comment 2 describes the buyer's duties under 2–602(2) with respect to rejected goods which arise "upon rejection." It follows the subsection's language in applying those duties to a "rejection," which may be rightful or wrongful. For these reasons, the material in 2–602's heading and Comment 3 to 2-602 which suggests that 2–602(1)'s mechanics for rejection apply only to rightful rejection is mistaken.

D.P. Technology Corp. v. Sherwood Tool, Inc.

United States District Court, District of Connecticut, 1990
751 F. Supp. 1038

■ ALAN H. NEVAS, UNITED STATES DISTRICT JUDGE

In this action based on diversity jurisdiction, the plaintiff seller, D.P. Technology ("DPT"), a California corporation, sues the defendant buyer, Sherwood Tool, Inc. ("Sherwood") a Connecticut corporation, alleging a breach of contract for the purchase and sale of a computer system. Now pending is the defendant's motion to dismiss, pursuant to Rule 12(b)(6), Fed. R. Civ. P., for failure to state a claim upon which relief can be granted. For the reasons that follow, the defendant's motion to dismiss is denied.

I.

A.

The facts of this case can be easily summarized. On January 24, 1989, the defendant entered into a written contract to purchase a computer system, including hardware, software, installation and training, from the plaintiff. The complaint alleges that the computer system was "specifically" designed for the defendant and is not readily marketable. The contract, executed on January 24, 1989, incorporates the delivery term set forth in the seller's Amended Letter of January 17, 1989 stating that the computer system would be delivered within ten to twelve weeks. The delivery period specified in the contract ended on April 18, 1989. The software was delivered on April 12, 1989 and the hardware was delivered on May 4, 1989. On May 9, 1989, the defendant returned the merchandise to the plaintiff, and has since refused payment for both the software and the hardware. Thus, the plaintiff alleges that the defendant breached the contract by refusing to accept delivery of the goods covered by the contract while the defendant argues that it was rather the plaintiff who breached the contract by failing to make a timely delivery.

* * * In the instant case, the contract comprised three writings: two letters from the seller, signed in California, and the letter of acceptance from the buyer, executed in Connecticut. Since the letter from the buyer stated "Ship it," it was arguably the letter of acceptance. Thus the contract under this interpretation was executed in Connecticut (the letter of acceptance by the buyer dated January 24, 1989). But even if it is unclear as to where the contract was executed, the contract was to have its place of operative effect or performance in Connecticut, since the computer system was to be delivered to and used in Connecticut. Thus, Connecticut law governs resolution of the instant dispute.

II.

Because the contract between the parties was a contract for the sale of goods,[1] the law governing this transaction is to be found in Article 2 of the Uniform Commercial Code ("UCC"); Conn. Gen. Stat. §§ 42a–2–101 et seq. In its motion to dismiss, the defendant argues that the plaintiff fails to state a claim upon which relief can be granted because the plaintiff breached the contract which provided for a delivery period of ten to twelve weeks from the date of the order, January 24, 1989. Since the delivery period ended on April 18, 1989, the May 4 hardware delivery was 16 days late. The defendant contends that because the plaintiff delivered the hardware after the contractual deadline, the late delivery entitled the defendant to reject delivery, since a seller is required to tender goods in conformance with the terms set forth in a contract. U.C.C. § 2–301; Conn. Gen. Stat. § 42a–2–301.

In its memorandum in opposition, the plaintiff contends that the defendant waived the original delivery schedule. The plaintiff points to its allegation in the complaint that it designed and developed the computer system pursuant to the contract, and argues that, in designing and developing a "specifically designed" computer system, consultations with the defendant took place which resulted in adjustment of the delivery schedule, and that the defendant waived the 10–12 week delivery requirement. In Bradford Novelty Co. v. Technomatic, 112 A.2d 214, 216 (1955) (pre-Code), where the buyer acquiesced to a delay in delivery, the court found that the buyer "by its conduct, waived its right to strict compliance with the provisions of the contract as to time of performance." In the instant case, however, the plaintiff failed to allege its waiver claim in the complaint. Consequently, the defendant's motion to dismiss cannot be denied on a claim of waiver.

The plaintiff also states that even if the computers were delivered late, the buyer could not reject the goods pursuant to Conn. Gen. Stat. § 42a–2–602 because the parties had an installment contract. The plaintiff contends that the contract was an installment one, which authorizes the delivery of goods in separate lots to be separately accepted, as illustrated by the separate deliveries of software and hardware. A buyer may reject an installment only if the non-conformity substantially impairs the value of the goods. Conn. Gen. Stat. § 42a–2–

---

[1]   Computer systems, including software, have been interpreted to be goods rather than services and thus subject to the Uniform Commercial Code.

612(2)–(3). The defendant has not asserted that the late delivery substantially reduced the computer system's value. Since the allegations in the complaint must be construed in favor of the nonmoving party in a motion to dismiss, if an installment contract was alleged, then UCC Section 2–601 would be superseded by UCC Section 2–612. However, the complaint lacks any reference to an installment contract. Therefore, the defendant's motion to dismiss cannot be denied on the grounds that there was an installment contract.

In addition, the plaintiff argues that the defendant relies on the perfect tender rule, allowing buyers to reject for any nonconformity with the contract. Plaintiff points out that the defendant has not cited one case in which a buyer rejected goods solely because of a late delivery, and that the doctrine of "perfect tender" has been roundly criticized. While it is true that the perfect tender rule has been criticized by scholars principally because it allowed a dishonest buyer to avoid an unfavorable contract on the basis of an insubstantial defect in the seller's tender, the basic tender provision of the Uniform Commercial Code continued the perfect tender policy developed by the common law and embodied in the Uniform Sales Act. Section 2–601 states that with certain exceptions, the buyer has the right to reject "if the goods or the tender of delivery fail in any respect to conform to the contract." Conn. Gen. Stat. § 42a–2–601. The courts that have considered the issue have agreed that the perfect tender rule has survived the enactment of the Code. See, e.g., Intermeat, Inc. v. American Poultry, Inc., 575 F.2d 1017, 1024 (2d Cir. 1978) ("There is no doubt that the perfect tender rule applies to measure the buyer's right of initial rejection of goods under UCC section 2–601."); Capitol Dodge Sales, Inc. v. Northern Concrete Pipe, Inc., 346 N.W.2d 535, 539 (1983) (adoption of 2–601 creates a perfect tender rule replacing pre-Code cases defining performance of a sales contract in terms of substantial compliance); Texas Imports v. Allday, 649 S.W.2d 730, 737 (Tex. App. 1983) (doctrine of substantial performance is not applicable under 2–601); Ingle v. Marked Tree Equip. Co., 428 S.W.2d 286, 289 (1968) (a buyer may accept or reject goods which fail to conform to the contract in any respect). Similarly, courts interpreting 2–601 have strictly interpreted it to mean any nonconformity, thus excluding the doctrine of substantial performance.[2] Astor v. Boulos, Inc., 451 A.2d 903, 906 (Me. 1982) (the generally disfavored "perfect tender rule" survives enactment of the UCC as respects a contract for sale of goods but does not control in the area of service contracts which are governed by the standard of substantial performance); Moulton Cavity & Mold, Inc. v. Lyn–Flex Indus., Inc., 396 A.2d 1024, 1027–28 (1979) (holding that the doctrine of substantial performance "has no application to a contract for the sale of goods"); Jakowski v. Carole Chevrolet, Inc., 433 A.2d 841, 843 (1981) (degree of nonconformity of goods is irrelevant in assessing buyer's concomitant right to reject them). These courts have thus found that

---

[2]   This interpretation allowing a buyer to cancel a contract for any nonconformity dates back to the common law interpretation of the perfect tender rule in the law of sales which differed from the law of contracts, which allows rescission only for material breaches. Thus, Judge Learned Hand stated in Mitsubishi Goshi Kaisha v. J. Aron & Co., Inc., 16 F.2d 185, 186 (2d Cir. 1926), that "there is no room in commercial contracts for the doctrine of substantial performance." While Judge Hand wrote in a pre-UCC context, modern courts have reiterated the view that perfect tender does not require substantial performance but complete performance.

the tender must be perfect in the context of the perfect tender rule in the sense that the proffered goods must conform to the contract in every respect. Connecticut, however, appears in this regard to be the exception. Indeed, in the one Connecticut case interpreting 2–601, Franklin Quilting Co., Inc. v. Orfaly, 470 A.2d 1228, 1229 (1984), in a footnote, the Appellate Court stated that "the 'perfect tender rule' requires a substantial nonconformity to the contract before a buyer may rightfully reject the goods." Thus, the Connecticut Appellate Court has adopted "the White and Summers construction of 2–601 as in substance a rule that does not allow rejection for insubstantial breach such as a short delay causing no damage." See also National Fleet Supply, Inc. v. Fairchild, 450 N.E.2d 1015, 1019 n. 4 (Ind. App. 1983) (despite UCC's apparent insistence on perfect tender, it is generally understood that rejection is not available in circumstances where the goods or delivery fail in some small respect to conform to the terms of the sales contract (citing White and Summers)); McKenzie v. Alla–Ohio Coals, Inc., 29 U.C.C. Rep. Serv. (Callaghan) 852, 856–57 (D.D.C. 1979) (there is substantial authority that where a buyer has suffered no damage, he should not be allowed to reject goods because of an insubstantial nonconform

As noted above, a federal court sitting in diversity must apply the law of the highest court of the state whose law applies. Since this court has determined that Connecticut law governs, the next task is to estimate whether the Connecticut Supreme Court would affirm the doctrine of substantial nonconformity, as stated in Orfaly, an opinion of the Connecticut Appellate Court. When the highest state court has not spoken on an issue, the federal court must look to the inferior courts of the state and to decisions of sister courts as well as federal courts. As noted, the weight of authority is that the doctrine of substantial performance does not apply to the sale of goods. However, as noted by White and Summers, in none of the cases approving of perfect rather than substantial tender was the nonconformity insubstantial, such as a short delay of time where no damage is caused to the buyer. White and Summers, Uniform Commercial Code (3rd Ed.), section 8–3 n. 8. In the instant case, there is no claim that the goods failed to conform to the contract. Nor is there a claim that the buyer was injured by the 16–day delay. There is, however, a claim that the goods were specially made, which might affect the buyer's ability to resell. Thus Connecticut's interpretation of 2–601 so as to mitigate the harshness of the perfect tender rule reflects the consensus of scholars that the rule is harsh and needs to be mitigated. Indeed, Summers and White state that the rule has been so "eroded" by the exceptions in the Code that "relatively little is left of it; the law would be little changed if 2–601 gave the right to reject only upon 'substantial' non-conformity," especially since the Code requires a buyer or seller to act in good faith. R. Summers and J. White, Uniform Commercial Code (3rd Ed. 1988), 8–3, at 357. See also Alden Press Inc. v. Block & Co., Inc., 527 N.E.2d 489, 493 (1988) (notwithstanding the perfect tender rule, the reasonableness of buyer's rejection of goods and whether such rejection of goods is in good faith are ultimately matters for the trier of fact); Printing Center of Texas v. Supermind Pub. Co., Inc., 669 S.W.2d 779, 784 (Tex. App. 1984) (if the evidence establishes any nonconformity, the buyer is entitled to reject the goods as long as it is in good faith); Neumiller Farms, Inc. v.

Cornett, 368 So. 2d 272, 275 (Ala. 1979) (claim of dissatisfaction with delivery of goods so as to warrant their rejection must be made in good faith, rather than in an effort to escape a bad bargain). A rejection of goods that have been specially manufactured for an insubstantial delay where no damage is caused is arguably not in good faith.

Although the Connecticut Supreme Court has not yet addressed the issue of substantial nonconformity, it has stated, in a precode case, Bradford Novelty Co. v. Technomatic, 112 A.2d 214, 216 (Conn. 1955), that although "the time fixed by the parties for performance is, at law, deemed of the essence of the contract," where, as here, goods have been specially manufactured, "the time specified for delivery is less likely to be considered of the essence . . . [since] in such a situation there is a probability of delay, and the loss to the manufacturer is likely to be great if the buyer refuses to accept and pay because of noncompliance with strict performance." But see Marlowe v. Argentine Naval Com'n, 257 U.S. App. D.C. 225, 808 F.2d 120, 124 (D.C. Cir. 1986) (buyer within its rights to cancel a contract for 6–day delay in delivery since "time is of the essence in contracts for the sale of goods") (citing Norrington v. Wright, 115 U.S. 188, 203 (1885) ("In the contracts of merchants, time is of the essence.")

After reviewing the case law in Connecticut, this court finds that in cases where the nonconformity involves a delay in the delivery of specially manufactured goods, the law in Connecticut requires substantial nonconformity for a buyer's rejection under 2–601, and precludes a dismissal for failure to state a claim on the grounds that the perfect tender rule, codified at 2–601, demands complete performance. Rather, Connecticut law requires a determination at trial as to whether a 16–day delay under these facts constituted a substantial nonconformity.

Conclusion

For the foregoing reasons, the defendant's rule 12(b)(6) motion to dismiss this one count complaint is denied.

NOTES AND QUESTIONS

1. The court, applying Connecticut law, found that the buyer could not rightly reject because of an insubstantial delay that caused it no damage, which arguably is not in good faith. The basis for this finding is unclear. Is the court denying that 2–601 permits rejection for even trivial nonconformities? Or is its view that 2–601's perfect tender rule is subject to an overriding obligation of good faith? The court's finding is consistent with both possibilities. The former possibility ignores 2–601's language, which entitles the buyer to reject if the goods fail to conform in any respect to the contract. Late delivery does not conform to the contract, even if it causes no damage to the buyer. In interpreting 2–601, the court relies on a Connecticut case, Franklin Quilting Co. v. Orfaly, 470 A.2d 1229 (Conn. App. Ct. 1984), which concluded that 2–601 "requires a substantial nonconformity to the contract before the buyer can rightfully reject the goods." Id. at 1129, n.3. The *Orfaly* court cites in support of its conclusion Professors White and Summers' summary of Article 2's provisions limiting 2–601's application and the case law applying 2–601. See James J. White &

Robert S. Summers, Uniform Commercial Code § 8.3 (at 305) (2d ed. 1980). Limitations on 2–601's application restrict without eliminating 2–601's perfect tender rule. White and Summers' survey of cases describes the ability of courts to manipulate 2–601 where the tender is trivially nonconforming. This result does not show (and is not intended to show) that 2–601's language allows rejection only if the nonconformity is substantial.

The other possibility is that the *D.P. Technology* court considers 2–601's perfect tender rule to be subject to an overriding obligation of good faith. According to this view, buyers who seize on trivial nonconformities act in bad faith and therefore cannot reject under 2–601. Some courts take this position to prevent buyers' strategic rejection of the goods. See, e.g., Y & N Furniture Inc. v. Nwabuoku, 190 Misc. 2d 402 (N.Y. Civ. Ct. 2001). The role of an obligation of good faith under the Code has been controversial. See Clayton P. Gillette, Limitations on the Obligation of Good Faith, 1981 Duke L. J. 619 (1981). Section 1–304 imposes "an obligation of good faith on the performance and enforcement" of contracts governed by the Code. The dispute is over whether good faith requires only the performance and enforcement of contractual obligations or whether it imposes obligations independent of the contract. "Contract" means the sum of obligations that arise from the parties' agreement, as determined by Code and extra-Code law. 1–201(b)(12). Section 2–601's perfect tender rule gives a buyer the right to reject, not an obligation to do so. In addition, rejection enforces the terms of the parties' agreement by allowing the buyer to refuse the goods when they do not conform to the contract. For both reasons, rejection of a trivially nonconforming tender is not bad faith under 1–304. Courts that allow rejection only in good faith understand the obligation of good faith to apply apart from the contract.

2. The Permanent Editorial Board of the UCC has rejected an independent obligation of good faith. According to PEB Commentary No. 10: Section 1–203 [1–304] (February 10, 1994): "The inherent flaw in the view that § 1–203 [§ 1–304] supports an independent cause of action is the belief that the obligation of good faith has an existence which is conceptually separate from the underlying agreement. . . . [T]his is an incorrect view of the duty. A party cannot simply 'act in good faith.' One acts in good faith relative to the agreement of the parties." The Commentary ends by amending the Comment to 1–203 [1–304] to read in relevant part: "This section [1–304] does not support an independent cause of action for failure to perform or enforce in good faith. Rather, this section means that a failure to perform or enforce, in good faith, a specific duty or obligation under the contract, constitutes a breach of that contract . . . This distinction makes it clear that the doctrine of good faith merely directs a court towards interpreting contracts within the commercial context in which they are created, performed and enforced, and does not create a separate duty of fairness and reasonableness which can be independently breached."

3. Alaska Pacific Trading Co. v. Eagon Forest Products, Inc., 933 P.2d 417 (Wash. Ct. App. 1997) applied 2–601's perfect tender rule even when the buyer's rejection appears strategic. In that case the market price of logs dropped and the seller feared that the buyer would not take delivery. The buyer's representative intimated to the seller that the buyer might not accept the logs. When the seller failed to ship the lumber by the date required by the contract, the buyer rejected the seller's tender (fashioning its rejection as an assertion of "no contract" in the face of the seller's breach). The court found the buyer's rejection rightful even if the time of delivery was a nonmaterial term of the contract. It described *D.P. Technology*'s substantial performance standard for rejection as a "minority rule" and refused to apply the standard. See also Ramirez v. Autosport, 88 N.J. 277, 285 (N.J. 1982); Moulton Cavity & Mold., Inc. v. Lyn–Flex Industries, 396 A.2d 1024, 1027 n.6 (Me.1979).

A strategic rejection of a tender that conforms in all respects to the contract is wrongful. In Neumiller Farms, Inc. v. Cornett, 368 So.2d 272 (Ala. 1979), the sales contract called for potatoes chipped to the buyer's satisfaction. When the market price of potatoes declined, the buyer rejected the delivery of potatoes it claimed were unsatisfactory, including the seller's tender of potatoes from the same fields as potatoes the buyer had recently purchased and found satisfactory. Finding that a claim of dissatisfaction must be made in good faith, the court upheld the jury's determination that the potatoes the seller tendered would chip satisfactorily. Because the potatoes tendered conformed to the contract, the buyer's rejection was wrongful. The buyer rejected the seller's tender because it regretted the deal, not because the potatoes tendered were unsatisfactory to it.

PROBLEM 7.2

Seller's contract with Buyer called for it to deliver two tons of wheat to Buyer's silo by truck. The contract price was $11 per bushel. When Seller delivered the wheat to Buyer's silo by train, Buyer refused to receive the wheat. Buyer had the capacity to receive deliveries by truck or train and would not be inconvenienced by taking delivery by train.

(a) Was Buyer's rejection rightful?

(b) Would it matter that the price of wheat declined to $10 per bushel between the time the contract was concluded and the date Seller delivered?

(c) Does 1–304 restrict Buyer's right to reject in the circumstances?

(d) Assume that the contract required that the wheat be satisfactory to Buyer. Assume also that Seller delivered the wheat to Buyer's silo by truck. Is Buyer's rejection rightful if it refused to receive the wheat after the price of wheat declined to $10 per bushel? Cf. 1–304.

PROBLEM 7.3

Buyer purchased 100 iPads from Seller. When Seller's shipment of iPads arrives, Buyer discovers that it contains 99 iPads. May Buyer reject the shipment? May Buyer keep 50 of the iPads, return the remaining 49 and adjust the contract price accordingly? 2–601, 2–105(6), 2–106(2), 2–717.

PROBLEM 7.4

Buyer's contract with Seller for widgets was on a F.O.B. Sellerville basis. Accordingly, Seller engaged a carrier and delivered the widgets to it at Sellerville, receiving bills of lading covering them in turn. Seller did not obtain insurance covering the widgets, and Buyer's insurance policy did not extend to the widgets. Because Seller was busy, it notified Buyer that the widgets had arrived at the carrier's warehouse in Buyerville five days after their arrival. Unfortunately, this was a day after the warehouse containing Buyer's widgets burned down. When Buyer viewed the burnt husks of the widgets, it refused to take them. (You may assume that the carrier is not liable for the loss; see 7–309.) Is Buyer's rejection rightful? 2–319(1), 2–504(c), 2–601.

PROBLEM 7.5

Buyer agreed to purchase 100 new widgets from Seller at $100 per widget. When the widgets arrived at Buyer's factory, it discovered that they were used widgets worth $460 per widget. Buyer immediately emailed Seller to the effect that "the widgets don't suit our purposes; further discussion to follow." Buyer and Seller had no further discussion. Instead, Buyer stored Seller's widgets and purchased 100 new widgets at $75 per widget, the now prevailing market price. When Seller later demanded payment of the $10,000 contract price ($100 × 100 = $10,000), Buyer refused. It argued that it had rejected Seller's widgets and offered to return them.

(a) Did Buyer reject Seller's widgets? 2–601, 2–602(1).

(b) Suppose Buyer's email stated that "the widgets are nonconforming; further discussion to follow." Did Buyer reject Seller's widgets?

(c) Suppose Buyer's email read as it did initially. Suppose too that Buyer proposed to retain the widgets and pay Seller the $10,000 contract price less $4,000 ($40 x 100), which is amount of its damages. Is Buyer entitled to reduce the contract price by any amount? 2–607(3)(a).

Midwest Mobile Diagnostic Imaging v. Dynamics Corp. of America

United States District Court, Western District of Michigan, 1997
965 F. Supp. 1003

■ Opinion: RICHARD ALAN ENSLEN, CHIEF JUDGE

* * *

I.   Introduction

Plaintiff Midwest Mobile Diagnostic Imagining, L.L.C. [hereinafter "MMDI"] brings this diversity action against defendant Ellis & Watts, d/b/a Dynamics Corporation of America [hereinafter "E&W"], seeking damages for 1) breach of a sales contract for the purchase of four mobile MRI units[1] * * *. Defendant, the seller, counterclaims for damages,

---

[1]   A mobile MRI unit is, in effect, a mobile MRI clinic. It is a semi tractor trailer which contains an MRI scanner and the computer equipment necessary to operate such a machine. It

alleging that the buyer is in breach. Having considered the evidence submitted and the legal arguments of the parties made during a three-day bench trial, and having reviewed the exhibits submitted, the Court enters the following Findings of Fact and Conclusions of Law pursuant to Federal Rule of Civil Procedure 52(a). To the extent that any findings of fact also constitute conclusions of law or vice versa, they are so adopted.

* * *

III. Contentions of the Parties

MMDI contends that, after its rightful rejection of a nonconforming trailer tendered by E&W on December 13, 1995, E&W repudiated the contract in its entirety. E&W's repudiation whether anticipatory or not, destroyed whatever right to cure E&W may have had and gave MMDI the right to cancel the contract, which it then did. Having rightfully canceled the contract, MMDI argues it is entitled to damages.

E&W counters that its tender on December 13, 1995 was both timely and in conformity with contract specifications. Consequently, MMDI's rejection was wrongful. E&W continues that, even if the trailer were not conforming, E&W had a right to cure pursuant to Uniform Commercial Code [hereinafter "UCC" or "Code"] § 2–508, and MMDI could not cancel the contract without first requesting adequate assurances from E&W in writing pursuant to UCC § 2–609. Since plaintiff did not satisfy § 2–609 and a reasonable time for performance had not expired, MMDI's cancellation of the contract on December 18, 1995 constituted anticipatory repudiation.

IV. Facts

Plaintiff Midwest Mobile Diagnostic Imaging, L.L.C. ("MMDI") is a Delaware limited liability company, with offices in Kalamazoo, Michigan, engaged in the business of furnishing equipment and personnel for magnetic resonance imaging (MRI) scans to hospitals in southwestern Michigan. In 1995, MMDI had three mobile MRI units servicing area facilities.

Defendant Ellis & Watts ("E&W") is a New York corporation whose principal place of business is in Cincinnati, Ohio, which engineers, designs, and manufactures trailers for mobile medical uses, including mobile MRI systems.

Under Michigan regulations, the number of mobile MRI scanners which may be licensed is strictly limited. Consequently, companies wishing to provide this service must seek a Certificate of Need from the State. In 1995, the demand for these mobile MRI units exceeded that which MMDI could supply. MMDI, therefore, sought and received a Certificate of Need to begin operating a fourth mobile MRI unit.

In April 1995, plaintiff commenced negotiations with defendant to purchase four mobile MRI trailers, each designed to house a state-of-the-art, ACS NT 1.5T MR scanner system, which plaintiff would purchase separately from Philips. During these initial negotiations, E&W became aware that MMDI had an immediate need for the first trailer because of the growing demand for its services. As a

_____

is designed to function as a temporary extension of the hospital which it is serving, with an interior which generally matches the hospital environment.

consequence, the parties agreed that delivery of the first trailer would occur in September 1995 with the rest to follow in monthly installments. However, during final negotiations in Kalamazoo on August 10, 1995, the parties agreed to delete a clause in the written contract requiring that all four trailers be delivered in 1995. While no specific delivery dates were ultimately included in the written contract, E&W understood that early delivery of the first trailer was of great importance to MMDI. At the time of signing, the parties expected delivery of the trailers to occur in October, November, December, 1995 and January, 1996. The delivery dates were, however, contingent upon coordination with Philips and agreement of the parties.

In addition to the timing of the project, during negotiations the parties also made representations concerning the design of the trailer. On April 17, 1995, Robert Freudenberger of E&W, faxed a signed purchase agreement to Jerry Turowski of MMDI. Attached to the form contract were two drawings. One of the drawings depicted a three-dimensional illustration of the interior of a mobile MRI system trailer upon which was written: "Spacious, efficient layout with clean, aesthetically pleasing interior." In addition, these drawings, and all others reviewed by MMDI both before and after contract signing, did not depict a bracing structure surrounding the scanner magnet.

On August 10, 1995, Mr. Turowski and Mr. Freudenberger executed a purchase agreement for four E&W trailers. With the signing of the contract, MMDI paid E&W a deposit in the amount of $63,000. On August 11, 1995, Mr. Andrew Pike, President of E&W, countersigned the purchase agreement in Cincinnati, Ohio. Under the parties' agreement, E&W was to construct the four trailers in accordance with Philips' specifications. Once certified by Philips, the trailers could be delivered.

On September 7, 1995, plaintiff and defendant met in Kalamazoo to discuss the delivery schedule. On September 21, 1995, MMDI sent a letter indicating that, as a result of that meeting, MMDI expected delivery of the first trailer on November 6, 1995. The letter also noted the parties' understanding that the trailer would be "show" ready for MMDI's open house in Kalamazoo, Michigan, on November 3, 1995. E&W did not respond to this letter. During the course of construction, the parties discussed several alterations to the trailer and consequently, again renegotiated the delivery date for the first trailer. Ultimately, the parties agreed upon a December 1, 1995 delivery date. Under the expectation that the trailer would be delivered on that date, MMDI scheduled patients assuming the trailer would be ready for use beginning December 4, 1995.

On November 3, 1995, indicating that the trailer was cosmetically complete, E&W presented the trailer to MMDI to show at its open house in Kalamazoo, during which representatives of MMDI and many of its customers, inspected the trailer. At that time, the scanner magnet was free from any metal, bracing structures. The trailer was then returned to E&W for final adjustments and testing.

As of mid-November 1995, the first E&W trailer was fully fabricated and substantially all equipment was installed and ready for testing by Philips. In anticipation of the December 1 delivery date, E&W invoiced MMDI on November 10, 1995 for the full purchase price of the first trailer. On November 16, 1995, E&W sent a follow-up letter requesting payment prior to shipment of the trailer on November 30 in accordance with the purchase agreement. MMDI paid $321,500 to E&W on November 17, 1995.

On November 28, 1995, the first trailer failed to meet contract specifications in a test conducted by Philips. The test indicated that the trailer did not comply with Philips' specifications for magnetic shielding in the sidewalls of the trailer. This failure occurred despite the fact that, throughout the construction of the trailer, Philips had repeatedly noted the importance of the proper fabrication of this feature in its correspondence with E&W.

When the parties discovered that the trailer had failed the test, they met to discuss potential solutions to the situation. At that time, E&W stated unequivocally that: 1) the trailer was defective; 2) the defect was entirely its fault and responsibility; and 3) it would cure the problem. E&W also indicated a willingness to reimburse MMDI for at least part of the expenses it might incur in renting another trailer to substitute for the one that E&W had not completed. As a result of the need for a cure, E&W failed to tender a conforming trailer on the December 1 delivery date and MMDI was forced to cancel appointments which had been scheduled with patients for December 4, 1995.

During the following two weeks, E&W designed a reinforcement structure to contend with the wall-flexing problem. The solution consisted of multiple, large, steel beams placed around the scanner magnet in a cage-like structure which prevented removal of the magnet's outer covers and dramatically changed its appearance. Such a bracing structure had never been used with a mobile MRI scanner by any manufacturer. During this period, E&W exchanged multiple letters and sketches with Philips in which Philips' representatives indicated several concerns with the bracing structure. E&W made adjustments to address some of these concerns. Ultimately, Philips approved the design as a temporary solution to the wall-flexing problem.

On December 7, 1995, E&W sent MMDI a schedule indicating that the decision whether to proceed with this design would be made on December 12, 1995. The letter indicated: "if no go at this point, alternate plans established." Although MMDI had reviewed drawings of the interior during the course of construction, E&W did not include a sketch of the reinforcement design in this correspondence.

On December 12, 1995, Philips' representatives retested the trailer with the bracing structure in place and found that the flexing problem had been remedied. Thus, the trailer was approved for use on a temporary basis. However, because the structure impaired service of the scanner magnet, Philips would not certify the trailer for permanent use with the structure in place.

On December 13, 1995, Mr. Turowski of MMDI arrived at E&W to inspect the new design for the first time. After viewing the trailer and speaking with Philips' representatives, Mr. Turowski concluded that the bracing structure was unacceptable for several reasons. Mr. Turowski and Mr. Andrew Pike of E & W then placed a telephone conference call to Dr. Azzam Kanaan and Dr. Ilydio Polachini at MMDI. At that time, Mr. Turowski indicated that, with the bracing structure, the trailer did not conform to the contract obligations because: 1) service of the scanner magnet would be impeded and, in cases, would be more dangerous; 2) its appearance was objectionable; and 3) the resale value of the trailer would be diminished.

Mr. Pike countered that the structure in place conformed to the parties' agreement, that this was the design that met the Philips' specification, that it had been approved by Philips, and told MMDI to accept it the way it was. Further, Mr. Pike stated that the materials had already been purchased to install this design in the second trailer, that this was the best design that one could come up with, and that he did not know if it could be done it any differently. Finally, Mr. Pike refused to pay rent for a replacement unit or to refund MMDI's previous payment.

The following day, December 14, 1995, Mr. Pike sent a letter to Dr. Kanaan at MMDI, indicating that E&W was working with "this design" to see if it could be made more aesthetically pleasing. The letter made no reference to the servicing problems, safety concerns, or concerns about a potential diminution in resale value resulting from the use of the bracing structure. Mr. Pike again asserted the validity of the contract, and refused to refund MMDI's payment for the trailer.

On December 18, 1995, acting in good faith, MMDI advised E&W in writing that the Purchase Agreement was canceled. On December 19, 1995, MMDI rented a mobile MRI unit to replace the one it had expected to receive from E&W. On December 21, 1995, MMDI executed a contract with a third party for the manufacture and construction of two trailers to house two of the Philips 1.5T MR scanner systems.

On December 22, 1995, Mr. Freudenberger sent a letter to Mr. Turowski, reiterating that the first trailer was ready for shipment and requesting instructions on how to ship it. In addition, the letter indicated that E&W was finalizing the design for an alternative bracing structure which would neither impede the servicing of the magnet components nor negatively impact the aesthetics of the trailer interior. Mr. Freudenberger also suggested that, after final testing and seeking MMDI's input regarding the aesthetics of the design, the design "would be considered the permanent solution" for the trailer. The design would then be incorporated into the second trailer at which time the first trailer would be returned to E&W and retrofitted with the new design at no cost to MMDI. E&W, however, maintained that the purchase agreement was still effective and continued to refuse to refund MMDI's payment. Soon after this correspondence, the parties ceased communication. Ultimately, E&W did remove the offending reinforcement structure and replaced it with an alternative design which was approved for permanent use by Philips. In the time since this replacement solution was fabricated and installed, E&W has sold two of the trailers to a third party.

On January 9, 1996, MMDI filed the instant suit for damages resulting from breach of contract and misrepresentation. E&W retained payments made by MMDI in the amount of $384,500. Further, MMDI incurred expenses in the amount of $185,250 for the lease of a mobile MRI scanner and trailer between December 19, 1995 and April 20, 1996.

V.   Analysis

A.   Breach of contract

The primary issue for resolution by the Court is whether MMDI rightfully rejected E&W's tender of the first trailer and then subsequently canceled the contract, or if its actions in mid-December constituted anticipatory repudiation of the contract. Having previously determined that Michigan law controls in the instant case, the Court simply notes that the Michigan version of the Uniform Commercial Code [hereinafter the "UCC"] applies to this sales contract. MCLA §§ 440.1101 et seq.

1.   Installment Contract

Before turning to the specific questions of rejection and cancellation, the Court must first resolve a threshold issue. Under the UCC, the parties' rights to reject, cure, and cancel under an installment contract differ substantially from those defined under a single delivery contract. Consequently, resolution of whether the contract is an installment contract is of primary concern. Section 2–612(1) defines an "installment contract" as "one which requires or authorizes the delivery of goods in separate lots to be separately accepted. . . ." The commentary following this section emphasizes that the "definition of an installment contract is phrased more broadly in this Article [than in its previous incarnation as the Uniform Sales Act] so as to cover installment deliveries tacitly authorized by the circumstances or by the option of either party." § 2–612, cmt. 1.

Plaintiff argues that the contract between itself and E&W does not constitute an installment contract because it authorizes delivery in commercial units, and not lots, as required by subsection (1). However, upon review of the Code section defining those terms, it becomes clear that those terms are not mutually exclusive. Section 2–105 defines a "lot" as a "parcel or single article which is the subject matter of a separate sale or delivery, whether or not it is sufficient to perform the contract." The same section defines a commercial unit as "such a unit of goods as by commercial usage is a single whole for purposes of sale and division of which materially impairs its character or value on the market or in use. A commercial unit may be a single article (as a machine) or a set of articles (as a suite of furniture or an assortment of sizes) or a quantity (as a bale, gross, or carload) or any other unit treated in use or in the relevant market as a single whole." Thus, a lot, which is the measure of goods that the contract states will be delivered together in one installment, can be a single commercial unit. Consequently, § 2–612 applies wherever a contract for multiple items authorizes the delivery of the items in separate groups at different times, whether or not the installment constitutes a commercial unit.

The contract between MMDI and E&W for the sale of four trailers authorizes the delivery of each trailer separately. While the written contract does not explicitly state this delivery schedule, it does authorize separate delivery. Paragraph 2 of the contract assumes separate delivery dates by setting out a payment schedule wherein the balance for each unit is due at the time of shipment. Furthermore, based on the parties testimony it is clear that both parties understood the trailers would be delivered in separate installments. Indeed, neither party disputes that they agreed to have the trailers delivered at four separate times. Therefore, the Court finds that the contract in dispute is an installment contract.

2. Right of Rejection

Section 2–612, therefore, is the starting point for the Court's analysis of MMDI's actions on December 13, 1995. Under § 2–612, the buyer's right to reject is far more limited than the corresponding right to reject under a single delivery contract defined under § 2–601. Under § 2–601, a buyer has the right to reject, "if the goods or tender of delivery fail in any respect to conform to the contract. . . . " Known as the "perfect tender" rule, this standard requires a very high level of conformity. Under this rule, the buyer may reject a seller's tender for any trivial defect, whether it be in the quality of the goods, the timing of performance, or the manner of delivery. To avoid injustice, the Code limits the buyer's correlative right to cancel the contract upon such rejection by providing a right to cure under § 2–508. § 2–508, cmt. 2. Under § 2–508, the seller has a right to cure if s/he seasonably notifies the buyer of the intent to do so, and either 1) the time for performance has not yet passed, or 2) the seller had reason to believe that the goods were in conformity with the contract. Thus, § 2–508's right to cure serves to temper the buyer's expansive right to reject under a single delivery contract.

Section 2–612 creates an exception to the perfect tender rule. Under subsection (2), a buyer may not reject nonconforming tender unless the defect substantially impairs the value of the installment. In addition, "if the nonconformity is curable and the seller gives adequate assurances of cure," the buyer must accept the installment. § 2–612, cmt. 5. But even if rejection is proper under subsection 2, cancellation of the contract is not appropriate unless the defect substantially impairs the value of the whole contract. § 2–612(3), cmt. 6. Because this section significantly restricts the buyer's right to cancel under an installment contract, there is no corresponding necessity for reference to § 2–508; the seller's right to cure is implicitly defined by § 2–612.[2]

a. Delivery Date

Before proceeding with the analysis of MMDI's December 13 rejection, the Court initially notes that E&W's tender on December 13 constituted a cure attempt for the wall-flexing defect which delayed the delivery of the first trailer beyond the agreed upon delivery date. Although under § 2–612 the delivery date does not cut off the seller's right to cure, it does have an effect on the rights of the parties.

In the instant case, the original, written contract included no definite delivery date. Instead, the contract left the delivery term to be agreed upon at a later date. At the time of execution, the parties both expected delivery of the first trailer to take place in October. During the months after the execution of the contract, however, the parties

---

[2] Courts of other jurisdictions have reached differing conclusions with regard to the interaction between §§ 2–612 and 2–508. This Court does not find the arguments of these other courts persuasive, however, and notes that their decisions are not binding on this Court. Nevertheless, the Court also notes that, since the time for delivery of the first installment had already passed on December 1, 1995 (see infra § 2(a)) and defendant could not have reasonably believed and, in fact, did not believe that the trailer was in conformity with the contract on that date, defendant had no right to cure under § 2–508.

modified the deadline for the first installment of the contract on several occasions. As noted above, upon review of the testimony and documentary evidence, the Court finds that, whatever delivery date the parties had agreed upon prior to November 1995, by early November they had renegotiated their agreement to establish a December 1, 1995 delivery date. See § 2–209 (sales contract may be modified by oral or written agreement without consideration, so long as agreement does not state otherwise).

Defendant argues, however, that, even if the parties had at one point agreed upon a December 1, 1995 deadline, when the first trailer failed the Philips road test on November 28, 1995, the parties renegotiated the delivery term to allow E&W a reasonable time to cure the defect. While E&W is correct that, as of December 1, it had a reasonable time in which to cure the wall-flexing problem, the Court disagrees that MMDI's willingness to wait for a cure constitutes an agreement to extend the delivery deadline. Because the parties believed that the defect was curable and E&W, without solicitation, unequivocally promised to cure it, under § 2–612, MMDI had no choice but to accept an offer of cure. To reject the installment on November 28 would have constituted a violation of § 2–612. The Court, therefore, finds that any negotiations the parties engaged in regarding delivery after discovery of the wall-flexing problem, did not constitute a modification of the delivery date for the first installment, but rather involved negotiation regarding cure. Since no specific date for delivery of a cure was agreed upon during those negotiations, under section 2–309(1), E&W had a reasonable time to effectuate a cure. Although there is some question as to whether further delay would have been reasonable, the Court finds that, as of December 13, 1995, a reasonable time had not yet passed. Therefore, defendant's tender of a cure was timely.

b.   Substantial Impairment of the Installment

The Court's conclusion that E&W's December 13 tender was an attempt to cure the November 28 breach raises another question: which standard of conformity applies to cure under an installment contract, perfect tender or substantial impairment? Looking to the rationale behind § 2–612, the Court notes that the very purpose of allowing the seller time to cure under this section is to permit it additional time to meet the obligations of the contract. The assumption is that, because the parties have an ongoing relationship, the seller should be given an opportunity to make up the deficiency. This section was not designed to allow the seller to have a never-ending series of chances to bring the item into conformity with the contract. Nor was it enacted to force the buyer to accept a nonconforming product as satisfaction of the contract. Consequently, it is logical that a tender of cure should be required to meet the higher "perfect tender" standard. On its face, however, § 2–612, which generally defines a buyer's right to reject goods under an installment contract, requires only substantial impairment in this context as well. Thus, there is some question as to which is the appropriate standard. The answer is not crucial, however, since the trailer in this case fails under both standards. Because a decision on this point will not affect the ultimate outcome in this case, the Court declines to address the issue. Instead, the Court proceeds with the substantial impairment analysis provided by § 2–612.

To establish substantial impairment of the value of an installment, the buyer " 'must present objective evidence that with respect to its own needs, the value of the goods was substantially impaired.' " Arkla Energy Resources v. Roye Realty & Dev., Inc., 9 F.3d 855, 862 (10th Cir. 1993). See also § 2–612, cmt. 4. The existence of such nonconformity depends on the facts and circumstances of each case, and "can turn not only on the quality of the goods but also on such factors as time . . . , and the like." § 2–612, cmt. 4. See, e.g., Colonial Dodge, Inc. v. Miller, 362 N.W.2d 704 (1984) (holding missing spare tire in new car had special devaluing effect for the buyer and thus could constitute substantial impairment). Finally, whether nonconformity rises to the level of substantial impairment may be judged by reference to the concept of material breach under traditional contract law.

In the instant case, plaintiff alleges several aspects in which defendant's December 13 tender failed to conform to contract obligations. Plaintiff contends that the trailer tendered on December 13 with the bracing structure did not conform to the parties' agreement because: 1) it was not and could not be certified by Philips without conditions for use with the 1.5T scanner and 2) its interior design did not conform with the parties' agreements. Because of these defects, MMDI argues that the value of trailer was reduced substantially. Defendant, on the other hand, contends that the contract required only that the trailer meet the technical specifications provided by Philips, and that, therefore, the December 13 trailer was in complete compliance with its terms.

The written contract signed by the parties in this case is relatively skeletal and thus, requires interpretation. The Court's fundamental purpose in interpreting the terms of the contract is to give effect to the intent of the parties as it existed at the time the agreement was made. " 'The meaning of the agreement of the parties is to be determined by the language used by them and by their action, read, and interpreted in the light of commercial practices and other surrounding circumstances.' " 1 WILLISTON ON SALES § 10–2, 431 (quoting 1 CORBIN ON CONTRACTS § 2.9 (rev. Ed.)). See also § 1–203 (setting out the requirement of good faith and requiring the Court to interpret "contracts within the commercial context in which they are created, performed, and enforced[ ]"). Furthermore, the Code explicitly authorizes courts to look to the parties' course of dealings and performance and to the usage of terms in trade in interpreting the terms of the contract. §§ 1–205, 2–202, and 2–208.

As instructed by the commentary to § 2–612, the Court begins the substantial impairment analysis by looking to the "normal and specifically known purposes of the contract." § 2–612, cmt. 4. Reviewing the evidence presented, the Court finds that the primary purpose of the contract was to provide the plaintiff with four trailers for use with the Philips 1.5T scanner. With that in mind, the parties agreed that the trailers would be constructed in accordance with the specifications provided by Philips and that the trailer would be not be ready for delivery until Philips certification had been received. Philips did not, however, ever certify the trailer for unconditional use with the bracing structure. Because the bracing structure prevented normal service of the scanner magnet, it was only approved as a temporary fix.

The general rule in cases where third party approval is required as a condition of performance is one of strict compliance. Such conditions will only be excused where the third party acts in bad faith or dishonestly. In the instant case, there was no credible evidence presented that Philips acted in bad faith by withholding approval. On the contrary, there was extensive evidence presented detailing the inherent problems with the long-term use of such a bracing solution, which demonstrated the reasonableness of Philips' refusal to certify the trailer. The bracing structure's shape and orientation prevented removal of the outer panels from the scanner magnet and made some repairs to the magnet more difficult and more dangerous. Furthermore, in order to perform certain repairs, the steel brace would have to be unbolted and removed. Once removed, the scanner magnet would have to be recalibrated and retested. Consequently, Philips' decision to refuse certification was entirely justified. Having found no evidence of bad faith or dishonesty on the part of Philips, the Court finds that defendant's failure to meet this condition constituted a breach of the parties' agreement. Given that the central purpose of the trailer was to house a Philips 1.5T scanner, the failure to meet the standard for Philips' certification substantially impaired the value of the trailer. The Court, therefore, finds that this failure to conform to the parties' agreement, in and of itself, constituted a material breach.

In addition to violating the requirement that the trailer receive certification from Philips, plaintiff correctly asserts that defendant breached yet another term of the contract. The Court notes that the bracing structure also violated the parties' implied agreement regarding the design of the interior of the trailer. During the course of the parties' dealings both before and after the contract signing, MMDI reviewed numerous representations of the trailer's interior layout and design. Many of these drawings showed the location of the scanner and detailed the location of every structure in the trailer. None of them, however, depicted a cage-like brace made up of multiple, large, steel beams surrounding the scanner magnet. These drawings, when coupled with E&W's own statement that the trailer was cosmetically complete without the brace when it was presented at the open house, convince the Court that there was an implied agreement that the trailer would not have such a structure.

Furthermore, it is clear that, when the contract was executed, the parties both understood that the trailer's interior was meant to be aesthetically pleasing. It is the very nature of a mobile MRI trailer to function as an extension of the hospital it services. Since E&W was in the business of constructing trailers for mobile medical uses, it no doubt understood that the appearance of the trailer's interior could impact the comfort of MMDI's patients. Indeed, it is apparent that E&W realized such aesthetics were important to the value of the trailer, since, in its initial negotiations with MMDI, E&W included a cut-away drawing of the interior of a mobile unit which read: "Spacious, efficient layout with clean, aesthetically pleasing interior." The Court, therefore, finds that the agreement between the parties required that the interior of the trailer be aesthetically pleasing.

Such a condition of satisfaction by one of the parties to the contract will only be excused if approval is withheld unreasonably. In the instant case, upon review of photographs of the bracing structure and testimony of those experienced in this industry, and in light of the fact that the interior of the trailer should match that of a hospital and not a construction site, the Court finds that plaintiff's refusal to approve the aesthetics of the design was commercially reasonable. Given that an integral aspect of the trailer's function is to serve as a clinic for patients undergoing medical procedures, and given MMDI's clients' expectations after having viewed the trailer at the open house, such a defect in the trailer's interior also reduced the value of the trailer substantially.

Upon review of the evidence, the Court finds that the bracing structure substantially impaired the value of the first trailer. Although the trailer met the express technical Philips' specifications for wall-flexing, it was never certified by the manufacturer. The failure of this condition does not relieve defendant of liability because it was defendant's failure to properly construct the trailer that prevented certification. In light of the specific facts and circumstances of this case, the Court finds that this deficiency substantially impaired the value of the installment. When coupled with the trailer's failure to conform with the aesthetic requirements of the contract and the delay caused by the cure attempt, the Court holds that the cure attempt clearly constitutes a substantial breach within the meaning of § 2–612(2).

Substantial impairment, however, does not in itself justify rejection of the installment. As noted above, the buyer must still accept tender if the defect can be cured and the seller gives adequate assurances. Under § 2–612, as opposed to § 2–609, it is incumbent upon the seller to assure the buyer that cure would be forthcoming. Defendant has failed in this regard. The Court notes that neither E&W's statements during the December 13 conference call nor the letter sent the following day constituted adequate assurances. On the contrary, during the December 13 conference call, Andrew Pike, the President of E&W denied the existence of a defect, disclaimed any continuing obligation to cure under the contract, and stated that he did not believe a better design could be made which would remedy the wall-flexing problem. Furthermore, on December 14, Mr. Pike again ignored the servicing problems that the bracing structure had caused, ignored the fact that the bracing structure had not been approved for permanent use by Philips, and reiterated his doubt that the design could be constructed in a more aesthetically pleasing manner. Under these circumstances, the Court finds that MMDI's rejection of E&W's cure on December 13 constituted a rightful rejection under § 2–612(2).[3]

---

[3] Defendant argues that, as of December 13, it still had a right to cure under § 2–508 and that it was not required to give assurances unless plaintiff requested them in writing under § 2–609. The Court reiterates that, under § 2–508, defendant's right to cure was cut off on December 1. Furthermore, § 2–612, unlike § 2–609, does not require the aggrieved party to request assurances. In an installment contract, where the seller's right to cure is more expansive it stands to reason that the burden would fall on the seller to show that it had the present ability and the intent to cure any remaining defect. In the instant case, defendant gave no indication that it either had the capability to satisfy the contract or the will to do so. On the contrary, E&W's President, gave MMDI the impression that cure was not possible and indicated clearly that he was not required to do anything more under the contract. Under such circumstances, MMDI's rejection was rightful.

3. Cancellation

a. Substantial Impairment of Contract as a Whole

The fact that rejection of one installment is proper does not necessarily justify cancellation of the entire contract. Under § 2–612(3) the right to cancel does not arise unless the nonconforming goods substantially impair the value of the entire contract. Indeed, as noted above, the very purpose of the substantial impairment requirement of § 2–612(3) is to preclude parties from canceling an installment contract for trivial defects.

Whether a breach constitutes "substantial impairment" of the entire contract is a question of fact. Bill's Coal Co. v. Board of Public Utilities, 887 F.2d 242, 247 (10th Cir. 1989). To make such a determination, the Court should consider "the cumulative effect of [the breaching party's] performance under the contract, based on the totality of the circumstances. . . . " Neufer v. Video Greetings, Inc., 931 F.2d 56 (6th Cir. 1991). Ultimately, "whether the non-conformity in any given installment justifies cancellation as to the future depends, not on whether such non-conformity indicates an intent or likelihood that future deliveries will also be defective, but whether the non-conformity substantially impairs the value of the whole contract." § 2–612, cmt. 6. Thus, the question is one of present breach which focuses on the importance of the nonconforming installment relative to the contract as a whole. If the nonconformity only impairs the aggrieved party's security with regard to future installments, s/he "has the right to demand adequate assurances but [ ] not an immediate right to cancel the entire contract." § 2–612, cmt. 6. The right to cancel will be triggered only if "material inconvenience or injustice will result if the aggrieved party is forced to wait and receive an ultimate tender minus the part or aspect repudiated." § 2–610, cmt.3 (noting the test for anticipatory repudiation under § 2–610 is the same as the test for cancellation under § 2–612(3)).

In the instant case, there is substantial evidence that one of the primary purposes of this contract was to provide MMDI with a fourth mobile MRI trailer so that it could meet the growing demand for its services. Thus, impairment of one of the four installments would have a substantial negative impact on MMDI. Moreover, an early delivery time was of primary importance to MMDI, as E&W was well aware. By failing to cure the November 28 breach on the first installment, E&W substantially delayed completion of the remainder of the contract which delayed MMDI's ability to begin use of the 1.5T MRI trailer it had promised to its customers at the open house on November 3. Having found that substantial injustice would be done to plaintiff if it were required to accept the remaining three trailers after substantial delay as satisfaction of the contract, the Court finds that plaintiff rightfully canceled the contract on December 18, 1995.

4. Damages

Having found that plaintiff rightfully rejected defendant's tender of cure on December 13, 1995, and subsequently properly canceled the contract, the Court finds that plaintiff is entitled to damages. Plaintiff has requested reimbursement of the amount it already paid for the nonconforming installment in the amount of $384,500 as well as damages in the amount of $185,250 incurred for the lease of a rental mobile MRI trailer between December 19, 1995 and April 20, 1996, to replace the trailer E&W failed to produce. Under § 2–711, a buyer who has rightfully canceled a contract may recover, among other things: 1) the amount that has already been paid, 2) damages for "cover" as defined in § 2–712, and 3) any damages of nondelivery, including consequential and incidental damages, as defined by § 2–715. Under § 2–715, incidental damages include "any [ ] reasonable expense incident to the delay or other breach." Thus, plaintiff is clearly entitled to return of the amount already paid for the item it never received. Plaintiff is also entitled to recover the amount paid for a replacement rental unit. Though this amount does not constitute cover it is allowable as incidental to the delay produced by E & W's breach. Had E&W made conforming tender on December 13, 1995, plaintiff would not have been forced to contract with another company for the trailers and to wait until spring for the first one. The court, therefore, finds plaintiff is entitled to both expectation and consequential damages under the Code and awards plaintiff a sum total of $569,250 for the breach of contract claim. * * *

VI. Conclusion

For the foregoing reasons, plaintiff is awarded expectation and incidental damages in the amount of $569,250. Plaintiff's claim of misrepresentation is deemed waived and dismissed. Defendant's counterclaim for damages is denied and its motion for judgment on partial findings pursuant to Federal Rule of Civil Procedure 52(c) is deemed moot.

NOTES

1. An installment contract is a single contract that calls for or allows separate deliveries. 2–612(1). Section 2–612 treats the single contract as if it were a series of independent contracts for separate deliveries. By contrast, unless the parties' agreement provides otherwise, a non-installment contract requires a single delivery. 2–307. Section 2–612's rules for rejection of an installment contract reflect an important economic difference between a single-delivery and installment contracts. Installment contracts are long-term contracts; single-delivery contracts are not. The seller's investment or other expenses incurred to perform a single-delivery contract are made before performance. In an installment contract the seller incurs these costs in performance over the course of the separate deliveries. As a result, the seller's investment is continuous. The seller's investment also is specific to the installment contract, so that it cannot be fully recovered by diverting it to other uses. For example, to make a series of deliveries, the installment seller might need to enter into a set of shipment contracts with a carrier in advance. The price of these contracts is lost if the buyer cancels the installment contract. Because the seller's investment is contract-specific and continuous, the seller risks losing its investment if the perfect tender rule applied to installment contracts. In that case the rule would allow the buyer to expropriate part of the investment by credibly threatening to reject a trivially nonconforming installment. Expropriation would occur through a renegotiation of the contract terms in the buyer's favor. Anticipating this risk, the installment seller would either underinvest in performance of the contract or incur costs in advance in contracting around the perfect tender rule. Both measures arguably produce an efficient installment contract.

Considered against this background, 2–612's special rules for the rejection of installment contracts make some sense. Section 2–601, by its terms, makes its perfect tender rule inapplicable to installment contracts ("Subject to the provisions of this Article on breach in installment contracts . . ."). Instead, 2–612(2) incorporates a substantial performance rule for the rejection of an installment, and 2–613(3) does the same for cancellation of the entire contract. Under the substantial performance rule the installment seller does not risk losing its investment if it make a trivially nonconforming delivery. The risk of expropriation of its investment therefore is lower than under the perfect tender rule. Accordingly, the installment seller will invest more in performing the installment contract than otherwise. Section 2–612(2) and (3)'s rules for rejection save the seller the cost of contracting for a rejection rule that protects its investment. Nonetheless, these rules were controversial when Article 2's provisions were drafted and some commentators remain unhappy with them. See 1 Report of the Law Revision Commission, Study of the Uniform Commercial Code 541–543 (1955); Permanent Editorial Board Study Group, Uniform Commercial Code: Article 2 178–180 (1990).

Although its special rules for rejection are defensible, 2-612 is poorly drafted and in places creates uncertainty. Subsection (2) applies to the buyer's rejection of an installment and describes two standards separated by a semicolon. The first standard appears in the part of the sentence before the semicolon. Under it the buyer "may reject" an installment if the nonconformity in the installment substantially impairs the value of that installment and cannot be cured or the nonconformity is in required documents of title. The second standard is stated in the part of subsection (2)'s sentence appearing after the semicolon ("but if . . . "). According to this standard, the buyer "must accept" an installment containing a nonconformity that substantially impairs the value of that installment if the nonconformity does not impair the value of the entire contract and the seller gives adequate assurances of its cure. An installment that the buyer "must accept" is one that the buyer "cannot reject." See 2–607(2). Thus, the first part of 2–612(2)'s sentence describes when the buyer may reject an installment; the second part following the semicolon describes when it cannot reject an installment. Neither 2–612 nor its Comments state whether substantial impairment is judged by a subjective or an objective standard. Cf. 2–608(1).

2.   *Midwest Mobile Diagnostic Imaging* is one of the few cases to construe 2–612(2)'s rules on rejection. There, MMDI (the buyer) and E&W (the seller) agreed on a December 1 delivery date for the first of four trailers. When the trailer E&W delivered on November 28 failed a road test, MMDI agreed to allow E&W more time to cure defects in it. Applying the second part of 2–612(2)'s sentence, the court concluded that MMDI could not reject the November 28 delivery. The court apparently assumed, reasonably enough, that the defects were curable because the parties believed they could be cured. The first part of 2–

612(2)'s sentence therefore was inapplicable. Although the defect in the delivered trailer substantially impaired its value, E&W promised to cure it. In these circumstances MMDI "had no choice but to accept an offer of cure," according to the court. Given this determination, E&W's offer must have constituted an adequate assurance of cure. Thus, under the second part of 2–612(2)'s sentence MMDI could not reject E&W's November 28 nonconforming delivery. MMDI later cancelled the contract after E&W's attempt to cure by a second tender on December 13 failed. The court found the cancellation proper under 2–612(3) because the uncured defects in the November 28 tender substantially impaired the value of the whole contract to MMDI.

    3. Section 2–612 does not state the conditions under which the installment seller has a right to cure a defective installment. It contains no reference to 2–508 or 2–508's restrictions on a seller's right to cure. The question therefore arises as to whether 2–508's restrictions control the installment seller's right to cure under 2–612(2) or whether 2–612 has its own implicit conditions of cure. This question matters because 2–612's implicit conditions for cure can differ from 2–508's conditions. Section 2–508(1) allows a seller to cure a defective tender if the contractual period for delivery has not passed. Section 2–508(2) allows cure even past the time for delivery if the seller tendered nonconforming goods with the belief that the tender would be acceptable to the buyer, with or without a money allowance. Both subsections require that cure be a substitute tender that conforms to the contract. Section 2–612 contains none of these limitations. Thus, a price adjustment for a defective installment, for example, can count as cure. See Comment 5 to 2–612. Price adjustments cannot constitute cure under 2–508, unless allowed by the contract.

    E&W's second tender on December 13 came after December 1, the date the contract called for delivery of the trailer. Thus, its cure came too late under 2–508(1). In addition, E&W did not believe at the time it first tendered the trailer on November 28 that the trailer conformed to the contract. Section 2–508(2) therefore does not give it the right to cure by making a second tender (at least as the *Midwest Mobile Diagnostic* understands the subsection; see footnote 3). Because 2–612 does not contain either of 2–508's limitations on cure, E&W's second tender on December 13 might be allowable.

    Courts can take two different positions on the relationship between 2–508 and 2–612(2)'s cure provisions. One position is that that 2–508's restrictions on cure regulate the installment seller's right to cure under 2–612(2). The second position is that 2–508's cure provisions govern single delivery contracts while 2–612's cure provision controls installment contracts. *Midwest Mobile Diagnostic* finds that the provisions are independent of each other and that 2–612 implicitly defines the installment seller's right to cure. Based on this implicit definition, the court concludes that E&W's second tender on December 13 was timely. A case can be made that the long-term character of installment contracts justifies a broader right of cure than for single-delivery contracts. The installment seller who has invested in performing the entire contract might be in a position to cheaply remedy a defective installment. The buyer's alternative of rejection and obtaining a substitute on the market can be more expensive. If so, giving the installment seller a more generous right to cure reduces the cost of breach. To be sure, a broad right to cure risks leaving the buyer undercompensated. This is particularly true if the seller can cure by providing something other than a conforming tender, such as a price adjustment. However, the relationship-specific investments already made by the installment seller leave it vulnerable to the buyer's strategic claims of damages. The right to cure avoids this risk. A broad right to cure under 2–612 is justified if the savings from breach are greater than the risk of the buyer being undercompensated by cure. The seller's right to cure under 2–508 is discussed in the next section.

4.   Under 2–612(3) the buyer may cancel the installment contract if the defect in the installment is substantial as to the entire contract. The subsection does not give the installment seller a right to cure. As noted, in *Midwest Mobile Diagnostic* MMDI relied on E&W's substantially defective tender of November 28 to cancel the entire contract. However, MMDI did not reject E&W's second tender of December 13. Does 2–612(2) require MMDI to accept the November 28 tender because it did not reject it, at the same time that 2–612(3) permits MMDI to cancel E&W's remaining deliveries under the contract? Then-Professor Ellen Peters' answer seems convincing: "Subsection (3)'s failure to mention 'cure' in the context of the specificity of 2–612(2) most likely indicates an intentional omission. . . . If cure were, in fact, tendered, however, nothing in subsection (2) expressly applies, since actual tender is certainly not identical with assurance. It would seem only sensible to consider this as a *casus omissus* and to allow complete rejection. The worst possible solution would be the one that a literal reading of the section would suggest, which would sanction rejection for the future while requiring acceptance of the particular installment which allowed the repudiation." Ellen A. Peters, Remedies for Breach of Contracts Related to the Sales of Goods Under the Uniform Commercial Code: A Roadmap for Article Two, 73 Yale L. J. 199, 227 (1963).

PROBLEM 7.6

Burton Cigars contracted with Smoke Corp. to buy five boxes of fine cigars each month over the course of a year. Smoke's January and February deliveries went well. Burton's customers were pleased with Smoke's cigars and asked for more. Smoke's March delivery went less well. Burton's customers soon complained that their cigars were dry and tasted unspeakably bad. Worried, Burton contacted Smoke, which acknowledged that one of the boxes of cigars delivered in March did not contain "fine" cigars. (Burton's complaining customers had purchased cigars from this box.) At the same time, Smoke promised that it would make sure that subsequent shipments of cigars would be of the quality of those delivered in January and February. Burton is not placated by Smoke's response. It is worried about its customers' continued loyalty and wants to look for another supplier of quality cigars.

(a) Burton still has four of the five boxes of cigars from Smoke's March delivery. May Burton reject Smoke's March delivery? 2–612(2), 2–601.

(b) May Burton cancel its contract with Smoke? 2–612(3). What risk does it take in doing so?

C. ACCEPTANCE

The buyer accepts the goods when it either signifies its acceptance to the seller, fails to make an effective rejection or does any act inconsistent with the seller's ownership. 2–606(1)(a)–(c). The first two ways of indicating acceptance are straightforward. The signification of acceptance need not be express; it can be inferred from the buyer's acts or silence in the appropriate circumstances. Comment 1 to 2–606. Acceptance through failure to reject occurs when the buyer does not make an effective rejection. 2–606(1)(b). Because acceptance in this manner cannot occur until a reasonable opportunity to inspect has passed, the failure to reject within this time constitutes an acceptance. Rejection requires giving the seller timely and adequate notice of the refusal to retain the goods. 2–602(1).

Acceptance indicated by acts inconsistent with the seller's ownership of the goods is more complicated. Rejection indicates to the seller that the buyer refuses to keep the goods. By rejecting, the buyer communicates that it does not want the goods and does not own them. Acts of control over the goods that typically are associated with ownership negates this communication. The buyer's continued control suggests to the seller that the buyer intends to retain the goods and use or dispose of them. It allows the seller to claim that the goods in fact belong to the buyer and indicate the buyer's acceptance. As case law puts it, acts inconsistent with the seller's ownership cancel or "waive" an earlier rejection. This inference from control fits with the signaling function acceptance and rejection serve under Article 2. As noted above in section A, the buyers' rejection signals to the seller that it is to retrieve and dispose of the goods; acceptance signals that the buyer will dispose of them itself. From this perspective, the buyer's continued control of the goods indicates its intent to dispose of the goods. Acts of control therefore indicate acceptance. Comment 2 to 2–601 recognizes the signaling feature of acceptance: ". . . [I]f the buyer attempts to accept . . . after his original rejection has the caused the seller to arrange for other disposition of the goods, the buyer must answer for any ensuing damage since the next section [2–602(2)(a)] provides that any exercise of ownership after rejection is wrongful as against the seller."

Section 2–606(1)(c) does not specify the acts which are "inconsistent with the seller's ownership." This sometimes makes it difficult to determine which acts are inconsistent with the seller's ownership of the goods, particularly when the buyer uses the goods after rejecting them. Under 2–602(2)(a), after rejection the buyer's exercise of ownership is wrongful against the seller. According to 2–606(1)(c), wrongful acts inconsistent with the seller's ownership operate as an acceptance if ratified by the seller. Taken together, the two sections treat these wrongful acts following rejection as constituting acceptance. Section 2–606(1)(c)'s failure to specify the "inconsistent acts" creates uncertainty as to whether the buyer accepts the goods when it uses them after rejection.

Consider in this regard the range of acts as to the goods, from the buyer's mere possession to its alteration of them. Article 2 does not count the rejecting buyer's retention of the goods, without more, as acceptance. Section 2–602(2)(b) obligates the buyer who has received the goods before it rejects to hold them with reasonable care at the seller's disposition. Merely retaining the goods therefore does not cancel an otherwise effective rejection. Even storing or reselling the goods for the seller's account following rejection does not constitute acceptance. Section 2–604 permits the rejecting buyer to either store or resell, failing reasonable instructions, and provides that "[s]uch action is not acceptance or conversion." A fair inference from 2–602(2)(b) and 2–604 is that retaining, storing or reselling the goods by themselves are not acts inconsistent with the seller's ownership. On the other hand, the buyer's fabrication or complete depletion of the goods arguably is inconsistent with the seller's ownership. Thus, the hard cases involve uses of the goods that go beyond mere possession or resale but fall short of their complete appropriation.

The first of the two following cases below involve the continued use of the goods by the buyer after rejection. In the second of the cases the buyer continued to use the goods after it revoked its acceptance. Under 2–608(3) the revoking buyer has the same rights and duties with respect to the goods as the rejecting buyer. The revoking buyer therefore is under the same "duty" as the rejecting buyer not to act with respect to the goods inconsistent with the seller's ownership. Both cases raise the same issue: what is the extent of continued use that renders an initially effective rejection or revocation no longer effective? Revocation is discussed in more detail below in section E.

Kuiper v. Wright

Texas Court of Appeals, 2001
2001 Tex. App. LEXIS 5519

■ Opinion by Moseley, Judge

Appellant Greg Kuiper f/k/a/ Advanced Cast Stone ("Kuiper") appeals a judgment in favor of appellees Dr. Damaris Young Wright, Don Knobler, and Don Knobler and Company, Inc. ("DKC"). Kuiper presents twenty issues generally contending the trial court erred in rendering judgment against him on his claims of breach of contract and unjust enrichment and in favor of appellees on their counterclaims for breach of contract, breach of warranty, and DTPA violations. For the reasons that follow, we reverse in part and affirm in part, and remand this case to the trial court for additional proceedings consistent with this opinion.

Background

Appellees Knobler and Wright are husband and wife and own a house in Dallas. Knobler also owns the corporate appellee DKC. Kuiper is an independent distributor of cast stone materials that are manufactured by Advanced Cast Stone, Inc.

In early 1996, Knobler contacted Kuiper about purchasing stone columns to replace wooden columns on his back porch and garage. The columns come in pieces, cross-sections of which are shaped like a "C." When two of the pieces are attached together by mortar, they create a hollow stone column with a round exterior. The hollow core allows the columns to be installed around a structural (load-bearing) pole, pipe, or rod.

Knobler had purchased columns from Kuiper in the past. At that time, Kuiper worked for American Cast Stone, but told Knobler he was leaving American Cast Stone and now owned his own business, "Advanced Cast Stone," which manufactured cast stone. However, contrary to Kuiper's representation, his business did not manufacture cast stone. Rather, Kuiper purchased cast stone from an unrelated company, Advanced Cast Stone, Inc.

On May 6, 1996, Kuiper sent a proposal to Knobler for the porch and garage columns, which were for purely decorative purposes. The proposal was for six sixteen-inch columns for the porch and four twelve-inch columns for the garage. The price quoted on the proposal was $8,080.00. The parties subsequently agreed on a contract price of $8,846.00. Knobler requested Kuiper to begin work on the columns. Before delivering the columns, Kuiper asked Knobler whether his existing columns had posts inside. Knobler determined the porch columns had four-inch square posts inside, but the garage columns had no posts. Kuiper told Knobler he should install four-inch square posts for the garage columns, and Knobler did so.

Knobler also requested bases for the garage columns. Kuiper suggested nineteen-inch bases, which was larger than his standard base, because the standard base would not fit over the existing concrete base. Knobler was concerned the larger base would not allow cars to safely enter and exit the garage, but Kuiper told Knobler the base would not be too large.

The columns and bases were delivered in December 1996. The porch columns were installed. The garage columns could not, however, be installed because the interior core was too small to fit around the four-inch square posts. Knobler had the four-inch posts replaced with smaller posts so that the columns could be installed. However, Knobler refused to install the columns because he said they were cracked. Although Knobler had already paid Kuiper $4,000, he refused to pay the remainder due until Kuiper replaced the garage columns. Kuiper refused to replace or repair the columns.

Meanwhile, Knobler installed the nineteen-inch bases for the garage columns. However, he complained to Kuiper that the bases were too large, causing Wright to run over them and damaging the bases and her car. Kuiper refused to replace the bases, asserting they were as small as he could make them for the columns. Another seller did, however, make smaller bases for the columns.

Because Kuiper did not retrieve the garage columns and because they were too heavy for Knobler to move, they remained in Knobler's driveway from December 1996 until January 1998. At that time, Knobler installed the columns because his homeowners association was threatening suit if the columns were not removed from the driveway. After the columns were installed, the cracks on them worsened.

Kuiper sued Wright, Knobler, and DKC for breach of contract and unjust enrichment. Knobler, Wright, and DKC counterclaimed for DTPA violations, breach of contract and breach of warranty. After hearing the evidence the trial court rendered judgment against Kuiper on his breach of contract and unjust enrichment claims, and in favor of appellees on their counterclaims for breach of contract, breach of warranty, and DTPA violations. The trial court awarded appellees $5,424.80 in damages, representing appellees' costs for: (1) installation of replacement posts; (2) the cost of replacement bases and their installation; (3) the cost of installing of the defective columns; and (4) the cost of replacement columns. The last item of damages was awarded only for the breach of warranty claim. In this appeal, Kuiper presents twenty issues, most of which attack the legal and factual sufficiency of the evidence to support the trial court's judgment. * * *

Application of Law to Facts

A. Privity

In his first issue, Kuiper contends the evidence is legally and factually insufficient to support a finding there was a contract between himself and Knobler and Wright. Specifically, Kuiper asserts the contract was only between him and DKC. Knobler testified he agreed to purchase the columns from Kuiper for his home in his individual capacity. Furthermore, Kuiper testified he knew the posts were for Knobler and Wright's home. Additionally, when asked whether there was a written agreement concerning the columns, Kuiper responded he received Knobler and Wright's "word" and a check from Wright's medical practice. Finally, Kuiper himself sued Knobler and Wright for breach of contract. We conclude the evidence is legally and factually sufficient to support a finding that Kuiper contracted with Knobler and Wright.

In this issue, Kuiper also asserts the evidence is legally and factually insufficient to support the trial court's finding that appellees contracted "only" for the four columns for the garage. He asserts the contract was for ten columns. The trial court did not, however, find appellees contracted to purchase only the four garage columns. We resolve the first issue against Kuiper.

B. Installation/Acceptance

In his second issue, Kuiper contends appellees' installation of the columns constitutes an acceptance of the columns, not a rejection. On this basis, he argues the evidence is legally and factually insufficient to support the trial court's findings that: appellees rejected the columns in a timely manner after they discovered the defects; the rejection was reasonable because the columns were not fit for their intended use; and appellees timely notified Kuiper of their rejection after they discovered the defects. Instead, Kuiper argues the undisputed evidence shows that appellees accepted the columns.

The undisputed evidence shows the columns were delivered in December 1996. When they were unwrapped for installation in January 1997, appellees found them to be unacceptable because they had cracks and because the interior cores were too small to fit around the four-inch posts that Knobler had installed. Appellees told Kuiper they were rejecting the columns; although they had paid a portion of the purchase price, they did not make any further payment. Kuiper refused to repair, replace, or pick up the columns, which sat in appellees' driveway for an extended period of time. Thereafter, in response to a threat that appellees would be sued by their homeowners' association if they did not install or move the columns, appellees had the columns installed on the garage.

However, appellees ultimately did not exercise any of the options allowed by the Code. Instead, appellees mortared pieces of the columns together and had them installed, putting them to their intended use as decorative vertical columns on appellees' garage. We agree with Kuiper that, as a matter of law, appellees' installation of the stone columns is an "act inconsistent with [Kuiper]'s ownership" of them, and thus constitutes an acceptance of the columns pursuant to the Code. § 2.606(a)(3); See also Bacchus Indus. Inc. v. Frontier Mechanical Contractors, 36 S.W.3d 579, 585 (Tex. App.–El Paso 2000) (buyer's post-rejection repair and modification of air conditioning units constituted acts inconsistent with the seller's ownership and constituted acceptance); Bowen v. Young, 507 S.W.2d 600, 603–05 (Tex. Civ. App.–El Paso 1974, no writ) (plaintiff's acts of moving in and repairing non-conforming mobile home after giving notice of rejection constitutes acceptance under section 2.606). This subsequent acceptance of the goods withdrew appellees' prior rejection.

Despite statements in appellees' brief that installation of the columns was "temporary," the portions of the record cited by appellees as support for those statements do not indicate there was anything temporary about mortaring the pieces of the columns together and installing them on appellees' garage. Although the trial court held that the columns would have to be replaced someday, we find no evidence in the record supporting the proposition that appellees' installation of the stone columns was temporary.

More importantly, what constitutes an acceptance of goods under the Code does not directly hinge on whether the buyer's actions were temporary or permanent. Such a rule would lead to uncertainty and disputes as to whether the buyer intended to act inconsistent with the seller's ownership in the tendered goods. Rather, the Code minimizes such uncertainties as to motivation and intent by providing a bright-line rule—a buyer accepts goods tendered if he or she "does any act inconsistent with the seller's ownership." § 2.606. Pursuant to this clear statutory standard, the undisputed evidence reveals that appellees accepted the columns by having them installed, regardless of their motives for doing so.

Because the undisputed evidence shows that appellees accepted the columns, we conclude the evidence is legally and factually insufficient to support the trial court's findings that appellees rejected the columns in a timely manner after they discovered the defects; that the rejection was reasonable because the columns were not fit for their intended use; and that appellees timely notified Kuiper of their rejection after they discovered the defects. We sustain Kuiper's second issue.

The trial court's determination that appellees rejected the columns was the foundation upon which many of its findings of fact and conclusions of law were based. Our conclusion that appellees accepted the columns as a matter of law impacts several of Kuiper's other issues, including the measure of damages awarded to appellees and determination of any amounts that Kuiper may be entitled to offset based upon his claims against appellees. However, we address each of Kuiper's remaining issues to the extent that they can be disposed of by this Court.

In his sixteenth issue, Kuiper attacks the trial court's conclusion of law that, as a result of Kuiper's breach of contract, he is not entitled to any additional payments. Because appellees ultimately accepted the columns, they "became obligated to pay at the contract price [under section 2.607]." *Bowen*, 507 S.W.2d at 603. Thus, the trial court's conclusion that Kuiper was not entitled to any additional payments is incorrect. However, because the trial court must reevaluate the appropriate measure of damages, we cannot determine in this appeal the extent of the offset to which Kuiper is entitled. That issue can and should be determined by the trial court on remand. We sustain Kuiper's sixteenth issue to the extent it complains of the trial court's conclusion that he is not entitled to any additional payments under the contract.

In his seventeenth issue, Kuiper asserts he is entitled to recover on his claim for breach of contract because he established all conditions precedent to his recovery. For the same reasons discussed in connection with the second and sixteenth issues, we sustain this issue to the extent it argues Kuiper is entitled to recover the contract price (less any offsets and credits) because appellees accepted the columns.

In his nineteenth issue, Kuiper contends appellees cannot recover for either breach of contract or breach of warranty because appellees accepted the columns and never paid the contract price. More specifically, Kuiper argues appellees "have no rights against Kuiper because they never paid for the goods at issue." The mere fact that appellees accepted the goods and are liable for the contract price does not negate their claims for breach of contract or breach of warranty. As discussed above, in the event the trial court determines appellees are entitled to recover under such claims, they would be entitled to damages or a set-off pursuant to section 2.714 and 2.715 of the Code. We resolve the nineteenth issue against Kuiper.

C. Evidence of Kuiper's Breach

As part of his sixteenth issue, Kuiper contends that because appellees installed, and thereby accepted, the columns, Kuiper did not breach his contract with appellees. Specifically, Kuiper attacks the trial court's conclusion of law that Kuiper's delivery of defective columns and failure to repair, replace or remove the columns constituted a breach of contract. Although appellees' installation of the columns constituted acceptance, it does not necessarily follow that Kuiper did not also breach the contract by delivering non-conforming goods, and appellees are not without a remedy under the Code. See §§ 2.607(b), 2.601 cmt. 1. They "retain[ ] such rights, if any, as existed for damages under [section] 2.714 and [section] 2.715." *Bowen*, 507 S.W.2d at 603; see also § 2.717 (deduction of damages from price). Accordingly, we overrule the remainder of Kuiper's sixteenth issue, in which he attacks the trial court's conclusion that his actions constituted a breach of contract.

In his fifth issue, Kuiper contends the evidence is legally and factually insufficient to support the trial court's findings that the columns were defective and that the columns had cracks, which continued to worsen after installation. Kuiper asserts: (1) the contract did not call for four-inch support posts, and he did not breach the contract by failing to deliver columns that would fit over such posts; and (2) there is no evidence the columns were cracked because no cracks were visible on any of the photographs taken of the columns after installation. There is evidence that before Kuiper delivered the columns, he told Knobler to install four-inch support posts. Numerous photographs of the columns before installation showed severe cracks. It follows the cracks remained after installation. Furthermore, Knobler testified the columns were cracked when they were delivered and the cracks worsened after delivery. We conclude there is legally and factually sufficient evidence to support the trial court's finding that the columns were defective.

In this issue, Kuiper also complains of the sufficiency of the evidence supporting the trial court's finding that the bases were too wide to allow a car to enter and exit the driveway. To support this contention, Kuiper merely argues the nineteen-inch bases were only two inches larger than the seventeen-inch garage separator, which did not impede entry and exit into the garage. Knobler testified that the new bases were too large, causing Wright to hit them when she entered the garage. We disagree with Kuiper's assumption that a two-inch difference is, as a matter of law, insignificant. The evidence is legally and factually sufficient to support the trial court's finding the bases were too large.

In his fifth issue, Kuiper also asserts Knobler's action of installing the columns is wholly inconsistent with the trial court's finding that the columns were valueless as decorative pieces. The record shows appellees tore down their existing columns to replace them with the stone columns. There is evidence Knobler did not install the columns initially because they were cracked and too small to fit over the four-inch posts. Knobler subsequently installed the columns; however, there was conflicting evidence as to the condition and value of the columns. We find some evidence in the record to support the trial court's determination that the columns were valueless as decorative pieces. Accordingly, Kuiper has not shown that the trial court's finding is so against the great weight and preponderance of the evidence that it is clearly wrong and unjust. We resolve Kuiper's fifth issue against him.

D. Damages

The trial court awarded appellees $5,424.80 in damages, representing appellees' costs for: (1) installation of replacement posts; (2) the cost of replacement bases and their installation; (3) the cost of installation of the defective columns; and (4) the cost of replacement columns. The cost of replacement columns was awarded only for appellees' breach of warranty claim. As previously discussed, the trial court's damage award is impacted greatly by our determination that appellees' action constituted an acceptance of the columns.

In his tenth issue, Kuiper contends appellees' damages in the amount of $1,600 for installing the columns was not caused by Kuiper's conduct. In light of our previous conclusions, we sustain Kuiper's tenth issue because it involves the amount of damages awarded to appellees for the installation of the defective columns. Additionally, the trial court's award of damages for installation is erroneous to the extent that it allows appellees to recover for replacement columns under their breach of warranty theory. Pursuant to section 2.714(b), the appropriate measure of damages for a breach of warranty under the Code is "the difference at the time and place of acceptance between the value of the goods accepted and the value they would have had if they had been as warranted, unless special circumstances show proximate damages of a different amount." § 2.714(b). Because appellees are limited to damages in the amount of the difference in value under their breach of warranty theory, they cannot recover damages arising out of appellees' purported need to replace the columns. Accordingly, Kuiper's tenth issue is sustained, and the trial court can determine the appropriate measure of damages pursuant to sections 2.714 and 2.715 on remand.

In his fifteenth issue, Kuiper contends appellees are not entitled to $5,424.80 in damages for breach of warranty or violation of the DTPA. For the reasons discussed in connection with Kuiper's tenth issue, Kuiper's fifteenth issue is also sustained.

In his sixth, seventh, and eighth issues, Kuiper attacks the trial court's award of damages arising from the replacement of the posts and bases for the garage columns. In these issues, Kuiper argues: (1) appellees' purported damages in the amount of $800 for the removal and replacement of the four-inch support posts were not caused by the size of the columns' interior cores; (2) Knobler's approval of the design for the bases on behalf of DKC makes DKC and Knobler responsible if the bases were designed too wide; and (3) appellees' purported damages in the amount of $600 for the removal and replacement of the bases were not caused by the size of the bases. Kuiper's sixth, seventh, and eighth issues merely make causation arguments and do not attack or discuss the theory under which the trial court awarded these damages. Accordingly, we resolve these issues against Kuiper. * * *

F. Misrepresentation and Warranty Issues

In his eleventh issue, Kuiper contends the evidence is legally and factually insufficient to support the trial court's finding that he: (1) misrepresented to appellees that he was an authorized agent or employee of Advanced Cast Stone, Inc. and (2) his use of the trade name Advanced Cast Stone was confusing and misled appellees into believing he had the sponsorship and approval of the manufacturers. There is evidence Kuiper told appellees he owned "Advanced Cast Stone" and he manufactured cast stone, when Kuiper in fact did not manufacture the cast stone and did not work for Advanced Cast Stone, Inc., the true manufacturer. We conclude the evidence is legally and factually sufficient to show Kuiper caused appellees to believe Kuiper had the sponsorship and approval of the manufacturer which he did not have. We resolve the eleventh issue against Kuiper.

In his twelfth issue, Kuiper contends the evidence is legally and factually insufficient to support the trial court's finding that he misled appellees into believing they would obtain any warranty coverage from American Cast Stone, Inc. that they did not actually receive. He asserts: (1) he made no express warranties, and (2) appellees are entitled to implied warranties from the actual manufacturer. To show he made no express warranties, Kuiper directs us to his own testimony to this effect. However, there is also evidence Kuiper told appellees: (1) the columns would fit over four-inch posts, and (2) the nineteen inch bases would not be too large. Kuiper has failed to provide any argument or authority to show these representations did not constitute express warranties. Kuiper has thus failed to show the evidence is legally and factually insufficient to support the trial court's finding. We resolve the twelfth issue against Kuiper.

In his thirteenth issue, Kuiper contends the evidence is legally and factually insufficient to support the trial court's finding that (1) Kuiper's misleading appellees into believing he was an authorized agent of Advanced Cast Stone, Inc. was the producing cause of lost warranty coverage and (2) he stipulated the lost warranty damages to be $2,424,80. Kuiper reiterates the argument made in the previous issue, of which we have disposed. Kuiper also complains he did not stipulate that value of the lost warranty coverage was $2,424.80. The trial court did not, however, find the value of the lost warranty coverage was stipulated. Rather, the trial court found the parties stipulated the cost of appellees replacing Kuiper's columns would be $2,424.80. We resolve the thirteenth issue against Kuiper.

In his fourteenth issue, Kuiper contends the evidence is legally and factually insufficient to support a finding that the stone columns were not fit for a particular purpose. The trial court did not find Kuiper breached the warranty of fitness for a particular purpose. Kuiper fails to show how the trial court's judgment is premised on such a finding. We resolve the fourteenth issue against Kuiper. [Resolution of remaining issues omitted.] * * *

Conclusion

In light of our holding that appellees' installation of the columns constituted acceptance of the columns despite their defects, we sustain in whole or in part the following issues: second, fifth, tenth, fifteenth, sixteenth, seventeenth, nineteenth, and twentieth. Because of our holdings, we do not need to reach Kuiper's third or ninth issue. All of Kuiper's other issues are overruled.

* * * [W]e reverse the judgment of the trial court and remand the case to the trial court for further proceedings consistent with this opinion.

Deere v. Johnson

United States Court of Appeals, Fifth Circuit, 2001
271 F.3d 613

■ E. Grady Jolly, Circuit Judge

Deere financed a combine its dealer, Parker Tractor & Implement Company ("Parker"), sold to Johnson. Johnson was unhappy with the combine because it would not do the job. Deere was unhappy with Johnson because he failed to make any payments on the loan. Johnson wrote Deere a letter revoking acceptance of the combine. Deere refused to take it back. Johnson continued to use the combine. Deere finally sued Johnson to collect the unpaid balance on the loan. Johnson counter-claimed against Deere, as the manufacturer of the combine, for breach of implied and express warranties, breach of the implied warranty of fitness for a particular purpose, and intentional misrepresentations. The jury returned a verdict that effectively awarded zero to both parties. The district court conformed the pleadings to the evidence and entered a quantum meruit award for Deere for the rental value of the combine while Johnson was using it.

Today's appeal addresses three issues: First, whether Johnson effectively revoked acceptance in the view of his continuing to assert ownership of the combine and failing to return it to Deere; second, whether the district court erred in conforming the pleadings to state a quantum meruit claim for Deere and awarding Deere a judgment on that basis; and finally, whether Deere presented sufficient evidence of the rental value of the combine. We hold that under the circumstances of this case, Johnson effectively revoked acceptance of the combine; that the district court erred in conforming the pleadings to state a quantum meruit claim and in entering a judgment for Deere; and that Deere presented evidence to support the jury's determination of the rental value of the combine. At the end of the day, this case is a "wash"— neither party receives anything. Accordingly, we reverse and remand for entry of a take-nothing judgment.

I

In 1994, Edward Johnson bought a combine from Parker, a retailer for Deere located in Tunica, Mississippi. Johnson made a down payment of $30,634.36. He financed the remainder of the purchase price with Deere, using the combine as security for the loan. The combine was a lemon. Throughout the harvest season of 1994, Johnson made service requests to Parker. Each time Parker sent its mechanic to Johnson's farm to repair the combine. Finally, on March 3, 1995, Johnson sent a letter to Deere, which revoked acceptance, tendered the combine, and asked for a replacement. In a letter dated May 12, 1995, Deere refused to take the combine back. It stated "Deere & Company certainly sees no reason to replace this combine and it is not willing to accept it back." Johnson continued to use the combine during the harvest season of 1995, as well as during the spring of 1996. After this lawsuit was initiated, Deere filed a replevin action, repossessed and sold the combine in July of 1997. Although Johnson used the combine from 1994 until the spring of 1996, he made no payments on the loan contract.

Moreover, even if we assumed that Deere, not Parker, had all the rights under the sale contract, this fact would still fail to explain why the parties vigorously litigated the validity of the underlying sale contract in this action for collection on a loan contract. The loan contract and the sale contract are independent unless there is a contractual provision which states otherwise. Neither contract contains such a provision.

Undaunted, our analysis of the issues proceeds as tried to the jury and briefed on appeal; that is, we assume Deere (not Parker) was potentially entitled to the reasonable rental rate of the combine and that Johnson's revocation of the sale contract (if effective) would have nullified his obligations under the loan contract.

II

On September 26, 1995, Deere filed a complaint seeking to collect on the contract. Johnson counter-claimed. He alleged breach of contract, breach of express and implied warranties, breach of the implied warranty of fitness for a particular purpose, and intentional misrepresentations. Johnson sought lost profits, punitive and consequential damages. The jury found for Johnson on his breach of warranty claim and against Deere on its breach of contract claim. The jury awarded Johnson the down payment that he had made on the combine, $30,634.86, but subtracted $70,000 from this award for the fair rental value of the combine for the period of Johnson's use. This calculation was exactly what the verdict form instructed the jury to do.

Deere then filed a post-verdict motion that sought (a) judgment as a matter of law under Rule 50 or, alternatively, (b) the amendment of the pleadings to conform to the evidence presented under Rule 15(b); that is, to state a claim against Johnson in quantum meruit. Johnson filed his own post-verdict motion. He sought (a) judgment notwithstanding the verdict, asking the court to set aside the jury's determination of the rental value of the combine and award him the full down payment, or (b) an alteration or amendment of the judgment to that same effect, or (c) a new trial on damages only, and (d) attorney's fees.

In resolving this barrage of post-verdict motions, the district court denied Johnson's motions in all respects except as to prejudgment interest on the down payment, denied Deere's motion for judgment as a matter of law, and granted Deere's motion to amend the pleadings.

Based on the legal theory of quantum meruit—raised for the first time in Deere's post-verdict 15(b) motion—the district court amended the pleadings and entered an amended judgment for Deere. The amended judgment awarded Deere $70,000 minus Johnson's down payment and any prejudgment interest on that down payment. Notwithstanding that (1) the jury had found in favor of Johnson and against Deere, and (2) the district court had found against Deere as a matter of law on all of its asserted claims, Deere walked away from the district court with about $35,000.

Both parties now appeal.

III

We first address Deere's appeal. Deere appeals the district court's denial of its motion for judgment as a matter of law with respect to its contract claim.

Deere moved for judgment as a matter of law twice—once during trial and once in its post-verdict motion. Deere's argument is that it was entitled to collect on the loan contract for the combine because Johnson's continued use of the combine nullified his revocation of acceptance as a matter of law. The district court denied both motions. Deere only appeals the denial of the post-verdict motion. This ruling of the district court is to be distinguished from its ruling granting Deere's 15(b) motion, which we address later in this opinion.

We review the denial of a motion for judgment as a matter of law de novo.

It is not surprising that Mississippi law requires that buyers pay the contract price for any goods accepted, unless that acceptance is later effectively revoked. MISS. CODE ANN. §§ 75–2–607(1), 75–2–608 (1999). Deere argues that because Johnson failed to revoke his acceptance of the combine, he is bound by the contract, and thus the jury erred in awarding Johnson the return of his down payment. On appeal, the question is whether, viewing the evidence in the light most favorable to Johnson, a reasonable jury could have found that Johnson revoked acceptance of the combine.

As we have noted, the Mississippi version of the UCC provides for the revocation of acceptance. A buyer revoking acceptance of goods has the same duties as a buyer rejecting a shipment of goods; in most cases, a buyer must discontinue asserting any ownership over the goods. MISS. CODE ANN. § 75–2–602(2)(a)(1999) ("after rejection any exercise of ownership by the buyer with respect to any commercial unit is wrongful as against the seller"). It is undisputed that Johnson notified Deere of his revocation in a letter of March 3, 1995. It is further undisputed that Johnson continued to use the combine after this letter of revocation. Still further, Johnson generated a tax benefit for himself by claiming depreciation of the combine on his tax forms in both 1995 and 1996. Without doubt, these two actions represent ownership activities by Johnson. The question remains: Do these activities nullify Johnson's revocation of acceptance as a matter of law?

Mississippi courts have addressed this question in several cases. In North River Homes v. Bosarge, 594 So. 2d 1153 (Miss. 1992) the court addressed whether a family's failure to move out of a "lemon" mobile home waived their revocation of acceptance. The court, in finding no waiver, reasoned that "[the family's] mistaken belief that North River would fulfill its assurances to repair the defects is but one reason why the Bosarges did not move out of their home. Another reason is simple and [understandable]: When you tie up all your savings into purchasing a home, you cannot take it and park it somewhere. You have got to live in it until you get the people to clear your lot so you can put another [mobile home] on it."

In a case involving a defective copier, however, the court held that the failure to return the copier did vitiate the revocation of acceptance. Nevertheless, the court noted in dicta that this might not always be true. J.L. Teel Co., Inc. v. Houston United Sales, Inc., 491 So. 2d 851, 859 (Miss. 1986) (stating "without doubt, failure to surrender the copier did not per se render ineffective Houston's revocation").

Other states agree that continued use of non-conforming goods does not, in all cases, waive the revocation of acceptance. See Wilk Paving, Inc. v. Southworth–Milton, Inc., 649 A.2d 778, 781–82 (Vt. 1994) (failure to return defective asphalt roller does not forfeit the revocation of acceptance); McCullough v. Bill Swad Chrysler–Plymouth, Inc., 449 N.E.2d 1289, 1291 (Ohio 1983) (failure to return automobile did not forfeit revocation); Aubrey's R.V. Center, Inc. v. Tandy Corp., 731 P.2d 1124, 1129 (Wash.App.Ct. 1987) (failure to return software did not forfeit revocation).

Allowing continued use of the good is not the general rule, however. Typically, the law requires that a buyer return a non-conforming good, purchase a replacement, if necessary, and then sue for breach. MISS. CODE ANN. §§ 75–2–602, 75–2–714 (1999). The rationale is that even non-conforming goods have value, and by requiring a prompt return of the goods, the law enables a seller to resell the goods before they substantially depreciate in value. As the Mississippi Supreme Court has noted, however, a buyer, with no ability to replace the defective good, suffers substantial injury if forced to cede ownership of that good. The law thus weighs the two effects; that is, where the cost of replacement is low, the injury to the seller from the depreciation of the good outweighs the injury to the buyer that results from surrendering ownership. Thus, in such a situation the law requires the return of the non-conforming good. On the other hand, when the cost of replacement is high, the injury resulting to the buyer from returning the good outweighs the seller's injury of depreciation; hence, in this situation the cases do not penalize the buyer when he reasonably retains the non-conforming good.

As we have noted, Mississippi case law employs this principle. In *North Rivers Homes*, the cost to the family of giving up the trailer was high. Hence, the court held that the failure to "move-out" did not waive revocation. On the other hand, in the Teel case, the company easily could have purchased another copier, and hence, the court held that the failure to surrender the copier nullified the attempt to revoke acceptance of the copier.

Here, the evidence shows that Johnson's cost of replacement was high. Johnson's credit was adversely affected when he failed to make payments on the loan for the combine. The record reflects that Johnson was operating close to the margin; he admittedly could not make but a few of the payments. It is unlikely that any combine dealer would have either rented or sold to Johnson under these circumstances. Without a combine, Johnson's ability to farm would be severely impaired. With little farm production, he could not mitigate the damages he suffered as a result of the defective combine. Thus, as with the mobile home owners in North River Homes, the record demonstrates that the damage to Johnson from ceding ownership of the combine would have been high.

Deere also maintains that Johnson continued to use the combine, which naturally caused depreciation, and that this change of the good rendered his revocation of acceptance ineffective. Other than depreciation, Deere does not allege that Johnson damaged the combine. Deere bases its depreciation-as-change argument on the language of the statute: "Revocation must occur within a reasonable time . . . and before any substantial change in the condition of the goods not caused by their defects." MISS. CODE ANN. § 75–2–608(2) (1999). Deere cites no cases in which depreciation by itself was deemed a substantial change under this section of the Mississippi UCC. It seems that in almost all cases involving a "substantial change" the buyer engaged in some activity which altered the goods. See Intervale Steel Corp. v. Borg & Beck Div., Borg–Warner Corp., 578 F. Supp. 1081 (E.D.Mich. 1984) (buyer broke up goods into parts); Trinkle v. Schumacher Co., 301 N.W.2d 255 (Wis.Ct.App. 1980) (buyer cut fabric); Toyomenka (America), Inc. v. Combined Metals Corp.,487 N.E.2d 1172 (Ill.App.Ct. 1985) (buyer cut goods into narrow strips).

That simple depreciation alone usually does not constitute a substantial change in the condition of the good is consistent with the doctrine of revocation of acceptance because the doctrine is meant to remedy a situation in which a latent defect arises. If simple depreciation of the non-conforming good was enough to nullify the revocation of acceptance, a buyer might not be able to revoke acceptance of a good with a latent defect.

Furthermore, Deere's refusal to accept the return of the combine undermines its argument that Johnson failed to revoke acceptance as a matter of law. How does one return a combine when the dealer refuses to take it back—park it, perhaps, illegally in their lot? We find unpersuasive the premise of Deere's argument: that a seller can refuse to accept the return of a non-conforming good, and then claim that the buyer nullified his revocation by not returning the good in question.

Most important for the case at hand, the issue of whether a buyer has effectively revoked acceptance is a factual one. For the reasons outlined above, we think that a reasonable jury could have concluded—despite Johnson's continued use of the combine—that he effectively revoked acceptance of the combine on March 5, 1995. The district court's denial of Deere's motion for judgment as a matter of law was thus correct. * * *

V

In sum, we hold: (1) that the district court committed no error when it denied Deere's motion for judgment as a matter of law because a reasonable jury could have concluded that Johnson revoked his acceptance of the combine; (2) that the district court erred when it amended the pleadings after the return of the jury verdict based on a legal theory that was not expressly or implicitly tried to the jury; and (3) that there was sufficient evidence to support the jury verdict.

Reversed and remanded for entry of judgment

NOTES

1. According to *Kuiper*, 2–606(1)(c) states a bright-line rule regarding acceptance: any act inconsistent with the seller's ownership constitutes acceptance. There seems nothing bright-line about a rule which does not specify which acts are inconsistent with ownership. *Kuiper* and *Deere* adopt different standards for when continued use constitutes an inconsistent act. *Kuiper* appears to hold that installation of the goods, with knowledge of the nonconformity, is an inconsistent act. Other courts disagree with *Kuiper*'s "installation" standard; see, e.g., Trident Steel Corp. v. Wiser Oil Co., 223 S.W.3d 520 (Tex. Ct. App. 2006). *Deere* holds that use of the goods, even with knowledge of the nonconformity, is consistent with ownership if the use is reasonable. Reasonableness, according to *Deere*, is judged by whether the buyer's use minimizes the total costs of disposing of the goods. As *Deere* notes, the buyer's use of the goods has two effects: it saves the buyer the cost of finding a replacement during the period of use while depreciating the goods' value or sacrificing opportunities to dispose of the goods. If financial constraints limit the buyer's ability to get a replacement, so that replacement cost is high, the depreciation or opportunity cost of continued use might be less than the cost of getting a replacement. Continued use is reasonable. On the other hand, if replacement costs are low, depreciation or opportunity costs produced by continued use might exceed replacement costs. In this situation continued use would be unreasonable. In principle installation of goods after rejection can minimize the total costs of disposition and therefore is not necessarily an act inconsistent with ownership.

Viewed in this way, continued use is consistent with ownership when it minimizes the costs of breach. The standard makes sense. Recall that rejection signals to the seller that the buyer does not want to retain the goods and that it is to retrieve and dispose of them. Because rejection may be wrongful or rightful, the goods may or may not conform to the contract. The breaching party will be liable for damages, whoever turns out to be the breacher. The buyer's use of the goods affects the size of the breacher's damage bill, by saving on replacement costs or diminishes the value of the good through use. The former reduces the buyer's incidental expenses or consequential damages if it is the breach-victim; the latter increases the seller's direct damages if it is the breach-victim. Continued use which minimizes breach costs minimizes the breacher's damage bill, whether the breacher is the buyer or the seller. For instance, suppose the buyer rejects goods delivered. Suppose too that the cost of replacing the goods is $10 and the buyer's use of the delivered goods decreases their value by $5. There are no other relevant costs associated with use. If the buyer replaces the delivered goods it will not use have to use them. Replacement therefore has a net cost of $10 ($10 − $0). If the buyer uses the delivered goods it will depreciate them but will not have to find a replacement. The net cost of using the goods is $5. Using the goods minimizes the breacher's damage bill, whether the buyer or the seller has breached. In this respect 2–606(1)(c) "acts inconsistent" rule for acceptance is similar to a duty of mitigation. The duty to mitigate induces the breach-victim to act to minimize the breacher's liability. For its part, 2–606(1)(c)'s rule also induces the buyer to use the goods only when doing so minimizes the breacher's liability, even before the identity of the breacher is established.

2. *Kupier* and *Deere* reflect the split among courts over the effect of continued use on the buyer's rejection or revocation. Some cases hold that use inconsistent with the seller's ownership cancels ("waives") a rejection or revocation and indicates acceptance. See Gerard Construction, Inc. v. Motor Vessel Virginia, 490 F. Supp. 475 (W.D. Pa. 1980), aff'd, 636 F.2d 1208 (3d Cir. 1980); Warner v. Reagan Buick, Inc., 483 N.W.2d 764 (Neb. 1992); H. G. Fischer X–Ray Co., Inc. v. Meredith, 433 A.2d 1306 (N.H. 1981). Other cases follow *Deere* in finding that reasonable use is consistent with ownership, leaving an initial rejection or revocation intact. Differences in the duration of use, the extent of buyer's alteration of the goods or the price of the goods do not account for the different results. Compare Minsel v. El Rancho Mobile Home Center, Inc., 188 N.W.2d 9 (Mich. Ct. App. 1971) (buyer dwelled in the mobile home for six weeks after having tendered it back to seller) with Jorgensen v. Pressnall, 545 P.2d 1382 (Or. 1976) (buyer dwelled in the mobile home for one year). Professors Schwartz and Scott conclude, based on a brief survey of cases decided before 1989, that "[t]he only accurate generalization is that a rejecting or revoking buyer who continues to occupy a mobile home will have a better chance in the courts than one who continues to use an automobile." Alan Schwartz & Robert E. Scott, Commercial Transactions: Principles and Policies 262 (2d ed. 1991). There are too few cases decided after 1989 to determine reliably whether that generalization remains accurate.

3. Section 2–711(3) gives the rejecting or revoking buyer a security interest in goods in its possession for any part of the contract price already paid. Under 9–110 the buyer's security interest is enforceable without a security agreement and is perfected automatically. 9–110(1),(2), 9–309(6). As a secured creditor in possession of collateral (the goods), the buyer has duties with respect to it. 9–207(a). Section 9–207(b)(4)(A) permits the buyer to use the collateral for the purpose of preserving it or its value. Plausibly, the buyer's permissible acts are not inconsistent with the seller-debtor's ownership of the goods. Thus, where the only feasible way of protecting the collateral is to use it, the buyer's use is not acceptance under 2–606(1)(c). For example, remaining in a mobile home after rejection or revocation to protect it from damage or theft is a reasonable way for a consumer buyer to preserve the mobile home. See Jorgensen v. Pressnall, 545 P.2d 1382 (Or. 1976). However, 9–207(b)(4)(A) will not always protect the buyer who continues to use the goods from a finding that its use amounts to acts inconsistent with ownership. Section 9–207(b)(4)(A) permits use to preserve the goods or their value. A buyer's continued use to avoid replacing the goods, or to generate revenues, is not an act of preservation. Continued use also typically depreciates the value of the goods. The buyers in both *Kuiper* and *Deere*, who had paid part of the contract price, did not use the goods to preserve them or their value. Their use was to avoid an expense if the goods were not used—being sued if the stone columns were not moved or installed (*Kuiper*) or having to finance a replacement combine (*Deere*).

D. THE SELLER'S RIGHT TO CURE

Section 2–508 gives the seller a right to cure an initially defective performance under prescribed conditions. The right to cure limits the effect of the perfect tender rule. When the right to cure applies, the buyer may reject nonconforming goods only if the seller fails to cure the nonconformity. A seller who cures can prevent the buyer from escaping the transaction because it regrets entering into the deal rather than because it is dissatisfied with the seller's performance. Buyers who resist cure when it is permitted are themselves in breach of the contract and therefore have no remedy for damages arising from the seller's breach. The parties' contract can displace the perfect tender rule by a remedy limitation clause that excludes the right to reject. 2–601, 2–719(1)(a). The remedy limitation may itself provide for cure, typically by repair or replacement of nonconforming goods. In this way the contract can tailor the conditions under which the buyer may reject to the parties' deal. By contrast, the right to cure is an off-the-rack default term that limits the buyer's right to reject under conditions described in 2–508.

Article 2's drafters assume that most contracting parties prefer the give the seller a right to cure. Although cure reduces the risk of the buyer's strategic rejection, it allows the seller to reduce its effort to tender conforming goods. Buyers might not discover the nonconformities in time to reject. If they are discovered, the seller will have to exert extra effort to provide conforming goods by cure. However, the cost of this extra effort discounted by the likelihood that the buyer will detect nonconformities in the initial tender can be less than the seller's savings in tendering nonconforming goods initially. In this case the seller will cut corners on the initial tender because its savings in doing so is greater than its expected cost of cure. If courts can easily observe strategic tenders, or non-legal constraints such as reputation operate, sellers have no incentive to cut corners. Because cure gives the buyer conforming goods and the seller the choice between curing and paying damages, the typical seller and buyer prefer to give the right to cure. Of course, if courts have difficulty observing strategic tenders and reputational constraints are weak, it is unclear whether the right to cure produces more or less strategic behavior than a perfect tender rule with no right to cure. Article 2's drafters appear optimistic about the informational capacities of courts or the effectiveness of reputation in products markets.

Section 2–508's requirements of cure are mostly straightforward. They depend on whether the time for tender or delivery set by the contract has expired. Under 2–508(1), a seller who makes a nonconforming tender or delivery before the time for performance has passed may cure by making a conforming delivery. The seller must seasonably notify the buyer of its intent to cure and cure within the time for performance set by the contract. Whether the seller decides to cure is completely within its discretion. It has a right but not an obligation to cure, as 2–508's language makes clear ("the seller may"). This means that the buyer cannot require cure under 2–508. A seller might decide that not curing and leaving the buyer to its remedies is the cheaper response to its own breach.

Section 2–508(2) permits cure even after the time for performance of the contract has expired. It gives the seller an opportunity to perform when 2–508(1) is inapplicable. Under 2–508(2) the seller has a "further reasonable time" to perform. However, this additional opportunity to cure is subject to two requirements. One is that the seller must have reasonable grounds to believe that the initial tender was acceptable to the buyer. The other requirement is that the seller must substitute a "conforming tender." The interpretation of both requirements has caused courts problems. Section 2–508(2)'s formulation of the first requirement is opaque: The seller may cure when "the buyer rejects a non-conforming tender which the seller has reasonable grounds to believe would be acceptable without or without money allowance . . . " It is unclear which part of the sentence in 2–508(2) the "which" modifies. "[W]hich the seller had reasonable grounds to believe would be acceptable" could modify either "tender" or "nonconforming tender." If the phrase modifies "tender", the seller must reasonably believe that the tender is acceptable. If it modifies "nonconforming tender," the seller reasonably must believe that the nonconforming tender is acceptable. In this latter case 2–508(2) gives a seller a right to cure only if it is aware that the goods are nonconforming. Courts and almost all commentators understand the quoted portion of 2–508(2) to refer to "tender," so that the seller need only reasonably believe that its tender is acceptable with or without money allowance. It need not believe that its tender is nonconforming. *Midwest Mobile Diagnostic Imaging*, reproduced above, is almost alone in understanding 2–508(2)'s relevant language to require the seller to reasonably believe that its tender is conforming. See p. 399 n.2. Proposed 2–508(2) eliminates the opaque language, simply requiring that the seller's initial tender be made in good faith.

The seller whose tender falls within 2–508(2) may cure only by making a conforming tender. In most cases, this means that the tender must comply with all of the terms of the contract. A tender that deviates from these terms will not be conforming. An offer of a price adjustment is not a conforming tender. Cf. Comment 5 to 2–612 (allowing price adjustment to cure a defective installment in an installment contract). Cure by repair is permissible under 2–508(2) only if repair constitutes a "substitute conforming tender." A repair that clearly diminishes the good's value to the buyer is not a conforming tender. For instance, an offer to install an additional air conditioner is not a substitute conforming tender when the contract called for a mobile home with a dual roof air conditioner and the installation would leave a hole in the middle of the mobile home. See Worldwide RV Sales & Service, Inc. v. Brooks, 534 N.E.2d 1132, 1133 (Ind. Ct. App. 1989).

In other cases it is harder to determine whether a conforming tender contemplates repair. In Wilson v. Scampoli, 228 A.2d 848 (D.C. 1967), the consumer buyer of a color television set refused to allow its seller to adjust or repair the color of the picture. The court determined that the seller had a right to cure the initial tender under 2–508(2), which included removing the television's chassis for a short period to determine the cause of the defect and to make minor necessary repairs. *Wilson*'s finding that cure permits repair is explainable by the nature of the goods and the likely terms of the sales contract for them. Some goods are complex enough that buyers will anticipate that some adjustment or repair might be necessary after delivery. The implicit term regarding tender in sales contracts for these goods is not "tender of the good that will function without adjustment." Rather, it is roughly "tender of the good that functions or will function after suitable adjustment or repair." The possible need for adjustment or repair presumably is factored into the price of the goods. On these facts a seller who repairs a defect in the goods provides a conforming tender. Color television sets sold in the early 1960s could well have been complex enough to require adjustment after tender, including by repair. In fact, the seller's expert testified that new color televisions frequently required adjustments. *Wilson*'s finding that cure permits repair recognizes that contracts for some sorts of goods define a conforming tender to include repair.

This focus on the conformity of the tender accounts for a range of cases involving what courts call "faith shaken." These are cases in which timely and effective repair is held not to constitute cure. The cases have produced what is sometimes called the faith shaken doctrine or theory. According to the doctrine, the buyer may reject without allowing cure when its faith in the goods is so shaken by a defect that remedying them would leave an ordinary buyer unsatisfied. Properly understood, the faith shaken doctrine is not an exception to the seller's right to cure. Rather, it describes contracts whose implicit terms do not allow a conforming tender by repair. In these cases cure by repair is ineffective because not allowed by the contract. Zabriski Chevrolet, Inc. v. Smith, 240 A.2d 195 (N.J. Super. Ct. 1968), a classic faith shaken case, illustrates the point. There the consumer buyer rejected a new car after the seller's replaced a defective transmission in it with a transmission of unknown origin. In finding the seller's cure ineffective, the court made the following, often quoted observation: "For a majority of people the purchase of a new car is a major investment, rationalized by the peace of mind that flows from its dependability and safety. Once their faith is shaken, the vehicle loses not only its real value in their eyes, but becomes an instrument whose integrity is substantially impaired and whose operation is fraught with apprehension." Id. at 205. However, the court based its finding of an ineffective cure on the terms of parties' agreement: "A 'cure' which endeavors by substitution to tender a chattel not within the agreement or contemplation of the parties is invalid." Id. The seller's replacement of the car's original transmission with a transmission of unknown origin was not a substitute conforming tender.

The hardest cases are those in which it is not easily determined what constitutes a substitute conforming tender. Suppose the contract calls for tender of good X in working order to a consumer buyer. The seller timely delivers good X, which it reasonably believes will be acceptable. When the buyer discovers that the good does not work, the seller immediately offers to substitute another good X in working order. The buyer refused the offer over the seller's objection. The question is whether the seller's the substitute good is a conforming tender for 2–508(2)'s purposes. Both parties have decent arguments for their opposite positions. The buyer can argue that the contract promised it a particular value from good X. When the seller delivered the defective good X, the buyer lost confidence in the good. It now places a lower value on good X, even a nondefective substitute, than it did initially. For this reason, the seller's offer of a substitute good X is not a conforming tender. It gives the buyer a good with a lower value than the contract entitled the buyer to expect. To require the buyer to accept a substitute good from the seller therefore reduces the buyer's profit from the deal.

Against this, the seller can argue that the offer of the substitute good is a conforming tender. Because the contract called for good X in working order, the offer gives the buyer what was promised. The buyer's refusal of a substitute good is opportunistic. It values the good less than it did originally not because of doubts about the good but because of factors unrelated to the qualities of the good, such as its market price, aesthetic appeal or changes in its plans for the good's use. These factors make the buyer regret entering into the deal. They do not make the tender of a substitute good X a nonconforming tender. Whether the buyer's rejection of cure is opportunistic or rightful obviously turns on the facts. However, the relevant facts can be difficult to verify. Where the buyer is commercial concern, market price is a reliable indicator of the value it places on the good. A constant market price for substitute goods likely indicates that the buyer's value for them remains unchanged. Correspondingly, a decline in market price after the contract is concluded is good evidence that the buyer regrets the deal. Similar inferences cannot be made for consumer purchasers. For a consumer buyer, the value it places on the goods is subjective and only loosely related to market price. Although it values the good at least at the market price, it might value the good at any amount above price too. The buyer's valuation might decline with a loss of confidence in the good but remain above market price, even when the price remains constant. Thus, there is no objective way to verify the buyer's assertions of faith shaken in the goods.

T.W. Oil, Inc. v. Consolidated Edison
Co. of New York, Inc.

New York Court of Appeals, 1982
443 N.E.2d 932

■ FUCHSBERG, JUDGE

In the first case to wend its way through our appellate courts on this question, we are asked, in the main, to decide whether a seller who, acting in good faith and without knowledge of any defect, tenders nonconforming goods to a buyer who properly rejects them, may avail itself of the cure provision of subdivision (2) of section 2–508 of the Uniform Commercial Code. We hold that, if seasonable notice be given, such a seller may offer to cure the defect within a reasonable period beyond the time when the contract was to be performed so long as it has acted in good faith and with a reasonable expectation that the original goods would be acceptable to the buyer.

The factual background against which we decide this appeal is based on either undisputed proof or express findings at Trial Term. In January, 1974, midst the fuel shortage produced by the oil embargo, the plaintiff (then known as Joc Oil USA, Inc.) purchased a cargo of fuel oil whose sulfur content was represented to it as no greater than 1%. While the oil was still at sea en route to the United States in the tanker *M T Khamsin*, plaintiff received a certificate from the foreign refinery at which it had been processed informing it that the sulfur content in fact was .52%. Thereafter, on January 24, the plaintiff entered into a written contract with the defendant (Con Ed) for the sale of this oil. The agreement was for delivery to take place between January 24 and January 30, payment being subject to a named independent testing agency's confirmation of quality and quantity. The contract, following a trade custom to round off specifications of sulfur content at, for instance, 1%, .5% or .3%, described that of the *Khamsin* oil as .5%. In the course of the negotiations, the plaintiff learned that Con Ed was then authorized to buy and burn oil with a sulfur content of up to 1% and would even mix oils containing more and less to maintain that figure.

When the vessel arrived, on January 25, its cargo was discharged into Con Ed storage tanks in Bayonne, New Jersey. In due course, the independent testing people reported a sulfur content of .92%. On this basis, acting within a time frame whose reasonableness is not in question, on February 14 Con Ed rejected the shipment. Prompt negotiations to adjust the price failed; by February 20, plaintiff had offered a price reduction roughly responsive to the difference in sulfur reading, but Con Ed, though it could use the oil, rejected this proposition out of hand. It was insistent on paying no more than the latest prevailing price, which, in the volatile market that then existed, was some 25% below the level which prevailed when it agreed to buy the oil.

The very next day, February 21, plaintiff offered to cure the defect with a substitute shipment of conforming oil scheduled to arrive on the *S. S. Appollonian Victory* on February 28. Nevertheless, on February 22, the very day after the cure was proffered, Con Ed, adamant in its intention to avail itself of the intervening drop in prices, summarily rejected this proposal too. The two cargos were subsequently sold to third parties at the best price obtainable, first that of the *Appollonian* and, sometime later, after extraction from the tanks had been accomplished, that of the *Khamsin*.[1]

There ensued this action for breach of contract,[2] which, after a somewhat unconventional trial course, resulted in a nonjury decision for the plaintiff in the sum of $1,385,512.83, essentially the difference between the original contract price of $3,360,667.14 and the amount received by the plaintiff by way of resale of the *Khamsin* oil at what the court found as a matter of fact was a negotiated price which, under all the circumstances,[3] was reasonably procured in the open market. To arrive at this result, the Trial Judge, while ruling against other liability theories advanced by the plaintiff, which, in particular, included one charging the defendant with having failed to act in good faith in the negotiations for a price adjustment on the *Khamsin* oil (Uniform Commercial Code, § 1–203 [1–304]), decided as a matter of law that subdivision (2) of section 2–508 of the Uniform Commercial Code was available to the plaintiff even if it had no prior knowledge of the nonconformity. Finding that in fact plaintiff had no such belief at the time of the delivery, that what turned out to be a .92% sulfur content was "within the range of contemplation of reasonable acceptability" to Con Ed, and that seasonable notice of an intention to cure was given, the court went on to hold that plaintiff's "reasonable and timely offer to cure" was improperly rejected (sub nom. The Appellate Division having unanimously affirmed the judgment entered on this decision, the case is now here by our leave. * * *

II

We turn then to the central issue on this appeal: Fairly interpreted, did subdivision (2) of section 2–508 of the Uniform Commercial Code require Con Ed to accept the substitute shipment plaintiff tendered? In approaching this question, we, of course, must remember that a seller's right to cure a defective tender, as allowed by both subdivisions of section 2–508, was intended to act as a meaningful limitation on the absolutism of the old perfect tender rule, under which, no leeway being allowed for any imperfections, there was, as one court put it, just "no room for the doctrine of substantial performance" of commercial obligations.

In contrast, to meet the realities of the more impersonal business world of our day, the code, to avoid sharp dealing, expressly provides for the liberal construction of its remedial provisions (§ 1–102) so that "good faith" and the "observance of reasonable commercial standards of fair dealing" be the rule rather than the exception in trade (see § 2–103,

---

[1]   Most of the *Khamsin* oil was drained from the tanks and sold at $10.75 per barrel. The balance was retained by Con Ed in its mixed form at $10.45 per barrel. The original price in January had been $17.875 per barrel.

[2]   The plaintiff originally also sought an affirmative injunction to compel Con Ed to accept the *Khamsin* shipment or, alternatively, the *Appollonian* substitute. However, when a preliminary injunction was denied on the ground that the plaintiff had an adequate remedy at law, it amended its complaint to pursue the latter remedy alone.

[3]   These circumstances included the fact that the preliminary injunction was not denied until April so that, by the time the *Khamsin* oil was sold in May, almost three months had gone by since its rejection.

subd. [1], par [b]), "good faith" being defined as "honesty in fact in the conduct or transaction concerned" (Uniform Commercial Code, § 1–201, subd. [19]). As to section 2–508 in particular, the code's Official Comment advises that its mission is to safeguard the seller "against surprise as a result of sudden technicality on the buyer's part" (Uniform Commercial Code, § 2–106, Comment 2).

Section 2–508 may be conveniently divided between provisions for cure offered when "the time for performance has not yet expired" (subd. [1]), a precode concept in this State, and ones which, by newly introducing the possibility of a seller obtaining "a further reasonable time to substitute a conforming tender" (subd. [2]), also permit cure beyond the date set for performance. In its entirety the section reads as follows:

"(1) Where any tender or delivery by the seller is rejected because non-conforming and the time for performance has not yet expired, the seller may seasonably notify the buyer of his intention to cure and may then within the contract time make a conforming delivery.

"(2) Where the buyer rejects a non-conforming tender which the seller had reasonable grounds to believe would be acceptable with or without money allowance the seller may if he seasonably notifies the buyer have a further reasonable time to substitute a conforming tender."

Since we here confront circumstances in which the conforming tender came after the time of performance, we focus on subdivision (2). On its face, taking its conditions in the order in which they appear, for the statute to apply (1) a buyer must have rejected a nonconforming tender, (2) the seller must have had reasonable grounds to believe this tender would be acceptable (with or without money allowance), and (3) the seller must have "seasonably" notified the buyer of the intention to substitute a conforming tender within a reasonable time.[4]

In the present case, none of these presented a problem. The first one was easily met for it is unquestioned that, at .92%, the sulfur content of the *Khamsin* oil did not conform to the .5% specified in the contract and that it was rejected by Con Ed. The second, the reasonableness of the seller's belief that the original tender would be acceptable, was supported not only by unimpeached proof that the contract's .5% and the refinery certificate's .52% were trade equivalents, but by testimony that, by the time the contract was made, the plaintiff knew Con Ed burned fuel with a content of up to 1%, so that, with appropriate price adjustment, the *Khamsin* oil would have suited its needs even if, at delivery, it was, to the plaintiff's surprise, to test out at .92%. Further, the matter seems to have been put beyond dispute by the defendant's readiness to take the oil at the reduced market price on February 20. Surely, on such a record, the trial court cannot be faulted for having found as a fact that the second condition too had been established.

---

4   Essentially a factual matter, "seasonable" is defined in subdivision (3) of section 1–204 [1–204(b)] of the Uniform Commercial Code as "at or within the time agreed or if no time is agreed at or within a reasonable time". At least equally factual in character, a "reasonable time" is left to depend on the "nature, purpose and circumstances" of any action which is to be taken (Uniform Commercial Code, § 1–204, subd [2] [1–204(a)]).

As to the third, the conforming state of the *Appollonian* oil is undisputed, the offer to tender it took place on February 21, only a day after Con Ed finally had rejected the Khamsin delivery and the *Appollonian* substitute then already was en route to the United States, where it was expected in a week and did arrive on March 4, only four days later than expected. Especially since Con Ed pleaded no prejudice (unless the drop in prices could be so regarded), it is almost impossible, given the flexibility of the Uniform Commercial Code definitions of "seasonable" and "reasonable", to quarrel with the finding that the remaining requirements of the statute also had been met.

Thus lacking the support of the statute's literal language, the defendant nonetheless would have us limit its application to cases in which a seller knowingly makes a nonconforming tender which it has reason to believe the buyer will accept. For this proposition, it relies almost entirely on a critique in Nordstrom, Law of Sales (§ 105), which rationalizes that, since a seller who believes its tender is conforming would have no reason to think in terms of a reduction in the price of the goods, to allow such a seller to cure after the time for performance had passed would make the statutory reference to a money allowance redundant.[5] Nordstrom, interestingly enough, finds it useful to buttress this position by the somewhat dire prediction, though backed by no empirical or other confirmation, that, unless the right to cure is confined to those whose nonconforming tenders are knowing ones, the incentive of sellers to timely deliver will be undermined. To this it also adds the somewhat moralistic note that a seller who is mistaken as to the quality of its goods does not merit additional time (Nordstrom, loc. cit.). Curiously, recognizing that the few decisions extant on this subject have adopted a position opposed to the one for which it contends, Con Ed seeks to treat these as exceptions rather than exemplars of the rule (e.g., Wilson v. Scampoli, 228 A2d 848 [DC App] [goods obtained by seller from their manufacturer in original carton resold unopened to purchaser; seller held within statute though it had no reason to believe the goods defective]; Appleton State Bank v. Lee, 33 Wis. 2d 690 [seller mistakenly delivered sewing machine of wrong brand but otherwise identical to one sold; held that seller, though it did not know of its mistake, had a right to cure by substitution]).[6]

That the principle for which these cases stand goes far beyond their particular facts cannot be gainsaid. These holdings demonstrate that, in dealing with the application of subdivision (2) of section 2–508, courts have been concerned with the reasonableness of the seller's belief that

---

[5] The premise for such an argument, which ignores the policy of the code to prevent buyers from using insubstantial remediable or price adjustable defects to free themselves from unprofitable bargains (Hawkland, Sales and Bulk Sales Under the Uniform Commercial Code, pp 120–122), is that the words "with or without money allowance" apply only to sellers who believe their goods will be acceptable with such an allowance and not to sellers who believe their goods will be acceptable without such an allowance. But, since the words are part of a phrase which speaks of an otherwise unqualified belief that the goods will be acceptable, unless one strains for an opposite interpretation, we find insufficient reason to doubt that it intends to include both those who find a need to offer an allowance and those who do not.

[6] The only New York case to deal with this section involved a seller who knowingly tendered a "newer and improved version of the model that was actually ordered" on the contract delivery date. The court held he had reasonable grounds to believe the buyer would accept the newer model (Bartus v. Riccardi, 55 Misc 2d 3 [Utica City Ct, Hymes, J.]).

the goods would be acceptable rather than with the seller's pretender knowledge or lack of knowledge of the defect.

It also is no surprise then that the afore-mentioned decisional history is a reflection of the mainstream of scholarly commentary on the subject.

White and Summers, for instance, put it well, and bluntly. Stressing that the code intended cure to be "a remedy which should be carefully cultivated and developed by the courts" because it "offers the possibility of conforming the law to reasonable expectations and of thwarting the chiseler who seeks to escape from a bad bargain" the authors conclude, as do we, that a seller should have recourse to the relief afforded by subdivision (2) of section 2–508 of the Uniform Commercial Code as long as it can establish that it had reasonable grounds, tested objectively, for its belief that the goods would be accepted. It goes without saying that the test of reasonableness, in this context, must encompass the concepts of "good faith" and "commercial standards of fair dealing" which permeate the code (Uniform Commercial Code, § 1–201, subd. [19] [1–201(b)(20)]; §§ 1–203 [1–304], 2–103, subd. [1], par [b]).[7]

III.

* * *

It has long been the law that agreement on a theory of damages at trial, even if only implied, must control on appeal.

For all these reasons, the order of the Appellate Division should be affirmed, with costs.

Order affirmed.

David Tunick, Inc. v. Kornfeld

United States District Court, Southern District of New York, 1993
838 F. Supp. 848

■ Opinion & Order: EDELSTEIN, DISTRICT JUDGE

This action arises from Mr. E. W. Kornfeld's and Galerie Kornfeld und Cie's (collectively "Kornfeld" or "defendants") sale of a signed Picasso print to plaintiff, David Tunick, Inc. Plaintiff alleges that defendants sold David Tunick, Inc. a print entitled Le Minotauromachie (the "Print") which defendants represented was signed by Pablo Picasso (the "Signature") but which, in fact, bears a forged signature. As a result, plaintiff brought this action alleging breach of warranties, fraud, reckless misrepresentation, breach of the duty of honesty and fair dealing, and breach of fiduciary duty. Defendants deny plaintiff's allegations, contend that the Signature is genuine, and have filed

---

[7] Except indirectly, on this appeal we do not deal with the equally important protections the code affords buyers. It is as to buyers as well as sellers that the code, to the extent that it displaces traditional principles of law and equity (§ 1–103), seeks to discourage unfair or hypertechnical business conduct bespeaking a dog-eat-dog rather than a live-and-let-live approach to the marketplace (e.g., §§ 2–314, 2–315, 2–513, 2–601, 2–608). Overall, the aim is to encourage parties to amicably resolve their own problems (Ramirez v. Autosport, 88 NJ 277, 285; compare Restatement, Contracts 2d, Introductory Note to chapter 10, p 194 ["the wisest course is ordinarily for the parties to attempt to resolve their differences by negotiations, including clarification of expectations [and] cure of past defaults"]).

counterclaims against plaintiff, David Tunick, Inc., and counterclaim defendant, David Tunick (collectively "Tunick" or "plaintiff"). Defendants' counterclaims allege breach of contract, unjust enrichment, and fraud. In the instant motion, defendants seek summary judgment on each of plaintiff's five claims for relief and on defendants' first counterclaim, which alleges breach of contract.

Discussion

* * *

1. Defendants' Motion for Summary Judgment on Plaintiff's First Claim for Relief

Defendants seek summary judgment on plaintiff's first claim for relief. Plaintiff's first claim for relief alleges that "Defendants have breached their express warranties to plaintiff (a) that the [signature on the Print] is authentic and (b) that the [Print] had been signed in 1942 and had gone directly from Picasso to a private collector whose widow consigned it to Defendants for sale at the action." Defendants contend that plaintiff is unable to demonstrate that the Signature is not genuine. Further, defendants contend that, even if the Signature is not authentic, plaintiff's refusal to accept a replacement print of Le Minotauromachie, that also was allegedly signed by Pablo Picasso, defeats plaintiff's ability to recover for breach of warranty.

Defendants' first contention is easily disposed of and, in fact, defendants in their reply memorandum concede that, for the purpose of this motion, the authenticity of the Signature is in dispute. Plaintiff, subsequent to the filing of defendants' motion for summary judgment, has identified a forensic document examiner, William J. Flynn, willing to testify that the Signature is a forgery. While the late date at which this expert was identified may appear odd in light of plaintiff's assertion in its complaint that "prior to the commencement of the present suit [in 1991], Plaintiff learned that numerous experts are of the opinion that the Signature [on the Print] is false," plaintiff has submitted sufficient evidence to place the authenticity of the Signature in dispute. Hence, summary judgment on this basis is not appropriate.

Defendants' second contention, that even if the Signature is not authentic, plaintiff's refusal to accept a replacement print of Le Minotauromachie defeats plaintiff's ability to recover for breach of warranty, appears to raise an issue of first impression. Plaintiff claims that, immediately upon learning that the Signature was forged, it demanded rescission of the sale and tendered the Print to defendants. Plaintiff thus revoked acceptance of the Print in accordance with Section 2–608 of the Uniform Commercial Code as enacted in New York ("N.Y.U.C.C."). Under the N.Y.U.C.C., a purchaser who in good faith revokes his acceptance of goods, has the same rights and duties with regard to the goods involved as if he had rejected them. See N.Y.U.C.C. § 2–608(3). One duty imposed upon the buyer pursuant to N.Y.U.C.C. Section 2–508 is that:

> (1) Where any tender or delivery by the seller is rejected because non-conforming and the time for performance has not yet expired, the seller may seasonably notify the buyer of his intention to cure and may then within the contract time make a conforming delivery.

(2) Where the buyer rejects a non-conforming tender which the seller had reasonable grounds to believe would be acceptable with or without money allowance the seller may if he seasonably notifies the buyer have a further reasonable time to substitute a conforming tender.

N.Y.U.C.C. § 2–508.

Defendants allege, and plaintiff does not contest, that shortly after Mr. Tunick informed Mr. Kornfeld that he believed the Signature to be a forgery, Mr. Kornfeld offered to exchange the Print for another print of Le Minotauromachie which also was allegedly signed by Pablo Picasso. Defendants contend that, in so doing, defendants exercised their right under N.Y.U.C.C. Section 2–508(2) to substitute conforming goods for the allegedly non-conforming tender rejected by plaintiff. Plaintiff rejected defendants' offer to replace the Print with another print of Le Minotauromachie and filed suit in this Court. Defendants aver that, because Mr. Kornfeld's offer met the standards of N.Y.U.C.C. Section 2–508, plaintiff could not properly reject the offer and look to alternative remedies. Plaintiff disputes the applicability of N.Y. U.C.C. Section 2–508 to prints. Plaintiff avers that:

In the world of fine art, however, there can be no legally meaningful doctrine of functional equivalence or substitution. . . . Prints vary, sometimes widely, in many ways and no two are the same. Purchasers obviously buy prints for different reasons. . . . Their choice of one print over another will be motivated by objective reasons, subjective reasons, whim, fancy and impulse.

Defendants' argument is novel. No court in this Circuit or in New York appears to have been presented with the question of whether a non-conforming tender of a work of art may be cured by an offer of a different but similar work. Furthermore, the legislative history of the relevant Uniform Commercial Code section is of no aid in answering this question. Indeed, this issue requires consideration of whether prints are substitutable for one another: Are two prints, printed from the same plates and by the same artist, sufficiently similar that one can be said to be a perfect substitute for another? Moreover, is any such similarity sufficient to burden a good faith purchaser of a print with the duty to accept, as fulfillment of a contract to purchase that print, another print that the purchaser did not view or bid upon?

After carefully considering this issue, I find that two prints, by the same artist and from the same plates, are not interchangeable. As such, N.Y.U.C.C. Section 2–508 does not, as a matter of law, obligate a buyer to accept in lieu of a non-conforming print, a substitute print from the same series of prints.

First, two prints from a series produced by an artist each possess distinctive qualities that may impact their aesthetic and economic value. Often, differences in the quality of impressions are observable as the plate used to make the prints wears during the course of printing. See Lee Rosenbaum, The Complete Guide to Collecting Art 134 (1982) (discussing potential for the "falling off in quality from the first to last" impression from a plate); Irwin W. Solomon, How to Start and Build an Art Collection 14 (1961) (As a print plate wears over time, later prints may become "fuzzy, lacking the fine definition and brilliant contrast of a superior print."). In addition, the price of a given print may be inflated by "some 'autograph' quality or quality of impression" not shared by other prints in the same series. Guy R. Williams, Collecting Pictures 86 (1968). Similarly, depending on the type of printing method used, coloration and contrast may vary among prints in a series. Each of these factors can substantially impact the value of a given print.

Second, prints, like other types of artwork, are fragile and their value can be diminished by the manner in which they are treated over time. Prints that are improperly stored easily can become damaged, fade or blur. See Christie's Guide to Collecting 110–11 (Robert Cumming ed., Prentice–Hall 1984). Any such occurrence substantially impacts the economic value of the print. See id. As one would expect, "the first factor [considered by collectors] is the general condition of the print. . . . Ideally, every print . . . purchased should look as nearly as possible as if it has just come straight from the press." Guy R. Williams, Collecting Pictures 102 (1968).[1]

Third, prints, unlike petroleum or produce, are not purchased for strictly utilitarian reasons. A print is selected by a purchaser because the traits of that print please the purchaser's aesthetic sensibilities. Thus, whether prints in a series are largely similar or slightly different is of no critical importance. The real fact to be considered is that the purchaser chose a given print because he viewed it as uniquely beautiful, interesting, or well suited to his collection or gallery. Nothing else will satisfy that collector but that which he bought. For these reasons, prints are not interchangeable.

Thus, each print is, by definition, unique. Hence, there can be no exact substitute for a given print purchased by a collector. In the case at bar, plaintiff did not enter into a contract to purchase a print of Le Minotauromachie signed by Picasso; rather, plaintiff bid for and purchased the specific print of Le Minotauromachie that Mr. Tunick viewed prior to the auction, which was signed by Picasso and in the condition Mr. Tunick observed at the time of purchase. In this context it would be fundamentally unfair, and unsound policy, to impose on plaintiff a duty to accept another—inherently different—print of Le Minotauromachie as a substitute for the one plaintiff actually viewed, bid for, and purchased.

A review of N.Y.U.C.C. Section 2–716 further demonstrates that New York courts would find that prints are intrinsically unique, rather than fungible or perfect substitutes for one another. N.Y.U.C.C. Section 2–716(1) provides that "Specific performance may be decreed where the goods are unique or in other proper circumstances." Official Comment 2 to N.Y.U.C.C. Section 2–716 indicates that specific performance historically has been available in connection with "contracts for the sale of . . . priceless works of art." Indeed, New York courts long have recognized the availability of the remedy of specific performance on facts analogous to those in this case. Accordingly, the trend in New York seems to be toward courts finding that prints are unique goods.

---

[1] The print at the center of this litigation is more than forty years old and has been under the ownership or control of at least two other persons. In addition, the print offered to plaintiff as a substitute is of the same age and also has passed through several hands. Thus, the condition of these prints clearly impacts their value and distinguishes one from the other.

Because prints are unique—both as a result of differences in impression quality and condition—N.Y.U.C.C. Section 2–508 is not applicable to prints. Even if a seller offers to substitute a print from a series from which a non-conforming tender was drawn, the buyer is not obligated to accept as a substitute the print that he did not view, bid upon, or purchase. Provided a buyer purchases a specific print, it is that print for which he has bargained. Unlike petroleum or other fungible goods, prints are inherently unique and are purchased for their aesthetic qualities and investment value. Such value is dictated by those attributes common only to the specific print purchased. Hence, N.Y.U.C.C. Section 2–508 does not provide defendants with a defense to plaintiff's first cause of action. Summary judgment on this claim must therefore be denied.

2. Defendants' Motion for Summary Judgment on Plaintiff's Second and Third Claims for Relief

Plaintiff's second claim for relief sounds in fraud. Plaintiff alleges that, at the time Kornfeld sold the Print to plaintiff, defendants knew that the Signature was not authentic and that the representations made to plaintiff regarding the provenance of the Print were false. Alternatively, in the third claim for relief, plaintiff alleges that defendants recklessly misrepresented facts concerning the Signature and the Print's provenance. In each claim, plaintiff contends that it justifiably relied, to its detriment, on defendants' representations and assurances.

Defendants aver that summary judgment should be granted on each of these claims because plaintiff is unable to establish that defendant acted with wrongful intent or utter disregard for the truth of their assertions in making representations concerning the Signature and provenance of the Print. Further, defendants claim entitlement to summary judgment because Mr. Kornfeld investigated the authenticity of the Signature and provenance of the Print. Defendants argue that, prior to the sale of the Print to Tunick, Mr. Kornfeld submitted the Print to Ms. Brigitte Baer for review, and reviewed a catalogue raisonne of Picasso prints ("Catalogue Raisonne") prepared by Ms. Baer, both of which indicated that the Signature was genuine.

Plaintiff alleges, however, that, at the time of defendants' alleged investigation, Ms. Baer was employed by defendants. This is disputed, and the veracity of this contention is unclear in the record. In addition, the Catalogue Raisonne purportedly consulted by Mr. Kornfeld was published by defendants. Furthermore, Mr. Kornfeld's deposition testimony indicates he was aware that another print of Le Minotauromachie, bearing a signature similar to that on the Print, has an annotation on the front of the print that was not written by Picasso or his printer, who Mr. Kornfeld knew were the only ones that properly could have written such an annotation. From these and other facts, plaintiff argues that defendants either knew or should have known that the Signature was forged.

While certain evidence submitted by defendants certainly seems to undermine plaintiff's second and third claims for relief, plaintiff has made a sufficient showing to place into question triable issues concerning Mr. Kornfeld's state of mind and defendants' intent at the time the Print was sold to plaintiff. On the record before the Court, disputed issues of material fact exist concerning whether the Signature is genuine, the provenance of the Print was accurately represented, and, if the Signature is not genuine or the provenance was inaccurately described, whether defendants acted recklessly or with scienter in making any inaccurate representations. These are issues for the jury.

3. Defendants' Motion for Summary Judgment on Plaintiff's Fourth Claim for Relief

Plaintiff's fourth claim for relief alleges that defendants breached their duties of "fair dealing, candor and honor" in connection with the sale of the Print to plaintiff. Defendants move for summary judgment on this claim because, they argue, plaintiff cannot sustain its burden with respect to the breach of warranty, fraud, or reckless misrepresentation claims. Hence, defendants contend, plaintiff is unable to sustain its burden of proof with respect to the fourth claim for relief.

As previously discussed, the merits of plaintiff's first, second, and third claims for relief must be evaluated by the trier of fact. A finding in favor of plaintiff on any of these claims would permit a reasonable jury also to find in favor of plaintiff on the fourth claim for relief. If, for example, the jury ultimately finds in favor of plaintiff on the fraud claim, the jury might find that defendants breached their duty of honesty and fair dealing under N.Y.U.C.C. Section 1–203. Summary judgment on this claim must therefore be denied.

* * *

5. Defendants' Motion for Summary Judgment on the First Counterclaim

Defendants' first counterclaim alleges breach of contract. Defendants contend that Mr. Tunick, on behalf of himself or David Tunick, Inc., breached his agreement to pay Kornfeld for the Print. By way of defense, plaintiff claims, inter alia, that the Signature is a forgery, and the authenticity of the Signature was misrepresented at the time the Print was purchased. Further, plaintiff claims that it validly revoked its acceptance of the Print upon discovering that the Signature was forged. Plaintiff thus claims that Tunick is not legally obligated to pay Kornfeld for the Print. Finally, plaintiff argues that the first counterclaim is barred by defendants' unclean hands, fraud, and other culpable acts.

Because I have denied defendants' motion for summary judgment on plaintiff's first, second, third, and fourth claims for relief, summary judgment on defendants' first counterclaim is not appropriate. Disputed issues of fact regarding defendants' first counterclaim exist, the most important of which concerns whether or not the Signature is authentic. These issues, and whether defendants are entitled to judgment on their first counterclaim, must be decided by the trier of fact. Accordingly, summary judgment on defendants' first counterclaim is denied.

Conclusion

For the reasons stated above, defendants' motion for summary judgment on plaintiff's first, second, third, and fourth claims for relief is denied. In addition, defendants' motion for summary judgment on their first counterclaim is denied. Summary judgment is granted in favor of defendants on plaintiff's fifth claim for relief. The Clerk of the Court is directed to unseal the briefs, exhibits and any other materials filed in connection with this motion.

NOTES

1. The *T.W. Oil* court gives two reasons for construing 2–508(2) not to require the seller to reasonably believe that its tender is nonconforming: policy and subsection (2)'s language. The policy reason is that requiring the seller to be aware about the nonconformity unjustifiably limits 2–508's ability to prevent strategic rejections by the buyer. This is a plausible reason for not requiring awareness of the nonconformity. The court's interpretation of 2–508(2)'s language is less convincing. As Professor Nordstrom argues, a seller who is unaware of the nonconformity in the tender has no reason to anticipate that the buyer will take the goods "with . . . a money adjustment." No money adjustment is anticipated because the seller believes the tender is conforming. Nordstrom infers that 2–508(2) therefore requires that the seller be aware of the nonconformity as a condition of cure. William Nordstrom, Handbook of the Law of Sales 321 (1970). The court rejects this inference. However, Comment 2 to 2–508 supports Nordstrom's reading by identifying 2–508(2)'s rationale as the avoidance of the effects of a "surprise" rejection. A seller can be "surprised" by the rejection only if it had been aware of the nonconformity while believing that the buyer would accept the goods. Of course, a seller can be surprised by a rejection of conforming goods. But in that case there is no nonconformity to cure.

Comment 2 adds a further confusion. It states that course of performance, course of dealing and trade usage can create reasonable grounds to believe the tender would be acceptable. This is true insofar as price adjustment in the face of nonconformities might be the practice in a trade, for instance. However, given the practice, the seller's tender arguably is conforming. This is because trade usage, course of performance and course of dealing form part of the terms of the agreement; see 1–201(b)(3), 1–303(d). Thus, a tender that deviates from the contract's specifications but falls within trade usage allowing for a price adjustment arguably is a conforming tender. The buyer's rejection is wrongful and there is no nonconformity to cure.

2. The effectiveness of the proposed cure is at issue in *Tunick*. After the buyer discovered that the print of Picasso's *Le Minatauromachie* bore a forged signature, it complained and demanded a refund. In response the seller offered to supply another print from the same print series with a genuine signature. The court found that the seller's offer was not a conforming tender, for two different reasons. First, art prints are unique, so that a print from the same print series cannot substitute for the initially tendered print. Second, prints in the same print series can be of different qualities depending on how they are framed, maintained or the integrity of the plate at the time the print is produced. The second reason implicitly concedes that prints can have substitutes but asserts that the substitutes offered are not close. Both reasons rest on factual claims, which the court does not substantiate in the case of the Picasso print. The production and sale of contemporary art prints suggests that the court's assertion of uniqueness might be mistaken. Plates from which prints of the age of the Picasso print sold in *Tunick* were produced (1935) apparently do not deteriorate with use. They produce a uniform set of prints. See Silvie Turner, Print Collecting 96 (1996); Theodore B. Donson, Prints and the Print Market 70, 89 (1977). Although prints are designated by a fraction representing the number of the print in a print series, the number of the print does not always indicate the order in which it is printed. See Jessica L. Darraby, 1 Art, Artifact, Architecture and Museum Law § 12.21 (2009). These facts suggest that contemporary art prints might be substitutes, at least when they are from the same series.

On the other hand, Picasso was not a trained printmaker and frequently reworked the etching plates he fabricated between 1900 and 1942 numerous times. This compromised the integrity of the etching and allowed for only a small run of prints from it. See Brigitte Baer, Picasso the Engraver 56 (1997). It is a further question whether prints of *Le Minotauromachie* within the same print series differ in quality from each other. Even if these prints are identical in quality, whether prints from the same series in fact are substitutes depends ultimately on the buyer's valuation of the print it purchased. The buyer might attribute significance to the print number that the market does not or to other characteristics of the particular print it purchased. In this case another signed print from the same print series would not be a substitute and therefore a conforming tender. The buyer in *Tunick* was a print gallery, which presumably did not attribute idiosyncratic value to a print. However, the print gallery's own customers might attach significance to the print number in the series. Because the court denied the seller's motion for summary judgment, it did not have to determine the buyer's different valuations of substitute prints.

3.   Article 2 does not specify, and courts do not squarely address, who bears the burden of proving that a substitute tender is conforming or nonconforming. *Tunick* involved an offer of cure after revocation of acceptance. The situation with revocation is a bit more complicated. Section 2–607(4) assigns to the buyer the burden of proving breach when it accepts the goods. Under 2–608(1) the buyer may revoke its acceptance if the tender is substantially nonconforming. The sections, taken together, require the buyer to proof breach as a condition of revoking its acceptance. However, 2–607(4) only assigns the buyer the burden of proving breach "with respect to goods accepted." The buyer who revokes its acceptance has already proven breach with respect to the accepted goods. Cure is not related to proving breach; rather, it is right the seller has after breach has been demonstrated. Thus, 2–607(4) does not put the burden on the buyer of establishing that the seller's substitute tender is nonconforming. Nonetheless, presumably under ordinary burden of proof assignments, the buyer must establish the nonconformity of a substitute tender offered by the seller.

PROBLEM 7.7

Buyer purchased a Model A dishwasher from Seller for his home. Before the purchase Buyer explained to Seller that he was having new flooring put in the kitchen and suspecting that the flooring could affect the tilt of an installed dishwasher. He added that the dishwasher might have to be installed before the flooring was complete. Seller was understanding and offered to level the dishwasher, if needed, after the flooring was in place. The sales contract called for Seller to deliver and install the unit by December 25. On December 15 Seller installed the Model A dishwasher, which had a scratched door. When Buyer complained, Seller replaced it with another Model A on December 20. On December 27, two days after Buyer's new kitchen floor was complete, Buyer discovered that the dishwasher was so tilted that it would not work. Fed up, Buyer told Seller that he no longer wanted the dishwasher and demanded that Seller remove it. Buyer refused Seller's offer to properly level the dishwasher immediately. Is Seller entitled to do so? 2–601, 2–508, 2–106(2). If so, under which subsection of 2–508?

Suppose that the Model A dishwasher installed on December 20 was properly leveled. Suppose too that the dishwasher's motor failed on December 27. When Buyer complained, Seller offered to replace the dishwasher with a Model AAA, a much more expensive and reliable model, at Buyer's convenience and at no extra charge. Buyer refused Seller's offer and insisted that Seller remove the Model A from his kitchen. Is Seller entitled to install the Model AAA (which has the same dimensions as the Model A)? 2–508(2).

E. REVOCATION OF ACCEPTANCE

The buyer who accepts the goods cannot reject them. 2–607(2). However, under conditions described in 2–608, it may revoke its acceptance and put the goods back with the seller. Section 2–608 states three requirements for revocation: one is substantive and two are procedural. The substantive requirement permits revocation only if prescribed circumstances excuse the buyer's acceptance and the nonconformity "substantially impairs" the value of the good to it. 2–608(1)(a), (b). The two procedural requirements are (1) that revocation occur within a reasonable time after the nonconformity was discovered or was discoverable and before any substantial change in the goods not caused by their own defects, and (2) that the buyer notify the seller of the revocation. 2–608(2).

Section 2–608(1)'s requirement of substantial impairment refers to a substantial impairment of the good's "value to him." This language suggests that there is a subjective test for substantial impairment. According to this test, the impairment must substantially reduce the goods' value in the buyer's eyes. Comment 2 to 2–608 supports the subjective test, which states that the test of impairment "is not what the seller had reason to know at the time of contracting; the question is whether the nonconformity is such as will in fact cause a substantial impairment of value to the buyer though the seller had no advance knowledge of the buyer's particular circumstances." Section 2–612(2)'s substantial impairment standard for installment contracts does not contain a "to him" qualification. On the other hand, 2–608(1) perhaps could be understood to require that the nonconformity substantially impair the goods' value to a reasonable purchaser. This is an objective standard. Some courts adopt a sort of "mixed" standard, which incorporates both the subjective and objective standards of impairment. See, e.g., Jorgenson v. Pressnall, 545 P.2d 1382 (Ore. 1976). The "mixed" standard requires both that the nonconformity impair the value of the goods to the buyer (the subjective component) and that the nonconformity in fact substantially impairs this value (the objective component). Strictly, this standard is not genuinely "mixed." Rather, it is a subjective standard that requires credible evidence of substantial impairment to the buyer. In any event, not too much should be made about the precise character of the substantial impairment test. In practice the fact finder will reach the same conclusion whether the test is subjective, objective or mixed. This is because the "substantiality" of a nonconformity will almost inevitably be vetted for reasonableness, in one way or another. For instance, the fact finder will meet the buyer's allegation of very significant loss of value in the face of a trivial nonconformity with disbelief.

Revocation must occur within a reasonable time after discovery of the grounds for it and before any substantial change in the condition of the goods that is not caused by their own defects. 2–608(2). Both conditions encourage the buyer to act quickly to put the goods back with the seller. Early action minimizes the seller's costs of breach. Barring revocation after a substantial change in the goods is consistent with this objective. The seller's advantage at salvaging defective goods by repairing or disposing of them probably is limited to goods in the condition it ordinarily handles. Once the goods have been altered while in the buyer's hands this advantage disappears. Because altered goods take them outside the seller's traditional market, the seller usually is no better at salvaging them than the buyer. It is cheaper (or at least no more expensive) for the buyer to dispose of them and recover damages from the seller rather than put the goods back with the seller and recover damages.

Section 2–608(2)'s requirement that revocation occur within a reasonable time after discovery of the grounds for it also minimizes the seller's breach costs. The longer the buyer waits to revoke after discovery of grounds for revocation, the more likely the seller loses opportunities to repair, replace or resell the defective goods. Fairly obviously, the measure of a "reasonable time" is vague. See 1–204(2). Comment 4 to 2–608 states that in most cases the reasonable time period will be beyond the time for discovery of the nonconformity after acceptance and beyond the time for rejection or acceptance. The buyer has a reasonable time to notify the seller of breach (2–607(3)(a)), and has a reasonable time after tender in which to reject or accept the goods (2–602(1); 2–606(1)(b)). Thus, the reasonable time in which to revoke comes later than the reasonable time to give notice of breach, which in turn is later than the reasonable time within which to accept or reject. The vagueness of these different periods of "reasonable time" can create disagreement as to whether the buyer has accepted the goods or revoked its acceptance. For instance, suppose the buyer purchases a car. While driving the car home the buyer notices significant mechanical problems in its operation. None of these problems were apparent at the time the buyer took delivery. A short time later, the buyer informs the seller that it is cancelling the deal. On these facts, the buyer could be found to have rejected the car under 2–602(1) because its rejection came within a reasonable time after it discovered the mechanical problems. Alternatively, the buyers could be found to have accepted the car, because the reasonable time for rejection ended when it took delivery. Nonetheless, the buyer's later cancellation came within a reasonable time after discovering the car's substantial defects and therefore effectively revoked its acceptance. Compare Rozmus v. Thompson's Lincoln–Mercury Co., 224 A.2d 782 (Pa. Super. Ct. 1966) (acceptance), with Zabriski Chevrolet, Inc. v. Smith, 240 A.2d 198 (N.J. Super. Ct. 1968) (rejection).

Although revocation and rejection both put the goods back with the seller, the remedies differ in their requirements. Revocation requires that the nonconformity substantially impairs the good's value. Thus, even if the buyer meets 2–608(2)'s procedural requirements, its revocation is ineffective if the nonconformity is minor. In this case the buyer has merely attempted (but failed) to revoke and its earlier acceptance continues to operate. By contrast, a procedurally proper rejection under 2–602(1) is effective even if the goods conform to the contract. In addition, the revocation and rejection differ with respect to the burden of proving their elements. Acceptance puts the burden of proving breach on the buyer. 2–607(4). Thus, to revoke its acceptance, the buyer must prove that there is a substantial nonconformity in the good. By contrast, 2–607(4)'s clear implication is that the seller must prove that the goods conform when the buyer rejects. The different assignments of the burden of proving breach matter in some cases. In the example above, for instance, if the buyer is found to have rejected the car, the seller must prove that the car conformed to the contract. In other words, it must prove that the buyer breached. On the other hand, if the buyer is found to have accepted the car, it must prove the grounds for its revocation. This requires it to prove that the car's mechanical problems constituted a nonconformity that substantially impaired the car's value to it.

A question which has arisen is whether the seller has a right to cure after the buyer has revoked its acceptance. Section 2–508, by its terms, gives the seller a right to cure when the buyer rejects. It says nothing about cure when the buyer revokes its acceptance. In addition, 2–608(2)(a) allows the buyer to revoke when it has accepted on the assumption that the nonconformity would be cured and it has not been seasonably cured. This recognizes a right to cure before revocation, which does not apply when the buyer is unaware of the nonconformity at the time it accepts the goods. For both reasons, the majority of courts have concluded that the seller does not have a right to cure after the buyer revokes. See Car Transport Brokerage Co. v. Blue Bird Body Co., 322 Fed. Appx. 891 (11th Cir. 2009) (collecting cases). A minority of courts find that Article 2 gives a right to cure even after revocation. The statutory basis supporting this right to cure is 2–608(3). Section 2–608(3) imposes on the revoking buyer the same duties with regard to the goods as the rejecting buyer. A buyer who rejects has a "duty" to accept cure under 2–508. Therefore, some courts infer, the buyer who has revoked its acceptance also has a "duty" to accept cure. This inference seems unjustified. The duties of a rejecting buyer to which 2–608(3) refers are duties to hold the goods with reasonable care (2–602(2)(c)) and, in the case of a merchant buyer, to make efforts to resell certain goods in the absence of the seller's instructions (2–603(1)). These are duties to hold or dispose of the goods. They are not duties to allow the seller to cure defects in them. Proposed 2–508 extends the seller's right to cure when the buyer revokes its acceptance.

Whether the seller should have a right to cure after revocation is a separate question. The answer turns on the two factors identified in section D, supra, in evaluating the seller's right to cure after the buyer rejects: the seller's incentive to offer a substandard product, and the buyer's incentive to revoke acceptance strategically when it regrets entering into the deal. The availability of cure gives the seller another opportunity to supply conforming goods; its initial tender does not have to be conforming. Because the buyer might not detect the nonconformity, the seller potentially saves costs by initially providing nonconforming goods. On the buyer's side, barring cure after revocation allows the buyer to end a deal that changed market conditions, rather than the seller's defective performance, make it regret. Two reasons, however, suggest that strategic revocations are unlikely. First, in order to revoke its acceptance, the buyer must prove that the revocation meets 2–608's requirements. The requirement that the nonconformity substantially impair value makes the standard for revocation higher than for rejection. As a result, the buyer will revoke only if the expected cost of proving substantial impairment is less than the loss to her of the defective good. (Otherwise, it will retain the good and recover damages.) Second, and related, the buyer bears its own litigation costs, which likely are higher in the case of revocation than rejection. Buyers who do not suffer a substantial impairment of value, while regretting their deal, are less likely to revoke acceptance. They risk having to keep the goods after incurring litigation costs. For both reasons, strategic revocations are likely to be less frequent than strategic rejections. There is therefore no need to allow cure in order to protect against strategic revocations, as there is with strategic rejections. Because cure encourages the seller to cut corners of its initial performance, a decent case can be made against allowing post-revocation cure.

Cissell Manufacturing Co. v. Park

Colorado Court of Appeals, 2001
36 P.3d 85

■ DAVIDSON, JUDGE

Defendant, Young Park, d/b/a Young's Equipment & Supplies (Park), appeals from the entry of partial summary judgment against him and the judgment of the trial court entered on a jury verdict in favor of plaintiff, Cissell Manufacturing Company. We affirm.

Park, a distributor for Cissell, bought 12 commercial clothing dryers from Cissell to lease to a laundromat owner. Park received and installed the dryers in April 1993, but never paid Cissell.

Difficulties with the dryers arose within days of installation, and Park alerted Cissell to the existence of these problems. After an unsuccessful attempt to meet with Cissell's representative in May 1993, Park and the laundromat owner sent a letter to Cissell on September 7, 1993, "rejecting and revoking acceptance" of the dryers under §§ 4–2–607 & 4–2–608, C.R.S. 2000, of the Colorado Uniform Commercial Code (UCC). Ultimately, the dryers were removed and placed in storage.

Cissell sued Park to collect the purchase price. Park counterclaimed for breach of contract, breaches of express and implied warranties, negligence, negligent misrepresentation, fraudulent misrepresentation, and fraudulent concealment, later adding a claim under the Colorado Consumer Protection Act (CCPA). The court granted partial summary judgment in favor of Cissell on its breach of contract claim and on Park's breach of contract counterclaim. Park's two motions for reconsideration—one immediately after the grant of partial summary judgment, and the other immediately preceding trial—were both denied.

At trial on Park's remaining counterclaims, the court granted Cissell's motion for directed verdict on Park's negligence claim. On the other counterclaims, the jury returned verdicts in favor of Cissell on all counts. Park's motion for new trial and for judgment notwithstanding the verdict was denied, and he now appeals.

I.

Park first argues that the trial court improperly granted Cissell's motion for summary judgment on Cissell's claim for payment and on Park's counterclaim for breach of contract. Park also argues that jury instructions based on the summary judgment ruling were incorrect. We agree. However, based on the jury verdicts on the remaining claims, we conclude that the errors were harmless.

A.

* * * According to the UCC, once a buyer has accepted goods, he or she cannot reject them and is obligated to pay for them at the contract rate. Section 4–2–607. In its order granting partial summary judgment, the trial court determined that, because Park's response to Cissell's summary judgment motion did not dispute that the dryers were accepted, under § 4–2–607, Park was obligated to pay for them. While acknowledging Park's argument that he had "rejected" acceptance under § 4–2–608 of the UCC, the court found that "because the dryers had been accepted in April 1993, [Park] did not provide in September a 'formal notice of rejection' pursuant to C.R.S. § 4–2–608. At most, he gave notice of an attempt to revoke acceptance." The court concluded that, although Park was free to "pursue other remedies," because he had accepted and was using the dryers, he was, nonetheless, obligated to pay. Thus, the court determined that no genuine issue of material fact remained regarding Cissell's claim for payment and Park's breach of contract counterclaim.

On appeal, Park argues that the trial court erred in concluding that § 4–2–608 does not allow revocation of goods with latent defects after acceptance of the goods; that a buyer remains obligated to pay the entire price even after a successful revocation of acceptance of the goods under § 4–2–608; and that any purported attempt to revoke was invalid as a matter of law because the required notice was inadequate. We agree with Park.

1.

Initially, to the extent Cissell argues that Park did not raise the issue of revocation of acceptance in the trial court and therefore has waived it, we disagree. Park asserted a counterclaim and defense under § 4–2–608 in his pleadings and in response to Cissell's motion for summary judgment. He also tendered an instruction on the same theory, which was rejected by the court on the ground that it was precluded by the grant of partial summary judgment to Cissell.

2.

Under the UCC, a buyer may either reject or accept delivered goods. Section 4–2–601, C.R.S. 2000. As discussed, once a buyer accepts goods, he or she is precluded from rejecting them, § 4–2–607(2), C.R.S. 2000, and is obligated to pay at the contract rate for goods accepted. Section 4–2–607(1), C.R.S. 2000.

However, even after accepting, the buyer may revoke such acceptance:

(1) The buyer may revoke his acceptance of a lot or commercial unit whose nonconformity substantially impairs its value to him if he has accepted it:

(a) On the reasonable assumption that its nonconformity would be cured and it has not been seasonably cured; or

(b) Without discovery of such nonconformity if his acceptance was reasonably induced either by the difficulty of discovery before acceptance or by the seller's assurances.

(2) Revocation of acceptance must occur within a reasonable time after the buyer discovers or should have discovered the ground for it and before any substantial change in condition of the goods which is not caused by their own defects. It is not effective until the buyer notifies the seller of it.

Section 4–2–608.

Revocation of acceptance is a relatively new concept in the UCC, instituted to resolve the ambiguities of the common law doctrine of rescission for the fact that rejection is exercised before acceptance and revocation after, the two have the same legal effect.

In its complaint, Cissell asserted an entitlement to payment and interest on the goods delivered. See § 4–2–709, C.R.S. 2000 (action for the price).

In such an action, the seller is entitled to recovery of the price of "goods accepted." Section 4–2–709(1)(a), C.R.S. 2000. However, the UCC limits the definition of "goods accepted" to "only goods as to which there has been no justified revocation of acceptance, for such a revocation means that there has been a default by the seller which bars his rights under this section." Section 4–2–709 comment 5, C.R.S. 2000.

Thus, a procedurally effective rejection or revocation "bars" acceptance, see J. White & R. Summers, Uniform Commercial Code § 7–3 (4th ed. 1995) (White & Summers), and revocation of acceptance, like rejection, allows the buyer to avoid the obligation to pay the price. To the extent the trial court determined otherwise in its summary judgment rulings, it was incorrect.

We also agree with Park that the trial court incorrectly determined that Park could not pursue a remedy under § 4–2–608 because he had not provided to Cissell a "formal" notice of rejection or revocation.

Contrary to the trial court's determination, there is no "formal notice of revocation" requirement under § 4–2–608, nor does it exist under § 4–2–607 (governing rejection). Indeed, § 4–2–608 does not require that a notice of revocation of acceptance assume any particular format, but rather that the content of the notice be determined by "considerations of good faith, prevention of surprise, and reasonable adjustment." Section 4–2–608 comment 5, C.R.S. 2000. The notice of revocation, to be sufficient, should fairly apprise the seller that the buyer wants to give back the goods and receive a substitute or money in return.

Here, Park's September 1993 letter was adequate. The letter described in detail the dryers' alleged defects, attempted to "reject acceptance" of the dryers, demanded that Cissell remove the machines from the premises, and requested that damages be paid to Park and the laundromat owner.

B.

Because the trial court erred in its grant of partial summary judgment [on Cissell's claim for payment, we agree with Park that its instruction to the jury that Park had breached the contract by failing to pay was error. Similarly, the trial court erroneously refused to instruct the jury on Park's revocation of acceptance counterclaim. However, we are convinced that, even if the jury had been instructed properly, the verdict against Park would have been the same. Thus, the errors were harmless.

As Cissell argues, to prove a valid revocation of acceptance, a buyer must show, inter alia, that the goods were nonconforming. Section 4–2–608(1). In this regard, revocation requires a greater showing than rejection: a buyer may reject goods if the tender fails "in any respect to conform to the contract," § 4–2–601, but, in order to revoke, a buyer must show, among other things, that the nonconformity of the goods substantially impairs their value to the buyer. Section 4–2–608 comment 2, C.R.S. 2000; see also Hawkland, supra, § 2–608:2 (clarifying the policy that "it makes good sense to require more from a buyer who has accepted the goods than from one who has rejected them").

Determination of an item's nonconformity hinges on whether it "substantially impairs its value to [the buyer]." See Hawkland, supra, § 2–608:2; see also Keen v. Modern Trailer Sales, Inc., 578 P.2d 668 (Colo. App. 1978) (although section 4–2–608 appears to create a subjective test in the sense that the requirements of the particular buyer must be examined and deferred to, impairment of the buyer's requirements must be substantial in objective terms). Whether goods are nonconforming requires reference to the terms of the contract and to the law of warranty. See § 4–2–106(2), C.R.S. 2000 (goods are conforming when they are in accordance with the obligations under the contract). In other words, if the goods are as contracted for and as warranted, they cannot be nonconforming.

Here, although Park's revocation of acceptance instruction was not presented to the jury, the jury was instructed on Park's remaining counterclaims for breach of express warranty, breach of implied warranty of fitness for a particular purpose, and breach of implied warranty of merchantability. Moreover, the evidence pertaining to the latter counterclaims was, as Park concedes, identical to that which would have supported his claim of revocation of acceptance.

By special verdict, however, the jury found against Park on all three counterclaims. Specifically, the jury found that the dryers' features satisfied all of Cissell's express warranties as set forth in the parties' contract. The jury also found that Park had failed to prove that the dryers were "not suitable for the particular purpose for which they were warranted." See § 4–2–315, C.R.S. 2000. Similarly, by rejecting Park's counterclaim of breach of implied warranty of merchantability, the jury found that the dryers were "of merchantable quality at the time of sale." See § 4–2–314, C.R.S. 2000.

Thus, by finding that the goods were "as warranted," "suitable," and "merchantable," the jury necessarily rejected any purported claim of nonconformity. See §§ 4–2–106 & § 4–2–608; see also Gulfwind South, Inc. v. Jones, 775 So. 2d 311 (Fla. Dist. Ct. App., 2000) ("before the trial court could find a valid revocation of acceptance, it had to find that there was, in fact, a contractual or warranty provision setting a standard of conformity, and the facts demonstrated nonconformity with that standard").

Moreover, because of the manner in which the jury was instructed, the verdict on the warranty claims could not have been tainted, as Park argues, by the court's errors.

Although the trial court erroneously instructed the jury that, by failing to pay, Park breached the contract, the jury could only consider that breach as an affirmative defense to Park's three breach of warranty claims. Specifically, for each of Park's breach of warranty claims, the structure of the verdict forms required the jury first to answer the question whether Park had proven his breach of warranty claim. Only if it had answered "yes" was it to answer the second question, whether Cissell had proved any of its affirmative defenses.

Thus, because the jury answered "no" to the first question on each of the three breach of warranty claims, we conclude that it did not consider Cissell's affirmative defense of breach of contract.

II.

The trial court directed a verdict against Park on his counterclaim for negligence on the grounds that it was barred by the "economic loss rule." Park contends that this was error. We disagree.

The "economic loss rule" prohibits a negligence claim when the breach of duty is contractual and the harm incurred is the "result of failure of the purpose of contract." Town of Alma v. AZCO Construction, Inc., 10 P.3d 1256 (Colo. 2000); Grynberg v. Agri Tech, Inc., 10 P.3d 1267 (Colo. 2000) (expressly adopting the economic loss rule in Colorado); Jardel Enterprises, Inc. v. Triconsultants, Inc., 770 P.2d 1301 (Colo. App. 1988). Under this rule, a party suffering purely economic loss from the breach of an express or implied contractual duty is barred from asserting a tort claim for such a breach, absent an independent duty of care under tort law.

Here, Park sought only economic damages. He claims, nevertheless, that Cissell's act of providing defective dryers was negligent and breached an independent duty of care.

However, the contract between the parties required that Cissell provide conforming goods to Park; its alleged failure to do so was the basis for Park's claim for breach of express warranty. Because Park's negligence claim was based on the existence of a duty that arose from the terms of the contract, his negligence and contract claims were equivalent.

Thus, since no duties independent of contractual duties were alleged to have been breached, the trial court correctly refused to submit Park's negligence claim to the jury.

* * * The judgment is affirmed.

NOTES AND QUESTIONS

1.   In his response to Cissell's summary judgment motion asking for the price, Park conceded that he had accepted the driers. Why do the facts the court recites force Park to make the concession? Put another way, why would Park's assertion that he rejected the driers be implausible even under a summary judgment standard? 2–606(1)(b), 2–602(1). A buyer can revoke its acceptance only if the nonconformity substantially impairs the value of the goods to him. 2–608(1). Finding that the driers Cissell delivered conformed to the contract, the court concluded that Park's revocation therefore was ineffective. Is there another basis on which the court could have found Park's revocation to be ineffective? Consult 2–608(2).

2.   The buyer's use of the goods after revocation of acceptance raises the same issue as their use following rejection. Section 2–608(2) imposes on the revoking buyer the same duties as are imposed on the rejecting buyer. Under 2–602(2)(a) after rejection the buyer's exercise of ownership of the goods is wrongful against the seller. Section 2–606(1)(c) considers an act inconsistent with the seller's ownership to be acceptance, if ratified by the seller. Thus, if the buyer's continued use after revocation is an act inconsistent with the seller's ownership, it constitutes re-acceptance of the goods. The division among courts over the legal effect of post-revocation use parallels the disagreement over the effect of post-rejection use. Some courts appear to take the view that any use after revocation is an act inconsistent with the seller's ownership and therefore constitutes re-acceptance. See Waltz v. Chevrolet Motor Div., 307 A.2d 815 (Del. Sup. Ct. 1973). Others hold that the buyer's continued reasonable use is not inconsistent with ownership and therefore the revocation remains effective. See Deere v. Johnson, 271 F.3d 613 (5th Cir. 2001). The latter courts allow the seller to offset damages for which it is liable by an amount reflecting the value of continued use, usually based on restitution. 1–103(b).

Although Article 2 does not expressly provide for an offset, both 2–712's cover measure of damages and 2–713's market price measure take it into account. These measures apply when the revoking buyer puts the goods back with the seller and measures its damages by a substitute transaction (cover) or directly by market price. Both 2–712 and 2–713 deduct from recoverable damages expenses that the buyer saves as a result of the seller's breach ("less expenses saved in consequence of the seller's breach"). Continued use after revocation saves the buyer the expense of obtaining substitute goods during this period. Some courts measure the offset by the rental cost of the goods for the period the buyer uses them; others measure it by the value of continued use to the buyer during this period. Compare rental cost cases, see e.g. Jorgensen v. Pressnall, 545 P.2d 1382, 1386 (Or. 1976) (setoff determined by rental value of the mobile home during plaintiffs' occupancy); Keen v. Modern Trailer Sales, Inc., 578 P.2d 668, 670 (Colo. Ct. App. 1978) with value to buyer cases, see e.g. Schaefer v. Spampinato, 1994 Ohio App. LEXIS 1523, at *6 (Ohio Ct. App. 1994) (set off valued at 10 cents for each mile buyer had driven); Johnson v. General Motors Corp., Chevrolet Motor Div., 668 P.2d 139, 146 (Kan. 1983) (10.7 cents per mile). Both measures overestimate the decline in the goods' value resulting from continued use. Rental cost reflects uses of rented goods that are more exacting or less careful than uses to which buyers put goods they purchase. It also does not take into account the inconvenience to the revoking buyer in using defective goods. Measuring the offset by the value of continued use to the buyer inflates the cost of continued use, because the buyer will use the goods only if the value to it exceeds cost. In addition, the value of use to the buyer is simply hard to verify.

3.   Sometimes a buyer attempts to revoke its acceptance against a remote seller in the distribution chain. This will occur when the buyer's immediate seller is insolvent, uncooperative or simply a less convenient source of recovery than the remote seller. The remote seller has no contractual relationship with the buyer. It does not receive the contract price from the buyer and might have disclaimed all liability with respect to the goods. The remote seller might not even have facilities to which the buyer can return the goods. A strong statutory argument suggests that revocation is impermissible against a remote seller. Section 2–711 includes among the buyer's remedies the buyer's right to revoke its acceptance against "the seller." Section 2–608(2) requires the revoking buyer to give notice to "the seller." According to 2–103(d), a "seller" is a "person who sells or contracts to sell goods." Finally, under 2–106(1), a "sale" consists of passage of title to the goods from the seller to the buyer. The last two provisions, taken together, restrict the term "seller" to the buyer's immediate seller. A reasonable inference is that the same restriction applies to the buyer's right to revoke its acceptance. Thus, revocation is permissible only against the seller with whom the buyer is in privity. Compare Seekings v. Jimmy GMC, Inc., 638 P.2d 210 (Az. 1981); Neal v. SMC, 99 S.W.3d 813 (Tex. Ct. App. 2003) (revocation against remote seller impermissible) with Gochey v. Bombardier, Inc., 572 A.2d 921 (Vt. 1990); Durfee v. Rod Baxter Imports, Inc., 262 N.W.2d 349 (Minn. 1977) (permissible).

F. PERFORMANCE UNDER THE CISG

1. INSPECTION AND NOTICE OF NONCONFORMITIES

The CISG's regulation of parties' performance of the contract is similar to the UCC, but with several important differences. Article 38(1) requires the buyer to examine, or have examined, the goods "within as short a period as is practicable in the circumstances." Where the contract involves carriage, examination may be deferred until the goods have arrived at their destination. Article 38(2). Unless the contract provides otherwise, the seller must make the goods available at its place of business. Article 31(c); cf. 2–308(a). Thus, unless otherwise provided, the buyer's inspection obligation begins when the goods have been delivered. In one respect Article 38 improves on its UCC counterpart, 2–513. While 2–513(1) is unclear as to the event which triggers the buyer's obligation to inspect (tender of the goods? delivery? identification of the goods?), Article 38 is precise: the obligation to inspect begins on delivery of the goods. Article 58(3) entitles the buyer, who is bound to pay the contract price when the goods are put at its disposal, to examine them prior to payment. As with other most other duties under the CISG, the contract can provide for payment prior to inspection. See Article 58(2). Even here Article 38(1) still requires the buyer to inspect the goods.

A failure to timely inspect by itself has no consequence. Instead, Article 39(1) sets a sanction of sorts for an untimely inspection. Under Article 39(1), the buyer loses the right to rely on a nonconformity it is fails to give notice within a reasonable time after it discovered or "ought to have discovered" the nonconformity. The buyer "ought to have discovered" nonconformities that a timely inspection in accordance with Article 38(1) would have revealed. Thus, the buyer cannot rely on a nonconformity it discovers on making a tardy inspection of the goods. Because the buyer will rely on nonconformities to obtain a remedy against the seller, Article 39's "sanction" for an untimely inspection is to bar the buyer from relief. For example, suppose the buyer fails to inspect the goods within the time set by Article 38(1). Later, it discovers a nonconformity that it would have discovered earlier had it timely inspected and informs the seller immediately. The buyer has given the seller proper notice within a reasonable time of discovering the nonconformity. However, the notice came after the time in which it "ought to have discovered" the nonconformity. Article 39(1) therefore bars the buyer from a remedy against the seller. The risk of this consequence sensibly encourages the buyer to timely inspect the goods. Early detection of nonconformities enables the seller to take measures to minimize the cost of its breach.

Other provisions qualify the buyer's obligation to give timely notice under Article 39(1). Article 40 does not allow the seller to rely on Article 39's notice requirements if the nonconformity relates to undisclosed facts that it knew or could not have been unaware of. Accordingly, under these conditions, a buyer who fails to give proper and timely notice is not barred from a remedy against the seller. For an illustration of Article 40's application, consult again BP Oil International, Ltd. v. Empresa Estatal Petroleos de Ecuador, 332 F.3d 333 (5th Cir. 2003), reproduced in Chapter 6 (p. 312). Article 40 is an efficient rule governing performance. A seller who knows of the nonconformity already is in a position to take measures to minimize the costs of its breach; it does not need notice of the nonconformity from the buyer. In fact, in the circumstances such notice is wasteful.

In addition, Article 44 entitles the buyer to limited remedies even when it fails to give proper and timely notice under Article 39(1). The Article allows the buyer to reduce the price according to Article 50's measure or recover damages (other than lost profits), "if he has a reasonable excuse for his failure to give the required notice." It is not clear that Article 44 has any independent application. A buyer who has a reasonable excuse for not giving timely notice nonetheless has given notice "within a reasonable time" in the circumstances. Otherwise, the buyer would not have a reasonable excuse for the delay in notice.

Similarly, a buyer whose tardy inspection reveals nonconformities nonetheless discovers nonconformities within the time in which it "ought to have discovered" them, given the circumstances. Otherwise, the buyer would not have a reasonable excuse for delaying its inspection. In both instances Article 44 is superfluous because timely notice has been given in accordance with Article 39. There might conceivably be instances in which Article 44 applies, such as when intervening events result in a delay in the buyer's notice reaching the seller. However, such instances will be rare. Finally, Article 39(2) puts an outer limit on the time in which the buyer must give notice. Under the Article the buyer loses the right to rely on conformities if it gives notice more than two years from the date the goods were handed over to the buyer. As usual, this period can be expanded or contracted by contract. Both Article 39(1) and Article 44 are subject to Article 39(2)'s time limit. Problem 7.8 below illustrates the operation of these three Articles.

PROBLEM 7.8

Seller, a Detroit manufacturer, contracted with a French buyer to sell it food processing machines. Buyer took delivery of the machines on January 1, 2005. Buyer's January 15 visual inspection revealed no apparent defects in the machines and Buyer put them to use. The machines worked well until April 20, 2007, when they malfunctioned. Buyer immediately notified Seller of the problem by letter sent the next day. Mishandling of the letter by postal workers delayed delivery of the letter until April 20, 2008. Both Buyer's large inventory of food processing machines and friendly relations with Seller gave it no reason to inquire of Seller before that date. In the circumstances Buyer's lack of inquisitiveness was reasonable. After Seller's refusal to do anything about the defective machines, relations between Seller and Buyer have become frosty. Buyer seeks to recover damages from Seller resulting from the defective, including lost profits. Alternatively, Buyer seeks to recover damages, without lost profits. Is Buyer entitled to either remedy? CISG Articles 27, 39(1), 39(2), 44.

2. AVOIDANCE OF THE CONTRACT AND CURE

The CISG does not determine performance rights by rejection or acceptance of the goods. In fact, aside from two references in Article 86, it does not refer to rejection at all. The CISG instead uses the notion of avoidance to determine performance rights. To avoid the contract is to end the contract for breach. Its counterpart under the UCC is "cancellation;" see 2–106(4). Cancellation ends the contract and allows recovery for breach of the remaining unperformed portion of the contract. See 703(1), 2–711(1). Avoidance under the CISG ends the contract too, but it also allows for recovery for breach of all obligations, performed or unperformed, including by restitution. Avoidance is a broader remedy than rejection of the goods in two respects. First, avoidance is a right held by both the seller and buyer. By contrast, rejection is the buyer's right only. Second, rejection applies only when the goods are tendered. While avoidance can apply when goods are tendered, it also can apply when the breaching party fails to perform any of its obligations. See Article 49(1)(a), 64(1)(a).

CISG's standard for avoidance is less generous to the injured party than the UCC's standard for rejection. Under 2–601's perfect tender rule, the buyer can reject the goods if they fail to conform in any respect to the contract. By contrast, under the CISG the buyer generally can avoid the contract only if the breach is fundamental. Article 49(1)(a). Article 25 in turn defines a breach as fundamental if it was reasonably foreseeable and "results in such detriment to the other party as substantially to deprive him of what he is entitled to expect under the contract." To avoid the contract, the aggrieved party must declare the contract avoided by notice to the other party. Article 26.

The substantiality or seriousness of the detriment to the buyer is determined by several factors. One factor is the terms of the contract. The parties may stipulate that certain terms are central or essential to their contract. For instance, the contractual provision to the effect that time is of the essence, or a document calling for delivery by a particular date, can make tardy delivery a fundamental breach. See Oberlandesgericht Hamburg (Germany), 28 February 1997, available at http://www.cisg.law.pace.edu/cases/970228g1.html. Even without such stipulation, construction of the contract may determine particular terms to be integral to it. A buyer is substantially deprived of what it is entitled to expect if it received goods with features that do not conform to the features called for by the contract. See Civil Court of Basil (Switzerland), 1 March 2002, available at http://cisgw3.law.pace.edu/cases/020301s1.html, Oberlandesgericht Stuttgart (Germany), 12 March 2001, available at http://www.cisg.law.pace.edu/cases/010312g1.html, China International Economic and Trade Arbitration Commission (China), 30 October 1991, available at http://www.cisg.law.pace.edu/cases/911030c1.html. Finally, the purpose for which the goods are bought also can determine the seriousness of the breach. A nonconformity that renders the goods unsalable but still useable is not a fundamental breach where the buyer purchased them only for its own use. See Oberster Gerichtshof (Austria), 21 June 2005, available at http://cisgw3.law.pace.edu/cases/050621a3.html.

Article 25's definition of fundamental breach is inevitably vague. This makes the determination of the character of a breach to some extent unpredictable in advance. Contractual stipulations of "fundamentality" or similar terms are only evidence of the centrality of a matter to the parties' contract. To be fundamental, the breach must in fact result in reasonably foreseeable and substantial detriment to the breached-against party. Such stipulations or terms therefore do not eliminate the legal uncertainty created by the notion of a fundamental breach. As a result, a party who makes the wrong guess about the character of a breach and declares the contract avoided on that basis risks itself being in breach. The declaration of avoidance gives its counterparty grounds for itself declaring the contract avoided. Parties who prize greater certainty than Article 25 provides can opt out of the CISG's standard for avoidance. Alternatively, they can provide for their own, more precise definition of fundamental breach. See Article 6.

Avoidance is a drastic remedy: it ends the contract and forces the seller to salvage the goods. In international trade salvage typically requires substantial transportation costs as well as costs associated with reselling or adapting the goods. To avoid or reduce these costs, the CISG's drafters and some courts want to preserve the contract. Accordingly, the strict standard for avoidance for fundamental breach restricts the occasions in which the buyer can put the goods back with seller. Buyers receiving defective performance that does not constitute a fundamental breach cannot end the contract. They instead must retain the goods and collect damages or reduce the contract price. While this may impose some uncompensated breach costs on buyers who are not fully compensated for their loss, the CISG's drafters apparently are more concerned with the prospect of the buyer's strategic behavior in international transactions.

In the case of non-delivery of the goods or nonpayment of the price, the breached-against party may avoid the contract even if the breach in not fundamental. Articles 49(1)(b) and 64(1)(b) describe a *Nachfrist* procedure borrowed from German law. These provisions allow the breached-against party to set an additional period—the *Nachfrist* period ("extended period" or "grace period")—within which the breaching seller or buyer must deliver or pay, respectively. If the breaching party does not perform within this period, the breached-against party may avoid the contract. Under Article 49(1)(b), for instance, if the seller has breached by not delivering within the time set by the contract, the buyer may fix an additional period of reasonable length within which the seller must deliver. See Article 47(1). If the seller does not deliver within that period, the buyer may declare the contract avoided. Articles 64(1)(b) and 63(1) together allow the seller to do the same when the buyer has breached by failing to pay or take delivery. Because Articles 49(1)(b) and 64(1)(b)'s *Nachfrist* procedure does not require a fundamental breach, the breached-against party can use it to avoid the contract without risking a court's ex post finding that avoidance was ineffective because the breach was not fundamental.

The CISG gives the seller a right to cure its defective tender. The right to cure is broad in both the conditions under which the seller is permitted to cure and the form that cure can take. Article 37 allows the seller to cure any deficiency at any time before the time for delivery has expired. Article 34 extends this right to cure deficiencies in documents as well. Both Articles allow cure only when it does not cause the buyer unreasonable inconvenience. Cure can take a variety of forms. Article 37 allows cure by replacement of missing parts, replacement of the goods or "remedy any lack of conformity in the goods delivered." The last phrase suggests that cure could be repair or even monetary compensation. Finally, Article 48(1) extends the seller's right to cure beyond the date for delivery. The only limitation is that cure must occur without unreasonable delay or causing the buyer unreasonable inconvenience or uncertainty of reimbursement. Nothing in Article 48(1) limits the form the seller's cure can take. Article 48 simply gives the seller a right to "remedy" its defective performance beyond the date of delivery. The unqualified reference to a "remedy," as well as Article 37's range of permissible forms of "remedy," suggests that the seller's cure can take similarly broad forms after the delivery date has passed.

Both Articles 37 and 48 provide that the seller "may" cure under prescribed conditions. This means that the buyer must allow the seller to cure. The seller's right therefore is not contingent on the buyer's consent. A seller might want to avoid the uncertainty of affecting a cure that the buyer finds unacceptable. Article 48(2) permits the seller to cure if the buyer does not timely respond to the seller's request that it make known whether it will find the cure acceptable. The seller's request does not entitle the buyer to refuse to allow cure that meets Articles 37 or 48(1)'s prescribed conditions. If the buyer's consent were necessary, the CISG's cure provisions would be superfluous: the parties could always bargain to allow the seller to cure (or not). There is no need to provide a right that the parties can provide themselves by contract, at no additional cost. Thus, Article 48(2) must be read to impose on the buyer a duty to accept the seller's cure even if it would rather not do so, as long as the cure is reasonable.

The CISG is unclear about the relationship between avoidance and cure. In particular, the impact of an offer of cure on the character of a breach as fundamental is not explicitly dealt with. The CISG leaves open whether the buyer may avoid the contract for fundamental breach even in the fact of the seller's reasonable offer of cure. To fix ideas, suppose the sales contract calls for delivery of laptops by March 1. Seller delivers printers to Buyer on February 25, who has no use for them or ability to resell them. On February 28 Seller makes a credible offer to deliver the laptops contracted for by March 2 and to retrieve the printers, without additional cost to the buyer. Delivery of printers which Buyer cannot use or resell, when the contract called for laptops, clearly is a serious breach. The delivery substantially deprives Buyer of what it is entitled to expect under the contract. Does Seller's timely and credible offer of cure make its breach not fundamental? If so, Buyer cannot avoid the contract under Article 49(1)(a). There are two views on the matter. One is that cure affects the character of the breach. A timely and credible offer of cure promises the buyer substantially what it was entitled to expect under the contract-laptops in the previous example. The offer therefore renders Seller's breach not fundamental under Article 25, unless Buyer has an immediate need for conforming goods. Thus, according to this view, to end the contract the buyer must avoid it before the seller makes a reasonable offer of cure. Most of commentary and cases take this view. See Peter Huber, Article 46, in UN Convention on Contracts for the International Sales of Goods (CISG): Commentary 693–694, 705–706 (S. Kröll, L. Mistelis & P.P. Viscasilles eds., 2011); Oberlandesgericht Koln (Germany), 14 October 2002, available at http://www.cisg.law.pace.edu/cases/970131g1.html; Handelsgericht des Kantons Aargau (Switzerland), 5 November 2002, available at http://www.cisg.law.pace.edu/cases/021105s1.html.

The other view is that cure has no effect on the character of a breach, so that whether the breach is fundamental is determined independently of cure. According to his view, the buyer can avoid the contract even after the seller makes an offer of cure under Article 48(1). This is because the seller's offer does not eliminate the buyer's grounds for avoidance based on fundamental breach. Two considerations favor this view. One is the language of the CISG's provisions. Article 48(1)'s introductory language makes the right to cure "[s]ubject to article 49." This clearly signals that the seller's right to cure is "subject" to the buyer's right to avoid the contract for fundamental breach. The other consideration goes to the contracting parties' performance of the contract. Other things being equal, parties want to know with some certainty when they can and cannot avoid the contract. If cure affects the character of the breach, they cannot have this knowledge. This is because the parties cannot know whether the breach is fundamental unless they know with confidence whether cure is forthcoming. If it is forthcoming, the breach is not fundamental and the buyer cannot avoid the contract. Article 25's standard for fundamental breach already is vague. Allowing cure to affect the character of a breach makes it much harder for the buyer to know in advance whether it has a right to avoid the contract. This increased uncertainty argues for determining the character of a breach independently of the seller's offer to cure. The buyer can more reliably establish whether the breach was fundamental just by comparing what was delivered to what it expected under the contract. See Clayton P. Gillette & Steven D. Walt, Sales Law: Domestic and International 266–267 (2d ed. 2009). On this view, in the previous example Seller's breach is fundamental, notwithstanding Seller's timely and credible offer to cure, and Buyer therefore may avoid the contract.

Uncitral Clout Case 171
Germany: Bundesgerichtschof (3 April 1996)

The Dutch plaintiff was the assignee of a Dutch company, which had sold four different quantities of cobalt sulphate to the defendant, a German company. It was agreed that the goods should be of British origin and that the plaintiff should supply certificates of origin and of quality. After the receipt of the documents, the defendant declared the contracts to be avoided since the cobalt sulphate was made in South Africa and the certificate of origin was wrong. The defendant also claimed that the quality of the goods was inferior to what was agreed upon. The plaintiff demanded payment. The German Supreme Court held that there were no grounds for avoidance of the contract and thus found for the plaintiff.

According to the Court, the declaration of avoidance could not be based on article 49(1)(b) CISG since the plaintiff had effected delivery. The delivery of goods which do not conform with the contract either because they are of lesser quality or of different origin does not constitute non-delivery.

The Court also found that there was no fundamental breach of contract since the defendant failed to show that the sale of the South African cobalt sulphate in Germany or abroad was not possible (article 49(1)(a) CISG). Thus, the defendant failed to show that it was substantially deprived of what it was entitled to expect under the contract (article 25 CISG).

Lastly, the Court held that the delivery of wrong certificates of origin and of quality did not amount to a fundamental breach of contract since the defendant could obtain correct documents from other sources. Accordingly, the defendant could not refuse payment under article 58.

NOTES

1. The terms of the sales contract in CLOUT Case 171 called for payment against documents. Accordingly, the German buyer was required to pay against the Dutch seller's tender of two documents: certificates of origin and quality. Article 58(3) entitles the buyer to inspect the goods before it pays, unless inspection is inconsistent with the procedures for delivery. The buyer paying against documents receives documents before the goods arrive to be inspected. Thus, prior to the arrival of the goods, the documents provide the only evidence that the goods conform to the contract. The court found that the seller's breach was no fundamental because the buyer could not show that it was unable to resell the cobalt sulphate in Germany or obtain accurate certificates of origin and quality. Apparently the court is requiring a buyer who pays against documents to determine before it pays the seriousness of a breach from the documents themselves. This puts buyers who have agreed to documentary sales in a tough position. They must take time before paying to ascertain the extent of breach, based only on the documents. A lengthy documentary examination to establish the seriousness of breach can slow the speed of documentary sales. Alternatively, the buyer who pays only to find after the goods arrive that the breach is serious risks difficulties in recovering the price from an insolvent or uncooperative seller.

2. The contract in CLOUT Case 171 was for the sale of a commodity. Commodities such as oil, grain or coffee are sold on volatile markets. Their publically available prices can change dramatically over very short periods. Commodities are sold through a series of documentary sales in which, in a typical case, the initial seller will ship the cargo and the last buyer will take physical delivery. Other parties will trade the cargo through a series of purchases and re-sales in intermediate contracts in which documents covering the cargo are transferred. They will trade paper only, speculating on the price of the commodity. The series of contracts constitutes a string sale: a sequence of contracts for a specific cargo with the same terms except for price. (In the oil trade string sales are called "daisy chains.") For a description of the practice, see Michael Bridge, The International Sale of Goods: Law and Practice ¶¶ 4.05–4.06, 4.22–4.25 (2d ed. 2007). The volatility of prices and multiple related contracts make it important for a contracting party to be able to determine quickly and easily its rights, including the right to avoid the contract. Delay in avoidance, or uncertainty as whether the contract may be avoided, can result in significant damages and affect the performance of other contracts in a string sale. For this reason, the notion of a fundamental breach is unsuitable for commodity sales. The parties instead prefer a crisp notion of breach that allows them to terminate the contract. The standard form contracts for commodities used by some predominant commodities trade associations opt out of the CISG entirely. See North American Export Grain Association (NAEGA) Contract No. 2, para. 27; Grain and Feed Trade Association (GFTA) Contract No. 100, para. 33. These exclusions suggest that commodity trades require greater precision in performance standards than the CISG provides. See, e.g., NAEGA para. 22 ("default"); GFTA para. 28 ("default"). CLOUT Case

121 is one of the relatively rare cases in CLOUT's database in which the CISG applies to a commodities contract.

Commentators have suggested different ways in which the CISG can be made more attractive to commodity traders. They all involve creating a presumption that a breach is fundamental. One suggestion is to distinguish between two different types of documents used in documentary sales. The first type is documents of title, such as bills of lading, which entitle the buyer to dispose of the goods. The second type is the accompanying documents, such as invoices or certificates of origin, quality or insurance, which can affect the value of the goods disposed without affecting the buyer's entitlement to dispose of them. A defect in documents of title is presumptively a fundamental breach. The buyer can avoid the contract without regard to the extent of harm the breach causes the buyer. No presumption applies for a defect in an accompanying document. See CISG Advisory Council Opinion No. 5: The Buyer's Right to Avoid the Contract in Case of Non–Conforming Goods or Documents (2005); Markus Muller-Chen, Article 49, in Schlechtriem & Schwenzer: Commentary on the UN Convention on the International Sale of Goods (CISG) 751–752 (I. Schwenzer ed., 3d ed. 2010); Peter Huber, Article 49, in UN Convention on Contracts for the International Sales of Goods (CISG): Commentary 735–736 (S. Kröll, L. Mistelis & P.P. Viscasillas eds., 2011). Another suggestion is to create an irrebuttable presumption that breaches of time clauses in the contract and all documentary conditions are fundamental. See Koji Takahashi, Right to Terminate (Avoid) International Sales of Commodities, [2003] J. Bus. L. 102, 128–129. The CISG does not allow an irrebuttable presumption of fundamental breach. An irrebuttable presumption is simply a rule that a certain consequence follows from certain facts. Strictly, it is not a presumption at all. Article 25's definition of a fundamental breach requires gauging the impact of the breach on the breached-against party's entitlement under the contract. Whether a breach is fundamental therefore depends on the extent of loss it causes the breached-against party. A breach of time clauses or documentary conditions will not always result in serious loss. Thus, Article 25 does not allow their breach to create an irrebuttable presumption that the breach is fundamental.

PROBLEM 7.9

Buyer Corp., located in Arizona, agreed to buy photocopiers from Manufacture, a German company. Under a separate contract it also agreed to purchase a quantity of fax machines from Manufacturer for its head office. Eager to increase its share of the retail market in fax machines, Buyer in turn contracted to sell these fax machines to some of its retail customers. Both items were to be delivered on March 1. The photocopiers Buyer ordered arrived on March 1 but came without instruction manuals. On the same day Manufacturer informed Buyer that production difficulties prevented it from delivering the fax machines before March 10. Because Buyer's customers were insisting that they receive their fax machines by March 6 (as their contracts with Buyer entitled them to do), Buyer gave Manufacturer until March 5 to deliver the machines to it. It also gave Manufacturer until that date to deliver the instruction manuals for its photocopiers. When Buyer did not receive the fax machines or the instruction manuals by March 5, it immediately notified Manufacturer that it was avoiding both contracts. Is Buyer's notice effective to end them? Articles 25, 26, 49(1)(a), (b).

Assume that Buyer did not give notice that it was avoiding the contract for the photocopiers. Instead it used them. After eighteen months Buyer discovered for the first time that the copiers presented health risks to employees who used them. Buyer immediately related its discovery to Manufacturer and gave notice that it was avoiding the contract. Is Buyer's notice effective to avoid the contract? Articles 25, 39(1), 49(1)(a), (2). Might Buyer's use bar avoidance? CISG Article 82(1), (2).

PROBLEM 7.10

Seller contracted to sell art reproductions to Buyer, a wholesaler of home furnishings. Their contract is governed by the CISG. Buyer has developed a reputation as a dealer in high quality, immaculate reproductions. On inspecting the reproductions it was purchasing at Seller's workshop, Buyer drew Seller's attention to some blemishes. Buyer refused Seller's offered to repair the blemishes after the reproductions were delivered. Instead, it wanted to avoid the contract and purchase blemish-free reproductions elsewhere. May Buyer avoid the contract? Articles 25, 49(1)(a). Assume that Seller persists and make sufficient repairs so that only minor blemishes remain. Seller informs Buyer that it is unable to repair these blemishes while reminding Buyer that it (Buyer) will be able to find buyers for the reproductions. Buyer does not want to sell reproductions with even minor blemishes. May Buyer avoid the contract? Would the result change if Seller credibly offered to pay for any loss Buyer sustained in selling the blemished reproductions?

G. EXCUSE FOR NONPERFORMANCE

Parties only enter into contracts each believes are profitable for them to perform. Their beliefs are based on assumptions about the conditions that will exist when they perform. A seller assumes that its production costs will remain below the contract price it charges, and that assets necessary to produce the goods contracted for will remain available. Buyers purchasing for resale assume that market prices will remain within a historical range of prices and above the contract price. When conditions change so significantly between the conclusion of the contract and the time for its performance that the assumptions no longer hold, one of the parties may profit from the contract's performance more than it anticipated and the other party may lose more from performance than it anticipated. Unsurprisingly, the party disadvantaged by the changed conditions will argue that the parties never intended the contract to apply in these changed conditions. It will urge that its performance is excused in the circumstances. Alternatively, the disadvantaged party will argue that a court should adjust the contract's terms in light of these conditions or require the parties to adjust them through negotiation.

The sales contract itself sometimes deals with the effect of changed circumstances on the parties' performance. Force majeure and "hardship" clauses are two of the most common provisions used to do so.

A force majeure clause entitles a party to suspend or terminate its performance on the occurrence of an event which is beyond its control and which prevents or impairs its ability to perform. A hardship clause entitles a party to terminate the contract on the occurrence of an event that renders its performance excessively burdensome. Well drafted clauses at a minimum define events covered by the clauses, often with nonexhaustive illustrations of them, and state the consequences that these events have on the affected party's obligations to perform. The stated consequences may include termination of the contract or renegotiation of the contract price. Force majeure and hardship clauses are frequently part of international sales contracts. They tend to be more common in domestic contracts governed by American or English law than in contracts governed by other domestic law. See Hubert Konarski, Force Majeure and Hardship Clauses in International Contractual Practice, 4 Int'l Bus. L. J. 405 (2003). The International Chamber of Commerce provides a model force majeure clause; see ICC Force Majeure Clause 2003 and ICC Hardship Clause 2003 (Pub. 650).

The law of excuse allocates the risk of changed circumstances when the contract is silent on the matter. It allows a court to terminate a contract that was expected to produce a surplus when concluded but will not produce one when performance is due. Default rules allowing excuse have a variety of effects on contracting parties' behavior. Excuse affects the willingness of parties to enter into contracts, because excusing a party's nonperformance reduces the profit the other party expects from the contract. It also affects the quality of performance of concluded contracts, because the performing party takes into account the prospect of changed circumstances allowing its performance to be excused. Finally, the availability of excuse affects the detail with which parties write excuse clauses in their contracts. Perhaps unsurprisingly, legal systems differ in their implicit judgments about the impact of excuse on the stability of contracts. English and American law allows changed circumstances to excuse under narrow conditions. Continental legal systems are more generous in the conditions under which a party's performance will be excused. See Hannes Rosler, Hardship in German Codified Private Law—In Comparative Perspective to English, French and International Contract Law, 3 Eur. Rev. Priv. L. 483 (2007).

1. UNDER THE UCC

Prior to the UCC, cases involving changed circumstances were decided under the doctrines of impossibility or frustration of purpose. The UCC integrates these doctrines to a large extent with a statutory based standard of "commercial impracticability." Sections 2–613 to 2–615 govern the grounds on which commercial impracticability excuses performance. Section 2–613, "Casualty to Identified Goods," describes a circumstance that used to be controlled by the traditional doctrine of impossibility. Under the section, the contract is terminated ("avoided") if the goods required for performance of the contract are destroyed before without fault of either party before risk of loss has passed to the buyer. Destruction of these goods makes the seller's performance impossible, not just more costly. Section 2–613 excuses the seller only if the goods the contract requires for performance are "identified when the contract is made." This qualification limits when impossibility excuses the seller. Consider two cases. In Case 1, the sales contract specifies that Seller is to manufacture a widget using a specific lot of wood. The wood is destroyed after the contract is concluded. The contract's specification of a particular lot of wood identifies the wood to the contract when the contract is made. See 2–501(1). Thus, if 2–613's other conditions are met, the contract is terminated and Seller is not liable for not producing the widget. Case 2 is identical to Case 1 except that the contract does not specify the lot of wood Seller is to use in the widget's manufacture. Instead, Seller and Buyer decide on a specific lot of wood after the contract is concluded. Although their decision identifies the wood to the contract (2–501(1)), the identification comes after the contract is made. Section 2–613 therefore does not apply to excuse Seller after the wood in Case 2 has been destroyed.

Section 2–615 excuses a seller's delay in delivery or nondelivery of goods "if performance as agreed has been made impracticable by the occurrence of a contingency the non-occurrence of which was a basic assumption on which the contract was made . . . " The seller's performance is excused under this test, unless the seller has assumed a greater obligation. The test for impracticability can cover cases in which intervening events make the seller's performance impossible, such as export bans or civil unrest. It is also broad enough to include instances where changed circumstances make performance not impossible but radically different than the parties anticipated. By its terms, 2–615 excuses only sellers, and Comment 1 explicitly mentions sellers but not buyers. The negative implication of both is that parallel relief is unavailable to buyers. However, Comment 9 allows 2–615 to excuse buyers in appropriate cases. Even without Comment 9, the doctrine of frustration remains available to buyers under 1–103(b).

As stated or applied by courts, 2–615's conditions are demanding but vague. Consider first the condition that the seller has not "assumed a greater obligation." 2-615. In other words, the seller is not excused if it has assumed the risk that supervening events make it regret entering into the contract on the terms it did. Determining whether the seller assumed this risk is easy when the risk allocation is explicit. For instance, the contract might state conditions of the seller's duties and provide that these duties are not subject to other conditions. Or the contract might expressly exclude force majeure events as excusing the seller's performance. Risk allocations are more difficult to determine when they are implicit. A common situation in which commercial impracticability is raised involves a long-term contract containing a price index used to adjust contract price over the contract's life. Regulatory or market changes may cause the price index to set contract price below market price. See, e.g., Eastern Air Lines, Inc. v. Gulf Oil Corp., 415 F. Supp. 429 (S.D. Fla. 1975). The seller can contend that the parties assumed that price fluctuations would parallel changes in the selected price index and that it did not assume the risk that they would deviate from that index. The buyer's contention would be that the selection of a particular price index implicitly puts on the seller the risk that the index will fail to remain an accurate index of price. Otherwise, the contract would not have relied on a price index to fix the price; instead it would have set price directly. See Missouri Public Service Co. v. Peabody Coal Co., 583 S.W.2d 721 (Mo. Ct. App. 1979).

Section 2–615's second condition is that a contingency occur the nonoccurrence of which was a "basic assumption" of the contract. The parties might not have considered the contingency or, if they had considered it, thought that it would not occur. In either case Comment 4 and courts ask whether the contingency was foreseeable by the parties. The foreseeability inquiry is inconclusive because the notion of foreseeability itself is slippery. Any event is foreseeable under a suitably general description. Suppose a fire on April 15 puts the seller's plant out of operation for a month. This contracting parties could foresee this event if it is described as "a disruption in the operation of the seller's plant" or "a fire in the seller's plant." The event might not be foreseeable if described as "a fire on April 15 in the seller's plant that renders it inoperable for month." In practice, cases ask whether the contingency was sufficiently foreseeable to make providing for it in the contract worthwhile. See, e.g., Opera Co. v. Wolf Trap Found., 817 F.2d 1094, 1101 (4th Cir. 1987). This is a risk-utility test. A seller who estimates that there is a 10% chance of a supervening event producing a $100 loss to it on the contract will spend no more than 10 cents to contract against the risk or otherwise avoid it. Courts seldom have reliable information about the parties' estimates of probability or loss. They must rely on self-serving and incomplete information supplied by the parties in litigation.

The third condition is that the supervening events render the seller's performance "impracticable." There are two obvious problems applying the condition. One problem is to determine when it is becomes impracticable for the seller to perform. In cases other than sheer impossibility of performance, a threshold of impracticability is required. Comment 4 unhelpfully states that "[i]ncreased cost alone does not excuse performance" and that a rise or collapse of market price does not "in itself" make performance impracticable. Section 2–615 does not clarify what exactly makes the seller's performance impracticable. The second problem is that multiple events can affect the seller's performance at the same time, some of which are do not violate the basic assumption of the contract and others which might do so. For instance, a price increase might be the result of both increased demand for the goods, which is not a basic assumption, and a regulatory restriction on supply of the goods, which is a basic assumption of the contract. To determine whether the seller's performance is excused, a court must separate the effect of these two events and determine the contract's assumptions with respect to them. Courts lack the information needed to do so. The inquiry into impracticability, like that into the basic assumption of a contract, risks judicial error.

Courts very seldom apply 2–615's vague conditions to excuse performance. Judicial intervention under comparable English law of frustration is similarly sparse. See Ewan McKendrick, Contract Law: Text, Cases and Materials 869, 928 (2d ed. 2005). This light judicial touch may improve the efficiency with which sales contracts are performed. Put the other way, judicial intervention can reduce the incentives of contracting parties best placed to avoid risk to take advantage of their position to do so. For instance, assume that the parties identify a risk that, if it materialized, would reduce the seller's profit from the contract by $100. The risk is remote. Assume also that the seller could avoid the loss by investing $80 in performance, while the buyer could avoid it by investing $105. Finally, assume that the seller believes that there is a 50% chance that a court would intervene to excuse the seller if the relevant risk materialized. As a result, given the chance of being excused, the seller's expected profit would decline by $50 (50% × $100). This expected loss is less than the $80 investment the seller would have to make to avoid it. Thus, although the seller's $80 investment would be efficient, the seller will not make it. A rule that does not excuse induces the seller to take make efficient investments in performing the contract. The judicial practice of not excusing under 2–615 comes close to the flat rule against excuse.

Specialty Tires of America, Inc. v. CIT Group/Equipment Financing, Inc.

United States District Court, Western District of Pennsylvania, 2000
82 F. Supp.2d 434

■ Memorandum opinion: D. BROOKS SMITH, DISTRICT JUDGE.

In this case, Specialty Tires, Inc. ("Specialty") has sued The CIT Group/Equipment Financing, Inc. ("CIT") for breach of contract arising out CIT's failure to deliver eleven tire presses that it had previously contracted to sell to Specialty. CIT, in turn, has filed a third-party complaint against Condere Corporation, Titan Tire Corporation and Titan International, Inc. (collectively "Condere") arising out of the latter's alleged wrongful refusal to permit those presses to be removed from its factory. Specialty has moved for partial summary judgment, arguing that CIT's defenses are without merit, while CIT has moved for full summary judgment on the ground that its performance was excused under the doctrine of impossibility or commercial impracticability, CIT has also moved, in the alternative, to dismiss the stay I previously entered in the third-party action. For the following reasons, I will grant CIT's motion based on impossibility and deny the other two motions as moot.

I.

The material facts of this case are simple and undisputed. In December 1993, CIT, a major equipment leasing company, entered into a sale/leaseback with Condere for eleven tire presses located at Condere's tire plant in Natchez, Mississippi, under which CIT purchased the presses from Condere and leased them back to it for a term of years. CIT retained title to the presses, as well as the right to possession in the event of a default by Condere. In May 1997, Condere ceased making the required lease payments and filed for Chapter 11 bankruptcy in the Southern District of Mississippi. In September 1997, Condere rejected the executory portion of the lease agreement, and the bankruptcy court lifted the automatic stay as to CIT's claim involving the presses.

CIT thus found itself, unexpectedly, with eleven tire presses it needed to sell. Maurice "Maury" Taylor, a former minor candidate for President of the United States and the CEO of Condere and Titan International, stated his desire that the presses be removed quickly and advised CIT on how they might be sold. Later, CIT brought two potential buyers to Condere's Natchez plant, where representatives of

Condere conducted them on a tour of the facility. Subsequently, Taylor and CIT negotiated concerning Condere's purchase of the presses, but negotiations fell through, after which Taylor again offered his assistance in locating another buyer.

When no buyer was found, CIT decided to advertise the presses. Specialty, a manufacturer of tires which sought to expand its plant in Tennessee, responded, and in early December 1997, representatives of Specialty, CIT and Condere met to conduct an on-site inspection of the equipment. Condere's representative discussed with CIT's personnel and in the presence of Specialty's agents the logistics concerning the removal of the presses. At that meeting, Condere's representative told CIT and Specialty that CIT had an immediate right to possession of the tire presses, and the right to sell them. At no time did any representative of Condere, whether by words or conduct, express any intent to oppose the removal of this equipment. The negotiations proved fruitful, and, in late December 1997, CIT and Specialty entered into a contract for the sale of the presses for $250,000. CIT warranted its title to and right to sell the presses.

Events then took a turn which led to this lawsuit. When CIT attempted to gain access to the presses to have them rigged and shipped to Speciality, Condere refused to allow this equipment to be removed from the plant. This refusal was apparently because Condere had just tendered a check to CIT for $224,000, without the approval of the bankruptcy court, in an attempt to cure its default under the lease. This unexpected change in position was rejected by CIT, which promptly filed a complaint in replevin in the Southern District of Mississippi to obtain possession. Condere then posted a bond and the replevin court removed the action from the expedited list, scheduling a case management conference for April 1998. It became clear at that juncture that Specialty was not going to obtain its tire presses expeditiously.

CIT then advised Specialty that the presses were subject to the jurisdiction of the bankruptcy court and suggested that Specialty either withdraw its claim to the equipment and negotiate with CIT for a sum of liquidated damages or make a bid for the presses at any auction that might be held by that court. Specialty, as was its right, rejected both suggestions and affirmed the existing contract, demanding performance. To date, Condere has refused to surrender to CIT, and CIT has failed to deliver to Specialty, the tire presses.

Subsequent to the briefing of these motions, the replevin court has issued findings of fact and conclusions of law to the effect that Condere wrongfully retained possession of the presses and that CIT is entitled to remove them immediately. Although Condere may appeal this ruling, CIT has informed Specialty that it is still willing to deliver the presses as soon as it gains possession, and Specialty has indicated its interest in accepting them, in "partial" settlement of its claims.

* * *

III.

In the overwhelming majority of circumstances, contractual promises are to be performed, not avoided: pacta sunt servanda, or, as the Seventh Circuit loosely translated it, "a deal's a deal." Waukesha

Foundry, Inc. v. Industrial Eng'g, Inc., 91 F.3d 1002, 1010 (7th Cir. 1996). This is an eminently sound doctrine, because typically a court cannot improve matters by intervention after the fact. It can only destabilize the institution of contract, increase risk, and make parties worse off.... Parties to contracts are entitled to seek, and retain, personal advantage; striving for that advantage is the source of much economic progress. Contract law does not require parties to be fair, or kind, or reasonable, or to share gains or losses equally. Industrial Representatives, Inc. v. CP Clare Corp., 74 F.3d 128, 131–32 (7th Cir. 1996) (Easterbrook, J.). Promisors are free to assume risks, even huge ones, and promisees are entitled to rely on those voluntary assumptions. Futures contracts, as just one example, are so aleatory that risk-bearing is their sole purpose, yet they are fully enforceable.

Even so, courts have recognized, in an evolving line of cases from the common law down to the present, that there are limited instances in which unexpectedly and radically changed conditions render the judicial enforcement of certain promises of little or no utility. This has come to be know[n], for our purposes, as the doctrines of impossibility and impracticability. Because of the unexpected nature of such occurrences, litigated cases usually involve, not interpretation of a contractual term, but the judicial filling of a lacuna in the parties agreement. Such "gap-filling," however, must be understood for what it is: a court-ordered, as opposed to bargained-for, allocation of risk between the parties.

Traditionally, there were three kinds of supervening events that would provide a legally cognizable excuse for failing to perform: death of the promisor (if the performance was personal), illegality of the performance, and destruction of the subject matter; beyond that the doctrine has grown to recognize that relief is most justified if unexpected events inflict a loss on one party and provide a windfall gain for the other or where the excuse would save one party from an unexpected loss while leaving the other party in a position no worse than it would have without the contract.[2] Thus, the Second Restatement of Contracts expresses the doctrine of impracticability this way:

> Where, after a contract is made, a party's performance is made impracticable without his fault by the occurrence of an event the non-occurrence of which was a basic assumption on which the contract was made, his duty to render that performance is discharged, unless the language or the circumstances indicate the contrary. Restatement (Second) of Contracts § 261 (1981). Article 2 of the U.C.C., which applies to the sale of goods presented by the case sub judice, puts it similarly:

Delay in delivery or non-delivery in whole or in part by a seller . . . is not a breach of his duty under a contract for sale if performance as agreed has been made impracticable by the occurrence of a contingency the non-occurrence of which was a basic assumption on

---

[2]   The second of these two grounds is what economists deem a "Pareto-optimal" move; that is, an adjustment that makes some parties better off and none worse off than they were initially. For an economic analysis of the law of impossibility, see Hon. Richard A. Posner, Economic Analysis of Law § 4.5 (5th ed. 1998).

which the contract was made. . . . U.C.C. § 2–615(1) (codified at 13 Pa. C.S. 2615(1)).

The principal inquiry in an impracticability analysis, then, is whether there was a contingency the non-occurrence of which was a basic assumption underlying the contract. It is often said that this question turns on whether the contingency was "foreseeable," 2 Farnsworth, supra § 9.6, at 616, on the rationale that if it was, the promisor could have sought to negotiate explicit contractual protection. This, however, is an incomplete and sometimes misleading test. Anyone can foresee, in some general sense, a whole variety of potential calamities, but that does not mean that he or she will deem them worth bargaining over. The risk may be too remote, the party may not have sufficient bargaining power, or neither party may have any superior ability to avoid the harm. As my late colleague Judge Teitelbaum recited two decades ago in a famous case of impracticability:

> Foreseeability or even recognition of a risk does not necessarily prove its allocation. Parties to a contract are not always able to provide for all the possibilities of which they are aware, sometimes because they cannot agree, often because they are too busy. Moreover, that some abnormal risk was contemplated is probative but does not necessarily establish an allocation of the risk of the contingency which actually occurs.

Aluminum Co. of Am. v. Essex Group, Inc., 499 F. Supp. 53, 76 (W.D. Pa. 1980) (applying Indiana law) (quoting Transatlantic Fin. Corp. v. United States, 124 U.S. App. D.C. 183, 363 F.2d 312 (D.C. Cir. 1966) (Skelly Wright, J.). So, while the risk of an unforeseeable event can safely be deemed not to have been assumed by the promisor, the converse is not necessarily true. See Restatement (Second) of Contracts § 261 cmt. c. Properly seen, then, foreseeability, while perhaps the most important factor, is at best one fact to be considered in resolving first how likely the occurrence of the event in question was and, second, whether its occurrence, based on past experience, was of such reasonable likelihood that the obligor should not merely foresee the risk but, because of the degree of its likelihood, the obligor should have guarded against it or provided for non-liability against the risk. Opera Co. v. Wolf Trap Found, 817 F.2d 1094, 1102–03 (quoted in Farnsworth, supra § 9.6, at 617–18).

It is also commonly said that the standard of impossibility is objective rather than subjective—that the question is whether the thing can be done, not whether the promisor can do it. 2 E. Allen Farnsworth, Farnsworth on Contracts § 9.6, at 619 (2d ed. 1998). This too is more truism than test, although Pennsylvania courts have couched their decisions in this rhetoric.[3] Indeed, the First Restatement took such an approach, but the Second simply applies "the rationale . . . that a party generally assumes the risk of his own inability to perform his duty." *Craig Coal*, 513 A.2d at 439 (quoting Restatement (Second) of Contracts § 261 cmt. e). This holds particularly when the duty is merely to pay money. It is therefore "preferable to say that such ["subjective"] risks as

---

[3] I do not mean to suggest that these courts in any way reached the wrong result or engaged in faulty analysis. Rather, in those cases the traditional formulation of the test yielded the unmistakably correct conclusion that the promisor had assumed the risk of his own inability to perform.

these are generally considered to be sufficiently within the control of one party that they are assumed by that party." 2 Farnsworth, supra § 9.6, at 619–20. It is, of course, essential that the impossibility asserted by the promisor as a defense not have been caused by the promisor.

Generally speaking, while loss, destruction or a major price increase of fungible goods will not excuse the seller's duty to perform, the rule is different when the goods are unique, have been identified to the contract or are to be produced from a specific, agreed-upon source. In such a case, the nonexistence or unavailability of a specific thing will establish a defense of impracticability. Thus, § 263 of the Second Restatement recites:

> If the existence of a specific thing is necessary for the performance of a duty, its failure to come into existence, destruction, or such deterioration as makes performance impracticable is an event the non-occurrence of which was a basic assumption on which the contract was made.

Moreover, the Supreme Court of Pennsylvania has interpreted this section's predecessor in the First Restatement to apply to, in addition to physical destruction and deterioration, interference by third parties with a specific chattel necessary to the carrying out of the agreement.

Thus, in Olbum v. Old Home Manor, Inc., 459 A.2d 757 (Pa. Super. Ct. 1983) the plaintiffs leased the mineral rights of specific portions of their land to a coal mining concern, in exchange for minimum royalty payments extending over four years. After successfully mining the land for a little over a year, defendant ceased its mining operations because the remaining coal had become unmineable and unmerchantable. 459 A.2d at 759. Plaintiffs then sued to recover the remaining royalty payments, but the court held that because the contract depended upon the "continued existence of a particular thing," specifically mineable coal, the contract was discharged for supervening impracticability.

In Yoffe v. Keller Indus., Inc., 443 A.2d 358 (Pa. Super. Ct. 1982), the promisor owed a contractual duty to file a securities registration statement with the SEC and effect registration within a set time. The SEC, however, unforeseeably undertook an investigation of its accounting practices, delaying the approval and causing damage to the promisee. The court held that, because the third party (SEC)'s actions were unforeseeable, the promisor was discharged. 443 A.2d at 363.

Likewise, in Selland Pontiac–GMC, Inc. v. King, 384 N.W.2d 490 (Minn. App. Ct. 1986), the promisor contracted to sell school bus bodies produced by a particular company, Superior. After the contract was entered into, and without the knowledge of any party, Superior became insolvent and the bodies were never delivered. The promisee then sued the promisor for breach of contract, but the court, applying § 2–615 of the U.C.C., held that the contract was discharged as impracticable. 384 N.W.2d at 492–93.

In Litman v. Peoples Natural Gas Co., 449 A.2d 720 (Pa. Super. Ct. 1982), the promisee contracted with defendant gas company to install gas service to an apartment building. Defendant-promisor was unable to perform, however, because the state utility commission subsequently forbade defendant from making any new connections. Plaintiff sued for breach, but the court held that performance was discharged as impossible, owing to the interference of the third-party regulatory body. 449 A.2d at 724–25.

Finally, in Waldinger Corp. v. CRS Group Eng'rs, Inc., 775 F.2d 781 (7th Cir. 1985), the court applied impracticability to a situation in which a third-party engineer unforeseeably required, contrary to industry custom, strict compliance with a standard, making the promisor-defendant's delivery of a compliant machine, as required by contract, impossible. 775 F.2d at 787–89.

The situation presented here is in accord with these cases. To recapitulate, CIT contracted to supply specific tire presses to Specialty. This was not a case of fungible goods; Specialty inspected, and bid for, certain identified, used presses located at the Natchez plant operated by Condere. All parties believed that CIT was the owner of the presses and was entitled to their immediate possession; Condere's representatives stated as much during the inspection visit. Neither Specialty nor CIT had any reason to believe that Condere would subsequently turn an about-face and assert a possessory interest in the presses. The most that can be said is that CIT had a course of dealings with Condere, but nowhere is it argued that there was any history of tortious or opportunistic conduct that would have alerted CIT that Condere would attempt to convert the presses to its own use.

Thus, whether analyzed traditionally in terms of foreseeability, as courts apply that term, or by the risk-exposure methodology outlined supra, it is clear that this is not the sort of risk that CIT should have expected to either bear or contract against. In economic terms, which I apply as a "check" rather than as substantive law, it cannot be said with any reliability that either Specialty or CIT was able to avoid the risk of what Condere did at a lower cost. It was "a bolt out of the blue" for both parties. On the other hand, Specialty was in a better position to know what consequences and damages would likely flow from nondelivery or delayed delivery of the presses. This suggests that Specialty is the appropriate party on which to impose the risk. Moreover, judicial discharge of CIT's promise under these circumstances leaves Specialty in no worse a position than it would have occupied without the contract; either way, it would not have these presses, and it has only been able to locate and purchase three similar used presses on the open market since CIT's failure to deliver. On the other hand, CIT is relieved of the obligation to pay damages. Accordingly, excuse for impracticability would appear to be a Pareto-optimal move, increasing CIT's welfare while not harming Specialty. This too is a valid policy reason for imposing the risk of loss on Specialty. Thus, economic analysis confirms as sound policy the result suggested by the caselaw discussed supra.

Plaintiff makes much of the argument that there was no "basic assumption" created by Condere upon which Specialty and CIT based their contract, stating that it relied upon CIT's representations alone. This is specious. As a matter of both law and logic, a basic assumption of any contract for the sale of specific, identified goods is that they are, in fact, available for sale. Accordingly, I reject this contention and conclude that the actions of Condere in detaining the presses presents sufficient grounds on which to base an impracticability defense.

Plaintiff also argues that this is a case only of subjective impossibility, presumably because Condere—which has been holding the presses essentially hostage—could deliver them up to Specialty. Thus, plaintiff contends that only CIT is incapable of performing and therefore should not be excused. This proves too much; in theory, at least, any hold-out party can be brought to the table if the price is high enough, including the parties in the cases discussed supra. Certainly, if CIT offered Condere $3 million to surrender the presses, there is little doubt that they would comply, but the law of impracticability does not require such outlandish measures. * * * This is simply not a case in which CIT became insolvent and could not perform, or in which the market price of tire presses spiked upward due to a shortage, making the contract unprofitable to CIT. While CIT did assume the risk of its own inability to perform, it did not assume the risk of Condere making it unable to perform by detaining the presses, any more than CIT assumed the risk that thieves would steal the presses from Condere before the latter could deliver them. In sum, this risk was not "sufficiently within the control of [CIT] that [it should be inferred that it was] assumed by that party." 2 Farnsworth, supra § 9.6, at 619–20. It was completely within the control of Condere.

Accordingly, I conclude on this record that CIT has made out its defense of impracticability. The ruling of the replevin court, however, indicates that CIT's performance is impracticable only in the temporary sense. Temporary impracticability only relieves the promisor of the obligation to perform as long as the impracticability lasts and for a reasonable time thereafter. Once it receives possession of the presses, CIT asserts that it stands ready and willing to perform its contract with Specialty. That issue is not ripe for adjudication and must await a separate lawsuit if CIT should fail to perform after obtaining possession. Suffice it to say that, to the extent Specialty seeks damages for nondelivery of the presses to date, CIT is excused by the doctrine of impracticability and is entitled to full summary judgment. * * *

Chainworks, Inc. v. Webco Industries

United States District Court, Western District of Michigan, 2006
2006 U.S. Dist. Lexis 9194

■ ROBERT HOLMES BELL, CHIEF UNITED STATES DISTRICT JUDGE

This dispute arises out of a requirements contract for steel tubing between Plaintiff Chainworks, Inc., and Defendant Webco Industries, Inc., governed by the Uniform Commercial Code. Chainworks seeks a declaration that it has not breached the contract and does not owe approximately $300,000 billed by Webco. The central issue in this case concerns Webco's ability to pass on certain additional costs incurred during the course of the contract. Although Webco offers a variety of creative arguments in support of its position, the Court is not persuaded from the view that this is a simple breach of contract case in which the parties agreed to a fixed and certain price for Chainworks' product requirements for an entire calendar year. As such, Webco could not unilaterally impose a new contract price. Accordingly, for the reasons stated below, Chainworks' motion for summary judgment is granted.

I.

Webco is a steel tubing manufacturer and supplier. Chainworks is a commercial broker of steel tubing which acts as an intermediary between Webco and third-party purchasers. The parties have had a commercial relationship since 1999. This case arises out of the parties' contract for 2004. In November 2004, Webco sent a memorandum regarding pricing for the 2004 calendar year. The memorandum provided price quotations for two types of steel tubing and specified that the prices were "firm for the period 1/1/04 through 12/31/04." Thereafter, following the federal government's removal of steel tariffs on foreign-made steel, Chainworks president, Andy Hinkley, inquired as to whether Webco's 2004 pricing would be affected. Jeff Williams, Webco's vice president of OEM sales, replied,

> The lifting of tariffs is seen as having no effect for the next 12–months. The worldwide market has shifted into a higher gear. Supplies are tightening and pricing is rising—mills now have all customers on allocation. We believe the economy, domestically and internationally, will continue to strengthen and demand, domestically and internationally, will continue to rise.

The result is that this will have no effect on our thinking for SSID tubing in 2004.

Following this exchange, on December 8, 2003, Chainworks issued a blanket purchase order incorporating the fixed prices provided by Webco. The blanket purchase order specified that it was a "requirements based blanket order." Under this arrangement, Chainworks would make purchases as its needs dictated throughout the year pursuant to the blanket purchase order and Webco would ship manufactured steel tubing to Chainworks' third-party purchaser (Tenneco Canada, Inc.). The blanket purchase order also incorporated Chainworks' published terms and conditions.

During the first week of January, 2004, Webco shipped the first series of steel products to Tenneco. Following the shipment, Webco mailed an invoice to Chainworks seeking payment at the price quoted in both Webco's initial price quotation and Chainworks' blanket purchase order. Webco's invoice also included its own conditions of sale. The conditions of sale included a paragraph stating: "All base prices, together with related extras and deductions, are subject to change without notice, and all orders are accepted subject to prices in effect at the time of shipment." Shortly after sending the invoice, Webco notified Chainworks that it was monitoring "dramatic developments in the steel industry" that were creating a "tight steel availability situation as well as dramatically higher prices." These "dramatic developments" eventually manifested themselves through a market shift that caused prices to soar. As a result, Wheeling Pittsburgh, Webco's supplier, imposed a raw material surcharge on all steel products and demanded payment by Webco in order to continue the production and shipment of steel. In response, Webco attempted to pass on the surcharge to Chainworks. On January 27, 2004, Jeff Williams notified Andy Hinkley that Webco would be assessing a surcharge on steel products shipped to Chainworks effective February 1, 2004. Webco advised that "in order . . . to maintain an uninterrupted supply of material to Chainworks; I must have, in writing, your acceptance of these charges

Throughout February, Webco sought Chainworks' acceptance of the surcharge, warning "if Chainworks does not wish to pay the surcharge, we will advise our material supplier that Webco cannot pay the surcharge for Chainworks raw material and we anticipate they will refuse to ship." On March 1, 2004, Hinkley sent the following memorandum to Williams:

> In the interest of maintaining an uninterrupted supply of your products for our customers, we feel that we have no other option but to accept the steel surcharge that you intend to impose on us, as described in your letter dated January 27, 2004. We sincerely hope that you will reconsider straddling us with these additional financial burdens, as we are not likely to obtain similar accommodation from our customers.

Given the current lack of alternatives and in the interest of mitigating our losses, we are making this concession under duress and reserve all rights and remedies that we may otherwise have under our original agreement.

Thereafter, Webco sent monthly notices of the surcharge amount to be applied to future shipments. Between March and August, Chainworks continued to authorize the manufacture and shipment of products to Tenneco as needed.

On August 23, 2004, Williams notified Hinkley that, in addition to the raw material surcharge, Webco was raising the price of its steel tubing products. Again, Williams cautioned that "Webco must have your agreement to accept this price revision or we will not be able to continue to order raw material or accept future releases for shipment." In a nearly identically worded memorandum to the March 1, 2004 letter, Hinkley agreed to the price increases, explaining that Chainworks believed it was conceding under duress and in order to mitigate its losses. Once again, Hinkley advised that Chainworks "reserved all rights and remedies that we may otherwise have under our original agreement." Thereafter, Chainworks again authorized Webco to manufacture and ship products to Tenneco through December.

Beginning in September and continuing through December, the parties attempted to negotiate a contract for the following year. Although the parties' discussed pricing arrangements for 2005, both parties agree that a contract was never entered into. In addition to the contract negotiations, in December 2004, Chainworks requested that three steel product shipments be sent to Chainworks' warehouse, rather than directly to Tenneco's facility.

On January 7, 2005, Chainworks notified Webco that it had entered into a requirements contract for 2005 with a Korean supplier and would not continue its relationship with Webco. Upon receipt of the final invoice for 2004, Chainworks discounted all surcharges and price increases assessed during the year from its final payment. This amounted to $301,949.78. The parties do not dispute that the amount allegedly owed only encompasses surcharges and price increases assessed during 2004. Chainworks contends that it is not required to pay this amount under the 2004 contract and seeks a declaratory judgment on this issue. Conversely, the failure to pay this amount provides the basis for Webco's counterclaim for breach of contract against Chainworks. Webco also alleges counterclaims for account stated, unjust enrichment, promissory estoppel, and fraudulent and/or negligent misrepresentation. The counterclaims stem from Chainworks' failure to inform Webco that it did not intend to enter into a contract for 2005 as well as Chainworks' alleged stock-piling of products at the end of 2004. Before the Court is Chainworks' motion for summary judgment on its declaratory judgment claim and on Webco's counterclaims.

Procedural Background

This Court previously denied Webco's motion to compel arbitration. The Court, applying MICH. COMP. LAWS § 440.2207(1), held that a contract was formed between the parties under the UCC. Chainworks' blanket purchase order constituted an offer and Webco's delivery of the products and issuance of an invoice constituted a definite and seasonable expression of acceptance, even though it stated terms additional to or different from those contained in the offer. Further, the Court determined that Webco's invoice and conditions of sale did not "clearly reveal that [Webco] was unwilling to proceed unless they were assured of [Chainworks] assent to the additional or different terms." Accordingly, a contract was formed between the parties under § 2–207(1).

The Court then applied § 2–207(2) and found that the arbitration provision contained in Webco's conditions of sale was an "additional term," and as such, did not become part of the contract because Chainworks' offer expressly limited acceptance to the terms of the offer. Because the arbitration clause was not part of the agreement between the parties, Webco's motion to compel arbitration was denied. * * *

III.

A.   Chainworks' Breach of Contract Claim

In its breach of contract claim, Chainworks alleges that Webco breached the 2004 contract by unilaterally imposing the surcharges and price increase. Chainworks' position can be summed up in a relatively simple fashion: a deal is a deal. That is, the parties agreed to a contract that would provide Chainworks with all the steel tubing it required during 2004 at a fixed price. When Webco sought to increase that price, it breached the contract. Accordingly, Chainworks seeks a declaration that it has fulfilled the terms of the original contract and, thus, does not owe the remaining balance.

Against this simple, straightforward analysis, Webco has offered numerous creative arguments, based on various provisions of the UCC and common law, in an attempt to justify its actions and avoid summary judgment. Webco's arguments include the following: 1) that under UCC § 2–207, the parties' contract included a term permitting Webco to alter the contract price, 2) that Chainworks' agreed to the surcharges and price increases, and 3) that the impracticability defense under UCC § 2–615 applies and permits Webco's failure to abide by the original, fixed contract price. Finally, Webco also alleges that Chainworks is barred from any recovery because it did not properly provide notice that it considered the price increase a breach of contract.

After reviewing the record in this case, the parties' briefs, and hearing oral argument, the Court is led to the conclusion that Chainworks' view is correct, as a matter of law, and summary judgment should be entered in its favor on the breach of contract claim. Webco's arguments to the contrary are unavailing. At its essence this is a simple breach of contract case. The parties entered into a contract under which Webco agreed to provide all of Chainworks' steel tubing needs for 2004 in exchange for a fixed price. After this contract was entered into, Webco attempted to unilaterally alter the price. This was a clear breach of contract and Chainworks is not required to pay the additional cost unilaterally imposed by Webco. A review of Webco's arguments to the contrary reveals that each lacks merit.

1.   The Battle of the Forms

Webco first contends that it had the authority to alter the contract price based on the price adjustment clause contained in its invoice. Because Webco relies on a clause contained in its invoice, the Court must determine whether the price adjustment clause is part of the contract. This requires a review of § 2–207 of the UCC * * * The parties agree and the Court has previously held that Chainworks' December 8, 2003 blanket purchase order was an offer. The blanket purchase order incorporated the fixed pricing terms provided by Webco to Chainworks on November 26, 2003. The blanket purchase order also specified the terms of acceptance: "This order can be accepted in writing or by delivery, the rendering of services, or commencement of work on supplies be (sic) manufactured for Buyer, pursuant to this order." Based upon this provision, Chainworks argues that Webco accepted the offer by shipping the first series of products in early January and that the subsequent invoice containing Webco's own terms and conditions is irrelevant and cannot modify the existing contract. While the Court finds that this argument is convincing and thus renders the "Battle of the Forms" analysis unnecessary, see MICH. COMP. LAWS § 440.2206, Litton Microwave Cooking Prods. v. Leviton Mfg. Co., Inc., 15 F.3d 790, 794 (8th Cir. 1994) (construing Minnesota's version of the UCC) ("For a 'battle of the forms' to arise and trigger the provisions of § 2–207, there must be conflicting forms to begin with. . . . "), for the purposes of the Court's analysis, the Court will assume that Webco's invoice was the acceptance and mandates an analysis under § 2–207.

Webco's invoice contained the same price term as Chainworks' blanket purchase order. In addition, the invoice also contained Webco's conditions of sale which included terms additional to or different from those contained in the offer. In the Court's previous opinion in this case, it held that the invoice was an acceptance under § 2–207(1), even though it included the additional or different terms. The Court also rejected Webco's argument that the acceptance was expressly made conditional on assent to the additional or different terms. The Court determined that Webco's invoice and conditions of sale did not clearly reveal an unwillingness to proceed absent assent to the additional or different terms. Therefore, Webco's invoice constituted a definite and seasonable expression of acceptance under § 2–207(1).

Despite the Court's previous findings regarding Webco's invoice, Webco appears to argue that it did clearly express its unwillingness to proceed unless Chainworks' accepted Webco's price adjustment clause. Webco's position is misguided and attempts to rely on events occurring after the contract was formed. Webco's argument is also based on the faulty assumption that the parties did not enter into a contract for the entire year, but rather agreed to a series of incremental contracts in which each production release during the year was a new offer and each invoice was a new acceptance.

Webco's argument is directly contrary to the Court's previous holding that the invoice was a definite and seasonable expression of acceptance and is contrary to the undisputed evidence in this case. First, the events relied upon by Webco to support its claim that it clearly expressed its unwillingness to proceed occurred after the first shipment and invoice. By its terms, § 2–207 precludes Webco's reliance on these post-acceptance letters. See MICH. COMP. LAWS § 440.2207(1). Second, Webco also appears to be attempting to circumvent this conclusion by raising the novel argument that the parties entered into a series of contracts throughout 2004.

The contract formed between the parties in January 2004 was a requirements contract for the entire year. The best evidence of this fact comes from the face of the blanket purchase order which states: "THIS IS A REQUIREMENTS BASED BLANKET ORDER. THIS IS NOT AN AUTHORIZATION TO MANUFACTURE. INDIVIDUAL PRODUCTION RELEASES WILL BE ISSUED AS REQUIRED VIA A SEPARATE DOCUMENT AGAINST THIS BLANKET ORDER." Nothing in the purchase order or in Webco's invoices indicates that the parties entered into a series of contracts, rather than a single contract for the entire year. Moreover, Webco, as the non-moving party on summary judgment, has the burden of bringing forth evidence to support a genuine issue of fact. Webco has not pointed to any evidence, whether in the form of the parties' prior course of dealing or their course of performance under the contract at issue, that would support its assertion that the parties' agreed to a series of contracts. Accordingly, the Court rejects Webco's argument that this contract was anything other than a requirements contract for the entire year and holds that Webco accepted Chainworks' offer through the January 6, 2004 invoice.

The next step in the § 2–207 analysis is to determine whether Webco's price adjustment clause is an additional or different term. If the term is additional, it becomes part of the contract unless: the offer expressly limited acceptance to the terms of the offer, the term materially alters the contract, or the buyer timely objects to the additional term. MICH. COMP. LAWS § 440.2207(2). If the clause is a different term, the conflicting terms cancel each other out and do not become part of the contract. The terms of the contract then consist of the terms agreed upon by the parties and other terms supplied by the UCC.

Webco's price adjustment clause provides "all base prices . . . are subject to change without notice, and all orders are accepted subject to prices in effect at the time of shipment." Webco argues that this term is different from and conflicts with a clause in Chainworks' terms and conditions which provides: "invoice payment terms, FOB point, part number, description and price are as listed on the face of the PO." Webco describes these clauses as conflicting "price terms." This is a mischaracterization of the terms. As stated previously, the blanket purchase order and invoice contained the same price term. In addition to the price term, however, Webco added its price adjustment clause.

The price adjustment clause is not a "price term" at all, but is a mechanism through which the price could be altered. This price adjustment mechanism was not addressed in the blanket purchase order and is clearly an additional term.[1]

In the Court's previous opinion, the Court applied § 2–207(2) to an additional arbitration clause contained in Webco's conditions of sale. In finding that the arbitration clause was not part of the parties' contract, the Court held that Chainworks' expressly limited acceptance to the terms of the offer. MICH. COMP. LAWS § 440.2207(2)(a). This analysis applies with equal force to Webco's price adjustment clause. Under § 2–207(2)(a), the price adjustment clause did not become part of the contract because it was an additional term and Chainworks' expressly limited acceptance to the terms contained in its offer.[2] Accordingly, Webco's price adjustment clause is not part of the contract between the parties. Therefore, Webco cannot rely on the clause to justify its unilateral assessment of surcharges and a price increase.

2.   Negotiation and Modification of the 2004 contract

Webco next argues that the surcharge and price increase were permissible because the parties negotiated the increases and agreed to modify the contract. In support of this argument, Webco points to a series of letters it sent to Chainworks following the rise of the market price for steel and Wheeling Pittsburgh's assessment of the raw material surcharge, as well as Chainworks eventual acceptance of the surcharge. A review of the record reveals that this argument is completely misguided and contrary to the undisputed evidence in this case.

The letters relied upon by Webco do not indicate a negotiation of a contract modification, but rather demonstrate Webco's attempt to force Chainworks into accepting the surcharge. In the January 27, 2004 letter, Jeff Williams explained to Andy Hinkley that Webco did not have any other choice but to assess a raw material surcharge on all steel product shipments. After explaining the amount of the surcharge and the method by which it would be assessed, Williams stated:

> Please allow me to be clear, the tactics being employed by our suppliers leave no room for negotiation. In order for Webco to maintain an uninterrupted supply of material to Chainworks; I must have, in writing, your acceptance of these charges.

---

[1]   At oral argument, Webco appeared to abandon its reliance on P6 of Chainworks' purchase order as the conflicting provision with the price adjustment clause and shifted its argument to P5 of the purchase order. Paragraph 5 specifies that any modification to the purchase order will be issued by Chainworks and reserves the right to modify the order in the future. Even assuming that P5 of the purchase order and Webco's price adjustment clause conflict, and therefore knock each other out, this result does not assist Webco in its assertion that the surcharge and price increase were permitted under the contract nor does it create an issue of fact as to price. The offer and acceptance agreed on the same fixed price. A determination that P5 and the price adjustment clause conflict merely precludes each party from unilaterally modifying the contract, it does not affect the agreed upon price.

[2]   Moreover, a strong argument can be made that § 2–207(2)(b) (additional terms that materially alter the contract do not become part of the contract) also precludes Webco's price adjustment clause from becoming part of the contract. It is quite apparent that a clause mandating that the contract price is subject to change without notice and through which one party attempted to unilaterally alter the price would be a material alteration of the contract terms.

* * *

Webco does not take these actions lightly, this is a position that is being forced upon us all. Webco cannot and will not, unilaterally, absorb these additional costs.

Two weeks later, Webco reiterated its position, explaining that it would not absorb the cost on Chainworks' behalf and "if Chainworks does not wish to pay the surcharge, we will advise our material supplier that Webco cannot pay the surcharge for Chainworks raw material and we anticipate they will refuse to ship. This will very quickly cause delivery problems."

The letters are not an attempt to negotiate with Chainworks. In fact, Williams' letter unequivocally states that there is no room to negotiate the surcharges. Rather than a negotiation, Webco's letters amount to a refusal to perform the parties' contract absent the inclusion of the surcharge. In effect, Webco threatened to breach the parties' contract if Chainworks did not agree to pay the surcharge. See e.g., MICH. COMP. LAWS § 440.2610, Official Comment 2 (explaining that a repudiation of a contract occurs when a demand by one party "amounts to a statement of intention not to perform except on conditions which go beyond the contract."). No other conclusion can be drawn from the reference in the letters to Chainworks' interest in maintaining an "uninterrupted supply" and "delivery problems" in the event Chainworks refuses to pay the surcharge.

Webco presented Chainworks with nothing more than a Hobson's choice, in which Chainworks was forced to choose between imposition of the surcharge or the prospect of its steel supply ending, with the resultant ill effect on Chainworks' agreement with its third-party purchaser, Tenneco. To construe such activity as negotiation and acceptance of a modification would stretch these concepts to their breaking point. Moreover, as will be discussed more fully below, Chainworks' purported acceptance of the surcharge clearly indicated that it had no other choice but to accept the charge and that it reserved any rights and remedies it had under the parties' original agreement. Therefore, Webco's reliance on the parties' correspondence as evidence of negotiations and acceptance of a modification to the contract is misplaced.

3.   Impracticability

Webco next argues that the surcharge and price increase were permissible because unforeseen market conditions rendered its performance impracticable under the original contract. Section 2–615 of the UCC allows a seller to raise impracticability as a defense in a sales contract. Section 2–615 provides in pertinent part:

Delay in delivery or non-delivery in whole or in part by a seller who complies with paragraphs (b) and (c) is not a breach of his duty under a contract for sale if performance as agreed has been made impracticable by the occurrence of a contingency the nonoccurrence of which was a basic assumption on which the contract was made or by compliance in good faith with any applicable foreign or domestic governmental regulation or order whether or not it later proves to be invalid.

MICH. COMP. LAWS § 440.2615. A party asserting the impracticability defense must prove the following: 1) that an unforeseeable event occurred; 2) the nonoccurrence of the event was a basic assumption underlying the agreement; and 3) the event rendered performance impracticable. Roth Steel Prods. v. Sharon Steel Corp., 705 F.2d 134, 149 (6th Cir. 1983) (interpreting Ohio's version of the UCC).

Webco argues that the dramatic rise in the market price for steel in early 2004 was not foreseeable and rendered its performance under its contract with Chainworks impracticable. Webco does not argue that it was unable to deliver product, that it was unable to obtain quality materials, or that there was a severe shortage of available material. Rather, it argues only that, due to the industry-wide surcharge, the cost to procure raw materials rose dramatically. It is abundantly clear to the Court, however, that increased cost, without more, does not support a claim of impracticability.[3] See *Roth Steel Prods.*, 705 F.2d at 149 n. 34 ("Increases in the cost of production, however, do not, absent more, support a claim of commercial impracticability."); Bernina Distributors, Inc. v. Bernina Sewing Machine Co., 646 F.2d 434, 439–40 (10th Cir. 1981) ("Cost increases alone, though great in extent, do not render a contract impracticable."). Moreover, Webco has failed to demonstrate that the shift in the market price was the result of an unforeseen contingency.

The undisputed evidence before the Court shows that the parties knew that the steel market was volatile and that an increase in raw material costs was foreseeable. First, Chainworks has provided a series of press releases from various steel companies announcing the imposition of surcharges due to the increase in raw material costs. The press releases were issued during December 2003, prior to Webco's acceptance, and explain that the surcharges are being assessed due to rapid increases in raw material prices. Further, the releases describe "recent volatility" in the steel market, a "perfect storm in the market," "enormous cost pressures" on all steel producers, and that "the major topic of conversation in and around the US steel industry" is the rapid increase in raw material costs. The sheer number of press releases filed in this case illustrates that the upward volatility of the market was clearly apparent prior to Webco's acceptance of Chainworks' offer. Further, as a sophisticated business entity and member of the steel industry, Webco was certainly aware of these volatile market conditions and the steps that steel companies were taking in response.

In fact there is undisputed evidence in the record that Webco was aware of the volatility in the marketplace prior to entering into the contract with Chainworks. In an email dated December 4, 2003, Jeff Williams stated "the worldwide market has shifted into a higher gear. Supplies are tightening and pricing is rising—mills now have all

---

[3] Webco's argument that the raw material surcharge is something other than an increased cost is unavailing. It is undisputed that the surcharge increased Webco's production costs. See Exhibit G, Def.'s Res. Br. (describing the surcharge assessed by Wheeling Pittsburgh as an "additional cost"). The form which the increase takes, whether a surcharge or price increase, is irrelevant and does not change the fact that the rise in the steel market and assessment of the surcharge resulted in increased costs for Webco.

customers on allocation." Nevertheless, Williams concluded that Webco's fixed pricing for 2004 would remain unchanged.[4]

Second, the parties' previous dealings also indicate that they understood that raw material pricing could fluctuate. In mid–2002, the parties attempted to negotiate a long term agreement that included a pricing adjustment clause that would allow the contract price to rise or fall if the raw material price rose above or fell below a certain percentage of the original contract price. While the parties' negotiations did not result in a long term contract, the discussion of a pricing adjustment clause indicates that the parties were well aware that raw material pricing could fluctuate during the course of their dealings with each other. This is further evidence that the increase in raw material costs was foreseeable prior to the parties' contract.[5]

In response to this evidence, Webco has offered a selection of news articles that it contends shows that the price increase did not occur until January 2004, after the parties entered into their contract. Rather than creating a genuine issue of fact for trial, the articles simply reinforce the conclusion that the raw material cost increase was foreseeable before the parties' contract. While the articles do indicate that steel pricing increased during January and February 2004, they also describe the historical volatility of the steel market as far back as 1995. According to the articles, steel pricing has fluctuated throughout the late 1990's and into 2003. This is simply further evidence that a market shift was foreseeable prior to the parties' agreement.

Webco has failed to allege a triable issue with respect to the foreseeability of the increased costs. The evidence demonstrates that, prior to the parties' contract, both Webco and Chainworks understood that the steel market was volatile and that steel manufacturers were imposing surcharges due to raw material price increases. Based on this evidence, it is clear that the increased costs incurred by Webco were not unforeseeable and do not support the assertion of the impracticability defense. At best, the evidence shows that while increased costs were foreseeable, Webco either misjudged or did not anticipate the degree of the increase. In the midst of this volatile market climate, the parties agreed to a contract that provided for the payment of a fixed, certain price. Webco cannot, after the fact, alter the contract based on impracticability simply because it may have misread the market and entered into a contract which became a greater financial burden than originally expected.[6] Neal–Cooper Grain C. v. Texas Gulf Sulfur Co.,

---

[4] The Court also notes that attached to Williams' email was a news article dated December 2, 2003, explaining that the global steel market faced a "roller coaster ride." The article predicted that steel export prices would reach unsustainable levels before entering into the "fifth pricing death spiral on the world steel export market since 1995." This is further evidence of Webco's knowledge of the market conditions prior to entering into the contract.

[5] Moreover, as Chainworks' points out, the negotiation and rejection of the pricing adjustment clause also indicates that the non-occurrence of a market shift was not a "basic assumption on which the contract was made." MICH. COMP. LAWS § 440.2615(a). To the contrary, by rejecting the adjustment clause in favor of fixed pricing, the parties assumed the risk that the price could rise or fall during the contract's duration.

[6] In reaching this conclusion, the Court recognizes that Webco's Chief Financial Officer has offered a financial forecast indicating that if Webco was forced to absorb the increased costs, it would have become insolvent during 2004. Given the fact that it was foreseeable that raw material pricing was on the rise during late 2003 and that the parties, as indicated by their previous dealings, understood that raw material pricing was volatile, it is of limited

508 F.2d 283, 294 (7th Cir. 1974) ("The buyer has a right to rely on the party to the contract to supply him with goods regardless of what happens to the market price. That is the purpose for which such contracts are made."); MICH. COMP. LAWS § 440.2615 Official Comment 4 ("Neither is a rise or a collapse in the market in itself a justification, for that is exactly the type of business risk which business contracts made at fixed prices are intended to cover."); 1 J. WHITE & R. SUMMERS, UNIFORM COMMERCIAL CODE § 3–10 (4th ed. 1995) (discussing increased costs as a basis for impracticability under § 2–615 and concluding "in our judgment an increase in price, even a radical increase in price, is the thing that contracts are designed to protect against.").

* * *

5.   Conclusion

As the foregoing analysis indicates, Webco's various attempts to justify its unilateral alteration of the fixed price contract term are without merit. Therefore, Chainworks is entitled to summary judgment. Finally, the Court cannot help but suspect that had the situation been reversed, and the steel market had collapsed and Chainworks attempted to escape the contract, this case would be before the Court in the opposite posture, with Webco asserting the binding nature of a requirements contract.

Leaving that aside, in the final analysis * * * Chainworks' presented Webco with an offer for a requirements contract for the term of one year at a fixed price. Webco accepted that offer in a manner consistent with the terms specified in the offer. At that time, there was an offer, an acceptance, and consideration, and consequently, a contract. Webco's attempt to unilaterally alter the contract after the fact is unavailing and amounts to a breach of contract. Such unilateral action is contrary to the well-known principles of contract law that guide this case. As succinctly summed up by the Third Circuit in another context, "the sanctity of a contract is a fundamental concept of our entire legal structure. Freedom of contract includes the freedom to make a bad bargain. 'It is a fundamental principle of contract law, therefore, that, wise or not, a deal is a deal.' " Chambers Dev. Co., Inc. v. Passaic County Utilities Authority, 62 F.3d 582, 589 (3d Cir. 1995). Accordingly, Chainworks' motion for summary judgment on its breach of contract claim is granted and the Court will enter an order declaring that Chainworks does not owe the total amount of the surcharges and price increase. * * *

Accordingly, Chainworks' motion for summary judgment on Webco's counterclaims is granted. An order will be entered consistent with this opinion.

NOTES AND QUESTIONS

1.   The court in *Specialty Tires of America* excused CIT on the basis of 2–615(a). Why did it not rely on 2–613 to do so? See 2–613(a) and Comment 5 to 2–615. Suppose the tire presses were destroyed by

---

relevance that Webco may have entered into a contract which eventually became an unprofitable venture.

fire while in the former lessee's factory. Under which section would CIT be excused? Comment 9 to 2–615.

2. There are broadly two categories of cases in which the seller raises 2–615's impracticability defense: cases in which the seller's cost of performance increases dramatically, and cases in which the seller is prevented from performing or unable to perform. The latter category includes cases in which an asset designed by the contract or parties as the source for performance becomes unavailable. Courts very seldom relieve a seller under 2–615 in the "cost increase" cases. *Chainworks'* result is typical for cases in this category. However, sellers frequently are excused in failure of source cases. These are cases in which the seller establishes a "sole source" defense, as in *Specialty Tires of America*. Where the contract specifies a particular source of supply or the parties understand the contract to be fulfilled from that source, the failure of the source excuses the seller. See Selland Pontiac–GMC, Inc. v. King, 384 N.W.2d 490 (Minn. Ct. App. 1986) (seller excused when supplier of buses specified in contract ceased operations); cf. Alamance County Board of Education v. Bobby Murray Chevrolet, Inc., 465 S.E.2d 306 (N.C. Ct. App. 1996) (seller not excused when specific manufacturer engaged by seller not an express or implied term of contract). Comment 5 to 2–615 requires that, to be excused under the sole source defense, the seller must have used "all due measures to assure himself that his source will not fail."

Is there a justification for the different judicial responses to these two sorts of cases? Consider in this regard the different burdens 2–615 puts on courts in "cost increase" and "sole source" cases. To determine that an increase in the seller's performance costs upsets a basic assumption of the contract, a court likely must determine the profit the seller expected from performance. Courts cannot reliably do so. The seller's profit is the difference between contract price and its performance costs. Although contract price is easily verifiable, a court cannot reliably verify the seller's cost. This information is not publically available, and the seller easily can manipulate to its advantage the information it reveals. By contrast, a court easily can verify whether the seller retains access to an asset the contract or parties specify as necessary to its performance. In *Specialty Tires of America*, for instance, the former lessee's unwillingness to surrender the tire presses to the seller could be determined. A seller's lack of access to a source of performance increases its performance costs so much as to allow a reliable inference that it will not profit from performing. Courts therefore can excuse the "sole source" seller under 2–615 based on verifiable variables. See Alan Schwartz, Relational Contracts in the Courts: An Analysis of Incomplete Contracts and Judicial Strategies, 21 J. Legal Stud. 271, 291–295 (1992).

3. Many airlines limit their exposure to increases in jet fuel costs by entering into swap contracts. These contracts use oil prices, because oil and fuel prices are highly correlated and jet fuel is not sold in liquid futures markets. A common "differential" fuel swap contract employs an index of a particular type of oil traded on a specified commodities exchange. The counterparty agrees to pay the airline a variable price equal to the average of prices of the specific oil grade traded on the commodities exchange over a stipulated time period. In exchange the airline will pay a fixed price for a specified grade and volume of oil over a stipulated period of time. The fixed price payment is the difference between the fixed price and the average of oil prices. The difference between the fixed and variable prices is settled in cash at the end of the stipulated time period.

The oil swap enables the airline to lock in the price it pays for jet fuel. The airline will purchase fuel at the market price. If the price of oil increases over the stipulated time period, the swap contract entitles the airline to a cash payment equal to the price increase. The airline therefore effectively pays for the jet fuel only the (lower) fixed price it paid under the oil swap contract. If the oil price declines, the airline loses on the swap contract because it pays the counterparty the difference between the fixed price and the (lower) variable price of oil sold on the commodities exchange. However, its loss is offset by the lower price it pays for fuel it purchases in the market. The airline therefore pays in total no more for fuel than the fixed price it paid under the swap contract. As a result, the oil swap contract allows the airline to fix the price it pays for fuel whether or not fuel prices rise or fall. See Dave Carter, Dan Rogers & Betty Sinkins, Fuel Hedging in the Airline Industry: The Case of Southwest Airlines, Case Research Journal (2001).

For example, suppose the airline wants to lock in at $3 per gallon the price of 10,000 gallons of jet fuel it will purchase on January 1. To do so, the airline concludes a swap contract in which it agree to pay $87 per barrel for 10,000 barrels of a specified type of oil and the counterparty agrees to pay it the average per barrel price of that oil over a stipulated period of time ending on January 1. Assume that the average price per barrel is $88 and the market price of a gallon of jet fuel on January 1 is $4. The airline purchases 10,000 gallons of fuel on that date at $4 per gallon. The counterparty on the swap contract pays the airline $1 per barrel of oil ($88 − $87). As a result, the airline's $1 gain on the swap contract for oil offsets the $1 increase in the price of jet fuel ($4 − $3). The airline therefore pays a net price of $3 per gallon for jet fuel. Now suppose that the average of oil prices over the time period stipulated in the swap contract is $86.50 per barrel and the market price of jet oil is $2.50 per gallon on January 1. The airline purchases 10,000 gallons of fuel on January 1 at $2.50 per gallon and must pay the counterparty $.50 per barrel of oil for 10,000 barrels on the swap contract ($87 − $86.50). However, even with the $.50 loss per barrel of oil on the swap contract, the airline pays no more than $3 per gallon for the jet fuel. (It pays $2.50 per gallon to the supplier of jet fuel and $.50 per barrel of oil to the counterparty on the oil swap contract.) Thus, whether the price of oil increases or decreases, the airline pays $3 per gallon of fuel.

The fuel oil swap fixes the airline's jet fuel price only if the prices of jet fuel and specified grade of oil are highly correlated. If the correlation between the two prices changes, the swap contract can leave the airline with significant losses on jet fuel it purchases. This has occurred fairly recently in the United States. The fuel oil swap contracts many domestic airlines enter into set price by a particular type of oil: West Texas Intermediate crude oil. For reasons having to do with transportation and storage costs, the price of West Texas crude has lagged behind the price of jet fuel. By contrast, Brent crude oil, a type of oil traded on European exchanges, has tracked jet fuel prices more closely. See Javier Blas and Pilita Clark, US Airlines Rethink Fuel Hedging Policy, Fin. Times, March 2, 1011, available at http://www.ft.com/cms/s/0/341bee96–4509–11e0–80e7–00144feab49a.html#axzz1 aE30BJba. Fuel costs are among the airline's largest costs, and the failure of a benchmark oil price index therefore can drastically affect their profits. Eastern Air Lines, Inc. v. Gulf Oil Corp., 415 F. Supp. 429, 441 (S.D. Fla. 1975) rejected the impracticability defense raised by a jet fuel supplier as follows: "But even if Gulf [the supplier] had established great hardship under UCC § 2–615, which it has not, Gulf would not prevail because the events associated with the so-called energy crisis were reasonably foreseeable at the time the contract was executed. If a contingency is foreseeable, it and its consequences are taken outside the scope of UCC § 2–615, because the party disadvantaged by fruition of the contingency might have protected himself in his contract." U.S. airlines are aware of divergence in prices between West Texas Intermediate and Brent crude oil. Blas and Clark, supra id.

4. In an early article on the role of economic considerations in assigning contractual liability, then-Professor Posner and Andrew Rosenfield argue that excuse doctrines reflect insurance considerations. See Richard A. Posner & Andrew M. Rosenfield, Impossibility and Related Doctrines in Contract Law: An Economic Analysis, 8 J. Legal Stud. 83 (1977). When impossibility, frustration or related doctrines discharge a contracting party, the other party bears the risk of the excusing event. The party to whom the risk is shifted insures against it ("insurance" being understood broadly). For example, if the seller's performance of a fixed price contract is discharged by impracticability when the market price exceeds the contract price, the seller loses the contract price while the buyer loses the amount by which the market price exceeds the contract price. The discharge insures the seller against the increase in market price above the contract price. Two factors are relevant to the cost of insurance: (1) the cost of accurately estimating the probability of the relevant event and the impact of its occurrence, and (2) the transaction costs of diversifying away its risk or purchasing market insurance. Posner and Rosenfield argue that the doctrines of excuse discharge a contracting party only when the other party is a cheaper insurer against the excused event than the discharged party. They maintain believe that the outcomes of most impossibility and frustration cases are consistent with this cheapest insurer rationale. In *Specialty Tires of America* Judge Smith uses their analysis to confirm—to "check," as he puts it—that 2–615 discharges CIT. See Richard A. Posner, Economic Analysis of Law § 4.5 (5th ed. 1998), which incorporates the analysis on which the court relies. Professor Atamer maintains that the same analysis is implicit in the CISG's exemption provision, discussed infra G. See Yesim M. Atamer, Article 79, in UN Convention on Contracts for the International Sales of Goods (CISG): Commentary 1054, 1072 (S. Kröll, L. Mistelis & P.P. Viscasellas eds., 2011).

A difficulty with Posner and Rosenfield's analysis (which they recognize) is that it is often inconclusive. This is because the factors relevant to identifying the cheapest insurer frequently point to different contracting parties. *Specialty Tires of America* might appear to be a case in which the buyer, Specialty Tires, clearly is the cheaper insurer. Neither the seller nor the buyer could forecast the lessee's unwillingness to part with the tire presses. This event was a "bolt out of the blue," as the court puts it. In addition, as the court also notes, Specialty Tires was better positioned to know about the impact not getting the presses would have on its business. So the factor of measurement costs identifies Specialty Tire as the cheapest insurer. But transaction costs might favor CIT. As a significant commercial lessor whose lessees might go into bankruptcy, CIT could spread the risk of its lessees refusing to surrender leased equipment, by charging them a premium. Alternatively, its comparative size might make it better able to absorb the loss than Specialty Tire. If so, CIT has the advantage in transaction costs. For this reason, it is not clear that Specialty Tire is the superior insurer. Even considered by itself, the criterion of transaction costs is inconclusive if applied to *Chainworks'* facts. Webco, the seller, could have spread the known risk of a rise in steel prices by hedging contracts with other steel suppliers. On the other hand, Chainworks also could have spread this risk by including a surcharge in contracts for steel products with its own customers. It is not apparent which party has an advantage with respect to transaction costs. For an influential criticism of Posner and Rosenfield's analysis along these lines, see Michael J. Trebilcock, The Role of Insurance Considerations in the Choice of Efficient Civil Liability Rules, 4 J. Law, Econ. & Org. 243, 249–255 (1988).

5. Section 2–615 is a default rule that excuses the seller's nonperformance when the parties' contract does not provide otherwise. The contract therefore can supply its own excuse term, such as with a force majeure clause, or not allow any excuse at all. See Wisconsin Electric Power v. Union Pacific R.R., 557 F.3d 504, 507 (7th Cir. 2009). The force majeure clause may expand or restrict the circumstances under which a party's performance is excused. It can contain entirely different excusing conditions than those given by 2–615(a). For instance, the typical force majeure clause only excuses when the force majeure event is "external"—an exogenously determined event over which the obligated party has no control—and therefore is not "internal." However, although unusual, the clause might excuse the seller when the event is internal, such as a strike at the seller's own factory that makes it unable to produce the goods. For its part, 2–615 excuses the seller only when its take due measures to assure its performance. See Comment 5 to 2–615. Because the seller can affect the likelihood of a strike at its own factory, 2–615 therefore might not excuse its nonperformance even though such nonperformance may nevertheless be excused by the force majeure clause. Whether and to what extent a force majeure clause in the sales contract displaces 2–615 is a matter of contract interpretation. See Perlman v. Pioneer Ltd. Partnership, 918 F.2d 1244 (5th Cir. 1990). If parties can expand the occasions in which their performance is excused, they also can limit the conditions in which 2–615(a) excuses. See Interpetrol Bermuda Ltd. v. Kaiser Aluminum Int'l Corp., 719 F.2d 992 (9th Cir. 1983).

2. UNDER THE CISG

The CISG has its own provision exempting sellers and buyers from performance. Although broad enough to accommodate commercial impracticability, the provision differs from 2–615 in its scope and terminology. Article 79 exempts the seller or buyer under prescribed conditions from liability for damages for failure to perform its contractual obligations. To be exempted, the party must meet three conditions: (1) its failure to perform was due to an impediment beyond its control, (2) that it could not reasonably be expected to have taken the impediment into account at the conclusion of the contract, and (3) that once the impediment occurred, the party could not reasonably have avoided it or its consequences. Article 79(1). Case law puts the burden of proving that these conditions obtain on the party seeking the exemption. See American Arbitration Association (USA), 23 October 2007, available at http://cisgw3.law.pace.edu/cases/071023a5.html.

Article 79's scope differs from 2–615 in two respects. First, by its terms, Article 79's exemption applies to "any of [the exempted party's] obligations." By contrast, 2–615 only operates to excuse the seller from its obligation of delivery; see 2–615(a). Because Article 79 can exempt the performance of any contractual obligation, its potential application is more extensive than 2–615. An instance in which Article 79's broader scope might make a difference concerns warranties. Assume the seller delivers goods that do not have the qualities required by the contract. The seller was obligated to deliver conforming goods. Section 2–615 would not excuse the seller, because the seller delivered the goods. However, Article 79 can apply. The seller's warranty is an obligation under the contract, and Article 79 exempts a party under prescribed conditions from liability for damages for failure to perform "any of his obligations." This includes the obligation to deliver conforming goods.

To date no court has decided whether Article 79 exempts a seller from delivering nonconforming goods. However, dicta in several cases suggest that the exemption could apply on appropriate facts. In one case a seller delivered powdered milk contaminated by lipase. Bundesgerichtshof (Germany), 9 January 2002, available at http://www. cisg.law.pace.edu/cases/020109g1.html. In response to the buyer's suit for damages, the seller invoked Article 79's exemption. The court did not decide whether Article 79 could exempt the seller. Instead, it remanded the case to the lower court to determine whether the seller met Article 79(1)'s requirements for an exemption. There was no need for the remand if Article 79 cannot apply to the seller's delivery of nonconforming goods.

The second difference in scope concerns the consequence of Article 79's exemption. Section 2–615 (and common law excuse doctrine) discharges the excused party's obligations under the contract. The discharge is total, so that the discharged party is not liable to the other contracting party for breach. By contrast, Article 79(1)'s exemption is limited. It only exempts a party from liability for damages resulting from its breach. The other party therefore retains remedies other than damages. Article 79(5) makes this explicit: "Nothing in this article prevents either party from exercising any right other than to claim damages under this Convention." "Nondamages" remedies include avoidance of the contract, reduction of the price (Article 50), recovery of interest where applicable, restitution, and specific relief when available. The continued availability of specific relief when damages are unavailable has an apparently odd consequence: A party can be forced to perform even when its performance is exempt from liability for damages. To understand the limited effect of the exemption, assume that the seller is temporarily prevented from delivering the goods and that Article 79(1) exempts it from making timely delivery. According to Article 79(3), the seller's exemption lasts as long as the impediment preventing delivery lasts. Thus, under Article 79(1), the buyer cannot recover damages it suffers from the delay in delivery. However, Article 79 does not prevent the buyer from avoiding the contract if the seller's delay constitutes a fundamental breach of the contract.

a. ARTICLE 79'S REQUIREMENTS

Article 79(1) essentially exempts a party from liability for damages when a supervening event impedes its performance. Taking Article 79(1)'s three requirements for the exemption in order, the first requirement is that the exempting event be an impediment beyond the party's control. Exogenously determined events such as hurricanes, civil unrest, export controls or governmental confiscation easily count as impediments whose occurrence a party cannot affect. These sorts of events can prevent performance. (They also are covered by traditional common law excuse doctrine of impossibility or frustration and the civil law doctrine of force majeure.) Harder to characterize are events which make a party's performance more expensive or difficult, such as increases in production costs or devaluations of currency in which the contract price is to paid. Article 79(1) is unclear as to whether such events count as impediments. To avoid national courts interpreting the CISG's exemption through the lens of domestic law, the CISG's drafters decided to use unfamiliar terminology. Article 79(1)'s novel and imprecise terminology leaves the notion of an impediment indeterminate at points. Worse, the relevant diplomatic history is inconclusive. Although some of it suggests that supervening events that merely increase the cost of performance cannot be impediments, most recent case law and commentary disagree. See Documentary History of the Uniform Law for International Sales 185, 631 (J. Honnold ed., 1989) (diplomatic history); Ingeborg Schwenzer, Article 79, in Schlechtriem & Schwenzer: Commentary on the UN Convention on the International Sales of Goods (CISG) 1076 (I Schwenzer ed., 3d ed. 2010); Yesim M. Atamer, Article 79, in UN Convention on Contracts for the International Sales of Goods (CISG): Commentary 1069 (S. Kröll, L. Mistelis & P.P. Viscasillas eds., 2011). In their view Article 79's terms can apply to instances of hardship or commercial impracticability.

The prevailing view counts as impediments events that make a party's performance extremely difficult or expensive. The difficulty, of course, is to determine the threshold at which increased difficulty or expense becomes an impediment for Article 79(1)'s purposes. As with 2–615's standard of impracticability, the threshold remains vague and the sparse case law on point does not help. Apparently a significant drop in market price does not exempt the buyer from payment. District Court Hasselt (Belgium), 2 May 1995, available at http://cisgw3.law.pace.edu/cases/950502b1.html. The buyer must purchase the minimum quantities required by the contract even if doing so increases its expenses by 100%. Cour d'Appel de Colmar (France), 12 June 2001, available at http://cisgw3.law.pace.edu/cases/010612f1.html. Even a 300% increase in the price of the commodity the seller promised its buyer does not exempt the seller's performance. Oberlandesgericht Hamburg (Germany), 28 February 1997, available at http://www.cisg. law.pace.edu/cases/970228g1.html. The cases leave completely unclear the point at which a price increase renders performance extremely difficult and therefore an impediment. One European commentator concludes that a 150–200% fluctuation in expenses or profits is an appropriate threshold. See Ingeborg Schwenzer, Force Majeure and Hardship in International Sales Contractors, 39 Victoria U. Welling. L. Rev. 709, 717 (2008). Nothing in Article 79 supports this stipulation.

Article 79(1)'s second requirement is that the impediment be one that the obligor could not reasonably be expected to have taken into account at the time the contract was concluded. The first requirement concerns an event that intervenes between the conclusion and performance of the contract; the second requirement concerns what the obligor could have done at the conclusion of the contract. To see the difference in the requirements, assume that the sales contract calls for the seller to ship railroad rails from the port of St. Petersburg, Russia to a US buyer. The rails are to be delivered to the buyer's U.S. plant by June 2002. Unusually low temperatures beginning in December 2001 froze the water in the port and prevented ice cutting vessels from clearing the port. The seller is unable to meet the June 2002 delivery date by shipment of the rails from the port after December 1, 2001. When the buyer sues for breach of contract, the seller seeks to exempt its failure to deliver under Article 79. Low winter temperature at the port easily is an impediment beyond the seller's control. Whether the seller could have taken the risk of the winter freeze into account at the conclusion of the contract is a separate question. It asks whether Article 79(1)'s second requirement is met.

These essentially are the facts presented in Raw Materials, Inc. v. Manfred Forberich GmbH & Co., KG, 53 UCC Rep. Serv.2d 878 (N.D. Ill. 2004). If the seller could reasonably have foreseen the risk of a unusually cold winter temperatures at the port, it could reasonably have taken the possibility into account at the time of the contract. In response the seller could have shifted the risk of freezing temperatures to the buyer through an appropriate force majeure clause. Article 79(1)'s second requirement is not met if the seller fails to take a foreseeable risk into account. The Raw Materials court for the most part followed this reasoning. Relying on 2–615 by analogy to interpret Article 79, the court asked whether the seller could have foreseen the unusually severe winter weather around the port in 2001. As noted supra in section F, foreseeability is a slippery notion: Under different descriptions, the same event can be foreseeable or unforeseeable. For instance, the freezing of waters around St. Petersburg port in December 2001 might be foreseeable if described as "low winter temperatures around St. Petersburg port" while unforeseeable if described as "temperatures low enough in December 2001 to freeze the waters around St. Petersburg port." Article 79(1)'s second requirement, however, is a bit more precise. It requires that the obligor could not "reasonably be expected to have taken the impediment into account." The qualification "reasonably" suggests that the standard is a rough risk-utility test, not a mere inquiry into foreseeability. Plausibly, to meet the second requirement, the seller must take measures at the time of the contract whose cost is less than the expected loss if the contingency materializes.

Under Article 79(1)'s third requirement, the obligor is exempt only if it could not have avoided or overcome the impediment or its consequences. Left unqualified, an obligor almost never meets the requirement. This is because, with enough expense, it can take measures to avoid or overcome almost any obstacle to its performance. For example, assume that the government bars export of the fungible goods the seller is about to dispatch overseas to its buyer. The seller still could purchase substitute goods to meet its delivery obligations, even if it must pay more for them than the contract price it receives from the buyer. Alternatively, the seller could negotiate with the buyer, at some price, to modify its delivery obligation. Even a seller would cannot take action to overcome an export ban once it becomes effective can take measures beforehand to avoid its effect. The problem, of course, is to determine the level of expense that an obligor should be expected to incur in avoiding or overcoming the impediment or its consequences. Although not entirely clear, Article 79(1) arguably requires only that the obligor act reasonably in response to the impediment. Article 79 requires that the obligor could not "reasonably be expected" to have taken the impediment into account. The phrase "reasonably expected" can be read to modify the obligation to "have avoided or overcome it or its consequences" as well. This means that Article 79(1)'s third requirement is met if the obligor's reasonable expenditures will not avoid or overcome the impediment or its consequences. While "reasonableness" is not defined, a cost-benefit test might inform the notion. An expenditure is reasonable if the cost to the obligor making it prevents a larger loss (a benefit) to the obligee.

Article 79(2) limits the exemption when the obligor relies on a third party to perform all or part of the contract. Under the subsection, the obligor is exempt from liability only if its nonperformance results from the third party's nonperformance and the third party would be exempt under Article 79(1) if it were applied to its own nonperformance. The terms of Article 79(2)'s limitation should be noted. For one thing, Article 79(2) applies only to sales contracts in which the obligor has subcontracted with the third party to perform all or part of its contract with the buyer ("a third person whom he has engaged to perform the whole or part of the contract"). It does not apply when the obligor merely engages a third party to supply it with materials or other means necessary to perform the contract. In addition, Article 79(2)(b) exempts the obligor only if the third party itself would be exempt if Article 79(1)'s requirement were applied to it. The test here is merely counterfactual. It asks whether the third party would meet the requirements for exemption had Article 79(1) applied to the third party. Article 79(1)'s requirements in fact may be inapplicable, either because the CISG does not apply to the subcontract or the subcontract's terms exclude Article 79. This does not matter. The obligor is exempted only if the third party's nonperformance itself would be exempted were Article 79(1) applied to that nonperformance.

Macromex SRL v. Globex International, Inc.

United States District Court, Southern District of New York, 2008
65 UCC Rep. Serv.2d 1033

■ Opinion and order: SHIRA A. SCHEINDLIN U.S.D.J.

I.   Introduction

Macromex SRL ("Macromex") has petitioned for confirmation of an arbitral award against Globex International, Inc. ("Globex"), and Globex has cross-petitioned to have that award vacated. Globex makes two main arguments. First, Globex argues that the arbitrator's application of the Uniform Commercial Code's ("U.C.C.") substituted performance provision constituted manifest disregard of the law. Second, Globex argues that if the arbitrator's use of the U.C.C. is upheld, it was irrational to base the lost profit damages on the Romanian market, where Globex's product was banned, instead of a substituted location. For the reasons discussed below, Globex's cross-petition is dismissed and the award is confirmed.

II.   Background

Globex is an American company that sells food products to countries around the world. Globex contracted to sell Macromex, a Romanian company, 112 containers of chicken parts to be delivered in Romania. That contract was governed by the United Nations Convention on Contracts for the International Sale of Goods ("CISG"). The contract required that Globex make the final shipment by May 29, 2006. However, by June 2, 2006, it had failed to ship sixty-two of the containers.

On June 2, 2006, the Romanian Government declared, without notice, that as of June 7, 2006, no chicken could be imported into Romania unless it was certified by the latter date. Between that announcement and June 7, 2006, Globex rushed out twenty of the remaining sixty-two containers it had contracted to sell. As of June 7, the remaining forty-two containers could not be shipped to Romania due to that regulation. Macromex then brought arbitration proceedings against Globex for breach of contract, demanding $608,323.00. Globex submitted to arbitration and lost.

Globex's principal argument was a force majeure defense. Globex argued that its delays in shipment were within the industry's informal standard of flexibility. The ban came within that period of flexibility without warning, completely blocking Globex from shipping the remaining chicken to Macromex.

The arbitrator found that the delay in shipment itself was not a fundamental breach. Because the ban on importing chicken into Romania made that non-delivery effectively indefinite, the arbitrator then examined whether Globex was exempted from performance by CISG Article 79, which covers excuses due to force majeure. That Article, as interpreted by the arbitrator, contains four elements: 1) an impediment beyond the party's control, 2) unforeseeable by that party, 3) that could not be reasonably avoided or overcome, and 4) an allegation by that party that nonperformance was due to that impediment. The arbitrator found that Globex satisfied the first two elements, may have satisfied the fourth, but failed to satisfy the third.

The arbitrator determined that the third element refers to the concept of substituted performance. The arbitrator found the language of the contract precluded an interpretation as to the third element based solely on a reading of the contract. He therefore turned to two extrinsic sources: authorities within the CISG's scope, including its commentary and caselaw, and material outside the CISG, such as the U.C.C. and caselaw interpreting the U.C.C. The arbitrator found that the materials within the CISG were of limited use, but suggested that Macromex's request for substituted performance was appropriate.[1] By contrast, the arbitrator found that section 2–614 of the U.C.C. was dispositive of the issue.

The arbitrator held that section 2–614 requires commercially reasonable alternatives to performance. Macromex proposed that Globex ship to a port in Georgia, a nearby country. The arbitrator noted that another of Macromex's American suppliers had accepted this offer, in the face of the same import ban. Globex, however, had refused, and instead took advantage of a contemporaneous jump in the market price of chicken.

Having decided for Macromex, the arbitrator set damages at the Romanian market price for the undelivered chicken—namely, the $606,323.00 sought by Macromex. The arbitrator also shifted all costs for the proceedings and attorneys' fees to Globex. The final award came to $876,310.58.

Globex made a "request for interpretation" of the award on the same issues it raises here: misuse of section 2–614 and miscalculation of the damages. The arbitrator doubted it had the power to revisit the substance of the award but nonetheless decided that Globex's complaints were without merit. Macromex then petitioned for confirmation of the award in this Court, and Globex cross-petitioned to vacate that award.

III. Legal Standard

A. Interpretation of Law

If the parties so agree, a contract may be governed by the CISG. Because the CISG is a self-executing treaty and the United States is a member, it is binding on this Court as federal law. However, "[b]ecause there is virtually no caselaw under the Convention, we look to its language and to 'the general principles' upon which it is based."[2] Further, "[c]aselaw interpreting analogous provisions of Article 2 of the [U.C.C.], may also inform a court where the language of the relevant CISG provisions tracks that of the U.C.C."[3] This rule of interpretation also applies to arbitrators examining a contract providing for the application of the CISG as governing law.

---

[1]   See Int. Award at 9 ("Thus, under this approach [referring to materials within the CISG] Seller should have explored possible alternatives in this regard with Buyer, but failed to do so to Buyer's detriment and Seller's enrichment.").

[2]   Id. at 1027–28 (citing CISG art. 7(1)).

[3]   Id. at 1028 (noting that such caselaw " 'is not per se applicable' " (quoting Orbisphere Corp. v. United States, 726 F. Supp. 1344, 1355, 13 Ct. Int'l Trade 866 (Ct. Int'l Trade 1989))).

B. Vacatur of Award

The confirmation of an arbitration award is a summary proceeding that converts a final arbitration award into a judgment of the court. "Arbitration awards are subject to very limited review in order to avoid undermining the twin goals of arbitration, namely, settling disputes efficiently and avoiding long and expensive litigation." Willemijn Houdstermaatschappij, BV v. Standard Microsystems Corp., 103 F.3d 9 (2d Cir. 1997). "A court is required to confirm the award unless a basis for modification or vacatur exists. The Federal Arbitration Act ("FAA") lists specific instances where an award may be vacated. In addition, the Second Circuit has recognized that a court may vacate an arbitration award that was rendered in " 'manifest disregard of the law.' " Wallace v. Butta, 378 F.3d 182, 189 (2d Cir. 2003). However, "review for manifest error is severely limited." Id.

Although "its precise boundaries are ill defined . . . its rough contours are well known." To find manifest disregard, the Second Circuit held in Duferco Int'l Steel Trading v. T. Klaveness Shipping A/S, 333 F.3d 383 (2d Cir. 2003), that the court must conduct a three step analysis. First, the court must find that the arbitrator ignored a law that was clearly and explicitly applicable to the case. Second, the court must find that the law was improperly applied, leading to an erroneous outcome. Third, the court must find that the arbitrator acted with the subjective knowledge that she was overlooking or misapplying the law.

"A federal court cannot vacate an arbitral award merely because it is convinced that the arbitration panel made the wrong call on the law. On the contrary, the award 'should be enforced, despite a court's disagreement with it on the merits, if there is a barely colorable justification for the outcome reached.' " *Wallace*, 378 F.3d at 190 (quoting Banco de Seguros deal Estado v. Mutual Marine Office, Inc., 344 F.3d 255, 260 (2d Cir. 2003)). In deciding whether to confirm an arbitration award, the court "should not conduct an independent review of the factual record" to check if facts support the panel's conclusion. Rather, "[t]o the extent that a federal court may look upon the evidentiary record of an arbitration proceeding at all, it may do so only for the purpose of discerning whether a colorable basis exists for the panel's award so as to assure that the award cannot be said to be the result of the panel's manifest disregard of the law." Id.

C. Lost Profits

Under the CISG, when a contract is breached, plaintiff may "collect damages to compensate for the full loss. This includes . . . lost profits, subject only to the familiar limitation that the breaching party must have foreseen, or should have foreseen, the loss as a probable consequence." Delchi Carrier SpA v. Rotorex Corp., 71 F.3d 1024, 1030 (2d Cir. 1995). The CISG allows damages to reach (although not exceed) the amount "which the party in breach foresaw or ought to have foreseen at the time of the conclusion of the contract . . . as a possible consequence of the breach of contract." CISG Article 74. Likewise, American law on lost profits supports the "general rule . . . that foreseeability should be assessed at the time of contracting," not at the time of breach. This prevents either party from exploiting favorable changes of circumstances.

IV. Discussion

A.   U.C.C. § 2–614

Globex does not contest the arbitrator's decision to use the U.C.C. to help clarify the CISG. Rather, Globex argues that the arbitrator misapplied the U.C.C. Globex argues that the official comment to the U.C.C. shows that section 2–614 is not intended to be applied to force majeure situations, which are covered instead by section 2–615. The official comment to section 2–614 states in relevant part, "[t]he distinction between [these sections] lies in whether the failure or impossibility of performance arises in connection with an incidental matter or goes to the very heart of the agreement." Comment 1 to section 2–614. Globex argues that the country of delivery as specified in the Contract "goes to the very heart of the agreement."

Section 2–614 is unambiguous. It covers unloading places that have "become unavailable" "without fault of either party." While—this may often be read to refer to specific facilities within a country, it is more than "barely colorable" to read this to include a country's facilities, blocked by regulation, when a nearby country's facilities are available. Indeed, as Macromex argues, there is no reason to overburden the significance of national ownership of a port (assuming Seller will not have to sustain whatever greater docking and importation fees there may be at the port of another country).

Globex instead argues that section 2–614 refers only to the technical details of contract performance. The official comment that Globex quotes, however, can easily be read to confirm the arbitrator's application. The comment's distinction between incidental matters and those going to the heart of the contract is better read as "surmountable impediments" and "insurmountable impediments." Nonperformance without substitution is only justified if the impediment is totally insurmountable, not just that it affects an important element of the contract. The comment cites to two cases as illustrative. In International Paper v. Rockefeller, 146 N.Y.S. 371 (3d Dep't 1914), the specific stand of trees Buyer wanted was accidentally destroyed. Because the requested product no long existed, the impediment to performance was insurmountable. In Meyer v. Sullivan, 181 P. 847 (Cal. App. 1919), however, Seller was to deliver certain goods to Buyer, but war regulations prohibited Seller from leaving port. Buyer was able to demand that Seller hold the goods at its warehouse so that Buyer could retrieve them at that location.

The instant case is closer to the second scenario. Globex had the product, but could not deliver it. The best substitution would be delivery to another port, as Globex intended to deliver the product by ship. In fact, in *Meyer v. Sullivan*, the Seller could not ship at all, but was still required to arrange substituted performance. Therefore, the arbitrator correctly applied section 2–614.

B.   The Damages

Globex argues that if it is liable for the breach, the arbitrator miscalculated the damages. According to Globex, the damages, calculated in accordance with CISG Article 74, should reflect the market prices in Georgia, not Romania. Globex reasons that if it breached, it did so by failing to complete the substituted performance (shipping to Georgia), not by failing to ship to Romania, which was impossible. Because shipment to Romania was impossible, Macromex could not have lost profits based on Romanian market prices.

The CISG defines damages in Section II, Articles 74 to 77. Article 74 discusses breached contracts; Articles 75 and 76 discuss avoided contracts. Finally, Article 77 discusses mitigation, an issue not raised in this case. Because the arbitrator rejected the force majeure defense, this contract was breached, rather than avoided. As a result, only Article 74 applies.

An unexcused breach fits squarely within Article 74. The arbitrator correctly read Article 74 to determine loss of profit as the amount foreseeable at the signing of the contract.

The arbitrator correctly applied Article 74, finding that "Buyer is entitled to lost profits caused by Seller that were foreseeable at the time of entry into the Contracts." The term "foreseeability" here is not the same as that used in the second element of force majeure, where it serves to protect the breaching party from unexpected impediments. The loss of profit foreseeable at the signing of the contract refers to circumstances similar to those raised here—preventing each side from using unforeseeable circumstances to modify the contract. Just as a Seller cannot require the buyer to pay an unexpected jump in market price for the contracted good, the seller is not required to accept less than the contract price even if the market crashes or a government regulation causes the price to drop.

Because lost profits are determined under the CISG as the amount foreseeable at the time the contract was executed, the arbitrator's calculation of damages was correct. The lost profits were based on the market value of the chickens in Romania, their intended place of sale.

V.   Conclusion

For the foregoing reasons, Macromex's petition to confirm the award is granted and Globex's cross-petition to vacate the award is denied. The Clerk of the Court is directed to close these motions and this case. * * *

NOTE

The arbitral award which the court confirmed is a bit more informative about Globex's motivations for refusing to deliver at a substitute port: "Buyer raised the prospect of accepting delivery of the product elsewhere to make subsequent shipment possible. Another American supplier facing the same Romanian ban as Seller shipped to another port. While that particular port may not have been a viable alternative for Seller, the evidence made clear there were ports where exclusivity arrangements would not have precluded such delivery. It was Seller's duty to do so here and it failed to do so, preferring to pocket the profit available in a market experiencing a dramatic rise in prices. In doing so Seller misappropriated a profit that should have been made available to Buyer through an alternative shipment destination. The law does not countenance such a result." International Centre for Dispute Resolution of the American Arbitration Association (USA), 23 October 2007, available at http://cisgw3.law.pace.edu/cases/071023a5. html. There is a long-running debate as to whether Article 7 imposes only a duty of good faith in interpreting the CISG provisions or whether it creates a broader duty of good faith that applies to the parties' performance of the contract. The latter duty sometimes is found among the principles underlying the CISG referred to in Article 7(2). Could the arbitral tribunal have relied on Article 7 to conclude that Globex's failure to deliver was not exempt under Article 79?

PROBLEM 7.11

Bright, a U.S. computer manufacturer, contracted to buy a lot of 5,000 computer chips from Sky, a Chinese chip producer. Under the sales contract Sky was to deliver the lot in Hong Kong by January 1 for shipment to the U.S. The contract included the following provision: "A party to this contract is not liable for a failure to perform any of his obligations if he proves that the failure was due to an impediment beyond his control and that he could not reasonably be expected to have taken into account at the time of the conclusion of the contract or to have avoided or overcome it or its consequences." In negotiations Bright had emphasized that the delivery date was crucial to its own ability to produce its new line of computers in time for the spring sales season.

Bright received three pieces of bad news in November. First, a hurricane destroyed its entire inventory of computer chips, as well as its factories that make them. Bright's competitors have limited supplies of the chips available but a shortage of chips has raised their price to three times the price Sky previously charged its own buyers. Second, new and unprecedented Chinese legislation imposed a 100% tax on sellers of certain computer-related items, including computer chips. The tax is assessed on the basis of the seller's cost for each chip sold. Third, the hurricane placed a significant financial strain on Sky, so that it risks insolvency in performing the contract. Accordingly, on November 15 Sky notified Bright that it would be unable to meet delivery the computer chips due to these circumstances. In response, Bright telephoned Sky cancelling the contract. Bright later obtained the computer chips it needed from another manufacturer at three times the price offered by Sky (the lowest available price). May Bright recover from Sky the amount by which the price of the substitute chips exceeds the contract price of Sky's chips? CISG Articles 6, 25, 49, 76, 79.

PROBLEM 7.12

Seller, a U.S. precision lens manufacturer, agreed to sell an industrial lens to Buyer, a Japanese company. The agreement recited that all aspects of the contract were governed by Virginia law. Because Seller did not produce lenses of the sort Buyer ordered, it contracted with Ajax, an Indian lens producer, to fabricate and deliver to Buyer the lens. A provision of their agreement required the lens to be made to the same specifications called for in Seller's contract with Buyer. The agreement also contained a provision calling for Indian law to govern all aspects of the contract. Japan is a signatory to the CISG; India is not a signatory.

Before Ajax could begin fabricating the lens, a fire destroyed its only manufacturing facility. Although lenses of the sort Ajax is to produce are available on the world market, Indian currency controls prevent Ajax from obtaining one. As a result, Ajax informed Seller and Buyer that it would not be in a position to make delivery to Buyer. Seller in turn informed Buyer that in the circumstances it too was unable to deliver the lens. When Buyer sued Seller for the additional cost it incurs in procuring a lens, Seller claimed that it was not liable for the amount. Assume that Indian law governs Seller's contract with Ajax. Also assume that Indian law excuses contracting parties in Ajax's position from all liability for nonperformance of their contractual obligations.

(a) Is Seller liable to Buyer for the additional cost Buyer seeks to recover?

(b) Suppose Ajax's contract with Seller called for it to provide Seller with the glass needed for Seller to produce Buyer's lens. Is the result different? Article 79(1), (2).

b. HARDSHIP DOCTRINE AND ARTICLE 79

A significant change in the market price of the goods can make the contract more expensive or burdensome to perform: a hardship. Hardship exempts a party from performing under Article 79(1) only if the change meets the Article's requirements for exemption. As noted above, some courts and commentators believe that Article 79 can apply when intervening events make the contract "excessively onerous" to perform. See CISG Advisory Council Opinion No. 7: Exemption of Liability for Damages Under Article 79 of the CISG (2007), available at http://www.cisg.law.pace.edu/cisg/CISG–AC-op7.html. A question that recently has arisen is whether Article 79 or another Article of the CISG authorizes a court to modify the terms of a contract that has become burdensome to the performing party.

To answer the question, consider first domestic law on the matter. Common law systems consider hardship to be merely a fact about the contract: changes in market price have made the contract burdensome to perform. If the hardship makes the contract commercially impracticable, performance is excused. Otherwise, nonperformance is breach. In either case common law excuse doctrine does not allow a court to modify the contract's terms in light of hardship. By contrast, a number of civil law systems recognize a doctrine of hardship, either by statute or decisional law. Hardship doctrine permits a court to order the parties to renegotiate specific contract terms that have become onerous as a result of events that fundamentally alter the "equilibrium of the contract." If renegotiation is unsuccessful, the court can terminate the contract or modify its terms. The following provisions of the UNIDROIT Principles of International Commercial Contracts (1994) are representative of the civil law hardship doctrine.

Principle 6.2.2 There is hardship where the occurrence of events fundamentally alters the equilibrium of the contract either because the cost of a party's performance has increased or because the value of the performance a party receives has diminished, and

(a) the events occur or become known to the disadvantaged party after the conclusion of the contract;

(b) the events could not reasonably have been taken into account by the disadvantaged party at the time of the conclusion of the contract;

(c) the events are beyond the control of the disadvantaged party; and

(d) the risk of the events was not assumed by the disadvantaged party.

Principle 6.2.3 (1) In case of hardship the disadvantaged party is entitled to request renegotiations. . . .

(3) Upon failure to reach agreement within a reasonable time either party may resort to the court.

(4) If the court finds hardship it may, if reasonable, (a) terminate the contract at a date and on terms to be fixed, or (b) adapt the contract with a view to restoring its equilibrium.

Principle 6.2.2's definition of hardship incorporates most of Article 79(1)'s requirements for exemption. However, unlike Principle 6.2.3(1) and (4), Article 79 does not authorize a court to order renegotiation or adapt the contract's terms in the case of hardship. Thus, seemingly the CISG does not allow the hardship relief allowed under Principle 6.2.3.

The Belgian Supreme Court concluded otherwise. In Scafom Int'l v. Lorraine Tubes S.A.S., Hof van Cassatie [Supreme Court] (Belgium), 19 June 2009, http://cisgw3.law.pace.edu/cases/090619b1.html, the Court ordered the buyer to renegotiate the price term of a contract governed by the CISG. The case is important and controversial. Its facts are simple. The parties in *Scafom* concluded a fixed price contract for the sale of steel tubes. The contract contained no price adjustment clause. When the price of steel increased by 70% the seller attempted to renegotiate a higher contract price. The buyer refused the seller's offer and insisted on delivery at the original price. In response the seller claimed that its liability for performance was exempt under Article 79. The Supreme Court found that hardship can be an impediment that exempts a party from liability for nonperformance. However, it also reasoned that neither Article 79 nor any of the CISG's other provisions address the authority of a court to order renegotiation or adapt contract terms in the case of hardship. The Court concluded that the CISG therefore contains a gap in its coverage: an issue that falls within the CISG's scope but which its provisions do not expressly address. In the jargon of European scholars, the Court found an "internal gap" in the CISG. The Court relied on Article 7(2) to fill this internal gap. Article 7(2) provides in relevant part that "[q]uestions concerning matters governed by this Convention which are not expressly settled in it are to be settled in conformity with the general principles on which it is based . . ." Applying Article 7(2), the Court concluded that the UNIDROIT Principle 6.2.3, quoted above, reflects a principle on which the CISG is based. The seller therefore was entitled under the CISG to ask that the contract price be renegotiated.

To see the weakness in the Belgian Supreme Court's reasoning, notice that it contains three steps:

1.   The CISG contains an internal gap concerning hardship relief.

2.   That gap is properly filled by principles underlying the CISG.

3.   UNIDROIT Principle 6.2.3 reflects these principles.

Each step is questionable. Considering step 3 first, here is how the Court justifies taking it: "Thus, to fill the gaps in a uniform manner[,] adhesion[ ] should be sought with the general principles which govern the law of international trade. Under these principles, as incorporated *inter alia* in the Unidroit Principles of International Commercial Contracts [Principle 6.2.3(1)], the party who invokes changed circumstances that fundamentally disturb the contractual balance . . . is also entitled to claim the renegotiation of the contract." This statement misreads Article 7(2). The Article requires resort to principles on which the CISG is based, not on general principles which "govern the law of international trade." The difference is important, because the CISG's underlying principles may be different from the principles operative in international trade. For instance, the compromise needed to ensure the CISG's wide adoption might require that the CISG's underlying principles be only a subset of principles at work in the trade. Innovations in international trade after the drafting of the CISG might even produce different principles governing international transactions than underlie the CISG. The Court identifies the wrong reference principles. In addition, UNIDROIT's Principles merely reflect the hardship doctrine in some civil law systems. Hardship doctrine is not so prevalent across legal systems for it to be among the (unspecified) general principles underlying the CISG or inferred from its provisions. The doctrine is unknown to common law systems, for example. In fact, practitioners sometimes advise adding an arbitration clause to contracts that incorporate the UNIDROIT Principles, fearing that common law courts will refuse to alter the contract's terms in response to an event of hardship. Even international contracts that contain their own hardship clauses frequently allow only for termination of the contract, not judicial adjustment of its terms. For these reasons, it would be surprising if significant legal principles foreign to the legal systems of a number of the CISG's signatories or contract practice underlie the CISG.

Step 2 is not inevitable even if the CISG contains an internal gap concerning hardship relief. Article 7(2) allows recourse to principles bearing on hardship relief underlying the CISG only if there are such principles. In the absence of these principles, Article 7(2)'s final clause requires that the internal gap be filled "in conformity with the applicable by virtue of the rules of private international law." Because the CISG's underlying principles do not support the hardship doctrine, the doctrine applies only if part of the domestic law selected by applicable principles of private international law (conflict of laws). This was the position taken by the intermediate appellate court in *Scafom*. Applying Article 7(2)'s final clause, the court found that Belgium's rules of private international law led to the application of French law. French decisional law apparently recognizes hardship relief where the party requesting it has acted in good faith.

Recourse to applicable domestic law or general principles underlying the CISG is proper only if the CISG contains an internal gap with respect to hardship relief. Step 1 asserts that there is an internal gap. However, more likely there is no gap at all. Article 79(1) deals with intervening events that occur between the conclusion of the contract and its performance, which affect the contract's value. It describes the requirements that must be met to exempt an obligor from liability for damages for nonperformance. The Article's drafters, well aware of differing domestic excuse doctrine, went out of their way to draft the

Article in terminology foreign to domestic law. Article 79 was controversial and its language discussed at different points in the Article's drafting. See Peter Schlechtriem, Commentary on the UN Convention on the International Sale of Goods (CISG) 601–602 (2d ed. 1998) (describing drafting history). If hardship relief were available under the CISG, it therefore would likely be found in Article 79. The relief would not be left to "general principles" underlying the CISG. Thus, a fair inference from the absence of hardship relief in Article 79(1) is that the Article displaces hardship doctrines, whether under applicable domestic law or the CISG. In Article 7(2)'s terms, Article 79(1) therefore "expressly settles" the matter of the continued availability of hardship relief—by making it unavailable. There is no gap in the CISG with respect to hardship doctrine.

A final position on the continued role of hardship doctrine under the CISG cannot be easily dismissed. Article 4(a) excludes from the CISG's scope "the validity of the contract or any of its provisions or of any usage." Issues of validity instead are resolved by applicable domestic sale law. (Article 4's exception for matters of validity "expressly provided" for in the CISG can be ignored here.) Thus, if hardship doctrine is a matter of validity under Article 4 and applicable domestic law deems hardship to invalidate the contract, the doctrine still applies to contracts governed by the CISG. In Professor Joseph Lookofsky's view, hardship doctrine is a matter of validity under Article 4. See Joseph Lookofsky, Not Running Wild with the CISG, 29 J. L. & Comm. 1, 16–28 (2011). Accordingly, on this view hardship doctrine continues to be available when applicable domestic law deems contracts invalid in response to an event of hardship. In Lookofsky's favor, Article 79(1) cannot be read to preempt such domestic law, because it concerns validity, which none of the CISG's provisions address. On the other hand, the position places a lot of weight on the precision of the notion of validity—perhaps too much. The trouble here, as discussed in Chapter 2, is that the CISG leaves the notion undefined and even unillustrated. Apart from easy cases such as fraud and incompetence, the application of the term is murky. It is far from clear that hardship doctrine is a matter of validity under the CISG. Clearly, domestic law labels cannot be conclusive. Otherwise, the label "validity" could defeat application of any of the CISG's provisions. For instance, domestic law might provide that a contract or contractual provision that calls for interest on payment of the contract price in arrears is "invalid." Article 78 nonetheless entitles the obligee to interest in these circumstances. Seemingly, domestic law's no-interest rule continues to apply, trumping Article 78. In addition, the position requires some way of determining when a domestic law rule is a matter of validity, when domestic law does not itself supply the label. The vagueness of the notion under the CISG makes validity an uncertain (and possibly weak) basis for applying hardship doctrine to contracts governed by the CISG.

CHAPTER 8

RISK OF LOSS

Goods may be damaged, destroyed or stolen. If one of these events occurs before the sales contract is concluded, the seller of course bears the loss. If damage, destruction or theft occurs after goods have been sold and delivered, the seller or the buyer bears the loss. The seller bears the loss if the damage or destruction results from a breach of the seller's warranty as to the goods. In all other cases, the buyer bears the loss after the goods have been delivered. Between the time the contract is concluded and the time the goods have been delivered, the goods may be damaged, destroyed or stolen. Sales law allocates the financial responsibility for the loss between the seller and buyer when one of these events occurs. It does so through a set of "risk of loss" rules. As with most rules of sale law, risk of loss rules are default rules; the sales contract can and often does alter them. Although the parties can shift the loss to third parties through insurance, sales law rules allocate loss between the seller and buyer.

A risk of loss is a cost to the contracting party exposed to it. The party exposed to the risk can deal with it in three ways: The party can bear the risk ("self-insure"), shift it through insurance or reduce its likelihood or impact by taking precautions. An efficient allocation of the risk of loss puts the risk on the contracting party who is in the best position to bear it, insure against it or avoid the loss. Putting the risk on this party optimally reduces the cost of the risk and therefore maximizes the net gains from the contract. As a result, if the contracting parties faced no bargaining costs, they would agree to allocate the risk of loss to the party in the superior position with respect to it. By allocating the risk in this way, the party in the superior position to deal with the risk has an incentive to take advantage of its position by caring for or insuring the goods. Usually, the contracting party who possesses or controls the goods can best reduce or avoid loss to them. In addition, the party in control often has more accurate information about the probability of loss to the goods, as well as its impact. This advantage in the measurement of risk and loss lowers the cost of obtaining insurance covering the goods.

National laws differ considerably in their basic risk of loss rules, even within common and civil law systems. See Alan Watson, Legal Transplants 83–87 (2d ed. 1993). Some countries adopt the Roman law rule, according to which risk of loss passes to the buyer at the conclusion of the contract; title to the goods passes on delivery of the goods. See Louis F. van Huyssteen et al., Contract Law in South Africa 222 (para. 540) (2010); Swiss Federal Code of Obligations § 185, Japanese Civil Code § 534(1). Under the law of other countries risk of loss and title passes to the buyer on delivery. See German Civil Code (BGB) § 446. The sales law of some countries makes passage of risk follow title, so that risk passes to the buyer when it acquires title. See English Sale of Goods Act § 20 (1979). The UCC and the CISG do not transfer risk of loss at the conclusion of the contract or transfer of ownership (title) in the goods. Instead, they identify different situations and state risk of loss rules for them, described below. These rules generally allocate risk to the party that has control or dominion over the goods, or control over others who themselves control the goods. The considerable diversity in risk of loss rules across nations is puzzling. The variety of rules might indicate reasonable disagreement over the efficiency effects of control over the goods.

Risk of loss rules must assign the financial responsibility for the loss in four different situations. In the first situation, the loss occurs while the seller remains in possession of the goods. In the second situation, the loss occurs while the goods are in possession of a third party bailee. The third situation, a specific instance of the second situation, is one in which the loss occurs while the goods are being transported to the buyer by a third party carrier. In the fourth situation, the loss occurs after the goods have been delivered to the buyer but before it has accepted them. Both the UCC and the CISG allocate risk of loss in each of these situations.

A. THE UCC'S RISK OF LOSS RULES

Article 2's risk of loss rules appear in 2–509 and 2–510, and 2A–219 contains the rule applicable to leases. As discussed below, 2-509 typically puts the risk of loss on the party in control of the goods on the assumption that it is best positioned to avoid the loss. Comment 3 to 2–509 identifies the control rationale underlying 2–509(3), 2–509's principal risk of loss provision: ". . . [T]he underlying theory of this rule is that a merchant who is to make physical delivery at his own place continues meanwhile to control the goods and can be expected to insure his interest in them. The buyer, on the other hand, has no control of the goods and it is extremely unlikely that he will carry insurance on goods not yet in his possession." The typical fire and casualty insurance policy available to sellers covers the contents of specified buildings, which would include inventory already sold or held for sale. Rather than instructing courts to place the loss on the party in the superior position to avoid or insure against it, 2–509 allocates risk of loss in circumstances described in 2–509(1)–(3).

1. LOSS WHEN THE SELLER RETAINS THE GOODS

Section 2–509(3) is 2–509's residual rule. It applies when none of 2–509's other rules allocating risk of loss apply ("In any case not within subsection (1) or (2) . . . "). Section 2–509(1) allocates loss when the sales contract calls for the seller to ship the goods by carriage, and 2–509(2) allocates it when the goods are being held by a bailee and are to be delivered without being moved. Thus, 2–509(3) allocates risk of loss when the seller retains the goods and is to deliver them to the buyer. Under the first part of 2–509(3), risk of loss passes to the buyer when it receives the goods if the seller is a merchant. This part of 2–509(3)'s rule is clear. "Receipt" requires physical possession of the goods; 2–103(1)(c). Thus, if the seller is a merchant, risk of loss passes to the buyer when it takes possession of the goods and therefore has control over them.

The second part of 2–509(3) provides that if the seller is not a merchant, risk of loss passes on tender of delivery. This part of the rule is less clear. Under 2–503(1), tender of delivery requires the seller to hold conforming goods at the buyer's disposition and give the buyer notification "reasonably necessary" for the buyer to take delivery. The goods must be kept available during this period; 2–503(1)(a). However, the subsection does not say when tender of delivery occurs. It only sets the requirements for tender. There are therefore two possibilities. Tender of delivery could occur at the time when the seller makes the goods available to the buyer, enabling it to take delivery, and gives the buyer the necessary notification. Call this point in time "tender on availability." Alternatively, tender could occur at the time the buyer breaches by not taking delivery after the seller has made the goods available and the requisite notice has been given. Call this point in time "tender on breach." Section 2–503(1) does not say whether tender of delivery occurs when goods are made available or when the buyer breaches by not taking delivery. The omission makes the second part of 2–509(3)'s rule sometimes hard to apply. For instance, assume that a buyer purchases a painting from a non-merchant seller at the seller's home. The seller and buyer agree that the buyer can retrieve the painting from the seller's home between January 1 and January 6, between 9 am and 5 pm. The painting is destroyed in a fire at the seller's home at 1 pm on January 3. Is the seller or the buyer responsible for the loss? The buyer bears the risk of loss only if the risk had passed to it as of 10 am on January 3. Under the "tender on availability" timing, tender of delivery occurred on January 1 (at 10 am). In this case risk of loss passed to the buyer on that date, before the painting was destroyed and therefore the buyer would bear the loss. By the "tender on breach" timing, tender of delivery occurs on the date at which the buyer breaches by not taking delivery. That date was January 6 (at 5 pm), the last day the buyer was entitled to pick up the painting from the seller. In this case the seller would tender delivery of the painting on January 6. The painting was destroyed before tender of delivery occurred, at the time the seller bore the loss.

Section 2–509's "best positioned to avoid loss" rationale might be in conflict with 2–503(1)'s language. A seller who retains possession of the goods is in a better position with respect to loss than the buyer, as matter of both control and insurance. This remains true even when the seller holds the goods at the buyer's disposition and has given the buyer reasonable notification. In fact, it argues for finding that tender does not occur until the buyer receives the goods. Section 9–503(1) does not allow this last conclusion, however, and it would eliminate the difference between tender and receipt of the goods, which 2–509(3) requires. But 2–509's underlying rationale at least supports delaying the start of the tender period, so that tender of delivery occurs under 2–503(1) when the buyer breaches by not taking delivery. Alternatively, 2–503(1)'s language could be read so that tender of delivery occurs at the beginning of the tender period. After all, 2–503(1) states requirements for tender, not breach, and it is plausible to find that tender occurs when the seller first meets those requirements. This reading would pass risk to the buyer under 2–509(3) even before the buyer takes possession of the goods. Proposed 2–509(3) eliminates the second part of 2–509(3). Thus, under the proposed rule, risk of loss passes on the buyer's receipt of the goods, whether the seller is a merchant or a non-merchant. It thereby avoids the need to determine when tender of delivery occurs.

The default rule for leases is different from 2–509(3)'s residual rule. Under 2A–219(1), except in the case of a finance lease, risk of loss remains with the lessor. It does not pass to the lessee even when the lessee receives the leased goods. This default rule may or may not be consistent with the rationale underlying 2–509's risk of loss rules. Arguments can be made on both sides. On the one hand, the lessor might be better positioned than the lessee to avoid loss to the goods. The lessor, who has experience with the leased goods, can use the information acquired to take precautions to avoid loss, even when the loss occurs while the goods are in the lessee's possession. By comparison, a lessee in a short-term lease has less information about the goods it can use to avoid the loss. Perhaps more importantly, the lessor has cost advantage in obtaining insurance. The lessor's experience with the goods gives it a more accurate actuarial basis on which to assess the risk of loss. It therefore can measure the expected value of the loss more accurately than the lessee. In addition, a lessor can take advantage of lower costs in arranging for insurance that come with insuring the range of goods it offers for lease. On the other hand, the lessee's possession of the goods might on balance give it an advantage at avoiding or insuring against loss, even taking into account other factors that favor the lessor. Significantly, most leases contain clauses shifting the risk of loss to the lessee after it accepts the goods. See, e.g., 1 Equipment Leasing ¶ 6.02[6][a] (at 6–11) (B. Dubin & J. Wong eds., 2004) (sample middle market master lease). Predominant contract practice is good evidence that an assignment of risk is efficient. This suggests that the cost associated with risk of loss is most often minimized when the lessee bears the risk. The "best positioned to avoid" rationale therefore argues against 2A–219(1)'s default rule. Both the argument for and against the rule seem strong.

The "best positioned to avoid" rationale clearly supports 2A–219(1)'s exception for finance leases. Finance lessors usually are financing companies or banks. Neither knows much about the goods they lease because they do not select, manufacturer or supply them. 2A–103(1)(g)(i). In fact, as a mere source of financing, the finance lessor will know less about the goods than the finance lessee, who selects them or approves the contract by which the lessor purchased them for lease. 2A–103(1)(g)(iii)(B). The finance lessor's inexperience with the goods puts it in a comparatively poor position to take precautions against loss. For the same reason, its inexperience gives it a poor basis for making reliable estimates of expected loss. Thus, the finance lessor does not have lower measurement costs that might make it a superior insurer to the lessee. By contrast, the lessee, not the finance lessor, has possession of the leased good during the lease term. The lessee's possession makes it well placed to use its superior information about the goods to avoid loss. Section 2A–219's default rule allocating risk to the lessee in a finance lease is consistent with this conclusion.

2.   LOSS WHEN THE GOODS ARE HELD BY A BAILEE

Goods may be sold while being held by a third party, usually a bailee such as a warehouseman. If the contract calls for the goods to be delivered without being moved from the bailee's premises, risk of loss passes to the buyer under 2–509(2) on the first of three events. First, risk of loss passes when the buyer receives possession or control of a negotiable document of title covering the goods. Rights in goods covered by a negotiable document are merged with the document, so that possession or control of the document gives control over the goods. See 7–502. Thus, the buyer controls the goods once it receives the negotiable document covering them. Second, risk of loss passes when the bailee acknowledges the buyer's right to possess the goods. Third, risk of loss passes when the buyer receives a non-negotiable document of title covering the goods or other written direction to deliver the goods and has had a reasonable time to present the document or direction to the bailee. See 9–503(4)(b). Receipt of the non-negotiable document constitutes tender of the goods covered by it under 2–503(4)(b), and the bailee's refusal to honor the document presented to it or direction for delivery defeats the tender. Thus, a bailee's agreement to honor the document or direction gives the buyer control over the goods. Therefore, once both events have occurred, the risk of loss passes to the buyer. However, if the bailee refuses to honor the document or direction given to it, the tender is defeated. The bailee's refusal to honor gives the buyer no control over the goods and prevents risk of loss from passing to it.

Sellers sometimes argue that they are bailees for purposes of 2–509(2). If the sales contract does not call for the seller to deliver the goods by moving them, the seller will urge that 2–509(2)(b) applies. Because the seller inevitably will have acknowledged the buyer's right to possession of the goods, it will conclude that its acknowledgment transfers the risk of loss to the buyer. Courts reject the argument that sellers are bailees under 2–509(2). Although Article 2 leaves "bailee" undefined, courts require that bailees be persons in the business of storing goods for hire-in other words, professional bailees. See Martins v. Meland's Inc., 283 N.W.2d 78 (N.D. 1979); Caudle v. Sherrard Motor Co., 525 S.W.2d 238 (Tex. Ct. App. 1975). The requirement is supported by Article 7 of the UCC's definition of "bailee" (7–102(1)), which essentially applies only to professional bailees. More important, allowing sellers to be bailees for 2–509(2)'s purposes makes no sense. It renders 2–509(3)'s residual risk of loss rule always inapplicable when the contract calls for the seller to deliver the goods without moving them. This is because sellers will always have acknowledged the buyer's right to possession of the goods, either in the sales contract or otherwise. Section 2–509(2)(b), if applicable, therefore passes risk to the buyer on the acknowledgment. If 2–509(2)(b) applies, 2–509(3)'s residual rule is inapplicable. As a result, the buyer has the risk of loss even before the seller tenders the goods or the buyer receives them. The UCC's drafters almost certainly did not intend this result. Limiting bailees to professional bailees excludes sellers and gets the intended (and defensible) result.

3. LOSS WHEN THE GOODS ARE IN TRANSIT

The sales contract often will call for or allow the seller to ship the goods by carrier. "Carrier" means an independent carrier: an entity other than the seller who will transport the goods. Cf. 7–

102(a)(2)(" 'carrier' means a person that issues a bill of lading"); United Nations Convention on Contracts for the International Carriage of Goods Wholly or Partly by Sea Art. 1(5) (" 'carrier' means a person that enters into a contract of carriage with a shipper") (2008). A seller who itself is to transport the goods to the buyer or other placed designated by the contract is not a "carrier." Although it transports the goods, 2–509(1)'s risk of loss rule applies only when the contract requires or allows the seller to ship the goods "by carrier." Because a seller who itself transports the goods does not ship them "by carrier," 2–509(1) is inapplicable. Instead, the seller will be deemed to retain possession of the goods and therefore 2–509(3)'s residual rule rather than 2–509(1)'s "carrier" rule applies.

There are two sorts of contracts of carriage: a "shipment" contract and a "destination" (or "arrival") contract. Section 2–509(1) recognizes both of them, and states different risk of loss rules corresponding to each. A "shipment" contract does not require the seller to deliver the goods to "a particular destination." Instead, it requires the seller to arrange a reasonable contract with the carrier for the transport of the goods. In addition, the seller must place the goods in the carrier's possession. 2–504(a). Importantly, under a shipment contract the seller bears the cost of delivering the goods to the carrier; the buyer bears the costs of carriage to the destination. The phrase "shipment contract" is unhappy because it suggests that the seller is not obligated to arrange to have the goods delivered to a particular destination, just to ship them. This of course is misleading: All shipments are destined for a particular destination. A "destination" contract requires the seller to deliver the goods to "a particular destination." The seller bears the cost of delivering the goods to the named place, including the costs of carriage. Sometimes the sales contract is unclear as to whether it calls for a shipment or destination contract. The presumption is that, absent contrary indication, a shipment contract is called for. Comment 5 to 2–503; see Stampede Presentation Prods., Inc. v. Productive Transp., Inc., 80 UCC Rep. Serv.2d 927 (W.D.N.Y. 2013).

Section 2–509(1)(a) allocates risk of loss when the sales contract calls for or permits a shipment contract. The subsection passes risk of loss to the buyer when the seller has duly delivered the goods to the carrier. Thus, under a shipment contract the buyer bears any loss to the goods that occurs while they are in transit. The requirement that the goods be "duly delivered" is important. Due delivery requires the seller to have arranged a reasonable carriage contract with the carrier and deliver the goods in accordance with the sales contract. If these vague terms are not met, 2–509(1)(a)'s rule does not apply to shift the risk of loss to the buyer. Section 2–509(1)(b) allocates risk of loss when the sales contract requires a destination contract. The subsection passes risk of loss to the buyer when the goods are duly tendered while in the carrier's possession at the destination.

The sales contract can expressly provide for the allocation of costs and risks in bringing the goods to the destination designated by the buyer. However, in many cases contracts instead incorporate abbreviations for shipment terms. These abbreviations are short-hand ways of allocating shipment costs and risk as well as other matters. Both the UCC and the International Chamber of Commerce's

International Commercial Terms ("Incoterms") define these abbreviations. A commonly used shipment term is "F.O.B." ("Free On Board"). For instance, a shipment term "F.O.B. place of shipment" (such as the city in which the seller is located) in the sales contract indicates that the parties intend a shipment contract, since no particular destination appears in the shipment term. Under 2–319(a) the seller bears the expense and risk of putting the goods into the possession of the carrier at the place of shipment. This allocates to the buyer the risk of loss to the goods in transit, after they are put into the carrier's possession. Section 2–319(a) therefore replicates 2–509(1)(a)'s risk of loss rule. Similarly, with the shipment term "F.O.B. vessel" (or other vehicle), the seller bears the cost and risk of bringing the goods to the named vessel or other vehicle and loading them. 2–319(1)(c). Risk of loss therefore passes to the buyer once the goods have been loaded. By contrast, if the shipment term is "F.O.B. place of destination" (such as the city in which the buyer is located), 2–319(b) puts on the seller the expense and risk of transporting the goods to that place and tendering delivery of them there. Because the risk of loss does not pass to the buyer until tender, in this case the seller bears the risk of loss while the goods are in transit. Section 2–319(b) therefore replicates 2–509(1)(b)'s risk of loss rule.

As should be apparent, shipment terms not only allocate the risk of loss in transporting the goods. They also allocate the cost of carriage and in some cases other services. A price always appears with a shipment term, such as "$100 F.O.B. New York" (the point of shipment). Under this term the $100 contract price includes the cost of delivering the goods to New York. The seller must arrange a reasonable contract of carriage, as 2–504(a) requires. However, because the F.O.B. term calls for a shipment contract, the buyer is responsible for freight and other costs, such as insurance and import licenses. If the seller pays the freight costs from New York, the place of shipment, the payment is for the buyer's account. Other shipment terms can allocate freight and other costs to the seller. "$100 C.I.F. Southhampton" (the port of destination) means that the $100 contract price includes the cost of delivering the goods to Southhampton and insuring the cargo. Under the C.I.F. term ("Cost, insurance and freight"), the cost of cargo insurance and freight is at the seller's expense. A C.I.F. term passes risk of loss to the buyer after the goods are put into the carrier's possession at the port of shipment. 2–320(2).

Developments in international trade have made the meaning of some shipment terms confusing. Incoterms are frequently used in international sales contracts, often being expressly incorporated into them. Incoterms defines a range of shipment terms, and the International Chamber of Commerce (ICC) updates their meanings in response to technological changes in international trade or perceived shortcomings in existing definition. Some Incoterms have no counterparts under Article 2 of the UCC. Others have definitions that are inconsistent with the UCC's definitions. For instance, an F.O.B. term under Incoterms is limited to F.O.B. named port of shipment. See ICC, Incoterms 2010 ("F.O.B."). An F.O.B. port of arrival (destination) has no meaning under Incoterms. Therefore, under Incoterms an F.O.B. term can create only a shipment contract, not a destination contract. This is not true under 2–319(1), which provides that an F.O.B. term can refer to any "named place." In addition, Incoterms limits the F.O.B. term to waterborne transportation. Thus, F.O.B. truck or car has no meaning under the Incoterms definition. Section 2–319(1)(c) does not restrict the F.O.B. definition to waterborne transportation. Finally, the Incoterms definition of F.O.B. passes risk to the buyer at a precise point: when the goods pass the ship's rail at the port of shipment. See ICC, Incoterms 2000 ("F.O.B."), A5. Passage of risk under 2–319(1)(c)'s counterpart term is less clear: risk is transferred when the goods have been loaded on the vessel at the port of shipment. Some courts consider the ship's rail to be an impractical point at which to shift risk. See, e.g., Pyrene v. Scindia Navigation, [1954] 2 Q.B. 402, 419 ("Only the most enthusiastic lawyer could watch with satisfaction the spectacle of liabilities shifting uneasily as the cargo sways at the end of a derrick across a notional perpendicular projecting from the ship's rail.") Incoterms 2010 apparently agrees. It transfers risk under an F.O.B. term at the point the goods have been loaded on board; see ICC, Incoterms 2010, B5, A4. Where the sales contract or trade usage is clear, the discrepancy between Incoterms and Article 2's definitions causes no difficulty. In other cases the discrepancy causes confusion. Proposed Article 2 eliminates the discrepancy by dropping definitions of shipment terms.

4. RISK OF LOSS ON BREACH

Under 2–510, breach alters the risk of loss allocated by 2–509. Section 2–510 places the risk of loss on the breaching party in three situations described by 2–510(1)–(3). The first two situations involve the seller's breach, and the third involves breach by the buyer. In the first situation the seller tenders goods that so fail to conform to the contract as to give the buyer a right to reject them. Section 2–510(1) keeps the risk of loss on the seller until cure or acceptance. Because the perfect tender rule gives the buyer the right to reject if the goods fail to conform in any respect to the contract, any uncured nonconformity leaves the risk of loss with the seller until the buyer accepts the goods. See Comment 2 to 2–106.

The second situation occurs when the buyer rightfully revokes its acceptance after discovering a non-conformity. Section 2–510(2) entitles the buyer to treat the risk of loss as resting on the seller from the beginning, to the extent of any deficiency in the buyer's insurance coverage. For instance, assume that the buyer rightfully revokes its acceptance of goods valued at $100 and that its insurance covers 25% of the value of the goods. Assume also that the goods are destroyed by a fire at the buyer's place of business, without the buyer's fault, before the seller can retrieve them. Under 2–510(2) the seller bears the risk of loss to the extent of $75, the deficiency in the buyer's insurance coverage, and the buyer bears the $25 insured portion of the loss. (The buyer's insurer ultimately bears the buyer's $25 loss.) The third situation occurs when the buyer breaches before the risk of loss has passed to it. Under 2–501(3) the seller may treat the risk of loss as resting on the buyer for a commercially reasonable period, to the extent of the deficiency in the seller's insurance coverage.

The meaning of the term "deficiency" as used in the second and third situations is clarified in the comments to 2-510. Comment 3 to 2–

510 states that "[t]he 'deficiency' referred to in the text [of 2–510(2) and (3)] means such deficiency in the insurance coverage as exists without subrogation. This section merely distributes the risk of loss as stated and is not intended to be disturbed by any subrogation of an insurer." This Comment assures that the breacher bears the uninsured portion of the loss (the "deficiency") and the insurer ultimately bears the insured portion of the loss. To illustrate, in the last example 2–510(2) allocates the $75 uninsured portion of the $100 loss to the breaching seller and the $25 insured portion of the loss to the buyer. The buyer in turn is indemnified by its insurer in the amount of $25. If the buyer's insurer were subrogated to the buyer's rights against the seller for the $25 loss, the insurer could recover $25 from the seller. In that case the breaching seller ultimately would bear the entire $100 loss. Comment 3 prevents the buyer's insurer from being subrogated to the buyer's rights against the seller. Thus, the insurer cannot recover the $25 loss from the seller, and the loss therefore is distributed between the seller ($75) and the insurer ($25).

Section 2–510's rules are inefficient. Breach has nothing to do with which party is best positioned to avoid or insure against loss. The party in possession or control of the goods is in the superior position to do so. This is the rationale underlining 2–509(3)'s transfer of risk of loss to the buyer when it receives the goods. Comment 3 to 2–509. The buyer's advantage with respect to avoiding or insuring against loss is unaffected by breach. Thus, breach should not prevent risk of loss from passing to the buyer. In keeping risk of loss or a portion of it on a party who no longer has possession or control of the goods, 2–510 increases the cost of performance. Although commentators have recommended that 2–510 be repealed (see PEB Study Group, Uniform Commercial Code Article 2: Preliminary Report 149 (1990)), Proposed Article 2 retained the section. Louisiana has not adopted Article 2 of the Uniform Commercial Code. Its statutory law dealing with risk of loss in sales contracts provides as follows:

The risk of loss of the thing sold owing to a fortuitous event is transferred from the seller to the buyer at the time of delivery.

That risk is so transferred even when the seller has delivered a nonconforming thing, unless the buyer acts in the manner required to dissolve the contract.

La. Civ. Code Art. 2467 (2011).

B. APPLICATIONS OF THE RISK OF LOSS RULES

Section 2–509(4) allows the parties to vary 2–509's rules by contrary agreement. Article 2A's drafters did not include a similar provision in 2A–219 for leases, apparently because they thought it "not necessary." 2A–219 Purposes. Lease agreements frequently allocate risk of loss differently than under 2A–219. See 1 Equipment Leasing ¶ 3.08[1] (at 3–48) (B.A. Dubin & J.J. Wong eds., 2004). With few exceptions inapplicable to risk of loss, 1–302(a) permits parties to vary by agreement any UCC provision. Parties to a lease therefore can opt out of 2A–219's allocation of risk of loss. Thus, 2A–219 states a default rule for leases. None of the agreements in the three cases below opt out of the UCC's default rules applicable to them. Two of the cases involve sales transactions to which 2–509 or 2–510 applies; the third involves a lease to which 2A–219 applies.

Jason's Foods, Inc. v. Peter Eckrich & Sons, Inc.

United States Court of Appeals, Seventh Circuit, 1985
774 F.2d 214

■ POSNER, CIRCUIT JUDGE.

The jurisdictional question that led us to order a limited remand in Jason's Foods, Inc. v. Peter Eckrich & Sons, Inc., 768 F.2d 189 (7th Cir. 1985), has been answered by the district judge: the defendant's principal place of business is Indiana, so there is diversity jurisdiction, and we can proceed to the merits of the appeal. Section 2–509(2) of the Uniform Commercial Code as adopted in Illinois (whose law, the parties agree, governs this diversity suit) provides that where "goods are held by a bailee to be delivered without being moved, the risk of loss passes to the buyer . . . (b) on acknowledgment by the bailee of the buyer's right to possession of the goods." Ill. Rev. Stat. ch. 26, para. 2–509(2). We must decide whether acknowledgment to the seller complies with the statute. There are no reported cases on the question, either in Illinois or elsewhere. Three commentators have opined that acknowledgment must be to the buyer, but without discussion. See Nordstrom, Handbook of the Law of Sales 404–05 (1970); Howard, Allocation of Risk of Loss Under the UCC: A Transactional Evaluation of Sections 2–509 and 2–510, 15 UCC L.J. 334, 347 n. 42 (1983); Comment, Risk of Loss Under Section 2509 of the California Uniform Commercial Code, 20 UCLA L. Rev. 1352, 1358 n. 30 (1973). The defendant submitted in the district court an affidavit from a professor of commercial law at Ohio State University (Professor Clovis), who also concluded, also without elaboration, that acknowledgment must be to the buyer. The plaintiff did not question the admissibility of expert testimony on a pure issue of domestic law—though well it might have [a]n alternative procedure would have been for the district judge to invite a disinterested expert on commercial law to submit a brief as amicus curiae. See Code of Judicial Conduct for United States Judges, Canon 3 (A) (4) and commentary thereto.

On or about December 30, 1982, Jason's Foods contracted to sell 38,000 pounds of "St. Louis style" pork ribs to Peter Eckrich & Sons, delivery to be effected by a transfer of the ribs from Jason's account in an independent warehouse to Eckrich's account in the same warehouse—which is to say, without the ribs actually being moved. In its confirmation of the deal, Jason's notified Eckrich that the transfer in storage would be made between January 10 and January 14. On January 13 Jason's phoned the warehouse and requested that the ribs be transferred to Eckrich's account. A clerk at the warehouse noted the transfer on its books immediately but did not mail a warehouse receipt until January 17 or January 18, and it was not till Eckrich received the receipt on January 24 that it knew the transfer had taken place. But on January 17 the ribs had been destroyed by a fire at the warehouse. Jason's sued Eckrich for the price. If the risk of loss passed on January 13 when the ribs were transferred to Eckrich's account, or at least before the fire, Jason's is entitled to recover the contract price;

otherwise not. The district judge ruled that the risk of loss did not pass by then and therefore granted summary judgment for Eckrich.

Jason's argues that when the warehouse transferred the ribs to Eckrich's account, Jason's lost all rights over the ribs, and it should not bear the risk of loss of goods it did not own or have any right to control. Eckrich owned them and Eckrich's insurance covered any ribs that it owned; Jason's had no insurance and anyway, Jason's argues, it could not insure what it no longer owned. (The warehouse would be liable for the fire damage only if negligent. Finally, Jason's points out that the draftsmen of the Uniform Commercial Code were careful and deliberate. Both subsections (a) and (c) of section 2–509(2)—the subsections that surround the "acknowledgment" provision at issue in this case—provide that the risk of loss passes to the buyer on or after "his receipt" of a document of title (negotiable in (a), nonnegotiable in (c)). If the draftsmen had meant that the acknowledgment of the buyer's right to possession of the goods—the acknowledgment that is subsection (b)'s substitute for a document of title—must be to the buyer, they would have said so.

Eckrich argues with great vigor that it cannot be made to bear the loss of goods that it does not know it owns. But that is not so outre a circumstance as it may sound. If you obtain property by inheritance, you are quite likely to own it before you know you own it. And Eckrich's position involves a comparable paradox: that Jason's continued to bear the risk of loss of goods that it knew it no longer owned. So the case cannot be decided by reference to what the parties knew or did not know; and neither can it be decided, despite Jason's urgings, on the basis of which party could have insured against the loss. Both could have. Jason's had sufficient interest in the ribs until then. You do not have to own goods to insure them; it is enough that you will suffer a loss if they are lost or damaged, as of course Jason's would if the risk of loss remained on it after it parted with title. Section 2–509(2) separates title from risk of loss. Title to the ribs passed to Eckrich when the warehouse made the transfer on its books from Jason's' account to Eckrich's but the risk of loss did not pass until the transfer was "acknowledged."

Thus, as is usually the case, insurability cannot be used to guide the assignment of liability. (The costs of insurance might sometimes be usable for its purpose, as we shall see, but not in this case.) Since whoever will be liable for the loss can insure against it, the court must determine who is liable before knowing who can insure, rather than vice versa. If acknowledgment to the seller is enough to place the risk of loss on the buyer, then Eckrich should have bought insurance against any losses that occurred afterward. If acknowledgment to the buyer is necessary (we need not decide whether acknowledgment to a third party may ever suffice), Jason's should have bought insurance against any losses occurring until then.

The suggestion that the acknowledgment contemplated by subsection (b) can be to the seller seems very strange. What purpose would it serve? When Jason's called up the warehouse and directed that the transfer be made, it did not add: and by the way, acknowledge to me when you make the transfer. Jason's assumed, correctly, that the transfer was being made forthwith; and in fact there is no suggestion that the warehouse clerk ever "acknowledged" the transfer to Jason's. If the draftsmen of subsection (b) had meant the risk of loss to pass when the transfer was made, one would think they would have said so, and not complicated life by requiring "acknowledgment."

A related section of the Uniform Commercial Code, section 2–503(4)(a), makes acknowledgment by the bailee (the warehouse here) a method of tendering goods that are sold without being physically moved; but, like section 2–509(2)(b), it does not indicate to whom acknowledgment must be made. The official comments on this section, however, indicate that it was not intended to change the corresponding section of the Uniform Sales Act, section 43(3). See UCC comment 6 to § 2–503. And section 43(3) had expressly required acknowledgment to the buyer. Rules on tender have, it is true, a different function from rules on risk of loss; they determine at what point the seller has completed the performance of his side of the bargain. He may have completed performance, but if the goods are still in transit the risk of loss does not shift until the buyer receives them, if the seller is a merchant. See UCC § 2–509(3) and UCC comment 3 to section 2–509. In the case of warehouse transfers, however, the draftsmen apparently wanted risk of loss to conform to the rules for tender. For comment 4 to section 2–509 states that "where the agreement provides for delivery of the goods as between the buyer and seller without removal from the physical possession of a bailee, the provisions on manner of tender of delivery apply on the point of transfer of risk." And those provisions as we have said apparently require (in the case where no document of title passes) acknowledgment to the buyer. The acknowledgment need not, by the way, be in writing, so far as we are aware. Jason's could have instructed the warehouse to call Eckrich when the transfer was complete on the warehouse's books. That is why Jason's case is not utterly demolished by the fact that the document of title—that is, the warehouse receipt—was not received by Eckrich till after the fire. Acknowledgment in a less formal manner is authorized; indeed, section 509(2)(b) would have no function if the only authorized form of acknowledgment were by document of title, whether negotiable or nonnegotiable.

The second sentence of comment 4 to section 509 is also suggestive: "Due delivery of a negotiable document of title covering the goods or acknowledgment by the bailee that he holds for the buyer completes the 'delivery' and passes the risk." The reference to a document of title is to subsections (a) and (c); and in both of those cases, of course, the tender involves notice to the buyer. It would be surprising if the alternative of acknowledgment did not.

All this may seem a rather dry textual analysis, remote from the purposes of the Uniform Commercial Code, so let us shift now to the plane of policy. The Code sought to create a set of standard contract terms that would reflect in the generality of cases the preferences of contracting parties at the time of contract. One such preference is for assignments of liability—or, what amounts to the same thing, assignments of the risk of loss—that create incentives to minimize the adverse consequences of untoward events such as (in this case) a warehouse fire. There are two ways of minimizing such consequences. One is to make them less painful by insuring against them. Insurance does not prevent a loss—it merely spreads it—but in doing so it reduces (for those who are risk averse) the disutility of the loss. So if one of the contracting parties can insure at lower cost than the other, this is an argument for placing the risk of loss on him, to give him an incentive to do so. But that as we have seen is not a factor in this case; either party could have insured (or have paid the warehouse to assume strict liability for loss or destruction of the goods, in which event the warehouse would have insured them), and so far as the record shows at equal cost.

The other method of minimizing the consequences of an unanticipated loss is through prevention of the loss. If one party is in a better position than the other to prevent it, this is a reason for placing the risk of loss on him, to give him an incentive to prevent it. It would be a reason for placing liability on a seller who still had possession of the goods, even though title had passed. But between the moment of transfer of title by Jason's and the moment of receipt of the warehouse receipt by Eckrich, neither party to the sale had effective control over the ribs. They were in a kind of limbo, until (to continue the Dantesque image) abruptly propelled into a hotter region. With Jason's having relinquished title and Eckrich not yet aware that it had acquired it, neither party had an effective power of control.

But this is not an argument for holding that the risk of loss shifted at the moment of transfer; it is just an argument for regarding the parties' positions as symmetrical from the standpoint of ability either to prevent or to shift losses. In such a case we have little to assist us besides the language of subsection (b) and its surrounding subsections and the UCC comments; but these materials do point pretty clearly to the conclusion that the risk of loss did not pass at the moment of transfer.

When did it pass? Does "acknowledgment" mean receipt, as in the surrounding subsections of 2–509 (2), or mailing? Since the evidence was in conflict over whether the acknowledgment was mailed on January 17 (and at what hour), which was the day of the fire, or on January 18, this could be an important question—but in another case. Jason's waived it. The only theory it tendered to the district court, or briefed and argued in this court, was that the risk of loss passed either on January 13, when the transfer of title was made on the books of the warehouse, or at the latest on January 14, because Eckrich knew the ribs would be transferred at the warehouse sometime between January 10 and 14. We have discussed the immateriality of the passage of title on January 13; we add that the alternative argument, that Eckrich knew by January 14 that it owned the ribs, exaggerates what Eckrich knew. By the close of business on January 14 Eckrich had a well-founded expectation that the ribs had been transferred to its account; but considering the many slips that are possible between cup and lips, we do not think that this expectation should fix the point at which the risk shifts. If you were told by an automobile dealer from whom you bought a car that the car would be delivered on January 14, you would not take out insurance effective that day, without waiting for the actual delivery.

Finally, Jason's argument from trade custom or usage is unavailing. The method of transfer that the parties used was indeed customary but there was no custom or usage on when the risk of loss passed to the buyer.

Affirmed.

Moser v. Conny
Ohio Court of Appeals, 2003
49 U.C.C. Rep. Serv.2d 1223

■ Opinion by: JUDGE JOSEPH J. VUKOVICH

* * *

Statement of Facts

In January 1998, Filnor, Inc. leased a 1997 Corvette through Lavery Chevrolet–Buick, Inc. in Alliance, Ohio for a two year term. The financing was provided by National City Bank, the lessor. Filnor was insured by State Farm. Soon thereafter, Filnor asked Lavery if it could help terminate the lease, but Lavery declined to assist. In July 1998, Filnor again asked Lavery for assistance in terminating the lease, and Lavery agreed to assist. On approximately July 7, 1998, Filnor brought the car to Lavery. On July 10, 1997, Lavery solicited defendant-appellant John Conny to test-drive the vehicle. Defendant-appellant, one of Lavery's good customers, was permitted to take the car without a salesperson for an unspecified length of time. That night, defendant-appellant drove the vehicle left of center on State Route 183 in Washington Township, colliding with the vehicle driven by plaintiff-appellee George Moser.

In June 1999, Moser filed a complaint against defendant-appellant, Lavery, and Nationwide Insurance Company, who was Moser's insurer. The complaint was later amended to add as defendants Filnor and two other insurance companies with whom Moser claimed to be insured. State Farm, who was Filnor's insurer, filed an intervening complaint for a declaratory judgment on three grounds. First, State Farm alleged that Filnor relinquished all insurable interest on the day Filnor surrendered the vehicle to Lavery and thus the policy terminated on that day. * * *

On April 27, 2001, defendant-appellant filed a motion for summary judgment on State Farm's complaint. He responded with the following arguments: the lease was still in effect, and thus, Filnor still had an insurable interest; he was driving as a permittee of a permittee; and he was not engaged in a car business. On May 8, 2001, the court denied various motions for summary judgment on these issues that had been filed by defendant-appellant, Nationwide, and others. The court found that Lavery became the owner for insurance purposes when Filnor dropped off the car. Thus, the court granted summary judgment in favor of State Farm with regards to State Farm's first argument and found State Farm's two remaining arguments moot. The court noted that not all issues in the case had been resolved.* * *

Assignment of Error

Appellant's sole assignment of error provides:

"THE TRIAL COURT ERRED AS A MATTER OF LAW IN DENYING APPELLANT'S MOTION FOR SUMMARY JUDGMENT AND IN FINDING THAT APPELLANT WAS NOT AN INSURED UNDER THE

STATE FARM POLICY ENTITLED TO COVERAGE FOR THE SUBJECT ACCIDENT."

This assignment of error is divided into the three alternative theories originally set forth by State Farm in its complaint for a declaratory judgment. The first sub-issue, which was the only one addressed by the trial court, asks: "At the time of the accident did Filnor (State Farm's insured) have an insurable interest in the Corvette?"

Filnor's lease agreement with National City Bank as the lessor provides that the lessee has no right to assign or sublease any rights or interests under the lease without the lessor's permission. The lease discloses the method and fees involved in early termination of a lease. The lease notes that the vehicle shall be returned to the lessor unless the purchase option is exercised. Here, National City Bank did not receive payment under the purchase option until mid-August 1998, one month after the alleged termination and accident, at which time Lavery provided the funds for the purchase.

The president of Lavery testified in a deposition that it was his intent to terminate the lease and relieve Filnor of all liability when he took possession of the car. He opined that he became the owner at that time. (We note it appears that his insurer had not reimbursed him for the value of the car as of the January 2000 deposition.) Nonetheless, he admitted that the president of Filnor agreed to reimburse Lavery for any losses sustained in the termination of the lease, but he claimed that he would not have asked for such reimbursement.

State Farm, Filnor's insurer, contends that transfer of possession of the car resulted in the loss of an insurable interest by Filnor. Appellant alleges that mere transfer of possession by a lessee does not result in a sale, an assignment, or a sublease. Appellant also points out that this is not a bona fide purchaser situation since Lavery was a dealer who was familiar with the lease agreement.

We first note that R.C. 4505.04(A) provides that no person acquiring a motor vehicle from its owner shall acquire any right, title, claim or interest until a certificate of title has been issued to that person and that possession plus consideration is not sufficient. Pure questions of ownership are answered with reference to this certificate of title law, instead of the Uniform Commercial Code. As appellee points out, however, the Supreme Court has held that the U.C.C., rather than the certificate of title law, applies to determine the owner of a vehicle for purposes of risk of loss/insurance coverage. Smith v. Nationwide Mut. Co. (1988), 524 N.E.2d 507.

Nevertheless, *Smith* is distinguishable from the case at hand. *Smith* dealt with the application of Section 2 of the U.C.C., or Chapter 1302 of the Ohio Revised Code. Those laws pertain to the sale of goods. The case before us deals with Section 2A of the U.C.C., or Chapter 1310 of the Ohio Revised Code. These laws pertain to the lease of goods. See R.C. 1310.02(A) (defining the scope of the chapter). There are clear differences in how the sale laws and the lease laws treat the application of the certificate of title law.

A lease does not include a sale. R.C. 1310.01(A)(10). A finance lease exists where, as here, the lessor does not select, manufacture, or supply the goods, the lessor acquires the right to possession in connection with the lease, and the lessee agrees to certain contractual terms. R.C. 1310.01(A)(7). The risk of loss passes to the lessee in a finance lease. R.C. 1310.26(A).

In *Smith*, there was a sale of a vehicle with title pending and a decision that risk of loss would be determined by the U.C.C. and thus at delivery. Here, we have an original lease which conformed to the statutes and which placed the risk of loss on the lessee as provided in R.C. 1310.26. We then have a subsequent action by the lessee which places the risk of loss in question.

It is important to realize that Chapter 1310 was enacted after the *Smith* decision. R.C. 1310.02(B)(1), specifically provides that a lease is subject to Chapter 4505 and any applicable certificate of title statutes of another jurisdiction. Moreover, R.C.1310.33(A) which is entitled, "Sale or Sublease of Goods by Lessee," states that the buyer or sublessee only obtains the interest in the goods that the lessee had power to transfer. Furthermore, R.C. 1310.33(C), provides:

"A buyer or sublessee from the lessee of goods that are subject to an existing lease contract and are covered by a certificate of title issued under Chapter 1548., 4505., or 4585. of the Revised Code or a similar law of another jurisdiction takes no greater rights than those provided by both this section and by the certificate of title law." [Emphasis omitted]

National City Bank was the owner/lessor at the time of the accident. The mere fact that Lavery decided it would help its customer out by attempting to sell or lease the car that was still under an existing lease does not make Lavery the owner where the certificate of title was not transferred. In fact, the process was not even begun, and National City Bank was not even consulted let alone paid off. Filnor remained the lessee at the time of the accident. Thus, the trial court erred in applying U.C.C. law that dealt with sales rather than leases.

The court also erred in its statement regarding the nonassignment clause of the lease. The trial court found that this was a consumer lease which can only be made nonassignable through a conspicuous clause. The court then stated that the clause in the lease before us is not conspicuous. See R.C. 1310.31(G) (which states that in a consumer lease, to prohibit transfer of an interest, the language shall be specific, written, and conspicuous).

A consumer lease is a type of finance lease where the lessor who is regularly engaged in the business of leasing makes a lease to a lessee who is an individual and who takes under the lease primarily for a personal, family, or household purpose. R.C. 1310.01(A)(5). However, in this case, one of the lessees was a corporation. Filnor, Inc.'s name was placed in the line of the lease which was specifically described as "business and commercial." This lease cannot be considered primarily for personal, family, or household purposes just because it was a Corvette used by the co-lessee/owner of the company rather than a utility truck. As such, the lease does not fit the definition of a consumer lease. In the case of a finance lease that is not a consumer lease, the lease is effective against third parties and is not subject to modification or termination without the consent of the party to whom the promises run. R.C. 1310.46(A) and (B). The language of R.C. 1310.31(G) would thus be inapplicable, and the language in the lease would have sufficiently prohibited an assignment.

As previously mentioned, the trial court erroneously applied Chapter 1302 dealing with sales. The appropriate law is found in Chapter 1310 which is specifically applicable and expressly deals with scenarios where a lessee attempts to sell or sublease its interest in the lease. Under R.C. 1310.25(E), the parties may determine by agreement which party shall have an obligation to obtain insurance. Here, the lessee was required to carry insurance on the vehicle.

The contract and the law, rather than the intent of the lessee and some third party, are determinative here. Still, as to intent, we note that although the Lavery representative claimed that Lavery's intent was to became the owner of the car, this person also admitted that Filnor agreed to reimburse Lavery for any loss, which establishes more of a consignment-like situation than that of a sale.

In conclusion, the lessee dropped off a leased vehicle at a dealership with hope the lease would be terminated one and a half years early. The lessee did not receive a different car and did not ask their insurer to cancel coverage. The lessee remained liable to the lessor/bank for payments. A pay off was not tendered to the bank by Lavery until one month after the accident. No paperwork was completed; no signatures were sought. The bank was not even notified of the situation. Finally, the certificate of title was not transferred.

State Farm, as the lessee's insurer, was not entitled to summary judgment on its argument that the lessee no longer had an insurable interest in the vehicle. Rather, appellant was entitled to summary judgment on its argument that State Farm's policy did not cease on the date that Filnor left its leased car with Lavery. In accordance, this sub-issue is sustained, and the trial court's judgment is reversed. * * *

For the foregoing reasons, the decision of the trial court on the main issue is reversed and this case is remanded to make decisions concerning the other two issues.

NOTES AND QUESTIONS

1. The court in *Jason's Foods* states that "[s]ection 2–509(2) separates title from risk of loss. Title to the ribs passed to Eckrich when the warehouse made the transfer on its books from Jason's account to Eckrich's, but the risk of loss did not pass until the transfer was 'acknowledged.'" Section 2–401 determines when title passes. The ribs at issue were delivered to Eckrich without being moved. Section 2–401(3) determines when title passes in this case. Delivery was not accomplished by delivery of a document of title covering the ribs. See 2–401(3)(a). Thus, under 2–401(3)(b), unless the parties agree otherwise, title to the ribs passed at the time and place of contracting. The parties apparently agreed otherwise, because in its confirmation Jason's notified Eckrich that the transfer would be made between January 10 and January 14. Jason's telephoned the warehouse on January 13 and requested that the ribs be immediately transferred to Eckrich's account. The warehouse complied. As a result, title to the ribs passed to Eckrich

on January 13. Chapter 9 discusses Article 2's default rules governing the passage of title in more detail.

Jason's Foods decides that risk of loss passes to the buyer under 2–509(2)(b) when the bailee acknowledges to the buyer its right to possess the goods. Proposed 2–509(2)(b) and 2–503(4)(a) agree. Does the bailee's acknowledgment occur when the bailee dispatches the acknowledgment? Or when the buyer receives it? Because Jason's did not raise the question, the court deemed it waived. The warehouse mailed a warehouse receipt to Eckrich on January 17, the day of the fire. Eckrich received the receipt on January 24. In determining whether 2–509(2)(b) requires the bailee's acknowledgment to the buyer, the court finds "little to asset us besides the language of [2–509(2)(b)] and its surrounding subsections and the UCC comments . . . " Nothing in this statutory material helps resolve the question as to whether the bailee's acknowledgment is effective on dispatch or on the buyer's receipt.

2. *Moser* involved a lawsuit against the lessee's insurer, State Farm, and others. State Farm sought a declaratory judgment that its insured (Filnor) had no insurable interest in the leased car at the time of the accident. Filnor had an insurable interest in the car only if it derived a financial or other benefit, or stood to lose, from the car during the lease term. Thus, Filnor had an insurable interest in the leased car if it bore the risk of loss with respect to the car at the time of the accident. On the facts described in *Moser*, would Filnor have an insurable interest in the car if its lease with National City Bank was a non-finance lease? 2A–219. If it sold the car to Lavery Chevrolet–Buick? 2–509.

3. Section 2–509 only allocates risk of loss between the parties to the sales contract. However, the contracting party bearing the risk might be able to recover its loss from a third party, such as a bailee. In this case the third party ultimately bears the risk of loss. Warehousemen and carriers are both bailees, and the law of bailments and tort law under some circumstances make them liable to a party to the sales contract. The common law imposes on a warehouseman a duty of due care with respect to warehoused goods. See R.H. Helmholtz, Bailment Theories and the Liability of Bailees: The Elusive Uniform Standard of Reasonable Care, 41 U. Kan. L. Rev. 97 (1992); Kurt P. Antor, Bailment Liability: Toward a Standard of Reasonable Care, 61 S. Cal. L. Rev. 2117 (1988). Article 7 of the UCC imposes the same standard of care on warehousemen when they issue warehouse receipts; 7–204(b). Some states increase the standard of care of warehousemen in prescribed instances; see, e.g., Cal. Civ. Code § 1630.5. Common law and statute make common carriers generally strictly liable for goods in their care; see, e.g., 7–309(a) (recognizing "rules of law" which set higher standards of care for carriers). A bailee also can be liable to a contracting party in tort, such as conversion. See Comment to 7–101.

4. Courts sometimes must determine whether the parties' agreement varies 2–509's risk of loss rules, as permitted by 2–509(4). In Caudle v. Sherrard Motor Co., 525 S.W.2d 238 (Tex. Ct. App. 1975), Caudle purchased a house trailer from Sherrard Motor Co. The sales contract provided that "[n]o transfer, renewal, extension or assignment of this agreement or any interest hereunder, and no loss, damage or destruction of said motor vehicle shall release buyer from his obligation hereunder." Caudle's house trailer was stolen from Sherrard's lot before Caudle retrieved it and Caudle refused to pay the contract price. In its suit to recover the price, Sherrard argued that the provision of the sales contract shifted risk of loss to Caudle before Caudle took delivery. The court rejected the argument: "We hold that this language [in the contract provision] is insufficient to constitute a 'contrary agreement' between the parties pursuant to UCC § 2–509(4). A contract which shifts the risk of loss to the buyer before he receives the merchandise is so unusual that a seller who desires to achieve this result must clearly communicate his intent to the buyer . . . This clause was apparently intended to fix responsibility for loss *after the defendant* [buyer] *had taken possession* of the trailer." Id. at 241. Is the court's interpretation of the provision in the sales contract persuasive? Section 2–509(3) passed risk of loss to Caudle after he took possession of the trailer. If so, would the parties draft a provision in the sales contract that provides for the same consequence? Other courts follow *Caudle*'s requirement that an agreement to opt out of 2–509's risk of loss rules must do so in clear and unequivocal language; see, e.g., McKenzie v. Omstead, 879 N.W.2d 873 (Minn. Ct. App. 1999); Hawkins v. Federated Mut. Insur. Co., 1996 U.S. Dist. LEXIS 21436 (N.D. Miss. 1996).

Multiplastics, Inc. v. Arch Industries, Inc.

Supreme Court of Connecticut, 1971
348 A. 618

■ Opinion by: BOGDANSKI, JUSTICE

The plaintiff, Multiplastics, Inc., brought this action to recover damages from the defendant, Arch Industries, Inc., for the breach of a contract to purchase 40,000 pounds of plastic pellets. From a judgment rendered for the plaintiff, the defendant has appealed to this court.

The facts may be summarized as follows: The plaintiff, a manufacturer of plastic resin pellets, agreed with the defendant on June 30, 1971, to manufacture and deliver 40,000 pounds of brown polystyrene plastic pellets for nineteen cents a pound. The pellets were specially made for the defendant, which agreed to accept delivery at the rate of 1000 pounds per day after completion of production. The defendant's confirming order contained the notation "make and hold for release." The plaintiff produced the order of pellets within two weeks and requested release orders from the defendant. The defendant refused to issue the release orders, citing labor difficulties and its vacation schedule. On August 18, 1971, the plaintiff sent the defendant the following letter: "Against P. O. 0946, we produced 40,000 lbs. of brown high impact styrene, and you have issued no releases. You indicated to us that you would be using 1,000 lbs. of each per day. We have warehoused these products for more than forty days, as we agreed to do. However, we cannot warehouse these products indefinitely, and request that you send us shipping instructions. We have done everything we agreed to do." After August 18, 1971, the plaintiff made numerous telephone calls to the defendant to seek payment and delivery instructions. In response, beginning August 20, 1971, the defendant agreed to issue release orders but in fact never did.

On September 22, 1971, the plaintiff's plant, containing the pellets manufactured for the defendant, was destroyed by fire. The plaintiff's fire insurance did not cover the loss of the pellets. The plaintiff brought this action against the defendant to recover the contract price.

The trial court concluded that the plaintiff made a valid tender of delivery by its letter of August 18, 1971, and by its subsequent requests for delivery instructions; that the defendant repudiated and breached the contract by refusing to accept delivery on August 20, 1971; that the period from August 20, 1971, to September 22, 1971, was not a commercially unreasonable time for the plaintiff to treat the risk of loss as resting on the defendant under General Statutes § 42a–2–510 (3); and that the plaintiff was entitled to recover the contract price plus interest.

General Statutes § 42a–2–510, entitled "Effect of breach on risk of loss," reads, in pertinent part, as follows: "(3) Where the buyer as to conforming goods already identified to the contract for sale repudiates or is otherwise in breach before risk of their loss has passed to him, the seller may to the extent of any deficiency in his effective insurance coverage treat the risk of loss as resting on the buyer for a commercially reasonable time." The defendant contends that § 42a–2–510 is not applicable because its failure to issue delivery instructions did not constitute either a repudiation or a breach of the agreement. The defendant also argues that even if § 42a–2–510 were applicable, the period from August 20, 1971, to September 22, 1971, was not a commercially reasonable period of time within which to treat the risk of loss as resting on the buyer. The defendant does not claim that the destroyed pellets were not "conforming goods already identified to the contract for sale," as required by General Statutes § 42a–2–510 (3), nor does it protest the computation of damages. With regard to recovery of the price of goods and incidental damages, see General Statutes § 42a–2–709 (1)(a).

The trial court's conclusion that the defendant was in breach is supported by its finding that the defendant agreed to accept delivery of the pellets at the rate of 1000 pounds per day after completion of production. The defendant argues that since the confirming order instructed the plaintiff to "make and hold for release," the contract did not specify an exact delivery date. This argument fails, however, because nothing in the finding suggests that the notation in the confirming order was part of the agreement between the parties. Since, as the trial court found, the plaintiff made a proper tender of delivery, beginning with its letter of August 18, 1971, the plaintiff was entitled to acceptance of the goods and to payment according to the contract. General Statutes §§ 42a–2–507 (1), 42a–2–307.

The defendant argues that its failure to issue delivery instructions did not suffice to repudiate the contract because repudiation of an executory promise requires, first, an absolute and unequivocal renunciation by the promisor, and, second, an unambiguous acceptance of the repudiation by the promisee. Anticipatory repudiation is now governed by General Statutes §§ 42a–2–609 to 42a–2–611, which in some respects alter the prior law on the subject. The present case does not involve repudiation of an executory promise, however, since the defendant breached the contract by failing to accept the goods when acceptance became due.

The defendant next claims that the plaintiff acquiesced in the defendant's refusal to accept delivery by continuing to urge compliance with the contract and by failing to pursue any of the remedies provided aggrieved sellers by General Statutes § 42a–2–703. In essence, the defendant's argument rests on the doctrines of waiver and estoppel, which are available defenses under the Uniform Commercial Code. The defendant has not, however, shown those defenses to apply. Waiver is the intentional relinquishment of a known right. Its existence is a question of fact for the trier. The trial court did not find that the plaintiff intentionally acquiesced in the defendant's breach of their agreement, thereby waiving its right to take advantage of that breach. Indeed, the plaintiff's repeated attempts to secure compliance seem inconsistent with the possibility of waiver.

Nor has the defendant made out a case of estoppel. "The two essential elements of estoppel are that 'one party must do or say something which is intended or calculated to induce another to believe in the existence of certain facts and to act on that belief; and the other party, influenced thereby, must change his position or do some act to his injury which he otherwise would not have done.' Dickau v. Glastonbury, 156 Conn. 437, 441, 242 A.2d 777. Neither element of estoppel is present in the record of this case. The plaintiff's requests for delivery instructions cannot be said to have misled the defendant into thinking that the plaintiff did not consider their contract breached. In fact, General Statutes § 42a–2–610, entitled "Anticipatory repudiation," specifically provides that the aggrieved seller may "resort to any remedy for breach as provided by section 42a–2–703 . . . , even though he has notified the repudiating party that he would await the latter's performance and has urged retraction." Although the present case is not governed by General Statutes § 42a–2–610, that section does demonstrate that the plaintiff's conduct after the defendant refused to accept delivery was not inconsistent with its claim that the contract was breached.

The remaining question is whether, under General Statutes § 42a–2–510 (3), the period of time from August 20, 1971, the date of the breach, to September 22, 1971, the date of the fire, was a "commercially reasonable" period within which to treat the risk of loss as resting on the buyer. The trial court concluded that it was "not, on the facts in this case, a commercially unreasonable time," which we take to mean that it was a commercially reasonable period. The time limitation in § 42a–2–510 (3) is designed to enable the seller to obtain the additional requisite insurance coverage. The trial court's conclusion is tested by the finding. Although the finding is not detailed, it supports the conclusion that August 20 to September 22 was a commercially reasonable period within which to place the risk of loss on the defendant. As already stated, the trial court found that the defendant repeatedly agreed to transmit delivery instructions and that the pellets were specially made to fill the defendant's order. Under those circumstances, it was reasonable for the plaintiff to believe that the goods would soon be taken off its hands and so to forgo procuring the needed insurance.

We consider it advisable to discuss one additional matter. The trial court concluded that "title" passed to the defendant, and the defendant attacks the conclusion on this appeal. The issue is immaterial to this case. General Statutes § 42a–2–401 states: "Each provision of this article with regard to the rights, obligations and remedies of the seller, the buyer, purchasers or other third parties applies irrespective of title to the goods except where the provision refers to such title." As one student of the Uniform Commercial Code has written: "The single most important innovation of Article 2 [of the Uniform Commercial Code] is its restatement of . . . [the parties'] responsibilities in terms of operative facts rather than legal conclusions; where pre-Code law looked to 'title' for the definition of rights and remedies, the Code looks to demonstrable realities such as custody, control and professional expertise. This shift in approach is central to the whole philosophy of Article 2. It means that disputes, as they arise, can focus, as does all of the modern law of contracts, upon actual provable circumstances, rather than upon a metaphysical concept of elastic and endlessly fluid dimensions." Peters, "Remedies for Breach of Contracts Relating to the Sale of Goods under the Uniform Commercial Code: A Roadmap for Article Two," 73 Yale L.J. 199, 201 [(1963)].

There is no error.

PROBLEM 8.1

Acme Tractor sold the tractor located in the showroom at its retail store to Farm Corp. on credit. To secure the purchase price, Acme retained title to the tractor until Farm paid it. The tractor operated with a swipe card. After Farm's representative signed the contract at Acme's store and was shown the tractor's location, Acme turned over the card. Pressing business forced the representative to leave just before he was going to take the tractor away. Two days later fire destroyed all of the contents in Acme's retail store, including Farm's tractor. An investigation established that Acme was not at fault. Farm has rejected Acme's demand that it honor its agreement to pay the tractor's purchase price. Is Farm entitled to the purchase price? 2–509(3), 2–709(1)(a). What result if the tractor was scratched at the time Farm's representative visited Acme's store?

Suppose the fire occurred the day before Farm's representative arrived at Acme's store. After the fire Farm immediately obtains a comparable tractor at a higher price than Acme's tractors from one of Acme's local competitors. When it demands that Acme pay the difference between the contract price and the price it paid for a replacement tractor, Acme refuses. Is Farm entitled to recover this amount from Acme? 2–613(a).

PROBLEM 8.2

In November Mr. Smith agreed to sell his valuable Christmas ornaments to Ms. Jones. Jones was to pay for the ornaments when she retrieved them from Smith's home between November 20 and November 25. Jones never came to pick the ornaments up and pay Smith. Worse, thieves broke into Smith's home and stole the ornaments. Smith does not carry insurance on his home or its contents.

(a) If the theft occurred on November 18, is Smith entitled to the recover the contract price from Jones? 2–503(1), 2–509(3), 2–709(1)(a).

(b) If the theft occurred on November 28, is he entitled to the price? 2–509(3), 2–719(1)(a).

(c) If the theft occurred three months later, is Smith entitled to the price? 2–509, 2–709(1)(a); 2–510(3).

(d) Assume that Jones' agreement with Smith required her to make a downpayment on the ornaments on November 18. Jones failed to make the downpayment. The facts being otherwise those in (c), is Smith entitled to the price? 2–509(3), 2–510(3), 2–709(1)(a).

PROBLEM 8.3

Sky contracted to sell Big Store a set of motion detectors for $5,000 F.O.B. Sky's place of business. Because the detectors were delicate, Sky agreed to take appropriate measures to protect the detectors while they were being transported to Big Store. Sky engaged Truck Corp. to deliver the detectors to Big Store. Sky's tight production schedule prevented it from informing Truck that the detectors were delicate and Truck handled them in the same way it handled books and used furniture it transported. Fortunately, the detectors arrived at Big Store undamaged. The day after they arrived, before Big Store unpacked the detectors, fire destroyed Big Store's warehouse that held them. Sky refused Big Store's demand that it refund the price it paid Sky for the detectors. Is Big Store entitled to the refund? 2–504(a), 2–509(1)(a), 2–510(1).

C. THE CISG'S RISK OF LOSS RULES

Articles 67–69 state default rules allocating the risk of loss. As with the UCC, these rules apply in the circumstances described in the respective Articles. It is worth emphasizing that the CISG's risk of loss rules are default rules only. They can vary by the parties' agreement; see Article 6. International sales contracts frequently allocate the loss between the seller and buyer. The value of these contracts and the likelihood of the goods having to travel over long distances make it worthwhile for the contracting parties to address risk of loss. For example, bulk oil contracts frequently deal expressly with risk, transferring it to the buyer at a specific point such as the hose connection at the loading port or the vessel's intake valve. Alternatively, parties may allocate risk by incorporating Incoterms into their contract. Recall that Incoterms defines the seller's delivery obligations and allocates risk for abbreviated shipment terms (e.g., F.O.B.). Thus, where the parties use Incoterms, Article 9(2) of the CISG likely will interpret their contract to allocate risk according to the shipment term they select. As noted above, international sales contracts often incorporate Incoterms. Some courts consider Incoterms to be trade usage. See, e.g., BP Oil Int'l, Ltd. v. Empresa Estatal Petroleos de Ecuador, 332 F.2d 333 (5th Cir. 2003); Citgo Petroleum Corp. v. Seachem, 2013 U.S. Dist. LEXIS 72898, at *1 (S.D. Tex. 2013). These courts might interpret a shipment term to allocate risk in accordance with Incoterms even if the sales contract governed by the CISG does not incorporate them. See Article 9(2). Where the parties expressly provide for risk or use Incoterms, the CISG's risk of loss rules do not apply.

Even when the CISG's loss rules do not apply, its other provisions continue to control contracts governed by the CISG. An important provision with continued application concerns the legal consequences of risk of loss passing. Although the parties' contract can determine when risk of loss passes, Article 66 determines when the seller can enforce the contract. The Article provides that loss or damage to the goods after risk has passed to the buyer does not discharge the buyer's obligation to pay for them, unless the loss or damage is due to the seller's act or omission. This provision entitles the seller to recover the contract price if the goods are damaged or destroyed after risk has passed to the buyer. Article 66's negative implication is that the seller is not entitled to the price if the damage or destruction occurs before risk has passed.

Article 66 does not entitle the seller to recover the contract price after risk of loss has passed if the loss was due to the seller's act or omission. The seller's breach counts as its act or omission. For example, assume that the sales contract called for the seller to place the goods in protective packing. The contract shifts risk to the buyer on delivery to the carrier, which the contract authorizes. The seller delivers the goods to the carrier without protective packing, and they are damaged in transit by carriage to the buyer. Had the goods been put in protective packing, they would not have been damaged. On these facts, the seller is not entitled to the price. The seller breached its express warranty under Article 35(1) by failing to pack the goods as required by the contract. Although the damage occurred after risk passed to the buyer, the damage resulted from the seller's omission—its failure to put the goods in protective packing. Article 66 therefore discharges the buyer from its obligation to pay the contract price.

Article 66's language appears to discharge the buyer even if the seller's "act or omission" is not a breach. (Some diplomatic history supports this interpretation; language in an early draft which limited the seller's "acts or omissions" to those in breach of contract was rejected. See [1977] Draft Convention on the International Sale of Goods, in Documentary History of the Uniform Law for International Sales 356 (para. 531) (J. Honnold ed., 1989).) For example, suppose the contract did not require protective packing and such packing was unusual in the circumstances. The seller's failure to provide protective packing therefore did not breach an express or implied warranty. See 35(1), (2)(d). Nonetheless, the seller was in a position to place the goods in protective packing at little cost but decided not to do so. The seller's failure to put the goods in protective packing arguably is an "omission." Article 66 does not entitle the seller to the contract price if the damage to the goods after risk passed to the buyer results from the seller's omission. Thus, the seller apparently is not entitled to the contract price, despite the fact that there was no breach.

Not everything the seller conceivably could do to avoid loss counts as an "act or omission" for purposes of Article 66. Otherwise, the seller effectively remains responsible for the goods after risk of loss has passed to the buyer. To see this, consider a final variant of the ongoing example. Assume that protective packing, although available, is very expensive and therefore not called for in contracts of the sort the seller concluded with the buyer. The facts are otherwise those of the ongoing example. Although the seller could have shipped the goods in protective packing, its failure to do is cost-justified. The seller's failure therefore arguably is not an "omission" under Article 66. Article 66's "unless" clause therefore does not apply and the buyer therefore is responsible for the contract price. To be sure, Article 66 speaks only of an "act or omission," not a cost-justified act or omission. However, sellers almost always can do something in advance, at enough expense, to avoid a later loss to the goods. Unless an "act or omission" is limited to cost-justified acts or omissions, Article 66's "unless" clause would apply and the buyer would not liable for the contract price even after the risk of loss has passed to it. The seller therefore effectively continues to bear the risk. To avoid this result, Article 66's "unless" clause is more plausibly read to apply only to cost-justified acts or omissions available to the seller.

The CISG's risk of loss provisions require close attention. Article 69 is the CISG's residual risk of loss rule. It determines the point at which risk passes when the CISG's other risk of loss rules are inapplicable ("(1) [i]n cases not within articles 67 and 68 . . . "). Article 67 allocates risk when the contract authorizes carriage. Article 68 allocates risk when goods are sold while afloat. The Article contemplates a sale while the goods are being transported by a carrier, so that it too applies when the goods are being shipped under a contract of carriage. Because Article 69 applies when Articles 67 and 68 are inapplicable, it allocates risk when the sales contract does not authorize shipment by carrier. Three sorts of sales contracts fit this description. One is a contract that calls for the buyer to take delivery at the seller's place of business. A second is a contract that calls for the seller itself to deliver the goods to the buyer rather than through a carrier. The third contract is one that calls for the buyer to take delivery of the goods being held by a bailee.

Article 69(1) deals with the first sort of sales contracts that do not call for shipment by carrier: contracts that call for delivery at the seller's place of business. Under Article 69(1) risk of loss passes to the buyer when it "takes over the goods." A buyer who takes over the goods has control of them and therefore is in a position to minimize risks to them. Article 69(1) is the counterpart of 2–509(3), the UCC's residual risk of loss rule. If the buyer fails to take delivery at the seller's place of business, risk of loss passes when the goods are placed at its disposal and it breaches by not taking delivery. Article 69(1) therefore keeps the risk on the seller even after the goods are placed at the buyer's disposal until the buyer breaches by not taking delivery.

Article 69(2) allocates risk when the buyer "is bound to take over the goods at a place other than a place of business of the seller." It therefore covers the remaining two sorts of sales contracts described above: contracts in which the seller either is to transport the goods or the buyer is to take delivery from a bailee. Under Article 69(2) risk passes when delivery is due and the buyer is aware that the goods have been placed at its disposal at the designated location. Risk does not pass until the goods have been identified to the contract, such as by marking them or otherwise connecting them with the contract. See Article 69(3).

Article 67 deals with sales contracts that call for carriage of the goods. "Carriage" means transportation by an entity independent of the seller. This is presupposed by Article 67(1)'s transfer of risk when the goods are "handed over" to a carrier. Article 67(1) covers two sorts of sales contracts: contracts calling for delivery of the goods to a carrier "at a particular place" and contract calling for delivery to a carrier but not at a particular place. With the first sort of contract, the first sentence of Article 67(1) passes risk to the buyer when the seller hands the goods over to the carrier at the particular place designated by the contract. With the second sort, risk passes when the seller hands the goods over to the first carrier.

There is a slight ambiguity in Article 67(1) concerning what it means for the seller to "hand over the goods" at a particular place. Must the seller personally hand over the goods to the carrier at the designated place? Or is it enough that the goods are handed over to the carrier at the designated place, whether by the seller or a carrier selected by it? For example, suppose the contract calls for the goods to be "sent by vessel X at Houston." The seller arranges with a carrier to take the goods by truck to Houston. The goods are destroyed en route to Houston. The contract's language does not require the seller personally to hand over the goods at Houston, but it does specify Houston as the place at which the goods are to be handed over. Thus, if Article 67(1)'s second sentence applies only when the seller must itself hand over the goods, the sentence is inapplicable. Instead, the first sentence applies. Under this sentence the contract does not require the seller to hand the goods over at a particular place (Houston). Risk therefore passes to the buyer when the seller hands the goods over to the first carrier for delivery to the ocean carrier in Houston. Because the first carrier was the truck carrier and the goods were destroyed after the goods were handed over to it, the buyer bears the loss. However, if Article 67(1)'s second sentence applies when the contract calls for the goods to be delivered to a particular place, regardless of whether it calls for the seller or a carrier selected by it to hand the goods over, the sentence applies to the example. The contract requires the goods to be handed over to the carrier (vessel X) at Houston, whether by the seller or its overland carrier. Risk therefore passes to the buyer when the seller or its overland carrier delivers the goods to the ocean carrier in Houston. Because the goods were destroyed before they were delivered to the ocean carrier in Houston, the seller bears the loss. Article 67(1)'s second sentence is best understood to apply when the contract calls for the seller or its selected carrier to deliver the goods to a designated location. Otherwise, the second sentence would apply only when the contract called for the seller personally to hand over the goods. In international trade, where carriers usually transport the goods during their entire journey to the buyer, such contracts are very seldom undertaken. The CISG's drafters are unlikely to have supplied a rule that would apply so infrequently.

Article 67's language might seem opaque and a bit arbitrary. It is very different from 2–509(1)'s terminology of a "particular destination," and 2–319 and 2–320's shipment terms, which are tied to particular modes of transportation (e.g., F.O.B. vessel). Article 67's terminology responds to technological changes in the transportation of goods during the last half century. Developments in multimodal transportation, especially in containerization, allow delivery to a carrier at an inland location. See Marc Levinson, The Box (2006). The goods can be transported by a combination of road, rail and water to their final destination by several different carriers. Containerization enables the seller to pack a container at its place of business, where it is retrieved by a land carrier and taken to an inland container terminal. The inland carrier in turn can arrange for the container's transport through different carriers, using possibly different modes of carriage, for ultimate delivery to the buyer. Current estimates are that about 90 percent of world non-bulk cargo is transported by container. Unlike the UCC's shipment and destination contracts, which specify a particular mode of transport or the buyer's location, Article 67(1) understandably focuses on the carrier's location. For goods that might be carried by multimodal transportation, passage of risk at the rail of the ship or on board a truck is infeasible. The seller and buyer might not even know in advance the particular modes of transport that will used to carry the goods. As important, the seller loses control over the goods on delivery of the packed container to the carrier. The use of several carriers creates proof of loss problems because it requires proof as to when the loss occurred. Article 67(1)'s first sentence eases the difficulty of proof, as between the seller and buyer, by shifting risk to the buyer after the seller hands the goods over to the first carrier.

The CISG contains a provision allocating risk when the goods are sold while they are in transit. For instance, a shipper might ship a quantity of bulk cargo such as wheat, corn or oil to a named destination. In taking the cargo the carrier in turn will issue documents of title to the shipper covering the cargo. While the cargo is in transit, the shipper might contract to sell some or all of the cargo. The sales contract usually will call for the seller to present certain documents to the buyer and the buyer to pay against their presentation. In the standard C.I.F. contract, the required documents are a negotiable bill of lading, an insurance certificate, and a commercial invoice indicating the price and describing the cargo. The buyer obtains these documents in exchange for paying the contract price. It may in turn resell the cargo to another buyer by delivering the shipping documents before the cargo arrives at its destination. In the bulk commodities trade, a series of sales of the same cargo while in transit are common. The series constitutes a "string sale": a sequence of contracts for a specific cargo with the same terms except for price. Only the final buyer takes physical delivery of the cargo at the destination. The intermediate sellers and buyers deal in the shipping documents while the cargo is in transit. At the time of a sale within the string, the goods in transit might be lost or damaged.

Under Article 68, risk passes at the conclusion of the contract where goods are sold in transit. This requires determining when the contract was concluded and when the goods were lost or damaged. The buyer bears the risk if the loss or damage occurred after the contract was concluded; the seller bears the risk if it occurred before the contract's conclusion. Obviously, determining the time at which these two events occur is difficult to verify when goods are sold while in transit. However, Article 68 also provides that "if the circumstances so indicate," risk passes retroactively to the buyer from the time the goods were handed to the carrier who issued the documents covering them. Although Article 68 is silent as to what these "circumstances" are, they might include cargo insurance for the buyer's benefit. See John O. Honnold, Uniform Law for International Sales Under the 1989 United Nations Convention 530 (H.M. Flechtner ed., 4th ed. 2009). The thought apparently is that a buyer fully protected by cargo insurance suffers no harm if risk is backdated to the point of delivery to the carrier. But at least one tribunal has refused to retroactively pass risk in a C.I.F. sale, even though the buyer was protected by cargo insurance. See China International Economic and Trade Arbitration Commission, Arbitration Proceeding, 1 April 1997, available at http://cisgw3.law.pace.edu/cases/970401c1.html. Article 68 does not backdate risk if at the contract's conclusion the seller knew and failed to disclose that the goods had been lost or damaged.

The UCC has a different rule for passage of risk for goods sold in transit. Section 2–509 does not address the situation. However, Comment 2 to 2–509 provides that "[t]o transfer the risk it is enough that a proper shipment and proper identification come to apply to the same goods although, aside from special agreement, the risk will not pass retroactively to the time of shipment in such a case." Article 68 does not require that the goods be identified to the contract before risk passes. More important, the Article backdates risk when "the circumstances so indicate." By contrast, Comment 2 does not pass risk retroactively in any circumstance. A "special agreement" to backdate risk is not a relevant circumstance, because as default rules both 2–509(4) and Article 6 of the CISG allow their respective risk allocations to be altered by agreement. By "circumstance" the CISG clearly means a situation that passes risk retroactively other than by contractual provision.

With one exception, the CISG's risk of loss rules apply without regard to breach. Article 36(1) provides that the seller is liable for any lack of conformity in the goods existing at the time risk passes to the buyer, even when the nonconformity only becomes apparent after that time. The seller's liability for breach does not prevent risk from passing. This makes good sense because the party in control of the goods usually can minimize the loss or damage to them. Breach by itself does not change control of the goods. By contrast, under 2–510 of the UCC breach can prevent risk from passing. The single exception to the CISG's "breach is irrelevant to passage of risk" rules is Article 69(1). Under Article 69(1), risk passes to the buyer if the seller places the goods at its disposal and the buyer breaches by failing to take timely delivery. The breaching buyer therefore can be liable for the contract price even if the goods are lost or damaged while in the seller possession. This result does not allocate risk inefficiently. The buyer owed the seller the contract price, according to Article 66. So, even if the risk had not passed to it, the buyer would be liable for the price. Article 74 entitles the seller to damages equal to the loss suffered from breach. Had the buyer not breached and taken delivery, the seller would be entitled to the contract price. Article 53. Thus, the seller's damages for breach are equal to (at least) the contract price, which is the amount it lost from the buyer's breach. Article 69(1) therefore puts on the buyer loss equal to the amount it owed the seller had it not breached.

The CISG's risk of loss rules are not perfect. They allow a buyer to shift risk that has passed to it back to the seller in certain circumstances. This "reshifting back" of risk can be inefficient. To see this, consider first Article 70. Article 70 provides that Article 67–69's risk of loss rules do not impair remedies available to the buyer on account of the seller's fundamental breach. One of the buyer's remedies on fundamental breach is to declare the contract avoided. Article 49(1)(a). Avoidance puts an end to all obligations under the contract, including the buyer's obligation to pay the contract price. Article 81(1). A buyer who avoids a contract on the seller's fundamental breach therefore can shift risk that has passed to it back to the seller. In this way avoidance can reallocate risks to the seller that the contract allocated to the buyer. The following example illustrates this possibility. Assume that the contract price is $100 and Seller delivers nonconforming goods with a market value of $80. Assume also that the nonconformity does not constitute a fundamental breach of Seller's obligations with respect to the goods. Finally, assume that the goods are damaged after they come into Buyer's hands and that the damage is unrelated to the good's nonconformity. The damaged goods have a market value of $50. Article 36 makes Seller liable for nonconformity because the nonconformity existed before risk passed to Buyer. Thus, Seller is liable to Buyer for $20 ($100 − $80). Under Article 69(1) risk passed to Buyer after it took delivery of the goods. As a result, Buyer bears the $30 loss ($80 − $50) resulting from damage to the goods. In sum, Seller bears the $20 loss and Buyer the $30 loss.

Now suppose that the nonconformity in the goods Seller delivered amounts to a fundamental breach. The facts of the example remain otherwise the same. Buyer can avoid the contract. Under Article 81(1) avoidance releases Buyer from all of its obligations under the contract. This includes its obligation to pay the contract price, less the $20 loss for which Seller is liable. Although Buyer must return the damaged goods (see Article 81(2)), it does not have to bear the $30 loss from damage to the goods after risk had passed to it. If it prepaid the $100 contract price, Article 81(2) entitles Buyer to a full refund. Avoidance allows Buyer to in effect reshift the risk it bore initially back to Seller. Seller therefore bears the entire $50 loss. This result arguably is inefficient. Buyer was in control of the goods when they were damaged. It could have taken measures to reduce the expected loss or insure against it. Article 70, by allowing Buyer to reshift risk back to Seller, allocates it to a party in an inferior position to minimize the risk or its impact. It gives Buyer an incentive to take inefficient precautions against risk.

St. Paul Guardian Ins. Co. v. Neuromed Medical Systems & Support

United States District Court, Southern District of New York, 2002
2002 WL 465312

■ Opinion & Order: STEIN, DISTRICT J.

Plaintiffs St. Paul Guardian Insurance Company and Travelers Property Casualty Insurance Company have brought this action as subrogees of Shared Imaging, Inc., to recover $285,000 they paid to Shared Imaging for damage to a mobile magnetic resonance imaging system ("MRI") purchased by Shared Imaging from defendant

Neuromed Medical Systems & Support GmbH ("Neuromed"). Neuromed has moved to dismiss the complaint on two grounds, namely that (1) the forum selection clause of the underlying contract requires the litigation to take place in Germany and (2) pursuant to Fed.R.Civ.P. 12(b)(6), the complaint fails to state a claim for relief. In an Order dated December 3, 2001, this Court first found that the contractual forum selection clause did not mandate that the action proceed in Germany and second, held the rest of the motion in abeyance pending submissions by the parties on German law, which, pursuant to the underlying contract, is the applicable law. The parties have now submitted affidavits from German legal experts.

The crux of Neuromed's argument is that it had no further obligations regarding the risk of loss once it delivered the MRI to the vessel at the port of shipment due to a "CIF" clause included in the underlying contract. Plaintiffs respond that (1) the generally understood definition of the "CIF" term as defined by the International Chamber of Commerce's publication, Incoterms 1990, is inapplicable here and (2) the "CIF" term was effectively superseded by other contract terms such that the risk of loss remained on Neuromed.

Pursuant to the applicable German law—the U.N. Convention on Contracts for the International Sale of Goods—the "CIF" term in the contract operated to pass the risk of loss to Shared Imaging at the port of shipment, at which time, the parties agree, the MRI was undamaged and in good working order. Accordingly, Neuromed's motion to dismiss the complaint should be granted and the complaint dismissed.

Background

Shared Imaging, an American corporation, and Neuromed, a German corporation, entered into a contract of sale for a Siemens Harmony 1.0 Tesla mobile MRI. Thereafter, both parties engaged various entities to transport, insure and provide customs entry service for the MRI. Plaintiffs originally named those entities as defendants, but the action has been discontinued against them by agreement of the parties. Neuromed is the sole remaining defendant.

According to the complaint, the MRI was loaded aboard the vessel "Atlantic Carrier" undamaged and in good working order. When it reached its destination of Calmut City, Illinois, it had been damaged and was in need of extensive repair, which led plaintiffs to conclude that the MRI had been damaged in transit.

The one page contract of sale contains nine headings, including: "Product;" "Delivery Terms;" "Payment Terms;" "Disclaimer;" and "Applicable Law." Under "Product" the contract provides, the "system will be delivered cold and fully functional." Under "Delivery Terms" it provides, "CIF New York Seaport, the buyer will arrange and pay for customs clearance as well as transport to Calmut City." Under "Payment Terms" it states, "By money transfer to one of our accounts, with following payment terms: US $93,000—downpayment to secure the system; US $744,000—prior to shipping; US $93,000—upon acceptance by Siemens of the MRI system within 3 business days after arrival in Calmut City." In addition, under "Disclaimer" it states, "system including all accessories and options remain the property of Neuromed till complete payment has been received." Preceding this clause is a handwritten note, allegedly initialed by Raymond Stachowiak of Shared Imaging, stating, "Acceptance subject to Inspection."

Discussion

Neuromed contends that because the delivery terms were "CIF New York Seaport," its contractual obligation, with regard to risk of loss or damage, ended when it delivered the MRI to the vessel at the port of shipment and therefore the action must be dismissed because plaintiffs have failed to state a claim for which relief can be granted. Plaintiffs respond that the generally accepted definition of the "CIF" term as defined in Incoterms 1990, is inapplicable. Moreover, plaintiffs suggest that other provisions of the contract are inconsistent with the "CIF" term because Neuromed, pursuant to the contract, retained title subsequent to delivery to the vessel at the port of shipment and thus, Neuromed manifestly retained the risk of loss.

* * *

2.   Applicable German Law

The parties concede that pursuant to German law, the U.N. Convention on Contracts for the International Sale of Goods ("CISG") governs this transaction because (1) both the U.S. and Germany are Contracting States to that Convention, and (2) neither party chose, by express provision in the contract, to opt out of the application of the CISG; see CISG, art. 1(1)(a).

The CISG aims to bring uniformity to international business transactions, using simple, non-nation specific language. To that end, it is comprised of rules applicable to the conclusion of contracts of sale of international goods. In its application regard is to be paid to comity and interpretations grounded in its underlying principles rather than in specific national conventions. See CISG art. 7(1), (2).

Germany has been a Contracting State since 1991, and the CISG is an integral part of German law. Where parties, as here, designate a choice of law clause in their contract-selecting the law of a Contracting State without expressly excluding application of the CISG–German courts uphold application of the Convention as the law of the designated Contracting state. To hold otherwise would undermine the objectives of the Convention which Germany has agreed to uphold.

C.   CISG, INCOTERMS and "CIF"

"CIF," which stands for "cost, insurance and freight," is a commercial trade term that is defined in Incoterms 1990, published by the International Chamber of Commerce ("ICC"). The aim of INCOTERMS, which stands for international commercial terms, is "to provide a set of international rules for the interpretation of the most commonly used trade terms in foreign trade." These "trade terms are used to allocate the costs of freight and insurance" in addition to designating the point in time when the risk of loss passes to the purchaser. Larry DiMatteo, The CISG and the Presumption of Enforceability: Unintended Contractual Liability in International Business Dealings, Yale J. Int'l L. 111, 188 (1997). INCOTERMS are incorporated into the CISG through Article 9(2) which provides that,

The parties are considered, unless otherwise agreed, to have impliedly made applicable to their contract or its formation a usage of which the parties knew or ought to have known and which in international trade is widely known to, and regularly observed by, parties to contracts of the type involved in the particular trade concerned. CISG, art. 9(2).

At the time the contract was entered into, Incoterms 1990 was applicable. INCOTERMS define "CIF" (named port of destination) to mean the seller delivers when the goods pass "the ship's rail in the port of shipment." The seller is responsible for paying the cost, freight and insurance coverage necessary to bring the goods to the named port of destination, but the risk of loss or damage to the goods passes from seller to buyer upon delivery to the port of shipment. Further, "CIF" requires the seller to obtain insurance only on minimum cover.

Plaintiffs' legal expert contends that INCOTERMS are inapplicable here because the contract fails to specifically incorporate them. Nonetheless, he cites and acknowledges that the German Supreme Court (Bundesgerichtshof [BGH])—the court of last resort in the Federal Republic of Germany for civil matters—concluded that a clause "fob" without specific reference to INCOTERMS was to be interpreted according to INCOTERMS "simply because the [INCOTERMS] include a clause 'fob'."

Conceding that commercial practice attains the force of law under section 346 of the German Commercial Code (Handelsgesetzbuch [HGB]), plaintiffs' expert concludes that the opinion of the BGH "amounts to saying that the [INCOTERMS] definitions in Germany have the force of law as trade custom." As encapsulated by defendant's legal expert, "It is accepted under German law that in case a contract refers to CIF-delivery, the parties refer to the INCOTERMS rules. . . . "

The use of the "CIF" term in the contract demonstrates that the parties "agreed to the detailed oriented [INCOTERMS] in order to enhance the Convention." Neil Gary Oberman, Transfer of Risk From Seller to Buyer in International Commercial Contracts: A Comparative Analysis of Risk Allocation Under CISG, UCC and Incoterms, at http:// www.cisg.law.pace.edu/cisg/thesis/Oberman.html. Thus, pursuant to CISG art. 9(2), INCOTERMS definitions should be applied to the contract despite the lack of an explicit INCOTERMS reference in the contract.

D.   INCOTERMS, the CISG, and the Passage of Risk of Loss and Title

Plaintiffs argue that Neuromed's explicit retention of title in the contract to the MRI machine modified the "CIF" term, such that Neuromed retained title and assumed the risk of loss. INCOTERMS, however, only address passage of risk, not transfer of title. Under the CISG, the passage of risk is likewise independent of the transfer of title. See CISG art. 67(1). Plaintiffs' legal expert mistakenly asserts that the moment of 'passing of risk' has not been defined in the CISG. Chapter IV of that Convention, entitled "Passing of Risk," explicitly defines the time at which risk passes from seller to buyer pursuant to Article 67(1).

If the contract of sale involves carriage of the goods and seller is not bound to hand them over at a particular place, the risk passes to the buyer when the goods are handed over to the first carrier for transmission to the buyer in accordance with the contract of sale. If the seller is bound to hand the goods over to a carrier at a particular place, the risk does not pass to the buyer until the goods are handed over to the carrier at that place. CISG, art 67(1).

Pursuant to the CISG, "[t]he risk passes without taking into account who owns the goods. The passing of ownership is not regulated by the CISG according to art. 4(b)." Annemieke Romein, The Passing of Risk: A Comparison Between the Passing of Risk under the CISG and German Law (Heidelberg, June 1999), at http://www.cisg.law.pace.edu/ cisg/biblio/romein.html. Article 4(b) provides that the Convention is not concerned with "the effect which the contract may have on the property in the goods sold." CISG art. 4(b). Moreover, according to Article 67(1), the passage of risk and transfer of title need not occur at the same time, as the seller's retention of "documents controlling the disposition of the goods does not affect the passage of risk." CISG art. 67(1).

Had the CISG been silent, as plaintiffs' expert claimed, the Court would have been required to turn to German law as a "gap filler." There again, plaintiffs' assertions falter. German law also recognizes passage of risk and transfer of title as two independent legal acts. In fact, it is standard "practice under German law to agree that the transfer of title will only occur upon payment of the entire purchase price, well after the date of passing of risk and after receipt of the goods by the buyer." Support for this proposition of German law is cited by both experts. They each refer to section 447 of the German Civil Code (Bügerliches Gesetzbuch [BGB]), a provision dealing with long distance sales, providing in part—as translated by plaintiff's expert—that "the risk of loss passes to the buyer at the moment when the seller has handed the matter to the forwarder, the carrier or to the otherwise determined person or institution for the transport."

Accordingly, pursuant to INCOTERMS, the CISG, and specific German law, Neuromed's retention of title did not thereby implicate retention of the risk of loss or damage.

E.   The Contract Terms

Plaintiffs next contend that even if the "CIF" term did not mandate that title and risk of loss pass together, the other terms in the contract are evidence that the parties' intention to supersede and replace the "CIF" term such that Neuromed retained title and the risk of loss. That is incorrect.

1.   "Delivery Terms"

Citing the "Delivery Terms" clause in the contract, plaintiffs posit that had the parties intended to abide by the strictures of INCOTERMS there would have been no need to define the buyer's obligations to pay customs and arrange further transport. Plaintiffs' argument, however, is undermined by Incoterms 1990, which provides that "[i]t is normally desirable that customs clearance is arranged by the party domiciled in the country where such clearance should take place." The "CIF" term as defined by INCOTERMS only requires the seller to "clear the goods for export" and is silent as to which party bears the obligation to arrange for customs clearance. The parties are therefore left to negotiate these obligations. As such, a clause defining the terms of customs clearance neither alters nor affects the "CIF" clause in the contract.

2.   "Payment Terms"

Plaintiffs also cite to the "Payment Terms" clause of the contract, which specified that final payment was not to be made upon seller's delivery of the machine to the port of shipment, but rather, upon buyer's acceptance of the machine in Calumet City. These terms speak to the final disposition of the property, not to the risk for loss or damage. INCOTERMS do not mandate a payment structure, but rather simply establish that the buyer bears an obligation to "[p]ay the price as provided in the contract of sale." Inclusion of the terms of payment in the contract does not modify the "CIF" clause.

3.   The Handwritten Note

Finally, plaintiffs emphasize the handwritten note, "Acceptance upon inspection." Based upon its placement within the contract and express terms, the note must serve to qualify the final clauses of the "Payment Terms," obliging buyer to effect final payment upon acceptance of the machine. As defendant's expert correctly depicts, "A reasonable recipient, acting in good faith, would understand that the buyer wanted to make sure that receipt of the GOOD should not be construed as the acceptance of the buyer that the GOOD is free of defects of design or workmanship and that the GOOD is performing as specified. This addition does not relate to the place of delivery." Accordingly, despite plaintiffs' arguments to the contrary, the handwritten note does not modify the "CIF" clause; it instead serves to qualify the terms of the transfer of title.

The terms of the contract do not modify the "CIF" clause in the contract such that the risk of loss remained with Neuromed. The fact remains that the CISG, INCOTERMS, and German law all distinguish between the passage of the risk of loss and the transfer of title. Thus, because (1) Neuromed's risk of loss of, or damage to, the MRI machine under the contract passed to Shared Imaging upon delivery of the machine to the carrier at the port of shipment and (2) it is undisputed that the MRI machine was delivered to the carrier undamaged and in good working order, Neuromed's motion to dismiss for failure to state a claim is hereby granted.

Conclusion

For the foregoing reasons, Neuromed's motion to dismiss for failure to state a claim is granted and the complaint is dismissed.

NOTES AND QUESTIONS

1. The sales contract in *St. Paul Guardian* incorporated a C.I.F. delivery term without referring to Incoterms. The court accepted the testimony of both parties' experts to the effect that under German law Incoterms had the status of trade custom. It concluded that under Article 9(2) of the CISG the C.I.F. term in the contract should be interpreted according to Incoterms. Accord Tribunal cantonal [Higher Cantonal Court] du Valais (Switzerland), 28 January 2009, available at http://cisgw3.law.pace.edu/cases/090128s1.html; BP Oil Int'l Ltd. v. Empresa Estatal Petroleos de Ecuador, 332 F.3d 333 (5th Cir. 2003);

Citgo Petroleum Corp. v. Seachem, 2013 U.S. Dist. LEXIS 72898, at *1 (S.D. Tex. 2013). Because this contract is governed by the CISG, not German domestic law, the treatment of undefined delivery terms under German law can at most have only persuasive authority. Is the court's conclusion about Article 9(2) compelled by the Article's language? Consider the final clause of the Article. Is a further finding needed to support the court's conclusion that the CISG incorporates Incoterms as a matter of trade usage?

2. As the court notes, Incoterms does not deal with transfer of title to the goods. Terms in the contract passing title does not therefore modify the meaning of the C.I.F. shipment term as defined by Incoterms. The UCC's definition of the C.I.F. is different. Unlike Incoterms (and the CISG; see Article 4(b)), 2–401(2)'s default rule is that title to the goods passes to the buyer when the seller physically delivers them. Comment 1 to 2–320 provides that "[d]elivery to the carrier is delivery to the buyer for purposes of risk and 'title.'" Thus, under 2–320's definition of the C.I.F. term, both risk and title pass to the buyer when the seller puts the goods into the carrier's possession at the port of shipment. If the UCC definition controlled the meaning of the C.I.F. term in the contract in *St. Paul Guardian*, the seller's retention of title until it was paid in full would modify the term's meaning.

3. Suppose the contract in *St. Paul Guardian* did not have a C.I.F. or any other shipment term. The facts otherwise being the same as in the case, would the defendant-seller be entitled to the contract price? CISG Articles 66–67. Does Article 67(1) pass risk at the same point as the C.I.F. term defined by Incoterms? See Incoterms 2010 "C.I.F.," A.5 ("The seller must . . . bear all risks of loss of or damage to the goods until such time as they are passed the ship's rail at the port of shipment.").

4. Suppose the CISG governed the contract in *Jason's Foods, Inc.* Which Article would allocate risk of loss? Would the result in the case change? In the case the warehouse mailed its acknowledgment to the buyer on January 17 or 18. The fire at the warehouse occurred on January 17 while the buyer received the acknowledgment on January 24. Would uncertainty about the date the acknowledgment was mailed affect the result under the CISG?

5. Under Article 66 loss or damage to the goods after risk has passed to the buyer does not discharge it from its obligation to pay the price, unless the loss or damage results from the seller's act or omission. Whether loss or damage to the goods being transported by carrier has occurred is easily determined when the goods arrive. Determining when the damage or loss occurred can be more difficult. The party bearing the burden of proof must establish whether it occurred before or after risk passed to the buyer. The CISG does not expressly deal with burden of proof generally. Based on unspecified "general principles" underlying the CISG (see Article 7(2)), Chicago Prime Packers, Inc. v. Northam Food Trading Co., 408 F.3d 894 (7th Cir. 2005) assigned the burden to the buyer. There, a trucking company, acting on the buyer's instructions, picked up ribs from an independent warehouse and delivered them to a sub-buyer. Neither the seller nor the buyer ever had possession of the ribs. The ribs were spoiled. When the seller sued for the price, the buyer argued that the ribs were spoiled when the trucking company received them, and that the seller's breach discharged it from its obligation to pay the contract price. The court relied on the UCC as the domestic law "analogue" of the CISG. Under 2–607(4) and associated caselaw, the buyer bears the burden of proving breach. The court concluded that the CISG's underlying "general principles" similarly assign to the buyer the burden of proving that the goods were nonconforming at the time risk passed to it. For criticism of resort to unspecified general principles to augment the CISG's scope, see Steven Walt, The CISG's Expansion Bias: A Comment, 25 Int'l Rev. L. & Econ. 342 (2005).

PROBLEM 8.4

Buyer, located in Paris, sent an email to Seller, located in Austin, requesting that Seller "send 100 coffee makers by ship at $1,000 per coffee maker." Seller agreed by return email to do so. Their agreement was governed by the CISG. The coffee makers suffered salt water damage while on board the ship. Is Buyer obligated to pay the contract price to Seller? CISG Articles 66, 67.

PROBLEM 8.5

Suppose Seller in Problem 8.4 quoted Buyer a price of $1,000 C.I.F. Houston (port of shipment), which Buyer accepted. Seller engaged Ace Trucking to take the coffee makers from its Austin factory to Houston. The coffee makers were damaged while in transit to Houston. (a) Who bears the loss? (b) Suppose the coffee makers were damaged while the carrier loaded them on board the designated vessel in Houston. Who bears the loss? CISG Articles 6, 67.

PROBLEM 8.6

Suppose in Problem 8.5 that the coffee makers Seller loaded on Ace's trucks had double thick glass. Buyer's agreement with Seller called for the items with thin glass, which were much less expensive but also less desirable to buyers. Seller had run out of the thin-glassed items and anticipated that Buyer would welcome the substitution. Although the coffee makers Buyer receives cannot be sold for as a high a price as unblemished coffee makers, they remain saleable. However, the market for coffee makers has also declined so that even unblemished coffee makers sell for less than the price Buyer agreed to pay Seller. In the circumstances Buyer would like to return the coffee makers to Seller and not pay the purchase price. May it?

PROBLEM 8.7

Who bears risk the risk of loss in the following circumstances? In all cases the CISG governs the sales contract described below. Consult CISG Article 69.

(a) A term in Seller and Buyers' sales contract called for Buyer to take delivery of coffee makers at Seller's factory at any time between June 1 and June 10. The coffee makers are stolen from Seller's factory on June 8.

(b) Suppose that the theft in (a) occurred on June 12. Does the result change if the theft occurred on July 30? See Article 85.

(c) The term in the sales contract called for Buyer to retrieve the coffee makers at Ace's warehouse between June 1 and June 10. The coffee makers are stolen from the warehouse on June 8, two after Seller instructed Ace to allow Buyer to take delivery of them. What result under Article 2 of the UCC?

(d) The sales contract calls for Seller to deliver the coffee makers to Buyer's store. Buyer later regretted making the purchase. When Seller arrived with the items, Buyer refused to take them. The coffee makers are stolen from Seller's delivery truck on its return to Seller's factory (without Seller's fault).

CHAPTER 9

CONFLICTING RIGHTS TO THE GOODS

A sale transfers title of the goods from the seller to the buyer, so that the buyer becomes their owner. See 2–106(1). Ordinarily the seller delivers the goods and the buyer pays the seller for them. However, through the buyer's fraud or insolvency, the seller sometimes goes unpaid. In this case the seller will assert a property right in the goods sold. There is no problem if it is the only person with a property right in them. Both the common law and Article 2 generally allow the seller to replevy the goods from the buyer in these circumstances. (The seller's right to reclaim goods under Article 2 is described in Chapter 10.) But things are more complicated if more than one person claims a property right in the goods sold. For instance, a third party might assert that it owns or has a security interest in them. In this case the law must determine whether the seller's property rights in the goods are superior to the third party's property rights. The legal rules which order property rights in the sold goods are priority rules. The UCC uses certain conveyancing principles to determine the priority of claims to the sold goods. Although these rules appear in different Articles of the UCC, depending on the asset or transaction, three sets of conveyancing rules may apply in sales transactions: a basic common law rule, Article 2's good faith purchase rules, and Article 7's purchase rule for negotiable documents of title covering goods.

A. GOOD FAITH PURCHASE RULES

1. COMMON AND CIVIL LAW GOOD FAITH PURCHASE RULES

Common law and civil law systems both contain good faith purchase rules. The common law adopts the rule that a transferor can transfer no better title in the goods than she has herself. This is an application of the principle stated in the Latin phrase "*nemo dat quod non habet*" ("one who hath not cannot give"). The *nemo dat* rule is a derivation rule: The transfer gives the transferee at most only the transferor's legal interest. Thus, if the transferor is a lessee or bailee, its transferee can acquire only a leasehold or bailment interest. Because a lease or bailment does not give title to the goods to the lessee or bailee, their transferees cannot acquire title to the goods. Likewise, because a transferee's legal interest derives from its transferor's interest, the buyer can acquire no better title to goods than its seller has.

An owner of goods cannot be deprived of title to them without her consent. Because theft of goods deprives their owner of title without her consent, the thief acquires no title in the stolen goods. As the common law puts it, the thief acquires only "void title." The UCC does not define the title acquired by a thief. However, courts construing 2–403(1) conclude that the subsection continues the common law view that a thief acquires void title. See, e.g., Marlow v. Conley, 787 N.E.2d 490, 493 (Ind. Ct. App. 2003). This means that under 2–403(1)'s derivation rule, a person with void title cannot convey good title ("valid title") to a purchaser, even when the purchaser takes in good faith. Although a sale passes title for a price (2–206(1)), a thief can only pass title it has in the stolen goods—void title. Thus, a purchaser from a thief, as well as those whose title derives from a thief, does not prevail against the original owner of the goods. This is the theft rule followed in Anglo–American law. See English Sales of Good Act of 1979 § 21(1) (1979). It places the entire risk of theft on the purchaser of the goods. To be sure, the purchaser whose goods are recovered by the owner will have a claim against her seller for breach of an implied warranty of good title. See 2–312(1). The claim enables her to shift the risk of theft to her seller. But the seller might be judgment proof or difficult to locate. For this reason, the theft rule often leaves the risk of theft on the purchaser.

From an economic point of view, the common law theft rule probably is inefficient. Where stolen goods are sold to a purchaser, both the true owner and the purchaser can take precautions: The owner can take measures to guard the goods against theft, and the purchaser can take measures to investigate title in the goods it is purchasing. Precautions by each party can prevent or reduce the prospect that goods will be stolen and purchased. Thus, up to a point, precautions by both parties reduce the chance of a priority contest between the true owner and the purchaser of the goods. An efficient rule therefore would assign responsibility for the loss by "double responsibility at the margin." See Robert Cooter, Unity in Tort, Contract and Property: The Model of Precautions, 73 Cal. L. Rev. 1 (1985). The rule would allocate the true owner's loss of the goods between the owner and the purchaser according to the portion of loss that the owner and purchaser each could have avoided by their taking optimal precautions against it. This would give both parties an incentive to take their respective optimal precautions against theft or its consequences.

However, the theft rule gives the true owner no incentive to take optimal precautions against theft, because the rule puts the entire loss of the goods on the purchaser. At the same time, the rule in many civil law systems also is inefficient. The predominant civil law rule allows a good faith purchaser of stolen goods to prevail against an owner after a stipulated period of time of the theft has passed. See, e.g., French Civil Code Article 2279 (2011); Swiss Civil Code Article 934 (2008). Even English sales law prior to 1994 recognized a limited exception to the theft rule, allowing the good faith purchaser in an open market (a "market overt") to prevail against the owner. See English Sale of Goods Act of 1979 § 22(1) (repealed by the Sales of Good (Amendment) Act of 1994). Both variants of the good faith purchase rule give the purchaser no incentive to take optimal precautions, because the rule allocates the entire loss of the goods to the true owner.

Whether more efficient alternatives to the common law or civil law rules are feasible is debatable. A rule that allocates loss from theft based on a negligence standard in principle can give both the owner and purchaser of goods optimal incentives to take precautions against theft or its consequences. See Alan Schwartz & Robert E. Scott, Rethinking the Laws of Good Faith Purchase, 111 Colum. L. Rev. 6 (2011). A comparative negligence rule improves their incentives: the owner suffers the loss of the goods to the extent that it does not exhibit reasonable care for them, while the purchaser suffers the loss to the extent that it does not take reasonable care in its purchase. The UCC already allocates loss from unauthorized payment of checks by comparative negligence. See 3–304(d), 3–405(b). Apportioning loss according to negligence in some cases could require selling the goods and distributing the proceeds between the owner and purchaser if the purchase does not have the liquidity to pay her portion of the loss to the owner. For instance, if the owner is 30% negligent in the theft of its $100 widget and the purchaser 70% negligent in buying it, the widget would have to be sold in order to give $70 to the owner, unless the purchaser has $70 otherwise available. An alternative rule suggested by Professors Alan Schwartz and Robert Scott is a "one-way" negligence rule: The true owner is entitled to the goods only if she is non-negligent with respect to their theft. See id. The rule incentivizes the owner to take more precautions because she cannot recover the goods if she is negligent in failing to take care of them. For its part, the buyer continues to have an incentive to take precautions, because it loses the goods to a non-negligent owner. Unlike the comparative negligence rule, which can require selling the stolen goods to allocate loss, Schwartz and Scott's "one-way" negligence rule awards the goods either to the owner (if non-negligent) or the purchaser (if the owner is negligent). The stolen goods never need be sold.

Legal systems might have rejected a negligence-based theft rule because the rule is believed to be difficult to administer. The precaution-taking capacities of parties can depend on information that is hard to verify across the range of circumstances in which goods might be stolen and purchased. In addition, standards of care are difficult to make precise and thus hard to apply consistently across adjudicators. More generally, there can be reasonable disagreement over the optimal level of precautions a given owner or purchaser is positioned to take against theft or its consequences. See Saul Levmore, Variety and Uniformity in the Treatment of the Good Faith Purchaser, 16 J. Legal Stud. 43 (1987). The considerable diversity in the comparative law of theft rules is consistent with doubt about the feasibility of administering negligence-based standards for allocating loss. For a recent case deciding whether Swiss law's good faith purchaser rule or New York's theft rule applies to the sale of art possibly expropriated by the Nazis, see Bakalar v. Vavra, 619 F.3d 136 (2d Cir. 2011).

2. ARTICLE 2'S GOOD FAITH PURCHASE RULES

Article 2's priority rules apply in two different situations. The first situation is one in which the seller, who owns the goods, sells and delivers them to the buyer. The buyer, without paying the seller, in turn sells the goods to a third party or grants it a security interest in them. Because the buyer is insolvent, the seller and third party both assert a property right in the goods. In the second situation the buyer purchases goods from the seller while allowing her to remain in possession. The buyer pays the seller all or part of the contract price. Later, the seller sells the goods to a third party or grants it a security interest in them. Because the seller is insolvent, the buyer and third party both assert a property right in the goods. The two situations look like this:

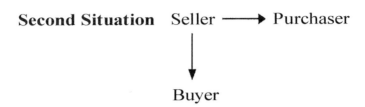

First Situation   Seller ⟶ Buyer ⟶ Purchaser

Second Situation   Seller ⟶ Purchaser

Buyer

Section 2–403(1) governs the transfer of title under Article 2 of the UCC. Its first sentence states a derivation rule: "A purchaser of goods acquires all title which his transferor had or had power to transfer, except that a purchaser of a limited interest acquires rights only to the extent of the interest purchased." The exception allows, consistent with the derivation rule, that a transferor can transfer a lesser legal interest than the one it has. Under 2–403(1)'s first sentence, a purchaser's title to the goods therefore is measured by her seller's title in them.

Section 2–403 contains both derivation and negotiation rules. Although 2–403(1)'s first sentence states a derivation rule, 2–403(1)'s second and third sentences contain a different sort of conveyancing rule. This is a rule that allows a transferee to acquire greater rights than its transferor has. The rule is a "negotiation" rule. It is a generalization of the rule of transfer recognized by the law of negotiable instruments. A transferee of a negotiable instrument takes free of most claims to the instrument when the transferee is a holder in due course. 3–302. Negotiation of the instrument therefore allows the holder to acquire greater rights in the instrument than its transferor may have. Similarly, a person who gives value for money takes free of competing claims to the money. Section 2–403(1)'s second sentence states a negotiation rule with respect to goods: "A person with voidable title has power to transfer a good title to a good faith purchaser for value." The third sentence of 2–403(1) gives the transferee the same power under "a transaction of purchase." It probably also is limited to sales transactions in which voidable title passes to the transferee ("purchaser"). "Purchaser" is defined broadly to include a party to a voluntary transaction that receives an interest in property. See 1–201(b)(29), (30).

Article 2 states default rules that determine when title passes. Under 2–401(2) title passes to the buyer when the seller has completed physical delivery of the goods, unless the parties explicitly agree otherwise. As noted in Chapter 8, where the sold goods are bailed and delivery is to occur without the goods being moved, 2–401(3) states a different default rule. If the goods are covered by a document of title, title passes to the buyer when the seller delivers the document. If the goods are not covered by a document of title, title passes when the sales contract is concluded. 2–401(3)(a), (b). At common law title is voidable when the contract is avoidable between the parties; avoidance revests title with the seller. Article 2 does not define when a transferee acquires good title and when it acquires only voidable title. Nonetheless, a fair inference from 2–401's default rules is that a sale passes at least voidable title to the buyer.

Under 2–403(1)'s good faith purchase rule, a buyer with voidable title can transfer good title to a good faith purchaser for value. As applied, it operates as a priority rule in the first priority contest described in the diagram above: that between a seller and a purchaser from the seller's buyer. In this contest the seller, who owns the goods, sells and delivers them to the buyer. The buyer fails to pay the seller and in turn sells the goods to a purchaser who purchases them in ignorance of the circumstances of the previous sale. The buyer has acquired voidable title from the seller and the purchaser has purchased in good faith for value. Under 2–403(1) the buyer's sale to the purchaser therefore passes good title to the goods. Thus, the sale cuts off seller's property right in the goods, and the purchaser has priority in the goods. The corollary to 2–403(1) is just as important: If the purchaser does not purchase in good faith and for value, the sale passes only voidable title. In a priority contest between the seller and the purchaser, the seller has priority in the goods and can replevy them from the purchaser.

Section 2–403(1)'s good faith purchase rule arguably is efficient. It increases the value of goods to qualifying purchasers and therefore the price they are willing to pay for them, because they acquire good title. Purchasers from buyers do not have to discount the value of the goods to them by the likelihood that the goods are subject to competing claims. At the same time, 2–403(1)'s negotiation rule increases the price a seller will demand to deliver goods to its buyer. Without 2–403(1), the seller would have the right to cancel the contract if the buyer did not pay. See 2–703(f). Cancellation revests title in the seller. Section 2–403(1) cuts off this right when the buyer transfers title to the goods to a good faith purchaser for value. This is a cost to the seller, which is reflected in the higher price the seller will charge to deliver goods on credit. Nevertheless, only sellers selling on credit must take measures to assure that they are paid, without relying on title in the goods. Without 2–403(1)'s protection, however, all purchasers for value must take precautions to avoid obtaining goods subject to competing claims. As a result, the increased price good faith purchasers are willing to pay for the goods when protected by 2–403(1)'s rule is greater than the increased cost the rule imposes on a subset of sellers. Article 2's drafters might have given little thought to the rule they drafted, and one UCC drafter later considered the rule a mistake. See Grant Gilmore, The Good Faith Purchase Idea and the Uniform Commercial Code: Confessions of a Repentant Draftsman, 15 Ga. L. Rev. 605 (1981).

West v. Roberts

Supreme Court of Colorado, 2006
143 P.3d 1037

■ Opinion by: JUSTICE BENDER

I.   Introduction

We review on certiorari an appellate decision from the district court, which construed Colorado Revised Statute section 18–4–405. We hold that this statute, which permits the rightful owner of stolen property to recover that property from the possession of another person, does not apply when the rightful owner intends to part with the property.

Kenneth James West relinquished his car in exchange for a cashier's check that appeared valid, but which thereafter proved to be a worthless counterfeit. When he later located the car in the possession of a subsequent purchaser, Tammy Roberts, West sued to recover the car under section 18–4–405. However, the trial court found that section 18–4–405 does not apply to situations, like this case, in which an owner voluntarily relinquishes the property, even if he is defrauded into doing so. Instead, the trial court applied Uniform Commercial Code (UCC) section 2–403, as enacted in Colorado as section 4–2–403, C.R.S. (2006). The trial court found that the UCC provision entitled Roberts, as a good faith purchaser for value, to retain ownership of the car. On appeal, the district court, acting as an appellate court, upheld the trial court's decision.

We agree with the district court's conclusion and hold that, although "theft" in our criminal code includes theft by deception, UCC section 2–403 abrogates section 18–4–405 so that "theft" in that provision does not include theft in which an owner voluntarily relinquishes property to a thief under a transaction of purchase.

Thus we affirm the district court and hold that Tammy Roberts, as a good faith purchaser for value, obtained good title to the car under C.R.S. section 4–2–403.

II.   Facts and Proceedings Below

West agreed to sell his car, a 1975 Corvette, to a man representing himself as Robert Wilson. In exchange for a cashier's check, West signed over the Corvette's title to Wilson and gave him the car. Ten days later, when West learned that the cashier's check was a forgery, he filed a stolen vehicle report with police. However, the police did not locate Wilson or the Corvette, and the case grew cold. Nearly two and a half years later, West asked the police to run a check on the Corvette's vehicle identification number. The check yielded the name and address of Tammy Roberts. Roberts, who holds certificate of title to the Corvette, had purchased the vehicle from her brother, who, in turn, had purchased it in response to a newspaper ad. West filed suit against Roberts in county court to establish legal ownership of the Corvette under Colorado's stolen property statute, C.R.S. section 18–4–405.[1]

The trial court determined that the stolen property statute did not apply in this case. Instead, the court found that the UCC, specifically C.R.S. section 4–2–403, governed the transaction and that Roberts was the rightful owner.

In reaching the conclusion that section 2–403 of the UCC applies in this case and that Roberts was the rightful owner of the Corvette, the trial court relied on Keybank Nat'l Ass'n v. Mascarenas, 17 P.3d 209

---

[1] The statute provides, in pertinent part: All property obtained by theft, robbery, or burglary shall be restored to the owner, and no sale, whether in good faith on the part of the purchaser or not, shall divest the owner of his right to such property. The owner may maintain an action . . . against any person in whose possession he finds the property.

§ 18–4–405, C.R.S. (2006).

(Colo. App. 2000). In Keybank, the court of appeals held that a theft in which the owner willingly entrusts his property to another is different than "ordinary theft," in which the owner is unaware of the taking and does not intend to part with the property. Id. at 214. The trial court found that, under the Keybank holding, theft by deception or fraud is not covered under the stolen property statute if the theft involves a transfer of goods in which the seller voluntarily parts with the goods in exchange for something else. Accordingly, the trial court held that the UCC applies in this case and that, because title can be legally transferred to a bona fide purchaser even if the transferor did not have proper authority to do so, Roberts possessed good title to the Corvette.

On appeal, the district court, acting as an appellate court, upheld the trial court's decision on two grounds. First, the court considered whether a theft had occurred for the purposes of the stolen property statute. Citing Keybank, the court found that a theft has not taken place if, as in this case, the owner was aware of a taking and had intended to part with the property. Thus, the court found the stolen property statute does not apply in this case. Second, the court found that the trial court correctly applied section 2–403 of the UCC. Even though the cashier's check from Wilson was later dishonored, the court held that Roberts was a bona fide purchaser and acquired a full property interest in the Corvette.

We accepted certiorari to reconcile the apparent conflict between the two statutes—section 2–403 of the UCC and the stolen property statute—and to determine which statute applies in this case. We first examine the stolen property statute and UCC section 2–403 and determine whether either statute applies in this case. We then reconcile the apparent conflict between the two statutes.

III. Analysis

The Stolen Property Statute

We begin by examining whether the stolen property statute applies in this case. Matters of statutory interpretation are questions of law, which we review de novo. When interpreting a statute, we look first to its plain language.

The stolen property statute permits the rightful owner of stolen property to recover that property from the possession of another person. § 18–4–405, C.R.S. For the stolen property statute to apply, "the owner of the property must prove that the taker ... committed acts constituting at least one of the statutory crimes" listed within the statute. Itin v. Ungar, 17 P.3d 129, 134 (Colo. 2000). However, the statute itself does not define theft. Because the stolen property statute is contained in the Colorado Criminal Code, terms contained in that statute may be defined within the scheme of the statutory framework. The criminal code defines theft as "knowingly obtain[ing] or exercis[ing] control over anything of value of another without authorization, or by threat or deception, and ... [i]ntend[ing] to deprive the other person permanently of the use or benefit of the thing of value." § 18–4–401(1)(a), C.R.S. (2006) (emphasis added). Theft by deception as set forth in subsection 18–4–401(1)(a) requires proof that the victim relied on a swindler's misrepresentations, which caused the victim to part with something of value.

The language of the stolen property statute states that the statute applies to property obtained by theft and that even a good faith purchaser of such property may be divested of it. The definition of theft contained in section 18–4–401 is clear. Use of the word "or" in a statute is presumed to be disjunctive. Thus, though a theft may occur when one takes property without the owner's authorization, the use of the word "or" indicates that a theft may also occur if the property is taken by deception, even with the owner's authorization.

The trial court found that Wilson deceived West into relinquishing the Corvette and its title in exchange for a fraudulent cashier's check and, accordingly, that Wilson could be charged with theft. A theft therefore occurred for the purposes of the stolen property statute. Hence, based upon the plain language of the stolen property statute and section 18–4–401, we determine that the stolen property statute appears to apply in this case.

Having analyzed the stolen property statute, we now examine section 2–403 of the UCC.

The Uniform Commercial Code

West asserts that the trial and district courts should not have applied section 2–403 of the UCC in this case. He offers two primary arguments in support of his position: (1) the entrustment provisions of section 2–403 only protect those who purchase from merchants; and (2) subsection 2–403(1) is also inapplicable because West did not pass voidable title to Wilson, the initial purchaser of the Corvette. We address each argument in turn.

West argues that, because Wilson was not a merchant, no entrustment occurred under section 2–403 and, therefore, Roberts did not acquire valid title to the car. We agree that an entrustment did not occur, which calls upon us to clarify the statute's relevance in merchant and non-merchant transactions.

We again turn to the statutory language as the starting point in our analysis. The language of section 2–403 does not indicate that all transactions falling within the statute's purview must involve a merchant; indeed, subsection (2) is the only portion of the statute that mentions the word "merchant."

Comments to a statute are relevant in its interpretation. As such, we turn to the official comments to section 2–403 for additional guidance in determining whether the statute applies to transactions involving non-merchants. The language of the official comments to section 2–403 strongly suggests that subsections (2), (3), and (4) apply specifically to merchant transactions, while subsection 2–403(1) is applicable to non-merchant transactions. Comment 2 states that subsections (2), (3), and (4) serve to protect persons who buy "in ordinary course out of inventory." The UCC defines a "buyer in ordinary course of business" as someone who buys "from a person . . . in the business of selling goods of that kind." § 4–1–201(9), C.R.S. (2006). Comment 4 indicates that the rights of purchasers who are not buyers in ordinary course—thus including those who did not buy from a merchant—are addressed in subsection (1) of the statute.

Comment 1, which applies to subsection (1), states that the provision protects "good faith purchaser[s] for value." Within the context of the UCC, the concept of good faith purchaser for value does not appear to require that the purchaser buy from a merchant or dealer. Several provisions of the UCC must be combined to define good faith purchaser for value. The UCC defines good faith as "honesty in fact and the observance of reasonable commercial standards of fair dealing." § 4–1–201(19), C.R.S. A purchaser is one who "takes by purchase." § 4–1–201(30), C.R.S. Purchase, in turn, means "taking by sale, lease, discount, negotiation, mortgage, pledge, lien, security interest, issue or reissue, gift, or any other voluntary transaction creating an interest in property." § 4–1–201(29), C.R.S. And a person gives value, generally, by providing "consideration sufficient to support a simple contract." § 4–1–204(4), C.R.S. (2006). The Kentucky Court of Appeals offered a more concise definition of good faith purchaser for value in the context of section 2–403 as "one who takes by purchase getting sufficient consideration to support a simple contract, and who is honest in the transaction of the purchase." United Rd. Machinery Co. v. Jasper, 568 S.W.2d 242, 244 (Ky. Ct. App. 1978).

When a Colorado statute is patterned after a model code, this court may draw upon outside authority in interpreting the provision. Leading treatises on the UCC support an interpretation of subsection 2–403(1) as applying beyond merchant transactions. The Uniform Commercial Code Series explains that, under subsection (2), a protected purchaser must be a buyer in the ordinary course of business, which is different than the type of purchaser addressed in subsection (1):

It should be noted that [a buyer in the ordinary course of business] is not the equivalent of the common law "bona fide purchaser" or the concept of "good faith purchaser for value" used in the voidable title situations addressed by Section 2–403(1). The principal difference between "buyer in the ordinary course of business" and these other terms lies [in] the fact that the buyer in the ordinary course must buy goods from a merchant in the business of selling goods of that kind and must buy them in the usual way in which such items of inventory are bought.

White & Summers's treatise also suggests that subsection (1) applies to non-merchant transactions. As its title implies, section 2–403 addresses three separate topics: (1) "the general powers of a transferor of goods to transfer title or interests [in subsection (1)]"; (2) "the title of a good faith purchaser of goods [in subsection (1)]"; and (3) "the rights of a buyer in ordinary course from a merchant to whom goods have been entrusted [in subsections (2) and (3)]." 1 James J. White & Robert S. Summers, Uniform Commercial Code § 3–12 (4th ed. 1995) (emphasis added). According to another treatise, for subsection 2–403(1), "the good faith of the purchaser is the focus of inquiry." Robert A. Hillman et al., Common Law and Equity Under the Uniform Commercial Code P 5.04[1] (1985). In contrast, Hillman's analyses of subsections 2–403(2) and (3) indicate that they apply to merchant transactions. For example, Hillman explains that the purpose of subsection 2–403(2) is " 'to enhance the reliability of commercial sales by merchants.' " Id. P 5.04[2]).

Finally, we note that courts in other jurisdictions have applied UCC section 2–403 to non-merchant sales transactions.

Because subsection 2–403(1) does not refer to merchant transactions or buyers in ordinary course, because the definition of good faith purchaser for value does not require purchase from a merchant or dealer, and because the official comments to UCC section 2–403 indicate that only subsections (2), (3), and (4) apply solely to merchant transactions, we conclude that subsection 2–403(1) applies to non-merchant transactions. Thus, we continue our analysis to determine whether subsection 2–403(1) applies in this case.

West also contends that, because the Corvette was stolen, he did not pass voidable title to the initial purchaser-cum-thief, Wilson. Thus, argues West, Roberts could not have obtained good title under subsection 2–403(1). West's primary argument in support of his assertion that he did not pass voidable title is that no purchase took place because he relinquished title to the car in exchange for a worthless cashier's check. We disagree.

Subsection 2–403(1) protects good faith purchasers for value. The provision requires that goods be "delivered under a transaction of purchase." § 4–2–403(1), C.R.S. (2006). As we have noted, under the UCC, a purchase is broadly defined as "taking by sale, lease, discount, negotiation, mortgage, pledge, lien, security interest, issue or reissue, gift, or *any other voluntary transaction creating an interest in property.*" § 4–1–201(29), C.R.S. (emphasis added). Voluntary means "proceeding from the will or from one's own choice or consent." Merriam–Webster's Collegiate Dictionary 1402 (11th ed. 2004). West freely chose to deliver the car and its title to Wilson. And he chose to do so even though he had neither attempted to cash the cashier's check nor obtained contact information for Wilson. Hence, we conclude that West's transfer of the Corvette and its title in exchange for a cashier's check, even though a worthless counterfeit, constitutes a voluntary transaction that is subject to subsection 2–403(1).

Indeed, the plain language of the statute itself bolsters this conclusion. Subsection 4–2–403(1) provides, in pertinent, that "[w]hen goods have been delivered under a transaction of purchase, the purchaser has such power [to transfer good title to a good faith purchaser for value] even though . . . [t]he delivery was in exchange for a check which is later dishonored, or . . . [t]he delivery was procured through fraud punishable as larcenous under the criminal law." § 4–2–403(1)(b), (d), C.R.S. This language indicates that a transaction of purchase is not thwarted simply because a purchaser failed to provide payment that met the seller's expectation. To employ West's rationale that exchanging goods for a fraudulent cashier's check does not constitute a delivery under a transaction of purchase would render the provision meaningless.

The addition of subsection 1.5 [to 2–403] by the legislature to Colorado's UCC statute also indicates that a transaction of purchase could encompass a fraud-based exchange. The General Assembly added subsection 1.5, which is not part of the UCC model code, in 1975. That provision specifies that, if a seller of livestock has not received payment, the purchaser "does not have power to transfer good title to a good faith purchaser for value until payment is made." § 4–2–403(1.5), C.R.S. We deem it significant that subsection 1.5 demarcates livestock transactions; its only effect is to require payment before a buyer has power to transfer title. This amendment to the Colorado UCC statute suggests that, by requiring payment before the power to transfer can attach, livestock transactions are to be treated differently than other transactions controlled by the statute. Therefore it is logical to conclude that a purchaser of non-livestock goods possesses the power to transfer those goods upon receipt of the goods from the seller, even if the purchaser's payment is invalid.

Various authorities provide additional support for our conclusion. "[T]he general rule seems to be that the physical delivery of the goods to a transferor-purchaser by the true owner sufficiently empowers that transferor-purchaser to transfer good title to a good faith purchaser for value even though the delivery was in exchange for a check which was later dishonored." 3 Patricia F. Fonseca & John R. Fonseca, Williston on Sales § 23:38 (5th ed. 1994). "Subsection 1(d) of 2–403 provides that even where delivery was procured through criminal fraud, voidable title passes." White & Summers, supra, § 3–12(b). The argument that the term "transaction of purchase" indicates that the true owner did not intend to enter such a fraudulent transaction fails "in light of the clear policy of Section 2–403(1) to enable the good-faith purchaser to prevail." Hillman, supra, P 5.04[2] n.95 (citing 3A R. Dusenberg & L. King, Sales & Bulk Transfers Under the Uniform Commercial Code § 10.06[1] (1982)).

We note that courts in other jurisdictions have applied subsection 2–403(1) to similar types of fraudulent, though voluntary, transactions. "A transfer that is fraudulently induced . . . is considered a 'purchase' under the Code, and meets the threshold of being 'voluntary.'" Demoulas v. Demoulas, 428 Mass. 555, 703 N.E.2d 1149, 1164 (Mass. 1998) (invoking subsection 2–403(1) to determine whether defendants were bona fide purchasers in a case in which a stock owner was defrauded into voluntarily transferring the stock). Accord Cooper, 603 P.2d at 283 (finding implicitly that a man who purchased a car with an invalid cashier's check obtained voidable title); Kenyon v. Abel, 2001 WY 135, 36 P.3d 1161, 1165–66 (Wyo. 2001) (explaining that subsection 2–403(1)(d) effectively provides that "voidable title is created whenever the transferor voluntarily delivers goods to a purchaser even though that delivery was procured through fraud" in ultimately holding that no voluntary transfer had occurred); Creggin Group, Ltd., 682 N.E.2d at 696–97 (holding that an exchange in which a man purchased an airplane using an invalid check was a transaction of purchase sufficient to confer voidable title to the purchaser regardless of the purchaser's larcenous intent).

Having concluded that West delivered the Corvette under a transaction of purchase, we continue our examination of subsection 2–403(1) in order to determine if Roberts obtained good title to the Corvette. The provision allows a person with voidable title to transfer good title to a good faith purchaser for value even under certain conditions, including when the transferor paid in cash or with a check that was later dishonored, or when the transferor otherwise procured the delivery through fraud punishable under criminal law. § 4–2–403(1), C.R.S. Specifically, subsection (1)(d) states that a good faith purchaser may obtain good title to property even if the transferor acquired the property "through fraud punishable as larcenous under the criminal law." We begin by noting that West does not dispute that Roberts is a good faith purchaser for value.

Section 18–4–403 of the Colorado Criminal Code provides that any Colorado law referring to larceny "shall be interpreted as if the word 'theft' were substituted therefore." As the trial court found, Wilson could be charged with theft for deceiving West into relinquishing the Corvette and its title in exchange for a fraudulent cashier's check. Accordingly, Wilson procured the Corvette through fraud punishable as larcenous under the criminal law. Because he obtained the car under a transaction of purchase, Wilson obtained voidable title to the car despite the fact that he paid with a fraudulent cashier's check. As such, Roberts, a subsequent good faith purchaser for value, obtained good title to the Corvette under subsection 2–403(1)(d). This result is opposite of that reached under the stolen property statute, which, pursuant to our earlier analysis, would allow West to recover the car from Roberts.

IV. Application

Because both the stolen property statute and subsection 2–403(1) of the UCC appear to apply in this case, we must next determine which statute prevails. When two statutes conflict, this Court favors a construction that avoids conflict between the provisions. If we cannot reconcile statutes passed at different legislative sessions, the statute with the latest effective date controls. And the more specific provision generally prevails over the more general provision.

The General Assembly enacted the UCC in 1965. The first version of the stolen property statute, which is effectively identical to the current provision, was enacted in 1861 as a territorial law. The UCC provision, which addresses in detail several types of scenarios, is more specific than the stolen property statute. We therefore hold that UCC section 2–403 prevails over the stolen property statute.

Further analysis bolsters our holding. The general rule, embodied in the stolen property statute, is that "[a] thief has no title and can pass none, not even to a buyer in the ordinary course." Fonseca & Fonseca, supra, § 23:35. See also, e.g., Thomas M. Quinn, Uniform Commercial Code Commentary and Law Digest P 2–403[A][5] (1978) ("Where the goods are stolen from the original owner, both the common law and the Code preserve the original owner's ownership rights . . . notwithstanding subsequent sales."). However, UCC section 2–403 provides an exception to that general rule. Comment 1 to section 2–403 hints at such an exception in the context of subsection (1), explaining that "subsection (1) provides specifically for the protection of the good faith purchaser for value in a number of specific situations which have been troublesome under prior law." § 4–2–403 official cmt. 1, C.R.S. Each of the specific situations listed in subsection 2–403(1) involves a voluntary transfer of goods, even though the intent to transfer the goods may have been induced by fraud. The language of the statute leads to the conclusion that goods delivered under a transaction of purchase, even when the seller is fraudulently induced to do so, can then be validly sold to a good faith purchaser for value, whereas goods that are stolen but not delivered under a transaction of purchase cannot.

Again, treatises on the UCC support this conclusion. White and Summers explain that theft by fraud should be distinguished from robbery-type theft because the original seller has a better opportunity to prevent that type of theft:

> In general voidable title passes to those who lie in the middle of the spectrum that runs from best faith buyer at one end to robber at the other. These are buyers who commit fraud, or are otherwise guilty of naughty acts (bounced checks), but who conform to the appearance of a voluntary transaction; they would never pull a gun or crawl in through a second story window. Presumably these fraudulent buyers get voidable title from their targets, but second story men get only void title because the targets of fraud are themselves more culpable than the targets of burglary.

White & Summers, supra, § 3–12(b). See also Quinn, supra, P 2–403[A][5] ("Where the original owner parts with the goods voluntarily in circumstances which, while deplorable, do not constitute outright theft, there is always the chance that the transferee will acquire apparent ownership or 'voidable title' and, thanks to this altered state, may be able to pass along better title to a good faith purchaser than he himself may have."). By relinquishing possession of the goods to the buyer, even when fraudulently induced to do so, the original seller cloaks the "thief" with the apparent authority to sell the goods. Fonseca & Fonseca, supra, § 23:35.

We note that other jurisdictions have distinguished theft by fraud that results in a voluntary transfer of the stolen property from theft by wrongful taking. This Court has also hinted at that distinction, explaining that the stolen property statute "allows an owner to regain only property 'obtained by theft, robbery, or burglary' rather than any property that has been 'wrongfully taken or detained.'" In re Marriage of Allen, 724 P.2d 651, 656 (Colo. 1986). Indeed, our court of appeals made this distinction in the context of section 2–403 in Keybank, upon which the trial and district courts relied in finding that Roberts acquired good title to the Corvette. Our decision today serves to extend the Keybank distinction beyond the context in which it was rendered—the entrustment provisions of subsections 2–403(2) and (3)—to transactions under subsection 2–403(1). However, we disagree with the Keybank rationale to the extent that it suggests that a distinction between theft and fraud exists within our criminal code.

We therefore hold that, although "theft" in our criminal code includes theft by deception, section 2–403 abrogates the stolen property statute so that "theft" in that provision does not include any theft in which an owner voluntarily relinquishes property to a thief under a transaction of purchase.

We acknowledge that such a rule can, as in this case, result in loss to an innocent party. But a determination that West is entitled to recover the car would also be a determination that Roberts, another innocent party, must relinquish a vehicle that she purchased in good faith. The policy behind subsection 2–403(1) is to protect the party least able to protect herself—the good faith purchaser for value.

Where an owner has voluntarily parted with possession of his chattel, even though induced by a criminal act, a bona fide purchaser can acquire good title, under the theory that where one of two innocent parties must suffer because of the wrongdoing of a third person, the loss must fall on the party who by his conduct created the circumstances which enabled the third party to perpetuate the wrong.

The original seller is better positioned to take precautions to prevent loss than a later purchaser. For example, West could have insisted upon cash or ensured that the check would clear before relinquishing the car and title. On the other hand, to place the onus on the good faith purchaser to fully investigate every purchase in order to determine whether it originated in fraud would unduly burden trade. We have acknowledged that this tenet "is in accord with the overall policy of the UCC's entrustment provision: to restrict impediments to the free flow of commerce when buyers in the ordinary course of business are involved." Cugnini v. Reynolds Cattle Co., 687 P.2d 962, 967 (Colo. 1984). It is equally applicable to good faith purchasers for value under subsection 2–403(1).

V.   Conclusion

For the reasons stated, we affirm the judgment of the district court acting as an appellate court.

* * *

NOTES

1.   The court decided that under 2–403(1)'s third sentence West passed voidable title to Roberts, even though Roberts paid with a bad check. The same result could be reached under 2–403(1)'s second sentence. According to 2–401(2), unless expressly agreed otherwise, the seller passes title to the buyer when he delivers the goods. West gave Roberts the car in exchange for a forged cashier's check and apparently did not retain title in the sales agreement. Thus, Roberts obtained voidable title in the car. Under 2–403(1)'s second sentence, Roberts therefore had the power to transfer good title in car to a good faith purchaser for value.

A seller who wants to assure payment will reserve a security interest in the goods sold. Section 2–401(1) provides that retention or reservation of title in the goods is limited in effect to a reservation of a security interest. Cf. 1–201(b)(35). This means that, even if the sales contract reserves title in the seller, the reservation does not prevent title from passing to the buyer on delivery of the goods. Reservation of title merely gives the seller a security interest in the goods, not an ownership interest in them. For the seller's security interest to be enforceable in the goods against third parties, the seller must perfect its interest. Perfection generally requires filing a financing statement covering the goods in the proper place. See 9–310(a). In the case of a motor vehicle covered by a certificate of title, perfection requires a notation of the security interest on the certificate. 9–311(a)(2), (b). Failure to do so allows a buyer of goods to take free of the security interest if it takes delivery without knowledge of the security interest and before it is perfected. 9–317(b).

2.   Section 2–403(1)'s third sentence is a response to vagueness in pre-Code law as to when a sale passes voidable title to a purchaser. The black letter rule was that the purchaser acquired voidable title only if her seller intended to pass title to her. See Phelps v. McQuade, 115 N.E. 441, 442 (N.Y. 1917). Courts disagreed over when this intent was present. One area of disagreement involved payment with bad checks. Some courts found that the seller who takes a check intends title to pass, title revesting in the seller if the check was bad and the seller rescinded the contract. Other courts concluded that the seller did not intent to pass title when it received a bad check. The other line of cases involved impersonation. A seller deceived by the identity of an imposter in her presence nonetheless was held to intend to pass title to the goods to the imposter. By contrast, a seller who is the victim of impersonation by letter intends not to pass title to the imposter but the person named in the letter. For a description of the pre-Code case law, see William D. Warren, Cutting Off Claims of Ownership Under the Uniform Commercial Code, 30 U. Chi. L. Rev. 469, 475–477 (1963); Grant Gilmore, The Commercial Doctrine of Good Faith Purchase, 63 Yale L. J. 1057, 1059–1060 (1954). The drafters of 2–403(1)'s third sentence added it to protect the good faith purchaser for value in cases that had been problematic under prior law. See 1956 New York Law Reform Commission, Report Relating to the Uniform Commercial Code 383 (1956). The sentence gives a transferee under a "transaction of purchase" the power to transfer good title to the goods even if the transferor was deceived as to the transferee's identity or delivery was in exchange for a bad check. See 2–403(1)(a), (b).

3. Section 2–403(1)'s third sentence does not specify the range of "transactions of purchase" to which it applies. The phrase "a transaction of purchase" is not limited to contracts of sale. "Purchase" means any interest voluntarily transferred, including lesser interests than ownership. 1–201(b)(29). A leasehold or bailment interest conveyed by an owner of goods therefore is a purchase. Accordingly, under 2–403(1)'s third sentence, can a lessee or bailee transfer the lessor or bailor's title to the leased or bailed goods to a good faith purchaser for value? Although a "transaction of purchase" is broad enough to apply to leases or bailments, the probable intent of 2–403(1)'s drafters suggests that it is limited to sales. As noted above, the 2–403(1)'s third sentence was added in response to uncertainty in some purported sales as to whether voidable title passed. The sentence was not intended to apply to non-sales transactions. Thus, a bailee cannot transfer the bailor's title to bailed goods to a good faith purchaser for value who does not buy the goods. See, e.g., In re Weiler, 2004 Bankr. LEXIS 2604, at *1 (Bankr. S.D. Iowa 2004). Sections 2A–305(1) similarly limits a lessee's power of transfer to the transfer of a good leasehold interest.

4. The CISG leaves conflicting claims to the goods to national law. Article 30 obligates the seller to transfer title ("property") in the goods as required by the contract and the Convention. However, the CISG does not control passage of title. Article 4 provides in relevant part that the Convention is not "concerned with . . . (b) The effect which the contract may have on the property in the goods sold." The CISG therefore does not determine whether, and under what circumstances, the sales contract passes title ("property") to the goods to the buyer. See, e.g., Oberlandesgericht München (Germany), 5 March 2008, available at http://www.cisg.law.pace.edu/cases/080305g1.html. It therefore also does not determine the circumstances under which the buyer's transfer of the goods passes voidable or good title to a purchaser. For the same reason, Article 4(b) excludes from the CISG's scope the priority of claims to the goods. Because the CISG does not address these issues, applicable national sales law controls. National laws governing transfer of title are diverse, even within Europe; see Ulrich Drobing, Transfer of Property, in Towards a European Civil Code 1003 (A. Hartkamp et al. eds., 4th ed. 2011).

PROBLEM 9.1

Sam has sewn three shirts that have won high praise and are in demand. His friends, Albert, Beatrice and Charles, appear at his house each wanting one of the shirts. Sam sells a shirt to Albert but keeps it until Albert returns with the money. On leaving Sam's house Albert immediately sells the shirt to Jones, who promises to pay Albert. Beatrice pays for her shirt by check and departs with it. She later gives the shirt to her friend, Zak, who is delighted. Sam decides to give away his third shirt to Charles, who is poor and has just lost his job. Also delighted, Charles departs with his shirt. In need of funds, he trades Landlord the shirt for a month's rent due on his apartment. Later events disappoint Sam. Albert does not return to pay him; instead Jones appears and demands the shirt Sam reserved for Albert. Beatrice's check bounces and Sam cannot bring himself to ask her for another check. However, Sam is pleased to learn that Zak's shirt is unworn. Although Sam and Charles are no longer friends, Sam has discovered that Landlord has not worn Charles' shirt either.

(a) Sam does not want to turn over Albert's shirt to Jones. He also wants to retrieve the shirts from Zak and Landlord. What rights does he have in these shirts? 2–403(1), 1–201(b)(20), (29), 1–204, 2–507(2), 2–511(3).

(b) If Sam does not have to turn over Albert's shirt to Jones, does Jones have any recourse against Albert?

(c) Assume that Jones promised to pay Albert a competitive price for Albert's shirt. Jones in turn received an extremely low price from Debbie for the shirt and instructed her to pick it up from Sam. Can Debbie retrieve the shirt from Sam?

Maryott v. Oconto Cattle Co.

Supreme Court of Nebraska, 2000
607 N.W.2d 820

■ CONNOLLY, J.

This case presents the following question: Under the Nebraska Uniform Commercial Code, is the interest of an unpaid cash seller in goods, already delivered to a buyer, superior or subordinate to the interest of a holder of a perfected security interest in those same goods?

The appellee, Ned Maryott, delivered cattle to Oconto Cattle Company, a limited partnership (Oconto), and was given two sight drafts drawn from lines of credit extended by the appellant, Farm Credit Services of the Midlands, PCA (Farm Credit). Before the drafts were presented for payment, Farm Credit declared the loans in default and refused payment on the drafts. Farm Credit held perfected security interests in cattle acquired by Oconto.

Maryott brought a replevin action against Oconto seeking return of the cattle, and Farm Credit intervened. The district court held that Maryott had a superior interest in the cattle and entered judgment in his favor. Farm Credit appeals, contending that regardless of whether Maryott retained title when he delivered the cattle to Oconto, all Maryott retained was a security interest in the cattle, which he failed to perfect. We conclude that under the Nebraska Uniform Commercial Code, an unpaid seller who reserves title in goods sold retains a security interest in the goods that, if perfected, will give the seller priority over creditors of the buyers. Because Maryott did not perfect his security interest as required by Neb. U.C.C. §§ 9–107 (Reissue 1992) and 9–312 (Cum. Supp. 1996), we conclude that Farm Credit has priority. Accordingly, we reverse.

Background

Farm Credit is composed of a production credit association (PCA) and a federal land credit association (FLCA). PCA makes operational loans secured by chattels, and FLCA makes longer term loans secured by real property. Oconto, a Nebraska limited partnership, owned a commercial cattle feedlot. At all relevant times, Warren E. Bierman, as general partner, operated the feedlot. Oconto's business included buying and selling cattle in its own name, custom feeding and marketing of cattle owned by others, and custom feeding and marketing of cattle purchased by others for which purchases Oconto supplied the financing.

Farm Credit was Oconto's lender. That relationship began in 1995 with the execution of several promissory notes. On July 25, 1996, the notes were renewed. At that time, two different notes provided Oconto with a line of credit up to $3,000,000 on each note. All notes were secured and cross-collateralized by security interests granted by Oconto in a security agreement and trust deed. The security agreement included in its description of collateral all livestock and inventory then owned by Oconto and thereafter acquired. The security agreement stated that the collateral secured all future and additional loans made to Oconto by Farm Credit.

Farm Credit's security interests were duly perfected by a financing statement filed with the Custer County clerk on June 1, 1995, and the Nebraska Secretary of State on June 5, and by a Nebraska effective financing statement filed with the Custer County register of deeds on June 1. The rights and obligations of Farm Credit and Oconto were contained in the promissory notes, security agreements, and trust deed described above, along with a loan agreement and several loan addendums (collectively the loan documents).

On and after July 25, 1996, under the loan documents, Farm Credit at its option could advance funds to Oconto under the line of credit loans to a maximum of $3,000,000 for each note. However, all advances were conditioned upon Oconto's being in compliance with the terms and conditions of the loan documents, including a borrowing base formula. The borrowing base formula, among other things, required Oconto to report monthly to Farm Credit. Such reports enabled Farm Credit to compute the ratio of debt to collateral. At the time of trial, Farm Credit had a nondischargeable judgment against Bierman.

For over 20 years, Maryott, a resident of Britton, South Dakota, sold cattle either to Bierman, individually, or to Oconto through Bierman. Maryott's practice was to deliver cattle by truck to the feedlot and present invoices for the cattle to Bierman or other feedlot personnel. Approximately 25 percent of the time, Maryott was paid immediately upon delivery of the cattle. Otherwise, Oconto would pay Maryott 2 to 3 weeks after delivery. In the industry, Oconto had the reputation of being a slow-pay client. With the exception of the cattle at issue, Oconto eventually paid Maryott for the cattle delivered.

When Maryott delivered cattle to Oconto, he did not restrict Oconto's ability to sell the cattle to others. He did not instruct Oconto regarding how to pen the cattle, how to feed or care for the cattle, or where, when, or at what price to sell the cattle. If cattle died after delivery but before Maryott received payment, the loss was born by Oconto.

Oconto paid Maryott for cattle with Farm Credit sight drafts payable through Norwest Bank Nebraska, N.A. The sight drafts were drawn on the lines of credit that Farm Credit had extended to Oconto under the loan documents. The loan documents provided that each sight draft that was honored by Farm Credit constituted an extension of credit to Oconto. Under the loan documents, Farm Credit had an absolute right to instruct Norwest not to honor a sight draft. Norwest would provide Farm Credit daily with a list of drafts presented for payment and obtain authorization from Farm Credit before payment. This form of payment is the customary method by which Farm Credit extends credit to borrowers with lines of credit.

From July 16 through August 29, 1996, Maryott, in several different deliveries, delivered 640 head of cattle to the feedlot. Although Oconto did not pay Maryott after each delivery, he continued to deliver cattle.

Maryott first learned there was a problem when two Farm Credit sight drafts dated August 26 and 28, 1996, issued by Oconto in partial payment for the cattle, were dishonored. Maryott called Bierman, who told Maryott to send the drafts through again. When Maryott did so, the drafts were dishonored a second time. Maryott called Bierman and was reassured that he would be paid. Maryott did not call or visit Farm Credit to inquire about the drafts until approximately September 19 or 23.

The reason for the dishonor was that on August 30, 1996, Farm Credit had declared Oconto in default of the loan documents and canceled Oconto's lines of credit. The lines were canceled because it appeared that Bierman had been double counting some receivables and that he was not in compliance with the borrowing base formula. There was also evidence of a check-kiting scheme. When Bierman failed to provide a satisfactory explanation, Farm Credit declared the Oconto loans to be in default and refused to extend any further credit with the exception of making some protective advances. At the time of Oconto's default, its indebtedness to Farm Credit was well in excess of the value of the cattle. The protective advances were made to cover costs in keeping up the feedlot and to ensure that cattle remaining on the lot were cared for until sold. Oconto subsequently filed bankruptcy.

Maryott came to the feedlot on September 23, 1996, inspected the cattle, and met with a Farm Credit representative, who did not allow him to take any of the cattle. Following a review of the records regarding the cattle, Farm Credit determined that Maryott could not prove a superior ownership and that there would likely be a dispute over it. However, there is some dispute in the record regarding whether a representative of Farm Credit told Maryott that "maybe" he would get either money or the cattle back.

Maryott subsequently filed a replevin action against Oconto, Bierman, and Bierman's wife, seeking a return of the cattle, and Maryott was granted relief from the automatic stay by the bankruptcy court. Farm Credit intervened. In both his petition and answer to Farm Credit's petition in intervention, Maryott alleged that as the owner of the cattle, he had a security interest in them. Maryott did not allege in his petition or answer to Farm Credit's petition in intervention that Farm Credit acted in bad faith. However, the court denied a motion for summary judgment on the basis that questions of fact remained regarding whether title to the cattle passed to Oconto upon delivery and whether Farm Credit acted in good faith when it stopped payment on the drafts.

At trial, Maryott contended that it was the industry standard that title would not pass until the seller of the cattle had been paid. As evidence of this, Maryott called three witnesses: a friend and neighbor of Maryott, a person who had a longstanding business relationship with Maryott, and a customer of Oconto who was in the same position as Maryott in relation to Oconto. The witnesses testified that the practice in the industry was that the buyer would not receive any rights in cattle until the seller was paid and that if there was no payment, the seller had the right to pick up the cattle.

Evidence introduced at trial indicated that Maryott was familiar with cattle financing and had given lenders, including Oconto, security interests in cattle as collateral for loans. Maryott did not require Oconto to execute any security documents in his favor with respect to the cattle, did not file any financing statement with respect to the cattle, did not check Oconto's credit record, and did not check county and state records for any security interests which might be claimed on Oconto's property. The record indicates that Farm Credit did not inquire about cattle delivered prior to declaring Oconto's loans in default. The record also reflects that Farm Credit did not know about Maryott's outstanding claim at the time it made the decision to cease extending credit under the loans. Farm Credit did not inquire about what the dishonored drafts were for when it refused to extend further credit.

The trial court concluded that Maryott and Oconto had established a course of business and custom that created an express agreement that a sale of cattle would not be complete until payment was made. The court also concluded that Maryott had a "special ownership or interest" in the cattle. The court then determined that Farm Credit had notice of Oconto's conduct in acquiring the cattle without payment, but that Farm Credit did not have a malicious motive in seizing the cattle. In addition, the court determined that Farm Credit's security interest did not attach to the cattle and that it did not advance funds for purchase of the cattle or change its financial position with respect to the cattle. As a result, the court entered a judgment in the amount of $348,479.94 for the value of the cattle and dismissed Farm Credit's petition in intervention with prejudice. Farm Credit appeals.

Assignments of Error

Farm Credit assigns that the trial court erred in determining that (1) title to the cattle did not pass to Oconto, (2) Farm Credit's security interest did not attach to the cattle, (3) Maryott had a superior interest in the cattle, and (4) Maryott was the real party in interest.

* * *

Analysis

Farm Credit contends that once the cattle were delivered to Oconto, all Maryott had was the reservation of a security interest, which he failed to perfect. As a result, Farm Credit contends that it has a superior right to the cattle because of its perfected security interests in the property of Oconto. However, Maryott argues that through either custom and usage in the trade, the course of dealing between himself and Oconto, or an oral contract, an express agreement existed that acted to reserve title in the cattle in Maryott until he was paid. He asserts that this interest defeats any interest that Farm Credit has in the cattle.

Before the adoption of the U.C.C., cash sales in some jurisdictions were governed by the "cash sales doctrine" under which a cash buyer did not receive title to goods purchased until the seller was paid in full. Under this doctrine, a cash buyer who had not paid the seller in full could not pass title to a bona fide purchaser and an unpaid cash seller could reclaim the goods. However, it was determined that the cash sales doctrine restricted the free flow of goods in commerce and was abolished by adoption of the provisions of the U.C.C.

Effect of Reservation of Title

The U.C.C. specifically limits a seller's ability to reserve title once he or she has surrendered possession to a buyer and dictates that even when title is reserved, the effect of such a reservation is the retention of a security interest. Neb. U.C.C. § 2–401 provides:

Each provision of this article with regard to the rights, obligations and remedies of the seller, the buyer, purchasers or other third parties applies irrespective of title to the goods except where the provision refers to such title. . . .

(1) . . . *Any retention or reservation by the seller of the title (property) in goods shipped or delivered to the buyer is limited in effect to a reservation of a security interest* . . .

(2) Unless otherwise explicitly agreed title passes to the buyer at the time and place at which the seller completes performance with reference to the physical delivery of the goods, despite any reservation of a security interest. . . . (Emphasis supplied.)

This section does not provide for a revesting of title for nonpayment of the purchase price alone, unless the contract of sale so provides. The theory behind § 2–401 is that " 'article [Two] deals with the issues between seller and buyer in terms of step-by-step performance or non-performance under the contract for sale and not in terms of whether or not "title" to the goods has passed.' " Matter of Samuels & Co., Inc., 526 F.2d 1238, 1246 (5th Cir. 1976).

In this case, even if Maryott could be determined to have explicitly reserved title in the cattle by a course of business or custom as the trial court found, under § 2–401, his interest was nonetheless limited to the reservation of a security interest subject to the provisions of article 9. A reservation of title does not automatically give Maryott rights to the cattle. Accordingly, the next question is whether Farm Credit's perfected security interest attached under Neb. U.C.C. § 9–203 to the cattle at issue and if that interest has priority over Maryott's unperfected security interest.

Attachment of Farm Credit's Security Interest

Under the U.C.C., attachment of an article 9 security interest takes place when (1) there is agreement that the interest attaches to the collateral, (2) the secured party has given the value of the collateral, and (3) the debtor has rights in the collateral sufficient to permit attachment.

In this case, there is no dispute that Farm Credit and Oconto had a specific agreement that allowed a lien on all of Oconto's after-acquired cattle and inventory. Value is defined to include "security for or in total or partial satisfaction of a preexisting claim." Neb. U.C.C. § 1–201(44)(b). This definition of value includes an article 9 security interest. The remaining question regarding attachment is whether Oconto had sufficient rights in the collateral to permit attachment.

The U.C.C. allows a buyer who has not paid for goods to transfer greater title to a good faith purchaser than he or she can claim. Further, a secured creditor of a buyer can be considered to be a good faith purchaser. Neb. U.C.C § 2–403 provides in part:

(1) A purchaser of goods acquires all title which his or her transferor had or had power to transfer except that a purchaser of a limited interest acquires rights only to the extent of the interest purchased. A person with voidable title has power to transfer a good title to a good faith purchaser for value. When goods have been delivered under a transaction of purchase the purchaser has such power even though

> (a) the transferor was deceived as to the identity of the purchaser, or
>
> (b) the delivery was in exchange for a check which is later dishonored[.]

Thus in a situation where a cash seller delivers goods to a buyer and is paid with a dishonored check, § 2–403 allows the buyer in this situation to pass greater title to a good faith purchaser than the buyer could claim. This rule is designed to promote the greatest range of freedom possible to commercial vendors and purchasers. the definition of "purchaser" found in the U.C.C. is broad and includes persons taking by mortgage, pledge, or lien. § 1–201[29] and [30]. The relationship between a lien creditor as a purchaser and attachment of a security interest were described by the Fifth Circuit in *Matter of Samuels & Co., Inc.*, 526 F.2d at 1243, as follows:

The existence of an Article Nine interest presupposes the debtor's having rights in the collateral sufficient to permit attachment. . . . Therefore, since a defaulting cash buyer has the power to transfer a security interest to a lien creditor, including an Article Nine secured party, the buyer's rights in the property, however marginal, must be sufficient to allow attachment of a lien.

In such cases, a secured creditor can qualify as a good faith purchaser for value and receive priority under article 9 over an unpaid seller. See, Cooperative Finance Ass'n v. B & J Cattle, 937 P.2d 915, 920 (Colo. App. 1997) ("a perfected security interest resulting from an after-acquired property clause prevails over the retained interest of an unpaid cash-seller"). We have held that between an unpaid seller and a secured party who qualifies as a good faith purchaser, the secured party has priority.

Lack of Good Faith

Maryott contends that Farm Credit is not a good faith purchaser because it can be inferred that Farm Credit had knowledge that the drafts would be used to purchase cattle. The trial court found that Farm Credit had notice that Oconto had acquired cattle from Maryott without payment.

Farm Credit did not notify Maryott or others of its actions before canceling Oconto's lines of credit and prevented payment for the cattle by dishonoring the drafts. However, the evidence at trial was clear that Farm Credit also did not have knowledge of the specific business transactions between Oconto and Maryott and was unaware that Maryott had not been paid for the cattle he had delivered to Oconto. The burden is on Maryott to show any bad faith on the part of Farm Credit. The record does not support any finding by the district court that Farm Credit had notice that Maryott had not been paid for deliveries of cattle at the time Oconto's lines of credit were canceled. Any such finding of fact is clearly erroneous.

Further, even if evidence established that Farm Credit had a general knowledge of Oconto's nonpayment and of Maryott's claim, Farm Credit's status as an article 2 good faith purchaser would be unaffected. The good faith provisions in the U.C.C. require "honesty in fact," § 1–201(19), which is further defined as "reasonable commercial standards of fair dealing in the trade," Neb. U.C.C. § 2–103(1)(b).

Lack of knowledge of outstanding claims is necessary to the common law [bona fide purchaser] and is similarly expressly required in many Code [bona fide purchaser] and priority provisions. . . . But the Code's definition of an Article Two good faith purchaser does not expressly or impliedly include lack of knowledge of third-party claims as an element. *Matter of Samuels & Co., Inc.*, 526 F.2d 1238, 1243–44 (5th Cir. 1976). In the context of the setoff of account funds, it has been held that actual knowledge that funds belong to a third party can limit the ability of a bank to setoff funds in good faith. However, general knowledge that an account was used for a feedlot's business transactions is not enough to charge a bank with bad faith on the basis that such a holding would act to make a bank liable every time it performed a setoff. Id.

In this case, lack of notice is not required under the U.C.C. in order for a purchaser to act in good faith. Further, Maryott did not specifically allege bad faith in either his petition or answer to Farm Credit's petition in intervention. In addition, there was no evidence at trial of specific notice on the part of Farm Credit. At most, any evidence of notice consisted of a general knowledge that advances of credit through the use of sight drafts were used by Oconto for its business transactions. As in the case of a setoff, a creditor would be subject to liability every time it refused to advance credit if general knowledge was sufficient to constitute bad faith. As another court has stated, "The Code's good faith provision requires 'honesty in fact' . . . it hardly requires a secured party to continue financing a doomed business enterprise." *Matter of Samuels & Co., Inc.*, 526 F.2d at 1243. Under these circumstances, Maryott did not prove bad faith on the part of Farm Credit.

Conclusion

In this case, Farm Credit's perfected security interest prevails over Maryott's unperfected interest. Article 9 does not provide an exception for an unpaid cash seller. Rather, it specifically provides a means for such a seller to perfect and achieve priority over previously perfected interests. Maryott could have protected his interest against Farm Credit's prior perfected interest by complying with the U.C.C.'s purchase-money provisions. Because Maryott failed to perfect his interest, Farm Credit has priority. Accordingly, the order of the trial court is reversed.

Reversed.

NOTES

1. *Maryott* finds that 2–403(1) gives the buyer's secured creditor priority over the unpaid seller. The secured creditor has priority under 2–403(1) only if it acquires good title to the goods from the buyer. The *Maryott* court is imprecise about the legal interest that the secured creditor acquires in the buyer's goods. It merely quotes *In re Samuels* to the effect that "[t]he existence of an Article Nine interest presupposes the debtor's having rights in the collateral sufficient to permit attachment." A security interest attaches only to the buyer's rights in the goods or its power to transfer rights in them. See 9–203(b)(2). A buyer who pays by check which is dishonored obtains voidable title in the goods. See 2–507(2), 2–511(3). However, a security interest does not by itself give the secured creditor title the goods (voidable or valid). In *Maryott*, for instance, Oconto's security agreement with Farm Credit did not make Farm Credit the owner of the cattle Oconto bought from Maryott. Instead, the security interest gives the creditor a specific property right: the right to satisfy its claim against the debtor from the collateral if the debtor defaults. Because the debtor continues to own the collateral, it is entitled to the proceeds from the disposition of the collateral in excess of the amount of the creditor's claim. See 9–615(d)(1). Section 2–403(1) refers to the buyer's "power to transfer" good title to a good faith purchaser for value. Implicit in this reference is the buyer's power to transfer lesser interests in the goods to a good faith purchaser for value. If a buyer with voidable title has the power to transfer good title, it also has the power to grant a security interest, a lesser property right, to a creditor. Under 2–403(1) the secured creditor's security interest in the goods therefore is superior to the unpaid seller's right in them.

2.   Section 1–201(b)(20) defines "good faith" to mean "honesty in fact and the observance of reasonable commercial standards of fair dealing." The "fair dealing" component of good faith, borrowed from 3–103(a)(6), was added as part of the 2001 amendments to Article 1. In finding that Farm Credit acted in good faith when it ordered the bank not to honor its sight drafts, the *Maryott* court focused on the "honesty in fact" component of good faith. Because Maryott did not allege that Farm Credit acted in bad faith, the court apparently thought it unnecessary to determine whether Farm Credit also satisfied the "fair dealing" component of 1–201(b)(20). Standards of fair dealing are norms of behavior, not standards of care with which a transaction is conducted. See Comment 2 to 3–103; Gerber & Gerber v. Regions Bank, 596 S.E.2d 174, 178 (Ga. Ct. App. 2004). The relevant standards of fair dealing are otherwise elusive. Courts have held that a merchant buyer does not act in accordance with these standards when it ignores warning signs that the sale might be suspect; see, e.g., Davis v. Carroll, 937 F. Supp.2d 390 (S.D.N.Y. 2013); Brown v. Mitchell-Innis & Nash, Inc., 68 UCC Rep. Serv.2d 599 (S.D.N.Y. 2009). There is no case law discussing the application of the "fair dealing" component of good faith to a secured creditor. In re Tucker, 329 B.R. 291 (Bankr. D. Ariz. 2005) is a rare case in which in which a court concluded that a secured creditor's failure to perfect its security interest violates reasonable commercial standards of fair dealing. The court did not reveal, however, the commercial standards that make the failure to give public notice of a security interest unfair dealing. In *Maryott*, Farm Credit perfected its security interest in Ocoto's inventory by filing a proper financing statement.

3.   Equitable principles, including estoppel, recognized under extra-UCC law continue to supplement Article 2, unless expressly displaced by its provisions. See 1–103(b). These principles can operate to allow a transferee to obtain good title or lesser interest in goods even when 2–403 is inapplicable. For instance, a true owner's failure to take action to prevent a seller from appearing to hold title in the goods can estop the owner from asserting ownership in them. Cf. United Rd. Mach. Co. v. Jasper, 568 S.W.2d 242 (Ky. Ct. App. 1978). Correspondingly, a purchaser's prior conduct might estop it from taking good title when it later purchases the goods in good faith and for value. In American Bank & Trust v. Shaull, 678 N.W.2d 779 (S.D. 2004), the South Dakota Supreme Court relied on estoppel to give priority to a bailee's secured creditor over the bailor. There, a cattle owner bailed his cattle with a bailee who also maintained his own herd of cattle. The bailee previously had granted a creditor a security interest in its existing and later acquired livestock. The bailor did not give public notice of the bailment (and was not required to do so). When the bailee defaulted on its obligations to its secured creditor, the creditor claimed a security interest in the bailee's herd, including the bailor's cattle. The Court held that the bailor was estopped from asserting ownership of the cattle in the bailee's possession. The bailee's apparent ownership of the cattle gave it sufficient rights to grant a security interest in the bailed cattle. The Court offered the following rationale for its holding, quoting from a previous case: "If the owner of collateral allows another to appear as the owner or to dispose of the collateral such that a third party is led into dealing with the apparent owner as though he were the actual owner, then the owner will be estopped from asserting that the apparent owner did not have rights in the collateral." Id. at 784.

PROBLEM 9.2

Solar Inc. manufactures energy efficient electrical units as well as fire detection devices. To enter the air conditioner market, it engaged Smith Corp. to market and sell only the air conditioners it would produce. Solar would continue to market its fire detection devices on its own. At the same time, Solar sent notice to customers who had purchased its products in the past to the effect that Smith was selling energy efficient products on Solar's behalf. Smith had never handled electrical products before. Nonetheless, it sold one of Solar's $10,000 fire detection devices to Battle, who had contacted Smith after receiving Solar's notice. Battle paid Smith by check, which was later dishonored. This occurred after Battle sold the fire detection device to Zeta Corp. for $3,000. Solar's products set the industry standard and sell for top dollar. Smith and Battle both are in bankruptcy and Solar wants to replevy the fire detection device in Zeta's hands. Can it? 2–403(1), (2), 2–511(2), 1–103(b), 1–201(b)(20).

3. BULK SALES LAWS

Buyers in a few jurisdictions need to worry about the purchase of all or a substantial portion of the seller's goods not in the ordinary course of business. These sales are called "bulk sales." Bulk sales typically involve the transfer of all or most of the seller's inventory. Section 6–102(c), for instance, defines a bulk sale as a sale not in the ordinary course of the seller's business of more than half of the seller's inventory, as measured by value. Bulk sales laws require the buyer to give the seller's creditors notice of the pending sale, although the seller remains responsible for paying its creditors. The notice puts the creditors in a position to be able to collect payment of their debts from the seller. Article 6 of the UCC governs bulk sales. Almost all states have repealed their bulk sales laws, as recommended by the Article 6's drafters and allowed by Article 6. See Article 6, Prefatory Note; § 1 (Alt.). The overwhelming view is that bulk sales law is unnecessary. The law of fraudulent conveyances is believed to adequately protect a seller's creditors from the seller disposing of its inventory and absconding with the sale proceeds. Bulk sales laws remain in only three states: California, Georgia, Maryland, and the District of Columbia.

The bulk sales laws retained in these few jurisdictions differ in several respects. The typical law restricts bulk sales to sales of inventory. See 6–102(c). California's law, however, applies to sales of equipment as well as inventory. Cal. Comm. Code § 6103(a) (2011). States also differ in the type of transactions exempted from their bulk sales laws. Cf. Md. Code Com. Law § 6–103(a)(3), Cal. Comm. Code § 6103(c)(5). In addition, the laws vary in the content and timing of the notice they require the buyer to give. Under 6–102(1)(e) the buyer must give notice to the seller's creditors, unless the seller has more than 200 creditors, in which case filing notice with the secretary of state suffices.

California requires the purchaser to record notice of the sale in the county recorder, deliver notice to the tax collector in the county in which the assets are located, and publish notice of the impending sale in a newspaper of general circulation. Cal. Comm. Code § 6–105(b). Section 6105(5) requires that the notice be given not less than 45 days before the date of the sale. California is less restrictive. It requires that notice be given not less than 12 days before the sale date. Cal. Comm. Code § 6–105(3).

The most important aspect of bulk sales laws is the consequence to the buyer of failing to comply with its notice requirements. Jurisdictions differ as to the consequence of noncompliance. Prior to revisions in Article 6, the buyer's failure to give proper notice rendered the sales transaction ineffective. Comment 2 to 6–107. The seller's protected creditors could set aside the transaction and satisfy their claims against the goods sold to the buyer. Georgia and Maryland law still provide for this result. Ga. Code Ann. § 11–6–104(1)(2011); Md. Code Comm. Law § 6–104(1) (2011). The law of other jurisdictions penalizes noncompliance less severely. California makes the buyer liable to the seller's creditors for the difference between the creditor's claim and the amount the creditor would have recovered had proper notice been given. Cal. Comm. Code §§ 6107(1); 6–107(1)(a). States also impose tax liabilities on buyers that do not give proper notice. A buyer who fails to give proper notice is liable for the seller's unpaid sales taxes due, less the amount the tax authorities would not have collected if the buyer had given proper notice. See, e.g. Cal. Comm. Code § 6107(a). Bulk sales liability for sales taxes remains even in a number of states that have repealed their bulk sales laws. See, e.g., N.Y Tax Law § 1141(c), N.J. Stat. Ann. § 54:50–38(c), Minn. Stat. § 270C.57.

4. ENTRUSTMENT OF THE GOODS

Section 2–403(1) codifies the common law doctrine of good faith purchase of goods. Section 2–403(2) goes beyond the common law doctrine in protecting certain transferees when they buy from a merchant entrustee. Agency law binds a principal when its agent with authority to sell sells goods to a buyer. The buyer has priority in the goods as against the principal. Section 2–403(2) allows a buyer to take free of competing claims to the goods even when agency principles do not apply. Under the subsection, entrusting of possession to a merchant who deals in goods of the kind gives him the power to transfer all of the entruster's rights in the goods to a buyer in the ordinary course of business. Section 2–403(2) states a negotiation rule. A merchant entrustee acquires whatever rights its entrustor gives it. Typically those rights are the limited rights of a bailee. Nonetheless, the subsection gives the merchant trustee to transfer greater rights (all of the entrustee's rights in the goods) to a buyer in the ordinary course of business.

The relevant notion of entrustment is defined very broadly by 2–403(3). Under 2–403(3), entrustment includes any delivery and acquiescence in retention of possession, regardless of any condition attached by the deliverer. As one of the UCC's drafters later characterized it, entrustment includes everything short of armed robbery. See Grant Gilmore, The Good Faith Purchase Idea and The

Uniform Commercial Code: Confessions of a Repentant Draftsman, 15 Ga. L. Rev. 605, 618 (1981). Entrustment clearly covers an ordinary bailment, under which goods are delivered to another for a specific purpose such as storage, transport or repair. But a buyer who leaves its seller in possession of the goods also has acquiesced in the seller's retention of them. The arrangement therefore is an entrustment, and the seller is the entrustee. Similarly, a debtor left by its secured creditor in possession of collateral is an entrustee. In both cases 2–403(2) gives the entrustee, if a merchant with respect to the goods, the power to transfer the entrustor's rights to a buyer in the ordinary course of business. Thus, a debtor left in possession of collateral can sell goods to a buyer in the ordinary course of business, who takes them free of the secured creditor's security interest. See 9–351(a); Comment 2 to 9–315.

Section 2–403(2) does not by its terms require that the entruster and buyer know that the entrustee is a merchant who deals in goods of the kind the buyer purchases. In a frequently cited case the court nonetheless takes the requirement to be implicit in the subsection: "Since the 'entrusting' provisions of UCC § 2–403 are an extension of the principle of estoppel, it would appear to be essential that the actual vocational status of the merchant be established, but also that the original owner and the ultimate purchaser must be shown to have been aware of the status." Atlas Auto Rental Corp. v. Weisberg, 281 N.Y.S.2d 400, 404 (N.Y. Civ. Ct. 1967). Commentators divide on whether such knowledge is implicit in 2–403(2)'s entrustment provision. Compare William D. Warren, Cutting Off Claims of Ownership Under the Uniform Commercial Code, 30 U. Chi. L. Rev. 469, 473, 474 (1963) (no) with Fairfax Leary Jr. & Warren F. Sperling, The Outer Limits of Entrusting, 35 Ark. L. Rev. 50, 84–85 (1981) (yes). A requirement of knowledge makes sense. Without the knowledge requirement, the entruster must take precautions against its entrustee selling its goods, because 2–403(2) protects the buyer if the entrustee is a merchant. Where the entruster does not know the merchant status of its entrustee, it will assume that the entrustee has the status of the average entrustee. Accordingly, it will take precautions in dealing with the average entrustee, the cost of which reflects the proportion of merchant and non-merchant entrustees with which it deals. The aggregate cost of these precautions is higher than the cost of precautions the entruster would take if precautions only had to be taken against an entrustee the entruster knows to be a merchant. This is because, without the knowledge requirement, the entruster takes precautions both when its entrustee is a merchant, where 2–403(2) protects its buyers, and when the entrustee is not a merchant, where its buyers are not protected by 2–403(2). With the requirement of knowledge, however, the entruster need only take precautions when it knows that its entrustee is a merchant. This is because entrustees about whose merchant status the entruster is ignorant cannot transfer all of the entruster's rights. The entruster therefore incurs lower precaution costs with the knowledge requirement.

It is not clear why 2–403(2) and 2–403(1) protect different classes of transferees. Section 2–403(2) protects only buyers in the ordinary course while 2–403(1) protects good faith purchasers for value. As a result, purchasers of goods who are not buyers only get the benefit of 2–403(1)'s good faith purchaser rule. Buyers in the ordinary course, on the other hand, as purchasers are protected by both 2–403(1) and 2–403(2). Section 2–403(2)'s working assumption is that an entruster is in a superior position to an ordinary course buyer to control misbehavior by the entrustee. But a non-buyer purchaser appears to have no advantage at taking precautions against competing claims to the goods, as compared to the entruster of the goods. Thus, the risk of the entrustee transferring the entruster's rights in them without its consent seemingly is not optimally minimized by allocating it to the non-buyer purchaser. For instance, a creditor with a security interest in bailed goods is a purchaser who is not a buyer of the goods. See 1–201(b)(9). The entruster is better positioned to avoid the risk of its entrustee encumbering the goods with a security interest than the secured creditor.

Canterra Petroleum v. Western Drilling & Mining Supply

Supreme Court of North Dakota, 1987
418 N.W.2d 267

■ Opinion By: ERICKSTAD, CHIEF JUDGE

NorthStar Equipment Corporation ["NorthStar"] appeals from a district court summary judgment awarding Western Drilling & Mining Supply ["Western"] $228,245.72 on its third-party claim against NorthStar. We reverse and remand for trial.

This multi-party litigation arises out of various transactions involving a certain quantity of oilfield pipe. The pipe was originally owned by Mitchell Energy Corporation ["Mitchell"]. In late 1981, Mitchell entrusted the pipe to Port Pipe Terminal, Inc. ["Port Pipe"] for storage.

Through paper transactions, two high-ranking employees of Port Pipe succeeded in fraudulently transferring apparent ownership of the pipe to Pharoah, Inc. ["Pharoah"], a "dummy" corporation which they had created to facilitate the fraudulent sale of merchandise stored at Port Pipe's facilities. On March 3, 1982, Pharoah sold the pipe owned by Mitchell to Nickel Supply Company, Inc. ["Nickel"]. On that same date, Nickel sold the pipe to Yamin Oil Supply ["Yamin"]. Five days later Yamin sold the pipe to NorthStar. On March 23, 1982, NorthStar sold it to Western, which a few days later sold it to Canterra Petroleum, Inc. ["Canterra"].

All of these intervening transactions, culminating in the sale to Canterra, were paper transactions only. The pipe never left Port Pipe's storage facility in Houston, Texas, until Canterra had it delivered to Getter Trucking in Dickinson sometime after its purchase in March 1982. The pipe remained stored at Getter Trucking until December 1983, when Canterra relinquished the pipe to Mitchell upon being informed by law enforcement agencies that the pipe was owned by Mitchell.

Canterra sued Western for breach of warranty of title seeking damages of $201,014.39, the price Canterra had paid for the pipe, plus interest. Western commenced a third-party action against NorthStar for breach of warranty of title, and NorthStar commenced a fourth-party action against Yamin.

Canterra moved for and received summary judgment against Western. Western then moved for summary judgment on its third-party claim against NorthStar. The court granted summary judgment to Western, awarding $228,245.72 in damages and interest. NorthStar has appealed from the judgment.

NorthStar contends that it did not breach the warranty of title, and that it presented sufficient evidence to demonstrate that material issues of fact remain to be resolved on the issue of title. NorthStar also contends that the trial court applied an incorrect measure of damages, and that material issues of fact need to be resolved by the factfinder to arrive at the proper amount of damages, if any.

* * *

I.   Liability

NorthStar contends that this case falls within the entrustment provision of the Uniform Commercial Code, codified at Section 41–02–48(2), N.D.C.C. [U.C.C. § 2–403]:

> "2. Any entrusting of possession of goods to a merchant who deals in goods of that kind gives him power to transfer all rights of the entruster to a buyer in ordinary course of business."

In essence, this statute contains three elements: (1) an entrustment of goods, (2) to a merchant who deals in goods of the kind, (3) followed by a sale to a buyer in the ordinary course of business. If all three elements are present, the rights of the entruster are transferred to the buyer in ordinary course of business. NorthStar argues that Mitchell entrusted the pipe to Port Pipe, a merchant who dealt in pipe, and that through Pharoah the pipe was sold to Nickel, a buyer in the ordinary course of business.

The trial court held that, based upon the affidavits presented, there was no factual dispute as to Port Pipe's status and that, as a matter of law, Port Pipe was merely a storage facility and not a merchant which dealt in pipe. "Merchant" is defined in Section 41–02–04(3), N.D.C.C. [U.C.C. § 2–104]:

> "3. 'Merchant' means a person who deals in goods of the kind or otherwise by his occupation holds himself out as having knowledge or skill peculiar to the practices or goods involved in the transaction or to whom such knowledge or skill may be attributed by his employment of an agent or broker or other intermediary who by his occupation holds himself out as having such knowledge or skill."

Although this definition provides several ways by which a party may acquire "merchant" status, the entrustment statute applies only to a "merchant who deals in goods" of the kind entrusted.

The determination whether a party to a transaction is a "merchant" under the Uniform Commercial Code is a question of fact.

Western contends that there is no dispute as to the facts regarding this issue, and that the court correctly determined as a matter of law that Port Pipe is a storage facility and not a merchant dealing in pipe.

Western relies primarily upon the affidavits of Bradley Beers, an assistant district attorney in Texas who prosecuted the two employees responsible for diverting materials stored at Port Pipe's facilities, and Janet Chisholm, former president of Port Pipe. These affidavits state in conclusory terms that Port Pipe was not a "merchant" dealing in oilfield pipe. Chisholm's affidavit, however, goes on to state that "Port Pipe . . . did sell small quantities of pipe from time to time, to clear odd lots, or to sell that pipe remaining after a substantial portion of a lot was sold."

The entrustment statute requires that goods be entrusted to a "merchant who deals in goods of that kind." Section 41–02–48(2), N.D.C.C. [U.C.C. § 2–403]. The requirement that the party "deals in goods" has been construed to mean one who is engaged regularly in selling goods of the kind.

The conclusory statements contained in the affidavits of Beers and Chisholm that Port Pipe was not a merchant which dealt in oilfield pipe are not dispositive of the issue. We have previously expressed our dissatisfaction with affidavits containing conclusory statements that are not supported by specific facts.

The relevant factual inquiry is whether Port Pipe was regularly engaged in selling pipe. The party opposing summary judgment, in this case NorthStar, is entitled to all favorable inferences which can reasonably be drawn from the evidence. Viewing Chisholm's affidavit in the light most favorable to NorthStar, we conclude that it does raise an inference that Port Pipe regularly sold pipe. Chisholm admits that Port Pipe did sell pipe "from time to time." It will be for the factfinder, after presentation of further evidence regarding the frequency and quantity of Port Pipe's sales of pipe, to determine whether Port Pipe regularly engaged in the sale of pipe and therefore was a merchant which dealt in pipe.

* * *

Western also contends that, even if a fact question remains unresolved regarding Port Pipe's merchant status, summary judgment is nevertheless appropriate. Western asserts that the entrustment doctrine of Section 41–02–48(2), N.D.C.C., applies only when the merchant who has been entrusted with the goods sells them in the ordinary course of business. Western contends that the doctrine does not apply where the goods are fraudulently transferred to a dummy corporation by employees of the entrustee and subsequently sold through the dummy corporation to a buyer in the ordinary course of business.

This is a troublesome issue, with neither party directing our attention to a case precisely on point. Both sides have, however, cited cases involving somewhat similar circumstances.

Western relies primarily upon * * * Olin Corp. v. Cargo Carriers, Inc., 673 S.W.2d 211 (Tex.Ct.App. 1984).

* * *

In *Olin*, Olin had entrusted fertilizer for storage at the warehouse of Cargo Carriers. The superintendent of Cargo Carriers' warehouse, Jerry Dollar, entered into a scheme with Charles Flowers to sell some of

Olin's fertilizer. Flowers would represent himself as the owner of the fertilizer, and Dollar would use his authority to release the fertilizer to the buyer. Several loads of fertilizer were sold in this manner to Ragsdale. When Olin sued Dollar, Flowers, Cargo Carriers, and Ragsdale for the misappropriated fertilizer, Ragsdale sought the protection of Section 2–403, U.C.C. The court held that the statute was inapplicable to Ragsdale because (1) his seller, Flowers, had no title,[1] (2) Olin never entrusted the fertilizer to Flowers, and (3) Flowers was not a merchant who dealt in the sale of fertilizer. *Olin*, supra, 673 S.W.2d at 216. These circumstances are materially distinguishable from the instant case. Flowers, Ragsdale's seller, was not an employee of Cargo Carriers but an outside party. Of even more significance is the court's finding that Flowers was not a merchant. Under those circumstances, the entrustment doctrine of Section 2–403, U.C.C., was inapplicable.

This case is readily distinguishable from Textile Supplies, Inc. v. Garrett, 687 F.2d 123 (5th Cir. 1982), and *Olin*. * * * In *Olin*, the court's holding was based upon the intervention of Flowers, who was not a merchant and was a party unrelated to either the entruster or the entrustee. In this case, however, there is no intervention by an unrelated party. The intervention was by two high-ranking employees of Port Pipe, the entrustee, who allegedly sold the pipe through their dummy corporation, Pharoah, to a buyer in the ordinary course of business.

We believe this case to be more closely analogous to Standard Leasing Corp. v. Missouri Rock Co., 693 S.W.2d 232 (Mo.Ct.App. 1985). In that case, Standard Leasing had entrusted two trucks to Herco for repair. Herco was a corporation in the business of leasing, selling, and repairing construction equipment. Herco's president, Robert Herring, transferred the trucks to Superior, a sham corporation created by Herring to fraudulently dispose of assets held by Herco. The trucks were sold by Superior to Dean, who in turn sold them to Missouri Rock. Standard Leasing sued Missouri Rock for replevin and conversion, and Missouri Rock claimed title under the entrustment doctrine. The court, in sustaining a jury verdict for Missouri Rock, held that the fraudulent transfer of the trucks from the entrustee, Herco, to a sham corporation controlled by Herco's president did not render the entrustment doctrine inapplicable. The court focused upon the underlying policies of Section 2–403:

> "Our conclusion is consistent with the policy of § 400.2–403(2) to increase the marketability of goods. See, Padgett, Uniform Commercial Code Section 2–403(2): The Authority of a Bailee to Convey Title, 21 U.Fla.L.Rev. 241, at 251 (1968–69). Section 2–403(2) places a greater burden on bailors than previous uniform commercial statutory enactments to exercise discretion in entrusting their goods to bailees. Id. In our case, both plaintiffs and defendants are innocent victims of fraudulent schemers. But under

---

[1] We are not certain why Flowers's lack of title was important. The entrustment statute presupposes that the seller to the buyer in ordinary course of business has no title to convey. If the seller had title, the buyer would not need the protection afforded by the statute, which allows the title of the entruster to pass to the buyer. Thus, in the classic entrustment example, when an owner entrusts goods to a merchant for repair and the merchant sells them to a buyer in the ordinary course of business, the merchant has no title but the title of the entruster passes to the buyer by operation of the statute.

UCC 2–403(2) Standard took the risk that its bailee might set up a sham corporation to aid it in its unlawful transfer of Standard's property. Where one of two innocent parties must suffer a loss occasioned by a third person, the person who enabled the acts of the wrongdoer must suffer the loss." *Standard Leasing*, supra, 693 S.W.2d at 237.

This rationale has also been expressed in 3 Anderson, Uniform Commercial Code § 2–403:4 (3d ed. 1983):

> " 'Section 2–403 was intended to determine the priorities between two innocent parties: (1) the original owner who parts with his goods through fraudulent conduct of another and (2) an innocent third party who gives value for the goods to the perpetrator of the fraud without knowledge of the fraud. By favoring the innocent third party, the Uniform Commercial Code endeavors to promote the flow of commerce by placing the burden of ascertaining and preventing fraudulent transactions on the one in the best position to prevent them, the original seller.' "

> We believe this policy also supports application of the entrustment doctrine to a situation where employees of the entrustee transfer the entrusted goods to their sham corporation, which in turn sells the goods to a buyer in the ordinary course of business. As between the two innocent parties in this case [Mitchell, which entrusted the pipe to Port Pipe, and Nickel, which bought the pipe in the ordinary course of business from Pharoah], the policy of the Code places the risk of the entrustee's employees fraudulently diverting and selling the goods upon the entruster, Mitchell, which had the opportunity to select its entrustee. Applying the doctrine to this case, Nickel would acquire the title of the entruster, Mitchell, and title would have passed on to the subsequent purchasers of the pipe.

> * * *

> We conclude that the trial court erred in holding that, as a matter of law, Port Pipe was not a "merchant" under Section 41–02–48(2), N.D.C.C., and that the entrustment doctrine was therefore inapplicable. Material issues of fact remain which require resolution upon trial.

> * * *

NOTES AND QUESTIONS

1.   *Canterra* finds that 2–403(2)'s entrustment provision can apply to the chain of transfers recited in the case. Mitchell entrusted pipe to Port Pipe. For 2–403(2) to apply, Port Pipe must be a merchant with respect to pipe. If Port Pipe is a merchant, 2–403(2) gives it the "power to transfer all rights" of Mitchell to a "buyer in ordinary course of business." Port Pipe is a merchant with respect to pipe. See 2–104(1). Did it "transfer" Mitchell's ownership interest or any other interest in the pipe to Pharoah? Suppose thieves broke into Port Pipe's storage facilities, stole Mitchell's pipe and sold it to Pharoah. Would Port Pipe have transferred the pipe to it? The *Canterra* court takes the position that an entrustee can act through its employees, so that the entrustee can sell bailed goods through them. Even if correct, 2–403(2) gives the entrustee the power to transfer all of the entruster's rights only to a buyer in the ordinary course of business. Is Pharoah a buyer in the

ordinary course of business? See 1–201(b)(9). Did Pharoah buy the pipe? See 2–103(1)(a). The court describes Pharoah as a "dummy" corporation, by which it meant that the corporation was created for the purpose of transferring assets located at Port Pipe. Pharoah did not have any assets or conduct any business. Pharoah in turn sold the pipe to Nickel, which in turn sold it to Yamin. Nickel might have bought the pipe in good faith from Pharoah. Could Nickel have bought the pipe in the ordinary course of business? See 1–201(b)(9). In *Canterra* the pipe was entrusted to a merchant (Port Pipe) and a buyer in the ordinary course of business (Yamin, North Star or Western) eventually might have purchased the entrusted goods, but this is not enough to divest the entruster of ownership under 2–403(2).

    2.   Goods covered by a certificate of title, such as motor vehicles, create problems for 2–403(2)'s application. These problems occur when the certificate of title does not accompany the sale of the titled vehicle in the dealer's possession. One question is whether a buyer from the dealer can be a buyer in the ordinary course of business if the dealer does not hand over the certificate of title covering the vehicle. Most courts allow it; see, e.g., Heartland Bank v. Nat'l City Bank, 171 Ohio App. 3d 132 (Ohio Ct. App. 2007). The other issue is whether ownership can pass without transferring the certificate of title. State certificate of title acts give different answers, as do some courts even in the same state. Compare Vibbert v. Par, Inc., 224 S.W.3d 317 (Tex. Ct. App. 2006) with Gallas v. Car Biz, Inc., 914 S.W.2d 692 (Tex. Ct. App. 1996). Some state certificate of title acts do not allow a person to acquire an interest in a motor vehicle until a certificate of title is issued to that person. Other title acts require issuance of a certificate of title only for a state resident to operate the motor vehicle in the state. These acts do not prevent a legal interest in the vehicle to pass without the certificate of title being transferred. See Madrid v. Bloomington Auto Co., Inc., 782 N.E.2d 386 (Ind. Ct. App. 2003). Under section 16(c) of the Uniform Certificate of Title Act (2005), transfer of ownership of a vehicle is effective even if unaccompanied by a certificate of title. Section 18(b) of the Act protects a buyer of the vehicle in the ordinary course of business if the buyer is protected under 2–403(2)'s entrustment provision. See Uniform Certificate of Title Act (2006), available at http://www.law. upenn.edu/bll/archives/ulc/ucota/2005AMAppText.pdf. To date no state has adopted the Act.

    3.   Section 2–403(2) does not say whether re-entrustment of the goods to a merchant gives the merchant the power to transfer the original entruster's rights in them to a buyer in the ordinary course of business. Porter v. Wertz, 421 N.E.2d 500 (N.Y. 1981), illustrates the unresolved issue. In *Porter*, Porter allowed Von Maker to take possession of a painting pending Von Maker's decision to buy it for his personal collection. Von Maker had identified himself to Porter as Peter Wertz, an art dealer. He was not an art dealer. Later, Von Maker delivered Porter's painting to the real Peter Wertz, who worked in a delicatessen, with instructions to sell it. Wertz sold the painting to the Feigen Gallery. The Feigen Gallery in turn sold the painting to a collector in South America. Because Von Maker was judgment proof and the painting was difficult to reach, Porter sued the Feigen Gallery for conversion to recover the value of the painting. To recover, 2–403(2) must not have divested Porter of title to it. The court concluded that title to the painting did not pass to the Feigen Gallery under 2–403(2). In doing so the court focused on the real Peter Wertz's non-merchant status and the Feigen's Gallery's lack of good faith. As a result, the court did not have to decide whether re-entrustment to a merchant gives it the power to pass the original owner's title to re-entrusted goods to a buyer in the ordinary course of business. Suppose that Peter Wertz in fact had been an art dealer and that the circumstances of the sale gave the Feigen Gallery no reason to suspect anything unusual. Does 2–403(2) give only the entrustee to whom the entruster delivers the goods the power to transfer good title? Or does it allow the entrustee to transfer all of the entruster's "rights," including the right to entrust the goods to another entrustee, so that the latter entrustee has the power to transfer good title?

PROBLEM 9.3

Ace Diamonds, a New York City operation, sells new jewelry to the public. Jones was in the market for a necklace, which he found at Ace's store. When Ace refused to accept Jones' check for the sale price, Jones asked if he could view the necklace on the store's saleswoman in the sun light. Ace's manager agreed and Jones, necklace in hand, followed the saleswoman outside. Once outside Jones ran away. A year later, Jewels Inc., located in San Diego, paid Jones cash for the necklace. Jones was well known to Jewels, but not to Ace, as a local seller of used necklaces. Jewels had been told that Jones was having financial problems and, to help, paid him a competitive price for the necklace. Ace has located the necklace in Jewels' display case and wants it back. Jewels is willing exchange the necklace for the price listed in the display. Can Ace retrieve the necklace without paying the price? 2–403(2), (3), 1–201(b)(9).

PROBLEM 9.4

Jewels Inc., the concern in Problem 9.3, had its own financial troubles. It was low on cash and needed to make a large interest payment on a loan or face closure. Fortunately, Stone had recently purchased a beautiful diamond from Jewels and paid by check, which has cleared. Because the diamond was very valuable, Stone asked Jewels to keep the diamond locked up until he could dispatch an armored car to retrieve it. Unfortunately, the diamond did not bring in enough cash for Jewels to pay the interest payment in full and Jewels needed funds quickly. Accordingly, it later sold the diamond to Zeta, an interested purchaser paid a competitive price. Zeta also decided to leave it with Jewels until arrangements for secure transport could be made. Although Jewels planned to make good on all of its obligations, it is now insolvent but stands ready to deliver the diamond to Stone or Zeta. To whom should Jewels deliver the diamond? 2–403(2), (3).

PROBLEM 9.5

Betty recently joined the company where Adam works. Learning that Betty needed floor coverings for her new apartment, Adam lent her one of his Persian carpets. Adam was too modest to tell Betty that the carpet was very valuable, and Betty believed that the carpet was worth little and easily replaceable. So when Betty's brother, Charles, bought a house and was considering wall to wall carpeting, Betty offered him Adam's carpet at a negligible price. Charles accepted and put the carpet in his living room. Later, he was annoyed to discover that one of the guests at his housewarming party had spilled wine on the carpet. Charles took the carpet to Mel's Rugs, which cleaned and sold Persian and other carpets. During Mel's annual carpet sale, Mel's manager placed Charles' cleaned carpet in the showroom by mistake. A rich customer noticed the carpet and offered Mel's salesman a price he could not refuse. He did not refuse and the customer left with the carpet. Adam has located Mel's customer and wants the carpet back. What rights do the parties have against each other? 2–403, 2–312(1).

B. GOOD FAITH PURCHASE OF DOCUMENTS OF TITLE

1. DOCUMENTARY SALES AND DOCUMENTS OF TITLE

Performance of the sales contract presents the risk that the seller might deliver nonconforming goods and the buyer might not pay. If a party performs and the other party does not perform, the performing party must litigate to receive the nonperforming party's performance or its value. During litigation the performing party is deprived either of the goods (buyer) or the contract price (seller). Simultaneous performance eliminates the risks of nonperformance and litigation. Article 2's default rules for performance ensure that the parties' performance is simultaneous. Section 2–511(1) requires the buyer to tender payment as a condition of the seller obligation to tender the goods, and 2–507(1) requires the seller to tender delivery of the goods as a condition of the buyer's obligation to pay. In addition, 2–513(1) allows the buyer to inspect the goods before it makes payment. The former two default rules ensure that the seller is not obligated to release the goods before it receives the contract price and that the buyer is not obligated to pay the contract price before the goods are available to it. The last rule ensures that the buyer does not have to pay for goods with nonconformities that inspection prior to payment would reveal.

Often a contract cannot be performed simultaneously. For financial or geographic reasons, performance instead must be sequential: Payment must be made before the goods are tendered, or the goods are tendered before payment is made. For instance, if the sales transaction involves physically distant parties, a face-to-face exchange of performance is infeasible. In such cases a party's superior bargaining power or its reputation for reliability can convince its contracting partner to pay before receiving the goods or to tender the goods before receiving payment. However, in relatively high-price sales transactions between strangers, an alternative arrangement protects both the buyer and seller's interests. A seller might be more willing to ship goods without advance payment if it has an instrument containing the buyer's obligation to pay independently of the seller's obligation to deliver the goods. For its part, the buyer might be more willing to pay in advance of delivery if it has assurances that at the time it pays conforming goods have been shipped to it. A documentary sale meets both the seller and buyer's needs. It is created by a term in the sales contract that calls for the exchange of payment for documents which reliably indicate that conforming goods have been shipped.

The simplest documentary sale involves two sorts of documents: (1) a negotiable document of title such as a negotiable bill of lading, and (2) a draft drawn on the buyer, typically a negotiable draft ordering it to pay the contract price. The law of documents of title governs the rights and obligations arising from a document of title, while negotiable instruments law governs the draft. To be a document of title ("document"), a writing or other record must meet two requirements. First, the record must purport to be issued by or addressed to a bailee and cover goods in the bailee's possession. Second, the record must in the regular course of business or financing be considered to adequately evidence that the person in possession of it is entitled to receive and dispose of the goods covered by the record. 1–201(b)(16). Although bills of lading and warehouse receipts are the most common types of documents of title, other sorts of documents issued by bailees also can meet these requirements. See Bank of New York v. Amoco Oil Corp., 35 F.3d 643 (2d Cir. 1994) ("holding certificates" issued by a lessee can count as documents of title).

Documents of title can be either negotiable or non-negotiable. As with negotiable instruments, the negotiability of a document is a matter of form. To be negotiable, the document must contain the language of negotiability. If the document states that the goods are to be delivered to the bearer or to the order of a named person, the document is negotiable. 7–104(a). If the document states that the goods are to be delivered to a named person, the document is non-negotiable or "straight." 7–104(b); cf. 49 U.S.C. § 80103. The bailee's obligation of delivery runs directly or "straight" to the named person alone. A negotiable document merges ownership of the goods with the document, so that it symbolizes the goods it covers. The person who holds the document therefore is entitled to receive the goods. 7–102(9); cf. 7–403(a), 1–201(b)(21). By contrast, the person named in the non-negotiable document is entitled to receive them. Thus, the seller retains control of the goods covered by a negotiable document issued to its order by retaining possession of the document. The buyer is not entitled to receive the goods or have them delivered until it holds the document. Very often when parties refer to a "document of title" in their contract they mean a "negotiable document of title."

The other document typically part of a documentary sale is the documentary draft. The draft is an instrument in which one party (the drawer) orders another party (the drawee) to pay a fixed amount of money on demand or at a specific time. In the draft used in a documentary sale, the seller is the drawer and the buyer is the drawee. The draft frequently used is negotiable, which means that the draft instructs the buyer to pay the contract price to the order of the seller. 3–104(a). Often the draft requires the draft to be payable on demand. This is called a "sight draft." The sight draft orders the buyer to pay the contract price to the order of the seller on demand ("sight"). If the draft is a sight draft, the buyer has three business days from the date payment is demanded in which to make payment. 3–502(c). Because the documentary sale usually calls for payment against negotiable documents, the buyer is obligated to pay the draft only if the seller tenders the documents covering the goods in exchange. Thus, on payment the buyer will receive the documents giving it control over the goods. As one court observed about the documentary sale, the transaction makes it possible for parties "to have the equivalent of a cash sale even though buyer and seller are hundreds of miles apart." Bunge v. First Nat'l Bank, 118 F.2d 427, 430 (3d Cir. 1941).

Consider the steps in a typical "sight draft against negotiable bill" documentary sale. The seller first delivers the goods to the carrier designated or allowed by the contract and receives a negotiable bill of lading in return. The negotiable bill describes the goods being shipped, the description being provided by the seller or carrier. 7–301(b). Under the bill of lading the carrier undertakes to deliver the goods. As a negotiable bill, the carrier is obligated to deliver them only to the holder of the document. To collect payment and transfer the bill, the seller and buyer previously will have engaged banks as their agents. Accordingly, the seller endorses the bill of lading and sends it through banking channels together with a sight draft drawn on the buyer for the contract price. These documents will be accompanied by a written instruction that the draft and bill of lading are to be delivered to the buyer only when it pays the draft. The draft and bill of lading are presented to the buyer through its bank. The buyer (and its bank) cannot obtain the bill, which is necessary to take delivery from the carrier, without paying the draft. Before it pays the draft, the buyer examines the bill of lading to determine whether the goods described in bill conform to the contract. On payment of the draft, the buyer's bank gives the bill to the buyer. The buyer in turn surrenders the bill to the carrier, which then delivers the goods to the buyer. Finally, the payment of the contract price is remitted through banking channels to the seller.

The diagram below describes the steps in the previous transaction:

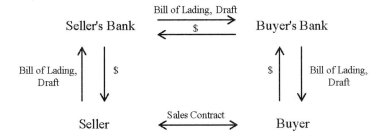

Documentary Sale Transaction

The diagram clearly shows how the documentary sale reduces performance and payment risks. At no point in the transaction does the seller or buyer, or their agents, have both the contract price and the bill of lading. At any stage in transaction either party might breach, the seller by not tendering the bill of lading or the buyer by not tendering the contract price. However, breach still leaves each party with their respective assets: the bill of lading (seller) and the contract price (buyer). The seller therefore can redirect the carrier to deliver the goods, and the buyer can use the contract price to make an alternative purchase. True, even a completed documentary sale does not eliminate the risk that the seller's performance will be nonconforming. This is because the buyer might discover that the goods covered by the bill are nonconforming only when they are delivered. A documentary sale leaves this risk with the buyer, as the buyer waives its right to inspection prior to payment. See 2–512(b), 2–513(3)(b). However, the description of the goods in the bill reduces the risk of receiving nonconforming goods somewhat. An inspection certificate, when required by the contract and issued by a third party, further reduces the risk of receiving nonconforming goods.

The regulation of documents of title is complex and involves different and in some cases overlapping laws. State and federal statutes principally control many of the legal aspects of the document. Article 7 of the UCC controls documents of title, unless preempted by federal law. The main federal statute governing warehouse receipts is the United States Warehouse Act, 7 U.S.C. § 71 et seq., applicable to goods stored for interstate or foreign commerce. Federal statute largely displaces Article 7's regulation of bills of lading. The Federal Bills of Lading Act ("FBLA"), 49 U.S.C. §§ 80101–80116, also known as the Pomerene Act, governs bills of lading issued by common carriers in the United States for the transportation of goods between states, from a state to a foreign country, or from a state through a foreign country or another state. Thus, Article 7 governs bills of lading only when they cover carriage entirely within a single state. The Carmack Amendment, 49 U.S.C. § 11706, applies to the interstate shipment of goods, as well as shipment from a state to an adjacent foreign country. The Act regulates the carrier's liability for loss or damage to the goods. Bills of lading issued by a common carrier for ocean carriage from a United States port are regulated by the Carriage of Goods by Sea Act, 46 U.S.C. § 30701 et seq. The Harter Act, 46 U.S.C. § 190–195, applies to ocean bills of lading issued in connection with waterborne carriage in the United States. The air carrier's liability for international shipments is governed by the Convention for the Unification of Certain Rules for International Carriage by Air, S. Treaty No. 106–45 (2000) (the "Montreal Convention").

2. PURCHASE OF DOCUMENTS

As with any transferable asset, a document can be purchased. The process by which the document is transferred, and the rights acquired by the purchaser, depends on the character of the document. If the document is non-negotiable, it is transferred in the same way any contractual rights are transferred. Because a non-negotiable document does not represent the goods, it can be transferred without transferring possession of the document. Article 7 does not regulate the process of transfer, and presumably the general law of assignment controls. Section 7–504(a) states the consequence of transferring a non-negotiable document (as well as a negotiable document that is not duly negotiated): The transferee of the document "acquires the title and rights that its transferor had or had actual to convey." This is a derivation rule and the counterpart for documents to 2–403(1)'s first sentence applicable to the sale of goods.

The process of transfer for negotiable documents is called "negotiation." It is similar to the process of transfer for negotiable instruments. "Negotiation" occurs when the person to whom the negotiable document is transferred becomes a holder of the document. If the document states that the goods are to be delivered "to bearer," any person in possession of the document is a holder. 7–501(a)(2); 1–201(b)(21). A thief therefore can negotiate a bearer document. If the document calls for delivery to the order of a named person, the document is negotiated when it is delivered to the named person. The named person's endorsement is unnecessary. 7–501(a)(3). For instance, if the document calls for delivery "to the order of Smith," the document is negotiated to Smith when it is delivered to him. However, for Smith to negotiate the document, his endorsement is necessary. Smith's endorsement can be "in blank," meaning that Smith signs the document "Smith." Endorsement in blank makes the document a bearer document, in which case further negotiation occurs by delivery alone. 7–501(a)(1). Smith's endorsement "deliver to Jones" is a special endorsement. The document is negotiated by delivery to Jones. 7–501(a)(4).

A holder to whom a document is negotiated obtains paramount rights in the goods covered by the document only if the document has been "duly negotiated" to it. Section 7–501(a)(5) defines when a negotiable document is "duly negotiated." Under the subsection, due negotiation requires that the document be negotiated to the holder that purchases it for value, in good faith and without notice of any defense against it or claims to it. In addition, due negotiation requires that the negotiation be in the regular course of business or financing and in a transaction other than the settlement or payment of a money obligation. Subsection (5) is unclear as to whether the required negotiation must be in the regular course of business or financing of the transferor or transferee, or both. Comment 2 to 7–501 suggests that it must be part of a commercial transaction in which the transferor regularly engages. ("No commercial purpose is served by allowing a tramp or a professor to 'duly negotiating' [a document]," according to the Comment.) The Comment indicates that a price "suspiciously below" market price takes the transaction out of the regular course. This observation is not very helpful, as a suspiciously low price for a document likely puts the purchaser on notice and might undermine its good faith in the purchase. The Federal Bill of Lading Act has no requirement of due negotiation. Cf. FBLA § 80105(a).

Section 7–501(a)(5)'s "regular course of business" requirement means that due negotiation cannot occur outside a fairly narrow commercial context. This impairs the negotiability of documents and therefore reduces their price. Purchasers of negotiable documents face the risk that a court will determine ex post that the document's negotiation occurred outside the transferor's regular course of business. To avoid this risk, the purchaser must have or obtain information about the frequency with which its transferor transfers documents. This information is costly to acquire, particularly when documents are purchased quickly and on an ongoing basis. Bills of lading covering some bulk cargo, for instance, are traded numerous times before the cargo arrives at its destination. In practice the "regular course of business" requirement forces the purchaser of documents to discount their value by the likelihood that the transfer is out of the regular course. The discount reduces the price they are willing to pay for documents, when those with legal interests in the documents arguably could easily prevent negotiation of the documents even outside the transferor's usual course of business. Probably in response to this concern, several states have enacted 7–501(a)(5) without its "regular course of business" requirement. See, e.g., Cal. Comm. Code § 7501(a)(4).

Due negotiation to the holder gives it title to the document and the goods, as well as rights against the issuer of the document to deliver the goods according to the document's terms. 7–502(a). Thus, a holder of a duly negotiated document takes free of prior legal interests in the document and goods covered by it. For instance, 7–501(a) cuts off prior claims of ownership in the document when it is duly negotiated. Section 7–502(a) therefore enables the holder to acquire greater rights in the document and goods covered by it than the transferor of the document had. Thus, a holder without title to the document or the goods covered by it may transfer good title to both the document and goods. As a result, due negotiation describes a negotiation rule of the sort found in 2–403(2). However, 7–503 limits 7–502(a)'s negotiation principle. Under 7–503(a) an unauthorized bailment of the goods does not give the bailor title in the documents or the goods. Section 7–503(a)(1) and (2) describe the circumstances in which a bailment is unauthorized. In these circumstances due negotiation of the document does not give the holder of the document title in the goods.

Section 7–502 makes duly negotiated documents more negotiable than goods but less fully negotiable than instruments. Under 2–403(2), entrustment to a merchant gives the merchant the power to transfer all of the entruster's rights in the goods to a buyer in the ordinary course. As a result, the buyer can acquire greater rights in the goods than the entrustee has in them. Although 2–403(2)'s negotiation rule makes goods negotiable, the rule is restricted to an entrustment to a merchant. This limits the negotiability of goods even within essentially commercial transactions. By contrast, the law of negotiable instruments makes instruments fully negotiable. A holder in due course of an instrument takes free of prior claims to the instrument, even if its delivery is not part of a commercial transaction. See 3–302, 3–306. So, for instance, delivery of a stolen instrument in a form negotiated by delivery allows its holder to take free of the owner's claim to the instrument.

Documents are less negotiable than instruments, because due negotiation requires that negotiation occur in the regular course of business or financing. Due negotiation therefore is limited to commercial settings. However, documents remain more negotiable than goods. This is because a document can be duly negotiated even if the person delivering it is not a merchant with respect to the goods covered by the document or entrusted with them. In addition, although due negotiation requires the holder to purchase the document, the purchaser need not buy it. "Purchase" is broader in meaning than "buy." See 1–201(b)(29). Thus, unlike 2–403(2), which applies to the sale of goods, a purchaser to whom a document is duly negotiated need not be a buyer in the ordinary course. For example, a secured creditor whose debtor negotiates a document as collateral for a secured loan "purchases" the document. For both reasons, documents are negotiable in a broader range of commercial transactions than the commercial transactions in which goods are negotiable. See William D. Warren, Cutting Off Claims of Ownership Under the Uniform Commercial Code, 30 U. Chi. L. Rev. 469, 483–484 (1963).

In the problems below, assume that the goods are stored in a local warehouse. The stored goods are for ultimate use in the state in which the warehouse is located.

PROBLEM 9.6

A, a wheat producer, stored some of its wheat in Warehouse, which issued to A a warehouse receipt. The receipt provided that the wheat would be delivered the bearer of the receipt. A's employee, B, stolen the warehouse receipt from the desk of A's chief financial officer, and sold and delivered it to C. C was a wheat merchant who knew that the receipt was stolen. C in turn sold and delivered the receipt to D, another wheat merchant who had no reason to believe that the receipt was not C's property. D retained the receipt without taking delivery of the wheat covered by it. Later, A learned of these facts and demanded that D turn over the receipt. Is A entitled to the receipt? 7–501(a)(2), 7–501(5), 7–502(a)(1), (2), 7–503(a)(1), (2), 1–201(b)(21). If Warehouse delivered the wheat to D on D's surrender of the warehouse receipt, would Warehouse be responsible to A? 7–403(1), (4).

PROBLEM 9.7

A, a wheat producer, stored some of its wheat in Warehouse, which issued to A a warehouse receipt to bearer. A's employee, B, stole the warehouse receipt from A and sold and delivered the receipt to M, a wheat merchant who knew that the receipt was stolen. M in turn surrendered the receipt to Warehouse and obtained delivery of the wheat. M then sold the wheat to Z, a wheat merchant who had no reason to know any of the previous facts. Later, while Z still has the wheat, A discovers the theft of the receipt and locates the wheat in Z's hands. It demands that Z turn over the wheat. Is A entitled to it? 7–502(a)(1), (2), 2–403(1).

PROBLEM 9.8

A, a wheat producer, owned wheat that was being transported in A's truck to its customer. B, A's truck driver stole the wheat and stored it with Warehouse, which issued to B a warehouse receipt in bearer form. B sold and delivered the receipt to M, a wheat merchant who knew that the receipt was stolen. Later, M sold and delivered the receipt to Z, who had no reason to know that the receipt and the wheat covered by it were not M's property. Z surrendered the receipt to Warehouse and took delivery of the wheat. It retained the wheat. When A learned all of these facts, it demanded that Z turn the wheat over. Is A entitled to the wheat? 7–503(a)(1), (2), St. Paul Fire & Marine Insurance Co. v. Leflore Bank & Trust Co., 181 So. 2d 913 (Miss. 1966). Suppose Z had been A's chief executive officer. Would the result change?

PROBLEM 9.9

A, a wheat producer, owned some wheat. Short of space to store the wheat, A asked Y, a competitor, to store it in its facilities until A could find a buyer for the wheat. Y agreed and A delivered the wheat to Y. A did not pay Y for the use of its facilities, and Y had never stored the goods of others. 7–501(5), 7–502(a), 7–503(a)(1), 7–504(a).

(a) Assume that Y, without A's permission or knowledge, sold the wheat to X, a wheat merchant who believed that the time of the purchase that the wheat was Y's property. What result if A demands that X return the wheat to it? 2–403(2).

(b) Assume that Y, without A's permission or knowledge, delivered A's wheat to Warehouse, which issue to Y a warehouse receipt covering the wheat in bearer form. Y in turn sold and delivered the receipt to C, a wheat merchant who had no reason to know of the previous facts. C obtained the wheat from Warehouse after surrendering to it the receipt purchased from Y. What result if A demands that C return the wheat to it? 7–501(4), 7–502(a)(1), (2), 7–503(a)(1).

(c) Assume that Y always dealt with wheat it produced on a "cash and carry" basis. That is, Y required its customers to pay cash and retrieve wheat they purchased at the time of the purchase. On (b)'s facts, is C entitled to the wheat?

CHAPTER 10

REMEDIES

A. INTRODUCTION: ARTICLE 2'S REMEDIES

Article 2's remedies for breach of the sales contract are intended to put the injured party in the position it would have been in had the breaching party performed. Section 1–305(a) confirms that their objective is to protect the injured party's expectation interest. It requires the UCC's remedies be liberally applied to put the injured party in the position that it would have been in had the breaching party performed. Putting the injured party in this position gives it the benefit of its bargain. For the seller the benefit of its bargain is its profit: the contract price minus its cost of performance. The buyer's profit is the value to it of the goods minus the contract price. If the buyer intends to resell the goods, market price measures their value to it; the subjective value of the goods is the value of the goods to the consumer buyer.

Sections 2–703 and 2–711 provide an incomplete catalogue of the seller and buyer's remedies, respectively. The table below lists all of the seller and buyer's remedies available under Article 2. Remedies that appear in the same numbered row are counterparts of each other. For example, the seller's action for the price (5.) is the sellers' counterpart of the buyer's right to specific performance (5.).

Seller's Remedies	Buyer's Remedies
1. Contract price—resale price (2–706)	1. Cover price—contract price (2–712)
2. Contract price—market price (2–708(1))	2. Market price—contract price (2–713)
3. Lost profits (2–708(2))	3. "Value difference" (2–714(1), (2)) reduction in price (2–717)
4. Incidental expenses (2–710)	4. Incidental expenses and consequential damages (2–715(1), (2))
5. Price action (2–709(1))	5. Specific performance or replevin (2–716)
6. Withhold delivery (2–702(1))	6. Inapplicable
7. Stop delivery (2–705(1))	7. Inapplicable
8. Reclaim goods (2–507(2), 2–702(2))	8. Claim goods upon payment (2–502(1))
9. Cancel the contract (2–703)	9. Cancel the contract (2–711)

Two features of the listed remedies are worth noticing. First, some remedies are substitutional and award money damages while others are specific and do not award money. Remedies 1.–4. award money damages; remedies 5.–9. give different sorts of specific or non-monetary relief. Second, some remedies are available only when the breaching party accepts the goods while other remedies are available when it rejects the goods or revokes its acceptance of them. For instance, the buyer can measure its damages by the cover-contract price difference or the market price-contract price difference, obtain specific performance in the appropriate case, or cancel the contract only if the seller "fails to make delivery or repudiates or the buyer rightfully rejects or justifiably revokes" its acceptance of the goods. 2-711(1). If the buyer accepts the goods and does not revoke its acceptance of nonconforming goods, it must measure its damages by 2–714's "value difference." Although it can reduce the contract price (if unpaid) by the amount of this difference under 2-717, the buyer cannot measure its damages by the cover-contract difference or the market price-contract difference. These measures are available only if the buyer rejects the goods or effectively revokes its acceptance.

The remedies in the above table all protect the injured party's expectation interest. To see this, assume that the buyer breaches without paying the contract price after the seller has completed production of the goods. Assume also that the market price and resale price of the goods are the same and less than the contract price. The seller's expectancy is its profit from performance: the contract price minus the cost of production. There are several ways in which the seller can recover its profit. First, 2–709(1) allows the seller under prescribed conditions to recover the contract price from the buyer. Since the seller has already incurred the cost of producing the goods, 2–709(1)'s action for the price enables it to receive its profit. Second, the seller gets its profit if its damages are measured by the contract-resale difference (1.). An easy rearrangement and substitution of terms shows this. Let K be the contract price, R the resale price, M the market price and D the seller's damages. Under 2–706(1), the seller recovers damages equal to the contract-resale difference: $D = K - R$. Rearranging terms, $K = D + R$. The seller's profit is the contract price (K) minus its cost of performance. Because the seller has already incurred the cost of performance, and substituting $D + R$ for K, 2–706(1)'s damages formula enables it to get its profit. This is because whatever profit the seller does not recover from re-selling the goods at the resale price (R) is included in the damages (D) it recovers from the breaching buyer. Third, the seller receives its profit by using 2–708(1)'s market price-contract price difference. Under 2–708(1) the seller recovers damages equal to the contract price-market price difference: $D = K - M$. Rearranging terms, $K = D + M$. Since D is equal to the difference between the contract price (K) and market price (M), the sum of the market price and the seller's damages equals the contract price. Again, the seller's profit is the contract price (K) minus its cost of performance. Because the seller has incurred the cost of performance, and substituting $D + M$ for K, it receives its profit. Similar to 2-706(1), this is because the profit the seller does not from receiving the market price (M) is included in the damages (D) it recovers from the breaching buyer.

The buyer's remedies also measure its profit from performance of the contract, which is its expectancy. The buyer's profit is equal to the value of the goods to it minus the contract price. Assume that the market price of the goods rises and the seller breaches by refusing to deliver the goods. The buyer has not paid the contract price. Assume too that the cover price of the goods is equal to the market price. As with the injured seller, the injured buyer can recover the benefit of its bargain in several ways. Section 2–716(1) gives the buyer a right to specific performance under prescribed conditions. By obtaining the goods, the buyer gets their value to it. Because the buyer trades the contract price for the goods, it receives its profit, which is the value of the goods to it minus the contract price (K). The buyer's damage remedies give the buyer its profit too. Section 2–712(1) measures the buyer's damages as the difference between the cover price (C) and contract price (K). That is, $D = C - K$. Rearranging terms, $K = C - D$. The buyer pays the higher cover price while recovering as damages the difference between the cover and contract price. It therefore pays on net the contract price to obtain goods with the same value as the contract goods. Substituting $C - D$ for K, the buyer obtains its profit, which is the value of the goods to it minus the contract price. Finally, 2–713 measures the buyer's damages as the difference between the market price (M) and contract price (K): $D = M - K$. Rearranging terms, $K = M - D$. Again, the buyer's profit is the value of the goods to it minus the contract price (K). Thus, substituting $M - D$ for K, 2–713(1)'s measure of damages preserves the buyer's profit. Although the buyer can purchase substitute goods only at the higher market price, it recovers in damages the difference between the market price and the contract price. It therefore can pay on net the contract price for substitute goods at the higher market price.

In practice different remedies can yield different recoveries. Article 2's damages remedies measure damages at different times. Section 2–708(1)'s contract-market price difference measures damages as of the time and place for tender, while 2–706(1)'s contract-resale difference measures damages by the resale price. Resale typically occurs after the time for tender and possibly at a different place. As a result, the relevant market price and resale price might diverge. In addition, remedies differ as to the costs incurred in proving their elements. Establishing that the goods are unique or substitute goods are unavailable often is more difficult than establishing the market price of goods. Similarly, market price sometimes might be established more easily than proving that a reasonable resale of contract goods was made. For both reasons, the injured party might prefer to rely on some remedies rather than others.

As with almost all of Article 2's rules, its remedies are default terms. See 1–302(a). Rather than dealing with the parties' performance, Article 2's remedies are implied terms that describe the remedies available on breach. They are available to the injured party unless the parties' agreement provides otherwise. Sales contracts frequently include terms that limit available remedies or substitute remedies that would be otherwise available under Article 2. An example of the former is the exclusion of the seller's liability for consequential damages. The exclusion limits the buyer's recoverable damages to loss other than consequential damages. A liquidated damages clause or a provision limiting the buyer's remedies to repair or replacement of the goods are examples of the latter. They substitute an agreed-upon sum or form of relief for those otherwise available under Article 2. The CISG's remedies also are default terms. Article 6 of the CISG allows the parties to derogate from almost all of its provisions, including its remedies provisions. Derogation can be by way of limiting or displacing the remedies available under the CISG. The material that follows focuses on the UCC's default remedies. The CISG scheme of remedies is discussed separately below.

B. SELLER'S REMEDIES

1. ACTION FOR THE PRICE

An action for the price gives the seller specific relief. It is the counterpart to the seller of the buyer's right of specific performance. Just as the specific performance gives the buyer the contract goods, a price action gives the seller what it bargained for from the buyer: the contract price. The buyer gets the goods in exchange for the price. See 2–709(2). As with a right to specific performance, the availability of an action for the price is restricted. Section 2–703(e) permits the seller to recover the price "in a proper case." According to 2–709(1), the seller may recover the price where the buyer has accepted the goods, the goods are damaged or destroyed within a reasonable time after the risk of loss has passed to the buyer, or when it is unable to resell the goods at a reasonable price. These are disjunctive conditions. The seller therefore may recover the price if any one of these conditions is met. Although 2–709(1) joins (1)(a) and (1)(b) with an "and," the subsections separately refer to "goods accepted," "goods identified . . ." and "goods which . . . " The seller may recover the price of "goods accepted," "goods identified" to the contract which are damaged or destroyed for which the buyer bears the financial responsibility, and "goods which" the seller is unable to resell at a reasonable price. These separate references to "goods" describe different circumstances in which the seller is entitled to the price. Thus, the seller may recover the price if the goods meet any of the conditions described in (1)(a) and (b). The "and" connecting (1)(a) and (b) therefore means "or."

Section 2–709(1)'s restriction on a price action has a straightforward justification. A price action minimizes the seller's damages when the seller's resale costs are greater than the buyer's resale costs. The buyer has breached either because it finds that the contract is not as profitable to perform as its next best alternative or through sheer mistake. In doing so the buyer has decided it does not want to retain the goods and adapt them for another purpose. Otherwise, it would keep the goods and not breach. Thus, given the breach, the goods must be resold either by the seller or the buyer. If the seller resells the goods, it can recover as incidental expenses the cost of resale (in addition to other damages). See 2–710. If the buyer resells them, it incurs resale costs but avoids having to pay for the seller's resale costs because none are incurred. Because the seller's resale costs are part of its recoverable damages, the seller's damages are minimized when the goods are resold by the party with the lowest resale costs. Thus, if the seller's resale costs are lower than the buyer's, the costs of breach are minimized by giving the seller the responsibility to resell the goods. Denying it a price action does this. If the buyer's resale costs are lower than the seller's, the breach costs are minimized by giving the buyer the responsibility of resale. Granting the seller a price action does this. The buyer receives the goods in exchange for the price and must decide how to dispose of them.

Viewed in these terms, 2–709(1)'s conditions are proxies for when the seller's resale costs are higher than the buyer's resale costs. Where the buyer has accepted the goods, it usually is in possession of them. The accepting buyer's proximity to the goods gives it an advantage at resale. A seller might not operate in a secondary market for goods. In this case, when the goods have been damaged or destroyed, the seller has no advantage at reselling them. Finally, where the seller is unable to resell at a reasonable price, it also has no advantage at resale.

<h1 style="text-align:center">Granvia Trading Ltd. v. Sutton Creations, Inc.</h1>

United States District Court, Southern District of New York, 2010
73 U.C.C. Rep. Serv.2d 50

■ SAND, DISTRICT JUDGE

Plaintiff Granvia Trading Ltd. brings this breach of contract action against Defendant Sutton Creations, Inc., based on Sutton's failure to accept a commercial shipment of winter coats. Plaintiff now moves for summary judgment finding Defendant liable for breach of contract and awarding Plaintiff damages in the amount of the price of the contract, $316,830.00, plus interest and incidental damages. Defendant cross-moves for summary judgment dismissing this action, arguing that Plaintiff has not established any recoverable damages, and that if Plaintiff can recover, it is only entitled to lost profits rather than the price of the contract.

The court finds that genuine issues of material fact exist regarding Defendant's rejection of the goods and Plaintiff's efforts to resell them. Accordingly, Plaintiff's and Defendant's motions for summary judgment are denied.

I. BACKGROUND

The following facts are not in dispute. Plaintiff Granvia Trading Ltd. is a Korean corporation engaged in garment imports and exports. From 2000 through 2008 Defendant Sutton Creations, Inc., a New York corporation, was a wholesale importer of men's, women's, and children's sportswear. WeiHai Foreign Trading Fuquan Garment Factory ("WeiHai") is a clothing manufacturer based in China. Four Third–Party Defendants are no longer parties to the dispute, but are mentioned in this Memorandum. Galihad Enterprises Ltd. is a New York corporation; in 2007 it was engaged as a purchasing agent for imported goods. Burlington Coat Factory Warehouse Corporation is a Delaware corporation engaged in the retail clothing industry. In 2007, Sherry Milkey was in the business of procuring goods for major national retail clothing operations, working independently through a New York limited liability company entitled Devin Industries, LLC. All claims against Third–Party Defendants Galihad, Burlington Coat Factory, Milkey, and Devin have been resolved or withdrawn.

In July 2007, Plaintiff received purchase orders issued by Defendant and Galihad, its partner in this joint venture, for the manufacture of four styles of women's coats at a contract price of $316,800.00. The coats were not custom or specialized goods; instead, they were routine, ordinary products for which a wide market exists. On July 30, 2007, Plaintiff entered into an agreement with WeiHai to manufacture the coats in Defendant's purchase orders. The parties understood that Galihad and Defendant would accept the shipment in China through their designated freight forwarder. Defendant's purchase order stated that Plaintiff would deliver the goods between October 8 and 20, 2007.

Between October 1 and 16, 2007, Plaintiff sent e-mail communications to Defendant and Galihad, requesting that they forward confirmation to their freight forwarder to take delivery of the garments from the manufacturer WeiHai. Defendant did not respond. Defendant never paid for or acquired the goods. They are currently being stored by WeiHai, which has sent a receipt of storage charges to Plaintiff totaling $7,500.00 as of March 28, 2009. Plaintiff has not paid WeiHai for the coats; nor has it paid fees for their storage. In October 2007, the coats had a market value of at least $317,000.00.

* * *

III. DISCUSSION

Plaintiff argues that it is entitled to recover the full purchase price of the goods pursuant to section 2–709(1) of the New York Uniform Commercial Code ("U.C.C."), known as the "action for the price," because either (1) Defendant accepted the goods because it failed to make an effective rejection of them through lack of notice, or (2) Plaintiff made reasonable yet unsuccessful efforts to resell the coats. Defendant argues that either (1) this transaction falls under U.C.C. section 2–708, and that pursuant to this section Plaintiff suffered no damages because the market price of the goods is equal to or greater than the contract price; or (2) Plaintiff should be classified as a "jobber" rather than a manufacturer pursuant to section 2–208(2), and consequently Plaintiff's potential damages are limited to lost profits.

A. Defendant's Rejection or Acceptance of the Goods

U.C.C. section 2–709(1)(a) allows sellers to recover the price "of goods accepted or of conforming goods lost or damaged within a commercially reasonable time after risk of their loss has passed to the buyer[.]" To recover under section 2–709(1)(a), "plaintiffs must show that 1) they had a contract; 2) the buyer failed to pay the purchase price; and 3) the buyer accepted the goods." Weil v. Murray, 161 F. Supp. 2d 250, 254–55 (S.D.N.Y. 2001). Defendant does not contest the first two elements of this test, but argues that section 2–709(1)(a) is inapplicable because it never accepted the goods. A finding of Defendant's acceptance through lack of seasonable notification of rejection would fall under section 2–709(1)(a), while a finding of rejection would fall under section 2–708.

Under the U.C.C., a buyer is deemed to have accepted goods when the buyer "fails to make an effective rejection, but such acceptance does not occur until the buyer has had a reasonable opportunity to inspect them[.]" N.Y. U.C.C. § 2–606(1)(b). Section 2–602(1) provides that "[r]ejection of goods must be within a reasonable time after their delivery or tender. It is ineffective unless the buyer seasonably notifies the seller." Id. § 2–602(2)(a). For a communication to serve as "notification" of rejection under section 2–602(1), it must be explicit and unequivocal. A "mere complaint" is not sufficient to constitute notice of rejection. Accordingly, even when there has been some communication, this does not guarantee that such communication will serve as notice for purposes of effective rejection.

Defendant has failed to show evidence that it notified Plaintiff of its rejection. Plaintiff cites its email correspondence with Defendant and its partner Galihad Enterprises from October 1 through 16, 2007, requesting them to forward confirmation to their designated freight forwarder to enable delivery. Defendant received copies of all this correspondence but never sent a response of its own. On October 16, Galihad reported that Defendant was "waiting for some info from Burlington" and would send approval as soon as Galihad received it. Galihad added that Defendant "fully understands that [Plaintiff] was not late" and that "Delay has been from the buyer side," asking Plaintiff to "wait for further instructions." Defendant has not offered evidence showing that it sent any notification of rejection to Plaintiff, even though it had contracted with Plaintiff through its purchase orders.

At the same time, Plaintiff has failed to show any evidence that Defendant did not timely notify Plaintiff of its rejection. While Plaintiff argues that Defendant's failure to communicate up to the scheduled delivery date on October 20, 2007 resulted in breach of the contract on that date, other correspondence shows that Defendant continued making arrangements with its partner Galihad for eventual shipment of the goods at least through November 1, 2007. The Complaint alleges that Defendant breached the contract on or about October 2007, but does not allege that Defendant refused all communication with Plaintiff or that it never rejected the goods. Plaintiff offered extensive deposition testimony from its Vice–President Jang Hoon Suh, a/k/a Steve Suh, but at no time did Suh claim that Defendant failed to notify Plaintiff of its rejection. Likewise, Plaintiff's Rule 56.1 Statement nowhere alleges that Defendant ceased contact with Plaintiff; it merely alleges that Defendant breached the contract as of October 20. Plaintiff never took the opportunity during discovery to offer evidence showing that Defendant never accepted the goods, and raised this claim only after discovery had concluded, in reply to Defendant's cross-motion for summary judgment.

The Court holds that a genuine issue of material fact exists as to whether Defendant notified Plaintiff that it was rejecting the goods.

B. Defendant's Efforts to Resell the Goods

Plaintiff argues that it made reasonable efforts to resell the goods at issue in this case, that these efforts proved unavailing, and that therefore recovery of the contract price is available under section 2–709(1)(b). This provision states that when a buyer fails to pay the contract price as it becomes due, the seller may recover the price of the goods "if the seller is unable after reasonable effort to resell them at a reasonable price or if the circumstances reasonably indicate that such effort will be unavailing." N.Y. U.C.C. § 2–709(1)(b).

To support its contention, Plaintiff offers a Certification from its Vice–President Suh listing the contacts he made in his attempts to re-sell the coats. In his deposition testimony, Suh also testified to contacts with buyers in Canada, the United States, and the Netherlands, and three or four agents in South Korea from the spring through the winter of 2008. He testified that he offered the goods at 60 to 70 percent of the contract price, and was willing to consider partial sales of the goods, but could not sell them. Plaintiff also cites correspondence with Claire Ma, an employee of a Korean company named Kenmnan Apparel, which made contacts on behalf of Plaintiff to re-sell the coats between March and July 2008.

Defendant argues that Plaintiff's efforts to resell the goods were cursory and therefore not reasonable. It contends that Suh testified to only four or so unsuccessful contacts with buyers. It notes that Plaintiff did not advertise the availability of the goods for sale. As for Plaintiff's sole contact with a United States buyer, Defendant points out that the potential buyer was in China on other business and did not carry the relevant category of merchandise. Defendant furthermore alleges that Plaintiff has failed to produce documentary evidence of the contacts mentioned by Suh in his deposition testimony. In other words, Defendant contends that Plaintiff took a perfunctory approach to identifying and contacting likely buyers.

Neither Plaintiff nor Defendant has offered dispositive evidence on the reasonableness of Plaintiff's efforts to resell the goods. Plaintiff offers evidence of between six and seven contacts in total, including buyers and agents. On the other hand, Defendant notes a lack of supporting documentary evidence—including emails and other correspondence—for the majority of these contacts. Defendant correctly notes that various recipients of the email correspondence between Plaintiff and Kenmnan Apparel are unidentified, and that the substance of the correspondence is difficult to discern, given the profusion of obscure terminology and the scarcity of references to the goods at issue. In other words, the record suggests that Plaintiff made some efforts to sell the goods, but the parties have offered conflicting and scanty evidence on their scope and substance.

Finally, Defendant contends that recovery under 2–709(1)(b) is generally limited to goods so specialized that virtually no resale market exists, and these goods—winter coats to be sold at a discount chain retailer—do not fall under this category. However, in cases of specialized goods the party seeking recovery is still required to demonstrate that the goods had "no value to other buyers." Emanuel Law Outlines, Inc. v. Multi–State Legal Studies, Inc., 899 F. Supp. 1081, 1089 (S.D.N.Y. 1995). While custom-made or specialized goods are more likely to fall under this category, courts require evidence of resale efforts even for custom-made goods where resale is a possibility. In other words, the character of goods as either specialized, custom-made, or standardized is not dispositive of liability under 2–709(1)(b). The party seeking recovery must offer evidence of either reasonable efforts to resell the goods or the impossibility of such efforts, and the relevant evidence in this case is not conclusive.

Accordingly, the Court holds that a genuine issue of material fact exists as to whether Plaintiff's efforts to resell the goods were reasonable.

* * *

For the foregoing reasons, the Court denies Plaintiff's and Defendant's motions for summary judgment.

NOTES

1. In ruling on the seller's summary judgment motion for the price under 2–709, the court in *Granvia Trading* assumed that Article 2 of the UCC governed the sales contract, not the CISG. The assumption is mistaken. Granvia Trading's complaint, not reproduced here, recites that the seller (Granvia Trading) was a South Korean corporation with its principal place of business in South Korea and the buyer (Sutton Creations) was a New York corporation with its principal place of business in New York City. Because South Korea and the United States are both Contracting States, Article 1(1)(a) of the CISG makes the CISG applicable to the sales contract. According to Article 62, Granvia Trading is entitled to the contract price. However, Article 28 limits the availability of specific relief under the CISG. The Article does not require the forum court to order specific relief unless it would do so under its own law with respect to sales contracts similar to those governed by the CISG. The forum is a New York federal court, and the domestic law applicable by the forum to sale of goods contracts not governed by the CISG is Article 2 of the UCC, as enacted in New York. Section 2–709(1) entitles a seller to the price only if one of its disjunctive conditions is met. Thus, Article 28 does not require the *Granvia Trading* court to award Granvia Trading the price unless a seller would be entitled to the price under 2–709(1) in sales contracts similar to the sales contract in the case. The court's reliance on 2–709 in disposing of the seller's summary judgment motion therefore ultimately is sound, even though the CISG governs the sales contract. Article 28's limitation on price actions is discussed in section C below.

The parties in *Granvia Trading* eventually settled their dispute. Suppose, however, that they did not. Suppose too that in further proceedings the court determined that none of 2–709(1)'s conditions were met. Could the court still award Granvia Trading the price? See CISG Articles 62, 28 ("is not bound").

2. Can the buyer's wrongful revocation of its acceptance deprive the seller of a price action? Article 2's provisions give conflicting answers. According to 2–608(1), the buyer may revoke its acceptance if the nonconformity in the goods substantially impairs its value to him. The revocation operates as a rejection; cf. 2–608(3). A rejection is inconsistent with an acceptance, according to 2–607(2). Thus, because the revocation operates as a rejection, the seller cannot recover the price under 2–709(1)(a). The problem comes when the goods conform to the contract or the nonconformity does not substantially impair their value to the buyer but the buyer nonetheless tries to revoke its acceptance. Section 2–608(1) does not allow the revocation to be effective if the goods are conforming or the nonconformity is insubstantial. Even a procedurally proper revocation therefore cannot operate as a rejection. Thus, a "wrongful" revocation remains an acceptance and the seller is entitled to the price under 2–709(1)(a). See Plateq Corp. of New Haven v. Machlette Labs., Inc., 35 UCC Rep. Serv. 1132 (Conn. 1983). However, 2–709(3) provides in relevant part that a seller is entitled to damages if it is not entitled to the price as against a

buyer who wrongfully rejects or revokes acceptance of the goods. This suggests that a seller might not have a price action even under 2–709(1)(a) against a buyer who has wrongfully revoked its acceptance. The seller would not have a price action in these circumstances only if the wrongful revocation was effective as a rejection. There is a conflict between 2–608(1) and 2–709(3).

3. Section 2–709(1) controls the seller's "duty" to mitigate its damages. The duty applies only when the seller tries to recover the price under subsection (1)(b). The subsection allows a price action with respect to identified goods if the seller is unable to resell them at a reasonable price or demonstrates that doing so would be unavailing. If the seller can mitigate its damages by reselling the goods at a reasonable price (with reasonable effort), it cannot recover the price under (1)(b). In this case the seller must dispose of the goods and recovering damages. The result makes sense. A seller who can make a reasonable resale has a presumptive advantage at doing so over its buyer. Denying the seller a price action in the circumstances minimizes the buyer's damage bill. By contrast, 2-709(1)(a) does not require the seller to mitigate its damages when the buyer accepts the goods. See Seimens Energy & Automation, Inc. v. Coleman's Electric Supply Co., Inc., 46 F.Supp.2d 217 (E.D.N.Y. 1999); Indust. Molded Plastic Products, Inc. v. J. Gross & Son, Inc., 398 A.2d 695 (Pa. Super. Ct. 1979). It does not contain the language of mitigation contained in subsection (1)(b). The seller therefore can maintain a price action for accepted goods even if it could dispose of them for a reasonable price with reasonable effort. Cf. Weil v. Murray, 161 F. Supp.2d 252 (S.D.N.Y. 2001) (seller not required to resell accepted painting in its possession). Although reselling accepted goods might expose the seller to a conversion action by the buyer's creditors, 2–709(1)(a) does not require the seller to demonstrate this risk. The seller can recover the price even if there is no risk of conflicting claims to the goods. The absence of a mitigation requirement from 2–709(1)(a) is justified, if at all, by the character of acceptance as a rough proxy. Buyers which have accepted the goods usually have possession. In these circumstances they usually are in a better position than their sellers at disposing of the goods. The sellers generally cannot mitigate their damages by reselling the goods from afar.

4. Section 2–709(1)(b)'s standard is one of "unsaleability": the seller must be unable after reasonable effort to resell the goods at a reasonable price or circumstances reasonably indicate that doing so will be unavailing. The triple appearance of "reasonable," particularly the reference to a "reasonable price," makes the standard vague and hard to apply. The court in *Granvia Trading* found that the seller's incomplete documentation failed to demonstrate that it had made reasonable efforts to dispose of the goods. The results in other cases turn on whether the seller demonstrated that it was unable to obtain a reasonable price for rejected goods. Based on a survey of these cases, Professors White and Summers conclude that the results reveal "apparently random interpretations" of the unsaleability standard; see James J. White & Robert S. Summers, Uniform Commercial Code § 8–5 (at 352) (6th ed. 2010).

PROBLEM 10.1

Seller contracted with Buyer to deliver on January 1 100 laptop computers at $500 per laptop. Payment was due on February 1. In November Buyer's marketing director learned that the popularity of tablets was reducing the demand for laptops. Laptops of the sort Buyer had ordered from Seller could be purchased or sold elsewhere for $400. On December 20 Buyer notified Seller that it was cancelling the contract and would not take delivery of Seller's laptops on January 1. After Buyer refused to pay for the laptops, Seller sued Buyer for the $50,000 contract price while retaining the laptops. Is Seller entitled to recover $50,000 price from Buyer? See 2–709(1)(a)–(b), 2–602(1); 2–706(1), 2–708(1).

Is Seller entitled to the price in the circumstances below?

(a) Assume that Seller delivered the laptops to Buyer on January 1. The same day Buyer notified Seller that it was cancelling the contract and demanded that Seller retrieve them. The laptops conformed in every respect to the contract. See 2–602(1), 2–607(2), 2–709(1)(a).

(b) Assume in (a) that Seller was not located in anywhere near Buyer. See 2–709(1)(b).

(c) Buyer visited Seller's plant on December 1, examined the laptops and approved them for the January 1 delivery. The facts are otherwise the same as above. 2–606(1)(a); 2–709(1)(a); see Unlaub Co., Inc. v. Sexton, 568 F.2d 72 (8th Cir. 1977).

(d) After Buyer refused delivery of the laptops, Seller placed them in its warehouse and waited until June to sue Buyer for the price. In May a freak snowstorm caused the roof in Seller's warehouse to tear and flooded the building. The laptops Seller stored there, including those labeled "Buyer's," became water logged and worthless. See 2–509(2); 2–709(1)(a).

2. RESALE AND MARKET PRICE MEASURES

a. CALCULATION OF DAMAGES

The seller whose buyer has wrongfully rejected the goods can measure its damages under either 2–706 or 2–708(1). See 2–703(d)–(e). Under 2–706, the seller may resell the goods and recover the difference between the contract price and the resale price. To recover the seller must meet three conditions. First, the resale must be done in good faith and in commercially reasonable manner. The resale may be by either private or public sale. Second, the seller must notify the buyer. In the case of a private sale the notice must state that the seller intends to resell. 2–706(2). In a public sale, where practicable, the notice must give the time and place of resale. 2–706(3)(c). Third, the resale contract must be "reasonably identified" to the breached contract. This requires that the resold goods be identified as the goods referred to by the breached contract. Although the resold goods need not be the same goods covered by the breached contract, 2–706(2) requires that they in some way be "reasonably identifiable" to it. *Apex Oil Co.*, reproduced below, explores what makes an identification "reasonable."

Section 2–708(1) gives an alternative means by which the seller can measure its damages. Under it the seller can recover the difference between the contract price and the market price of the goods at the time and place for tender. The market price sometimes might be difficult or impossible to determine. In this case 2–723(2) allows the market price prevailing within a reasonable time before or after the time and place for tender to suffice. If the buyer repudiates the contract and the case comes to trial before the time for tender, 2–723(1) deems the relevant market price to be the market price at the time the seller learned of the repudiation. Although resale and market measures of damages give the same recovery when resale and market price remain the same, resale and market price can differ when resale occurs after the time and place for tender of the goods. The seller's recovery under 2–706's resale measure in this case might be more or less than its recovery under 2–708(1)'s resale measure.

Although 2–703 allows the seller to measure its damages either by the contract-resale or contract-market price difference, the measures have different costs associated with their use. To rely on the contract-market price difference, the seller must prove the market price of the goods at the time and place for tender. If market prices are volatile or the relevant market thin, the costs of proving market price can be high. By comparison, the seller need not prove market price if it relies on the contract price-resale difference. It can set its damages instead by making a resale in accordance with 2–706's requirements. However, to do so the seller must prove in litigation that its resale was commercially reasonable and that it gave the buyer proper notice. Proof of these fact-dependent elements also can be difficult. Thus, a seller deciding to measure its damages by 2–706's resale formula or 2–708(1)'s market formula has to estimate the comparative size of the proof costs associated with each measure. Other things being equal, the seller will prefer the measure under which it will incur the lowest proof costs.

Apex Oil Co. v. Belcher Co. of New York, Inc.

United States Court of Appeals, Second Circuit, 1988
855 F.2d 997

■ WINTER, CIRCUIT JUDGE:

This diversity case, arising out of an acrimonious commercial dispute, presents the question whether a sale of goods six weeks after a breach of contract may properly be used to calculate resale damages under Section 2–706 of the Uniform Commercial Code, where goods originally identified to the broken contract were sold on the day following the breach. Defendants The Belcher Company of New York, Inc. and Belcher New Jersey, Inc. (together "Belcher") appeal from a judgment, entered after a jury trial before Judge McLaughlin, awarding plaintiff Apex Oil Company ("Apex") $432,365.04 in damages for breach of contract and fraud in connection with an uncompleted transaction for heating oil. Belcher claims that the district court improperly allowed Apex to recover resale damages and that Apex failed to prove its fraud claim by clear and convincing evidence. We agree and reverse.

BACKGROUND

Apex buys, sells, refines and transports petroleum products of various sorts, including No. 2 heating oil, commonly known as home heating oil. Belcher also buys and sells petroleum products, including No. 2 heating oil. In February 1982, both firms were trading futures contracts for No. 2 heating oil on the New York Mercantile Exchange ("Merc"). In particular, both were trading Merc contracts for February 1982 No. 2 heating oil—i.e., contracts for the delivery of that commodity in New York Harbor during that delivery month in accordance with the Merc's rules. As a result of that trading, Apex was short 315 contracts, and Belcher was long by the same amount. Being "short" one contract for oil means that the trader has contracted to deliver one thousand barrels at some point in the future, and being "long" means just the opposite—that the trader has contracted to purchase that amount of oil. If a contract is not liquidated before the close of trading, the short trader must deliver the oil to a long trader (the exchange matches shorts with longs) in strict compliance with Merc rules or suffer stiff penalties, including disciplinary proceedings and fines. A short trader may, however, meet its obligations by entering into an "exchange for physicals" ("EFP") transaction with a long trader. An EFP allows a short trader to substitute for the delivery of oil under the terms of a futures contract the delivery of oil at a different place and time.

Apex was matched with Belcher by the Merc, and thus became bound to produce 315,000 barrels of No. 2 heating oil meeting Merc specifications in New York Harbor. Those specifications required that oil delivered in New York Harbor have a sulfur content no higher than 0.20%. Apex asked Belcher whether Belcher would take delivery of 190,000 barrels of oil in Boston Harbor in satisfaction of 190 contracts, and Belcher agreed. At trial, the parties did not dispute that, under this EFP, Apex promised it would deliver the No. 2 heating oil for the same price as that in the original contract—89.70 cents per gallon—and that the oil would be lifted from the vessel *Bordeaux*. The parties did dispute, and vigorously so, the requisite maximum sulfur content. At trial, Belcher sought to prove that the oil had to meet the New York standard of 0.20%, while Apex asserted that the oil had to meet only the specifications for Boston Harbor of not more than 0.30% sulfur.

The *Bordeaux* arrived in Boston Harbor on February 9, 1982, and on the next day began discharging its cargo of No. 2 heating oil at Belcher New England, Inc.'s terminal in Revere, Massachusetts. Later in the evening of February 10, after fifty or sixty thousand barrels had been offloaded, an independent petroleum inspector told Belcher that tests showed the oil on board the *Bordeaux* contained 0.28% sulfur, in excess of the New York Harbor specification. Belcher nevertheless continued to lift oil from the ship until eleven o'clock the next morning, February 11, when 141,535 barrels had been pumped into Belcher's terminal. After pumping had stopped, a second test indicated that the oil contained 0.22% sulfur—a figure within the accepted range of tolerance for oil containing 0.20% sulfur. (Apex did not learn of the second test until shortly before trial.) Nevertheless, Belcher refused to resume pumping, claiming that the oil did not conform to specifications.

After Belcher ordered the *Bordeaux* to leave its terminal, Apex immediately contacted Cities Service. Apex was scheduled to deliver heating oil to Cities Service later in the month and accordingly asked if it could satisfy that obligation by immediately delivering the oil on the *Bordeaux*. Cities Service agreed, and that oil was delivered to Cities Service in Boston Harbor on February 12, one day after the oil had been rejected by Belcher. Apex did not give notice to Belcher that the oil had been delivered to Cities Service.

Meanwhile, Belcher and Apex continued to quarrel over the portion of the oil delivered by the *Bordeaux*. Belcher repeatedly informed Apex, orally and by telex, that the oil was unsuitable and would have to be sold at a loss because of its high sulfur content. Belcher also claimed, falsely, that it was incurring various expenses because the oil was unusable. In fact, however, Belcher had already sold the oil in the ordinary course of business. Belcher nevertheless refused to pay Apex the contract price of $5,322,200.27 for the oil it had accepted, and it demanded that Apex produce the remaining 48,000 barrels of oil owing under the contract. On February 17, Apex agreed to tender the 48,000 barrels if Belcher would both make partial payment for the oil actually accepted and agree to negotiate as to the price ultimately to be paid for that oil. Belcher agreed and sent Apex a check for $5,034,997.12, a sum reflecting a discount of five cents per gallon from the contract price. However, the check contained an endorsement stating that "the acceptance and negotiation of this check constitutes full payment and final settlement of all claims" against Belcher. Apex refused the check, and the parties returned to square one. Apex demanded full payment; Belcher demanded that Apex either negotiate the check or remove the discharged oil (which had actually been sold) and replace it with 190,000 barrels of conforming product. Apex chose to take the oil and replace it, and on February 23 told Belcher that the 142,000 barrels of discharged oil would be removed on board the *Mersault* on February 25.

By then, however, Belcher had sold the 142,000 barrels and did not have an equivalent amount of No. 2 oil in its entire Boston terminal. Instead of admitting that it did not have the oil, Belcher told Apex that a dock for the *Mersault* was unavailable. Belcher also demanded that Apex either remove the oil *and* pay terminalling and storage fees, or accept payment for the oil at a discount of five cents per gallon. Apex refused to do either. On the next day, Belcher and Apex finally reached a settlement under which Belcher agreed to pay for the oil discharged from the *Bordeaux* at a discount of 2.5 cents per gallon. The settlement agreement also resolved an unrelated dispute between an Apex subsidiary and a subsidiary of Belcher's parent firm, The Coastal Corporation. It is this agreement that Apex now claims was procured by fraud.

After the settlement, Apex repeatedly contacted Belcher to ascertain when, where and how Belcher would accept delivery of the remaining 48,000 barrels. On March 5, Belcher informed Apex that it considered its obligations under the original contract to have been extinguished, and that it did not "desire to purchase such a volume [the 48,000 barrels] at the offered price." Apex responded by claiming that the settlement did not extinguish Belcher's obligation to accept the 48,000 barrels. In addition, Apex stated that unless Belcher accepted the oil by March 20, Apex would identify 48,000 barrels of No. 2 oil to the breached contract and sell the oil to a third party. When Belcher again refused to take the oil, Apex sold 48,000 barrels to Gill & Duffus Company. This oil was sold for delivery in April at a price of 76.25 cents per gallon, 13.45 cents per gallon below the Belcher contract price.

On October 7, 1982, Apex brought this suit in the Eastern District, asserting breach of contract and fraud. The breach-of-contract claim in Apex's amended complaint contended that Belcher had breached the EFP, not in February, but in March, when Belcher had refused to take delivery of the 48,000 barrels still owing under the contract. The amended complaint further alleged that "at the time of the breach of the Contract by Belcher the market price of the product was $.7625 per gallon," the price brought by the resale to Gill & Duffus on March 23. In turn, the fraud claim asserted that Belcher had made various misrepresentations—that the *Bordeaux* oil was unfit, and unusable by Belcher; and that consequently Belcher was suffering extensive damages and wanted the oil removed—upon which Apex had relied when it had agreed to settle as to the 142,000 barrels lifted from the *Bordeaux*. Apex asserted that as a result of the alleged fraud it had suffered damages of 2.5 cents per gallon, the discount agreed upon in the settlement.

The case went to trial before Judge McLaughlin and a jury between February 3 and February 13, 1986. As it had alleged in its pleadings, Apex asserted that its breach-of-contract claim was based on an alleged breach occurring *after* February 11, 1982, the day Belcher rejected the oil on board the *Bordeaux*. Judge McLaughlin, however, rejected this theory as a matter of law. His view of the case was that Belcher's rejection of the *Bordeaux* oil occurred under one of two circumstances: (i) either the oil conformed to the sulfur specification, in which case Belcher breached; or (ii) the oil did not conform, in which case Apex breached. Judge McLaughlin reasoned that, if Belcher breached on February 11, then it could not have breached thereafter. If on the other hand Apex breached, then, Judge McLaughlin reasoned, only under the doctrine of cure, see U.C.C. § 2–508, could Belcher be deemed to have breached. Apex, however, waived the cure theory by expressly disavowing it (perhaps because it presumes a breach by Apex). Instead, Apex argued that, regardless of whether the *Bordeaux* oil had conformed, Belcher's refusal throughout February and March 1982 to accept delivery of 48,000 barrels of conforming oil, which Belcher was then still demanding, had constituted a breach of contract. Judge McLaughlin rejected this argument, which he viewed as simply "an attempt to reintroduce the cure doctrine."

In a general verdict, the jury awarded Apex $283,752.94 on the breach-of-contract claim, and $148,612.10 on the fraud claim, for a total of $432,365.04. With the addition of prejudgment interest, the judgment came to $588,566.29.

Belcher appeals from this verdict. Apex has not taken a cross-appeal from Judge McLaughlin's dismissal of its post-February 11 breach theories, however. The parties agree, therefore, that as the case comes to us, the verdict concerning the breach can be upheld only on the theory that, if Belcher breached the contract, it did so only on February 11, 1982, and that the oil sold to Gill & Duffus on March 23 was identified to the broken contract.

DISCUSSION

* * *

Belcher's principal argument on appeal is that the district court erred as a matter of law in allowing Apex to recover resale damages under Section 2–706. Specifically, Belcher contends that the heating oil Apex sold to Gill & Duffus in late March of 1982 was not identified to the broken contract. According to Belcher, the oil identified to the contract was the oil aboard the *Bordeaux*—oil which Apex had sold to Cities Service on the day after the breach. In response, Apex argues that, because heating oil is a fungible commodity, the oil sold to Gill & Duffus was "reasonably identified" to the contract even though it was not the same oil that had been on board the *Bordeaux*. We agree with Apex that, at least with respect to fungible goods, identification for the purposes of a resale transaction does not necessarily require that the resold goods be the exact goods that were rejected or repudiated. Nonetheless, we conclude that as a matter of law the oil sold to Gill & Duffus in March was not reasonably identified to the contract breached on February 11, and that the resale was not commercially reasonable.

Resolving the instant dispute requires us to survey various provisions of the Uniform Commercial Code. * * * The *Bordeaux* oil was unquestionably identified to the contract under Section 2–501(b), and Apex does not assert otherwise. Nevertheless, Apex argues that Section 2–501 "has no application in the context of the Section 2–706 resale remedy," because Section 2–501 defines identification only for the purpose of establishing the point at which a buyer "obtains a special property and an insurable interest in goods." U.C.C. § 2–501. This argument has a facial plausibility but ignores Section 2–103, which contains various definitions, and an index of other definitions, of terms used throughout Article 2 of the Code. With regard to "identification," Section 2–103(2) provides that the "definition[ ] applying to *this Article*" is set forth in Section 2–501. Id. § 2–103 (emphasis added).

Section 2–501 thus informs us that the *Bordeaux* oil was identified to the contract. It does not end our inquiry, however, because it does not exclude as a matter of law the possibility that a seller may identify goods to a contract, but then substitute, for the identified goods, *identical* goods that are then identified to the contract. . . .

In particular, Belcher relies upon Section 2–706's statement that "the seller may resell the *goods concerned*," U.C.C. § 2–706(1) (emphasis added), and upon Section 2–704, which states that "an aggrieved seller . . . may . . . identify to the contract conforming goods *not already identified* if at the time he learned of the breach they are in his possession or control." § 2–704(1) (emphasis added). According to Belcher, these statements absolutely foreclose the possibility of reidentification for the purpose of a resale. Apex, on the other hand, points to Section 2–706's statement that "it is not necessary that the goods be in existence or that any or all of them have been identified to the contract before the breach." According to Apex, this language shows that "the relevant inquiry to be made under Section 2–706 is whether the resale transaction is reasonably identified to the breached contract and not whether the goods resold were originally identified to that contract."

None of the cited provisions are dispositive. First, Section 2–706(1)'s reference to reselling "the goods concerned" is unhelpful because those goods are the goods identified to the contract, but which goods are so identified is the question to be answered in the instant case. Second, as to Section 2–704, the fact that an aggrieved seller may identify goods "not already identified" does not mean that the seller may not identify goods as substitutes for previously identified goods. Rather, Section 2–704 appears to deal simply with the situation described in Section 2–706(2) above, where the goods are not yet in existence or have not yet been identified to the contract. Belcher thus can draw no comfort from either Section 2–704 or Section 2–706(1). Third, at the same time, however, Section 2–706(2)'s reference to nonexistent and nonidentified goods does not mean, as Apex suggests, that the original (prebreach) identification of goods is wholly irrelevant. Rather, the provision regarding nonexistent and nonidentified goods deals with the special circumstances involving anticipatory repudiation by the buyer. Under such circumstances, there can of course be no resale remedy unless the seller is allowed to identify goods to the contract after the breach. That is obviously not the case here.

* * *

We agree with Servbest Foods, Inc. v. Emessee Industries, Inc., 403 N.E.2d 1 (Il. Ct. App. 1980) that fungible goods resold pursuant to Section 2–706 must be goods identified to the contract, but need not always be those originally identified to the contract. In other words, at least where fungible goods are concerned, identification is not always an irrevocable act and does not foreclose the possibility of substitution. . . . Thus, Section 2–706 should not be construed as always proscribing the resale of goods other than those originally identified to the broken contract. Nevertheless, as that Section expressly states, "the resale must be *reasonably* identified as referring to the broken contract," and "every aspect of the sale including the method, manner, time, place and terms must be commercially reasonable." U.C.C. § 2–706(2) (emphasis added). Moreover, because the purpose of remedies under the Code is to put "the aggrieved party . . . in as good a position as if the other party had fully performed," id. § 1–106(1) [§ 1–305(a)], the reasonableness of the identification and of the resale must be determined by examining whether the market value of, and the price received for, the resold goods "accurately reflects the market value of the goods which are the subject of the contract." *Servbest,* 403 N.E.2d at 8.

* * *

Here, Apex's delay of nearly six weeks between the breach on February 11, 1982 and the purported resale on March 23 was clearly unreasonable, even if the transfer to Cities Service had not occurred. . . . In view of the long delay and the apparent volatility of the market for No. 2 oil, the purported resale failed to meet the requirements of Section 2–706 as a matter of law.

Nor do we find Apex's delay justified on any other ground. Apex does not assert, for example, that "the time for resale [should] be appropriately lengthened" because Belcher sought an "inspection . . . [to] preserv[e] evidence of [the] goods in dispute," U.C.C. § 2–706 comment 5; Belcher of course made no such request, and Apex immediately disposed of the *Bordeaux* oil in any event. Apex's only asserted justification, which the district court accepted in denying Belcher's motion for judgment notwithstanding the verdict, was that the delay was caused by continuing negotiations with Belcher. We find that ruling to be inconsistent with the district court's view that Belcher's breach, if any, occurred on February 11. The function of a resale was to put Apex in the position it would have been on that date by determining the value of the oil Belcher refused. The value of the oil at a later date is irrelevant because Apex was in no way obligated by the contract or by the Uniform Commercial Code to reserve 48,000 gallons for Belcher after the February 11 breach. Indeed, that is why Apex's original theory, rejected by the district court and not before us on this appeal, was that the breach occurred in March.

The rule that a "resale should be made as soon as practicable after breach" should be stringently applied where, as here, the resold goods are not those originally identified to the contract. In such circumstances, of course, there is a significant risk that the seller, who may perhaps have already disposed of the original goods without suffering any loss, has identified new goods for resale in order to minimize the resale price and thus to maximize damages. That was not the case in *Servbest*, for example, where the resale consisted of the first sales made after the breach. Here, by contrast, the oil originally identified to the contract was sold the day after the February 11, 1982 breach, and no doubt Apex sold ample amounts thereafter in the six weeks before the purported resale. We note that in its complaint and throughout the trial Apex asserted that it was suing on a breach that occurred as late as three days before the resale. This is not surprising given *Servbest*, the length of Apex's delay, and the drop in the market price for No. 2 oil. But, as noted, the district court held, in a ruling not appealed from, that the only viable theory available to Apex was that involving a breach on February 11. Because the sale of the oil identified to the contract to Cities Service on the next day fixed the value of the goods refused as a matter of law, the judgment on the breach-of-contract claim must be reversed.

*   *   *

NOTE

Sections 2–706 and 2–708(1) both allow the seller to recover incidental expenses in addition to the contract-resale or contract-market price difference, respectively. However, neither section mentions consequential damages, and no other provision in Article 2 allows the seller to recover these damages. Thus, consequential damages are not a seller's remedy. See Afram Export Corp. v. Metallurgiki Halyps, S.A., 772 F.2d 1358 (7th Cir. 1985). By contrast, under 2–715(1) the buyer may recover consequential damages resulting from the seller's breach. Compare 2–708(1), 2–706 (seller's damages include incidental expenses) with 2–712 and 2–713 (buyer's damages include both incidental expenses and consequential damages). This limitation on the seller's recoverable damages forces a distinction between incidental expenses and consequential damages. In the buyer's case, unless the contract contains a liability limitation clause, the distinction does not usually matter. In the seller's case, it often does.

The divide between incidental expenses and consequential damages sometimes is unclear. According to 2–710, incidental damages include commercially reasonable charges, expenses or commissions incurred in transporting, caring for or reselling the goods resulting from breach. Section 2–710's reference to "charges, expenses, or commissions incurred" suggests that the incidental expenses are out-of-pocket expenses expended as a result of breach. Opportunity costs, on the other hand, are valuable opportunities lost as a result of the breach rather than outlays. Discounts, tax benefits or investment returns lost on breach are types of opportunity costs. It therefore might appear that incidental expenses are certain outlays resulting from breach ("charges, expenses, or commissions") while consequential damages are opportunity costs that result from it. However, the distinction does not accurately classify the two sorts of loss. For example, personal injury or foreseeable contract liability to third parties resulting from the seller's breach, although not forgone opportunities, are recoverable by the buyer as consequential damages; see 2–715(2). In addition, courts disagree about how to classify some expenses incurred by the seller, such as interest payments on loans in connection with the goods between the breach and the date they are resold. Some consider these payments, where foreseeable, to be consequential damages, not "reasonable expenses or charges" incurred in connection with resale of the goods. See, e.g., S.C. Gray, Inc. v. Ford Motor Co., 286 N.W.2d 34 (Mich. Ct. App. 1979). Other courts treat the payments as "reasonable expenses" recoverable as incidental expenses; see Bulk Oil (U.S.A.), Inc. v. Sun Oil Trading Co., 697 F.2d 481 (2d Cir. 1983).

Even if the distinction between incidental damages and consequential damages is clear, not allowing recovery of consequential damages undercompensates the seller. The seller incurs an opportunity cost when the money invested in the contract goods cannot be used to obtain a return in an alternative use. If its damages do not reflect this cost, its expectation interest is not fully protected. The PEB Study Group recommended that Article 2 be revised to give the seller a remedy of consequential damages. See PEB Study Group, Preliminary Report on Uniform Commercial Code Article 2 221–222 (1990); cf. Proposed 2–710.

b. ELECTION OF REMEDIES

A question arises when the market price at the time of tender is lower than the price at which the seller resold the goods. In this case the contract-market price difference is greater than the contract-resale difference and therefore the seller would prefer its damages to be calculated by the former measure if given the choice. May a seller who makes a proper resale under 2–706 choose to measure its damages by 2–708(1)'s contract-market price difference rather than by 2–706's contract-resale difference? Article 2 does not say. Some of its provisions and Comments allow the choice among remedies; others seem to bar election. Section 2–703, which lists both damages remedies, is ambiguous. It can be read to mean (i) that the seller may measure its damages under either 2–706 or 2–708(1) or (ii) that the seller may resell and use 2–706 to measure its damages or not resell and use 2–708(1) to measure its damages. The former interpretation allows the seller to elect its remedy, so that the remedies are cumulative; the latter interpretation does not. Comment 5 to 2–713 addresses the question of the election of remedies for the buyer. In the buyer's case the question arises when the buyer properly covers at below the market price but above the contract price. May the buyer measure its damages by 2–713's market price-contract difference rather than the 2–712(1)'s cover-contract price difference? Comment 5 states that 2–712(1)'s market price measure is available "only when and to the extent that the buyer has not covered." But no similar Comment deals with the seller's election of remedies. More important, the language of 2–703 and 2–711, which lists the seller and buyer's remedies respectively, does not support Comment 5. Both sections say that the seller and buyer "may" rely on the remedies listed. Neither section restricts access to the market price measure if the seller has resold or the buyer covered. Supporting the same conclusion is Comment 1 to 2–703, which states that Article 2 rejects the election of remedies.

Unsurprisingly, courts and commentators disagree about the permissibility and wisdom of allowing an election of remedies. Compare Peace River Seed Coop., Ltd. v. Proseeds Mktg., 253 Ore. App. 704 (Ore. Ct. App. 2012) (election allowed) with Tesoro Petroleum Corp. v. Holborn Oil Co., Ltd., 547 N.Y.S.2d 1012 (N.Y. Sup. Ct. 1989) (election barred). Opponents of election rely on 1–305(a)'s instruction that the UCC remedies be administered to put the injured party in the position it would be in had the breaching party performed. They claim that the seller who has resold and recovers damages based on the lower market price receives a "windfall": the recovery puts the seller in a better position than it would be in had the buyer not breached. See James J. White & Robert S. Summers, Uniform Commercial Code § 8–7 (at 421) (6th ed. 2010); Roy Ryden Anderson, Pitfalls for Seller and Buyers Under the Market Formula of 2–708, 4 Rev. Litig. 251, 264 (1985); *Tesoro Petroleum*, 547 N.Y.S.2d, at 1016. Whether the seller receives a "windfall" depends on what it bargained for. A decent argument can be made that the seller bargained for a fixed price, which the market-contract difference protects. A contract with a fixed price sets the price for delivery at a later time. The fixed price allocates to the buyer the risk that the market price at that time falls below the contract price. As a result, if the seller resells at a price above market price, the contract-resale difference does not make the seller whole. It keeps on the seller a portion of the risk of a decline in market price that the fixed price contract shifted to the buyer. By contrast, the seller's recovery of the contract-market price difference makes the seller whole, even if it the resale price is above the market price. The seller retains the goods with the reduced market price and recovers the contract-market price difference in damages, so that it receives in total what the buyer promised: the price fixed by the contract. Because the seller bargained for the fixed price, it does not receive a "windfall." For different arguments for the same conclusion, see Victor Goldberg, Framing Contract Law 225–226 (2006); Robert E. Scott, The Case for Market Damages: Revisiting the Lost Profits Puzzle, 74 U. Chi. L. Rev. 1155, 1175–1179 (1990).

PROBLEM 10.2

In March Buyit, located in Houston, agreed to purchase 10 tractors from Supply, located in New York City. The agreement called for payment of "$100,000 C.I.F. Houston" and for payment to be made against presentation of negotiable bills of lading covering the tractors. Shipment to be made by December 1. Supply delivered the tractors to the carrier on November 27 and received the proper bills of lading from the carrier. When the shipment of tractors arrived in Houston on December 15, Supply presented the bills of lading to Buyit and demanded payment. Between March and December the price of tractors in Los Angeles fell. As of December 10 tractors of the sort Buyit had ordered could be purchased there for $90,000. The same tractors could be purchased in New York during the same period for $75,000. If Supply decides not to resell the tractors, what amount can it recover damages from Buyit? See 2–320(1), 2–503, 2–504, 2–708(1). What amount can Buyit recover if Supply's agreement with Buyit did not call for presentation of a document of title?

PROBLEM 10.3

Sell contracted with Buy to deliver 20 tons of fertilizer between January and June at $1,000 per ton for a total price of $20,000. Payment was due within a week of delivery. Buy took delivery of 10 tons of fertilizer from Sell in January. Immediately after it did so Buy discovered that the price of fertilizer had dropped to $500 per ton. Although fertilizer prices were extremely volatile, Buy was not confident that they would increase in the short term. Accordingly, it refused to pay Sell for the shipment, repudiated the contract, and demanded that Sell retrieve the fertilizer it had delivered. In February, after retrieving the fertilizer, Sell sued Buy. Can Sell recover the $20,000 contract price from Sell? Assuming that it cannot, in what amount can it recover in damages? See 2–709(1)(a), (b), 2–708(1), 2–723(1).

PROBLEM 10.4

Mobley regretted having agreed to purchase from Ace Gallery an original oil painting for $5,000 after he discovered that the current price of the painting was $3,000. When Ace tried to deliver the painting, Mobley refused to receive or pay for it. After Ace sent Mobley a note stating that "we regret that you chose to refuse to accept delivery and pay us. A deal is a deal," it had no further contact with Mobley. A short time later Ace sent emails to art dealers throughout the country offering the painting to the highest bidder and setting a date within which bids were to be received. The emails also informed the dealers that they could inspect the painting at their convenience. After receiving a number of bids, Ace sold the painting to the highest bidder for $1,000. The bidder was not willing to pay more because the painting's current price had declined to $1,000 after Mobley had refused the painting. In what amount can Ace Gallery recover as damages from Mobley? See 2–706(1), (3), (4); Comment 2 to 2–706, 2–708(1); Comment 7 to 9–610.

PROBLEM 10.5

Assume in Problem 10.4 that Ace Gallery informed Mobley that "we will resell the painting and hold you responsible for the consequences" after Mobley refused to take delivery or pay the $5,000 contract price. Assume also that the highest bidder offered $4,000, which Ace accepted. May Ace measure its damages by 2–708(1)'s market price formula? See Comment 2 to 2–706, Comment 1 to 1–305; cf. Comment 5 to 2–713.

PROBLEM 10.6

Power is a wholesale supplier of cork. It agreed to sell Wine, a manufacturer of corks for wine bottles, 1000 pounds of cork for $5,000. Later, on April 15, Wine repudiated the contract after it decided to produce only twist caps. At the time Power had on hand 2000 pounds of cork in its inventory. When two buyers each expressed interest in purchasing 1000 pounds of cork, Power informed Wine that it would try to sell cork to them after May 1. On May 7 Power sold 1000 pounds of cork for $4,000 to one of the buyers. The same day the other buyer, in urgent need of cork, agreed to pay $4,500 for 1000 pounds. The market price of cork, which had declined, remained at $4,000 throughout the relevant period. Power can establish that the cork delivered to the two buyers came from its inventory. If Power does not want to rely on the market price to recover damages, how much can it recover in damages from Wine? See 2–706(2), 2–501.

3. DAMAGES MEASURED BY LOST PROFITS

The seller's profit is its net gain from performing the contract. Its net gain in turn is equal to the contract price minus its cost of performance. As noted at the beginning of the Chapter, all damage remedies when available give the injured party its profit. For example, the injured seller who resells the goods at a market price below the contract price and recovers under 2–706(1) obtains its profits. It recovers the contract price-resale price difference in damages from the breaching buyer and receives the resale price from the buyer to whom it resells the goods. The sum of these two amounts equals the contract price. Because the seller incurs the costs of producing the goods, 2–706(1)'s resale measure gives the seller its profits. But sometimes the seller cannot use 2–706(1) or 2–708(1) to recover its profit. This can occur in two different circumstances. One occurs when the seller decides not to complete production or acquire the goods from its supplier after the buyer breaches. See 2–704. Because the seller does not have the goods in a deliverable form, it cannot resell them or measure their value by their market price. In "uncompleted goods" cases the seller therefore cannot measure its damages by the contract-resale or the contract-market price difference.

The second circumstance is one in which the seller completes or acquires the goods and resells them after the buyer breaches. Had the buyer not breached, the seller would have sold goods to this second buyer too. The sale to the second buyer is an additional sale, not a substitute sale for the breached contract. Thus, had the buyer performed, the seller would have made two sales and received two profits—one from the first buyer and another from the second buyer.

Because the buyer breached, the seller makes only one sale and one profit. It has "lost volume" and therefore lost a profit on the breached contract. Sections 2–706(1) and 2–708(1)'s damage measures do not compensate the seller for the lost profit. To see this, suppose the market price on tender of delivery and resale price remained the same as the contract price. Both 2–706(1)'s resale formula and 2–708(1)'s market price formula would give the seller no damages. Nonetheless, the seller still has lost a profit on the breached contract.

In both of the circumstances just described, 2–706(1)'s resale and 2–708(1)'s market price formulas are inadequate because they do not give the seller its lost profit. This is easily seen in the second, "lost volume" case where neither formula gives the seller damages. But 2–706(1) and 2–708(1)'s damage formulas are inadequate in the first, "uncompleted goods" case too because they are inapplicable there. Under 2–708(2), where 2–708(1)'s damage formula is inadequate the seller can recover its lost profit according to the formula described there. Although strictly 2–708(2) applies only when 2–708(2)'s market price formula is inadequate, it is not much of a stretch to make 2–708(2) applicable too when 2–706(1)'s resale formula is inadequate. In both cases 2–708(2) measures the seller's lost profits. The presentation below relies on Clayton P. Gillette & Steven D. Walt, Sale Law: Domestic and International 286–295 (2d ed. 2009).

a. CALCULATING LOST PROFIT

Section 2–708(2) raises two questions. First, how does 2–708(2) measure the seller's lost profit? Second, when is a seller entitled to recover lost profits under the subsection? Taking the questions in order, 2–708(2)'s formula measuring lost profits does not work in some circumstances. To see this, begin with the seller's profit. The seller's profit is the contract price minus its variable costs. Variable costs are costs which the seller incurs in performing the contract and would not otherwise occur. By contrast, costs that the seller bears even if the contract were never entered into or performed are fixed costs. The seller's fixed costs include labor costs, taxes and other financial charges that the seller incurs irrespective of the contract. Although in calculating its profit the seller may include in its costs a portion of fixed costs as "overhead," the treatment is for accounting purposes only. Fixed costs do not affect the seller's economic profit from performance. Strictly, fixed costs are part of the seller's economic profit. A simple rearrangement of terms shows this. Let K be the contract price, VC the variable costs of the seller's performance, FC the seller's fixed costs and P the seller's profit. The contract price is the sum of the variable costs, fixed costs and the seller's profit: $VC + FC + P = K$. Rearranging terms, $FC + P = K - VC$. Given this equality, the seller's profit (P) could be redefined as equal to the contract price minus the seller's variable costs. Defined in this way, the seller's profits include its fixed costs. Section 2–708(2)'s measurement recognizes this by allowing the seller to recover "the profit (including reasonable overhead)." Whether profit is defined narrowly to exclude fixed costs or broadly to include it is merely a matter of accounting practices. The seller's economic gain from performance $(K - VC)$ remains the same. Courts calculating lost profits under 2–708(2) consistently consider overhead part of the seller's fixed costs and do not deduct it from profit. See Vitex Manufacturing v.

Caribtex Corp., 377 F.2d 795 (3d Cir. 1967). For some reason, courts divide in their treatment of overhead in calculating lost profits in copyright infringement cases. Compare Hamil America, Inc. v. GFI, 193 F.3d 92 (2d Cir. 1999) (overhead deducted from gross revenues) with Saxon v. Blann, 968 F.2d 676 (8th Cir. 1992) (overhead not deductible).

Now consider how 2–708(2) measures the recovery of lost profits. The subsection provides that the seller's damages as "the profit (including reasonable overhead) . . . together with any incidental damages . . . due allowance for costs reasonably incurred and due credit for payment or proceeds of resale." It has long been acknowledged that this formula gives the seller no damages when the seller completes production of the goods and resells them for a price equal to the contract price. See John A. Sebert, Jr., Remedies Under Article Two of the Uniform Commercial Code: An Agenda for Review, 130 U. Pa. L. Rev. 360, 393–394 (1981). For example, assume that the contract price is $100 and the seller's total cost of performance is $80. The buyer breaches without paying any portion of the contract price after the seller has produced the goods. Assume also that the seller incurs no incidental expenses in reselling them for $100. Section 2–708(2) measures the seller's damages as follows:

Profit +   Overhead + Incidental expenses + Costs incurred – Payments – Proceeds of resale

$20   +   0   + $80   –   0   – $100   =   0

The seller's profit is equal to the contract price ($100) minus its variable costs. Because the seller's $80 costs incurred in producing the goods are variable costs, its profit is $20. Section 2–708(2) adds the $80 in costs incurred to the $20 in profit and deducts the $100 the seller receives on reselling the goods. The subsection therefore gives the seller no damages, as shown just above. Where the seller has completed production, courts therefore ignore the "costs incurred" and "proceeds of resale" parts of 2–708(2). See Neri v. Retail Marine Corp., 30 N.Y.2d 393, 399 (N.Y. 1971). They calculate profit instead in this case as the difference between the contract price and the seller's variable costs.

Section 2–708(2)'s measure of lost profits works for sellers in "uncompleted goods" cases, as is widely recognized. Sellers of uncompleted goods are of two types. One type is the "components" seller. This is a seller who partially performs but reasonably does not complete performance after the buyer breaches. Because the seller has not completed performance, its costs incurred will not equal its variable costs and the proceeds of resale will not equal the contract price. For example, if the seller in the ongoing illustration stopped production after incurring $60 in costs and resold the uncompleted goods for scrap for $60, 2–708(2)'s formula gives the seller its $20 in lost profit: $20 (Profit) + 0 (Incidental expenses) + $60 (Costs incurred) – 0 (Payments) – $60 (Proceeds of resale) = $20. The other type of seller is the "jobber": a middleman who acquires from a supplier the goods it has contracted to sell. If the seller does not acquirer the goods after the buyer's breach, it incurs no costs and obtains no proceeds from reselling the goods. Thus, 2–708(2) measures the seller's damages as its profit (the contract price minus the seller's variable costs).

b.   RECOVERING LOST PROFIT UNDER 2–708(2): THE LOST VOLUME
      SELLER

It is harder to determine when a seller should be entitled to recover
lost profits under 2–708(2), however lost profits are measured. The
problem arises in "completed goods" cases. If the seller makes a sale
after the buyer breached and would have made the sale even had the
buyer not breached, the second sale does not replace the first sale. In
this case the seller has "lost volume" as a result of the breach. If the
buyer had not breached the seller would have made two sales and
enjoyed two profits. As a result of the breach, the seller has made only
one sale and obtained only one profit. The profit from the second sale
therefore does not give the seller the economic gain from the breached
contract. Thus, the price received in the second sale should not be
considered "proceeds of resale" under 2–708(2) and deducted from the
seller's profit on the breached contract. The question of course is when a
seller is a "lost volume" seller.

Courts take two different views. A number of them hold that the
seller has lost volume if it has the capacity to make two sales and in
fact made a sale to a third party after its buyer breached. These courts
consider the second sale an additional sale, not a substitute sale for the
breached contract. They reason that if the seller in fact made a second
sale and had the capacity to make two sales, the second sale would have
been made regardless of the buyer's breach. The seller therefore loses
volume as a result of the buyer's breach. Other courts maintain that it
is not enough that the seller is operating at below full capacity. They
require the seller to establish two things in addition. First, it must
prove that it could have made a profit on the second sale. In addition, it
must show that it probably would have made the second sale had the
buyer not breached. The seller has lost volume if it could profitably
make two sales and in fact made a sale to a third party after the buyer's
breach. The seller's variable costs of performing the second sale are its
marginal costs of making the sale. Thus, the seller apparently must
establish that the marginal costs of making the second sale are below or
equal to the contract price (the marginal revenue) of that sale.

These two views have very different implications for the award of
lost profits damages. Courts that define lost volume by the seller's
capacity to obtain the goods tend to assume that the seller can acquire
an unlimited supply; see Note 1 below. A seller that has an unlimited
supply available can make an unlimited number of sales. Thus, it can
supply both the breaching buyer and the second buyer. The buyer's
breach therefore causes the seller to lose a sale and a profit. Thus, it
can recover lost profits under 2–708(2). By contrast, courts that define
lost volume by the seller's profit-making capacity restrict the recovery
of lost profits damages. This is because the number of profitable sales is
limited by the structure of the market in which the seller operates. In a
competitive market a seller maximizes profits when it produces goods
up the point where its marginal costs equal its marginal revenue. Its
production decision is made without regard to the number of sales
contracts breached by its buyers. For this reason, the seller does not
lose a sale and a profit when it sells to a second buyer after the buyer
breaches. The seller therefore is not entitled to lost profits damages
under 2–708(2). At a minimum, to recover lost profits, the seller must

establish that it is operating at less than full capacity or pricing its goods at below marginal cost.

In an imperfectly competitive market the result is more complicated. Whether the seller is entitled to lost profits damages depends on how it prices the sales contract. At least three situations are possible. First, if the monopolistic seller sets quantity and price without regard to the possibility of breach, it loses a sale when one of its buyers breaches. A second sale does not replace the breached contract because the seller can supply every buyer in the relevant market. Thus, the seller loses volume and is entitled to recover its lost profit under 2–708(2). Second, again assuming that the seller sets price without regard to the buyer's breach, the breach gives the seller a choice: It can resell the goods at a lower price or not resell them at all. If the seller resells, the sale replaces the breached contract and its volume of sold goods remains the same. However, the resale is at a lower price, reflecting the lower value the second buyer puts on the goods. (The demand curve for the seller's goods slopes downward.) The resale therefore reduces the seller's profit on the resold goods. Because the seller receives a reduced profit on the resold goods, it is entitled to recover from the breaching buyer the amount by which its profit is reduced. Only this amount should be recoverable under 2–708(2) as lost profits on the breached contract. If the seller decides not to resell, it loses volume. It therefore is entitled to recover its lost profits on the breached contract under 2–708(2). See Robert Cooter & Melvin Aron Eisenberg, Damages for Breach of Contract, 73 Cal. L. Rev. 1432, 1451–1455 (1985). Third, the seller in an imperfectly competitive market might offer contracts that do not allow for the seller's recovery of lost profits if the buyer breaches. The price of the contracts offered takes the bar on recovery into account. In this case the seller loses a sale when its buyer breaches. However, the contract price compensates the seller for the loss and therefore it is not entitled to recover its lost profit under 2–708(2). Given the sensitivity of the recovery of lost profits to assumptions about market structure and the seller's pricing decisions, you might wonder if courts are well equipped to take them into account in applying 2–708(2).

R.E. Davis Chemical Corp. v. Diasonics, Inc.

United States Court of Appeals, Seventh Circuit, 1987
826 F.2d 678

■ CUDAHY, CIRCUIT JUDGE

* * *

I.

Diasonics is a California corporation engaged in the business of manufacturing and selling medical diagnostic equipment. Davis is an Illinois corporation that contracted to purchase a piece of medical diagnostic equipment from Diasonics. On or about February 23, 1984, Davis and Diasonics entered into a written contract under which Davis agreed to purchase the equipment. Pursuant to this agreement, Davis paid Diasonics a $300,000 deposit on February 29, 1984. Prior to entering into its agreement with Diasonics, Davis had contracted with

Dobbin and Valvassori to establish a medical facility where the equipment was to be used. Dobbin and Valvassori subsequently breached their contract with Davis. Davis then breached its contract with Diasonics; it refused to take delivery of the equipment or to pay the balance due under the agreement. Diasonics later resold the equipment to a third party for the same price at which it was to be sold to Davis.

Davis sued Diasonics, asking for restitution of its $300,000 down payment under section 2–718(2) of the Uniform Commercial Code (the "UCC" or the "Code"). Diasonics counterclaimed. Diasonics did not deny that Davis was entitled to recover its $300,000 deposit less $500 as provided in section 2–718(2)(b). However, Diasonics claimed that it was entitled to an offset under section 2–718(3). Diasonics alleged that it was a "lost volume seller," and, as such, it lost the profit from one sale when Davis breached its contract. Diasonics' position was that, in order to be put in as good a position as it would have been in had Davis performed, it was entitled to recover its lost profit on its contract with Davis under section 2–708(2) of the UCC.

* * *

The court held that lost volume sellers were not entitled to recover damages under 2–708(2) but rather were limited to recovering the difference between the resale price and the contract price along with incidental damages under section 2–706(1). Davis was awarded $322,656, which represented Davis' down payment plus prejudgment interest less Diasonics' incidental damages. Diasonics appeals the district court's decision respecting its measure of damages as well as the dismissal of its third-party complaint.

II.

* * *

We conclude that the Illinois Supreme Court, if presented with this question, would adopt the position of these other jurisdictions and would conclude that a reselling seller, such as Diasonics, is free to reject the damage formula prescribed in 2–706 and choose to proceed under 2–708.

Concluding that Diasonics is entitled to seek damages under 2–708, however, does not automatically result in Diasonics being awarded its lost profit. Two different measures of damages are provided in 2–708. Subsection 2–708(1) provides for a measure of damages calculated by subtracting the market price at the time and place for tender from the contract price. The profit measure of damages, for which Diasonics is asking, is contained in 2–708(2). However, one applies 2–708(2) only if "the measure of damages provided in subsection (1) is inadequate to put the seller in as good a position as performance would have done. . . . " Diasonics claims that 2–708(1) does not provide an adequate measure of damages when the seller is a lost volume seller. To understand Diasonics' argument, we need to define the concept of the lost volume seller. Those cases that have addressed this issue have defined a lost volume seller as one that has a predictable and finite number of customers and that has the capacity either to sell to all new buyers or to make the one additional sale represented by the resale after the breach. According to a number of courts and commentators, if the seller would have made the sale represented by the resale whether or not the breach occurred, damages measured by the difference between the contract price and market price cannot put the lost volume seller in as good a position as it would have been in had the buyer performed. The breach effectively cost the seller a "profit," and the seller can only be made whole by awarding it damages in the amount of its "lost profit" under 2–708(2).

We agree with Diasonics' position that, under some circumstances, the measure of damages provided under 2–708(1) will not put a reselling seller in as good a position as it would have been in had the buyer performed because the breach resulted in the seller losing sales volume. However, we disagree with the definition of "lost volume seller" adopted by other courts. Courts awarding lost profits to a lost volume seller have focused on whether the seller had the capacity to supply the breached units in addition to what it actually sold. In reality, however, the relevant questions include, not only whether the seller could have produced the breached units in addition to its actual volume, but also whether it would have been profitable for the seller to produce both units. Goetz & Scott, Measuring Sellers' Damages: The Lost–Profits Puzzle, 31 Stan. L. Rev. 323, 332–33, 346–47 (1979). As one commentator has noted, under

> the economic law of diminishing returns or increasing marginal costs[,] . . . as a seller's volume increases, then a point will inevitably be reached where the cost of selling each additional item diminishes the incremental return to the seller and eventually makes it entirely unprofitable to conclude the next sale.

Shanker, The Case for a Literal Reading of UCC Section 2–708(2) (One Profit for the Reseller), 24 Case W. Res. 697, 705 (1973). Thus, under some conditions, awarding a lost volume seller its presumed lost profit will result in overcompensating the seller, and 2–708(2) would not take effect because the damage formula provided in 2–708(1) does place the seller in as good a position as if the buyer had performed. Therefore, on remand, Diasonics must establish, not only that it had the capacity to produce the breached unit in addition to the unit resold, but also that it would have been profitable for it to have produced and sold both. Diasonics carries the burden of establishing these facts because the burden of proof is generally on the party claiming injury to establish the amount of its damages; especially in a case such as this, the plaintiff has easiest access to the relevant data. Finance America Commercial Corp. v. Econo Coach, Inc., 118 Ill. App. 3d 385, 390, 454 N.E.2d 1127, 1131, 73 Ill. Dec. 878 (2d Dist. 1983) ("A party seeking to recover has the burden not only to establish that he sustained damages but also to establish a reasonable basis for computation of those damages.") (citation omitted).

* * *

We therefore reverse the grant of summary judgment in favor of Davis and remand with instructions that the district court calculate Diasonics' damages under § 2–708(2) if Diasonics can establish, not only that it had the capacity to make the sale to Davis as well as the sale to the resale buyer, but also that it would have been profitable for it to make both sales. Of course, Diasonics, in addition, must show that it would probably have made the second sale absent the breach.

* * *

NOTES

1. *R.E. Davis* rejects the rule followed by courts that define a lost volume seller as one which has the physical capacity to make a sale in addition to the breached contract. In Neri v. Retail Marine Corp., 30 N.Y.2d 393 (1972), after the buyer repudiated the contract the seller resold the boat ordered by its buyer for the contract price and sued the buyer for its profit on the breached contract. The court awarded the seller its profit under 2–708(2). In doing so it relied on an illustration in which the seller was assumed to have an unlimited supply of the goods of the sort it is selling. The court's rationale is that if the seller has an unlimited supply of boats available to it, it could make an additional sale regardless of whether the buyer breached. The court in Famous Knitwear Corp. v. Drug Fair, Inc., 493 F.2d 251 (4th Cir. 1974), had to decide whether the seller had lost volume. The buyer contended that the seller lacked the inventory to sell to both the buyer and a third party after the buyer breached. For its part, the seller countered that it could have bought additional units from other suppliers for sales to third parties. Determining that the trial judge made no finding of facts about the seller's capacity to procure additional units, the court remanded the issue. Apparently the seller lost volume if it had the capacity to make an additional sale. For a non-UCC case applying this definition of lost volume to the recovery of lost profits in a breached personal services contract, see Gianetti v. Norwalk Hospital, 833 A.2d 891 (Conn. 2003).

2. After holding that the lost volume seller must demonstrate that it profitably could make a second sale, the court in *R.E. Davis* remanded the issue to the District Court. On remand, the District Court determined that the seller met its burden by presenting average cost data. The Seventh Circuit upheld the finding on appeal. See R.E. Davis Chemical Corp. v. Diasonics, Inc., 924 F.2d 709, 712 (7th Cir. 1991). Presumably the seller presented data on its average variable costs. Average variable costs, as the term suggests, are total variable costs divided by total output. Over a range of output average costs may be lower or higher than the marginal costs of producing a particular unit of goods. They therefore do not establish the seller's variable costs in making a second sale, which alone are relevant to the seller's profit from the sale. Although easier to prove, average variable costs may overestimate or underestimate the seller's profit. Neither court insisted that the seller produce evidence of its marginal costs in making a second sale. Accord Scullin Steel Co. v. Paccar Inc., 710 S.W.2d 910 (Mo. Ct. App. 1988).

3. Courts applying the CISG also have to determine when a seller has lost volume as result of the buyer's breach. Article 74 states the CISG's general rule for recovering damages. It provides that damages "consist of a sum equal to the loss, including the loss of profit, suffered by the other party as a consequence of breach." A seller reselling the goods after the buyer has breached might argue that it would have made the second sale regardless of the buyer's breach. Article 74's general rule, it might conclude, allows it to recover lost profit on the breached contract. The Austrian Supreme Court, relying on the view that a commercial seller has an unlimited supply of goods available to it, has accepted the argument: "[B]usinesspersons, who regularly trade with goods as the ones involved in the avoided contract, will—as a general rule—always be in a position to replace the failed transaction by a substitute transaction selling the goods of the avoided contract or different goods on the basis of the current market price." Oberster Gerichtshof (Austria), 28 April 2000, available at http://cisgw3.law.pace.edu/cisg/CISG-AC-op6.html; accord CISG Advisory Council Opinion No. 6, Calculation of Damages Under CISG Article 74 para. 3.20 (2006), available at http://cisgw3.law.pace.edu/cisg/CISG-AC-op6.html. Other courts might define the seller's lost volume by its capacity to make a profitable sale to both the breaching buyer and the second buyer.

The different definitions of a lost volume seller create a potential problem for Article 74's application. Article 7(1) directs that the CISG's provisions be interpreted with regard to its international character and the need to promote uniformity in international trade. The CISG's international character requires that its provisions be given what European scholars call an "autonomous interpretation": an interpretation that avoids reliance on domestic law. Article 7(1)'s directive to promote uniformity arguably also requires courts to take into account ("regard") the construction of the CISG's provisions given by foreign courts. The demand for an autonomous interpretation means that a court cannot use domestic law to define a lost volume seller to award lost profits damages under Article 74. In addition, Article 7(1)'s interpretive directive to promote uniformity requires courts calculating lost profits under Article 74 to give some (unspecified) weight to the definitions of lost volume foreign courts have used in calculating lost profits under the Article. Although the Austrian Supreme Court's decision is the only reported case to date on the matter, the potential for divergent definitions of lost volume among courts remains.

4. THE SELLER'S POWER OVER THE GOODS

The remedies discussed so far give the seller rights against the breaching buyer. They are in personam in character. Sometimes the seller prefers to have rights over the goods that it can exercise if the buyer breaches or is likely to breach. If the buyer breaches by refusing to pay on tender of the goods, the seller would prefer to withhold the goods rather than deliver them and sue for damages. Similarly, the seller usually will like to stop delivery or reclaim goods delivered if the buyer is insolvent. A damages claim against an insolvent buyer is unlikely to be worth much. Article 2 gives the seller under prescribed circumstances the right to reclaim goods delivered or stop their delivery. Sections 2–507(2) and 2–702(2) control the seller's reclamation right, and 2–705(2) controls its right to stop delivery of the goods.

a. RECLAMATION RIGHTS

The seller's right to reclaim goods delivered differs according to when the sales contract calls for payment. If it requires payment at a time after delivery of the goods, the sale is a "credit sale." If payment must be made at the time of delivery, the sale is a "cash sale." When the buyer pays by check on delivery, the sale is a "cash sale." Section 2–507(2) governs the cash seller's reclamation right. Although 2–507(2) does not expressly give a seller in a cash sale by check that is later dishonored a right to reclaim the goods, courts conclude that the right is implied in the subsection. Under 2–507(2), where payment is due on delivery, the buyer's right to retain the goods delivered is conditional on making payment. Section 2–511(3) provides that payment by check is conditional and is defeated by dishonor of the check. Taken together, the sections plausibly give the cash seller a right to reclaim the goods when the buyer's check is subsequently dishonored. The seller's remedy is to rescind the transaction and retake the goods. Unlike 2–702(2), which is discussed below and allows the seller to reclaim good delivered on credit on learning of the buyer's insolvency, under 2–507(2) the cash seller can reclaim the goods whether or not the buyer is insolvent. Nonetheless, in most cases the cash seller relies on 2–507(2) to reclaim the goods when its buyer is insolvent.

Section 2–507(2) leaves unanswered two questions about the cash seller's reclamation right. One is the time limit within which the seller may reclaim goods delivered. By comparison, 2–702(2), which governs the credit seller's reclamation rights, requires it to make the demand for a return of the goods within ten days of delivery. Prior to 1990, Comment 3 to 2–507 stated that 2–702(2)'s ten day limitation also applied to 2–507, and many courts relied on the Comment to put a ten day limit on the cash seller's exercise of its reclamation right. In 1990 the Permanent Editorial Board of the UCC removed the statement from Comment 3 and substituted a sentence that stated that there was no time limit within which the cash seller must demand the return of the goods. Although Official Comments are not binding on courts (except in the several states that have enacted them into law), courts appear to have taken the substituted sentence seriously and now rely on it. See, e.g., In re Edgerton, 186 B.R. 143 (Bankr. M.D. Fla. 1995); Continental Grain Co. v. Heritage Bank, 548 N.W.2d 507 (S.D. 1996). A second question 2–507(2) leaves unanswered is the priority of the cash seller's reclamation right as against third parties' rights to the goods. By comparison, 2–702(3) expressly makes the credit seller's reclamation right under 2–702(2) "subject to" the rights of good faith purchasers of the goods for value under 2–403(1). This means that the good faith purchaser for value has priority in the goods over the reclaiming creditor seller. Comment 3 to 2–507 states that 2–507 also protects good faith purchasers for value under 2–403(1) as against the reclaiming cash seller. However, nothing in 2–507(2)'s language suggests this priority rule.

Section 2–702(2) gives a seller who has sold goods on credit the right to reclaim them. The right applies when the buyer has received the goods while insolvent. To exercise the right the seller must make a demand to reclaim the goods within ten days after the buyer's receipt. No time limit applies if the buyer has misrepresented its solvency in writing within three months of delivery. As noted above, 2–702(3) subordinates the credit seller's reclamation right to the rights of a good faith purchaser of the goods for value, including a buyer in the ordinary course. Many of the litigated cases in which the buyer has received goods are transactions in which the buyer fraudulently induced the seller to extend credit. A typical sort of fraud involves the buyer misrepresenting its financial condition or solvency. The common law gave the seller in such cases the right to rescind the transaction for fraud and retake the goods. Section 2–702(2) displaces the common law rule to the extent that the circumstances described in the subsection apply. Thus, a seller who delivers goods on credit while the buyer is insolvent can rescind the transaction and reclaim the goods. The buyer need not have fraudulently or even innocently misrepresented its solvency or other financial condition. Section 2–702(2)'s preemption of the common law rule also means that the seller may still rely on the reclamation right based on the buyer's fraudulent misrepresentation of its solvency. However, 2–702(2)'s displacement of the common law rescission rule is limited. It does not displace the rule (or any other common law rules of restitution) when the buyer's fraud is unrelated to its insolvency.

Bankruptcy law limits both the cash and credit seller's reclamation rights. Because buyers whose checks bounce or are insolvent often go into bankruptcy, the impact of bankruptcy law on these rights is important. A brief description of relevant bankruptcy law is enough to show its impact. The Bankruptcy Code ("BC") gives the bankruptcy trustee avoidance powers which it can use to set aside transfers by the debtor or rights others have in the debtor's property. One of these powers is the trustee's "strong arm" powers under BC 544(a)(1). Under BC 544(a)(1), the trustee has the rights of a judicial lien creditor to the goods, which it can use to avoid interests in them. Although the reclaiming seller has an "interest" in the goods it has sold—the right to reclaim them under prescribed conditions—BC 544(a)(1) does not give the trustee the rights of a bona fide purchaser for value. For this reason, the trustee cannot avoid the seller's right to reclaim goods it has delivered to the bankrupt buyer. However, another avoidance power applies to the seller's reclamation rights: the trustee's power to avoid statutory liens under 545 of the Bankruptcy Code. BC 545(1) allows the trustee to avoid statutory liens that first become effective when the debtor is insolvent. In addition, BC 545(2) allows the trustee to avoid a statutory lien if it is not enforceable against a bona fide purchaser of property subject to the lien. A lien is a property right that secures performance of an obligation or payment of a debt; see BC 101(37). The seller's reclamation right is a lien because it gives the seller property rights to secure performance of an obligation: payment of the contract price. The lien also is statutory because it is created by 2–702(2) and 2–507(2); BC 101(54). Finally, 2–702(2) gives the credit seller a reclamation right only if the buyer is insolvent when it receives the goods. Section 2–702(3), and 2–507(2) by implication, subordinates the seller's reclamation rights to the rights of a good faith purchaser of the goods for value. For both reasons, subject to BC 546(c), the trustee can avoid the seller's reclamation rights.

BC 546(c) limits the trustee's power to avoid statutory liens under 545. The trustee cannot avoid statutory liens in the circumstances described by 546(c). Prior to 2005 these circumstances were clear. Section 546(c) in relevant part provided that the trustee's avoidance power under 545 "are subject to any statutory or common law right of a seller of goods . . . in the ordinary course of such seller's business, to reclaim such goods if the debtor received such goods while insolvent." The provision also required the seller to make a written demand to reclaim the goods within ten days of the buyer's receipt of them. If the ten day period had expired after the commencement of the bankruptcy case, the seller had 10 days after the buyer-debtor's receipt of the goods in which to make the written demand. Section 546(c)'s requirements of an ordinary course sale and a written demand limited in bankruptcy the seller's reclamation rights given by 2–702(2) and 2–507(2).

The Bankruptcy Abuse Prevention and Consumer Protection Act ("BAPCPA") of 2005 amends 546(c) to extend the ten day period to 45 days. BAPCPA extends the ten day period for giving a written reclamation demand to 20 days if the 45 day period expires after the commencement of the case. It also eliminated the language quoted above and replaces it with the following language: the trustee's powers under 545 ". . . are subject to the right of a seller of goods that has sold the goods to the debtor, in the ordinary course of such seller's business, to reclaim such goods while insolvent . . . " Gone is the reference to "any statutory or common law right" of reclamation. The effect of the elimination of this language is unclear. Does amended 546(c) create a federal reclamation right in bankruptcy that displaces the cash and credit seller's reclamation rights under 2–702(2) and 2–507(2)? Or does the subsection create a federal reclamation right with the same content as 2–702(2) and 2–507(2), and subject to 546(c)'s limitations? Or did Congress merely intend to recognize these reclamation rights in 546(c), referring to them in a clumsy way as "statutory," while limiting their effect? Courts tend to hold that 546(c) continues to limit state reclamation rights rather than supplanting them. See Incredible Auto Sales LLC, 62 UCC Rep. Serv.2d 357 (Bankr. D. Mont. 2007); In re Dana Corp., 367 B.R. 409 (Bankr. S.D.N.Y. 2006).

BAPCPA added a provision to the Bankruptcy Code that makes the reclamation right less important in the buyer's bankruptcy. BC 503(b)(9) gives the seller an administrative expense for the value of goods received by the debtor within 20 days of the bankruptcy filing. An administrative expense is paid before almost all unsecured claims against the buyer; see BC 507(a)(2). This priority does not depend on whether or not the seller has a reclamation right under state law. It also does not depend on whether 546(c) creates a federal reclamation right. Thus, a seller who has delivered goods on credit on the eve of the buyer's bankruptcy does not have to rely on a right to reclaim them. Its administrative expense priority generally assures that it will receive the value of the goods. A reclamation right matters to the seller only when the buyer's estate is administratively insolvent, which means that there are insufficient assets to pay all administrative expense priorities.

b.   STOPPAGE IN TRANSIT

On discovering that its buyer is insolvent the credit seller has a choice. It can deliver the goods and risk having to assert its right to be paid in the buyer's insolvency proceeding. Alternatively, 2–702(1) and 2–705(1) allow the seller to withhold the goods or stop delivery of the goods in transit. Withholding the goods or stopping delivery may give the seller a better chance of being paid by the buyer. Section 2–702(1) permits the credit seller who discovers its buyer to be insolvent before the goods are delivered to unilaterally reform the contract. The subsection allows the seller to refuse delivery except for cash. Section

2–705(1) complements the rights 2–702(1) gives to the seller. It allows the seller who discovers its buyer to be insolvent to stop the bailee of the goods from delivering them and require cash for delivery. Section 2–705(1) also permits stoppage of a carload or larger shipments when the buyer's prospectively fails to perform, even when the buyer is not insolvent. Withholding or stopping delivery on the buyer's insolvency does not end the contract. The seller still must tender the goods if the buyer pays in cash. Similarly, the contract is not ended when the seller stops delivery of the goods based on the buyer's prospective nonperformance. The seller cannot resell or divert the goods if the buyer gives adequate assurance of payment. See Comment 2 to 2–705.

The seller's has a right to withhold or stop delivery even if ownership of the goods has passed to the buyer. Section 2–401 states that Article 2's provisions apply "irrespective of title to the goods except where the provision refers to such title." The seller's rights to withhold or stop delivery under 2–702(1) and 2–705(1) do not refer to title and these rights therefore do not depend on the location of title in the goods. See Comment 1 to 2–702. The sections give the seller rights of possession, not ownership. Thus, the seller can withhold or stop delivery even if the sales contract made the buyer the owner of the goods before they were to be delivered. Section 2–705(2) cuts off the seller's right of stoppage in described conditions. Problems 10.10 and 10.11, following *National Sugar Refining* below, explore some of them. When the buyer is in bankruptcy, bankruptcy law determines whether the seller can exercise its right of stoppage. *National Sugar Refining* addresses the issue. Although the case was decided before BAPCPA's amendments to BC 546(c), the court's reasoning and result is unaffected by them.

In re National Sugar Refining Co.

United States District Court, Southern District of New York, 1983
27 B.R. 565

■ SAND, DISTRICT JUDGE.

* * *

I.   FACTS

Appellant purchased 6,550 long tons of raw sugar from Czarnikow pursuant to two contracts dated August 12, 1981 and August 26, 1981, both of which called for September delivery. On August 27, 1981, Czarnikow advised appellant that 6,550 tons of sugar then on board the vessel M/V Edispsos and for which Czarnikow held the negotiable bill of lading would be used to fulfill its obligations under the two contracts. At that point, title to the sugar passed from Czarnikow to appellant.

On September 3, 1981, appellant filed a Chapter 11 petition pursuant to the Bankruptcy Reform Act of 1978, 11 U.S.C. (the "Bankruptcy Code" or "Code") § 101 et seq. in the United States Bankruptcy Court for the Southern District of New York.

On September 11, 1981, Czarnikow applied to the bankruptcy court and obtained on even date an order requiring appellant to show cause why it should not be required to assume or reject the two "executory" sugar contracts forthwith and, if the contracts were assumed, why appellant should not be required to provide Czarnikow with adequate assurance of payment. Czarnikow's application further stated that it was exercising its right of stoppage in transit pursuant to Uniform Commercial Code ("UCC") §§ 2–702(1), 2–705(1).

* * *

Appellant's answer and counterclaim to the Czarnikow application, filed September 16, 1981, asserted that the contracts were nonexecutory; that Czarnikow had no right of stoppage in transit; that the sugar should immediately be delivered to appellant; and that Czarnikow was restrained by the automatic stay provisions of Code § 362 from interfering with delivery of the sugar.

* * *

II. ISSUES

The central issue presented herein, one of apparent first impression, is whether Czarnikow's exercise of its right of stoppage in transit, under UCC § 2–702(1), subsequent to appellant's filing of a petition in bankruptcy constituted the creation of a "statutory lien" avoidable by the trustee or debtor-in-possession under Bankruptcy Code § 545 or resulted in the creation of interest in the sugar in favor of Czarnikow subordinate to the rights of appellant under Bankruptcy Code § 544(a) and UCC § 9–301.

* * *

III. DISCUSSION

A. Stoppage of Goods in Transit

1. Generally

Section 2–703(1) of the Uniform Commercial Code provides:

"Where the seller discovers the buyer to be insolvent he may refuse delivery except for cash including the payment for all goods theretofore delivered under the contract, and stop delivery under this Article . . .

See also UCC 2–705(1) ("The seller may stop delivery of goods in possession of a carrier or other bailee when he discovers the buyer to be insolvent . . . ").

The right accorded a seller of goods pursuant to this provision is premised on the inequity of permitting the buyer to obtain possession of goods when there has been a prospective failure of the buyer's performance. When the buyer is insolvent and thus impaired in fulfilling its contractual obligation to pay, the seller rather than deliver the goods and seek to recover on the price, may withhold or stop in transit the delivery of the goods—i.e., suspend his performance, see UCC § 2–705 Comment 1—until and unless he is assured of the buyer's payment in cash upon delivery, even though the contract may call for the extension of credit. This right persists so long as the goods are in the hands of a carrier or any other bailee not holding for the buyer and is cut off by the buyer's attainment of actual or constructive possession. See UCC § 2–705(2).

The fact that Czarnikow had passed to appellant title to the sugar did not affect the former's right to stop in transit. As one commentator notes, "Under strict legal terminology, the right to stop goods where title has *not* passed should not be called stoppage *in transitu*. The vendor's rights are then much greater." 4A Collier on Bankruptcy para. 70.40, at 481 n.2 (14th ed. 1978).

    2.   Bankruptcy Code § 545

Appellant asserts, however, that Czarnikow's stoppage in transit constitutes a statutory lien avoidable under Code § 545.

Section 545 provides, in relevant part:

> "Statutory liens. The trustee may avoid the fixing of a statutory lien on property of the debtor to the extent that such lien—
>
> (1) first becomes effective against the debtor—
>
>   . . . .
>
> (D) when the debtor becomes insolvent;
>
>   . . . .
>
> (2) is not perfected or enforceable on the date of the filing of the petition against a bona fide purchaser that purchases such property on the date of the filing of the petition, whether or not such a purchaser exists. . . ."

11 U.S.C. § 545(1)(D), (2).

A "statutory lien" is defined in the Bankruptcy Code as a "lien arising solely by force of a statute on specified circumstances or conditions, or lien of distress for rent, whether or not statutory, but does not include a security interest or judicial lien, whether or not such interest or lien is provided by or is dependent on a statute or whether or not such interest of lien is made fully effective by statute;" 11 U.S.C. § [101(53)].

Appellant maintains that the exercise of the right of stoppage in transit pursuant to UCC § 2–702(1) merely confers a vendor's lien upon the seller. In support of this position, appellant cites the following commentary:

> "When delivery of goods is rightfully stopped by the seller, he is thereby revested with a lien in the same way as if possession of the goods had never been surrendered. The sale is not cancelled; if title had passed to the buyer. . . . it remains in the buyer unless the seller thereafter makes a proper cancellation by virtue of the [Uniform Commercial] Code § 2–703."

2 Anderson, Uniform Commercial Code § 2–705:28, at 371 (2d ed. 1981). . . . Because the right of stoppage in transit and the "lien" resulting from the exercise of such right become effective under UCC § 2–702(1) only at the time of the buyer's insolvency, appellant asserts that as a debtor-in-possession, it may avoid the "lien" under § 545(1).

    * * *

    4.   Relevancy of Code § 546(c)

We are of the opinion, however, that appellant's arguments under both Code §§ 545 and 544(a) neglect the significance of Bankruptcy Code § 546(c) which states:

"Limitations on avoiding powers

> . . . .
>
> The rights and powers of the trustee under sections 544(a), 545, 547, and 549 of this title are subject to any statutory right or common-law right of a seller, in the ordinary course of such seller's business, of goods to the debtor to reclaim such goods if the debtor has received such goods while insolvent. . . . "

* * *

In light of this provision's denial of the avoidance powers conferred on a trustee under Bankruptcy Code §§ 544(a) and 545 as against a seller who delivers goods and then reclaims, we find it hardly likely that Congress intended to grant these very same powers as against a seller who succeeds in "reclaiming" the goods *prior* to delivery, by means of stopping them in transit. In both instances, the property interest of the buyer in the goods that is affected by the post-petition acts of the seller is the same, namely, defeasible title. There appears no rationale either in the legislative history or in case law construing UCC § 2–702(1) and the statutory antecedents to Code §§ 544(a) and 545, and appellant has suggested none, for holding that a seller's acts pursuant to UCC § 2–702(2) do not constitute the creation of a statutory lien, while those under UCC § 2–702(1) do.

Indeed, adoption of appellant's position would result in the anomaly of placing an unpaid seller who had withheld from the buyer constructive possession of the goods in a worse condition than one who has transferred such possession to the buyer, and would suggest that Czarnikow should have engaged in the rather absurd behavior of proceeding to deliver the goods to appellant and immediately thereafter issuing a written demand for reclamation pursuant to Code § 546(c).

Congress' silence in Code § 546(c) on the validity in bankruptcy law of a seller's right of stoppage in transit does not, as appellant argues, compel by negative implication a determination that Congress intended to subject such right to the trustee's avoidance powers. The more probable explanation for this silence lies in the apparently complete absence of case law, noted by both parties, suggesting that the seller's exercise of rights under subsection (1) of UCC § 2–702 constitutes the creation of a statutory lien or of lienor's rights junior to those enjoyed by the debtor-in-possession as a hypothetical lien creditor.

* * *

In summary, if, as appellant contends, stoppage in transit revests the unpaid seller with a vendor's lien, surely reclamation is to the same effect. Congress' determination, as expressed in Code § 546(c), that the latter should not be countermanded by the Bankruptcy Code's statutory-lien provision or strong-arm clause persuades us that Congress would likewise have recognized the validity of a seller's right of stoppage as against a debtor-in-possession had the matter been placed in issue. Accordingly, the bankruptcy court correctly ruled that Czarnikow possessed the right to stop the delivery of the sugar in transit.

* * *

NOTE

In an omitted portion of the opinion, the court considers and rejects the debtor-buyer's contention that the seller's stoppage of the goods in transit violated the automatic stay provisions of the Bankruptcy Code. BC 362(a)(3) in relevant part stays acts to obtain possession of the property of the estate or exercise control over estate property. "Property of the estate" is a technical notion under the Bankruptcy Code. It includes all of the debtor's legal and equitable interests in property as of the commencement of the bankruptcy case; BC 541(a)(1). The buyer's rights under the sales contract become property of its bankruptcy estate. These rights include the right to take delivery of the goods on payment of the contract price. They do not include the right to the goods themselves; see In re Coast Trading Co., Inc., 744 F.2d 686, 693 (9th Cir. 1984). Stoppage in transit, while preventing delivery, does not interfere with the buyer's contract rights. Thus, it does not violate the automatic stay. The *National Sugar Refining* court notices that the practical effect of finding that the seller's stoppage right is subject to the automatic stay is to deny the right. The goods usually will have arrived at the buyer, thereby cutting off the stoppage right, by the time the bankruptcy court grants the seller relief from the stay. *National Sugar Refining*, 27 B.R. at 573.

The consequence of the seller stopping delivery of the goods in transit is that the sales contract becomes an executory contract under the Bankruptcy Code. See BC 365(a); In re Coast Trading Co., Inc., 744 F.2d 686, 693 (9th Cir. 1984); *National Sugar Refining*, 27 B.R., at 573 n.5. This is because material obligations remain unperformed on both the seller and the buyer's part: the seller to deliver the goods and the buyer to pay the contract price. Because a bankruptcy trustee generally has the power to assume or reject an executor contract, the buyer's bankruptcy estate has right to delivery only if the trustee assumes the contract. BC 365(a). To assume the contract, the trustee must provide the seller with adequate assurances that seller will receive the contract price. See BC 365(b)(1)(C); *National Sugar Refining*, 27 B.R., at 573 n.5.

PROBLEM 10.7

Sell manufactured fashionable running shoes that had become popular. Buy, a large sports equipment store, was interested in purchasing a large shipment of Sell's shoes. Its problem was that it had expanded its business recently and had little cash flow. Sell had cash flow problems of its own as a result of its increased production of running shoes and was setting tight price terms for retailers purchasing its products. Accordingly, it usually required payment within 10 days of delivery of shipments of its running shoes. Buy needed more generous payment terms. To convince Sell to allow it to pay within 20 days of delivery, on May 1 Buy showed Sell's sales representative around its warehouse, touting its healthy inventory and quick sales activity. It failed to tell Sell's representative that most of the inventory in the warehouse was owned by another retailer and that Buy was storing the inventory there only for a short time. During the tour Buy gave Sell's representative a letter stating that it had $4 million in sales of running shoes that year. In fact it had only $2 million in sales. Impressed by what he had seen, the representative recommended that Sell

sell Buy running shoes under terms which allowed Buy to pay the purchase price within 20 days of delivery. On June 1 Sell agreed to these terms and shipped the shoes Buy ordered, which arrived at Buy's store the same day. Although the value of Buy's assets exceeded its liabilities, Buy had trouble making payments on its contracts in May and June. When June 20 passed without Buy paying Sell, Sell demanded the return of the running shoes it had delivered. What result? See 2–507(2), 2–702(2), 1–102(b)(23), Restatement (Third) of Restitution and Unjust Enrichment § 54 (2011).

PROBLEM 10.8

Large sold 10 tractors to Behemoth and instructed Railroad to deliver them to Behemoth, as required by the sales agreement. The agreement called for Behemoth to pay Large by depositing at its bank the contract price on the day Railroad delivered the tractors to Behemoth. Three days after Railroad delivered the tractors and Behemoth failed to make the deposit, Large demanded that Behemoth return them. Large did not know that Lien, one of Behemoth's judgment creditors, had levied on the tractors two days earlier. It also did not know that a year before Lender had made a loan to Behemoth secured by all of Behemoth's existing and after-acquired inventory, which included the tractors. Lender had asserted rights in Behemoth's tractors after Behemoth defaulted on its loan obligations. May Large retrieve the tractors in Behemoth's hands? Who is entitled to them? See 2–507(2), Comment 3 to 2–507, 2–403(1), 1–201(b)(29), (30), 9–102(a)(52), 9–317(a)(2), 1–204(a)(1), (4).

PROBLEM 10.9

Seller sold a shipment of cell phones to Wholesale on credit and received in return Wholesale's promissory note and a signed document granting Seller a security interest in the phones to secure their purchase price. In need of funds, on June 1 Seller sold the note along with the document to Local Loan without recourse and delivered both to it in exchange for a check. The sale gave Local all of Seller's rights in the note and the document. Although the transaction was unusual for Seller, its financial condition required the sale and Wholesale had no objections. After Local's bank refused to honor its check on June 5, Seller demanded in a letter to Local the same day that it return Wholesale's note and signed document. Local filed for bankruptcy protection on June 10 without returning them. Seller argues that Article 2 of the UCC allows it to reclaim the note and signed document, and that bankruptcy law does not disturb this right. What result? See 2–102, 2–507(2), 1–205(1); 9–102(a)(11), BC 546(c).

PROBLEM 10.10

Sell, located in Houston, contracted to sell Buy, located in Los Angeles, 5,000 pounds of steel. The sale terms called for a price of $5,000 C.I.F. Los Angeles, payment to be made within days of delivery. Sell properly arranged with an ocean carrier to transport the steel to Los Angeles and handed it over to the carrier in Houston. In exchange Sell received from the carrier a nonnegotiable bill of lading consigning the steel to Buy. While the steel was at sea, Sell discovered that Buy had become insolvent and was unlikely to pay the $5,000 contract price. When the steel arrived at the Port of Los Angeles, Sell instructed the carrier not to deliver the steel to Buy.

(a) Assuming that the carrier will act on Sell's instruction, has the instruction come too late? See 2–504, 2–320(a), Comment 1 to 2–320, 2–702(1), 2–103(1)(c), 2–705(2)(a). (For the nonnegotiable bill of lading, see 7–104, supra Chapter 9; for the carrier's right to follow the consignor's instructions, see 7–303(1).)

(b) Assume that the carrier had issued a bill of lading covering the steel to Sell's order. Later, Sell endorsed and delivered the bill to Buy while the steel was at sea bound for Los Angeles. Has Sell's instruction come too late? See 2–705(2)(d), 7–501(a)(1); see also 7–303(a)(1).

PROBLEM 10.11

Wholesaler sold on credit a set of watches to Retailer, who needed them to fill an order Jones had placed with it. The agreement between Wholesaler and Retailer passed title to the watches to Retailer at the conclusion of the contract, and Retailer's agreement with Jones in turn passed title to Jones. Wholesaler's agreement with Retailer required it to ship the watches to Retailer under a nonnegotiable bill of lading. When Wholesaler discovered that Retailer was insolvent and before the watches arrived, it instructed the carrier to return the watches to it. (a) May Wholesaler stop delivery to Retailer? 7–205(2); In re Pester Refining, 66 B.R. 801 (Bankr. S.D. Idaho 1986). (b) May Wholesaler stop delivery if Wholesaler had shipped the watches directly to Jones? See Comment 2 to 2–705.

C. THE CISG'S SCHEME OF REMEDIES

The remedies available under the CISG are comparable to those available under Article 2 of the UCC, with a few important differences. Under prescribed conditions the CISG allows the injured party to avoid the contract, reduce the contract price, recover damages, obtain specific relief, or suspend its own performance. Articles 44 and 61 refer to the buyer and seller's remedies, respectively. Restitution, available under Article 81, is an additional remedy not mentioned in Article 44 and 61. Also not referred to in Article 61 is the seller's right to withhold the goods or stop them in transit. The following index lists the CISG's remedies.

		Seller	**Buyer**
1.	Avoidance	Article 64(1)	Article 49(1)
2.	Specific relief	Article 62	Article 46
3.	Price reduction	Inapplicable	Article 50
4.	Damages:		
	General rule	Article 74	Article 74
	Substitute performance measure	Article 75	Article 75

	Market price measure	Article 76	Article 76
5.	Stop delivery	Article 71(1), (2)	Inapplicable
6.	Restitution	Article 81(2)	Article 81(2)

The list reveals some familiar distinctions among remedies. Some remedies do not require judicial intervention, such as avoidance of the contract, reduction of the contract price, and stoppage of delivery. Other remedies, such as damages and specific relief, require judicial recognition. A distinction peculiar to the CISG's scheme of remedies is its division between remedies that are available only when the contract is avoided and remedies available only when the contract is not avoided. As described in Chapter 7, avoidance puts an end to the contract for breach. To allow avoidance, the breach must either be fundamental or nonperformance does not occur within the *Nachfrist* period set by the injured party. Both damages measured by market price or a substitute transaction and restitution, for instance, require avoidance. Avoidance also is required for restitution of the goods or the price. Article 81(2). On the other hand, specific relief and price reduction are available only if the contract is not avoided. Finally, damages measured by loss under Article 74 are available whether or not the injured party avoids the contract.

As is apparent, avoidance channels the access to remedies. In this respect the CISG differs from the scheme of remedies under Article 2. Under Article 2 acceptance, not avoidance, controls the injured party's access to remedies. Article 2 makes certain remedies available if the buyer accepts the goods, while others are available only if the buyer has rejected them or revoked its acceptance. If the injured buyer has accepted the goods, it must measure its damages by 2–714(2)'s "value difference." It cannot measure its damages by the market price or cover difference. If the breaching buyer has accepted the goods, the seller can recover the contract price. Acceptance of the goods does not channel access to remedies under the CISG. Under the CISG the injured buyer can avoid the contract and put the goods back with the breaching seller even after it has accepted them. The avoiding buyer in this case has three options. It can measure its damages under Article 74. Alternatively, it can obtain substitute performance by purchasing substitute goods and measure its damages under Article 75. The buyer's third option is to forgo a substitute purchase and measure its damages under Article 76. For its part, the injured seller can recover the contract price if it does not avoid the contract. If the seller has avoided the contract, it can recover the goods in restitution even after they have been accepted by the breaching buyer. See Article 81(2). In addition, the avoiding seller has three options available to it. It can measure its damages under Article 74. Alternatively, the seller can make a substitute sale and measure its damages under Article 75. The avoiding seller's third option is to forgo a substitute sale and measure its damages under Article 76. The subsections below describe the seller's rights to goods and the CISG's damage measures; section D, subsection 4 below deals with the buyer's remedies under the CISG.

1. RECOVERY OF THE PRICE

The seller's remedy of specific performance is the right to the contract price from the buyer. Article 62 entitles the seller to the price, subject to two limitations. One limitation, stated in Article 62, is that the seller has not resorted to an inconsistent remedy. Avoidance of the contract, for instance, is an inconsistent remedy. The seller cannot at the same both demand the price, which presupposes that the contract continues, and avoid the contract, which ends it. Article 62 places no other restriction on the seller's right to recover the price. In particular, it contains none of the limitations 2–709(1) puts on a price action. Thus, the seller may recover the price even if it can resell the goods for a reasonable price. Compare 2–709(1)(b). By giving the seller a right to the price, Article 62 puts the burden of disposing or adapting goods the buyer no longer wants on the buyer, even when the seller is in a better position to do so.

However, Article 28 in effect puts a second, more serious limitation on the seller's recovery of the price. Article 28 provides that a court is "not bound to" order specific performance unless the court would do so under its own law for similar sales contracts not governed by the CISG. The Article refers to "specific performance," not more generally to "specific relief," and specific performance is a buyer's remedy only. Nonetheless, Article 28's limitation is sensibly understood to apply to all forms of specific relief, including a price action, not just to specific performance. After all, requiring the buyer to pay the contract price is specific performance for the price. Thus, under Article 28, if the forum would not order the buyer to pay the contract price in similar sales contracts under its domestic law, it is not obligated to ("not bound to") order it for the contract governed by the CISG. The forum court still has the discretion to order the buyer to pay the price, but Article 28 does not require it to do so. However, the court must order the buyer to pay the price if its domestic law requires the order with respect to sales contracts similar to those governed by the CISG.

Accordingly, to determine whether Article 28 requires a court to order the buyer to pay the price, two questions must be answered. First, is the seller entitled to the price under Article 62 of the CISG? Second, if the seller is entitled to the remedy under Article 62, would the forum court order it for like contracts ("similar contracts") otherwise governed by the substantive domestic law of the forum ("its own law")? Article 28's limitation represents a compromise between the delegates from civil and common law legal systems to the Vienna Conference that approved the CISG. Civil law systems, with some variation, generally make specific relief routinely available while common law systems treat the relief as an extraordinary remedy. Article 28 in effect only requires the forum to award specific relief when its domestic law requires the relief (if requested). Its application to the buyer's right to specific performance under the CISG is discussed separately below. For more details on Article 28's operation, see Clayton P. Gillette & Steven D. Walt, The UN Convention on Contracts for the International Sales of Goods: Practice and Theory 9–26–9–31 (2013).

PROBLEM 10.12

Seller, located in Switzerland, agreed to manufacture and deliver design furniture for Buyer, located in the United States. Payment was due on delivery to Buyer's New York headquarters. After Buyer merged with a furniture manufacturer, it decided to produce the design furniture for itself. When Seller's furniture arrived at Buyer's headquarters, Buyer told Seller that it no longer needed the furniture and refused to pay or take delivery. Seller, which warehoused the furniture in New York, regularly sold to New York clients and its design furniture fetched a premium. Nonetheless, Seller insisted on Buyer paying the contract price. If Seller sues Buyer in New York, can it recover the price? See CISG Articles 62, 28; 2–709(1)(b). Can Seller recover the price if it sues Buyer in Switzerland? Cf. Swiss Law of Obligations Article 211 (2011); Commercial Court Bern (Switzerland), 22 December 2004, available at http://cisgw3.law.pace.edu/cases/041222s1. html (Swiss law entitles seller to require the contract price).

2. RECLAMATION AND STOPPAGE RIGHTS

The CISG gives the seller a generous right to reclaim the goods from the buyer. Article 81(2) allows a party who has avoided the contract to obtain restitution of what it supplied the other party. If both parties have performed, they must make restitution concurrently. Article 81 places no other restrictions on restitution. In the seller's case, the most likely basis for avoidance is the buyer's failure to pay the contract price, and the claim for restitution is for the return of the goods it delivered to the buyer under the sales contract. Thus, if the seller avoids the contract after the buyer fails to pay for delivered goods, Article 81(2) entitles it to reclaim them from the breaching buyer. In these circumstances the seller is not limited to recovering the contract price. Instead, it may recover the goods and recover damages under the damage measures given by Articles 74–76, discussed below. By contrast, the seller's reclamation right under the UCC is more limited. Section 2–702(2) entitles the seller to reclaim the goods, on a timely demand, only if it delivered them to the buyer on credit while the buyer was insolvent. In addition, a seller reclaiming the goods has no other remedies with respect to them. See 2–702(3). Neither of these limitations applies to the seller's reclamation right under the CISG.

Article 81(2)'s reclamation right operates only against the buyer. The Article says nothing about the seller's right to reclaim the goods when third parties have competing claims to them. This is unsurprising because the CISG defines the rights and obligations only of the seller and buyer against each other. See Article 4 ("This Convention governs only . . . the rights . . . of the seller and the buyer arising from such a contract."). Thus, the CISG does not determine whether the seller's reclamation right is cut off by the buyer's sale of the goods to a good faith purchaser. It also does not determine whether, or the extent to which, this right survives in the buyer's bankruptcy. Instead, applicable domestic law controls both matters. See 2–702(3); BC 546(c).

The CISG also gives the seller the power to control the goods when there is a prospective breach by the buyer. Article 71(1) allows the seller to suspend its own performance if "it becomes apparent" that the buyer will not perform a substantial part of its obligations, as a result of a serious financial deficiency or a serious deficiency in its ability to perform. The seller's suspension of its performance includes the power to prevent a carrier or other bailee from handing over the goods to buyer, if the goods are out of the seller's control when the buyer's prospective breach becomes apparent. The seller has this power even if the buyer holds a document of title covering the goods that is duly negotiated to it. See Article 71(2). This gives the seller a broader right to stop goods in transit than under 2–705. Under 2–705(1)(d) negotiation of a document of title to the buyer cuts off the seller's stoppage right. By contrast, according to Article 71(2), the seller retains this right under the same circumstances.

The right of stoppage does not have much practical use to the seller. This is because the bailee under most applicable transport law has no obligation to comply with the seller's stoppage order when the buyer holds a negotiable document covering the goods. To see this, notice that there are two contracts involved: the sales contract and the contract of carriage (or other bailment contract). The contracts are independent of each other and governed by different law. While the sales contract is between the seller and buyer, and governed by the CISG, the carriage contract is between the carrier and the seller, and controlled by other domestic or treaty transport law. In the United States, for example, the Federal Bill of Lading Act ("FBLA") controls interstate carriage of goods and outgoing carriage to a foreign country.

The independence of the sales and carriage contracts from each other means that the seller's powers under the sales contract may not be good against the bailee under the carriage contract. For this reason, although Article 71(2) gives the seller the power to stop goods in transit, the power operates only against the buyer. See Article 71(2) (final sentence); cf. Article 4. Applicable transport law determines whether the bailee is obligated to heed the seller's order not to deliver the goods. Most transport law gives the good faith purchaser for value of a negotiable document negotiated to it priority over the seller's right to stop the goods in transit. See FBLA 49 U.S.C. § 80105(b). The seller therefore loses its stoppage rights in these circumstances. Even if the seller retains a stoppage right, the carrier is permitted to deliver the goods to the seller only on its surrender of the negotiable document of title covering the goods. FBLA § 80105(a). Thus, the carrier may not deliver the goods to a seller who, having negotiated the document, is not in a position to surrender it. For both reasons, a carrier will seldom have to comply with the stoppage order of a seller when its buyer holds the negotiable document covering the goods.

3.   ARTICLE 74'S GENERAL DAMAGES RULE

a.   THE RULE

Article 74 states the general rule for recovering damages for breach. The rule measures damages whether or not the injured party has avoided the contract. According to the Article, "[d]amages for breach of contract by one party consist of a sum equal to the loss, including loss of profit, suffered by the other party as a consequence of breach." The Article makes clear that damages are equal to all loss resulting from breach, not just lost profits. Thus, consequential and incidental damages resulting from the breach also are recoverable under Article 74. Because "loss" includes lost profit and consequential and incidental damages, Article 74's objective is to put the injured party in the position in which performance would have put it in. Its measurement of damages therefore protects the injured party's expectation interest. As it is sometimes put, Article 74 states a rule of full compensation. Damages can be recovered under Article 74 whether or not the injured party avoids the contract.

Both the injured seller and buyer can measure their damages by Article 74's general rule. Articles 44(1)(b) allows the buyer to recover damages under Article 74 if the seller "fails to perform any of his obligations" under the contract, while Article 61(1)(b) allows the seller to recover damages under the Article if the buyer "fails to perform any of his obligations" under the contract. The injured party need not rely on the substitute transaction and market price calculations provided by Articles 75 and 76, respectively. In fact, to recover damages, sometimes the injured party must rely on Article 74's general rule. If the party cannot avoid the contract, Article 75 and 76's measures are unavailable to it. Even if it is entitled to avoid the contract, the party might decide not to do so. For instance, the buyer might decide the retain nonconforming goods and recover damages rather than avoid the contract and turn the goods back to the breaching seller. Where the injured party has not avoided the contract, it can measure its damages only under Article 76's general rule. Finally, consequential damages can recovered only under Article 74. This is because neither Article 75 nor Article 76's damages measures provide for their recovery. Thus, even an injured party relying on one of these damages measures must also rely on Article 74 to recover consequential damages resulting from breach. Unlike 2–715(2), the Article allows both the seller and buyer to recover consequential damages.

Article 74 does not state a formula for measuring damages. It only provides a general rule or principle of full compensation by which damages are to be calculated. Nonetheless, the general rule is not trivial. Its language does not allow for the award of punitive damages, which give the injured party more than it lost from the breach. Article 74's rule that damages include lost profit also requires that the injured party's expectation interest be protected. The rule therefore does not allow the exclusion of lost profit in the calculation of loss, as in some legal systems. More generally, against the rule in some legal systems, Article 74 makes clear that damages are recoverable for loss from breach regardless of the breaching party's fault. Nonetheless, the absence of a formula for calculating damages under Article 74's general rule makes it hard to apply in some cases. Unlike 2–708(2), the Article does not specify how lost profit is calculated.

Uncitral Clout Case 348

Germany: Oberlandesgericht Hamburg (26 November 1999)

Brazilian seller, the plaintiff, delivered jeans to a German buyer, the defendant. When inspecting the delivered jeans the buyer found the quantity to be incorrect. The jeans were also incorrectly labeled and the sizes were wrong. Some pairs had also become moldy. The buyer declared the contract avoided and placed the jeans at the seller's disposal. When the seller refused to take the jeans back, the buyer sold them. The seller sued the buyer for the original purchase price and the buyer offset the claims with its own claim for damages. The lower court granted the seller the resale price reduced by the buyer's loss of profit and dismissed the counterclaim.

On appeal, the court dismissed the claim entirely. The court held that the buyer was entitled to declare the contract avoided pursuant to Art. 49(1) CISG and that it was therefore released from the obligation to pay the purchase price under Art. 81(1) CISG. By delivering the defective jeans, the seller committed a fundamental breach of contract. The buyer gave notice about the lack of conformity specifying the nature of the lack within a reasonable time and declared the contract avoided (Art. 49(1) CISG in time (Art. 49(2) CISG).

The court stated that the buyer was discharged from its obligation to pay the resale price to the seller (Art. 88(3) CISG) due to set-off. The buyer was entitled to claim damages under Art. 45 and 74 CISG despite the avoidance of the contract (Art. 81(1) CISG). The court found, unlike the lower court, that damages under Art. 74 CISG were not limited to the loss of profit. As damages cover the whole loss resulting from non-performance, the buyer was entitled to claim the difference between its interest in the performance of the contract and its saved costs. The interest in the performance of the contract was calculated on the basis of the total profit reduced by the original purchase price. The difference had to be established in a concrete calculation, differing from Art. 76 CISG, where the current price was decisive. The court held that the fixed costs (so-called general expenses) could not be considered as being part of the saved costs. The seller had to prove that the fixed costs in case of performance exceeded the fixed costs in case of non-performance. The interest in the performance had to be reduced by saved value-added tax and costs for taking delivery and resale of the goods (so-called special expenses). The buyer's interest in the performance reduced by the value-added tax and the special expenses exceeded by far the benefit from the resale of the jeans.

The court stated that the CISG governed the issue of set-off (Art. 7(2) CISG) as long as the set-off was to concern claims arising under the CISG. Therefore the buyer was entitled to set-off. The court left however open the question of whether the buyer's right to keep the benefit of the resale could be directly inferred from the CISG or whether this issue was governed by the applicable German law, according to which set-off was also admissible.

NOTES

1.   CLOUT Case 348 agrees with other courts that in calculating lost profits under Article 74 fixed costs are not to be deducted from the value of performance to the injured party. See Delchi Carrier SpA v. Roterex Corp., 71 F.3d 1024, 1030 (2d Cir. 1995); TeeVee Toons, Inc. v. Gerhard Schubert, GmbH, 2006 WL 2463537 (S.D.N.Y. 2006). Only the buyer's variable costs saved as the result of the seller's breach, such as taxes and delivery expenses, are deducted. Because the buyer withheld the contract price owed, it too is a saved cost.

2. The court ruled that the injured buyer was entitled to setoff its damages claim from both the contract price it owed the breaching seller and the proceeds of the jeans it resold. Setoff is the right of parties owing debts to each other arising to apply their mutual debts to each other. Recoupment gives a party a defense to payment that arises from the same transaction as the right to payment. The buyer in the case had a damages claim against the seller that arose from the same sales transaction as the seller's right to the purchase price against the buyer. Thus, although the court refers to the buyer's right in the case as a right of "setoff," strictly the right is one of recoupment. Setoff or recoupment rights are created by decisional law, statute or contract.

It is controversial whether the CISG regulates setoff or recoupment. The court in the case found that the CISG regulates recoupment ("setoff") when the mutual claims both arise from the CISG: "The set-off is considered a general principle in the meaning of article 7(2) CISG in any case in so far as two reciprocal claims arising from the CISG are facing each other." See http://cisgw3.law.pace.edu/cases/ 991126g1.html (full case). It is careful to take no position on whether the CISG regulates setoff generally. Case law and commentary divide over whether the CISG governs setoff or recoupment. Compare Tribunale di Padova (Italy), 25 February 2004, available at http:// cisgw3.law.pace.edu/cases/040225i3.html, Peter Huber & Alastair Mullis, The CISG 30 (2007), John O. Honnold, Uniform Law for International Sales Under the 1980 United Nations Convention 656–57 (H.M. Flechtner ed., 4th ed. 2009) (neither setoff nor recoupment covered) with Ingeborg Schwenzer & Pascal Hachem, Article 7, in Schlechtriem & Schwenzer: Commentary on the UN Convention on the International Sales of Goods (CISG) 120, 135 (I. Schwenzer ed., 3d ed. 2010) (limited coverage). Although the court allowed setoff also against the proceeds of the resold jeans, it was agnostic about the basis of setoff. It did not decide whether the buyer's setoff right arose under the CISG or applicable German law. The court is rightly careful here. Article 88(3) allows the party selling the goods to retain out of the sale proceeds the expenses of preserving and selling the goods. The subsection does not fairly allow an inference that the party may retain from the sale proceeds the sum of its damages claim against the counterparty.

3. Are attorney's fees and other litigation expenses recoverable as loss under Article 74? Courts disagree. Compare Turku Court of Appeal (Finland), 12 April 2002, available at http://cisgw3.law.pace.edu/cases/020412f5.html (fees recoverable under Article 74) with Norfolk Southern Railway Co. v. Power Source Supply, Inc., 66 UCC Rep. Serv.2d 680 (W.D. Pa. 2008) (not recoverable). Article 74's principle of full compensation seemingly allows their recovery, on the rationale that litigation expenses are foreseeable loss resulting from breach. Against recovery is the argument that litigation expenses are the result of litigation to recover damages for breach, not themselves the result of breach. More persuasive is a consideration based on the likely intent of Contracting States. Contracting States whose domestic law adopts the American, "litigants pay their own way" rule are unlikely to have agreed to a "loser pays" rule. Given their likely strong views about a "loser pays" rule, the absence of an express reference to litigation expenses in Article 74 suggests that the expenses are not recoverable loss. Litigation expenses are recoverable, if at all, only by contract or under the forum's domestic law. For a version of this argument, see Zapata Hermanos Sucesores v. Hearthside Baking Co., 313 F.3d 385 (7th Cir. 2002).

b. ARTICLE 74'S FORESEEABILITY LIMITATION

Article 74 limits the damages recoverable under its general rule according to the foreseeability of loss from breach. According to the Article, damages "may not exceed the loss for which the party in breach foresaw or ought to have foreseen at the time of the conclusion of the contract... as a possible consequence of the breach of contract." The limitation is comparable to the foreseeability requirement for consequential damages applicable under American law. Although stated in slightly different terms, it is similar to *Hadley v. Baxendale*'s foreseeability limitation. Article 74's limitation on recoverable damages also is similar to 2–715(2)(a), which permits the buyer's recovery of consequential damages resulting for the seller's breach for any loss of which the seller has "reason to know" at the time contracting. By negative implication, 2–715(2)(a) does not allow recovery of loss of which the seller had no reason to know. For both Article 74 and 2–715(2)(a), facts which the breaching party discovers or should have discovered after the contract's conclusion have no effect on recoverable damages.

There is debate as to whether Article 74's foreseeability limitation differs from the foreseeability limitation under American law. The precise terms in which the limitation is formulated are not those American law usually uses to state the limitation. Article 74 excludes loss that the breaching party did not and could not reasonably foresee as a "possible consequence" of breach. By contrast, general contract law in the United States excludes loss that the breaching party did not have reason to foresee as a "probable result" of the breach. See Restatement (Second) of Contracts § 351(1) (1981). For its part, by implication the non-breaching buyer cannot recover loss under 2–715(2)(a) that the breaching seller had no "reason to know" would result from its breach. In addition, *Hadley*'s rule usually is stated in terms of loss both parties foresaw or should have foreseen, while Article 74's limitation is put in terms of loss the breaching party foresaw or should have foreseen. Despite these differences, several courts nonetheless find that Article 74's foreseeability limitation states *Hadley v. Baxendale*'s limitation on recoverable damages. See, e.g., Delchi Carrier SPA v. Rotorex Corp., 71 F.3d 1024, 1029 (2d Cir. 1995); cf. Bendesgericht (Switzerland), 28 October 1998, available at http://cisgw3.law.pace.edu/cases/981028s1.html. Article 74's different terminology ("possible consequence") makes this unlikely. See Franco Ferrari, *Hadley v. Baxendale* v. Foreseeability Under Article 74 CISG, in Contract Damages: Domestic and International Perspectives 305 (D. Saidov & R. Cunnington eds., 2008).

In principle the different verbal formulations of the foreseeability limitation allow for different recoveries of loss from breach. Limiting recoverable loss to the "possible consequence" of breach excludes only loss that the breaching party could not foresee as possible. Because minimally informed parties can foresee almost any loss as possible, the "possible consequence" limitation makes the breaching parties' liability close to strict. By contrast, limiting recoverable loss to the "probable consequence" of breach excludes more loss, because not every loss can be forecast as probable to an even moderately informed party. This limitation is closer to a negligence standard of liability. Article 74's relevant language states the "possible consequence" limitation. However, courts applying Article 74's foreseeability limitation appear to adopt neither a "possible consequence" nor a "probable consequence" standard. The little case law to date seems to limit loss according to whether it was reasonably foreseeable to the breaching party at the conclusion of the contract. In a 2000 Russian arbitration, the tribunal denied the nonbreaching buyer lost profit it would have realized on a sale to a subpurchaser on the ground that the breaching seller had not been informed of the sale. See Tribunal of International Commercial Arbitration (Russia), 6 June 2000, available at http://cisgw3.law.pace.edu/cases/000606r1.html. The tribunal concluded that in the circumstances the buyer's lost profit was unforeseeable. Clearly, the loss of profit in a sale to a subpurchaser is a possible consequence of breach. The court in *Delchi Carrier* found that profit from sales lost as a result of breach was recoverable because the sales were "objectively foreseeable" to the breaching seller. Similarly, the court in TeeVee Toons, Inc. v. Gerhard Schubert GmbH, 2006 WL 2463537, at *1 (S.D.N.Y. 2006) inferred foreseeability from the nonbreaching buyer's intent to resell the goods. Neither court inquired into the probability that the nonbreaching buyer would have made these sales.

4. SUBSTITUTE PERFORMANCE AND MARKET PRICE MEASURES

An injured party that has avoided the contract and obtained substitute performance may measure its damages under Article 75. Article 75 in turn measures these damages as the difference between the price of the substitute performance and the contract price. If the injured party is buyer, the substitute performance is the price the buyer paid for comparable goods. If the seller is the injured party, the substitute performance is the price at which the seller resold the goods. Article 75 is comparable to 2–712 and 2–706's cover and resale measures for the buyer and seller, respectively. Article 76 makes available another measure of damages to a party that has avoided the contract and not obtained substitute performance. The Article measures damages as the difference between the market price ("current price") at the time of avoidance and the contract price. The market price is the price prevailing at the place where the goods were to be delivered. Article 76(2). Article 76 is comparable to 2–713 and 2–708's market price measures for the buyer and seller, respectively. Both Article 75 and 76 allow the recovery of additional damages ("as well as") under Article 74's general rule for damages. Incidental expenses and consequential damages are the most likely sort of recoverable additional damages.

Both Articles 75 and 76 put restrictions on their respective damages measurements. Most obviously, both measurements are available only if the injured party has avoided the contract. An injured party that has not avoided the contract, or is not entitled to do so, must measure its damages under Article 74's general rule. Article 75 and 76's measurements are not available to it. In addition, Article 75 requires that the injured party obtain substitute performance in a comparable transaction ("reasonable manner") within a reasonable time after avoidance. For its part, Article 76 requires that there be a market price for the goods under contract. Thus, the injured party cannot calculate its damages under Article 76 if there is no prevailing price for the goods. Finally, Article 76 explicitly prevents the injured party from electing its remedy. The injured party may decide whether or not to obtain substitute performance. However, if it decides to obtain substitute performance under Article 75, it may not measure its damages under Article 76's market price measure (". . . if he has not made a purchase or resale under Article 75 . . ."). In this case the injured party must measure its damages under either Article 75 or Article 74. Consider the restrictions on Article 75 and 76's measurements in connection with the case abstract below and the notes following it.

Uncitral Clout Case 395

Spain: Tribunal Supremo (28 January 2000)

The matters at issue in this case are diverse and on all of them the ruling of the Supreme Court establishes case law.

In the first place, the ruling states that the contract of sale was completed by the exchange of faxes in early 1993 between the parties with regard to the subject matter of the contract—800,000 sacks of jute and the price payable for each of them (US $55.90 per 100 bags)—and to the conformity of the goods with the subject matter: "the literal terms of the faxes unequivocally indicate the acceptance of the offer by the buyer, defendant, thus given rise to a contractual agreement binding on the parties."

Moreover, any subsequent proposal made by the buyer to the seller to renegotiate the contract terms at which the agreement had been made—in the present case, the price—cannot be regarded as altering the conclusion of the contract, which had already occurred. It is precisely because it was subsequent to the unconditional acceptance of the offer—and to the delivery of a first consignment of the purchased sacks—that the proposal has to be regarded as a proposal of novation amending the contract with regard to the price. That proposal was not accepted by the seller and the buyer refused to pay.

In such circumstances, the seller arranged a substitute sale of the sacks to a third party at terms far lower than those agreed with the Spanish buyer, namely US $0.30 per sack, pursuant to article 75 of the Convention. Furthermore, the amount of the substitute sale was far below the renegotiation price offered by that original buyer. Thereupon, the seller claimed from the Spanish buyer the difference between the original price agreed and the price of the substitute sale, in accordance with articles 74 and 75.

The Court held that the buyer was in breach of its obligation to mitigate the loss, as stipulated in article 77 of the Convention, and consequently made an appropriate reduction in the amount of damages claimed.

NOTES

1. The Court reports that the seller resold the jute at a "far lower" price than the buyer previously offered to pay. Article 77 requires a party seeking damages take reasonable measures to mitigate its loss. Finding that the seller failed to mitigate its loss by refusing the buyer's offer to pay a higher price for the jute, the Court measured the seller's damages under Article 75 while reducing them by the amount of mitigable loss. Is the Court's reliance on both Articles 75 and 77 consistent? Consider Article 75's requirement that the seller to have resold the jute in a "reasonable manner." Has the seller in the case done so when it refused the buyer's previous offer to purchase the jute at a far higher price than it ultimately sold the jute for? On what other Articles should the Court have relied to measure the seller's damages?

2. The Court's reliance on Article 75's damages measure, although mistaken, probably is harmless. The same damages award would result if the seller were forced to measure its damages under either Article 74 or Article 75 while deducting mitigable loss. However, the particular damages measure used may matter in other circumstances. This is because the different measures require proof of different facts, such as the reasonableness of a substitute transactions (Article 75), market price (Article 76) or loss from breach (Article 74). A party may be in a better or worse position to prove or contest some of these facts.

3. ICC Case No. 8740 (1996), available at http://cisgw3.law.pace. edu/cases/968740i1.html, involved a contract for the delivery of specified quantity of coal. The seller breached by delivering nonconforming coal and failing to deliver the entire order. After the buyer avoided the contract, it made a substitute purchase of part of the quantity ordered. When the buyer tried to setoff its damages from the contract price owed the seller, the arbitral tribunal had to measure the buyer's damages. The tribunal decided that the buyer could not recover damages for the portion of the undelivered coal it did not replace. In doing so it made three findings. First, the buyer could measure its damages under Article 75 only for the portion of the undelivered coal it replaced with a substitute purchase. Second, the buyer could not measure its damages under Article 76 for the portion not replaced because there was no market price for the contracted coal. Third, Article 74 could not be used to measure the buyer's damages for the portion of coal it did not replace. Is the tribunal's third finding correct? Although the absence of a market price for the contracted coal prevents Article 76 from measuring these damages, Article 75 might be used to help measure damages under Article 74. After all, the higher price the buyer paid to replace some of the undelivered coal can be extrapolated to apply to the quantities of undelivered coal that the buyer did not replace with a substitute purchase. The difference between the higher replacement price and the (lower) contract price in turn can be used to calculate the buyer's loss under Article 74 with respect to quantities not replaced.

PROBLEM 10.13

Comair, a U.S. firm, contracted to manufacture and deliver 10 standard industrial air conditioning units ("units") to Biotex, a French firm, at its Paris factory for $20,000 per unit. Later, after Comair had produced the units and placed them in a Paris warehouse to await delivery, Biotex closed its factory and decided that it no longer needed the units. At the end of April it notified Comair that it would not receive them. In response, on May 1 Comair informed Biotex by email that it "considered our contract ended in light of your refusal to take the units. We are holding you responsible."

The price of standard industrial air conditioning units showed regional differences. Throughout May a unit could be purchased for $10,000 in the U.S. and $15,000 throughout Europe. However, by June 1 their price was volatile, ranging between $25,000 per unit at the top and $15,000 at the bottom in both regions. In September, when Comair first made efforts to sell Biotex's 10 units, it found a French buyer willing to pay $18,000 per unit. This was the highest price Comair was offered in September. Comair paid the warehouse $1,000 in storage costs between May and September and a carrier $2,000 to deliver the units to the buyer. Comair argues that it is entitled to damages as measured by Article 76 plus $3,000 in expenses. Biotex, which concedes its liability to Comair, insists that Comair must measure its damages by Article 75. It also contends that Comair is not entitled to recover $3,000 in expenses. (a) Who is right? (b) Suppose Comair's May 1 email merely acknowledged receipt of Biotex's notice that it would not receive the units. How may Comair measure its damages? See CISG Articles 25, 26, 74.

PROBLEM 10.14

Structure, a Miami manufacturer of custom-made furniture, contracted with Center, a Berlin wholesale furniture concern, to produce a wooden table for Center's Berlin showroom. Center submitted the design and Structure agreed to deliver the table for $10,000 at its Miami workshop in time for Center's annual design show. Structure's products were in demand and a number of retailers had approached Center to express interest in placing orders with Structure if they liked what they saw at Center's annual design event. Before Structure began to build the table for Center, Center cancelled the contract without excuse. Given the customized nature of its products, Structure reasonably decided not to produce the table. Structure can establish the following facts: The materials and utilities to be used to produce Center's table cost $6,000, and only Structure's full time employees fabricate its products during regular hours. In addition, fabrication occurs at a rented workshop under a long-term lease. Finally, Center knew that is was very likely that a retailer would have asked Structure to produce a table for it after viewing Structure's table at Center's annual design event. For its part, Center can prove that Structure realizes an average profit of 10 percent on its products, taking into its labor costs, lease obligations and other long-term commitments. How much can Structure recover from Center? See CISG Article 74.

D. BUYER'S REMEDIES

Most of the buyer's remedies are close counterparts to the seller's remedies described above. One difference, already noted, is the availability of consequential damages. Consequential damages can be recovered by the buyer but not the seller. See 2–715(2). The buyer's available remedies divide according to whether or not the buyer has accepted the goods. If it has accepted nonconforming goods, it must measure its damages by 2–714. If the buyer has rejected or revoked its acceptance of nonconforming goods, it can measure its damages under 2–712 or 2–713. Finally, if the seller has breached by not delivering the goods so that the buyer has neither accepted nor rejected them, the buyer can recover the goods under prescribed conditions. Where these conditions are not met, the buyer can recover money damages as measured under 2–712 or 2–713.

1. RECOVERY OF THE GOODS

The buyer can recover the goods on three different bases: specific performance, replevin and replevin after payment of at least part of the contract price. Specific performance may be available if the seller has breached by not delivering the goods. According to 2–716(1) specific performance "may be decreed where the goods are unique or in other proper circumstances." The traditional rule is that specific performance is unavailable where the buyer's legal remedies are adequate to compensate for the loss from breach. See Comment 1 to 2–716. Section 2–716(1)'s allowance of specific performance where the goods are unique endorses this rule, because legal remedies such as damages cannot replace unique goods. They are by definition irreplaceable. Section 2–716(1)'s allowance of specific performance "in other proper circumstances" arguably goes beyond the traditional irreparable injury rule. It permits the remedy in circumstances where goods are fungible. Comment 1 to 2–716 states that "this Article seeks to further a more liberal attitude that some courts have shown in connection with the specific performance of contracts of sale."

"In other proper circumstances" is a separate basis for allowing specific performance. Comment 2 to 2–716 notes this and adds that "inability to cover is strong evidence of 'other proper circumstances.'" If the buyer cannot cover by making a substitute purchase, even ordinary goods under the contract are irreplaceable. Although ordinary goods are not family heirlooms or one-of-a-kind paintings, market conditions, the buyer's needs or financial condition may prevent it from replacing them. Unique goods therefore are only one instance in which goods cannot be replaced with substitutes. Thus, replaceability, not uniqueness, is the basis for specific performance under 2–716(1). See Comment 2 to 2–716 (first sentence).

Except when the goods are unique, they can be replaced through a substitute purchase. In these cases buyers must expend different amounts of effort and pay a price to replace them. The replaceability of ordinary goods therefore is a matter of degree. The court in *Bander v. Grossman*, reproduced below, relies on cases that, taken together, stand for the proposition that an extreme price increase does not preclude specific performance while a "mere" price increase does not merit the remedy. Fairly interpreted, the proposition considers goods irreplaceable when the price of a substitute purchase is extremely high and replaceable when the substitute purchase can be made at price modestly above the contract price. Courts disagree as to what standard of replaceability required is for a grant of specific performance. The majority grant the remedy when the goods are difficult to replace, taking into account the effort and price of doing so. See Douglas Laycock, Death of the Irreparable Injury Rule, 103 Harv. L. Rev. 685, 710 (1990). Some courts deny the remedy if the goods can be replaced, without regard to the difficulty or the price of doing so.

As an alternative to specific performance, 2–716(3) allows the buyer to replevy the goods. Under 2–716(3) the buyer has the right to replevy goods if they are identified to the contract and it cannot reasonably cover. Replevin traditionally permits the owner of goods to recover them from one who is wrongly in possession. Section 2–716(3)'s right of replevin differs from the traditional remedy, because it allows replevin even when the buyer does not own the goods (title not having passed to it). It is enough that the goods are identified to the contract, 2–501, and cover is infeasible. This change in the right of replevin is consistent with Article 2 of the UCC's reduced reliance on title in allocating rights under the contract; see 2–401, Comment to 2–101; cf. 1 New York Law Revision Commission Report, Study of the Uniform Commercial Code 577 (1955). Nevertheless, 2–716(3)'s right of replevin is odd. Only part of the right makes sense. Under 2–716(3), the buyer also may replevy identified goods if they have been shipped under reservation and the buyer satisfies or tenders satisfaction of the seller's security interest in them. A shipment under reservation gives the seller a security interest in the goods to secure the contract price; see 2–505(1). Accordingly, payment of the contract price satisfies the seller's security interest—or, more accurately, satisfies the buyer's obligation secured by the seller's security interest. It is therefore unsurprising that 2–716(3) gives the buyer a right to replevy the goods in these circumstances.

The odd part of 2–716(3) is the buyer's right to replevy identified goods when it cannot cover reasonably. Section 2–716(1) already permits the buyer to obtain specific performance when it cannot cover. The inability to cover is among the circumstances Comment 2 to 2–716 considers "other proper circumstances" allowing the remedy. Thus, 2–716(3)'s right of replevin is superfluous when the buyer cannot cover reasonably. In addition, replevin is a more restrictive remedy than specific performance when cover is unavailable, because it requires that the goods be identified to the contract. Specific performance under 2–716(1) does not require that they be identified. Finally, modern replevin statutes frequently give courts a contempt power to enforce their replevin orders, so that the traditional distinction between the enforcement of specific performance and replevin has disappeared. For these reasons, 2–716(3)'s right of replevin seems to be useless to the buyer. Nonetheless, 2–716(3) still might play a useful role in the buyer's scheme of remedies. Specific performance under 2–716(1) is a discretionary remedy: the court may but need order the remedy when the buyer requests it. Section 2–716(3)'s right of replevin is non-discretionary. This means that the buyer has a right to recover the contract goods when the subsection's conditions are met. Thus, the trier of fact, which may be a court or jury, must allow the buyer to recover identified goods if it cannot effect reasonable cover. The court does not have the discretion to deny the buyer's request to recover goods, as it does under 2–716(1). There are very few reported cases in which a buyer seeks replevin rather than specific performance.

Specific performance and replevin are remedies that allow the buyer to recover the goods. Section 2–502 gives the buyer a right to recover them directly. Under 2–502(1) the buyer may recover goods identified to the contract when it has paid at least part of the contract price. Recovery requires the buyer to pay the unpaid portion of the price. Section 2–502(1)(b) allows the commercial buyer to recover the goods only if the seller has become insolvent within ten days after receiving the first installment of the contract price. This condition does not apply to the consumer buyer. See 2–502(1)(a). Thus, the consumer buyer who has paid at least part of the purchase price can recover the goods from the seller whether or not, and whenever, the seller becomes insolvent. An insolvent seller likely will go into bankruptcy. In this case the goods become part of the seller's bankruptcy estate but continue to be subject to the buyer's right to recover them under 2–502(1). The buyer's right to recover the goods from the seller's bankruptcy trustee remains effective, subject to the trustee's avoidance powers and the automatic stay.

Bander v. Grossman

New York Supreme Court, 1994
611 N.Y.S.2d 985

■ LEBEDEFF, JUDGE:

Following a jury trial on a claim that the defendant, a sports car dealer, repudiated plaintiff's contract to purchase a rare Astin–Martin automobile, plaintiff moves for judgment on its alternative request for monetary specific performance in the form of a judgment approximately 10 times greater than the breach of contract damages awarded by the jury. In opposition, defendant moves to set aside the breach of contract jury verdict in favor of plaintiff. Both motions are consolidated for purposes of this decision.

* * *

I

The attack on the verdict requires an amplification of the underlying facts. In the summer of 1987, plaintiff looked for a sports car to purchase for interim personal use and to sell when the price rose (a practice in which he had previously engaged). The defendant had in his inventory the subject 1965 DB5 Astin–Martin convertible with left-hand drive. Plaintiff learned this particular model was one of only 20 in existence, with only 40 having been made, although those 20 cars seem to turn over with more frequency than their number might suggest. Plaintiff testified he thought the car was undervalued, based upon his knowledge of sports car prices, and anticipated a price rise. A contract of sale was reached with a purchase price of $40,000, with plaintiff depositing $5,000.

The commercial agreement proceeded to unwind thereafter. The dealer could not obtain the title documents from the wholesaler from whom he had agreed to purchase the vehicle; the deposition testimony of the out-of-State wholesaler was read into evidence and confirmed that the title had been misplaced. The defendant did not transmit this explanation to plaintiff, but instead told a story about problems of getting title from a different individual. In August of 1987, the defendant attempted to return the deposit, but advised that he would continue to try to resolve the title problems. Plaintiff pursued the purchase until, ultimately, in December of 1987, plaintiff's lawyer wrote defendant that the contract had been breached and plaintiff would commence litigation. However, no further action was taken by plaintiff until this case was commenced in 1989, four months after defendant sold the car.

There was no dispute that the contract had been canceled. It was agreed that contract damages were to be given to the jury under the standard of UCC 2–713, applicable to a buyer who does not cover: the difference between the market price when the buyer learned of the breach, and the contract price. The jury did not accept the defendant's claim that he could not deliver title, which would have excused his performance under the concept of "commercial impracticability" and the defendant does not challenge this aspect of the jury verdict.

The jury fixed plaintiff's knowledge of the breach as the time his attorney announced it, and did not accept plaintiff's insistence that the contract remained in effect thereafter. Given the continued assurances of defendant that he would pursue title, which proved to be a hollow promise, it was a fair view of the evidence that plaintiff could no longer claim ignorance of breach after his attorney proclaimed one.

The jury concluded that the market price had increased $20,000 by December, which defendant urges is unsupported. The jury was presented with evidence that the price remained basically flat at $40,000 throughout 1987, and by January of 1988 was in a range from $0,000 to $100,000. The jury clearly rejected the proposition that there was no upward curve in value toward the end of 1987. Accordingly, as of December of 1987, $60,000 was a fair and logical assessment of the value of the car and the jury, as it was instructed to do, deducted from the value the purchase price of the car, to reach an award of $20,000.

Plaintiff's final protest is that there was no specific car on the market in December of 1987. It cannot be ignored that the evidence before the jury fully portrayed an intimate community of Astin–Martin enthusiasts, linked by membership in an Astin–Martin club and supported by an Astin–Martin speciality dealer located in New Jersey. The jury's verdict is soundly premised on the conclusion that, had plaintiff attempted to offer to purchase a comparable Astin–Martin within this community, one would have surfaced with a price of $60,000. After all, the same seller who sold a vehicle in January would only have to be lured into the market a month earlier, somewhat before the market price ascent.

* * *

II

The request for specific performance raises a novel issue under the Uniform Commercial Code concerning entitlement to specific performance of a contract for the sale of unique goods with a fluctuating price. Section 2–716(1) of the Uniform Commercial Code, which is controlling, provides that "[s]pecific performance may be decreed where the goods are unique or in other proper circumstances." The jury's advisory determined that the Astin–Martin car at issue was unique.

As noted above, the car was sold prior to the commencement of this litigation for a price of $185,000 more than the $40,000 contract price, and plaintiff requests that he be granted specific performance in the form of a constructive trust impressed upon the proceeds of sale, plus interest from the date of sale. As it developed, the defendant had not sold at the "top of the market," which peaked in July of 1989, approximately two years after the original contract, when the car had a value of $335,000, which was $295,000 over the contract price. Thereafter, collectible automobile values slumped and the sale price of a comparable Astin–Martin vehicle by January of 1990 was $225,000 and, by the time of trial, was $80,000.

Clearly, plaintiff's request for an award of specific performance monetary damages is legally cognizable, for every object has a price and even rare goods are subject to economic interchangeability. Plaintiff urges that specific performance is particularly appropriate here for UCC 2–716 has been viewed as a statute enacted to liberalize the availability of specific performance of contracts of sale as a buyers' remedy. Nonetheless, this change does not lessen the UCC's "emphasis on the commercial feasibility of replacement" as the most desirable approach (UCC 2–716, Comment 2), nor does it mean that typical equitable principles are inapplicable to consideration of the remedy.

However, both on the facts and the law, the court determines that, if equitable monetary damages are to be awarded here, that award must be based upon value at the time of trial, rather than on an earlier valuation. Traditionally, equity "give[s] relief adapted to the situation at the time of the decree" (Union Bay & Paper Co. v. Allen Bros. Co., 107 App Div 529, 539 [3d Dept 1905]). This position is consistent with the explicit goal of the Uniform Commercial Code that its remedies are to "be liberally administered to the end that the aggrieved party may be put in as good a position as if the other party had fully performed" (UCC 1–106[1]), which, in the case of specific performance, has led to confining the remedy to restoration of the equivalent of the subject goods to a plaintiff's possession. Here, if plaintiff were to be awarded enough to be able to acquire another Astin–Martin at current prices, he would achieve the requisite equivalent.

Plaintiff has fervently, but ultimately unconvincingly, argued that the larger amount is his due. While every litigant wishes to gain a maximum economic benefit, a court of equity should not grant an award which would be " 'disproportionate in its harm to defendant and its assistance to plaintiff' " (Van Wagner Adv. Corp. v. S & M Enters., 67 NY2d 186, 195 (N.Y. 1986) [citation omitted]). On the plaintiff's side of this equation, a higher award would give plaintiff more than the current equivalent of the automobile. On the defendant's side, the court found credible the dealer's testimony that he put the funds derived from the sale into his stock, which then decreased in value in the same measure as the car in question, so that a higher award would cause a disproportionate harm. This testimony was uncontroverted by plaintiff and it was undisputed that neither party saw a rise in price of the dimensions present here. The court rejects the request for monetary specific performance to the extent that more than the current market price is sought.

This conclusion limits the debate to the current price of the automobile, which is approximately $40,000 more than the contract price. As to interest in an equitable matter, generally, where damages are fixed as of the date of trial, interest is to commence as of the date judgment is entered, although the court must consider the facts of the case in determining the calculation of interest. There is a certain factual irony in that, by reason of market factors, the contract remedy plus interest would result in a specific performance monetary damages award only somewhat short of the current price.

The issue of monetary specific performance remains, despite this conclusion, because such an award would be somewhat higher than the contract measure of damages. Plaintiff's position that specific performance must follow a determination that an object is "unique" misperceives the law.

First, specific performance rests upon the discretion of the trial court, reviewable under an abuse of discretion standard. The use of a permissive "may" in the text of UCC 2–716 does not modify that standard in any way or change the accepted concept, as set forth in Da Silva v. Musso (53 NY2d 543, 547 [1981]), that specific performance may be declined if it is concluded such relief "would be a 'drastic' or harsh remedy." It should be noted in relation to price fluctuations that even an extreme rise in price is an insufficient reason, as a matter of law, to decline to consider this equitable remedy, but, on the other hand, neither does a mere "increase in the cost of a replacement . . . merit the remedy" (Klein v. PepsiCo, Inc., 845 F2d 76, 80 [4th Cir 1988] [citation omitted]).

Second, a factual determination that an object is "unique," as the jury determined here in an advisory verdict, is an ingredient which has the greatest significance when an action for specific performance is commenced immediately after the breach, and is more complex when other factors or delays are present. In cases concerning the sale of goods promptly commenced after the breach, specific performance is frequently granted and turns primarily upon uniqueness.

Once beyond this simple factual threshold, under New York law, "uniqueness" must be considered as it bears upon the adequacy of the legal remedy. It is noted that not all jurisdictions take this view.

With the passage of time, specific performance becomes disfavored. For example, because goods are subject to a rapid change in condition, or the cost of maintenance of the goods is important, time may be found to have been of the essence, and even a month's delay may defeat specific performance, notwithstanding that risk of loss under title concepts is generally irrelevant under the UCC, which considers whether an item has been identified to a contract. Even absent such special circumstances, with a greater delay, where a defendant has changed position or taken any economic risk, the court may conclude that "the plaintiff will lose nothing but an uncontemplated opportunity to gather a windfall" (Concert Radio v. GAF Corp., 108 AD2d 273, 278 [1st Dept 1985], affd 73 NY2d 766 [1988]). Particularly where some other transactions are available, it has been held that a " 'customer [for resale] may not . . . refuse to cover . . . and thereby speculate on the market entirely at the risk of the [defendant]' " (Saboundjian v. Bank Audi [USA], 157 AD2d 278, 284 [1st Dept 1990], referring in part to UCC 1–106 [UCC 1–305(a)] which limits damages under UCC 2–713 to a buyer's expected profit where the purchase is for resale, quoting Brown v. Pressner Trading Corp., 101 AD2d 761, 762 [1st Dept 1984]).

Turning to the facts in the instant case, the plaintiff did not sue in December of 1987, when it is likely a request for specific performance would have been granted. At that point, the defendant had disclaimed the contract and plaintiff was aware of his rights. The plaintiff was not protected by a continued firm assurance that defendant definitely would perfect the car's title, and it was established that New York is an automobile "title" State, so that title is a specific impediment upon which complete legal possession must turn. The court does not accept plaintiff's protest that he believed the commercial relationship was intact; the parties had already had a heated discussion and were communicating through attorneys. A more likely explanation of plaintiff's inaction is that he proceeded to complete the purchase in April of 1988 of Ferrari Testarrosa for $28,000 and a Lamborghini for $40,000 in 1989.

In short, the plaintiff abandoned any active claim of contract enforcement by late spring of 1988. Moreover, to the extent that his two sports cars constituted "cover," he did not present any evidence as to his treatment of those cars such that the court could evaluate damages or quantify what profits he expected to make on the Astin–Martin which he regarded, in significant part, as a business transaction. Finally, the court determines, as a matter of credibility, that plaintiff would not have pursued this matter had the price fallen below the contract price.

On this point, it is helpful to note that the initial burden of proving the proper remedy remains on the buyer (UCC 2–715, Comment 4). In this instance, plaintiff's very attempt to prove qualifiable special performance damages has also proved: (a) the value of the disputed automobile was readily established by expert sources; (b) the adequacy of legal contract damages; and (c) the availability of "a substitute transaction [which] is generally a more efficient way to prevent injury than is a suit for specific performance . . . [and gives] a sound economic basis for limiting the injured party to damages" (see, Restatement [Second] of Contracts § 360, comment c).

In closing, the court does not fault plaintiff for his valiant attempt to reach for a higher level of damages. As two leading commentators have pointed out, in relation to the use of uniqueness as a basis for specific performance, the "exact dimensions [of the concepts] are not fully known" (3A Hawkland & Miller, UCC Series § 2A–521:03 [1993]). If only in the interest of commercial certainty, there is great wisdom in a rule of thumb that "uniqueness continues to cover one-of-a-kind goods and items of special sentimental value, [and] goods that have particular market significance, such as goods covered by an output contract or which are being specially manufactured" (ibid.; nn omitted).

After full consideration of these factors, the court is satisfied that it would be inequitable and improper to grant specific performance in the form of a constructive trust upon the proceeds of sale.

Accordingly, the motion to fix the specific performance damages and the motion to vacate the jury verdict are denied.

NOTES

1. By ordering specific performance a court avoids the need to measure the buyer's expectation interest. The remedy assures that the buyer obtains its profit from the goods it receives. Section 2–716(1) does not say whether, at the buyer's request, a court may require the breaching seller to turn over the proceeds of the sale when the contract goods are sold to another buyer. This is sometimes called "monetary specific performance." "Monetary specific performance" is another name for a constructive trust impressed on the proceeds of the sale to another buyer. If granted, monetary specific performance gives the buyer the seller's gain from the sale, which might be more than the buyer's loss from the seller's breach. The court in *Bander* had to determine whether the buyer was entitled to the proceeds from the sale of a rare Aston–Martin car to a third party. The court refused to order the seller to pay the buyer more than the difference between the market price of the car at the time the buyer learned of the breach ($60,000) and the contract price ($40,000). Are there circumstances in which the court likely would have ordered the seller to pay the entire amount it received from the sale of the car to another buyer ($185,000)? Suppose the buyer had sued for specific performance soon after the seller's breach.

2. Specific performance may or may not be an efficient remedy. The seller's breach of contract is efficient when the gains from breach exceed the buyer's loss from not receiving the goods. Specific performance might induce the seller to perform when the transaction costs of renegotiating the contract to share the gains from breach are high. In this case the seller might perform even when gains from breach exceed the loss to the buyer from breach. On the other hand, denying the buyer the right to specific performance can induce the seller to inefficiently breach the contract. This occurs when the buyer's loss from breach is measured inaccurately to undercompensate it. The seller in this case will breach even when the buyer's gain from receiving the goods exceeds the seller's loss from performance. Whether specific performance is efficient depends on whether the risk of inefficient nonperformance is greater than the risk of inefficient performance. The comparative size of these risks ultimately is an empirical matter on which there is almost no evidence.

Potentially relevant are data about parties' efforts to contract for specific performance. Specific performance increases the seller's expected cost of performance, because it must forego a more valuable transaction that later arises. The seller therefore will include a charge in the price it demands for a contract that allows for specific performance. Buyers willing to pay this charge presumptively value the specific performance right more than the amount of the charge. A study of a variety of high value commercial contracts by Professors Theodore Eisenberg and Geoffrey Miller finds frequent specific performance clauses in corporate merger and asset sales agreements, and infrequent use of these clauses in corporate loan agreements. They also find specific performance clauses, where present, highly correlated with forum selection, arbitration and attorney's fees clauses. See Theodore Eisenberg & Geoffrey P. Miller, Damages Versus Specific Performance: Evidence From Commercial Contracts (March 29, 2013), available at http://papers.ssrn.com/sol3/papers.cfm?abstract_id=2241654. Simple inferences from this data about the efficiency of specific performance as a default remedy for sales of goods are unsafe. The preferences of parties to sales of goods contracts could differ from those of parties to other sorts of contracts. The correlation of specific performance clauses with other clauses in Eisenberg and Miller's sample, which are not found in typical sale of goods contracts, might be indirect evidence of this difference. In addition, unlike the range of sales of goods, close substitutes might be unavailable in the case of corporate mergers or asset sales. Measuring damages also could be more difficult in the former sort of transaction than the latter sort of transaction.

3. Case law tends to refuse to give automatic effect to contractual provisions that call for specific performance. See, e.g., In re Mitchell, 249 B.R. 55, 59 (Bankr. S.D.N.Y. 2000), Stokes v. Moore, 262 Ala. 59 (1955), Restatement (Second) of Contracts § 359 comm. *a* (1979). Nonetheless some courts allow parties to contract for specific performance; see, e.g., Ash Park, LLC v. Alexander & Bishop, Ltd., 783 N.W.2d 294 (Wis. 2010), Martin v. Sheffer, 403 S.E.2d 555 (N.C. Ct. App. 1991). Commentators generally favor enforcement of specific performance clauses; see, e.g., Dan B. Dobbs, 3 The Law of Remedies 12.5 at 117 (2d ed. 1993); Alan Schwartz, The Case for Specific Performance, 89 Yale L.J. 271, 277 (1979); Anthony T. Kronman, Specific Performance, 43 U. Chi. L. Rev. 351, 376 (1978).

2. COVER AND MARKET PRICE MEASURES OF DAMAGES

a. THE MEASURES

The injured buyer who has rejected or revoked its acceptance of the goods has a choice. It can make a substitute purchase and measure its damages under 2–712(2) as the difference between the cover price and the contract price. Alternatively, it can abstain from making a substitute purchase and measure its damages by 2–713(1) as the difference between the market price and the contract price. To recover under 2–712(2), the cover transaction must be made within a reasonable time after the seller's breach ("without unreasonable delay"). 2–712(1). In addition, cover must be by way of a substitute purchase. This requires the purchase to be connected in some way with the breached contract. The requirement prevents the buyer from making a series of purchases and selecting the highest purchase price as the cover price. Finally, the cover purchase must be a reasonable substitute purchase for the contract goods. Although the goods purchased need not be identical, they must be comparable to the contract goods in the circumstances. See Comment 2 to 2–712. A buyer who fails to satisfy 2–713(1)'s requirements must measure its damages under 2–713(1)'s market price-contract difference. According to 2–713(1), the relevant market price is the market price at the time the buyer learned of the breach. The buyer will elect to rely on the cover or market price to fix its damages based on the cost of proving the respective elements of 2–712(2) and 2–713(1).

A question that has arisen under 2–712(1) is whether the buyer can cover by either producing the substitute goods itself or by substituting goods it has in its inventory. This is "self-cover." Cover involves the buyer making a substitute purchase in another contract. Can the buyer engage in self-cover and measure its damages under 2–712(1)'s cover formula? Although some case law and commentary allows the possibility (see, e.g., Dura–Wood Treatment Co. v. Century Forest Indus., Inc., 675 F.2d 745 (5th Cir. 1982); Cives Corp. Callier Steel Pipe & Tube, Inc., 482 A.2d 852 (Me. 1984)), a decent argument can be made against self-cover. For one thing, 2–712(2)'s requirement of a cover "purchase" by definition demands that substitute goods be acquired in a transaction with another party. See 1–201(b)(29) ("purchase"). Self-cover does not count as a "purchase." In addition, the price of the goods the buyer uses to self-cover is likely to be equal to the market price at the time the buyer learned of the breach. In this case 2-713(1)'s market price formula therefore would give the same measure of damages as 2–712(2)'s cover formula. The buyer therefore need not rely on 2–712(2)'s cover formula to measure its damages. Finally, at the time the contract is concluded it is as likely that the self-cover price will be above the cover and market price as below them. The buyer does not have information that systematically allows it to outguess the market. Thus, the buyers' expected recovery is the same under both the market price (2-713(1)) and cover price (2-712(2)) measures of damages regardless of whether self-cover is permitted. Self-cover therefore does not reduce the expected liability of the breaching seller.

The time at which 2–713(1) sets market price is a problem when the seller repudiates the contract before its performance is due. In a case of the seller's anticipatory repudiation, 2–610(b) allows the buyer to measure its damages by 2–713(1)'s market price formula. According to 2–713(1), the market price is of the time at which "the buyer learned of the breach." Case law has interpreted that phrase as giving three different times: the time at which the buyer learns of the seller's repudiation, the last point in time within which the buyer could cover, and the time at which the seller's performance is due under the contract. The first alternative is inconsistent with 2–723(1). Section 2–723(1) provides that if an action based on anticipatory repudiation comes to trial before the date performance is due, market price is determined as of time the injured party learned of the repudiation. The section's negative implication is that if the action comes to trial after the date performance is due, market price is *not* determined as of this time. The third alternative allows the buyer to speculate at the seller's expense. This is because it allows the buyer to observe the market price between the time it learns of the repudiation and the time the seller's performance is due. If market price is below the cover price, the buyer will cover. If market price is above the cover price, the buyer can abstain from cover and fix its damages under 2–713(1) as of the time performance. The second alternative is defensible: the market price under 2–713(1) is determined at a reasonable time after the seller's repudiation in which the buyer could cover, but not beyond the time performance is due.

PROBLEM 10.15

Selco, a Los Angeles wholesaler, and Tonex, a retailer located in New York City, contracted for Selco to deliver 100 plastic toner cartridges to Tonex "$1,000 F.O.B. Port of Los Angeles." Selco in turn arranged for the cartridges to be transported by a carrier on a vessel designated by Tonex. Later, it loaded the cartridges on its truck to transport to the Port of Los Angeles. While in transit, the truck caught fire. The fire was quickly brought under control, but not before smoke discolored the cartridge casings. Selco nonetheless delivered the cartridges at the Port of Los Angeles and had them put on board the vessel selected by Tonex. When Tonex took delivery of the cartridges in New York City, it noticed their discolored appearance and immediately notified Selco that it could not sell them. It also instructed Selco to retrieve the cartridges. Selco is not in a position to deliver any other cartridges to Tonex, and Tonex has decided not to obtain replacements on the open market. The prevailing price for a comparable 100 lot of toner cartridges in Los Angeles is $1,500. The same lots sell for $1,200 in New York City. (a) How much can Tonex recover from Selco in damages? 2–509(1), 2–319(1)(a), 2–713(1), (2). (b) Suppose that after the fire Selco decided not to transport the cartridges to Los Angeles and destroyed them. The facts otherwise remaining the same, how much can Tonex recover from Selco in damages? See 2–504, 2–713(1), (2).

PROBLEM 10.16

In January Chemco's contracted with Argo to deliver to Argo two tons of grade AA fertilizer by April 1. The contract price was $10,000, payment on delivery. Production problems prevented Chemco from making delivery on time for the foreseeable future, and April 1 passed without Argo receiving fertilizer from Chemco. Argo began looking for a replacement supply in April. Argo's inquiries extended into June, when the summer planting season approached and fertilizer prices began to rise as a result of increased demand. In July, unable to find AA fertilizer available any longer, Argo purchased two tons of AAA premium fertilizer for $13,000. This was $2,000 more than the price of two tons of AA fertilizer that prevailed between February and April. Argo seeks to recover $3,000 in damages from Chemco. Chemco in turn concede its liability to Argo but contests the amount Argo seeks to recover. May Argo recover $3,000 from Chemco? If not, how much can Argo recover? See 2–712(1), (2), 2–713(1).

b.   LOST PROFITS AS A LIMIT ON MARKET PRICE DAMAGES?

A simple question can be asked about 2–713(1)'s market price formula: Can the buyer rely on 2–713(1)'s market price-contract difference to measure its damages when that difference gives it more than its lost profits from the seller's breach? Article 2's provisions do not provide a definitive answer to this question. To understand the problem, consider the following example. Suppose Seller agrees to deliver a widget to Buyer for a price of $10. On the same date Buyer agrees to deliver the widget to Jones for $12. Buyer's agreement with

Jones gives Buyer the right to cancel the contract if Seller fails to deliver the widget to it. Suppose also that the market price of the widget increases from $10 to $15 and Seller refuses delivery to Buyer. Buyer in turn cancels its contract with Jones and sues Seller to recover damages for Seller's breach. Seller's breach caused Buyer to lose a net profit of $2 in its contract with Jones ($12 − $10). However, 2–713(1)'s market price formula gives Buyer $5 in damages ($15 − $10). May Buyer rely on its formula to recover these damages when they exceed its lost profit of $2? Or is Buyer's recovery under 2–713(1)'s market price formula limited to its $2 in lost profit?

Article 2's provisions give different answers to these questions. On the one hand, 2–713(1)'s language allows Buyer to rely on its market price formula. The provision does not limit the buyer's recovery by its lost profit on breach. It calculates damages simply as the difference between the market price at the time the buyer learned of the breach and the contract price. Section 2–708(2) allows the seller to recover its lost profit when 2–708(1)'s market price formula is inadequate to put the seller in the same position as performance would have done. By comparison, Section 2–713(1) does not say that 2–713(1)'s market price formula is inapplicable to the extent that it puts the buyer in a better position than performance would have done. Because the section calculates damages by market price without regard to the actual loss the buyer suffers from the seller's breach, it gives what are sometimes called "statutory liquidated damages." On the other hand, 1–305(a) provides that the UCC's remedies are to be liberally administered to the end that the injured party be put in the same position as if the breaching party had performed. Had Seller performed, Buyer would have delivered the widget to Jones, received in return $12 and obtained a net profit of $2 from the transaction. A "liberal" application of 2–713(1)'s market price formula, according to most courts, limits Buyer's recovery to its $2 in lost profit. Allowing Buyer to recover the additional $3 under the formula puts it in a better position than had Seller delivered. Courts divide over whether 2–713(1)'s language prevails over 1–305(a)'s general injunction, as the next two cases illustrate.

TexPar Energy, Inc. v. Murphy Oil USA, Inc.

United States Court of Appeals, Seventh Circuit, 1995
45 F.3d 1111

■ REAVLEY, CIRCUIT JUDGE:

In this contract dispute, appellant Murphy Oil USA, Inc. complains of the jury charge and the damages awarded to appellee TexPar Energy, Inc. Finding no reversible error, we affirm.

BACKGROUND

On May 29, 1992, TexPar contracted to purchase 15,000 tons of asphalt from Murphy at an average price of $53 per ton. On the same day, TexPar contracted to sell the 15,000 tons to Starry Construction Company at an average price of $56 per ton. Hence, TexPar stood to profit by $45,000 if both contracts were performed.

During the first half of 1992, the price of asphalt varied widely. Evidence was presented of prices ranging from $40 to $100 per ton. The wide range of prices reflected volatile market forces. From the supply standpoint, asphalt is one of the end products of petroleum refining, and must be sold or stockpiled to accommodate the production of more valuable petroleum products. Demand depends in large measure on the availability of government funding for highway construction. Weather also affects asphalt supply and demand. The price rose rapidly in June of 1992, and consequently, the sale price of $53 per ton lost its attractiveness to Murphy.

In May and early June TexPar took delivery of 690 tons of asphalt; but, on June 5, Murphy stopped its deliveries and notified TexPar that its sales manager lacked authority to make the contract. By then, the price of asphalt had risen to $80 per ton. Starry insisted that TexPar deliver the full 15,000 tons at $56 per ton as TexPar and Starry had agreed. Ultimately, with TexPar's approval, Starry and Murphy negotiated directly and agreed on a price of $68.50 per ton. This arrangement was reached several weeks after the repudiation by Murphy. By this time the market price had dropped, according to TexPar. TexPar agreed to pay Starry the $12.50 difference between the new price of $68.50 per ton and the original $56 per ton price. TexPar therefore paid Starry approximately $191,000 to cover the price difference.

The jury found that the difference between the market price ($80) and the contract price ($53) of the undelivered asphalt (14,310 tons) on the date of repudiation (June 5), amounted to $386,370. The court entered judgment for this amount.

DISCUSSION

The parties agree that Wisconsin law, and particularly Wisconsin's version of the Uniform Commercial Code, applies to this dispute.

A. Damages Under UCC § 2–713

The district court applied UCC § 2–713, which provides a measure of the buyer's damages for nondelivery or repudiation:

> Subject to § 2.723 with respect to proof of market price, the measure of damages for nondelivery or repudiation by the seller is the difference between the market price at the time when the buyer learned of the breach and the contract price together with any incidental and consequential damages provided in § 2.715, but less expenses saved in consequence of the seller's breach.

Murphy does not dispute that if this provision is applied, the damages awarded are proper, since Murphy does not dispute the quantity of goods, the market price or the date of notice of repudiation used by the jury to calculate damages. Instead, Murphy argues that the general measure of damages in a breach of contract case is the amount needed to place the plaintiff in as good a position as he would have been if the contract had been performed. Murphy argues that since TexPar's award—$386,370—far exceeds its out-of-pocket expenses ($191,000) and lost profits ($45,000) occasioned by the repudiation, the court erred in instructing the jury merely to find the difference in market price and entering judgment in that amount.

We cannot quarrel with Murphy that the general measure of damages in contract cases is the expectancy or "benefit of the bargain" measure. The UCC itself embraces such a measure in § 1–106, providing that the UCC remedies "shall be liberally administered to the end that the aggrieved party may be put in as good a position as if the other party had fully performed. . . . "

Nevertheless, we do not believe that the district court erred in awarding damages based on a straightforward application of § 2.713. That provision is found in the article on the sale of goods, and specifies a remedy for the circumstances presented here—the seller's nondelivery of goods for which there is a market price at the time of repudiation.

We can see no sound reason for looking to an alternative measure of damages. Murphy argues that TexPar shouldn't be awarded a "windfall" amount in excess of its out-of-pocket damages. Since it depends on the market price on a date after the making of the contract, the remedy under § 2.713 necessarily does not correspond to the buyer's actual losses, barring a coincidence. Our problem with Murphy's suggested measure of damages is that limiting the buyer's damages in cases such as this one to the buyer's out-of-pocket losses could, depending on the market, create a windfall for the seller. If the price of asphalt had fallen back to $56 per ton by the time Starry and Murphy had arranged for replacement asphalt, TexPar's damages would have been zero by this measure, and Murphy could have reaped a windfall by selling at the market price of $80 in early June instead of the $53 price negotiated with TexPar.

Murphy argues that it did not in fact realize a windfall, since its cost of production was $70 per ton and it eventually agreed to sell to Starry for $68.50. We find this argument unpersuasive. Applying the market value measure of damages under UCC § 2–713, as the district court did, is expressly allowed under the Code. Since § 2–713 addresses the circumstances of a seller's nondelivery of goods with a market price, we see no error in applying this specific provision over the more general remedies provision found at [§ 1–305(a)]. See Tongish v. Thomas, 251 Kan. 728, 840 P.2d 471, 474 (1992) ("[B]ecause it appears impractical to make [§ 1–106] and [§ 2–713] harmonize in this factual situation, [§ 2–713] should prevail as the more specific statute according to statutory rules of construction."). The UCC § 2–713 remedy serves the purpose of discouraging sellers from repudiating their contracts as the market rises, if the buyer should resell as did TexPar, or gambling that the buyer's damages will be small should the market drop. It also has the advantage of promoting uniformity and predictability in commercial transactions, by fixing damages on the date of the breach, rather than allowing the vicissitudes of the market in the future to determine damages. Id. at 476 ("Damages computed under [§ 2–713] encourage the honoring of contracts and market stability.").

* * *

AFFIRMED.

NHF Hog Marketing, Inc. v. Pork–Martin, LLP

Minnesota Court of Appeals, 2012
76 U.C.C. Rep. Serv.2d 480

■ PETERSON, JUDGE:

In this appeal from a judgment for breach-of-contract damages awarded after respondent breached the parties' contract by failing to deliver hogs, appellant argues that (1) the district court erred when it held that appellant is entitled only to its lost commission on the resale of the hogs; and (2) under Minn. Stat. § 336.2–713 (2010), appellant is entitled to damages for the difference between the contract price and the market price at the time the hogs were to be delivered. We affirm.

FACTS

Appellant NHF Hog Marketing Inc. is a hog-marketing business, and respondent Pork–Martin LLP is a business that owns and finishes hogs. In November 2005, appellant entered into a master hog-procurement contract (master contract) with third-party J.B.S. Swift, under which appellant agreed to deliver approximately 750,000 hogs to Swift each year from January 2006 through December 2010. The master contract required that the hogs come from designated production facilities specified in the contract and that the hogs meet specified quality requirements. The contract provided that appellant would be paid a base price equal to market price, subject to adjustments if the market price per carcass hundred weight fluctuated above or below a specified range. To meet the requirements of the master contract, appellant entered into contracts with operators of designated production facilities, including respondent.

In January 2006, appellant and respondent entered into a hog-procurement contract, under which respondent agreed to deliver 2,333 market-weight hogs per month to appellant. The price terms of the hog-procurement contract and the master contract were the same, except that respondent was paid $0.33 less per carcass hundredweight than appellant received from Swift. The $0.33 difference between the price that appellant paid respondent and the price that appellant received from Swift was appellant's commission for negotiating and coordinating respondent's delivery of hogs to Swift. In May 2008, the market price for hogs increased, and respondent stopped delivering hogs under the hog-procurement contract and sold its hogs to another buyer.

Appellant brought this breach-of-contract action against respondent, seeking damages equal to the difference between the hog-procurement-contract price and the market price at the time the hogs were to have been delivered to Swift. Appellant sought total damages of $439,844.95. Of this amount, $396,647.45 was for damages incurred by Swift under the master contract due to respondent's failure to deliver hogs. This amount is the difference between the market price on the day the hogs were to be delivered to Swift and the sale price under the master contract; it is the additional amount that Swift would have had to pay to buy hogs when respondent failed to deliver. The remaining $43,197.50 in damages sought was for the commission that appellant lost when respondent failed to deliver and no sale occurred.

The case was tried to the court. At the time of trial, Swift had not started any action against appellant to enforce the terms of the master contract, and appellant presented no evidence indicating that Swift was likely to insist on performance. The district court awarded appellant $43,197.50 in damages. This appeal followed.

ISSUE

Did the district court err in limiting appellant's damages to its lost commission?

ANALYSIS

* * *

Appellant argues that, under the Uniform Commercial Code (U.C.C.), in addition to its lost commission, it is entitled to damages in the amount of the difference between the master-contract price and the market price at the time respondent failed to deliver the hogs. The U.C.C. states:

> (1) Subject to the provisions of this article with respect to proof of market price (section 336.2–723), the measure of damages for nondelivery or repudiation by the seller is the difference between the market price at the time when the buyer learned of the breach and the contract price together with any incidental and consequential damages provided in this article (section 336.2–715), but less expenses saved in consequence of the seller's breach.

> (2) Market price is to be determined as of the place for tender or, in cases of rejection after arrival or revocation of acceptance, as of the place of arrival.

Minn. Stat. § 336.2–713 (2010).

Minnesota's appellate courts have not addressed whether a buyer is entitled to market-differential damages under this statute when those damages exceed actual damages. Courts in other jurisdictions are divided on the issue. See Allied Canners & Packers, Inc. v. Victor Packing Co., 162 Cal. App.3d 905, 912, 209 Cal. Rptr. 60 (1984) (noting division). One view is that U.C.C. § 2–713, codified in Minnesota as section 336.2–713, is a statutory liquidated-damages provision and, therefore, damages should not be limited to a plaintiff's actual economic loss.

The other view, which is urged by respondent, is that a buyer's damages should be limited to actual damages. This view is consistent with the U.C.C. policy that

> remedies provided by the Uniform Commercial Code must be liberally administered to the end that the aggrieved party may be put in as good a position as if the other party had fully performed but neither consequential or special damages nor penal damages may be had except as specifically provided in the Uniform Commercial Code or by other rule of law.

Minn. Stat. § 336.1–305 (2010).

Respondent's position was adopted in H–W–H Cattle Co. v. Schroeder, 767 F.2d 437 (8th Cir. 1985). In *H–W–H*, the buyer contracted to buy cattle from the seller and resell them to a third party. *H–W–H*, 767 F.2d at 438. The market price of cattle increased, the seller breached the contract, and the buyer sought damages under U.C.C. § 2–713 as codified in Iowa, and corresponding to Minn. Stat. § 336.2–713. Id. at 439. The United States Court of Appeals for the Eighth Circuit upheld the district court's award of lost-profits damages, stating that adopting the buyer's position would result in a windfall to the buyer and violate the general principle of remedies underlying the statutory provision corresponding to Minn. Stat. § 336.1–305.

* * *

The position taken by *H–W–H* and *Allied* is favored by commentators James J. White and Robert S. Summers. After noting that the *Allied* court "relied substantially" on the policy of U.C.C. section 1–305, White and Summers state:

> Courts should take care to apply the *Allied* and *H–W–H* limitation narrowly. First, it should be applied only when the defendant proves that the plaintiff's expected resale profit was less than the 2–713 differential; we would not impose the burden of proving the negative on the plaintiff as part of its case in chief. Second, in any case in which the buyer's resale purchaser will likely insist upon performance, the buyer's damages should not be limited to the buyer's expected resale profit, for in that case the buyer will be liable in damages to its own purchaser equal to the difference between the buyer's resale contract price and the market price (or will have to cover at market price in order to make delivery).
>
> . . . We recognize that the prospect of a reduction in damages may have some impact upon a seller's willingness to perform, and may make the security of a buyer's expectations somewhat smaller than would otherwise be the case. Arguably, too, our position will unjustly enrich an occasional seller and may also make the trial more complicated. Even so, we think our overall position is more faithful to the idea that the contract plaintiff should recover only his lost expectancy. That idea is deeply entrenched in Anglo–American common law and is adopted in section 1–305 of Revised Article One and its predecessor section 1–106 of the Uniform Commercial Code. Limiting the plaintiff to expectation damages also preserves the possibility of what economists call efficient breach, an idea endorsed by one of your authors.

1 James J. White & Robert S. Summers, Uniform Commercial Code § 6–4, at 413–14 (5th ed. 2006).

We are persuaded that the position adopted in *H–W–H* and *Allied* and favored by White and Summers is the better approach. The damages awarded by the district court put appellant in as good a position as if respondent had fully performed. We, therefore, hold that a buyer's damages under Minn. Stat. § 336.2–713 are limited to the buyer's actual damages when the breaching seller shows that the buyer's expected resale profit was less than market-differential damages and the buyer fails to show a likelihood that the resale purchaser will enforce the resale contract.

DECISION

Because appellant's actual damages were limited to its lost commission and there was no showing of a likelihood of enforcement of the master contract, the district court properly awarded appellant damages of $43,197.50 for its lost commission.

Affirmed.

NOTE

TexPar Energy and *NHF Hog* above are representative of the split among courts over the relationship between 1–301(a)'s general instruction and 2–713(1)'s measure of damages. Although the cases are fairly evenly divided, a slight majority of courts take *TexPar Energy*'s approach to the question. See Tongish v. Thomas, 840 P.2d 471, 476 (Kan. 1992). Both *TexPar Energy* and *NHF Hog* assume that 2–713(1) and 1–305(a) conflict: *TexPar Energy* holds that 2–713(1) prevails over 1–305(a), so that damages fixed by its market price formula are not limited by the buyer's actual damages. *NHF Hog* rules that 1–305(a) prevails over 2–713(1), so that the buyer's damages under 2–713(1)'s formula cannot exceed its actual damages. However, the two sections may be consistent. Section 1–305(a) demands that Article 2's remedies be applied to put the injured party in the position performance would have put it. According to the *NHF Hog* court, this "policy" requires limiting the buyer's damages under 2–713(1)'s market price formula to its lost profit. But 1–305(a) does not compel this result. The buyer in *NHF Hog*, NHF Hog, was acting as a middleman. It contracted with Pork–Martin for a supply of hogs that it was to provide to Swift under a separate contract. Thus, there are two contracts involved: Pork–Martin's contract with NHF Hog, and NHF Hog's contract with Swift. Pork–Martin breached by refusing to deliver when the market price of hogs increased. Section 1–305(a) requires administering 2–713(1) to put NHF Hog in the same position that it would be in had Pork–Martin performed its contract with NHF Hog. If Pork–Martin had performed, NHF would have received hogs whose market price was above the contract price of the NHF Hog–Pork–Martin contract. Thus, NHF Hog's recovery of the market price-contract price difference under 2–713(1) is consistent with 1–305(a)'s policy. Section 1–305(a)'s policy appears to limit the buyer to its lost profit because the court focuses on the wrong contract: the NHF Hog–Swift contract. Whether or not NHF Hog entered in this contract does not affect Pork–Martin's liability under the contract it breached. Cf. Victor Goldberg, Framing Contract Law 236 (2006).

The seller's breach of one contract might cause the buyer to breach its contract with the subpurchaser. In that case the buyer is liable to the subpurchaser under the second contract if the subpurchaser suffers loss as a result of the breach. In *NHF Hog* NHF Hog was not liable to Swift because it had the privilege, but was not obligated, to deliver hogs to Swift. Thus, NHF Hog's failure to deliver hogs to Swift was not a breach. On the other hand, the buyer in *TexPar* (Texpar) was liable to its subpurchaser (Starry) as a result of the seller's (Murphy's) breach of the original contract. Damages for which the buyer is liable under the second contract are recoverable as consequential damages under the first contract in addition to the market price-contract price difference. See 2–713(1) (". . . together with any . . . consequential damages").

The consistency of 1–305(a) and 2–713(1) aside, most parties would not want the buyer's damages limited by its lost profits. For one thing, proving lost profits sometimes is hard and often costly. Although the contract price is verifiable, the buyer's value from performance is not. Litigants have to invest in supplying or contesting evidence of value. This may make the trial "more complicated," as White and Summers concede in a passage the court quotes in *NHF Hog*. Although the *NHF Hog* court puts the burden of proving the amount of lost profit on the breaching seller, thereby reducing the buyer's proof costs, the buyer still has to rebut evidence of lost profit introduced by the seller. The buyer's proof costs therefore are not eliminated. In addition, buyers sometimes prefer to keep private information about the contract price or the value they attach to performance. Disclosing the information might give others a competitive advantage or disadvantage the buyer in its own future dealings with the seller. See Omri Ben–Sharar & Lisa Bernstein, The Secrecy Interest in Contract Law, 109 Yale L.J. 1885 (2000). By withholding the information, the buyer risks having its lost profits calculated inaccurately. For both reasons, the trier of fact might underestimate the amount of the buyer's lost profits. (In fact, proof problems might be so severe as to dissuade a buyer from bringing suit for the seller's breach at all.) This has both ex post and ex ante effects. Ex post the buyer's damage award is undercompensatory. Ex ante the prospect of an undercompensatory award of lost profits encourages the seller to inefficiently breach when the gain from breach exceeds the expected (undercompensatory) award of lost profits.

By comparison, 2–713(1)'s market price formula relies on verifiable variables. Market price is relatively easily determined based on objective evidence. The formula puts fewer proof costs on the buyer than does the need to produce, or rebut evidence, about its lost profits. Also, because the formula relies on objective evidence, the buyer can measure its damages without an unwanted disclosure of private information about the value it attaches to performance. Although some buyers might not want to disclose information about contract price, contract price is an element of 2–713(1)'s market price formula too. Thus, the information must be disclosed in any case to recover damages under it. Because parties are likely to be both seller and buyers in different transactions, most parties prefer that damages under 2–713(1) not be limited by the buyer's lost profits.

3. DAMAGES FOR BREACH OF WARRANTY

An injured buyer that has accepted the goods cannot measure its damages by 2–712's cover formula or 2–713's market price formula. Both formulas apply only when the buyer either has not received the goods or has rejected or revoked its acceptance of them. Cover damages are available when the buyer makes a substitute purchase, while market price damages measure the price at which the buyer could have made a substitute purchase. A buyer that has accepted nonconforming goods without revoking its acceptance retains them. Thus, cover or market price measures cannot protect its expectation interest. The buyer instead must recover its damages under 2–714. Section 2–714 has two different formulas for measuring the accepting buyer's damages. Under 2–714(1) the buyer may recover as damages "the loss resulting in the ordinary course of events from the seller's breach as determined in any manner which is reasonable." Under 2–714(2) the measure of damages for breach of warranty is the difference between the value of the goods accepted and the value they would have if they had been as warranted. Section 2–714(3) allows recovery of incidental expenses and consequential damages under 2–714(1) and (2). According to 2–607(3)(a), the buyer's failure to give notice of breach within a reasonable time after it discovers or ought to have discovered the breach bars it from any remedy. To recover damages under either of 2–714's formulas, the buyer therefore must give timely and proper notice of breach.

Section 2–714(1) states the general formula measuring damages when the buyer accepts nonconforming goods. By its terms, the formula calculates damages for "any non-conformity of tender." Section 2–714(2)'s difference in value formula is a specific measure of damages for breach of warranty. Although a breach of warranty is a type of nonconforming tender, not all nonconforming tenders are breaches of warranty. For example, the seller's failure to pay warehousing costs necessary to enable the buyer to take delivery of the goods, as agreed, makes its tender nonconforming. The failure is not a breach of the seller's warranty as to the goods tendered. Comment 2 to 2–714 states that 2–714(2)'s difference in value formula is the "usual, standard" method of measuring damages for breach of warranty. The Comment implicitly recognizes that the buyer in "unusual" or "atypical" cases may measure these damages by 2–714(1)'s general formula. Neither the Comment nor 2–714(2) gives a hint as to what these cases might be.

Section 2–714(2) measures warranty damages as the difference between the "value" of the goods as warranted and the "value" of the goods accepted. It does not say what "value" means. Is "value" the value of the goods to most buyers or to a reasonable buyer (an objective standard)? Or is it the value to the particular buyer, taking into account its preferences and specific circumstances (a subjective standard)? Arguments based on statutory construction do not favor either standard of value. Sections 2–708(1) and 2–713(1) both mention "market value," while 2–714(2)'s reference to "value" omits reference to "market value." An inference from the omission of "market value" in 2–714(2) might be that "value" refers to subjective value. On the other hand, 2–608(1) refers to a nonconformity that substantially impairs its "value to him." By comparison, Section 2–714(2)'s mention of "value" is unqualified. An inference from the unqualified reference is that "value" refers to objective value. Considered alone, statutory arguments therefore are inconclusive.

The case for applying 2–714(2)'s difference in value formula based on an objective standard of value is that the objective standard likely produces efficient terms in the contract. The argument for this conclusion is similar to the justification for *Hadley v. Baxendale*'s foreseeability limit on consequential damages described in Chapter 1. Buyers have better information about the subjective value they attach to the goods than their sellers. A seller will price the goods on the assumption that its buyer's subjective value is equal to the average value placed on them by all of its buyers. Buyers whose subjective values are below the average value subsidize buyers with subjective values above the average value. Measuring damages by an objective standard of value, such as market price, induces buyers to disclose the subjective value they place on the goods to their seller when the subjective value is above market price. This is because 2–714(2)'s difference in value formula undercompensates an injured buyer who has failed to disclose its subjective value in these circumstances. In response to the buyer's disclosure, the seller can adjust the contract price, disclaim warranties or exclude damages. Measuring damages by a subjective standard of value gives the buyer no incentive to disclose information about its subjective valuation. Without this information, the seller will charge "low" value buyers an inefficiently high price and "high" value buyers an inefficiently low price. (For present purposes, the contract price for goods is efficient if it takes into account all information about the seller's expected liability from breach.)

Measuring value by an objective standard still allows subjective value to figure in the calculation of damages under 2–714(2)'s difference in value formula. According to 2–714(2), the measure of damages is the difference between the value of the goods as warranted and their value as accepted, unless "special circumstances" show damages of a different amount. Information about the buyer's subjective value known to the seller can count as a "special circumstance." Damages in this case can be calculated as the difference between the subjective value the buyer placed on the goods as warranted and the subjective value of the goods to the buyer as accepted. Section 2–714(2)'s reference to "special circumstances" appears in the last clause of the subsection, while its reference to "value" occurs in the subsection's main clause. Although the last clause can allow 2–714(2)'s difference in value formula based on subjective value in the appropriate ("special") circumstances, the formula is calculated based on an objective standard of value in "ordinary" circumstances.

In many cases, the cost of repair measures the difference in value between the goods as warranted and the value of the goods as accepted. The cost of repair is verifiable and puts the injured buyer in the position that it would be in had it received conforming goods. However, in some cases repair cost cannot measure the difference in value. Repair cost cannot be measure this difference when the good cannot be repaired or repair cannot entirely make the goods conform to the contract. In addition, where repair costs exceed the value of the goods as warranted, repair is possible but inefficient. In both cases 2–714(2)'s difference in value is measured in some other way. The contract price is a verifiable measure of the fair market value of the goods as warranted, as is the fair market value of the nonconforming goods at the time of acceptance. Neither 2–714(2) nor 2–714's Comments describe the "special circumstances" appropriate to calculate the difference in value differently than 2–714(2) requires. Nonetheless, 2–714(2)'s "special circumstances" clause is broad enough to allow a buyer with subjective values that differ from fair market value to prove that it values the goods as warranted above fair market value or values nonconforming goods below it.

Mayberry v. Volkswagen of America, Inc.

Supreme Court of Wisconsin, 2005
692 N.W.2d 226

■ WILCOX, J.

* * *

I. ISSUE

The issue on appeal concerns the proper measure of damages under Wisconsin's Uniform Commercial Code in a breach of warranty action. We must determine what constitutes the appropriate measure of damages where the buyer alleges that the product was defective and not worth what she paid for it at the time of acceptance but nonetheless used the product for a significant period of time and later resold the product for more than its fair market value after the manufacturer made several attempts at repairing the product. Specifically, the issue before us is whether the "special circumstances" clause in Wis. Stat. § 402.714(2) requires damages in a breach of warranty action to be calculated based on the difference between the fair market value of the defective product at resale and the price the consumer actually obtained, such that a consumer's claim may be barred if she receives more than the fair market value for the defective product upon resale. This is an issue of first impression in Wisconsin.

We reject Volkswagen's claim that the "special circumstances" language in § 402.714(2) prevents the plaintiff from maintaining her action by calculating damages based on the difference in market value and actual price at the time of resale. We hold that pursuant to § 402.714(2), the appropriate method for measuring damages in this case is the difference between the warranted value of the vehicle in question and its actual value at the time and place of acceptance. When the plaintiff has established a prima facie case of damages under this standard, the "special circumstances" clause of § 402.714(2) should not be construed so as to completely bar her breach of warranty claim simply because she used the defective product for a period of time and later resold it for more than its fair market value. We have found no authority that stands for the proposition that the proper measure of damages under the Uniform Commercial Code in such circumstances is the difference between the market value and actual price obtained for the defective product at the time and place of resale. However, the price of the defective product upon resale may be relevant insomuch as it constitutes circumstantial evidence of the actual value of the product in its defective condition at the time and place of acceptance.

Because the circuit court applied an incorrect standard for measuring damages, we affirm the decision of the court of appeals reversing the circuit court's order of summary judgment.

II. FACTUAL BACKGROUND

On October 14, 2000, the plaintiff, Jessica Mayberry, purchased a new 2001 galactic blue Volkswagen Jetta GLS from Van Dyn Hoven Imports in Appleton, Wisconsin. The cash price of the vehicle was $17,800. After sales tax, registration, title, and other fees, the price of the vehicle came to $18,526. However, according to Mayberry, the total purchase price of the vehicle came to $22,548 after adding finance charges. As part of the vehicle purchase, the manufacturer, Volkswagen, issued a two-year or 24,000 mile limited warranty for the Jetta. Under the terms of the written warranty, Volkswagen agreed to repair any manufacturer's defect in material or workmanship and replace defective parts free of charge for the warranty period. However, the warranty did not give Mayberry the right to a refund or replacement of the vehicle if it was defective.

Shortly after taking possession of the Jetta, Mayberry began experiencing problems with the vehicle. Service records from Van Dyn Hoven indicate that Mayberry brought the vehicle in for service on a number of occasions for various problems. The problems consisted of a broken armrest, intermittent illumination of the "check engine" light, and burning and leaking oil. The engine problems culminated in the replacement of a piston ring in the engine on November 29, 2001. On all occasions, the vehicle was inspected or repaired free of charge under the warranty. Thereafter, Mayberry attempted to revoke acceptance of the vehicle in writing. Volkswagen refused the revocation.

On June 3, 2002, Mayberry filed suit against Volkswagen under the federal Magnuson–Moss Warranty Act, 15 U.S.C. § 2301 et seq. (2000), asserting three causes of action. First, Mayberry alleged that Volkswagen breached its written warranty for the vehicle. Second, Mayberry contended that Volkswagen breached its implied warranty of merchantability under 15 U.S.C. §§ 2301(7) & 2308. Finally, Mayberry claimed that she revoked her acceptance under 15 U.S.C. § 2310.

Subsequently, Mayberry traded in her Volkswagen for a 2003 Mazda Tribute at Mazda Knoxville. Mayberry received $15,100 as a trade-in allowance for the Jetta. The total purchase price of the Mazda Tribute was $24,149.32. At the time of the trade-in, the mileage on the Jetta was 32,737. On November 8, 2002, Mayberry amended her complaint to reflect the trade-in of the Jetta. As an affirmative defense to the amended complaint, Volkswagen alleged that Mayberry "suffered no damages as she received more than the full fair market value for the vehicle which is the subject of the action at the time of the trade in."

III. PROCEDURAL POSTURE

On February 18, 2003, Volkswagen moved for summary judgment on the ground that Mayberry did not suffer any damages as a result of the allegations set forth in her complaint. Specifically, Volkswagen argued that Mayberry was "unable to prove that she suffered any compensable damages" because "Mayberry traded in the vehicle for more than fair market value." In addition, Volkswagen argued that Mayberry's extended use of the vehicle and subsequent trade-in for more than fair market value invalidated her revocation of acceptance claim because she could not demonstrate that the value of the Jetta was substantially impaired.

* * *

[O]n May 28, 2003, the circuit court entered judgment in favor of Volkswagen, dismissing Mayberry's complaint in its entirety.

The court of appeals reversed, concluding that the circuit court utilized an incorrect standard for measuring damages and that genuine issues of material fact concerning damages existed. The court of appeals concluded that under § 402.714(2), the proper measure of damages for breach of warranty is the difference between the value of goods as accepted and the value as warranted at the time and place of acceptance. The court stated that the evidence demonstrated that the warranted value of the vehicle was $18,000 and that Mayberry's own testimony as to the actual value of the car was sufficient to survive summary judgment. The court of appeals also noted that Volkswagen might be entitled to an offset for the mileage Mayberry put on the vehicle under the "special circumstances" clause of Wis. Stat. § 402.714(2). Therefore, the court of appeals reversed the circuit court order for summary judgment because the circuit court failed to apply the correct measure of damages in Wis. Stat. § 402.714(2) and a genuine issue of material fact existed regarding damages insomuch as Mayberry had provided testimony as to the actual value of the vehicle and Volkswagen had "offered evidence suggesting 'proximate damages of a different amount.'"

* * *

V. ANALYSIS

* * *

We begin by noting that we are not presented with any issue concerning whether Volkswagen actually breached any of its warranties in this case. Rather, the appeal concerns only the issue of what measure of damages is appropriate in this case. Thus, for purposes of this appeal, we will assume that Mayberry's allegations regarding Volkswagen's breach of warranties are true.

* * *

Volkswagen argues that while § 402.714(2) provides that the usual means for calculating damages for breach of warranty is the difference in value at the time and place of acceptance between the product as warranted and the product as received, the statute specifically allows for an alternate damage calculation when special circumstances show proximate damages in a different amount. Volkswagen contends that special circumstances are present here because under the standard calculation, Mayberry would reap a windfall, as Volkswagen repaired the vehicle free of charge under the warranty, Mayberry was able to use the vehicle for a substantial period of time, and Mayberry later resold the vehicle for more than its fair market value. Volkswagen points to a series of cases that allow damages to be calculated at the time and place of replacement and asserts that we should follow the Illinois Court of Appeals' decision in Valenti, which held that a consumer cannot prove damages when she resells the vehicle for more than its fair market value. Volkswagen contends that because Mayberry received more than fair market value for the Jetta on resale, she has no damages and thus has no case.

In contrast, Mayberry argues that we should follow the default rule for calculating damages as contained in § 402.714(2). * * * Mayberry notes that she presented a prima facie case of damages by presenting evidence of the value of the vehicle as warranted (its purchase price) and testified as to the actual value of the vehicle at the time and place of acceptance. Thus, the crux of the dispute before us is the interpretation of the "special circumstances" language contained in § 402.714(2) and what effect, if any, a purchaser's use and subsequent resale of an allegedly defective vehicle has on her ability to recover damages.

* * *

[W]e have found no authority that stands for the proposition that the proper measure of damages under the Uniform Commercial Code is the difference between the market value and actual price of the defective product at the time and place of resale when the plaintiff alleges a breach of the manufacturer's written warranty and implied warranty of merchantability. Breach of contract remedies under the Uniform Commercial Code are designed to put the aggrieved party "in as good a position as if the other party had fully performed." Wis. Stat. § 401.106(1). Section 2–714 of the Uniform Commercial Code is designed to compensate " 'damage flowing directly from insufficient product quality.' " *Beyond the Garden Gate,* 526 N.W.2d at 309 (quoting James J. White & Robert S. Summers, Uniform Commercial Code § 11– 5, at 536 (3d ed. 1988)).

Mayberry has alleged that she suffered damages because her vehicle was defective when she accepted it and she did not receive a vehicle of the quality for which she paid. The fact that Mayberry later resold the vehicle for more than its fair market value does not totally negate the fact that she did not receive the benefit of her bargain. While the amount of profit realized on the resale may be relevant to the issue of mitigation, construing the "special circumstances" clause of § 402.714(2) to completely bar the plaintiff from maintaining a claim would defeat the manifest purpose of the remedies under the Uniform Commercial Code, which are to compensate the plaintiff for her direct economic loss and place her in as good a position as if the seller had fully performed.

Therefore, we hold that pursuant to Wis. Stat. § 402.714(2), the appropriate method for measuring damages in this case is the difference between the warranted value of the vehicle in question and its actual value at the time and place of acceptance. Further, we conclude that Mayberry has established a prima facie case of damages sufficient to survive summary judgment under this standard.

The standard measure of damages under § 402.714(2) requires evidence of two values: (1) the value of the product as warranted at the time and place of acceptance and (2) the actual value of the vehicle with defects at the time and place of acceptance. As to the first value, courts generally hold that the contract price is relevant but not conclusive evidence of the value of the goods as warranted at the time and place of acceptance.

The record in the present case contains a copy of the sales contract for the Jetta that indicates the cash price of the vehicle was $17,800 and that after taxes and fees the price came to $18,526. In addition, Mayberry alleged in her complaint that after finance charges, the total cost of the Jetta was $22,548. The parties dispute which figure— $17,800, $18,526, or $22,548—correctly represents the value of the Jetta as warranted. This issue is not directly before us and therefore we do not directly address it. Because the record contains evidence of the purchase price of the vehicle, Mayberry has presented sufficient evidence of the value of the vehicle as warranted at the time and place of acceptance.

As to the second value—the actual value of the vehicle with defects at the time and place of acceptance—Mayberry submitted an affidavit stating that she believed the value of the Jetta with all of its defects was only $12,526. Volkswagen challenges whether this constitutes sufficient evidence of the actual value of the vehicle to survive summary judgment.

* * *

While Mayberry's opinion as to the value of her vehicle may be sufficient for her to survive summary judgment, it does not necessarily follow that it will be persuasive to a jury. Although we have held that the fact that Mayberry traded in her vehicle for more than fair market value does not bar her claim, the price she obtained for the Jetta at resale may be probative as to the value of the vehicle with defects at the time and place of acceptance. A reasonable jury could conclude that her testimony that the vehicle was worth only $12,526 at the time of acceptance is inherently incredible, given that the vehicle was sold two years and 30,000 miles later for $15,100.

* * *

We hold that pursuant to Wis. Stat. § 402.714(2), the appropriate method for measuring damages in this case is the difference between the warranted value of the vehicle in question and its actual value at the time and place of acceptance. When the plaintiff has established a prima facie case of damages under this standard, the "special circumstances" clause of § 402.714(2) should not be construed so as to completely bar her breach of warranty claim simply because she used the defective product for a period of time and later resold it for more than its fair market value.

* * *

Because the circuit court applied an incorrect standard for measuring damages, we affirm the decision of the court of appeals reversing the circuit court's order of summary judgment.

■ WILCOX, J. (concurring)

I write separately because while I agree that the "special circumstances" clause of Wis. Stat. § 402.714(2) may not be used to bar Mayberry's claim by calculating damages based on the difference between the market value and actual price of her vehicle at resale, the "special circumstances" clause of § 402.714(2) is still relevant to this case.

Despite Volkswagen's attempt to sustain the circuit court's order for summary judgment, what the parties are really arguing over is the amount of Mayberry's damages. Volkswagen is concerned that the standard method for calculating damages under § 402.714(2) will allow Mayberry to reap a windfall because her actual damages are less than the difference between the warranted value of the Jetta and actual value of the Jetta at the time and place of acceptance. Volkswagen argues that the standard measure for calculating damages cannot be an inflexible rule because Mayberry has mitigated her damages and thus has actual damages of a different amount. Volkswagen's concerns do not fall on deaf ears.

While I wholeheartedly agree with the majority that the "special circumstances" clause of § 402.714(2) should not be construed to completely bar a plaintiff from maintaining a claim, I would further hold, in accordance with the numerous authorities that have addressed the issue, that the "special circumstances" clause of § 402.714(2) may be utilized to adjust a plaintiff's damages—as calculated under the difference in value at acceptance standard—to reflect any damages mitigated by the plaintiff. In other words, I would hold that while the difference between the warranted value and actual value at the time and place of acceptance is the "starting point" for calculating damages, this figure may be adjusted upwards or downwards in appropriate circumstances to reflect the actual amount of plaintiff's damages under the "special circumstances" clause of § 402.714(2).

* * *

One recognized category of cases in which the plaintiff's damages may be adjusted downward from the standard difference in value formulation is *"where the buyer has mitigated damages to less than those provided by the value differential formula."* Roy Anderson, 1 Damages Under UCC § 10:10, at 10–47 (2003) (emphasis added). Thus:

Circumstances may exist in which the buyer is fully indemnified although the buyer does not obtain the full recovery authorized by UCC § 2–714. In such case, the buyer will not be allowed to recover the damages authorized by the Code but only so much as is required to indemnify the buyer for his or her actual loss.

Ronald A. Anderson, 4A Anderson on the Uniform Commercial Code § 2–714:219, at 487 (3d ed. rev. vol. 4A 1997).

This application of "special circumstances" is consistent with the purpose underlying the remedies in the Uniform Commercial Code, which is to place the aggrieved party "in as good a position as if the other party had fully performed." Wis. Stat. § 401.106(1). As noted by the majority, . . . the remedies under the Uniform Commercial Code for breach of warranty are designed to compensate an injured party for her "direct economic loss." In other words, under the Uniform Commercial Code " 'an injured party should be fully compensated for losses suffered through the fault of another, but . . . he should not be allowed a windfall.' " James J. White & Robert S. Summers, 1 Uniform Commercial Code § 10–2, at 555–56 (4th ed. 1995) (quoting Cmty. Television Servs., Inc. v. Dresser Indus., Inc., 435 F. Supp. 214, 217 (D.S.D. 1977)). The plaintiff is entitled to be compensated for her actual damages, no more, no less. As such, § 1–106 [§ 1–305(a)] of the Uniform Commercial Code "requires mitigation of damages." Cates v. Morgan Portable Bldg. Corp., 780 F.2d 683, 688 (7th Cir. 1985).

* * *

Here, in an attempt to mitigate her damages, Mayberry resold the vehicle to another dealer for $15,100. However, Mayberry conceded that the fair market value of the vehicle at the time of trade-in was $14,200. Thus, assuming Mayberry is successful in convincing a jury that Volkswagen breached its warranties and that she suffered damages, Mayberry's damages should be reduced to reflect the net profit she obtained as a result of the resale of the vehicle. If this amount were not deducted from Mayberry's damages, the duty to mitigate would be meaningless. While Mayberry is entitled to the difference between the warranted value of the vehicle and its actual value at the time and place of acceptance, she mitigated these damages by selling the vehicle for a profit. If she were entitled to keep both the profit from the resale and the total benefit of the bargain damages, she would be placed in a better position than had the Jetta not been defective.

* * *

As such, I would hold that pursuant to § 402.714(2), the starting point for calculating damages in this case is the difference in value at the time and place of acceptance, but that figure may be adjusted downward to take into account any damages that Mayberry mitigated under the "special circumstances" clause.

NOTES AND QUESTIONS

1. The seller in *Mayberry* argued that the buyer's continued use and later resale of the car for more than its fair market value constituted "special circumstances" that made 2–714(2)'s difference in value formula inapplicable. The court refused to find that 2–714(2)'s "special circumstances" clause barred the buyer from measuring her damages by 2–714(2)'s formula. It reasoned that the buyer was seeking to recover damages for the car's diminished value to her at the time she accepted it. What she did with the car after that time is irrelevant to the measurement of warranty damages under 2–714(2). Would 2–714(1) allow the buyer to recover the same amount in damages as 2–714(2)? Section 2–714(1) measures the buyer's damages as the loss resulting "in the ordinary course of events" from the nonconforming tender. The seller's breach of warranty was a nonconforming tender, and the diminished value of the car to the buyer on her acceptance was a loss in the ordinary course resulting from the breach.

2. The damage measures under 2–714(1) and (2) occasionally can give different recoveries. Suppose the seller's breach of warranty results in foreseeable consequential damages to the buyer. Assume also that the contract contains a valid damage exclusion clause that bars the recovery of consequential damages. The clause prevents recovery of consequential damages under 2–714(3). As a result, these damages cannot supplement damages recoverable under 2–714(2)'s difference in value formula. Nonetheless, because the damages are a foreseeable result of breach, they are arguably "ordinary loss" under 2–714(1). Thus, the buyer's recovery under 2–714(1) can include consequential damages notwithstanding the damage exclusion clause. The court in Hill v. BASF Wyandotte Corp., 311 S.E.2d 734 (S.C. 1984), accepted this argument and allowed the buyer to recover its lost profits from breach even though the agreement's damage exclusion clause excluded their recovery. In doing so the court characterized the buyer's lost profits as "direct damages." The court in Wright Schuchart, Inc. v. Cooper Industries, 1994 U.S. App. 31520 (9th Cir.) refused to allow the buyer to recover its lost profits under 2–714(2) when the agreement contained a valid damage exclusion clause that excluded consequential damages. It found lost profits to be consequential damages, not direct damages. Given the finding, the court likely would not have allowed their recovery under 2–714(1) either. Which characterization of lost profits respects the parties' allocation of risk of loss from the seller's breach?

3. The buyer in *Mayberry* made a profit by reselling the car for an amount above its fair market value. According to the majority, profit from resale is not a "special circumstance" that bars the buyer from measuring its damages by 2–714(2)'s difference in value formula. It nevertheless allows that these damages may be reduced by the buyer's profit on resale. The concurrence holds that the buyer's profit from resale constitute a "special circumstance," to be deducted from damages calculated under 2–714(2) by the difference in value. Thus, according to both the majority and the concurrence, profit from resale mitigates the buyer's damages. Is this correct? The buyer's "duty" of mitigation, applicable under general contract law principles, requires it to take reasonable measures to reduce its damages. Both the majority and concurrence conclude that reselling the car at a profit is a reasonable measure that reduces the buyer's damages recoverable under 2–714(2). Does the duty of mitigation deprive the buyer of profits from the seller's breach, such as profits from resale of nonconforming goods that the buyer has accepted? Would the buyer be found to have failed to mitigate its damages if it decided not to resell the car even when it could do so at a profit? To answer both questions, compare the situation of the injured seller who resells goods its buyer has wrongly rejected. Under 2–706(6) the seller is not accountable to the buyer for any profit it realized on the resale. The subsection effectively considers the seller to own the goods. As an owner the seller is entitled to the profits from resale. Accordingly, 2–706(6) does not impose a duty of mitigation on the seller with respect to these profits. It may resell the goods for its own account or not resell them at all and recover damages under 2–708(1). An injured buyer who resells goods it has accepted is in the same position as the injured seller.

PROBLEM 10.17

Supply's agreement with Zeit, a contemporary watch store, called for it to sell and deliver to Zeit by December 1, High Glow lighting fixtures for $10,000. Zeit selected the fixtures to install in its carefully planned showroom. Increased demand for High Glow lighting depleted Supply's inventory, and it was unable to get more in time to fill Zeit's order. However, the superior but more expensive Ultra Light lighting fixtures, at $15,000, were not nearly in as much in demand, and Supply had plenty in stock. Wanting to fill Zeit's order by December 1, Supply delivered the Ultra Light lighting at the price of the High Glow lighting. Business was booming and Zeit was so busy that it discovered only much later, when it opened the packaging, that Supply filled its order with the Ultra Light lighting. Even with the $10,000 invoice price, Zeit was not pleased and immediately let Supply know. Zeit claims (truthfully) that the Ultra Light lighting is of no use to it in its showroom. It wants to cancel the contact and return the fixtures to Supply. Alternatively, Zeit wants to recover damages from Supply. What result? What result if Zeit had told Supply that its showroom was designed to suit only High Glow lighting fixtures? See 2–606(1)(b), 2–607(1), 2–714(1), (2).

PROBLEM 10.18

Anxious to secure a computerized sign for its new venture, Buyer made the rounds of potential sellers. In doing so it explained that it needed an entirely scratch-free sign in time for the launch party for its venture. Buyer eventually accepted Seller's proposal to supply it with the sign for $500 more than the $2,000 going rate. Buyer's launch party came and went without a sign. With apologies, Seller delivered the sign the day after the party. Although Buyer noticed that the sign had a few scratches, it immediately put the sign to use in its showroom. At the same time it notified Seller by email to the effect that "the late delivery and the scratches both are unacceptable; holding you responsible." The prevailing price for a sign of the sort and condition Buyer received sells for $1,500. What damages, if any, can Buyer recover? See 2–714(1), (2), 2–606(1)(b), 2–607(3)(a).

4. BUYER'S REMEDIES UNDER THE CISG

a. DAMAGES

The injured buyer may recover damages according to the CISG's damage measures, described above. If the buyer avoids the contract and makes a reasonable substitute purchase, Article 75 measures its damages as the difference between the price of the substitute purchase and the contract price. Article 75 is the counterpart of the 2–712(2)'s cover measure of damages. If the buyer avoids the contract and does not make a reasonable substitute purchase, Article 76 measures its damages as the difference between the current price at the time of avoidance and the contract price. This measure corresponds to 2–713(1)'s market price measure of damages. In addition, in either case the buyer may recover its incidental expenses and consequential damages under Article 74. Because the price of a substitute purchase may differ from the current price of the goods at the time of avoidance, Articles 75 and 76's measures can give different recoveries.

Under Article 76, the current price of the goods is its price as of the time of avoidance if avoidance occurs before the injured buyer takes over the goods. However, if the buyer avoids the contract after taking over the goods, current price is at the time they are taken over. Article 76 does not define "taking over" the goods. Arguably the phrase does not mean "delivery." The CISG refers to "delivery" in other Articles (e.g., Articles 30, 31 and 33), so that the different terms likely refer to different events. The buyer "takes over" the goods when it gets actual possession of them. "Delivery" occurs when the goods are put at the buyer's disposal at a particular location; see, e.g., Article 31(c). Although goods may be delivered by putting them into the buyer's possession, sometimes they may be delivered even before the buyer receives them. For instance, Article 31(a) provides that, if the sales contract involves carriage of the goods and the seller is not obligated to deliver them to a particular place, the seller delivers the good when it hands them over to the first carrier for transmission to the buyer. In this case the seller has delivered the goods even before the buyer "takes over" them.

This turn of phrase matters. Construing "taking over" as getting actual possession fixes the market ("current") price at the time the buyer is in a position to detect a nonconformity in the goods that justifies avoidance of the contract. By contrast, fixing market price under Article 76 at the time of delivery forces the buyer to make a decision to avoid the contract even before it can examine the goods. For example, assume that a sales contract with a contract price of $50 calls for carriage and does not specify a particular place at which the seller is to deliver the goods. The market price of the goods increases to $55 at the time the seller hands over nonconforming goods to the first carrier for transmission to the buyer. When the buyer eventually receives the goods, the market price has increased further to $60. The buyer immediately examines them, discovers that the nonconformity constitutes a fundamental breach and avoids the contract. Because the buyer avoided the contract after taking over the goods, Article 76 fixes the current price of the goods as of the time the buyer took over them. According to Article 31(a), the seller delivered the goods to the buyer when it handed them over to the first carrier. Thus, if the buyer took over the goods on their delivery, Article 76 calculates the buyer's damages at $5 ($55 − $50 = $5). However, if the buyer took over the goods when it received them, the Article calculates its damages at $10 ($60 − $50 = $10). In most cases the buyer cannot detect nonconformities in the goods before it receives them. It is in a position to make a timely and informed decision with respect to avoidance only on receiving the goods. By comparison, 2–713(1) sets the market price as of the time the buyer learned of the breach. Buyers usually cannot learn of the breach before they get the goods. Case law under the CISG has not construed the meaning of "taking over" of the goods for purposes of Article 76's damages formula.

Both Article 75 and 76's measures apply only when the buyer avoids the contract. If the buyer retains nonconforming goods and does not or cannot avoid the contract, it must measure its damages under Article 74's general rule. As noted above, Article 74's rule does not state how damages are to be calculated. Article 74 measures damages when the seller breaches a warranty with respect to the goods and the buyer does not avoid the contract. Although Article 74's general rule is consistent with 2–714(2)'s difference in value formula measuring damages for breach of warranty, it does not compel use of that formula. Unsurprisingly, diplomatic history and some scholarly commentary recommends that warranty damages under Article 74 be measured as the difference between the price of conforming goods and the price of the nonconforming goods. See Secretariat Commentary on the [1978] Draft Convention on Contracts for the International Sale of Goods, in Documentary History of the Uniform Law for International Sales 449 (para. 7, Ex. 70D) (J. Honnold ed., 1989); Ingeborg Schwenzer, Article 74, in Schlechtriem & Schwenzer: Commentary on the UN Convention on the International Sale of Goods (CISG) 999, 1006 (I. Schwenzer ed., 3d ed. 2010). Courts have measured damages from breach of warranty by the cost of repair. See Court of Appeals Koln (Germany), 8 January 1997, available at http://cisgw3.law.pace.edu/cases/970108g1.html.

b. SPECIFIC PERFORMANCE

The CISG gives the injured buyer a broad right to specific performance. Under Article 46(1) the buyer may require the seller to perform its obligations under the contract. The only limitation is that the buyer must not have resorted to a remedy inconsistent with specific performance. Avoidance of the contract, for instance, is a remedy inconsistent with the demand that the seller perform. Article 46(2) allows the buyer to require the seller to deliver substitute goods if the seller has delivered nonconforming goods that fundamentally breach the contract. Under Article 46(3) the buyer may require the seller to repair a nonconformity in the goods if repair is reasonable in the circumstances. Importantly, specific performance is available under Article 46 even if the buyer could obtain substitute goods from another seller or otherwise reduce its loss from breach. This is because the Article does not require the buyer to mitigate its loss. Article 77 entitles the breaching party to "claim a reduction in the damages" for which it is liable if the injured party does not take reasonable measures to mitigate its loss from breach. The remedy of specific performance is not "damages." Thus, the buyer can obtain specific performance from its seller even if it could mitigate its loss by purchasing substitute goods elsewhere without inconvenience. Specific performance often is an expensive remedy for buyers to pursue. Litigation to enforce performance can be costly and protracted. There also is delay between the initiation of suit and enforcement, during which the buyer is without the goods. For both reasons, buyers seldom ask for specific performance even in legal systems that make the remedy routinely available. See Henrik Lando & Caspar Rose, On the Enforcement of Specific Performance in Civil Law Countries, 24 Int'l Rev. L. & Econ. 473 (2004); The Myth of Specific Performance in Civil Law Countries (November 21, 2003), available at http://papers.ssrn.com/sol3/papers.cfm?abstract_id=462700. Nonetheless, Article 46 makes specific relief generally available to the injured buyer. There are very few reported cases under the CISG in which specific performance is at issue.

Article 46's broad right to specific performance reflects the routine availability of the remedy in many civil law systems. Civil law systems differ in the extent to which they give a right to specific performance. See Gerard De Vries, Right to Specific Performance: Is There a Divergence Between Civil– and Common–Law Systems and, If So, How Has it Been Bridged in the DCFR?, 17 Eur. Rev. Priv. L. 581 (2009); Specific Performance in Contract Law: National and Other Perspectives (J. Smits, D. Haas & G. Hesen eds., 2008). Nonetheless, in most civil law systems the remedy remains more widely available than in common law systems. For example, 2-716(1) considers specific performance to be an exceptional remedy. It is available only when the goods are unique or "in other proper circumstances." By contrast, in most civil law and mixed systems the buyer can require the seller to deliver goods it has available even if the buyer easily could replace them with a substitute purchase. See De Vries, at 589–590; Ronald J. Scalise Jr., Why No Efficient Breach in the Civil Law: A Comparative Assessment of the Doctrine of Efficient Breach of Contract, 55 Am. J. Comp. L. 721 (2007); La. Civ. Code Ann. Article 1986; Quebec Civ. Code Article 1590.

As a compromise between civil law systems that routinely allow specific performance and common law systems that restrict the remedy, Article 28 limits the availability of specific performance under the CISG. Article 28 provides in relevant part that "a court is not bound to enter a judgment for specific performance unless the court would do so under its own law in respect of similar contracts of sale not governed by this Convention." Accordingly, to determine whether it must order specific performance at the buyer's request, the court must ask two questions. First, is the buyer entitled to specific performance under Article 46 of the CISG? Second, if the buyer is entitled to the remedy under Article 46, would the forum court order it for like contracts ("similar contracts") otherwise governed by the substantive domestic law of the forum ("its own law")? If both questions have affirmative answers, the forum court must order the seller to perform its obligations under the contract. Otherwise, Article 28 permits the court to refuse to order the seller to perform. Although the court nonetheless may decide in its discretion to order performance, the Article does not require the court to do so. For further discussion of Article 28's application, see Clayton P. Gillette & Steven D. Walt, The UN Convention on Contracts for the International Sale of Goods: Practice and Theory 9–26–9–31 (2013).

Magellan International Corp. v. Salzgitter Handel GmbH

United States District Court, Northern District of Illinois, 1999
76 F. Supp.2d 919

■ SHADUR, DISTRICT JUDGE

MEMORANDUM OPINION AND ORDER

Salzgitter Handel GmbH ("Salzgitter") has filed a motion pursuant to Fed.R.Civ.P. ("Rule") 12(b)(6) ("Motion"), seeking to dismiss this action brought against it by Magellan International Corporation ("Magellan"). Because the allegations in Complaint Counts I and II state claims that are sufficient under Rule 8(a), Salzgitter's Motion must be and is denied as to those claims. Count III, however, is deficient and is therefore dismissed without prejudice.

Facts

* * *

Magellan is an Illinois-based distributor of steel products. Salzgitter is a steel trader that is headquartered in Dusseldorf, Germany and maintains an Illinois sales office. In January 1999 Magellan's Robert Arthur ("Arthur") and Salzgitter's Thomas Riess ("Riess") commenced negotiations on a potential deal under which Salzgitter would begin to act as middleman in Magellan's purchase of steel bars—manufactured according to Magellan's specifications—from a Ukrainian steel mill, Dneprospetsstal of Ukraine ("DSS").

By letter dated January 28, Magellan provided Salzgitter with written specifications for 5,585 metric tons of steel bars, with proposed pricing, and with an agreement to issue a letter of credit ("LC") to Salzgitter as Magellan's method of payment. Salzgitter responded two weeks later (on February 12 and 13) by proposing prices $5 to $20 per ton higher than those Magellan had specified.

* * *

On February 15 Magellan accepted Salzgitter's price increases, agreed on 4,000 tons as the quantity being purchased, and added $5 per ton over Salzgitter's numbers to effect shipping from Magellan's preferred port (Ventspills, Latvia). Magellan memorialized those terms, as well as the other material terms previously discussed by the parties, in two February 15 purchase orders. Salzgitter then responded on February 17, apparently accepting Magellan's memorialized terms except for two "amendments" as to prices. Riess asked for Magellan's "acceptance" of those two price increases by return fax and promised to send its already-drawn-up order confirmations as soon as they were countersigned by DSS. Arthur consented, signing and returning the approved price amendments to Riess the same day.

On February 19 Salzgitter sent its pro forma order confirmations to Magellan. But the general terms and conditions that were attached to those confirmations differed in some respects from those that had been attached to Magellan's purchase orders, mainly with respect to vessel loading conditions, dispute resolution and choice of law.

Contemplating an ongoing business relationship, Magellan and Salzgitter continued to negotiate in an effort to resolve the remaining conflicts between their respective forms. While those fine-tuning negotiations were under way, Salzgitter began to press Magellan to open its LC for the transaction in Salzgitter's favor. On March 4 Magellan sent Salzgitter a draft LC for review. Salzgitter wrote back on March 8 proposing minor amendments to the LC and stating that "all other terms are acceptable." Although Magellan preferred to wait until all of the minor details (the remaining conflicting terms) were ironed out before issuing the LC, Salzgitter continued to press for its immediate issuance.

On March 22 Salzgitter sent amended order confirmations to Magellan. Riess visited Arthur four days later on March 26 and threatened to cancel the steel orders if Magellan did not open the LC in Salzgitter's favor that day. They then came to agreement as to the remaining contractual issues. Accordingly, relying on Riess's assurances that all remaining details of the deal were settled, Arthur had the $1.2 million LC issued later that same day.

Three days later (on March 29) Arthur and Riess engaged in an extended game of "fax tag" initiated by the latter. Essentially Salzgitter demanded that the LC be amended to permit the unconditional substitution of FCRs for bills of lading—even for partial orders—and Magellan refused to amend the LC, also pointing out the need to conform Salzgitter's March 22 amended order confirmations to the terms of the parties' ultimate March 26 agreement. At the same time, Magellan requested minor modifications in some of the steel specifications. Salzgitter replied that it was too late to modify the specifications: DSS had already manufactured 60% of the order, and the rest was under production.

Perhaps unsurprisingly in light of what has been recited up to now, on the very next day (March 30) Magellan's and Salzgitter's friendly fine-tuning went flat. Salzgitter screeched an ultimatum to Magellan: Amend the LC by noon the following day or Salzgitter would "no longer feel obligated" to perform and would "sell the material elsewhere." On April 1 Magellan requested that the LC be canceled because of what it considered to be Saltzgitter's breach. Salzgitter returned the LC and has since been attempting to sell the manufactured steel to Magellan's customers in the United States.

Magellan's Claims

Complaint Count I posits that—pursuant to the Convention—a valid contract existed between Magellan and Salzgitter before Salzgitter's March 30 ultimatum. Hence that attempted ukase is said to have amounted to an anticipatory repudiation of that contract, entitling Magellan to relief for its breach.

Count II seeks specific performance of the contract or replevin of the manufactured steel. That relief is invoked under the Illinois version of the Uniform Commercial Code ("UCC," specifically 810 ILCS 5/2–716) because Magellan is "unable to 'cover' its delivery commitments to its customers without unreasonable delay."

     * * *

Count I: Breach of Contract

* * * Because the transaction involves the sale and purchase of steel—"goods"—the parties acknowledge that the governing law is either the Convention or the UCC. Under the facts alleged by Magellan, the parties agreed that Convention law would apply to the transaction, and Salzgitter does not now dispute that contention. That being the case, this opinion look to Convention law.

Pleading Requirements

* * * [T]he specification of the pleading requirements to state a claim for breach of contract under the Convention truly poses a question of first impression. Despite that clean slate, even a brief glance at the Convention's structure confirms what common sense (and the common law) dictate as the universal elements of any such action: formation, performance, breach and damages. Hence under the Convention, as under Illinois law (or the common law generally), the components essential to a cause of action for breach of contract are (1) the existence of a valid and enforceable contract containing both definite and certain terms, (2) performance by plaintiff, (3) breach by defendant and (4) resultant injury to plaintiff. In those terms it is equally clear that Magellan's allegations provide adequate notice to Salzgitter that such an action is being asserted.

* * * [T]he requisite contractual joinder could reasonably be viewed by a factfinder as having jelled on March 26. In that respect Convention Art. 18(a) requires an indication of assent to an offer (or counteroffer) to constitute its acceptance. Such an "indication" may occur through "a statement made by or other conduct of the offeree." And at the very least, a jury could find consistently with Magellan's allegations that the required indication of complete (mirrored) assent occurred when Magellan issued its LC on March 26. So much, then, for the first element of a contract: offer and acceptance.

Next, the second pleading requirement for a breach of contract claim—performance by plaintiff—was not only specifically addressed by Magellan but can also be inferred from the facts alleged in Complaint P43 and from Magellan's prayer for specific performance. Magellan's performance obligation as the buyer is simple: payment of the price for the goods. Magellan issued its LC in satisfaction of that obligation, later requesting the LC's cancellation only after Salzgitter's alleged breach. Moreover, Magellan's request for specific performance implicitly confirms that it remains ready and willing to pay the price if such relief were granted.

As for the third pleading element—Salzgitter's breach—Complaint P38 alleges:

> Salzgitter's March 30 letter (Exhibit G) demanding that the bill of lading provision be removed from the letter of credit and threatening to cancel the contract constitutes an anticipatory repudiation and fundamental breach of the contract.

It would be difficult to imagine an allegation that more clearly fulfills the notice function of pleading.

Convention Art. 72 addresses the concept of anticipatory breach:

> (1) If prior to the date for performance of the contract it is clear that one of the parties will commit a fundamental breach of contract, the other party may declare the contract avoided.

> (2) If time allows, the party intending to declare the contract avoided must give reasonable notice to the other party in order to permit him to provide adequate assurance of his performance.

> (3) The requirements of the preceding paragraph do not apply if the other party has declared that he will not perform his obligations.

And Convention Art. 25 states in relevant part:

> A breach of contract committed by one of the parties is fundamental if it results in such detriment to the other party as substantially to deprive him of what he is entitled to expect under the contract. . . .

That plain language reveals that under the Convention an anticipatory repudiation pleader need simply allege (1) that the defendant intended to breach the contract before the contract's performance date and (2) that such breach was fundamental. Here Magellan has pleaded that Salzgitter's March 29 letter indicated its pre-performance intention not to perform the contract, coupled with Magellan's allegation that the bill of lading requirement was an essential part of the parties' bargain. That being the case, Salzgitter's insistence upon an amendment of that requirement would indeed be a fundamental breach.

Lastly, Magellan has easily jumped the fourth pleading hurdle—resultant injury. Complaint P40 alleges that the breach "has caused damages to Magellan."

Count II: Specific Performance or Replevin

Convention Art. 46(1) provides that a buyer may require the seller to perform its obligations unless the buyer has resorted to a remedy inconsistent with that requirement. As such, that provision would appear to make specific performance routinely available under the Convention. But Convention Art. 28 conditions the availability of specific performance:

> If, in accordance with the provisions of this Convention, one party is entitled to require performance of any obligation by the other party, a court is not bound to enter judgment for specific performance unless the court would do so under its own law in respect of similar contracts of sale not governed by this Convention.

Simply put, that looks to the availability of such relief under the UCC. And in pleading terms, any complaint adequate to provide notice under the UCC is equally sufficient under the Convention.

Under UCC § 2–716(1) a court may decree specific performance "where the goods are unique or in other proper circumstances." That provision's Official Commentary instructs that inability to cover should be considered "strong evidence" of "other proper circumstances." UCC § 2–716 was designed to liberalize the common law, which rarely allowed specific performance. Basically courts now determine whether goods are replaceable as a practical matter—for example, whether it would be difficult to obtain similar goods on the open market.

Given the centrality of the replaceability issue in determining the availability of specific relief under the UCC, a pleader need allege only the difficulty of cover to state a claim under that section. Magellan has done that (Complaint P42).

* * *

Conclusion

It may perhaps be that when the facts are further fleshed out through discovery, Magellan's claims against Salzgitter will indeed succumb either for lack of proof or as the consequence of some legal deficiency. But in the current Rule 12(b)(6) context, Salzgitter's motion as to Counts I and II is denied, and it is ordered to file its Answer to the Complaint on or before December 20, 1999. As to the Count III trade secret claim, however, Salzgitter's motion to dismiss is granted without prejudice.

NOTES

1. Does the *Magellan* court conclude that 2–716(1) would entitle the buyer to compel the seller to deliver the steel were it applicable to their contract? Or does it merely decide to allow the case to go forward?

2. By its terms, Article 28's limitation on specific performance applies only to courts. Arbitral tribunals are not courts. They are not organs of sovereign states. Because many, and perhaps most, sales contracts governed by the CISG contain arbitration clauses, only Article 46's limitation qualifies the buyer's broad right to specific performance in arbitration. The rules of arbitral institutions seldom address the remedies an arbitral award may provide. For an exception, see AAA Commercial Arb. Rule 43(a). Arbitral awards issued under the rules of major arbitral institutions have included specific relief. See Performance as a Remedy: Non–Monetary Relief in International Arbitration (M.E. Schneider & J. Kroll eds., 2011). A further question is whether courts uphold arbitral awards of specific performance. Born finds the practice routine; see Gary B. Born, International Commercial Arbitration 2480 (2009).

3. Article 28 might induce forum shopping to obtain specific performance or preempt it. To preserve the option of specific performance, the injured buyer could file suit in a jurisdiction in which the remedy is routinely available. Anticipating this, and wanting avoid the prospect of being compelled to perform, the seller might preemptively sue the injured buyer in a jurisdiction that considers specific performance an extraordinary remedy. For an argument that Article 28 is unlikely to induce forum shopping, see Steven Walt, For Specific Performance Under the United Nations Sales Convention, 21 Tex. Int'l L.J. 211, 230 (1991). To avoid the ex post litigation costs of forum shopping, the parties can include an appropriate forum selection clause in their contract. In doing so they can select a forum that makes specific performance routinely available or a forum that considers it an extraordinary remedy. Alternatively, they can contract out of specific performance under the CISG or perhaps contract for the remedy without Article 28's limitation.

The first option in the alternative clearly is possible. Article 6 allows the parties to derogate from the CISG's provisions (with exceptions irrelevant here), including its remedial provisions. The parties' contract therefore can make Article 46's right to specific performance unavailable to the buyer. However, the ability to contract for specific performance without Article 28's limitation is harder to assess and might not be possible. Article 6 seemingly allows the parties to derogate from Article 28 and therefore from its limitation on specific performance. After all, it allows the parties to vary the effect of "any of [the CISG's] provisions." On the other hand, Article 28 is addressed to courts and its limitation therefore does not depend on the parties' rights under the contract. Even if Article 28's limitation can be altered by the parties' contract, the enforceability of a contractual provision excluding the limitation might be considered a matter of "validity." Article 4 leaves issues of validity, except those "expressly provided for" by the CISG, to applicable domestic law. The CISG does not expressly deal with the validity of derogating from Article 28, and the forum's domestic law might consider a provision to contract around Article 28's limitation invalid.

4. Article 28's limitation on specific performance might be less restrictive than its language suggests. The Article requires a court to order specific performance only if it would do so under its own domestic law with respect to "similar" sales contracts not governed by the CISG. International sales contracts have two characteristic features: either the goods sold are nonstandard goods in the buyer's local market or the supply of standard goods is inelastic in that market. This is because an international purchase would be unnecessary if a price-equivalent substitute were available domestically. Customized sophisticated goods, commodities or trademarked goods are instances of goods that can be in short supply in the buyer's local market. Thus, the "similar" domestic sales contracts referred in Article 28 are contracts for the sale of goods with these features. In addition, the delay and cost of obtaining specific performance assures that buyers seek specific performance under the CISG only when the goods do not have close local substitutes. For both reasons, the relevant domestic comparison dictated by Article 28 is with sales of goods in short supply in the buyer's local market. Article 28 requires an American court to grant specific performance if, applying 2–716(1), it would do so when the sales contract involves goods that are in short supply or entirely unavailable in the buyer's local market. According to Comment 2 to 2–716, the buyer's inability to cover is a "proper circumstance" warranting specific performance under 2–716(1). *Magellan* follows other courts in allowing specific performance when cover is difficult. Article 28 therefore is likely to require American courts to order, at the buyer's request, the specific performance of contracts governed by the CISG.

c.   REDUCTION OF THE PRICE

Article 50 gives the buyer a form of monetary relief, familiar in some civil law systems, that has no counterpart in the UCC or common law. It allows the buyer to reduce the contract price in the same proportion as the value of the non-conforming goods had on the date of the delivery bears to the value that the goods would have had on the same date had they conformed to the contract. The proportionate reduction in price is the amount by which the buyer may reduce the price it owes the seller. If the buyer has already paid the seller the contract price, it can recover from the seller the amount by which the contract price may be reduced. Article 50's measure can be stated in an easy formula as follows:

> Reduced price/Contract price = Value of the non-conforming goods on delivery/Value of conforming goods on delivery

Rearranging terms,

> Reduced price = Value of non-conforming goods on delivery/Value of conforming goods on delivery × Contract price

Recall that Article 50's remedy is stated in terms of the proportion by which the contract price may be reduced. The rearranged formula just given calculates the reduced price the buyer owes the seller. The difference between the contract price and the reduced price is the amount of the reduction in price to which Article 50 entitles the buyer.

The following example illustrates Article 50's calculation of the reduction in price. Assume that the seller and buyer conclude a contract for the sale of goods with a contract price of $90. The contract calls for the buyer to pay the price after the goods have been delivered. Later, the price of the goods declines, so that at the time of delivery they sell for $60. Assume also that the seller delivers non-conforming goods that have a value of $20. The seller refuses to do anything about the non-conformity and the buyer, needing the goods, retains them rather than avoiding the contract. Under these circumstances the buyer need not pay the entire $90 contract price or rely on Article 74 to recover damages. Instead, it may rely on Article 50 to pay a reduced price. Article 50 allows the buyer to reduce the contract price by the proportion the value that the non-conforming goods on delivery has to the value that they would have had on delivery had they conformed to contract. This proportion is 1/3 in the example ($20/$60). Thus, the buyer may pay only 1/3 of the $90 contract price, or $30. This is the reduced price calculated by the last formula above ($30 = $20/$60 × $90). Article 50 therefore allows the buyer to reduce the $90 contract price by $60.

The CISG does not consider Article 50's reduction in price to be a form of damages. Article 45's list of the buyer's remedies is careful to identify the remedies in Articles 74–76 as "damages" and distinguish these damage remedies from the buyer's "rights provided in articles 46 to 52." See Article 45(1)(a), (b); "Section II. Damages" (heading following Article 73). The right to reduce is price is "provided" in Article 50. Thus, the reduction in price, although a monetary remedy, is not "damages." This terminological point has two important remedial consequences. One is that the CISG permits the buyer to reduce the price in accordance with Article 50 without mitigating its loss. As noted above, Article 77 requires the buyer to mitigate its loss only when it claims damages. Because a reduction in price is not a damages remedy, the requirement does not apply to a buyer who relies on Article 50 to measure its loss from breach. The other remedial consequence concerns the foreseeability limitation on recoverable damages. Article 74's general rule limits recoverable damages to loss that is foreseeable by the breaching party at the time of the conclusion of the contract as a possible result of breach. Because a reduction in price is not damages, the buyer's recovery is not limited by the foreseeability of the loss. As a result, the buyer can reduce the price under Article 50 without regard to whether the seller could reasonably have foreseen the loss as a consequence of its breach. Of course, the seller's breach might both diminish the value of the goods and result in consequential damages to the buyer. In that case the buyer may recover consequential damages under Article 74 in additional to reducing the price in accordance with Article 50. See Article 45(2). To recover consequential damages, they must have been foreseeable to the seller as a possible result of its breach.

European courts, which have had more experience with Article 50 than American courts, have had to decide whether Article 50's measure is available to a buyer who has received worthless goods. Article 50's language does not bar a buyer from reducing the price to zero when it receives non-conforming goods that have no value at the time of delivery. At the same time, the seller's delivery of worthless goods constitutes a fundamental breach, entitling the buyer to avoid the contract. Avoidance relieves the buyer from paying the contract price (and allows for its recovery from the seller if payment has been made). See Article 81(1). Thus, it normally does not have to rely on Article 50 to reduce the contract price to zero. However, a buyer who fails to give timely and sufficient notice of avoidance in accordance with Articles 26 and 49(2) cannot avoid the contract. It might therefore need to rely on Article 50 to avoid paying the contract price for worthless goods. In these circumstances both the Austrian Supreme and German Supreme Courts have permitted the buyer to reduce the contract price to zero. See Oberster Gerichtshof (Austria), 23 May 2005, available at http://cisgw3.law.pace.edu/cases/050523a3.html;   Bundesgerichtshof (Germany), 2 March 2005, available at http://cisgw3.law.pace.edu/cases/050302g1.html. According to the Austrian Supreme Court, even if the right to reduce the price under Article 50 were "subordinate" to the right to avoidance, "it could in no way lead to the result that a buyer of goods that are totally worthless because of a defect is worse off than a buyer of goods that are grossly defective but anyway have some minor worth;" http://cisgw3.law.pace.edu/cases/050523a3.html (translation).

Article 74's damage measure, as applied, calculates the buyer's loss as the difference between the value of the conforming goods and the value of the non-conforming goods. This also is the "difference in value" measure for breach of warranty damages under 2–714(2). When common lawyers think of the injured buyer reducing the price by its damages, they think of it reducing the price by the difference in value between conforming and the non-conforming goods. This is true under 2–717, which permits the buyer to deduct from the price still due damages resulting from breach. Article 50, however, calculates the reduction in price differently. Its reduction in price often is called "proportional": it reduces the contract price by the proportion of the value of the non-conforming goods on delivery to the value that conforming goods would have on delivery. By contrast, Article 74's (and 2–714(2)'s) damage measure often is "linear": damages increase directly—are linear—with loss from breach because they are equal to the loss.

While a "linear" damage measure allocates to the seller all of the loss from its breach, a "proportional" measure can leave some of this loss on the buyer. For instance, suppose the contract price is $90 and the seller breaches by delivering non-conforming goods. Suppose too that the market price of the goods has increased on the date of delivery, so that price of conforming goods is $100 and the price of the non-conforming goods delivered is $95. The buyer's damages under Article 74 are $5 ($5 = $100 − $95). Article 50 reduces the price by $4.50, so that the reduced price the buyer must pay is $85.50 ($85.50 = $95/$100 × $90). Article 74 puts on the seller the entire $5 loss from its breach. By comparison, Article 50 allocates to the seller only $4.50 of the $5 loss, the injured buyer bearing $.50 of the loss.

The CISG also allows the injured buyer to recover damages rather than reduce the price. See Article 45(1). If the buyer avoids the contract, Article 50 is unavailable to it. It must rely on Articles 75 or 76's avoidance-based measures of damages. If the buyer does not avoid the contract, it may elect between recovering damages under Article 74 and reducing the price in accordance with Article 50. This raises the question as to when the buyer will prefer to reduce the price in accordance with Article 50 rather than recovering damages, when both remedies are available to it. As Article 50's terms suggest, the attractiveness of a price reduction depends on the closeness of the value of the goods to the contract price. The Problem below works through some cases in which the buyer can choose between damages and a reduction in price.

PROBLEM 10.19

Seller sold an assembly robot to Buyer for $50,000, which Buyer prepaid, for use in Buyer's factory. Although the robot Seller delivered fell far short of the performance standards called for by the contract, Buyer's tight production schedule required it to continue using the robot. Buyer has notified Seller that the robot is non-conforming and that it demands compensation. In the following three Cases assume that market price measures the relevant values. Should Buyer calculate its loss by damages or by Article 50's formula?

Case 1: The robot Buyer received has a market price of $40,000 at the time of delivery. At that time conforming comparable industrial robots sell for $50,000.

Case 2: The robot Buyer received has a market price of $60,000 at the time of delivery. Conforming comparable industrial robots sell for $70,000 at that time.

Case 3: The robot Buyer received has a market price of $20,000 at the time of delivery. At that time conforming comparable industrial robots sell for $40,000.

Suppose that in Case 3 Buyer's production schedule does not require use of the robot. What is Buyer's best option, assuming that it can give Seller the proper notice?

E. LIQUIDATED DAMAGES

The remedies supplied by the UCC are default terms. They compensate the injured party for its loss from breach unless the sales contract provides other remedies. Cf. 1–302(a). For a variety of reasons, parties sometimes prefer to stipulate damages from breach at the time of contracting. A damage stipulation reduces the risk of judicial error in computing damages as well as the litigation expenses incurred in proving them. It also allows the recovery of elements of damage not otherwise recoverable under the UCC's default remedies. In addition, a stipulation of damages allows the parties to increase their liability from breach, by relieving the injured party from a duty to mitigate its loss. Finally, it may signal a party's reliability as a contracting partner or its attitude towards breach. A damage stipulation can provide a remedy in addition to those provided by the UCC and therefore be optional or replace remedies available under the UCC and therefore be exclusive. Under 2–719(1)(b) a stipulated remedy is optional unless it is expressly agreed to be exclusive. Courts sometimes take a relaxed view of the requirement and allow a stipulated remedy to be exclusive if the circumstances indicate that the parties intend it to be exclusive. See, e.g., Farmers Union Grain Terminal Ass'n v. Nelson, 223 N.W.2d 494 (N.D. 1974); Dow Corning Corp. v. Capital Aviation, Inc., 411 F.2d 622 (7th Cir. 1969).

Rules on unconscionability, mistake and good faith regulate the enforceability of damage stipulations, as they regulate other contract terms. However, unlike other terms, the UCC subjects damage stipulations to additional judicial scrutiny. Section 2–718(1) provides that damages may be liquidated by agreement "but only at an amount which is reasonable in the light of the anticipated or actual harm caused by the breach, the difficulties of proof of loss, and the inconvenience or infeasibility of otherwise obtaining an adequate remedy." A damage stipulation that meets these conditions is enforceable as liquidated damages; stipulations that violate they conditions are void as penalties. It is not obvious why damage stipulations are singled out for special judicial regulation. Warranty terms, risk of loss allocations and other terms bearing on performance can affect the value of the contract as much as stipulations about remedies on breach. Article 2 of the UCC allows parties to set these terms as they like, subject to general rules applicable to other terms as well (e.g., unconscionability, good faith). Its underlying assumption is that courts cannot systematically improve on the parties' allocation of the risks of performance. Cf. XCO Int'l. Inc. v. Pac. Scientific Co., 369 F.3d 998, 1001 (7th Cir. 2004) ("[E]ven if damages wouldn't be difficult to determine after the fact, it is hard see why the parties shouldn't be allowed to substitute their own ex ante determination for the ex post determination of a court. Damages would be just another contract provision that parties would be permitted to negotiate under the general rubric of freedom of contract."). Neither Article 2 nor general contract law has a "performance terms" rule restricting the performance terms of the contract, as both have with respect to damage stipulations. Section 2–718(1)'s assumption is that courts can do a better job than the parties at forecasting damages when the contract is concluded and measuring them when loss from breach occurs.

As is apparent from 2–718(1)'s language, its basic test is disjunctive. A damages stipulation is enforceable if the stipulation bears a reasonable relation either to the anticipated or actual damages. The first part of this disjunctive test is an ex ante standard. It asks whether the forecast of damages is reasonable in relation to actual damages. The second part of the test is an ex post standard. It inquires whether the amount of damages stipulated is reasonable in relation to the actual damages. Because 2–718(1)'s test is disjunctive, a damage stipulation is enforceable if it satisfies either the ex ante or ex post standard. Thus, even if damages stipulated are unreasonable forecast of damages, the stipulation is enforceable as liquidated damages if the actual damages in fact bear a reasonable relation to the damages stipulated. By contrast, the common law test uses only an ex post standard: a damage stipulation is enforceable as liquidated damages only if it bears a reasonable relation to actual damages.

Section 2–718(2) gives the seller statutory liquidated damages when the buyer has made payments to the seller and the seller justifiably withholds delivery of the goods because of the buyer's breach. The liquidated damages are "statutory" because (unsurprisingly) they are created by 2–718(2), not by the parties' agreement. According to 2–718(2)(b), the buyer is entitled to restitution of any amount by which its payments exceeds the lesser of twenty percent of the obligations under the contract for which the buyer is liable or $500. Basically, this allows the buyer to recover amounts it has paid the seller in excess of twenty percent of the contract price or $500, whichever is less. The buyer also is entitled to restitution of any amount by which its payments exceed the contractually stipulated liquidated damages; 2–718(b)(1). Section 2–718(2) puts the seller's statutory liquidated damages in terms of the buyer's right to "restitution" of payments it has made. Amounts the buyer is entitled to by restitution leave the seller with an amount the buyer is *not* entitled to recover by restitution. This is the amount that the seller may retain as statutory liquidated damages.

Finally, 2–718(3)(a) provides that the buyer's right to restitution under 2–718(2) is subject to offset against the seller's damages, other than as contractually stipulated liquidated damages. For example, assume that the buyer breaches a sales contract with a $1,000 price after it has paid the seller $300. The contract does not stipulate damages. Assume also that the seller incurs damages of $250 as a result of the buyer's breach. The lesser of twenty percent of the $1,000 contract price ($200) or $500 is $200. This is the amount of the seller's statutory liquidated damages. Thus, 2–718(2)(b) entitles the buyer to restitution of the amount by which its $300 payment to the seller exceeds $200—in this case $100. However, 2–718(3)(a) allows the seller to offset against the $100 its $250 in damages. The seller therefore may retain the $100 and owes the buyer nothing. This leaves the seller with $200 in statutory liquidated damages plus $100 to offset against its damages. Taken together, 2–718(2) and (3) apparently allow the seller to retain a total of $300, which is more than its damages of $250. Presumably the buyer may recover from the seller the $50 in excess of its damages, based on ordinary principles of restitution. Section 2–718(3)'s justification is obscure and there is almost no case law construing the provision.

The CISG does not regulate damages stipulations set by the sales contract. It leaves their regulation to applicable domestic law. Article 6 allows the parties to make inapplicable to their contract almost all of the CISG's provisions, including all of the CISG's remedies. However, the CISG says nothing about the enforceability of the parties' own provision of recoverable damages resulting from breach. The enforceability of such provisions is a matter of "validity," according to the ordinary understanding of the term. Article 4(a) excludes issues of "validity" from the CISG's scope, unless the CISG expressly provides otherwise. This leaves issues of validity to applicable domestic law. Tracking the ordinary understanding of "validity," case law considers the enforceability of damages stipulations to be an issue of their validity governed by domestic law. See, e.g., ICC Case 9978, 4 UNILEX E.199–6.1 (M.J. Bonell ed., 2008) (full text); American Mint LLC v. Gosoftware, 2006 U.S. LEXIS 1569, at 19* (M.D. Pa. 2006).

The CISG's exclusion of the regulation of damages exclusions from its scope is unsurprising. It reflects the diversity among national laws with respect to damage stipulations. Legal systems tend to take three different approaches to their regulation. A few civil law systems enforce damage stipulations even if they are penalties. Other civil law systems enforce penalties if they are not "manifestly excessive" in relation to the loss from breach or put an upper limit on the amount of the enforceable penalty. See, e.g., Civil Code of Mexico Article 1843. The law of some countries in this group allow courts to reform the penalty sum so that it is no longer "excessive." See, e.g., Civil Code of France Article 1152; Principles of European Contract Law Article 9:509(2) (2002). Common law systems take a third approach, enforcing damages stipulations only when the stipulated sum does not exceed actual loss (the common law rule) or when it does not exceed the actual or reasonably anticipated loss from breach (2–718(1)). The diversity of approaches to damages stipulations makes it unlikely that the delegates to the Vienna Conference could have agreed on the proper regulation of stipulated damages as part of a uniform sales law. The decision of the CISG's drafters to exclude the issue from the CISG's scope therefore is understandable.

Kvassay v. Murray

Kansas Court of Appeals, 1991
808 P.2d 896

■ WALKER, J.

Plaintiff Michael Kvassay, d/b/a Kvassay Exotic Food, appeals the trial court's finding that a liquidated damages clause was unenforceable and from the court's finding that damages for lost profits were not recoverable. Kvassay contends these damages occurred when Great American Foods, Inc., (Great American) breached a contract for the purchase of baklava. . . .

On February 22, 1984, Kvassay, who had been an independent insurance adjuster, contracted to sell 24,000 cases of baklava to Great American at $19.00 per case. Under the contract, the sales were to occur over a one-year period and Great American was to be Kvassay's only customer. The contract included a clause which provided: "If Buyer refuses to accept or repudiates delivery of the goods sold to him, under this Agreement, Seller shall be entitled to damages, at the rate of $5.00 per case, for each case remaining to be delivered under this Contract."

Problems arose early in this contractual relationship with checks issued by Great American being dishonored for insufficient funds. Frequently one of the Murrays issued a personal check for the amount due. After producing approximately 3,000 cases, Kvassay stopped producing the baklava because the Murrays refused to purchase any more of the product.

* * *

In April 1985, Kvassay filed suit for damages arising from the collapse of his baklava baking business. . . . The trial court ruled that liquidated damages could not be recovered and that Great American's corporate veil could be pierced by Kvassay. The court also held "as a matter of law" that Kvassay would not be able to recover damages for lost profits in the action because they were too "speculative and conjectural." * * *

Kvassay first attacks the trial court's ruling that the amount of liquidated damages sought by him was unreasonable and therefore the liquidated damages clause was unenforceable.

Kvassay claimed $105,000 in losses under the liquidated damages clause of the contract, representing $5 per case for the approximately 21,000 cases of baklava which he was not able to deliver. The trial court determined that Kvassay's use of expected profits to formulate liquidated damages was improper because the business enterprise lacked duration, permanency, and recognition. The court then compared Kvassay's previous yearly income (about $20,000) with the claim for liquidated damages ($105,000) and found "the disparity becomes so great as to make the clause unenforceable."

Since the contract involved the sale of goods between merchants, the Uniform Commercial Code governs. * * *

Liquidated damages clauses in sales contracts are governed by K.S.A. 84–2–718, which reads in part:

"(1) Damages for breach by either party may be liquidated in the agreement but only at an amount which is reasonable in the light of the anticipated or actual harm caused by the breach, the difficulties of proof of loss, and the inconvenience or nonfeasibility of otherwise obtaining an adequate remedy. A term fixing unreasonably large liquidated damages is void as a penalty."

To date, the appellate courts have not interpreted this section of the UCC in light of facts similar to those presented in this case. In ruling on this issue, the trial court relied on rules governing liquidated damages as expressed in U.S.D. No. 315 v. DeWerff, 6 Kan. App. 2d 77, 626 P.2d 1206 (1981). *DeWerff*, however, involved a teacher's breach of an employment contract and was not governed by the UCC. Thus, the rules expressed in that case should be given no effect if they differ from the rules expressed in 84–2–718.

In *DeWerff*, this court held a "stipulation for damages upon a future breach of contract is valid as a liquidated damages clause if the set amount is determined to be reasonable and the amount of damages is difficult to ascertain." 6 Kan. App. 2d at 78. This is clearly a two-step test: Damages must be reasonable and they must be difficult to ascertain. Under the UCC, however, reasonableness is the only test. K.S.A. 84–2–718. K.S.A. 84–2–718 provides three criteria by which to measure reasonableness of liquidated damages clauses: (1) anticipated or actual harm caused by breach; (2) difficulty of proving loss; and (3) difficulty of obtaining an adequate remedy.

In its ruling, the trial court found the liquidated damages clause was unreasonable in light of Kvassay's income before he entered into the manufacturing contract with Great American. There is no basis in 84–2–718 for contrasting income under a previous unrelated employment arrangement with liquidated damages sought under a manufacturing contract. Indeed, the traditional goal of the law in cases where a buyer breaches a manufacturing contract is to place the seller " 'in the same position he would have occupied if the vendee had performed his contract.' " Outcault Adv. Co. v. Citizens Nat'l Bank, 118 Kan. 328, 330–31, 234 Pac. 988 (1925). Thus, liquidated damages under the contract in this case must be measured against the anticipated or actual loss under the baklava contract as required by 84–2–718. The trial court erred in using Kvassay's previous income as a yardstick.

* * *

Kvassay produced evidence of anticipated damages at the bench trial showing that, before the contract was signed between Kvassay and Great American, Kvassay's accountant had calculated the baklava production costs. The resulting figure showed that, if each case sold for $19, Kvassay would earn a net profit of $3.55 per case after paying himself for time and labor. If he did not pay himself, the projected profit was $4.29 per case. Nevertheless, the parties set the liquidated damages figure at $5 per case. In comparing the anticipated damages of $3.55 per case in lost net profit with the liquidated damages of $5 per case, it is evident that Kvassay would collect $1.45 per case or about 41 percent over projected profits if Great American breached the contract. If the $4.29 profit figure is used, a $5 liquidated damages award would allow Kvassay to collect 71 cents per case or about 16 1/2 percent over projected profits if Great American breached the contract.

An examination of these pre-contract comparisons alone might well lead to the conclusion that the $5 liquidated damages clause is unreasonable because enforcing it would result in a windfall for Kvassay and serve as a penalty for Great American. A term fixing unreasonably large liquidated damages is void as a penalty under 84–2–718.

A better measure of the validity of the liquidated damages clause in this case would be obtained if the actual lost profits caused by the breach were compared to the $5 per case amount set by the clause. However, no attempt was made by Kvassay during the bench trial to prove actual profits or actual costs of production. Thus, the trial court could not compare the $5 liquidated damages clause in the contract with the actual profits lost by the breach. It was not until the jury trial that Kvassay attempted to prove his actual profits lost as part of his damages. Given the trial court's ruling that lost profits were not recoverable and could not be presented to the jury, it is questionable whether the court would have permitted evidence concerning lost profits at the bench trial.

The trial court utilized an impermissible factor to issue its ruling on the liquidated damages clause and the correct statutory factors were not directly addressed. We reverse the trial court on this issue and remand for further consideration of the reasonableness of the liquidated damages clause in light of the three criteria set out in 84–2–718 * * *

Given the quantity of evidence offered to prove the profitability of Kvassay's business, it is clear the trial court was premature in ruling, as a matter of law, that lost profits could not be proved. Kvassay should have been permitted to offer his evidence and meet his burden of proof on damages.

* * *

NOTES

1. The court in *Kvassay* relied on the ex post part of 2–718(1)'s test to remand the case to the trial court to determine the validity of the seller's liquidated damages clause. In doing so the court required the seller to prove that its lost profits resulting from the buyer's breach approximated the damages stipulated in its clause. Is the seller in the case likely to be able to prove its lost profits? The seller had never produced the product before, and it stopped production when the buyer repudiated the contract, making its production costs difficult to establish. The seller's liquidated damages clause relieved it of having to prove its lost profits from breach, when these profits are hard to prove. Testing the validity of the seller's liquidated damages clause by its lost profits undermines the utility of the clause.

2. Section 2–718(1)'s ex ante part is justified only if courts can more accurately forecast loss from breach at the time the contract is made than the contracting parties. Courts might do a comparatively bad job of predicting loss from breach. Lee Oldsmobile, Inc. v. Kaiden, 363 A.2d 270 (Md. Ct. App. 1976) invalidated a liquidated damages clause that allowed the car dealer to keep its breaching buyer's $5,000 deposit. The court concluded that the clause was a penalty because the dealer's damages of $2,075.07 were capable of accurate estimation at the time the contract was concluded. These damages consisted of incidental expenses based on evidence the dealer provided. However, the damages did not include the seller's lost profits, which the seller did not try to recover directly and could be hard to prove. The dealer's stipulated damages clause allowing it to retain the buyer's deposit might be a reasonable forecast of the sum of incidental expenses and profits lost from the buyer's breach. See Garden Ridge, L.P. v. Advance Int'l, Inc., 80 UCC Rep. Serv.2d 548 (Tex. Ct. App. 2013) (Frost J., concurring) ("Hindsight has a way of making estimations that were reasonable at the time [of contracting] seem unreasonable after a breach. By the time a breach has occurred . . . honest estimates made at the inception of the contract might prove to be too high or too low").

3. Penalty regulation is potentially applicable to "take-or-pay" clauses common in certain parts of the energy industry. A take-or-pay clause requires the buyer to accept the entire quantity contracted for at the contract price or pay for a stipulated minimum quantity at a unit price. If the buyer declines to accept the entire quantity, the seller is saved the production and transportation costs of supplying the quantity not taken. By requiring the buyer to pay for the minimum quantity, the take-or-pay clause therefore arguably overcompensates the seller. Courts therefore ask whether a take-or-pay clause is a damages stipulation or part of the buyer's performance obligations under the contract. If it is a damages stipulation, it is void as a penalty; if part of performance obligations, the clause is not a damages stipulation at all. Instead, in the latter case, the clause allows the buyer to perform by paying for a minimum quantity as an alternative to taking the entire quantity. The clauses do not therefore set a remedy on the buyer's breach. Courts tend to consider take-or-pay clauses to describe an alternative means of performance rather than to stipulate damages. See, e.g., Willsten Basin Interstate Pipeline Co. v. F.E.R.C., 931 F.2d 948 (D.C. Cir. 1991); Roye Realty & Dev., Inc. v. ARKLA, Inc., 863 P.2d 1150 (Okla. 1993). The predominant judicial refusal to consider take-or-pay clauses as damages stipulations might be an implicit acknowledgment of their inability to accurately estimate or predict actual damages.

4. Section 2–718(1) regulates "overliquidated damages": damages stipulations that exceed the amount of actual damages from breach. The section deems as void a contractual provision that fixes unreasonably large liquidated damages. Section 2–718(1) therefore does not apply to the less frequent case of "underliquidated damages": contractual clauses that stipulate damages that are below the actual damages resulting from breach. Underliquidated damage stipulations limit the liability of the breaching party rather than fixing damages. They set the maximum amount of damages the injured party can recover rather than setting the sum it can recover. An underliquidated damage clause has the same effect as a damage exclusion clause, limiting liability to specified damages; see 2–719(3). Section 2–719 regulates contractual limitations on remedies and liability generally, including clauses that limit the amount of recoverable damages; see 2–719(1)(a),(3). As applied to underliquidated damages, 2–719(1)(b) allows the injured party to resort to the UCC's remedies, unless the damages stipulation is expressly agreed to be exclusive. In addition, where the damages stipulation is an exclusive remedy, 2–719(2) allows resort to the UCC's remedies where the stipulation "fails of its essential purpose." Finally, underliquidated damages are unenforceable if they are unconscionable. See 2–302; cf. 2–719(3).

5. Under certain conditions a penalty clause can increase the joint value of the contract to the parties by encouraging efficient investment in the contract. Investment in the contract may increase the value of performance or reduce its cost, or both. For example, the buyer's advertisements in advance of purchase might increase its own sales of the product, and an improved manufacturing technique can reduce the seller's production costs. To see how a penalty clause can encourage investment in the contract, recognize that expectation damages induce inefficiently high investment. This is because the injured party recovers its investment whether or not the contract is breached. If the contract is breached, expectation damages give the injured party its profit net of investment had the contract been performed. If the contract is performed, the party receives the profit from its investment. Because the injured party receives the same return whether or not the contract is breached, it will not discount its investment by the probability that the contract will be breached. As a result, it will make an inefficiently high investment in performing the contract. See Steven Shavell, Damage Measures for Breach of Contract, 11 Bell J. Econ. 466 (1980).

Stipulated damages separate recoverable damages from investment: the injured party receives the same damages without regard to the investment it has made in the contract. This forces the injured party to take the probability of breach into account in deciding to invest, because a dollar invested reduces its net recovery from breach by a dollar. Thus, the injured party will calibrate the cost of an investment with the additional value the investment produces to it (discounted by the probability of breach). As a result, stipulated damages force it to efficiently invest in its performance of the contract. Parties can design a contract in which a penalty clause assures efficient investment. The simplest case is one in which only one of the parties can invest and the investment benefits only the investing party. In this case a penalty gives the investing party efficient incentives to invest if three conditions are met. First, the contract price is set below the investing party's marginal cost. Otherwise, the non-investing party might breach and the investing party will not be assured the value of its investment. Second, the non-investing party makes a nonrecoverable payment, or a promise of one, to the investing party large enough to make the contract profitable for the investing party. This is the "penalty," because the payment is unrelated to the investing party's damages from breach. Third, the level of contractual performance is set so high that renegotiation of the contract is infeasible. Otherwise, the non-investing party might appropriate through renegotiation the returns from investment. See Aaron S. Edlin & Alan Schwartz, Optimal Penalties in Contract, 78 Chi–Kent L. Rev. 33 (2003).

These conditions are restrictive and unlikely to be satisfied in many cases. Investment by one party to a contract in many cases benefits both of the parties, not just the investing party. In addition, a court may ex post find that the payment or payment obligation undertaken by the non-investing party void as unenforceable penalty.

The parties cannot assure that this will not occur. Aware of the possibility that the contract's penalty payment may be unenforceable and that in this case expectation damages are recoverable, the investing party's incentive to invest inefficiently in the contract is reinstated. More generally, in regulating damage stipulations, 2–718(1) does not take investment into account. It applies to all sales contracts without regard to whether investment by a party can increase the contract's value to it or a penalty clause is written to encourage investment.

PROBLEM 10.20

Jones purchased an ordinary used computer for $400 from Second Wind to use in her home. Because the home was being renovated and would not be ready until the end of month, Jones asked Second Wind to hold the computer until that time. Second Wind agreed to do so if Jones made a partial payment of $100 and undertook to pick up the computer at the end of the month. In addition, Second Wind insisted that it have the right to sell the computer and retain the $100 if Jones did not take delivery of the computer on that date. Jones agreed to Second Wind's terms. At the end of the month Jones notified Second Wind that she would not pay for the computer or take delivery. She also demanded the return of her $100 payment. Second Wind resold the computer for $400 but refused to return the $100. What result? What result if Jones and Second Wind's agreement said nothing about what would be done with Jones' $100 payment? See 2–718(1), (2).

CHAPTER 11

LETTERS OF CREDIT

A. INTRODUCTION

Letters of credit are important and versatile financial instruments.[*] They frequently are involved in a wide range of different transactions and play different roles in them. Letters of credit customarily are used to pay for goods or services in cross-border and sometimes in domestic transactions. But they also are used as a credit enhancement to secure the performance of leases, insurance, construction projects or financial obligations. Simply put, a letter of credit is an undertaking by one person to pay a specified person a stated amount of money or other value if that person presents documents that comply with the conditions specified by the undertaking. See 5–102(a)(10). In its most basic form the instrument involves three parties: the issuer, the applicant (or "customer") and the beneficiary. The issuer is the party making the undertaking, often but not always a bank. The applicant is the party requesting the issuer, for a fee, to make the undertaking, and the beneficiary is the party entitled to payment if it satisfies the documentary conditions stated in the undertaking.

To understand the letter of credit's function, consider its role in a contract for the sale of goods. Four sorts of risks affect whether the seller receives the purchase price called for by the contract. One is commercial risk: the prospect that the buyer will refuse or be unable to pay the price. Even if the contract requires payment against the seller's presentation of negotiable documents covering the goods, the seller is left with the documents if the buyer does not or cannot pay against them. Negotiating them another buyer does not guarantee the seller the purchase price in the breached contract. Political risk is a second risk. Political instability might prevent the buyer from paying the purchase price or the seller from receiving payment. A third risk is legal: capital controls or other regulatory restrictions might prevent the buyer from paying for the goods. Litigation is a fourth risk. This is the prospect that the seller will have to sue the buyer to recover the recover the purchase price.

When a letter of credit is used to pay the purchase price, the issuer undertakes to pay the seller on the seller's presentation of specified documents. The credit represents the issuer's own undertaking to the seller. It therefore gives the seller a (usually) reliably solvent source of payment of the purchase price. This shifts the four payment risks identified from the seller to the issuer. Because the credit entitles the seller to payment from the issuer if it presents specified documents, the seller looks to the issuer to be paid, not the buyer. It therefore no longer bears the risk that the buyer will refuse or be unable to pay. For the same reason, the seller also does not bear political or legal risk. Intervening events or legal restrictions that might prevent the buyer

---

[*] Some of the material in this Chapter is adapted from Chapter 10 of William D. Warren & Steven D. Walt, Commercial Law (9th ed. 2013).

from paying the purchase price do not by themselves prevent the issuer from paying the seller. Finally, the issuer's undertaking relieves the seller of the burden of having to litigate to recover the purchase price from the buyer. The seller gets the purchase price by drawing on the credit. The buyer instead must sue the seller to recover damages for the seller's breach of the underlying sales contract. Although the buyer ultimately risks receiving goods that do not conform to the contract, the documents called for by the letter of credit can provide reliable evidence of the seller's performance of the contract, including the condition of the goods delivered.

The letter of credit also shifts the four risks identified when it secures performance of a contract. This is the case where the credit obligates the issuer to pay the beneficiary upon the party's documentary certification that the issuer's applicant has defaulted on its obligation to the beneficiary. Because the beneficiary is entitled to payment from the issuer in these circumstances, the credit secures the applicant's performance of its obligation. The issuer, not the beneficiary, therefore bears the commercial or financial risk of its applicant's default. Political and legal risks that affect the applicant's performance of its obligation by themselves have no effect on the issuer's obligation or ability to pay the beneficiary. Litigation risk also is not borne by the beneficiary, because it obtains payment on documentary certification of default. The beneficiary therefore does not have to sue the applicant on the applicant's default on its obligation.

When a letter of credit is issued, three separate relationships are present. One is the agreement between the beneficiary and the applicant that calls for the establishment of the credit or gives rise to it. This is the underlying transaction. The sale of goods contract is an example. A second relationship is the agreement between the issuer and applicant which states the terms of the credit and provides for the issuer's reimbursement by the applicant. This is the reimbursement agreement. The third is the relationship between the issuer and the beneficiary in which the issuer makes the credit undertaking to the beneficiary. Some courts and scholars refer to this relationship as the letter of credit "contract." Strictly, the letter of credit relationship is not a contract at all. See In re Montgomery Ward LLC, 292 B.R. 49, 54 (Bankr. Del. 2003). There is no bargained-for exchange between the beneficiary and the issuer, and the beneficiary owes no obligation to the issuer, as a contract requires. Instead, the issuer's undertaking to the beneficiary gives the beneficiary certain rights against the issuer.

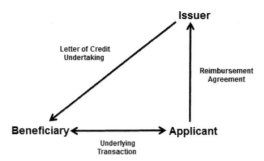

Frequently two other parties are involved in a letter of credit. One is an advisor. 5–102(a). Beneficiaries often want assurance that the credit is authentic and its terms are accurately communicated. To provide assurance, the issuer engages a person familiar to the beneficiary, usually a local bank, which verifies the credit through a secure communication system. The advising bank in turn advises the beneficiary of the credit and its terms. The obligations of the advising bank are modest. It must satisfy itself that the credit is authentic and that the advice accurately reflects the credit's terms. See 5–107(c). The advisor's responsibilities are limited to those of communication. Importantly, by advising the beneficiary the advisor does not obligate itself under the credit. Thus, it is not obligated to honor documentary presentations that comply with the terms of the credit. The other party frequently involved in the letter of credit is a confirmer, usually a bank. The confirming bank, at the issuer's request, adds its own undertaking to the beneficiary to that of the issuer. 5–102(a)(4). By adding its confirmation the confirmer undertakes to honor documentary presentations that comply with the terms of the main credit. See 5–107(a). The confirmer may also advise as to the existence and terms of the credit. In doing so it takes on two different obligations: to confirm and to advise. A confirmed letter of credit gives the beneficiary two sources of payment: the issuer and the confirmer. Beneficiaries worried about the issuer's own solvency or political and legal risks affecting the issuer may insist that the letter of credit be confirmed.

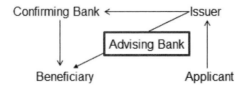

There are two types of letters of credit: commercial (or "documentary") credits and standby credits. They are distinguished by their financial purposes and the sorts of documentary conditions specified by them. Commercial credits are issued to pay for goods or services obtained by the applicant. For instance, the sales contract might require the buyer-applicant to establish a credit naming the seller as the beneficiary. The terms of credit established in turn will require the issuer to pay a stated sum equal to the contract price to the beneficiary if the beneficiary presents documents described in the credit. The described documents can be of any sort. Usually the commercial credit requires some documents that evidence the beneficiary's performance of the underlying sales or services contract. In the case of a sale of goods, the documents typically include a draft drawn by the seller on the buyer, a commercial invoice, a negotiable bill of lading or other document of title, a certificate or origin and an inspection certificate. Where the underlying contract involves a sale of assets other than goods, such as real estate or securities, different documentation will be required. The issuer pays the seller-beneficiary the contract price if it presents document that comply with the terms of the credit.

A standby letter of credit serves as security for the applicant's performance of the underlying contract or transaction with the beneficiary. It is not a mechanism for payment of the contract price. Typically a standby credit provides that the issuer will pay the beneficiary if the beneficiary presents specified documentary evidence of default by the applicant or some other party in the underlying contract or transaction. Thus, presentation of these documents allows the beneficiary to obtain payment from the issuer. In this way the issuer's obligation to the beneficiary guarantees the applicant's or another's obligation under the underlying contract or transaction. The standby credit thereby shifts the risk of the applicant's default from the beneficiary to the issuer. Standby credits in turn are of two sorts: "payment" (or "financial") and "performance" standbys. A "payment" standby credit calls for payment on presentation of documentary certification of default on a financial obligation. A "performance" standby credit calls for payment on presentation of documentary certification of default on a non-financial obligation. Sometimes a credit is issued that requires no documents certifying default to be presented or requires merely a certificated demand for payment. These are "clean" credits. Finally, a "direct pay" standby letter of credit is a hybrid of a commercial and standby credit. It serves as security for the applicant's payment obligations. However, the credit also serves as a primary source of payment. For example, a direct-pay standby credit secures payment of principal and interest owed by the applicant on bonds it has issued. At the same time, the credit provides for the payment of principal and interest without the applicant's default.

Standby credits serve a guarantee function in a wide range of different underlying transactions. Issuers of commercial paper can market the paper at a higher price by backing it up with a standby letter of credit. Purchasers of limited partnerships on credit can guarantee their partnership interests by having a standby credit issued that undertakes to pay the beneficiaries-sellers on documentary certification of the purchasers' default on their payment obligations. In securitization transactions a standby credit serves to guarantee the payment of interest and principal on debt securities issued by the securitization vehicle. This enhances the credit rating of these securities. A standby credit can play a guarantee role in a sale of goods contract too. There, the credit might allow the seller-beneficiary to draw on its certification that the buyer has failed to pay the invoice price of the goods. A standby credit can be used even when the buyer prepays for the goods. The credit here might entitle the buyer-beneficiary to draw on the credit on documentary presentation of the seller-applicant's breach of the underlying sales contract, such as a breach of warranty. The wide range of uses for standby credits and the comparatively low fees charged to issue them make them an attractive financial instrument. Standby credits dwarf commercial credits in their financial importance. In 2011 U.S. FDIC-insured depository banks issued slightly more than $525 billion in standby credits. During the same period they issued about $25 billion in commercial credits. See FDIC Statistics in Banking (2011).

A sample commercial letter of credit appears below. *Van Zeeland Oil Co.*, which appears in section C below, reproduces a standby letter of credit at p. 698.

Sample Commercial Letter of Credit

Letter of Credit No. 1234

State Bank

500 High Street

Grand Rapids, Michigan 49503

September 1, 2013

Beneficiary: Universal Exports   Applicant: Ace Imports

657 Main Street   152 Regent's Park Road

Grand Rapids, Michigan 49503   London NW1, England

Dear Universal Exports:

We hereby open an irrevocable letter of credit in your favor, for the account of Ace Imports, 152 Regent's Park Road, London NW1, England, in the amount of $50,000 (US). This letter of credit is available by your sight draft on us accompanied by the following required documents:

1. Commercial invoice in triplicate

2. Marine Insurance policy for 110% of the invoice amount

3. Certificate of Origin in triplicate

4. Full set 3/3 of clean on board negotiable bills of lading consigned to the order of State Bank, Grand Rapids, Michigan.

5. The original of this letter of credit

The merchandise must be described in the invoice as "50 maple wood tables, Design 480." Invoice must indicate total amount of $50,000 C.I.F. Southhampton, England.

Partial shipments and transshipment are not allowed.

All drafts must be marked "drawn under Letter of Credit No. 1234." Drafts must be presented to us no later than November 1, 2013.

We hereby engage with the drawer, indorsers, and bona fide holders of drafts to duly honor on presentation drafts drawn in compliance with this letter of credit and accompanied by conforming documents. This credit is subject to the Uniform Customs and Practice for Documentary Credits, Publication No. 600 (UCP 600).

Sincerely,

State Bank
Authorized signature: s/State Bank

A final distinction concerns the parties to whom the issuer's undertaking runs. In some credits the issuer undertakes to pay only the beneficiary or its agents. Credits of this sort are called "straight credits": the issuer's engagement is to the beneficiary alone. In other credits the issuer undertakes to pay the beneficiary or those who have purchased the beneficiary's draft and documents that comply with the credit's terms. These credits are called "negotiation credits." The issuer may engage to honor conforming drafts and documents presented by anyone or it may restrict the persons whose presentations it will honor. A negotiation credit enables the beneficiary to discount its draft, which suits beneficiaries in need of immediate funds. Whether a credit is straight or negotiation is a matter of the credit's language. If the credit is silent on the matter, it is a straight credit. Language in a credit stating that the issuer "engages with you [the beneficiary] that drafts drawn in compliance with the terms and conditions of this letter of credit and accompanied by conforming documents will be honored on presentation" creates a straight credit. A statement in a credit providing that issuer "engages with the drawer, indorsers, and bona fide holders of drafts to honor drafts drawn in compliance with this letter of credit and accompanied by conforming documents" makes the credit a negotiation credit. This statement appears in the sample letter of credit above.

B. LETTERS OF CREDIT: THEIR LEGAL CHARACTER AND SOURCES OF LAW

Letters of credit have a unique or at least peculiar legal character. They are subject to special legal rules, not to the ordinary rules that apply to other contracts. For instance, unlike a contract, the issuer's undertaking to the beneficiary is enforceable without consideration. 5–105. Other rules of general contract law also do not apply to the letter of credit. For example, the issuer's obligation to the beneficiary is not the created by the beneficiary's acceptance of an offer by the issuer. Rules about third party beneficiaries do not apply to the letter of credit beneficiary, because the issuer cannot raise defenses the applicant might have against the beneficiary to resist paying it. In addition, the letter of credit is not subject to legal rules applicable to special sorts of contracts. For instance, a credit is not a negotiable instrument because it is does not satisfy the requirements of negotiability for such instruments under the UCC. See 3–104. It therefore is not governed by negotiable instruments law. The legal principles applicable to guarantees also are inapplicable to letters of credit. A guarantor's liability on its guarantee is secondary. It is liable on the guarantee only if the principal obligor has defaulted. See Restatement (Third) of Suretyship and Guaranty § 34 (1996). The guarantor also may rely on the defenses to payment available to the principal obligor.

By contrast, the issuer's liability under the credit is "primary." Its payment obligation is conditioned only on the documentary terms described in the credit. Those terms alone govern the issuer's obligation. Facts extrinsic to the documents, including default, therefore can have no effect on the issuer's obligation to the beneficiary. For same reason, the issuer cannot rely on defenses available to the applicant against the beneficiary to resist honoring its undertaking to the beneficiary. A letter of credit therefore is not a guarantee because the issuer's payment obligation is not conditional on the applicant's default; the issuer's liability is not secondary. In short, the legal rules central to letter of credit law cannot be assimilated to rules that operate in other areas of law.

Most letter of credit law consists of domestic law and institutional rules, and much of the law is uniform across jurisdictions. It has five potential sources: (1) In the United States Article 5 of the UCC and common law; (2) the Uniform Customs and Practice for Documentary Credits (International Chamber of Commerce, Publication 600) ("UCP 600" or "UCP"); (3) the International Standby Practices (International Chamber of Commerce, Publication 590) ("ISP 98"); (4) the Uniform Rules for Demand Guarantees (International Chamber of Commerce, Publication 758) ("URDG"); and (5) the United Nations Convention on Independent Guarantees and Standby Letters of Credit ("U.N. Convention"). Although eight countries have ratified the U.N. Convention, neither the United States nor other countries with large financial sectors have done so. Thus, domestic law such as Article 5 of the UCC and the International Chamber of Commerce's rules remain the most important sources of letter of credit law.

Article 5 of the UCC governs both commercial and standby letters of credit. The UCP 600 and ISP 98 are the institutional rules most frequently incorporated into credits. By its terms, the UCP 600 applies only to credits issued by banks, although non-bank issuers can make its rules applicable by incorporating the UCP into the credits they issue. Because the International Chamber of Commerce has no legislative authority and therefore does not produce law, its rules apply only if the credits make them applicable. International credits usually incorporate the UCP, as do many domestic credits. To govern the credit, the UCP 600, ISP 98 and the URDG all require that the incorporation be express. UCP 600 art. 1; ISP 98 Rule 1.01(b); URDG art. 1. The ISP 98 and the URDG are made applicable only to standby credits; the UCP 600 is incorporated into both commercial and standby credits. The trend is in favor of making standby credits subject to the ISP 98 rather than to the UCP 600. Several courts have held that the UCP can govern the credit as a matter of trade usage, even when the credit does not expressly provide for the UCP's application.

In most cases the UCP 600, ISP 98 and URDG 758's rules are consistent with UCC Article 5's provisions. They usually either say the same thing or address a matter that Article 5 does not address. However, there are a few instances in which Article 5 and the

International Chamber of Commerce's rules conflict. UCC 5–116(c) is clear about which rule controls in these cases. The subsection provides that if the credit is subject to the UCP or other "rules of custom or practice," the UCP or other rules of custom or practice displace UCC Article 5 if the conflicting rule is not a mandatory rule under Article 5. If the conflicting rule is mandatory, Article 5's rule continues to apply. Very few of Article 5's rules are mandatory; almost all can be varied by the terms of the credit. Section 5–103(c) lists the following mandatory rules: the definition of a letter of credit, formal requirements, restrictions on the stipulation of an expiration date, the independence principle, limits on the issuer's ability to withhold its consent to the assignment of letter of credit proceeds, rights of subrogation, and obligations of good faith. See UCC 5–102(a)(9), (10), 5–106(d), 5–103(d), 5–114(d), 5–117(d), 1–302(b). In every other matter the issuer and applicant are free to set the terms of the credit. In fact, even Article 5's mandatory rules in effect are default rules too. This is because 5–116(a) allows the parties to select the law of the jurisdiction that governs the liability of the issuer, nominated person or adviser. Section 5–116(a) adds that the law selected "need not bear any relation to the transaction." Thus, parties can select applicable law that does not contain Article 5's mandatory rules. Put another way, Article 5's mandatory rules therefore apply only if affected parties fail to select the law of a jurisdiction that does not contain the same rules. See Comment 2 to 5–103 (second paragraph). This makes these rules in effect only default rules.

There are instances in which domestic law must supplement the International Chamber of Commerce's sets of rules. These occur when the rules incorporated into a credit are silent about a particular matter bearing on the credit. For example, the UCP 600 says nothing about when the letter of credit becomes effective. It also has nothing to say about implied warranties the beneficiary or other presenter of documents makes to issuer, the remedies for wrongful dishonor of a documentary presentation, the issuer or applicant's rights of subrogation, or the effect of fraud on the issuer's obligations to the beneficiary. And the UCP 600 is silent about the circumstances in which an applicant can enjoin an issuer from honoring a documentary presentation or the beneficiary from making one. Article 5 has provisions that address these matters. See 5–106(a), 5–110, 5–111, 5–117, 5–109.

C. FORMAL REQUIREMENTS

1. FORM

To be a letter of credit, a financial instrument must take a certain form. Section 5–104 states the formal requirements a credit must satisfy. It requires that the credit instrument be a record authenticated by the issuer. See 5–102(a)(14), 1–201(b)(7). In addition, to be a letter of credit in the first place (whether or not in authenticated record form), the financial instrument must state a particular sort of undertaking. Because the essential feature of a letter of credit is that the issuer's obligations under the credit are independent of the underlying transaction, the instrument must reflect this fact. Form must follow function. This means that an instrument is a letter of credit only if it conditions the issuer's obligations on the satisfaction of documentary conditions. Section 5–102(a)(10) defines a letter of credit as a "definite undertaking . . . to honor a documentary presentation by payment or delivery of an item of value." This definition describes a mandatory rule; see 5–103(c). Thus, an agreement to treat an instrument that is not a letter of credit under Article 5 of the UCC therefore is ineffective.

For example, suppose as part of its construction contract with Owner, Contractor induced Bank to notify Owner by letter. The letter read in relevant part:

LETTER OF CREDIT

We hereby establish a letter of credit in your favor, under the following terms: We will pay to you $50,000 on your demand in the event Contractor has defaulted on its obligations to you under your construction contract. Signed: x/Bank.

This instrument is a guarantee, not a letter of credit. Under 5–102(a)(10), to be a letter of credit, the issuer's obligation of payment must be conditioned on compliance with documentary conditions. See also UCP 600 art. 2 ("credit"). Whether an instrument is a letter of credit therefore depends on the nature of the issuer's undertaking, not the label given to it. For this reason, the designation as a "letter of credit" in Bank's letter is irrelevant. (European banks issue instruments called "bank guarantees" or "independent guarantees." The instruments are standby letters of credit.) In its letter Bank undertakes to pay Owner $50,000 on Owner's demand in the event Contractor has defaulted. Contractor's default is a nondocumentary condition: a condition stated in Bank's letter that the letter does not require to be evidenced by a document. Bank's undertaking to pay Owner therefore is not made conditional on compliance with documentary conditions. Thus, its undertaking is not a letter of credit.

The legal character of the instrument is easy to identify in the example just given. It can be harder to identify when an instrument contains both documentary and nondocumentary conditions. Section 5–102(a)(10) does not prevent an instrument that contains both sorts of conditions from being a letter of credit. It merely requires that the issuer's definite undertaking be conditioned on compliance with documentary conditions ("to honor a documentary presentation by payment"). Section 5–108(g) directs that nondocumentary conditions in a letter of credit be disregarded. See also UCP 600 art. 14(h), ISP 98 Rule 4.11. This instruction makes sense. Issuing banks deal with documents, not with extrinsic facts. The expertise and time needed to verify compliance with nondocumentary conditions impairs the speed and certainty of administering a letter of credit. This delay and uncertainty increases the price an issuer will charge to issue the credit. However, 5–108(g)'s instruction applies only to a letter of credit that contains nondocumentary conditions. A more difficult question of characterization is presented when the inclusion of a nondocumentary condition prevents an instrument from being a letter of credit in the first place. The following case and Notes inquire about the nondocumentary conditions in a written undertaking that undermine the writing's character as a letter of credit. The Problems following the case investigate 5–104's other formal requirements.

Wichita Eagle & Beacon Publishing Co. v. Pacific National Bank of San Francisco

United States Court of Appeals, Ninth Circuit, 1974
493 F.2d 1285

■ PER CURIAM:

[Summary by Ed. Lessors leased a site on which Lessee (Circular Ramp Garages), under the terms of the lease, undertook to build a parking garage. In order to assure Lessors that Lessee would perform, Lessee obtained from Bank (Pacific National Bank) a writing addressed to Lessors in which Bank established its "Letter of Credit No. 17084" in favor of Lessors for payment of $250,000. Bank's "letter of credit" obligated Bank to make payment on the satisfaction of a number of conditions. Three of the condition were: (1) that Lessee has failed to perform the terms of the lease; (2) that Lessors have sent the Lessee written notice specifying how Lessee has failed to perform its lease; and (3) that either Lessee or its contractor has failed to cure defaults under the lease during a period of thirty days after receiving Lessor's notice. Lessee failed to obtain the financing necessary to build the parking garage and defaulted on the lease. Lessors' assignee (Plaintiff) presented to Bank a draft for $250,000 drawn upon Letter of Credit No. 17084, together with the required documents. When Bank refused payment, Plaintiff sued Bank. The district court concluded that "[a]lthough the question is not free from doubt, the Instrument denominated 'Letter of Credit No. 17084' should be treated as a letter of credit and be subject to the law respecting letters of credit to the extent applicable and appropriate." Wichita Eagle & Beacon Publishing Co. v. Pacific National Bank, 343 F. Supp. 332, 339 (N.D. Cal. 1975).]

We do not agree with the district court that the instrument sued upon is a letter of credit, though it is so labeled. Rather, the instrument is an ordinary guaranty contract, obliging the defendant bank to pay whatever the lessee Circular Ramp Garages, Inc., owed on the underlying lease, up to the face amount of the guaranty. Since the underlying lease clearly contemplated the payment of $250,000 in case of default, and since this provision appears to be a valid liquidated damages clause, the judgment below must be modified to award the plaintiff $250,000 plus interest.

We do not base our holding that the instrument is not a letter of credit on the fact that payment was triggered by default rather than performance or on the fact that the instrument was written in a lease context, for we recognize that the commercial use of letters of credit has expanded far beyond the international sales context in which it originally developed. . . .

The instrument involved here strays too far from the basic purpose of letters of credit, namely, providing a means of assuring payment cheaply by eliminating the need for the issuer to police the underlying contract. . . . The instrument neither evidences an intent that payment be made merely on presentation on a draft nor specifies the documents required for termination or payment. To the contrary, it requires the actual existence in fact of most of the conditions specified: . . . for payment, that the lessee have failed to perform the terms of the lease and have failed to correct that default, in addition to an affidavit of notice.

True, in the text of the instrument itself the instruments is referred to as a "letter of credit," and we should, as the district court notes, "giv[e] effect wherever possible to the intent of the contracting parties." 343 F. Supp. at 338. But the relevant intent is manifested by the terms of the agreement, not by its label. . . . And where, as here, the substantive provisions require the issuer to deal not simply in documents alone, but in facts relating to the performance of a separate contract (the lease, in this case), all distinction between a letter of credit and an ordinary guaranty contract would be obliterated by regarding the instrument as a letter of credit.

It would hamper rather than advance the extension of the letter of credit concept to new situations if an instrument such as this were held to be a letter of credit. The loose terms of this instrument invited the very evil that letters of credit are meant to avoid—protracted, expensive litigation. If the letter of credit concept is to have value in new situations, the instrument must be tightly drawn to strictly and clearly limit the responsibility of the issuer.

NOTES

1. The conceptual issue presented in *Witchita Eagle* concerns the character of the instrument issued by the Bank: is it a guarantee or a standby letter of credit? *Wichita Eagle* was decided under the 1962 version of Article 5, in effect before its revision in 1995. Pre-1995 5–103(a) defined a "letter of credit" in relevant part as an engagement by a person to "honor . . . demands for payment upon compliance with the conditions specified in the credit." How would this case be decided under the current version of Article 5? See 5–102(a)(10) ("letter of credit") and Comment 6 to 5–102. How could the document in *Wichita Eagle* be rewritten to remove all doubt about its status as a letter of credit? Does 5–108(g) allow the court in this case to find that the writing is a valid letter of credit by disregarding the two nondocumentary conditions? Comment 9 to 5–108. If the undertaking is a letter of credit, the disregard of nondocumentary conditions does not mean that the issuer can ignore them. As a matter of the reimbursement agreement between the applicant and the issuer, their honor might be required. Section 5–108(g)'s injunction only means that the issuer's obligations to the beneficiary under the letter of credit do not depend on the satisfaction of nondocumentary conditions. See Comment 9 to 5–108.

2. In approving of the result in *Witchita Eagle*, Comment 6 to 5–102 in so many words says that 5–102(a)(10)'s definition of a letter of credit requires that the instrument not contain fundamental nondocumentary conditions. See also Comment 9 to 5–108. The distinction between fundamental and nonfundamental nondocumentary conditions presents a line-drawing problem for courts. Comment 6 gives as examples of nonfundamental conditions a term prohibiting "shipment on vessels more than 15 years old" or a term requiring an arbitral award by a "duly appointed arbitrator." A term requiring performance of the underlying contract by the beneficiary is a fundamental condition, according to the Comment. Aside from the authority of the Comment, it gives no help in drawing the distinction between fundamental and nonfundamental nondocumentary conditions. Perhaps no usable distinction can be made, because the "fundamentality" of a condition appears to depend on the condition's contribution to the value of the underlying transaction. Nondocumentary conditions that if unfulfilled diminish the value of the contract significantly seem to be fundamental, while unfulfilled conditions that have a lesser effect on the contract's value are not fundamental. The trouble is that this inquiry requires courts and issuers to go beyond the face of the instrument to determine the instrument's character. The inquiry disturbs the quick and reliable payment provided by letters of credit. For a different way of distinguishing between fundamental and nonfundamental nondocumentary conditions, see Richard F. Dole Jr., The Essence of a Letter of Credit Under Revised U.C.C. Article 5: Permissible and Impermissible Nondocumentary Conditions Affecting Honor, 35 Hous. L. Rev. 1079, 1112–1116 (1995).

ISP 98 avoids some of the difficulty in distinguishing between fundamental and nonfundamental nondocumentary conditions. It does so by defining nondocumentary conditions to exclude certain extrinsic facts while including certain others. Under ISP 98 Rule 4.11(b), terms or conditions are nondocumentary "if the standby does not require presentation of a document in which they are to be evidenced and if their fulfillment cannot be determined by the issuer from the issuer's own records or within the issuer's normal operations." The last part of this definition therefore counts as a documentary condition an extrinsic condition that is verifiable by the issuer from its own records or within its normal operations. As a documentary condition, ISP 98 Rule 4.11(a)'s directive that nondocumentary conditions be ignored does not apply. For example, a standby credit might condition payment on the applicant having a deposit account with the issuer with a certain minimum balance on the date payment is demanded. The condition is factual, not documentary. Nonetheless, the issuer can determine whether the condition is fulfilled based on its records of its customers and their account balances. Thus, although the condition need not be evidenced by a document, it is a documentary condition according to Rule 4.11(b)'s definition. Rule 4.11(a) therefore does not allow the issuer to ignore the condition.

3. The legal character of an instrument can be important for bank regulation. National banks in the United States generally are not permitted to issue guarantees. They are permitted, however, to issue letters of credit, subject to regulatory restrictions. In function guarantees and standby letters of credit are indistinguishable. Both involve the enhancement of an obligor's promise by adding the promise of a creditworthy third party. However, conceptually standbys and guarantees are distinguishable by the nature of the issuer's obligation and the conditions under which its obligation attaches. The issuer's obligation under the standby credit is primary while the guarantor's obligation under the guarantee is secondary. Thus, the issuer cannot invoke defenses against the beneficiary available to the applicant to resist honoring the credit. A guarantor's obligation is secondary: it can invoke defenses available to the obligor to resist payment to the obligee.

Because banks generally can only issue letters of credit, the conceptual distinction between credits and guarantees is crucial.

The Office of the Comptroller of the Currency regulates the issuance of letters of credit by focusing on documentary conditions. By the Comptroller's interpretive ruling, national banks may issue letters of credit, including standby letters of credit, only if the obligation to honor "depends upon the presentation of specified documents and not upon nondocumentary conditions or resolution of questions of fact or law at issue between the applicant and the beneficiary." 12 C.F.R. § 7.1016(a) (1998). State chartered banks usually are subject to a similar sort of regulation.

An important question is the effect of a bank issuing a guarantee in violation of bank regulations. Issuing banks or applicants sometimes adopt the odd litigation posture of urging the illegal issuance of a guarantee as a defense to enforcement of the guarantee. This is the "ultra vires" defense to honor. See Republic Nat'l Bank v. Northwest Nat'l Bank, 578 S.W.2d 109 (Tex.1978); *Wichita Eagle.* Although a few courts have accepted the ultra vires defense, the majority of case law has rejected it. See, e.g., Fed. Dep. Ins. Corp. v. Freudenfeld, 492 F.Supp. 763 (E.D. Wis.1980); First Am. Nat'l Bank v. Alcorn, Inc., 361 So.2d 481 (Miss.1978); John F. Dolan, 1 The Law of Letters of Credit ¶ 12.03[2] (4th ed. 2007). In *Wichita Eagle*, for instance, the court enforced the instrument as a guarantee. As a matter of policy, the rejection of the ultra vires defense makes sense. The issuer or applicant almost always is in a better position than the beneficiary to avoid violating applicable bank regulations or to detect their violation. Bank regulating agencies also are better positioned than beneficiaries to monitor issuers and applicants. Accordingly, not allowing the defense to enforcement increases the cost to issuers of violating the regulation against the issuance of guarantees. It serves as a partial substitute for closer monitoring of a bank's investment activities by bank regulating agencies.

4. Section 5–104 recognizes that the day of an exclusively paper based system of letter of credit transactions has long since passed. Comment 3 notes: "Many banking transactions, including the issuance of many letters of credit, are now conducted mostly by electronic means. . . . By declining to specify any particular medium in which the letter of credit must be established or communicated, Section 5–104 leaves room for future developments." See the definitions of "document" (5–102(a)(6)) and "record" (5–102(a)(14)). The documents to be presented to the issuer of the letter of credit to obtain payment usually include a draft drawn by the beneficiary (5–102(a)(3)) on the issuing bank (5–102(a)(9)) payable "at sight" (that is on presentment) to the order of the beneficiary. A sight draft is merely a demand for payment that may be negotiable in form, thus conferring upon the beneficiary the power to transfer the draft to a third person who may take the rights of a holder in due course. Comment 11 to 5–102. Some letters of credit either do not require presentation of a draft or do not call for a draft at all.

PROBLEM 11.1

Seller contracted with Buyer to manufacture and deliver air conditioners for a total price of $50,000. The agreement allowed Buyer to pay the contract price within 30 days of delivery, but required it have issued a letter of credit to guarantee payment. Accordingly, Buyer later induced Bank to notify Seller by letter and Seller delivered the air conditioners. Bank's letter read in relevant part:

GUARANTEE

We hereby establish a guarantee in you [Seller's] favor, under the following terms: We will pay to you $50,000 on your presentation of your draft in the amount of $50,000 drawn on us and written statement to the effect that Buyer has failed to pay the $50,000 contract price due within 30 days of delivery of the air conditioners by you under your sales contract with Buyer. Signed: x/Bank

Bank refused to pay Seller when Seller presented the draft and written statement called for in the letter because the air conditioners Seller delivered were defective. Assuming that the air conditioners were defective, may Bank refuse to pay Seller? See 5–102(a)(10), Comment 6 to 5–102, 5–102(a)(6).

PROBLEM 11.2

Bank sent a letter to XYZ Corporation that read in relevant part as follows:

LETTER OF CREDIT

Applicant: ABC Corporation

Expiration: December 31, 2013

Dear XYZ Corporation:

We hereby establish our letter of credit in your favor, at the request of ABC Corporation [address], to pay up to the amount of 10,000. Signed: x/Bank

(a) Is the instrument a letter of credit? See 5–102(a)(10); Comment 6 to 5–102; cf. Transparent Products Corp. v. Paysaver Credit Union, 864 F.2d 60 (7th Cir. 1988).

(b) Would the result change if Bank undertook in its letter "to pay up to the amount of $10,000"?

(c) What would be the result if the letter had provided: "We hereby establish our letter of credit, at the request of ABC Corporation [address], up to the aggregate amount of $10,000 (U.S.) on which you may draw through December 31, 2013 by presentation of a draft payable at sight for any amount up to the credit limit"? See 5–105(a)(6), (10), (12), Comment 1 to 5–104.

2. DURATION

As noted, most of Article 5's rules are default rules. An important default rule is the irrevocability of the letter of credit. Section 5–106(a) provides that a credit is irrevocable unless it states otherwise. Accord UCP 600 art. 7b; ISP 98 Rule 1.06(a). Irrevocability means that the issuer cannot cancel or amend the credit once it is issued without the beneficiary's consent. See 5–106(b). This rule makes sense for most beneficiaries, who will rely on the credit before they draw on it. Section 5–106(a) provides that the credit is issued and becomes enforceable when the issuer sends or transmits it to the beneficiary. Because a credit is "sent" when it is mailed or delivered for transmission by the usual means (1–201(b)(36)(A)), the credit becomes enforceable upon its dispatch. Section 5–106(a)'s dispatch rule does not expressly deal with confirmed letters of credit. However, 5–107(a) imposes on the confirmer the obligations to the issuer "as if . . . the confirmer had issued the letter of credit at the request and for the account of the issuer." In addition, Comment 1 to 5–107 provides that the terms "confirmation" and "letter of credit" are interchangeable throughout Article 5. Because the confirmer issues its own confirmed letter of credit, it is reasonable to infer that 5–106(a)'s dispatch rule applies to both the main and confirmed credits.

One of Article 5's few mandatory rules concerns the duration of the letter of credit. A letter of credit must have a date at which it expires. Section 5–106(c) provides that if there is no stated expiration date in the credit, the credit expires one year after its issuance, and 5–106(d) provides that if the credit states that it is perpetual, it expires five years after its issuance. The latter is a mandatory rule. It is not uncommon for a standby letter of credit to have a clause that provides that the credit is automatically renewed at the stipulated expiration date. The clause is called an "evergreen clause." The following is an example of an evergreen clause: "This letter of credit expires on March 1, 2013 but shall be automatically extended, without written amendment, to March 1, 2014 and for an additional one year period from the present or any future expiration dates, unless on or before March 1, 2013 or any future expiration date we [the issuer] notify you in writing that this letter of credit will not be extended." Comment 4 to 5–106 deems credits renewable at the option of the issuer, which are common, not to be perpetual. The Problem below asks about 5–106(d)'s application to a credit which by its terms the issuer cannot terminate.

PROBLEM 11.3

The credit issued by Bank to Company in 2008 stated in relevant part:

All drafts on this Letter of Credit shall be honored on presentation and delivery of the above-specified documents on or before the expiration of this Letter of Credit. The initial term of this credit shall extend to and include December 31, 2012, after which this Letter of Credit shall automatically renew on a month to month basis. Bank shall not be permitted to terminate or in any manner reduce or limit this Letter of Credit during the initial term or any renewal term.

Company presented complying documents to Bank in 2014. Bank dishonored the presentation on the ground that the the duration clause above makes the duration period "perpetual." According to it, even though the clause did not use the term "perpetual," the credit's duration was five years under 5–106(d). Company's presentation therefore came too late. In support Bank argues that Comment 4 to 5–106 does not require a different result. Its credit, unlike the credit described in the Comment, does not give Bank the option to renew the credit. Does Bank's credit have a perpetual duration under 5–106(d)? See Michigan Commerce Bank v. TDY Indus., Inc., 76 UCC Rep. Serv.2d 279 (W.D. Mich. 2011); accord Golden West Refi. Co. v. Suntrust Bank, 538 F.3d 1233 (9th Cir. 2008).

NOTE

Does an evergreen clause create a letter of credit of perpetual duration when it does not give the issuer the right not to renew the credit? The court in *Michigan Commerce Bank* concluded, on facts similar to those in Problem 11.3, that the credit did not have a perpetual duration. Its conclusion relies on 5–106(d)'s language. Section 5–106(d) deems a credit to have a duration of five years if the credit "states" that it is perpetual. Although a credit that does not allow for termination effectively makes its duration perpetual, 5–106(d) deals only with credits that state that they are perpetual. A credit that does not allow for termination, although functionally perpetual, is not perpetual in form. It does not "state" that it is perpetual in duration. Comment 4 to 5–106 deems a credit non-perpetual when the credit is renewable at the option of the issuer. This goes beyond 5–106(d)'s language, which addresses the duration only of credits that "state" that they are perpetual. In addition, the Comment says nothing about the duration of a credit that automatically renews and cannot be terminated. The *Golden West Refining* court declined to draw any inferences about 5–106(d)'s construction from the relevant portion of Comment 4: "We will not speculate what the drafters intended by electing not to comment on a particular type of letter of credit." 538 F.3d at 1241.

Section 5–106(d), as construed by *Michigan Commerce Bank* and *Golden West Refining*, recites a sensible rule. It adopts a formal test of duration: a credit expires after five years if it states that it is perpetual. Otherwise, the credit expires after its stated date. From an operational perspective, this formal test has a lot to be said for itself. For one thing, it allows parties to the credit to determine easily whether the credit has a duration of five years or not, when the credit does not so state. By contrast, a functional test that asks whether the terms of the credit in effect make the credit perpetual makes the credit harder to administer. For instance, qualifying language stating conditions under which the issuer has the option not to renew the credit may be complex enough that it would be difficult even for the parties to determine the credit is perpetual or not. Parties (and courts) easily can determine that a credit is perpetual when it so states. Formal requirements make the letter of credit cheaper to administer and therefore more attractive to potential users.

D. Issuer's Duty to Honor

1. The Strict Compliance Standard

A letter of credit is a very efficient instrument by which beneficiaries get quick and reliable payment on their presentation of prescribed documents. Indirect evidence of the credit's efficiency is the comparatively low fees issuers charge compared to fees charged for other comparable instruments. Although large banks do not generally publish their fees, they appear to charge between slightly more than a tenth of a percent (0.125%) and a quarter of a percent of the face amount (usually with a minimum of $20 million) per year to issue a standby letter of credit. By comparison, a surety issuing a performance bond might charge between half a percent and two percent of the same face amount. Central to the credit's cost advantage is the issuer's duty to honor complying documentary presentations. Under 5–108(a), the standard of documentary compliance is strict: ". . . [A]n issuer shall honor a presentation that, as determined by the standard practice referred to in subsection (e), appears on its face strictly to comply with the terms and conditions of the letter of credit." Section 5–108(a) requires the issuer to compare the documents presented ("on their face") to the terms of the credit. In doing so, as provided by 5–108(e), the issuer must take into account the standard practice of financial institutions that issue credit. Based on the documents and this standard practice, the strict compliance standard requires the issuer to honor a presentation if it strictly complies with the credit's terms. Otherwise, the issuer honors the presentation at its own risk. The letter of credit law of most legal systems apparently also adopts the strict compliance standard. See Boris Kozolchyk, Commercial Letters of Credit in the Americas 72, 259 (1966).

Neither the UCP 600 nor ISP 98 expressly adopts a standard of documentary compliance. UCP 600 article 14a merely states that "the issuing bank must examine a presentation to determine, on the basis of the documents alone, whether or not the documents appear on their face to constitute a complying presentation." ISP 98 Rule 4.01b is even less specific. It simply provides that "[w]hether a presentation appears to comply is determined by examining the presentation on its face against the terms and conditions in the standby . . . to be read in the context of standard standby practice." Article 14d of the UCP 600 seems to suggest that the standard of compliance is strict. The Article recites that data in a document, read with the credit and taking into account international standard banking practice, need not be identical to, but must not conflict with any data in other required documents or in that document. And some observers believe that Article 14a implicitly adopts the strict compliance standard. Whether the UCP 600 does or does not incorporate the strict compliance standard is not terribly important. If a credit is subject to the UCP 600 and the UCP implicitly adopts the standard, the standard controls the issuer's duty to honor. If the UCP does not implicitly adopt the strict compliance standard and the credit does not address the standard of compliance, domestic standards apply. The predominant standard under domestic letter of credit law is strict compliance.

Under the strict compliance standard the importance of a documentary discrepancy is irrelevant. As a Law Lord put it in Equitable Trust Co. of New York v. Dawson Partners Ltd., (1927) 27 L.L.Rep. 49, 52, a leading letter of credit case, "[t]here is no room for documents which are almost the same, or which will do just as well." Of course, facts about the underlying transaction also are irrelevant to the issuer's duty to the beneficiary. If the documents presented correspond to the terms of the credit, the issuer must pay. Otherwise, not. As discussed below, an issuer who honors a noncomplying documentary presentation risks not being reimbursed by the applicant.

The strict compliance standard resists an informative and precise statement. Strict compliance does not require literal, letter for letter correspondence between the contents of prescribed documents and the credit's terms. Comment 1 to 5–108 states that the standard does not mean "slavish conformity to the terms of the credit." On the other hand, both the strict compliance standard and Comment 1 reject a substantial compliance standard, which judges compliance by an undefined measure of the degree to which documents comply with the credit's terms. Thus, the strict compliance standard seems to treat documents as complying if they less than literally, but more than substantially, comply with the credit's terms. Courts and commentators have had trouble identifying the permissible range of less-than-perfect compliance. Even courts that do not insist on absolute compliance sometimes disagree on what is strict but less than literal compliance. A rough working notion of compliance under 5–108(a) finds that documents strictly comply when the issuer, using the standard practices of letter of credit issuers, determines that they correspond on their face with the credit's terms. Put another way, the notion is that the documents comply if a reasonable issuer, examining only the documents and the credit and charged with knowledge of the practices of issuers, would decide that a documentary discrepancy is insubstantial.

What standard practice considers an insubstantial documentary discrepancy might not be obvious to those who do not deal with letters of credit. For example, the International Chamber of Commerce has attempted to describe some of the specific "best practices" for examining documents among international banks. See ICC, International Standard Banking Practice for the Examination of Documents Under UCP 600 (Pub. No. 745) (2013) ("ISBP 2013"). The ISBP 2013 finds acceptable a description of the quantity of goods in the invoice that varies +/–5% from the quantity required by the credit. ISBP 2013 C13. It also considers a credit that calls for "one invoice" or "invoice in 1 copy," without more, to require an original invoice rather than a copy. ISBP 2013 A29(d)(i). Neither discrepancy likely would be regarded as insubstantial by non-issuers. Under 5–108(e) the determination of the standard practice of letter of credit issuers is to be decided by the court, not a jury.

Section 5–108(e) does not allow the issuer to take into account practices other than those of letter of credit issuers. As a result, the issuer is not charged with knowledge of practices in the trade or industry involved in the underlying transaction. This means that a reference in a document that differs from the reference required by the credit may not satisfy the strict compliance standard, even if the relevant trade considers them synonyms. J.H. Rayner & Co. v. Hambros Bank, Ltd., [1943] 1 K.B. 37 (C.A.), a classic English letter of credit case, illustrates the point. There, the credit called for bills lading covering "about 1400 tons Coromandel groundnuts." The bills of lading presented described the goods as "bags machine-shelled groundnuts" and referred to them as "O.T.C. C.R.S. Aarhus." In the nut trade in London "C.R.S." was an abbreviation for "Coromandel." The beneficiary sued for wrongful dishonor after the issuing bank refused to pay the draft drawn under the credit. In ruling that the documents presented did not strictly comply with the terms of the credit, the court found it "quite impossible" that the issuer is charged with knowledge of the trades involved in the transactions from which letters of credit arises. The court therefore concluded that the bank was not required to take into account in determining documentary compliance the practice of those who deal in nuts in Mincing Lane.

Much of the litigation over the issuer's duty to honor involves the application of the strict compliance standard. Typographical differences and abbreviations in documents are at issue in some of these cases. Strict compliance tests these documentary discrepancies by the standard practice of financial institutions that regularly issue credits. The credit in In New Braunfels National Bank v. Odiorne, 780 S.W.2d 313 (Tex. Ct. App. 1989), called for drafts to refer to "Letter of Credit No. 86B122B5." The beneficiary presented a draft referring to "Letter of Credit No. 86B122BS." The court found that the discrepancy in the last letter "S" to be an obvious typographical error that strictly complied with the credit's terms. In Tosco Corp. v. FDIC, 723 F.2d 1242 (6th Cir. 1983), the credit required presentation of a draft that recited "drafts Drawn under Bank of Clarksville Letter of Credit Number 105." The court ruled that the issuer's honor was proper when it honored the beneficiary presentation of a draft that stated "drawn under Bank of Clarksville, Tennessee letter of Credit No. 105." The lower case "l," abbreviation of "Number" and addition of "Tennessee" in the draft were discrepancies that the found did not justify dishonor. Although the Tosco court applied the substantial compliance standard, Comment 1 to 5–108 approves the results in both New Braunfels and Tosco as proper under the strict compliance standard.

Van Zeeland Oil Co., Inc. v. Lawrence Agency, Inc.

United States District Court, Western District of Michigan, 2010
704 F. Supp.2d 711

■ OPINION BY: R. ALLAN EDGAR, DISTRICT JUDGE

MEMORANDUM

* * *

I.   Background

The central issue in this action is whether Plaintiff Van Zeeland complied with the strict terms of a letter of credit implicating the Bank's duty to honor the letter by submitting to Van Zeeland the amount of fifty thousand dollars ($50,000). The parties agree on the material facts. According to the complaint, Plaintiff operates a business that sells and distributes petroleum products. Defendant Lawrence Agency operated a gas station in Manistique, Michigan. The Lawrence Agency and Plaintiff entered into a ten-year agreement entitled the Detailed Dealer Motor Fuel Agreement ("Agreement") that operated from June 27, 2008 until June 27, 2018. Although the specific terms of the Agreement are not legally relevant to this matter, the Agreement's provisions contained Lawrence's commitment to purchase from Plaintiff 100% of the gasoline it sold during the ten-year term of the Agreement. The Agreement further required the Lawrence Agency to provide Plaintiff with a letter of credit in the amount of $50,000. Todd Van Zeeland and Gary Grams signed the Agreement on behalf of Van Zeeland. Rudolph Lawrence signed the Agreement without indicating for which entity he signed, but the parties appear to agree that he signed on behalf of the Lawrence Agency. He also indicated the word "Pres." after his name apparently indicating his status as President of Defendant Lawrence Agency.

On June 30, 2008 the Bank issued "Irrevocable Standby Letter of Credit No. 691." The Letter of Credit states that Van Zeeland is the "Beneficiary" and that the "Applicant" is "Van Zeeland Oil Customer Daryl E. and Michele A. Lawrence." The parties agree that Daryl Lawrence is the son of Rudolph Lawrence. The Letter of Credit states in its entirety:

> We hereby establish our Irrevocable Standby Letter of Credit No. 691 in your favor at the request and for the account of Van Zeeland Oil Company, Inc. (the "Applicant") in the amount of $50,000.00 U.S. dollars effective June 30, 2008.
>
> This Letter of Credit is available with the People State Bank of Munising by payment against presentation of your sight draft(s) drawn on the Peoples State Bank of Munising of Credit No. 691 dated June 30, 2008, and accompanied by your signed and dated statement stating:
>
> "Van Zeeland Oil Company, Inc. hereby represents, certifies, and warrants that the amount of the accompanying draft represents funds due and owing to Van Zeeland Oil Company, Inc. by the Applicant for purchases of products and services by Applicant from Van Zeeland Oil Company, Inc. according to such terms as are established by Van Zeeland Oil Company, Inc. from time to time or pursuant to a Retail Supply Agreement and/or Image Rebate Reimbursement Agreement executed by Van Zeeland Oil Company, Inc. and the Applicant.["]
>
> Partial drawings under this Letter of Credit are allowed and each such partial drawing will reduce the amount thereafter available hereunder for drawings under this Letter of Credit.
>
>   * * *

Richard Nebel signed the Letter of Credit on behalf of the Bank as its chief executive officer ("CEO").

Plaintiff asserts that Defendant Lawrence Agency accepted a final delivery of gasoline on December 8, 2008, only six months into the contract. According to the Complaint, the Lawrence Agency breached the terms of the Agreement by failing to continue to purchase gasoline from Plaintiff for a remaining 114 months under the terms of the Agreement.

On January 8, 2009 Todd Van Zeeland wrote Richard Nebel at the Bank requesting that the Bank honor the Letter of Credit and quoted the specified language required under paragraph 3 of the Letter of Credit. The letter attached a draft and summary of alleged debt owed to Plaintiff, including amounts totaling $113,712.28 for such items as uniforms, materials, services, Cenex image elements, freight, installation, and labor. The Complaint asserts that the Bank verbally refused to honor the submitted Letter of Credit because the applicant for the Letter of Credit differed from the company that signed the Agreement.

On May 29, 2009 Mr. Van Zeeland again wrote Mr. Nebel at the Bank and quoted the requested language from the Letter of Credit asking the Bank to honor the Letter of Credit by paying Plaintiff $50,000. The request pursuant to the Letter of Credit was accompanied by a document entitled "Sight Draft" in the amount of $50,000.

On June 10, 2009 Mr. Nebel responded to Plaintiff's request by writing a letter to Plaintiff's attorney, Clifford Knaggs. The letter states:

> Thank you for your letter dated June 2, 2009. Unfortunately, the bank cannot honor the most current sight-draft dated May 29, 2009 for the same reason that existed back in January, 2009.
>
> It is the position of the bank and our customer that the letter of credit you reference required the "Applicant" of the letter of credit owe money to Van Zeeland Oil Company. Our applicant that sought the letter of credit was Daryl Lawrence and his wife, Michele Lawrence. The letter of credit states as follows: "Van Zeeland Oil Company, Inc. hereby represents, certifies, and warrants that the amount of the accompanying draft represents funds due and owing to Van Zeeland Oil Company, Inc., by the Applicant for purchases of products and services by Applicant from Van Zeeland Oil Company, Inc. according to such terms as are established by Van Zeeland Oil Company, Inc. from time to time or pursuant to a Retail Supply Agreement and/or Image Rebate Reimbursement Agreement executed by Van Zeeland Oil Company, Inc. and the Applicant."
>
> Our applicants (customers) in this situation were Daryl Lawrence and Michele Lawrence, not Lawrence Agency, Inc., d.b.a. Centex [sic] Pit Stop. The letter of credit is void of any reference to Lawrence Agency, Inc., d.b.a. Centex [sic] Pit Stop as the "applicant". Do our customers (applicants) of the letter of credit, Daryl Lawrence and Michele Lawrence currently owe Van Zeeland Oil Company for any product and/or service?
>
> We agree that the beneficiary in the letter of credit is Van Zeeland Oil Company and the Peoples State Bank of Munising is the referenced bank, however, we disagree that our "applicant" for the letter of credit owes any money for product or services to Van Zeeland Oil Company. . . .

Following the Bank's second refusal to honor the Letter of Credit, Plaintiff brought this suit against the Lawrence Agency and the Bank.

Plaintiff claims that the Bank breached its obligation under the Letter of Credit and seeks $50,000 from the Bank.

* * *

III. Analysis

Letters of credit under Michigan law are governed by Article 5 of Michigan's version of the Uniform Commercial Code ("UCC"), Mich. Comp. Laws § 440.5101 et seq. . . . Article 5 makes clear that except in cases involving fraud:

> [A]n issuer shall honor a presentation that, as determined by the standard practice referred to in subsection (5), appears on its face strictly to comply with the terms and conditions of the letter of credit. Except as otherwise provided in section 5113 and unless otherwise agreed with the applicant, an issuer shall dishonor a presentation that does not appear to comply.

Mich. Comp. Laws § 440.5108(1). An issuer, however, "is not responsible for: [t]he performance or nonperformance of the underlying contract, arrangement, or transaction" or "[a]n act or omission of others." Mich. Comp. Laws § 440.5108(6)(a)–(b).

* * *

Michigan courts have not had very many opportunities to address letters of credit pursuant to Article 5. However, two relevant decisions exist that provide further guidance regarding the legal interpretation of letters of credit. In Toyota Tsusho Corp. v. Comerica Bank the federal district court explained the law pertaining to letters of credit in Michigan in general terms. 929 F.Supp. 1065, 1070–71 (E.D. Mich. 1996). It noted that:

> A [letter of credit] is a contract between a bank and a beneficiary of credit that is separate and distinct from the commercial contract between the beneficiary (usually a seller), and the bank's customer (usually a buyer). The [letter of credit] is not dependent upon the underlying commercial transaction, and in determining whether to pay, the bank looks only at the [letter of credit] and the documentation presented by the beneficiary to determine whether it meets the [letter of credit's] requirements.

> The majority view, which has been expressly adopted by Michigan courts, is a standard of "strict compliance" with a [letter of credit's] presentment requirements. . . . The purpose behind this "strict compliance" standard is to promote the predictability and swiftness of a determination to honor or dishonor a draw request on [a letter of credit] and to make the processing of [letters of credit] more efficient. Id. (citing Osten Meat Co. v. First of America Bank– Southfield Michigan, 517 N.W.2d 742 (Mich. Ct. App. 1994).

* * *

In this case the letter of credit required Plaintiff to assert that:

> Van Zeeland Oil Company, Inc. hereby represents, certifies, and warrants that the amount of the accompanying draft represents funds due and owing to Van Zeeland Oil Company, Inc. by the Applicant for purchases of products and services by Applicant from Van Zeeland Oil Company, Inc. according to such

terms as are established by Van Zeeland Oil Company, Inc. from time to time or pursuant to a Retail Supply Agreement and/or Image Rebate Reimbursement Agreement executed by Van Zeeland Oil Company, Inc. and the Applicant.

Before honoring the Letter of Credit, the Bank would have been entitled to check with the applicants named in the Letter of Credit, Daryl and Michele Lawrence, to determine whether they personally owed funds to Van Zeeland based on a contract they entered with Plaintiff or other purchases from Plaintiff. Otherwise honoring the Letter of Credit might have exposed the Bank to liability for wrongful honor. Nowhere in the Letter of Credit does it mention the name of the Lawrence Agency, Cenex Pit Stop, or Rudolph Lawrence. This appears to have been by design as the Bank indicates that it did not wish to extend credit to Lawrence, and it appears that Daryl Lawrence also did not intend to be responsible for his father's business.

* * *

Under Michigan law the Bank's role is a ministerial one. It must make a prompt decision regarding whether to honor the letter of credit. The Bank's role was not to analyze the potential relationship between the applicants and the Lawrence Agency, but was rather to determine if the applicants personally owed anything to Plaintiff. As Plaintiff could not demonstrate strict compliance by showing funds owed to it by the applicants, the Bank was within its rights to refuse to honor the Letter of Credit.

Plaintiff's failure to investigate the law of strict compliance in Michigan regarding letters of credit and to peruse the Letter of Credit more carefully requires that it bear the loss of the Lawrence Agency's default.

* * *

IV. Conclusion

For the reasons explained supra, Plaintiff's motion for summary judgment will be DENIED. The Bank's motion for summary judgment will be GRANTED. Plaintiff's claims against the Bank will be DISMISSED in their entirety with prejudice.

Uniloy Milacron Inc. v. PNC Bank, N.A.

United States District Court, Western District of Kentucky, 2008
2008 U.S. Dist. LEXIS 33063

■ OPINION BY: CHARLES R. SIMPSON III, DISTRICT JUDGE

MEMORANDUM OPINION

This matter is before the court upon cross motions of the plaintiff, Uniloy Milacron Inc. ("Uniloy"), and defendants PNC Bank, N.A. and PNC Financial Services Group (collectively "PNC Bank" or the "Bank") for partial summary judgment.

BACKGROUND

The facts relevant to the motions before the court are not disputed. On October 20, 2005, Uniloy entered into a contract with defendant MAB, LLC ("MAB") to manufacture two plastic bottling machines for

MAB's use (the "Contract"). The total price of the machines was $1,320,050. After making a $232,050 down payment on the machines, MAB obtained $800,000 of the outstanding balance of the purchase price from a venture capital firm. MAB remained responsible for the remaining outstanding balance of $388,000.

As a condition to obtaining the venture capital funding, MAB was required to obtain a letter of credit to cover the $388,000 for which it remained responsible. On April 10, 2006, PNC Bank issued a letter of credit to Uniloy on behalf of MAB for $388,000 (the "Letter of Credit"). By its terms, the Letter of Credit was to expire at 5:00 p.m. on July 31, 2006. In order for Uniloy to obtain payment from PNC Bank under the terms of the Letter of Credit, Uniloy was required to present three items to the Bank: first, a dated signed certification by an authorized Uniloy representative stating that Uniloy had not received payment from MAB within sixty days of shipment of "1) Uniloy Model UR8X7–7PNE CBTR Blow Molding Machine Including Molds and Material Corporationing—Serial Number: N01A010088 and 1) Uniloy Model UR6X9–7PNE CBTR Blow Molding Machine Including Molds and Material Corporationing—Serial Number: N01A0100089;" second, copies of the unpaid invoices for the merchandise described above; and third, a copies of the bills of lading for the merchandise described above evidencing the shipment date.

On May 3, 2006, Uniloy shipped the machines to MAB. MAB failed to pay the remaining $388,000 of the purchase price and on Friday, July 28, 2006, Uniloy sent a demand for payment under the Letter of Credit to PNC Bank by Federal Express (the "Draw Request"). PNC Bank received the Draw Request on July 31, 2006. Upon review of the documents submitted by Uniloy, PNC Bank discovered that the signed certification was undated and that the serial number on one invoice was listed as "N01A0100088." PNC Bank also discovered that the bills of lading contained the following descriptions of the merchandise shipped:

Customer Order No. 12	Customer Order No. 13
(1) Uniloy R2000 B.M.M.	(1) Uniloy R2000 B.M.M.
S/N N01A0100089	S/N N01A0100088

At 4:24 p.m. the Bank faxed a "Notice of Discrepancies" to Uniloy stating that it was refusing to honor Uniloy's Draw Request due to discrepancies between the format of the Draw Request and the format required by the Letter of Credit. Specifically, PNC Bank informed Uniloy that:

> (1) the certification of Uniloy's representative was not dated as required by the Letter of Credit;

> (2) the serial number shown on one invoice did not match the serial number on the Letter of Credit; and

> (3) the description of the merchandise on the bills of lading did not match the description of the merchandise on the Letter of Credit.

* * *

* * * In the declaratory judgment count of its complaint Uniloy alleges that any discrepancies between the Draw Request and Letter of Credit were minor and that PNC Bank has not, and cannot, be prejudiced by these discrepancies. In the equitable estoppel count Uniloy alleges that it relied on the Bank's representation that it would contact MAB to determine if the discrepancies could be waived, and the Bank did not contact, nor had any intention of contacting, MAB. Uniloy, therefore, claims the Bank should be estopped from relying on the discrepancies to refuse its Draw Request.

DISCUSSION

* * *

The parties disagree as to the standard that a demand for payment is required to meet in order to comply with a letter of credit. PNC contends that a letter of credit must be strictly complied with while Uniloy contends that substantial compliance should suffice. The parties agree, however, that neither Kentucky state courts nor the Sixth Circuit has opined on the standard for compliance under Kentucky law. The parties also agree that the Uniloy's compliance with the Letter of Credit should be viewed in light of the Uniform Customs and Practice for Documentary Credits ("UCP"), a set of rules, standards, and commercial policy promulgated by the International Chamber of Commerce ("ICC") which frequently governs letters of credit. This court finds that even if Kentucky were to adopt a "strict compliance" standard, Uniloy's Draw Request would satisfy such a standard.

Under the strict compliance standard, courts have held that documents presented in connection with a demand for payment that are "nearly the same" as required by the letter of credit will not suffice. However, even under the strict compliance standard, nonmeaningful errors, such as obvious typographical errors, will not justify a bank's refusal to honor a letter of credit. Additionally, under the strict compliance standard, discrepancies between the demand for payment and the terms of the letter of credit will also not justify a bank's refusal to honor the letter of credit when there is no possibility that the bank could have been misled by the discrepancies to its detriment.

The UCP provides that upon receipt of a demand for payment under a letter of credit a bank "must determine on the basis of the documents [presented in the demand] alone whether or not they appear on their face to be in compliance with the terms and conditions of the [letter of] [c]redit." International Chamber of Commerce, ICC Uniform Customs and Practice for Documentary Credits, ICC Publication 500. "[D]ocuments which appear on their face to be inconsistent with one another will be considered as not appearing on their face to be in compliance with the terms and conditions of the [letter of] [c]redit." Id. Courts interpreting the UCP have held that individual documents presented in a demand for payment must be viewed in light of all documents presented in order to determine whether the documents obviously relate to the same transaction. Voest–Alpine Trading USA Corp. v. Bank of China, 167 F.Supp.2d 940, 947 (S.D.Tex. 2000).

In the instant case, the court finds that the documents presented by Uniloy in its Draw Request obviously relate to the same transaction, and that there is no possibility that PNC Bank could have been misled by the discrepancies between the presented documents and the Letter of Credit. Thus, even under the strict compliance standard, the discrepancies which the Bank relied upon to refuse Uniloy's Draw Request did not justify such refusal.

With respect to the undated signed certification presented by Uniloy, PNC Bank argues that inasmuch as the Letter of Credit only authorized Uniloy to obtain payment from the Bank if MAB failed to make payment to Uniloy within sixty days of shipment of the machines, the absence of a date on the certification could have drawn its validity into question. We disagree. Although[ ] the certification presented by Uniloy in its Draw Request was undated, the cover letter attached to the Draw Request was dated July 28, 2006. The cover letter expressly referred to the Letter of Credit and was signed by the same Uniloy representative that signed the certification. Clearly, PNC Bank could not have been misled by the absence of a date on the signed certification. Accordingly, the undated certification does not justify the Bank's refusal to honor Uniloy's Draw Request.

With respect to the discrepancy between the serial number on one of the invoices and the serial number on the Letter of Credit, a mere examination of the entire face of the invoice makes it clear that PNC Bank could not have been misled by the discrepancy. The serial number at issue was listed on the Letter of Credit as "N01A010088." Invoice number 423–X–152 listed the serial number as "N01A0100088."[1] Absent additional evidence, the differing serial numbers could possibly be viewed as having the potential to mislead the Bank. However, invoice number 423–X–152 also contained a description of the merchandise identified by serial number "N01A0100088." The description of the merchandise in the invoice was identical to the description of the merchandise in the Letter of Credit. Given that the serial numbers differed by one "0" and that the merchandise description was identical, the court finds that the differing serial numbers were the product of an obvious typographical error. Such a discrepancy does not justify the Bank's refusal to honor Uniloy's Draw Request.

With respect to the discrepancy between the merchandise descriptions on the bills of lading and the Letter of Credit, when the bills of lading are viewed in light of the additional documents presented by Uniloy this discrepancy also cannot be said to have had the potential to mislead the Bank. The court agrees with PNC Bank insofar as the description of the merchandise in the bills of lading, "Uniloy R2000 B.M.M," is not the same as the description in the Letter of Credit, "Uniloy Model UR6X9–7PNECBTR Blow Molding Machine" or "Uniloy Model UR8X7–7PNECBTR Blow Molding Machine." However, although the description of the merchandise on the bills of lading differs from the description of the merchandise on the Letter of Credit, the serial numbers on the bills of lading match the serial numbers on the Letter of Credit.[2] Moreover, the serial numbers on the bills of lading also match the serial numbers on the invoices. The bills of lading and the invoices clearly relate to the same transaction. Such invoices contain a

---

[1]   The court also notes that the bill of lading presented by Uniloy that corresponds with the Invoice number 423–X–152 also lists the serial number as "N01A0100088."

[2]   With the exception of the typographical error discussed above.

merchandise description identical to the merchandise description in the Letter of Credit. Given that the bills of lading, when viewed in light of the invoices, clearly relate to MAB's purchase of one "Uniloy Model UR8X7–7PNE CBTR Blow Molding Machine" and one "Uniloy Model UR6X9–7PNE CBTR Blow Molding Machine" this court cannot find that the Bank could have been misled based on the discrepancy between the merchandise description on the bills of lading and the Letter of Credit.

For the above stated reasons the court finds that Uniloy's Draw Request was in strict compliance with the Letter of Credit and, therefore, PNC Bank was obligated to honor the Draw Request. Accordingly, the court will grant Uniloy's motion for partial summary judgment as to the declaratory judgment claim. . . .

NOTES AND QUESTIONS

1.   In finding that the Bank rightfully dishonored the beneficiary's documentary presentation, the *Van Zeeland Oil* court faulted the beneficiary for failing "to investigate the law of strict compliance in Michigan regarding letters of credit and to peruse the Letter of Credit more carefully." Who failed to understand 5–108(a)'s strict compliance standard and its application: the beneficiary or the court? That standard provides in relevant part that the issuer shall honor a presentation that appears "on its face" strictly to comply with the terms and conditions of the letter of credit. The third paragraph of the Bank's credit, reproduced and referred to by the court, required the beneficiary's draft to recite that the amount of the draft represents the amount that the "Applicant" owes the beneficiary and that is past due. Van Zeeland Oil Company was the beneficiary and Daryl and Michele Lawrence the applicants ("the Applicant"). Van Zeeland's draft recited the language of the third paragraph. Although Daryl and Michele owed no obligations to Van Zeeland, 5–108(a)'s strict compliance standard does not allow the Bank to rely on this fact to refuse to honor Van Zeeland's documentary presentation. In doing so the Bank has gone beyond the face of the relevant documents to take account of facts extrinsic to them. Under limited circumstances bearing on the beneficiary's fraud, the issuer may refuse honor of a strictly conforming presentation. The Bank alleged no such facts. The fraud exception to the independence principle is discussed in section E below.

2.   Whether a documentary discrepancy is a typographical error is not always clear. A letter, word or numeral in a name or description might refer to the goods or a person referred to in the credit. Or it might refer to different goods or a different person. In Voest–Alpine Trading USA Corp. v. Bank of China, 167 F. Supp.2d 940 (S.D. Tex. 2000), the letter of credit required that the beneficiary be identified as "Voest–Alpine Trading USA Corp." Several documents presented identified the beneficiary as "Voest–Alpine USA Trading Corp." In a suit against the issuer for wrongful dishonor, the court held that the documents presented, although discrepant with the credit's terms, strictly complied. The court found that, taking the documents as a whole, they appeared to refer to the same beneficiary (Voest–Alpine Trading USA Corp.). The *Uniloy Milacron* court relies on *Voest–Alpine*'s "documents as a whole" approach to conclude that the different serial number in an

invoice was a typographical error. Is the court's conclusion obviously correct? The description of the goods in the bills of lading differed from the description in the credit. In addition, one of the invoices the beneficiary presented contained an additional zero in the serial number of the goods. The court concluded that the issuer's document examiners, reading the description of the goods in the invoice and the bills of lading together, would know that the additional zero in the serial number was an error. But isn't it possible that the serial number appearing in the invoice correctly identified goods that were shipped and the serial number without the additional zero in the remaining invoices referred to different (or nonexistent) goods? In that case the different description of the goods in the bills of lading and the serial number in the single invoice would not be a typographical error at all. Perhaps more to the point, is a document examiner likely to know which is the more likely possibility, based just on standard banking practice? Cf. UCP 600 art. 14d.

3.   Section 5–108(a)'s strict compliance standard is a default rule. As with most aspects of the letter of credit, it can be varied by the reimbursement agreement between the applicant and the issuer when their interests and capabilities favor doing so. See 5–103(c); Comment 2 to 5–103; Comment 1 to 5–108. Some reimbursement agreements either qualify or supplant the strict compliance standard. ISP 98 Rule 4.09(c), which requires exact compliance in the documentary presentation when the credit calls for "exact" or "identical" wording in documents. Even when the parties do not opt out of the default rule, 1–302(b) allows the reimbursement agreement to set standards of documentary compliance. Thus, whether a strict compliance standard is preferable to an alternative compliance standard depends on the preferences and capacities of typical parties to a letter of credit. Which rule is likely to minimize the costs of effecting payment under a credit for the typical applicant?

4.   Does the strict compliance standard enhance the reliability of letters of credit as payment mechanisms? Or does it encourage an issuing bank to find a minor defect in the documents in instances in which the bank does not want to pay, such as when the applicant has gone into bankruptcy and reimbursement of the bank's claim against the applicant may be difficult? Observers have consistently found a high frequency of noncomplying documentary presentations, typically exceeding 50%. In an informal survey of selected banks issuing commercial credits, the issuers reported that 73% of the documentary presentations contained discrepancies. See Ronald J. Mann, The Role of Letters of Credit in Payment Transactions, 98 Mich. L. Rev. 2494 (2000). Concerned about the number of discrepant presentations, the ICC has tried to reduce their incidence by publishing a description of international banking practices for handling documentary discrepancies. See ISBP 2013, Introduction.

In assessing the wisdom of the strict compliance standard, recognize three points. First, in most commercial credits the beneficiary does not care if the documents presented contain discrepancies because the issuer will honor the presentation anyway. Where the market price of goods contracted for in the underlying transaction is stable or rising, the applicant buyer will want the goods and, therefore, will have the issuer waive its right to insist on conforming documents. Alternatively, under these markets conditions, the issuer may waive the discrepancy at its own risk. Thus, most of the time obtaining conforming documents isn't cost justified for beneficiary sellers. See John F. Dolan, Why High Discrepancy Rates Do Not Discourage L/C Use, 2003 Ann. Survey Letter Credit L. & Prac. 36. The few beneficiaries who are concerned about the prospect of a falling market can opt out of strict compliance by insisting that the reimbursement agreement provide a more forgiving standard of compliance.

Second, there is a powerful market mechanism controlling strategic rejections of discrepant documents by issuers. Issuers operate in a market in which reputation matters. Because issuance fees are comparatively low, an issuer's profit from operating a credit department depends on generating a high volume of credits. The issuer therefore must both obtain repeat business and attract potential applicants and beneficiaries. The number of issuers is relatively small, and information about their handling of credits often can be obtained from other issuers. An issuer may seize on a discrepancy to avoid honor because it fears not being reimbursed or is undercollaterized or wants to avoid involvement in the applicant's bankruptcy or simply wants to placate its applicant. But doing so risks a loss of credit business since potential beneficiaries will insist that credits be issued by issuers that are reliable sources of payment. The presenting beneficiary also is unlikely to do business with the issuer again. Thus, prospect of a loss in reputation often suffices to prevent issuers from strategic rejections even under a strict compliance standard.

Third, less stringent standards of compliance require enhanced judicial scrutiny of the underlying transaction, and courts are poorly positioned to scutinize it. For instance, the court in Voest–Alpine Trading USA Corp. v. Bank of China, 167 F.Supp.2d 940 (S.D. Tex. 2000), considers and rejects a standard that finds documentary discrepancies when the deviation in the document risks harming the applicant in the underlying transaction. Application of this standard encourages parties to litigate the issuer's decision to honor or dishonor a documentary presentation. Courts and issuers may be unfamiliar with the facts necessary to make this determination of harm at the time the issuer must decide to honor the presentation. They may know nothing about industry practices bearing on the underlying transaction. Standards less stringent than strict compliance, therefore, undermine the credit's efficient payment function. Professors White and Summers reach the same conclusion and state, without remorse, that "the issuer may examine the documents microscopically and may assert small discrepancies to excuse its duty to pay." 3 James J. White & Robert S. Summers, Uniform Commercial Code, § 26–5 (at 164) (5th ed. 1995).

PROBLEM 11.4

In its letter of credit application to a New York bank ("Bank"), the applicant listed the name of the beneficiary as "Sung Jin." The beneficiary's name in fact was Sung Jun. Acting on the application Bank issued its credit subject to UCP 600, naming the beneficiary as "Sung Jin". The credit, which allowed for negotiation of the documents, required the beneficiary's name, "Sung Jin," to appear on documents presented. (By allowing for negotiation Bank undertook to honor a presentation by the purchaser of complying documents.) Later, Sung Jun negotiated documents to Hanil in which the beneficiary's name appeared as "Sung Jun." Hanil sued Bank for wrongful dishonor after Bank refused to pay against Hanil's presentation of the documents it had purchased. What result? See Hanil Bank v. PT Bank Negara Indonesia, 41 U.C.C. Rep. Serv.2d 618 (S.D.N.Y. 2000).

PROBLEM 11.5

Buyer was lucky enough to acquire from Seller a first edition of Thomas Hobbes, *Leviathan* (1651), in mint condition for $20,000. To pay for her purchase, Buyer had Bank issue a letter of credit in the amount of the purchase price and naming Seller as the beneficiary. The terms of the credit required Seller to present an invoice and a written appraisal which described the book as a "first edition of Thomas Hobbes, *Leviathan* (1651)." When Seller presented to Bank a draft for $20,000 drawn on Buyer along with an invoice and a written appraisal, Bank noticed that both the invoice and appraisal described the book as "Thomas Hobbs, *Leviathan*, the Head edition." Fortunately, by chance Bank's document examiner is Smith, who has a doctorate in the history of political thought and collects rare books. Smith recognizes that "the Head edition" is a common and unmistakable reference to the 1651 first edition of *Leviathan*. Although Smith's superiors believe him, Bank refuses to pay Seller, informing him immediately by a letter that pointed out the discrepancies in his documentary presentation. Is Bank's refusal wrongful? See 5–108(a), (e); cf. UCP 600 arts. 14b, 14c, 18c.

2. WAIVER, ESTOPPEL AND PRECLUSION

When the beneficiary of a letter of credit seeks payment, it presents the letter of credit and other documents, which often will include a draft demanding payment, usually on sight. An issuer can respond to a documentary presentation in either of two ways: by honoring or dishonoring it. To honor the presentation is to pay or otherwise give value, as required by the credit. See 5–102(a)(8). If the documents comply with the credit's terms, both 5–108(a) and UCP 600 article 8a. require the issuer to honor the presentation. However, the issuer can still have a duty to honor even a noncomplying documentary presentation. This occurs if the issuer waives its right to rely on the documentary discrepancies to dishonor the presentation or is estopped or precluded from doing so.

Waiver is an intentional relinquishment of a known legal right and applies to Article 5 via 1–103(b), as a supplementing principle of extra UCC common law. It is not an amendment of the credit. An amendment requires the agreement of all parties (5–106(b); UCP art. 10a); waiver requires the consent only of the party relinquishing its rights. In addition, unlike an amendment of the credit, a waiver can be oral, unless the reimbursement agreement requires otherwise. Cf. 5–104. An issuer who waives a documentary discrepancy does so at its own risk, unless the applicant has agreed to the waiver. Comment 7 to 5–108 construes waiver narrowly, so that waiver of one or more presentations does not waive subsequent discrepant presentations. UCP 600 article 16b allows the issuer to approach the applicant for a waiver. The UCP is silent as to the effect of the issuer's waiver against the beneficiary. A few courts have divided over whether common law doctrines such as waiver apply to credits subject to the UCP. Compare Banco General Runinahui, S.A. v. Citibank Int'l, 97 F.3d 480 (11th Cir. 1996) (waiver inapplicable), with Alaska Textile Co., Inc. v. Chase Manhattan Bank, N.A., 982 F.2d 813 (2d Cir. 1992) (applicable).

In deciding whether to waive a documentary discrepancy, prudent issuers usually approach their applicants to obtain their consent. This is because the reimbursement agreement conditions the issuer's reimbursement on its honoring a complying documentary presentation. The applicant's consent relinquishes its right to insist on documentary compliance as a condition of the issuer's reimbursement. Sometimes issuers waive discrepancies at their own risk, without the consent of their applicants. In all cases, waiver is a right of the issuer that it can exercise within its discretion. The issuer has no obligation to waive a discrepancy, even if the applicant consents to the waiver. See Suntex Indus. Corp., Ltd. v. CIT Group/BBC, Inc., 2001 WL 34401367 (D. Del. 2001). It need not even approach the applicant to elicit the applicant's consent. UCP article 16b and ISP 98 Rules 5.05 and 5.06(a) are to the same effect.

Both Article 5 and the UCP require the issuer to give proper notice of dishonor and attach a consequence to the failure to give it. Article 5 follows the UCP's approach both to the sufficiency of notice that must be given to the presenter and the effect of the failure to give timely notice and sufficient notice of dishonor. Section 5–108(b) requires that, in the case of dishonor, the issuer must communicate both the fact and grounds of dishonor to the presenter. See Comment 2 to 5–108 (second paragraph); cf. UCP 600 art. 16d.i, and ii. Thus, 5–108(b) contemplates two possibilities: either the issuer fails to make a timely decision to honor or dishonor, or the issuer's timely decision fails to give timely notice of the grounds for dishonor. In both cases, 5–108(c) precludes the issuer from relying as a ground for dishonor on discrepancies it has delayed communicating to the presenter within 5–108(b)'s prescribed time limit.

Section 5–108(b)'s preclusion rule is not a rule concerning waiver or estoppel. Estoppel in letter of credit law requires the beneficiary to reasonably rely to its detriment on the issuer's handling of documentary discrepancies. For example, the issuer's delay in giving the beneficiary notice of discrepancies may prevent the beneficiary from curing them before the credit expires. In these circumstances the issuer is estopped from relying on the discrepancies to refuse honor. Like waiver, estoppel is an extra-UCC principle applicable to Article 5 via 1–103(b). Estoppel and preclusion are exceptions to the strict compliance standard. However, although both obligate the issuer to honor a noncomplying presentation when they apply, the notions are different. Courts tend to mix waiver and estoppel together, and sometimes treat both as preclusion. See, e.g., American Coleman v. Intrawest Bank of Southglenn, N.A., 887 F.2d 1382, 1387 (10th Cir. 1989) ("waiver estoppel rule"); Banco General Runinahui, S.A., 97 F.3d at 480, 485 n.11 (preclusion as "strict estoppel"). Preclusion is not waiver because it does not require the issuer to intentionally relinquish its right to a complying presentation. Section 5–108(b)'s preclusion rule applies when the issuer simply fails to give timely notice of the grounds for dishonor within the prescribed period. Preclusion also is not estoppel because estoppel requires detrimental reliance and 5–108(b)'s rule does not require reliance. It therefore requires no showing that the presenter has been harmed by the issuer's failure to give timely notice of the fact or grounds of dishonor. Unlike waiver and estoppel, Article 5's preclusion rules avoid the proof costs associated with litigating over relinquishment of a right to a complying presentation (waiver) or detrimental reliance on a failure to give timely notice of a discrepancy (estoppel). The UCP's rules are similar.

PROBLEM 11.6

1. Over the period of a year, Beneficiary presented three drafts for payment to Bank. Each presentation contained the same discrepancy. The first two times Bank paid the draft without objection after receiving permission of the Applicant to pay despite the nonconformity. The third time Applicant refused to consent to payment and Bank dishonored the draft on the ground that the presentation was nonconforming. Has Bank wrongfully dishonored? Comment 7 to 5–108.

2. Bank issued a letter of credit subject to UCP 600. The credit recited that it was also "subject to provisions of Article 5 of the UCC to the extent that they are consistent with UCP 600." Among the documents required was a commercial invoice covering "toys." Beneficiary presented to Bank documents, including a commercial invoice covering "construction equipment," on Day 1. Bank delayed examining the documents until Day 9. On that date, it properly notified Beneficiary of the documentary discrepancy and stated that it was refusing to honor Beneficiary's presentation. Assume that issuing banks in these circumstances always examine documents the day after they are presented. May Bank nonetheless rely on the documentary discrepancy to dishonor Beneficiary's presentation? If not, why? See UCP 600 arts. 14b, 16f; 5–116(c). Suppose Bank examined the documents on Day 5 and notified Beneficiary on the same date. Can it make a plausible argument based on UCP 600 article 14b for a different result? Cf. ISP 98 Rule 5.01(a)(i) (notice given within three business days deemed not unreasonable).

PROBLEM 11.7

Bank issued a letter of credit subject to UCP 600 and with an expiration date of January 9. The credit obligated Bank to pay Beneficiary $100,000 (U.S.) upon Beneficiary's presentation of three documents: a commercial invoice, a bill of lading and a certificate of inspection. The terms of the credit required the documents to cover "100 pounds of widgets," and invoice and certificate of inspection to state that the widgets were "quality 100%." On January 1, Beneficiary presented all three documents to Bank. The commercial invoice described the goods as "105 pounds of widgets of 95% quality." The bill of lading described the goods as "105 pounds of widgit . . . all received on board for shipment."

Bank notified Beneficiary on January 2 to the effect that it "rejects the invoice presented by you based on discrepancies going to the quantity and quality of widgets described. The descriptions do not accord with the terms of the credit." On January 5, Bank notified Beneficiary that it "finds that the description of the goods in the bill ('105 pounds of widgit') does not accord with the terms of the credit." Each notice was accompanied by Bank's statement that it was returning the documents to Beneficiary, and Bank did so. This did Beneficiary no good because Beneficiary was unable to make another presentation by January 9, the date on which the credit expired. Bank refused to pay Beneficiary $100,000.

(1) Did Beneficiary's documentary presentation comply with the terms of the credit? Consult ISBP 2013 A23 and C13 reproduced below. (2) If not, is Bank entitled to dishonor Beneficiary's noncomplying documentary presentation? See UCP 600 arts. 16c.i, ii, f.

ICC, International Standard Banking Practices (ISBP) (2013):

A23 A misspelling or typing error that does not affect the meaning of a word or the sentence in which it occurs does not make a document discrepant. . . . However, a description as "model 123" instead of "model 321" would not be regarded as a typing error and would constitute a discrepancy.

C13 The quantity of the goods required in the credit may be indicated on an invoice within a tolerance of +/–5%. . . . The tolerance of +/–5% in the quantity of the goods will not apply when:

    a.   a credit states that the quantity in terms of a stipulated number of packing units or individual items.

E. THE INDEPENDENCE PRINCIPLE AND THE FRAUD EXCEPTION

1. THE INDEPENDENCE PRINCIPLE

Basic to letter of credit law is the principle that the letter of credit undertaking is separate from and independent of all other relationships, including the relationships out of which it arises. This is the independence (or "autonomy") principle. Given the principle, the issuer's obligations are completely unaffected by facts concerning the performance or breach of the underlying transaction or the reimbursement agreement. Section 5–103(d) states the independence principle: "[r]ights and obligations of an issue to a beneficiary . . . under a letter of credit are independent of the existence, performance, or nonperformance of a contract or arrangement out of which the letter of credit arises or which underlies it . . . " UCP 600 article 4a states the principle more succinctly: "A credit by its nature is a separate transaction from the sale or other contract on which it may be based." The other sets of rules produced by the International Chamber of Commerce governing letters of credit have similar provisions; see, e.g., ISP 98 Rule 1.07; URDG 758 art. 5.

The independence principle is a mandatory rule under Article 5. See 5–103(c), (d). Accordingly, the issuer's undertaking to the beneficiary may not qualify or eliminate the principle. The principle has a number of implications both outside and within letter of credit law. Outside letter of credit law, the Comptroller of the Currency's Interpretive Ruling 7.1016 relies on the principle to regulate the issuance of letters of credit. The Ruling permits national banks, subject to other conditions, to issue letters of credit "and other independent undertakings." 12 C.F.R. § 7.1016(a). Thus, the Ruling regulates a national bank's permissible engagements by their separateness ("independence") from other relationships. Where a standby credit obeys the independence principle, the Ruling permits its issuance. A national bank generally cannot issue a guarantee because it is not an "independent undertaking."

As important are the implications of the independence principle within letter of credit law. Most basic, the principle makes the credit a distinct financial product, different from a guarantee or negotiable instrument. The credit issuer's obligation to the beneficiary is primary in part because it does not depend on any other relationships or transactions, or facts about them. Thus, the issuer's obligation is unaffected by whether the underlying transaction has been performed or breached. It therefore cannot rely on defenses to the applicant arising from the underlying transaction to refuse to honor its obligation under the credit. Given the independence principle, the credit issuer's obligation depends only on the presentation of documents called for in the issuer's undertaking. As a result, there are fewer circumstances under which the beneficiary will not be paid by the issuer. This makes the credit more valuable to the beneficiary than a guarantee. Without the independence principle, letters of credit would not be legally distinctive instruments.

In addition, the independence principle underlies two more specific rules that deal with the issuer's right of reimbursement. One rule applies to the confirmer's right to reimbursement from the issuer. Where a bank confirms a credit at the request of an issuer, the original issuer is the applicant and the confirming bank the issuer of the confirmed credit. See 5–107(a). The independence principle applies to the confirmed credit, so that the confirmed credit is separate from the original credit. Thus, if the documentary conditions of the confirmed credit differ from those of the original credit, the beneficiary is entitled to have its presentation honored by the confirming bank only if the presentation conforms to the conditions set by the confirmed credit. However, unless otherwise provided, a confirming bank that in turn presents documents that do not comply with the conditions of the original credit is not entitled to reimbursement. 5–107(a) (second sentence).

The other specific rule concerns the issuer's right to insist on terms of the credit even when the applicant agrees to waive or modify them. As noted above, it is not uncommon for a beneficiary's initial documentary presentation to deviate from conditions of the credit. In response the applicant sometimes will agree to waive the discrepancy and request that the issuer honor the discrepant documentary presentation. The applicant might even offer to modify its reimbursement agreement with the issuer accordingly. The issuer nonetheless does not have a duty to waive the discrepancy or agree to the modification. See Suntex Indus. Corp., Ltd. v. CIT Group/BBC, Inc., 2001 WL 34401367 (D. Del. 2001); Bombay Industries, Inc. v. Bank of N.Y., 649 N.Y.S.2d 784 (N.Y. App. Div. 1996). The independence principle underlies this result. The letter of credit undertaking is separate from the reimbursement agreement or any other transaction. Thus, the conditions of the credit are unaffected by the applicant's waiver or willingness to modify the reimbursement agreement to allow payment against discrepant documents. The issuer therefore may continue to insist on a conforming documentary presentation.

2. THE FRAUD EXCEPTION

Fraud is the single exception to the independence principle. It is explicitly recognized under decisional law and 5–109(a). The U.N. Convention on Independent Guarantees recognizes the exception too. See U.N. Convention art. 19(1). The UCP does not address the fraud exception. Its silence on the issue allows two opposite inferences: the failure to address fraud implicitly displaces the exception or the failure to do so leaves unaffected fraud as a basis for dishonoring a complying documentary presentation. Courts and commentators tend to accept the latter inference. See Mid–America Tire, Inc. v. PTZ Trading Ltd., 768 N.E.2d 619 (Ohio 2005), reproduced below; John F. Dolan, 1 The Law of Letters of Credit 4.06[2][e] (at 4–61) (4th ed. 2007). In their view, where the credit is subject to the UCP, applicable domestic law such as 5–109 controls the fraud exception and its application.

Although some of 5–109's crucial terms are imprecise, its structure is clear. When fraud has been committed, 5–109(a) allows the issuer to refuse payment to some presenters while requiring payment to other presenters. Section 5–109(a)(2) identifies the class of presenters the issuer may but need not pay, and 5–109(a)(1) identifies the class of presenters the issuer must pay. Section 5–109(b) prevents a court from enjoining payment of the latter, "protected" class of presenters. The subsection allows a court to enjoin payment of the former, "unprotected" class of presenters. An injunction against them may be issued only if the conditions generally required for the relief are met. 5–109(b)(3).

Section 5–109(a) allows the issuer to refuse to honor a presentation by an unprotected presenter if a required document is materially fraudulent or that presentation would facilitate a material fraud on the issuer. The provision does not define "material fraud" because Article 5's drafting committee was unable to agree on a definition. Comment 1 to 5–108 states: "Material fraud by the beneficiary occurs only when the beneficiary has no colorable right to expect honor and where is no basis in fact to support such a right to honor." However, the addition of the adjective "material" does not help determine when there is fraud in the first place (material or non-material). In Sztejn v. J. Henry Schroder Banking Corp., 31 N.Y.S.2d 631, 634–35 (N.Y. Sup. Ct. 1941), an influential pre-Code case, the court distinguished between what it called "active fraud" and a "mere breach of warranty" without precisely characterizing the distinction. To see the difficulty with the distinction, consider a sales contract calling for Seller to deliver new widgets and a letter of credit requiring documents describing the goods delivered as "new widgets." Is there fraud in Seller's performance of the sales contract in the following four circumstances? (1) Seller intentionally delivers a car, not new widgets. (2) Seller intentionally delivers new widgets with very minor scratches. (3) The same as (2) except the market price for widgets has increased so that scratched widgets sell for more than new widgets were previously sold. (4) Seller intentionally delivers seriously malfunctioning new widgets. Notice that Seller has breached an express warranty in all four circumstances. Circumstance (4) arguably is an easy case: deliberately delivering seriously defective goods is egregious behavior characteristic of fraud. The extent of breach differs in the other three circumstances, and a standard is needed to find fraud nonarbitrarily in one or more of them. Article 5 apparently decided not to provide one.

Section 5–109(a) applies when "a required document is forged or materially fraudulent, or honor of the presentation would facilitate a material fraud by the beneficiary on the issuer or applicant." This language refers to two different sorts of fraud. One sort involves fraud with respect to a required document. This is fraud in the letter of credit (or "documentary") transaction. The other sort of fraud involves fraud in the performance of the underlying transaction: behavior that "would facilitate a material fraud by the beneficiary." Fraud in the letter of credit transaction can occur without fraud in the underlying transaction. For instance, a required document may be intentionally altered to comply with the terms of the credit without effecting performance of the underlying contract. Conversely, fraud in the underlying transaction can occur without fraud in the letter of credit transaction. Worthless goods intentionally can be delivered even though the required documents state nothing about their quality. Section 5–109(a) allows the issue, in prescribed conditions, to refuse to pay when there is fraud in either the letter of credit or in the underlying transaction. Fraud in the letter of credit transaction is not an exception to the independence principle, because credit itself requires genuine documents. Thus, the issuer may dishonor the documentary presentation because the documents presented do not comply with credit's terms. Because fraud in the underlying transaction allows a fact about a separate transaction to affect the issuer's obligations under the letter of credit, it is an exception to the independence principle.

Finally, as noted, 5–109(a)(1) protects certain presenters against dishonor. Fraud does not allow the issuer to dishonor their conforming presentations. The members of the class of protected presenters have one thing in common: they are all transferees of documents under the letter of credit. See 5–109(a)(1)(i)–(iv). For instance, a negotiating bank, a holder of a draft, and a purchaser of documents all are presenters that have received required documents from the beneficiary or the beneficiary's transferee. To be protected, the presenter must take the documents or draft in good faith and without notice of the fraud. See 5–109(a)(1)(i)–(iv). All other presenters are not protected, and the issuer therefore in good faith can dishonor conforming presentations by them. Because a beneficiary under the credit does not purchase the draft or documents, it is a not transferee and therefore not a protected presenter.

Note how 5–109(a) allocates the risk of fraud. In the case of a protected presenter, the applicant bears this risk. This is because the issuer honoring the draw is entitled to be reimbursed by the applicant either by contract or by statute, or both. 5–108(i)(1). The applicant therefore must recover from the beneficiary. Because the issuer can dishonor an unprotected presenter's conforming presentation, the presenter bears the risk of the beneficiary's fraud when dishonor occurs. It must recover from the beneficiary (or its transferor, who ultimately must recover from the beneficiary). Thus, the unprotected presenter bears the risk of the beneficiary's fraud. Article 5's implicit judgment is that protected presenters are in an inferior position to the applicant or issuer to detect the beneficiary's fraud. Allocating fraud risk to either the applicant or unprotected presenters but never to protected presenters is thought to be the cost minimizing solution. Is this judgment sound? In support, it is usually observed that the applicant has dealt with the beneficiary whereas a presenter may have purchased a draft or documents from a remote transferor and never have dealt directly with the applicant. See United Bank Ltd. v. Cambridge Sporting Goods Corp., 360 N.E.2d 943, 949 n.6 (N.Y.1976). The applicant's costs in taking appropriate precautions, therefore, are thought generally to be lower than those facing the ultimate transferee's precaution costs. The observation has no force when the presenter purchases directly from the beneficiary. Consider also that often issuers or confirmers are local banks who know the beneficiary or can easily acquire information about it. Article 5's allocation of fraud risk is justifiable only if most documentary drafts are discounted in markets to strangers to the underlying contract. Neither the Comments to 5–109 nor its drafting history discuss this assumed empirical generalization.

Mid–America Tire, Inc. v. PTZ Trading Ltd.

Supreme Court of Ohio, 2002
768 N.E.2d 619

■ OPINION: ALICE ROBIE RESNICK, J.

I.   FACTS

* * *

B.   Parties and Participants

Given the multilateral nature of the negotiations and arrangements in this case, it is beneficial to provide a working list of the various parties and key participants and their relationships to one another and the transactions at hand.

The American parties and participants are as follows:

(1) Plaintiff-appellant and cross-appellee, Mid–America Tire, Inc. ("Mid–America"), is an Ohio corporation doing business as a tire wholesaler. Mid–America provided the financing for the purchase of the tires in this case and was the named applicant by whose order and for whose account the LC was issued.

(2) Arthur Hine is the president of Mid–America and signatory to the LC application.

(3) Plaintiff-appellant and cross-appellee, Jenco Marketing, Inc. ("Jenco"), is a Tennessee corporation doing business as a tire

wholesaler. Jenco formed a joint venture with Mid–America to purchase the tires at issue.

(4) Fred Alvin "F.A." Jenkins is the owner of Jenco and also acted as Mid–America's agent in the underlying negotiations.

(5) Paul Chappell is an independent tire broker who resides in Irvine, California. Chappell works as an independent contractor for Tire Network, Inc., a company owned by his wife, and acted throughout most of the negotiations as an agent for Jenco.

(6) First National Bank of Chicago ("First National"), on behalf of NBD Bank Michigan, is the issuer of the LC in this case. First National was a defendant below, but is not a party to this appeal.

The European parties and participants are as follows:

(1) Defendant-appellee and cross-appellant, PTZ Trading Ltd. ("PTZ"), is an offshore import and export company established in Guernsey, Channel Islands. PTZ is the seller in the underlying transaction and the beneficiary under the LC.

(2) Gary Corby is an independent tire broker operating as Corby International, a trading name of Corby Tyres (Wholesale) Ltd., in Wales, United Kingdom. Corby was the initiator of the underlying negotiations. The trial court's findings with regard to Corby's status as PTZ's agent form the subject of PTZ's cross-appeal.

(3) John Evans is the owner of Transcontinental Tyre Company located in Wolverhampton, England, and PTZ's admitted agent in the underlying negotiations.

(4) Aloysius Sievers is a German tire broker to whom PTZ owed money from a previous transaction unconnected to this case. Sievers, also an admitted agent for PTZ, procured and shipped the subject tires on behalf of PTZ, and signed and presented the draft for payment under the LC.

(5) Patrick Doumerc is the son of the proprietor of Doumerc SA, a French company that is authorized to sell Michelin overstock or surplus tires worldwide. Doumerc is the person from whom Sievers procured the mud and snow tires for sale to Jenco and Mid–America.

(6) Barclays Bank PLC in St. Peter Port, Guernsey, is the bank to which Sievers presented the invoice and shipping documents for payment under the supporting LC. Barclays Bank was a defendant below, but is not a party to this appeal.

C.   Events Leading to the Issuance of the LC

In October 1998, Corby approached Evans about obtaining large quantities of Michelin winter tires. Evans contacted Sievers, to whom PTZ owed money. Evans knew that Sievers had a relationship with a sole distributor of Michelin surplus tires out of France. Eventually, an arrangement was worked out under which Sievers would buy the tires from Doumerc's warehouse in France and Evans would sell them on behalf of PTZ through Corby to an American purchaser.

Meanwhile, Corby contacted Chappell in California and asked whether he was interested in importing Michelin tires on the gray market for sale in the United States. "Gray imports" are tires that are imported without the knowledge or approval of a manufacturer into a market that the manufacturer serves, at a greatly reduced price. Corby told Chappell that he had a large client who negotiated an arrangement directly with Michelin to handle all of its overstock blem tires from France and who could offer 50,000 to 70,000 Michelin tires per quarter at 40 to 60 percent below the United States market price on an exclusive and ongoing basis. Chappell contacted Jenkins in Tennessee, who called Hine in Ohio, and it was arranged that Jenco and Mid–America would pursue the deal through Chappell.

On October 28, 1998, Corby faxed Chappell a list of Michelin mud and snow tires that were immediately available for shipment and Chappell forwarded the list to Jenkins. The list was arranged in columns for quantity, size, pattern, and other designations applicable to the European market with which Chappell and Jenkins were unfamiliar. In particular, many of the tires on the list bore the designation "DA/2C." Chappell and Jenkins understood that DA meant "defective appearance," a European marking for a blem, but they were not familiar with the "/2C" portion of the designation. When they asked for clarification, Corby told Chappell that "DA/2C" means the same thing as "DA," but since all of the listed tires are not warehoused at a single location, "/2C" is used merely to indicate that those blemished tires are located in a different warehouse.

Chappell also asked Corby whether he could procure and offer summer or "highway" tires, along with the winter tires. Chappell, Jenkins, and Hine had no interest in purchasing strictly snow tires, as it was already too late in the season to market them profitably. However, they would have an interest in buying both winter and highway tires and marketing them together as a package deal.

Corby told Chappell that 50,000 to 70,000 highway tires would be made available on a quarterly basis at 40 to 60 percent below the United States market price. However, when Chappell received another list of available tires from Corby on November 11, 1998, he complained to Corby that this list contained no summer tires and nowhere near 50,000 units. Corby responded that Michelin was anxious to get rid of these tires first, as the market for snow tires in Europe was coming to a close, that a list of summer highway tires would be made available over the next few weeks, and that Chappell and appellants would not have an opportunity to procure the highway tires unless they first agreed to purchase the snow tires. Corby explained that Michelin does not list available summer tires in the mid-month of a quarter. Instead, it waits for these tires to accumulate in a warehouse and then puts out the list at the end of the month. Thus, a list of summer tires would be available over the next few weeks.

In a transmission dated November 13, 1998, Corby wrote to Chappell:

"The situation is as I explained yesterday, there are no summer tyres available at all but, if, and a very big if, this deal goes ahead we will get all surplus stocks at the end [of] each quarter from now on, but if this deal does not go, then I know we can kiss any future offers good buy [sic]."

On November 20, 1998, Corby faxed Chappell a list of summer tires available for immediate shipment, but the listed units were not priced, were composed of many small "odd ball sizes" unmarketable in the United States, and did not approach the 50– to 70,000–range in aggregate quantity. In his cover letter, Corby assured Chappell that "I have of course been in contact with Michelin regarding the list of summer tyres" and "they have confirmed that in the next three/four weeks we have exclusive to us the new list of Michelin summer tyres, quantity unknown as yet, but they believe to be anything from 50,000/70,000 tyres, which would not be too bad for Jan sales." The letter also stated that Michelin was offering the tires at "the price of $1.50 per tyre more than the M & S tyres * * * based on taking the whole lot."

On November 23, 1998, Corby faxed the following letter to Jenkins:

"Subject: Michelin Tyre Programme.

"Dear F.A.

"I would just like to confirm our current position with the Off–Shore marketing company that have been authorized to sell all Michelin factory 'Over Stock' tyres. That is, from now on the tyres will only be offered for sale to us through PTZ Trading Ltd., these tyres will come available every two/three months which I have been informed by my contact the next large consignment (not including the current stock of winter/summer tyres) will be in the next three/four weeks time of around 50,000/70,000 tyres.

"If our business with the winter tyres goes well, then I see this as [an] extremely excellent opportunity to tap into large consignments of tyres direct from the factory on a regular long term basis.

"Just to confirm once again, I have been assured by PTZ Trading who are acting on behalf of the factory that we will have exclusivity to all tyres that come available from now on."

On December 1, 1998, Evans faxed a letter and "pro forma invoice" (an invoice that sets out in rough terms what the eventual invoice will look like) to Jenkins. The letter stated, "We understand from Gary Corby that you are now about to open the Letter of Credit for the Michelin M&S Tyres."

However, Chappell and Jenkins were hesitant to have Hine proceed with the financing for the winter tires because they had not yet received concrete information as to the cost and availability of the initial 50,000 to 70,000 summer tires. As Chappell and Jenkins held out for the list of summer tires, Corby and Evans pressed for the LC. While continually assuring Chappell and Jenkins that large stocks of Michelin summer tires would be made available in a short time, Corby and Evans became increasingly insistent about conditioning the offer of summer tires upon the issuance of an acceptable LC in favor of PTZ for the winter tires.

From early December 1998, through late January 1999, Corby made repeated, often daily, telephone calls to Chappell insisting that Jenkins confirm the issuance of the LC or forfeit the deal entirely. During this time, Corby also sent a number of faxes to Chappell, each one proclaiming that without confirmation of the LC by the end of the day, the offer for the winter tires would be withdrawn and there would be no future offers for winter or summer tires.

In addition, Evans faxed two messages to Jenkins on January 7, 1999. In the first, Evans wrote:

"There are large stocks of Michelin summer pattern tyres being made available within the next 7/10 days and we will be pleased to offer these to you when an acceptable Letter of Credit is received for the winter pattern tyres. We will be very happy to work with you on Michelin tyres on a long term basis and give you first option on offers.

"May we once again stress the urgency of letting us have the Letter of Credit for the Michelin winter tyres so that we can commence business on a long term basis."

In the second message, Evans informed Jenkins:

"Further to our fax of today we understand that you would like clarification on future offers made by PTZ Trading Ltd. of Michelin tyres.

"As we have already indicated we wish to commence a long term business relationship with Jenco Marketing Ltd. [Sic.] We assure you that we will not offer any Michelin tyres that we obtain to any other party in the United States of America provided Jenco Marketing Inc. agree to purchase in a reasonable time."

D.   The Issuance of the LC

By the end of January 1999, Jenkins and Hine were convinced that they had to open the LC for the winter tires as a show of good faith towards the quarterly acquisition of summer tires and that, upon doing so, PTZ would honor its end of the bargain.

Effective February 1, 1999, and expiring in Guernsey, Channel Islands, on April 2, 1999, First National issued an irrevocable credit at Hine's request in favor of PTZ and for the account of Mid–America in the amount of $517,260.33. The LC provided, among other things:

"COVERING SHIPMENT OF:

"14,851 MICHELIN TYPES AT USD 34.83 PER TIRE IN ACCORDANCE WITH SELLER'S PROFORMA INVOICE 927–98 DATED 11–19–98

"SHIPPING TERMS: EXWORKS ANY EUROPEAN LOCATION

* * *

"THE CREDIT IS SUBJECT TO THE UNIFORM CUSTOMS AND PRACTICE FOR DOCUMENTARY CREDITS (1993 REVISION), INTERNATIONAL CHAMBER OF COMMERCE—PUBLICATION 500."

E.   Events Following the Issuance of the LC

Over the next month, Corby and Evans pushed for shipping arrangements under the supporting LC for the winter tires, while Chappell and Jenkins continued to insist on a conforming price list for the summer tires. As the final LC shipping date approached, and several nonconforming lists of summer tires emerged, the negotiations grew increasingly volatile until they were hostilely terminated.

A week after the issuance of the LC, Chappell wrote to Corby, "Without the list and pricing [for the summer tires], we are at a standstill with the clock ticking on the winters. Please make every effort to send list during your workday, so we can compile our list for combined sales of both winter and summer units." Corby then faxed Chappell a list of summer tires but, as before, this list contained no prices and fell considerably short of 50,000 units. When Chappell complained, Corby sent another list, which he noted to be six out of 15 sheets of an "original list from Michelin." The other nine sheets, however, were never sent. In any event, this list once again failed to contain the promised quantities of tires, and a considerable number of the listed units were snow tires. Although this list did set forth unit prices, those prices were represented in French francs, and when the French francs were converted into United States dollars, it became apparent that the prices for these units were equal to or in excess of the maximum market prices for a like product in the United States.

On the morning of February 17, 1999, Evans telephoned Jenkins to inform him that no price list for summer tires would be sent until Barclays Bank received the LC for the winter tires. This caught Jenkins by surprise, as the LC had been in place since the first of the month and all information pertaining thereto had previously been sent to Evans, but Jenkins nevertheless faxed Evans the LC confirmation number. Throughout that day, Evans made repeated requests for Jenkins to provide him with shipping instructions and orders to release the winter tires. Jenkins responded with several letters that he faxed to Evans on February 17. In these letters, Jenkins informed Evans that he would not authorize the shipment of any winter tires in the absence of a conforming list of summer tires, that any attempt by Evans to ship the winter tires without Jenkins's written consent would be met with legal action, and that the deal would be voided and the LC recalled unless a complete list of competitively priced summer tires arrived in Jenkins's office by February 19.

On February 19, 1999, Evans faxed the following message to Jenkins:

"We appreciate your feeling of frustration at the delay in giving you the price for the Summer Tyres but assure you it is only in your best interests to obtain the most favorable prices.

* * *

"Further urgent negotiations are due to take place with Michelin on Monday February 22nd 1999 to see if we can arrive at an acceptable packaged price but of course the final desission [sic] is yours.

"In the meantime in the interests of all concerned please do not give a specific time for completion if you want us to obtain the most favorable price."

On February 23, 1999, Corby faxed Chappell another list of summer tires, but this list was illegible in places and irreconcilable with the previous list. Chappell complained and Corby sent another list the following day. However, once again, this list fell well short of 50,000 units, contained many European sizes not used in the United States and various tires not manufactured by Michelin, and stated prices that were often higher than the cost of purchasing the tires one at a time from most United States dealers. The list also provided that, in addition to the stated prices, appellants were required to pay all shipping, handling, duty, and freight charges. Moreover, Jenkins was now informed that he could no longer pick and choose from among the listed tires, but instead must purchase the entire lot or none at all.

On March 1, 1999, Jenkins wrote to Evans, "We are with drawing [sic] our offer effective immediately to purchase the snow package, as PTZ has failed to meet their agreed commitment on the Michelin summer tire offer." (Emphasis deleted.) Jenkins stated that the listed prices for the tires are "not competitive" and "TOTALLY UNACCEPTABLE," and that "we have gone from a reported 50,000 tires to a total offer of about 12,000 tires of which approximately 2,500 of those are TRX tires not sold in this country."

Between March 1 and March 5, 1999, Chappell and Jenkins discovered that it was Doumerc, not PTZ, who all along had the direct and exclusive relationship with Michelin to sell all of its overstock and blem tires. They also discovered that Corby had misrepresented the "DA/2C" designation, which attached to many of the tires on the summer lists as well as on the original winter list. Rather than indicating the warehousing location for those tires, "/2C" actually meant that the Department of Transportation serial numbers had been buffed off those units, rendering them illegal for import or sale in the United States.

During this time, Jenkins informed Evans that he would notify the United States Customs Service if the DA/2C tires were shipped, and Evans confirmed that he would not ship those tires to the United States. Also, Chappell informed Doumerc of the entire course of events, and Doumerc agreed not to ship the tires until Chappell and Jenkins had the opportunity to come to France, inspect the tires, and resolve the situation.

Chappell and Jenkins made arrangements to fly to France, but when they called Doumerc on March 11, Sievers answered the phone. They explained the entire matter to Sievers and offered to extend the LC expiration date in order to allow for a peaceful resolution. Sievers rejected the offer, however, stating that the winter tires belonged to him, not Doumerc, that he did not care what Doumerc had agreed to, and that "I have a letter of credit and I am shipping the tires."

The following day, Mid–America instituted the present action to enjoin payment under the LC. The complaint was later amended to add Jenco as a plaintiff. The trial court granted a temporary restraining order on March 16, 1999, and a preliminary injunction on April 8, 1999.

On July 14 and 15, 1999, a trial was held on appellants' motion for a permanent injunction. In a final judgment entry dated October 8, 1999, the trial court granted a permanent injunction against honor or presentment under the LC pursuant to R.C. 1305.08(B). In its separate findings of fact and conclusions of law, the trial court found that the documents presented to Barclays Bank on behalf of PTZ appeared on their face to be in strict compliance with the terms and conditions of the LC. However, the court also found by clear and convincing evidence that PTZ, acting through Evans and Corby, fraudulently induced appellants to open the LC, and that such fraud was sufficient to vitiate the LC. In this regard, the trial court was "satisfied that fraud in the inducement of the issuance of a letter of credit is grounds for a court to grant injunctive relief against the payment of such letter of credit to the beneficiary who perpetrated such fraud."

In a split decision, the court of appeals reversed the judgment of the trial court. . . .

* * *

The cause is now before this court pursuant to the allowance of a discretionary appeal and cross-appeal.

* * *

III. MID–AMERICA AND JENCO'S APPEAL

* * *

B. Governing Law

R.C. Chapter 1305 is Ohio's version of Article 5 of the Uniform Commercial Code ("UCC"). It was enacted in its current form, effective July 1, 1998, to reflect the 1995 revision of Article 5, and is applicable to any LC that is issued on or after its effective date.

The parties in this case have specifically adopted the UCP as applicable to the present undertaking. . . . The question that naturally arises from such an incorporation is whether and to what extent R.C. Chapter 1305 will continue to apply to the undertaking. In other words, when a particular LC states that it is subject to the UCP, what is the resulting relationship between the UCP and R.C. Chapter 1305 with regard to that transaction?

* * *

. . . This is not a situation where one complete set of rules is substituted for another. The scope of the UCP is basically different from that of Article 5. "Because of their different scope, Article 5 [of the UCC] covers some important areas not covered by the UCP, and the UCP covers some important areas not covered by Article 5." 6B Hawkland & Miller (Rev.2001), at 5–46 to 5–47, Section 5–103:3. Each of these bodies of rules will apply to govern the undertaking in their respective areas of coverage, and both will apply concurrently in the event of any overlapping consistent provisions. Id. at 5–47, Section 5–103:3.

It is only when the UCP and R.C. Chapter 1305 contain overlapping inconsistent provisions on the same issue or subject that the UCP's terms will displace those of R.C. Chapter 1305. Thus, when a particular LC states that it is subject to the UCP, the UCP's terms will replace those of R.C. Chapter 1305 only to the extent that "there is a direct conflict between a provision of the UCP and an analogous provision of R.C. Chapter 305." Mantua Mfg. Co. v. Commerce Exchange Bank (1996), 75 Ohio St. 3d 1, 661 N.E.2d 161, paragraph one of the syllabus.

* * *

The UCP also adopts the independence principle, but does not provide for a fraud exception.

* * *

In adopting the UCP, "the International Chamber of Commerce undertook to fill in operational details for documentary letter of credit transactions by stating a consensus view of the customs and practice for documentary credits." 6B Hawkland & Miller (Rev.2001), at 5–44, Section 5–103:3. Because "the UCP 'is by definition a recording of practice rather than a statement of legal rules,' [it] does not purport to offer rules which govern the issuance of an injunction against honor of a draft." Intraworld Indus., Inc. v. Girard Trust Bank (1975), 336 A.2d 316, quoting Harfield, Practice Commentary (McKinney's Consol. Laws of N.Y., 1964), Comment 38. Thus, the UCP's silence on the issue of fraud "should not be construed as *preventing* relief under the 'fraud in the transaction' doctrine, where applicable law permits it." (Emphasis sic.)

* * *

We hold, therefore, that when a letter of credit expressly incorporates the terms of the UCP, but the UCP does not contain any rule covering the issue in controversy, the UCP will not replace the relevant provisions of R.C. Chapter 1305. Since the UCP does not contain any rule addressing the issue of injunctive relief where fraud occurs in either the credit documents or the underlying transaction, R.C. 1305.08(B) remains applicable in credit transactions made subject to the UCP.

Accordingly, the rights and obligations of the parties in this case are governed by R.C. 1305.08(B), and the judgment of the court of appeals is reversed as to this issue.

C.   Establishing Fraud Under R.C. 1305.08(B)

Having determined the applicability of R.C. 1305.08(B), we must now consider its boundaries. In this regard, we have been asked to decide whether an issuer may be enjoined from honoring a presentation on the basis of beneficiary's fraud in the underlying transaction and to characterize the fraudulent activity justifying such relief.

1.   Fraud in the Underlying Transaction

May the issuer be enjoined from honoring a presentation under R.C. 1305.08(B) on the basis of the beneficiary's fraudulent activity in the underlying transaction? The short answer is yes, since R.C. 1305.08(B) authorizes injunctive relief where "honor of the presentation would facilitate a material fraud by the beneficiary on the * * * applicant."

* * *

We hold, therefore, that material fraud committed by the beneficiary in either the letter of credit transaction or the underlying sales transaction is sufficient to warrant injunctive relief under R.C. 1305.08(B). Accordingly, the judgment of the court of appeals is reversed as to this issue.

2.   Measure of Fraud

Another controversy that surrounded the "fraud in the transaction" language of UCC 5–114(2) involved the degree or quantity of fraud necessary to warrant injunctive relief.

* * *

As another court adhering to this standard explained, the applicant must show that the letter of credit was, in fact, being used by the beneficiary "as a vehicle for fraud," or in other words, that the beneficiary's conduct, if rewarded by payment, "would deprive the [applicant] of any benefit of the underlying contract and * * * transform the letter of credit * * * into a means for perpetrating fraud." GATX Leasing Corp. v. DBM Drilling Corp., 657 S.W.2d 178, 183 (Tex. App. 1983).

Thus, we hold that "material fraud" under R.C. 1305.08(B) means fraud that has so vitiated the entire transaction that the legitimate purposes of the independence of the issuer's obligation can no longer be served.

3.   PTZ's Actions

The trial court found the following facts to have been established by clear and convincing evidence:

"6. Gary Corby represented to F.A. Jenkins that PTZ Trading, Ltd. was in fact the sole distributor for surplus Michelin tires and that there was a direct relationship between PTZ Trading, Ltd. and Michelin. Corby further represented to Jenkins that there would be 50,000 to 70,000 summer tires available to Jenco per quarter at a price 40 to 60 percent below the U.S. market price within weeks of Jenco showing good faith by purchasing in excess of five hundred thousand dollars worth of mud and snow tires currently offered by PTZ Trading, Ltd.

"7. The Court further finds that John Evans, as agent for PTZ Trading, Ltd., was aware that Corby was making such representations to Jenco and that such representations were false. Mr. John Evans, as an agent for PTZ, knew that Jenco considered the purchase of the summer tires to be necessary in order to make the winter snow and mud tires saleable in the U.S. market. Mr. Evans did nothing to correct Mr. Corby's misrepresentations. Mr. Evans affirmed the misrepresentations and attempted to buttress them in correspondence with Jenco.

"8. Mr. Evans conveyed this information to Mr. Sievers who also acknowledged that he understood that the purchase of the summer tires by Jenco was critical to the conclusion of the sale of the mud and snow tires and without which the winter tire sale would not occur.

"9. John Evans and Aloysius Sievers also knew that a large portion of the mud and snow tires they were attempting to sell were not capable of being imported into the United States or sold here because the United States Department of Transportation identification number had been 'buffed' off of such tires. Both Sievers and Evans knew that Jenco and Mid America Tire intended to sell the snow tires in the United States, but neither advised Jenco or Mid America Tire of the existence of the 'buffed' tires.

"10. Prior to the issuance of the letter of credit, John Evans knew Mid America Tire, Inc. and Jenco were operating under intentionally false and inaccurate representations made by Corby and reinforced by John Evans."

* * *

"12. The Court finds, specifically, that the representation that PTZ had a direct relationship with Michelin Tire, the representation that PTZ was the exclusive distributor for surplus Michelin Tires, the representation that a substantial quantity of between fifty and seventy thousand tires would be available quarterly on an exclusive basis to Jenco and Mid America Tire, Inc. at 40 to 60 percent of the U.S. market price were all material statements inducing Plaintiffs to issue the underlying letter of credit and were in fact false and made with knowledge of their falsity."

* * *

Given these facts, we are compelled to conclude that PTZ's actions in this case are sufficiently egregious to warrant injunctive relief under the "material fraud" standard of R.C. 1305.08(B). The trial court's findings demonstrate that PTZ sought to unload a large quantity of surplus winter tires on appellants by promising a large number of bargain-priced summer tires, without which the winter tires would be virtually worthless to appellants. Keenly aware that appellants would not agree to purchase the winter tires without the summer tires, PTZ made, participated in, and/or failed to correct a series of materially fraudulent promises and representations regarding the more lucrative summer tires in order to induce appellants to commit to purchasing the winter tires and to open an LC in PTZ's favor to secure payment. Dangling the prospect of the summer tires just beyond appellants' reach, PTZ sought first the issuance of the LC, and then shipping instructions, in an effort to cash in on the winter deal before appellants could discover the truth about the "DA/2C" tires and PTZ's lack of ability and intention ever to provide summer tires at the price and quantity represented. Indeed, when appellants learned of PTZ's fraud after opening the LC, and PTZ was no longer able to stall for shipping instructions with nonconforming lists of summer tires, Sievers proclaimed, "I have a letter of credit and I am shipping the tires."

Under these facts, it can truly be said that the LC in this case was being used by PTZ as a vehicle for fraud and that PTZ's actions effectively deprived appellants of any benefit in the underlying arrangement. In this sense, PTZ's conduct is comparable to the shipment of cow hair in Sztejn v. J. Henry Schroder Banking Corp., 31 N.Y.S.2d 631 (N.Y. Sup. Ct. 1941), the shipment of old, ripped, and mildewed boxing gloves in United Bank Ltd. v. Cambridge Sporting Goods Corp., 360 N.E.2d 943 (N.Y. 1976) and the failure to disclose nonconforming performance specifications for the stereo receivers in NMC Ent., Inc. v. Columbia Broadcasting System, Inc., 14 U.C.C. Rep.Serv. 1427 (N.Y. Sup. Ct. 1974).

PTZ's demand for payment under these circumstances has absolutely no basis in fact, and it would be pointless and unjust to permit PTZ to draw the money. PTZ's conduct has so vitiated the entire transaction that the only purpose served by invoking the independence principle in this case would be to transform the LC into a fraudulent seller's Holy Grail, which once obtained would provide cover for fraudulent business practices in the name of commercial expedience.

* * *

V. CONCLUSION

Based on all of the foregoing, the judgment of the court of appeals is hereby reversed, and the permanent injunction as granted by the trial court is reinstated.

NOTES

1. Section 5–109(a)(2) permits an issuer acting in good faith to honor or dishonor a demand for payment made by an unprotected presenter. "Good faith" is defined in 5–102(a)(7) as "honesty in fact." This is a subjective standard. Section 1–201(b)(20) contains the operative standard of good faith in the Articles of the UCC: " 'Good faith,' except as otherwise provided in Article 5, means honesty in fact and the observance of reasonable commercial standards of fair dealing." The generally applicable definition includes both subjective and objective elements. Why is the "commercially reasonable standards" language not included in the Article 5 definition of good faith? See Comment 3 to 5–102. Professor White reports that in Article 5's drafting, representatives of a banking industry trade group argued that "Europeans and other non-Americans were frightened by the threat of a runaway good faith doctrine, particularly by American courts' applying good faith in unforeseen cases." James J. White, The Influence of International Practice on the Revision of Article 5 of the UCC, 16 Nw. J. Int'l L. & Bus. 189, 205 (1995).

Comment 3 finds 5–102(a)(7)'s subjective standard of good faith appropriate because it creates greater certainty in the issuer's obligations. The finding goes against the usual assessment of the effects of subjective standards. Standards such as "honesty in fact" make potentially relevant large bodies of evidence, encourage prelitigation coaching of witnesses, and potentially extend the course of judicial proceedings going to the issue of good faith. Objective standards of good faith, by contrast, typically involve more limited evidence, less prelitigation jockeying, and more truncated proceedings. The usual assessment is that subjective standards produce indeterminacy and high costs in the application of otherwise clear rules. See, e.g., Richard A. Epstein, Simple Rules for a Complex World (1995); Robert D. Cooter & Edward L. Rubin, A Theory of Loss Allocation for Consumer Payments, 66 Tex. L. Rev. 63 (1987). Comment 3's different assessment depends on a confidence that the requisite showing of "honesty in fact" is so easy (and a showing of "dishonesty in fact" so hard) as to discourage investment in litigation of the issue.

2. Section 5–109(b)(3) allows a court to enjoin honor of a credit based on fraud only if the applicable conditions for an injunction are met. Traditionally recognized among these conditions is the requirement that the party seeking the injunction is likely to suffer irreparable injury if the injunction is not issued. Applicants sometimes argue that their business reputation will suffer if the standby credit is drawn on and that this damage constitutes an irreparable injury to them. Their theory is that the draw adversely signals to the applicant's potential contracting partners that it has breached the underlying contract and that it therefore will be an unreliable contracting partner. Although courts count loss of business reputation as an injury not adequately compensated by money damages, they refuse to find that a draw on a credit by itself results in injury to business reputation. In reversing a district court's injunction based on likely irreparable injury to the applicant of the beneficiary's draw on a standby credit, the Sixth Circuit noted: "This finding misunderstands the nature of letters of credit. Under the so-called 'independence principle,' a bank's duty to pay on letters of credit is independent of whether or not the applicant (here Langley) and the beneficiary (here Prudential) have performed on the underlying contract. In other words, the bank 'must pay on a proper demand from the beneficiary even though the beneficiary may have breached the underlying contract with the applicant' [3 White & Summers, Uniform Commercial Code § 26–2, at 138 (5th ed. 2008)]. Consequently, payment on the letters of credit in no way suggests that Langley breached or otherwise failed to perform under the contracts with Prudential. It therefore strains credulity to think that Langley's reputation or goodwill would be tarnished upon payment of the letters." Langley v. Prudential Mortg. Capital Co., LLC, 554 F.3d 647, 649 (6th Cir. 2009).

3. Some international letter of credit law recognizes exceptions to the independence principle in addition to fraud. In Daughin Offshore Engineering & Trading Pte Ltd. v. Private Office of HRH Sheikh Sultan bin Kalifa bin Azyed al Nahyan, [2000] S.L.R. 657, the Singapore Court of Appeals ruled that payment under the credit could be enjoined based on unconscionable conduct in the underlying transaction. Similarly, the Ontario Court of Appeal imposed under the credit a fiduciary duty as well as a duty of good faith to see that the underlying transaction is performed; see Nareerux Import Co. v. Canadian Imperial Bank of Commerce, 2009 Rep. LEXIS 206. An English court ruled that the beneficiary's participation in an illegal scheme in violation of securities laws gives the issuer a defense against honor; see Mahonia Ltd. v. J.P. Morgan Chase Bank, [2004] EWHC 1938. Although these decisions impair the value and smooth operation of letters of credit, the same charge can be made against the fraud exception itself. American courts do not recognize exceptions to the independence principles based on unconscionability, good faith or illegality in the underlying transaction. See James G. Barnes, "Illegality" as Excusing of Dishonour of LC Obligations, 2006 Ann. Rev. Int'l Banking L. & Prac. 23 (illegality).

4. Certain "sanctions clauses" that banks involved in international trade increasingly include in their credits violate the independence principle. For reasons of foreign policy or national security, countries enforce economic and trade boycotts. U.S. sanction regulations, administered by the Treasury Department's Office of Foreign Assets Control, prohibit trade or its facilitation with designated countries, assets or persons. The prohibition is broad enough to include the issuance or honor of a letter of credit made in connection with an underlying transaction that violates U.S. sanctions. In response banks issuing international credits sometimes include in their engagement to their credit beneficiaries wording to the effect that applicable sanctions laws override the conditions of the credit and might prevent honor of their obligations under the credit.

The application of sanctions laws to the letter of credit does not by itself threaten the independence principle. Sanction laws that prohibit the issuer from honoring a complying documentary presentation have priority over the duties imposed on the issuer under Article 5 of the UCC or other rules. Their priority no more compromises the independence principle than do criminal laws that prohibit the issuer from murdering its competitors or stealing their property. However, some sanctions clauses give the issuer the discretion to pay under the credit based on its internal policy or its belief that payment might violate a sanctions law, whether or not that law applies to the payment. These clauses condition the issuer's payment obligation on facts extrinsic to documents required by the credit—facts about its internal policy or beliefs—even when applicable law allows payment. Clauses of this sort therefore violate the independence principle. Because the independence principle is a mandatory rule under Article 5 of the UCC, inclusion of such clauses in an instrument has one of two consequences: either the clause describes a nonfundamental nondocumentary condition that must be ignored or the instrument is not a letter of credit. The International Chamber of Commerce has become concerned enough about the use of sanctions clauses to recommend that issuers incorporating the UCP into their credits omit them. See ICC Banking Commission, Guidance Paper on Sanctions Clauses for Trade Related Products (e.g., Letters of Credit, Documentary Collections and Guarantees) Subject to ICC Rules (470/1129, March 2010). Perhaps understandably, issuing banks apparently have been reluctant to act on the recommendation.

PROBLEM 11.8

Retailer purchased 500 pairs of running shoes from Foot for $20,000. To pay for the shipment Retailer had Bank issue a $20,000 letter of credit naming Foot as the beneficiary. In the credit Bank undertook to pay Foot or purchasers of documents required by the credit. The documents required by the credit included a bill of lading listing the shoes that indicated that they had been loaded "on board" the vessel transporting them. Short on running shoes, Foot delivered boxes of running shorts to the carrier and received in return an "on board" bill of lading covering running shoes. Retailer discovers this fact before the boxes arrive. Worse, Foot has also filed for bankruptcy and is unlikely to pay its creditors in full.

(1) May Retailer prevent Bank from paying Foot? (2) Assume that Foot discounted the bill of lading and other required documents to Ace. Ace knew nothing about the circumstances in which the bill of lading was issued. May Retailer prevent Bank from paying Ace? (3) Assume that Foot shipped 500 pairs of running shoes. Assume also that the carrier issued an "on board" bill of lading even though the running shoes had not been loaded on a vessel. Foot knew nothing about the carrier's behavior. May Retailer prevent Bank from paying Foot? See 5–109(a)(1), (2), (b)(3), (4); 5–102(a)(11).

F. DAMAGES FOR BREACH

Under 5–111(a), the beneficiary or other presenter can recover from the issuer the face amount of the draw under the credit if the issuer wrongfully dishonors the draw. The presenter also can recover incidental damages, but not consequential damages. Section 5–111(a) does not require the presenter to mitigate its loss in these circumstances. However, if the presenter does mitigate its loss, recoverable damages are reduced by the amount of damages avoided by mitigation. The right to recover the face amount of the credit is effectively a remedy of specific performance. Section 5–111(a) confirms this by giving the presenter the right to elect specific performance when the issuer breaches its obligation to deliver something other than money. Because the issuer will have paid or otherwise given value to the presenter according to the credit's terms, as required by 5–111(a) (the dishonor was wrongful), the issuer's reimbursement agreement requires the applicant to reimburse it. The applicant, in turn, is left to recover from the beneficiary or other presenter in a separate action.

Section 5–111(b) governs the remedies of the applicant against the issuer. Under 5–111(b), the applicant can recover damages from the issuer who wrongfully dishonors or wrongfully honors a draft or other presentation under the credit. Unlike 5–111(a)'s recovery, the applicant may only recover damages "resulting" from the issuer's breach. It is therefore not entitled to the face amount of the credit unless the issuer's breach caused loss in that amount. See Comment 2 to 5–111. As under 5–111(a), incidental damages are recoverable but not consequential damages. Unlike 5–111(a)'s recovery, the applicant is required to mitigate its damages under 5–111(b).

The differences in the remedies available to the presenter and the applicant under 5–111 reflect differences in the loss from breach and possibly the influence of issuers in Article 5's drafting. A beneficiary or other presenter's loss from the issuer's wrongful dishonor usually approximates the face amount of the credit. In these cases requiring proof of the amount of damages is wasteful and 5–111(a) does not require it. In addition, even if the beneficiary is in a position to mitigate its loss, proving this fact often is costly and protracts litigation. Perhaps for this reason, 5–111(a) does not require the beneficiary to mitigate its loss. By comparison, in most cases the applicant's loss from the issuer's wrongful dishonor is not equal to the face amount of the credit. Usually its loss is much less. For instance, the applicant typically will not have reimbursed the issuer in advance of the issuer's honor of a presentation. Thus, when the issuer dishonors the presentation, the applicant does not lose more than the fee it has paid the issuer to issue the letter of credit. Because the applicant's loss bears no close relation to the face amount of the credit, 5–111(b) justifiably allows damages only in the amount of loss caused by the issuer's breach. Section 5–111(b) requires the applicant to mitigate its loss, perhaps because proving mitigation will not materially extend litigation that already requires proof of loss from breach.

Finally, both 5–111(a) and (b) do not allow the recovery of consequential damages from the issuer, unless otherwise agreed. See 5–103(c). Section 4A–305(c) adopts the same rule for banks making funds transfers. Presenters and applicants are thought to be in a better position than the issuer to forecast or avoid consequential damages resulting from the issuer's breach. See Comment 4 to 5–111; Comment 2 to 4A–305 (fourth paragraph). For this reason, the exclusion of consequential damages might be an efficient default term. Alternatively, it might be an inefficient default term produced by a drafting process over which the bankers' trade association had a powerful influence. The Reporter for Article 5, however, does not list the exclusion of consequential damages among the issues on which the banker's representatives had an impact; see James J. White, The Influence of International Practice on Revised Article 5 of the UCC, 16

Nw. Int'l L. & Bus. 189 (1995). Even if Article 5–111's exclusion of consequential damages is not the product of interest group influence, there can be reasonable disagreement over its impact on the total cost of a letter of credit.

Section 5–111(e) requires courts to award reasonable attorney's fees and other litigation expenses to the prevailing party for any action in which a remedy is sought under Article 5. The subsection overrules the "American rule" under which each party bears its own litigation costs. Section 5–111(e)'s mandatory award is not limited to remedies available under 5–111. The operative language of 5–111(e) is "under this Article." Thus, a party prevailing on a breach of warranty claim against a beneficiary under 5–110, for instance, must be awarded reasonable attorney's fees and other litigation expenses. Would an injunction issued to prevent a materially fraudulent draw, discussed below, be a "remedy . . . sought under Article 5"? Unsurprisingly, both 5–111(e) and the exclusion of consequential damages have proven controversial. Connecticut and Louisiana have adopted nonuniform amendments to 5–111 allowing recovery of consequential damages, and several states have enacted nonuniform versions of 5–111(e). New Jersey and Texas, for instance, simply allow the award of attorney's fees and litigation expenses. New York's enactment of Article 5, significantly, omits 5–111(e) entirely. See 2B Unif. L. Ann. § 5–111 (2003).

PROBLEM 11.9

1. Applicant planned to develop a recreational community. County approval of Applicant's subdivision was conditional on Applicant's agreement to provide a standby letter of credit payable to the County as beneficiary to ensure that Applicant would complete roads and related improvements in accordance with subdivision design specifications. The required letter of credit was obtained from Issuer. Applicant never commenced construction of the roads or other improvements. Issuer wrongfully dishonored the letter of credit upon presentation. The County sued Issuer for the face amount of the credit plus interest from the date of the demand for payment. Issuer defended on the ground that the County would receive a windfall since it had not expended or committed itself to expend any funds to complete the improvements. The facts are based on Colorado National Bank v. Board of County Commissioners, 634 P.2d 32 (Colo.1981). What result? See 5–111(a).

2. Material Corp. bought two tons of metal from Ace. To pay for its purchase Material had Bank issue a letter of credit for $10,000 in Ace's favor. Bank in turn debited Material's deposit account in the amount of the $100 fee for issuing the credit. When Ace presented complying documents to Bank, Bank refused to pay Ace under the credit. For its part Ace did not release the documents and Material never received the metal listed in them. This result did not bother Ace because it quickly found another buyer willing to pay the same price for the metal. However, although Bank offered to credit its account in the amount of the $100 issuance fee, Material still was unhappy with Bank's behavior. It had a contract with Jones to sell the metal it received from Ace. When Material was unable to deliver the metal, Jones cancelled the contract and turned to another seller

to supply him. As a result Material lost $5,000 in profits. Material accurately estimates that it will have to incur $3,000 in attorney's fees to recover damages from Bank. How much can Material recover if it chooses to sue Bank? Does Material have an incentive to sue? See 5–111(b), (e).

INDEX

References are to Pages